Index of American Periodical Verse: 1989

Rafael Catalá

and

James D. Anderson

assisted by

Sarah Park Anderson

and

Martha Park Sollberger

The Scarecrow Press, Inc.
Metuchen, N.J., & London
1991

Library of Congress Catalog Card No. 73-3060
ISBN 0-8108-2456-6
Copyright © 1991 by Rafael Catalá and James D. Anderson
Manufactured in the United States of America

Ref
016.8115
In38
1989   Contents

Preface

This, the nineteenth annual volume of the *Index of American Periodical Verse*, was produced with the cooperation of 269 participating periodicals from Canada, the United States, and the Caribbean. More than 6,000 entries for individual poets and translators are included, with more than 18,000 entries for individual poems. A separate index provides access by title or first line.

The importance of the *Index* grows as its necessity becomes more apparent in circles of contemporary poetry research. The increasing demand for inclusion corroborates this fact. The *Index* constitutes an objective measure of poetry in North America, recording not only the publication of our own poets in Canada, the U.S. and the Caribbean, but also those from other lands and cultures and from other times. Of course, the *Index*'s primary purpose is to show what poems have been published by particular poets, what poems have been translated by particular translators, and who wrote poems with particular titles or first lines. But taken together, the *Index* reveals trends and influences: the ebb and flow of particular poets, as well as the influence of cultures of other lands and times as represented by their poets published in North American journals.

James D. Anderson has made a major contribution to the *Index* by designing and refining computer programs that have greatly facilitated the indexing process, control of necessary cross references, and typesetting. Also, I want to express my sincere appreciation to Sarah Park Anderson and Martha Park Sollberger, librarians *emeritae*, for their valuable assistance.

Rafael Catalá
Co-Editor

Introduction

Scope

The *Index of American Periodical Verse* indexes poems published in a broad cross-section of poetry, literary, scholarly, popular, general, and "little" magazines, journals and reviews published in the United States, Canada, and the Caribbean. The periodicals included are listed in the "Periodicals Indexed" section, together with name of editor(s), address, issues indexed in this volume, and subscription information. Selection of periodicals to index is the responsibility of the editors, based on recommendations of poets, librarians, literary scholars and publishers. Publishers participate by supplying copies of all issues to the editors. Criteria for inclusion include the quality of poems and their presentation and the status or reputation of poets. Within these very broad and subjective guidelines, the editors attempt to include a cross-section of periodicals by type of publisher and/or publication, place of publication, language, and type of poetry. Periodicals published outside of North America are included only if they have North American editors.

Compilation

Citation data are compiled using the WordStar word-processing program, version 4, on a 286 MS/DOS computer. "Shorthand" macro programs are used to repeat author headings for multiple poems by the same poet, create translator entries from author entries for translated poems, and transform complex author names into cross-reference entries. Sorting is done by "IOTA Big Sort," a fast program for sorting very large files written by Fred A. Rowley. Title entries were extracted from the original author entries and sorted, and formatted author and title entries were transferred to a Macintosh computer with laser printer for typesetting and page formatting using MacWrite and PageMaker programs.

Persons interested in the precise details of compilation, including the computer programs used for error checking, sorting and formatting, should write to the editors at P.O. Box 38, New Brunswick, NJ 08903-0038. The *Indexes* for 1982 through 1989 are available from the editors on micro-computer disks.

Names and Cross References

Because many poets have compound surnames and surnames containing various prefixes, we recognize the need for systematic provision of cross references from alternative forms of surname to the form chosen for entry in the *Index*. We have included cross references whenever the form used for entry does not fall under the last part or element of the name. In addition, many poets publish under different forms of the same name, for example, with or without a middle initial. When poets are known to use different forms of the same name, alternative forms may be indicated using the format authorized by the *Anglo-American Cataloguing Rules*, Second Edition. For example:

WHEATLEY, Pat (Patience)

This heading indicates that this poet has poems published under two forms of name: Pat Wheatley and Patience Wheatley.

When two or more different names refer to the same poet, one name will be chosen, with "see" references to the chosen name from other names. When it is not possible to determine with assurance whether a single poet is using variant forms of name or different poets have similar names, both names will be used. In such cases, "see also" references may be added to headings to remind users to check the variant name forms which might possibly refer to the same poet.

Format and Arrangement of Entries

The basic format and style of the *Index* remain unchanged. Poets are arranged alphabetically by surname and forenames. In creating this alphabetical sequence, we have adopted principles of the filing rules issued in 1980 by the American Library Association and the Library of Congress. Names are arranged on the basis of their spelling, rather than their pronunciation, so that, for example, names beginning with "Mac" and "Mc" are no longer interfiled. Similarly, the space consistently counts as a filing element, so that similar compound and prefixed surnames are often separated by some distance, as illustrated in the following examples. Note that "De BOLT" precedes "DeBEVOISE" by a considerable number of entries.

De ANGELIS	Van BRUNT
De BOLT	Van DUYN
De GRAVELLES	Van HALTEREN
De LOACH	Van TOORN
De PALCHI	Van TROYER
De RONSARD	Van WERT
De VAUL	Van WINCKEL
DEAL	VANCE
DeBEVOISE	Vander DOES
DeFOE	VANDERBEEK
DEGUY	VanDEVENTER
Del VECCHIO	
DeLISLE	
DeMOTT	
DENNISON	
Der HOVANESSIAN	
DESY	
DeYOUNG	

Abbreviations are also arranged on the basis of spelling, rather than pronunciation, so that "ST. JOHN" is *not* filed as "SAINT JOHN", but as "S+T+space+JOHN". Punctuation, signs and symbols other than alphabetic letters and numerals are not considered; a hyphen is filed as if it were a space and apostrophes and accents are ignored for purposes of filing. In title entries, initial articles are also ignored. Numerals are arranged in numerical order preceding alphabetical letters rather than as if they were spelled out.

Under each poet's name, poems are arranged alphabetically by title or, if there is no title, by first line. Poems with only "Untitled" printed as if it were the title are entered as "Untitled" plus the first line of the poem under the name of the poet. In the title index, two entries are provided, one under "Untitled" plus the first line, and one directly under the first line. Numbered poems are handled in the same way. Under poets, initial numbers are treated as the first part of titles, and they are so entered. In the title index, they are entered both under their initial numbers and under the part following the number, if any.

Poem titles and first lines are placed within quotation marks. All significant words of titles are capitalized, but in first lines, only the first word and proper nouns are capitalized. Incomplete excerpts from larger works are followed by the note "Excerpt" or "Excerpts", or, if they consist of complete sections, by "Selection" or "Selections". The title, first line or number of excerpts or selections may follow if given in the publication. For example:

WALCOTT, Derek
    "Midsummer" (Selections: XXXIV-XXXVI). [Agni] (18) 83, p. 5-7.

WEBB, Phyllis
    "The Vision Tree" (Selection: "I Daniel"). [PoetryCR] (5:2) Wint
        83-84, p. 11.

WAINWRIGHT, Jeffrey
    "Heart's Desire" (Excerpt: "Some Propositions and Part of a
        Narrative"). [Agni] (18) 83, p. 37.

WATTEN, Barret
    "One Half" (Excerpts). [ParisR] (24:86) Wint 82, p. 112-113.

If an excerpt is treated as a complete "sub-work", it receives an independent entry, with reference to the larger work in a note. For example:

ANDERSON, Jack
    "Magnets" (from "The Clouds of That Country"). [PoNow] (7:2,
        #38) 83, p. 23.

Notes about dedications, joint authors, translators, and sources follow the title, enclosed in parentheses. A poem with more than one author is entered under each author. Likewise, a translated poem is entered under each translator, as well as its author(s). Each entry includes the names of all authors and all translators. Multiple authors or translators are indicated by the abbreviation "w.", standing for "with". Translators are indicated by the abbreviation "tr. by", standing for "translated by", and original authors are indicated by the abbreviation "tr. of", standing for "translation of". For example:

AGGESTAM, Rolf
    "Old Basho" (tr. by Erland Anderson and Lars Nordström).
    [NewRena] (16) Spr 83, p. 25.

ANDERSON, Erland
    "Old Basho" (tr. of Rolf Aggestam, w. Lars Nordström).
    [NewRena] (16) Spr 83, p. 25.

NORDSTRÖM, Lars
    "Old Basho" (tr. of Rolf Aggestam, w. Erland Anderson).
    [NewRena] (16) Spr 83, p. 25.

The journal citation includes an abbreviation standing for the journal title, followed by volume and issue numbers, date, and pages. The journal abbreviation is enclosed in square brackets. An alphabetical list of these journal abbreviations is included at the front of the volume, followed by the full journal title, name of editor(s), address, the numbers of the issues indexed for this volume of the *Index*, and subscription information. A separate list of indexed periodicals is arranged by full journal title, with a reference to the abbreviated title. Volume and issue numbers are included within parentheses, e.g., (16:5) stands for volume 16, number 5; (21) refers to issue 21 for a journal which does not use volume numbers. Dates are given using abbreviations for months and seasons. Year of publication is indicated by the last two digits of the year, e.g., 89. Please see the separate list of abbreviations at the front of the volume.

Compiling this year's *Index* has been an adventure into the wealth and variety of poetry published in U. S., Caribbean and Canadian periodicals as well as the intricacies of bringing this richness together and organizing it into a consistent index. The world of poetry publication is a dynamic one, with new journals appearing, older journals declining, dying, reviving and thriving. This year saw the loss of 11 journals and the addition of 20 new ones, with a net gain of 9 journals. Both deleted and newly added journals are listed at the front of the volume. Keeping up with these changes is a big job, and we solicit our readers' suggestions as to journals which should be included in future volumes of the *Index*, and also, journals which could be dropped. Editors who would like their journals considered for inclusion in future volumes should send sample issues to:

Rafael Catalá, Editor
Index of American Periodical Verse
P.O. Box 38
New Brunswick, NJ 08903-0038

Although indexing is indispensable for the organization of any literature so that particular works can be found when needed and scholarship and research facilitated, it is a tedious business. I know that we have made mistakes. We solicit your corrections and suggestions, which you may send to me at the above address.

James D. Anderson
Co-Editor

Abbreviations

dir., dirs.	director, directors
ed., eds.	editor, editors
(for.)	price for foreign countries
(ind.)	price for individuals
(inst.)	price for institutions
(lib.)	price for libraries
NS	new series
p.	page, pages
po. ed.	poetry editor
pub.	publisher
(stud.)	price for students
tr. by	translated by
tr. of	translation of
U.	University
w.	with

Months

Ja	January	Jl	July
F	February	Ag	August
Mr	March	S	September
Ap	April	O	October
My	May	N	November
Je	June	D	December

Seasons

Aut	Autumn	Spr	Spring
Wint	Winter	Sum	Summer

Years

86	1986	88	1988
87	1987	89	1989

Periodicals Added

Periodical acronyms are followed by titles. Full information may be found in the list of periodicals indexed.

Aerial: AERIAL

AnthNEW: THE ANTHOLOGY OF NEW ENGLAND WRITERS

ApalQ: APALACHEE QUARTERLY

BrooklynR: BROOKLYN REVIEW

ChangingM: CHANGING MEN

EmeraldCR: EMERALD COAST REVIEW

EvergreenC: THE EVERGREEN CHRONICLES

FreeL: FREE LUNCH

HeavenB: HEAVEN BONE

Journal: THE JOURNAL

Kalliope: KALLIOPE

Manoa: MANOA

Mildred: MILDRED

Ometeca: OMETECA

OxfordM: OXFORD MAGAZINE

PaperAir: PAPER AIR

Screens: SCREENS AND TASTED PARALLELS

SoCoast: SOUTH COAST POETRY JOURNAL

Tribe: TRIBE

WashR: WASHINGTON REVIEW

Periodicals Deleted

ArizQ: ARIZONA QUARTERLY, Albert Frank Gegenheimer, ed., U. of Arizona, Main Library B-541, Tucson, AZ 85721. "Under a change of editorial policy and staff, Arizona Quarterly is now exclusively a journal of American literature, culture and theory, and will no longer publish poetry or fiction."

CrescentR: THE CRESCENT REVIEW, Guy Neal Williams, ed., P.O. Box 15065, Winston-Salem, NC 27113. "No longer publishes poetry."

Electrum: ELECTRUM MAGAZINE, Roger Suva, ed., 2222 Silk Tree Drive, Tustin, CA 92680-7129. No 1988 or 1989 issues received; letters returned by post office.

Gambit: GAMBIT MAGAZINE: A Journal of the Ohio Valley, a joint publication of the Ohio Valley Literary Group and Parkersburg Community College, Jane Somerville, ed., P.O. Box 1122, Marietta, OH 45750. No 1989 issues received. Letter returned by post office.

Germ: GERMINATION, Allan Cooper, ed. & pub., Leigh Faulkner, Assoc. ed., 428 Yale Ave., Riverview, New Brunswick E1B 2B5, Canada. No 1988 or 1989 issues received; letters not answered.

LittleM: THE LITTLE MAGAZINE, Kathryn Cramer, et al ., eds, Dragon Press, P.O. Box 78, Pleasantville, NY 10570. No longer published.

Pax: PAX: A Journal for Peace through Culture, Bryce Milligan, ed., Center for Peace through Culture, 217 Pershing Ave., San Antonio, TX 78209. No 1987, 1988 or 1989 issues received; letters not answered.

Phoenix: PHOENIX, Joan Shaddox Isom, ed., Division of Arts & Letters, Northeastern State U., Tahlequah, OK 74464. "We are having publishing problems that must be sorted out. Just drop us for the time being."

PoeticJ: POETIC JUSTICE: Contemporary American Poetry, Alan Engebretsen, ed., 8220 Rayford Dr., Los Angeles, CA 90045. No 1988 or 1989 issues received; letters not answered.

Puerto: PUERTO DEL SOL, English Dept., Box 3E, New Mexico State U., Las Cruces, NM 88003. No 1988 or 1989 issues received; letters not answered.

SnapD: SNAPDRAGON, Gail Eckwright, D'Wayne Hodgin, Ron McFarland, Tina Foriyes, eds., Dept. of English, U. of Idaho, Moscow, ID 83843. No 1988 or 1989 issues received; letters not answered.

Periodicals Indexed

Arranged by acronym, with names of editors, addresses, issues indexed, and subscription information. New titles added to the *Index* in 1989 are marked with an asterisk (*).

Abraxas: ABRAXAS, Ingrid Swanberg, ed., 2518 Gregory St., Madison, WI 53711. Issues indexed: No 1989 issues published. Subscriptions: $12/4 issues; Single issues: $3; Double issues: $6.

Acts: ACTS: A Journal of New Writing, David Levi Strauss, ed. & pub., 514 Guerrero St., San Francisco, CA 94110. Issues indexed: (10). Subscriptions: $12/yr. (2 issues, ind.), $16/yr. (2 issues, inst. & for.); $20/2 yrs. (4 issues, ind.), $28/2 yrs. (4 issues, inst. & for.); Single issues: $10.

*Aerial: AERIAL, Rod Smith, ed., P.O. Box 25642, Washington, DC 20007. Issues indexed: (5). Subscriptions: $15/3 issues; Single issues: $7.50.

Agni: AGNI, Askold Melnyczuk, ed., Creative Writing Program, Boston U., 236 Bay State Rd., Boston, MA 02115. Issues indexed: (28). Subscriptions: $12/yr., $23/2 yrs., plus $5/yr. (for.); Single issues: $6.

AlphaBS: ALPHA BEAT SOUP, Dave Christy, ed., 68 Winter Ave., Scarborough, Ont. M1K 4M3 Canada. Issues indexed: (5-6). Subscriptions: $5/yr. (2 issues); Single issues: $3.

Amelia: AMELIA, Frederick A. Raborg, Jr., ed., 329 "E" St., Bakersfield, CA 93304. Issues indexed: (5:3, issue 14). Subscriptions: US, Canada, Mexico, $20/yr. (4 issues), $38/2 yrs., $56/3 yrs.; $36/yr., $70/2 yrs., $104/3 yrs. (for. air mail); Single issues: $6.50, $10 (for. air mail).

Americas: THE AMERICAS REVIEW, A Review of Hispanic Literature and Art of the USA, Julián Olivares, ed., U. of Houston, Houston, TX 77204-2090. Issues indexed: 17:1-3/4). Subscriptions: $15/yr. (ind.), $20/yr. (inst.); Single issues: $5.

AmerPoR: THE AMERICAN POETRY REVIEW, David Bonanno, Stephen Berg, Arthur Vogelsang, eds., 1704 Walnut St., Philadelphia, PA 19103. Issues indexed: (18:1-6). Subscriptions: $11/yr., $19/2 yrs., $26/3 yrs.; $13/yr., $23/2 yrs., $31/3 yrs. (for.); classroom rate $6/yr. per student; Single issues: $2.25.

AmerS: THE AMERICAN SCHOLAR, Joseph Epstein, ed., The Phi Beta Kappa Society, 1811 Q St. NW, Washington, DC 20009. Issues indexed: (58:1-4). Subscriptions: $19/yr., $34/2 yrs., $48/3 yrs. plus $3/yr. (for.); Single issues: $5.50.

AmerV: THE AMERICAN VOICE, Sallie Bingham, Frederick Smock, eds., The Kentucky Foundation for Women, Inc., 332 West Broadway, Suite 1215, Louisville, KY 40202. Issues indexed: (14-17). Subscriptions: $12/yr. Single issues: $4.

AnotherCM: ANOTHER CHICAGO MAGAZINE, Lee Webster, Barry Silesky, eds. & pubs., Box 11223, Chicago, IL 60611. Issues indexed: (19-20). Subscriptions: $15/yr., $60/5 yrs., $149.95/lifetime; Single issues: $8.

Antaeus: ANTAEUS, Daniel Halpern, ed., The Ecco Press, 26 W. 17th St., New York, NY 10011. Issues indexed: (61-63). Subscriptions: $30/4 issues; Single issues: $10.

*AnthNEW: THE ANTHOLOGY OF NEW ENGLAND WRITERS, Walter Mendoza, ed., New England Writers (Vermont Poets Association), 151 Main St., Windsor, VT 05089. Issues indexed: (1).

Periodicals Indexed

AntigR: THE ANTIGONISH REVIEW, George Sanderson, ed., St. Francis Xavier U., Antigonish, Nova Scotia B2G 1C0 Canada. Issues indexed: (76, 77/78, 79). Subscriptions: $16/4 issues; Single issues: $4.50.

AntR: THE ANTIOCH REVIEW, Robert S. Fogarty, ed., David St. John, po. ed., P.O. Box 148, Yellow Springs, OH 45387. Issues indexed: (47:1-4). Subscriptions: $20/yr. (4 issues), $38/2 yrs., $54/3 yrs. (ind.); $30/yr., $58/2 yrs., $86/3 yrs. (inst.); plus $5/yr. (for.); Single issues: $5. Subscription address: P.O. Box 3011, Ridgefield, NJ 07657-3011.

*ApalQ: APALACHEE QUARTERLY, Barbara Hamby, Pam Ball, Bruce Boehrer, Claudia Johnson, Paul McCall, eds., P.O. Box 20106, Tallahassee, FL 32316. Issues indexed: (31-32). Subscriptions: $12/yr. (2 issues, ind.), $15/yr. (inst.), $20/yr. (for.); Single issues: $5.

Areíto: AREITO, Andrés Gómez, Director, P.O. Box 44-1403, Miami, FL 33144. Issues indexed: Segunda Epoca (2:5/6). Subscriptions: $12/yr. (ind.), $20/yr. (inst.), $18/yr. (for. ind.), $30/yr. (for. inst.).

ArtfulD: ARTFUL DODGE, Daniel Bourne, Karen Kovacik, eds., Dept. of English, College of Wooster, Wooster, OH 44691. Issues indexed: (16/17). Subscriptions: $10/4 issues (ind.), $16/4 issues (inst.); Single issues: $5.

Ascent: ASCENT, Carol Pagliara, ed. secretary, English Dept., U. of Illinois, 608 South Wright St., Urbana, IL 61801. Issues indexed: (14:3). Subscriptions: $3/yr. (3 issues), $4.50/yr. (for.); Single issues: $1 (bookstore), $1.50 (mail).

Atlantic: THE ATLANTIC, William Whitworth, ed., Peter Davison, po. ed., 745 Boylston St., 7th fl., Boston, MA 02116-2603. Issues indexed: (263:1-6, 264:1-6). Subscriptions: $14.95/yr., $27.95/2 yrs., $39.95/3 yrs., plus $4/yr. (Canada), $6/yr. (for.); Single issues: $2.50, $2.95 (Canada). Subscription address: Atlantic Subscription Processing Center, Box 52661, Boulder, CO 80322.

BallSUF: BALL STATE UNIVERSITY FORUM, Bruce W. Hozeski, ed., Darlene Mathis-Eddy, po. ed., Ball State U., Muncie, IN 47306. Issues indexed: (30:1-4). Subscriptions: $20/yr. (4 issues), Single issues: $6.

BambooR: BAMBOO RIDGE: The Hawaii Writers' Quarterly, Eric Chock, Darrell H. Y Lum, eds., P.O. Box 61781, Honolulu, HI 96839-1781. Issues indexed: (41, 42/43, 44, 45/46). Subscriptions: $12/yr. (4 issues), $22/2 yrs., $30/3 yrs.; Single issues, $3-$8.

BellArk: BELLOWING ARK, Robert R. Ward, ed., P.O. Box 45637, Seattle, WA 98145. Issues indexed: (5:1-6). Subscriptions: $12/yr. (6 issues), $20/2 yrs.; Single issues: $2.

BellR: THE BELLINGHAM REVIEW, Shelley Rozen, ed., 1007 Queen St., Bellingham, WA 98226. Issues indexed: (12:1-2, #25-26). Subscriptions: $4/yr. (2 issues), $7.50/2 yrs., $10.50/3 yrs.; through agencies, $4.50/yr.; Single issues: $2.

BelPoJ: THE BELOIT POETRY JOURNAL, Marion K. Stocking, ed., RFD 2, Box 154, Ellsworth, ME 04605. Issues indexed: (39:3-4, 40:1-2). Subscriptions: $8/yr. (4 issues, ind.), $22/3 yrs.; $12/yr., $33/3 yrs. (inst.); plus $2.96/yr. (Canada), $3.20/yr. (for.); Single issues: $2.

BilingR: THE BILINGUAL REVIEW / LA REVISTA BILINGÜE, Gary D. Keller, ed., Hispanic Research Center, Arizona State U., Tempe, AZ 85287. Issues indexed: No 1989 issues received. Subscriptions: $15/yr., $28/2 yrs., $39/3 yrs. (ind.); $24/yr. (inst.).

BlackALF: BLACK AMERICAN LITERATURE FORUM, Division on Black American Literature and Culture, Modern Language Association, Joe Weixlmann, ed., Thadious David, Pinkie Gordon Lane, Sterling Plumpp, po. eds., Dept. of English, Indiana State U., Terre Haute, IN 47809. Issues indexed: (23:1-4). Subscriptions: $18/yr. (ind.), $28/yr. (inst.), $23/yr. (for.), $33/yr. (for. inst.). Single issues: $7.50.

BlackWR: BLACK WARRIOR REVIEW, Mark Dawson, ed., Glenn Mott, po. ed., U. of Alabama, P.O. Box 2936, Tuscaloosa, AL 35487-2936. Issues indexed: (15:2, 16:1). Subscriptions: $7.50/yr. (ind.), $11/yr. (inst.); Single issues: $4.

BlueBldgs: BLUE BUILDINGS: An International Magazine of Poetry, Translations and Art, Ruth Doty, Kelly Van Diver, Tom Urban, Guillaume Williams, eds., Dept. of English, Drake U., Des Moines, IA 50311. Issues indexed: (11). Subscriptions: $6 per issue; Back issues: $4.

Blueline: BLUELINE, Anthony Tyler, ed., English Dept., Potsdam College, SUNY, Potsdam, NY 13676. Issues indexed: (10:1/2). Single issues: $6.

Bogg: BOGG, John Elsberg, ed., 422 N. Cleveland St., Arlington, VA 22201. Issues indexed: (61). Subscriptions: $10/3 issues; Single issues: $4.

Bomb: BOMB MAGAZINE, Betsy Sussler, ed. & pub., Roland Legiardi-Laura, po. ed., New Art Publications, P.O. Box 2003, Canal Station, New York, NY 10013. Issues indexed: (27-30). Subscriptions: $16/yr., $30/2 yrs.; $26/yr. (for.); Single issues: $4.

BostonR: BOSTON REVIEW, Margaret Ann Roth, ed. & pub., 33 Harrison Ave., Boston, MA 02111. Issues indexed: (14:1-6). Subscriptions: $12/yr., $20/2 yrs. (ind.); $15/yr., $25/2 yrs. (inst.); plus $6/yr. (for.); Single issues: $3.

Boulevard: BOULEVARD, Richard Burgin, ed., 2400 Chestnut St., Apt. 3301, Philadelphia, PA 19103. Issues indexed: (4:1-2, #10-11). Subscriptions: $12/3 issues, $20/6 issues, $25/9 issues; Single issues: $5.

Bound: BOUNDARY 2, William V. Spanos, ed., Dept. of English, State U. of New York, Binghamton, NY 13901. Issues indexed: (16:2/3). Subscriptions: $25/yr. (inst.), $15/yr. (ind.), $13/yr (stud.), plus $2 (for.); Single issues: $8, Double issues: $10. "As of the 1990 volume, no longer publishes poetry."

*BrooklynR: BROOKLYN REVIEW, Peter Catapano, Karen Kelly, managing eds., Mary Greene, David Trinidad, po. eds., Dept. of English, Brooklyn College, Bedford & H Avenues, Brooklyn, NY 11210. Subscriptions: $5/issue.

Caliban: CALIBAN, Lawrence R. Smith, ed., P.O. Box 4321, Ann Arbor, MI 48106. Issues indexed: (6-7). Subscriptions: $8/yr., 2 issues (ind.), $15/yr. (inst.); $11/yr. (ind.), $15/yr. (inst.), Canadian currency; $12/yr. (for. ind.), $21/yr. (for. inst.). Single issues: $5.

Callaloo: CALLALOO: A Journal of Afro-American and African Arts and Letters, Charles H. Rowell, ed., Dept. of English, Wilson Hall, U. of Virginia, Charlottesville, VA 22903. Issues indexed: (12:1-4; #38-41). Subscriptions: $20/yr. (ind.), $41/yr. (inst.); plus $3.50 (Canada, Mexico); plus $14 (outside North America, airfreight); The Johns Hopkins University Press, Journals Publishing Division, 701 W. 40th St., Suite 275, Baltimore, MD 21211.

CalQ: CALIFORNIA QUARTERLY, Elliot L. Gilbert, ed., Carlos Rodriguez, po. ed., 100 Sproul Hall, U. of California, Davis, CA 95616. Issues indexed: No 1988 or 1989 issues received. Subscriptions: $10/yr. (4 issues); Single issues: $2.50.

Calyx: CALYX: A Journal of Art and Literature by Women, Margarita Donnelly, Managing ed., Catherine Holdorf, Beverly McFarland, Linda Varsell Smith, eds, P.O. Box B, Corvallis, OR 97339-0539. Issues indexed: (12:1-2); Note: 11:2/3 (Fall 1988) was indexed in the 1988 volume, but was accidentally omitted from the "issues indexed" section of the entry for Calyx in that volume. Subscriptions: $18/3 issues, $32/6 issues, $42/9 issues, plus $4/3 issues (for.), $9/3 issues (for. airmail); $22.50/3 issues (inst.); $15/3 issues (low income individual); Single issues: $8, Double issues: $16, plus $1 postage.

CanLit: CANADIAN LITERATURE, W. H. New, ed., U. of British Columbia, 2029 West Mall, Vancouver, B.C. V6T 1W5 Canada. Issues indexed: (120, 121, 122/123). Subscriptions: $25/yr. (ind.), $35/yr. (inst.) plus $5/yr. outside Canada; Single issues: $10.

Periodicals Indexed

CapeR: THE CAPE ROCK, Harvey Hecht, ed., Southeast Missouri State U., Cape Girardeau, MO 63701. Issues indexed: (24:1-2). Subscriptions: $5/yr. (2 issues); Single issues: $3.

CapilR: THE CAPILANO REVIEW, Pierre Coupey, ed., Capilano College, 2055 Purcell Way, North Vancouver, B.C. V7J 3H5 Canada. Issues indexed: (Series 1, No. 50; Series 2, No. 1). Subscriptions: $16/yr. (3 issues), $36/3 yrs.; $25/yr. (inst.); same rates in U.S. funds (U.S.A.); plus $3/yr. (for.); Single issues: $8.

CarolQ: CAROLINA QUARTERLY, Barnhouse, Rebecca, ed., David Kellogg, po. ed., Greenlaw Hall CB#3520, U. of North Carolina, Chapel Hill, NC 27599-3520. Issues indexed: (41:2-3, 42:1). Subscriptions: $10/yr. (ind.), $12/yr. (3 issues) (inst.), $11/yr. (for.); Single issues: $4, plus $1 postage.

CentR: THE CENTENNIAL REVIEW, R. K. Meiners, ed., College of Arts and Letters, 110 Morril Hall, Michigan State U., East Lansing, MI 48824-1036. Issues indexed: (33:1-4). Subscriptions: $10/yr., $15/2 yrs., plus $3/yr. (for.); Single issues: $3.

CentralP: CENTRAL PARK, Stephen-Paul Martin, Eve Ensler, Richard Royal, eds., Box 1446, New York, NY 10023. Issues indexed: (15-16). Subscriptions: $9/yr., 2 issues (ind.), $10/yr. (inst.); Single issues: $5 (ind), $5.50 (inst).

ChamLR: CHAMINADE LITERARY REVIEW, Loretta Petrie, ed., Jim Kraus, po. ed., Chaminade U. of Honolulu, 3140 Waialae Ave., Honolulu, HI 96816. Issues indexed: (2:2, 3:1; #4-5). Subscriptions: $10/yr.; $18/2 yrs.; plus $2 (for.).; Single issues: $5.

*ChangingM: CHANGING MEN: Issues in Gender, Sex and Politics, Michael Biernbaum, Rick Cote, managing eds., 306 N. Brooks St., Madison, WI 53715, Daniel Garrett, po. ed. (105-63 135th St., Queens, NY 11419). Issues indexed: (20). Subscriptions: $16/4 issues, $30/4 issues (inst.); $12/4 issues (limited income); $18/4 issues (Canada & Mexico); $27/4 issues (for., air mail); Single issues: $4.50.

CharR: THE CHARITON REVIEW, Jim Barnes, ed., Northeast Missouri State U., Kirksville, MO 63501. Issues indexed: (15:1-2). Subscriptions: $9/4 issues; Single issues: $2.50.

ChatR: THE CHATTAHOOCHEE REVIEW, Lamar York, ed., DeKalb College, 2101 Womack Road, Dunwoody, GA 30338-4497. Issues indexed: (9:2-4, 10:1). Subscriptions: $15/yr. (4 issues), $25/2 yrs.; Single issues: $3.50.

Chelsea: CHELSEA, Sonia Raiziss, ed., P.O. Box 5880, Grand Central Station, New York, NY 10163. Issues indexed: (48). Subscriptions: $11/2 issues or double issue, $13 (for.); Single issues: $6, $7 (for.).

ChiR: CHICAGO REVIEW, Elizabeth Arnold, Jane Hoogestraat, Emily McKnight, eds., Jane Hoogestraat, po. eds., 5801 South Kenwood, Chicago, IL 60637. Issues indexed: (36:3/4). Subscriptions: $16/ yr. (ind.); $20/yr. (inst.), $40/2 yrs., $60/3 yrs., plus $4/yr. (for.); Single issues: $5.

ChrC: THE CHRISTIAN CENTURY, James M. Wall, ed., 407 S. Dearborn St., Chicago, IL 60605. Issues indexed: (106:1-39). Subscriptions: $28/yr.; Single issues: $1.50. Christian Century Subscription Service, 5615 W. Cermak, Cicero, IL 60650.

CimR: CIMARRON REVIEW, Gordon Weaver, ed., Jack Myers, po. ed., 205 Morrill Hall, Oklahoma State U., Stillwater, OK 74078-0135. Issues indexed: (86-89). Subscriptions: $12/yr., $15 (Canada); $30/3 yrs., $40 (Canada); plus $2.50/yr. (for.); Single issues: $3.

CinPR: CINCINNATI POETRY REVIEW, Dallas Wiebe, ed., Dept. of English, ML 069, U. of Cincinnati, Cincinnati, OH 45221. Issues indexed: (19-20). Subscriptions: $9/4 issues; Single issues: $3.

ClockR: CLOCKWATCH REVIEW: A Journal of the Arts, James Plath, ed., Dept. of English, Illinois Wesleyan Univ., Bloomington, IL 61702. Issues indexed: (5:1-2). Subscriptions: $8/yr. (2 issues); Single issues: $4.

ColEng: COLLEGE ENGLISH, National Council of Teachers of English, James C. Raymond, ed., James Tate, po. ed., P.O. Drawer AL, Tuscaloosa, AL 35487. Issues indexed: (51:1-8). Subscriptions: $35/yr. (ind.), $40/yr. (inst.), plus $4/yr. (for.); Single issues: $5.; NCTE, 1111 Kenyon Rd., Urbana, IL 61801.

ColR: COLORADO REVIEW, Bill Tremblay, ed., English Dept., Colorado State U., 360 Eddy Bldg., Fort Collins, CO 80523. Issues indexed: (NS 16:1-2). Subscriptions: $9/yr. (2 issues), $17.50/2 yrs.; Single issues: $5.

Colum: COLUMBIA: A Magazine of Poetry & Prose, Elizabeth Osborne, ed., Cynthia Atkins, po. ed., 404 Dodge Hall, Columbia Univ., New York, NY 10027. Issues indexed: (14). Subscriptions: $4.50/yr. (1 issue).

Comm: COMMONWEAL, Margaret O'Brien Steinfels, ed., Rosemary Deen, po. ed., 15 Dutch St., New York, NY 10038. Issues indexed: (116:1-22). Subscriptions: $32/yr., $34/yr. (Canada), $37/yr. (for.); $57/2 yrs., $61/2 yrs. (Canada), $67/2 yrs. (for.), ; Single issues: $1.50.

Cond: CONDITIONS: A Feminist Magazine of Writing by Women with an Emphasis on Writing by Lesbians, Cheryl Clarke, Melinda Goodman, Paula Martinac, Pam A. Parker, Dorothy Randall Gray, Mariana Romo-Carmona, eds., P.O. Box 159046, Van Brunt Station, Brooklyn, NY 11215-9046. Issues indexed: (16). Subscriptions: $24/3 issues (ind.), $34/3 issues (inst.), $32 (for.); Single issues: $8.95 (ind.), Back issues: $7-10.

Confr: CONFRONTATION, Martin Tucker, ed., English Dept., C. W. Post Campus of Long Island U., Brookville, NY 11548. Issues indexed: (39/40, 41). Subscriptions: $10/yr., $20/2 yrs., $30/3 yrs.; Single issues: $6-7.

Conjunc: CONJUNCTIONS: Bi-Annual Volumes of New Writing, Bradford Morrow, ed., P.O. Box 199, Youngsville, NY 12791. Issues indexed: (13-14). Subscriptions: $18/yr. (2 issues), $32/2 yrs.; $25/yr., $45/2 yrs. (inst., for.); $45/yr., $85/ 2 yrs. (cloth binding); Single issues: $9.95.

ConnPR: THE CONNECTICUT POETRY REVIEW, J. Clair White, James Wm. Chichetto, eds., P.O. Box 3783, Amity Station, New Haven, CT 06525. Issues indexed: (8:1). Single issues: $3 (including postage).

Contact: CONTACT II: A Poetry Review, Maurice Kenny, J. G. Gosciak, eds., P.O. Box 451, Bowling Green, New York, NY 10004. Issues indexed: (9:50/51/52, 53/54/55). Subscriptions: $8/yr. (ind.); $14/yr. (inst.); Single issues: $6.

CrabCR: CRAB CREEK REVIEW, Linda Clifton, ed., 4462 Whitman Ave. N., Seattle WA 98103. Issues indexed: (6:1-2). Subscriptions: $8/yr. (3 issues), $15/2 yrs.; Single issues: $3.

Crazy: CRAZYHORSE, K. Z. Derounian-Stodola, managing ed., Dept. of English, U. of Arkansas, 2801 S. University, Little Rock, AR 72204. Send poetry to: Lynda Hull, David Wojahn, Dean Young, po. eds., Dept. of English, Ballantine Hall, Indiana Univ., Bloomington, IN 47405. Issues indexed: (36-37). Subscriptions: $8/yr. (2 issues), $15/2 yrs., $22/3 yrs. Single issues: $4.

CreamCR: CREAM CITY REVIEW, Ron Tanner, ed., Marilyn Taylor, po. ed., Dept. of English, U. of Wisconsin, P.O. Box 413, Milwaukee, WI 53201. Issues indexed: (13:1-2). Subscriptions: $10/yr. (2 issues), $14/2 yrs.; Single issues: $4; Double issues: $5.

CrossC: CROSS-CANADA WRITERS' MAGAZINE, Ted Plantos, ed., George Swede, po. ed., Box 277, Station F, Toronto, Ontario M4Y 2L7 Canada. Issues indexed: (11:1-3). Subscriptions: $14/yr. (3 issues), $24/2 yrs. (ind.); $20/yr. (Canada inst.), $24/yr (for. inst.); Single issues: $3.

CrossCur: CROSSCURRENTS, Linda Brown Michelson, ed., 2200 Glastonbury Road, Westlake Village, CA 91361. Issues indexed: (8:2-4). Subscriptions: $18/yr. (4 issues), $25/2 yrs., $30/3 yrs.; Single issues: $6.

Periodicals Indexed

CuadP: CUADERNOS DE POÉTICA, Diógenes Céspedes, Director, Apartado Postal 1736, Santo Domingo, República Dominicana; US Editors: Kate Nickel, 1111 Oldfather Hall, U. of Nebraska, Lincoln, NE 68588-0315, Rafael Catalá, P.O. Box 450, Corrales, NM 87048. Issues indexed: (6:17-19). Subscriptions: America & Europe, $25/yr. (ind.), $30/yr. (inst.); Africa, Asia & Oceania, $30/yr. (ind.), $40/yr. (inst).

CumbPR: CUMBERLAND POETRY REVIEW, Ingram Bloch, Bob Darrell, Sherry Bevins Darrell, Malcolm Glass, Jeanne Gore, Thomas Heine, Laurence Lerner, Anthony Lombardy, Alison Touster-Reed, Eva Touster, eds., Poetics, Inc., P.O. Box 120128, Acklen Station, Nashville, TN 37212. Issues indexed: (8:2, 9:1). Subscriptions: $12/yr, $22/2 yrs. (ind.); $15/yr., $27/2 yrs. (inst.); $21/yr., $33/2 yrs. (for.); Single issue: $6.

CutB: CUTBANK, Paul S. Piper, ed., Dept. of English, U. of Montana, Missoula, MT 59812. Issues indexed: No 1989 issues received. Subscriptions: $9/yr.

Dandel: DANDELION, John McDowell, managing ed., Christopher Wiseman, Debra Godin, po eds., Alexandra Centre, 922 - 9th Ave., S.E., Calgary, Alberta T2G 0S4 Canada. Issues indexed: (16:1-2). Subscriptions: $10/yr. (2 issues), $18/2 yrs.; $15/yr. (inst.); Single issues: $6.

DeKalbLAJ: THE DEKALB LITERARY ARTS JOURNAL, Charleise T. Young, ed., DeKalb College, 555 N. Indian Creek Dr., Clarkston, GA 30021. Issues indexed: (22:1/4). "Final issue."

DenQ: DENVER QUARTERLY, Donald Revell, ed., U. of Denver, Denver, CO 80208. Issues indexed: (23:3/4, 24:1-2). Subscriptions: $15/yr., $18/yr. (inst.); $28/2 yrs.; plus $1/yr. (for.); Single issues: $5.

Descant: DESCANT, Karen Mulhallen, ed., P.O. Box 314, Station P, Toronto M5S 2S8, Ontario, Canada. Issues indexed: (20:1/2-3/4, issues 64/65-66/67). Subscriptions: $21/yr., $38/2 yrs., $55/3 yrs. (ind.); $29/yr., $58/2 yrs., $83/3 yrs. (inst.); plus $6/yr. (for.); Single/double issues: $7.50-$15.

*EmeraldCR: EMERALD COAST REVIEW: A Collection of Works of West Florida Writers, Ronald B. Cannon, ed., West Florida Literary Federation, P.O. Box 1644, Pensacola, FL 32597-1644. Issues indexed: (1989, c1988).

EngJ: ENGLISH JOURNAL, National Council of Teachers of English, Ben F. Nelms, ed., 215-216 Townsend Hall, U. of Missouri, Columbia, MO 65211; Paul Janeczko, po. ed., P.O. Box 1079, Gray, ME 04039. Issues indexed: (78:1-8). Subscriptions: $40/yr. (inst.), $35/yr. (ind.), plus $4/yr. (for.); Single issues: $5; Subscription address: 1111 Kenyon Rd., Urbana, IL 61801.

Epoch: EPOCH, C. S. Giscombe, ed., 251 Goldwin Smith Hall, Cornell U., Ithaca, NY 14853-3201. Issues indexed: (38:1-3). Subscriptions: $11/yr.; Single issues: $4.

Event: EVENT: The Douglas College Review, Dale Zieroth, ed., Douglas College, P.O. Box 2503, New Westminster, B.C., V3L 5B2 Canada. Issues indexed: (18:1-3). Subscriptions: $12/yr., $20/2 yrs.; $20/2 yrs. (lib.); Single issue: $5.

*EvergreenC: THE EVERGREEN CHRONICLES: A Journal of Gay and Lesbian Writers, Barrie Jean Borich, Keith Gann, eds., P.O. Box 8939, Minneapolis, MN 55408. Issues indexed: (4:3-4, 5:1). Subscriptions: $12/yr.; Single issues: $3.50; Back issues: $2.50.

Farm: FARMER'S MARKET, Jean C. Lee, John E. Hughes, Lisa Ress, Susan Swartwout, eds., Midwest Farmer's Market, Inc., P.O. Box 1272, Galesburg, IL 61402. Issues indexed: (6:1-2). Subscriptions: $7/yr. (2 issues).

Field: FIELD: Contemporary Poetry and Poetics, Stuart Friebert, David Young, eds., Rice Hall, Oberlin College, Oberlin, OH 44074. Issues indexed: (40-41). Subscriptions: $10/yr., $16/2 yrs.; Single issues: $5.; Back issues: $10.

Periodicals Indexed

FiveFR: FIVE FINGERS REVIEW, Aleka Chase, Elizabeth Claman, Marsha Drummond, J. Malcolm Garcia, John High, eds., 553 - 25th Ave., San Francisco, CA 94121. Issues indexed: (7). Subscriptions: $23/4 issues, $12/2 issues, plus $5 (for.); $24/4 issues, $13/2 issues (inst.); Single issues: $7; Sample issues: $5.

FloridaR: THE FLORIDA REVIEW, Pat Rushin, ed., Tom George, po. ed., Dept. of English, U. of Central Florida, Orlando, FL 32816. Issues indexed: (16:2/3) Fall-Wint 89, c1988. Subscriptions: $7/yr., $11/2 yrs.; Single issues: $4.50.

Footwork: FOOTWORK: The Paterson Literary Review, A Literary Collection of Contemporary Poetry, Short Fiction, and Art, Maria Mazziotti Gillan, ed., Passaic County Community College, College Boulevard, Paterson, NJ 07509. Issues indexed: (1989). Subscriptions: $5/issue + $1 for postage and handling.

FourQ: FOUR QUARTERS, John J. Keenan, ed., La Salle U., Philadelphia, PA 19141. Issues indexed: Second Series (3:1-2). Subscriptions: $8/yr. (2 issues), $13/2 yrs.; Single issues: $4.

*FreeL: FREE LUNCH: A Poetry Journal, Free Lunch Arts Alliance, Ron Offen, ed., P.O. Box 7647, Laguna Niguel, CA 92607-7647. Issues indexed: (1-4). Subscriptions: $10/3 issues; $13/3 issues (for.); Single issues: $4, $5 (for.).

Gargoyle: GARGOYLE MAGAZINE, Richard Peabody, Peggy Pfeiffer, eds., Paycock Press, P.O. Box 30906, Bethesda, MD 20814. Issues indexed: No paper issues published in 1989; Nos. 34 & 36 were published on audio cassette and were not indexed. Nos. 37/38 (1990) will be the last issue. Subscriptions: $15/2 issues (ind.), $20/2 issues (inst.). Single issues: $5.95-7.95.

GeoR: GEORGIA REVIEW, Stanley W. Lindberg, ed., U. of Georgia, Athens, GA 30602. Issues indexed: (43:1-4); Note error in 1988 volume listing, which should have read (42:1-4) rather than (41:1-4). Volume 41 was indexed in the 1987 volume. Subscriptions: $12/ yr., $20/2 yrs., plus $3/yr. (for.); Single issues: $5, $6 (for.).

GettyR: GETTYSBURG REVIEW, Peter Stitt, ed., Gettysburg College, Gettysburg, PA 17325-1491. Issues indexed: (2:1-4). Subscriptions: $12/yr., $22/2 yrs., $30/3 yrs., plus $4 (for.); Single issues: $4.

GrahamHR: GRAHAM HOUSE REVIEW, Peter Balakian & Bruce Smith, eds., Colgate U. Press, Box 5000, Colgate U., Hamilton, NY 13346; Issues indexed: (12). Subscriptions: $14/2 yrs. (2 issues); Single issues: $7.50.

Grain: GRAIN, Saskatchewan Writers Guild, Mick Burrs, ed., Mary Shepperd, po. ed., Box 1154, Regina, Saskatchewan S4P 3B4 Canada. Issues indexed: (17:1-4). Subscriptions: $12/yr., $20/2 yrs.; Single issues: $4.

GrandS: GRAND STREET, Ben Sonnenberg, ed., 50 Riverside Dr., New York, NY 10024. Issues indexed: (8:2-4, 9:1). Subscriptions: $24/yr. (ind.), $28/yr. (for.); $28/yr. (inst.), $32/yr. (for. inst.); Single issues: $6; Back issues, $8.

GreensboroR: THE GREENSBORO REVIEW, Jim Clark, ed., Sheila P. Donohue, po. ed., Dept. of English, U. of North Carolina, Greensboro, NC 27412. Issues indexed: (46-47). Subscriptions: $5/yr. (2 issues), $12/3 yrs.; Single issues: $2.50.

HampSPR: THE HAMPDEN-SYDNEY POETRY REVIEW, Tom O'Grady, ed., P.O. Box 128, Hampden-Sydney, VA 23943. Issues indexed: Wint 1989. Subscriptions: $5/yr. (single issue).

HangL: HANGING LOOSE, Robert Hershon, Dick Lourie, Mark Pawlak, Ron Schreiber, eds., 231 Wyckoff St., Brooklyn, NY 11217. Issues indexed: (54-55). Subscriptions: $9/3 issues, $17.50/6 issues, $25/9 issues (ind.); $10.50/3 issues, $21/6 issues, $31.50/9 issues (inst.); Single issues: $3.50 plus $1 postage and handling.

Periodicals Indexed

Harp: HARPER'S MAGAZINE, Lewis H. Lapham, ed., 666 Broadway, New York, NY 10012. Issues indexed: (278:1664-1669, 279:1670-1675). Subscriptions: $18/yr., plus $2/yr. (USA possessions, Canada), plus $3/yr. (for.); Single issues: $2; Subscription address: P.O. Box 1937, Marion, OH 43305.

HarvardA: THE HARVARD ADVOCATE, Rebecca Zorach, Managing ed., Jenny Schuessler, po. ed., 21 South St., Cambridge, MA 02138. Issues indexed: (123:2-4, 124:1). Subscriptions: $15/yr. (ind.), $17/yr. (inst.), $20/yr. (for.).

HawaiiR: HAWAI'I REVIEW, Dellzell Chenoweth, ed., T. M. Goto, po. ed., Dept. of English, U. of Hawai'i, 1733 Donaghho Rd., Honolulu, HI 06822. Issues indexed: (13:1-32, #25-27). Subscriptions: $10/yr. (3 issues); Single issue: $4.

HayF: HAYDEN'S FERRY REVIEW, Salima Keegan, Managing ed., Catherine French, Wendy White-Ring, po. eds., Matthews Center, Arizona State U., Tempe, AZ 85287-1502. Issues indexed: (4-5). Subscriptions: $10/yr. (2 issues), $18/2 yrs.; $13/yr., $26/2 yrs. (inst.); Single issues: $5 plus $1 postage.

*HeavenB: HEAVEN BONE, Steven Hirsch, ed., pub., P.O. Box 486, Chester, NY 10918. Issues indexed: (6-7). Subscriptions: $14.95/2 yrs. (4 issues); Single issue: $4.50.

HeliconN: HELICON NINE: The Journal of Women's Arts & Letters, Gloria Vando Hickok, ed., P.O. Box 22412, Kansas City, MO 64113. Issues indexed: (20). Subscriptions: $18/yr. (3 issues), $33/2 yrs., $22/yr. (inst.), plus $1/issue (for.); Single issues: $8-12.

HighP: HIGH PLAINS LITERARY REVIEW, Robert O. Greer, Jr., ed., Joy Harjo, po. ed., 180 Adams St., Suite 250, Denver, CO 80206. Issues indexed: (4:1-3). Subscriptions: $20/yr. (3 issues), $38/2 yrs., plus $5/yr. (for.); Single issues: $7.

HiramPoR: HIRAM POETRY REVIEW, English Dept., Hiram College, Hale Chatfield & Carol Donley, eds., P.O. Box 162, Hiram, OH 44234. Issues indexed: (46) plus supplement #10. Subscriptions: $4/yr. (2 issues); Single issues: $2; Supplements, $4.

HolCrit: THE HOLLINS CRITIC, John Rees Moore, ed., Hollins College, VA 24020. Issues indexed: (26:1-5). Subscriptions: $6/yr., $10/2 yrs., $14/3 yrs.; $7.50/yr., $11.50/2 yrs., $15.50/3 yrs. (for.).

Hudson: THE HUDSON REVIEW, Paula Deitz, Frederick Morgan, eds., 684 Park Ave., New York, NY 10021. Issues indexed: (41:4, 42:1-3). Subscriptions: $20/yr., $38/2 yrs., $56/3 yrs., plus $4/yr. (for.); Single issues: $6; Recent back issues: $5.

IndR: INDIANA REVIEW, Jon Tribble, ed., Will Farmer, J. D. Scrimgeour, po. eds., 316 N. Jordan Ave., Bloomington, IN 47405. Issues indexed: (12:2-3, 13:1). Subscriptions: $12/3 issues, $15/3 issues (inst.); $22/6 issues (ind.), $25/6 issues (inst.); plus $5/3 issues (for.). Single issues: $5.

Interim: INTERIM, A. Wilber Stevens, ed., Dept. of English, U. of Nevada, Las Vegas, NV 89154. Issues indexed: (8:1-2). Subscriptions: $5/yr. (2 issues), $8/2 yrs., $10/3 yrs. (ind.); $8/yr. (lib.), $10/yr. (for.); Single issues: $3, $5 (for.).

InterPR: INTERNATIONAL POETRY REVIEW, Evalyn P. Gill, ed., Box 2047, Greensboro, NC 27402. Issues indexed: (15:2); v. 15 no. 1 not received. Subscriptions: $8/yr. (2 issues); Single issues: $4.

Inti: INTI, Revista de Literatura Hispanica, Roger B. Carmosino, ed., Dept. of Modern Languages, Providence College, Providence, RI 02918. Issues indexed: (29/30). Subscriptions: $25/yr. (2 issues, ind.), $35/yr. (inst.); Single issues: $20, $30 (double issues).

Iowa: IOWA REVIEW, David Hamilton, ed., 308 EPB, U. of Iowa, Iowa City, IA 52242. Issues indexed: (19:1-3). Subscriptions: $15/yr. (3 issues, ind.), $20/yr. (inst.), plus $3/yr. (for.); Single issues: $6.95.

Jacaranda: THE JACARANDA REVIEW, Bruce Kijewski, ed., Dept. of English, U. of California, Los Angeles, CA 90024. Issues indexed: (4:1). Subscriptions: $8/yr. (2 issues, ind.), $12/yr. (inst.).

JamesWR: THE JAMES WHITE REVIEW, A Gay Men's Literary Journal, Greg Baysans, ed., P.O. Box 3356, Traffic Station, Minneapolis, MN 55403. Issues indexed: (6:2-4, 7:1); 6:2, Winter 1989, has "volume 5, number 2" in error. Subscriptions: $12/yr., $20/2 yrs.; $14/yr. (Canada); $17/yr. (other for.); Single issues: $3.

JlNJPo: THE JOURNAL OF NEW JERSEY POETS, Sander Zulauf, ed., County College of Morris, Route 10 & Center Grove Rd., Randolph, NJ 07869. Issues indexed: 1989 (vol. 11, but issue not labeled). Subscriptions: $5/2 issues; Single issues: $4.

*Journal: THE JOURNAL: The Literary Magazine of The Ohio State University, David Citino, ed., The Ohio State U., Dept. of English, 164 W. 17th Ave., Columbus, OH 43210. Issues indexed: (12:2, 13:1). Subscriptions: $5/yr. (2 issues), $10/2 yrs., $15/3 yrs.; Single issues: $3.

Kaleid: KALEIDOSCOPE, International Magazine of Literature, Fine Arts, and Disability, Darshan Perusek, ed., Chris Hewitt (228 W. 71 St., Apt. F, New York, NY 10023), po. ed., United Cerebral Palsy and Services for the Handicapped, 326 Locust St., Akron, OH 44302. Issues indexed: (18-19). Subscriptions: $9/yr. (2 issues, ind.), $12/yr. (inst.), plus $5/yr. (for.); Single issues: $4.50, $7 (for.); Sample issue: $2.

*Kalliope: KALLIOPE: A Journal of Women's Art, Mary Sue Koeppel, ed., Florida Community College at Jacksonville, 3939 Roosevelt Blvd., Jacksonville, FL 32205. Issues indexed: (10:1/2-3, 11:1-3). Subscriptions: $10.50/1 yr. (3 issues), $20/2 yrs.; $18/yr. (inst.); plus $6/yr. (for.); free to women in prison; Single issues: $7; Back issues: $4-8.

KanQ: KANSAS QUARTERLY, Harold Schneider, Ben Nyberg, W. R. Moses, John Rees, Paul McCarthy, eds., Dept. of English, Denison Hall, Kansas State U., Manhattan, KS 66506-0703. Issues indexed: (21:1/2-4). Subscriptions: $20/yr., $35/2 yrs. (USA, Canada, Latin America); $21/yr., $37/2 yrs. (other countries); Single issues: $6; Double issues: $7.50.

KenR: KENYON REVIEW, David H. Lynn, acting ed., David Baker, po. ed., Kenyon College, Gambier, OH 43022. Issues indexed: (NS 11:1-4). Subscriptions: Kenyon Review, P.O. Box 837, Farmingdale, NY 11735; $20/yr., $35/2 yrs., $45/3 yrs. (ind.); $23/yr. (inst.); plus $5 (for.); Single issues: $7; Back issues: $10.

KeyWR: KEY WEST REVIEW, William J. Schlicht, Jr., ed., 9 Ave. G, Key West, FL 33040. Issues indexed: (2:1/2). Subscriptions: P.O. Box 2082, Key West, FL 33045-2082, $17/yr. (4 issues); Single issues: $5, double issues: $10.

Lactuca: LACTUCA, Mike Selender, ed., P.O. Box 621, Suffern, NY 10901. Issues indexed: (12-13). Subscriptions: $10/yr. (3 issues), $13/yr. (for.); Single issues: $3.50, plus $1 (for.).

LakeSR: THE LAKE STREET REVIEW, Kevin FitzPatrick, ed., Box 7188, Minneapolis, MN 55407. Issues indexed: (22). Subscriptions: $4/2 yrs. (2 issues); Single issues: $2.

LaurelR: LAUREL REVIEW, Craig Goad, ed., Green Tower Press, Dept. of English, Northwest Missouri State U., Maryville, MO 64468. Issues indexed: (23:1-2). Subscriptions: $8/yr. (2 issues), $14/2 yrs.; Single issues: $5; Back issues: $4.50.

LetFem: LETRAS FEMENINAS, Asociación de Literatura Femenina Hispánica, Adelaida López de Martínez, ed., Dept. of Modern Languages, U. of Nebraska-Lincoln, Lincoln, NE 68588-0315. Issues indexed: No 1989 issues received. Membership/Subscription: $20/yr; $25/yr. (lib.).

LightY: LIGHT YEAR: The Biennial of Light Verse & Witty Poems, Robert Wallace, ed., Bits Press, Dept. of English, Case Western Reserve U., Cleveland, OH 44106. Issues indexed: not published in 1989. Subscriptions: '87, $13.95; '88/9, $15.95.

Periodicals Indexed

LindLM: LINDEN LANE MAGAZINE, Heberto Padilla, Belkis Cuza Malé, eds., P.O. Box 2384, Princeton, NJ 08543-2384. Issues indexed: (8:1-4). Subscriptions: $12/yr. (ind.), $18/yr. (inst.), $22/yr. (Latin America, Europe); Single issues: $2.

Lips: LIPS, Laura Boss, ed., P.O. Box 1345, Montclair, NJ 07042. Issues indexed: No 1989 issues received. Subscriptions: $9/yr. (3 issues), $12/yr. (inst).; Single issues: $3, $4 (inst.).

LitR: THE LITERARY REVIEW, Walter Cummins, ed., Fairleigh Dickinson U., 285 Madison Ave., Madison, NJ 07940. Issues indexed: (32:2-4, 33:1). Subscriptions: $18/yr., $21/yr. (for.); $30/2 yrs., $36/2 yrs. (for.); Single issues: $5, $6 (for.).

LittleBR: THE LITTLE BALKANS REVIEW: A Southeast Kansas Literary and Graphics Quarterly, Gene DeGruson, ed., 601 Grandview Heights Terrace, Pittsburg, KS 66762. Issues indexed: No 1989 issues received. Subscriptions: $15/yr.; Single issues: $4.

Lyra: LYRA, Lourdes Gil, Iraida Iturralde, eds., P.O. Box 3188, Guttenberg, NJ 07093. Issues indexed: (2:1/2). Subscriptions: $15/yr. (4 issues, ind.), $20/yr. (inst.), plus $5/yr. (for.); Single issues: $4, $6 (for.).

Mairena: MAIRENA: Revista de Crítica y Poesía, Manuel de la Puebla, director, Himalaya 257, Urbanización Monterrey, Río Piedras, PR 00926. Issues indexed: (12:27); "El No. 26 no incluyó ningún verso" -- No. 26 included no poetry. Subscriptions: $6/yr. (2 issues), $10/yr. (inst.), $10/yr. (for.), $15/yr. (for. inst.).

MalR: THE MALAHAT REVIEW, Constance Rooke, ed., P.O. Box 1700, Victoria, B. C., Canada V8W 2Y2. Issues indexed: (86-89). Subscriptions: $15/yr. (4 issues), $40/3 yrs., (ind., USA, Canada); $25/yr. (inst., USA, Canada); $20/yr., $50/3 yrs. (other countries); $10/yr. (stud., USA, Canada); Single issues: $7 (USA, Canada), $8 (other countries).

ManhatPR: MANHATTAN POETRY REVIEW, Elaine Reiman-Fenton, ed., P.O. Box 8207, New York, NY 10150. Issues indexed: No 1989 issues received. Subscriptions: $12/yr. (2 issues); Single issues: $7.

ManhatR: THE MANHATTAN REVIEW, Philip Fried, ed., 440 Riverside Dr., #45, New York, NY 10027. Issues indexed: No 1989 issues published; next issue 5:1, 1990. Subscriptions: $8/2 issues (ind.), $12/2 issues (inst.), plus $2.50/2 issues (outside USA & Canada); Back issues: $4 (ind.), $6 (inst).

*Manoa: MANOA: A Pacific Journal of International Writing, Robert Shapard, ed., English Dept., U. of Hawaii, Honolulu, HI 96822. Issues indexed: (1:1/2). Subscriptions: $12/yr. (2 issues), $22/2 yrs., $30/3 yrs. (ind.); $18/yr., $34/2 yrs., $48/3 yrs. (inst.); plus $12/yr. for airmail; $15/yr. (for. ind.), $18/yr. (for. inst.).

Margin: MARGIN: A Quarterly Magazine for Imaginative Writing and Ideas, Orion Ross, USA ed., 1430 Massachusetts Ave., #306-17, Cambridge, MA 02138-3810. Issues indexed: (8-9). Subscriptions: $20/4 issues; $24/4 issues (Canada); Single issues: $7.

MassR: THE MASSACHUSETTS REVIEW, Mary Heath, Paul Jenkins, Fred Robinson, eds., Anne Halley, Paul Jenkins, po. eds., Memorial Hall, U. of Massachusetts, Amherst, MA 01003. Issues indexed: (30:1-4). Subscriptions: $14/yr. (4 issues, ind.), $17/yr. (lib.), $20/yr. (for.); Single issues: $4.50.

MemphisSR: MEMPHIS STATE REVIEW: name changed to RiverC: RIVER CITY.

Mester: MESTER, Silvia Rosa Zamora, ed., Dept. of Spanish and Portuguese, U. of California, Los Angeles, CA 90024-1532. Issues indexed: (18:1-2). Subscriptions: $12/yr. (2 issues, ind.), $20/yr. (inst.), $8/yr. (stud.), plus $2/yr. outside U.S., Canada, Mexico.

MichQR: MICHIGAN QUARTERLY REVIEW, Laurence Goldstein, ed., 3032 Rackham Bldg., U. of Michigan, Ann Arbor, MI 48109. Issues indexed: (28:1-4). Subscriptions: $13/yr., $24/2 yrs. (ind.), $15/yr. (inst.); Single issues: $3.50; Back issues: $2.

Periodicals Indexed

MidAR: MID-AMERICAN REVIEW, Ken Letko, ed., John Bradley, po. ed., 106 Hanna Hall, Dept. of English, Bowling Green State U., Bowling Green, OH 43403. Issues indexed: (9:1-2). Subscriptions: $6/yr. (2 issues), $10/2 yrs., $14/3 yrs.

MidwQ: THE MIDWEST QUARTERLY: A Journal of Contemporary Thought, James B. M. Schick, ed., Stephen E. Meats, po. ed., Pittsburg State U., Pittsburg, KS 66762-5889. Issues indexed: (30:2-4, 31:1). Subscriptions: $10/yr. plus $3 (for.); Single issues: $3.

*Mildred: MILDRED, Ellen Biss, Kathryn Poppino, eds., P.O. Box 9252, Schenectady, NY 12309. Issues indexed: (3:1-2). Subscriptions: $12/yr. (2 issues), $20/2 yrs., $28/3 yrs.; $14/yr., $24/2 yrs., $30/3 yrs. (inst.); Single issues: $6.

MinnR: THE MINNESOTA REVIEW, Helen Cooper, Marlon Ross, Michael Sprinker, Susan Squier, eds, Helen Cooper, William J. Harris, po. eds., Dept. of English, State U. of New York, Stony Brook, NY 11794-5350. Issues Indexed: (NS 32-33). Subscriptions: $8/yr. (2 issues), $14/2 yrs. (ind.); $16/yr., $28/2 yrs. (inst. & for.); Single issues: $4.50.

MissouriR: THE MISSOURI REVIEW, Speer Morgan, ed., Sherod Santos, Garrett Kaoru Hongo, Lunne McMahon, po. eds., Dept. of English, 107 Tate Hall, U. of Missouri, Columbia, MO 65211. Issues indexed: (12:1-3). Subscriptions: $12/yr. (3 issues), $21/2 yrs.; Single issues: $5.

MissR: MISSISSIPPI REVIEW, Frederick Barthelme, ed., The Center for Writers, U. of Southern Mississippi, Southern Station, Box 5144, Hattiesburg, MS 39406-5144. Issues indexed: (17:1/2-3, 18:1, issues 49/50-52); in the 1988 index, issues 46-48 were incorrected listed as 15:1-2/3 instead of 16:1-2/3. The 1988 issue numbers were correct. Subscriptions: $15/yr. (2 issues), $28/2 yrs., $40/3 yrs., plus $2/yr. (for.); Single issues: usually $7.50.

MoodySI: MOODY STREET IRREGULARS, Joy Walsh, ed., P.O. Box 157, Clarence Center, NY 14032. Issues indexed: (20/21). Subscriptions: $10/4 single, 2 double issues (ind.), $15/4 single, 2 double issues (lib.); Single issues: $3, double issues: $5.

MSS: MSS, L. M. Rosenberg, ed., Box 530, State U. of NY at Binghamton, Binghamton, NY 13901. Issues indexed: (6:3); superseded by New Myths, Robert Mooney, ed., State U. of New York, Binghamton, NY 13901.

Nat: THE NATION, Victor Navasky, ed., Grace Schulman, po. ed., 72 Fifth Ave., New York, NY 10011. Issues indexed: (248:1-24, 249:1-22). Subscriptions: $36/yr., $64/2 yrs., plus $14/yr. (for.); Single issues: $1.75; Back issues: $3, $4 (for.). Send subscription correspondence to: P.O. Box 1953, Marion, OH 43305.

NegC: NEGATIVE CAPABILITY, Sue Walker, ed., 62 Ridgelawn Dr. East, Mobile, AL 36608. Issues indexed: (9:1-2). Subscriptions: $12/yr. (3 issues, ind.), $16/yr. (inst., for.); Single issues: $5.

NewAW: NEW AMERICAN WRITING, Maxine Chernoff, Paul Hoover, eds., OINK! Press, 2920 West Pratt, Chicago, IL 60645. Issues indexed: (5). Subscriptions: $12/yr. (2 issues); Single issues: $6.

NewEngR: NEW ENGLAND REVIEW AND BREAD LOAF QUARTERLY, T. R. Hummer, senior ed, Maura High, ed., Middlebury College, Middlebury, VT 05753. Issues indexed: (11:3-4, 12:1-2). Subscriptions: $12/yr. (4 issues), $22/2 yrs., $33/3 yrs. (ind.); $18/yr., $26/2 yrs., $33/3 yrs. (inst.); plus $3/yr. (for.); Single issues: $4-6.

NewL: NEW LETTERS, James McKinley, ed., U. of Missouri-Kansas City, 5100 Rockhill Rd., Kansas City, MO 64110. Issues indexed: (55:3-4, 56:1-2/3). Subscriptions: $17/yr. (4 issues), $28/2 yrs., $55/5 yrs. (ind.); $20/yr., $34/2 yrs., $65/5 yrs. (lib.); Single issues: $4.

NewOR: NEW ORLEANS REVIEW, John Biguenet, John Mosier, eds., Box 195, Loyola U., New Orleans, LA 70118. Issues indexed: (16:1-4). Subscriptions: $25/yr. (ind.), $30/yr. (inst.), $35/yr. (for.); Single issues: $9.

Periodicals Indexed

NewRena: THE NEW RENAISSANCE, Louise T. Reynolds, ed., James E. A. Woodbury, po. ed., 9 Heath Road, Arlington, MA 02174. Issues indexed: (7:3, #23). Subscriptions: $11.50/3 issues, $22/6 issues; $13.50/3 issues, $25/6 issues (Canada, Mexico, Europe); $14.50/3 issues, $27/6 issues (elsewhere); Single issues: $7.30, $7.60 (Europe, Mexico, Canda), $7.75 (elsewhere).

NewRep: THE NEW REPUBLIC, Martin Peretz, ed., Richard Howard, po. ed., 1220 19th St. N.W., Washington, DC 20036. Issues indexed: (200:1-26, 201:1-26). Subscriptions: $59.97/yr., $74.97/yr. (Canada), $89.97/yr. (elsewhere). Back issues: $3.50. Single issues: $2.95. Subscription Service Dept., The New Republic, P.O. Box 56515, Boulder, CO 80322.

NewYorker: THE NEW YORKER, 25 W. 43rd St., New York, NY 10036. Issues indexed: (64:46-52, 65:1-45). Subscriptions: $32/yr., $52/2 yrs.; $50/yr. (Canada); $56/yr. (other for.); Single issues: $1.75; Subscription correspondence to: Box 56447, Boulder, CO 80322.

NewYRB: THE NEW YORK REVIEW OF BOOKS, Robert B. Silvers, Barbara Epstein, eds., 250 W. 57th St., New York, NY 10107. Issues indexed: (35:21/22, 36:1-20). Subscriptions: $37.50/yr.; Single issues: $2.25; NY Review of Books, Subscription Service Dept., P.O. Box 940, Farmingdale, NY 11737.

Nimrod: NIMROD, Francine Ringold, ed., Joan Flint, Manly Johnson, Dee Ann Short, Mary Cantrell, po. eds., Arts and Humanities Council of Tulsa, 2210 S. Main St., Tulsa, OK 74114. Issues indexed: (32:2, 33:1). Subscriptions: $10/yr. (2 issues), $13/yr. (for.); Single issues: $6.95.

NoAmR: THE NORTH AMERICAN REVIEW, Robley Wilson, Jr., ed., Peter Cooley, po. ed., U. of Northern Iowa, Cedar Falls, IA 50614. Issues indexed: (274:1-4). Subscriptions: $11/yr., $14/yr. (Canada, Latin America), $15/yr. (elsewhere); Single issues: $3, $4 (Canada).

NoDaQ: NORTH DAKOTA QUARTERLY, Robert W. Lewis, ed., Jay Meek, po. ed., Box 8237, U. of North Dakota, Grand Forks, ND 58202. Issues indexed: (57:1-4). Subscriptions: $10/yr., $14/yr. (for.); Single issues: $5.

Northeast: NORTHEAST, John Judson, ed., Juniper Press, 1310 Shorewood Dr., La Crosse, WI 54601. Issues indexed: (Ser. 5:1). Subscriptions: $33 (2 issues, ind.), $38 (inst.), includes 2-4 books in addition to NORTHEAST; Single issues: $3.

Notus: NOTUS, New Writing, Pat Smith, ed., 2420 Walter Dr., Ann Arbor, MI 48103. Issues indexed: (4:1-2). Subscriptions: $10/yr. (2 issues, U.S. & Canada, ind.), $14/yr. (elsewhere), $20/yr. (inst.).

NowestR: NORTHWEST REVIEW, John Witte, ed. & po. ed., 369 PLC, U. of Oregon, Eugene, OR 97403. Issues indexed: (27:1-3). Subscriptions: $11/yr. (3 issues), $21/2 yrs., $30/3 yrs.; $10/yr., $20/2 yrs. (stud.); plus $2/yr. (for.); Single issues: $4.

Obs: OBSIDIAN II: Black Literature in Review, Gerald Barrax, ed., Dept. of English, Box 8105, North Carolina State U., Raleigh, NC 27695-8105. Issues indexed: (2:1, 3; 3:1-3; 4:1-3); 1:3, 2:2 & 3:1 not received; 3:1 indexed from table of contents. Subscriptions: $12/yr. (3 issues), $20/2 yrs.; $13/yr. (Canada), $15/yr. (other for.); Single issues: $5; Double issues: $10.

OhioR: THE OHIO REVIEW, Wayne Dodd, ed., Ellis Hall, Ohio U., Athens, OH 45701-2979. Issues indexed: (43-44). Subscriptions: $12/yr. (3 issues), $30/3 yrs.; Single issues: $4.25.

*Ometeca: OMETECA: Ciencia y Literatura, Science & Literature, Ciência e literatura, Rafael Catalá, ed., P.O. Box 450, Corrales, NM 87048. Issues Indexed: (1:1). Subscriptions: $16/yr. (2 issues) (USA, Canada, Mexico); $20/yr. (elsewhere).

OntR: ONTARIO REVIEW, Raymond J. Smith, ed., 9 Honey Brook Dr., Princeton, NJ 08540. Issues indexed: (30-31). Subscriptions: $10/yr. (2 issues), $18/2 yrs., $24/3 yrs., plus $2/yr. (for.); Single issues: $4.95.

Os: OSIRIS, Andrea Moorhead, ed., Box 297, Deerfield, MA 01342. Issues indexed: (28-29); the 1988 Index included numbers 26 & 27, not 26 & 26 as stated. Subscriptions: $8/2 issues, $10/2 issues (inst.). Single issues: $4.

Outbr: OUTERBRIDGE, Charlotte Alexander, ed., Linda Principe, po. ed., English Dept. (A323), College of Staten Island, 715 Ocean Terrace, Staten Island, NY 10301. Issues indexed: (20). Subscriptions: $5/yr. (1 issue).

*OxfordM: OXFORD MAGAZINE, Constance Pierce, editorial advisor, Bachelor Hall, Miami U., Oxford, OH 45056. Issues indexed: (5:1-2). Subscriptions: No information.

PacificR: THE PACIFIC REVIEW: A Magazine of Poetry and Prose, Allison Deputy, ed., Matt Cofer, Po. ed., Rodney Simard, , faculty ed., Dept. of English, California State U., 5500 University Parkway, San Bernardino, CA 92407-2397. Issues indexed: (7). Single issues: $4; $6.50 (inst.). Published annually.

Paint: PAINTBRUSH: A Journal of Poetry, Translations, and Letters, Ben Bennani, ed., Division of Language and Literature, Northeast Missouri State U., Kirksville, MO 63501. Issues indexed: (vol. 16); Note: in the 1988 volume, "(14:29-30)" should have been listed as (15:29-30). Subscriptions: $9/yr. (2 issues, ind.), $12/yr. (inst.); Single issues: $7; Back issues: $7.

PaintedB: PAINTED BRIDE QUARTERLY, Louis Camp, Joanna DiPaolo, eds., Painted Bride Arts Center, 230 Vine St., Philadelphia, PA 19106. Issues indexed: (37-39). Subscriptions: $16/yr. (4 issues), $28/2 yrs., $20/yr. (lib, inst.); Single issues: $5. Distributed free to inmates.

*PaperAir: PAPER AIR, Gil Ott, ed. and pub., Singing Horse Press, P.O. Box 40034, Philadelphia, PA 19106. Issues indexed: (4:2). Subscriptions: $12/3 issues (ind.), $24/3 issues (lib.); Single issues: $7.

ParisR: THE PARIS REVIEW, George A. Plimpton, Peter Matthiessen, Donald Hall, Robert B. Silvers, Blair Fuller, Maxine Groffsky, eds., Patricia Storace, po. ed., 541 East 72nd St., New York, NY 10021. Issues indexed: (31:110-113). Subscriptions: $20/4 issues, $40/8 issues, $60/12 issues, $1000/life, plus $5/4 issues (for.); Single issues: $6; Subscription address: 45-39 171 Place, Flushing, NY 11358.

PartR: PARTISAN REVIEW, William Phillips, ed., Boston U., 236 Bay State Rd., Boston, MA 02215. Issues indexed: (56:1-4). Subscriptions: $18/yr. (4 issues), $33/2 yrs., $47/3 yrs.; $21/yr., $36/2 yrs. (for.); $28/yr. (inst.); Single issues: $5 plus $1 per issue postage and handling.

PassN: PASSAGES NORTH, Elinor Benedict, ed., Bay Arts Writers' Guild of the William Bonifas Fine Arts Center, Inc., Escanaba, MI 49829. Issues indexed: (10:1-2). Subscriptions: $2/yr., $5/3 yrs; Single issues: $1.50.

Pembroke: PEMBROKE MAGAZINE, Shelby Stephenson, ed., Box 60, Pembroke State U., Pembroke, NC 28372. Issues indexed: (21). Subscriptions: $3/issue (USA, Canada, Mexico), $3.50/issue (for.).

PennR: THE PENNSYLVANIA REVIEW, Ed Ochester, executive ed., Jan Beatty, po. ed., 526 Cathedral of Learning, U. of Pittsburgh, Pittsburgh, PA 15260. Issues indexed: No 1989 issues published. Subscriptions: $9/yr., $15/2 yrs.; Single issues: $5.

Pequod: PEQUOD, Mark Rudman, ed., Dept. of English, Room 200, New York U., 19 University Place, New York, NY 10003. Issues indexed: (26/27, 28/29/30). Subscriptions: $10/yr. (2 issues, ind.), $18/2 yrs.; $17/yr., $30/2 yrs. (inst.); plus $3/yr. (for.); Single issues: $5.

Pig: PIG IRON, Jim Villani, Naton Leslie, Rose Sayre, eds., Pig Iron Press, P.O. Box 237, Youngstown, OH 44501. Issues indexed: (15). Subscriptions: $8/yr., $15/2 yrs. (ind.); $10/yr., $19/2 yrs. (inst.); Single issues: $8.95.

Periodicals Indexed

PikeF: THE PIKESTAFF FORUM, Robert D. Sutherland, James R. Scrimgeour, eds./pubs., P.O. Box 127, Normal, IL 61761. Issues indexed: No 1989 issues received. Subscriptions: $10/6 issues; Single issues: $2.

Plain: PLAINSONGS, Dwight Marsh, ed., Dept. of English, Hastings College, Hastings, NE 68902. Issues indexed: (9:2-3, 10:1). Subscriptions: $8/yr. (3 issues).

Ploughs: PLOUGHSHARES, DeWitt Henry, executive director, Joyce Peseroff, po. ed., Div. of Writing, Publishing and Literature, Emerson College, 100 Beacon St., Boston, MA 02116. Issues indexed: (15:1, 2/3, 4). Subscriptions: $15/yr. (ind.), $19/yr. (for. ind.); $18/yr. (inst.), $22/yr. (for. inst.). Single issues: $5.95-$7.95.

Poem: POEM, Huntsville Literary Association, Nancy Frey Dillard, ed., c/o English Dept., U. of Alabama, Huntsville, AL 35899. Issues indexed: (61-62). Subscriptions: $10/yr.; Back issues: $5; subscription address: Huntsville Literary Association, P.O. Box 919,, Huntsville, AL 35804.

PoetC: POET AND CRITIC, Neal Bowers, ed., 203 Ross Hall, Iowa State U., Ames, IA 50011. Issues indexed: (20:2-3, 21:1). Subscriptions: Iowa State U. Press, South State St., Ames, IA 50010, $16/yr., plus $3/yr. (for.); Single issues: $6.

PoetL: POET LORE, Philip K. Jason, Roland Flint, Executive eds., The Writer's Center, 7815 Old Georgetown Rd., Bethesda, MD 20814. Issues Indexed: (84:1-4). Subscriptions: $8/yr. (Writer's Center members); $12/yr. (ind.); $20/yr. (inst.), plus $5/yr. (for.); Single issues: $4.50; Samples: $4.

Poetry: POETRY, Joseph Parisi, ed., 60 W. Walton St., Chicago, IL 60610. Issues indexed: (153:4-6, 153:1-6, 155:1/2-3). Subscriptions: $25/yr. (ind.); $31/yr. (for.); $27/yr. (inst.); $33/yr. (for. inst.); Single issues: $2.50 plus $1 postage; Back issues: $3 plus $1 postage.

PoetryE: POETRY EAST, Richard Jones, Kate Daniels, eds., Dept. of English, 802 W. Belden Ave., DePaul Univ., Chicago, IL 60614. Issues indexed: (27-28). Subscriptions: $10/yr.; Single issues: $6.

PoetryNW: POETRY NORTHWEST, David Wagoner, ed., U. of Washington, 4045 Brooklyn Ave., NE, Seattle, WA 98105. Issues indexed: (30:1-4); Note: vol. 29 was indexed in the 1988 volume, not vol. 28 as was printed there; vol. 28 was indexed in the 1987 volume. Subscriptions: $10/yr., $12/yr. (for.); Single issues: $3, $3.50 (for.).

PottPort: THE POTTERSFIELD PORTFOLIO, Peggy Amirault, Barbara Cottrell, Donalee Moulton-Barrett, eds., Crazy Quilt Press, c/o 19 Oakhill Drive, Halifax, Nova Scotia B3M 2V3 Canada. Issues indexed: None; vol. 11 not received. Subscriptions: $12/3 yrs. (ind.), $15/3 yrs. (inst.); $15/3 yrs. (USA, for. ind.), $18/3 yrs. (USA, for. inst., USA); Single issues: $4.50.

PraF: PRAIRIE FIRE, Andris Taskans, managing ed., Kristjana Gunnars, po. ed., 423-100 Arthur Street, Winnipeg, Manitoba R3B 1H3 Canada. Issues indexed: (10:1-4, #46-49). Subscriptions: $22/yr., $40/2 yrs. (ind.); $28/yr. (inst.), plus $8 (for.); Single issues: $6.95.

PraS: PRAIRIE SCHOONER, Hilda Raz, ed., 201 Andrews Hall, U. of Nebraska, Lincoln, NE 68588-0334. Issues indexed: (63:1-4). Subscriptions: $15/yr., $28/2 yrs., $39/3 yrs. (ind.); $19/yr. (lib.); Single issues: $4.

Prima: PRIMAVERA, Lisa Grayson, Elizabeth Harter, Ruth Young, eds., U. of Chicago, 1212 East 59th, Chicago, IL 60637. Issues indexed: (13). Single issues: $6; Back issues: $5.

Quarry: QUARRY, Steven Heighton, ed., Box 1061, Kingston, Ontario K7L 4Y5 Canada. Issues indexed: (38:1-4). Subscriptions: $18/yr. (4 issues), $30/2 yrs. (8 issues); Single issues: $5.

QRL: QUARTERLY REVIEW OF LITERATURE, T. & R. Weiss, 26 Haslet Ave., Princeton, NJ 08540. Issues indexed: (Poetry eries 9: vol. 28/29). Subscriptions: $20/2 volumes (paper), $20/volume (cloth, inst.).

15

Periodicals Indexed

QW: QUARTERLY WEST, Tom Hazuka, Kevin J. Ryan, eds.; C. F. Pinkerton, po. ed., 317 Olpin Union, U. of Utah, Salt Lake City, UT 84112. Issues indexed: (28-29). Subscriptions: $8.50/yr. (2 issues), $16/2 yrs.; $12.50/yr., $24/2 yrs. (for.); Single issues: $4.50.

RagMag: RAG MAG, Beverly Voldseth, ed., Box 12, Goodhue, MN 55027. Issues indexed: (7:1). Subscriptions: $8/yr. (2 issues), $12/yr. (inst.); Single issues: $4.50.

Rampike: RAMPIKE, Karl Jirgens, Jim Francis, James Gray, eds., 95 Rivercrest Road, Toronto, Ontario M6S 4H7 Canada. Issues indexed: (6:1-3). Subscriptions: $14/yr. (2 issues); Single issues: $7.

Raritan: RARITAN, Richard Poirier, ed., Rutgers U., 165 College Ave., New Brunswick, NJ 08903. Issues indexed: (8:3-4, 9:1-2). Subscriptions: $16/yr., $26/2 yrs. (ind.); $20/yr., $30/2 yrs. (inst.); plus $4/yr (for.); Single issues: $5; Back issues: $6.

RedBass: RED BASS, Jay Murphy, ed., 2425 Burgundy St., New Orleans, LA 701 17. Issues indexed: (14). Subscriptions: $10/2 issues (ind.), $15 (inst., for.); Single issues: $5.

RiverC: RIVER CITY (formerly MemphisSR: MEMPHIS STATE REVIEW), Sharon Bryan, ed., Dept. of English, Memphis State U., Memphis, TN 38152. Issues indexed: (9:1, 10:1). Subscriptions: $6/yr. (ind., 2 issues), $7/yr. (inst).; Single issues: $4.

RiverS: RIVER STYX, Jennifer Atkinson, ed., 14 South Euclid, St. Louis, MO 63108. Issues indexed: (28-30). Subscriptions: $14/3 issues (ind.); $24/3 issues (inst.); Single issues: $5.

Rohwedder: ROHWEDDER, Nancy Antell, Robert Dassanowsky-Harris, Hans Jurgen Schacht, eds., P.O. Box 29490, Los Angeles, CA 90029. Issues indexed: No 1989 issues published. Subscriptions: $12/4 issues (USA, Canada, Mexico, ind.); $18/4 issues (inst.); $16/4 issues (other for., surface mail, plus $1/copy airmail); Single issues: $4.

Salm: SALMAGUNDI, Robert Boyers, ed., Skidmore College, Saratoga Springs, NY 12866. Issues indexed: (81, 82/83, 84). Subscriptions: $12/yr., $18/2 yrs. (ind.); $16/yr., $25/2 yrs. (inst.); Plus $2/yr. (for.); Single issues: $6.

*Screens: SCREENS AND TASTED PARALLELS, Terrel Hale, ed. & pub., 3032 Emerson St., Palo Alto, CA 94306. Issues indexed: (1). Subscriptions: $10/2 issues (ind.); $15 (inst.); Single issues: $6.

SenR: SENECA REVIEW, Deborah Tall, ed., Hobart & William Smith Colleges, Geneva, NY 14456. Issues indexed: (19:1-2). Subscriptions: $8/yr. (2 issues), $15/2 yrs.; Single issues: $5.

Sequoia: SEQUOIA: The Stanford Literary Journal, Annie Finch, po. ed ., Storke Publications Building, Stanford, CA 94305. Issues indexed: (32:2, 33:1). Subscriptions: $10/yr. (2 issues), $11/yr. (for.), $15/yr. (inst.); Single issues: $5.

SewanR: THE SEWANEE REVIEW, George Core, ed., U. of the South, Sewanee, TN 37375. Issues indexed: (97:1-4). Subscriptions: $15/yr., $27/2 yrs., $38/3 yrs. (ind.); $20/yr., $37/2 yrs., $54/3 yrs. (inst.); plus $4/yr. (for.); Single issues: $5; Back issues: $6-10.

Shen: SHENANDOAH, Dabney Stuart, ed., Washington and Lee U., Box 722, Lexington, VA 24450. Issues indexed: (39:1-4). Subscriptions: $11/yr., $18/2 yrs., $25/3 yrs.; $14/yr., $24/2 yrs., $33/3 yrs. (for.); Single issues: $3.50; Back issues: $6.

SilverFR: SILVERFISH REVIEW, Rodger Moody, ed., P.O. Box 3541, Eugene, OR 97403. Issues indexed: (16-18). Subscriptions: $9/3 issues (ind.), $12/3 issues (inst.), Single issues: $4.

SingHM: SING HEAVENLY MUSE!: Women's Poetry and Prose, Sue Ann Martinson, ed., P.O. Box 13299, Minneapolis, MN 55414. Issues indexed: (16). Subscriptions: $17/3 issues (ind.), $21/3 issues (inst.); Single issues: $7 + $2 postage & handling.

Periodicals Indexed

TriQ: TRIQUARTERLY, Reginald Gibbons, ed., Northwestern U., 2020 Ridge Ave., Evanston, IL 60208. Issues indexed: (74-77). Subscriptions: $18/yr., $32/2 yrs., $250/life (ind.); $26/yr., $44/2 yrs., $300/life (inst.), plus $4/yr. (for.); Single issues: usually $7.95; Sample copies: $4.

Turnstile: TURNSTILE, Jill Benz, Lindsey Crittenden, Ann Biester Deane, Twisne Fan, Sara Gordonson, Mitchell Nauffts, Paolo Pepe, Lisa Samson, Amit Shah, eds., 175 Fifth Avenue, Suite 2348, New York, NY 10010. Issues indexed: No 1989 issues published. Subscriptions: $12/2 issues, $24/4 issues; Single issues: $6.50.

US1: US 1 WORKSHEETS, Sondra Gash, ed., David A. Heinlein, Virginia Lockwood, Norma Voorhees Sheard, po eds., US 1 Poets' Cooperative, 21 Lake Dr., Roosevelt, NJ 08555. (22/23). Subscriptions: $6/2 issues; Single issues: $4.

Verse: VERSE, Henry Hart, U. S. ed., Dept. of English, College of William and Mary, Williamsburg, VA 23185. Issues indexed: (6:1-3). Subscriptions: $12/yr. (3 issues); Single issues: $4.

VirQR: THE VIRGINIA QUARTERLY REVIEW, Staige D. Blackford, ed., Gregory Orr, po. consultant, One West Range, Charlottesville, VA 22903. Issues indexed: (65:1-4). Subscriptions: $15/yr., $22/2 yrs., $30/3 yrs. (ind.); $22/yr., $30/2 yrs., $50/3 yrs. (inst.); plus $3/yr. (for.); Single issues: $5.

Vis: VISIONS INTERNATIONAL, Bradley R. Strahan, po. ed./pub., Black Buzzard Press, 4705 South 8th Rd., Arlington, VA 22204. Issues indexed: (29-31). Subscriptions: $11/yr., $21.50/2 yrs. (ind.); $33/3 yrs. (lib.); Single issues: $4-$4.50.

*WashR: WASHINGTON REVIEW, Clarissa K. Wittenberg, ed., P.O. Box 50132, Washington, DC 20091. Issues indexed: (14:4-6. 15:1-4). Subscriptions: $12/yr. (6 issues), $20/2 yrs.; Single issues: $3.

WeberS: WEBER STUDIES: An Interdisciplinary Humanities Journal, Neila Seshachari, ed., Weber State College, School of Arts and Humanities, Ogden, UT 84408-1904. Issues indexed: (6:1-2). Subscriptions: $5/yr. (2 issues), $10/yr. (inst.); plus actual postage extra per year (for.); Back issues: $5; Single issues: $2.75.

WebR: WEBSTER REVIEW, Nancy Schapiro, ed., Pamela White Hadas, Jerred Metz, po. eds., Webster U., 470 E. Lockwood, Webster Groves, MO 63119. Issues indexed: (14:1). Subscriptions: $5/yr. (2 issues); Single issues: $2.50.

WestB: WEST BRANCH, Karl Patten, Robert Taylor, eds., Bucknell Hall, Bucknell U., Lewisburg, PA 17837. Issues indexed: (23-25). Subscriptions: $5/yr. (2 issues), $8/2 yrs.; Single issues: $3; double issues $5.

WestCR: WEST COAST REVIEW, a Literary Quarterly, Harvey De Roo, ed., Dept. of English, Simon Fraser U., Burnaby, B.C. V5A 1S6 Canada. Issues indexed: (23:3-4). Subscriptions: $14/yr. (ind., 4 issues), $18/yr. (inst.); Single issues: $4.

WestHR: WESTERN HUMANITIES REVIEW, Barry Weller, Charles Berger, eds., Richard Howard, po. ed., U. of Utah, Salt Lake City, UT 84112. Issues indexed: (43:1-4). Subscriptions: $18/yr. (4 issues, ind.), $24/yr. (inst.); Single issues: $5.

WilliamMR: THE WILLIAM AND MARY REVIEW, William Clark, ed., Susan Taylor, Christopher Vitiello, po. eds., College of William and Mary, Williamsburg, VA 23185. Issues indexed: (27). Subscriptions: $4.50/issue, plus $1.50 (for.); Single issues: $5.

WillowS: WILLOW SPRINGS, Gillian Conoley, ed., Paige Kenney, po. ed., PUB P.O. Box 1063, MS-1, Eastern Washington U., Cheney, WA 99004. Issues Indexed: (23-24). Subscriptions: $7/yr. (2 issues), $13/2 yrs.; Single issues: $4.

Wind: WIND, Quentin R. Howard, ed., RFD Route 1, Box 809K, Pikeville, KY 41501. Issues indexed: (19:64-65). Subscriptions: $7/3 issues (ind.), $8/3 issues (inst.), $12/3 issues (for.); Single issues: $2.50; $5 (for.).

Periodicals Indexed

WindO: THE WINDLESS ORCHARD, Robert Novak, ed., English Dept., Indiana-Purdue U., Fort Wayne, IN 46805. Issues indexed: (51-52). Subscriptions: $8/yr. (4 issues), $20/3 yrs.; Single issues: $3.

Witness: WITNESS, Peter Stine, ed., 31000 Northwestern Highway, Suite 200, Farmington Hills, MI 48018. Issues indexed: (2:1, 2/3, 4; 3:1, 2/3). Subscriptions: $16/yr. (4 issues), $28/2 yrs.; $22/yr., $40/2 yrs. (inst.); plus $4/yr. (for.); Single copies: $5.

WorldO: WORLD ORDER, Firuz Kazemzadeh, Betty J. Fisher, Howard Garey, James D. Stokes, eds., National Spiritual Assembly of the Baha'is of the United States, 415 Linden Ave., Wilmette, IL 60091. Issues indexed: (21:3/4-22:1/2). Subscriptions: $10/yr., $18/2 yrs. (USA, Canada, Mexico); $15/yr., $28/2 yrs. (elsewhere); $20/yr., $38/2 yrs. (for. airmail); Single issues: $3.

WormR: THE WORMWOOD REVIEW, Marvin Malone, ed., P.O. Box 8840, Stockton, CA 95208-0840. Issues indexed: (29:1, 2/3, 4; #113, 114/115, 116). Subscriptions: $8/4 issues (ind.), $10/4 issues (inst.); Single issues: $4.

Writ: WRIT, Roger Greenwald, ed., Innis College, U. of Toronto, 2 Sussex Ave., Toronto, ON M5S 1J5 Canada. Issues indexed: No 1989 issues published; No. 21 published in 1990. Subscriptions: $12/2 issues (US funds outside Canada); Back issues: $5-10.

Writer: THE WRITER, Sylvia K. Burack, ed. & pub., 120 Boylston St., Boston, MA 02116. Issues indexed: (101:1-2, 4-5, 7; 102:1-12); in the 1987 Index Volume, vol. "103" should have been vol. "101". Subscriptions: $23/yr., $45/2 yrs., $66/3 yrs.; plus $8/yr. (for.); $10/6 issues for new subscribers; Single issues: $2.

WritersF: WRITERS' FORUM, Alexander Blackburn, Victoria McCabe, Craig Lesley, Bret Lott, eds., P.O. Box 7150, U. of Colorado, Colorado Springs, CO 80933-7150. Issues indexed: (15). Subscriptions: $8.95/yr. plus $1.05 postage and handling; Back issue sample: $5.95 plus $1.05 postage and handling.

YaleR: THE YALE REVIEW, Penelope Laurans, ed., J. D. McClatchy, po. ed., Yale U., 1902A Yale Station, New Haven, CT 06520. Issues indexed: (78:2-4, 79:1). Subscriptions: $18/yr. (ind.), $27/yr. (inst.), plus $3/yr. (for.); Single issues: $7; Back issues: Prices on request; Subscription office: Yale University Press, 92A Yale Station, New Haven, CT 06520.

YellowS: YELLOW SILK, Journal of Erotic Arts, Lily Pond, ed., pub., P.O. Box 6374, Albany, CA 94706. Issues indexed: (29-32). Subscriptions: $24/yr. (ind.), $30/yr. (lib., inst.), plus $6/yr. (for. surface) or $20/yr. (for. air). Single issues: $6.

Zyzzyva: ZYZZYVA: The Last Word, West Coast Writers & Artists, Howard Junker, ed, 41 Sutter St., Suite 1400, San Francisco, CA 94104. Issues indexed: (5:1-4, #17-20). Subscriptions: $20/yr. (4 issues), $32/2 yrs; $28/yr. (inst.); $30/yr. (for.); Single copies: $8 post paid.

Alphabetical List of Journals Indexed, with Acronyms

Abraxas : Abraxas
Acts: A Journal of New Writing : Acts
Aerial : Aerial
The Agni Review : Agni
Alpha Beat Soup : AlphaBS
Amelia : Amelia
The American Poetry Review : AmerPoR
The American Scholar : AmerS
The American Voice : AmerV
The Americas Review : Americas
Another Chicago Magazine : AnotherCM
Antaeus : Antaeus
The Anthology of New England Writers : AnthNEW
The Antigonish Review : AntigR
The Antioch Review : AntR
Apalachee Quarterly : ApalQ
Arefto : Arefto
Artful Dodge : ArtfulD
Ascent : Ascent
The Atlantic : Atlantic

Ball State University Forum : BallSUF
Bamboo Ridge : BambooR
The Bellingham Review : BellR
Bellowing Ark : BellArk
The Beloit Poetry Journal : BelPoJ
The Bilingual Review/La Revista Bilingüe : BilingR
Black American Literature Forum : BlackALF
Black Warrior Review : BlackWR
Blue Buildings : BlueBldgs
Blueline : Blueline
Bogg : Bogg
Bomb Magazine : Bomb
Boston Review : BostonR
Boulevard : Boulevard
Boundary 2 : Bound
Brooklyn Review : BrooklynR

Caliban : Caliban
California Quarterly : CalQ
Callaloo : Callaloo
Calyx : Calyx
Canadian Literature : CanLit
The Cape Rock : CapeR
The Capilano Review : CapilR
Carolina Quarterly : CarolQ
The Centennial Review : CentR
Central Park : CentralP
Chaminade Literary Review : ChamLR
Changing Men : ChangingM
The Chariton Review : CharR
The Chattahoochee Review : ChatR
Chelsea : Chelsea
Chicago Review : ChiR
The Christian Century : ChrC
Cimarron Review : CimR

Cincinnati Poetry Review : CinPR
Clockwatch Review : ClockR
College English : ColEng
Colorado Review : ColR
Columbia : Colum
Commonweal : Comm
Conditions : Cond
Confrontation : Confr
Conjunctions : Conjunc
The Connecticut Poetry Review : ConnPR
Contact II : Contact
Crab Creek Review : CrabCR
Crazyhorse : Crazy
Cream City Review : CreamCR
Cross-Canada Writers' Quarterly : CrossC
Crosscurrents : CrossCur
Cuadernos de Poética : CuadP
Cumberland Poetry Review : CumbPR
Cutbank : CutB

Dandelion : Dandel
The Dekalb Literary Arts Journal : DekalbLAJ
Denver Quarterly : DenQ
Descant : Descant

Emerald Coast Review : EmeraldCR
English Journal : EngJ
Epoch : Epoch
Event: Journal of the Contemporary Arts : Event
The Evergreen Chronicles : EvergreenC

Farmer's Market : Farm
Field: Contemporary Poetry and Poetics : Field
Five Fingers Riview : FiveFR
The Florida Review : FloridaR
Footwork : Footwork
Four Quarters : FourQ
Free Lunch : FreeL

Gargoyle Magazine : Gargoyle
Georgia Review : GeoR
Gettysburg Review : GettyR
Graham House Review : GrahamHR
Grain : Grain
Grand Street : GrandS
The Greensboro Review : GreensboroR

The Hampden-Sydney Poetry Reivew : HampSPR
Hanging Loose : HangL
Harper's Magazine : Harp
The Harvard Advocate : HarvardA
Hawaii Review : HawaiiR
Hayden's Ferry Review : HayF
Heaven Bone : HeavenB
Helicon Nine : HeliconN
High Plains Literary Review : HighP
Hiram Poetry Review : HiramPoR
The Hollins Critic : HolCrit
The Hudson Review : Hudson

Indiana Review : IndR
Interim : Interim
International Poetry Review : InterPR
Inti : Inti
Iowa Review : Iowa

Alphabetical List of Journals

The Jacaranda Review : Jacaranda
The James White Review : JamesWR
The Journal : Journal
The Journal of New Jersey Poets : JlNJPo

Kaleidoscope : Kaleid
Kalliope : Kalliope
Kansas Quarterly : KanQ
Kenyon Review : KenR
Key West Review : KeyWR

Lactuca : Lactuca
The Lake Street Review : LakeSR
Laurel Review : LaurelR
Letras Femeninas : LetFem
Light Year : LightY
Linden Lane Magazine : LindLM
Lips : Lips
The Literary Review : LitR
The Little Balkans Review : LittleBR
Lyra : Lyra

Mairena : Revista de Crítica y Poesía
The Malahat Review : MalR
Manhattan Poetry Review : ManhatPR
The Manhattan Review : ManhatR
Manoa : Manoa
Margin : Margin
The Massachusetts Review : MassR
Memphis State Review : *Name changed to* River City : RiverC
Mester : Mester
Michigan Quarterly Review : MichQR
Mid-American Review : MidAR
The Midwest Quarterly : MidwQ
Mildred : Mildred
The Minnesota Review : MinnR
Mississippi Review : MissR
The Missouri Review : MissouriR
Moody Street Irregulars : MoodySI
Mss : MSS

The Nation : Nat
Negative Capability : NegC
New American Writing : NewAW
New England Review And Bread Loaf Quarterly : NewEngR
New Letters : NewL
New Orleans Review : NewOR
The New Renaissance : NewRena
The New Republic : NewRep
The New York Review Of Books : NewYRB
The New Yorker : NewYorker
Nimrod : Nimrod
The North American Review : NoAmR
North Dakota Quarterly : NoDaQ
Northeast : Northeast
Northwest Review : NowestR
Notus : Notus

Obsidian II : Obs
The Ohio Reivew : OhioR
Ometeca : Ometeca
Ontario Review : OntR
Osiris : Os
Outerbridge : Outbr
Oxford Magazine : OxfordM

Pacific Review : PacificR
Paintbrush : Paint
Painted Bride Quarterly : PaintedB
Paper Air : PaperAir
The Paris Review : ParisR
Partisan Review : PartR
Passages North : PassN
Pembroke Magazine : Pembroke
The Pennsylvania Review : PennR
Pequod : Pequod
Pig Iron : Pig
The Pikestaff Forum : PikeF
Plainsongs : Plain
Ploughshares : Ploughs
Poem : Poem
Poet And Critic : PoetC
Poet Lore : PoetL
Poetry : Poetry
Poetry East : PoetryE
Poetry Northwest : PoetryNW
The Pottersfield Portfolio : PottPort
Prairie Fire : PraF
Prairie Schooner : PraS
Primavera : Prima

Quarry : Quarry
Quarterly Review of Literature : QRL
Quarterly West : QW

Rag Mag : RagMag
Rampike : Rampike
Raritan : Raritan
Red Bass : RedBass
River City : RiverC
River Styx : RiverS
Rohwedder : Rohwedder

Salmagundi : Salm
Screens and Tasted Parallels : Screens
Seneca Review : SenR
Sequoia : Sequoia
The Sewanee Review : SewanR
Shenandoah : Shen
Silverfish Review : SilverFR
Sing Heavenly Muse! : SingHM
Sink : Sink
Sinister Wisdom : SinW
Slipstream : SlipS
The Small Pond Magazine of Literature : SmPd
Sonora Review : Sonora
South Carolina Review : SoCaR
South Coast Poetry Journal : SoCoast
South Dakota Review : SoDakR
Southern Humanities Review : SouthernHR
Southern Poetry Review : SouthernPR
Southern Review : SouthernR
Southwest Review : SouthwR
Sparrow Press Poverty Pamphlets : Sparrow
Spirit : SpiritSH
The Spirit That Moves Us : Spirit
The Spoon River Quarterly : SpoonRQ
Stand : Stand
Stone Country : StoneC
Sulfur : Sulfur
Swamp Root : SwampR

Alphabetical List of Journals

Talisman : Talisman
Tampa Review : TampaR
Tar River Poetry : TarRP
Temblor : Temblor
Texas Review : TexasR
Three Rivers Poetry Journal : ThRiPo
The Threepenny Review : Thrpny
Timbuktu : Timbuktu
Translation : Translation
Tribe : Tribe
Triquarterly : TriQ
Turnstile : Turnstile

Us 1 Worksheets : US1

Verse : Verse
The Virginia Quarterly Review : VirQR
Visions : Vis

Washington Review : Wash
Weber Studies : WeberS
Webster Review : WebR
West Branch : WestB
West Coast Review : WestCR
Western Humanities Review : WestHR
The William and Mary Review : WilliamMR
Willow Springs : WillowS
Wind : Wind
The Windless Orchard : WindO
Witness : Witness
World Order : WorldO
The Wormwood Review : WormR
Writ : Writ
The Writer : Writer
Writers' Forum : WritersF

The Yale Review : YaleR
Yellow Silk : YellowS

Zyzzyva : Zyzzyva

The Author Index

1. AAL, Katharyn Machan
"The Electric Pig." [ChamLR] (3:1, #5) Fall 89, p. 89-90.
"The Night Orion Offered Me a Rose." [ChamLR] (3:1, #5) Fall 89, p. 88.
2. AARNES, William
"Dishes." [AmerS] (58:4) Aut 89, p. 509-510.
"Routes of Escape." [Pembroke] (21) 89, p. 63.
"Spirea." [PoetC] (20:2) Wint 89, p. 10-12.
"Thinking Better of It." [PoetC] (20:2) Wint 89, p. 8-9.
"To a Familiar." [SouthernR] (25:4) Aut 89, p. 904-907.
3. ABBE, Kate
"Barbarians." [WestB] (23) 89, p. 33.
"Eight Poems of China." [WestB] (23) 89, p. 29-32.
"The Sun-Bather" (for S.A.). [Kalliope] (10:1/2) 88, p. 88.
"That One Day Only." [Nimrod] (33:1) Fall-Wint 89, p. 72.
4. ABBOTT, Anthony S.
"Incarnation." [StoneC] (16:3/4) Spr-Sum 89, p. 65.
5. ABBOTT, Keith
"Portrait of Childhood." [Talisman] (3) Fall 89, p. 104.
6. ABBOTT, Tony
"At the Table." [Confr] (39/40) Fall 88-Wint 89, p. 225.
7. ABEL, Kathy
"The Developer." [AnthNEW] (1) 89, p. 1.
"To Jami on Her Second Birthday." [AnthNEW] (1) 89, p. 2.
8. ABELL, M. J.
"From a Kertesz Photograph." [US1] (22/23) Spr 89, p. 44.
9. ABERNETHY, Hugh (Hugh C., Jr.)
"Bears and Drums." [MinnR] (NS 33) Fall 89, p. 15-17.
"God in the Coffee Cup." [NegC] (9:1) 89, p. 80.
"Pick-Up." [MidwQ] (30:2) Wint 89, p. 189.
"Silent Survivor." [MidwQ] (30:2) Wint 89, p. 192.
"Sugaring." [MidwQ] (30:2) Wint 89, p. 208.
"Summer Storm Before the War." [MinnR] (NS 33) Fall 89, p. 15.
10. ABESHOUSE, Nancy
"Wayne Steele, 1969." [EngJ] (78:5) S 89, p. 96.
11. ABESSINIO, Gino M.
"The Weight of a Journal." [EngJ] (78:4) Ap 89, p. 100.
12. ABINADER, Elmaz
"The Burden of History." [CharR] (15:2) Fall 89, p. 43.
13. ABRAHMS, Judith
"Dog Jam" (for Terry K.). [Sequoia] (32:2) Wint-Spr 89, p. 70-71.
14. ABSE, Dannie
"Dog on a Rubbish Tip." [GeoR] (43:2) Sum 89, p. 345-346.
"Last Words." [NoDaQ] (57:2) Spr 89, insert p. 42.
"Peachstone." [NoDaQ] (57:2) Spr 89, insert p. 43.
"Return to Cardiff." [NoDaQ] (57:2) Spr 89, insert p. 41-42.
15. ABU-JABER, Diana
"The Beetroot." [CimR] (86) Ja 89, p. 85.
ACEVEDO, Manuel Silva
See SILVA ACEVEDO, Manuel
16. ACHTENBERG, Anya
"Breath" (Guy Owen Poetry Prize Winner, David Bottoms, Judge). [SouthernPR] (29:2) Fall 89, p. 5.
17. ACKERMAN, Diane
"Dinner at the Waldorf." [PraS] (63:2) Sum 89, p. 25-26.
"Portrait without Pose." [PraS] (63:2) Sum 89, p. 19-23.
"Song of the Trilobite." [PraS] (63:2) Sum 89, p. 24-25.
18. ACKERMAN, Kathy Cantley
"Surviving the Fire." [SouthernPR] (29:2) Fall 89, p. 58.

19. ACKERMAN, Stephen
    "Effortless Affection." [Boulevard] (4:1, #10) Spr 89, p. 185.
    "Nets" (for J.A., L.H.). [PartR] (56:3) Sum 89, p. 450.
20. ACOSTA, Juan David
    "Poem for a Future Departure" (for J. F. J.). [EvergreenC] (4:3) Spr 89, p. 23.
21. ACUFF, Gale
    "Lines to the Sun." [HeavenB] (7) Wint 89, p. 40.
22. ADAM, Ian
    "The Parents: A Sequence" (Excerpt). [Dandel] (16:1) Spr-Sum 89, p. 36-42.
    "War and Peace." [PraF] (10:4, #49) Wint 89-90, p. 30-39.
23. ADAMS, Barbara
    "Survivors (For Sylvia Plath)." [MinnR] (NS 32) Spr 89, p. 81-82.
24. ADAMS, Chelsea
    "Through Lightning Skies." [PoetL] (84:4) Wint 89-90, p. 5-6.
    "Unnamed in China (1983)." [PoetL] (84:4) Wint 89-90, p. 7.
25. ADAMS, David
    "Long Distance." [StoneC] (16:3/4) Spr-Sum 89, p. 47.
    "Presque Isle: Two Lovers Skipping Stones." [StoneC] (16:3/4) Spr-Sum 89, p. 47.
26. ADAMS, Deborah
    "Lay of the Land." [Vis] (31) 89, p. 20.
27. ADAMS, Erika B.
    "Fishing at Twilight." [BellArk] (5:6) N-D 89, p. 7.
    "A Homecoming in March." [BellArk] (5:3) My-Je 89, p. 9.
    "Imbolc: A Feast of Light" (for John Jech, et al). [BellArk] (5:3) My-Je 89, p. 5.
    "Song of Myself at Dawn." [BellArk] (5:6) N-D 89, p. 8.
28. ADAMS, Keith
    "Attending a Demonstration in the United States." [Bomb] (28) Sum 89, p. 89.
    "Southern Town." [Bomb] (28) Sum 89, p. 89.
29. ADAMS, Kurt
    "The Quest." [Mildred] (3:1) Spr-Sum 89, p. 33.
30. ADAMS, Michelene
    "Nate By De Sea." [Event] (18:2) Sum 89, p. 22.
    "Nate Mudder, Nate Granmudder an Nate." [Event] (18:2) Sum 89, p. 23.
31. ADAMS, Monica
    "Kitchen Table Poem." [CarolQ] (42:1) Fall 89, p. 49.
32. ADAMS, Terry
    "Point of View." [Witness] (2:2/3) Sum-Fall 88, p. 119.
    "Writing Home." [Witness] (2:2/3) Sum-Fall 88, p. 118.
33. ADAMS, Vicky
    "House, Deep River, April 1986" (A photograph of rural Iowa by David Plowden).
        [Farm] (6:2) Fall 89, p. 96.
    "Plains Song." [Farm] (6:2) Fall 89, p. 93-95.
34. ADCOCK, Fleur
    "Cattle in Mist." [Pequod] (26/27) 89, p. 71-72.
    "Happiness." [Descant] (20:3/4, #66/67) Fall-Wint 89, p. 213.
35. ADDISON, William
    "Munch Meets Grieg." [NegC] (9:2) 89, p. 29-30.
36. ADDONIZIO, Kim
    "Pantoum: At Mount Hebron" (for Zelman). [ParisR] (31:111) Sum 89, p. 222.
    "The Philosopher's Club." [Thrpny] (36) Wint 89, p. 20.
37. ADELMAN, Mitch
    "Bone Marrow Memory." [AmerPoR] (18:1) Ja-F 89, p. 47.
    "Headache for the Ages." [AmerPoR] (18:1) Ja-F 89, p. 47.
38. ADILMAN, Mona Elaine
    "Petting Zoo." [CanLit] (122/123) Aut-Wint 89, p. 25.
39. ADISA, Opal Palmer
    "Let Us Speak." [Sequoia] (33:1) Sum 89, p. 38.
    "Planning for My Great Grandchildren Seven Generations Ahead." [Sequoia] (33:1)
        Sum 89, p. 33-35.
    "Practise." [Sequoia] (33:1) Sum 89, p. 36-37.
40. ADKINS, Gilbert R.
    "A Seasonable Man." [SewanR] (97:3) Sum 89, p. 398.
41. ADLER, Cori
    "For Viktor Frankl." [Lactuca] (13) N 89, p. 39.
    "Jewlove." [Lactuca] (13) N 89, p. 37-39.

42. ADLER, Fran
     "Wood Floor Rising." [HayF] (5) Fall 89, p. 49-50.
43. AFIF, Fatimah
     "Tell the President, It's My Day Off!" [Footwork] 89, p. 44-45.
44. AGOSIN, Marjorie
     "The Captive Woman and the Light II" (tr. by Cola Franzen). [Pig] (15) 88, p. 94.
     "Disappeared Woman I" (tr. by Cola Franzen). [Pig] (15) 88, p. 94.
     "Last More Than Round" (tr. by Cola Franzen). [NewAW] (5) Fall 89, p. 66-67.
     "Letters" (tr. by Cola Franzen). [NewAW] (5) Fall 89, p. 65-66.
     "The Red Shoes" (For Marylin, tr. by Sara Heikoff Woehrlen). [CumbPR] (9:1) Fall
          89, p. 54-55.
     "Los Zapatos Rojos" (para Marylin). [CumbPR] (9:1) Fall 89, p. 53-54.
45. AGRICOLA, Sandra
     "A Sort of Adagio." [ThRiPo] (31/32) 88, p. 7.
     "Warping Up." [DenQ] (24:1) Sum 89, p. 6-7.
AGUDELO, Dario Jaramillo
     See JARAMILLO AGUDELO, Dario
46. AGUEROS, Jack
     "Sonnet for Maddog." [HangL] (55) 89, p. 5.
     "Sonnet for Willie Classen." [HangL] (55) 89, p. 6.
AGUIAR, Fred d'
     See D'AGUIAR, Fred
47. AHERN, Donal
     "On the Spot." [Vis] (29) 89, p. 46.
48. AHLSCHWEDE, Margrethe
     "Letters from the Dead." [SoDakR] (27:4) Wint 89, p. 71.
49. AI
     "Blue Suede Shoes" (A Fiction). [NewL] (56:2/3) Wint 89-Spr 90, p. 13-18.
     "Conversation" (For Robert Lowell). [NewL] (56:2/3) Wint 89-Spr 90, p. 19.
     "The Detective." [NewL] (56:2/3) Wint 89-Spr 90, p. 20-23.
     "General George Armstrong Custer: My Life in the Theater." [HayF] (5) Fall 89, p.
          7-9.
     "Jimmy Hoffa's Odyssey" (for Ron Vawter). [Agni] (28) 89, p. 58-61.
     "Little America Confidential" (Selection: 6-7). [Callaloo] (12:2, #39) Spr 89, p.
          391-395.
     "The Shadowboxer." [Manoa] (1:1/2) Fall 89, p. 162-165.
50. AIELLO, Kate
     "Friends on Rio Coco." [Bogg] (61) 89, p. 22-23.
51. AIGLA, Jorge H.-
     "El Monje a Solas." [Americas] (17:2) Sum 89, p. 52.
     "El Reloj, el Jarro y el Espejo." [Americas] (17:2) Sum 89, p. 53.
52. AINSWORTH, Alan
     "A Letter Not Sent to Leslie When I Found Out She Was Pregnant But She Didn't
          Know That I Knew." [BlueBldgs] (11) 89, p. 30.
53. AISENBERG, Katy
     "Dusk Falling." [BostonR] (14:3) Je 89, p. 13.
     "First Will." [AntR] (47:1) Wint 89, p. 72.
54. AISENBERG, Nadya
     "Holdfast." [Agni] (28) 89, p. 282-283.
55. AJAY, Stephen
     "How Is It." [YellowS] (32) Wint 89, p. 10.
     "Morning Shift in Banaras." [Caliban] (7) 89, p. 58-60.
56. AKAKA, Jonah Hau'oli
     "Manoa Chant." [Hawai'iR] (13:3) Fall 89, p. 23.
     "Oli Manoa." [Hawai'iR] (13:3) Fall 89, p. 22.
57. AKERS, Ellery
     "Missing My Grandmother." [AmerPoR] (18:6) N-D 89, p. 18.
     "Night: Volcano, California." [ThRiPo] (31/32) 88, p. 8-9.
AKIKO, Yosano (ca. 1900)
     See YOSANO, Akiko (ca. 1900)
58. Al-DINE, Jawdat Fakhr
     "Beware of Our Death in the South" (tr. by Sabah Ghandour). [Jacaranda] (4:1)
          Spr-Sum 89, p. 60.
59. Al-MAGHUT, Muhammad
     "A Face Between Two Shoes" (tr. by John Asfour). [Chelsea] (48) 89, p. p. 15-17.

60. Al-MUTAMID, Abu 'l-Kasim Mohammed Ibn-Abbad
    "To Abu Bakr ben Ammar Going to Silves" (tr. by Christopher Middleton of Emilio
        García Gómez' Spanish version). [SouthwR] (74:2) Spr 89, p. 225-226.
61. ALABAU, Magali
    "Y estoy segura que si supieras que tu amor me resucita." [Lyra] (2:1/2) 88, c89, p.
        42-43.
62. ALARCON, Francisco X.
    "Orden en la Casa." [Zyzzyva] (5:2, #18) Sum 89, p. 77.
    "Order in the Home" (tr. by Francisco Aragon). [Zyzzyva] (5:2, #18) Sum 89, p. 76.
63. ALBERTI, Rafael
    "Botticelli" (Arabesco, in Spanish). [Sequoia] (32:2) Wint-Spr 89, p. 21.
    "Botticelli" (Arabesque, tr. by Carolyn L. Tipton). [Sequoia] (32:2) Wint-Spr 89, p.
        22.
64. ALBRECHT, Laura
    "Ethel." [Kalliope] (11:2) 89, p. 66.
65. ALCOSSER, Sandra
    "Flame." [IndR] (13:1) Wint 89, p. 34.
    "Glory Monster." [Manoa] (1:1/2) Fall 89, p. 120.
    "Spittle Bug." [Manoa] (1:1/2) Fall 89, p. 121.
66. ALCUIN
    "Epitaph" (tr. by William Alfred). [Trans] (22) Fall 89, p. 202-203.
67. ALDAN, Daisy
    "The Clown Reproved (Le Pitre Chatié)" (Tournan, 1864, tr. of Stéphane Mallarmé).
        [AmerPoR] (18:2) Mr-Ap 89, p. 14.
    "Sea Breeze (Brise Marine)" (Tournan, May 1865, tr. of Stéphane Mallarmé).
        [AmerPoR] (18:2) Mr-Ap 89, p. 14.
    "Windows (Les Fenêtres)" (London, 1863, tr. of Stéphane Mallarmé). [AmerPoR]
        (18:2) Mr-Ap 89, p. 14.
68. ALDRICH, Marcia
    "Asking for a Little More Time." [GreensboroR] (47) Wint 89-90, p. 38-39.
69. ALEGRIA, Claribel
    "Little Cambray Tamales (5,000,000 Bite-Size Tamales)" (for Eduardo and Helena, tr.
        by Louise Popkin). [TriQ] (77) Wint 89-90, p. 273-274.
    "Snapshots" (to Eliseo Diego, tr. by Louise Popkin). [TriQ] (77) Wint 89-90, p. 275.
70. ALEJANDRO, Ann
    "Adobe." [Sonora] (17) Spr-Sum 89, p. 131-132.
    "Paseo." [Sonora] (17) Spr-Sum 89, p. 129-130.
71. ALENIER, Karren L.
    "Dialectic of the Census Takers." [NegC] (9:2) 89, p. 31-32.
72. ALESHIRE, Joan
    "Air Show." [Nat] (249:12) 16 O 89, p. 434.
    "Cheek to Cheek." [IndR] (12:2) Spr 89, p. 104-105.
    "Cheek to Cheek." [NewL] (56:2/3) Wint 89-Spr 90, p. 27-28.
    "Color." [NewL] (56:2/3) Wint 89-Spr 90, p. 26-27.
    "Full Flower Moon." [NewL] (56:2/3) Wint 89-Spr 90, p. 29.
    "Just Looking at the Bones." [NewL] (56:2/3) Wint 89-Spr 90, p. 25.
    "Notes for a Dark Winter." [NewL] (56:2/3) Wint 89-Spr 90, p. 24-25.
    "Wake." [SenR] (19:1) 89, p. 12-13.
73. ALEXANDER, Charles
    "A Book of Hours" (Selections: "Prime -- The First Age," "Vespers -- Speaking in
        Tongues"). [PaperAir] (4:2) 89, p. 109-110.
74. ALEXANDER, Constance
    "Mammogram Blues." [Calyx] (12:2) Wint 89-90, p. 6-7.
75. ALEXANDER, Craig
    "The Long Way." [PraS] (63:4) Wint 89, p. 71.
76. ALEXANDER, Elizabeth
    "Boston Year." [PraS] (63:3) Fall 89, p. 53-54.
    "Deadwood Dick." [Obs] (2:3) Wint 87, p. 89-90.
    "John Col." [Obs] (2:3) Wint 87, p. 88-89.
    "Nineteen." [IndR] (12:2) Spr 89, p. 36.
    "Ode." [BlackALF] (23:3) Fall 89, p. 495.
    "A Poem for Nelson Mandela." [Callaloo] (12:2, #39) Spr 89, p. 269.
    "Preliminary Sketches: Philadelphia." [PraS] (63:3) Fall 89, p. 54-55.
    "Robeson at Rutgers." [IndR] (12:2) Spr 89, p. 37.
    "Today's News." [IndR] (12:2) Spr 89, p. 38.
    "The Venus Hottentot (1825)." [Callaloo] (12:2, #39) Spr 89, p. 265-268.

"West Indian Primer" (for Clifford L. Alexander, Sr., 1897-1989). [Callaloo] (12:2, #39) Spr 89, p. 270.
77. ALEXANDER, Floyce
"Abiquiu." [Contact] (9:50/51/52) Fall-Wint 88-Spr 89, p. 18-19.
78. ALEXANDER, Meena
"Night-Scene, the Garden" (in her mother's voice. For my sisters, Anna and Elsa). [Chelsea] (48) 89, p. 37-63.
79. ALEXANDER, Pamela
"Aububon Takes Inventory" (Amerian Harbor, Labrador). [Margin] (8) 89, p. 20-21.
"Audubon Aboard the *Ripley*." [Margin] (8) 89, p. 21.
"Audubon at 13, As Revolution Begins in France." [Margin] (8) 89, p. 19.
"Audubon Writes to His Future Wife" (Excerpt). [Margin] (8) 89, p. 22.
"Safe." [Poetry] (153:4) Ja 89, p. 202.
"Six." [Poetry] (153:4) Ja 89, p. 201.
80. ALEXANDER, Paul
"John Clare Going Home." [SewanR] (97:4) Fall 89, p. 501-502.
81. ALEXANDROU, Aris
"Cherephon [sic] to Pindar." [GrandS] (8:2) Wint 89, p. 127.
"In Camp." [GrandS] (8:2) Wint 89, p. 125.
"The Knife." [GrandS] (8:2) Wint 89, p. 123.
"Meditations of Flavius Marcus." [GrandS] (8:2) Wint 89, p. 126.
82. ALEXIS, Austin
"Igor." [KeyWR] (2:1/2) Fall-Wint 89, p. 139.
"Spiders." [KeyWR] (2:1/2) Fall-Wint 89, p. 138.
83. ALFRED, William
"Epitaph" (tr. of Alcuin). [Trans] (22) Fall 89, p. 202-203.
84. ALGARIN, Miguel
"7th Street & Ave. A." (On Seeing Miky's Body). [Contact] (9:50/51/52) Fall-Wint 88-Spr 89, p. 11.
"Lucky Talks." [Contact] (9:50/51/52) Fall-Wint 88-Spr 89, p. 10.
85. ALI, Agha Shahid
"Before You Came" (tr. of Faiz Ahmed Faiz). [PoetryE] (27) Spr 89, p. 114.
"Black Out" (written during the India-Pakistan war of 1965, tr. of Faiz Ahmed Faiz). [PoetryE] (27) Spr 89, p. 108.
"The City from Here" (tr. of Faiz Ahmed Faiz). [PoetryE] (27) Spr 89, p. 103.
"City of Lights" (tr. of Faiz Ahmed Faiz). [PoetryE] (27) Spr 89, p. 104.
"Crucifixion" (for Christopher Merrill). [VirQR] (65:4) Aut 89, p. 655-656.
"Don't Ask Me for That Love Again" (tr. of Faiz Ahmed Faiz). [PoetryE] (27) Spr 89, p. 110.
"Ghazal: Ask no more about separation" (tr. of Faiz Ahmed Faiz). [PoetryE] (27) Spr 89, p. 109.
"Ghazal: He bet both this life and the next" (tr. of Faiz Ahmed Faiz). [PoetryE] (27) Spr 89, p. 111.
"Ghazal: Let the breeze pour colors" (tr. of Faiz Ahmed Faiz). [PoetryE] (27) Spr 89, p. 112-113.
"The Heart Gives Up" (tr. of Faiz Ahmed Faiz). [PoetryE] (27) Spr 89, p. 105.
"Last Night" (tr. of Faiz Ahmed Faiz). [PoetryE] (27) Spr 89, p. 116.
"A Last Speaker" (corrected reprint from 31:2, 1988). [Nimrod] (33:1) Fall-Wint 89, p. 139-140.
"Leaving Sonora" (for Richard Shelton). [QW] (28) Wint-Spr 89, p. 86.
"A Letter from Prison" (tr. of Faiz Ahmed Faiz's Urdu version of a poem by Nazim Hikmet). [PoetryE] (27) Spr 89, p. 101.
"Photograph in Sedona." [QW] (28) Wint-Spr 89, p. 87-88.
"A Prison Daybreak" (tr. of Faiz Ahmed Faiz). [PoetryE] (27) Spr 89, p. 99-100.
"A Prison Evening" (tr. of Faiz Ahmed Faiz). [PoetryE] (27) Spr 89, p. 98.
"The Rain of Stones Is Finished" (Elegy for Hassan Nasir, tortured to death, tr. of Faiz Ahmed Faiz). [PoetryE] (27) Spr 89, p. 97.
"So Bring the Order for My Execution" (tr. of Faiz Ahmed Faiz). [PoetryE] (27) Spr 89, p. 106.
"Solitude" (tr. of Faiz Ahmed Faiz). [PoetryE] (27) Spr 89, p. 107.
"Vista" (tr. of Faiz Ahmed Faiz). [PoetryE] (27) Spr 89, p. 115.
86. ALIESAN, Jody
"Divination." [PoetryNW] (30:4) Wint 89-90, p. 25.
87. ALKALAY-GUT, Karen
"'Dante' Coffee House in New York -- 1" (tr. of Yehuda Amichai). [Amelia] (5:3, #14) 89, p. 126.

"'Dante' Coffee House in New York -- 2" (tr. of Yehuda Amichai). [Amelia] (5:3, #14) 89, p. 126.
"'Dante' Coffee House in New York -- 3" (tr. of Yehuda Amichai). [Amelia] (5:3, #14) 89, p. 127.
"Flowers." [WebR] (14:1) Spr 89, p. 66.
"A Poet Writes." [WebR] (14:1) Spr 89, p. 67.
"Poets in Their Youth." [WebR] (14:1) Spr 89, p. 66.
"What I Learned in the Wars" (tr. of Yehuda Amichai). [AmerV] (16) Fall 89, p. 74-75.

88. ALLAN, A. T.
"Poem: Singing out all over." [ChamLR] (2:2, #4) Spr 89, p. 117.

89. ALLAN, Rob
"Karitane Postcards." [Descant] (20:3/4, #66/67) Fall-Wint 89, p. 199-200.

90. ALLBERY, Debra
"In the Dream She Doesn't Tell Him" (Prizewinning Poets -- 1989). [Nat] (248:20) 22 My 89, p. 708.

91. ALLEGRA, Donna
"Before I Dress and Soar Again." [Cond] (16) 89, p. 40.

92. ALLEN, Beverly
"The Baby-Talk Elegy" (tr. of Andrea Zanzotto). [Poetry] (155:1/2) O-N 89, p. 57-61.
"Don't Jump Out of Your Skin" (tr. of Marica Larocchi). [Poetry] (155:1/2) O-N 89, p. 116.
"The Flowers Come As Gifts" (tr. of Amelia Rosselli). [Poetry] (155:1/2) O-N 89, p. 85.
"If It Were a Sea, This Immense Wind" (tr. of Maria Luisa Spaziani). [Poetry] (155:1/2) O-N 89, p. 67.
"In Ancient China" (tr. of Amelia Rosselli). [Poetry] (155:1/2) O-N 89, p. 87.
"In This Way" (Selection: VI, tr. of Marica Larocchi). [Poetry] (155:1/2) O-N 89, p. 115.
"Sailing to Aphinar" (For Stefano Agosti, tr. of Marica Larocchi). [Poetry] (155:1/2) O-N 89, p. 117.
"Sunday in the Provinces" (tr. of Maria Luisa Spaziani). [Poetry] (155:1/2) O-N 89, p. 69.
"There's Something Like Pain in the Room" (tr. of Amelia Rosselli). [Poetry] (155:1/2) O-N 89, p. 86.
"Your Life Is a Baby Not Yet Born" (tr. of Maria Luisa Spaziani). [Poetry] (155:1/2) O-N 89, p. 68.

93. ALLEN, Connie S.
"My Mother Triumphant" (The Full Cycle). [KanQ] (21:1/2) Wint-Spr 89, p. 248.
"With Love from the Tattoo Lady." [KanQ] (21:1/2) Wint-Spr 89, p. 248-249.

94. ALLEN, Dick
"At Brown." [CrossCur] (8:2) Ja 89, p. 167.
"The Narrow Mind." [Poetry] (154:6) S 89, p. 324.

95. ALLEN, Gilbert
"A Change in the Weather." [SouthernHR] (23:4) Fall 89, p. 358.
"He's Up." [Interim] (8:1) Spr 89, p. 41.
"Jesus May Save But He Doesn't Signal" (for Theron Price, Th.D.). [Pembroke] (21) 89, p. 51.
"The News for Tonight." [SoCaR] (22:1) Fall 89, p. 120-121.
"Noah's Fish." [WilliamMR] (27) 89, p. 20.
"Twelve Words on a Windy Day." [AmerS] (58:1) Wint 89, p. 76-78.
"The Unseen." [Pembroke] (21) 89, p. 50.

96. ALLEN, Jeffrey Renard
"Festival of Corn and Tobacco" (for Victor Montejo). [Caliban] (7) 89, p. 63-64.

97. ALLEN, Paul
"American Crawl." [Ascent] (14:3) 89, p. 29-31.
"Letting the Rabbit Scream." [Ascent] (14:3) 89, p. 28-29.
"The Man with the Hardest Belly." [OntR] (30) Spr-Sum 89, p. 99-102.

98. ALLEN, Paula Gunn
"The Text Is Flesh." [AmerV] (14) Spr 89, p. 13-15.

99. ALLEN, William
"Notes on Poetry and Art, 1987-1988." [Pequod] (28/29/30) 89, p. 211-216.

ALLESSIO, Andreas di
See Di ALLESSIO, Andreas

100. ALLEY, Rick
"Primary Detail." [HayF] (4) Spr 89, p. 66.

101. ALLIN, Louise
   "A Canadian in Merida." [AntigR] (79) Aut 89, p. 7.
   "The Death of Ice." [CapeR] (24:1) Spr 89, p. 43.
102. ALMON, Bert
   "By the Wayside." [HighP] (4:1) Spr 89, p. 21.
   "A Critique of Pure Happiness." [Dandel] (16:2) Fall-Wint 89, p. 7.
   "A Cup of Greek Coffee in Burnaby." [Dandel] (16:2) Fall-Wint 89, p. 5.
   "Olga's Hydrangeas." [Grain] (17:4) Wint 89, inside back cover.
   "One Spring in Delphi." [Dandel] (16:2) Fall-Wint 89, p. 6.
   "Theoretically Speaking." [PoetryE] (28) Fall 89, p. 9.
103. ALOHA, Kalina
   "Ka Wai O Kulanihako'i." [Hawai'iR] (13:3) Fall 89, p. 54.
   "The water of Kulanihako'i spills." [Hawai'iR] (13:3) Fall 89, p. 55.
104. ALTHAUS, Keith
   "Early Days." [VirQR] (65:4) Aut 89, p. 652-654.
   "Winter Dawn." [WillowS] (23) Wint 89, p. 52-53.
105. ALTIZER, Nell
   "Ave." [Ploughs] (15:4) Wint 89-90, p. 8.
   "Binding." [ChamLR] (3:1, #5) Fall 89, p. 6.
   "Exchange." [ChamLR] (3:1, #5) Fall 89, p. 1-2.
   "For A. in the Season of Deprivation." [ChamLR] (3:1, #5) Fall 89, p. 3.
   "For Desdemona and Love and Myrrh." [Ploughs] (15:4) Wint 89-90, p. 6.
   "Moral Theology." [Ploughs] (15:4) Wint 89-90, p. 9.
   "Quintet in C Major." [Ploughs] (15:4) Wint 89-90, p. 7.
   "Sestina *Perdonare*." [ChamLR] (3:1, #5) Fall 89, p. 4-5.
106. ALTSCHUL, Carlos
   "And Now on to Sensible Explanations" (tr. of Alfredo Vieravé, w. Monique
      Altschul). [LitR] (32:4) Sum 89, p. 593.
   "La Casa Grande" (eleven poems, tr. of Tamara Kamenszain, w. Monique Altschul).
      [LitR] (32:4) Sum 89, p. 512-517.
   "Description of the Monster She or the Cannon Woman" (tr. of Alfredo Vieravé, w.
      Monique Altschul). [LitR] (32:4) Sum 89, p. 592.
   "History and Sociology" (tr. of Alfredo Vieravé, w. Monique Altschul). [LitR] (32:4)
      Sum 89, p. 588-590.
   "Madame Bovary" (tr. of Alfredo Vieravé, w. Monique Altschul). [LitR] (32:4) Sum
      89, p. 591-592.
   "Poem: Claudia Cardinale bird of imperial plumage and her breasts" (tr. of Alfredo
      Vieravé, w. Monique Altschul). [LitR] (32:4) Sum 89, p. 590-591.
107. ALTSCHUL, Monique
   "And Now on to Sensible Explanations" (tr. of Alfredo Vieravé, w. Carlos Altschul).
      [LitR] (32:4) Sum 89, p. 593.
   "La Casa Grande" (eleven poems, tr. of Tamara Kamenszain, w. Carlos Altschul).
      [LitR] (32:4) Sum 89, p. 512-517.
   "Description of the Monster She or the Cannon Woman" (tr. of Alfredo Vieravé, w.
      Carlos Altschul). [LitR] (32:4) Sum 89, p. 592.
   "History and Sociology" (tr. of Alfredo Vieravé, w. Carlos Altschul). [LitR] (32:4)
      Sum 89, p. 588-590.
   "Madame Bovary" (tr. of Alfredo Vieravé, w. Carlos Altschul). [LitR] (32:4) Sum 89,
      p. 591-592.
   "Poem: Claudia Cardinale bird of imperial plumage and her breasts" (tr. of Alfredo
      Vieravé, w. Carlos Altschul). [LitR] (32:4) Sum 89, p. 590-591.
108. ALVAREZ BRAVO, Armando
   "Notations." [KeyWR] (2:1/2) Fall-Wint 89, p. 133-135.
109. AMABILE, George
   "The Artist As Historian." [Margin] (9) 89, p. 60-61.
   "How Do You Spell Relief?" [Margin] (9) 89, p. 53.
   "How to Kill Time on the Prairies." [Margin] (9) 89, p. 54.
   "Landlocked Lighthouse Railway Train" (for Alison). [Margin] (9) 89, p. 56, 58.
110. AMADOR RODRIGUEZ, Monica
   "Adios." [Mairena] (11:27) 89, p. 70.
111. AMARA, Lamia Abbas
   "Frouzanda Mahrad" (tr. by Mike Maggio). [Pig] (15) 88, p. 28.
112. AMDAHL, Kenn
   "Met Before." [ChatR] (9:3) Spr 89, p. 45.
113. AMICHAI, Yehuda
   "'Dante' Coffee House in New York -- 1" (tr. by Karen Alkalay-Gut). [Amelia] (5:3,

#14) 89, p. 126.
"'Dante' Coffee House in New York -- 2" (tr. by Karen Alkalay-Gut). [Amelia] (5:3,
#14) 89, p. 126.
"'Dante' Coffee House in New York -- 3" (tr. by Karen Alkalay-Gut). [Amelia] (5:3,
#14) 89, p. 127.
"Dog After Love" (tr. by W. D. Snodgrass). [GrandS] (9:1) Aut 89, p. 264.
"What I Learned in the Wars" (tr. by Karen Alkalay-Gut). [AmerV] (16) Fall 89, p.
74-75.
114. AMMONS, A. R.
"Castaways." [ChatR] (9:3) Spr 89, p. 48.
"Enfield Falls." [GettyR] (2:2) Spr 89, p. 330.
"Lofty Calling." [MichQR] (28:1) Wint 89, p. 118.
"Obsession." [MichQR] (28:1) Wint 89, p. 119.
"A Part of the Whole." [SouthwR] (74:1) Wint 89, p. 39-40.
"Resolve." [Epoch] (38:2) 89, p. 138.
"Weightlessness." [MichQR] (28:1) Wint 89, p. 120.
115. AMOROSE, Thomas
"Autumn." [Blueline] (10:1/2) 89, p. 52.
116. AMPRIMOZ, Alexandre L.
"Pavese's Tomb." [FreeL] (3) Aut 89, p. 8.
"Something to Gain." [FreeL] (3) Aut 89, p. 7.
117. AMSBERRY, Jan
"Voices of Silence." [NegC] (9:2) 89, p. 33.
118. AN, Jing
"To Be Sent to the Shadow of the Sun" (tr. of Ding Yu Ping, w. Rex A. McGuinn).
[LitR] (32:2) Wint 89, p. 168.
AN-SHIH, Wang
See WANG, An-shih
An tSAOI, Máire Mhac
See Mhac an tSAOI, Máire
119. ANAGNOSTOPOULOS, Athan
"Diary Entries" (tr. of George Seferis). [Pequod] (28/29/30) 89, p. 105-107.
120. ANDERS, Shirley
"First Snow, with Sunlight" (for Betsy Gregg). [Pembroke] (21) 89, p. 133-134.
"The Owl Against the Glass." [PraS] (63:1) Spr 89, p. 104-107.
121. ANDERSON, Barbara
"Meat Never Cooks in the House of the Murderer." [AmerPoR] (18:3) My-Je 89, p.
31.
"Over Easy." [Crazy] (36) Spr 89, p. 30-31.
122. ANDERSON, Catherine
"Midwifery." [AmerV] (15) Sum 89, p. 33.
123. ANDERSON, Doug
"For John Clellon Holmes" (because "the debt one human being owes another . . .
should be paid"). [MoodySI] (20/21) Spr 89, p. 32.
124. ANDERSON, Fortner
"I Hold a Package in My Hand." [Rampike] (6:3) 88, p. 53.
125. ANDERSON, Jack
"The Feasts." [Caliban] (7) 89, p. 150.
"Some Things You Can Do with Your Hair." [Caliban] (7) 89, p. 151.
126. ANDERSON, Kathleen
"It Happens to Us All." [PaintedB] (38) 89, p. 71.
"This Is What You Wanted." [PaintedB] (38) 89, p. 72.
127. ANDERSON, Lori
"On the Last Page of Her Diary She Said She Was Two Severed Selves." [DenQ]
(24:2) Fall 89, p. 15-17.
128. ANDERSON, Maggie
"Doing My Part." [IndR] (12:3) Sum 89, p. 4.
"The Long Evenings." [IndR] (12:3) Sum 89, p. 3.
"Setting Out." [IndR] (12:3) Sum 89, p. 1-2.
129. ANDERSON, Mark
"The End of Summer." [CumbPR] (8:2) Spr 89, p. 21.
"Power." [KanQ] (21:1/2) Wint-Spr 89, p. 241.
130. ANDERSON, Mia
"Spirit Level" (for Jane Rule). [MalR] (89) Wint 89, p. 53-56.
131. ANDERSON, Murray
"When You're Away" (To my daughter in a group home). [Kaleid] (18) Wint-Spr 89,

p. 23.
132. ANDERSON, Nathalie
"Red Sea." [DenQ] (24:1) Sum 89, p. 8.
133. ANDERSON, Robert R.
"Pas de Deux." [Ploughs] (15:4) Wint 89-90, p. 11.
"Poppies" (for R. H.). [Ploughs] (15:4) Wint 89-90, p. 10.
134. ANDERSON, Rod
"And the Evening and the Morning Were the Sixth Day" (Verbatim from *Scientific American*, Apr 87). [AntigR] (77/78) Spr-Sum 89, p. 225.
"Le Chien Englouti." [Grain] (17:4) Wint 89, p. 41.
"Dream of First Dawn." [Grain] (17:4) Wint 89, p. 42.
"Size." [AntigR] (77/78) Spr-Sum 89, p. 223.
"TTTT" (Editors' First Prize Winner, Poetry). [CrossC] (11:1) 89, p. 16.
"Weather Eye." [AntigR] (77/78) Spr-Sum 89, p. 224.
135. ANDERSON, Susan
"Humboldt's Caves and Lakes." [Caliban] (7) 89, p. 40.
136. ANDERSON, T. J., III
"The Basic Training of Randall Ferguson." [IndR] (12:2) Spr 89, p. 52-53.
"Corner Court." [IndR] (12:2) Spr 89, p. 55.
"Firstling." [IndR] (12:2) Spr 89, p. 54.
"Income." [Obs] (4:3) Wint 89, p. 52.
"Lone Lantern in a Bamboo Grove." [IndR] (12:2) Spr 89, p. 49-50.
"Myself When I Am Real" (-- Charles Mingus). [Obs] (4:3) Wint 89, p. 51.
"Naima." [IndR] (12:2) Spr 89, p. 51.
"River to Cross." [Obs] (4:3) Wint 89, p. 49-50.
137. ANDERSON, Vicky
"Even Here." [RiverC] (10:1) Fall 89, p. 54.
"Familiar." [RiverC] (10:1) Fall 89, p. 52-53.
"Health." [RiverC] (10:1) Fall 89, p. 50-51.
"Playing for Keeps" (for my mother). [RiverC] (10:1) Fall 89, p. 55.
138. ANDERSON, Warwick
"Indochina Diary." [SenR] (19:2) Fall 89, p. 37.
139. ANDERSON-JONES, Teruko
"Travelling the Fairgrounds." [AntigR] (77/78) Spr-Sum 89, p. 184-185.
140. ANDRADE, Carlos Drummond de
"Love Beats in the Aorta" (tr. by Hess, David). [GrahamHR] (12) Spr 89, p. 51-52.
141. ANDRADE, Eugenio de
"Beauty" (tr. by Alexis Levitin). [HampSPR] Wint 89, p. 47.
"Boulevard Delessert" (tr. by Alexis Levitin). [HampSPR] Wint 89, p. 46.
"Call" (tr. by Alexis Levitin). [CentralP] (15) Spr 89, p. 176.
"Childhood" (tr. by Alexis Levitin). [Trans] (22) Fall 89, p. 234.
"Confidence" (tr. by Alexis Levitin). [Trans] (22) Fall 89, p. 234.
"Conto de Inverno." [StoneC] (17:1/2) Fall-Wint 89-90, p. 20.
"Da Poesia Japonesa." [BlackWR] (15:2) Spr 89, p. 104.
"The day clean as a deserted churchyard" (tr. by Alexis Levitin). [AmerPoR] (18:6) N-D 89, p. 48.
"The Flower of Thessaly" (tr. by Alexis Levitin). [OxfordM] (5:1) Spr-Sum 89, p. 52.
"The Flute" (tr. by Alexis Levitin). [Chelsea] (48) 89, p. 26-27.
"The Harmony of the World" (tr. by Alexis Levitin). [ConnPR] (8:1) 89, p. 34.
"I No Longer Know" (tr. by Alexis Levitin). [CreamCR] (13:2) Fall 89, p. 162.
"If the Wind Comes" (tr. by Alexis Levitin). [CentralP] (15) Spr 89, p. 176.
"It is within that the mouth is luminous" (tr. by Alexis Levitin). [AmerPoR] (18:6) N-D 89, p. 48.
"Melancholy" (tr. by Alexis Levitin). [Chelsea] (48) 89, p. 26.
"Night had brought him round" (tr. by Alexis Levitin). [AmerPoR] (18:6) N-D 89, p. 48.
"Old Music" (tr. by Alexis Levitin). [Trans] (22) Fall 89, p. 234.
"On Japanese Poetry" (tr. by Alexis Levitin). [BlackWR] (15:2) Spr 89, p. 105.
"The open book forgotten in the grass" (tr. by Alexis Levitin). [AmerPoR] (18:6) N-D 89, p. 48.
"Porto" (in Portuguese). [BlackWR] (15:2) Spr 89, p. 106.
"Porto" (tr. by Alexis Levitin). [BlackWR] (15:2) Spr 89, p. 107.
"Praca da Alegria" (tr. by Alexis Levitin). [HampSPR] Wint 89, p. 46.
"Solar Matter" (Selections: 20-22, tr. by Alexis Levitin). [NowestR] (27:1) 89, p. 37-39.

"Solar Matter" (tr. by Alexis Levitin). [OxfordM] (5:2) Fall-Wint 89, p. 50.
"That Sheet" (tr. by Alexis Levitin). [Trans] (22) Fall 89, p. 233.
"There must be somewhere where one arm" (tr. by Alexis Levitin). [AmerPoR] (18:6) N-D 89, p. 48.
"Winter's Tale" (tr. by Alexis Levitin). [StoneC] (17:1/2) Fall-Wint 89-90, p. 20.
"A Working Hypothesis" (tr. by Alexis Levitin). [Chelsea] (48) 89, p. 27.
"You can almost see it from here, the summer" (tr. by Alexis Levitin). [AmerPoR] (18:6) N-D 89, p. 48.
142. ANDRÉS, Cira
"The Temporary Madness of Quixote" (tr. by Bonnie Jefferson). [Pig] (15) 88, p. 64.
143. ANDREW, Victor
"Having a Ball." [AntigR] (76) Wint 89, p. 123.
"Rainwind." [WindO] (51) Spr 89, p. 23.
144. ANDREWS, Bruce
"Divestiture -- A" (Excerpts). [CentralP] (16) Fall 89, p. 14-16.
"Divestiture -- A" (Excerpts). [Screens] (1) 89, p. 114-116.
"I Am Your Problem." [MinnR] (NS 32) Spr 89, p. 56-57.
"I Don't Have Any Paper So Shut Up (or, Social Romanticism" (Selections: 3 poems). [Aerial] (5) 89, p. 9-15.
"Untitled: Can be summarized in the following diagram." [Caliban] (6) 89, p. 206.
145. ANDREWS, Claudia Emerson
"Accidents." [GreensboroR] (47) Wint 89-90, p. 41.
146. ANDREWS, Linda
"In Blossom." [CreamCR] (13:2) Fall 89, p. 157.
147. ANDREWS, Nin
"The Armadilloes." [Plain] (10:1) 89, p. 8.
148. ANDREWS, Shari
"What Is Dying." [AntigR] (79) Aut 89, p. 12.
149. ANDREWS, Tom
"The Hemophiliac's Motorcycle." [Field] (41) Fall 89, p. 79-85.
"Yellow Grass: An Elegy." [VirQR] (65:2) Spr 89, p. 248-256.
150. ANGEL, George
"Food and Beverage Management in Hotels (Illus.)." [Caliban] (7) 89, p. 96-98.
151. ANGELINE, Mary
"The Regular Work of Splendor." [Talisman] (3) Fall 89, p. 47.
ANGELIS, Milo de
See De ANGELIS, Milo
152. ANGELL, Roger
"Greetings, Friends!" [NewYorker] (65:45) 25 D 89, p. 36.
153. ANGLESEY, Zoe
"Hair Cut Like Gabriela Mistral's." [MassR] (30:2) Sum 89, p. 321-322.
"El Mundo Machimbre." [MassR] (30:2) Sum 89, p. 322-323.
"Peace Over the City." [WillowS] (23) Wint 89, p. 61.
154. ANONYMOUS
"Androtion built me to give room" (tr. by James Michie). [GrandS] (8:4) Sum 89, p. 83.
"Deor" (in Gaelic[?]). [CumbPR] (8:2) Spr 89, p. 86,88.
"Deor" (tr. from the Gaelic[?] by Fike, Francis). [CumbPR] (8:2) Spr 89, p. 87, 89.
"Drunken Villagers" (tr. from the Chinese by J. P. Seaton). [LitR] (32:3) Spr 89, p. 413.
"Early morning glows" (Kokinshu 637, tr. by Sam Hamill). [PoetryE] (28) Fall 89, p. 200.
"Fortune and Hope, a long goodbye" (tr. by James Michie). [GrandS] (8:4) Sum 89, p. 85.
"The Frog Who Was King" (Aboriginal narrative of New South Wales, collected by Roland Robinson, related by Tom Whaddy, Gumbangirr Tribe). [PraS] (63:3) Fall 89, p. 77-78.
"I, Lais, whose proud beauty" (tr. by James Michie). [GrandS] (8:4) Sum 89, p. 81.
"If you who use this path catch sight" (tr. by James Michie). [GrandS] (8:4) Sum 89, p. 83.
"The Large Beak Finches" (tr. from the Korean by Constantine Contogenis and Wolhee Choe). [ChiR] (36:3/4) 89, p. 18.
"O Apple-Tree, O" (from "Eilean Fraoich," tr. by Iain Crichton Smith). [Stand] (30:1) Wint 88-89, p. 15.
"The Pillow: a Transylvanian Folk Song" (tr. by Bruce Berlind). [PoetryE] (28) Fall 89, p. 205.

"Plum Scent" (From the First Imperial Anthology, Kokinwakashu, of 905, tr. by
Graeme Wilson). [Jacaranda] (4:1) Spr-Sum 89, p. 72.
"Proximity" (tr. from the Japanese by Graeme Wilson). [DenQ] (24:1) Sum 89, p. 87.
"The Ruin" (tr. from the Anglo-Saxon by Roger Nash). [AntigR] (79) Aut 89, p. 95.
"The Seafarer" (tr. from the Anglo-Saxon by Roger Nash). [AntigR] (79) Aut 89, p.
94.
"Second Thoughts" (From the First Imperial Anthology, Kokinwakashu, of 905, tr.
by Graeme Wilson). [Jacaranda] (4:1) Spr-Sum 89, p. 72.
"Selections from Ancient Middle-American Poetry Inscribed on Walls of the
Anthropological Museum in Mexico City" (tr. by Mary Prentice Lillie).
[InterPR] (15:2) Fall 89, p. 27-29.
"To a Worthless Magistrate" (tr. by James Michie). [GrandS] (8:4) Sum 89, p. 84.
"Uncle Abraham Whose Blackfeller's Name Was Minah" (Aboriginal narrative of
New South Wales, collected by Roland Robinson, related by Percy Mumbulla,
Wallaga Lake). [PraS] (63:3) Fall 89, p. 78-82.
"Under the sky's broad reaches" (Kokinshu 542, tr. by Sam Hamill). [PoetryE] (28)
Fall 89, p. 201.
"Wulf and Eadwacer" (from the Exeter Book, tr. from Old English by Richard Ryan).
[Trans] (22) Fall 89, p. 235-236.
155. ANONYMOUS (Six Dynasties)
"All Year Long" (tr. from the Chinese by Kenneth Rexroth). [LitR] (32:3) Spr 89, p.
304.
156. ANOS, Joanna
"We Have No Need." [AmerS] (58:4) Aut 89, p. 563.
157. ANTHONY, Frank
"Antony's Dream." [AnthNEW] (1) 89, p. 3.
"The Leaves Are Still" (for Robert Penn Warren). [AnthNEW] (1) 89, front matter.
"Making Way for Meadowlarks." [AnthNEW] (1) 89, p. 4.
158. ANTIPATER OF THESSALONICA
"Everywhere the sea is the sea" (tr. by James Michie). [GrandS] (8:4) Sum 89, p. 81.
159. ANTLER
"All the Breaths." [BellR] (12:2, #26) Fall 89, p. 19.
160. ANTON, K. H.
"Seven Trees Against Sunset" (tr. of Pablo Antonio Cuadra, w. Todd Frederickson).
[AnotherCM] (19) 89, p. 31-49.
161. ANZALDUA, Gloria
"Nightvoice." [SinW] (38) Sum-Fall 89, p. 55-57.
162. APPEL, Cathy
"The Agate Ring." [PoetryE] (28) Fall 89, p. 84.
"Crying in School." [PassN] (10:2) Sum 89, p. 27.
163. APPEL, Dori
"Detective Story." [NewRena] (7:3, #23) 89, p. 164.
"Focus." [NewRena] (7:3, #23) 89, p. 163.
164. APPLEBY, Frank W.
"The Immolation of Icarus." [InterPR] (15:2) Fall 89, p. 95.
"The Unfolding." [InterPR] (15:2) Fall 89, p. 95.
"Within the Moat." [Vis] (31) 89, p. 22.
165. APPLEWHITE, James
"Back Then." [ChatR] (9:3) Spr 89, p. 44.
"The Descent." [BostonR] (14:2) Ap 89, p. 21.
"The Giant Familiar Tree, Stranger at Nightfall." [Shen] (39:2) Sum 89, p. 25-26.
"The Pageant." [VirQR] (65:3) Sum 89, p. 453.
"The Runner, Pursued." [Verse] (6:3) Wint 89, p. 72.
"The Runner, Pursued." [VirQR] (65:3) Sum 89, p. 452.
"Stopping for Gas." [Verse] (6:3) Wint 89, p. 66-67.
"Working Around the Grease Rack." [Shen] (39:2) Sum 89, p. 24-25.
AQUINO, Luis Hernandez
See HERNANDEZ AQUINO, Luis
166. ARAGON, Francisco
"Order in the Home" (tr. of Francisco X. Alarcón). [Zyzzyva] (5:2, #18) Sum 89, p.
76.
"The Poet Speaks with His Beloved on the Telephone" (tr. of Federico Garcia Lorca,
w. J. K. Walsh). [ChamLR] (3:1, #5) Fall 89, p. 76.
"The Poet Tells the Truth" (tr. of Federico Garcia Lorca, w. J. K. Walsh). [ChamLR]
(3:1, #5) Fall 89, p. 75.
"Sonnet of the Sweet Complaint" (tr. of Federico Garcia Lorca, w. J. K. Walsh).

[ChamLR] (3:1, #5) Fall 89, p. 77.
167. ARANDA, Alejandro
"Encuentro." [Inti] (29/30) Primavera-Otoño 89, p. 261-262.
168. ARBELAEZ, Fernando
"La Lluvia de Oro." [LindLM] (8:2) Ap-Je 89, p. 3.
169. ARBUTHNOT, Nancy
"In Provence." [HiramPoR] (46) Spr-Sum 89, p. 7.
"Nice: Morning During Rain." [HiramPoR] (46) Spr-Sum 89, p. 8.
170. ARCHER, Anne
"If Not for You." [Quarry] (38:2) Spr 89, p. 40.
"Orpheus (After D.G. Jones)." [Quarry] (38:2) Spr 89, p. 41.
171. ARCHER, Nuala
"Edge Skool." [Vis] (29) 89, p. 11.
"From a Mobile Home: Bohemian Waxwings." [NoDaQ] (57:1) Wint 89, p. 55.
"From a Mobile Home: Dream in a Species of Opera." [NoDaQ] (57:1) Wint 89, p. 56.
"Giant Irish Deer." [Vis] (29) 89, p. 11.
"Subtitles Cont'd: The Ellipses Between Pa & Ma." [Epoch] (38:3) 89, p. 215-220.
172. ARCHIAS
"Here, a small Priapus, I stand" (tr. by James Michie). [GrandS] (8:4) Sum 89, p. 82.
ARCY, Michael James d'
   See D'ARCY, Michael James
173. ARELLANO, Marc
"In Two." [AntigR] (79) Aut 89, p. 23.
"Just Too Kosher." [AntigR] (79) Aut 89, p. 22-23.
174. ARENA, Adri
"Rational Anarchy." [StoneC] (16:3/4) Spr-Sum 89, p. 16.
175. ARENAS, Marion
"Late Afternoon." [CreamCR] (13:2) Fall 89, p. 214.
"Lecture with Music." [PoetL] (84:1) Spr 89, p. 30.
"On Being Unable to Find Mother's Burial Place." [PoetL] (84:1) Spr 89, p. 31-32.
"Why She Doesn't Tell." [PoetL] (84:4) Wint 89-90, p. 14.
176. ARGENTARIOS, Markos
"V. 104" (in Greek and English, tr. by Richard Dauenhauer). [YellowS] (30) Sum 89, p. 5.
177. ARGÜELLES, Ivan
"(Angel)." (for sarah). [Talisman] (3) Fall 89, p. 52-53.
"Argot." [HeavenB] (7) Wint 89, p. 7.
"Cipango." [YellowS] (29) Spr 89, p. 24.
"The Continent of Distant Women." [YellowS] (29) Spr 89, p. 25.
"Empty Mind." [Aerial] (5) 89, p. 152-153.
"Hieroglyph Spells Desire" (for Sarah). [YellowS] (30) Sum 89, p. 40.
"Homer Son of Telemachus" (for CZ). [HeavenB] (7) Wint 89, p. 17.
"The Hymn to Circe" (Excerpt). [AnotherCM] (19) 89, p. 7-8.
"Jade Bordering on Black" (for Sarah). [Caliban] (7) 89, p. 32-34.
"Playing Piano with You." [Caliban] (7) 89, p. 35-36.
"Sainte Eglyse." [Caliban] (7) 89, p. 30-31.
"Tireisias" (for sarah). [SilverFR] (16) Spr 89, p. 18-19.
"White Stockings." [YellowS] (31) Aut 89, p. 12-13.
ARGÜLLES, Ivan
   See ARGÜELLES, Ivan
178. ARGYROS, Alex
"Bloodsport." [Hawai'iR] (13:1, #25) Spr 89, p. 101.
179. ARIWARA NO NARIHIRA (825-880)
"Spending the whole night" (tr. by Sam Hamill). [PoetryE] (28) Fall 89, p. 202.
180. ARKEKETA, Annette
"The Absence." [Nimrod] (32:2) Spr-Sum 89, p. 76.
"Elegy for Mary Pat." [Nimrod] (32:2) Spr-Sum 89, p. 76.
"So You Think You Are Crazy Horse." [Nimrod] (32:2) Spr-Sum 89, p. 75.
181. ARM, Hector
"Comiendose una Fruta el Escribano Recuerda Su Isla." [LindLM] (8:3) Jl-S 89, p. 8.
182. ARMANTROUT, Rae
"Paris." [Screens] (1) 89, p. 101.
"You." [Screens] (1) 89, p. 101.
ARMAS, Paula de
   See DeARMAS, Paula

183. ARMITAGE, Barri
"Double Helix." [Poetry] (153:5) F 89, p. 263-266.
184. ARMSTRONG, Gene
"Beyond All Reason." [BellArk] (5:1) Ja-F 89, p. 9.
"Current Flow." [BellArk] (5:4) Jl-Ag 89, p. 6.
"Dining Room on Lincoln Ave." [BellArk] (5:5) S-O 89, p. 20.
"Full-Blown." [BellArk] (5:5) S-O 89, p. 9.
"Lupine Flowers, Blowing." [BellArk] (5:5) S-O 89, p. 4.
"Marjorie." [BellArk] (5:4) Jl-Ag 89, p. 7.
"Radiance." [HampSPR] Wint 89, p. 29.
"Simply." [HampSPR] Wint 89, p. 28.
"Skipping Stones." [BellArk] (5:4) Jl-Ag 89, p. 5.
"Variations on a Supermarket Sign." [OxfordM] (5:1) Spr-Sum 89, p. 41.
"Walnut Canyon, Arizona." [BellArk] (5:6) N-D 89, p. 9.
185. ARMSTRONG, Glen
"I Want the Girl." [CreamCR] (13:2) Fall 89, p. 9.
186. ARNETT, Carroll
"Grandma Rema." [Nimrod] (32:2) Spr-Sum 89, p. 50.
187. ARNOD, Bob
"Barred Owl" (for Janine Pommy-Vega). [HeavenB] (7) Wint 89, p. 14.
188. ARNOLD, Heidi
"Sub-ter-fuge." [Rampike] (6:3) 88, p. 70.
ARPINO, Tony d'
See D'ARPINO, Tony
189. ARROWSMITH, William
"At This Point" (tr. of Eugenio Montale). [AmerPoR] (18:4) Jl-Ag 89, p. 3.
"Changing Color" (tr. of Eugenio Montale). [AmerPoR] (18:4) Jl-Ag 89, p. 4.
"The Diver" (tr. of Eugenio Montale). [AmerPoR] (18:4) Jl-Ag 89, p. 3.
"Hiding Places" (tr. of Eugenio Montale). [AmerPoR] (18:4) Jl-Ag 89, p. 3.
"Imitation of Thunder" (tr. of Eugenio Montale). [AmerPoR] (18:4) Jl-Ag 89, p. 4.
"The Imponderable" (tr. of Eugenio Montale). [AmerPoR] (18:4) Jl-Ag 89, p. 3.
190. ARTHUR, Elizabeth
"Compass Bearings" (for Steven). [IndR] (13:1) Wint 89, p. 36.
191. ARTMAN, Deborah
"I Catch Her Mid-Swing." [HeliconN] (20) 89, p. 22.
"Romance." [HeliconN] (20) 89, p. 23.
192. ASAPH, R. Philip
"After the Hurricane." [CumbPR] (9:1) Fall 89, p. 34.
"Grandmother Walks in the Night." [CumbPR] (9:1) Fall 89, p. 35-36.
"Precious Metal." [ChatR] (10:1) Fall 89, p. 66.
193. ASCHMANN, Charles
"Card Game." [DeKalbLAJ] (22:1/4) 89, p. 42.
"Fall Match." [KanQ] (21:3) Sum 89, p. 86.
"Genesis." [KanQ] (21:3) Sum 89, p. 87.
194. ASCLEPIADES
"Three times, dear lamp, she swore here by your fire" (tr. by James Michie).
[GrandS] (8:4) Sum 89, p. 79.
195. ASEKOFF, L. S.
"Blind." [TriQ] (77) Wint 89-90, p. 271-272.
"Crows" (for Meyer Schapiro). [Pequod] (28/29/30) 89, p. 126.
"Lily Photographed by Moonlight, 1863." [Pequod] (28/29/30) 89, p. 125.
"Reading After Dark." [Sulfur] (9:1, #24) Spr 89, p. 70.
"The Sled." [Witness] (3:1) Spr 89, p. 9.
"Tsung Ping" (Tsung Ping, exiled from his homeland in old age, painted purely from
memory). [Pequod] (28/29/30) 89, p. 123-124.
196. ASFOUR, John
"A Face Between Two Shoes" (tr. of Muhammad al-Maghut). [Chelsea] (48) 89, p. p.
15-17.
197. ASH, John
"Boulevard Solitude." [Bomb] (30) Wint 89-90, p. 66.
"In a Rainy Country." [NewYorker] (65:45) 25 D 89, p. 46-47.
198. ASHANTI, Asa Paschal
"New York 1987" (from *Heart of the Father*). [Obs] (3:2) Sum 88, p. 94-95.
199. ASHBERY, John
"Autumn on the Thruway." [Conjunc] (13) 89, p. 22-26.
"In Another Time." [NewYorker] (65:10) 24 Ap 89, p. 81.

"It Is Not Visible." [BrooklynR] (6) 89, p. 44.
"Notes from the Air." [NewYorker] (65:37) 30 O 89, p. 44-45.
"Still-Life with Stranger." [NewYorker] (65:31) 18 S 89, p. 48.
"Words and Smiths." [BrooklynR] (6) 89, p. 45.
200. ASHBURY, Susan
"The Giant." [AmerV] (16) Fall 89, p. 27-28.
"When We Walked Past the DeAndrea." [Hawai'iR] (13:2, #26) Sum 89, p. 117.
201. ASHEAR, Linda
"Elegy for Ruth" (for Ruth Lisa Schechter). [Footwork] 89, p. 52.
"Testing the Water." [Vis] (31) 89, p. 33.
202. ASHLEY, Renée A.
"Burning the Sheets." [SoCoast] (7) Spr-Fall 89, p. 11.
"Warrington Ave." [SouthernPR] (29:2) Fall 89, p. 54-55.
"What Makes the Dead Rejoice." [NegC] (9:2) 89, p. 9-10.
203. ASHTON, Jennifer
"In Your South American Dream." [NewRep] (200:18) 1 My 89, p. 37.
204. ASHWORTH, D. J.
"The Abandoned Cabin." [AnthNEW] (1) 89, p. 6.
"Paradise Found." [AnthNEW] (1) 89, p. 5.
"This Spring." [AnthNEW] (1) 89, p. 6.
205. ASHWORTH, Kathryn R.
"About Trees." [WeberS] (6:2) Fall 89, p. 55-56.
"Deer Hunt." [WeberS] (6:2) Fall 89, p. 54.
"The Gypsy." [WeberS] (6:2) Fall 89, p. 53-54.
"It Is November." [WeberS] (6:2) Fall 89, p. 54.
206. ASIM, Jabari
"Days Ahead and Journeys" (for G'Ra Asim). [Obs] (3:3) Wint 88, p. 98-99.
"Dred Scott Square." [Obs] (3:3) Wint 88, p. 101-102.
"The Flying Afrikan." [PaintedB] (38) 89, p. 5-6.
"A Photograph of My Mother." [Obs] (3:3) Wint 88, p. 100.
"Sunwoman, Earthchild" (for Joyce Ella Smith). [Obs] (3:3) Wint 88, p. 103.
"Your Mother." [Obs] (3:3) Wint 88, p. 99-100.
207. ASNER, Marie
"First Day of Spring." [PassN] (10:2) Sum 89, p. 27.
208. ASPENBERG, Gary
"Autumn." [Lactuca] (12) F 89, p. 32.
"By the Road." [Vis] (31) 89, p. 29.
"June Evening." [Lactuca] (12) F 89, p. 32.
209. ASPINWALL, Dorothy
"Brother of the Prodigal Son" (tr. of Jean-Pierre Lemaire). [WebR] (14:1) Spr 89, p.
19.
"Ry th ming" (tr. of Roger Aralamon Hazoumé). [WebR] (14:1) Spr 89, p. 20.
"To the Ten Thousand Years" (tr. of Victor Segalen). [WebR] (14:1) Spr 89, p. 18.
210. ASSIS, Luiza
"O album de fotografias." [InterPR] (15:2) Fall 89, p. 60.
"Cavalos selvagens correm livres." [InterPR] (15:2) Fall 89, p. 64.
"Guitarras tangem ondulantes sons." [InterPR] (15:2) Fall 89, p. 62.
"Guitars strum undulant sounds" (tr. by the author). [InterPR] (15:2) Fall 89, p. 63.
"In our bed, only bodies exist" (tr. by the author). [InterPR] (15:2) Fall 89, p. 63.
"Na nossa cama, só corpos existem." [InterPR] (15:2) Fall 89, p. 62.
"Onde existe em nós a gente anônima." [InterPR] (15:2) Fall 89, p. 66.
"The photograph album" (tr. by the author). [InterPR] (15:2) Fall 89, p. 61.
"Where in us do anonymous people exist" (tr. by the author). [InterPR] (15:2) Fall
89, p. 67.
"Wild horses run free" (tr. by the author). [InterPR] (15:2) Fall 89, p. 65.
211. ATKINS, Kathleen
"Avowals." [CinPR] (20) Fall 89, p. 55.
"Crocus." [NowestR] (27:1) 89, p. 31.
"In the Window, Forsythia." [NowestR] (27:1) 89, p. 30.
"Summer Places." [SouthernR] (25:1) Wint 89, p. 140-142.
212. ATKINS, Priscilla
"Cornflower." [Hawai'iR] (13:2, #26) Sum 89, p. 31.
"December Rain." [BambooR] (41) Wint 89, p. 5.
"Nasturtiums." [ChamLR] (3:1, #5) Fall 89, p. 122-123.
"Turtles" (for M.J.M.). [ChamLR] (3:1, #5) Fall 89, p. 121.
"Why Haitians Speak to Their Water Buffalo in Chinese." [BambooR] (41) Wint 89,

39

p. 6-7.
213. ATKINSON, Alan
"Black Bread." [Margin] (9) 89, p. 92.
214. ATKINSON, Charles
"Anniversary Song." [CumbPR] (9:1) Fall 89, p. 17-18.
"Cancer" (for Ben Clark). [RiverC] (10:1) Fall 89, p. 108-109.
"Laid Off." [TarRP] (28:2) Spr 89, p. 26.
"Local Parades." [NegC] (9:1) 89, p. 98-99.
"Nicaraguan Ceremonial" (For the Sandanistas). [NegC] (9:1) 89, p. 100.
"Stanley" (for my sons). [CumbPR] (9:1) Fall 89, p. 19-20.
215. ATKINSON, Donald
"Whale Bone Man." [Stand] (30:4) Aut 89, p. 31.
216. ATKINSON, Jennifer
"Rain." [PraS] (63:4) Wint 89, p. 89-90.
217. ATKINSON, Michael
"3.28.88." [RiverC] (9:1) Spr 89, p. 89.
"Aurora" (For the Irish). [InterPR] (15:2) Fall 89, p. 97.
"A Dialectic." [Outbr] (20) 89, p. 18.
"Homeward." [InterPR] (15:2) Fall 89, p. 96-97.
"What the Lightning's Like." [Outbr] (20) 89, p. 16.
218. ATLIN, Gary
"Selling Seed for a Living." [MalR] (89) Wint 89, p. 65.
"Spring Thaw." [MalR] (89) Wint 89, p. 64.
219. ATTINASI, Pietro
"The Madonie" (tr. by Nat Scammacca). [Footwork] 89, p. 31.
220. AUBERT, Alvin
"All Singing in a Pie." [BlackALF] (23:3) Fall 89, p. 441.
"Baptism." [BlackALF] (23:3) Fall 89, p. 442-443.
"Nat Turner in the Clearing." [BlackALF] (23:3) Fall 89, p. 443.
"South Louisiana." [BlackALF] (23:3) Fall 89, p. 442.
221. AUFRAY, Gil
"The Thomas P. Manuscript." [Rampike] (6:3) 88, p. 64-65.
222. AUGUSTINE, Laura M.
"Splitting Up" (for TSR). [HiramPoR] (46) Spr-Sum 89, p. 9.
223. AUSTIN, Dave
"After the Poetry Reading." [JINJPo] [11] 89, p. 5-6.
"Don't Show Me Your Poem." [Footwork] 89, p. 43-44.
"Monuments." [Footwork] 89, p. 43.
224. AUSTIN, David Craig
"Saint Francis & the Elephants." [GettyR] (2:4) Aut 89, p. 658.
"The Tattooed Man." [NegC] (9:1) 89, p. 91.
"Tern's Song." [SouthwR] (74:4) Aut 89, p. 514.
225. AUSTIN, Jerry
"At My Mother's Day Care." [BellArk] (5:2) Mr-Ap 89, p. 29.
"Irish." [BellArk] (5:2) Mr-Ap 89, p. 29.
"My Triton Shell." [BellArk] (5:2) Mr-Ap 89, p. 29.
"Our Walk." [BellArk] (5:5) S-O 89, p. 10.
"Red Admiral Butterfly." [BellArk] (5:2) Mr-Ap 89, p. 29.
226. AUSTIN, Penelope
"Advice to Mothers." [Journal] (12:2) Fall-Wint 88-89, p. 6-7.
"Heedless." [NewRep] (200:24) 12 Je 89, p. 34.
"Liberty: An Aubade" (for Sydney McCall). [Journal] (12:2) Fall-Wint 88-89, p. 5.
"Lie." [Journal] (12:2) Fall-Wint 88-89, p. 8-9.
"Romance of the Road." [Journal] (12:2) Fall-Wint 88-89, p. 10-11.
227. AVERILL, Diane
"His Fence of Women." [Kalliope] (11:2) 89, p. 6.
"Leaf Tongues." [MidwQ] (31:1) Aut 89, p. 45.
"The Soil Wants Us" (After "Upright" by Tomas Tranströmer). [MidwQ] (31:1) Aut 89, p. 46.
"Steps in Composition: Four Students." [TarRP] (29:1) Fall 89, p. 12.
"While Moving We." [Kalliope] (11:2) 89, p. 59.
228. AVISON, Margaret
"Ode to Bartok" (tr. of Gyula Illyés, w. Ilonn Duczynska). [CanLit] (120) Spr 89, p. 46-49.
229. AWAD, Joseph
"Checkpoint." [Sparrow] (56) 89, p. 9.

"For Jude's Lebanon." [Sparrow] (56) 89, p. 4-5.
"Repeating Pattern." [Sparrow] (56) 89, p. 11.
"Richmond." [Sparrow] (56) 89, p. 10.
"Snapshot." [Sparrow] (56) 89, p. 6.
"Stonework." [Sparrow] (56) 89, p. 14.
"Storm at Sandbridge." [Sparrow] (56) 89, p. 12-13.
"The Two of Us." [Sparrow] (56) 89, p. 7-8.
230. AWANA, Les
"The Brand New Day." [Hawai'iR] (13:3) Fall 89, p. 66.
231. AXELROD, David B.
"Black Dream." [Footwork] 89, p. 16.
"Geraci Sicolo, Sicily." [Footwork] 89, p. 17.
"He Waters His Plants at 1:15 AM" (for Nat Scammacca). [Footwork] 89, p. 17.
"The Universal Language." [Footwork] 89, p. 16.
232. AXINN, Donald Everett
"The Antelope" (for Jay Parini). [WritersF] (15) Fall 89, p. 21-22.
"Tiwa Pueblo, Taos." [WritersF] (15) Fall 89, p. 22.
233. AYCOCK, Estelle
"Keep Passing the Open Windows" (with thanks to John Irving, *The Hotel New Hampshire*). [EngJ] (78:6) O 89, p. 93.
234. AYYILDIZ, Judy Light
"Cappadocia" (Central Turkey). [Pig] (15) 88, p. 36.
"Lake Drained for Aesthetic Values." [NewRena] (7:3, #23) 89, p. 29.
235. AZRAEL, Mary
"Sitting Out, in Bat Light." [KanQ] (21:4) Fall 89, p. 120.
236. AZZOPARDI, Mario
"Plants" (tr. by Oliver Friggieri). [Vis] (31) 89, p. 10.
237. BAATZ, Ronald
"Against the World." [WormR] (29:4, #116) 89, p. 111.
"Around the Edges." [WormR] (29:4, #116) 89, p. 112-113.
"Back at the Panda." [WormR] (29:4, #116) 89, p. 112.
"Before I Sit Down to write." [WormR] (29:4, #116) 89, p. 114-115.
"Exotic Japanese." [WormR] (29:4, #116) 89, p. 109-110.
"Frozen Pizza." [WormR] (29:4, #116) 89, p. 113-114.
"I Have Completely Given Up Cooking." [WormR] (29:4, #116) 89, p. 108-109.
"Insecure." [WormR] (29:4, #116) 89, p. 110-111.
"My Mozart Series." [WormR] (29:4, #116) 89, p. 114.
"Poetry Has Ruined Me." [WormR] (29:4, #116) 89, p. 115.
"When I Leave Here." [WormR] (29:4, #116) 89, p. 111.
"Womanless Tuesday." [YellowS] (32) Wint 89, p. 29.
BACA, Jimmy Santiago
See SANTIAGO-BACA, Jimmy
238. BACHMANN, Ingeborg
"Every Day" (tr. by Peter Filkins). [TriQ] (74) Wint 89, p. 214.
"The Landscape Around Vienna" (tr. by Lisa Ress). [GrahamHR] (12) Spr 89, p. 48-50.
"No Delicacies" (tr. by Peter Filkins). [TriQ] (74) Wint 89, p. 215-216.
239. BACHNER, Jane
"Autumn Day." [CentR] (33:1) Wint 89, p. 56-57.
240. BACHSTEIN, Michael
"As She Left It." [Poem] (61) My 89, p. 52.
"Limb for Limb." [Poem] (61) My 89, p. 51.
241. BACK, Rachel Tzvia
"After Love." [PaintedB] (38) 89, p. 48.
"Night Song." [PaintedB] (38) 89, p. 50.
"Where Grief Hovers" (for Ouma & Oupa). [PaintedB] (38) 89, p. 49.
242. BACKER, Sara
"Maybe You're the Man Who Can Make Me Come, But First, Your Bank Balance." [Vis] (30) 89, p. 46.
"Veteran." [OxfordM] (5:1) Spr-Sum 89, p. 67.
243. BAD, Bill E.
"Dogs." [WormR] (29:1, #113) 89, p. 4.
"An Even Score." [WormR] (29:1, #113) 89, p. 4.
244. BADEJO, Diedre L.
"Tokunbo: A Divination Poem." [BlackALF] (23:3) Fall 89, p. 486-489.

41

245. BADIKIAN, B.
    "At the Exhibit" (for Georgia O'Keeffe, 1887-1986). [SpoonRQ] (14:3) Sum 89, p.
        14-15.
    "Reading Denise Levertov." [SpoonRQ] (14:3) Sum 89, p. 15.
246. BADILLA, Sergio
    "It Frequently Happens" (tr. by Sara Heikoff Woehrlen). [SoDakR] (27:2) Sum 89,
        p. 85.
    "Skin" (tr. by Sara Heikoff Woehrlen). [SoDakR] (27:2) Sum 89, p. 86.
247. BAECHLER, Lea
    "Hyperbola." [SouthernR] (25:4) Aut 89, p. 900-902.
    "Taking a Life." [SouthernR] (25:4) Aut 89, p. 902-903.
248. BAER, Daniel
    "Facades Beneath." [HarvardA] (123:3) Mr 89, p. 22.
249. BAER, Thomas
    "Peter Bowles' Piscine Pusses." [Rampike] (6:3) 88, p. 55-57.
250. BAGLEY, Alice Ann
    "Aunt Nell." [Calyx] (12:1) Sum 89, p. 11.
    "Bones." [Calyx] (12:1) Sum 89, p. 9.
    "Finding." [Calyx] (12:1) Sum 89, p. 10.
251. BAGLOW, John
    "The Pterodactyl's Nest." [Grain] (17:1) Spr 89, p. 44.
    "Reductio." [CanLit] (121) Sum 89, p. 124-125.
252. BAHAN, Lee Harlin
    "Almanac." [Ploughs] (15:4) Wint 89-90, p. 13-14.
    "Canonicity." [PaintedB] (37) 89, p. 17.
    "Invisible Lids: A Revison of Petrarch" (Selection: No. 74). [ArtfulD] (16/17) Fall 89,
        p. 12.
    "John Cougar Really Has Cousins Here." [Ploughs] (15:4) Wint 89-90, p. 12.
    "Mid-Winter Thaw, New England." [ArtfulD] (16/17) Fall 89, p. 13.
253. BAHLER, Beth
    "There Are Times." [Footwork] 89, p. 35.
254. BAHM, Jim
    "Being There." [Plain] (10:1) 89, p. 28.
255. BAI, Hua
    "A Book" (tr. by Dong Jiping). [Footwork] 89, p. 26.
256. BAI, Juyi
    "At the Tomb of Li Bai" (tr. by Anthony Piccione and Carol Zhigong Chang). [LitR]
        (32:3) Spr 89, p. 392.
    "Evening River Song" (tr. by Anthony Piccione and Carol Zhigong Chang). [LitR]
        (32:3) Spr 89, p. 392.
    "Grasses" (tr. by Chuan Y. Fu and Nick Otten). [RiverS] (30) [89], p. 79.
    "Love Long-Enduring" (tr. by Burton Watson). [LitR] (32:3) Spr 89, p. 436.
    "On Board Ship: Reading Yüan Chen's Poems" (tr. by Arthur Waley). [LitR] (32:3)
        Spr 89, p. 305.
    "A Question Addressed to Liu Shih-Chiu" (tr. by Burton Watson). [LitR] (32:3) Spr
        89, p. 436.
    "Spring Outing" (tr. by Burton Watson). [LitR] (32:3) Spr 89, p. 437.
BAI, Li
    See LI, Po
BAIG, Sandi Blakemore
    See BLAKEMORE-BAIG, Sandi
257. BAILEY-WOFFORD, Jan
    "After the Divorce." [SingHM] (16) 89, p. 44.
258. BAKER, David
    "1962." [NoAmR] (274:4) D 89, p. 37.
    "After the Reunion." [Nat] (249:3) 17 Jl 89, p. 100.
    "Called Back." [GettyR] (2:3) Sum 89, p. 426.
    "Cardinals in Spring" (After Whitman). [KenR] (NS 11:3) Sum 89, p. 101-104.
    "Domestic of Hope" (a pastoral). [MissouriR] (12:1) 89, p. 228-229.
    "Domestic of Terror" (a confession). [MissouriR] (12:1) 89, p. 230-231.
    "Music in the Smokehouse." [PoetryNW] (30:3) Aut 89, p. 43-47.
    "Sweet Home, Saturday Night." [SouthernR] (25:4) Aut 89, p. 918-935.
259. BAKER, Dean
    "The Slow Gathering" (for Maria). [Bogg] (61) 89, p. 24.
260. BAKER, June Frankland
    "Antique Car Show, Columbia Center." [KanQ] (21:4) Fall 89, p. 22.

"Cypridina." [CrossCur] (8:3) Apr 89, p. 102-103.
"Flying a Piper Cub J-3." [ThRiPo] (33/34) 89, p. 27.
"Listening In." [ThRiPo] (33/34) 89, p. 26.
261. BAKER, T. M.
"Bob White." [Nimrod] (32:2) Spr-Sum 89, p. 77.
"A Song for Two Voices and Four Worlds." [Nimrod] (32:2) Spr-Sum 89, p. 78-79.
"A Stitch in Time." [Nimrod] (32:2) Spr-Sum 89, p. 77.
262. BAKER, Winona
"Exorcism." [Bogg] (61) 89, p. 52.
263. BAKOWSKI, Peter
"The Farmer Ploughs the Earth of His Piano" (for Thelonious Monk). [MoodySI]
(20/21) Spr 89, p. 44.
"I Am Vagabond in Every Room of the World." [AlphaBS] (5) Jl 89, p. 22-26.
"Love Poem for the Thin Girls" (for Jayne). [AlphaBS] (6) Wint 89-90, p. 49-50.
"Piece for Solo Piano (Looking for Angels in the Nicotine)." [AlphaBS] (5) Jl 89, p.
27-28.
"This Thing Goes On for As Many Rounds As You Live" (for Eugene Carchesio).
[AlphaBS] (6) Wint 89-90, p. 28.
264. BALABAN, John
"Words for My Daughter" (From Ploughshares, vol. 14, no. 1). [Harp] (278:1664) Ja
89, p. 42.
265. BALAKIAN, Peter
"The Color of Pomegranates." [Poetry] (154:5) Ag 89, p. 257.
"Jersey Fog." [KenR] (NS 11:2) Spr 89, p. 40-44.
"A Toast" (For Bruce Smith). [Poetry] (154:5) Ag 89, p. 256.
266. BALAN, Jars
"Circus" (for Tamarka and Katrusia, from Autobiographica). [CanLit] (120) Spr 89,
p. 105-109.
267. BALASHOVA, Elena
"Observation of a Fallen Leaf as the 'Ultimate Basis' of Landscape" (a reading, tr. of
Arkadii Dragomoshchenko, w. Lyn Hejinian). [PaperAir] (4:2) 89, p. 63-66.
"Opsis" (from "Syn tax," tr. of Arkadii Dragomoshchenko, w. Lyn Hejinian).
[MichQR] (28:4) Fall 89, p. 734-736.
268. BALAZ, Joseph P. (Joe)
"Da Mainland to Me." [ChamLR] (2:2, #4) Spr 89, p. 109.
"Da New Kahiko." [Hawai'iR] (13:1, #25) Spr 89, p. 41.
"The Industrial Poet." [ChamLR] (3:1, #5) Fall 89, p. 184-185.
"Kala Talks." [Hawai'iR] (13:1, #25) Spr 89, p. 42.
"Mokuahana." [Hawai'iR] (13:3) Fall 89, p. 28.
"No Moking." [Hawai'iR] (13:3) Fall 89, p. 26.
"Protestant Hawaiian." [Hawai'iR] (13:3) Fall 89, p. 27.
269. BALAZS, Mary
"Afterwards to Stop Our Scolding." [KanQ] (21:3) Sum 89, p. 131.
"Elder Son." [KanQ] (21:3) Sum 89, p. 130.
270. BALDWIN, Beth Williams
"Free Fall." [GreensboroR] (47) Wint 89-90, p. 72-73.
271. BALDWIN, Neil
"Occupational Hazards." [Contact] (9:53/54/55) Sum-Fall 89, p. 28.
"Psalm." [Contact] (9:53/54/55) Sum-Fall 89, p. 28.
272. BALDWIN, Sy Margaret
"The Desert Is Not the Enemy" (for the Salvadorans who died in Organ Pipe National
Monument 7/80). [Cond] (16) 89, p. 107-108.
"I Work Underground" (for the woman miner killed by a falling slab of slate,
Coalport, Pennsylvania, October 1979). [Cond] (16) 89, p. 155-156.
273. BALESTRI, Ray A.
"Wallace Stevens in a Photograph." [CapeR] (24:2) Fall 89, p. 29.
274. BALESTRIERI, Elizabeth
"Salad Days." [ApalQ] (31) 89, p. 54-55.
"Torch Lake." [ApalQ] (31) 89, p. 52-53.
275. BALI, Brigitta
"Biography -- 1981" (in Hungarian & English, tr. by Wally Keeler). [Rampike] (6:2)
88, p. 66.
"Replacement" (in Hungarian & English, tr. by Wally Keeler). [Rampike] (6:2) 88, p.
66-67.
276. BALL, Angela
"The Artist Who Became Colorblind." [Outbr] (20) 89, p. 66.

"Body." [Poetry] (153:4) Ja 89, p. 199.
"Cobweb." [MalR] (89) Wint 89, p. 25.
"During Great Pain." [Journal] (13:1) Spr-Sum 89, p. 40.
"Elegy for Edgar Allan Poe." [MalR] (89) Wint 89, p. 24.
"Four Poems for Anton Checkov." [MalR] (88) Fall 89, p. 20-25.
"I Don't Know." [Journal] (13:1) Spr-Sum 89, p. 41-43.
"A Language" (For Michael Ondaatje). [KenR] (NS 11:3) Sum 89, p. 25-26.
"Leaf Hour." [MalR] (89) Wint 89, p. 26-27.
"Necessary Wood." [PoetryE] (28) Fall 89, p. 167.
"The New City." [NewOR] (16:3) Fall 89, p. 95.
"Nina" (for Tomaz Salamun). [DenQ] (23:3/4) Wint-Spr 89, p. 77.
"Possession." [Poetry] (154:6) S 89, p. 325-326.
"The Prayer Meeting." [NowestR] (27:2) 89, p. 56.
"Tandem." [Poetry] (153:4) Ja 89, p. 197-198.
"Touch." [MalR] (89) Wint 89, p. 28-29.
"Verge." [Journal] (13:1) Spr-Sum 89, p. 44-46.
277. BALL, David
"Les Ravagés" (Selections: 2, 4, 7, 12, 21, tr. of Henri Michaux). [MassR] (30:3)
Aut 89, p. 396-398.
278. BALL, Joseph H.
"Drive-In Movie." [WindO] (51) Spr 89, p. 48-49.
279. BALL, Richard
"Alphabet." [Pembroke] (21) 89, p. 58.
"Billy." [Pembroke] (21) 89, p. 57.
"Pain" (Oswestry Cottage Hospital, 15th October, 1984). [Pembroke] (21) 89, p. 55.
"Quarryman at the Pandy, CLWYD." [Pembroke] (21) 89, p. 56-57.
"Tree Pipits." [Pembroke] (21) 89, p. 55-56.
280. BALLARD, Rae
"Eve to Her Daughters." [ChrC] (106:14) Ap 26, 89, p. 436.
281. BALON, Brett
"Eiffel." [Grain] (17:1) Spr 89, p. 60.
"Whirlwind." [Grain] (17:1) Spr 89, p. 60.
282. BALTENSPERGER, Peter
"Lake Huron Suite." [CanLit] (122/123) Aut-Wint 89, p. 65-68.
283. BAMFORTH, Iain
"Men on Fire." [Verse] (6:1) Mr 89, p. 19.
"Pisces Ascendant" (for D. J. S.). [Verse] (6:1) Mr 89, p. 20-21.
284. BANDYOPADHYAY, Sanjukta
"Death Beside the Ganges" (tr. by Paramita Banerjee and Carolyne Wright, w. the
author). [MichQR] (28:2) Spr 89, p. 230-231.
"Kitchen" (tr. by Paramita Banerjee and Carolyne Wright, w. the author). [MichQR]
(28:2) Spr 89, p. 229-230.
285. BANERJEE, Paramita
"Beginning and End" (in Bengali and English, tr. of Nabaneeta Dev Sen, w. Carolyn
Wright and the author). [BlackWR] (15:2) Spr 89, p. 82-83.
"The Carriers of Fire" (tr. of Mallika Sengupta, w. Carolyne Wright). [NewEngR]
(11:4) Sum 89, p. 460.
"Death Beside the Ganges" (tr. of Sanjukta Bandyopadhyay, w. Carolyne Wright and
the author). [MichQR] (28:2) Spr 89, p. 230-231.
"Engraving" (in Bengali and English, tr. of Anuradha Mahapatra, w. Carolyn Wright
and the author). [BlackWR] (15:2) Spr 89, p. 86-87.
"Home" (tr. of Mallika Sengupta, w. Carolyne Wright). [Iowa] (19:2) Spr-Sum 89,
p. 120.
"Kitchen" (tr. of Sanjukta Bandyopadhyay, w. Carolyne Wright and the author).
[MichQR] (28:2) Spr 89, p. 229-230.
"Living in Disguise" (tr. of Anuradha Mahapatra, w. Carolyne Wright). [Iowa] (19:2)
Spr-Sum 89, p. 119.
"Marriage Vessel" (tr. of Pratima Ray, w. Carolyne Wright). [NewEngR] (11:4) Sum
89, p. 459.
"The Peacock" (tr. of Anuradha Mahapatra, w. Carolyne Wright). [Iowa] (19:2)
Spr-Sum 89, p. 118.
"Return" (in Bengali and English, tr. of Nabaneeta Dev Sen, w. Carolyn Wright and
the author). [BlackWR] (15:2) Spr 89, p. 84-85.
"Ritual Sacrifice" (tr. of Mallika Sengupta, w. Carolyne Wright). [Iowa] (19:2)
Spr-Sum 89, p. 120-121.
"Village Nocturne" (tr. of Anuradha Mahapatra, w. Carolyne Wright). [Iowa] (19:2)

Spr-Sum 89, p. 117.
"You" (in Bengali and English, tr. of Anuradha Mahapatra, w. Carolyn Wright and the author). [BlackWR] (15:2) Spr 89, p. 88-89.
286. BANGS, Carol Jane
"Jomon Sho" (Yoshiyuki Takada fell 80 feet to his death while performing a "hanging" dance entitled "Jomon Sho"). [IndR] (13:1) Wint 89, p. 20-22.
287. BANKS, Kenneth
"Almost Unnoticed, Till the Snow." [AntigR] (76) Wint 89, p. 10.
"Only a Week Ago They Would." [AntigR] (76) Wint 89, p. 8.
"You Rummaged Through the High Cliffs Like." [AntigR] (76) Wint 89, p. 9.
288. BANUS, Maria
"Across Bucarest After Rain" (tr. by Mary Mattfield). [GrahamHR] (12) Spr 89, p. 45.
"Gemütlich" (tr. by Mary Mattfield). [GrahamHR] (12) Spr 89, p. 42-43.
"In the Forest" (tr. by Mary Mattfield). [GrahamHR] (12) Spr 89, p. 47.
"Letter" (tr. by Mary Mattfield). [GrahamHR] (12) Spr 89, p. 44.
"Song Beneath Tanks" (tr. by Mary Mattfield). [GrahamHR] (12) Spr 89, p. 46.
289. BARAKA, Amiri
"Ancient Music." [BlackALF] (23:3) Fall 89, p. 465.
"Chuck." [BlackALF] (23:3) Fall 89, p. 465.
"Masked Angel Costume." [BlackALF] (23:3) Fall 89, p. 463-465.
290. BARANCZAK, Stanislaw
"Above Us" (tr. of Julia Hartwig, w. Clare Cavanagh). [PartR] (56:2) Spr 89, p. 282.
"Aniela in the Town of Folino" (tr. of Miron Bialoszewski, w. Clare Cavanah). [Trans] (21) Spr 89, p. 38-39.
"Atlantyda" (tr. by Michael and Aleksandra Parker). [Verse] (6:1) Mr 89, p. 39.
"Barricade" (tr. of Julian Kornhauser, w. Clare Cavanah). [Trans] (21) Spr 89, p. 78.
"Clothes" (tr. of Wislawa Szymborska, w. Clare Cavanagh). [SenR] (19:2) Fall 89, p. 20.
"Don't Use the Word 'Exile'" (tr. by the author). [SenR] (19:2) Fall 89, p. 6.
"Ex-Jewish Things" (tr. of Jerzy Ficowski, w. Clare Cavanagh). [SenR] (19:2) Fall 89, p. 25.
"Facing the Wall" (tr. of Ryszard Krynicki, w. Clare Cavanagh). [PartR] (56:2) Spr 89, p. 288.
"Fascist Nations" (tr. of Wiktor Woroszylski, w. Clare Cavanagh). [PartR] (56:2) Spr 89, p. 283-285.
"Fate the Clerk Lays Down a New Set of By-Laws" (tr. of Artur Miedzyrzecki, w. Clare Cavanagh). [PartR] (56:2) Spr 89, p. 281.
"From the Gulf Stream of Sleep" (tr. of Ewa Lipska, w. Clare Cavanah). [Trans] (21) Spr 89, p. 77.
"Funny" (tr. of Anna Kamienska, w. Clare Cavanah). [Trans] (21) Spr 89, p. 20.
"The Great Man's House" (tr. of Wislawa Szymborska, w. Clare Cavanah). [Trans] (21) Spr 89, p. 42-43.
"How to Spoil Cannibals' Fun" (tr. of Jerzy Ficowski, w. Clare Cavanah). [Trans] (21) Spr 89, p. 44-45.
"Hymn" (tr. of Jan Polkowski, w. Clare Cavanagh). [PartR] (56:2) Spr 89, p. 290.
"In Broad Daylight" (tr. of Wistawa Szymborska, w. Clare Cavanagh). [PartR] (56:2) Spr 89, p. 278-279.
"Indictment" (tr. of Wiktor Woroszylski, w. Clare Cavanagh). [PartR] (56:2) Spr 89, p. 285-286.
"Indiscretions" (tr. of Piotr Sommer, w. Clare Cavanagh). [SenR] (19:2) Fall 89, p. 29.
"Into the Ark" (tr. of Wislawa Szymborska, w. Clare Cavanagh). [SenR] (19:2) Fall 89, p. 21-22.
"It Takes Just a Few Minutes" (tr. of Bronislaw Maj, w. Clare Cavanah). [Trans] (21) Spr 89, p. 82.
"The Jesus of Nonbelievers" (tr. of Jan Twardowski, w. Clare Cavanah). [Trans] (21) Spr 89, p. 18.
"Mandelstam Street" (tr. of Jaroslaw Marek Rymkiewicz, w. Clare Cavanagh). [SenR] (19:2) Fall 89, p. 28.
"Mantegna's Christ" (tr. of Mieczyslaw Jastrun, w. Clare Cavanah). [Trans] (21) Spr 89, p. 17.
"Medicine" (tr. of Piotr Sommer, w. Clare Cavanah). [Trans] (21) Spr 89, p. 79.
"Mendacity" (tr. of Witold Wirpsza, w. Clare Cavanah). [Trans] (21) Spr 89, p. 19.
"My Sweet Motherland" (tr. of Jan Polkowski, w. Clare Cavanagh). [PartR] (56:2) Spr 89, p. 289.

"A New Day" (tr. of Ryszard Krynicki, w. Clare Cavanah). [Trans] (21) Spr 89, p.
   67.
"The Offspring of Heraclitus" (tr. of Adam Wazyk, w. Clare Cavanah). [Trans] (21)
   Spr 89, p. 16.
"Our Ancestors' Short Lives" (tr. of Wistawa Szymborska, w. Clare Cavanagh).
   [PartR] (56:2) Spr 89, p. 277-278.
"The Padlock Speaks" (From the "Diary of Internment, II," tr. of Wiktor
   Woroszylski, w. Clare Cavanagh). [PartR] (56:2) Spr 89, p. 286.
"Pastoral Psalm" (for Zosia, tr. of Tadeusz Nowak, w. Clare Cavanah). [Trans] (21)
   Spr 89, p. 60-61.
"Philately" (tr. of Wiktor Woroszylski, w. Clare Cavanah). [Trans] (21) Spr 89, p.
   58-59.
"The Poet Grows Weaker" (tr. of Tadeusz Rozewicz, w. Clare Cavanah). [Trans]
   (21) Spr 89, p. 36-37.
"Possibilities" (tr. of Wislawa Szymborska, w. Clare Cavanagh). [SenR] (19:2) Fall
   89, p. 23-24.
"Psalm with No Answer" (tr. of Tadeusz Nowak, w. Clare Cavanagh). [SenR] (19:2)
   Fall 89, p. 26.
"A Question of Rhythm" (tr. by Michael and Aleksandra Parker). [Verse] (6:1) Mr 89,
   p. 38.
"The Reason of Existence" (tr. of Artur Miedzyrzecki, w. Clare Cavanah). [Trans]
   (21) Spr 89, p. 40-41.
"Report" (tr. of Leszek A. Moczulski, w. Clare Cavanah). [Trans] (21) Spr 89, p. 66.
"The Restaurant 'Arcadia,' Central Square, Nowa Huta" (tr. of Jan Polkowski, w.
   Clare Cavanah). [Trans] (21) Spr 89, p. 81.
"Smoke" (tr. of Tomasz Jastrun, w. Clare Cavanah). [Trans] (21) Spr 89, p. 80.
"Socialist Realism" (tr. of Ryszard Krynicki, w. Clare Cavanagh). [PartR] (56:2) Spr
   89, p. 287.
"Some Time, Years Later" (tr. by Michael and Aleksandra Parker). [Verse] (6:1) Mr
   89, p. 38.
"Song of a Crust of Bread Thown to Sparrows on Victory Square . . ." (tr. of Jan
   Prokop, w. Clare Cavanagh). [SenR] (19:2) Fall 89, p. 27.
"Song of Four-Egg Enriched Ribbon Noodles" (tr. of Jan Prokop, w. Clare
   Cavanah). [Trans] (21) Spr 89, p. 62.
"Soot" (tr. of Ernest Bryll, w. Clare Cavanah). [Trans] (21) Spr 89, p. 63.
"A Stop" (tr. of Ryszard Krynicki, w. Clare Cavanagh). [PartR] (56:2) Spr 89, p.
   287.
"A Tale Begun" (tr. of Wistawa Szymborska, w. Clare Cavanagh). [PartR] (56:2) Spr
   89, p. 280-281.
"This city died. Blue streetcars moan" (tr. of Bronislaw Maj, w. Clare Cavanagh).
   [PartR] (56:2) Spr 89, p. 291.
"The Three Magi" (To Lech Dymarski, tr. by the author). [SenR] (19:2) Fall 89, p. 5.
"The War of Nerves" (tr. of Artur Miedzyrzecki, w. Clare Cavanagh). [PartR] (56:2)
   Spr 89, p. 282.
"What Can They" (tr. of Julia Hartwig, w. Clare Cavanagh). [PartR] (56:2) Spr 89,
   p. 283.
"When I Woke Up" (tr. of Jaroslaw Marek Rymkiewicz, w. Clare Cavanah). [Trans]
   (21) Spr 89, p. 64-65.
"Who Says" (tr. of Julia Hartwig, w. Clare Cavanah). [Trans] (21) Spr 89, p. 35.
"Who will bear witness to these times?" (tr. of Bronislaw Maj, w. Clare Cavanagh).
   [PartR] (56:2) Spr 89, p. 290.
"You're Free" (tr. of Ryszard Krynicki, w. Clare Cavanagh). [PartR] (56:2) Spr 89,
   p. 287.
291. BARANOW, Joan
   "Looking Out of a Window." [US1] (22/23) Spr 89, p. 3.
292. BARATTA, Edward
   "Hips." [PoetryE] (28) Fall 89, p. 10.
293. BARBARESE, J. T.
   "Cross." [Boulevard] (4:2, #11) Fall 89, p. 176.
   "Full Moon." [SewanR] (97:2) Spr 89, p. 173-174.
   "Kite Flying, 29 August" (for Marianna Moore: 1954-1987). [AntR] (47:1) Wint 89,
      p. 63.
   "New Science." [SewanR] (97:2) Spr 89, p. 175.
   "You." [SewanR] (97:2) Spr 89, p. 174-175.
294. BARBER, J. Delayne
   "Imagining the Photo Album." [HighP] (4:1) Spr 89, p. 90-91.

295. BARBOSA, Jorge
"Children" (tr. by Jean R. Longland). [Pig] (15) 88, p. 52.
"Island" (tr. by Jean R. Longland). [Pig] (15) 88, p. 51.
"Lullaby" (tr. by Jean R. Longland). [Pig] (15) 88, p. 51.
296. BARBOUR, Doug
"How do we speak of the dead." [Dandel] (16:1) Spr-Sum 89, p. 34-35.
"Two Chinese Tracings." [Dandel] (16:1) Spr-Sum 89, p. 31-33.
297. BARCLAY, Connon
"Attention: Mr. President: Washington, D.C., or A Sonnet for Three." [Writer]
(102:9) S 89, p. 22.
298. BARDWELL, Leland
"Them's Your Mother's Pills." [FourQ] (2d series 3:2) Fall 89, p. 43-44.
299. BARENDSEN, Kristin
"A Way of Seeing" (Winner of the Michael Jasper Gioia Undergraduate Award in
Poetry for 1989). [Sequoia] (33:1) Sum 89, p. 41.
300. BARGEN, Walter
"The Bates Method of Eye Exercises." [Farm] (6:1) Wint-Spr 88-89, p. 120-121.
"Concessions." [LaurelR] (23:2) Sum 89, p. 66-67.
"Kristallnacht." [CharR] (15:2) Fall 89, p. 80-81.
"Rumors of Your Death." [MissouriR] (12:1) 89, p. 218-219.
"The Terms." [CapeR] (24:1) Spr 89, p. 5.
"Waif Time." [Ascent] (14:3) 89, p. 45-46.
"Yet Other Waters" (for Bobette). [MissouriR] (12:1) 89, p. 217.
301. BARKAN, Stanley H.
"In the Back of the Grocery Store." [Footwork] 89, p. 32.
"On the Milkboxes" (for Howard Strassman). [Footwork] 89, p. 32-33.
"The Trees of My Childhood." [Footwork] 89, p. 31-32.
"Words My Father Left Me" (for Rabbi Jeremiah Wohlberg). [Footwork] 89, p. 31.
302. BARKER, David
"Mercy." [Poetry] (154:5) Ag 89, p. 280.
"Red Shift." [Poetry] (154:5) Ag 89, p. 279-280.
"The Supernatural: A Love Poem" (1963-1988). [Poetry] (154:5) Ag 89, p. 278-279.
303. BARKER, Diane
"Spooked." [KanQ] (21:1/2) Wint-Spr 89, p. 130.
304. BARKER, Sebastian
"On the Rocks" (Selections: XVII, XXI, L). [Pequod] (26/27) 89, p. 73-74.
305. BARKER, Sue Tamminga
"My Child." [Poetry] (154:2) My 89, p. 90.
"A Woman's Song." [Poetry] (154:2) My 89, p. 89.
306. BARKER, Wendy
"Giving Up the Dead." [Poetry] (155:3) D 89, p. 222-223.
"My Mother's Dream Winter." [PoetL] (84:1) Spr 89, p. 27-28.
"My Mother's Sewing Machine." [TarRP] (29:1) Fall 89, p. 34-35.
"Requiescat, for My Father." [AmerS] (58:4) Aut 89, p. 578-580.
"White Chair Before Summer." [MSS] (6:3) 89, p. 68.
"Why We Went to the Ocean." [CrossCur] (8:3) Apr 89, p. 168-169.
307. BARLOW, Mailin L.
"On Seeing Robin Williams at the Royal Gala." [CrossCur] (8:3) Apr 89, p. 39.
308. BARNARD, Sylvia
"The Museum." [Mildred] (3:2) 89, p. 124.
"St. Patrick's Day." [Mildred] (3:2) 89, p. 125.
309. BARNES, C. F.
"At the Supermarket." [CumbPR] (8:2) Spr 89, p. 22-23.
"The Traveler." [ConnPR] (8:1) 89, p. 9.
"With Horses, an Elegy" (for my mother). [CreamCR] (13:2) Fall 89, p. 145-146.
310. BARNES, Christopher R.
"For Sydney" (g.g. grandfather, 1828-1864). [WestB] (24) 89, p. 27.
BARNÉS, Gladys Vila
See VILA BARNÉS, Gladys
311. BARNES, Jane
"Discovery." [HangL] (55) 89, p. 8.
"Got to Go." [HangL] (55) 89, p. 10.
"Within Hearing." [HangL] (55) 89, p. 9.
312. BARNES, Jim
"After the Funeral" (In memory of Bessie Vernon Adams Barnes). [PoetryE] (28) Fall
89, p. 82-83.

"The Chicago Odyssey." [NewL] (56:2/3) Wint 89-Spr 90, p. 30-31.
"Crossing the Kiamichis Again." [LaurelR] (23:2) Sum 89, p. 19.
"For the Suicide." [LaurelR] (23:2) Sum 89, p. 20.
"The Game." [CinPR] (19) Spr 89, p. 34.
"Gill Netting the Beaver Pond." [MissouriR] (12:1) 89, p. 222-224.
"La Plata, Missouri: Bandstand." [KenR] (NS 11:1) Wint 89, p. 78-79.
"La Plata, Missouri: Sante Fe Depot, Sundown." [KenR] (NS 11:1) Wint 89, p. 78.
"Return to La Plata, Missouri." [NewL] (56:2/3) Wint 89-Spr 90, p. 31.
"Touching the Rattlesnake." [NewL] (56:2/3) Wint 89-Spr 90, p. 32-33.
"The War Over Holson Valley." [LaurelR] (23:2) Sum 89, p. 18.
"The War Over Holson Valley." [NewL] (56:2/3) Wint 89-Spr 90, p. 33.

313. BARNES, Kate
"The White Mare." [BelPoJ] (40:1) Fall 89, p. 1.

314. BARNES, Mary Ellen
"Aretha, Rodney, and Me." [WormR] (29:1, #113) 89, p. 12-13.
"The Last Japanese Soldier to Emerge from the Jungle." [WormR] (29:1, #113) 89, p. 12.
"Not Quite Making the Grade." [WormR] (29:1, #113) 89, p. 13.

315. BARNES, W. J.
"Being in Hospital." [Quarry] (38:4) Fall 89, p. 62-63.
"Birth Poem" (for Ian Christopher). [Quarry] (38:4) Fall 89, p. 59.
"On the Death of My Father." [Quarry] (38:4) Fall 89, p. 57-58.
"Sister Irene on Johnson 4." [Quarry] (38:4) Fall 89, p. 60-61.

316. BARNETT, Cathy
"Waiting for Deer." [BallSUF] (30:4) Aut 89, p. 6.

317. BARNSTONE, Tony
"25. Don't spy at the window" (tr. of Miguel Hernández). [InterPR] (15:2) Fall 89, p. 47.
"30. You in white, I in black" (tr. of Miguel Hernández). [InterPR] (15:2) Fall 89, p. 47.
"31. The ardent firefly" (tr. of Miguel Hernández). [InterPR] (15:2) Fall 89, p. 47.
"32. I can't forget" (tr. of Miguel Hernández). [InterPR] (15:2) Fall 89, p. 49.
"38. The two doors catch fire" (tr. of Miguel Hernández). [InterPR] (15:2) Fall 89, p. 49.
"71. The cemetery is near" (tr. of Miguel Hernández). [InterPR] (15:2) Fall 89, p. 49.
"Composed on Horseback for My Younger Brother Cui the Ninth on His Departure to the South" (tr. of Wang Wei, w. Willis Barnstone and Xu Haixin). [LitR] (32:3) Spr 89, p. 337.
"Going to the Country in the Spring" (tr. of Wang Wei, w. Willis Barnstone and Xu Haixin). [LitR] (32:3) Spr 89, p. 338.
"Lady Pan" (tr. of Wang Wei, w. Willis Barnstone and Xu Xaixan). [CentR] (33:3) Sum 89, p. 250.
"Missing the Loved One" (tr. of Wang Wei, w. Willis Barnstone and Xu Xaixan). [CentR] (33:3) Sum 89, p. 250.
"Moaning about My White Hair" (tr. of Wang Wei, w. Willis Barnstone and Xu Haixin). [LitR] (32:3) Spr 89, p. 337.
"The Stillness of Meditation" (tr. of Wang Wei, w. Willis Barnstone and Xu Haixin). [LitR] (32:3) Spr 89, p. 338.
"Written in My Garden in Spring" (tr. of Wang Wei, w. Willis Barnstone and Xu Xaixan). [CentR] (33:3) Sum 89, p. 250.

318. BARNSTONE, Willis
"Christmas Morning on Plato Street." [NewL] (56:2/3) Wint 89-Spr 90, p. 35.
"Composed on Horseback for My Younger Brother Cui the Ninth on His Departure to the South" (tr. of Wang Wei, w. Tony Barnstone and Xu Haixin). [LitR] (32:3) Spr 89, p. 337.
"Going to the Country in the Spring" (tr. of Wang Wei, w. Tony Barnstone and Xu Haixin). [LitR] (32:3) Spr 89, p. 338.
"Gospel of the Goddess of Democracy." [NewL] (56:2/3) Wint 89-Spr 90, p. 37.
"If My Hands Could Undress the Moon" (a variation on Lorca's theme, tr. of Bronislava Volkova, w. the author). [InterPR] (15:2) Fall 89, p. 20-21.
"Lady Pan" (tr. of Wang Wei, w. Tony Barnstone and Xu Xaixan). [CentR] (33:3) Sum 89, p. 250.
"Missing the Loved One" (tr. of Wang Wei, w. Tony Barnstone and Xu Xaixan). [CentR] (33:3) Sum 89, p. 250.
"Moaning about My White Hair" (tr. of Wang Wei, w. Tony Barnstone and Xu Haixin). [LitR] (32:3) Spr 89, p. 337.

354. BATEMAN, Meg
  "Aotromachd." [Verse] (6:3) Wint 89, p. 42.
  "As Aonais Drochaid." [Verse] (6:3) Wint 89, p. 42.
  "Lightness." [Verse] (6:3) Wint 89, p. 42.
  "There Being No Bridge." [Verse] (6:3) Wint 89, p. 42.
355. BATHANTI, Joseph
  "The Death of East Liberty." [WestB] (24) 89, p. 28.
  "Evening Late Summer." [Pembroke] (21) 89, p. 171.
  "Kyrie." [SouthernHR] (23:1) Wint 89, p. 52.
  "October." [SoDakR] (27:4) Wint 89, p. 12.
  "On the Road to White Store." [LaurelR] (23:1) Wint 89, p. 29.
356. BATTRAM, Michael R.
  "Argument." [WindO] (52) Wint 89-90, p. 24.
  "The Cuckold's Song." [WindO] (52) Wint 89-90, p. 23.
357. BAUDELAIRE, Pierre Charles
  "La Voix" (tr. by Richard Howard). [SouthwR] (74:2) Spr 89, p. 152-153.
358. BAUER, Grace
  "Poem for a Stranger I've Been Dreaming About." [OxfordM] (5:1) Spr-Sum 89, p.
     53.
  "She Has Days." [Outbr] (20) 89, p. 3-5.
  "Women of the Night." [PassN] (10:1) Wint 89, p. 21.
359. BAUER, Steven
  "Digging the Grave." [HighP] (4:1) Spr 89, p. 48-49.
  "Reading." [HighP] (4:1) Spr 89, p. 47.
360. BAUMEL, Judith
  "In the Shadow of a Metaphor" (tr. of Patrizia Cavalli). [Poetry] (155:1/2) O-N 89, p.
     135.
  "Now That Time Seems All Mine" (tr. of Patrizia Cavalli). [Poetry] (155:1/2) O-N 89,
     p. 137.
  "Someone Told Me" (tr. of Patrizia Cavalli). [Poetry] (155:1/2) O-N 89, p. 135.
  "This Time I Won't Permit the Blue" (tr. of Patrizia Cavalli). [Poetry] (155:1/2) O-N
     89, p. 136-137.
  "To Simulate the Burning of the Heart" (tr. of Patrizia Cavalli). [Poetry] (155:1/2)
     O-N 89, p. 136.
  "Together Eternity and Death Threaten Me" (tr. of Patrizia Cavalli). [Poetry] (155:1/2)
     O-N 89, p. 135.
361. BAUMGAERTNER, Jill P.
  "From an Old House in Illinois." [ChrC] (106:21) Jl 5-12, 89, p. 654.
  "Jephthah's Daughter" (Judges 11-12). [ChrC] (106:19) Je 7-14, 89, p. 590.
362. BAWER, Bruce
  "California." [CrossCur] (8:2) Ja 89, p. 133-138.
  "Communion." [Chelsea] (48) 89, p. 137.
  "Mount Hope" (to the memory of Ruth Hines Thomas, 1898-1985). [KanQ] (21:1/2)
     Wint-Spr 89, p. 68-69.
  "Sixty-Fifth Street Poems." [ParisR] (31:113) Wint 89, p. 150-151.
  "The Snow Boy." [Boulevard] (4:1, #10) Spr 89, p. 123.
363. BAXTER, Charles
  "Construction in Black and White." [Pequod] (28/29/30) 89, p. 262.
  "Imaginary Painting: *River Rogue*." [Pequod] (28/29/30) 89, p. 261.
364. BAYSA, Fred O.
  "A Study of Protea in a Basket Under White Light" (for Daryl K.). [Hawai'iR] (13:1,
     #25) Spr 89, p. 93.
365. BAYSANS, Greg
  "Biography." [JamesWR] (5:2 [i.e. 6:2]) Wint 89, p. 15.
  "Cute Pub Tempers (September Cut-Up)." [JamesWR] (7:1) Fall 89, p. 15.
  "Fat." [JamesWR] (5:2 [i.e. 6:2]) Wint 89, p. 15.
  "There Is a Poem in Here Called Random Light." [JamesWR] (7:1) Fall 89, p. 15.
366. BAZETT, Susan
  "Confessions 1." [Kalliope] (11:1) 89, p. 48.
367. BEACH, Jack
  "Three-Mile Bridge II: Noon." [EmeraldCR] (1989) c1988, p. 81.
  "Three-Mile Bridge III: Sunset." [EmeraldCR] (1989) c1988, p. 81.
368. BEAM, Jeffery
  "After Love-Making." [YellowS] (30) Sum 89, p. 11.
369. BEAMS, John
  "Ahimsa." [ChangingM] (20) Wint-Spr 89, p. 27.

370. BEASLEY, Bruce
"The Fear of God." [MissouriR] (12:2) 89, p. 30-32.
"Ghost Elegy." [DenQ] (24:2) Fall 89, p. 18-19.
"Noel." [SouthernR] (25:4) Aut 89, p. 940-941.
"Tracing the Angel." [SouthernR] (25:4) Aut 89, p. 938-940.
371. BEASLEY, Sherry
"The Moment." [SouthernPR] (29:1) Spr 89, p. 7.
372. BEATTY, Paul
"EP's." [BrooklynR] (6) 89, p. 13.
"From the Mysterious Blue Planet." [BrooklynR] (5) 88, p. 28.
"A Lot Less Than Zero." [BrooklynR] (5) 88, p. 25-27.
"Please No Unnecessary Talking in the Auditorium." [BrooklynR] (6) 89, p. 12.
373. BEAUBIEN, Kathleen
"On Hearing Gwendolyn Brooks in Hauck Theatre." [ColR] (NS 16:1) Spr-Sum 89,
p. 52.
374. BEAUMONT, Jeanne
"All Night." [PoetryNW] (30:4) Wint 89-90, p. 22-23.
"Into the Storm." [CapeR] (24:1) Spr 89, p. 1.
"A Lesson." [Caliban] (7) 89, p. 118-119.
"The Others." [SenR] (19:1) 89, p. 14-15.
375. BEAUREGARD, Christophe
"Five Rooms" (w. Giovanni Tovt, inspired by the paintings of Yvonne Hawker,
Edinburgh, 5.12.87). [AlphaBS] (5) Jl 89, p. 44.
376. BEAUSOLEIL, Claude
"A l'Auteur du Spleen de Paris." [Os] (28) 89, p. 14-15.
377. BEAVER, Bruce
"Homage." [Descant] (20:3/4, #66/67) Fall-Wint 89, p. 165.
"In the Act." [Descant] (20:3/4, #66/67) Fall-Wint 89, p. 162.
"Median Strip." [Descant] (20:3/4, #66/67) Fall-Wint 89, p. 161.
"Round-up." [Descant] (20:3/4, #66/67) Fall-Wint 89, p. 163.
"Vegetable Egotism." [Descant] (20:3/4, #66/67) Fall-Wint 89, p. 164.
378. BEAVERS, Herm
"An Old Man Remembers the Guitar." [CinPR] (20) Fall 89, p. 64-66.
"There Was the Time." [CinPR] (20) Fall 89, p. 62-63.
379. BEBENSEE, George
"God Regretting the Moon." [AntigR] (76) Wint 89, p. 38.
"Watching the Buildings." [AntigR] (76) Wint 89, p. 38.
380. BECK, Art
"And Still Another Ressurection [sic]." [SwampR] (1:4) Sum 89, p. 12.
381. BECK, Marion
"Norma." [Grain] (17:2) Sum 89, p. 30.
"Psychic." [Grain] (17:2) Sum 89, p. 31.
382. BECKER, Anne
"And There Was Light." [SouthernPR] (29:2) Fall 89, p. 45-49.
"House Work." [WashR] (15:2) Ag-S 89, p. 12.
383. BECKER, Carol
"The Emu" (Stadspark, Leuven, Belgium). [ColEng] (51:1) Ja 89, p. 47.
384. BECKER, Jürgen
"Before the Crisis" (tr. by John Linthicum). [LitR] (33:1) Fall 89, p. 122.
"Far and Near" (tr. by John Linthicum). [LitR] (33:1) Fall 89, p. 121.
"In the Vicinity" (tr. by John Linthicum). [LitR] (33:1) Fall 89, p. 122.
"Legends" (tr. by John Linthicum). [LitR] (33:1) Fall 89, p. 118.
"Season" (tr. by John Linthicum). [LitR] (33:1) Fall 89, p. 118.
"Two Nights" (tr. by John Linthicum). [LitR] (33:1) Fall 89, p. 118.
"Two Windows" (tr. by John Linthicum). [LitR] (33:1) Fall 89, p. 119.
"Wahner Heath" (tr. by John Linthicum). [LitR] (33:1) Fall 89, p. 120.
"Weekend" (tr. by John Linthicum). [LitR] (33:1) Fall 89, p. 120.
385. BECKER, Robin
"The Children's Concert." [PraS] (63:4) Wint 89, p. 91-92.
"Hiking Gold Hills Ridge." [SoDakR] (27:3) Aut 89, p. 104.
"In Pompano Beach, FL." [PraS] (63:4) Wint 89, p. 90-91.
"Overdose." [Ploughs] (15:4) Wint 89-90, p. 18.
386. BECKER, Therese
"Raccoons at the Window." [PassN] (10:2) Sum 89, p. 19.
387. BECKETT, Larry
"Paul Bunyan" (Selections: 3 poems). [NowestR] (27:1) 89, p. 68-70.

388. BECKETT, Tom
    "Seems." [Talisman] (3) Fall 89, p. 73-75.
389. BECKMAN, Madeleine
    "Sunday." [Confr] (39/40) Fall 88-Wint 89, p. 202.
    "Take Out." [Confr] (39/40) Fall 88-Wint 89, p. 203.
390. BEDWELL, Carol
    "Hay Barge, in Summer Current, Touched" (tr. of Christoph Meckel). [MidAR] (9:1)
        89, p. 162.
391. BEECHHOLD, Henry F.
    "Day and Night." [US1] (22/23) Spr 89, p. 21.
392. BEEDE, Gayle Jansen
    "Hejira." [NegC] (9:1) 89, p. 75.
    "Sonogram." [PoetC] (20:3) Spr 89, p. 26.
393. BEHM, Richard
    "On Not Taking the Cemetery Road." [SewanR] (97:1) Wint 89, p. 21.
    "The Prayer of the Middle Class, Middle-Aged Man Getting Ready for Work."
        [KanQ] (21:1/2) Wint-Spr 89, p. 50.
    "Seduction in the Produce Aisle." [SewanR] (97:1) Wint 89, p. 20.
394. BEHRENDT, Stephen C.
    "Bird Point." [SewanR] (97:2) Spr 89, p. 181-182.
    "Elegy." [KanQ] (21:3) Sum 89, p. 37.
    "The Fisherman in the Ice." [TexasR] (10:3/4) Fall-Wint 89, p. 30.
    "Herb Garden." [SewanR] (97:2) Spr 89, p. 179-180.
    "The Stone Man" (for Robert McEwen). [TexasR] (10:3/4) Fall-Wint 89, p. 28-29.
    "Victoria Street Idyll." [SewanR] (97:2) Spr 89, p. 180-181.
395. BEI, Dao
    "Accomplices" (tr. by Donald Finkel and Xueliang Chen). [LitR] (32:3) Spr 89, p.
        340.
    "Echo" (tr. by Dong Jiping). [Footwork] 89, p. 25.
    "Elegy" (tr. by Donald Finkel and Xueliang Chen). [LitR] (32:3) Spr 89, p. 342.
    "The Host" (tr. by Donald Finkel and Xueliang Chen). [LitR] (32:3) Spr 89, p. 343.
    "I'm Forever a Stranger" (tr. by Donald Finkel and Xueliang Chen). [LitR] (32:3) Spr
        89, p. 340.
    "Love Story" (tr. by Dong Jiping). [Footwork] 89, p. 25.
    "Memory" (tr. by Donald Finkel and Xueliang Chen). [LitR] (32:3) Spr 89, p. 343.
    "Night: Theme and Variations" (tr. by Donald Finkel and Xueliang Chen). [LitR]
        (32:3) Spr 89, p. 341.
    "No Tomorrow" (tr. by Donald Finkel and Xueliang Chen). [LitR] (32:3) Spr 89, p.
        339.
    "Shore" (tr. by Donald Finkel and Xueliang Chen). [LitR] (32:3) Spr 89, p. 342.
    "SOS" (tr. by Dong Jiping). [Footwork] 89, p. 26.
    "Temptation" (tr. by Dong Jiping). [Footwork] 89, p. 26.
    "Toast" (tr. by Donald Finkel and Xueliang Chen). [LitR] (32:3) Spr 89, p. 339.
396. BEINING, Guy R.
    "Stoma 1846." [Caliban] (7) 89, p. 114.
    "Stoma 1848." [Caliban] (7) 89, p. 114.
    "Stoma 1849." [Caliban] (7) 89, p. 115.
    "Stoma 1850." [Caliban] (7) 89, p. 116.
397. BELAMRI, Rabah
    "Take Me Between Your Eyelashes" (tr. by Eric Sellin). [Pig] (15) 88, p. 37.
398. BELFIELD, Judy
    "Do No." [Plain] (9:2) Wint 89, p. 36.
399. BELGUIM, Erik
    "Intensive Care." [RedBass] (14) 89, p. 8-14.
400. BELIECH, Mamie Alexander
    "The Best Poem." [EmeraldCR] (1989) c1988, p. 87.
    "Use Your Talent." [EmeraldCR] (1989) c1988, p. 88.
401. BELIN, Mel
    "Jael." [SoCoast] (5) Spr 88, p. 10.
402. BELITT, Ben
    "Alcohol and Syllables" (tr. of Gonzalo Rojas). [Salm] (82/83) Spr-Sum 89, p. 300.
    "Bed with Mirrors" (tr. of Gonzalo Rojas). [Salm] (82/83) Spr-Sum 89, p. 299-300.
    "Don't Copy Pound" (tr. of Gonzalo Rojas). [Salm] (82/83) Spr-Sum 89, p.
        297-298.
    "Latin and Jazz" (tr. of Gonzalo Rojas). [Salm] (82/83) Spr-Sum 89, p. 298-299.

403. BELL, Marvin
"3 Horses Facing the Saskatchewan Sun." [AmerPoR] (18:2) Mr-Ap 89, p. 28.
"After Tu Fu (They Say You're Staying in a Mountain Temple)." [Iowa] (19:3) Fall
      89, p. 23.
"Average American." [NegC] (9:1) 89, p. 22.
"The Body Breaking." [Iowa] (19:3) Fall 89, p. 18.
"The Book of the Dead Man" (Selections: 1, 2). [MassR] (30:4) Wint 89, p. 566-567.
"Cargo Moving to Gaza." [AmerPoR] (18:2) Mr-Ap 89, p. 29.
"The Cat Who Caught a Pigeon." [AmerPoR] (18:2) Mr-Ap 89, p. 28.
"Climbing Mt. Baldy at the Dunes." [Iowa] (19:3) Fall 89, p. 21.
"Comb and Rake." [Atlantic] (263:6) Je 89, p. 70.
"Cornet." [AmerPoR] (18:2) Mr-Ap 89, p. 28.
"Dark Brow." [MassR] (30:4) Wint 89, p. 568.
"Darts." [AmerPoR] (18:2) Mr-Ap 89, p. 31.
"A Dream, or Was It?" [Iowa] (19:3) Fall 89, p. 23.
"An Elegy for the Past." [AmerPoR] (18:2) Mr-Ap 89, p. 31.
"Frankenstein." [AmerPoR] (18:2) Mr-Ap 89, p. 30.
"How I Grew Up." [AmerPoR] (18:2) Mr-Ap 89, p. 29.
"I, or Someone Like Me." [NewRep] (201:16) 16 O 89, p. 40.
"I Shed My Blood on Unimportant Battlefields." [AmerPoR] (18:2) Mr-Ap 89, p. 28.
"Ice." [WestHR] (43:2) Sum 89, p. 101-102.
"Inklings." [NegC] (9:1) 89, p. 25.
"Jay's Almosts." [AmerPoR] (18:2) Mr-Ap 89, p. 30.
"A Man May Change." [WestHR] (43:2) Sum 89, p. 100.
"Marco Polo." [AmerPoR] (18:2) Mr-Ap 89, p. 30.
"Northwest Passage." [AmerPoR] (18:2) Mr-Ap 89, p. 27.
"An Old Trembling." [NewYorker] (65:27) 21 Ag 89, p. 60.
"Pioneer Night." [AmerPoR] (18:2) Mr-Ap 89, p. 30.
"A Play by Saroyan (1939)." [NegC] (9:1) 89, p. 24.
"Poem After Carlos Drummond de Andrade." [AmerPoR] (18:2) Mr-Ap 89, p. 27.
"Portrait." [Iowa] (19:3) Fall 89, p. 21-22.
"Report from the Writers' Convention." [Iowa] (19:3) Fall 89, p. 19-20.
"Report to the Fulbright Commission." [NegC] (9:1) 89, p. 23.
"The Retaliatarians." [GettyR] (2:4) Aut 89, p. 597.
"Riddle." [NegC] (9:1) 89, p. 21.
"Street Fair: The Quartet." [AmerPoR] (18:2) Mr-Ap 89, p. 29.
"To Logan in the Grave." [PaintedB] (39) 89, p. 90.
"Two Difficult Images." [AmerPoR] (18:2) Mr-Ap 89, p. 30.
"Using Some Words That Showed Up Recently." [Iowa] (19:3) Fall 89, p. 24-26.
"Victim of Himself." [Atlantic] (263:5) My 89, p. 61.
"Washing Our Hands of the Rest of America." [AmerPoR] (18:2) Mr-Ap 89, p. 28.
"We Have Lived With It." [AmerPoR] (18:2) Mr-Ap 89, p. 29.
404. BELL, Melissa
"Summer." [Vis] (31) 89, p. 28.
405. BELLEN, Martine
"Deception." [Conjunc] (14) 89, p. 46-47.
"Hole." [Caliban] (6) 89, p. 155.
"Home Warming." [CentralP] (16) Fall 89, p. 145.
406. BELLINI LUIS, Sara
"La Cosa Amada." [Os] (28) 89, p. 24.
407. Ben JELLOUN, Tahar
"The Girls of Tangier" (tr. by Eric Sellin). [Pig] (15) 88, p. 38.
408. BEN-LEV, Dina
"Spinning." [GettyR] (2:1) Wint 89, p. 177-179.
"The Unfound." [OxfordM] (5:2) Fall-Wint 89, p. 27-28.
409. BEN-TOV, S.
"Clouds Over Jerusalem, in Winter." [ParisR] (31:113) Wint 89, p. 226.
410. BENDALL, Molly
"The Hairdresser." [NewAW] (5) Fall 89, p. 117.
"Late, Late Bachelorette." [NewAW] (5) Fall 89, p. 116.
"Laughter and Diamonds." [Crazy] (37) Wint 89, p. 48-49.
"Letter." [DenQ] (24:2) Fall 89, p. 20.
411. BENDON, Chris
"Swifts." [Margin] (8) 89, p. 51.
412. BENEVENTO, Joe
"Alone." [Footwork] 89, p. 55.

413. BENFEY, Christopher
    "A Broken Bowl." [ParisR] (31:111) Sum 89, p. 127.
    "Cutting My Niece's Nails." [ParisR] (31:111) Sum 89, p. 126.
    "Noborigama." [Pequod] (28/29/30) 89, p. 32.
414. BENJAMIN, Pat
    "Drink Me." [SpiritSH] (54) Spr-Sum 89, p. 4.
    "Frozen Waterfall." [SpiritSH] (54) Spr-Sum 89, p. 6.
    "Icarus Falling" (for poet G.S.). [SpiritSH] (54) Spr-Sum 89, p. 5.
    "The Lip-Reader." [SpiritSH] (54) Spr-Sum 89, p. 3.
415. BENNANI, Ben
    "Psalms for Palestine" (Selections: "Psalm One," "Psalm Nine," tr. of Mahmud
        Darwish). [CharR] (15:2) Fall 89, p. 76-79.
416. BENNETT, Allyson
    "Humpty Dumpty." [MinnR] (NS 32) Spr 89, p. 63-65.
417. BENNETT, Bruce
    "A Story about a Wolf." [LaurelR] (23:2) Sum 89, p. 60.
418. BENNETT, Frederick R.
    "Morning Song." [StoneC] (16:3/4) Spr-Sum 89, p. 27.
419. BENNETT, John (John M.)
    "The Blur." [Rampike] (6:2) 88, p. 70.
    "The Corpse." [Caliban] (6) 89, p. 172.
    "Dig Its." [Caliban] (6) 89, p. 173.
    "Eating." [Caliban] (7) 89, p. 121.
    "Exito." [Bogg] (61) 89, p. 20.
    "I Care Its Us." [Caliban] (6) 89, p. 172.
    "Pico Mojado." [Caliban] (7) 89, p. 120.
    "Scaling Oh Scaling." [Caliban] (6) 89, p. 173.
    "Short Choke." [Rampike] (6:2) 88, p. 70.
    "Showering." [Caliban] (7) 89, p. 120.
    "Snow Screen." [Rampike] (6:2) 88, p. 70.
    "Wet Veteran." [CentralP] (16) Fall 89, p. 70.
420. BENNETT, Paul
    "Third Man in the Ring: Arthur Donovan." [Journal] (12:2) Fall-Wint 88-89, p.
        44-45.
421. BENSE, Robert
    "Footprints." [Poem] (62) N 89, p. 23.
    "They Have Gathered" (The Carter Family). [Poem] (62) N 89, p. 21.
    "Tonight the Moon Is Blue" (for Bill Monroe). [Poem] (62) N 89, p. 22.
422. BENSEN, Robert
    "Blue Room." [ParisR] (31:111) Sum 89, p. 219.
423. BENSKO, John
    "After *A Day in the Country*" (on the film by Jean Renoir). [Ploughs] (15:1) 89, p.
        24-25.
    "Growing Up on the Lively Art of Painting." [Ploughs] (15:1) 89, p. 23.
424. BENSON, R. Michael
    "Atomic Lullaby" (To José Martf). [Pig] (15) 88, p. 90.
425. BENSON, Steve
    "Reverse Order" (Excerpt). [NewAW] (5) Fall 89, p. 84-86.
    "Reverse Order" (Excerpt). [Screens] (1) 89, p. 47-50.
426. BENTLEY, Beth
    "Choices." [RiverC] (9:1) Spr 89, p. 32-34.
    "Domestic Interiors." [RiverC] (9:1) Spr 89, p. 28-29.
    "Getting the Picture." [RiverC] (9:1) Spr 89, p. 30-31.
    "Stuck." [PoetryNW] (30:4) Wint 89-90, p. 46.
427. BENTLEY, Nelson
    "Kalaloch: Looking Toward Destruction Island." [BellArk] (5:5) S-O 89, p. 10.
    "The Mermaid and the Dragon." [BellArk] (5:5) S-O 89, p. 5.
    "Orcas Island Apocalypse." [BellArk] (5:2) Mr-Ap 89, p. 27-29.
428. BENTLEY, Roy
    "The Heart Has Its Reasons." [Pig] (15) 88, p. 86.
    "The Picture My Father Promised." [ArtfulD] (16/17) Fall 89, p. 36-37.
429. BENTLEY, Sean
    "The Boy Who Was the Suitor of Electricity." [WindO] (52) Wint 89-90, p. 15.
    "Zorro Falls Asleep." [WindO] (52) Wint 89-90, p. 16.
430. BENTTINEN, Ted
    "The Breath of Whales" (Race Point, Provincetown). [KenR] (NS 11:2) Spr 89, p.

55

BENTTINEN

120-121.
"Four Messages for Radio Telescope." [BallSUF] (30:4) Aut 89, p. 64-65.
"Keiko." [YellowS] (30) Sum 89, p. 26.
"Prayer and Vision in the Stave Church at Røldal." [KenR] (NS 11:2) Spr 89, p.
121-123.
BERAS, Carlos Roberto Gomez
See GOMEZ, Beras, Carlos Roberto
431. BERECK, Patricia
"Not Even Hard Work Will Save Us Now." [Farm] (6:2) Fall 89, p. 40-41.
432. BERENGUER, Carmen
"At Half Mast / A Media Asta" (tr. by Lake Sagaris). [Rampike] (6:1) 87, p. 64.
"The Great Speech (MM)" (Selection: "The Crazy Woman from the Alley / La Loca
del Pasaje," tr. by Lake Sagaris). [Rampike] (6:1) 87, p. 64-65.
433. BERG, K. J.
"Growing Images of a Garden." [BellArk] (5:5) S-O 89, p. 4.
"Winter Sequence." [BellArk] (5:3) My-Je 89, p. 5.
434. BERG, Stephen
"First Song / Bankei / 1653." [DenQ] (24:2) Fall 89, p. 21-25.
"Porno Diva Numero Uno" (Selections: Sections 9 & 11). [CimR] (89) O 89, p.
78-81.
"Shoeshine." [Thrpny] (39) Fall 89, p. 27.
"Writing Class." [DenQ] (24:2) Fall 89, p. 26-27.
435. BERGAMIN, José
"Lofty Solitudes" (tr. by David Garrison). [LitR] (32:2) Wint 89, p. 162.
"Snow" (tr. by David Garrison). [LitR] (32:2) Wint 89, p. 162.
"Time Crystal" (tr. by David Garrison). [LitR] (32:2) Wint 89, p. 161.
"Your Voice" (tr. by David Garrison). [LitR] (32:2) Wint 89, p. 161.
436. BERGAMINO, Gina
"Frankfurt Bahnhof." [PoetL] (84:4) Wint 89-90, p. 13.
437. BERGER, Bruce
"Acquired Taste." [ApalQ] (31) 89, p. 56.
"Rubato." [StoneC] (16:3/4) Spr-Sum 89, p. 72.
438. BERGER, Hedwig
"Some Kind of Way Back Home." [Sequoia] (33:1) Sum 89, p. 50.
439. BERGER, Jamie
"The Other Day My Girlfriend." [NegC] (9:2) 89, p. 34.
440. BERGMAN, David
"Abel's Story." [JamesWR] (6:3) Spr 89, p. 5.
"Along Hadrian's Wall." [WestHR] (43:1) Spr 89, p. 66.
"Death and the Young Man" (after Schubert). [NewRep] (201:17) 23 O 89, p. 30.
"A Father's Blessings." [AmerS] (58:1) Wint 89, p. 103-104.
"My Father Almost Ascending." [AmerS] (58:1) Wint 89, p. 102.
441. BERGON, Holly St. John
"Rain." [ColEng] (51:8) D 89, p. 836.
"San Cristóbal de las Casas." [ColEng] (51:8) D 89, p. 835.
442. BERGSTROM, Vera
"Two Half-Baked Crows." [Bogg] (61) 89, p. 43.
443. BERKE, Judith
"Acting Problems: The Subtext." [Field] (40) Spr 89, p. 59.
"Custody." [Poetry] (153:5) F 89, p. 292.
"Dachau '44." [MassR] (30:4) Wint 89, p. 569.
"Delmore." [Poetry] (153:4) Ja 89, p. 204.
"A Disciple of Stanislavsky." [PraS] (63:2) Sum 89, p. 53-54.
"Dress Rehearsal." [Field] (40) Spr 89, p. 58.
"On the Radio." [PraS] (63:2) Sum 89, p. 52-53.
"Persona." [Field] (40) Spr 89, p. 56.
"The Retreat." [Poetry] (153:4) Ja 89, p. 203.
"Sloth." [PraS] (63:2) Sum 89, p. 54-55.
"The Tattoo." [MassR] (30:4) Wint 89, p. 570.
"Triple Toe Loop." [Atlantic] (263:3) Mr 89, p. 73.
"Trying Out for the Class Production of 'A Streetcar Named Desire'." [Field] (40) Spr
89, p. 57.
"Village at the Foot of the Volcano." [DenQ] (24:1) Sum 89, p. 9.
444. BERKE, Nancy
"Giving a Language." [CentralP] (15) Spr 89, p. 34.
"On the Road." [Pig] (15) 88, p. 48.

445. BERKSON, Bill
    "Serious Moment" (for Nathaniel Dorsky). [Talisman] (3) Fall 89, p. 99.
446. BERLIND, Bruce
    "After We Broke Up" (tr. of Imre Oravecz, w. Mária Körösy). [TriQ] (77) Wint
        89-90, p. 296.
    "Autumn in the Midwest" (tr. of Imre Oravecz, w. Mária Körösy). [ArtfulD] (16/17)
        Fall 89, p. 66.
    "Ebb Tide" (tr. of Gyula Illyes, w. Maria Korosy). [Colum] (14) 89, p. 125.
    "Evening Song" (tr. of Gyula Illyes, w. Maria Korosy). [Colum] (14) 89, p. 124.
    "It Was Still Summer" (tr. of Imre Oravecz, w. Mária Körösy). [TriQ] (77) Wint
        89-90, p. 297.
    "The Pillow: a Transylvanian Folk Song" (tr. of anonymous poem). [PoetryE] (28)
        Fall 89, p. 205.
    "When Now and Then We Run Into Each Other" (tr. of Imre Oravecz, w. Mária
        Körösy). [TriQ] (77) Wint 89-90, p. 295.
447. BERMAN, David
    "Advice to a Gossip." [Amelia] (5:3, #14) 89, p. 131.
    "Disinclined to Think." [Amelia] (5:3, #14) 89, p. 131.
448. BERMAN, Ruth
    "Mortal and Triton." [KanQ] (21:1/2) Wint-Spr 89, p. 71.
    "Sale Air and the Cause of Colds." [KanQ] (21:1/2) Wint-Spr 89, p. 70.
449. BERNARD, April
    "Blackbird Bye Bye." [Bomb] (28) Sum 89, p. 80-82.
450. BERNARD, Betty
    "Elegy." [FloridaR] (16:2/3) Fall-Wint 89, p. 144-145.
    "Mirages" (for the muralist, Mame Cohalan). [CapeR] (24:1) Spr 89, p. 9.
451. BERNARDI, Adria
    "Authority Has Played" (tr. of Gregorio Scalise). [Poetry] (155:1/2) O-N 89, p. 106.
    "The Mind and Body Are Angels" (tr. of Gregorio Scalise). [Poetry] (155:1/2) O-N
        89, p. 105.
    "Now to Reopen a Text" (tr. of Gregorio Scalise). [Poetry] (155:1/2) O-N 89, p. 105.
    "Saying Again That Flowers" (tr. of Gregorio Scalise). [Poetry] (155:1/2) O-N 89, p.
        107.
452. BERNHARD, Jim
    "Summer Conversations on a Concrete Path." [BellArk] (5:1) Ja-F 89, p. 10.
453. BERNHEIMER, Alan
    "Kiosk." [Zyzzyva] (5:3, #19) Fall 89, p. 46-47.
454. BERNSTEIN, Carole
    "The Charm Machine, 1965." [YaleR] (79:1) Aut 89, p. 125.
    "Figure of a Man." [AntR] (47:1) Wint 89, p. 59.
    "Ricordo di Venezia" (Panorama from Isola S. Giorgio). [Poetry] (153:6) Mr 89, p.
        315.
455. BERNSTEIN, Charles
    "The Absent Father in Dumbo." [Screens] (1) 89, p. 179.
    "The Age of Correggio and the Carracci." [AmerPoR] (18:5) S-O 89, p. 14.
    "American Boy with Bat." [MinnR] (NS 32) Spr 89, p. 55.
    "At the Reading (2)." [Talisman] (3) Fall 89, p. 9.
    "Common Stock." [Conjunc] (14) 89, p. 40-43.
    "Egg Under My Feet." [Rampike] (6:2) 88, p. 72.
    "External Market Constraints." [NewAW] (5) Fall 89, p. 82.
    "Freud's Butcher." [AmerPoR] (18:5) S-O 89, p. 14.
    "Hard Feelings." [Epoch] (38:1) 89, p. 11.
    "I'll Call You When I Get There." [Epoch] (38:1) 89, p. 12.
    "Internal Loss Control." [NewAW] (5) Fall 89, p. 83.
    "Plausibly Deniable Link." [Epoch] (38:1) 89, p. 13.
    "Precisely and Moreover." [Talisman] (2) Spr 89, p. 64-65.
    "Soapy Water." [Witness] (2:4) Wint 88, p. 129.
    "Sunsickness." [Sulfur] (9:1, #24) Spr 89, p. 97-101.
    "Through the Motions" (w. Ray DiPalma). [Caliban] (6) 89, p. 123-129.
    "Trill." [Talisman] (3) Fall 89, p. 9.
    "Vault and Volley." [Screens] (1) 89, p. 179.
456. BERNSTEIN, Lisa
    "Camp." [Caliban] (6) 89, p. 130.
    "The Envelope." [PoetL] (84:3) Fall 89, p. 36-37.
    "Falcon." [Calyx] (12:2) Wint 89-90, p. 12-13.
    "A Girl in Winter." [PoetL] (84:3) Fall 89, p. 39-41.

"Glimpse of the Other World." [Caliban] (6) 89, p. 132.
"Hawk." [Field] (40) Spr 89, p. 45-46.
"Hen." [Field] (40) Spr 89, p. 43-44.
"Single Woman." [Kalliope] (10:1/2) 88, p. 72.
"Sounding the Passage." [Field] (40) Spr 89, p. 47-53.
"To Pick a Self." [Caliban] (6) 89, p. 131.
"Two Childhood Fables." [Caliban] (6) 89, p. 133-134.
457. BEROLD, Robert
"Eclipse of the Moon." [AmerPoR] (18:4) Jl-Ag 89, p. 34.
458. BERRIGAN, Ted
"A Certain Slant of Sunlight." [Talisman] (3) Fall 89, p. 83-84.
"Christmas in September" (for Mark Hillringhouse). [Talisman] (3) Fall 89, p. 97.
"Down on Mission." [Talisman] (3) Fall 89, p. 90.
"In Your Fucking Utopias." [Talisman] (3) Fall 89, p. 96.
"Paris, Frances." [Talisman] (3) Fall 89, p. 88.
"People Who Change Their Names." [Talisman] (3) Fall 89, p. 85.
"Poem: Yea, though I walk." [Talisman] (3) Fall 89, p. 83.
"The Public-School Windows Song" (after Vachel Lindsay). [Talisman] (3) Fall 89,
    p. 93.
"Salutation." [Talisman] (3) Fall 89, p. 87.
"To Jacques Roubaud." [Talisman] (3) Fall 89, p. 86.
"To Sing the Song, That Is Fantastic." [Talisman] (3) Fall 89, p. 94.
"Tough Cookies." [Talisman] (3) Fall 89, p. 91-92.
"Two Sonnets" (XXXVI, LXXVI). [AlphaBS] (6) Wint 89-90, p. 45-46.
"Via Air." [Talisman] (3) Fall 89, p. 88.
459. BERRY, David
"After Adultery." [TexasR] (10:3/4) Fall-Wint 89, p. 81.
"Blondes." [TexasR] (10:3/4) Fall-Wint 89, p. 80.
"Oranges." [TexasR] (10:3/4) Fall-Wint 89, p. 82.
460. BERRY, Jake
"Untitled: To let bloods divide." [Rampike] (6:3) 88, p. 18.
461. BERSSENBRUGGE, Mei-Mei
"Ghost Essay." [Temblor] (10) 89, p. 22-24.
"Gold." [Sulfur] (9:1, #24) Spr 89, p. 104-105.
"Hiddenness." [Pequod] (28/29/30) 89, p. 96-102.
"Irises." [Conjunc] (14) 89, p. 256-258.
462. BERTON, Melissa
"Disjunction." [Jacaranda] (4:1) Spr-Sum 89, p. 30-31.
463. BERTRAM, Anne
"An Anthropological Expedition" (for Weasel and Jade). [Lactuca] (12) F 89, p.
    17-18.
464. BESCHTA, Jim
"Imagining My Daughter's Boyfriends As She Turns 13." [ChatR] (9:3) Spr 89, p.
    52-53.
465. BESS, Robert
"Noon Horn: Salem, VA." [Amelia] (5:3, #14) 89, p. 55.
466. BETT, Stephen
"Lucy Kent XIX" (a history lesson / a lesson in history). [Rampike] (6:2) 88, p.
    52-55.
467. BETTENCOURT, Michael
"Driving Through the Fog." [NegC] (9:1) 89, p. 40.
468. BEUM, Robert
"524." [ChrC] (106:4) F 1-8, 89, p. 101.
"April Morning." [CanLit] (122/123) Aut-Wint 89, p. 56.
"First Grade: End of Term." [ChrC] (106:20) Je 21-28, 89, p. 623.
"Rain Years." [ChrC] (106:21) Jl 5-12, 89, p. 646.
469. BEVELL, Brett
"Clown." [MoodySI] (20/21) Spr 89, p. 32.
BEY, Brenda Connor
    See CONNOR-BEY, Brenda
470. BEYER, Richard G.
"Crop Duster" (For Phillip Champlain). [NegC] (9:1) 89, p. 60-61.
471. BEZNER, Kevin
"Cutting Wood: Vermont, 1977." [PassN] (10:1) Wint 89, p. 22.
"Madison Avenue,Summer Morning." [Kalliope] (10:3) 88, p. 30.
"Streets." [Kalliope] (10:3) 88, p. 29-30.

"Walking to the Moon." [Kalliope] (10:3) 88, p. 27-28.
472. BIAGIONI, Amelia
"To Say" (tr. by Renata Treitel). [MidAR] (9:1) 89, p. 163-164.
473. BIALOCK, D. T.
"Forest Words." [Poem] (61) My 89, p. 43.
"The Garden." [Poem] (61) My 89, p. 44-45.
"A Northern Village." [Poem] (61) My 89, p. 42.
474. BIALOSKY, Jill
"Carousel." [Pequod] (26/27) 89, p. 173.
475. BIALOSZEWSKI, Miron
"Aniela in the Town of Folino" (tr. by Stanislaw Baranczak and Clare Cavanah).
[Trans] (21) Spr 89, p. 38-39.
476. BIALY, Harvey
"Odyssey" (Book VI, tr. of Homer). [Notus] (4:1) Spr 89, p. 29-38.
477. BIANOR
"O greedy boatman of the Styx" (tr. by James Michie). [GrandS] (8:4) Sum 89, p. 81.
478. BIARUJIA, Javant
"Charles Blackman in the Vicinity of Rue des Beaux Arts." [AlphaBS] (5) Jl 89, p.
21.
"Ian Hance." [AlphaBS] (5) Jl 89, p. 20.
"Listening to 'Ole' by John Coltrane" (for Gwenn Carter). [AlphaBS] (5) Jl 89, p. 28.
479. BICH, Nguyen Ngoc
"The Final Freedom" (tr. of Tran Kha). [Vis] (31) 89, p. 21.
480. BICHET, Yves
"L'Ouvrier" (à Philippe Jaccottet). [Os] (29) 89, p. 24-32.
481. BICKERSTAFF, Patsy Anne
"Accident in Albemarle." [CapeR] (24:1) Spr 89, p. 25.
"Five O'Clock Shadow." [CapeR] (24:1) Spr 89, p. 24.
482. BIDGOOD, Ruth
"Chimneys." [NoDaQ] (57:2) Spr 89, insert p. 38.
"Lighting Candles." [NoDaQ] (57:2) Spr 89, insert p. 39.
"Tourists." [NoDaQ] (57:2) Spr 89, insert p. 40.
483. BIELSKI, Alison
"Forest Song" (for Richard Ball). [Pembroke] (21) 89, p. 169.
484. BIEN, Jeff
"The First Poetry Reading." [Grain] (17:3) Fall 89, p. 48-49.
485. BIERDS, Linda
"For the Sake of Retrieval." [Atlantic] (264:4) O 89, p. 58.
"The Shakers." [NewYorker] (65:8) 10 Ap 89, p. 44-45.
486. BIERMANN, Wolf
"Apple" (tr. by John Linthicum). [LitR] (33:1) Fall 89, p. 32.
"Crossing" (tr. by John Linthicum). [LitR] (33:1) Fall 89, p. 32.
"Eternal Peace" (tr. by John Linthicum). [LitR] (33:1) Fall 89, p. 33.
"High Water in Paris" (tr. by John Linthicum). [LitR] (33:1) Fall 89, p. 34.
487. BIGGINS, Michael
"Artist and Model" (tr. of Veno Taufer). [NewEngR] (11:3) Spr 89, p. 246-247.
"At Evening the Nomads" (tr. of Milan Jesih). [NewEngR] (11:3) Spr 89, p. 238.
"Buffaloes" (tr. of Kajetan Kovic). [NewEngR] (11:3) Spr 89, p. 242.
"City by Night" (tr. of Bozo Vodusek). [NewEngR] (11:3) Spr 89, p. 252-253.
"The Classless Society" (tr. of Gustav Janus). [NewEngR] (11:3) Spr 89, p.
236-237.
"The Crow's Song" (tr. of Andrej Kokot). [NewEngR] (11:3) Spr 89, p. 241.
"The Fish" (tr. of Tomaz Salamun). [NewEngR] (11:3) Spr 89, p. 248-249.
"Grass" (tr. of Tomaz Salamun). [ColR] (NS 16:1) Spr-Sum 89, p. 102.
"Hands" (tr. of Edvard Kocbek). [NewEngR] (11:3) Spr 89, p. 240.
"Hunger II" (tr. of Braco Rotar). [NewEngR] (11:3) Spr 89, p. 245.
"The Lighthouse" (tr. of Svetlana Makarovic). [NewEngR] (11:3) Spr 89, p. 243.
"Moon Shining onto Fenced Pastures" (tr. of Edvard Kocbek). [NewEngR] (11:3)
Spr 89, p. 240.
"Noonday Bells in Trnovo" (tr. of Majda Kne). [NewEngR] (11:3) Spr 89, p. 239.
"Relics: The Family" (tr. of Sasa Vegri). [NewEngR] (11:3) Spr 89, p. 251.
"Their Genius" (tr. of Jure Potokar). [NewEngR] (11:3) Spr 89, p. 244.
"A Tiny Poem" (tr. of Milan Jesih). [NewEngR] (11:3) Spr 89, p. 238.
"The Wheel" (tr. of Tomaz Salamun). [ColR] (NS 16:1) Spr-Sum 89, p. 101.
"When There Is No More" (tr. of Tomaz Salamun). [NewEngR] (11:3) Spr 89, p.
250.

"You're Not" (tr. of Dane Zajc). [NewEngR] (11:3) Spr 89, p. 254.
488. BILGERE, George
"After Dickinson's 'The Lightning Is a Yellow Fork'." [NewEngR] (12:1) Aut 89, p. 90.
"Pfeifer, Kansas." [LitR] (32:2) Wint 89, p. 178.
489. BINGHAM, Sallie
"The Last Plane Out of Key West." [AmerV] (14) Spr 89, p. 56.
490. BINNING, Sadhu
"The First Encounter." [MinnR] (NS 33) Fall 89, p. 21.
491. BIRD, Gloria
"In Chimayo." [HighP] (4:3) Wint 89-90, p. 23-24.
"Train Home." [HighP] (4:3) Wint 89-90, p. 21-22.
"The Twinning." [HighP] (4:2) Fall 89, p. 78-79.
492. BIRO, Lindsey D.
"At the Wellington County Detention Centre." [Quarry] (38:4) Fall 89, p. 44-45.
493. BIRTHA, Becky
"Houseguest." [EvergreenC] (4:4) Sum 89, p. 33.
494. BISHOP, Bonnie
"Ontogenesis Toward the Thirty-Sixth Year." [Dandel] (16:1) Spr-Sum 89, p. 44.
"The Spinster." [Dandel] (16:1) Spr-Sum 89, p. 44.
495. BISHOP, Elizabeth
"Insomnia." [Lyra] (2:1/2) 88, c89, p. 3.
"Insomnio" (tr. by Orlando José Hernández). [Lyra] (2:1/2) 88, c89, p. 2.
"Paisaje Marino" (tr. by Orlando José Hernández). [Lyra] (2:1/2) 88, c89, p. 4.
"Seascape." [Lyra] (2:1/2) 88, c89, p. 5.
496. BISHOP, Judith
"First Sweat." [Kalliope] (11:3) 89, p. 20-23.
"You Are Crossing Long Island Sound" (Honorable Mention). [StoneC] (17:1/2) Fall-Wint 89-90, p. prelim. p. 3.
497. BISHOP, Neil B.
"Bivalve" (tr. of Michel Savard). [AntigR] (79) Aut 89, p. 43.
"In winter the flies rest, a few bad whistles" (tr. of Michel Savard). [AntigR] (79) Aut 89, p. 47.
"Observe attentively observe this season" (tr. of Michel Savard). [AntigR] (79) Aut 89, p. 45.
498. BISHOP, Rand
"Mrs. Mallarmés Prayer." [WindO] (52) Wint 89-90, p. 25.
499. BISHOP, Wendy
"Chichicastenango." [EngJ] (78:7) N 89, p. 92.
"Coral Monuments." [TexasR] (10:3/4) Fall-Wint 89, p. 116.
"December Roofs: Alaska." [LaurelR] (23:1) Wint 89, p. 91.
"Geraniums, Pisac, Peru." [MinnR] (NS 32) Spr 89, p. 77.
"A Life." [ColEng] (51:4) Ap 89, p. 386.
"A Man and a Woman Are Not an Island." [ColEng] (51:4) Ap 89, p. 387.
"A Vaudeville Woman Remembers Love." [DenQ] (24:1) Sum 89, p. 10-11.
"Waldo Resurgent." [PoetC] (20:3) Spr 89, p. 3-4.
500. BISS, Ellen
"The Squash Blossom World." [Blueline] (10:1/2) 89, p. 36.
501. BISSETT, Bill
"Subtr Fugue." [Rampike] (6:3) 88, p. 62.
502. BIXBY, Robert
"The house has burned." [Amelia] (5:3, #14) 89, p. 35.
"Mantra to Technological Delight." [GreensboroR] (46) Sum 89, p. 153.
"Out of Nothing." [SoCoast] (6) Fall 88, p. 42.
503. BIZEK, Barbara
"Toward Commonness." [AnotherCM] (19) 89, p. 9.
504. BIZZARO, Patrick
"Pine Cones." [OxfordM] (5:2) Fall-Wint 89, p. 26.
"Second Chance." [OxfordM] (5:1) Spr-Sum 89, p. 16.
"A Tornado Watch, a Thunderstorm Warning" (for Krissy). [OxfordM] (5:1) Spr-Sum 89, p. 14-15.
505. BLACK, Candace
"A Gift." [ThRiPo] (31/32) 88, p. 10.
"Postpartum: Shantung Province." [ThRiPo] (31/32) 88, p. 11.
506. BLACK, Harold
"The Air Cries Out" (tr. of Mendel Lifshitz). [Vis] (31) 89, p. 22.

507. BLACK, Patricia
   "Wake Like an Egyptian" (for Bob). [GreensboroR] (46) Sum 89, p. 93.
508. BLACK, Ralph
   "Nicaraguan Pastorale." [Pequod] (26/27) 89, p. 31-32.
509. BLACK, Sophie Cabot
   "Express." [Ploughs] (15:4) Wint 89-90, p. 19-20.
   "February." [Field] (40) Spr 89, p. 11.
   "Into Dark." [Field] (40) Spr 89, p. 10.
   "Northwest Passage." [Agni] (28) 89, p. 92-93.
   "She Drives." [Field] (40) Spr 89, p. 12.
510. BLACK, Star
   "The Silent Saboteur." [Boulevard] (4:2, #11) Fall 89, p. 175.
511. BLACKHAWK, Terry
   "February Teacher." [PassN] (10:2) Sum 89, p. 10.
   "Margaret Atwood & the Filmmaker (A Review)." [PassN] (10:1) Wint 89, p. 16.
512. BLACKLEDGE, Adrian
   "Waiting Outside with the Children." [Verse] (6:3) Wint 89, p. 79.
513. BLACKMAN, Roy
   "The Robin." [Margin] (8) 89, p. 47.
514. BLACKSTONE, Alice
   "Chokecherry." [Plain] (10:1) 89, p. 6.
   "Parson's Wife." [Plain] (9:3) Spr 89, p. 34.
515. BLACKWOOD, Jean A.
   "The Rock's Progress." [Farm] (6:2) Fall 89, p. 19.
516. BLADES, Joe
   "Scallops." [CrossC] (11:1) 89, p. 3.
517. BLAICH, Beryl
   "Apparition." [BambooR] (42/43) Spr-Sum 89, p. 158-159.
518. BLAIR, John
   "Cicada." [Poetry] (153:4) Ja 89, p. 211-212.
   "Winter Storm, New Oleans." [Poetry] (153:4) Ja 89, p. 213.
519. BLAIR, Sam
   "Up and Down." [PoetryNW] (30:4) Wint 89-90, p. 43.
520. BLAIS, Hélene
   "Katujak." [PraF] (10:1, #46) Spr 89, p. 34-35.
   "Lionne Ailée" (à Madeleine Gagnon). [PraF] (10:1, #46) Spr 89, p. 36.
521. BLAKE, George
   "I Think I Climbed Trees." [KanQ] (21:3) Sum 89, p. 40.
   "The Raker." [KanQ] (21:3) Sum 89, p. 40.
522. BLAKE, Jonathan
   "In America" (Selections: 1, 4, 6). [Mildred] (3:1) Spr-Sum 89, p. 111-112.
523. BLAKE, William
   "Eternity." [LakeSR] (23) 89, p. 38.
524. BLAKEMORE-BAIG, Sandi
   "The Sunset." [Lactuca] (12) F 89, p. 35.
525. BLANCO, Alberto
   "Blue Tryptich" (tr. by John Oliver Simon). [Lactuca] (12) F 89, p. 14-15.
   "Green Tryptich" (tr. by John Oliver Simon). [Lactuca] (12) F 89, p. 16-17.
   "Red Tryptich" (tr. by John Oliver Simon). [Lactuca] (12) F 89, p. 13-14.
   "Trípitco Azul." [Lactuca] (12) F 89, p. 14-15.
   "Trípitco Rojo." [Lactuca] (12) F 89, p. 13-14.
   "Trípitco Verde." [Lactuca] (12) F 89, p. 16-17.
526. BLAND, Celia
   "Byzantine Icon." [Pequod] (28/29/30) 89, p. 110.
   "Conception." [Colum] (14) 89, p. 146.
   "Painting Prostheses." [Pequod] (28/29/30) 89, p. 108-109.
527. BLANDIANA, Ana
   "Ceausescu: No Little Prince" (tr. of "A Star in My Street" from "Events in My
        Street"). [Harp] (279:1675) D 89, p. 16, 18-19.
528. BLANKENSHIP, Richard
   "God Bless Our Electric Vampire." [SpoonRQ] (14:2) Spr 89, p. 45-52.
529. BLASER, Robin
   "Poppycock & Druthers." [CapilR] (1st series: 50) 89, p. 12-15.
530. BLASING, Mutlu Konuk
   "9-10 P.M. Poems" (tr. of Nazim Hikmet, w. Randy Blasing). [PoetryE] (27) Spr
        89, p. 31-46.

"Istanbul House of Detention" (tr. of Nazim Hikmet, w. Randy Blasing). [PoetryE]
    (27) Spr 89, p. 17-20.
"Letters from Chankiri Prison" (tr. of Nazim Hikmet, w. Randy Blasing). [PoetryE]
    (27) Spr 89, p. 24-30.
"One Night of Knee-Deep Snow" (tr. of Nazim Hikmet, w. Randy Blasing).
    [PoetryE] (27) Spr 89, p. 14-16.
"Since I Was Thrown Inside" (tr. of Nazim Hikmet, w. Randy Blasing). [PoetryE]
    (27) Spr 89, p. 21-23.
"Some Advice to Those Who Will Serve Time in Prison" (tr. of Nazim Hikmet, w.
    Randy Blasing). [PoetryE] (27) Spr 89, p. 12-13.
531. BLASING, Randy
    "9-10 P.M. Poems" (tr. of Nazim Hikmet, w. Mutlu Konuk Blasing). [PoetryE] (27)
        Spr 89, p. 31-46.
    "Istanbul House of Detention" (tr. of Nazim Hikmet, w. Mutlu Konuk Blasing).
        [PoetryE] (27) Spr 89, p. 17-20.
    "Letters from Chankiri Prison" (tr. of Nazim Hikmet, w. Mutlu Konuk Blasing).
        [PoetryE] (27) Spr 89, p. 24-30.
    "One Night of Knee-Deep Snow" (tr. of Nazim Hikmet, w. Mutlu Konuk Blasing).
        [PoetryE] (27) Spr 89, p. 14-16.
    "Since I Was Thrown Inside" (tr. of Nazim Hikmet, w. Mutlu Konuk Blasing).
        [PoetryE] (27) Spr 89, p. 21-23.
    "Some Advice to Those Who Will Serve Time in Prison" (tr. of Nazim Hikmet, w.
        Mutlu Konuk Blasing). [PoetryE] (27) Spr 89, p. 12-13.
    "Triptych." [Poetry] (154:2) My 89, p. 77-78.
    "White Bread." [Poetry] (154:2) My 89, p. 79-80.
    "Within Limits." [Poetry] (153:6) Mr 89, p. 340.
532. BLAUNER, Laurie
    "The Art of Translation." [Poetry] (155:3) D 89, p. 213.
    "Discussions of Marriage by Strangers Among Fireflies." [AmerPoR] (18:3) My-Je
        89, p. 8.
    "What We Don't See." [NewOR] (16:1) Spr 89, p. 75.
533. BLAZEK, Douglas
    "The Butcher" (After a Photograph by Ralph Sutton). [FreeL] (1) 89, p. 25-26.
    "In the Narrow Wooden Room Baudelaire Aimed the Camera Directly at Himself."
        [FreeL] (1) 89, p. 24-25.
534. BLAZEVIC, Neda-Miranda
    "Mississippi" (tr. by Ellen Elias-Bursac). [ColR] (NS 16:1) Spr-Sum 89, p. 94.
535. BLESSING, Tom
    "At the Track in Paducah." [Bogg] (61) 89, p. 40.
536. BLESSINGTON, Francis
    "Forms in Contemporary Poetry." [SouthernR] (25:3) Sum 89, p. 632.
537. BLEWETT, Peter
    "Coming Home at Night on the Freeway." [LitR] (32:2) Wint 89, p. 214.
538. BLITCH, Lynn
    "Woman." [NegC] (9:1) 89, p. 78-79.
539. BLOCH, Chana
    "The Family." [Poetry] (154:2) My 89, p. 88.
    "A Future." [Poetry] (154:2) My 89, p. 87.
    "Learning Fire." [SouthernPR] (29:2) Fall 89, p. 57.
540. BLOCK, Laurie
    "The Sprint." [PraF] (10:4, #49) Wint 89-90, p. 44.
541. BLODGETT, E. D.
    "Pavanes." [Dandel] (16:1) Spr-Sum 89, p. 63-67.
542. BLOMAIN, Karen
    "Magna Carta." [Footwork] 89, p. 48.
    "The Migrants in Suburbia." [Mildred] (3:1) Spr-Sum 89, p. 108-110.
    "Rain and Memory." [WindO] (51) Spr 89, p. 25.
543. BLONSTEIN, Anne
    "Behind the Times." [AntigR] (77/78) Spr-Sum 89, p. 28.
544. BLOOMFIELD, Maureen
    "The Meeting of Dante and Beatrice." [SouthernR] (25:1) Wint 89, p. 146-147.
    "To Be Childless Is an Error?" [Ploughs] (15:4) Wint 89-90, p. 21-22.
545. BLOSSOM, Laurel
    "Landscape Painting." [Pequod] (28/29/30) 89, p. 254.
546. BLOSSOMHOUSE, Amelia
    "A Dedication for H.J.B." [Bomb] (28) Sum 89, p. 89.

547. BLOYD, Rebekah
    "Hurricane Jane." [CinPR] (20) Fall 89, p. 22-23.
    "The Sky Vanishes." [CinPR] (20) Fall 89, p. 24.
548. BLUE, Savana
    "While Making a Pencil Sketch of Eggs with the Sun So Perfectly Burning." [Prima]
        (13) 89, p. 43.
549. BLUM, Ann Marie
    "Missionary." [WorldO] (22:1/2) Fall-Wint 87-88, c90, p. 26-27.
550. BLUMENREICH, Julia
    "Ingathering Text 1 Feb - 15 Feb 1988." [PaperAir] (4:2) 89, p. 102-105.
    "Ingathering text 1 Sept - 27 Oct 88." [Screens] (1) 89, p. 64-65.
    "Non/Purchase #4." [Aerial] (5) 89, p. 16-17.
    "Non/Purchase #9." [Aerial] (5) 89, p. 18.
    "Non/Purchase #11." [Aerial] (5) 89, p. 19.
551. BLUMENTHAL, Jay (Jay A.)
    "The Alchemist As Poet." [JINJPo] [11] 89, p. 7.
    "Annus Mirabilis, 1969-1970." [SoCaR] (22:1) Fall 89, p. 39.
    "At War with Particulars." [CarolQ] (41:3) Spr 89, p. 52.
    "Brief Encounter." [NoDaQ] (57:3) Sum 89, p. 148.
    "Brief Encounter." [Outbr] (20) 89, p. 6.
    "The Canonization: August 16, 1948." [GrahamHR] (12) Spr 89, p. 31-32.
    "Capitalism on the Moon." [NowestR] (27:3) 89, p. 53.
    "Death at the Chocolatier's." [Plain] (9:2) Wint 89, p. 16.
    "The Dover Sole." [WestB] (23) 89, p. 100-101.
    "Dream Just Before Morning." [InterPR] (15:2) Fall 89, p. 99.
    "The Frontier of Hindsight." [WormR] (29:1, #113) 89, p. 3.
    "God Watches the Orient Express, Does Nothing." [CarolQ] (41:3) Spr 89, p. 51.
    "Hail, Sister, Keeper of the Spirit." [SoCaR] (21:2) Spr 89, p. 28.
    "The Last Great Age of Breakfast." [Hawai'iR] (13:2, #26) Sum 89, p. 1.
    "The Midnight Shark." [DenQ] (24:2) Fall 89, p. 28-29.
    "Monday Morning, Eastbound." [SoCaR] (22:1) Fall 89, p. 40.
    "Old Ways and Former Gods." [WormR] (29:1, #113) 89, p. 3-4.
    "On First Looking into Freshman Composition." [InterPR] (15:2) Fall 89, p. 98.
    "Parallel Universe." [Jacaranda] (4:1) Spr-Sum 89, p. 157.
    "Parallel Universe." [SenR] (19:1) 89, p. 73.
    "The Princess of the Silver Bullet." [SoCaR] (21:2) Spr 89, p. 29.
    "Pygmalion." [BallSUF] (30:4) Aut 89, p. 63.
    "The Retirement of Ulysses." [BrooklynR] (6) 89, p. 16.
    "Reunion." [BallSUF] (30:4) Aut 89, p. 57.
    "Reunion." [Interim] (8:2) Fall 89, p. 39.
    "Reunion." [SoCaR] (22:1) Fall 89, p. 38.
    "Stopping at Nothing." [CumbPR] (9:1) Fall 89, p. 10.
    "Swan Song." [InterPR] (15:2) Fall 89, p. 98.
    "When Worlds Collide." [WashR] (15:4) D 89-Ja 90, p. 18.
    "Wit's End." [NowestR] (27:3) 89, p. 54.
552. BLUMENTHAL, Michael
    "Cambridge." [BostonR] (14:2) Ap 89, p. 3.
553. BLY, Robert
    "Melancholy inside Families" (tr. of Pablo Neruda, w. James Wright). [Quarry]
        (38:2) Spr 89, p. 76-77.
    "Take a pitcher full of water and set it down on the water" (tr. of Kabir). [Mildred]
        (3:2) 89, p. 132.
    "The United Fruit Company" (tr. of Pablo Neruda). [PoetryE] (27) Spr 89, p.
        119-120.
    "Waking from Sleep." [SouthwR] (74:4) Aut 89, p. 522.
554. BLYLER, Diane
    "Preparations for the Life Ahead" (from An Honest Account). [SinW] (38) Sum-Fall
        89, p. 45-46.
555. BLYTHE, Randy
    "Hornman's Jubilee." [WindO] (51) Spr 89, p. 16.
    "Spaghetti-O's." [WindO] (51) Spr 89, p. 17.
556. BOBRICK, James
    "Bank." [OxfordM] (5:1) Spr-Sum 89, p. 72.
    "Job-Hunting." [NewRena] (7:3, #23) 89, p. 173-174.
    "Shave." [CumbPR] (8:2) Spr 89, p. 83.

557. BOBROWSKI, Johannes
    "Cemetery" (tr. by Patricia Pollock Brodsky). [NewL] (55:3) Spr 89, p. 43.
    "Memorial for a River Fisherman" (tr. by Patricia Pollock Brodsky). [NewL] (55:3)
        Spr 89, p. 41.
    "Pruzzian Elegy" (tr. by Patricia Pollock Brodsky). [NewL] (55:3) Spr 89, p. 43-45.
    "Village" (tr. by Patricia Pollock Brodsky). [NewL] (55:3) Spr 89, p. 42.
558. BOCCIA, Michael
    "A Curse Upon the Reader of These Words." [WindO] (51) Spr 89, p. 15.
559. BOE, Marilyn J.
    "He Skates From Me." [PassN] (10:1) Wint 89, p. 18.
    "Sorting Mother's Things." [ChrC] (106:3) Ja 25, 89, p. 78.
    "Telephone Call." [SoCoast] (6) Fall 88, p. 17.
    "Wild Swans at Christmas" (Nantwich, England, 1985). [ChrC] (106:39) D 20-27,
        89, p. 1200.
560. BOGAN, James
    "Mar-ahu" (tr. of Max Martins). [RiverS] (30) [89], p. 77.
    "Time" (tr. of Max Martins). [RiverS] (30) [89], p. 75.
561. BOGEN, Don
    "The Machines." [NewRep] (201:12/13) 18-25 S 89, p. 50.
    "A Muse." [YaleR] (79:1) Aut 89, p. 40-41.
    "Necklace." [NewRep] (200:14) 3 Ap 89, p. 34.
    "Three Cradle Songs" (Norman Dinerstein, composer, 1937-1982). [PartR] (56:3)
        Sum 89, p. 455-456.
562. BOGIN, George
    "At Sixty-Four." [Ploughs] (15:4) Wint 89-90, p. 23-25.
563. BOHANAN, Audrey
    "Accretion." [VirQR] (65:1) Wint 89, p. 74.
    "Draft Animals." [BelPoJ] (39:4) Sum 89, p. 29-31.
    "Eula and April." [BelPoJ] (39:4) Sum 89, p. 28.
    "View from Webhannet Marsh." [DenQ] (24:2) Fall 89, p. 30-31.
    "Winter Burial." [VirQR] (65:1) Wint 89, p. 74-75.
564. BOISSEAU, Michelle
    "Eurydice." [Crazy] (37) Wint 89, p. 41-42.
    "Persephone." [RiverS] (28) 89, p. 4.
BOK, Yi Sung
    See YI, Sung Bok
565. BOLAND, Eavan
    "The Black Lace Fan My Mother Gave Me." [NoDaQ] (57:1) Wint 89, p. 57.
    "Dark Flowers." [NewYorker] (65:32) 25 S 89, p. 56.
    "In Exile." [TriQ] (77) Wint 89-90, p. 253.
    "Nights of Childhood." [NewYorker] (65:15) 29 My 89, p. 33.
    "Our Origins are in the Sea." [NewYorker] (65:15) 29 My 89, p. 33.
    "Outside History." [TriQ] (77) Wint 89-90, p. 252.
    "The Photograph on My Father's Desk." [Pequod] (26/27) 89, p. 75.
    "The Rooms of Other Women Poets." [Ploughs] (15:4) Wint 89-90, p. 26-27.
    "The Rooms of Other Women Poets." [TriQ] (77) Wint 89-90, p. 249-250.
    "We Are Human History. We Are Not Natural History." [TriQ] (77) Wint 89-90, p.
        251.
    "What We Lost." [NewYorker] (65:15) 29 My 89, p. 33.
    "White Hawthorn in the West of Ireland." [NewYorker] (65:6) 27 Mr 89, p. 111.
566. BOLDT, Christine
    "(For My Son Sharaf, and for the Bahá'ís Suffering Persecution in Iran) 7 Jalal 140
        B.E." [WorldO] (22:1/2) Fall-Wint 87-88, c90, p. 33.
    "Gardenia." [WorldO] (22:1/2) Fall-Wint 87-88, c90, p. 35.
567. BOLDUC, David
    "Honeymoon Suite" (Excerpt, w. Victor Coleman). [CapilR] (1st series: 50) 89, p.
        27-31.
568. BOLIN, Randall
    "Whisper Jeezus." [EvergreenC] (4:3) Spr 89, p. 33.
569. BOLLIER, Philip
    "Observations on a Black and White Tile." [NegC] (9:1) 89, p. 30-31.
570. BOLLING, Madelon
    "The Last Grandparent." [BellArk] (5:6) N-D 89, p. 5.
    "Mohnkuchen." [BellArk] (5:3) My-Je 89, p. 10.
    "On the Way to Language." [BellArk] (5:3) My-Je 89, p. 3.

571. BOLLS, Imogene (Imogene L.)
    "The Dance." [SoDakR] (27:3) Aut 89, p. 75.
    "Early Mimbres Bowl" (Ca. 650 A.D.). [SoDakR] (27:3) Aut 89, p. 74.
    "Finding the Remains of a Dead Sheep at Wild Oughtershaw." [KanQ] (21:1/2)
        Wint-Spr 89, p. 113.
    "Freshly Plowed." [SoDakR] (27:3) Aut 89, p. 76.
    "Holy Dirt" (Reflections at Santuario de Chimayo). [SoDakR] (27:2) Sum 89, p.
        55-56.
572. BOLSTRIDGE, Alice
    "Covenant." [CinPR] (19) Spr 89, p. 46-47.
    "Mating Habits of Waterfowl." [CinPR] (19) Spr 89, p. 44-45.
573. BOLT, Jeffrey
    "Monday Morning." [Interim] (8:2) Fall 89, p. 15.
574. BOLT, Thomas
    "Field with Large Stones." [Bomb] (29) Fall 89, p. 72.
    "Meditation in Loudoun County." [SouthwR] (74:1) Wint 89, p. 36.
    "Trainyard at Noon." [Bomb] (29) Fall 89, p. 72.
    "Unauthorized Dump." [SouthwR] (74:1) Wint 89, p. 37-38.
    "Unpolluted Creek." [Bomb] (29) Fall 89, p. 72.
575. BOLTEN, André Michael
    "Breath" (tr. by John Linthicum). [LitR] (33:1) Fall 89, p. 66.
    "I Want to Know" (tr. by John Linthicum). [LitR] (33:1) Fall 89, p. 66.
    "Poetry" (tr. by John Linthicum). [LitR] (33:1) Fall 89, p. 67.
    "The Tomcat" (tr. by John Linthicum). [LitR] (33:1) Fall 89, p. 67.
576. BOLTON, Joe
    "And If in the History of Man" (tr. of Enrique Huaco). [Pig] (15) 88, p. 92.
    "August Elegy." [CumbPR] (9:1) Fall 89, p. 41.
    "The Beginning of Summer." [QW] (28) Wint-Spr 89, p. 84.
    "Contemplating a Landscape in Spring." [ConnPR] (8:1) 89, p. 25-26.
    "Daisy Miller in the Colosseum." [Thrpny] (37) Spr 89, p. 11.
    "Diptych" (Improvisations on a Theme by Jiménez). [AntR] (47:3) Sum 89, p.
        328-329.
    "Elegy for Roland Barthes." [Poetry] (154:2) My 89, p. 63-64.
    "The Green Diamonds of Summer." [ApalQ] (32) 89, p. 92-97.
    "Hurricane." [IndR] (12:2) Spr 89, p. 109-110.
    "Justification of a War" (tr. of Enrique Huaco). [Pig] (15) 88, p. 91.
    "Little Testament." [IndR] (12:2) Spr 89, p. 111-112.
    "The Parthenon at Nashville." [CumbPR] (9:1) Fall 89, p. 40.
    "Sherwood Anderson, 1912." [NoAmR] (274:2) Je 89, p. 27.
    "There Is an Instant" (tr. of Guillermo Valencia). [Pig] (15) 88, p. 92.
    "Trilce XV" (tr. of César Vallejo). [Pig] (15) 88, p. 90.
    "Wild Horses." [QW] (28) Wint-Spr 89, p. 83.
    "Your Sex" (after César Vallejo). [StoneC] (16:3/4) Spr-Sum 89, p. 39.
577. BOLZ, Jody
    "Last Costume." [FreeL] (2) Sum 89, p. 7.
578. BOMBA, Bernard
    "Prick Song." [OxfordM] (5:1) Spr-Sum 89, p. 8-9.
    "Stairwell, the Kelsey Building." [SoCoast] (6) Fall 88, p. 49.
    "Terminal." [JINJPo] (11) 89, p. 8.
579. BONACCI, Michael
    "And the Strength of the Hills to Uphold Me" (Paiute Song, for Kevin). [EvergreenC]
        (4:4) Sum 89, p. 34.
580. BONAFFINI, Luigi
    "The Crossroads" (tr. of Eugenio Cirese). [WebR] (14:1) Spr 89, p. 22.
    "Nothing" (tr. of Eugenio Cirese). [WebR] (14:1) Spr 89, p. 23.
    "The Snowstorm" (tr. of Eugenio Cirese). [WebR] (14:1) Spr 89, p. 23.
581. BOND, Bruce
    "Cézanne: *Apples and Oranges*." [SouthwR] (74:1) Wint 89, p. 77.
    "Elsewhere." [SoCoast] (6) Fall 88, p. 40.
    "The Final Days of Robert Schumann." [PoetC] (21:1) Fall 89, p. 24-25.
    "Hospice." [Ploughs] (15:4) Wint 89-90, p. 28.
    "The Ivory Hours." [Shen] (39:4) Wint 89, p. 71-72.
    "Kurt Weill." [AntR] (47:2) Spr 89, p. 189.
    "Mahler: *Kindertotenlieder*." [NegC] (9:1) 89, p. 43.
    "The Oracle of Remembered Things." [MidwQ] (30:4) Sum 89, p. 437.
    "Stravinsky." [WestB] (25) 89, p. 45.

"The Weathercock" (Literary Wards: Honorable Mention). [GreensboroR] (47) Wint
89-90, p. 120.
582. BOND, Cynthia
"Buoy." [Epoch] (38:3) 89, p. 213.
"A Romance." [Epoch] (38:3) 89, p. 214.
"See Joy." [Epoch] (38:3) 89, p. 212.
583. BONDS, Diane
"The Cup of Tea" (a painting by Mary Cassatt). [SouthernHR] (23:4) Fall 89, p. 342.
"Monarchs." [SouthernHR] (23:3) Sum 89, p. 240.
584. BONIFAY, Kurt E.
"Beachcomber." [EmeraldCR] (1989) c1988, p. 115-116.
585. BONNEFOY, Yves
"The Hawk" (tr. by Emily Grosholz). [Hudson] (42:3) Aut 89, p. 447.
"The Trees" (tr. by Emily Grosholz). [Hudson] (42:3) Aut 89, p. 448.
586. BONTA, David
"Bessie's Blues." [WestB] (23) 89, p. 38.
587. BOOK, M. K.
"Clown Death, 1." [WormR] (29:1, #113) 89, p. 41.
"Clown Death, 2." [WormR] (29:1, #113) 89, p. 41.
588. BOOTH, Philip
"Calling." [AmerPoR] (18:3) My-Je 89, p. 34.
"Dear Life." [AmerPoR] (18:3) My-Je 89, p. 35.
"Directions." [PoetryNW] (30:2) Sum 89, p. 45-46.
"Fallback." [AmerPoR] (18:3) My-Je 89, p. 34.
"Farview Home." [AmerPoR] (18:3) My-Je 89, p. 35.
"Girl in a Gallery." [PoetryNW] (30:2) Sum 89, p. 46-47.
"Glove." [Poetry] (154:1) Ap 89, p. 13.
"Heading Out." [Poetry] (154:1) Ap 89, p. 15.
"Longings." [PoetryNW] (30:2) Sum 89, p. 44-45.
"March." [AmerPoR] (18:3) My-Je 89, p. 35.
"Petition." [Talisman] (2) Spr 89, p. 62.
"A Postcard from Portsmouth." [PoetryNW] (30:2) Sum 89, p. 47.
"Provisions." [AmerPoR] (18:3) My-Je 89, p. 36.
"Reaching In." [DenQ] (23:3/4) Wint-Spr 89, p. 11.
"Rule One." [Poetry] (153:4) Ja 89, p. 220-221.
"Sea Level." [AmerPoR] (18:3) My-Je 89, p. 35.
"Sentence." [DenQ] (23:3/4) Wint-Spr 89, p. 10.
"Thanksgiving." [NewEngR] (12:2) Wint 89, p. 153-155.
"Times." [Poetry] (154:1) Ap 89, p. 14.
"Words Made from Letters." [GeoR] (43:2) Sum 89, p. 296-297.
"Zeros." [AmerPoR] (18:3) My-Je 89, p. 35.
589. BORCZON, Matthew
"An American Ritual." [HangL] (54) 89, p. 5.
BORDA, J. G. Cobo
See COBO BORDA, J. G.
590. BORDEN, William
"To All My Former Lovers." [CinPR] (20) Fall 89, p. 14-15.
"Wyoming Cows." [CinPR] (20) Fall 89, p. 12-13.
591. BORDERS, Andrew
"Pond Draining." [TarRP] (29:1) Fall 89, p. 28-30.
592. BORINSKY, Alicia
"Compraventa de la Marioneta." [AnotherCM] (19) 89, p. 12.
"Don't Jump" (tr. by Cola Franzen). [Pig] (15) 88, p. 93.
"Home" (tr. by Cola Franzen). [Pig] (15) 88, p. 91.
"Justificacion." [AnotherCM] (19) 89, p. 10.
"Justification" (tr. by Cola Franzen). [AnotherCM] (19) 89, p. 11.
"Purchase and Sale Agreement for the Marionette" (tr. by Cola Franzen).
[AnotherCM] (19) 89, p. 13.
"Visits to the Doctor" (tr. by Cola Franzen). [Pig] (15) 88, p. 92.
593. BORN, Anne
"An Old-World Norseman" (tr. of Olav Hauge). [Verse] (6:1) Mr 89, p. 46.
"Pigs" (tr. of Olav Hauge). [Verse] (6:1) Mr 89, p. 45.
"Scent of Apples" (tr. of Solveig von Schoultz). [Verse] (6:1) Mr 89, p. 47.
"Three Sisters" (tr. of Solveig von Schoultz). [Verse] (6:1) Mr 89, p. 47.
594. BORNEMAN, W. R.
"Signals Without an Intrinsic Content." [PaperAir] (4:2) 89, p. 117.

595. BOROQUE, Ben
"Banquet II." [EmeraldCR] (1989) c1988, p. 103.
"Spring Fever." [EmeraldCR] (1989) c1988, p. 103.
596. BORROFF, Marie
"Houses." [Sequoia] (32:2) Wint-Spr 89, p. 5.
"Solitude." [Sequoia] (32:2) Wint-Spr 89, p. 4.
597. BORUCH, Marianne
"Argument, with Migration." [Field] (40) Spr 89, p. 9.
"Holy Cards." [Field] (40) Spr 89, p. 7-8.
"Inventing the Train." [Field] (40) Spr 89, p. 6.
"Maps." [NewYorker] (65:20) 3 Jl 89, p. 36.
"Moss Burning." [GeoR] (43:4) Wint 89, p. 729-730.
"Snow." [Field] (40) Spr 89, p. 5.
598. BOSCH, Daniel
"From a Thank You Note." [WestHR] (43:2) Sum 89, p. 121.
"Jesu Meine Freude" (after BWV 227). [BelPoJ] (40:1) Fall 89, p. 4-7.
599. BOSS, Laura
"The Great Falls of Paterson." [Footwork] 89, p. 76-77.
"I Feel Like Madonna." [Footwork] 89, p. 77.
"Portrait of Bebe." [Footwork] 89, p. 77.
"Tradition: Struga Poetry Outing" (XXVI Annual International Poetry Week at Struga
in Macedonia, Yugoslavia, 1987). [Footwork] 89, p. 77.
600. BOSTRUM, Annette
"Landscape in Black and White." [CentralP] (16) Fall 89, p. 185.
601. BOSWELL, Robin Mary
"The Jeweled Christ" (Upper cover of binding, from the Lindau Gospels). [MassR]
(30:2) Sum 89, p. 274-275.
"The Rotting of the Playhouse." [MassR] (30:2) Sum 89, p. 269-274.
"The Virgin General." [MassR] (30:2) Sum 89, p. 275-276.
602. BOSWORTH, David
"The Critic Waits for the Poet to Clear His Throat." [CrossCur] (8:3) Apr 89, p.
29-34.
"Ice Out." [CrossCur] (8:3) Apr 89, p. 35-38.
603. BOTTOMS, David
"Last Nickel Ranch: Plains, Montana." [ParisR] (31:112) Fall 89, p. 65.
604. BOUCHER, Alan
"Folk Verse" (tr. of Olafur Johann Sigurdsson). [Vis] (31) 89, p. 19.
"Running Water" (tr. of Stein Steinarr). [Vis] (31) 89, p. 36.
605. BOUGH, Michael
"School Days." [Screens] (1) 89, p. 46.
606. BOUGHN, Mike
"The Boat" (for Tom Dubree). [Notus] (4:2) Fall 89, p. 79.
"Geographeme: Ge-Ode" (for Susan Barnes). [Notus] (4:2) Fall 89, p. 80.
"Geographeme: Riveredge" (for Jack Clarke). [Notus] (4:2) Fall 89, p. 81.
607. BOURNE, Daniel
"A Bird Gets the Death Sentence" (tr. of Tomasz Jastrun). [OhioR] (44) 89, p. 27.
"Breath" (tr. of Ryszard Holzer). [AnotherCM] (19) 89, p. 111.
"Cat Hunters #1" (tr. of Ryszard Holzer). [AnotherCM] (19) 89, p. 107.
"Cat Hunters #2" (tr. of Ryszard Holzer). [AnotherCM] (19) 89, p. 109.
"Cleaning Out the Nest." [Shen] (39:4) Wint 89, p. 102-103.
"The Country We Are Living In." [PoetryE] (28) Fall 89, p. 105.
"The Death of Literature." [Salm] (81) Wint 89, p. 94.
"Each Night" (tr. of Tomasz Jastrun). [ColR] (NS 16:2) Fall 89-Wint 90, p. 87.
"Eyes" (tr. of Tomasz Jastrun). [Chelsea] (48) 89, p. 22.
"Fatherland" (tr. of Tomasz Jastrun). [LitR] (32:2) Wint 89, p. 167.
"Fire" (tr. of Tomasz Jastrun). [LitR] (32:2) Wint 89, p. 167.
"Five Before Twelve" (tr. of Tomasz Jastrun). [AntigR] (79) Aut 89, p. 8.
"The Flip Side of the Medal" (tr. of Tomasz Jastrun). [GrahamHR] (12) Spr 89, p.
59.
"Fruitless" (tr. of Tomasz Jastrun). [Chelsea] (48) 89, p. 20.
"Good Fences." [Salm] (81) Wint 89, p. 93.
"The Great Emigration" (tr. of Tomasz Jastrun). [OhioR] (44) 89, p. 27.
"Ground Cover" (tr. of Tomasz Jastrun). [AntigR] (79) Aut 89, p. 9.
"Guardian Angel" (tr. of Tomasz Jastrun). [BelPoJ] (39:3) Spr 89, p. 30.
"In a Cage" (tr. of Tomasz Jastrun). [CumbPR] (9:1) Fall 89, p. 26.
"The Language of the Dead" (Warsaw, October 1985). [Shen] (39:4) Wint 89, p. 101.

"The Last Days of My Guardian Angel" (tr. of Tomasz Jastrun). [BelPoJ] (39:3) Spr 89, p. 31.
"A Letter from Prison" (tr. of Tomasz Jastrun). [Shen] (39:2) Sum 89, p. 54.
"The Life Left." [Shen] (39:4) Wint 89, p. 100.
"Lights" (tr. of Tomasz Jastrun). [Chelsea] (48) 89, p. 21.
"Nothing" (tr. of Tomasz Jastrun). [Chelsea] (48) 89, p. 19.
"Our Table of Desire" (tr. of Tomasz Jastrun). [ConnPR] (8:1) 89, p. 17.
"Outage." [SpoonRQ] (14:1) Wint 89, p. 64.
"Peasant Farmer" (tr. of Tomasz Jastrun). [ConnPR] (8:1) 89, p. 18.
"Possessed" (tr. of Tomasz Jastrun). [SoCaR] (21:2) Spr 89, p. 73.
"Postcard from Martial Law" (to Edward Nowak, the Lenin Steelmills, tr. of Ryszard Holzer). [Pequod] (26/27) 89, p. 14.
"Power" (tr. of Tomasz Jastrun). [LitR] (32:2) Wint 89, p. 166.
"The Retreat of the Home Army" (tr. of Tomasz Jastrun). [GrahamHR] (12) Spr 89, p. 58.
"Returning from the Dance." [Mildred] (3:2) 89, p. 19.
"Sex Song for Our Second Year in Warsaw." [YellowS] (29) Spr 89, p. 21.
"Sheepskin." [PoetryE] (28) Fall 89, p. 108.
"Silence" (tr. of Tomasz Jastrun). [LitR] (32:2) Wint 89, p. 166.
"A Single Drop" (tr. of Tomasz Jastrun). [LitR] (32:2) Wint 89, p. 167.
"Solar Eclipse" (tr. of Irén Négyesy, w. Nicholas Kolumban). [ArtfulD] (16/17) Fall 89, p. 76.
"Straw" (tr. of Tomasz Jastrun). [ColR] (NS 16:2) Fall 89-Wint 90, p. 86.
"Street of Dobermen." [CrossCur] (8:3) Apr 89, p. 49.
"Translated from the Polish of 1986." [PoetryE] (28) Fall 89, p. 106.
"Unburied Shoes." [TarRP] (28:2) Spr 89, p. 13.
"Wall" (tr. of Tomasz Jastrun). [AntigR] (79) Aut 89, p. 11.
"We Rebuild Warsaw (Reprise, 1986)." [PoetryE] (28) Fall 89, p. 107.
"We'll Breathe Quietly" (tr. of Ryszard Holzer). [AnotherCM] (19) 89, p. 113.
"Wigilia." [Salm] (81) Wint 89, p. 95-96.
"Wing Span." [CrossCur] (8:3) Apr 89, p. 51.
"Yet Another Time" (tr. of Tomasz Jastrun). [AntigR] (79) Aut 89, p. 10.
"Zomo" (tr. of Tomasz Jastrun). [CumbPR] (9:1) Fall 89, p. 25.
608. BOURNE, Lesley-Anne
"The First and the Next." [Grain] (17:1) Spr 89, p. 67.
"Man on a Tenth Floor Balcony Feeding the Birds One Evening." [Grain] (17:1) Spr 89, p. 65.
"The Orange Canoe." [Grain] (17:1) Spr 89, p. 65.
"Ranchman." [Grain] (17:1) Spr 89, p. 66.
"Wanting & Chance." [Grain] (17:1) Spr 89, p. 66.
609. BOURNE, Louis
"Elegy from Simancas" (Towards History, tr. of Claudio Rodríguez). [InterPR] (15:2) Fall 89, p. 39-45.
"Just a Smile" (tr. of Claudio Rodríguez). [InterPR] (15:2) Fall 89, p. 33, 35.
"The Poppy's Shadow" (tr. of Claudio Rodríguez). [InterPR] (15:2) Fall 89, p. 31.
"Right There" (tr. of Claudio Rodríguez). [InterPR] (15:2) Fall 89, p. 35, 37.
"A Startling Sight" (tr. of Claudio Rodríguez). [InterPR] (15:2) Fall 89, p. 31, 33.
"With No Good-Bye" (tr. of Claudio Rodríguez). [InterPR] (15:2) Fall 89, p. 37, 39.
BOUTILLIER, Michelle le
    See LeBOUTILLIER, Michelle
610. BOUVARD, Marguerite
"Like Years." [MidwQ] (30:4) Sum 89, p. 440.
"Ways of Looking at the Ocean." [MidwQ] (30:4) Sum 89, p. 438-439.
611. BOWDEN, Michael
"Miller Canyon Trail No. 106." [CarolQ] (42:1) Fall 89, p. 28-29.
612. BOWDRING, Paul
"Silent Piano." [Grain] (17:1) Spr 89, p. 69.
"Vanishing Point." [Grain] (17:1) Spr 89, p. 68.
613. BOWERS, Brad
"Demeaning." [KeyWR] (2:1/2) Fall-Wint 89, p. 80.
BOWERS, Cathy Smith
    See SMITH-BOWERS, Cathy
614. BOWERS, Edgar
"A Defense of Poetry." [Thrpny] (37) Spr 89, p. 8.
"On Clive Wilmer's Visit to the Wildfowl Refuge." [Raritan] (9:1) Sum 89, p. 27-28.
"On Dick Davis' Reading, California State University, Los Angeles." [Raritan] (9:1)

Sum 89, p. 30.
"Richard." [Raritan] (9:1) Sum 89, p. 29.
615. BOWERS, Neal
"Apology for Solitude." [Poetry] (154:4) Jl 89, p. 210.
"Dark Vision." [FreeL] (1) 89, p. 7-8.
"Extremities." [Poetry] (154:4) Jl 89, p. 208.
"Feet" (for James Mahoney, D.P.M.). [GeoR] (43:3) Fall 89, p. 529.
"Out of the Blue." [SouthernR] (25:1) Wint 89, p. 162-163.
"Pockets." [Poetry] (154:4) Jl 89, p. 209.
"Putting Out the Trash." [FreeL] (1) 89, p. 9.
"The Rescue." [Poetry] (154:4) Jl 89, p. 209-210.
"The Resurrection Ball." [GeoR] (43:3) Fall 89, p. 530.
"Rites." [TarRP] (29:1) Fall 89, p. 41.
"The Woman in Charge of Night." [SouthernR] (25:1) Wint 89, p. 163.
616. BOWERS, Stan
"These Things Won't Do Ya No Good in Chicago at 5 A.M." [SlipS] (9) 89, p. 49.
617. BOWIE, Robert
"Photographs: The Past." [KanQ] (21:1/2) Wint-Spr 89, p. 56.
"Up to the Point of Truth-Ache." [SmPd] (26:1, #75) Wint 89, p. 6-7.
618. BOWLING, Tim
"In Defence of My Country." [Bogg] (61) 89, p. 11.
619. BOWMAN, Catherine
"Pot Roast." [RiverS] (29) [89], p. 59.
620. BOWMAN, Elizabeth
"At Sesame Place." [US1] (22/23) Spr 89, p. 7.
621. BOWMAN, W. R., Sr.
"Bettycan." [EmeraldCR] (1989) c1988, p. 98.
"Dawn." [EmeraldCR] (1989) c1988, p. 96.
622. BOYCE, Scott
"Luweero Triangle, Uganda." [Event] (18:2) Sum 89, p. 27.
"They Call It a Road." [Event] (18:2) Sum 89, p. 28-29.
"To Mbae Wakirika, Whom I Met Again by Chance." [AntigR] (76) Wint 89, p. 128.
623. BOYCHUK, Bohdan
"The Image" (tr. of Boris Pasternak, w. Mark Rudman). [Pequod] (28/29/30) 89, p. 273-274.
624. BOYER, Patsy
"The Sketch as Poem" (tr. of Alberto Girri, w. Mary Crow). [LitR] (32:4) Sum 89, p. 495-496.
625. BOZANIC, Nick
"Years." [YellowS] (29) Spr 89, p. 38.
626. BRACHO, Coral
"In a Delicate Mimicry of Rain" (9 Poems in Spanish & English, Translation Chapbook Series, tr. by Thomas Hoeksema and Romelia Enríquez). [MidAR] (9:1) 89, p. 81-115.
627. BRACKENBURY, Alison
"Detour." [Stand] (30:3) Sum 89, p. 34.
"Hippo Pool." [Stand] (30:3) Sum 89, p. 35-36.
"Mrs Taynton." [Stand] (30:3) Sum 89, p. 35.
628. BRACKENRIDGE, Valery
"Coloring the Tree of Night." [Footwork] 89, p. 34.
"Computer Chip I." [Footwork] 89, p. 33-34.
"Death Desires." [Footwork] 89, p. 34.
"Kathy." [Footwork] 89, p. 34-35.
"This One's for You. Max." [Footwork] 89, p. 34.
629. BRACKETT, Donald
"A Forest of Obelisks." [Rampike] (6:2) 88, p. 61.
630. BRADEN, David
"Reconnoiter" (Commended). [StoneC] (17:1/2) Fall-Wint 89-90, p. prelim. p. 6.
631. BRADLEY, George
"The 4th of July, and." [ParisR] (31:112) Fall 89, p. 28-33.
"Ideal City." [NewYorker] (65:3) 6 Mr 89, p. 36.
"More Perils of Pauline." [WestHR] (43:3) Aut 89, p. 204.
"Nostalgie de la Boue." [NewYorker] (65:37) 30 O 89, p. 40.
632. BRADLEY, Jane
"Defence." [Grain] (17:1) Spr 89, p. 53.

633. BRADLEY, John
"The Admirers of Vasko Popa." [HayF] (5) Fall 89, p. 96.
"After Lorca." [HighP] (4:3) Wint 89-90, p. 130.
"Black Rock with Blue." [BellR] (12:2, #26) Fall 89, p. 5.
634. BRADLEY, Robert
"Whistlestop: Central Kansas" (for Jeffrey Myers). [GettyR] (2:3) Sum 89, p.
476-477.
635. BRADY, J. Clancy
"The Baying of the Beast." [EmeraldCR] (1989) c1988, p. 139-140.
636. BRADY, Philip
"There Are No Political Prisoners" (Lubumbashi, Zaire). [PoetL] (84:4) Wint 89-90,
p. 15-16.
637. BRAGGS, Earl S. (Earl Sherman)
"Forsyth Co., Georgia, 1912" (from *From the Hands of a Fish Scaler's Son*). [Obs]
(3:2) Sum 88, p. 117.
"Hats." [ColR] (NS 16:1) Spr-Sum 89, p. 71-72.
"An Impressario of Hats." [ColR] (NS 16:1) Spr-Sum 89, p. 73-74.
"Street Corner Man." [ColR] (NS 16:1) Spr-Sum 89, p. 75-76.
638. BRAMHALL, Rick
"Blind Panorama of New York" (an interpretation of the original by Federico Garcia
Lorca). [PacificR] (7) 89, p. 35-37.
639. BRAND, Alice (Alice G.)
"How Coral Evolves." [Confr] (39/40) Fall 88-Wint 89, p. 60-61.
"How Coral Evolves." [Pig] (15) 88, p. 13.
"The Poet Does Laundry." [MinnR] (NS 33) Fall 89, p. 29-31.
640. BRAND, Madeleine
"A Belle Revue of *Bogg* 56." [Bogg] (61) 89, p. 16.
641. BRANDI, John
"Shadow Play." [RiverS] (28) 89, p. 63.
642. BRANDT, Di
"On the Terrace of the Porta Nigra" (for Stephan & Barbara). [PraF] (10:3, #48) Aut
89, p. 15.
"Piecing together the alphabet." [PraF] (10:3, #48) Aut 89, p. 17.
"Prairie Love Song." [PraF] (10:3, #48) Aut 89, p. 16.
"Teaching in Prison" (for all my students at Rockwood). [PraF] (10:3, #48) Aut 89,
p. 14.
643. BRANDT, Gus
"Embrace an Art Major." [EmeraldCR] (1989) c1988, p. 129.
"Humbert." [EmeraldCR] (1989) c1988, p. 128.
"Schastleebovo Pootee." [EmeraldCR] (1989) c1988, p. 129.
644. BRANNEN, Jonathan
"Last Rites." [Pembroke] (21) 89, p. 103.
"Renting the Air." [Pembroke] (21) 89, p. 103.
645. BRAQUE, G.
"Cahier de 1947" (Selections, tr. by Roger Shattuck). [Salm] (81) Wint 89, p. 6-18.
646. BRASCH, Thomas
"Babel's Death" (tr. by Michael Hamburger). [Stand] (30:2) Spr 89, p. 18.
647. BRASFIELD, James
"Off the Path." [ChiR] (36:3/4) 89, p. 40.
648. BRAUN, G. K.
"Trophy Hunter." [Grain] (17:1) Spr 89, p. 21.
649. BRAUN, Henry
"To Fat Boy, the Bomb." [AmerPoR] (18:1) Ja-F 89, p. 48.
650. BRAUN, Jenifer
"1. In Response to Field's 'A Bill to My Father'." [Footwork] 89, p. 63.
"Scraps: A Portfolio." [Footwork] 89, p. 61-63.
651. BRAUN, Volker
"Avignon." [Stand] (30:2) Spr 89, p. 28-29.
"Consultation." [Stand] (30:2) Spr 89, p. 28.
"Noon." [Stand] (30:2) Spr 89, p. 28.
"Volker Braun's Curriculum Vitae." [Stand] (30:2) Spr 89, p. 26-27.
652. BRAVERMAN, Kate
"Wailua River." [Jacaranda] (4:1) Spr-Sum 89, p. 28-29.
BRAVO, Armando Alvarez
See ALVAREZ BRAVO, Armando

70

BRAVO, Jorge de
    See DEBRAVO, Jorge
653. BRAXTON, Charlie R.
    "In Grandma's Eyes." [BlackALF] (23:3) Fall 89, p. 474.
    "Juking at Miz Annie's Café." [BlackALF] (23:3) Fall 89, p. 475.
654. BREBNER, Diana
    "The Chair." [Event] (18:3) Fall 89, p. 43.
    "For My Sister in Spirit River, Alberta." [Grain] (17:3) Fall 89, p. 13.
    "Immolation." [Event] (18:3) Fall 89, p. 42.
655. BREHM, John
    "Before Morning." [KanQ] (21:3) Sum 89, p. 97.
656. BREIDENBACH, Tom
    "The Communist Revolution." [ColEng] (51:2) F 89, p. 147.
    "Daytrip to Subtlety." [ColEng] (51:2) F 89, p. 148.
    "From 'Hints to Epics'." [ColEng] (51:2) F 89, p. 149.
    "Narrative Isle." [DenQ] (23:3/4) Wint-Spr 89, p. 78.
    "Near El Condorla." [ColEng] (51:2) F 89, p. 150.
657. BREINER, Laurence
    "In the Great Rift Valley" (for Jacob Bronowski). [PartR] (56:3) Sum 89, p. 456-457.
    "Sonettina: At the Murano Glassworks." [ParisR] (31:113) Wint 89, p. 120.
658. BRENNAN, Matthew
    "Autumn Landscape." [KanQ] (21:3) Sum 89, p. 130.
    "The Gravity of Love." [KanQ] (21:3) Sum 89, p. 129.
    "The Music of Exile." [PassN] (10:1) Wint 89, p. 17.
    "Spring Fever." [CapeR] (24:1) Spr 89, p. 44.
    "When You Don't Come Home." [Wind] (19:64) 89, p. 35.
659. BRESLIN, Paul
    "The Stairs of the House." [TriQ] (77) Wint 89-90, p. 280-281.
    "Text and Scholar" (for Harry Hayford). [TriQ] (77) Wint 89-90, p. 283.
    "Time and the Tide." [TriQ] (77) Wint 89-90, p. 282.
    "Two Doors Down." [TriQ] (77) Wint 89-90, p. 284.
660. BRETT, Peter
    "Carson Valley" (Eastern Sierra, near Minden, NV). [Lactuca] (13) N 89, p. 20.
    "Deadwood." [Wind] (19:64) 89, p. 1.
    "Drought." [Lactuca] (13) N 89, p. 20.
661. BREWER, Gay
    "Artillery." [Vis] (30) 89, p. 45.
    "Beaver." [Bogg] (61) 89, p. 29.
    "Big Jesus." [SlipS] (9) 89, p. 21.
    "Blondes." [SlipS] (9) 89, p. 22.
    "Dear Raymond." [WormR] (29:1, #113) 89, p. 35.
    "Hemingway's Birthday." [WormR] (29:1, #113) 89, p. 35-36.
662. BREWSTER, Elizabeth
    "Garden Cantos: A Month of Poems" (Selections: 13, 14, 17, 19-21). [MalR] (86)
        Spr 89, p. 102-111.
    "Nausicaa Cantos: A Continuation." [AntigR] (79) Aut 89, p. 35-39.
    "Nausicaa Cantos, an Argument with Ezra" (Selections: 3. Juice (May 15), 6. On
        Minor Poets (May 23), 8. Nobody (May 26)). [Grain] (17:1) Spr 89, p. 17-19.
    "Waiting for Rain (May 29, May 31)." [PraF] (10:3, #48) Aut 89, p. 42.
    "Weeding (June 9)." [PraF] (10:3, #48) Aut 89, p. 43.
663. BREWTON, Catherine
    "Resuscitation." [SouthernR] (25:1) Wint 89, p. 183-184.
664. BRICCETTI, Lee Ellen
    "Devotion." [MSS] (6:3) 89, p. 204.
    "First Year in America." [SenR] (19:1) 89, p. 57-58.
    "For Christ's Sake and All the Angels and Saints in Florence." [SenR] (19:1) 89, p.
        60.
    "Madonna of the Meadow." [MSS] (6:3) 89, p. 205.
    "To You, My Hands." [SenR] (19:1) 89, p. 59.
665. BRIDGFORD, Kim
    "The American Dream." [LaurelR] (23:2) Sum 89, p. 49.
    "Greater Than or Less Than a Tree." [BallSUF] (30:4) Aut 89, p. 29-30.
    "The Honor of the Body." [LitR] (32:2) Wint 89, p. 180.
    "Just a Little Fight." [BallSUF] (30:4) Aut 89, p. 39.
    "Leaning Toward the Night." [BallSUF] (30:4) Aut 89, p. 66.
    "The Lesson." [SouthernPR] (29:2) Fall 89, p. 17.

"Otherworldly." [NoDaQ] (57:3) Sum 89, p. 205-206.
"Outsaying the Green." [CimR] (86) Ja 89, p. 12-13.
"Picture This." [NewOR] (16:3) Fall 89, p. 24.
"A Simple Matter." [CumbPR] (8:2) Spr 89, p. 77-78.
"A Weather." [CreamCR] (13:2) Fall 89, p. 220-221.
666. BRIEGER, Randy
"Boiled Peanuts." [WestB] (23) 89, p. 60.
667. BRINT, Armand
"Ohio Tops the List of License Plates Traded in for California Plates." [FiveFR] (7)
89, p. 19.
668. BRISTOL, David
"Huck Finn." [Aerial] (5) 89, p. 146.
669. BRIXIUS, Elizabeth
"Avoiding the Fanfare of Being Found." [ColEng] (51:6) O 89, p. 584.
"Hardware." [ColEng] (51:6) O 89, p. 588.
"Letter Home." [ColEng] (51:6) O 89, p. 586.
"The School of Incredible Replicas." [ColEng] (51:6) O 89, p. 587.
"Where There Is No Well Enough to Leave Alone." [ColEng] (51:6) O 89, p. 585.
670. BROADHEAD, Marlis Manley
"Fortunes" (From "Catching Up the Baby Books"). [KanQ] (21:1/2) Wint-Spr 89, p.
82-83.
"Sleeping Closer to the Edge." [Kalliope] (10:1/2) 88, p. 95-96.
671. BROBST, Richard
"The Water Is Wide." [Pembroke] (21) 89, p. 116-119.
672. BROCKMAN, Gary G.
"Sunday: 3 A.M." [Amelia] (5:3, #14) 89, p. 90.
673. BROCKWELL, Stephen
"Helicoid." [AntigR] (79) Aut 89, p. 77.
"Klein Bottle." [AntigR] (79) Aut 89, p. 79.
"Monkey Saddle." [AntigR] (79) Aut 89, p. 78.
674. BRODERICK, Richard
"In Praise of Polonius." [StoneC] (16:3/4) Spr-Sum 89, p. 13.
675. BRODSKY, Joseph
"A Song." [NewYorker] (65:6) 27 Mr 89, p. 40.
676. BRODSKY, Louis Daniel
"The Perfect Crime." [CapeR] (24:2) Fall 89, p. 27.
"Seasons of Summer." [BallSUF] (30:4) Aut 89, p. 70-74.
677. BRODSKY, Patricia Pollock
"Cemetery" (tr. of Johannes Bobrowski). [NewL] (55:3) Spr 89, p. 43.
"Memorial for a River Fisherman" (tr. of Johannes Bobrowski). [NewL] (55:3) Spr
89, p. 41.
"Pruzzian Elegy" (tr. of Johannes Bobrowski). [NewL] (55:3) Spr 89, p. 43-45.
"Village" (tr. of Johannes Bobrowski). [NewL] (55:3) Spr 89, p. 42.
678. BROF, Janet
"Mother Feet." [MSS] (6:3) 89, p. 42.
679. BROGAN, Jacque Vaught
"Friday Nights." [Kalliope] (11:1) 89, p. 57.
680. BROMIGE, David
"Ancient Riff." [Talisman] (3) Fall 89, p. 7.
"By Drawing a Line" (Selections). [Sulfur] (9:1, #24) Spr 89, p. 106-112.
"Reality, of Continuing Interest" (Excerpt from suite from *Tiny Courts*,
book-in-progress). [Screens] (1) 89, p. 26.
"A Set of Twelve." [Sulfur] (9:1, #24) Spr 89, p. 113-125.
681. BROMLEY, Anne (Anne C.)
"Cobbs Hill." [Mildred] (3:1) Spr-Sum 89, p. 82-83.
"The Ghost in My House." [Mildred] (3:1) Spr-Sum 89, p. 84.
"Hammer." [PraS] (63:2) Sum 89, p. 87-88.
"Phoenix Summer Blues." [PraS] (63:2) Sum 89, p. 86-87.
"Slow Night." [PraS] (63:2) Sum 89, p. 85-86.
"Watching Regina." [Mildred] (3:1) Spr-Sum 89, p. 80-81.
682. BRONK, William
"All in the Family." [Talisman] (2) Spr 89, p. 47.
"At Four in the Morning." [Talisman] (2) Spr 89, p. 52.
"At Last." [Talisman] (2) Spr 89, p. 50.
"Image and Likeness." [Talisman] (2) Spr 89, p. 53.
"The Import-Export Ratio." [Talisman] (2) Spr 89, p. 49.

"The License." [Talisman] (2) Spr 89, p. 45.
"May Card." [Talisman] (2) Spr 89, p. 51.
"Mundane." [Talisman] (2) Spr 89, p. 48.
"On *Credo ut Intelligam*" (from "The Empty Hands"). [Talisman] (2) Spr 89, p. 93-95.
"Real Estate." [Talisman] (2) Spr 89, p. 46.
"The Smile on the Face of a Kouros" (from "The Empty Hands"). [Talisman] (2) Spr 89, p. 96-97.
683. BRONSON, Lisa Marie
"Untitled: I wanna meet some witch women" (To Vetti and Maria). [SinW] (38) Sum-Fall 89, p. 67.
684. BROOKS, Andrew
"Sweetmeats." [CanLit] (122/123) Aut-Wint 89, p. 68.
685. BROOKS, David
"Anima, Animus and Everybody." [WestB] (25) 89, p. 16.
"Divertimento for Various Alter Egos." [WestB] (23) 89, p. 102-103.
"Kindling the Lights." [WestB] (25) 89, p. 19.
"A Loaf of Bread, A Jug of Wine and Things That Are Best Avoided." [WestB] (25) 89, p. 17.
"Saturday Night at Krishna High." [WestB] (25) 89, p. 18-19.
"What to Do" (Rites for the Divorced). [WestB] (25) 89, p. 20.
686. BROOKS, Gwendolyn
"Art." [NewAW] (5) Fall 89, p. 63.
687. BROSMAN, Catharine Savage
"Note Left on the Front Table, 1940." [SouthernR] (25:1) Wint 89, p. 145.
688. BROTHERSON, John
"In a Permanent Place" (tr. of Pablo Fernando Hernandez). [PoetryE] (28) Fall 89, p. 190.
"Learning to Die" (tr. of Pablo Fernando Hernandez). [PoetryE] (28) Fall 89, p. 187-188.
"Parable" (tr. of Pablo Fernando Hernandez). [PoetryE] (28) Fall 89, p. 185-186.
"What I Know" (tr. of Pablo Fernando Hernandez). [PoetryE] (28) Fall 89, p. 189.
689. BROTZ, Jo
"To B.H." (In Memoriam). [NegC] (9:1) 89, p. 13.
690. BROUGHTON, T. Alan
"A Brilliant Parenthesis." [GrahamHR] (12) Spr 89, p. 74-75.
"Conversion." [NewOR] (16:3) Fall 89, p. 14.
"Don Giovanni's Dream." [Poetry] (154:1) Ap 89, p. 24.
"In the Country of Elegies." [SenR] (19:1) 89, p. 19-31.
"It Is the Sky That Changes." [GrahamHR] (12) Spr 89, p. 78.
"Listening to Sorrow." [TarRP] (28:2) Spr 89, p. 22.
"Lost Treasure." [SouthernHR] (23:2) Spr 89, p. 136.
"Message from Herculaneum." [Poetry] (154:1) Ap 89, p. 21-23.
"Musical Girls." [BelPoJ] (39:4) Sum 89, p. 1.
"Reconstructions." [GrahamHR] (12) Spr 89, p. 76-77.
"A Season's Edge." [TarRP] (28:2) Spr 89, p. 23.
"Visiting an Old Friend on Butternut Mountain and Not Finding Him There." [CharR] (15:2) Fall 89, p. 13.
691. BROUMAS, Olga
"After Lunch." [AmerPoR] (18:1) Ja-F 89, p. 4.
"After *The Little Mariner*." [AmerPoR] (18:1) Ja-F 89, p. 3.
"Amberose Triste." [AmerPoR] (18:1) Ja-F 89, p. 5.
"Attitude." [AmerPoR] (18:1) Ja-F 89, p. 5.
"Etymology." [BellR] (12:2, #26) Fall 89, p. 17.
"The Massacre." [NewL] (56:2/3) Wint 89-Spr 90, p. 42-45.
"The Masseuse." [Antaeus] (62) Spr 89, p. 45-46.
"The Masseuse." [NewL] (56:2/3) Wint 89-Spr 90, p. 41-42.
"Mercy." [AmerPoR] (18:1) Ja-F 89, p. 5.
"Mercy." [NewL] (56:2/3) Wint 89-Spr 90, p. 40.
"Mitosis." [BellR] (12:2, #26) Fall 89, p. 15-16.
"The Moon of Mind Against the Wooden Louver." [AmerPoR] (18:1) Ja-F 89, p. 5.
"Next to the *Café Chaos*." [AmerPoR] (18:1) Ja-F 89, p. 4.
"On Earth." [AmerPoR] (18:1) Ja-F 89, p. 3.
"The Pealing." [AmerPoR] (18:1) Ja-F 89, p. 6.
"Remember This." [Cond] (16) 89, p. 1.
"Walk on the Water." [AmerPoR] (18:1) Ja-F 89, p. 4.

"The Way a Child Might Believe." [AmerPoR] (18:1) Ja-F 89, p. 4.
"Wedding Song." [NewL] (56:2/3) Wint 89-Spr 90, p. 38-39.
692. BROWN, Angus
"Movie Extract." [Rampike] (6:2) 88, p. 73.
693. BROWN, Arthur
"Doxy." [Contact] (9:50/51/52) Fall-Wint 88-Spr 89, p. 28.
"I am the tune." [Contact] (9:50/51/52) Fall-Wint 88-Spr 89, p. 28.
"Message from the Early Worm." [Contact] (9:50/51/52) Fall-Wint 88-Spr 89, p. 29.
"You think that you a tree." [Contact] (9:50/51/52) Fall-Wint 88-Spr 89, p. 29.
694. BROWN, Berkeley
"Global Concepts." [DenQ] (24:1) Sum 89, p. 12.
"In a Storm." [NowestR] (27:2) 89, p. 57.
695. BROWN, Betsy
"The Mirror to Deal With." [ColEng] (51:3) Mr 89, p. 280.
"Rivera Live at Cyrano's." [ColEng] (51:3) Mr 89, p. 281.
"Ruthless Use of Men as Dictionaries." [ColEng] (51:3) Mr 89, p. 282.
"Wisconsin." [DenQ] (23:3/4) Wint-Spr 89, p. 79-80.
696. BROWN, Bill
"Appalachian Poems" ("Omen," "East Tennessee Eulogy"). [PassN] (10:1) Wint 89,
    p. 3.
"Birth Root" (Lay one tansy leaf on the navel to promote childbearing). [Kalliope]
    (10:3) 88, p. 67.
"Event." [Kalliope] (10:3) 88, p. 66.
"Hymenoptera: an Ode." [ChatR] (9:2) Wint 89, p. 39.
"Winter Telescope." [DeKalbLAJ] (22:1/4) 89, p. 43.
697. BROWN, Celia
"The Procession." [Vis] (29) 89, p. 17.
"St Brigid's Day" (For my Father). [Vis] (29) 89, p. 16.
698. BROWN, Clarence "Gatemouth"
"Sometimes I Slip." [ClockR] (5:1) 89, p. 30.
699. BROWN, Cory
"Double Digging." [WestB] (24) 89, p. 69.
"The Fear of No Center." [ClockR] (5:1) 89, p. 31.
"A Fine Dust." [WestB] (24) 89, p. 67.
"Rain Last Night." [Farm] (6:2) Fall 89, p. 72.
"Summer View." [WestB] (24) 89, p. 68.
"Today's Limbs." [Farm] (6:1) Wint-Spr 88-89, p. 125.
700. BROWN, Dan
"Approached at a Hotdog Stand." [PoetryNW] (30:3) Aut 89, p. 11-12.
701. BROWN, Evangeline
"Each House Will Have a Memory." [Sequoia] (33:1) Sum 89, p. 51.
702. BROWN, Gregory R.
"America." [MoodySI] (20/21) Spr 89, p. 43.
703. BROWN, Harriet
"At Dusk." [ClockR] (5:1) 89, p. 15.
704. BROWN, Julie
"Las Vegas Cousin." [CreamCR] (13:2) Fall 89, p. 218-219.
705. BROWN, Linda
"To a Physicist." [ClockR] (5:1) 89, p. 47.
706. BROWN, Robert
"The Barefoot and the Pious: Santa Teresa de Avila." [Poem] (62) N 89, p. 36.
"Grace." [WilliamMR] (27) 89, p. 102-103.
"Notes on *Walking Man I*." [Poem] (62) N 89, p. 34-35.
"A Poem Which Resists Freudian Interpretation." [CreamCR] (13:2) Fall 89, p.
    112-113.
"Sleepwalking with Mayakovsky." [HighP] (4:2) Fall 89, p. 72-73.
"Where Eroticism Goes Awry." [Poem] (62) N 89, p. 37.
707. BROWN, Sterling A.
"After Winter." [IndR] (12:2) Spr 89, p. 22-23.
"Lone Gone." [IndR] (12:2) Spr 89, p. 15-16.
"Ma Rainey." [IndR] (12:2) Spr 89, p. 20-21.
"Salutamus." [IndR] (12:2) Spr 89, p. 24.
"Strong Men." [IndR] (12:2) Spr 89, p. 17-19.
708. BROWN, Steven Ford
"An Astonishing World" (tr. of Angel Gonzalez, w. Pedro Gutierrez Revuelta).
    [SenR] (19:2) Fall 89, p. 75.

"The Battlefield" (tr. of Angel Gonzalez, w. Pedro Gutierrez Revuelta). [NegC] (9:1)
89, p. 191, 193.
"Before I Could Call Myself Angel González" (10 Poems in Spanish & English,
Translation Chapbook Series, tr. of Angel González, w. Gutierrez Revuelta).
[MidAR] (9:2) 89, p. 97-123.
"Diatribe Against the Dead" (tr. of Angel Gonzalez, w. Pedro Gutierrez Revuelta).
[SenR] (19:2) Fall 89, p. 73.
"Horoscope for a Forgotten Dictator" (tr. of Angel Gonzalez, w. Pedro Gutierrez
Revuelta). [SenR] (19:2) Fall 89, p. 74.
"Sonata for Violin Solo" (Johann Sebastian Bach, tr. of Angel Gonzalez, w. Pedro
Gutierrez Revuelta). [NegC] (9:1) 89, p. 189.
"A Traveler's Notes" (tr. of Angel Gonzalez, w. Pedro Gutierrez Revuelta). [PoetL]
(84:3) Fall 89, p. 47-49.
709. BROWN, Tom
"Heavy Weights." [InterPR] (15:2) Fall 89, p. 100.
"Heroes Die Too, with Difficulty" (For Jenni). [InterPR] (15:2) Fall 89, p. 100-101.
710. BROWN, William J.
"Lost Dogs." [ClockR] (5:1) 89, p. 17.
"The Magic Show" (a Valentine poem for d). [ClockR] (5:1) 89, p. 20.
"To a Mathematics Major" (for Greta Stangeland). [ClockR] (5:1) 89, p. 18-19.
711. BROWN-DAVIDSON, Terri
"Doppelganger." [CentR] (33:2) Spr 89, p. 133-134.
"Pig Heaven." [Outbr] (20) 89, p. 13-14.
"Sherwood Cafe." [Plain] (10:1) 89, p. 25.
"Stillborn." [Outbr] (20) 89, p. 15.
"They Usually Die." [GreensboroR] (47) Wint 89-90, p. 134.
712. BROWNE, Michael Dennis
"Evensong." [TriQ] (76) Fall 89, p. 102.
"Road Overgrown." [TriQ] (76) Fall 89, p. 103.
713. BROWNSTEIN, Michael H.
"Erotic." [Bogg] (61) 89, p. 24.
714. BROXSON, Perry
"The Cathe of the Tongue-Thwollen Thiren." [EmeraldCR] (1989) c1988, p. 90.
"Pyramid." [EmeraldCR] (1989) c1988, p. 91.
715. BRUCE, Debra
"Blessed and Brooding." [VirQR] (65:4) Aut 89, p. 657-658.
"The Fitting." [NewEngR] (11:3) Spr 89, p. 338.
716. BRUCHAC, Joseph
"Anthology Indians" (For Lance Henson). [Nimrod] (32:2) Spr-Sum 89, p. 53.
"Four Poems for Ndakinna." [Pig] (15) 88, p. 55.
"Louis Oliver and Carroll Arnett at the Grave of John Ross." [Nimrod] (32:2)
Spr-Sum 89, p. 51.
"Old Woman, Dancing." [Kalliope] (10:3) 88, p. 31-32.
"Wotge." [Nimrod] (32:2) Spr-Sum 89, p. 52.
717. BRUCK, Julie
"Cautious." [MalR] (86) Spr 89, p. 56-57.
"House Sitter, 4 A.M." [MalR] (86) Spr 89, p. 58.
"Still Life." [MalR] (86) Spr 89, p. 59-60.
"The Woman Downstairs Used to Be Beautiful." [MalR] (86) Spr 89, p. 55.
718. BRUEY, Alfred J.
"How to Pick Up a Person." [Amelia] (5:3, #14) 89, p. 59.
"Kites Are Flying in Washington DC." [Amelia] (5:3, #14) 89, p. 141-142.
"This Poem Will Not Live Up To Its Expectations." [Amelia] (5:3, #14) 89, p. 142.
719. BRUGALETTA, John J.
"Conceiving Ovid." [NegC] (9:2) 89, p. 24.
"Things to Be Forgiven." [NegC] (9:1) 89, p. 29.
720. BRUMBAUGH, Thomas
"There Is a Chinese Bronze." [CumbPR] (8:2) Spr 89, p. 2.
721. BRUMER, Andy
"That Perfect Planet: Sleep." [RiverC] (10:1) Fall 89, p. 115.
722. BRUMMELS, J. V.
"Bastards." [PraS] (63:4) Wint 89, p. 82-83.
"Iron." [CharR] (15:2) Fall 89, p. 84-85.
"Lumps of Clay" (for Kate Shuttleworth). [PraS] (63:4) Wint 89, p. 81-82.
"What Be and Ain't in Omaha" (for Larry Holland and Red Shuttleworth). [WestB]
(25) 89, p. 65-67.

723. BRUNK, Juanita
    "Green Waters." [AmerPoR] (18:5) S-O 89, p. 38.
    "This World." [AmerPoR] (18:5) S-O 89, p. 37.
BRUNO, Michael La
    See LaBRUNO, Michael
BRUNT, Lloyd van
    See Van BRUNT, Lloyd
724. BRUSH, Thomas
    "Night Skiing." [PoetryNW] (30:2) Sum 89, p. 41.
725. BRUTUS, Dennis
    "October 31, 1987: Newberry Library." [Pig] (15) 88, p. 48.
726. BRYAN, Roy
    "Letter to Pablo Neruda." [PoetryE] (28) Fall 89, p. 97.
727. BRYAN, Sharon
    "Belie." [SenR] (19:1) 89, p. 10-11.
    "Dead Air." [Ploughs] (15:1) 89, p. 26.
    "Indirect Objects." [Ploughs] (15:1) 89, p. 27.
    "Slip of the Tongue." [DenQ] (24:2) Fall 89, p. 32.
    "Theory." [MissouriR] (12:1) 89, p. 29.
728. BRYANT, Daniel
    "Early Autumn" (tr. of Meng Hao-jan). [LitR] (32:3) Spr 89, p. 398.
    "I Am Not in Time to Say Farewell to Hsin Chih-o" (tr. of Meng Hao-jan). [LitR]
        (32:3) Spr 89, p. 398.
    "On Reaching Ying on My Return Trip" (tr. of Meng Hao-jan). [LitR] (32:3) Spr 89,
        p. 398.
729. BRYANT, Philip S.
    "Booker T. Washington's Metaphor About Spring." [IndR] (12:2) Spr 89, p. 28-29.
    "Children of Ham." [IndR] (12:2) Spr 89, p. 34-35.
    "Eleven Short Scenes from My Life." [IndR] (12:2) Spr 89, p. 25-26.
    "Folks vs. People." [IndR] (12:2) Spr 89, p. 32.
    "Incident on a Hot Spring Day." [IndR] (12:2) Spr 89, p. 30.
    "The New Negro." [IndR] (12:2) Spr 89, p. 33.
    "The Park Worker." [IndR] (12:2) Spr 89, p. 27.
    "Requiem" (To My Father). [IndR] (12:2) Spr 89, p. 31.
730. BRYANT, Suzanne
    "Keeping My Mother's Tears" (Selection: 2). [Outbr] (20) 89, p. 48.
731. BRYLL, Ernest
    "Soot" (tr. by Stanislaw Baranczak and Clare Cavanah). [Trans] (21) Spr 89, p. 63.
732. BUBY, Andrea Hollander
    "Jack Sprat." [CharR] (15:1) Spr 89, p. 64-65.
BUCHLER, Judith Lewis von
    See Von BUCHLER, Judith Lewis
733. BUCKHOLTS, Claudia
    "What Has Been Given." [ConnPR] (8:1) 89, p. 27.
734. BUCKLEY, Christopher
    "After a Theme by Vallejo, after a Theme by Justice." [KenR] (N 11:4) Fall 89, p.
        46-47.
    "Apologues of Winter Light." [Poetry] (155:3) D 89, p. 227-228.
    "Corot at Mantes-La-Jolie" (Le Pont de Mantes, 1868-70). [Pequod] (28/29/30) 89, p.
        209-210.
    "Crows in Coatesville" (for Tim Geiger). [DenQ] (23:3/4) Wint-Spr 89, p. 82-83.
    "Dark Time." [Poetry] (153:5) F 89, p. 255-257.
    "Last Train East." [BlackWR] (16:1) Fall-Wint 89, p. 107-109.
    "The Past." [Poetry] (153:5) F 89, p. 258-259.
735. BUDBILL, David
    "I'm Worried." [OhioR] (44) 89, p. 110-112.
736. BUDEK, M.
    "Captain Video (1953)." [SpiritSH] (54) Spr-Sum 89, p. 32.
737. BUDY, Andrea Hollander
    "Forth of July." [Farm] (6:2) Fall 89, p. 73.
    "Full Moon at Caddo Lake." [OxfordM] (5:1) Spr-Sum 89, p. 37.
    "On Learning to Break the Rules." [Ascent] (14:3) 89, p. 31.
    "Trying Not to Listen." [TarRP] (29:1) Fall 89, p. 10.
    "What I Want." [OhioR] (44) 89, p. 94.
738. BUELL, Frederick
    "Benares." [Pembroke] (21) 89, p. 36-38.

"Chronometrics." [Pembroke] (21) 89, p. 35-36.
"Mythopoeia." [LaurelR] (23:1) Wint 89, p. 73-75.
739. BUELL, T. C.
"Piano Piece for One Hand" (for Carl at eighty). [SmPd] (26:3 #77) Fall 89, p. 12.
740. BUENO, Raúl
"Día tras Día." [Os] (29) 89, p. 38.
741. BUFFETT, Josephine D.
"Old Mrs. Bedell." [DeKalbLAJ] (22:1/4) 89, p. 44.
"Papa Played Violin." [DeKalbLAJ] (22:1/4) 89, p. 44-45.
742. BUGEJA, Michael (Michael J.)
"The Art of Amnesia." [PoetC] (21:1) Fall 89, p. 11.
"The Fast." [CinPR] (20) Fall 89, p. 50.
"Forgiveness." [PoetC] (21:1) Fall 89, p. 12-13.
"Holy War: Stillwater, Oklahoma." [Wind] (19:64) 89, p. 2.
"How to End a Romance." [KenR] (NS 11:1) Wint 89, p. 80-81.
"The Last Napkin." [CimR] (87) Ap 89, p. 21.
"Man in the Kitchen." [KenR] (NS 11:1) Wint 89, p. 81-82.
"Stay." [HolCrit] (26:5) D 89, p. 14.
"What the Waitress Sees." [SouthernPR] (29:2) Fall 89, p. 28.
743. BUHROW, Bonnie
"Carny Man." [PassN] (10:1) Wint 89, p. 20.
744. BUKOWSKI, Charles
"The Beggars." [AlphaBS] (6) Wint 89-90, p. 58-59.
"Comments Upon My Last Book of Poesy." [Antaeus] (62) Spr 89, p. 49-50.
"Dear Paw and Ma." [WormR] (29:4, #116) 89, p. 143.
"The Factory Crew of Southeast L.A." [WormR] (29:4, #116) 89, p. 141-143.
"Freaky Time." [Antaeus] (62) Spr 89, p. 47-48.
"I Dreamt." [AlphaBS] (6) Wint 89-90, p. 60-61.
"Justice." [WormR] (29:1, #113) 89, p. 44.
"The Media." [WormR] (29:1, #113) 89, p. 44-45.
"My Doctor." [WormR] (29:1, #113) 89, p. 45-46.
"The State and That Begging Motherfucker, Art." [WormR] (29:4, #116) 89, p. 140.
745. BULLINGTON, Mary
"The Power Lines Above Carvin's Cove." [GreensboroR] (46) Sum 89, p. 137.
746. BULMER, April
"Irish Woman, My Neighbour." [CrossC] (11:3) 89, p. 12.
747. BUNSE, Lois
"Right in *The Kalavala* It Says." [Calyx] (12:1) Sum 89, p. 5.
748. BURAK, Kathryn
"The Clairvoyant in the Seat Behind Me." [GettyR] (2:3) Sum 89, p. 440.
749. BURDEN, Jean
"Sleepwalker." [PoetC] (20:3) Spr 89, p. 38.
750. BURGESS, Lynne
"Breaking Drought by Lake Superior." [RagMag] (7:1) 89, p. 6.
"Pictures." [RagMag] (7:1) 89, p. 7.
751. BURGGRAF, Linda P. (Linda Parsons)
"The Chance of a Life." [HeliconN] (20) 89, p. 82-83.
"Confessions of a Courteous Southern Woman: Saying the Magic Words." [Kalliope]
(11:2) 89, p. 63.
"Feste's Song." [NegC] (9:2) 89, p. 27-28.
"Sadness." [GeoR] (43:2) Sum 89, p. 311.
752. BURK, Ronnie
"Pluto 23° Libra Retrograde" (after Kabir). [Caliban] (6) 89, p. 122.
753. BURKARD, Michael
"Adultery." [WillowS] (23) Wint 89, p. 20-21.
"And the Two -- the Raindrop and Man." [NewL] (56:2/3) Wint 89-Spr 90, p. 52-54.
"Because." [AmerPoR] (18:6) N-D 89, p. 48.
"Bird of Paradise" (for Mary Hackett). [NewL] (56:2/3) Wint 89-Spr 90, p. 48-49.
"Bridges with People on Them." [WillowS] (23) Wint 89, p. 19.
"Each of Them Icons." [Iowa] (19:1) Wint 89, p. 27-37.
"A Feeling from the Sea." [NewL] (56:2/3) Wint 89-Spr 90, p. 47.
"The Fires They Kept." [NewL] (56:2/3) Wint 89-Spr 90, p. 49.
"A Hint of Grief." [NewL] (56:2/3) Wint 89-Spr 90, p. 51.
"January 24, 1986." [Iowa] (19:1) Wint 89, p. 37-38.
"My Mother Orders a Children's Book." [SouthernPR] (29:1) Spr 89, p. 13.
"Out There." [NewL] (56:2/3) Wint 89-Spr 90, p. 50.

"Singing in the Rain." [WillowS] (23) Wint 89, p. 22-23.
"A Song of Death." [Iowa] (19:1) Wint 89, p. 38-39.
"To Maria." [AmerPoR] (18:6) N-D 89, p. 47.
"Two Faces." [Agni] (28) 89, p. 266.
"Untitled: Honest appraisal of life: dryness." [Iowa] (19:1) Wint 89, p. 39-40.
"Wanted." [WillowS] (23) Wint 89, p. 16-18.
"When Given in the Darkness." [NewL] (56:2/3) Wint 89-Spr 90, p. 46.
"The White Moon Night." [AmerPoR] (18:6) N-D 89, p. 47.
754. BURKE, Anne
"Emergency Room II -- Admittance." [CrossC] (11:2) 89, p. 4.
755. BURKE, Brian
"Past Midnight." [Bogg] (61) 89, p. 25.
"Sapling." [CanLit] (122/123) Aut-Wint 89, p. 41.
"Teach Me to Step Through Sorrow." [Bogg] (61) 89, p. 19.
"Woman in the Smithrite." [AlphaBS] (5) Jl 89, p. 61.
756. BURKE, Cate
"Jerusalem Hill" (for Aaron on his 16th birthday). [PoetL] (84:3) Fall 89, p. 8.
757. BURKE, Daniel
"Boxes." [FourQ] (2d series 3:1) Spr 89, p. 50.
758. BURKE, Linda Joy
"Afrikaner Part I." [Obs] (3:1) Spr 88, p. 76-77.
"Afrikaner Part II." [Obs] (3:1) Spr 88, p. 78-79.
"For Carlotta Who Died at the Age of 20." [Obs] (3:1) Spr 88, p. 80-81.
"The Peace Poem." [Obs] (3:1) Spr 88, p. 82.
"We shall not have a face today." [Obs] (2:1) Spr 87, p. 69.
759. BURKETT, Katherine E.
"Frances Farmer Confesses." [DenQ] (24:2) Fall 89, p. 33.
760. BURNHAM, Deborah
"Folding." [WestB] (25) 89, p. 110.
"Thrift." [WestB] (25) 89, p. 111.
761. BURNS, Cullen Bailey
"Sorting." [PassN] (10:2) Sum 89, p. 18.
762. BURNS, Gerald
"Double Sonnet for Mickey." [Temblor] (10) 89, p. 111.
"Fretting an Upscale Themis." [Temblor] (10) 89, p. 105-109.
"Madox Brown's 'Work'." [Temblor] (10) 89, p. 110.
"The Myth of Accidence, Book VII (lines 85-99)." [AnotherCM] (19) 89, p. 19.
"The Passions of Being." [Temblor] (9) 89, p. 14-23.
763. BURNS, Michael
"After the Annual Convention" (for Michael Heffernan and Mickey at St. Jude's
        Children's Hospital). [MissouriR] (12:1) 89, p. 50-51.
"Entering Puberty." [PoetC] (21:1) Fall 89, p. 33.
"For an Old Pear Tree." [PoetC] (21:1) Fall 89, p. 32.
"Last Tuesday." [LaurelR] (23:1) Wint 89, p. 78.
"Stroke" (for T.N., my father-in-law). [LaurelR] (23:1) Wint 89, p. 76-77.
"Sunday Evening, 1962." [Journal] (12:2) Fall-Wint 88-89, p. 21.
"This Side of the River." [SouthernR] (25:1) Wint 89, p. 171-172.
764. BURNS, Ralph
"Anniversary of Wood." [IndR] (13:1) Wint 89, p. 23.
"Barbed Wire." [Atlantic] (264:2) Ag 89, p. 60.
"The Distance" (for Clint). [OhioR] (44) 89, p. 95-99.
"Luck." [OhioR] (43) 89, p. 40-47.
"The Shimmer of Influence." [Ploughs] (15:1) 89, p. 28-29.
765. BURNSIDE, John
"Annunciations." [Verse] (6:3) Wint 89, p. 35-39.
"At Pittenweem." [Verse] (6:3) Wint 89, p. 40.
"Domestic." [Verse] (6:1) Mr 89, p. 5.
"The Forest of Beguilement." [Verse] (6:2) Je 89, p. 5.
"Thrush." [Verse] (6:3) Wint 89, p. 40.
"To love you is a dialect." [Verse] (6:2) Je 89, p. 5.
766. BURNSIDE, Sam
"Her Recipe" (For Mary, Myra, Sive and Cathy). [Vis] (29) 89, p. 8.
"Mary Anne McCraken." [Vis] (29) 89, p. 9-10.
767. BURR, Gray
"High School Reunion." [Northeast] (ser. 5:1) Wint 89-90, p. 3.

768. BURRELL, Clarice Arnold
"First Person Singular." [EmeraldCR] (1989) c1988, p. 126.
"Gypsy Song." [EmeraldCR] (1989) c1988, p. 126-127.
"A Rendezvous." [EmeraldCR] (1989) c1988, p. 126.
769. BURRIS, Dorothy
"Heathcliff visits the Arizona Desert." [CapeR] (24:1) Spr 89, p. 12.
770. BURRIS, Sidney
"The Death and Life of Jesse James." [KenR] (NS 11:2) Spr 89, p. 110-112.
"Flamingo, Frog, and Aunt." [KenR] (NS 11:2) Spr 89, p. 107-108.
"The New Bicycles." [KenR] (NS 11:2) Spr 89, p. 108-110.
"Of Learning What I Was Taught Was Taught." [NewEngR] (11:3) Spr 89, p. 339.
771. BURROUGHS, William S.
"Dream Voices of Technical Tilly." [AlphaBS] (6) Wint 89-90, p. 30.
772. BURROWS, E. G.
"Ancient Burials." [CharR] (15:1) Spr 89, p. 56-57.
"Bull Calf." [SoCoast] (6) Fall 88, p. 19.
"Cradle of Reeds." [SoCoast] (6) Fall 88, p. 43.
"How They Brought God to Easter." [CharR] (15:1) Spr 89, p. 58.
"Minor Afflictions." [PoetryNW] (30:4) Wint 89-90, p. 44.
"North Babylon River." [CharR] (15:1) Spr 89, p. 55-56.
"Since the First Speakers." [CharR] (15:1) Spr 89, p. 58-59.
773. BURRS, Mick
"Missing Persona Report" (A Document of Secrets, Part III). [CanLit] (121) Sum 89,
p. 7-10.
BURSAC, Ellen Elias
See ELIAS-BURSAC, Ellen
774. BURT, Brian
"Heimat: A Cycle" (10 poems). [SpoonRQ] (14:2) Spr 89, p. 21-37.
"Heimat: A Cycle" (10 poems). [SpoonRQ] (14:4) Fall 89, p. 29-45.
775. BURTON, Elizabeth Ann
"Heavy Women." [JINJPo] [11] 89, p. 9.
776. BURWELL, Michael
"Making the Island." [PacificR] (7) 89, p. 90.
777. BUSAILAH, R. (Reja-e)
"Beyond." [Mildred] (3:1) Spr-Sum 89, p. 86.
"Dafoura." [Pig] (15) 88, p. 29.
"Just Three G's and One F." [Pig] (15) 88, p. 29.
"Like Two Pears." [Mildred] (3:1) Spr-Sum 89, p. 87.
"Topsy-Turvy." [Mildred] (3:1) Spr-Sum 89, p. 87.
778. BUSCH, Trent
"Elena." [ColEng] (51:6) O 89, p. 583.
"Glorious to Find an Uncle." [BlueBldgs] (11) 89, p. 56.
"St. Louis." [ColEng] (51:6) O 89, p. 581.
"Woman Asleep in Chair" (Variation on Renoir's *Sleeping Girl*). [ColEng] (51:6) O
89, p. 582.
779. BUSHKOWSKY, Aaron
"Middle-Aged." [Grain] (17:3) Fall 89, p. 35.
"Sunday Cat." [Grain] (17:3) Fall 89, p. 34.
780. BUSTAMANTE, Cecilia
"La Araña sobre el Lecho." [Inti] (29/30) Primavera-Otoño 89, p. 253.
"Arco Voltaico." [Inti] (29/30) Primavera-Otoño 89, p. 254-255.
"Limpieza." [Inti] (29/30) Primavera-Otoño 89, p. 254.
"Ventisca." [Inti] (29/30) Primavera-Otoño 89, p. 255.
BUSTILLO, Camilio Pérez
See PÉREZ-BUSTILLO, Camilio
781. BUTCHER, Grace
"Bricks" (Honorable Mention, 1989 Poetry Competition). [PassN] (10:2) Sum 89, p.
8.
"Getting What We Want." [Poetry] (154:1) Ap 89, p. 25.
"Going for Tests." [CapeR] (24:2) Fall 89, p. 39.
"If You Want to Catch Fish, You've Got to Go Fishing" (-- William Stafford).
[StoneC] (16:3/4) Spr-Sum 89, p. 44-45.
"If You Want to Catch Fish, You've Got to Go Fishing" (--William Stafford. The
Phillips Award, Spring Summer 1989). [StoneC] (17:1/2) Fall-Wint 89-90, p.
87.
"Leaving." [Wind] (19:64) 89, p. 3.

"The Stork Bringeth, the Stork Taketh Away." [CapeR] (24:2) Fall 89, p. 38.
782. BUTLER, Jack
"Daughters." [CrossCur] (8:2) Ja 89, p. 17.
783. BUTLER, Lynn
"Beginning the Poem." [BellArk] (5:3) My-Je 89, p. 1.
"Poetry" (for Marina Tsvetaeva). [BellArk] (5:3) My-Je 89, p. 5.
"Where Do You Get Your Subjects?" [BellArk] (5:3) My-Je 89, p. 18.
784. BUTLER, Lynne (Lynne B.)
"The Friends Meet to Work." [CapeR] (24:2) Fall 89, p. 20.
"A Minor Gift." [Blueline] (10:1/2) 89, p. 15.
"Reflection." [DeKalbLAJ] (22:1/4) 89, p. 46.
"Reflection on the Beauty of Bats." [NegC] (9:1) 89, p. 93.
"Sea Lions at Fisherman's Wharf." [Plain] (9:2) Wint 89, p. 35.
"The Worst Thing." [CapeR] (24:2) Fall 89, p. 19.
785. BUTLIN, Ron
"Arrivals: Hamburg" (tr. of Ninon Schubert). [Verse] (6:2) Je 89, p. 29.
"Divided Islands" (tr. of Ninon Schubert). [Verse] (6:2) Je 89, p. 29.
786. BUTTON, Greg
"The Wonder." [Grain] (17:3) Fall 89, inside front cover.
787. BUTTRESS, Derrick
"A Brief History of the Planet." [Bogg] (61) 89, p. 20.
788. BUTTS, W. E.
"Martin's Nursing Home." [PoetL] (84:1) Spr 89, p. 40.
789. BYER, Kathryn Stripling
"The Exotics." [GreensboroR] (46) Sum 89, p. 95-96.
"Jericho's" (from *Voices from Blood Mountain*). [SouthernPR] (29:2) Fall 89, p. 50.
790. BYNNER, Witter
"On Meeting Li Kuei-nien Down the River" (tr. of Tu Fu). [LitR] (32:3) Spr 89, p. 306.
BYONG, Ha Hwang
See HWANG, Byong Ha
791. BYRD, Sigman
"Kindling." [Pequod] (28/29/30) 89, p. 31.
792. BYRNE, Edward
"First Love." [Outbr] (20) 89, p. 17.
793. BYRNE, Joseph
"To Osip Mandelstam." [SpiritSH] (54) Spr-Sum 89, p. 20.
794. BYRNES, Fred
"Hey Jack." [MoodySI] (20/21) Spr 89, p. 6.
795. BYRON, Catherine
"Damson-Fall in the Study at Dove Cottage" (for Dorothy). [RiverC] (10:1) Fall 89, p. 60.
"Gravity." [RiverC] (10:1) Fall 89, p. 61.
"Naming Remains -- Mayo." [RiverC] (10:1) Fall 89, p. 62-63.
"Turning the Butter, County Donegal." [AntigR] (77/78) Spr-Sum 89, p. 46.
796. BYRON, Su
"While Men Sleep." [NegC] (9:2) 89, p. 35.
797. BYRUM, John
"Anathemas." [Talisman] (3) Fall 89, p. 123.
"Repeat." [Talisman] (3) Fall 89, p. 121.
"Rimage." [Talisman] (3) Fall 89, p. 124.
"Syzygy." [Talisman] (3) Fall 89, p. 122.
798. CABACUNGAN, Darryl Keola
"He Inoa No John" (in Hawaiian). [ChamLR] (3:1, #5) Fall 89, p. 152.
"His Name Is John." [ChamLR] (3:1, #5) Fall 89, p. 153.
"Kaiko'o at Kupikipiki'o" (in English). [ChamLR] (3:1, #5) Fall 89, p. 149.
"Kaiko'o Ma Kupikipiki'o" (in Hawaiian). [ChamLR] (3:1, #5) Fall 89, p. 148.
"Lunar New Year '89." [ChamLR] (3:1, #5) Fall 89, p. 150.
"Overwhelmed." [ChamLR] (3:1, #5) Fall 89, p. 151.
799. CABALLERO SAMPER, Cristina
"Melorabilia." [Mairena] (11:27) 89, p. 69.
800. CABLE, Gerald
"Awake." [PraS] (63:3) Fall 89, p. 85-86.
"The Bees." [CreamCR] (13:2) Fall 89, p. 215-216.

"Counterweight." [CimR] (89) O 89, p. 97-98.
"The Farm." [Shen] (39:1) Spr 89, p. 88.
"Mortality Tables." [SouthernPR] (29:1) Spr 89, p. 52-53.
"Pentecost." [SoCoast] (7) Spr-Fall 89, p. 28.
"Someday." [PraS] (63:3) Fall 89, p. 84-85.
801. CABRAL, Olga
"A Cricket." [Contact] (9:50/51/52) Fall-Wint 88-Spr 89, p. 25.
"The Double Portrait." [Contact] (9:50/51/52) Fall-Wint 88-Spr 89, p. 22.
"Landscape with Figure in Snowstorm" (from a news photo). [Contact] (9:50/51/52)
        Fall-Wint 88-Spr 89, p. 23.
"The Letter." [Contact] (9:50/51/52) Fall-Wint 88-Spr 89, p. 26.
"The Whistler in the Street." [Contact] (9:50/51/52) Fall-Wint 88-Spr 89, p. 24.
802. CACCIUTTO, Franklin C.
"My Foot." [EngJ] (78:4) Ap 89, p. 101.
803. CADER, Teresa
"Gulag." [Agni] (28) 89, p. 279-280.
804. CADNUM, Michael
"Anatomy of the Uterus." [WestB] (24) 89, p. 105.
"Aphasia." [WestB] (24) 89, p. 104.
"Book." [CrabCR] (6:1) 89, p. 26.
"Dawn Heat." [Wind] (19:64) 89, p. 4.
"The Drive-In By Day." [Pembroke] (21) 89, p. 12.
"Escaping the Party." [RiverC] (9:1) Spr 89, p. 23.
"Escaping the Party." [Wind] (19:64) 89, p. 4.
"Foreign Garden." [RiverC] (9:1) Spr 89, p. 22.
"The Governess, Preparing Her Lecture on Sex." [LitR] (32:2) Wint 89, p. 194-195.
"The Lighthouse at Pigeon Point." [CrabCR] (6:1) 89, p. 26.
"Night in the Thur Valley." [Pembroke] (21) 89, p. 12.
"Niles' Heart Attack." [WritersF] (15) Fall 89, p. 23.
"Pigeons." [BelPoJ] (39:3) Spr 89, p. 24.
"To the Publisher Who Ruined My Book." [PoetC] (21:1) Fall 89, p. 15.
805. CAFAGNA, Marcus
"First Scent." [HiramPoR] (46) Spr-Sum 89, p. 10-11.
"White Frosting." [BellR] (12:1, #25) Spr 89, p. 8.
806. CAGE, John
"Painting Relates to Any Moment." [Talisman] (3) Fall 89, p. 10-15.
807. CAI, Qi-jiao
"The Han River Under Fog" (tr. by Edward Morin and Dai Fang). [MichQR] (28:3)
        Sum 89, p. 399.
"Seagull" (tr. by Edward Morin and Dai Fang). [MichQR] (28:3) Sum 89, p. 399.
808. CAINE, Shulamith Wechter
"Penelope." [DenQ] (23:3/4) Wint-Spr 89, p. 81.
"What I Know About Clair." [NegC] (9:1) 89, p. 66.
809. CAIRNS, Scott
"Embalming." [NewRep] (200:26) 26 Je 89, p. 34.
"False Angels." [ColEng] (51:7) N 89, p. 706.
"The Mummy Viewed." [NewRep] (201:20) 13 N 89, p. 36.
"Still Waiting." [NewRep] (200:1) 2 Ja 89, p. 34.
810. CALBERT, Cathleen
"Babysitting." [NoAmR] (274:4) D 89, p. 29.
"Babysitting." [SouthernPR] (29:2) Fall 89, p. 56-57.
"Floating." [WestHR] (43:2) Sum 89, p. 120.
"When Nights Were Full of Sex and Churches." [NewRep] (201:25[i.e.26]) 25 D 89,
        p. 32.
811. CALDERWOOD, James L.
"Borders." [AmerS] (58:1) Wint 89, p. 39-40.
812. CALHOUN, E. Frank
"Sun-Scape." [EmeraldCR] (1989) c1988, p. 111.
813. CALHOUN, Harry
"In the Hallway Outside the Dean's Office at the College of Fine Arts." [Bogg] (61)
        89, p. 47.
814. CALLAHAN, Bridget
"Solitary Crossing." [NewRena] (7:3, #23) 89, p. 92.

815. CALVERLY, Ruthe
"Like Always Talking About the Weather." [CrossC] (11:2) 89, p. 7.
816. CALVILLO, M. Kimberly
"Poor Thunder on the Rosebud." [NoAmR] (274:2) Je 89, p. 12.
CAMBRA HO'OIPO DE
See DeCAMBRA Ho'oipo
817. CAMERON, Juan
"Plaza Echaurren" (tr. by Cola Franzen). [Pig] (15) 88, p. 94.
818. CAMILLO, Victor
"Soccer." [Footwork] 89, p. 10-11.
"The Wind." [Farm] (6:1) Wint-Spr 88-89, p. 79.
819. CAMMER, Les
"Better to be free." [WormR] (29:4, #116) 89, p. 136.
"If you jumped off the empire state building." [WormR] (29:4, #116) 89, p. 136.
"Im walking along this car stops." [WormR] (29:4, #116) 89, p. 135.
"Looks like it's going to be a jackoff day." [WormR] (29:4, #116) 89, p. 136.
"Want to sit around." [WormR] (29:4, #116) 89, p. 136.
820. CAMPBELL, Anne
"The Itinerary" (from *The Croatian Journal*). [Event] (18:2) Sum 89, p. 21.
"Monte Cassino" (from *The Croatian Journal*). [Event] (18:2) Sum 89, p. 20.
"What a Welcome" (from *The Croatian Journal*). [Event] (18:2) Sum 89, p. 20.
"Wisdom on the Hydrofoil" (from *The Croatian Journal*). [Event] (18:2) Sum 89, p. 21.
821. CAMPBELL, Carolyn
"Expectancy." [BellArk] (5:3) My-Je 89, p. 3.
822. CAMPBELL, Elizabeth
"Nude Cleaning a Bathtub." [ClockR] (5:2) 89, p. 11.
823. CAMPBELL, Joan
"Salmon-Fishing on the Chilkoot River." [SouthernPR] (29:2) Fall 89, p. 44-45.
824. CAMPBELL, P. Michael
"My Father's Tumbleweed Story." [Thrpny] (39) Fall 89, p. 30.
825. CAMPIGLIO, Stephen
"The Dead Fall Through." [Mildred] (3:1) Spr-Sum 89, p. 105.
"Morning at the Center of Four Dimensions." [Mildred] (3:1) Spr-Sum 89, p. 105.
826. CAMPION, Dan
"The Annoyances of Scholars." [LakeSR] (23) 89, p. 34.
827. CAMPO, Rafael
"The Lost Plaza Is Everywhere." [Field] (41) Fall 89, p. 60.
"The Test." [Field] (41) Fall 89, p. 61.
828. CANGIALOSI, Karen
"What You Cannot Leave Behind." [PaintedB] (37) 89, p. 27.
829. CANNON, Maureen
"Pal and Pal's Pal." [Amelia] (5:3, #14) 89, p. 39.
830. CANNON, Melissa
"Aunt Barbara." [SingHM] (16) 89, p. 2.
"Mysteries at Granny's." [SingHM] (16) 89, p. 1.
831. CANTERA, Judy
"Untitled: The closest I ever got to god was pillows." [SingHM] (16) 89, p. 94-95.
832. CANTRELL, Charles
"Memory's Hard Way Out." [Confr] (39/40) Fall 88-Wint 89, p. 134.
833. CANTWELL, Kevin
"The Darwin Decades." [NewRep] (201:3/4) 17-24 Jl 89, p. 32.
834. CAPRONI, Giorgio
"I Coltelli." [Poetry] (155:1/2) O-N 89, p. 33.
"Delizia (e Saggezza) del Bevitore." [Poetry] (155:1/2) O-N 89, p. 24.
"Drinker's Delight (and Wisdom)" (tr. by Michael Palma). [Poetry] (155:1/2) O-N 89, p. 35.
"The Elevator" (tr. by Michael Palma). [Poetry] (155:1/2) O-N 89, p. 30-32.
"The Knives" (tr. by Michael Palma). [Poetry] (155:1/2) O-N 89, p. 33.
"Le Parole." [Poetry] (155:1/2) O-N 89, p. 34.
"The Words" (tr. by Michael Palma). [Poetry] (155:1/2) O-N 89, p. 35.
835. CARBAUGH, Amie
"Green Shoes Mean I Love You." [BellR] (12:1, #25) Spr 89, p. 51.

CARBEAU, Mitchell Les
    See LesCARBEAU, Mitchell
836. CARDEA, Caryatis
    "Tremors." [SinW] (37) Spr 89, p. 48-49.
837. CARDILLO, Joe
    "The Death of Descartes." [Lactuca] (12) F 89, p. 5.
    "Field." [Lactuca] (12) F 89, p. 2-4.
    "North Road." [RagMag] (7:1) 89, p. 8.
    "Sometime After 11 p.m." [RagMag] (7:1) 89, p. 9.
    "Stillness." [Lactuca] (12) F 89, p. 6-8.
838. CARDOZO, Nancy
    "The Middle Distance." [Hudson] (42:2) Sum 89, p. 281.
839. CARDOZO LUNA, Hernando
    "Instrucciones para Jugar la Vida." [Mairena] (11:27) 89, p. 73.
840. CAREAU, Rachel
    "Itineraries" (Selections: 2-13). [Notus] (4:2) Fall 89, p. 19-21.
841. CARELLA, Richard
    "Tutorial." [Talisman] (2) Spr 89, p. 76.
842. CAREY, Michael (Michael A.)
    "Elmer and Betsy." [NoAmR] (274:2) Je 89, p. 7.
    "The Sandhill Crane" (for John and Marsha Nelson). [MidwQ] (30:2) Wint 89, p.
        203.
    "Starless." [Plain] (9:2) Wint 89, p. 34.
    "Witness." [NoAmR] (274:2) Je 89, p. 6.
843. CAREY, Tom
    "Ted." [BrooklynR] (6) 89, p. 51.
844. CARLETON, Augustus
    "Diverted Sonnets" (Selections: "Twenty-Eight," "Fifty-Three"). [Epoch] (38:3) 89,
        p. 221-222.
845. CARLILE, Henry
    "For Walt Whitman." [NowestR] (27:2) 89, p. 13.
    "The Girlfriend." [LaurelR] (23:2) Sum 89, p. 83.
    "Hunting, Hazards, and Holiness." [LaurelR] (23:2) Sum 89, p. 82-83.
    "The Poet's Neighbor Talks Back." [Poetry] (153:5) F 89, p. 294-295.
846. CARLIN, Lisa
    "As Love Is a House." [SinW] (38) Sum-Fall 89, p. 53.
847. CARLISLE, S. E.
    "The Life Preserver." [StoneC] (16:3/4) Spr-Sum 89, p. 43.
848. CARLOS, Edward
    "Layers." [BallSUF] (30:4) Aut 89, p. 15.
849. CARLOS, Susan V.
    "Eavesdropper." [BlueBldgs] (11) 89, p. 55.
    "Sorcery." [BlueBldgs] (11) 89, p. 55.
850. CARLSON, Barbara Siegel
    "For the Workshop." [MidwQ] (30:4) Sum 89, p. 441.
851. CARLSON, Michael
    "Crystals in Their Hearts" (for Rania). [MissR] (18:1, #52) 89, p. 67-68.
852. CARLSON, R. S.
    "Thinking I Could Learn to Love Her." [CapeR] (24:2) Fall 89, p. 42.
853. CARNERO, Guillermo
    "Avila" (tr. by Frederick H. Fornoff). [AmerPoR] (18:2) Mr-Ap 89, p. 32.
    "Dawn in Burgos" (Las Huelgas, tr. by Frederick H. Fornoff). [AmerPoR] (18:2)
        Mr-Ap 89, p. 32.
    "Embarking for Cythera" (tr. by Frederick H. Fornoff). [ChiR] (36:3/4) 89, p. 31-32.
854. CARON, Phillip
    "Viet Vet." [NegC] (9:2) 89, p. 89-90.
855. CARPENTER, Bogdana
    "Landscape" (tr. of Zbigniew Herbert, w. John Carpenter). [PartR] (56:1) Wint 89, p.
        113.
    "The Nepenthe Family" (tr. of Zbigniew Herbert, w. John Carpenter). [PartR] (56:1)
        Wint 89, p. 113-114.
856. CARPENTER, Carol
    "Frozen Fantasies." [Vis] (31) 89, p. 46.

857. CARPENTER, John
"Landscape" (tr. of Zbigniew Herbert, w. Bogdana Carpenter). [PartR] (56:1) Wint 89, p. 113.
"The Nepenthe Family" (tr. of Zbigniew Herbert, w. Bogdana Carpenter). [PartR] (56:1) Wint 89, p. 113-114.
858. CARPER, Thomas
"The Inseparables at the Rink." [FreeL] (1) 89, p. 27.
"Talking with Charlot." [FreeL] (1) 89, p. 28.
"The Tranquil Life." [Poetry] (154:5) Ag 89, p. 277.
859. CARR, Dana Elaine
"Rearview." [Kalliope] (10:1/2) 88, p. 94.
860. CARRACINO, Nicholas
"These Eyes." [Footwork] 89, p. 14.
"Used To." [Footwork] 89, p. 14.
861. CARRADICE, Phil
"Channel Tunnel Blues." [Bogg] (61) 89, p. 36.
862. CARRANZA, Eduardo
"Galeron." [LindLM] (8:2) Ap-Je 89, p. 3.
863. CARRANZA, Maria Mercedes
"Maldicion." [LindLM] (8:2) Ap-Je 89, p. 4.
864. CARRICABURU, Sally
"Grandma's Bed." [Interim] (8:1) Spr 89, p. 36.
865. CARRIER, Lois
"Mockingbird." [KanQ] (21:3) Sum 89, p. 178.
"Requiem for an Elephant." [KanQ] (21:3) Sum 89, p. 178.
866. CARROLL, Paul
"Shams." [AnotherCM] (20) 89, p. 80-84.
867. CARROLL, Rhoda
"The Discursive Aspects of Sherry in Evening Light." [TarRP] (28:2) Spr 89, p. 14.
"Drive, She Said." [PoetL] (84:4) Wint 89-90, p. 11-12.
868. CARROTHERS, Pat
"The Militiaman Speaks" (tr. of Manuel Díaz-Martínez, w. Armando Romero). [Pig] (15) 88, p. 69.
"Parabola" (tr. of Pablo Armando Fernández, w. Armando Romero). [Pig] (15) 88, p. 75.
869. CARRUTH, Hayden
"August." [GrandS] (8:4) Sum 89, p. 43-44.
"Balance." [Thrpny] (38) Sum 89, p. 14.
"Block." [Ploughs] (15:4) Wint 89-90, p. 30-31.
"Catalogue." [Sulfur] (9:1, #24) Spr 89, p. 131-132.
"Clearing." [ParisR] (31:113) Wint 89, p. 61.
"The Codgers." [Talisman] (2) Spr 89, p. 8.
"Crucifixion." [AmerPoR] (18:2) Mr-Ap 89, p. 56.
"Essay." [SilverFR] (16) Spr 89, p. 25.
"Figment." [Sulfur] (9:1, #24) Spr 89, p. 130-131.
"Forth." [GrandS] (8:4) Sum 89, p. 45.
"Goes." [Ploughs] (15:4) Wint 89-90, p. 29.
"Houses." [SouthernR] (25:2) Spr 89, p. 483-484.
"Ideal." [KenR] (NS 11:3) Sum 89, p. 100.
"Listen." [SouthernR] (25:3) Sum 89, p. 597-598.
"Pessimism." [SouthernR] (25:3) Sum 89, p. 598-599.
"Purity." [SouthernR] (25:2) Spr 89, p. 481-482.
"Renaissance." [SenR] (19:1) 89, p. 5-6.
870. CARSON, Anne
"The Life of Towns." [GrandS] (8:3) Spr 89, p. 182-194.
871. CARSON, Ciarán
"Ambition." [NewYorker] (65:38) 6 N 89, p. 58-59.
"Bedtime Story." [NewYorker] (65:29) 4 S 89, p. 44.
"The Hand." [Pequod] (26/27) 89, p. 78.
"Jump Leads." [Pequod] (26/27) 89, p. 76.
"Portrait of Youth I" (for Annie Bowen/Julia Brien, tr. of Liam O Muirthile). [Trans] (22) Fall 89, p. 128-129.
"Yes." [Pequod] (26/27) 89, p. 77.

872. CARSON, Jeffrey
      "The Almond of the World" (tr. of Odysseus Elytis, w. Nikos Sarris). [PartR] (56:1)
          Wint 89, p. 125-132.
873. CARSON, Julia
      "Amanda." [Vis] (30) 89, p. 33-35.
874. CARSON, Meredith (Meredith S.)
      "Spring Green Up." [Blueline] (10:1/2) 89, p. 50.
      "These Plankton, Jellyfish, Winged Sea Snails and Pelagic Worms." [ChamLR] (3:1,
          #5) Fall 89, p. 124.
      "Who You Are." [ChamLR] (2:2, #4) Spr 89, p. 26.
875. CARTAÑA, Luis
      "Hoy sangro sobre la playa, sobre las ardientes arenas de la dulzura." [LindLM] (8:1)
          Ja-Mr 89, p. 12.
876. CARTER, Anne Babson
      "Bells of Taiwan." [Nat] (249:11) 9 O 89, p. 396.
877. CARTER, Chauncey
      "At an arboretum." [Hawai'iR] (13:3) Fall 89, p. 40.
      "The heart examines." [Hawai'iR] (13:3) Fall 89, p. 41.
878. CARTER, Jared
      "Catalpa." [SoDakR] (27:4) Wint 89, p. 61-64.
      "Double Jacquard Coverlet." [LaurelR] (23:2) Sum 89, p. 93-94.
      "Foundling." [PraS] (63:3) Fall 89, p. 50-51.
      "Getting It Right." [PraS] (63:3) Fall 89, p. 52-53.
      "Moment of Silence." [Witness] (2:4) Wint 88, p. 87.
      "Shortcut." [NoDaQ] (57:4) Fall 89, p. 91-92.
      "Triage." [Poetry] (154:3) Je 89, p. 140-142.
      "Tuning" (for Diane). [MidwQ] (31:1) Aut 89, p. 47-49.
      "The Visual Display of Qualitative Information" (for Rolf Meyn). [Witness] (2:1) Spr
          88, p. 34-36.
879. CARUSO, Lucia V.
      "Ode to a Dove Flying (For Teachers of the Cause)." [WorldO] (22:1/2) Fall-Wint
          87-88, c90, p. 23.
880. CARVER, Beverly
      "6 x 6" (w. Sheila Murphy). [CentralP] (15) Spr 89, p. 152-158.
881. CARVER, Lydia
      "Fucking Japanese Style." [YellowS] (29) Spr 89, p. 20.
882. CARVER, Raymond
      "Afterglow." [NewYorker] (65:10) 24 Ap 89, p. 36.
      "Another Mystery." [Poetry] (154:1) Ap 89, p. 3.
      "Cherish." [HayF] (4) Spr 89, p. 134.
      "Hummingbird" (For Tess). [Poetry] (154:1) Ap 89, p. 4.
      "Letter." [MichQR] (28:1) Wint 89, p. 73-74.
      "No Need." [Poetry] (154:1) Ap 89, p. 4.
      "One More." [HayF] (4) Spr 89, p. 135-137.
      "Proposal" (From "A New Path by the Waterfall: Poems"). [Harp] (278:1666) Mr 89,
          p. 32.
      "Wake Up." [MichQR] (28:1) Wint 89, p. 71-72.
      "Wake Up." [Poetry] (154:1) Ap 89, p. 1-2.
883. CASAVIS, Dave
      "Downsizing." [Lactuca] (13) N 89, p. 43.
884. CASCIATO, Art
      "Red Wagon." [OxfordM] (5:1) Spr-Sum 89, p. 75-76.
885. CASE, David
      "Palms at Christmas." [SouthernR] (25:1) Wint 89, p. 185.
886. CASEY, Crysta
      "Guarantee." [BellArk] (5:5) S-O 89, p. 7.
      "Rocking Chair." [BellArk] (5:5) S-O 89, p. 3.
887. CASEY, Deb
      "Attic Sister Wails. She Sings. In Four Parts, She Advances." [PraS] (63:3) Fall 89,
          p. 59-60.
888. CASEY, Philip
      "Morning Prayer" (tr. of Michael Davitt). [Trans] (22) Fall 89, p. 118.
      "O My Two Palestinians" (Palestinian massacre in Beirut, 18/9/'82, tr. of Michael
          Davitt). [Trans] (22) Fall 89, p. 119.

889. CASKIE, Mark
  "Black Snake." [SoCoast] (5) Spr 88, p. 54.
890. CASPERS, Nona
  "Litany, Amy of." [EvergreenC] (4:4) Sum 89, p. 19.
891. CASSELLS, Cyrus
  "Fleur." [Ploughs] (15:4) Wint 89-90, p. 32-35.
892. CASSELMAN, Barry
  "Comets and Emeralds." [LakeSR] (23) 89, p. 24.
893. CASSIAN, Nina
  "Night Must Fall" (tr. by Dana Gioia). [WilliamMR] (27) 89, p. 49.
  "On an Old Theme." [Verse] (6:3) Wint 89, p. 76.
  "Poetry" (tr. by William Jay Smith). [NewYorker] (64:50) 30 Ja 89, p. 71.
894. CASTELLANOS, Rosario
  "Self-Portrait" (tr. by Beth Miller). [Jacaranda] (4:1) Spr-Sum 89, p. 68-69.
CASTELLON, Manuel Garcia
  See GARCIA CASTELLON, Manuel
895. CASTERTON, Julia
  "Birthday Wishes." [Margin] (9) 89, p. 94.
  "Mrs Thatcher Presides Over the Death of Tragedy." [Margin] (9) 89, p. 93-94.
896. CASTILLO, Sandra M.
  "Foreigners" (for my father). [FloridaR] (16:2/3) Fall-Wint 89, p. 146.
  "Inheritances." [ApalQ] (32) 89, p. 81-84.
897. CASTLE, Luanne
  "The Dentist." [Lactuca] (12) F 89, p. 49.
  "Down by the River." [Lactuca] (12) F 89, p. 50.
  "Ramona Palace." [Lactuca] (12) F 89, p. 49-50.
  "Walkup Under the El." [Lactuca] (12) F 89, p. 48-49.
898. CASTLEBURY, John
  "White Trash in Vacationland." [HeavenB] (7) Wint 89, p. 52.
899. CASTLEMAN, D.
  "Epitaph." [Hawai'iR] (13:2, #26) Sum 89, p. 29.
900. CATALA, Rafael
  "Epitafio para el Siglo XX." [Ometeca] (1:1) 89, p. 25-26.
  "La Espontaneidad del Panadero." [Ometeca] (1:1) 89, p. 24.
901. CATANOY, Nicholas
  "Notes on a Prison Wall" (Fragment). [CanLit] (121) Sum 89, p. 100-106.
902. CATERINA, Angela
  "House." [Outbr] (20) 89, p. 26.
  "Photos." [Outbr] (20) 89, p. 27.
903. CATLIN, Alan
  "If Ché Guevara Had Lived." [Lactuca] (13) N 89, p. 53.
  "A J.B. Scott's Dream." [SlipS] (9) 89, p. 65-66.
  "A Lifetime of Abnormal." [Lactuca] (13) N 89, p. 51-52.
  "On Hearing of the Death of a Misfit." [Lactuca] (13) N 89, p. 50-51.
  "Sixty Cents Worth." [SlipS] (9) 89, p. 67-69.
904. CATLIN, Janet Green
  "Driving Sunnylane." [Pembroke] (21) 89, p. 51.
905. CATTAFI, Bartolo
  "A Noi Due." [BlueBldgs] (11) 89, p. 43.
  "Cammino." [InterPR] (15:2) Fall 89, p. 68.
  "Commino." [BlueBldgs] (11) 89, p. 40.
  "E Qui Che Dio." [InterPR] (15:2) Fall 89, p. 70.
  "Folate di Primavera." [InterPR] (15:2) Fall 89, p. 70.
  "Here" (tr. by Rina Ferrarelli). [InterPR] (15:2) Fall 89, p. 69.
  "In the Mediterranean Stain" (tr. by Dana Gioia). [Poetry] (155:1/2) O-N 89, p. 55.
  "Into Its Cold" (tr. by Rina Ferrarelli). [InterPR] (15:2) Fall 89, p. 69.
  "It's Here That God" (tr. by Rina Ferrarelli). [InterPR] (15:2) Fall 89, p. 71.
  "Mio Amore Non Credere." [Poetry] (155:1/2) O-N 89, p. 52.
  "Missed Opportunity" (tr. by Rina Ferrarelli). [BlueBldgs] (11) 89, p. 41.
  "Missed Opportunity" (tr. by Rina Ferrarelli). [InterPR] (15:2) Fall 89, p. 73.
  "My Love, Don't Believe" (tr. by Dana Gioia). [Poetry] (155:1/2) O-N 89, p. 53.
  "Nel Suo Gelo." [InterPR] (15:2) Fall 89, p. 68.
  "Nella Macchia Mediterranea." [Poetry] (155:1/2) O-N 89, p. 54.
  "Occasione Mancata." [BlueBldgs] (11) 89, p. 41.

"Occasione Mancata." [InterPR] (15:2) Fall 89, p. 72.
"Path" (tr. by Rina Ferrarelli). [BlueBldgs] (11) 89, p. 40.
"Path" (tr. by Rina Ferrarelli). [InterPR] (15:2) Fall 89, p. 69.
"Pyracantha" (in Italian). [InterPR] (15:2) Fall 89, p. 72.
"Pyracantha" (tr. by Rina Ferrarelli). [InterPR] (15:2) Fall 89, p. 73.
"Questi Piccoli Uccelli." [Poetry] (155:1/2) O-N 89, p. 52.
"Qui." [InterPR] (15:2) Fall 89, p. 68.
"Spring Breezes" (tr. by Rina Ferrarelli). [InterPR] (15:2) Fall 89, p. 71.
"These Little Birds" (tr. by Dana Gioia). [Poetry] (155:1/2) O-N 89, p. 53.
"To the Two of Us" (tr. by Rina Ferrarelli). [BlueBldgs] (11) 89, p. 42.
"Il Tuo Rilievo." [InterPR] (15:2) Fall 89, p. 70.
"Your Relief" (tr. by Rina Ferrarelli). [InterPR] (15:2) Fall 89, p. 71.

906. CAUCHI, Alfred
"Somos Agua Viva" (tr. of Oliver Friggieri). [Mairena] (11:27) 89, p. 91.

907. CAUSLEY, Charles
"I Am the Great Sun" (from a Norman crucifix of 1632). [TriQ] (75) Spr-Sum 89, p. 102.

908. CAVALIERI, Grace
"The Afterward Kiss." [EmeraldCR] (1989) c1988, p. 103-104.
"The Bluebird of Happiness." [PoetL] (84:4) Wint 89-90, p. 21-22.
"The Devoted Dead." [PoetL] (84:2) Sum 89, p. 49-50.

909. CAVALLI, Patrizia
"All'Ombra di una Metafora." [Poetry] (155:1/2) O-N 89, p. 134.
"Eternità e Morte Insieme Mi Minacciano." [Poetry] (155:1/2) O-N 89, p. 134.
"In the Shadow of a Metaphor" (tr. by Judith Baumel). [Poetry] (155:1/2) O-N 89, p. 135.
"Now That Time Seems All Mine" (tr. by Judith Baumel). [Poetry] (155:1/2) O-N 89, p. 137.
"Qualcuno Mi Ha Detto." [Poetry] (155:1/2) O-N 89, p. 134.
"Someone Told Me" (tr. by Judith Baumel). [Poetry] (155:1/2) O-N 89, p. 135.
"This Time I Won't Permit the Blue" (tr. by Judith Baumel). [Poetry] (155:1/2) O-N 89, p. 136-137.
"To Simulate the Burning of the Heart" (tr. by Judith Baumel). [Poetry] (155:1/2) O-N 89, p. 136.
"Together Eternity and Death Threaten Me" (tr. by Judith Baumel). [Poetry] (155:1/2) O-N 89, p. 135.

910. CAVANAGH, Clare
"Above Us" (tr. of Julia Hartwig, w. Stanislaw Baranczak). [PartR] (56:2) Spr 89, p. 282.
"Aniela in the Town of Folino" (tr. of Miron Bialoszewski, w. Stanislaw Baranczak). [Trans] (21) Spr 89, p. 38-39.
"Barricade" (tr. of Julian Kornhauser, w. Stanislaw Baranczak). [Trans] (21) Spr 89, p. 78.
"Clothes" (tr. of Wislawa Szymborska, w. Stanislaw Baranczak). [SenR] (19:2) Fall 89, p. 20.
"Ex-Jewish Things" (tr. of Jerzy Ficowski, w. Stanislaw Baranczak). [SenR] (19:2) Fall 89, p. 25.
"Facing the Wall" (tr. of Ryszard Krynicki, w. Stanislaw Baranczak). [PartR] (56:2) Spr 89, p. 288.
"Fascist Nations" (tr. of Wiktor Woroszylski, w. Stanislaw Baranczak). [PartR] (56:2) Spr 89, p. 283-285.
"Fate the Clerk Lays Down a New Set of By-Laws" (tr. of Artur Miedzyrzecki, w. Stanislaw Baranczak). [PartR] (56:2) Spr 89, p. 281.
"From the Gulf Stream of Sleep" (tr. of Ewa Lipska, w. Stanislaw Baranczak). [Trans] (21) Spr 89, p. 77.
"Funny" (tr. of Anna Kamienska, w. Stanislaw Baranczak). [Trans] (21) Spr 89, p. 20.
"The Great Man's House" (tr. of Wislawa Szymborska, w. Stanislaw Baranczak). [Trans] (21) Spr 89, p. 42-43.
"How to Spoil Cannibals' Fun" (tr. of Jerzy Ficowski, w. Stanislaw Baranczak). [Trans] (21) Spr 89, p. 44-45.
"Hymn" (tr. of Jan Polkowski, w. Stanislaw Baranczak). [PartR] (56:2) Spr 89, p. 290.
"In Broad Daylight" (tr. of Wistawa Szymborska, w. Stanislaw Baranczak). [PartR]

(56:2) Spr 89, p. 278-279.
"Indictment" (tr. of Wiktor Woroszylski, w. Stanislaw Baranczak). [PartR] (56:2) Spr 89, p. 285-286.
"Indiscretions" (tr. of Piotr Sommer, w. Stanislaw Baranczak). [SenR] (19:2) Fall 89, p. 29.
"Into the Ark" (tr. of Wislawa Szymborska, w. Stanislaw Baranczak). [SenR] (19:2) Fall 89, p. 21-22.
"It Takes Just a Few Minutes" (tr. of Bronislaw Maj, w. Stanislaw Baranczak). [Trans] (21) Spr 89, p. 82.
"The Jesus of Nonbelievers" (tr. of Jan Twardowski, w. Stanislaw Baranczak). [Trans] (21) Spr 89, p. 18.
"Mandelstam Street" (tr. of Jaroslaw Marek Rymkiewicz, w. Stanislaw Baranczak). [SenR] (19:2) Fall 89, p. 28.
"Mantegna's Christ" (tr. of Mieczyslaw Jastrun, w. Stanislaw Baranczak). [Trans] (21) Spr 89, p. 17.
"Medicine" (tr. of Piotr Sommer, w. Stanislaw Baranczak). [Trans] (21) Spr 89, p. 79.
"Mendacity" (tr. of Witold Wirpsza, w. Stanislaw Baranczak). [Trans] (21) Spr 89, p. 19.
"My Sweet Motherland" (tr. of Jan Polkowski, w. Stanislaw Baranczak). [PartR] (56:2) Spr 89, p. 289.
"A New Day" (tr. of Ryszard Krynicki, w. Stanislaw Baranczak). [Trans] (21) Spr 89, p. 67.
"The Offspring of Heraclitus" (tr. of Adam Wazyk, w. Stanislaw Baranczak). [Trans] (21) Spr 89, p. 16.
"Our Ancestors' Short Lives" (tr. of Wistawa Szymborska, w. Stanislaw Baranczak). [PartR] (56:2) Spr 89, p. 277-278.
"The Padlock Speaks" (From the "Diary of Internment, II," tr. of Wiktor Woroszylski, w. Stanislaw Baranczak). [PartR] (56:2) Spr 89, p. 286.
"Pastoral Psalm" (for Zosia, tr. of Tadeusz Nowak, w. Stanislaw Baranczak). [Trans] (21) Spr 89, p. 60-61.
"Philately" (tr. of Wiktor Woroszylski, w. Stanislaw Baranczak). [Trans] (21) Spr 89, p. 58-59.
"The Poet Grows Weaker" (tr. of Tadeusz Rozewicz, w. Stanislaw Baranczak). [Trans] (21) Spr 89, p. 36-37.
"Possibilities" (tr. of Wislawa Szymborska, w. Stanislaw Baranczak). [SenR] (19:2) Fall 89, p. 23-24.
"Psalm with No Answer" (tr. of Tadeusz Nowak, w. Stanislaw Baranczak). [SenR] (19:2) Fall 89, p. 26.
"The Reason of Existence" (tr. of Artur Miedzyrzecki, w. Stanislaw Baranczak). [Trans] (21) Spr 89, p. 40-41.
"Report" (tr. of Leszek A. Moczulski, w. Stanislaw Baranczak). [Trans] (21) Spr 89, p. 66.
"The Restaurant 'Arcadia,' Central Square, Nowa Huta" (tr. of Jan Polkowski, w. Stanislaw Baranczak). [Trans] (21) Spr 89, p. 81.
"Smoke" (tr. of Tomasz Jastrun, w. Stanislaw Baranczak). [Trans] (21) Spr 89, p. 80.
"Socialist Realism" (tr. of Ryszard Krynicki, w. Stanislaw Baranczak). [PartR] (56:2) Spr 89, p. 287.
"Song of a Crust of Bread Thown to Sparrows on Victory Square . . ." (tr. of Jan Prokop, w. Stanislaw Baranczak). [SenR] (19:2) Fall 89, p. 27.
"Song of Four-Egg Enriched Ribbon Noodles" (tr. of Jan Prokop, w. Stanislaw Baranczak). [Trans] (21) Spr 89, p. 62.
"Soot" (tr. of Ernest Bryll, w. Stanislaw Baranczak). [Trans] (21) Spr 89, p. 63.
"A Stop" (tr. of Ryszard Krynicki, w. Stanislaw Baranczak). [PartR] (56:2) Spr 89, p. 287.
"A Tale Begun" (tr. of Wistawa Szymborska, w. Stanislaw Baranczak). [PartR] (56:2) Spr 89, p. 280-281.
"This city died. Blue streetcars moan" (tr. of Bronislaw Maj, w. Stanislaw Baranczak). [PartR] (56:2) Spr 89, p. 291.
"The War of Nerves" (tr. of Artur Miedzyrzecki, w. Stanislaw Baranczak). [PartR] (56:2) Spr 89, p. 282.
"What Can They" (tr. of Julia Hartwig, w. Stanislaw Baranczak). [PartR] (56:2) Spr 89, p. 283.

"When I Woke Up" (tr. of Jaroslaw Marek Rymkiewicz, w. Stanislaw Baranczak).
[Trans] (21) Spr 89, p. 64-65.
"Who Says" (tr. of Julia Hartwig, w. Stanislaw Baranczak). [Trans] (21) Spr 89, p.
35.
"Who will bear witness to these times?" (tr. of Bronislaw Maj, w. Stanislaw
Baranczak). [PartR] (56:2) Spr 89, p. 290.
"You're Free" (tr. of Ryszard Krynicki, w. Stanislaw Baranczak). [PartR] (56:2) Spr
89, p. 287.
911. CAVITCH, Joanna Byrne
"I follow an Ambulance This Morning." [BelPoJ] (40:2) Wint 89-90, p. 1.
912. CAY, Marilyn
"A Pure and Startled Second" (a poem to my son). [Grain] (17:2) Sum 89, p. 78.
913. CAYAN, Phyllis Coochie
"Hakioawa Bay." [Hawai'iR] (13:3) Fall 89, p. 46.
914. CECIL, Richard
"American Movie Classics." [AmerPoR] (18:3) My-Je 89, p. 8.
"Appalachian Fall." [WestB] (24) 89, p. 102-103.
"Reply to the Goslar Letter." [Ploughs] (15:1) 89, p. 33-34.
"San Francisco Modern Language Convention." [Ploughs] (15:1) 89, p. 30-32.
915. CELAN, Paul
"Abend der Wortef." [InterPR] (15:2) Fall 89, p. 84.
"And the Beauty" (tr. by Lauren Hahn). [ColR] (NS 16:2) Fall 89-Wint 90, p. 88.
"And the Beauty" (tr. by Lauren Hahn). [InterPR] (15:2) Fall 89, p. 83.
"Breton Beach" (tr. by Lauren Hahn). [InterPR] (15:2) Fall 89, p. 85.
"Bretonischer Strand." [InterPR] (15:2) Fall 89, p. 84.
"The Bright Stones move through the air" (From *Niemandsrose*, tr. by Bernard
Frank). [AntigR] (76) Wint 89, p. 125.
"Du Wirfst Mir Ertrinkendem" (From *Zeitgehöff*). [AntigR] (76) Wint 89, p. 126.
"Evening of Words" (tr. by Lauren Hahn). [InterPR] (15:2) Fall 89, p. 85.
"Der Gast." [InterPR] (15:2) Fall 89, p. 82.
"The Guest" (tr. by Lauren Hahn). [InterPR] (15:2) Fall 89, p. 83.
"Die Hellen Steine Gehn durch die Luft" (From *Niemandsrose*). [AntigR] (76) Wint
89, p. 124.
"Schneepart" (Selections: 6 poems, tr. by Bernhard Frank). [AntigR] (79) Aut 89, p.
130-135.
"Und das Schöne." [InterPR] (15:2) Fall 89, p. 82.
"The Way I wear the ring's shadow" (From *Zeitgehöff*, tr. by Bernard Frank).
[AntigR] (76) Wint 89, p. 127.
"Wie Ich den Ringschatten Trage" (From *Zeitgehöff*). [AntigR] (76) Wint 89, p. 126.
"You Toss Gold after me" (From *Zeitgehöff*, tr. by Bernard Frank). [AntigR] (76)
Wint 89, p. 127.
916. CELANO, Ellen
"Ice Skating." [Lactuca] (13) N 89, p. 21-22.
"Trainyard, Santa Fe." [Lactuca] (13) N 89, p. 21.
917. CENDRARS, Blaise
"Clair de Lune (Moonlight)" (tr. by Elisabeth Frost). [Jacaranda] (4:1) Spr-Sum 89,
p. 58.
CERTAIN, Miguel Falquez
See FALQUEZ-CERTAIN, Miguel
918. CERTOV, Jozica
"As You Become" (tr. by Tom Priestly). [ColR] (NS 16:1) Spr-Sum 89, p. 92.
"Universitatsstrasse" (tr. by Tom Priestly). [ColR] (NS 16:1) Spr-Sum 89, p. 91.
919. CERVANTES, Lorna Dee
"Blue Full Moon in Witch." [Americas] (17:3/4) Fall-Wint 89, p. 44.
"The Captive's Verses" (after Neruda). [Americas] (17:3/4) Fall-Wint 89, p. 50.
"Colorado Ave." [Americas] (17:3/4) Fall-Wint 89, p. 48-49.
"Continental Divide" (For Jay). [Americas] (17:3/4) Fall-Wint 89, p. 47.
"From the Cables of Genocide." [Americas] (17:3/4) Fall-Wint 89, p. 45.
"On Love and Hunger." [Americas] (17:3/4) Fall-Wint 89, p. 46.
"The Poet Is Served Her Papers." [Americas] (17:3/4) Fall-Wint 89, p. 43.
920. CERVO, Nathan
"Abide with: Me." [SpiritSH] (55) Fall-Wint 89 [90 on cover], p. 40-41.
"The Hell You Say." [SpiritSH] (55) Fall-Wint 89 [90 on cover], p. 38-39.
"Menstruum of the Dragon." [SpiritSH] (55) Fall-Wint 89 [90 on cover], p. 37.

"Nest of the Kingfisher." [SpiritSH] (55) Fall-Wint 89 [90 on cover], p. 41.
"Pseudonica's Veil." [SpiritSH] (54) Spr-Sum 89, p. 21.
"Subiaco." [SpiritSH] (55) Fall-Wint 89 [90 on cover], p. 36.
"Teratoma." [SpiritSH] (55) Fall-Wint 89 [90 on cover], p. 39-40.
921. CÉSAIRE, Aimé
"C'est l'Obligé Passage." [Callaloo] (12:1, #38) Wint 89, p. 72.
"Dyâli" (For Léopold Sédar Senghor, tr. by Lee Hildreth). [Callaloo] (12:1, #38)
Wint 89, p. 53, 55.
"Dyâli" (Pour Leopold Sédar Senghor). [Callaloo] (12:1, #38) Wint 89, p. 52, 54.
"It Is the Necessary Passage" (tr. by Lee Hildreth). [Callaloo] (12:1, #38) Wint 89, p.
73.
"References." [Callaloo] (12:1, #38) Wint 89, p. 68.
"References" (tr. by Lee Hildreth). [Callaloo] (12:1, #38) Wint 89, p. 69.
"Supreme Mask" (tr. by Lee Hildreth). [Callaloo] (12:1, #38) Wint 89, p. 71.
"Supreme Masque." [Callaloo] (12:1, #38) Wint 89, p. 70.
922. CESAREO, Mario
"A Papá." [Mester] (18:1) Spr 89, p. 51.
923. CETRANO, Sal
"Cathy's Room, Morning Round." [KanQ] (21:3) Sum 89, p. 76.
924. CHACE, Joel
"Ghost Lightning." [Pembroke] (21) 89, p. 152.
"The Pros." [Pembroke] (21) 89, p. 152.
925. CHADWICK, Jerah
"Lessons of Bread." [ChangingM] (20) Wint-Spr 89, p. 21.
926. CHADWICK, Joseph
"Hospital Call" (for Jack). [ChamLR] (3:1, #5) Fall 89, p. 154.
927. CHAIKIN, Joseph
"Struck Dumb" (w. Jean-Claude van Itallie). [Kaleid] (19) Sum-Fall 89, p. 10-18.
"Thank You" (acceptance speech, 5th annual Edwin Booth Award, City University of
New York). [Kaleid] (19) Sum-Fall 89, p. 8-9.
928. CHALGREN, Jim
"Untitled: sweet nectar of the lotus." [EvergreenC] (4:3) Spr 89, p. 34.
929. CHALLENDER, Craig
"Walt." [Northeast] (ser. 5:1) Wint 89-90, p. 23.
930. CHAMBERS, Carole
"Escape from the Net." [Grain] (17:4) Wint 89, p. 32.
931. CHAMBERS, George
"Baskets of Asparagus" (Literary Award Poem). [GreensboroR] (47) Wint 89-90, p.
107-108.
"Shadblow." [GreensboroR] (47) Wint 89-90, p. 109-110.
932. CHAMBERS, Henry Tim
"Lover Boy." [NegC] (9:1) 89, p. 83.
933. CHANDLER, Tom
"Book Burning." [CumbPR] (8:2) Spr 89, p. 7.
"World's Saddest Song." [HampSPR] Wint 89, p. 14.
934. CHANDRA, G. S. Sharat
"Awards." [NewL] (56:2/3) Wint 89-Spr 90, p. 55-56.
"Confusion." [NewL] (56:2/3) Wint 89-Spr 90, p. 58.
"Dear Editor." [PoetC] (20:2) Wint 89, p. 48.
"For My Mother Who Died Before My Children Visited Her." [NewL] (56:2/3) Wint
89-Spr 90, p. 59-60.
"Hawaiian Zen Fleas." [NewL] (56:2/3) Wint 89-Spr 90, p. 60-61.
"Love Poem." [PoetC] (20:2) Wint 89, p. 47.
"Midlife." [NewL] (56:2/3) Wint 89-Spr 90, p. 57.
"Peasants Waiting for Rain." [Poetry] (154:5) Ag 89, p. 264.
935. CHANEY, Joseph
"Shaving Again." [BelPoJ] (40:2) Wint 89-90, p. 20.
"What Is an Editor?" [BelPoJ] (40:2) Wint 89-90, p. 21.
936. CHANG, Carol Zhigong
"At the Tomb of Li Bai" (tr. of Bai Juyi, w. Anthony Piccione). [LitR] (32:3) Spr 89,
p. 392.
"Autumn and a Woman's Room" (tr. of Li Yu, w. Anthony Piccione and Li Young
Lee). [LitR] (32:3) Spr 89, p. 390.
"Drinking at a Lake on a Clear Day Followed by Rain" (tr. of Su Shih, w. Anthony

Piccione). [LitR] (32:3) Spr 89, p. 391.
"Evening River Song" (tr. of Bai Juyi, w. Anthony Piccione). [LitR] (32:3) Spr 89,
    p. 392.
"Past Thoughts" (tr. of Li Yu, w. Anthony Piccione and Li Young Lee). [LitR] (32:3)
    Spr 89, p. 390.
"Rising Late" (tr. of Meng Hao-jan, w. Anthony Piccione and Li Young Lee). [LitR]
    (32:3) Spr 89, p. 389.
"Separation" (tr. of Su Shih, w. Anthony Piccione and Li Young Lee). [LitR] (32:3)
    Spr 89, p. 389.
CHANG, Chi
    See ZHANG, Ji
937. CHANG, Diana
    "Bird, Woman and Leaves." [CrossCur] (8:3) Apr 89, p. 101.
    "Like Wind." [StoneC] (16:3/4) Spr-Sum 89, p. 59.
938. CHANG, Lisa
    "Boy by Choice." [Sequoia] (32:2) Wint-Spr 89, p. 69.
    "If I Came." [Sequoia] (32:2) Wint-Spr 89, p. 68.
CHANG, Soo Ko
    See KO, Chang Soo
939. CHANG, Yang-hao
    "A Sigh for Life" (tr. by J. I. Crump). [LitR] (32:3) Spr 89, p. 418.
940. CHANG, Yüeh
    "Written When Drunk" (tr. by Burton Watson). [LitR] (32:3) Spr 89, p. 435.
CH'ANG-LING, Wang
    See WANG, Ch'ang-ling
941. CHAPMAN, R. S. (Robin S.)
    "Catching Rabbits." [Poetry] (154:5) Ag 89, p. 275.
    "Haystacks at Sunset" (after Monet). [BelPoJ] (39:4) Sum 89, p. 37.
    "Rookery." [Nimrod] (33:1) Fall-Wint 89, p. 73.
    "Summer Jobs" (for JFM). [BelPoJ] (39:4) Sum 89, p. 36.
    "The Way of Your Going" (for my mother). [Shen] (39:4) Wint 89, p. 46.
942. CHARINHO, Pai Gomes
    "Song for a Lover What Went to Sea (Cantiga d'Amigo)" (tr. by Richard Zenith).
        [PoetryE] (28) Fall 89, p. 194.
    "Song of the Parting Flowers (Cantiga d'Amigo)" (tr. by Richard Zenith). [PoetryE]
        (28) Fall 89, p. 192-193.
CHARITY, Ralph la
    See La CHARITY, Ralph
943. CHARLIE-2
    "Day after Day" (Poems of Vietnam Combat). [MichQR] (28:2) Spr 89, p. 176.
    "December 24, 1969" (Poems of Vietnam Combat). [MichQR] (28:2) Spr 89, p.
        174-175.
    "Sweep Spot" (Poems of Vietnam Combat). [MichQR] (28:2) Spr 89, p. 177-178.
944. CHARRY LARA, Fernando
    "Serenata." [LindLM] (8:2) Ap-Je 89, p. 3.
945. CHARTERS, Samuel
    "Vermeer" (tr. of Tomas Tranströmer). [Quarry] (38:2) Spr 89, p. 81-82.
946. CHASE, Karen
    "What You Can't See." [Caliban] (7) 89, p. 8.
947. CHATFIELD, Hale
    "In Charge of Death." [Wind] (19:65) 89, p. 1-2.
948. CHATTERJEE, Enakshi
    "Curse" (tr. of Kabita Sinha, w. Carolyne Wright). [Trans] (21) Spr 89, p. 150.
    "Waterfall" (tr. of Kabita Sinha, w. Carolyne Wright). [Trans] (21) Spr 89, p. 149.
949. CHATTERJEE, Monish R.
    "I Am Lost" (tr. of Rabindranath Tagore). [InterPR] (15:2) Fall 89, p. 86.
    "The Touch" (tr. of Premendra Mitra). [InterPR] (15:2) Fall 89, p. 87.
950. CHATTORAJ, Partha
    "Love Poem with Repetition." [HarvardA] (123:4) My 89, p. 34.
951. CHAVES, Jonathan
    "Don't Read Books!" (tr. of Yang Wan-li). [LitR] (32:3) Spr 89, p. 429.
    "Echoing Mountain Recluse Ho Ching's Poem on *Hai-T'ang* Blossoms" (tr. of Wen
        T'ung). [LitR] (32:3) Spr 89, p. 433.
    "First Day of the Second Month: Rain and Cold" (tr. of Yang Wan-li). [LitR] (32:3)

Spr 89, p. 430.
"Irritated by the Insects" (tr. of Wen T'ung). [LitR] (32:3) Spr 89, p. 434.
"Late Winter -- Describing Scenes" (tr. of Wen T'ung). [LitR] (32:3) Spr 89, p. 433.
"On Receiving My Letter of Termination" (tr. of Yüan Hung-tao). [LitR] (32:3) Spr
     89, p. 431.
"Reading" (tr. of Yang Wan-li). [LitR] (32:3) Spr 89, p. 428.
"Things Seen on Spring Days" (tr. of Yüan Hung-tao). [LitR] (32:3) Spr 89, p. 432.
"West Lake" (tr. of Yüan Hung-tao). [LitR] (32:3) Spr 89, p. 431.
"A Woman's Room in Autumn" (tr. of Yüan Hung-tao). [LitR] (32:3) Spr 89, p. 432.
952. CH'EN, Tzu-lung
"The Little Cart" (tr. by Arthur Waley). [LitR] (32:3) Spr 89, p. 305.
953. CHEN, Xueliang
"Accomplices" (tr. of Bei Dao, w. Donald Finkel). [LitR] (32:3) Spr 89, p. 340.
"Elegy" (tr. of Bei Dao, w. Donald Finkel). [LitR] (32:3) Spr 89, p. 342.
"The Host" (tr. of Bei Dao, w. Donald Finkel). [LitR] (32:3) Spr 89, p. 343.
"I'm Forever a Stranger" (tr. of Bei Dao, w. Donald Finkel). [LitR] (32:3) Spr 89, p.
     340.
"Memory" (tr. of Bei Dao, w. Donald Finkel). [LitR] (32:3) Spr 89, p. 343.
"Night: Theme and Variations" (tr. of Bei Dao, w. Donald Finkel). [LitR] (32:3) Spr
     89, p. 341.
"No Tomorrow" (tr. of Bei Dao, w. Donald Finkel). [LitR] (32:3) Spr 89, p. 339.
"Shore" (tr. of Bei Dao, w. Donald Finkel). [LitR] (32:3) Spr 89, p. 342.
"Toast" (tr. of Bei Dao, w. Donald Finkel). [LitR] (32:3) Spr 89, p. 339.
954. CHENG, Anne A.
"Waterlilies" (tr. of Te-Ho Li). [Jacaranda] (4:1) Spr-Sum 89, p. 71.
CHENG, Gu
     See GU, Cheng
955. CHENOWETH, Goldie
"Chasing the Water." [Hawai'iR] (13:1, #25) Spr 89, p. 65.
"No Place Called Forever (A Dio)." [Hawai'iR] (13:1, #25) Spr 89, p. 66-67.
"La Vita Nova." [Hawai'iR] (13:1, #25) Spr 89, p. 68.
956. CHERKOVSKI, Neeli
"Aleph." [AlphaBS] (5) Jl 89, p. 15-16.
"Lost." [AlphaBS] (5) Jl 89, p. 14.
"Viva la Causa." [AnotherCM] (19) 89, p. 20.
957. CHERRY, Kelly
"The Caverns of Unacknowledged Fears." [FourQ] (2d series 3:1) Spr 89, p. 20.
"Galilee." [SouthernPR] (29:2) Fall 89, p. 6.
"I'm Out of My Head." [FourQ] (2d series 3:1) Spr 89, p. 22.
"Learned from a Poet" (for Robert Watson). [GreensboroR] (46) Sum 89, p. 91.
"Remembering." [AmerS] (58:3) Sum 89, p. 428.
"Seclusion Room, a Tabula Rasa." [FourQ] (2d series 3:1) Spr 89, p. 21.
958. CHETWYND, Richard
"The Grave." [Ploughs] (15:1) 89, p. 35-36.
CHI, Chang
     See ZHANG, Ji
CH'I, Kao
     See KAO, Ch'i
CHI, Wang
     See WANG, Chi
CHI-FANG, Chu
     See CHU, Chi-fang
959. CHICHETTO, James William (J. Wm.)
"Augustine Conversing with Albee" (Excerpt). [ConnPR] (8:1) 89, p. 29-30.
960. CHIDESTER, E. Leon
"Capricorn." [WeberS] (6:1) Spr 89, p. 54.
"If This House Should Burn." [WeberS] (6:1) Spr 89, p. 53-54.
"With My Son in the Principal's Office, Public School 317." [WeberS] (6:1) Spr 89,
     p. 52-53.
CH'IEN, T'ao
     See T'AO, Ch'ien
CHIEN-WU, Shih
     See SHIH, Chien-wu

961. CHIESA, Carmen
    "Suplica." [Mairena] (11:27) 89, p. 72.
CHIH-YÜAN, Ma
    See MA, Chih-yüan
962. CHIN, Justin
    "Sold." [BelPoJ] (40:1) Fall 89, p. 2-3.
963. CH'IN, Kuan
    "Another to the Tune 'All the Garden's Fragrance'" (tr. by David Young and William
        McNaughton). [LitR] (32:3) Spr 89, p. 374.
    "A Third to the Tune 'As Though Dreaming'" (tr. by David Young and William
        McNaughton). [LitR] (32:3) Spr 89, p. 373.
    "To the Tune 'As Though Dreaming'" (tr. by David Young and William
        McNaughton). [LitR] (32:3) Spr 89, p. 372.
    "To the Tune 'Welcome Spring Music'" (tr. by David Young and William
        McNaughton). [LitR] (32:3) Spr 89, p. 373.
964. CHIN, Marilyn
    "Old Asian Hand." [RiverS] (30) [89], p. 52.
    "Until Suddenly, a Small Jet Crosses Her Vision." [RiverS] (30) [89], p. 51.
965. CHING, Laureen
    "Fever" (for Mona). [BambooR] (42/43) Spr-Sum 89, p. 196.
CH'ING-CHAO, Li
    See LI, Ch'ing-chao
966. CHINOWETH, Okey
    "William David Soneton Canfield, The Third." [Footwork] 89, p. 70-72.
967. CHIPASULA, Frank (Frank M., Frank Mkalawile)
    "A Harp of Heartstrings: II" (for Hesse & Esther). [Pig] (15) 88, p. 40.
    "Manifesto on Ars Poetica." [PaperAir] (4:2) 89, p. 12.
    "Manifesto on Ars Poetica." [Pig] (15) 88, p. 41.
    "A Momument to a Tyrant." [Pig] (15) 88, p. 41.
    "Nightmare." [Bomb] (28) Sum 89, p. 87.
    "A Poem for Martyrs' Day." [Bomb] (28) Sum 89, p. 87.
    "This Island Now" (for Rene Belance). [Pig] (15) 88, p. 44.
    "Wizard." [Bomb] (28) Sum 89, p. 87.
968. CHITWOOD, Michael
    "Hard Surface Road." [SouthernPR] (29:2) Fall 89, p. 11.
    "Signs." [SouthernPR] (29:1) Spr 89, p. 50.
969. CHMIELARZ, Sharon
    "Two Sonnets: Daughter's and Mother's." [SingHM] (16) 89, p. 29.
970. CHOCHOLAK, Misha
    "Prayers of Steel." [Rampike] (6:2) 88, p. 62.
971. CHOCK, Eric
    "Chinese Fireworks Banned in Hawaii" (for Uncle Wongie, 1987). [BambooR]
        (42/43) Spr-Sum 89, p. 187-188.
    "Chinese New Year." [BambooR] (42/43) Spr-Sum 89, p. 194.
    "Last Days Here" (Special double issue: 46 poems). [BambooR] (45/46) Wint-Spr
        89-90, 88 p.
    "Looking Back from a Small Hill to Downtown Honolulu." [BambooR] (42/43)
        Spr-Sum 89, p. 189-190.
    "Poem for My Father." [BambooR] (42/43) Spr-Sum 89, p. 193.
    "What? Another Chinese Holiday?!" [BambooR] (42/43) Spr-Sum 89, p. 195.
972. CHOE, Wolhee
    "Iron, We Were Told" (Three Poems by Kisang, tr. of Jin-ock, w. Constantine
        Contogenis). [BelPoJ] (39:4) Sum 89, p. 32.
    "The Large Beak Finches" (tr. of anonymous Korean poem, w. Constantine
        Contogenis). [ChiR] (36:3/4) 89, p. 18.
    "Let My Cassia Boat" (Three Poems by Kisang, tr. of Kae-ju, w. Constantine
        Contogenis). [BelPoJ] (39:4) Sum 89, p. 33.
    "Old Plum Trees" (tr. of Mae-wha, w. Constantine Contogenis). [ChiR] (36:3/4) 89,
        p. 19.
    "What Blight" (Three Poems by Kisang, tr. of Mae-wha, w. Constantine
        Contogenis). [BelPoJ] (39:4) Sum 89, p. 32.
973. CHOI, Kathleen T.
    "Butcher Block." [BambooR] (44) Fall 89, p. 6.
    "Day Break." [BambooR] (44) Fall 89, p. 5.

974. CHORLTON, David
    "The Alchemist." [ChamLR] (2:2, #4) Spr 89, p. 61.
    "August 27th, Night" (tr. of Hans Raimund). [Os] (29) 89, p. 15.
    "Che Solo Puoi Afferrare Bricioli di Ricordi" (tr. of Hans Raimund). [Os] (29) 89, p.
        17.
    "Dwarf Steps." [DeKalbLAJ] (22:1/4) 89, p. 47.
    "Experiments." [CapeR] (24:2) Fall 89, p. 44.
    "Grace." [SoCoast] (5) Spr 88, p. 9.
    "Planctus." [PoetL] (84:2) Sum 89, p. 39-40.
    "Raincoat." [ChamLR] (2:2, #4) Spr 89, p. 62.
    "San Virila." [StoneC] (17:1/2) Fall-Wint 89-90, p. 36.
    "Trakl's Dream." [PoetL] (84:2) Sum 89, p. 38.
CHOU, Hsi
    See HSI, Chou
975. CHOUDHURI, Pradip
    "China Soup." [AlphaBS] (5) Jl 89, p. 37.
    "Dream-Machine" (For Theo Green: in Brion's Memory). [AlphaBS] (5) Jl 89, p.
        35-36.
    "Prelude to a Nightmare." [AlphaBS] (6) Wint 89-90, p. 25-27.
976. CHRISTAKOS, Margaret
    "September 13." [Rampike] (6:2) 88, p. 70.
977. CHRISTHILF, Mark
    "Full Hands." [NoDaQ] (57:3) Sum 89, p. 218.
    "The Ladder." [HighP] (4:1) Spr 89, p. 42.
    "Letter from Illinois." [MidwQ] (30:2) Wint 89, p. 179.
    "The Sentence." [HighP] (4:1) Spr 89, p. 45.
    "Town Crier." [HighP] (4:1) Spr 89, p. 43-44.
978. CHRISTIANSON, Norah
    "Wet, Awaiting Blue." [KanQ] (21:1/2) Wint-Spr 89, p. 228.
979. CHRISTINA, Martha
    "Haymow." [SingHM] (16) 89, p. 3.
    "The Long Posing." [Kalliope] (11:1) 89, p. 58-59.
    "Photographing Yusef and the Children." [SingHM] (16) 89, p. 4.
980. CHRISTINA-MARIE
    "Origami." [ChiR] (36:3/4) 89, p. 73.
981. CHRISTOPHER, Michael
    "Saying It Is So" (A Design for an Art Space). [Nimrod] (33:1) Fall-Wint 89, p.
        133-135.
982. CHRISTOPHER, Nicholas
    "In the Country." [NewYorker] (65:27) 21 Ag 89, p. 36.
    "Nine Cities." [NewRep] (200:15) 10 Ap 89, p. 32.
    "South of the Border." [SouthwR] (74:3) Sum 89, p. 337-339.
983. CHU, Chi-fang
    "Outside the Dust" (tr. by Paul Hansen). [LitR] (32:3) Spr 89, p. 355.
CHU-I, Po
    See BAI, Juyi
CHÜ-YI, Po
    See BAI, Juyi
CHU-YI, Po
    See BAI, Juyi
CHUAN, Y. Fu
    See FU, Chuan Y.
984. CHUBBS, Boyd
    "Maria." [AntigR] (76) Wint 89, p. 24.
CHUILLEANAIN, Eileán Ni
    See Ni CHUILLEANAIN, Eileán
985. CHUN, Herbert K. K.
    "Pa-ke." [BambooR] (42/43) Spr-Sum 89, p. 215-216.
CHUN, Soo Kim
    See KIM, Chun-Soo
CHUN-JIAN, Xue
    See XUE, Chun-jian
CHUNG, Li
    See LI, Chung

986. CHURA, David
"Foxes." [Blueline] (10:1/2) 89, p. 26.
"From Winslow Homer's Notebook: Frog on Mink Pond, 1891." [Blueline] (10:1/2)
89, p. 27.
"Grieving." [EvergreenC] (4:3) Spr 89, p. 14.
"Winslow Homer in Hipboots." [Blueline] (10:1/2) 89, p. 25.
987. CHUTE, Robert M.
"Actaeon in the Tunnel of Leaves." [TexasR] (10:3/4) Fall-Wint 89, p. 114.
"Agnostic." [SmPd] (26:3 #77) Fall 89, p. 31.
"Blackbirds Bathing." [TexasR] (10:3/4) Fall-Wint 89, p. 115.
"Hang by the Neck 'till the World Is Dead." [SmPd] (26:3 #77) Fall 89, p. 29.
"Measure of the Earth." [LitR] (32:2) Wint 89, p. 172.
"The Monster Escapes Once More." [SmPd] (26:3 #77) Fall 89, p. 30.
"Note on the Occasion of a New Moon." [CapeR] (24:2) Fall 89, p. 23.
"October Meditation." [StoneC] (16:3/4) Spr-Sum 89, p. 68.
"Past Is Present." [SmPd] (26:3 #77) Fall 89, p. 28.
"Pine Plantation: October." [SmPd] (26:3 #77) Fall 89, p. 31.
"Puritan Intermission." [AntigR] (77/78) Spr-Sum 89, p. 196.
"Sap-Run Days." [SmPd] (26:3 #77) Fall 89, p. 27.
"Shaker Village: Recent Photographs." [BelPoJ] (39:4) Sum 89, p. 5.
"Tracks." [LitR] (32:2) Wint 89, p. 173.
"The Western." [Ascent] (14:3) 89, p. 13.
"The Winter Den." [SmPd] (26:3 #77) Fall 89, p. 27.
"Working Up Wood." [SmPd] (26:1, #75) Wint 89, p. 7.
CI, Song
    See SONG, Ci
988. CIESLINSKI, L. John
"Gathering." [StoneC] (17:1/2) Fall-Wint 89-90, p. 58-59.
989. CIHLAR, Jim
"Half-Dead Pigeon in a Warehouse Parking Lot." [Plain] (9:2) Wint 89, p. 32.
990. CIMA, Annalisa
"Hypotheses on Love" (Selections: 1, 2, 4, 9, 11, tr. by Jonathan Galassi). [Poetry]
    (155:1/2) O-N 89, p. 109-113.
"Ipotesi d'Amore" (Selections: 1, 2, 4, 9, 11). [Poetry] (155:1/2) O-N 89, p.
    108-112.
991. CIMON, Anne
"Marketplace." [CanLit] (121) Sum 89, p. 84.
992. CIORAN, E. M.
"From: Ulysses" (tr. of Benjamin Fondane, w. Leonard Schwartz). [PartR] (56:1)
    Wint 89, p. 120-121.
993. CIORDIA, Javier
"Isla-Eden." [Mairena] (11:27) 89, p. 73.
994. CIRESE, Eugenio
"The Crossroads" (tr. by Luigi Bonaffini). [WebR] (14:1) Spr 89, p. 22.
"Nothing" (tr. by Luigi Bonaffini). [WebR] (14:1) Spr 89, p. 23.
"The Snowstorm" (tr. by Luigi Bonaffini). [WebR] (14:1) Spr 89, p. 23.
995. CIRESI, Rita
"Everywhere, Protect Me." [PoetL] (84:2) Sum 89, p. 23-24.
"First Stop, Miami." [PraS] (63:3) Fall 89, p. 62-63.
"Five Girls and a Ouija." [PraS] (63:3) Fall 89, p. 61-62.
996. CIRINO, Leonard
"The Poet." [WestB] (24) 89, p. 65.
"Somewhere in the Moonlight." [WestB] (25) 89, p. 25.
997. CITINO, David
"Developers Announce Plans for Largest Shopping Mall in the Nation." [CinPR] (19)
    Spr 89, p. 59.
"He Realizes His Own Worst Fears." [CharR] (15:1) Spr 89, p. 66.
"M.S." [CinPR] (19) Spr 89, p. 58.
"Meditation on I Kings." [WestB] (25) 89, p. 26.
"One Hundred Percent Chance of Snow, Accumulating Eight to Twelve Inches by
    Morning." [SouthernR] (25:1) Wint 89, p. 181-182.
"Sister Mary Appassionata Addresses the Urologists' Convention." [TexasR] (10:3/4)
    Fall-Wint 89, p. 60-61.
"Sister Mary Appassionata Delivers an Impromptu Speech at the Local Ponderosa."

[TexasR] (10:3/4) Fall-Wint 89, p. 58-59.
"Sister Mary Appassionata on the Excommunication of the Locusts." [WestB] (24) 89, p. 86-87.
"Sister Mary Appassionata to the Sociobiology Class." [WestB] (24) 89, p. 88-89.
CLAES, Astrid Gehlhoff
    See GEHLHOFF-CLAES, Astrid
CLAIR, Mary Ellen le
    See LeCLAIR, Mary Ellen
998. CLAIR, Maxine
    "Daughter." [Obs] (2:1) Spr 87, p. 73.
    "The Flying Africans." [Obs] (2:1) Spr 87, p. 70-71.
    "The Other Lady." [Obs] (2:1) Spr 87, p. 71.
    "Running." [Obs] (2:1) Spr 87, p. 71-72.
999. CLAMPITT, Amy
    "Amherst, May 15, 1987." [GrandS] (8:3) Spr 89, p. 31-32.
    "Geese." [GrandS] (8:2) Wint 89, p. 226.
    "The Halloween Parade." [GrandS] (9:1) Aut 89, p. 105-107.
    "My Cousin Muriel." [NewYorker] (65:1) 20 F 89, p. 33.
    "A Note from Leiden." [NewYorker] (65:42) 4 D 89, p. 50.
    "Nothing Stays Put." [NewYorker] (65:10) 24 Ap 89, p. 40-41.
    "Savannah." [NewYorker] (64:48) 16 Ja 89, p. 70.

1000. CLAPS, Robert
    "Clam-Digger." [SmPd] (26:3 #77) Fall 89, p. 26.
1001. CLARK, Arthur
    "A Certain Hat." [AntigR] (77/78) Spr-Sum 89, p. 9.
    "Intersection." [Grain] (17:3) Fall 89, p. 20-21.
    "Origami." [AntigR] (77/78) Spr-Sum 89, p. 10.
    "Tiny Alice" (The reader in Codresculand). [CrossC] (11:1) 89, p. 8.
1002. CLARK, Irene Grayce
    "At the Airport: Why I Said 'I Love You, Dad'." [Plain] (9:3) Spr 89, p. 10.
1003. CLARK, J. Wesley
    "Alba." [Wind] (19:64) 89, p. 10.
    "Blue Prairie Motel." [Notus] (4:2) Fall 89, p. 41.
    "In Mary's Bowl." [Notus] (4:2) Fall 89, p. 40.
    "Kid Curry" (Knox County Jail, June 27, 1903). [Notus] (4:2) Fall 89, p. 42.
1004. CLARK, Jeanne E.
    "Everything About Men." [OxfordM] (5:2) Fall-Wint 89, p. 42.
    "Staying Dressed." [OxfordM] (5:1) Spr-Sum 89, p. 50.
1005. CLARK, Jim
    "Letter to Ciardi: April 3, 1986." [DenQ] (24:2) Fall 89, p. 34-35.
1006. CLARK, Kevin
    "Conversion" (From Coccapani's *La Maddalena in Estasi*). [BellR] (12:2, #26) Fall 89, p. 38-42.
    "Eros in Middle Age." [BellR] (12:2, #26) Fall 89, p. 35-37.
1007. CLARK, Mary
    "Breasts." [Iowa] (19:2) Spr-Sum 89, p. 70-72.
    "The Curious." [RiverS] (29) [89], p. 53.
    "The Fish Lovers." [RiverS] (29) [89], p. 55.
    "The Guinea Hen." [Iowa] (19:2) Spr-Sum 89, p. 72-74.
    "The Late-Shift Workers." [RiverS] (29) [89], p. 54.
1008. CLARK, Miriam Marty
    "A Child of Air." [PraS] (63:1) Spr 89, p. 28.
    "February." [PraS] (63:1) Spr 89, p. 27.
    "January." [PraS] (63:1) Spr 89, p. 26.
1009. CLARK, Naomi
    "A Dark Hill." [CimR] (86) Ja 89, p. 50.
    "The Language of Doors" (for Burnie). [CimR] (86) Ja 89, p. 48-49.
    "The Sleeper." [HayF] (5) Fall 89, p. 64-65.
    "Spinning." [BelPoJ] (40:2) Wint 89-90, p. 36.
    "The Sun! The Sun!" [IndR] (13:1) Wint 89, p. 40-43.
    "To My Mother." [BelPoJ] (40:2) Wint 89-90, p. 37-38.
    "Vivaldi and the Braille-Writer" (For my student Nancy, who died by suicide).
        [PoetryNW] (30:2) Sum 89, p. 21-22.

1010. CLARK, Tom
    "After Thomas Hardy." [NewAW] (5) Fall 89, p. 106.
    "Inside the Redwood." [Temblor] (10) 89, p. 133.
    "The Pure Products of America, Much Later." [NewAW] (5) Fall 89, p. 105.
    "Society." [NewAW] (5) Fall 89, p. 104.
1011. CLARKE, Adrian
    "2 Terminal Preludes." [PaperAir] (4:2) 89, p. 113-114.
1012. CLARKE, Amanda M.
    "The October Promise." [InterPR] (15:2) Fall 89, p. 121.
    "The Russian Romance." [InterPR] (15:2) Fall 89, p. 121.
1013. CLARKE, Catherine
    "Jim Shannon's Lesson." [Blueline] (10:1/2) 89, p. 76.
    "Learning to Love It Here." [GrahamHR] (12) Spr 89, p. 69.
    "Night." [Blueline] (10:1/2) 89, p. 77.
1014. CLARKE, Cheryl
    "Committed Sex." [Cond] (16) 89, p. 167.
1015. CLARKE, Gillian
    "Blaen Cwrt." [NoDaQ] (57:2) Spr 89, insert p. 60.
    "The Hare" (i. m. Frances Horovitz, 1938-1983). [NoDaQ] (57:2) Spr 89, insert p.
        62-63.
    "Harvest at Mynachlog." [NoDaQ] (57:2) Spr 89, insert p. 61.
1016. CLARKE, John
    "Alabaster Gypsum." [Temblor] (10) 89, p. 85.
    "Bees of the Aether." [Temblor] (10) 89, p. 84.
    "Black Garters of the Deadlock." [Notus] (4:1) Spr 89, p. 3.
    "The Flare for Being Right." [Temblor] (10) 89, p. 85.
    "Four American Ones for Clark." [Talisman] (3) Fall 89, p. 60.
    "Glasnost AND Perestroika." [Temblor] (10) 89, p. 86.
    "God Bless You, Art Blakey" (Memorial Day, 1984). [Talisman] (3) Fall 89, p. 63.
    "Green Is the Color of Islam." [Temblor] (10) 89, p. 84.
    "Heritage Unmixed." [Screens] (1) 89, p. 143.
    "Hewn Interjacence." [Notus] (4:1) Spr 89, p. 6.
    "I Knew Madame de Stael, and You're No Madame de Stael" (for R.D.). [Screens]
        (1) 89, p. 144.
    "The Identity of Things Changed by Growth." [Notus] (4:1) Spr 89, p. 5.
    "In Everyman's Despite." [Notus] (4:1) Spr 89, p. 7.
    "The Last First Coming." [Notus] (4:1) Spr 89, p. 4.
    "The Lotus Eaters." [Temblor] (10) 89, p. 88.
    "The Minarets, So Named, Not to be Parted With." [Temblor] (10) 89, p. 90.
    "Nobody Is Coming After Us." [Temblor] (10) 89, p. 87.
    "One Police Against Another" (for Robin, "of such listening"). [Temblor] (10) 89, p.
        89.
    "Poem Beginning with a Line from Margaret Johnson." [Temblor] (10) 89, p. 89.
    "Skull and Bones." [Screens] (1) 89, p. 145.
    "Straight Pulse, No Chase Her." [Talisman] (3) Fall 89, p. 61.
    "The Thunder of Bees." [Screens] (1) 89, p. 145.
    "Tibetan Nuts" (for Liz Willis). [Temblor] (10) 89, p. 88.
    "Two's Company" (for Robert Creeley). [Screens] (1) 89, p. 143.
    "Under the Mighty Flow from the Great Celestial Sea" (for John Thorpe). [Screens]
        (1) 89, p. 144.
    "Wood Pussy" (to Tina). [Temblor] (10) 89, p. 86.
    "World Baedeker" (for Fred). [Temblor] (10) 89, p. 90.
    "The World Stage." [Talisman] (3) Fall 89, p. 62.
    "The Zebraiad." [Temblor] (10) 89, p. 87.
1017. CLAVIJO, Uva
    "Isla Mia" (A Lisandro Pérez, que también recuerda la infancia de trópico y
        disparos). [LindLM] (8:1) Ja-Mr 89, p. 7.
1018. CLAY, Russell
    "The Bream Sea." [Poem] (61) My 89, p. 49.
    "Goodbye to Kindling and Soul." [Poem] (61) My 89, p. 50.
1019. CLEARY, Michael
    "Bewley's Cafe." [NegC] (9:2) 89, p. 36-37.
1020. CLEARY, Suzanne
    "Girl in Mourning" (After Paul Klee). [Poetry] (153:6) Mr 89, p. 345.
    "Listening to the Poem" (For P. Schultz and National Public Radio). [Poetry]
        (153:6) Mr 89, p. 343-344.

"Stock Footage." [Poetry] (153:6) Mr 89, p. 345-346.
1021. CLEMENTS, Arthur L.
"Baptisms." [Footwork] 89, p. 73.
"A Knotty Metaphysical Sonnet." [Footwork] 89, p. 73.
"Learning How to Start" (for Ruth Stone). [Footwork] 89, p. 73.
1022. CLEMENTS, Susan Hauptfleisch
"Beauty of Masks." [Footwork] 89, p. 8-9.
"Cardinals" (for Nat and Nina Scammacca). [Footwork] 89, p. 9.
"Fragments for a Found Lover." [Footwork] 89, p. 8.
"The Helmsman." [GreensboroR] (47) Wint 89-90, p. 71.
"Movie House." [Footwork] 89, p. 7-8.
"Visitation at Passaic Falls." [Footwork] 89, p. 8.
"Witch Hazel." [Footwork] 89, p. 9.
1023. CLENMAN, Donia
"I Had Forgotten That I Loved You." [CrossC] (11:1) 89, p. 10.
1024. CLEVE, E.
"Aubad December 25." [SpiritSH] (55) Fall-Wint 89 [90 on cover], p. 17.
"Autumn." [SpiritSH] (55) Fall-Wint 89 [90 on cover], p. 19.
"Sea Serpents." [SpiritSH] (55) Fall-Wint 89 [90 on cover], p. 18.
1025. CLEVIDENCE, Carin
"Not Dated" (for Kafka, tr. of Blanca Varela). [Field] (41) Fall 89, p. 58-59.
1026. CLEWELL, David
"From the Other Side, Houdini Tries to Come Through for Bess." [Poetry] (153:5) F
89, p. 278-281.
"This Book Belongs to Susan Someone" (on finding a copy of a friend's book,
heavily marked and underlined, in a second-hand bookshop -- for Bill
Kloefkorn). [CimR] (89) O 89, p. 91-92.
"We Never Close." [GeoR] (43:1) Spr 89, p. 14-18.
CLIFF DWELLER
See DWELLER, Cliff
1027. CLIFTON, Harry
"Dag Hammarskjold." [NoDaQ] (57:1) Wint 89, p. 59-60.
"Spring at Thirty." [NoDaQ] (57:1) Wint 89, p. 58-59.
1028. CLIFTON, Lucille
"Eyes" (for Clarence Fountain and The Five Blind Boys of Alabama . . .). [Callaloo]
(12:2, #39) Spr 89, p. 379-381.
"Peeping Tom." [Zyzzyva] (5:2, #18) Sum 89, p. 49.
"Poem Beginning in No and Ending in Yes." [Zyzzyva] (5:2, #18) Sum 89, p. 48.
1029. CLINTON, DeWitt
"Going to Sleep." [BellR] (12:2, #26) Fall 89, p. 10.
"Man Falls with Unfinished Story." [ApalQ] (32) 89, p. 85-87.
"Topeka." [BellR] (12:2, #26) Fall 89, p. 11.
1030. CLINTON, Michelle T.
"009." [Zyzzyva] (5:2, #18) Sum 89, p. 83.
"Solitude Ain't Loneliness." [Zyzzyva] (5:2, #18) Sum 89, p. 82.
"Traditional Postmodern Neo-HooDoo Afra-Centric Sister in a Purple Head Rag
Mourning Death and Cooking." [Zyzzyva] (5:2, #18) Sum 89, p. 85-88.
CLUE, Charlotte de
See DeCLUE, Charlotte
1031. CLUYSENAAR, Anne
"Landfall at Porthceri" (In memory of the Irish craftsmen). [Pequod] (26/27) 89, p.
79-81.
1032. COBEAN, Charles S.
"Finally." [CumbPR] (8:2) Spr 89, p. 68.
1033. COBO BORDA, J. G.
"La Guaira, 1812." [LindLM] (8:2) Ap-Je 89, p. 4.
1034. COCHRAN, Brian
"First." [SouthernPR] (29:2) Fall 89, p. 7.
1035. COCHRAN, Leonard
"The Art of Dying" (for L.M.C.). [SpiritSH] (55) Fall-Wint 89 [90 on cover], p. 12.
"A Bethlehem." [SpiritSH] (54) Spr-Sum 89, p. 1.
"The Deer's Cry" (Variation on a 6th Century Irish Poem). [SpiritSH] (55) Fall-Wint
89 [90 on cover], p. 10.
"Husbandman." [SpiritSH] (55) Fall-Wint 89 [90 on cover], p. 11.
"Museum." [SpiritSH] (55) Fall-Wint 89 [90 on cover], p. 11.
"Second Son." [SpiritSH] (55) Fall-Wint 89 [90 on cover], p. 11.

"The Testing." [ChrC] (106:14) Ap 26, 89, p. 445.
1036. COCHRANE, Shirley
"Long Time Passing" (for my sons). [PassN] (10:2) Sum 89, p. 19.
1037. CODY, Charlie
"Why a Modern Adam Makes the Same Choice." [Plain] (10:1) 89, p. 24-25.
1038. COE, Dina
"Puddles." [MSS] (6:3) 89, p. 202.
"To Fix Those Four." [SenR] (19:2) Fall 89, p. 86-87.
1039. COFER, Judith Ortiz
"The Campesino's Lament." [SouthernPR] (29:1) Spr 89, p. 20.
"Counting." [PassN] (10:2) Sum 89, p. 16.
"Lessons of the Past" (for my daughter). [GeoR] (43:1) Spr 89, p. 157-158.
1040. COFER, Matt
"Contemporary Nomad." [PacificR] (7) 89, p. 51.
1041. COFFMAN, Lisa
"Cathedral." [WestB] (25) 89, p. 15.
1042. COGSWELL, Kelly Jean
"Augusta." [CinPR] (20) Fall 89, p. 48-49.
"Cincinnati." [CinPR] (20) Fall 89, p. 47.
1043. COHEN, Helen Degen
"And the Airplanes Fly." [SpoonRQ] (14:3) Sum 89, p. 23.
"And the Airplanes Fly." [SpoonRQ] (14:4) Fall 89, p. 49.
"And the Snow Kept Falling" (For my sister, who died at the age of two).
[SpoonRQ] (14:3) Sum 89, p. 24-26.
"And the Snow Kept Falling" (For my sister, who died at the age of two).
[SpoonRQ] (14:4) Fall 89, p. 50-52.
"Bad Money" (After seeing *L'Argent*). [SpoonRQ] (14:3) Sum 89, p. 39-40.
"Bad Money" (After seeing *L'Argent*). [SpoonRQ] (14:4) Fall 89, p. 65-66.
"Drought." [SpoonRQ] (14:3) Sum 89, p. 41-42.
"Drought." [SpoonRQ] (14:4) Fall 89, p. 67-68.
"Fourth Grade" (poet in residence, on her back, daydreaming). [SingHM] (16) 89,
p. 31-33.
"Poem for Angelina." [SpoonRQ] (14:3) Sum 89, p. 33-34.
"Poem for Angelina." [SpoonRQ] (14:4) Fall 89, p. 59-60.
"Poem Upon Hearing Part of Marguerite Duras' *The War* on the Radio." [SpoonRQ]
(14:3) Sum 89, p. 31-32.
"Poem Upon Hearing Part of Marguerite Duras' *The War* on the Radio." [SpoonRQ]
(14:4) Fall 89, p. 57-58.
"So Many Parades, Mirenka" (In memory of 1942). [SpoonRQ] (14:3) Sum 89, p.
27-28.
"So Many Parades, Mirenka" (In memory of 1942). [SpoonRQ] (14:4) Fall 89, p.
53-54.
"The Star in the Window Is Yellow." [SpoonRQ] (14:3) Sum 89, p. 26.
"The Star in the Window Is Yellow." [SpoonRQ] (14:4) Fall 89, p. 52.
"There Are Men." [SpoonRQ] (14:3) Sum 89, p. 29-30.
"There Are Men." [SpoonRQ] (14:4) Fall 89, p. 55-56.
"When You Finally Marry." [SpoonRQ] (14:3) Sum 89, p. 35-38.
"When You Finally Marry." [SpoonRQ] (14:4) Fall 89, p. 61-64.
1044. COHEN, Ira
"Blue Train." [Caliban] (7) 89, p. 85.
"Even the King of the Ginza Must Sometimes Sleep" (for Yamaguchi Kenjiro).
[Caliban] (6) 89, p. 80-81.
"Osaka Diary" (for Tetsuya Taguchi). [Caliban] (6) 89, p. 84-85.
"Tokyo Birdhouse" (for Kazuko Shiraishi). [Caliban] (6) 89, p. 82-83.
"White Ashes." [Caliban] (7) 89, p. 86.
1045. COHEN, Marc
"Blue Lonely Dreams." [ParisR] (31:113) Wint 89, p. 92-95.
"Violets in Mapland." [ParisR] (31:113) Wint 89, p. 96.
1046. COHEN, Rhea L.
"These Friends." [NewYorker] (65:24) 31 Jl 89, p. 66.
1047. COHEN, Sascha Benjamin
"This Tree." [BellArk] (5:4) Jl-Ag 89, p. 6.
"Willie." [BellArk] (5:4) Jl-Ag 89, p. 3.
1048. COKINOS, Christopher
"Orbits." [MidwQ] (30:2) Wint 89, p. 200-202.

1049. COLBURN, Don
"In the Workshop after I Read My Poem Aloud." [Iowa] (19:2) Spr-Sum 89, p.
169-170.
1050. COLE, Carole
"Scattered Patterns." [Kalliope] (11:2) 89, p. 57.
1051. COLE, Henri
"American Girl." [OntR] (30) Spr-Sum 89, p. 76-77.
"The Annulment for My Nephew." [Atlantic] (264:6) D 89, p. 78.
"Ascension on Fire Island." [Antaeus] (62) Spr 89, p. 51-52.
"The Best Man." [Colum] (14) 89, p. 39-41.
"Boy's Life." [NewYorker] (65:22) 17 Jl 89, p. 38.
"Caesar." [SouthwR] (74:4) Aut 89, p. 510-511.
"Crayola." [OntR] (30) Spr-Sum 89, p. 75.
"Lines on Seeing the First Color Photograph of Planet Mars." [Boulevard] (4:2, #11)
Fall 89, p. 18-19.
"Lost in Venice" (David Kalstone, 1932-1986). [YaleR] (78:3) Spr 89, p. 462-465.
"O." [Boulevard] (4:2, #11) Fall 89, p. 16-17.
"Tuxedo." [GettyR] (2:4) Aut 89, p. 690-691.
"The Zoo Wheel of Knowledge" (for Christopher Bram and Draper Shreeve).
[GettyR] (2:4) Aut 89, p. 692-693.
1052. COLE, James
"A Guileless Air." [ChatR] (9:3) Spr 89, p. 49.
"The Scholar in the Hospital." [Comm] (116:5) Mr 11, 89, p. 146.
1053. COLE, Michael
"Then" (for Charles Simic). [ArtfulD] (16/17) Fall 89, p. 95.
1054. COLE, Norma
"After Arthur, or Please Let Me Be Misunderstood." [Screens] (1) 89, p. 99-100.
"Erotema." [Acts] (10) 89, p. 41-47.
"It Then" (Part I, tr. of Danielle Collobert). [Temblor] (10) 89, p. 175-181.
1055. COLE, Richard
"Quiet Days Beside the Ocean." [DenQ] (23:3/4) Wint-Spr 89, p. 84-85.
1056. COLEMAN, Jane
"Neighbors." [WestB] (23) 89, p. 11.
1057. COLEMAN, John
"Postcard of My Father." [WestB] (24) 89, p. 49.
1058. COLEMAN, Mary Ann
"Still Life with Rain and Nectarines." [NegC] (9:1) 89, p. 84-85.
1059. COLEMAN, Victor
"Brief Gaudy Hour." [CapilR] (1st series: 50) 89, p. 32.
"Honeymoon Suite" (Excerpt, w. David Bolduc). [CapilR] (1st series: 50) 89, p.
27-31.
"The Swimming Pool." [CapilR] (1st series: 50) 89, p. 33-34.
1060. COLEMAN, Wanda
"AI 1968." [Obs] (4:1) Spr 89, p. 23.
"America." [Bound] (16:2/3) Wint-Spr 89, p. 253.
"American Sonnet." [BlackALF] (23:3) Fall 89, p. 556.
"Becuz of My Blood" (for P. Armando Fernandez). [Bound] (16:2/3) Wint-Spr 89,
p. 253.
"Black Isis" (for Michael Palmer). [BlackALF] (23:3) Fall 89, p. 557.
"Blue Period." [Contact] (9:53/54/55) Sum-Fall 89, p. 58-59.
"Blues for the Man on Sax (2)." [Bound] (16:2/3) Wint-Spr 89, p. 254.
"Bojack Sam Dealin' Man." [BlackALF] (23:3) Fall 89, p. 555.
"Figueroa." [Contact] (9:53/54/55) Sum-Fall 89, p. 57.
"The First Day of Spring 1985" (polemic for Tim & Kathy Joyce). [Contact]
(9:53/54/55) Sum-Fall 89, p. 60-61.
"The First Day of Spring 1985" (polemic for Tim & Kathy Joyce). [Obs] (4:1) Spr
89, p. 20-22.
"Hollywood Theology." [Contact] (9:53/54/55) Sum-Fall 89, p. 62.
"Homage to an Old White Lady Grown Ill." [Obs] (4:1) Spr 89, p. 22-23.
"How to Pop a Roach." [Obs] (4:1) Spr 89, p. 24.
"The Midas Touch." [Contact] (9:53/54/55) Sum-Fall 89, p. 57.
"Prove It Why Don't You." [BlackALF] (23:3) Fall 89, p. 556.
"Steel." [Contact] (9:53/54/55) Sum-Fall 89, p. 56.
"They'll Starve You" (from me to me). [Contact] (9:53/54/55) Sum-Fall 89, p.
54-55.
"Treadmill." [Contact] (9:53/54/55) Sum-Fall 89, p. 59.

1061. COLETTA, Caroline
"He dressed in high heels and polyester skirts." [ChangingM] (20) Wint-Spr 89, p. 21.
1062. COLEY, John
"The House." [JamesWR] (5:2 [i.e. 6:2]) Wint 89, p. 14.
"Landscape and History." [JamesWR] (6:4) Sum 89, p. 4.
1063. COLLAZO, Hiram
"Mas Alla de los Pajaros." [Mairena] (11:27) 89, p. 61.
"Viejo Capitan." [Mairena] (11:27) 89, p. 61.
1064. COLLIER, Michael
"The Cave." [PartR] (56:3) Sum 89, p. 446-447.
"The Heavy Light of Shifting Stars." [MissouriR] (12:1) 89, p. 149.
"The Lights." [IndR] (12:3) Sum 89, p. 55-56.
"Night Swimming." [AmerPoR] (18:4) Jl-Ag 89, p. 31.
1065. COLLINS, Andrea
"Inez." [PraS] (63:3) Fall 89, p. 57-59.
"Shooting Flamingos Near Buenos Aires." [PraS] (63:3) Fall 89, p. 55-57.
1066. COLLINS, Billy
"Candle Hat." [Field] (41) Fall 89, p. 100-101.
"The Dead." [Boulevard] (4:2, #11) Fall 89, p. 177.
"The Dead." [Jacaranda] (4:1) Spr-Sum 89, p. 3.
"First Reader." [Poetry] (153:6) Mr 89, p. 327-328.
"The Hunt." [FreeL] (1) 89, p. 6.
"Koan in the Rain." [Jacaranda] (4:1) Spr-Sum 89, p. 4.
"The Last Man on Earth." [Jacaranda] (4:1) Spr-Sum 89, p. 4.
"Last Sunday in October." [SouthernPR] (29:1) Spr 89, p. 57.
"The Norton Anthology of English Literature." [Jacaranda] (4:1) Spr-Sum 89, p. 2-3.
"The Perfect Drink." [FreeL] (1) 89, p. 5.
"Purity." [Jacaranda] (4:1) Spr-Sum 89, p. 1-2.
"A Wonder of the World." [Field] (41) Fall 89, p. 99.
1067. COLLINS, Floyd
"Piano Player." [GettyR] (2:3) Sum 89, p. 547.
1068. COLLINS, Jane
"This Is About Romance." [PaintedB] (37) 89, p. 83.
1069. COLLINS, Judy
"At the Streamliner Diner." [BellArk] (5:5) S-O 89, p. 1.
1070. COLLINS, Martha
"2 A.M." [Journal] (12:2) Fall-Wint 88-89, p. 40.
"Beech." [Journal] (12:2) Fall-Wint 88-89, p. 41.
"Cover." [Journal] (12:2) Fall-Wint 88-89, p. 39.
"Dickinson." [FiveFR] (7) 89, p. 59.
"Morning." [FiveFR] (7) 89, p. 58.
"On Your Wall." [CarolQ] (41:3) Spr 89, p. 19.
"Wherever You Find It." [Ploughs] (15:4) Wint 89-90, p. 36-37.
1071. COLLINS, Robert
"Deluge." [SoCoast] (5) Spr 88, p. 38-39.
1072. COLLOBERT, Danielle
"It Then" (Part I, tr. by Norma Cole). [Temblor] (10) 89, p. 175-181.
1073. COLON RUIZ, José O.
"La Espera." [Mairena] (11:27) 89, p. 91.
1074. COLON SANTIAGO, José Luis
"Si fuera tu voz como una casa." [Mairena] (11:27) 89, p. 74.
1075. COLTMAN, Paul
"Mistress." [CumbPR] (9:1) Fall 89, p. 30.
1076. CONDE, Gil Peres
"Song of Thy My Money" (Galician-Portuguese Troubadour poem, tr. by Richard Zenith). [SenR] (19:1) 89, p. 80.
1077. CONDINI, Ned
"If Only" (tr. of Mario Luzi). [Trans] (21) Spr 89, p. 186.
"Mother and Son" (tr. of Mario Luzi). [Trans] (21) Spr 89, p. 187.
1078. CONKLIN, Dennis
"Saying that he knows." [FiveFR] (7) 89, p. 15.
1079. CONKLING, Helen
"The Enemy." [PraS] (63:4) Wint 89, p. 46-47.
"Midsummer." [PraS] (63:4) Wint 89, p. 45-46.

"Transient." [PraS] (63:4) Wint 89, p. 47-48.
1080. CONN, Christopher
"The Convenience Store." [KanQ] (21:1/2) Wint-Spr 89, p. 148.
1081. CONN, Jan
"Fusion." [Quarry] (38:1) Wint 89, p. 55-56.
"In This Photograph of My Parents and Their Two Eldest Children." [Quarry] (38:1)
Wint 89, p. 52-53.
"Separation." [Quarry] (38:1) Wint 89, p. 54.
1082. CONN, Jeanne
"Monologue: Warden-Controlled." [AlphaBS] (5) Jl 89, p. 39.
"The Site." [AlphaBS] (5) Jl 89, p. 38.
1083. CONN, Jeffrey D.
"Undercover." [EngJ] (78:2) F 89, p. 97.
1084. CONNELL, Frances Garrett
"Tashkurghan, Afghanistan" (September 1973-June 1975). [Pig] (15) 88, p. 26-27.
1085. CONNELLY, Karen
"Family Reunions." [AntigR] (79) Aut 89, p. 24.
"For Junwei Qi, Who Went Home." [AntigR] (79) Aut 89, p. 25-26.
"The Singing Beggars, Chiang Mai." [Event] (18:2) Sum 89, p. 61.
1086. CONNOLLY, Brian (Brian A)
"Hunns Lake Poems" (5 poems). [Lactuca] (12) F 89, p. 66-67.
"An Owl Calls." [ChamLR] (2:2, #4) Spr 89, p. 27.
1087. CONNOLLY, Geraldine
"Elk Horn, Montana." [WestB] (25) 89, p. 100.
"Ghost Ranch." [WestB] (25) 89, p. 101.
"Our Mother Tongue." [DenQ] (24:2) Fall 89, p. 36.
1088. CONNOLLY, J. F.
"God Watching." [CapeR] (24:2) Fall 89, p. 3.
"Growing Up in a Funeral Home." [CapeR] (24:2) Fall 89, p. 4.
1089. CONNOLLY, Tristanne
"The Old Man and His Orchids." [AntigR] (77/78) Spr-Sum 89, p. 76.
1090. CONNOR-BEY, Brenda
"Crossroad of the Serpent" (for Quint-Rose and Janemarie). [Obs] (3:3) Wint 88, p.
107-108.
"He Who Turns His Back Is Lost" (for Albert). [Obs] (3:3) Wint 88, p. 106-107.
"Maria Louisa" (for Theresa). [Obs] (3:3) Wint 88, p. 104-106.
1091. CONNORS, Marie
"Sister of Mercy." [SoCoast] (7) Spr-Fall 89, p. 29.
1092. CONOLEY, Gillian
"O'Keeffe's Black Iris." [PoetryE] (28) Fall 89, p. 81.
"The Parrots." [Crazy] (37) Wint 89, p. 50-51.
"Skinhead." [GettyR] (2:3) Sum 89, p. 509-510.
"Tall Stranger." [DenQ] (23:3/4) Wint-Spr 89, p. 12-13.
"Walt Whitman in the Car Lot, Repo or Used." [NoAmR] (274:2) Je 89, p. 56-57.
"A Window to the Private Life." [GettyR] (2:3) Sum 89, p. 507-508.
1093. CONOVER, Carl
"The Black Tulip." [Journal] (13:1) Spr-Sum 89, p. 24.
"Cobwebs." [Bound] (16:2/3) Wint-Spr 89, p. 174.
"The Glover's Son." [NewRep] (201:5) 31 Jl 89, p. 34.
"Looking at Narcissus" (after the statue by Cellini). [SouthernHR] (23:1) Wint 89,
p. 63.
"Stalking the Wild Marigolds in C Minor." [Outbr] (20) 89, p. 75.
"Woman with a Book" (after Braque). [Bound] (16:2/3) Wint-Spr 89, p. 174.
1094. CONRAN, Tony
"Elegy for the Welsh Dead, in the Falkland Islands, 1982." [NoDaQ] (57:2) Spr 89,
insert p. 52-53.
"Gooseberries" (for Mike Donahue, killed in a car crash August 1985). [Stand]
(30:2) Spr 89, p. 42-46.
"Research." [NoDaQ] (57:2) Spr 89, insert p. 54.
1095. CONSTANTINE, David
"The Pitman's Garden" (For Bill and Diane Williamson). [Verse] (6:2) Je 89, p. 27.
1096. CONTE, Giuseppe
"After Marx, April" (tr. by Lawrence Venuti). [Poetry] (155:1/2) O-N 89, p. 129.
"Dopo Marx, Aprile." [Poetry] (155:1/2) O-N 89, p. 128.
"Lei Mi Diceva Proprio Cosi" (Excerpt). [Poetry] (155:1/2) O-N 89, p. 126.
"This Is Exactly What She Told Me" (Excerpt, tr. by Lawrence Venuti). [Poetry]

(155:1/2) O-N 89, p. 127.
"Trans-Europe-Express" (in Italian). [Poetry] (155:1/2) O-N 89, p. 130.
"Trans-Europe-Express" (tr. by Lawrence Venuti). [Poetry] (155:1/2) O-N 89, p. 131.
1097. CONTI, Edmund
"Tennyson, Anyone?" [NegC] (9:1) 89, p. 36.
1098. CONTOGENIS, Constantine
"Iron, We Were Told" (Three Poems by Kisang, tr. of Jin-ock, w. Wolhee Choe). [BelPoJ] (39:4) Sum 89, p. 32.
"The Large Beak Finches" (tr. of anonymous Korean poem, w. Wolhee Choe). [ChiR] (36:3/4) 89, p. 18.
"Let My Cassia Boat" (Three Poems by Kisang, tr. of Kae-ju, w. Wolhee Choe). [BelPoJ] (39:4) Sum 89, p. 33.
"Old Plum Trees" (tr. of Mae-wha, w. Wolhee Choe). [ChiR] (36:3/4) 89, p. 19.
"What Blight" (Three Poems by Kisang, tr. of Mae-wha, w. Wolhee Choe). [BelPoJ] (39:4) Sum 89, p. 32.
1099. COOK, Jane W.
"Apology to Cyndi Lauper." [DeKalbLAJ] (22:1/4) 89, p. 48.
1100. COOK, Jeanne
"The Old Bards Say" (tr. of Heberto Padilla, w. Anthony Kerrigan). [Salm] (82/83) Spr-Sum 89, p. 320.
"A Swim Off Havana" (tr. of Heberto Padilla, w. Anthony Kerrigan). [Salm] (82/83) Spr-Sum 89, p. 320.
1101. COOK-LYNN, Elizabeth
"My Flight." [Contact] (9:53/54/55) Sum-Fall 89, p. 51.
"Tourists Shouldn't Write Home That Indians Aren't 'Real' Anymore" (a poem for the Crown Butte Singers). [Contact] (9:53/54/55) Sum-Fall 89, p. 52.
"Widowhood." [Contact] (9:53/54/55) Sum-Fall 89, p. 53.
1102. COOKE, Robert P.
"A Week Off, Mathesen Bay, Canada, Fishing Trip." [WritersF] (15) Fall 89, p. 67.
1103. COOKSHAW, Marlene
"Miniota, Manitoba." [Event] (18:2) Sum 89, p. 24-25.
"Quarter Section." [Event] (18:2) Sum 89, p. 26.
"Sempre Amore." [MissR] (17:3, #51), p. 36-37.
1104. COOLEY, Dennis
"I Think." [Rampike] (6:3) 88, p. 39.
"Perishable Light." [Quarry] (38:1) Wint 89, p. 100.
"Sun Is." [Quarry] (38:1) Wint 89, p. 102.
1105. COOLEY, Peter
"Auspices." [WilliamMR] (27) 89, p. 76.
"Evensong." [DenQ] (24:2) Fall 89, p. 37.
"Ground Fog." [WilliamMR] (27) 89, p. 7.
"In the Warehouse District." [ColR] (NS 16:2) Fall 89-Wint 90, p. 71.
"Little Ode." [AntR] (47:3) Sum 89, p. 324.
"One Step, Two Step." [ColR] (NS 16:2) Fall 89-Wint 90, p. 70.
"To a Mockingbird." [WilliamMR] (27) 89, p. 75.
"Wormwood." [DenQ] (24:2) Fall 89, p. 38.
"Wunderkind." [WilliamMR] (27) 89, p. 74.
1106. COOLIDGE, Clark
"Boat House Yards" (for Bob Perelman). [Screens] (1) 89, p. 156-161.
"The Devil's Slide." [Sonora] (17) Spr-Sum 89, p. 20.
"Dodge's Bluff, Grand River Canyon." [Sonora] (17) Spr-Sum 89, p. 19.
"Echo." [Witness] (2:4) Wint 88, p. 108.
"The Going On." [Witness] (2:4) Wint 88, p. 109.
"In Nora's House with Rilke's Apollo." [Talisman] (3) Fall 89, p. 64-72.
"In the Rooms of Guston." [Sulfur] (9:1, #24) Spr 89, p. 41-45.
"Registers (People in All)" (Selections: 1-8). [Temblor] (10) 89, p. 59-67.
1107. COONEY, Ellen
"Chemin de Jerusalem." [SmPd] (26:1, #75) Wint 89, p. 10-11.
1108. COOPER, Allan
"The Black Flying Insect." [HighP] (4:2) Fall 89, p. 96-97.
"The Mud Dauber Wasp." [HighP] (4:2) Fall 89, p. 94-95.
1109. COOPER, Evin Nelle
"The Ice Web" (Mainstreet Elementary Poetry Contest, 5th Grade, 1st Place). [DeKalbLAJ] (22:1/4) 89, p. 104.

1110. COOPER, Jane
    "The Winter Road." [Ploughs] (15:4) Wint 89-90, p. 38-41.
1111. COOPER, Lisa
    "Beacon." [MidAR] (9:2) 89, p. 153.
    "The Winding Room." [SouthernPR] (29:1) Spr 89, p. 55-56.
1112. COOPER, Lora
    "Demeter in a Garden State." [US1] (22/23) Spr 89, p. 46.
1113. COOPER, M. Truman (Marsha Truman)
    "By a Disappearing Path." [Kalliope] (10:1/2) 88, p. 29.
    "Common Rue." [Blueline] (10:1/2) 89, p. 85.
    "Contractions." [SingHM] (16) 89, p. 92-93.
    "Fearing Paris." [RiverC] (9:1) Spr 89, p. 35.
    "Going to the Wall." [KanQ] (21:1/2) Wint-Spr 89, p. 240.
    "Lemons." [CentR] (33:3) Sum 89, p. 244-245.
    "Living without Euclid." [Kalliope] (10:1/2) 88, p. 27-28.
    "Momentum." [Kalliope] (10:1/2) 88, p. 26-27.
    "On Judging Children." [RiverC] (9:1) Spr 89, p. 36-37.
    "Opening the New Pool." [KanQ] (21:1/2) Wint-Spr 89, p. 239.
1114. COOPER, Mary
    "Owl Ears." [Obs] (2:1) Spr 87, p. 82.
1115. COOPER, Michele F.
    "Hey, Man, Where's My Lines." [WorldO] (22:1/2) Fall-Wint 87-88, c90, p. 28-29.
1116. COOPER, Reid
    "And there, turning her motor over slowly." [Writer] (102:12) D 89, p. 25.
1117. COOPER, Scottie Joel
    "Seraphyre." [EmeraldCR] (1989) c1988, p. 125.
1118. COOPERMAN, Robert
    "Ajax in Hades." [OxfordM] (5:2) Fall-Wint 89, p. 15-16.
    "Assent." [Outbr] (20) 89, p. 7.
    "Byron Comes to Terms with Shelley Concerning Claire Clairmont, August 1816."
        [SoCoast] (6) Fall 88, p. 38-39.
    "Cut Dead." [Comm] (116:9) My 5, 89, p. 266.
    "Distant Estella." [CumbPR] (9:1) Fall 89, p. 51-52.
    "Dream." [PoetC] (20:2) Wint 89, p. 13-14.
    "Early December Afternoon." [Wind] (19:64) 89, p. 6-7.
    "The Emigrants' Buffalo Hunt." [CimR] (87) Ap 89, p. 75-76.
    "Emmett Moore, the First Man to Use a Telephone in Silver Dollar." [Wind] (19:64)
        89, p. 5-6.
    "Eva Kanturkova in the Rezne Prison, Czechoslovakia." [ChatR] (9:2) Wint 89, p.
        40-41.
    "The Executioner's Downfall." [SoCoast] (5) Spr 88, p. 26.
    "Extravagant Endings" (The Phillips Award, Fall/Winter 1988/89). [StoneC]
        (16:3/4) Spr-Sum 89, p. 2.
    "Filler." [StoneC] (17:1/2) Fall-Wint 89-90, p. 14.
    "For Your Thirty-Seventh Birthday." [InterPR] (15:2) Fall 89, p. 90.
    "The Frail Magic of Ice." [SwampR] (1:4) Sum 89, p. 13.
    "From the Ballad, 'The Railroad Boy'." [DeKalbLAJ] (22:1/4) 89, p. 49.
    "Henry James and the Price of Art." [AntigR] (76) Wint 89, p. 62-63.
    "Hers Was a Beauty." [Lactuca] (13) N 89, p. 40.
    "The Honourable Robert Leeson Answers the Charges of Percy Bysshe Shelley."
        [SoCoast] (7) Spr-Fall 89, p. 16-17.
    "In Later Life, Fanny Brawne Remembers John Keats." [AntigR] (77/78) Spr-Sum
        89, p. 191-192.
    "The Instruments of Logic" (for my mother). [InterPR] (15:2) Fall 89, p. 91.
    "Jack Tanner, After His Attack on Shelley's House, Tremadoc, Wales, 1813."
        [SoCoast] (7) Spr-Fall 89, p. 18-19.
    "John Keats Remembers His First Meeting with the Family of Leigh Hunt."
        [InterPR] (15:2) Fall 89, p. 93-94.
    "Ladybird Beetles." [SpoonRQ] (14:3) Sum 89, p. 43.
    "The Man Who Killed Himself by Jumping into Niagara Falls." [SoCaR] (22:1) Fall
        89, p. 70.
    "Mary McCormick Talks to a Lawyer, Five Years After Being Seduced by Three
        Priests." [LitR] (32:2) Wint 89, p. 169.
    "The Measurement of Love." [Poem] (61) My 89, p. 11.
    "Mrs. Lynch Talks of Mary McCormick, the Girl Who Accused Three Priests of
        Seducing Her." [LitR] (32:2) Wint 89, p. 170.

"Mrs. Miller Talks of the Priests Who Seduced Mary McCormick." [LitR] (32:2) Wint 89, p. 171.
"The Music of Motion." [SpoonRQ] (14:3) Sum 89, p. 19.
"My Mother, Ann." [Poem] (61) My 89, p. 12.
"Odysseus Recalls Cassandra." [OxfordM] (5:2) Fall-Wint 89, p. 14-15.
"Orchids" (for Hugh Ruppersburg). [HampSPR] Wint 89, p. 32.
"Percy Bysshe Shelley, After the Night Attack, Tremodoc, Wales, 1813." [SoCoast] (7) Spr-Fall 89, p. 14-15.
"Pranks." [DeKalbLAJ] (22:1/4) 89, p. 50.
"Saint Rose of Lima Catholic School." [SmPd] (26:3 #77) Fall 89, p. 19.
"Scott's Ghost Pony of the South Pole" (for Bud Fogerty). [StoneC] (17:1/2) Fall-Wint 89-90, p. 15.
"The Sculptor's Art." [Grain] (17:3) Fall 89, p. 12.
"St. Patrick's Day in Grade School." [AntigR] (76) Wint 89, p. 63.
"Theodora, Empress of the Eastern Empire, A.D. 533." [InterPR] (15:2) Fall 89, p. 91-92.
"Thomas Jefferson Hogg Rationalizes His Failed Seduction of Harriet Westbrook Shelley, 1811." [BellR] (12:2, #26) Fall 89, p. 32-33.
"Uncle Phil's Saxophone." [SoCaR] (22:1) Fall 89, p. 69.
"The Visions of the Nun Hildegarde of Bingen, 1098-1179." [CapeR] (24:2) Fall 89, p. 12.
"The Wild Boys of the Locker Room." [SoCaR] (22:1) Fall 89, p. 68.
"Years Later, Coleridge Remembers Meeting Keats on Hamstead Heath." [NegC] (9:1) 89, p. 38-39.

1119. COPE, Clarence E.
"Autumn." [Wind] (19:64) 89, p. 8.
1120. COPE, Steven R.
"Homecoming." [Wind] (19:64) 89, p. 9-10.
"Nightwalker." [CinPR] (20) Fall 89, p. 42-43.
"Of Whitman, Reclining." [KanQ] (21:1/2) Wint-Spr 89, p. 134.
"Touting the Flag." [AnotherCM] (19) 89, p. 30.
1121. COPELLO, Fernando
"La Frontera." [CuadP] (7:19) S-D 89, p. 71-73.
1122. CORBETT, Michael
"Maximum Sanctuary." [MSS] (6:3) 89, p. 139.
"Tarsane." [SlipS] (9) 89, p. 20.
1123. CORBETT, William
"9 April" (drawing by Philip Guston). [Notus] (4:2) Fall 89, p. 6.
"12 April" (drawing by Philip Guston). [Notus] (4:2) Fall 89, p. 7.
"14 February Valentine's Day" (drawing by Philip Guston). [Notus] (4:2) Fall 89, p. 4.
"14 May" (drawing by Philip Guston). [Notus] (4:2) Fall 89, p. 8.
"Easter" (drawing by Philip Guston). [Notus] (4:2) Fall 89, p. 5.
"Ed." [Notus] (4:1) Spr 89, p. 8-9.
"February 29, 1988." [Agni] (28) 89, p. 51-54.
"Jack Gilbert." [NewAW] (5) Fall 89, p. 100.
"The Kid With." [NewAW] (5) Fall 89, p. 101-102.
"Memorial Day" (drawing by Philip Guston). [Notus] (4:2) Fall 89, p. 9.
"A Palimpsest." [Notus] (4:1) Spr 89, p. 11.
"The Richard Nixon Story" (drawing by Philip Guston). [Notus] (4:2) Fall 89, p. 10.
"Rosso Fortuna." [NewAW] (5) Fall 89, p. 103.
"Trotting Horse." [Notus] (4:1) Spr 89, p. 10.
1124. CORDING, Robert
"Gestures." [RiverC] (10:1) Fall 89, p. 68-69.
"Going to Sea in a Sieve." [Poetry] (154:6) S 89, p. 335-337.
"Local Song." [RiverC] (10:1) Fall 89, p. 66-67.
"September 3." [Poetry] (154:6) S 89, p. 332-333.
"Thoor Ballylee." [Poetry] (154:6) S 89, p. 333-335.
1125. COREY, Chet
"Bath Waters." [KanQ] (21:1/2) Wint-Spr 89, p. 72.
"Visitors." [Plain] (9:3) Spr 89, p. 22.
1126. COREY, Stephen
"For the Spreading Laurel Tree" (to my daughter Heather). [LaurelR] (23:1) Wint 89, p. 107.
"Hunger." [KenR] (NS 11:3) Sum 89, p. 53-54.

"I Find That Mother Begins." [LaurelR] (23:1) Wint 89, p. 108-109.
"Town and Country Losses." [LaurelR] (23:1) Wint 89, p. 105-106.
1127. CORINO, Karl
"Bengali, 12/31" (tr. by John Linthicum). [LitR] (33:1) Fall 89, p. 42.
"The Divorcée" (tr. by John Linthicum). [LitR] (33:1) Fall 89, p. 42.
"Grape and Olive" (tr. by John Linthicum). [LitR] (33:1) Fall 89, p. 41.
"In the South" (tr. by John Linthicum). [LitR] (33:1) Fall 89, p. 41.
"Lapsed" (tr. by John Linthicum). [LitR] (33:1) Fall 89, p. 43.
"The Unexpected" (tr. by John Linthicum). [LitR] (33:1) Fall 89, p. 43.
1128. CORMAN, Cid
"A Batch of Late Poems" (9 poems, tr. of Kusano Shimpei, w. Kamaike Susumu).
    [Sulfur] (9:1, #24) Spr 89, p. 60-69.
"The Friends Who Know Me" (tr. of T'ao Ch'ien). [LitR] (32:3) Spr 89, p. 379.
"Moving I" (tr. of T'ao Ch'ien). [LitR] (32:3) Spr 89, p. 380.
"Moving II" (tr. of T'ao Ch'ien). [LitR] (32:3) Spr 89, p. 380.
"My Home Here" (tr. of T'ao Ch'ien). [LitR] (32:3) Spr 89, p. 379.
"Of" (Selections: 2 poems). [TriQ] (76) Fall 89, p. 111-112.
"The Past at Yüeh" (tr. of Li Po). [LitR] (32:3) Spr 89, p. 376.
"A Sequence" (for Pat & Marla). [Notus] (4:1) Spr 89, p. 12-13.
"Set Piece" (tr. of Li Po). [LitR] (32:3) Spr 89, p. 376.
"Sundown at Shih-hao and the" (tr. of Tu Fu). [LitR] (32:3) Spr 89, p. 378.
"Ten Years Living Dying Alone" (tr. of Su Tung-p'o). [LitR] (32:3) Spr 89, p. 375.
"We Drink" (tr. of Li Po). [LitR] (32:3) Spr 89, p. 377.
"Yea" (Selections: 4 poems). [TriQ] (76) Fall 89, p. 109-110.
"Young Strong and Willing" (tr. of Li Po). [LitR] (32:3) Spr 89, p. 376.
CORMIER-SHEKERJIAN, Regina de
    See DeCORMIER-SHEKERJIAN, Regina
1129. CORN, Alfred
"After Rilke." [Nat] (249:5) 7-14 Ag 89, p. 176.
"Law of Reciprocal Force." [CinPR] (20) Fall 89, p. 19.
"Somerset Alcaics." [Ploughs] (15:4) Wint 89-90, p. 42.
"A Village Walk under Snow." [NewYorker] (64:47) 9 Ja 89, p. 28.
1130. CORRIE, Daniel
"Hourglass Parables." [SouthernR] (25:3) Sum 89, p. 628-629.
1131. CORRIGAN, Paul
"November Beeches." [Blueline] (10:1/2) 89, p. 37-38.
1132. CORRINGTON, John William
"Old Man Among His Flowers." [SouthernR] (25:3) Sum 89, p. 595-596.
1133. CORSERI, Gary
"Destruction of Poetry." [SouthernHR] (23:3) Sum 89, p. 215.
"Girl in a Photo." [ChatR] (9:4) Sum 89, p. 64.
1134. CORSO, Gregory
"30th Year Dream." [AmerPoR] (18:6) N-D 89, p. 56.
"The Day After Humankind -- a Fragment" (Night of 5th-6th March, 1960).
    [AlphaBS] (6) Wint 89-90, p. 40.
"Down Old Greece Way." [Contact] (9:53/54/55) Sum-Fall 89, p. 35.
"Last Night in Milano" (Night of 5th-6th March, 1960). [AlphaBS] (6) Wint 89-90,
    p. 40.
1135. CORWIN, Phillip
"American Thoughts at Xi'an." [KanQ] (21:1/2) Wint-Spr 89, p. 181.
1136. CORY, Jim
"Last Days of Oscar Wilde." [WormR] (29:1, #113) 89, p. 36.
"Memoir: Spring, '77." [EvergreenC] (4:4) Sum 89, p. 27-28.
"Part of the Game" (To: Phoebe Penrod, Faculty Advisor). [EvergreenC] (4:4) Sum
    89, p. 4-5.
"Taxi." [WormR] (29:1, #113) 89, p. 36-37.
1137. COSENS, Susan M.
"Lilies." [YellowS] (30) Sum 89, p. 8.
"My Womb Fills with Light." [RagMag] (7:1) 89, p. 10.
1138. COSGROVE, Ed
"Migration." [Shen] (39:4) Wint 89, p. 20.
1139. COSHOW, Karen
"The Passive Act of Self-Forgiving." [BellArk] (5:3) My-Je 89, p. 20.
1140. COSIER, T.
"Photo of the Schoolmarm at Owl's Head." [Blueline] (10:1/2) 89, p. 16.
"Teacher at White Lake." [CapeR] (24:1) Spr 89, p. 35.

1141. COSTANZO, Gerald
"Washington Park." [PraS] (63:4) Wint 89, p. 25-26.
1142. COTA, Raúl Antonio
"Of Fierce Origin" (tr. by John Oliver Simon). [Caliban] (7) 89, p. 78.
"The Possible Myth" (tr. by John Oliver Simon). [Caliban] (7) 89, p. 79-81.
1143. COUGHLIN, K.
"Oarswoman." [Hawai'iR] (13:2, #26) Sum 89, p. 69.
1144. COULEHAN, Jack
"Banana Bread." [KanQ] (21:1/2) Wint-Spr 89, p. 218.
"Building Beds" (For Eric Cassell). [NegC] (9:1) 89, p. 46-47.
"The Dead Wait Like Pelicans" (after *El Fatasma* by Enrique Anderson Imbert).
[NegC] (9:1) 89, p. 52.
"Don't Be Afraid, Gringo." [CumbPR] (9:1) Fall 89, p. 15-16.
"For the First Time." [PraS] (63:4) Wint 89, p. 87-88.
"The Lima Bean." [CentR] (33:3) Sum 89, p. 246.
"The Power of Inclination." [PraS] (63:4) Wint 89, p. 88-89.
"Sweathouse." [NegC] (9:1) 89, p. 48-49.
"These Shards Are Wrist Bones." [NegC] (9:1) 89, p. 50-51.
1145. COULTER, Page
"Equilibrium." [KanQ] (21:1/2) Wint-Spr 89, p. 102.
"New England Weather." [KanQ] (21:1/2) Wint-Spr 89, p. 101.
COURCY, Lynne H. de
See DeCOURCY, Lynne H.
1146. COWING, Sue
"Artemisia Gentileschi: Self-Portrait, 1632." [ChamLR] (3:1, #5) Fall 89, p. 95-96.
"Corona Smith's Elevator Adventure." [WormR] (29:4, #116) 89, p. 106-107.
"Coronoa Smith Buys Violets." [WormR] (29:4, #116) 89, p. 106.
"'Infant Nursing,' Sketch by Paula Modersohn-Becker." [VirQR] (65:4) Aut 89, p.
657.
"Painting One Another." [VirQR] (65:4) Aut 89, p. 656-657.
1147. COX, Andrew
"Around These Parts." [BrooklynR] (5) 88, p. 50-51.
"Call In, That Number Is." [LaurelR] (23:2) Sum 89, p. 62.
"The Evangelical." [Witness] (3:1) Spr 89, p. 41.
"Funny." [RiverS] (29) [89], p. 11-12.
"How've Y'all Been." [LaurelR] (23:2) Sum 89, p. 61.
"In Your Face." [RiverS] (29) [89], p. 6-8.
"Nothing Changes Like the Weather in Missouri." [RiverS] (29) [89], p. 9-10.
1148. COX, Ed
"These Two: Ezra and Agnes" (Dedicated to Rudd Fleming). [WashR] (15:3) O-N
89, p. 16-18.
1149. COX, Mark
"Body Hair." [CimR] (89) O 89, p. 89-90.
"Fugitive Love." [NoAmR] (274:3) S 89, p. 42-43.
"The Good War." [CimR] (89) O 89, p. 85-88.
"The Lido." [AmerPoR] (18:5) S-O 89, p. 47.
"Long-Lighted Evenings in the Garden." [BrooklynR] (6) 89, p. 48.
"Nothing Like Us Ever Was." [AmerPoR] (18:5) S-O 89, p. 47.
"Sorrow Bread." [Crazy] (36) Spr 89, p. 37-39.
1150. COX, Wayne
"So Solemn" (tr. of Miquel Martí i Pol, w. Lourdes Manye i Martí). [Shen] (39:3)
Fall 89, p. 46.
"Things" (tr. of Miquel Martí i Pol, w. Lourdes Manye i Martí). [Shen] (39:3) Fall
89, p. 46.
CRABBE, Chris Wallace
See WALLACE-CRABBE, Chris
1151. CRAGO, William
"Canadian Vacation." [Wind] (19:65) 89, p. 33.
1152. CRAIG, Christine
"Diary of a Disturbance, February 1985." [Callaloo] (12:2, #39) Spr 89, p. 288-289.
1153. CRAIG, Ford M.
"At 40." [Plain] (10:1) 89, p. 27.
1154. CRAMER, Steven
"The Battle of the Bands" (For Thom Swiss). [Poetry] (154:6) S 89, p. 317-318.
"Creosote." [IndR] (12:3) Sum 89, p. 43.
"First Kiss." [IndR] (12:3) Sum 89, p. 44-45.

"For the Bullies of West Morris High." [Poetry] (154:6) S 89, p. 318-319.
"The Haircut." [NewEngR] (11:4) Sum 89, p. 418-419.
"Hibiscus" (John Cramer, 1916-1987). [PraS] (63:3) Fall 89, p. 83-84.
"The Hotel at Mount Freedom." [IndR] (12:3) Sum 89, p. 46-47.
"A Sudden Change in Temperature" (John Cramer, 1916-1987). [GrahamHR] (12)
    Spr 89, p. 90.
"Terrorists." [GrahamHR] (12) Spr 89, p. 93-94.
"Truce." [PraS] (63:3) Fall 89, p. 83.
"The World Book." [GrahamHR] (12) Spr 89, p. 91-92.
1155. CRAPSEY, Adelaide
"Blue Hyacinths." [PraS] (63:4) Wint 89, p. 117.
"Lunatick." [PraS] (63:4) Wint 89, p. 117.
1156. CRATE, Joan
"The Appearances of Fresh Fruit." [Grain] (17:1) Spr 89, p. 80.
1157. CRAVEN, Gary B.
"Shake a Mean Pan of Eggs." [SoCoast] (6) Fall 88, p. 55.
1158. CRAWFORD, Robert
"For My Daughter." [NegC] (9:1) 89, p. 63.
"Photonics." [Verse] (6:1) Mr 89, p. 18.
"A Scottish Assembly." [Verse] (6:1) Mr 89, p. 18.
1159. CRAWFORD, Tom
"Farmer Creek." [PoetryE] (28) Fall 89, p. 17.
"The Franklin Expedition / 1855." [PoetryE] (28) Fall 89, p. 19-20.
"Wave." [PoetryE] (28) Fall 89, p. 18.
1160. CREAMER, Colleen
"Anyway." [PaintedB] (37) 89, p. 77.
1161. CREELEY, Robert
"Eight Plus" (Inscriptions for Eight Bollards at 7th & Figueroa, Los Angeles, for
    James Surls). [Temblor] (9) 89, p. 3-6.
"Ever Since Hitler." [Acts] (10) 89, p. 31.
"Fading Light." [Conjunc] (14) 89, p. 260.
"For J.L." [PaintedB] (39) 89, p. 6.
"Help." [RiverS] (28) 89, p. 33.
"Later" (for Bill Bronk). [Talisman] (2) Spr 89, p. 9.
"Oh." [Antaeus] (62) Spr 89, p. 53.
"Reading of Emmanuel Levinas." [Antaeus] (62) Spr 89, p. 54-55.
"Small Time." [RiverS] (28) 89, p. 34.
"So." [RiverS] (28) 89, p. 32.
"So Much." [Conjunc] (14) 89, p. 260.
"Water." [Antaeus] (62) Spr 89, p. 56.
"What." [Antaeus] (62) Spr 89, p. 57.
"What." [Conjunc] (14) 89, p. 259.
"Winter Night." [Conjunc] (14) 89, p. 259.
1162. CRENNER, James
"In the Public Library." [KanQ] (21:1/2) Wint-Spr 89, p. 182-183.
"Upon Julia's Clothes" (for Professor Julia Watson). [KanQ] (21:1/2) Wint-Spr 89,
    p. 182.
1163. CREW, Louie
"Sport." [ConnPR] (8:1) 89, p. 11.
1164. CREWS, Judson
"A Black Sash Was All She Had. Okay." [Lactuca] (12) F 89, p. 38.
"Blood Devisable by Sand -- Isn't It Soon." [Interim] (8:1) Spr 89, p. 40.
"A Descent into the Depths Would Have Changed." [Lactuca] (12) F 89, p. 37.
"If He Swam at All It Was in a Religion." [Lactuca] (12) F 89, p. 38.
"If the Bark Comes Off the Sheen of Branch." [Lactuca] (12) F 89, p. 39.
"I've Seen Worse, As They Say, Without Even." [Lactuca] (12) F 89, p. 39.
"Skin or Sheen As It Fails to Coalesce." [Lactuca] (12) F 89, p. 38.
"These Suicidal Caresses -- Is That What." [Interim] (8:1) Spr 89, p. 40.
"The Windows I Have Stared Out of Looking." [Lactuca] (12) F 89, p. 37.
1165. CRIENJAK, Jill
"Friends" (Mainstreet Elementary Poetry Contest, 3rd Grade, 2nd Place).
    [DeKalbLAJ] (22:1/4) 89, p. 102.
1166. CROCKER, Jean-Marie J.
"The Measure of March." [BallSUF] (30:4) Aut 89, p. 60.
1167. CROCKETT, Andy
"Chagall." [MidAR] (9:2) 89, p. 147.

1168. CROFT, Sally
    "Small Matters." [SpoonRQ] (14:1) Wint 89, p. 12.
1169. CRONWELL, Brian
    "Those of Us Afraid of Praise." [Contact] (9:50/51/52) Fall-Wint 88-Spr 89, p. 36.
    "The Way Dreams Are Not Quite the Same." [Contact] (9:50/51/52) Fall-Wint
        88-Spr 89, p. 36.
1170. CROOKER, Barbara
    "The Last Woman in America to Wash Diapers." [Footwork] 89, p. 16.
    "Rites of Passage." [Footwork] 89, p. 16.
    "Still Another Poem for Nuclear Disarmament." [StoneC] (16:3/4) Spr-Sum 89, p.
        68.
    "Walking in the Snow." [WestB] (23) 89, p. 98-99.
1171. CROSS, Mary
    "Vis-à-vis" (Chapbook of Poems, for my family: 11 poems). [OhioR] (43) 89, p.
        47-62.
1172. CROSSON, Robert
    "Egypt" (A First Recital, from "Field Notes." To Lily). [Temblor] (9) 89, p.
        194-197.
1173. CROW, Mary
    "After Days" (tr. of Olga Orozco). [BlackWR] (15:2) Spr 89, p. 109, 111.
    "Dreaming of the Land." [AmerPoR] (18:2) Mr-Ap 89, p. 46.
    "The Four Seasons" (tr. of Marco Martos). [NewOR] (16:3) Fall 89, p. 39.
    "In the End Was the Word" (tr. of Olga Orozco). [LitR] (32:4) Sum 89, p. 555.
    "Kragujevac" (Yugoslavia). [OxfordM] (5:1) Spr-Sum 89, p. 59-60.
    "A Mother's Insomnia" (After a poem by Charles Simic that begins with the same
        line). [Journal] (12:2) Fall-Wint 88-89, p. 20.
    "The Other Side" (tr. of Olga Orozco). [LitR] (32:4) Sum 89, p. 554.
    "Reference Point" (tr. of Olga Orozco). [LitR] (32:4) Sum 89, p. 552-553.
    "The Sketch as Poem" (tr. of Alberto Girri, w. Patsy Boyer). [LitR] (32:4) Sum 89,
        p. 495-496.
    "Songs for D.H. Lawrence" (To Teresa Parodi, tr. of Francisco Madariaga). [LitR]
        (32:4) Sum 89, p. 526-527.
    "Survival" (tr. of Bogomil Gjuzel, w. the Author). [ColR] (NS 16:1) Spr-Sum 89,
        p. 100.
    "Vertical Poetry" (six poems from "Novena poesía vertical," tr. of Roberto Juarroz).
        [LitR] (32:4) Sum 89, p. 508-511.
    "Wailing Wall" (tr. of Olga Orozco). [LitR] (32:4) Sum 89, p. 556.
1174. CROW, Pamela
    "Still Life." [SouthernPR] (29:2) Fall 89, p. 37.
1175. CROW, Steve
    "Bluejay." [KanQ] (21:1/2) Wint-Spr 89, p. 117.
    "For the Three Fires." [Caliban] (7) 89, p. 165.
    "Remaking Chants" (Selections: I, II, IV). [Nimrod] (32:2) Spr-Sum 89, p.
        117-119.
    "Songs: Becoming Beautiful" (Selection: VI. "The wind winters"). [Caliban] (7) 89,
        p. 164.
    "Sunrise Lake" (for the Grandfather). [KanQ] (21:1/2) Wint-Spr 89, p. 117.
1176. CROWN, Kathy
    "Fingers." [SouthernPR] (29:2) Fall 89, p. 24-25.
1177. CROZIER, Lorna
    "Living Day by Day." [CanLit] (122/123) Aut-Wint 89, p. 92.
CRUALAOICH, Gearóid O
    See O CRUALAOICH, Gearóid
1178. CRUM, Robert
    "The Bat in the Bedroom." [MSS] (6:3) 89, p. 137-138.
    "Children's Ward." [ChiR] (36:3/4) 89, p. 39.
    "The Hereford." [ChiR] (36:3/4) 89, p. 37-38.
    "Sleeping in the Evening." [MSS] (6:3) 89, p. 138.
1179. CRUMP, Charles H.
    "Trap." [BellArk] (5:3) My-Je 89, p. 4.
1180. CRUMP, J. I.
    "A Sigh for Life" (tr. of Chang Yang-hao). [LitR] (32:3) Spr 89, p. 418.
    "Vast the World and Its Forge of Time" (tr. of Liu Yin). [LitR] (32:3) Spr 89, p.
        419.
    "You Left" (tr. of Ma Chih-yüan). [LitR] (32:3) Spr 89, p. 417.

109

1181. CRUNK, T.
"Souvenirs" (for my father). [PoetL] (84:3) Fall 89, p. 33-34.
1182. CRUSZ, Rienzi
"The Sandwich-Maker." [Grain] (17:4) Wint 89, p. 50-51.
1183. CRUZ, Grethel
"Ceferino, the Peasant" (tr. by Diane Kendig). [Pig] (15) 88, p. 88.
1184. CRYER, James M.
"Bamboo and Rock" (tr. of Hsü Wei). [LitR] (32:3) Spr 89, p. 412.
"Butterflies on a Fan" (tr. of Hsü Wei). [LitR] (32:3) Spr 89, p. 411.
"Cloud Gate Temple: Painting Plum Trees" (tr. of Hsü Wei). [LitR] (32:3) Spr 89, p. 409.
"Crabs" (tr. of Hsü Wei). [LitR] (32:3) Spr 89, p. 411.
"Dark Stream: Album Leaf" (tr. of Hsü Wei). [LitR] (32:3) Spr 89, p. 410.
"Painting Bamboo" (tr. of Hsü Wei). [LitR] (32:3) Spr 89, p. 410.
"Pear Blossoms" (tr. of Hsü Wei). [LitR] (32:3) Spr 89, p. 409.
"Two Locusts" (tr. of Hsü Wei). [LitR] (32:3) Spr 89, p. 412.
1185. CSAMER, Mary Ellen
"For Anne Sexton." [Quarry] (38:4) Fall 89, p. 26-27.
1186. CSOORI, Sándor
"Apparition" (tr. by Len Roberts). [InterPR] (15:2) Fall 89, p. 23.
"Darkly from the Darkness" (tr. by Len Roberts). [InterPR] (15:2) Fall 89, p. 24.
"The Day Has Passed (Elmút a nap)" (tr. by Len Roberts and László Vertes). [IndR] (12:2) Spr 89, p. 100.
"Esztergom Summer" (tr. by Len Roberts and Anita Senyi). [InterPR] (15:2) Fall 89, p. 26.
"Farewell to Finland" (tr. by Len Roberts). [InterPR] (15:2) Fall 89, p. 22.
"Postponed Nightmare (Elmaradt lázálom)" (tr. by Len Roberts and László Vertes). [IndR] (12:2) Spr 89, p. 101.
"Winter's Voice Has Softened" (tr. by Len Roberts and Calduia Zimmermann). [InterPR] (15:2) Fall 89, p. 25.
1187. CUADRA, Pablo Antonio
"E. T." (tr. by Phillipa Leddy). [KeyWR] (2:1/2) Fall-Wint 89, p. 142.
"The New Time" (tr. by Phillipa Leddy). [KeyWR] (2:1/2) Fall-Wint 89, p. 143.
"Seven Trees Against Sunset" (tr. by K. H. Anton and Todd Frederickson). [AnotherCM] (19) 89, p. 31-49.
1188. CUADROS, Gil
"Valencia." [JamesWR] (6:4) Sum 89, p. 4.
1189. CUCCHI, Maurizio
"I Am Awakened" (tr. by Michael Palma). [Poetry] (155:1/2) O-N 89, p. 124.
"Il Mio Risveglio E Stato Nel Tuo Nome." [Poetry] (155:1/2) O-N 89, p. 124.
"Sorrow" (tr. by Michael Palma). [Poetry] (155:1/2) O-N 89, p. 125.
1190. CUDDIHY, Michael
"The Deepest Part of the Forest." [AntR] (47:1) Wint 89, p. 71.
1191. CULHANE, Brian
"History of the Mediterranean." [Antaeus] (62) Spr 89, p. 58.
1192. CUMBERLAND, Sharon
"Ars Poetica." [Iowa] (19:1) Wint 89, p. 96-98.
1193. CUMMINGS, Darcy
"Years Later, Alice Dreams of Rabbits." [CarolQ] (41:3) Spr 89, p. 83.
1194. CUMMINS, James
"The Critic." [Ploughs] (15:4) Wint 89-90, p. 44.
"The Passion." [ParisR] (31:110) Spr 89, p. 188.
"The Poet-in-Residence." [Ploughs] (15:4) Wint 89-90, p. 43.
"To My Daughter." [ParisR] (31:110) Spr 89, p. 192.
"The Voices." [ParisR] (31:110) Spr 89, p. 189-191.
1195. CUMMINS, Paul
"One: Two." [Lactuca] (12) F 89, p. 53.
1196. CUMPIAN, Carlos
"El Cinco de Mayo / L Sinko Day My-O." [Pig] (15) 88, p. 57.
"The Gift." [Pig] (15) 88, p. 58.
"Muralist Incantation." [Pig] (15) 88, p. 58.
"Understanding My Feet All Day." [Pig] (15) 88, p. 57.
1197. CUMPIANO, Ina
"Jacaranda." [BlackWR] (16:1) Fall-Wint 89, p. 85.
1198. CUNNIFF, Christopher
"Fugitive." [PacificR] (7) 89, p. 96.

1199. CUNNINGHAM, Julia
"South Dakota, 1989." [SoDakR] (27:4) Wint 89, p. 66-67.
1200. CUNNINGHAM, Mark
"September: Against Intensity." [RiverC] (9:1) Spr 89, p. 90.
1201. CUNNINGHAM, Tom
"The Third Disaster." [JamesWR] (6:4) Sum 89, p. 11.
1202. CUOCO, Lorin
"Just Intonation." [RiverS] (29) [89], p. 47.
"Pump." [RiverS] (29) [89], p. 48.
1203. CURBELO, Silvia
"Birds" (for Andre Kertezs). [Caliban] (7) 89, p. 111-112.
"Christa: A Monologue, Jan. 28, 1986" (Cape Canaveral). [IndR] (13:1) Wint 89, p.
    85-86.
"First Shift at Hersheys, 4 a.m." [TampaR] (2) 89, p. 13.
"First Snow" (For Laura, 1954-1986). [TampaR] (2) 89, p. 14.
"Floating." [IndR] (13:1) Wint 89, p. 84.
"Hit and Run." [FloridaR] (16:2/3) Fall-Wint 89, p. 34.
"I Turn Out All the Lights and Pretend It's Raining." [Caliban] (7) 89, p. 109-110.
"Natural Causes." [FloridaR] (16:2/3) Fall-Wint 89, p. 32-33.
"When It Rains Every Road Washes Clean." [FloridaR] (16:2/3) Fall-Wint 89, p.
    31.
1204. CURISTON, Nora
"Crush." [Grain] (17:3) Fall 89, p. 62.
1205. CURTIS, David
"Circumference." [Poem] (61) My 89, p. 36.
"We Go on Trust." [Poem] (61) My 89, p. 35.
1206. CURTIS, G. L.
"The Balloon Man" (Dublin Circa 1948). [NoDaQ] (57:1) Wint 89, p. 61.
1207. CURTIS, John
"Hard Boiled Ex-Pate." [Bogg] (61) 89, p. 44.
1208. CURTIS, Tony
"Great Uncle Charlie 1893-1986." [SoDakR] (27:2) Sum 89, p. 87-89.
"Preparations." [NoDaQ] (57:2) Spr 89, insert p. 67.
"Public Sale." [SoDakR] (27:2) Sum 89, p. 90.
"Return to the Headland." [NoDaQ] (57:2) Spr 89, insert p. 69.
"Soup." [NoDaQ] (57:2) Spr 89, insert p. 68.
1209. CUSHING, James
"If You Could See Me Now." [Plain] (10:1) 89, p. 38.
"Nature Boy." [BellR] (12:2, #26) Fall 89, p. 30.
"Too Marvelous for Words." [Jacaranda] (4:1) Spr-Sum 89, p. 153.
"You Go to My Head." [Nimrod] (33:1) Fall-Wint 89, p. 74.
"You'd Be So Nice to Come Home To." [Plain] (9:2) Wint 89, p. 8.
1210. CUTLER, Bruce
"The Book of Naples" (Selections: 4 poems). [BelPoJ] (40:1) Fall 89, p. 10-18.
"The Insurrection" (Naples, September 27-30, 1943). [KanQ] (21:3) Sum 89, p.
    94-95.
"Otherwise, Or." [PoetryNW] (30:3) Aut 89, p. 4.
"Performance." [SpoonRQ] (14:2) Spr 89, p. 53-55.
"What the Sibyl Says." [PoetryNW] (30:3) Aut 89, p. 3-4.
1211. CUTULY, Joan
"Las Vegas Poem." [Interim] (8:1) Spr 89, p. 20-22.
"Waking Up in the Wrong Room" (For Margaret Mee). [Interim] (8:1) Spr 89, p.
    23.
1212. CZURY, Craig
"Alternating Direct Current." [PaintedB] (37) 89, p. 85.
"X." [MinnR] (NS 33) Fall 89, p. 26.
Da PONTE, Pero
    See PONTE, Pero da
1213. DABNEY, Janice
"Half Moon Bay." [HayF] (4) Spr 89, p. 45.
1214. DABROCK, Martha
"Unseen Circles." [NegC] (9:1) 89, p. 82.
1215. DACEY, Florence (Florence Chard)
"Finders / Keepers." [LakeSR] (23) 89, p. 15.
"Undone." [Vis] (30) 89, p. 35.

1216. DACEY, Philip
"Black Snow." [NewL] (56:2/3) Wint 89-Spr 90, p. 67.
"Coke." [FreeL] (2) Sum 89, p. 8-9.
"Comic Hopkins" (July 25, 1880, Liverpool). [NewL] (56:2/3) Wint 89-Spr 90, p.
    65.
"Coupon Love." [NewL] (56:2/3) Wint 89-Spr 90, p. 64-65.
"Dead Letters." [NewL] (56:2/3) Wint 89-Spr 90, p. 66.
"Freud in London, 1938." [OxfordM] (5:1) Spr-Sum 89, p. 54.
"I'm Calling About Your Ad for the Golden Retriever." [PassN] (10:1) Wint 89, p.
    8.
"The No." [NewL] (56:2/3) Wint 89-Spr 90, p. 62-63.
"On the Island of Korcula" (Yugoslavia, May 20, 1988). [Shen] (39:1) Spr 89, p.
    20-21.
"The Train." [NoDaQ] (57:4) Fall 89, p. 60.
"Troy." [Shen] (39:1) Spr 89, p. 21-22.
1217. DAGAMA, Steven
"Carmen's Poem." [YellowS] (32) Wint 89, p. 12.
"Granada." [YellowS] (29) Spr 89, p. 29.
"Portuguese Boy." [YellowS] (32) Wint 89, p. 13.
"A Room" (Trois-Rivieres, Québec). [YellowS] (29) Spr 89, p. 29.
"There Was No Paper." [YellowS] (32) Wint 89, p. 13.
1218. D'AGUIAR, Fred
"Airy Hall Isotrope." [Stand] (30:1) Wint 88-89, p. 31.
"Airy Hall Leave-Taking." [Stand] (30:1) Wint 88-89, p. 31.
"Airy Hall's Common Denominators." [Stand] (30:1) Wint 88-89, p. 30.
1219. DAHL, Chris
"Cub Scout Meeting at Which We Learn America Has Just Bombed Libya." [RiverC]
    (9:1) Spr 89, p. 74-75.
"The Tooth Fairy." [CrabCR] (6:2) Wint 89, p. 21.
"While My Grandfather Is Dying." [RiverC] (9:1) Spr 89, p. 73.
1220. DAHLEN, Beverly
"Three Poems on the Main Idea." [PaperAir] (4:2) 89, p. 106-108.
1221. DAHLQUIST, Daniel
"The Armadillo." [RiverS] (30) [89], p. 64-65.
"Whirlwind." [RiverS] (30) [89], p. 66.
1222. DAHLSTEDT, Kate
"Breasts." [Mildred] (3:2) 89, p. 62-63.
DAI, Fang
    See FANG, Dai
1223. DAIGON, Ruth
"How Old Would You Be If You Didn't Know How Old You Was" (Satchel Paige).
    [OxfordM] (5:1) Spr-Sum 89, p. 57-58.
"The Promise." [StoneC] (16:3/4) Spr-Sum 89, p. 69.
"The Search." [Vis] (31) 89, p. 19.
1224. DAILEY, Joel
"Audience, Ambience, Ambulance." [Timbuktu] (4) Sum-Fall 89, p. 54.
"Unlimited Limo." [Timbuktu] (4) Sum-Fall 89, p. 55.
1225. DALE, Karen
"Choosing." [MSS] (6:3) 89, p. 140.
1226. DALEY, Michael
"Blue Heaven." [CrabCR] (6:2) Wint 89, p. 27.
1227. DALLAS, Jonathan
"The Quarry." [Blueline] (10:1/2) 89, p. 84.
1228. DALTON, Anne B.
"An Unsent Letter to Emily: Constellations of Desire." [SinW] (38) Sum-Fall 89, p.
    98-99.
"The Woman Whose Garden Becomes the Whole World." [SinW] (38) Sum-Fall 89,
    p. 119-120.
1229. DALTON, Roque
"Elegia Vulgar para Francisco Sorto." [Contact] (9:50/51/52) Fall-Wint 88-Spr 89,
    p. 57-58.
"Jubilant Poem" (Homage to a poem of Andre Breton, tr. by James Graham).
    [Contact] (9:50/51/52) Fall-Wint 88-Spr 89, p. 55-56.
"Poema Jubiloso" (Homenage a un poema de André Bretón). [Contact] (9:50/51/52)
    Fall-Wint 88-Spr 89, p. 54-55.
"Seeing You Naked" (To Maria del Carmen, tr. by James Graham). [Contact]

(9:50/51/52) Fall-Wint 88-Spr 89, p. 56.
"Vernacular Elegy for Francisco Sorto" (tr. by James Graham). [Contact]
(9:50/51/52) Fall-Wint 88-Spr 89, p. 58-59.
"Verte Desnuda" (A Maria de Carmen). [Contact] (9:50/51/52) Fall-Wint 88-Spr 89,
p. 56.
1230. DALY, Daniel
"The Inheritors." [ChamLR] (3:1, #5) Fall 89, p. 120.
"Little Fish." [SpiritSH] (54) Spr-Sum 89, p. 13.
"Martha." [SpiritSH] (54) Spr-Sum 89, p. 12.
"Milk Cartons." [Poetry] (154:2) My 89, p. 91.
"Pine Cones." [SpiritSH] (54) Spr-Sum 89, p. 11-12.
"Walking Dogs." [TarRP] (28:2) Spr 89, p. 30.
1231. DALY, Doris C.
"A Lost Love." [EmeraldCR] (1989) c1988, p. 134-135.
1232. "DALY, Mary Ann
"Forgetting the Three-Faced God." [PoetL] (84:4) Wint 89-90, p. 9.
1233. DALY, Mary Ann
"Old Gold." [PoetL] (84:4) Wint 89-90, p. 10.
1234. DAMACION, Kenneth Z. (Kenneth Zamora)
"In the Loire Valley." [ChamLR] (2:2, #4) Spr 89, p. 104.
"Shinju." [ChamLR] (3:1, #5) Fall 89, p. 35-36.
1235. DAME, Enid
"Vildeh Chaya." [Cond] (16) 89, p. 26-27.
1236. DAMERON, Chip
"Three Designs." [MidwQ] (30:4) Sum 89, p. 442.
1237. DAMIAN, Christian
"Afrika screams, Aspen dance." [Rampike] (6:2) 88, p. 74.
1238. DANA, Robert
"Hard Souls." [GeoR] (43:4) Wint 89, p. 782-783.
1239. DANAHY, Michael
"Accidental Poem on Two Works of Art." [WindO] (51) Spr 89, p. 45.
"City Garden." [WindO] (51) Spr 89, p. 46.
1240. DANIEL, Hal (Hal J., III)
"C Squared Vision." [ChatR] (9:4) Sum 89, p. 67.
"For Whom the Bells Toll." [Mildred] (3:2) 89, p. 18.
"National Nugatory Day." [Lactuca] (12) F 89, p. 29.
"Tool Boxing." [Mildred] (3:2) 89, p. 17.
"Why I Like My Father." [PoetC] (21:1) Fall 89, p. 21.
1241. DANIEL, Yuli
"5.1.66" (in Russian). [StoneC] (17:1/2) Fall-Wint 89-90, p. 24.
"16.1.66" (in Russian). [StoneC] (17:1/2) Fall-Wint 89-90, p. 24.
"January 5, 1966" (tr. by B. Z. Niditch). [StoneC] (17:1/2) Fall-Wint 89-90, p. 24.
"January 16, 1966" (tr. by B. Z. Niditch). [StoneC] (17:1/2) Fall-Wint 89-90, p. 24.
1242. DANIELS, Celia A.
"Moving" (for Lori). [Farm] (6:1) Wint-Spr 88-89, p. 126-127.
1243. DANIELS, Jim
"Bucket." [Iowa] (19:1) Wint 89, p. 81.
"Elephants." [Iowa] (19:1) Wint 89, p. 80.
"Handling Empty Boxes." [KanQ] (21:1/2) Wint-Spr 89, p. 27.
"Night Light" (for Mrs. Francis). [KenR] (N 11:4) Fall 89, p. 59-60.
"Parked Car." [NoDaQ] (57:3) Sum 89, p. 199-200.
"Paul Pakowski Was Here." [LaurelR] (23:2) Sum 89, p. 44.
"Protection." [OhioR] (44) 89, p. 84.
"Skilled Trades." [Contact] (9:53/54/55) Sum-Fall 89, p. 26.
"Slush." [CinPR] (20) Fall 89, p. 59.
"Spring Sap." [GettyR] (2:4) Aut 89, p. 672.
"Tag Teams" (Third Award Poem, 1988/1989). [KanQ] (21:1/2) Wint-Spr 89, p.
26.
"Taking Stock." [MinnR] (NS 33) Fall 89, p. 27.
"Temporary / Help." [Iowa] (19:1) Wint 89, p. 81.
"Vocabulary Test." [Contact] (9:53/54/55) Sum-Fall 89, p. 26.
"Weekend Warrior." [Contact] (9:53/54/55) Sum-Fall 89, p. 26.
"You Bet." [Iowa] (19:1) Wint 89, p. 79-80.
1244. DANISON, Tracy
"Bad Angels." [YellowS] (29) Spr 89, p. 37.

"Psalm 8" (tr. by Lena Jayyusi and Anselm Hollo). [PoetryE] (27) Spr 89, p. 77.
"Psalm 9" (tr. by Lena Jayyusi and Christopher Middleton). [PoetryE] (27) Spr 89,
      p. 78.
"Psalm 13" (tr. by Lena Jayyusi and Anselm Hollo). [PoetryE] (27) Spr 89, p. 79.
"Psalms for Palestine" (Selections: "Psalm One," "Psalm Nine," tr. by Ben
      Bennani). [CharR] (15:2) Fall 89, p. 76-79.
"There Is a Night" (tr. by Lena Jayyusi and Jeremy Reed). [PoetryE] (27) Spr 89, p.
      93.
"You Will Carry the Butterfly's Burden" (tr. by Lena Jayyusi and W. S. Merwin).
      [PoetryE] (27) Spr 89, p. 90-92.

DASHI, Kobo
      See KUKAI
1261. DASSANOWSKY-HARRIS, Robert
      "The Local Color" (Joshua Tree, California). [WritersF] (15) Fall 89, p. 77.
      "Mata Hari Considers a Response." [Jacaranda] (4:1) Spr-Sum 89, p. 150-151.
      "What Happens When You Recognize a Face." [Os] (29) 89, p. 37.
1262. DATTA, Jyotirmoy
      "Undesired" (tr. of Anuradha Mahapatra, w. Carolyne Wright). [NewEngR] (11:4)
            Sum 89, p. 457.
1263. DAUENHAUER, Richard
      "V. 104" (tr. of Markos Argentarios). [YellowS] (30) Sum 89, p. 5.
1264. DAUNT, Jon
      "Naming Our Child." [Mildred] (3:1) Spr-Sum 89, p. 71.
1265. DAUPHIN, Jacques
      "Remembering / Remembered" (to James Baldwin, tr. by Ron Offen). [StoneC]
            (17:1/2) Fall-Wint 89-90, p. 42.
      "Se Souvenant / Souvenu" (à James Baldwin). [StoneC] (17:1/2) Fall-Wint 89-90,
            p. 42.
1266. DAURIO, Bev
      "The Breaking Down Dream." [Rampike] (6:1) 87, p. 61.
1267. DAVEY, Frank
      "Postcard Poems." [Rampike] (6:1) 87, p. 6.
1268. DAVID, Hess,
      "Love Beats in the Aorta" (tr. of Carlos Drummond de Andrade). [GrahamHR] (12)
            Spr 89, p. 51-52.
1269. DAVIDSON, Scott
      "Spitting It Back." [CumbPR] (8:2) Spr 89, p. 51-52.
DAVIDSON, Terri Brown
      See BROWN-DAVIDSON, Terri
1270. DAVIES, Alan
      "Jackson Mac Low: Premises for the Appreciation." [PaperAir] (4:2) 89, p. 78-81.
1271. DAVIES, Hilary
      "Interior" (after Bonnard, tr. of Jean Joubert). [Verse] (6:2) Je 89, p. 17.
1272. DAVIES, John
      "Flight Patterns" (for Rich). [CumbPR] (8:2) Spr 89, p. 11-14.
      "How to Write Anglo-Welsh Poetry." [NoDaQ] (57:2) Spr 89, insert p. 65-66.
      "The Leaning Tree." [CumbPR] (8:2) Spr 89, p. 10.
      "Port Talbot." [NoDaQ] (57:2) Spr 89, insert p. 64.
1273. DAVIES, Robert A.
      "4:00 AM." [FreeL] (2) Sum 89, p. 20.
      "Elegy to an Imagined Man." [FreeL] (2) Sum 89, p. 19.
1274. DAVIES, Sheila
      "Serpent Worship." [Rampike] (6:3) 88, p. 25-28.
1275. DAVIS, Alan R.
      "Dillon, Bouncing on the Bounce-a-Baby." [BallSUF] (30:4) Aut 89, p. 10.
1276. DAVIS, Barbara
      "In the Garden of the Women." [Vis] (31) 89, p. 44.
1277. DAVIS, Becky
      "Christmas Portrait." [Plain] (9:2) Wint 89, p. 31.
      "Horse Catcher." [Plain] (9:3) Spr 89, p. 7.
1278. DAVIS, Christopher
      "Anarchy." [Sonora] (17) Spr-Sum 89, p. 4.
1279. "DAVIS, Christopher
      "Coconut Oil Near the Sun." [Sonora] (17) Spr-Sum 89, p. 1-3.
1280. DAVIS, Christopher
      "Compressor." [JamesWR] (6:3) Spr 89, p. 7.

"Grief, Fading" (after a lover's death). [Sonora] (17) Spr-Sum 89, p. 5.
"Little Crisis Framed in My Window." [RiverC] (10:1) Fall 89, p. 58-59.
"A Map Made of Air." [RiverC] (10:1) Fall 89, p. 56-57.
"Middle Class Prayer." [JamesWR] (6:3) Spr 89, p. 7.
"Postcard." [JamesWR] (6:3) Spr 89, p. 7.
"Sunday Afternoon, After a Funeral, One Can't Change?" [AmerPoR] (18:4) Jl-Ag 89, p. 18.
1281. DAVIS, Glover
"Illuminating Manuscripts." [MissouriR] (12:1) 89, p. 178-179.
1282. DAVIS, Jennifer
"Withdrawal." [Amelia] (5:3, #14) 89, p. 9.
1283. DAVIS, John
"Jim." [EngJ] (78:4) Ap 89, p. 101.
1284. DAVIS, Jon
"The Story of My Life by Angela Winona Smith." [OntR] (31) Fall-Wint 89-90, p. 86.
1285. DAVIS, Jordan
"Bearing the Legend." [PaintedB] (37) 89, p. 18.
"Cursing Softly at the Foot of the Government." [PaintedB] (37) 89, p. 19.
1286. DAVIS, Kate
"Old House." [SouthernPR] (29:2) Fall 89, p. 36.
1287. DAVIS, Margo
"Ol Time Religion." [Kalliope] (11:3) 89, p. 16.
1288. DAVIS, Michael C.
"Hallgerd's Husband." [PoetL] (84:2) Sum 89, p. 11-12.
1289. DAVIS, R. M.
"Missouri Farmers at the Louvre." [CharR] (15:1) Spr 89, p. 70.
1290. DAVIS, William Virgil
"The Boathouse at Laugharne." [Bogg] (61) 89, p. 43.
"Crimes and Crimes." [CharR] (15:2) Fall 89, p. 82.
"The Dead Man." [Chelsea] (48) 89, p. 103.
"Detective Work." [HampSPR] Wint 89, p. 26.
"A Journey." [KanQ] (21:1/2) Wint-Spr 89, p. 249.
"A Long Return." [CharR] (15:2) Fall 89, p. 83.
"The Meeting" (-- Elizabeth Bishop). [PoetC] (21:1) Fall 89, p. 36.
"An Ordered Universe." [TexasR] (10:3/4) Fall-Wint 89, p. 70.
"A Tour of the City of the Dead" (St. Louis cemetery No. 1, New Orleans / All Hallow's Eve). [Chelsea] (48) 89, p. 100-102.
"A True Story." [HampSPR] Wint 89, p. 27.
"The Wall." [Pequod] (26/27) 89, p. 145-146.
"Windows" (For my mother, in memory). [Poetry] (154:2) My 89, p. 98.
1291. DAVISON, Peter
"Autobiographer." [AmerS] (58:2) Spr 89, p. 288.
"Generations of Swan." [Atlantic] (264:1) Jl 89, p. 59.
"The Passing of Thistle." [Atlantic] (264:3) S 89, p. 71.
1292. DAVISON, Steven
"Give and Rise." [US1] (22/23) Spr 89, p. 38.
1293. DAVITT, Michael
"August" (tr. by Paul Muldoon). [Trans] (22) Fall 89, p. 121.
"In the Convent of Mercy" (tr. by Seán O Tuama). [Trans] (22) Fall 89, p. 120.
"The Mirror" (in memory of my father, tr. by Paul Muldoon). [Trans] (22) Fall 89, p. 124-125.
"Morning Prayer" (tr. by Philip Casey). [Trans] (22) Fall 89, p. 118.
"O My Two Palestinians" (Palestinian massacre in Beirut, 18/9/'82, tr. by Philip Casey). [Trans] (22) Fall 89, p. 119.
"Rust and Rampart of Rushes" (for Máire, tr. by Gabriel Rosenstock and Michael Hartnett). [Trans] (22) Fall 89, p. 126-127.
"Stillborn 1943: A Call to Limbo" (tr. of Derry O'Sullivan). [Trans] (22) Fall 89, p. 100-101.
"To Pound, from God" (tr. by Paul Muldoon). [Trans] (22) Fall 89, p. 122-123.
1294. DAVOLE, Franke
"Helen Is the Sun." [BlueBldgs] (11) 89, p. 34-35.
"Songs of the Gargoyles." [BlueBldgs] (11) 89, p. 36-37.
1295. DAWE, Gerald
"Elocution Lesson." [NoDaQ] (57:1) Wint 89, p. 62.
"Hostage" (for Brian Keenan). [NoDaQ] (57:1) Wint 89, p. 63.

DAWSON

1296. DAWSON, Hester
"Zebras." [StoneC] (17:1/2) Fall-Wint 89-90, p. 61.
1297. DAY, Holly
"Mental Ward." [SmPd] (26:1, #75) Wint 89, p. 13.
De . . .
See also names beginning with "De" without the following space, filed below in their alphabetic positions, e.g., DeFOE.
De ANDRADE, Carlos Drummond
See ANDRADE, Carlos Drummond de
De ANDRADE, Eugenio
See ANDRADE, Eugenio de
1300. De ANGELIS, Milo
"Annuario." [Poetry] (155:1/2) O-N 89, p. 154.
"Chi Ha Osato." [Poetry] (155:1/2) O-N 89, p. 152.
"He Who Has Dared" (tr. by Lawrence Venuti). [Poetry] (155:1/2) O-N 89, p. 153.
"The Narrator" (tr. by Lawrence Venuti). [Poetry] (155:1/2) O-N 89, p. 155.
"Il Narratore." [Poetry] (155:1/2) O-N 89, p. 154.
"Ti Benderai?" [Poetry] (155:1/2) O-N 89, p. 152.
"Will You Put on the Blindfold?" (tr. by Lawrence Venuti). [Poetry] (155:1/2) O-N 89, p. 153.
"Year" (tr. by Lawrence Venuti). [Poetry] (155:1/2) O-N 89, p. 151.
"Yearbook" (tr. by Lawrence Venuti). [Poetry] (155:1/2) O-N 89, p. 155.
De DIOS, Maria Jesus Diez
See DIEZ DE DIOS, Maria Jesus
De la HOZ, León
See HOZ, León de la
De la VEGA, Garcilaso
See VEGA, Garcilaso de la
De LACERDA, Alberto
See LACERDA, Alberto de
1301. De MARIS, Ron
"In the Tetons." [Nat] (249:8) 18 S 89, p. 286.
De OTERO, Blas
See OTERO, Blas de
De QUEVEDO, Francisco
See QUEVEDO, Francisco de
1302. De RUGERIS, C. K.
"Balls, Bells and the Failure of Money." [JamesWR] (7:1) Fall 89, p. 13.
"Empty Ice Box." [JamesWR] (7:1) Fall 89, p. 13.
1304. De STEFANO, John
"In Memory R.D.H." [AnotherCM] (19) 89, p. 62-63.
"On the Open-Air Asylum." [NowestR] (27:1) 89, p. 72.
"Springfever." [NowestR] (27:1) 89, p. 71.
De TAVEIROS, Pai Soares
See TAVEIROS, Pai Soares de
De UNGRIA, Ricardo M.
See UNGRIA, Ricardo M. de
1305. De VEAUX, Alexis
"Forward Looking Strategies." [Obs] (4:2) Sum 89, p. 55-56.
"New Body: New Life." [Obs] (4:2) Sum 89, p. 56-57.
"Physical Therapy." [Obs] (4:2) Sum 89, p. 57.
De VINCK, Christopher
See DeVINCK, Christopher
1306. De VITO, E. B.
"Graduates." [AmerS] (58:2) Spr 89, p. 282.
1307. De WIT, Johan
"Encounter." [Bogg] (61) 89, p. 41.
1308. DEAL, Susan Strayer
"Palpating." [OxfordM] (5:1) Spr-Sum 89, p. 69.
1309. DEAN, Benjamin Tucker
"Oh, I've seen the sights of the Arctic nights." [EmeraldCR] (1989) c1988, p. viii-x.
1310. DEAN, Debi Kang
"Fidelity." [TarRP] (28:2) Spr 89, p. 15.

1311. DEAN, Virginia M.
"The Hurricane." [EmeraldCR] (1989) c1988, p. 110.
1312. DEANE, John F.
"Fall." [Vis] (29) 89, p. 7.
"The Poor Ladies of San Damiano." [Vis] (29) 89, p. 5-7.
1313. DEANE, Seamus
"Omerta." [NoDaQ] (57:1) Wint 89, p. 64.
1314. DEANE, Sheila
"Hand Creatures" (for Petra). [Quarry] (38:2) Spr 89, p. 26-30.
1315. DeARMAS, Paula
"Fireflies Revisited." [BellArk] (5:3) My-Je 89, p. 6.
"Learning the Mountain." [BellArk] (5:5) S-O 89, p. 10.
"The Living." [BellArk] (5:3) My-Je 89, p. 4.
"Planetary Behavior." [BellArk] (5:3) My-Je 89, p. 18.
"Walking to the Store with Beth." [BellArk] (5:5) S-O 89, p. 8.
1316. DEBRAVO, Jorge
"Poem of Inevitable Love" (tr. by Michael L. Johnson). [BlueBldgs] (11) 89, p. 10.
"Poema de Amor Inevitable." [BlueBldgs] (11) 89, p. 11.
1317. DeCAMBRA, Ho'oipo
"I've Been to India and Back." [Hawai'iR] (13:3) Fall 89, p. 33-35.
"Magic America." [Hawai'iR] (13:3) Fall 89, p. 36-37.
1318. DECEMBER, John
"Letter to the Arctic." [PoetL] (84:2) Sum 89, p. 25-26.
"Suns." [Poem] (61) My 89, p. 23.
"Two Letters from a Mute." [Poem] (61) My 89, p. 22.
1319. DeCLUE, Charlotte
"Definition." [Contact] (9:53/54/55) Sum-Fall 89, p. 13.
"LI(teracy) Is a LI Word" (to the ikons of the LI world). [Contact] (9:53/54/55)
      Sum-Fall 89, p. 11.
"A Redefinition" (for all those who give life to the street). [Contact] (9:53/54/55)
      Sum-Fall 89, p. 12-13.
1320. DeCORMIER-SHEKERJIAN, Regina
"Childhood." [PoetryE] (28) Fall 89, p. 113-114.
"A Garland of Straw." [HeliconN] (20) 89, p. 32-33.
"A Mouth Full of Hunger" (for H.S.). [HeliconN] (20) 89, p. 33.
"A Mouth Full of Hunger" (for H.S.). [PoetryE] (28) Fall 89, p. 111-112.
"The Way It Is." [PoetryE] (28) Fall 89, p. 109-110.
1321. DeCOURCY, Lynne H.
"At Bedtime." [PraS] (63:3) Fall 89, p. 107-108.
"Autumn Drive." [CinPR] (19) Spr 89, p. 24.
1322. "DeCOURCY, Lynne H.
"Fear." [Kalliope] (11:2) 89, p. 33-34.
1323. DeCOURCY, Lynne H.
"Leaving." [MinnR] (NS 32) Spr 89, p. 70.
"The Pearls." [MidAR] (9:1) 89, p. 165.
"Recognition." [NegC] (9:1) 89, p. 55-56.
"Taking Him from the Cell." [ThRiPo] (33/34) 89, p. 38-39.
"Walking Toward the Light." [NegC] (9:1) 89, p. 53-54.
1324. DEE, Mandy
"Night." [SinW] (39) Wint 89-90, p. 64-65.
DEELEY, Lois Roma
      See ROMA-DEELEY, Lois
1325. DEEN, Rosemary
"Applied Art." [Ploughs] (15:4) Wint 89-90, p. 49.
"Fascination of the Line of Transit" (for Leonard). [Ploughs] (15:4) Wint 89-90, p.
      47-48.
"Infant and Martyrs" (For Anne Robertson). [Comm] (116:22) D 15, 89, p. 700.
1326. DeFOE, Mark
"Coming Home Late." [ColEng] (51:1) Ja 89, p. 44.
"Evening Rain: Frank's Porch." [StoneC] (16:3/4) Spr-Sum 89, p. 75.
1327. DeFREES, Madeline
"Denby Romany." [NewL] (56:2/3) Wint 89-Spr 90, p. 70-75.
"Dialogue Partly Platonic." [MassR] (30:2) Sum 89, p. 215-216.
"From the Clerestorey." [NewL] (56:2/3) Wint 89-Spr 90, p. 68-69.
"The Garden of Botanical Delights." [MassR] (30:2) Sum 89, p. 212-215.
"Hanging the Pictures." [NewL] (56:2/3) Wint 89-Spr 90, p. 69.

"What I Mistook for Heather." [NewL] (56:2/3) Wint 89-Spr 90, p. 75.
1328. DeGRAZIA, Emilio
"Good Friday Blue." [WestB] (25) 89, p. 79.
1329. DEGUY, Michel
"Now you will see everything is going to happen very slowly" (tr. by David
Kinloch). [Verse] (6:2) Je 89, p. 16.
1330. DeGUZMAN, Maria
"Substitution." [CapeR] (24:1) Spr 89, p. 10.
1331. DeKELVER, Sue
"Deer Killing." [CapeR] (24:1) Spr 89, p. 42.
"A Pear for My Teacher." [CapeR] (24:1) Spr 89, p. 41.
1332. Del GRECO, Robert
"Dakota Poem." [SoDakR] (27:1) Spr 89, p. 122.
1333. DELANO, Page Dougherty
"The Marilyn Monroe Photographs." [Crazy] (37) Wint 89, p. 38-40.
1334. DELFFS, C. J.
"Freshman Love Poem." [MSS] (6:3) 89, p. 208.
1335. DELGADO, Juan
"Cat's Eyes." [SilverFR] (16) Spr 89, p. 16.
1336. Della ROCCA, Lennie
"Washing Machine." [NegC] (9:1) 89, p. 90.
1337. DELLABOUGH, Robin
"Genetic Code." [Footwork] 89, p. 11-12.
"Lullaby." [Footwork] 89, p. 11.
"Shutter." [Footwork] 89, p. 12.
DellaROCCA, Lennie
    See Della ROCCA, Lennie
1338. DELORME, Alain Gilles
"Black and White." [AntigR] (79) Aut 89, p. 76.
1339. DELP, Michael
"Hunting for Arrowheads." [PassN] (10:1) Wint 89, p. 12.
1340. DeLUCA, Geraldine
"Mother's Day." [CapeR] (24:1) Spr 89, p. 29.
1341. DEM, Dev
"Pride's Ride." [AnthNEW] (1) 89, p. 7.
1342. DeMARS, Douglas
"Did Man Get Here by Evolution or Creation?" [KanQ] (21:1/2) Wint-Spr 89, p. 34.
1343. DEMPSTER, Barry
"Working Together." [CrossC] (11:1) 89, p. 10.
1344. DENBERG, Ken (Kenneth)
"Caressed by Stones and Others." [StoneC] (16:3/4) Spr-Sum 89, p. 64.
"Full Moon over My Papa's Eye." [SilverFR] (16) Spr 89, p. 22-23.
1345. DeNIORD, Chard
"Graffito." [AntR] (47:4) Fall 89, p. 467.
"Horse Heart." [TarRP] (28:2) Spr 89, p. 4-5.
"Recovery." [StoneC] (16:3/4) Spr-Sum 89, p. 17.
"The Woman Clothed with the Sun." [Nimrod] (33:1) Fall-Wint 89, p. 75-76.
"Zephyr." [AmerPoR] (18:3) My-Je 89, p. 47.
1346. DENNIS, Carl
"Adventure." [DenQ] (23:3/4) Wint-Spr 89, p. 86-88.
"The Boat." [PraS] (63:3) Fall 89, p. 20-21.
"If I Need to See You." [Poetry] (154:2) My 89, p. 67-68.
"Indian Meadows." [ThRiPo] (31/32) 88, p. 14.
"The Miracle." [ThRiPo] (31/32) 88, p. 13.
"More Snow." [PraS] (63:3) Fall 89, p. 21-22.
"No Shame." [Poetry] (154:1) Ap 89, p. 27-28.
"Nuts and Raisons." [ThRiPo] (31/32) 88, p. 12.
"The Photograph." [PraS] (63:3) Fall 89, p. 18-19.
1347. "DENNIS, Carl
"Soon." [Poetry] (154:2) My 89, p. 66-67.
1348. DENNIS, Carl
"Thanksgiving." [GeoR] (43:4) Wint 89, p. 675-676.
"Unfinished Symphony." [AmerPoR] (18:3) My-Je 89, p. 31.
"Waking on Sunday." [Poetry] (154:2) My 89, p. 65-66.
"We and They." [GeoR] (43:4) Wint 89, p. 674-675.

1349. DENNIS, Pascal
"Autumn Cemetery." [Grain] (17:3) Fall 89, p. 25.
"For Gina." [Grain] (17:3) Fall 89, p. 24.
1350. DENSON, Howard
"The Last Entry." [Kalliope] (10:3) 88, p. 55.
1351. D'EPIRO, Peter
"Inferno" (Canto IX, tr. of Dante Alighieri). [PraS] (63:4) Wint 89, p. 72-75.
1352. DEPPE, Theodore
"Breaking and Entering." [Crazy] (37) Wint 89, p. 52-53.
"Les Enfants du Paradis." [Crazy] (37) Wint 89, p. 54-55.
"Richmond Avenue." [NegC] (9:1) 89, p. 88-89.
1353. DEPTA, Victor M.
"Band Supper." [Outbr] (20) 89, p. 46.
"The Club and the Harley." [Poem] (61) My 89, p. 5.
"Driving Lessons." [Outbr] (20) 89, p. 47.
"The Fever of Any House." [Poem] (61) My 89, p. 4.
"The New South." [Poem] (61) My 89, p. 3.
"Sunrise Service." [Poem] (61) My 89, p. 2.
"Thor and the Golden Bell." [HolCrit] (26:5) D 89, p. 15-16.
"Where the Pines Groom Heaven." [Poem] (61) My 89, p. 1.
1354. DEPUTY, Allison
"Her Face." [PacificR] (7) 89, p. 55-56.
"Idée Fixe." [PacificR] (7) 89, p. 52-54.
1355. DER-HOVANESSIAN, Diana
"Fractals." [AmerS] (58:3) Sum 89, p. 382.
"Salt." [Agni] (28) 89, p. 207-209.
DERICOTTE, Toi
See DERRICOTTE, Toi
1357. DERNIER, Ann
"The Piano." [Thrpny] (39) Fall 89, p. 30.
1358. DERRICOTTE, Toi
"Abuse." [ColR] (NS 16:1) Spr-Sum 89, p. 44.
"Aerial Photograph Before the Atomic Bomb." [MichQR] (28:3) Sum 89, p. 324-325.
"Boy at the Paterson Falls." [ColR] (NS 16:1) Spr-Sum 89, p. 45.
"Captivity: The Minks." [ColR] (NS 16:1) Spr-Sum 89, p. 46-47.
"Captivity: The Singing Bugs." [ColR] (NS 16:1) Spr-Sum 89, p. 48.
"Christmas Eve: My Mother Dressing." [NewEngR] (12:1) Aut 89, p. 69-70.
"Dead Baby Speaks." [Ploughs] (15:4) Wint 89-90, p. 50-57.
"For a Godchild, Regina, on the Occasion of Her First Love." [Cond] (16) 89, p. 61-62.
"High School." [Caliban] (6) 89, p. 48.
"The House on Norwood." [Caliban] (6) 89, p. 47.
"On the Turning Up of Unidentified Black Female Corpses." [Callaloo] (12:2, #39) Spr 89, p. 389-390.
"St. Peter Claver." [ColR] (NS 16:1) Spr-Sum 89, p. 49.
"The Wedding" (For Dinah Berland). [ColR] (NS 16:1) Spr-Sum 89, p. 50.
"Whitman, Come Again to the Cities." [ColR] (NS 16:1) Spr-Sum 89, p. 51.
1359. DERRY, Alice
"When the Warmth Comes." [RiverC] (10:1) Fall 89, p. 119-121.
1360. DERSCHAU, Christoph
"Thirty Running Haikus" (for Allen Ginsberg, in German & English, tr. by Thomas Schaller. Special Translation Feature). [MidAR] (9:1) 89, p. 1-23.
DeRUGERIS, C. K.
See De RUGERIS, C. K.
1361. DESIDERIO, Mark
"Ascension." [RiverS] (28) 89, p. 31.
"In the Pantheon." [RiverS] (28) 89, p. 30.
"Reconstruction." [RiverS] (28) 89, p. 29.
1362. DESNOS, Robert
"A la Faveur de la Nuit." [PaintedB] (38) 89, p. 60.
"Arbitrary Fate" (tr. by Edouard Roditi). [Caliban] (7) 89, p. 117.
"Under Cover of Night" (tr. by Karl Patten). [PaintedB] (38) 89, p. 61.
1363. DESSASO, Deborah A.
"The Bag." [Obs] (4:3) Wint 89, p. 72-73.

"Death of a Sage in the City of God's Team." [Obs] (4:3) Wint 89, p. 72.
"Etosha." [Obs] (4:3) Wint 89, p. 71.

1364. DESY, Peter
"Anniversary." [Quarry] (38:4) Fall 89, p. 18.
"Camping." [BallSUF] (30:4) Aut 89, p. 38.
"Corner Garden." [PoetC] (20:2) Wint 89, p. 30.

1365. "DESY, Peter
"Dream Water." [NoDaQ] (57:3) Sum 89, p. 103.

1366. DESY, Peter
"Homo Corpulos." [Iowa] (19:2) Spr-Sum 89, p. 67-68.
"Intimations." [PoetC] (20:2) Wint 89, p. 29.
"Late October." [Mildred] (3:2) 89, p. 59.
"Late Winter Blues." [Iowa] (19:2) Spr-Sum 89, p. 66.
"Martyr." [SoCoast] (6) Fall 88, p. 24.
"Naming." [Northeast] (ser. 5:1) Wint 89-90, p. 21.
"Nostalgic." [Mildred] (3:2) 89, p. 60.
"Notes Toward a Theory of Ecstatic Language" (for Dave Heaton and Ray Fitch).
    [Mildred] (3:2) 89, p. 57.
"On the Fifth Anniversary of My Father's Death." [Mildred] (3:2) 89, p. 58.
"Out of Body." [Iowa] (19:2) Spr-Sum 89, p. 69.
"The Right Word." [TampaR] (2) 89, p. 25.
"Safeway, 3 A.M., July" (after Allen Ginsberg). [KeyWR] (2:1/2) Fall-Wint 89, p.
    145.
"Spring of '42." [BallSUF] (30:4) Aut 89, p. 7.
"St. Theresa's." [Iowa] (19:2) Spr-Sum 89, p. 68-69.
"Suppose Dogs." [GrahamHR] (12) Spr 89, p. 95.
"The Touch." [HolCrit] (26:2) Ap 89, p. 15.
"Winter Bread." [Mildred] (3:2) 89, p. 61.
"Yard Sale." [KeyWR] (2:1/2) Fall-Wint 89, p. 144.

1367. DETLEFSEN, Karen
"Afternoon Walk, Day Before Leaving." [Dandel] (16:1) Spr-Sum 89, p. 54.
"Settling Woman." [Dandel] (16:1) Spr-Sum 89, p. 53.

1368. DEV SEN, Nabaneetä
"Beginning and End" (in Bengali and English, tr. by Paramita Banerjee and Carolyn
    Wright, w. the author). [BlackWR] (15:2) Spr 89, p. 82-83.
"Full Moon" (tr. by Sunil B. Ray and Carolyne Wright, w. the author). [NewEngR]
    (11:4) Sum 89, p. 456.
"Return" (in Bengali and English, tr. by Paramita Banerjee and Carolyn Wright, w.
    the author). [BlackWR] (15:2) Spr 89, p. 84-85.
"Welcome Angel" (tr. by Sunil B. Ray and Carolyne Wright, w. the author). [MalR]
    (89) Wint 89, p. 31-33.

1369. DEVET, Rebecca McClanahan
"Yes." [NegC] (9:2) 89, p. 75.

1370. DeVINCK, Christopher
"Azure." [Footwork] 89, p. 59.

1371. DeVRIES, Judith A.
"Hedge Life" (Honorable Mention). [StoneC] (17:1/2) Fall-Wint 89-90, p. prelim. p.
    4.

1372. DEVRIES, Rachel Guido
"Blue." [YellowS] (32) Wint 89, p. 38.

1373. DEWDNEY, Chris
"The Secular Grail." [CapilR] (1st series: 50) 89, p. 24.
"Time Travel II." [CapilR] (1st series: 50) 89, p. 26.
"Untitled: D.N.A. is the selective mutational interface between cosmic noise and
    survival." [CapilR] (1st series: 50) 89, p. 25.

1374. DeWIT, Sonja
"Chinese Poem by Li Ho (791-817)." [Dandel] (16:1) Spr-Sum 89, p. 26.

1375. DeWITT, Jim
"You'll Agree, How Helplessly." [Mildred] (3:2) 89, p. 63.

1376. DeZURKO, Edward
"Mousepiece, or What the Little Eye Sees When Closed." [KanQ] (21:1/2) Wint-Spr
    89, p. 214.

1377. DHARWADKER, Vinay
"The Alphabet" (tr. of Arun Kolatkar). [TriQ] (77) Wint 89-90, p. 184.
"An Argument About Horses" (tr. of Kedarnath Singh). [TriQ] (77) Wint 89-90, p.
    149-150.

"Bread" (tr. of Arun Kolatkar). [TriQ] (77) Wint 89-90, p. 182.
"Buildings" (tr. of Arun Kolatkar). [TriQ] (77) Wint 89-90, p. 180.
"The Carpenter and the Bird" (tr. of Kedarnath Singh). [TriQ] (77) Wint 89-90, p. 145.146.
"The City, Evening, and an Old Man: Me" (tr. of Dhoomil). [TriQ] (77) Wint 89-90, p. 160-161.
"Distance" (tr. of G. M. Muktibodh). [TriQ] (77) Wint 89-90, p. 166-167.
"The Forest of Yellow Bamboo Trees" (tr. of B. S. Mardhekar). [TriQ] (77) Wint 89-90, p. 202.
"Ghalib." [CumbPR] (9:1) Fall 89, p. 64.
"The Green Dress" (tr. of P. S. Rege). [TriQ] (77) Wint 89-90, p. 194-195.
"Her Dream" (tr. of Indira Sant). [TriQ] (77) Wint 89-90, p. 208.
"Khyber" (tr. of Shrikant Verma). [TriQ] (77) Wint 89-90, p. 172-173.
"The Knot" (tr. of Vinda Karandikar). [TriQ] (77) Wint 89-90, p. 187-190.
"Licked Clean" (tr. of Arun Kolatkar). [TriQ] (77) Wint 89-90, p. 183.
"Lifetime" (tr. of Narayan Surve). [TriQ] (77) Wint 89-90, p. 205.
"Mirror" (tr. of P. S. Rege). [TriQ] (77) Wint 89-90, p. 192.
"On Reading a Love Poem" (tr. of Kedarnath Singh). [TriQ] (77) Wint 89-90, p. 143-144.
"Our Hindi" (tr. of Raghuvir Sahay). [TriQ] (77) Wint 89-90, p. 135-136.
"Poem at Midnight" (tr. of P. S. Rege). [TriQ] (77) Wint 89-90, p. 196.
"Process of Change" (tr. of Shrikant Verma). [TriQ] (77) Wint 89-90, p. 170-171.
"The Rats Died in a Wet Barrel" (tr. of B. S. Mardhekar). [TriQ] (77) Wint 89-90, p. 200.
"Salaam" (tr. of Mangesh Padgaonkar). [TriQ] (77) Wint 89-90, p. 211-214.
"Sanskrit" (tr. of Raghuvir Sahay). [TriQ] (77) Wint 89-90, p. 138.
"Seven Forty-five in the Morning" (tr. of Mangesh Padgaonkar). [TriQ] (77) Wint 89-90, p. 210.
"Signature" (tr. of Kedarnath Singh). [TriQ] (77) Wint 89-90, p. 140-141.
"Touch and Sight." [CumbPR] (9:1) Fall 89, p. 62-63.
"Towards Delhi" (tr. of Kunwar Narayan). [TriQ] (77) Wint 89-90, p. 153.
"Twenty Years After Independence" (tr. of Dhoomil). [TriQ] (77) Wint 89-90, p. 157-158.
"An Unusual Day" (tr. of Kunwar Narayan). [TriQ] (77) Wint 89-90, p. 154.
"The Visit" (tr. of P. S. Rege). [TriQ] (77) Wint 89-90, p. 197.
"The Void" (tr. of G. M. Muktibodh). [TriQ] (77) Wint 89-90, p. 163-164.
1378. DHASAL, Namdeo
"Ambedkar, 79" (tr. by Laurie Hovell and Asha Mundlay, w. Jayant Karve). [Trans] (21) Spr 89, p. 234-235.
"Just a Bit More Time" (tr. by Laurie Hovell and Jayant Karve). [Trans] (21) Spr 89, p. 235.
DHOMHNAILL, Nuala Ni
See Ni DHOMHNAILL, Nuala
1379. DHOOMIL
"The City, Evening, and an Old Man: Me" (tr. by Vinay Dharwadker). [TriQ] (77) Wint 89-90, p. 160-161.
"Twenty Years After Independence" (tr. by Vinay Dharwadker). [TriQ] (77) Wint 89-90, p. 157-158.
Di . . .
See also names beginning with "Di" without the following space, filed below in their alphabetic positions, e.g., DiPALMA
1380. Di ALLESSIO, Andreas
"For (from) Bernard Welt." [WashR] (15:1) Je-Jl 89, p. 17.
1381. Di BIASIO, Rodolfo
"Poem of the Dawn and the Night" (tr. by Stephen Sartarelli). [Poetry] (155:1/2) O-N 89, p. 95, 97.
"Poemetto dell'Alba e della Notte." [Poetry] (155:1/2) O-N 89, p. 94, 96.
1382. Di MICHELE, Mary
"The Afterlife of Shoes" (for Gary Geddes). [MalR] (87) Sum 89, p. 33-35.
"Invitation to Darkness." [MalR] (87) Sum 89, p. 30-32.
"The Light from Stars" (Santiago, Chile). [Quarry] (38:1) Wint 89, p. 17-19.
"Luminous Emergency." [MalR] (88) Fall 89, p. 26-35.
"Magi." [Quarry] (38:1) Wint 89, p. 13-14.
"Who by Literature." [Quarry] (38:1) Wint 89, p. 15-16.
1383. Di PIERO, W. S.
"1944-1947" (tr. of Franco Fortini). [Poetry] (155:1/2) O-N 89, p. 37-38.

"After the Sacrifice." [Thrpny] (39) Fall 89, p. 12.
"One September Night" (tr. of Franco Fortini). [Poetry] (155:1/2) O-N 89, p. 40.
"Out of China" (tr. of Franco Fortini). [Poetry] (155:1/2) O-N 89, p. 36.
"The Restorers" (Strozzi Chapel, Santa Maria Novella). [Pequod] (28/29/30) 89, p. 64-66.
"Thrasher." [NewYorker] (65:12) 8 My 89, p. 76.
"The Trees" (tr. of Franco Fortini). [Poetry] (155:1/2) O-N 89, p. 39.
"An Unwritten Letter to My Daughter." [SouthwR] (74:2) Spr 89, p. 257-258.
"You Look Out and See" (tr. of Franco Fortini). [Poetry] (155:1/2) O-N 89, p. 41.
Di STEFANO, John
   See De STEFANO, John
DIAZ, René Vazquez
   See VÁZQUEZ DIAZ, René
1384. DIAZ ARTINEZ, Manuel
"Give, Claudia, My Regards to Lenin" (tr. by Lourdes González and Ofelia Martínez). [Pig] (15) 88, p. 68.
"Those Brief Goodbyes" (tr. by Lourdes González and Ofelia Martínez). [Pig] (15) 88, p. 68.
1385. DIAZ-MARTINEZ, Manuel
"The Militiaman Speaks" (tr. by Pat Carrothers and Armando Romero). [Pig] (15) 88, p. 69.
1386. DIB, Mohammed
"Time's Stake" (tr. by Eric Sellin). [Pig] (15) 88, p. 37.
1387. DIBUZ, Balazs
"Between the Furrows." [BellArk] (5:3) My-Je 89, p. 9.
1388. DICKEMAN, Nancy
"Comfort." [RiverC] (9:1) Spr 89, p. 6-7.
"Resilience and the Improbability of Escape." [RiverC] (9:1) Spr 89, p. 4-5.
"Separations." [RiverC] (9:1) Spr 89, p. 8-9.
1389. DICKENSON, Joan
"The Allegany Hills." [NegC] (9:2) 89, p. 38-39.
1390. DICKEY, James
"Eagles." [Vis] (30) 89, p. 9-10.
1391. DICKINSON, Stephanie
"Slicker's Third Day." [Rampike] (6:2) 88, p. 41.
1392. DICKINSON, Steve
"Cannot Help." [Screens] (1) 89, p. 119.
1393. DICKLER, Howard
"Mutilated Me, or Alban Berg Visits the Soul of Dostoevsky in Hell." [Jacaranda] (4:1) Spr-Sum 89, p. 152.
1394. DICKSON, John
"Brave New World." [PassN] (10:1) Wint 89, p. 6.
"The Casualty." [StoneC] (17:1/2) Fall-Wint 89-90, p. 23.
"Good Old Boy." [Poetry] (154:3) Je 89, p. 143.
"Preservation of the Species." [Poetry] (153:5) F 89, p. 285-286.
1395. DICKSON, Ray Clark
"Amerika" (for William Willis). [BelPoJ] (40:1) Fall 89, p. 25-27.
"Dutch Wife: A Sailor's Odyssey." [BelPoJ] (40:1) Fall 89, p. 24.
"The Last Whale." [BelPoJ] (40:1) Fall 89, p. 28-30.
"The New Immigrants." [YellowS] (29) Spr 89, p. 28.
"To the Swooping Loop of His Libido." [YellowS] (32) Wint 89, p. 22.
1396. DIEGO, Eliseo
"Dibujando." [Areíto] (2:5/6) Julio 89, p. 80.
"No Es Mas" (for selva oscura). [Areíto] (2:5/6) Julio 89, p. 76.
"Nostalgia de Por la Tarde" (A Bella). [Areíto] (2:5/6) Julio 89, p. 78.
"Oigo Tu Fragil Vocecita Ahumada." [Areíto] (2:5/6) Julio 89, p. 79.
"La Pagina en Blanco." [Areíto] (2:5/6) Julio 89, p. 81.
"Riesgos del Equilibrista." [Areíto] (2:5/6) Julio 89, inside front cover.
"Todo el Ingenuo Disfraz, Toda la Dicha." [Areíto] (2:5/6) Julio 89, p. 81.
"Versiones." [Areíto] (2:5/6) Julio 89, p. 76.
"Y Nosotros Donde Siempre Estamos." [Areíto] (2:5/6) Julio 89, inside back cover.
1397. DIEZ DE DIOS, Maria Jesus
"Escualido Hogar." [Mairena] (11:27) 89, p. 68.
DIFAN, Zou
   See ZOU, Difan

1398. DIFFIN, Daniel
"Doing It Like the Animals." [PoetryE] (28) Fall 89, p. 11.
1399. DIGBY, John
"To a Linnet" (After Pedro Soto de Rojas, 1585-1658). [Margin] (8) 89, p. 40.
1400. DIGGES, Deborah
"The Flower Thief." [NewYorker] (65:13) 15 My 89, p. 48-49.
"A Greeting." [Pequod] (26/27) 89, p. 9-13.
"Media Years." [MissouriR] (12:1) 89, p. 225-227.
"Oaxacan Stories." [Pequod] (28/29/30) 89, p. 33-34.
"Resurrection Garden." [Antaeus] (62) Spr 89, p. 68-69.
"The Rockettes." [NewYorker] (65:4) 13 Mr 89, p. 34.
1401. DILLARD, Gavin Geoffrey
"The Naked Poet." [EvergreenC] (5:1) Fall 89, p. 19.
"Untitled: Last night he stayed over and we hardly slept at all." [EvergreenC] (5:1)
Fall 89, p. 20.
1402. DILLARD, Jennifer O.
"At Such Young Age." [CrabCR] (6:1) 89, p. 20.
1403. DILLON, Andrew
"Busted Twice in One Night." [NegC] (9:2) 89, p. 40.
"The Fall into Words." [CumbPR] (8:2) Spr 89, p. 9.
"For a Creative Writing Class." [Confr] (39/40) Fall 88-Wint 89, p. 106.
"An Outdoor Production of Sophocles" (For Constantine Santas). [KanQ] (21:3)
Sum 89, p. 145.
"Searching." [InterPR] (15:2) Fall 89, p. 102.
"Teaching with Lint in My Pockets." [CumbPR] (8:2) Spr 89, p. 8.
"To the Office on a Sunday." [InterPR] (15:2) Fall 89, p. 102.
"Trinity Cemetery, Columbia, S.C." [SouthernPR] (29:1) Spr 89, p. 17.
1404. DILLON, Enoch
"Jogging on St. Stephen's Green" (for Dolores, Dublin 8-27-88). [Vis] (29) 89, p.
21.
1405. DIMAGGIO, Jill
"Juan." [SmPd] (26:3 #77) Fall 89, p. 18.
1406. DIMEO, Gregory
"Laborhood." [PaintedB] (37) 89, p. 86.
1407. DINE, Carol
"The Killing." [Kalliope] (11:3) 89, p. 68.
DINE, Jawdat Fakhr Al
    See Al-DINE, Jawdat Fakhr
1408. DING, Dennis
"The Circular Expressway and Straight Lines of the Ancient City" (tr. of Ye
Yan-bing, w. Edward Morin and Dai Fang). [Pig] (15) 88, p. 6.
"Flint" (tr. of Gao Fa-lin, w. Edward Morin and Dai Fang). [Pig] (15) 88, p. 6.
"The Girl I Knew Is Dead" (tr. of Huang Yong-yu, w. Edward Morin). [Pig] (15)
88, p. 6.
"I'll Always Remember" (tr. of Yan-Xiang Shao, w. Edward Morin). [DenQ] (24:2)
Fall 89, p. 69.
"The Trolley Car Goes On" (tr. of Yan Yi, w. Edward Morin). [MinnR] (NS 32) Spr
89, p. 79.
1409. DING, Yu Ping
"To Be Sent to the Shadow of the Sun" (tr. by An Jing and Rex A. McGuinn).
[LitR] (32:2) Wint 89, p. 168.
1410. DINGS, Fred
"After the Solstice." [DenQ] (24:2) Fall 89, p. 39-40.
"Redwing Blackbirds." [NewRep] (201:2) 10 Jl 89, p. 31.
"Swallows at a Quarry Lake." [CarolQ] (41:3) Spr 89, p. 86.
"Sycamores." [NewRep] (200:20) 15 My 89, p. 34.
1411. DIONYSIUS
"Rose with the roses, tell me, what do you sell?" (tr. by James Michie). [GrandS]
(8:4) Sum 89, p. 81.
1412. DIOP, Alioune (David)
"Certainty" (tr. by J. Kates). [StoneC] (17:1/2) Fall-Wint 89-90, p. 25.
"Certitude." [StoneC] (17:1/2) Fall-Wint 89-90, p. 25.
DIOS, Maria Jesus Diez de
    See DIEZ DE DIOS, Maria Jesus
1413. DiPALMA, Ray
"Metropolitan Corridor" (Selections: 6 poems). [Aerial] (5) 89, p. 122-127.

DiPALMA

"Raik" (Excerpts). [CentralP] (15) Spr 89, p. 68.
"Through the Motions" (w. Charles Bernstein). [Caliban] (6) 89, p. 123-129.
DIREAIN, Máirtín O
   See O DIREAIN, Máirtín
1414. DISCH, Tom
"The Crumbling Infrastructure." [SouthwR] (74:3) Sum 89, p. 359-360.
"Garage Sale." [LakeSR] (23) 89, p. 32.
"Ritin'" (a Manifesto). [CrossCur] (8:2) Ja 89, p. 58-59.
"Summer of '88." [TampaR] (2) 89, p. 58-59.
"Tales of the Forebears." [LakeSR] (23) 89, p. 31.
"The Varieties of Oneiric Experience." [TampaR] (2) 89, p. 60-61.
1415. DISCHELL, Stuart
"Between Two Storms." [GrahamHR] (12) Spr 89, p. 108.
"Columbus: Chorus & Monologue." [PartR] (56:3) Sum 89, p. 453-454.
"Of Women and Men." [GrahamHR] (12) Spr 89, p. 106.
"Where Angels Dance." [GrahamHR] (12) Spr 89, p. 107.
1416. DISSANAYAKE, Wimal
"The Old Poet." [BambooR] (44) Fall 89, p. 9.
1417. DITSKY, John
"Kinships." [Interim] (8:2) Fall 89, p. 10.
"The Naked Man Has the Run of the House." [LakeSR] (23) 89, p. 39.
"'S Teeth." [AntigR] (77/78) Spr-Sum 89, p. 74.
"Sheikh." [AntigR] (77/78) Spr-Sum 89, p. 75.
"Wilson's Song." [MalR] (86) Spr 89, p. 97.
"Wine Time." [MalR] (86) Spr 89, p. 96.
1418. DITTMER, Mike
"Looking at Daddy, Looking at Me." [ChangingM] (20) Wint-Spr 89, p. 26.
1419. DIVAKARUNI, Chitra
"Magritte Knew." [Kalliope] (11:3) 89, p. 18.
"Making Samosas." [Prima] (13) 89, p. 26-27.
1420. DIXON, Andrea
"Far Below Stars." [Interim] (8:1) Spr 89, p. 11.
"Midnight and Winter." [Interim] (8:1) Spr 89, p. 13.
"With the Sailing of the Moon." [Interim] (8:1) Spr 89, p. 12.
1421. DIXON, Ivey
"Afterthought" (Selections: 3 poems). [Obs] (3:2) Sum 88, p. 92-93.
1422. DIXON, Kent R.
"The Deeper Green." [GreensboroR] (47) Wint 89-90, p. 106.
"Leeway." [GreensboroR] (46) Sum 89, p. 186.
"Perseids." [GreensboroR] (46) Sum 89, p. 185.
1423. DIXON, Melvin
"Aunt Ida Pieces a Quilt." [Ploughs] (15:4) Wint 89-90, p. 59-61.
"Into Camp Ground" (James Arthur Baldwin, 1924-1987). [Ploughs] (15:4) Wint
   89-90, p. 58.
1424. DJANIKIAN, Gregory
"Mrs. Caldera's House of Things." [Poetry] (154:2) My 89, p. 92-93.
1425. DJERASSI, Carl
"I Have Nothing Left to Say." [NegC] (9:1) 89, p. 65.
"Spider at an Exhibition" ("Skulptur im 20. Jahrhundert" -- Basel, 1984). [PoetC]
   (20:3) Spr 89, p. 15-17.
1426. DLUGOS, Tim
"West 22nd Street." [BrooklynR] (6) 89, p. 46.
1427. DOBBS, Kevin
"Reno, Nevada." [CarolQ] (41:3) Spr 89, p. 53-54.
1428. DOBLER, David
"In Maine." [WebR] (14:1) Spr 89, p. 62-64.
1429. DOBLER, Patricia
"Effigy." [CarolQ] (41:2) Wint 89, p. 9.
1430. DOBYNS, Stephen
"Adam." [Poetry] (154:3) Je 89, p. 125-126.
"The Body's Strength." [ParisR] (31:111) Sum 89, p. 34-35.
"Eyelids." [ParisR] (31:111) Sum 89, p. 39.
"Fingernails." [ParisR] (31:111) Sum 89, p. 36.
"The Music One Looks Back On." [GettyR] (2:1) Wint 89, p. 140-141.
"Rootless." [Poetry] (154:3) Je 89, p. 126-127.
"Slipping Away." [ParisR] (31:111) Sum 89, p. 38.

"Summer Evenings." [GettyR] (2:1) Wint 89, p. 139.
"Sweat." [ParisR] (31:111) Sum 89, p. 37.
"Utopian Melodies." [Poetry] (154:6) S 89, p. 316.
1431. DODD, Elizabeth
"Debsconeag Deadwater." [DenQ] (23:3/4) Wint-Spr 89, p. 89-90.
1432. DODD, Wayne
"Desuetude." [TarRP] (29:1) Fall 89, p. 32-33.
"Echoes of the Unspoken." [ThRiPo] (31/32) 88, p. 15-24.
"Homage to Marcel Duchamp." [DenQ] (23:3/4) Wint-Spr 89, p. 93.
"Hylocichla Mustelina." [TarRP] (29:1) Fall 89, p. 31-32.
"In January." [DenQ] (23:3/4) Wint-Spr 89, p. 91-92.
1433. DODIADAS, x
"Altar" (tr. by Stanley Lombardo). [Temblor] (10) 89, p. 203.
1434. DODSON, Keith (Keith A.)
"It's All in the Timing." [WormR] (29:4, #116) 89, p. 135.
"The Majestic Diner, Pittston, PA." [WormR] (29:4, #116) 89, p. 135.
"Picked This Woman Up." [Lactuca] (13) N 89, p. 24-25.
1435. DODSON, Mayhew Wilson (Pat), III
"Warning to a Young Writer." [EmeraldCR] (1989) c1988, p. 14-16.
1436. DOEBLER, Bettie Anne
"The Divided Self." [PassN] (10:1) Wint 89, p. 18.
1437. DÖERFLER, R. Eric
"Who Says Spirits Can't Hear a Cry for Help?" [Footwork] 89, p. 41.
1438. DOERING, Steven
"Music from a Dead Radio." [SlipS] (9) 89, p. 31.
1439. DOLCIMASCO, Celia
"Retaliation" (Creative Writing Club Contest, Honorable Mention). [DeKalbLAJ]
(22:1/4) 89, p. 79.
1440. DOLLING, Susan
"Thinking of You: To the tune of 'Grateful for New Favors, II'" (tr. of Li Yu).
[LitR] (32:3) Spr 89, p. 347.
"To Be Delivered to My Twelfth Brother, the Lord of Zheng . . ." (tr. of Li Yu).
[LitR] (32:3) Spr 89, p. 347.
"To the Tune of 'Gathering Mulberries'" (tr. of Li Yu). [LitR] (32:3) Spr 89, p. 346.
"To the Tune of 'Song of Sand-Sifting Waves'" (tr. of Li Yu). [LitR] (32:3) Spr 89,
p. 346.
1441. DOMEK, Tom
"A Union Chief Offers Good Advice to a Young Switchman." [GettyR] (2:3) Sum
89, p. 424-425.
1442. DOMIN, Hilde
"Abel Stand Up" (tr. by John Linthicum). [LitR] (33:1) Fall 89, p. 30-31.
"Crossing" (tr. by John Linthicum). [LitR] (33:1) Fall 89, p. 29.
"Guarded Hope" (tr. by John Linthicum). [LitR] (33:1) Fall 89, p. 27.
"Many" (tr. by John Linthicum). [LitR] (33:1) Fall 89, p. 30.
"Sorting Walls" (tr. by John Linthicum). [LitR] (33:1) Fall 89, p. 26.
"That's Not It" (tr. by John Linthicum). [LitR] (33:1) Fall 89, p. 28-29.
1443. DOMINA, Lynn
"The Orange." [OxfordM] (5:2) Fall-Wint 89, p. 53.
"Rahab Remembers." [NegC] (9:2) 89, p. 41-42.
"Sponge Bath." [OxfordM] (5:1) Spr-Sum 89, p. 49.
1444. DONAHUE, Joseph
"Adam, in Hell." [Notus] (4:2) Fall 89, p. 85.
"A Curse Upon the Saintly Corpse of Luis Buñuel." [Notus] (4:2) Fall 89, p. 86-87.
"Desire." [Talisman] (2) Spr 89, p. 67-75.
1445. DONALDSON, Dick
"Pulltabs Now at Jolly's Bar." [LakeSR] (23) 89, p. 40.
1446. DONALDSON, Lee
"Abandoned Building." [Obs] (2:3) Wint 87, p. 91-92.
DONG, Han
    See HAN, Dong
1447. DONG, Jiping
"Autumn" (tr. of Duo Duo). [Footwork] 89, p. 28.
"Autumn" (tr. of Wang Jiaxin). [Footwork] 89, p. 25.
"Being Missing" (tr. of Meng Lang). [Footwork] 89, p. 25.
"A Book" (tr. of Bai Hua). [Footwork] 89, p. 26.
"Byzantium, Byzantium" (tr. of Lu Lu). [Footwork] 89, p. 26.

"Crime and Punishment" (tr. of Song Ci). [Footwork] 89, p. 29.
"Echo" (tr. of Bei Dao). [Footwork] 89, p. 25.
"Experience." [Footwork] 89, p. 22.
"Fate" (tr. of Xiao Qing). [Footwork] 89, p. 27.
"In This Spacious and Bright World" (tr. of Gu Cheng). [Footwork] 89, p. 27.
"Landscape" (tr. of Wang Jiaxin). [Footwork] 89, p. 25.
"Law Case" (tr. of Gu Cheng). [Footwork] 89, p. 27.
"The Lost Horizon" (tr. of Xiao Qing). [Footwork] 89, p. 27.
"Love Story" (tr. of Bei Dao). [Footwork] 89, p. 25.
"Matisse, the Wild Beast" (tr. of Lu Lu). [Footwork] 89, p. 26.
"Old Song" (tr. of Lu Lu). [Footwork] 89, p. 26-27.
"A Praise" (tr. of Wang Jiaxin). [Footwork] 89, p. 25.
"The Queen in a Coin" (tr. of Gu Cheng). [Footwork] 89, p. 28.
"Ravens" (tr. of Duo Duo). [Footwork] 89, p. 28.
"Shadow and Crime" (tr. of Song Ci). [Footwork] 89, p. 28.
"Sitting All Alone" (tr. of Guo Hong). [Footwork] 89, p. 24.
"Someone Brings Flowers Today" (tr. of Han Dong). [Footwork] 89, p. 29.
"The Song You Want to Hear" (tr. by the author). [Footwork] 89, p. 22.
"SOS" (tr. of Bei Dao). [Footwork] 89, p. 26.
"The Steps We Face To" (tr. of Song Ci). [Footwork] 89, p. 28-29.
"Temptation" (tr. of Bei Dao). [Footwork] 89, p. 26.
"Time" (tr. of Xiao Qing). [Footwork] 89, p. 27.
"To Dusk, or Grief" (tr. of Han Dong). [Footwork] 89, p. 29.
"Today" (tr. of Yu Yu). [Footwork] 89, p. 29.
"A View-Point to an International Congress" (tr. of Yu Yu). [Footwork] 89, p. 29.
"The West" (tr. of Xu Jingya). [Footwork] 89, p. 28.
"Yesterday Was a Black Snake" (tr. of Gu Cheng). [Footwork] 89, p. 27.
1448. DONIO, Greg
"Haiku -- Neighborhood Cuisine." [Writer] (102:6) Je 89, p. 27-28.
1449. DONLAN, John
"After the Beep" (for Liz Paton). [Caliban] (7) 89, p. 132.
"Cinderella." [CanLit] (120) Spr 89, p. 144.
"Home Improvements." [AntigR] (77/78) Spr-Sum 89, p. 87.
"Messenger." [MalR] (89) Wint 89, p. 30.
"Missing." [AntigR] (77/78) Spr-Sum 89, p. 88.
"Now." [Event] (18:2) Sum 89, p. 75.
"Orderly." [Caliban] (7) 89, p. 131.
"The Past." [Event] (18:2) Sum 89, p. 74.
"Spiral Jetty." [AntigR] (77/78) Spr-Sum 89, p. 89.
1450. DONNELLY, Susan
"Why I Can't." [MassR] (30:3) Aut 89, p. 423-432.
1451. DONOHUE, Sheila
"Voices." [SouthernPR] (29:1) Spr 89, p. 11-12.
1452. DONOHUE, Timothy
"20 Footnotes Found in a Text on Blood." [YellowS] (29) Spr 89, p. 8-9.
1453. DONOVAN, Deborah
"Color Blind." [AnthNEW] (1) 89, p. 9.
"Portland Streets." [AnthNEW] (1) 89, p. 8.
1454. DONOVAN, Laurence
"Moments." [SpiritSH] (55) Fall-Wint 89 [90 on cover], p. 9.
"The Sandflats" (St. Petersburg, Florida, 1935). [LindLM] (8:4) O-D 89, p. 6.
"Sidewalks" (Bird Road, Miami, 1990). [LindLM] (8:4) O-D 89, p. 6.
"Sunday Afternoon." [LindLM] (8:4) O-D 89, p. 6.
"Variations of Some Lines from Ungaretti." [SpiritSH] (55) Fall-Wint 89 [90 on cover], p. 8.
"The Walk" (For my Father, New York, 1946). [SpiritSH] (55) Fall-Wint 89 [90 on cover], p. 6.
"What We Have Here." [SpiritSH] (55) Fall-Wint 89 [90 on cover], p. 7.
1455. DONOVAN, Loretta
"A Thin Fish Swimming." [Vis] (31) 89, p. 43.
1456. DOPLICHER, Fabio
"A Diderot." [Poetry] (155:1/2) O-N 89, p. 98-102.
"To Diderot" (tr. by Stephen Sartarelli). [Poetry] (155:1/2) O-N 89, p. 99-103.
1457. DOR, Moshe
"Abishag" (tr. by Barbara Goldberg). [WebR] (14:1) Spr 89, p. 34.
"Alternate Possibilities" (tr. by Barbara Goldberg). [Trans] (21) Spr 89, p. 126-127.

"Coalman" (tr. by Barbara Goldberg). [Trans] (21) Spr 89, p. 128.
"The Count of Monte Cristo" (tr. by Barbara Goldberg). [WebR] (14:1) Spr 89, p.
   31-32.
"Dream-Life" (tr. by Barbara Goldberg). [WebR] (14:1) Spr 89, p. 33.
"Khamsin" (tr. by Barbara Goldberg). [WebR] (14:1) Spr 89, p. 34.
"Toward Evening" (tr. by Barbara Goldberg). [Trans] (21) Spr 89, p. 127.
"When You Are With Me" (tr. by Barbara Goldberg). [WebR] (14:1) Spr 89, p. 32.
1458. DORESKI, William
"Blizzard in Fitzwilliam." [Wind] (19:65) 89, p. 5-6.
"A Congeries of Form." [Wind] (19:65) 89, p. 4-5.
"Modern Times." [Pembroke] (21) 89, p. 66.
"A T.S. Eliot Centennial Lecture." [WindO] (51) Spr 89, p. 9-10.
"Turtle Things." [Pembroke] (21) 89, p. 65.
"Vorticism." [Wind] (19:65) 89, p. 3-4.
1459. DORF, Marilyn
"The Sun Speaks Intermittent." [Plain] (10:1) 89, p. 13.
"Waiting Out the Wind" (a Plainsongs Award Poem). [Plain] (9:3) Spr 89, p. 20-21.
1460. DORION, Hélène
"Je Ne Sais Pas Encore" (extraits). [Os] (28) 89, p. 18-21.
1461. DORN, Alfred
"Air." [Amelia] (5:3, #14) 89, p. 52.
1462. DORRIS, Michael
"Felt." [PraS] (63:3) Fall 89, p. 14-15.
"Fiction." [PraS] (63:3) Fall 89, p. 16.
"Weather." [PraS] (63:3) Fall 89, p. 15.
1463. DORSETT, Robert
"Night Song" (tr. of Wen Yi-duo). [LitR] (32:3) Spr 89, p. 345.
"Spring Glow" (tr. of Wen Yi-duo). [LitR] (32:3) Spr 89, p. 344.
"You Point to the Sun and Swear" (tr. of Wen Yi-duo). [LitR] (32:3) Spr 89, p. 344.
1464. DORSETT, Thomas
"The Scales." [Verse] (6:1) Mr 89, p. 57.
1465. DOTY, Mark
"Beginners." [Crazy] (36) Spr 89, p. 5-7.
"Cemetery Road." [Crazy] (36) Spr 89, p. 8-10.
"The Garden of the Moon." [MissR] (17:3, #51) 89, p. 41-43.
"Night Ferry." [SouthwR] (74:4) Aut 89, p. 512-514.
"Noir." [MissR] (17:3, #51), p. 38-40.
1466. DOUGHERTY, Jay
"Carrot-Talk." [Amelia] (5:3, #14) 89, p. 40.
"New on the Job." [Amelia] (5:3, #14) 89, p. 41.
"On Poetry and Suffering." [Amelia] (5:3, #14) 89, p. 42.
"Physical." [Amelia] (5:3, #14) 89, p. 40.
"Voice." [Amelia] (5:3, #14) 89, p. 43.
1467. DOUGLAS, Jim
"Saigon Sidewalk." [BallSUF] (30:4) Aut 89, p. 42-43.
"These Elephants." [BallSUF] (30:4) Aut 89, p. 41.
1468. DOUGLASS, Karen
"Surfacing." [FreeL] (3) Aut 89, p. 10.
1469. DOUSKEY, Franz
"Kubla Redux." [DenQ] (24:1) Sum 89, p. 13-16.
"Ocean Drive." [MinnR] (NS 33) Fall 89, p. 12-13.
"Up From the Mud." [MinnR] (NS 33) Fall 89, p. 10-12.
"The Wall." [MinnR] (NS 33) Fall 89, p. 13-14.
1470. DOVE, Rita
"A l'Opera." [SouthwR] (74:2) Spr 89, p. 174-175.
"Alfonso Prepares to Go Over the Top" (Belleau Wood, 1917). [RiverS] (30) [89],
   p. 35.
"And Counting" (Bellagio, Italy). [TriQ] (76) Fall 89, p. 88.
"The Breathing, the Endless News." [Poetry] (153:4) Ja 89, p. 196.
"Dialectical Romance." [Chelsea] (48) 89, p. 130.
"In a Neutral City." [TriQ] (76) Fall 89, p. 89.
"The Island Women of Paris." [TriQ] (76) Fall 89, p. 86.
"Lint." [SouthwR] (74:2) Spr 89, p. 173-174.
"Melencolia I" (Albrecht Dürer, 1514). [Field] (40) Spr 89, p. 37.
"Missing." [Ploughs] (15:4) Wint 89-90, p. 63.
"Particulars." [Chelsea] (48) 89, p. 131.

"Political" (for Breyten Breytenbach). [TriQ] (76) Fall 89, p. 87.
"The Royal Workshops." [SouthwR] (74:2) Spr 89, p. 172-173.
"Rusks." [Ploughs] (15:4) Wint 89-90, p. 64.
"Sonnet." [Ploughs] (15:4) Wint 89-90, p. 62.
"Uncle Millet." [RiverS] (30) [89], p. 36.
"Used." [Atlantic] (264:1) Jl 89, p. 61.
1471. DOW, Mark
"Arm's Length." [Thrpny] (39) Fall 89, p. 27.
1472. DOW, Philip
"Ducks of the Heart" (A parody of John Logan, 1967). [PaintedB] (39) 89, p.
41-43.
1473. DOWDEN, Kaviraj George
"Flying." [AlphaBS] (5) Jl 89, p. 31-34.
"I Lay in Whitman's Deathbed." [AlphaBS] (5) Jl 89, p. 29-31.
"Today Is the First Day of the Rest of Your Life!" [AlphaBS] (6) Wint 89-90, p.
62-69.
1474. DOWNES, Claire van Breemen
"Mother's Day at Her Daughter's (1887-1988)." [TampaR] (2) 89, p. 90.
1475. DOWNES, Jeremy M.
"Tory." [PoetL] (84:2) Sum 89, p. 32.
1476. DOWNES, Melissa K.
"Kalypso." [PoetL] (84:2) Sum 89, p. 27-28.
1477. DOWNIE, Glen
"Occupations of the Material World." [Rampike] (6:2) 88, p. 77.
1478. DOWNING, Ben
"Two Poems About Touching from the End of October." [HarvardA] (123:3) Mr 89,
p. 7.
1479. DOWNS, Buck
"Drink too fast and smoke too much I end up." [Colum] (14) 89, p. 38.
1480. DOYLE, Bonnie G.
"Tides." [JINJPo] [11] 89, p. 10.
1481. DOYLE, James
"The Advice." [ChamLR] (2:2, #4) Spr 89, p. 63.
1482. DOYLE, Lunn
"News from the Outside World -- January 1986." [VirQR] (65:2) Spr 89, p.
261-262.
1483. DOYLE, Sally
"Shepherding" (Selections: 5 poems). [Temblor] (10) 89, p. 153-157.
1484. DOZIER, Brent
"The Willows of Wisconsin." [SouthernHR] (23:1) Wint 89, p. 37.
1485. DRAGNEA, Gabriela
"And Everything Slips Easily Away" (tr. of Marin Sorescu, w. Stuart Friebert and
Adriana Varga). [Timbuktu] (4) Sum-Fall 89, p. 25.
"Between Stars" (tr. of Marin Sorescu, w. Stuart Friebert and Adriana Varga).
[MalR] (88) Fall 89, p. 79.
"Dream" (tr. of Marin Sorescu, w. Stuart Friebert and Adriana Varga). [Timbuktu]
(4) Sum-Fall 89, p. 27.
"Game" (tr. of Marin Sorescu, w. Stuart Friebert and Adriana Varga). [Timbuktu]
(4) Sum-Fall 89, p. 29.
"Hide and Seek" (tr. of Marin Sorescu, w. Stuart Friebert and Adriana Varga).
[Field] (40) Spr 89, p. 40.
"Horoscope" (tr. of Marin Sorescu, w. Stuart Friebert and Adriana Varga).
[Timbuktu] (4) Sum-Fall 89, p. 35.
"The House" (tr. of Marin Sorescu, w. Stuart Friebert and Adriana Varga).
[Timbuktu] (4) Sum-Fall 89, p. 31.
"Hyena" (tr. of Marin Sorescu, w. Stuart Friebert and Adriana Varga). [Field] (40)
Spr 89, p. 42.
"Laocoon" (tr. of Marin Sorescu, w. Stuart Friebert and Adriana Varga). [Timbuktu]
(4) Sum-Fall 89, p. 29.
"Launching" (tr. of Marin Sorescu, w. Stuart Friebert and Adriana Varga). [MalR]
(88) Fall 89, p. 83.
"Lightning Passed" (tr. of Marin Sorescu, w. Stuart Friebert and Adriana Varga).
[Field] (40) Spr 89, p. 41.
"Paintings" (tr. of Marin Sorescu, w. Stuart Friebert and Adriana Varga). [Field]
(40) Spr 89, p. 38-39.
"Paper" (tr. of Marin Sorescu, w. Stuart Friebert and Adriana Varga). [MalR] (88)

Fall 89, p. 80-81.
"Passport" (tr. of Marin Sorescu, w. Stuart Friebert and Adriana Varga). [MalR]
    (88) Fall 89, p. 78.
"Spiral" (tr. of Marin Sorescu, w. Stuart Friebert and Adriana Varga). [MalR] (88)
    Fall 89, p. 82.
"Subjectivism" (tr. of Marin Sorescu, w. Stuart Friebert and Adriana Varga).
    [Timbuktu] (4) Sum-Fall 89, p. 33.
"Vibrations" (tr. of Marin Sorescu, w. Stuart Friebert and Adriana Varga).
    [Timbuktu] (4) Sum-Fall 89, p. 33.
1486. DRAGOMOSHCHENKO, Arkadii
"Observation of a Fallen Leaf as the 'Ultimate Basis' of Landscape" (a reading, tr.
    by Lyn Hejinian and Elena Balashova). [PaperAir] (4:2) 89, p. 63-66.
"Opsis" (from "Syn tax," tr. by Lyn Hejinian and Elena Balashova). [MichQR]
    (28:4) Fall 89, p. 734-736.
1487. DRAKE, Barbara
"Coda." [WormR] (29:4, #116) 89, p. 105.
"Cut Her Hair." [WormR] (29:4, #116) 89, p. 104-105.
"The Hens That Came with the Place." [WormR] (29:4, #116) 89, p. 102-104.
"My Clothes." [WormR] (29:4, #116) 89, p. 101-102.
1488. DRAKE, Jeannette
"For My First Husband and the War We Missed." [Obs] (3:3) Wint 88, p. 96-97.
"Forecast." [Obs] (3:3) Wint 88, p. 95.
"A Room of Her Own" (In Memory of "Miss Patience"). [Obs] (3:3) Wint 88, p.
    94-95.
"Suicide of a Young Girl, Summer 1985." [Obs] (3:3) Wint 88, p. 95-96.
1489. DRESSEL, Jon
"Thursday." [NoDaQ] (57:2) Spr 89, insert p. 57.
"You, Benjamin Jones." [NoDaQ] (57:2) Spr 89, insert p. 55-56.
1490. DREW, George
"The Death of Robert Brower." [TexasR] (10:3/4) Fall-Wint 89, p. 45-47.
1491. DREXEL, John
"Loose Chippings." [US1] (22/23) Spr 89, p. 31.
"October in Durham." [SouthernR] (25:3) Sum 89, p. 617.
"Winter Day in Bath." [SouthernR] (25:3) Sum 89, p. 618.
1492. DRISCOLL, Frances
"No One Writes Me" (tr. of Therese Plantier). [WillowS] (23) Wint 89, p. 26.
"So That Fur and Water and My Dreams Surround You" (tr. of Therese Plantier).
    [WillowS] (23) Wint 89, p. 28.
"This Being the Season" (tr. of Therese Plantier). [WillowS] (23) Wint 89, p. 27.
"Unpurchased Batteries." [WillowS] (23) Wint 89, p. 24-25.
1493. DRISKELL, Kathleen Mason
"A Mother Considers Housework." [GreensboroR] (47) Wint 89-90, p. 92.
"The Rate That Girls Mature." [GreensboroR] (47) Wint 89-90, p. 93.
1494. DRISKELL, Leon
"Growing Pains." [NegC] (9:1) 89, p. 26-27.
1495. DRIZHAL, Peter
"And on This." [Lactuca] (13) N 89, p. 53-54.
"I Am This." [Lactuca] (13) N 89, p. 54-55.
"In." [Lactuca] (13) N 89, p. 55-56.
1496. DRUMMOND, Robbie Newton
"Baby Boy in Mamma's Lap." [Dandel] (16:2) Fall-Wint 89, p. 26.
"Einstein's Poisoned Mushrooms." [Grain] (17:4) Wint 89, p. 60.
"Trout Tickles." [Grain] (17:3) Fall 89, p. p33.
"Wind Trick." [PraF] (10:4, #49) Wint 89-90, p. 40.
DRUMMOND de ANDRADE, Carlos
    See ANDRADE, Carlos Drummond de
1497. DRURY, John
"Against Regret." [CinPR] (20) Fall 89, p. 52.
"The Angel on the Wall." [CinPR] (20) Fall 89, p. 53.
"Crossing the Border." [WestHR] (43:1) Spr 89, p. 60-63.
"Embassy Row." [DenQ] (24:2) Fall 89, p. 41-42.
"Interrupted Song." [RiverS] (30) [89], p. 49.
"The Maid Train." [GettyR] (2:3) Sum 89, p. 438-439.
"Postmodern Love." [NewRep] (201:23) 4 D 89, p. 36.
"The Slopes." [RiverS] (30) [89], p. 50.

1498. DRUSKA, John
"Ways of Staying Faithful." [WorldO] (22:1/2) Fall-Wint 87-88, c90, p. 19.
DU . . .
See also names beginning with "Du" without the following space, filed below in their alphabetic positions, e.g., DuPLESSIS.
1499. DU, Fu
"Adviser to the Court" (tr. by Carolyn Kizer). [LitR] (32:3) Spr 89, p. 325.
"Broken Boat" (tr. by Stephen Owen). [LitR] (32:3) Spr 89, p. 427.
"Dejeuner sur l'Herbe" (tr. by Carolyn Kizer). [LitR] (32:3) Spr 89, p. 323.
"Drunk I Fell, Sober They Bring Me Wine" (adaption by Kenneth O. Hanson).
    [LitR] (32:3) Spr 89, p. 329-330.
"For Wei Pa, in Quiet" (tr. by David Gordon). [LitR] (32:3) Spr 89, p. 382.
"House Cricket" (tr. by J. P. Seaton). [LitR] (32:3) Spr 89, p. 414.
"I Go Too" (tr. by Carolyn Kizer). [LitR] (32:3) Spr 89, p. 321.
"Jade-Blossom Palace" (tr. by David Hinton). [LitR] (32:3) Spr 89, p. 423.
"Leaving Kung-An at Dawn" (tr. by David Hinton). [LitR] (32:3) Spr 89, p. 424.
"Moonlit Night Thinking of My Brothers" (tr. by David Hinton). [LitR] (32:3) Spr
    89, p. 426.
"The New Moon" (tr. by David Hinton). [LitR] (32:3) Spr 89, p. 423.
"Old Field" (tr. by David Gordon). [LitR] (32:3) Spr 89, p. 381.
"On Meeting Li Kuei-nien Down the River" (tr. by Witter Bynner). [LitR] (32:3) Spr
    89, p. 306.
"On the Way Out" (tr. by Carolyn Kizer). [LitR] (32:3) Spr 89, p. 322.
"Premier of Shu" (tr. by Chuan Y. Fu and Nick Otten). [RiverS] (30) [89], p. 78.
"Reply to a Friend's Advice" (tr. by Carolyn Kizer). [LitR] (32:3) Spr 89, p. 322.
"Returning Late" (tr. by David Hinton). [LitR] (32:3) Spr 89, p. 424.
"Song at Year's End" (tr. by David Hinton). [LitR] (32:3) Spr 89, p. 425.
"Song for Silkworms and Grain" (tr. by David Hinton). [LitR] (32:3) Spr 89, p.
    426.
"Song of the Bound Chicken" (tr. by J. P. Seaton). [LitR] (32:3) Spr 89, p. 414.
"Spring Goes" (tr. by Carolyn Kizer). [LitR] (32:3) Spr 89, p. 321.
"Sundown at Shih-hao and the" (tr. by Cid Corman). [LitR] (32:3) Spr 89, p. 378.
"Thwarted" (tr. by Carolyn Kizer). [LitR] (32:3) Spr 89, p. 324.
"A Traveler From " (tr. by David Hinton). [LitR] (32:3) Spr 89, p. 425.
"Winter Dawn" (tr. by Kenneth Rexroth). [LitR] (32:3) Spr 89, p. 303.
"Yen-Chou City Wall Tower" (tr. by Sam Hamill). [LitR] (32:3) Spr 89, p. 351.
1500. DU, Wei Ping
"My Father and the Sea" (tr. by Paulette Giles). [GrahamHR] (12) Spr 89, p. 40-41.
1501. DUARTE, Matt
"Mike Tyson." [Hawai'iR] (13:2, #26) Sum 89, p. 51.
1502. DUBIE, Francesca
"Goddess Litany." [Sequoia] (33:1) Sum 89, p. 18.
1503. DUBIE, Norman
"Amen" (for Patrick & Robert). [NewL] (56:2/3) Wint 89-Spr 90, p. 79.
"Anagram Born of Madness at Czernowitz, 12 November 1920." [AmerPoR] (18:6)
    N-D 89, p. 27.
"Angela." [AmerPoR] (18:6) N-D 89, p. 28.
"The Apocrypha of Jacques Derrida." [NewL] (56:2/3) Wint 89-Spr 90, p. 80.
"The Clergyman's Daughter." [AmerPoR] (18:2) Mr-Ap 89, p. 44.
"Coyote Creek." [NewL] (56:2/3) Wint 89-Spr 90, p. 78-79.
"A Depth of Field" (for David St. John). [NewEngR] (12:2) Wint 89, p. 123.
"The Desert Deportation of 1915." [AmerPoR] (18:2) Mr-Ap 89, p. 45.
"The Diatribe of the Kite." [AmerPoR] (18:6) N-D 89, p. 26.
"A Dream of Three Sisters." [NewEngR] (12:2) Wint 89, p. 122.
"The Evening of the Pyramids." [AmerPoR] (18:6) N-D 89, p. 25.
"The Fish." [AmerPoR] (18:2) Mr-Ap 89, p. 45.
"The Garden Asylum of Saint-Paul-de-Mausole." [AmerPoR] (18:2) Mr-Ap 89, p.
    45.
"The Ghosts, Saratoga Springs." [AmerPoR] (18:6) N-D 89, p. 26.
"Hummingbirds." [NewL] (56:2/3) Wint 89-Spr 90, p. 76-77.
"Inside the City Walls." [NewEngR] (12:2) Wint 89, p. 121.
"Looking Up from Two Renaissance Paintings to the Massacre at Tiananmen
    Square." [AmerPoR] (18:6) N-D 89, p. 26.
"Margaret." [NewEngR] (12:2) Wint 89, p. 120-121.
"Near the Bridge of Saint-Cloud" (after Rousseau). [AmerPoR] (18:2) Mr-Ap 89, p.
    44.

"Northwind Escarpment." [NewL] (56:2/3) Wint 89-Spr 90, p. 77.
"Of Politics, & Art." [AmerPoR] (18:2) Mr-Ap 89, p. 45.
"The Open Happens in the Midst of Beings" (-- Martin Heidegger). [AmerPoR] (18:6) N-D 89, p. 27.
"Radio Sky." [KenR] (N 11:4) Fall 89, p. 132.
"Thomas Merton and the Winter Marsh." [AmerPoR] (18:6) N-D 89, p. 28.
"Tomb Pond" (for Dave Smith). [AmerPoR] (18:6) N-D 89, p. 25.
1504. DUBNOV, Eugene
"At the Moscow Zoo" (tr. by the author and John Heath-Stubbs). [HolCrit] (26:2) Ap 89, p. 20.
1505. DUBRAVA, Patricia
"On Attending a Lecture on the Poetry of Su Tung-po." [HighP] (4:3) Wint 89-90, p. 133.
1506. DUCZYNSKA, Ilonn
"Ode to Bartok" (tr. of Gyula Illyés, w. Margaret Avison). [CanLit] (120) Spr 89, p. 46-49.
1507. DUDIS, Ellen Kirvin
"Waiting for You on the Farm Road." [StoneC] (16:3/4) Spr-Sum 89, p. 67.
1508. DUDLEY, Betty
"Swimming Lessons." [SinW] (37) Spr 89, p. 81.
1509. DUDLEY, Ellen
"The Doctor and the Doctor's Wife." [StoneC] (17:1/2) Fall-Wint 89-90, p. 33.
"Ice Fishing" (Honorable Mention, 3rd Annual Contest). [SoCoast] (6) Fall 88, p. 44.
1510. DUEHR, Gary
"History." [CinPR] (20) Fall 89, p. 54.
"Late." [RiverS] (28) 89, p. 35.
"True" (for G.). [RiverS] (28) 89, p. 36.
1511. DUEHR, Gloria Mindock
"Feast." [RiverS] (29) [89], p. 56.
1512. DUER, David
"Of Two Minds." [Poetry] (154:4) Jl 89, p. 187-188.
"That Quotidian Decency." [LakeSR] (23) 89, p. 5.
1513. DUESING, Laurie
"Let It Go." [Kalliope] (10:1/2) 88, p. 23-24.
1514. DUFAULT, Peter Kane
"Reductio." [NewYorker] (65:2) 27 F 89, p. 34.
1515. DUFFY, Carol Ann
"Liar." [Pequod] (26/27) 89, p. 82.
"Le Pére-Lachaise." [Pequod] (26/27) 89, p. 83.
"Somewhere Someone's Eyes." [Pequod] (26/27) 89, p. 84.
1516. DUGAN, Alan
"American Tourist to a Guatemalan Tarantula." [AmerPoR] (18:5) S-O 89, p. 4.
"Autobiographical Libation to Erato Muse of Lyric Poetry." [AmerPoR] (18:5) S-O 89, p. 3.
"Criticism of Berson and Darwin." [Antaeus] (62) Spr 89, p. 71.
"Elegy for a Magician." [AmerPoR] (18:5) S-O 89, p. 4.
"Lament for Cellists and Jacqueline DuPré." [Antaeus] (62) Spr 89, p. 73-74.
"On Plumbing After an Air Raid." [AmerPoR] (18:5) S-O 89, p. 3.
"Oxymoronic Hospital Blues." [Antaeus] (62) Spr 89, p. 70.
"Provincetown Totentanz." [AmerPoR] (18:5) S-O 89, p. 4.
"Sexist Lament: Ruin by Monitor." [Antaeus] (62) Spr 89, p. 72.
"Soliloquy: Ghost Dance for a Cripple." [AmerPoR] (18:5) S-O 89, p. 3.
"Speech for Auden." [AmerPoR] (18:5) S-O 89, p. 4.
"Speech to the Student Clowns at the Circus Clown School at Sarasota, Florida." [AmerPoR] (18:5) S-O 89, p. 4.
DUGGAN, Devon Miller
See MILLER-DUGGAN, Devon
1517. DUGGAN, Laurie
"II.vii. You'll tackle anything" (tr. of Martial). [TriQ] (74) Wint 89, p. 221.
"II.xii. Your sweet breath tells me" (tr. of Martial). [TriQ] (74) Wint 89, p. 221.
"III.xii. The perfumed anorexics of L.A." (tr. of Martial). [TriQ] (74) Wint 89, p. 222.
"VIII.iii. Sixty epigrams are too many" (tr. of Martial). [TriQ] (74) Wint 89, p. 222.
1518. DUHAMEL, Denise
"Doing Cartwheels." [SouthernPR] (29:1) Spr 89, p. 8.

"From Lorca's Deli, New York City." [MinnR] (NS 32) Spr 89, p. 66.
"The Long Drive Home." [AnotherCM] (19) 89, p. 65.
"October." [SoCoast] (5) Spr 88, p. 15.
1519. DUMARAN, Adele
"Why This Conversion." [Manoa] (1:1/2) Fall 89, p. 175.
1520. DUMARS, Denise
"Phoneme." [PoetL] (84:3) Fall 89, p. 11-12.
1521. DUMBRAVEANU, Anghel
"Only the Blank Page" (tr. by Adam J. Sorkin and Irina Grigorescu). [NewOR]
(16:2) Sum 89, p. 92.
"Runes" (tr. by Adam J. Sorkin and Irina Grigorescu). [NewOR] (16:2) Sum 89, p.
96.
1522. DUNCAN, Graham
"Climbing the Run." [CrabCR] (6:1) 89, p. 13.
"Confession." [Confr] (39/40) Fall 88-Wint 89, p. 23.
"The Face." [Poem] (62) N 89, p. 46.
"Homemade Doll." [SoCoast] (5) Spr 88, p. 20.
"Jugglers" (suggested by Alice Hudson's tiny sculpture . . .). [Poem] (62) N 89, p.
44.
"Nuisances." [Poem] (62) N 89, p. 47.
"Skin Show." [Poem] (62) N 89, p. 45.
"Witness." [WindO] (52) Wint 89-90, p. 12-13.
1523. DUNCAN, Michaeline
"Grady's Feed and Groceries." [Pembroke] (21) 89, p. 134-135.
1524. DUNETZ, Lora
"Sinkhole." [Footwork] 89, p. 59.
1525. DUNGEY, Christopher
"Ducking Araki-Alcock." [SenR] (19:1) 89, p. 63.
"Maundy Thursday." [Jacaranda] (4:1) Spr-Sum 89, p. 143.
"New Stove." [SoCaR] (21:2) Spr 89, p. 74.
1526. DUNKELBERG, Kendall
"The Heart's Time." [Farm] (6:1) Wint-Spr 88-89, p. 106.
"There Is No Danger." [Farm] (6:1) Wint-Spr 88-89, p. 107.
"This Is Not a Poem." [Farm] (6:1) Wint-Spr 88-89, p. 108.
1527. DUNN, Raucous Robert
"Pandowdy." [Plain] (9:2) Wint 89, p. 33.
1528. DUNN, S. P.
"The Road to the Mountain" (Pueblo to Aspen 8/6-7/60). [Kaleid] (18) Wint-Spr 89,
p. 38-39.
1529. DUNN, Sharon
"Refugees in the Garden." [Agni] (28) 89, p. 67-68.
1530. DUNN, Stephen
"About the Elk and the Coyotes That Killed Her Calf" (For Richard Selzer).
[ThRiPo] (33/34) 89, p. 22.
"After the Resolution." [Shen] (39:4) Wint 89, p. 44-45.
"Bringing It Down." [GeoR] (43:4) Wint 89, p. 767-768.
"Clarities." [GeoR] (43:1) Spr 89, p. 115-116.
"Each from Different Heights." [Iowa] (19:2) Spr-Sum 89, p. 77.
"Forgiveness." [Iowa] (19:2) Spr-Sum 89, p. 76-77.
"Grey." [AmerPoR] (18:2) Mr-Ap 89, p. 50.
"The Guardian Angel." [Iowa] (19:2) Spr-Sum 89, p. 75-76.
"Midwest" (After the paintings of David Ahlstead). [Shen] (39:4) Wint 89, p. 42-43.
"Mon Semblable." [GeoR] (43:1) Spr 89, p. 113-114.
"On the Death of a Colleague" (The Mary Elinore Smith Poetry Prize). [AmerS]
(58:3) Sum 89, p. 352-353.
"Privilege." [GrahamHR] (12) Spr 89, p. 23-24.
"Room, House, Country, Planet." [GrahamHR] (12) Spr 89, p. 27.
"Sadness." [AmerPoR] (18:2) Mr-Ap 89, p. 50.
"Wanting to Get Closer." [AmerPoR] (18:2) Mr-Ap 89, p. 50.
"White Flamingos at 37,000 Feet." [GrahamHR] (12) Spr 89, p. 25-26.
1531. DUO, Duo
"Autumn" (tr. by Dong Jiping). [Footwork] 89, p. 28.
"Ravens" (tr. by Dong Jiping). [Footwork] 89, p. 28.
1532. DUPANGA, Shania
"Freedom Dreams." [BlackALF] (23:3) Fall 89, p. 504.

1533. DUPIN, Jacques
"Dans Cet Oubli." [InterPR] (15:2) Fall 89, p. 76.
"L'Eau Ruisselle." [InterPR] (15:2) Fall 89, p. 76.
"Hands Smooth" (tr. by Glenn W. Fetzer). [InterPR] (15:2) Fall 89, p. 79.
"In This Oblivion" (tr. by Glenn W. Fetzer). [InterPR] (15:2) Fall 89, p. 77.
"Let the Words Take Hold in the Air" (tr. by Glenn W. Fetzer). [InterPR] (15:2) Fall 89, p. 81.
"Livre Delacéré." [InterPR] (15:2) Fall 89, p. 76.
"Les Mains Lisse." [InterPR] (15:2) Fall 89, p. 78.
"Maintenant Je Parle." [InterPR] (15:2) Fall 89, p. 76.
"The Mineral Kingdom" (tr. by Elton Glaser). [StoneC] (17:1/2) Fall-Wint 89-90, p. 67.
"Now I Speak" (tr. by Glenn W. Fetzer). [InterPR] (15:2) Fall 89, p. 77.
"Pierre Dressés." [InterPR] (15:2) Fall 89, p. 78.
"Plonger." [InterPR] (15:2) Fall 89, p. 78.
"Plunging" (tr. by Glenn W. Fetzer). [InterPR] (15:2) Fall 89, p. 79.
"The Prisoner" (tr. by Elton Glaser). [StoneC] (17:1/2) Fall-Wint 89-90, p. 66.
"Le Prisonnier." [StoneC] (17:1/2) Fall-Wint 89-90, p. 66.
"Que les Mots Fassent Souche dans l'Air." [InterPR] (15:2) Fall 89, p. 80.
"Raised Stones" (tr. by Glenn W. Fetzer). [InterPR] (15:2) Fall 89, p. 79.
"Récit du Voyageur." [InterPR] (15:2) Fall 89, p. 76.
"Le Règne Minéral." [StoneC] (17:1/2) Fall-Wint 89-90, p. 67.
"Story of the Traveler" (tr. by Glenn W. Fetzer). [InterPR] (15:2) Fall 89, p. 77.
"Torn Book" (tr. by Glenn W. Fetzer). [InterPR] (15:2) Fall 89, p. 77.
"Water Streams" (tr. by Glenn W. Fetzer). [InterPR] (15:2) Fall 89, p. 77.
1534. DuPLESSIS, Rachel Blau
"Draft #7: Me." [Notus] (4:1) Spr 89, p. 39-41.
"Gap." [Conjunc] (13) 89, p. 40-44.
1535. DuPREE, Don Keck
"An Importance of Place." [MissouriR] (12:2) 89, p. 174.
DURAN, Laura Gonzalez
See GONZALEZ DURAN, Laura
1536. DURBIN, Martina
"Neutrinos." [SouthernPR] (29:1) Spr 89, p. 42-43.
1537. DURKIN, Andrew
"Here in Charlottesville the roads ring" (tr. of Bronislava Volkova, w. the author). [InterPR] (15:2) Fall 89, p. 20.
1538. DURRELL, Lawrence
"Endpapers and Inklings." [Antaeus] (61) Aut 88, p. 88-95.
1539. DUVAL, Quinton
"Red Hair." [HayF] (4) Spr 89, p. 37.
DUYN, Mona van
See Van DUYN, Mona
1540. DWELLER, Cliff
"Musical Chairs." [SlipS] (9) 89, p. 99-101.
"The Seed." [Caliban] (7) 89, p. 56-57.
1541. DWYER, David
"A Love Letter." [SoDakR] (27:1) Spr 89, p. 134.
"Nicht Wahr?" [VirQR] (65:3) Sum 89, p. 450-451.
"Old Books." [VirQR] (65:3) Sum 89, p. 450.
1542. DYBEK, Stuart
"Entrance Hall." [Witness] (2:1) Spr 88, p. 122.
"Goathead." [MichQR] (28:2) Spr 89, p. 232-233.
"Grasshoppers." [Witness] (2:1) Spr 88, p. 120.
"Louvers." [MichQR] (28:2) Spr 89, p. 234.
"Menu for a Last Supper." [ArtfulD] (16/17) Fall 89, p. 98.
"Mowing." [TriQ] (76) Fall 89, p. 94-95.
"Portrait." [Witness] (2:1) Spr 88, p. 121.
1543. DYE, Bru
"Light Years." [JamesWR] (6:3) Spr 89, p. 11.
1544. EADIE, Tom
"Dead Letters." [AntigR] (79) Aut 89, p. 108.
"You're So Neat." [AntigR] (79) Aut 89, p. 109.
1545. EADY, Cornelius
"Car Alarm." [WilliamMR] (27) 89, p. 38.
"Charlie Chaplin Impersonates a Poet." [WilliamMR] (27) 89, p. 37.

"Dental Hygiene." [Ploughs] (15:4) Wint 89-90, p. 67-68.
"Hank Mobley's." [Obs] (3:3) Wint 88, p. 92-93.
"The Sheets of Sound" (for Xam). [SenR] (19:2) Fall 89, p. 49-62.
"The Solos." [Obs] (3:3) Wint 88, p. 91.
"Thrift." [Obs] (3:3) Wint 88, p. 89-90.
"The View from the Rooftop, Waverly Place." [Obs] (3:3) Wint 88, p. 90.
"West Third Street, the First Weekend in June." [Obs] (3:3) Wint 88, p. 91.
"The Wrong Street." [Ploughs] (15:4) Wint 89-90, p. 65-66.

1546. EARLY, Gerald
"The Autobiographies of Ex-Colored Men, Part III" (for Sugar Ray Robinson . . .,
    for Muhammad Ali, . . .). [BlackALF] (23:3) Fall 89, p. 471-472.
"Carrying Water for an Elephant." [Obs] (3:1) Spr 88, p. 22.
"The Difference Between Six and a Half-Dozen." [Obs] (3:1) Spr 88, p. 21.
"Down South Camp Meeting." [BlackALF] (23:3) Fall 89, p. 473.
"Lester Leaps in or Blues for Orpheus." [Obs] (3:1) Spr 88, p. 22.
"Listening to Frank Sinatra." [PraS] (63:3) Fall 89, p. 108-110.
"Pragmatism or Jehovah's Witnessing" (for my uncle, a Jehovah's Witness). [SenR]
    (19:2) Fall 89, p. 33-34.
"The Quality of Being Poor." [Obs] (3:1) Spr 88, p. 20.
"Satyagraha" (for black British middleweight Randy Turpin . . .). [BlackALF] (23:3)
    Fall 89, p. 472-473.
"Stairway to the Stars" (for Bill "Bojangles" Robinson, known for dancing on
    stairs). [RiverS] (30) [89], p. 70.
"Standards Vol. 1." [Obs] (3:1) Spr 88, p. 21.
"Ulysses as the King of Spades" (for Bill "Bojangles" Robinson). [SenR] (19:2) Fall
    89, p. 32.

1547. EARNHART, Brady
"March 31st." [Ascent] (14:3) 89, p. 33-34.
"Tips for City Living." [Ascent] (14:3) 89, p. 32-33.
"To a Friend Just Back from Tannersville." [Blueline] (10:1/2) 89, p. 51.

1548. EASTON, Jean Anaporte
"The Cut Flower of Our Flesh." [Mildred] (3:1) Spr-Sum 89, p. 76-77.
"When My Daughter Was a Child." [Mildred] (3:1) Spr-Sum 89, p. 77.

1549. EATON, Charles Edward
"Bayou." [CentR] (33:1) Wint 89, p. 53-54.
"The Cane." [HolCrit] (26:2) Ap 89, p. 17.
"A Charmed Life." [WebR] (14:1) Spr 89, p. 80.
"The Cobra." [InterPR] (15:2) Fall 89, p. 88.
"The Hinge." [LaurelR] (23:2) Sum 89, p. 91-92.
"Leaning Tower." [CreamCR] (13:2) Fall 89, p. 28.
"The Magician." [InterPR] (15:2) Fall 89, p. 89.
"The Magnet." [Pembroke] (21) 89, p. 38-39.
"Picasso's Egg." [Pembroke] (21) 89, p. 39.

1550. EBERHART, Richard
"History and Mystery." [NewL] (56:2/3) Wint 89-Spr 90, p. 87-88.
"Old Tree by the Penobscot." [NewL] (56:2/3) Wint 89-Spr 90, p. 81-82.
"Sea Storm." [NewL] (56:2/3) Wint 89-Spr 90, p. 83-86.
"So Much to Say." [AnthNEW] (1) 89, front matter.
"To Molly on Her Seventh Birthday." [NewL] (56:2/3) Wint 89-Spr 90, p. 88.

1551. EDDY, Elizabeth
"Avocado." [SpoonRQ] (14:3) Sum 89, p. 60.

1552. EDDY, Gary
"The Moment, the Lightning." [LaurelR] (23:1) Wint 89, p. 72.
"The Supplement to the Theory of Dreams." [LaurelR] (23:1) Wint 89, p. 71.

1553. EDELMANN, Carolyn Foote
"Crimes of the Heart." [Footwork] 89, p. 55.
"Raccoon." [US1] (22/23) Spr 89, p. 8.

1554. EDELSON, Noah
"Sonnet for a Cookie Thief." [Writer] (102:9) S 89, p. 21.

1555. EDFELT, Johannes
"Autumnal Journey" (tr. by David Ignatow and Leif Sjöberg). [Pequod] (26/27) 89,
    p. 26.
"This Is You" (tr. by David Ignatow and Leif Sjöberg). [Pequod] (26/27) 89, p. 26.

1556. EDGINGTON, Amy
"Boogeywoman." [SinW] (39) Wint 89-90, p. 110.

1557. EDKINS, Anthony
    "Life As It Comes." [SpiritSH] (55) Fall-Wint 89 [90 on cover], p. 32-33.
    "Rear-View Mirror." [SpiritSH] (55) Fall-Wint 89 [90 on cover], p. 31.
1558. EDSON, Russell
    "The Art of the Fugue." [Witness] (2:1) Spr 88, p. 105.
    "Balloons." [Caliban] (6) 89, p. 70.
    "The Chances." [Caliban] (6) 89, p. 71.
    "The Crying Hyena." [Witness] (2:1) Spr 88, p. 105.
    "Electric Insects." [Caliban] (6) 89, p. 70.
    "The Garden Party." [Witness] (2:1) Spr 88, p. 106.
    "Portrait of a Realist." [Witness] (2:1) Spr 88, p. 106.
1559. EDWARDS, J. H.
    "A Failure of Imagination" (Guernica, April 1987). [AntigR] (77/78) Spr-Sum 89, p.
        112-113.
1560. EDWARDS, Ken
    "Blaze, for Joseph Beuys." [CentralP] (16) Fall 89, p. 63-66.
    "Good Science." [CentralP] (16) Fall 89, p. 67-68.
1561. EDWARDS, Robert
    "Espanol 101." [WillowS] (23) Wint 89, p. 39-40.
    "What I Know and What I Need to Know." [Caliban] (6) 89, p. 190-191.
1562. EDWARDS, Thomas S.
    "Dream in Exile" (tr. of Reiner Kunze, w. Ken Letko, Thomas Schaller, and Jeff
        Gearing). [Nimrod] (33:1) Fall-Wint 89, p. 111.
    "On the Danube in the Fog" (tr. of Reiner Kunze, w. Ken Letko, Thomas Schaller,
        and Jeff Gearing). [Nimrod] (33:1) Fall-Wint 89, p. 111.
    "The Silhouette of Lübeck" (tr. of Reiner Kunze, w. Ken Letko, Thomas Schaller,
        and Jeff Gearing). [Nimrod] (33:1) Fall-Wint 89, p. 111.
1563. EGAN, Dennis
    "Felicite" (tr. of Gaston Miron). [Vis] (30) 89, p. 19.
1564. EGERMEIER, Virginia
    "Leaning." [CrossCur] (8:3) Apr 89, p. 159.
    "Library." [CrossCur] (8:3) Apr 89, p. 157.
    "Lodovicus." [Vis] (30) 89, p. 19.
    "New Chapel." [Vis] (31) 89, p. 35.
1565. EHRHART, W. D.
    "For Anne, Approaching Thirty-Five." [ConnPR] (8:1) 89, p. 37.
    "Just for Laughs." [VirQR] (65:3) Sum 89, p. 444-445.
    "Keeping My Distance." [VirQR] (65:3) Sum 89, p. 445-446.
    "Lenin" (On the outskirts of Managua, Nicaragua, July 1986). [PoetryE] (28) Fall
        89, p. 104.
    "Not Your Problem." [ConnPR] (8:1) 89, p. 36.
1566. EHRLICH, Shelley
    "Note How a Story Conceals a Story, Last Poems" (12 poems). [PraS] (63:4) Wint
        89, p. 100-114.
    "Pumpkin" (for E.). [KanQ] (21:1/2) Wint-Spr 89, p. 81.
1567. EIBEL, Deborah
    "Making Fun of Travelers." [CanLit] (121) Sum 89, p. 53-54.
    "Retirement." [CanLit] (121) Sum 89, p. 54.
1568. EICHER, Margaret Flanagan
    "First Communion." [Footwork] 89, p. 36.
1569. EIMERS, Nancy
    "Basic Treatments." [WestHR] (43:4) Wint 89, p. 293-294.
    "Edith Frank." [Crazy] (37) Wint 89, p. 65-66.
    "Training Films, Nevada, 1953." [Crazy] (37) Wint 89, p. 64.
1570. EINZIG, Barbara
    "After John Cage's *Europeras 1 & 2*." [Conjunc] (13) 89, p. 27-32.
1571. EISELE, Midge
    "Night Train to Edinburgh." [GettyR] (2:3) Sum 89, p. 427-428.
1572. EISELE, Thomas
    "I have forever been amazed." [PoetryE] (28) Fall 89, p. 170.
    "I see it there before me." [PoetryE] (28) Fall 89, p. 171.
    "It is Christmas." [PoetryE] (28) Fall 89, p. 168.
    "When I was a young man." [PoetryE] (28) Fall 89, p. 169.
1573. EISER, Mary
    "I Dream About Marriage, After the Fight." [Hawai'iR] (13:2, #26) Sum 89, p. 30.

1574. EISIMINGER, Skip
"The Psychic Income of Teaching." [LitR] (32:2) Wint 89, p. 213.
1575. EISNER, J. Guy
"My Rat." [CrabCR] (6:2) Wint 89, p. 20.
1576. EKHOLM, John
"In-Yan-Teopa" (Frontenac State Park, Lake Pepin). [LakeSR] (23) 89, p. 13.
"The Permanent Scars of Dreams" (in memory of Primo Levi). [NegC] (9:2) 89, p. 43.
1577. EKLUND, George
"The Great Dreams." [NegC] (9:1) 89, p. 57.
1578. ELDER, Karl
"The Carhop' Complaint." [Wind] (19:64) 89, p. 11.
"My Signature." [Wind] (19:64) 89, p. 11-13.
1579. ELDER, Mary
"Lake Montebello." [AntR] (47:1) Wint 89, p. 69.
1580. ELDRED, Charlotte
"Black Dress." [EngJ] (78:1) Ja 89, p. 92.
"Gone for Good." [EngJ] (78:5) S 89, p. 96.
1581. ELDRIDGE, Kevin Joe
"Cheating." [PoetryNW] (30:2) Sum 89, p. 38-39.
"Message." [DenQ] (24:1) Sum 89, p. 17-18.
1582. ELEISH, Parinaz
"How Lucky Persimmons Are." [StoneC] (16:3/4) Spr-Sum 89, p. 28-29.
1583. ELENBOGEN, Dina
"Jabotinsky Street." [PraS] (63:3) Fall 89, p. 30-32.
"Trains." [PraS] (63:3) Fall 89, p. 27-30.
1584. ELGARRESTA, Jose
"El Exposito." [WindO] (52) Wint 89-90, p. 34.
"The Foundling" (tr. by Sara Heikoff Woehrlen). [WindO] (52) Wint 89-90, p. 33.
"El Suicida." [WindO] (52) Wint 89-90, p. 34, 36.
"The Suicide" (tr. by Sara Heikoff Woehrlen). [WindO] (52) Wint 89-90, p. 33, 35.
1585. ELIAS, Karen
"Sharp Turning" (A Crown of Sonnets in 4 Parts). [SinW] (38) Sum-Fall 89, p. 85-86.
1586. ELIAS-BURSAC, Ellen
"Mississippi" (tr. of Neda-Miranda Blazevic). [ColR] (NS 16:1) Spr-Sum 89, p. 94.
1587. ELIZABETH, Martha
"Lot's Wife." [Interim] (8:2) Fall 89, p. 46.
"Ode to Knees" (for Sharon Olds). [MidwQ] (30:4) Sum 89, p. 443-444.
1588. ELKIN, Roger
"Engineering Apprentices." [AntigR] (76) Wint 89, p. 22.
"The Fellowship of Hedges." [AntigR] (76) Wint 89, p. 23.
"Keeping Distances" (For Sarah). [SpoonRQ] (14:1) Wint 89, p. 60.
"The Naming of James's Fantail Fish." [SpoonRQ] (14:1) Wint 89, p. 59.
"Oriental Poppies." [SpoonRQ] (14:1) Wint 89, p. 57-58.
1589. ELKIND, Sue Saniel
"Jerusalem of My Dream." [DeKalbLAJ] (22:1/4) 89, p. 51.
"A Language I Don't Understand." [Kalliope] (10:1/2) 88, p. 89.
"A New Creation." [KanQ] (21:1/2) Wint-Spr 89, p. 272.
"A Part of Me." [Kalliope] (11:3) 89, p. 19.
"When the Red Rage Comes." [KanQ] (21:1/2) Wint-Spr 89, p. 260.
1590. ELLEDGE, Jim
"Ciao." [DenQ] (23:3/4) Wint-Spr 89, p. 94.
"Other Side of the Tracks." [PoetC] (20:2) Wint 89, p. 18-21.
"The Rivoire." [AntR] (47:3) Sum 89, p. 316-318.
"The Vigilant." [SpoonRQ] (14:2) Spr 89, p. 62-63.
1591. ELLIOTT, Jeanne
"Skin." [SoCoast] (6) Fall 88, p. 48.
1592. ELLIS, Frances
"The Call." [DeKalbLAJ] (22:1/4) 89, p. 52.
"The Truth About Frost's Wood-Pile." [DeKalbLAJ] (22:1/4) 89, p. 53.
1593. ELLIS, Ron
"Brandy" (A Dramatic Monologue: Excerpts). [SlipS] (9) 89, p. 7476.
1594. ELLMAN, Kitsey
"Hazy." [BelPoJ] (39:3) Spr 89, p. 27-28.
"Mamu in Heaven." [ColR] (NS 16:2) Fall 89-Wint 90, p. 65.

1595. ELLSWORTH, Priscilla
"Speaking with My Sister." [CapeR] (24:1) Spr 89, p. 31.
1596. ELOVIC, Barbara
"Sposabella." [FreeL] (3) Aut 89, p. 22.
1597. ELROD, John
"He Stops to Tie His Shoelace." [BellArk] (5:4) Jl-Ag 89, p. 10.
"The Magical Power of Wild Mountain Air." [BellArk] (5:5) S-O 89, p. 5.
"Soft Cloth." [BellArk] (5:5) S-O 89, p. 9.
"The Wanderer." [BellArk] (5:4) Jl-Ag 89, p. 18.
1598. ELSBERG, John
"Item" (Based loosely on an item in the *Guardian*). [HangL] (55) 89, p. 11.
"The Southern Campaign" (for Robert Boyce). [Bogg] (61) 89, p. 15.
1599. ELSON, Rebecca A. W.
"Chess Game in a Garden." [US1] (22/23) Spr 89, p. 21.
1600. ELSON, Virginia
"Harrier." [PraS] (63:4) Wint 89, p. 76.
1601. ELUARD, Paul
"The Dog" (tr. by Antony Oldknow). [WebR] (14:1) Spr 89, p. 16.
"Fish" (tr. by Antony Oldknow). [WebR] (14:1) Spr 89, p. 17.
"In Order to Live Here" (tr. by Antony Oldknow). [WebR] (14:1) Spr 89, p. 17.
1602. ELYTIS, Odysseus
"The Almond of the World" (tr. by Jeffrey Carson and Nikos Sarris). [PartR] (56:1)
Wint 89, p. 125-132.
1603. EMANS, Elaine V.
"Blue Cheese." [KanQ] (21:3) Sum 89, p. 144.
"Caraway." [KanQ] (21:3) Sum 89, p. 144.
"For Celia Thaxter." [BallSUF] (30:4) Aut 89, p. 76.
"Poem to Brain." [KanQ] (21:1/2) Wint-Spr 89, p. 153.
"Timberdoodle." [KanQ] (21:1/2) Wint-Spr 89, p. 154.
"Words and Music." [CapeR] (24:2) Fall 89, p. 30.
1604. EMINESCU, Mihai
"Din Noaptea" (tr. by W. D. Snodgrass, w. Dona Rosu and Radu Lupan).
[AmerPoR] (18:6) N-D 89, p. 32.
"If Boughs Tap" (tr. by W. D. Snodgrass). [SenR] (19:2) Fall 89, p. 76.
"Sonnets" (I, II, III, tr. by W. D. Snodgrass, w. Dona Rosu and Radu Lupan).
[AmerPoR] (18:6) N-D 89, p. 32.
"Star" (tr. by W. D. Snodgrass). [SenR] (19:2) Fall 89, p. 77.
1605. ENGELL, John
"Saying a Prayer to Him -- Twenty Months." [Pembroke] (21) 89, p. 126.
1606. ENGELS, John
"Black Dog." [KenR] (NS 11:2) Spr 89, p. 28-29.
"Brooding Duck." [KenR] (NS 11:2) Spr 89, p. 27-28.
"Ghost." [Boulevard] (4:2, #11) Fall 89, p. 42.
"A Little Night Music for My Mother." [NewEngR] (12:1) Aut 89, p. 49.
"Long Ago." [NewEngR] (12:1) Aut 89, p. 50.
"Moonset." [KenR] (NS 11:2) Spr 89, p. 28.
"Naturist Beach." [NewEngR] (12:1) Aut 89, p. 51.
"Poem on My Birthday." [KenR] (NS 11:2) Spr 89, p. 24-27.
"Resurrection." [Boulevard] (4:2, #11) Fall 89, p. 43-44.
"Silent Film" (For David Huddle). [NewEngR] (12:1) Aut 89, p. 52-53.
1607. ENGLER, Robert Klein
"How We Live." [Vis] (31) 89, p. 18.
"Moroccan Elegies." [JamesWR] (6:4) Sum 89, p. 6-7.
"Summer Threnody" (for Carol Kyros Walker). [Farm] (6:2) Fall 89, p. 16-17.
1608. ENGMAN, John
"Darkness." [PraS] (63:2) Sum 89, p. 19.
"Friends." [PraS] (63:2) Sum 89, p. 17-18.
"A Little Poem About the Rain." [PoetryE] (28) Fall 89, p. 12.
1609. ENNS, Victor Jerrett
"Bathing." [Grain] (17:1) Spr 89, p. 82.
"He Would Rather Not Worry." [Grain] (17:1) Spr 89, p. 83.
"Levitations." [Grain] (17:1) Spr 89, p. 81.
"Light Enough." [Grain] (17:1) Spr 89, p. 86.
"The Multicultural Sport Coat." [Grain] (17:1) Spr 89, p. 84-85.
"Under Your Wings." [Grain] (17:1) Spr 89, p. 85.

1610. ENRIQUEZ, R. (Romelia)
"Gray emptiness" (tr. of Adriana Yanez, w. T. Hoeksema). [Jacaranda] (4:1)
Spr-Sum 89, p. 63.
"In a Delicate Mimicry of Rain" (9 Poems, Translation Chapbook Series, tr. of Coral
Bracho, w. Thomas Hoeksema). [MidAR] (9:1) 89, p. 81-115.
"Robinson Pursued" (tr. of Francisco Hinojosa, w. Thomas Hoeksema). [Nimrod]
(33:1) Fall-Wint 89, p. 129, 131.
1611. ENSING, Riemke
"Composition" (for Katherine Mansfield). [Descant] (20:3/4, #66/67) Fall-Wint 89,
p. 196.
"Fate of a Dove" (for Joseph Wright, of Derby). [Descant] (20:3/4, #66/67)
Fall-Wint 89, p. 198.
"Finding the Ancestors" (for Brigit Pike). [Descant] (20:3/4, #66/67) Fall-Wint 89,
p. 194.
"Katherine Mansfield Contemplates a Painting of Elizabeth I (1533-1603)."
[Descant] (20:3/4, #66/67) Fall-Wint 89, p. 195.
"Zen and the Art of Gurdjieff" (for Katherine Mansfield). [Descant] (20:3/4, #66/67)
Fall-Wint 89, p. 197.
1612. ENSLER, Eve
"Goodbye Abbie from Bermuda." [CentralP] (16) Fall 89, p. 11-12.
1613. ENTREKIN, Charles
"*Goodbye* Is" (for Andy Grossbardt, 1979). [CharR] (15:1) Spr 89, p. 67.
"Goodbye, Is" (for Andy Grossbardt, 1979). [CumbPR] (8:2) Spr 89, p. 76.
"Hold Me." [CumbPR] (8:2) Spr 89, p. 75.
1614. ENZENSBERGER, Hans Magnus
"Arrière-Pensée" (tr. by Reinhold Grimm). [LitR] (33:1) Fall 89, p. 23.
"The Divorce" (tr. by Felix Pollak and Reinhold Grimm). [LitR] (33:1) Fall 89, p.
19.
"The Dresses" (tr. by Felix Pollak and Reinhold Grimm). [LitR] (33:1) Fall 89, p.
22.
"Isolated House" (for Günter Eich, tr. by Sammy McLean). [AnotherCM] (19) 89,
p. 66.
"Shit" (tr. by Felix Pollak and Reinhold Grimm). [LitR] (33:1) Fall 89, p. 21.
"Short History of the Bourgeoisie" (tr. by Felix Pollak and Reinhold Grimm). [LitR]
(33:1) Fall 89, p. 20.
EPIRO, Peter d'
See D'EPIRO, Peter
1615. EPSTEIN, Elaine
"Room in a Dutch House" (a painting by Pieter Janssens Elinga). [Pequod]
(28/29/30) 89, p. 275.
1616. EPSTEIN, Henrietta
"Letter." [DenQ] (24:2) Fall 89, p. 43.
1617. EPSTEIN, Renee
"I Was Unborn to Your Time." [FreeL] (3) Aut 89, p. 27.
"The Quiltmaker." [FreeL] (3) Aut 89, p. 26.
1618. EPSTEIN, Richard
"Catalogue." [BallSUF] (30:4) Aut 89, p. 55.
1619. EQUI, Elaine
"Becoming Worldly." [CentralP] (15) Spr 89, p. 23.
"Being Sick Together." [ParisR] (31:111) Sum 89, p. 155.
"Fable." [BrooklynR] (6) 89, p. 49.
"Invoice." [ParisR] (31:111) Sum 89, p. 156.
"Live Bats Attack Moviegoers in New Jersey." [Aerial] (5) 89, p. 8.
"Reversal" (after Roni Horn). [Pequod] (28/29/30) 89, p. 37.
"Surface Tension." [ParisR] (31:111) Sum 89, p. 152-154.
"Tao." [Aerial] (5) 89, p. 7.
"To La Rochefoucauld." [BrooklynR] (6) 89, p. 50.
"What We Look Forward To." [CentralP] (15) Spr 89, p. 24-25.
1620. ERATOSTHENES
"To you, Bacchus, Xenophon the sot" (tr. by James Michie). [GrandS] (8:4) Sum
89, p. 85.
1621. ERB, Lisa
"Arizona Monsoon." [ChamLR] (3:1, #5) Fall 89, p. 78.
"Finally." [Manoa] (1:1/2) Fall 89, p. 122.
"Hilo Bay." [ChamLR] (3:1, #5) Fall 89, p. 79.
"Late Afternoon, Volcano." [ChamLR] (3:1, #5) Fall 89, p. 80.

"Marriage Is Not Form." [Manoa] (1:1/2) Fall 89, p. 123.
"Trying to Be Married: Mauna Loa." [Manoa] (1:1/2) Fall 89, p. 122.
1622. ERBA, Luciano
"The Forties" (tr. by Charles Wright). [Poetry] (155:1/2) O-N 89, p. 65.
"La Grande Jeanne" (in Italian). [Poetry] (155:1/2) O-N 89, p. 62.
"La Grande Jeanne" (tr. by Charles Wright). [Poetry] (155:1/2) O-N 89, p. 63.
"Vanitas Varietatum." [Poetry] (155:1/2) O-N 89, p. 64.
1623. ERDRICH, Louise
"Bidwell Ghost." [PraS] (63:3) Fall 89, p. 13-14.
"Birth." [ParisR] (31:111) Sum 89, p. 221.
"The Fence." [ParisR] (31:111) Sum 89, p. 220.
"The Flood." [PraS] (63:3) Fall 89, p. 11-12.
"Fooling God." [Poetry] (154:4) Jl 89, p. 223-224.
"The Return." [PraS] (63:3) Fall 89, p. 12-13.
"The Ritual." [MassR] (30:3) Aut 89, p. 433-434.
"The Sacraments." [NowestR] (27:3) 89, p. 9-14.
"Sunflowers." [Iowa] (19:3) Fall 89, p. 50.
"Translucence." [Iowa] (19:3) Fall 89, p. 51-52.
1624. EREMENKO, Aleksandr
"And Schubert on the water, and Pushkin living on rations" (tr. by John High and
Katya Olmsted). [FiveFR] (7) 89, p. 97.
"I look at you from such deep graves" (To Hieronymus Bosch, inventor of the
projector, tr. by John High). [FiveFR] (7) 89, p. 98-101.
"Philological Verse" (tr. by John High). [MichQR] (28:4) Fall 89, p. 722-723.
1625. ERLICH, Richard D.
"The Serpent's Tale." [Outbr] (20) 89, p. 8.
1626. ERMINI, Flavio
"Blei." [Os] (28) 89, p. 3.
"Ottilia." [Os] (28) 89, p. 3.
1627. ERNO, Patricia
"Landlords." [Plain] (9:3) Spr 89, p. 10.
1628. ERNST, Myron
"At the Broome County Board of Realtors." [WestB] (24) 89, p. 46-47.
"Florida." [ChiR] (36:3/4) 89, p. 69-70.
"Florida." [HampSPR] Wint 89, p. 10-11.
"A Jew Plays the Recorder in the United Methodist Church." [HiramPoR] (46)
Spr-Sum 89, p. 12.
"A Song of Florida." [CumbPR] (9:1) Fall 89, p. 29.
"Susquehanna, St. Clair, & Frackville, Pennsylvania." [CumbPR] (8:2) Spr 89, p.
28.
"What About Those Old Faces in the Puffy Clouds of Summer?" [CumbPR] (8:2)
Spr 89, p. 27.
"The Wife in the Mural at Pompeii." [HampSPR] Wint 89, p. 9.
1629. ERON, Don
"The Four Rivers." [CinPR] (19) Spr 89, p. 48-49.
"Her Henrik." [CinPR] (19) Spr 89, p. 50.
1630. ESENIN, Sergei
"Song About a Dog" (tr. by Robert L. Smith). [Sequoia] (32:2) Wint-Spr 89, p. 30.
1631. ESHE, Aisha
"For My Grandmothers." [BlackALF] (23:3) Fall 89, p. 468.
"I Expect a Call Each Day" (cocaine abuse). [BlackALF] (23:3) Fall 89, p. 468.
"A Picture" (for the better care of children). [BlackALF] (23:3) Fall 89, p. 468.
ESHELMAN, Clayton
See ESHLEMAN, Clayton
1632. ESHLEMAN, Clayton
"At the Cleveland Museum of Art." [Contact] (9:53/54/55) Sum-Fall 89, p. 23.
"The Bison Keyboard." [Sequoia] (33:1) Sum 89, p. 19.
"Les Eyzies Nights." [Notus] (4:1) Spr 89, p. 42-45.
"Guyton Place." [Sulfur] (9:2, #25) Fall 89, p. 111-115.
"Just Before Sunday Morning." [Contact] (9:53/54/55) Sum-Fall 89, p. 24-25.
"Looking Up Through the Christmas Tree at 51." [Screens] (1) 89, p. 123-124.
"Minotaur Grief." [Agni] (28) 89, p. 82-84.
"Sixteen Years in Los Angeles." [Temblor] (10) 89, p. 130-132.
"Sulfur : imagination as an instrument in change" (Notes taken during James
Hillman's two-day seminar on Alchemy, Los Angeles, 1985). [Sulfur] (9:1,
#24) Spr 89, p. 4-6.

"Thanksgiving with Maya." [Screens] (1) 89, p. 120-122.
"Twomb." [Agni] (28) 89, p. 85-86.
1633. ESPADA, Martín
"Cross Plains, Wisconsin." [HangL] (55) 89, p. 13.
"Federico's Ghost." [RiverS] (30) [89], p. 31-32.
"Nando Meets Papo" (Somerset County, Maryland, August 1983). [Agni] (28) 89,
p. 65-66.
"The New Bathroom Policy at English High School." [HangL] (55) 89, p. 12.
"Niggerlips." [MinnR] (NS 33) Fall 89, p. 22.
"The Promised Land" (Selection: Section 35, tr. of Clemente Soto Vélez, w. Camilo
Pérez-Bustillo). [MinnR] (NS 33) Fall 89, p. 39-42.
"Two Mexicanos Lynched in Santa Cruz, California, May 3, 1877." [Agni] (28) 89,
p. 64.
1634. ESPAILLAT, Rhina P.
"Undelivered Mail." [Amelia] (5:3, #14) 89, p. 101.
1635. ESPOSITO, Nancy
"Chemical Examination" (Primo Levi, 1919-1987). [DenQ] (24:2) Fall 89, p. 44.
"The Country, After the Revolution." [IndR] (12:3) Sum 89, p. 60-61.
"A Day in the Country." [AntR] (47:4) Fall 89, p. 460-461.
"Explosion at the Military Hospital, Managua." [IndR] (12:3) Sum 89, p. 58-59.
"Playa del Carmen." [IndR] (12:3) Sum 89, p. 57.
"Snake Charmer." [SouthwR] (74:4) Aut 89, p. 530-531.
1636. ESSARY, Loris
"A." [Aerial] (5) 89, p. 92.
"What the English channel." [Aerial] (5) 89, p. 91.
1637. ESSINGER, Cathryn
"The Mathematician, Counting." [NegC] (9:1) 89, p. 74.
1638. ESTEBAN, Cooper
"Bald Knob." [PoetryE] (28) Fall 89, p. 14.
"Lies." [PoetryE] (28) Fall 89, p. 13.
1639. ESTES, Carolyn
"Auction." [EngJ] (78:1) Ja 89, p. 92.
1640. ESTOK, Michael
"Killing the Porcupine." [JamesWR] (7:1) Fall 89, p. 10.
1641. ESTROFF, Nadine F.
"Out There." [HolCrit] (26:4) O 89, p. 19.
1642. ETTER, Dave
"Honeysuckle Rose." [FreeL] (1) 89, p. 30-31.
"Too Late to Turn Back Now." [ClockR] (5:2) 89, p. 60.
1643. EUBANK, Ilona M.
"Neighbors." [PacificR] (7) 89, p. 57.
1644. EUENUS
"So, bee-eating swallow with the chattering tongue" (tr. by James Michie). [GrandS]
(8:4) Sum 89, p. 82.
"The Vine Speaks" (tr. by James Michie). [GrandS] (8:4) Sum 89, p. 82.
1645. EVANS, Bradford
"After I Leave the House the Telephone Rings." [ArtfulD] (16/17) Fall 89, p. 111.
"Star Explodes in a Nearby Galaxy." [ArtfulD] (16/17) Fall 89, p. 110.
1646. EVANS, David Allan
"Exit." [CharR] (15:1) Spr 89, p. 70-71.
"Grandmother." [SoDakR] (27:1) Spr 89, p. 118.
1647. EVANS, Kevin
"What Does Not Happen." [BlueBldgs] (11) 89, p. 44-45.
1648. EVARTS, Prescott, Jr.
"Wood." [KanQ] (21:1/2) Wint-Spr 89, p. 217.
1649. EVERDING, Kelly
"How to Get a Haircut." [DenQ] (23:3/4) Wint-Spr 89, p. 95.
1650. EVEREST, Beth
"In the Tent" (for Karen). [Dandel] (16:1) Spr-Sum 89, p. 19-20.
1651. EWART, Gavin
"Entrance and Exit Wounds Are Silvered Clean" (-- Robert Graves). [RiverC] (10:1)
Fall 89, p. 65.
"Nearly There: W. B. Yeats and Maud Gonne." [GrandS] (8:4) Sum 89, p. 243.
1652. EWING, Margaret S.
"Either Organelle." [CimR] (87) Ap 89, p. 97.

1653. EWING, Sharon
    "'Thalidomide,' I Said to Myself When I Noticed." [NegC] (9:1) 89, p. 64.
1654. EXNER, Kirk
    "Quincunx" (for my father). [Grain] (17:3) Fall 89, p. 36.
EYCK, Richard Ten
    See TENEYCK, Richard
1655. EYTAN, Ella
    "Mindfully." [PoetL] (84:4) Wint 89-90, p. 27.
    "You Like Me Cool." [PoetL] (84:4) Wint 89-90, p. 26.
FA-LIN, Gao
    See GAO, Fa-lin
1656. FABIAN, Jamie
    "Maintaining Stability." [Kalliope] (11:2) 89, p. 62.
1657. FAGLES, Robert
    "Hector Returns to Troy: The *Iliad*, Book VI" (tr. of Homer). [TriQ] (77) Wint
        89-90, p. 302-319.
    "Medical History." [SewanR] (97:4) Fall 89, p. 503-504.
    "The Shield of Achilles" (*The Iliad*, Book XVIII, tr. of Homer). [GrandS] (8:3) Spr
        89, p. 147-165.
    "Wild Geese." [SewanR] (97:4) Fall 89, p. 505.
1658. FAHRLAND, Bridget
    "What Is Past." [PartR] (56:3) Sum 89, p. 452.
1659. FAINLIGHT, Ruth
    "Flower Feet." (Silk shoes in the Whitworth Art Gallery, Manchester, England).
        [NewYorker] (65:21) 10 Jl 89, p. 36.
    "String." [YaleR] (79:1) Aut 89, p. 42.
    "That Presence." [Hudson] (42:1) Spr 89, p. 97.
    "The Wittersham Sibyl." [YaleR] (79:1) Aut 89, p. 42.
1660. FAIRCHILD, B. H.
    "The Messengers." [SouthernPR] (29:2) Fall 89, p. 62-63.
1661. FAISON, Jody
    "Bulbs." [CumbPR] (9:1) Fall 89, p. 27.
1662. FAIZ, Faiz Ahmed
    "Before You Came" (tr. by Agha Shahid Ali). [PoetryE] (27) Spr 89, p. 114.
    "Black Out" (written during the India-Pakistan war of 1965, tr. by Agha Shahid Ali).
        [PoetryE] (27) Spr 89, p. 108.
    "The City from Here" (tr. by Agha Shahid Ali). [PoetryE] (27) Spr 89, p. 103.
    "City of Lights" (tr. by Agha Shahid Ali). [PoetryE] (27) Spr 89, p. 104.
    "Don't Ask Me for That Love Again" (tr. by Agha Shahid Ali). [PoetryE] (27) Spr
        89, p. 110.
    "Ghazal: Ask no more about separation" (tr. by Agha Shahid Ali). [PoetryE] (27)
        Spr 89, p. 109.
    "Ghazal: He bet both this life and the next" (tr. by Agha Shahid Ali). [PoetryE] (27)
        Spr 89, p. 111.
    "Ghazal: Let the breeze pour colors" (tr. by Agha Shahid Ali). [PoetryE] (27) Spr
        89, p. 112-113.
    "The Heart Gives Up" (tr. by Agha Shahid Ali). [PoetryE] (27) Spr 89, p. 105.
    "Last Night" (tr. by Agha Shahid Ali). [PoetryE] (27) Spr 89, p. 116.
    "A Letter from Prison" (tr. by Agha Shahid Ali of an Urdu version of a poem by
        Nazim Hikmet). [PoetryE] (27) Spr 89, p. 101.
    "A Prison Daybreak" (tr. by Agha Shahid Ali). [PoetryE] (27) Spr 89, p. 99-100.
    "A Prison Evening" (tr. by Agha Shahid Ali). [PoetryE] (27) Spr 89, p. 98.
    "The Rain of Stones Is Finished" (Elegy for Hassan Nasir, tortured to death, tr. by
        Agha Shahid Ali). [PoetryE] (27) Spr 89, p. 102.
    "So Bring the Order for My Execution" (tr. by Agha Shahid Ali). [PoetryE] (27) Spr
        89, p. 106.
    "Solitude" (tr. by Agha Shahid Ali). [PoetryE] (27) Spr 89, p. 107.
    "Vista" (tr. by Agha Shahid Ali). [PoetryE] (27) Spr 89, p. 115.
1663. FAJARDO, Miguel
    "Si tan sólo Tuviéramos." [Mairena] (11:27) 89, p. 86.
1664. FALCO, Edward
    "While Cold Medicine Made My Heart and Mind Race." [Wind] (19:65) 89, p. 18.
FALERO, Luis Martinez
    See MARTINEZ-FALERO, Luis
1665. FALLA, Jeffrey
    "A Chill at the Edge of an Intersection." [RagMag] (7:1) 89, p. 11.

"Earth Poem: Fear of Clarity." [CinPR] (19) Spr 89, p. 25.
"Maniac Manifesto." [MinnR] (NS 32) Spr 89, p. 89-90.
"The Woman, Dream, and Lazy Circus." [RagMag] (7:1) 89, p. 12-13.
1666. FALLON, Peter
"Windfalls." [NoDaQ] (57:1) Wint 89, p. 65.
"The Woman of the House." [NoDaQ] (57:1) Wint 89, p. 66.
1667. FALLON, Teresa
"At the Women's Correctional Institution." [Kalliope] (10:1/2) 88, p. 46-47.
1668. FALQUEZ-CERTAIN, Miguel
"Cananeos." [LindLM] (8:2) Ap-Je 89, p. 25.
"Ganimedes." [LindLM] (8:2) Ap-Je 89, p. 25.
1669. FANG, Dai
"The Circular Expressway and Straight Lines of the Ancient City" (tr. of Ye
        Yan-bing, w. Edward Morin and Dennis Ding). [Pig] (15) 88, p. 6.
"Flint" (tr. of Gao Fa-lin, w. Edward Morin and Dennis Ding). [Pig] (15) 88, p. 6.
"The Han River Under Fog" (tr. of Cai Qi-jiao, w. Edward Morin). [MichQR] (28:3)
        Sum 89, p. 399.
"The Pledge" (tr. of Li-hong Zhao, w. Edward Morin). [CharR] (15:2) Fall 89, p.
        60.
"Seagull" (tr. of Cai Qi-jiao, w. Edward Morin). [MichQR] (28:3) Sum 89, p. 399.
1670. FANNING, Roger
"Story." [VirQR] (65:1) Wint 89, p. 75-76.
1671. FANTHORPE, U. A.
"The Comforters" (for Philip Gross). [Stand] (30:1) Wint 88-89, p. 29.
1672. FARAM, Lois
"Preemption." [PassN] (10:2) Sum 89, p. 23.
1673. FARAWELL, Martin Jude
"Accident." [Footwork] 89, p. 45.
"Another Night at the Fights." [Footwork] 89, p. 45.
"Around." [SouthernR] (25:2) Spr 89, p. 497-498.
"Night." [Amelia] (5:3, #14) 89, p. 6.
1674. FARBMAN, Evelyn
"Gift Exchange." [SingHM] (16) 89, p. 42-43.
1675. FARGNOLI, Patricia
"Anniversaries" (for Donald Sheehan). [Kalliope] (11:3) 89, p. 28-29.
"The Offer." [StoneC] (16:3/4) Spr-Sum 89, p. 66.
1676. FARGUE, Leon-Paul
"Aeternae Memoriae Patris." [Caliban] (6) 89, p. 60-62.
1677. FARLEY, Blanche
"In Her Suite at The Hotel St. Regis, Amy Lowell Muses at Midnight." [Kalliope]
        (10:1/2) 88, p. 44.
"Lament to Sylvia." [Kalliope] (10:1/2) 88, p. 45.
1678. FARLEY, Joseph
"Chinese Tea." [BallSUF] (30:4) Aut 89, p. 14.
"The Lesson." [PaintedB] (38) 89, p. 38.
"Letters from Canada." [PaintedB] (38) 89, p. 37.
"Untitled: Blue sari turns." [BallSUF] (30:4) Aut 89, p. 14.
1679. FARLEY, Rebecca M.
"Eternity." [EmeraldCR] (1989) c1988, p. 136.
1680. FARMER, Harold
"Cicada" (For Sharon Olds). [Grain] (17:1) Spr 89, p. 58.
"Okavango Dawn." [Grain] (17:1) Spr 89, p. 59.
1681. FARMILOE, Dorothy
"In the Beginning Was the Line." [Dandel] (16:2) Fall-Wint 89, p. 33.
"Whatever Happened to the Real Real Thing?" [Dandel] (16:2) Fall-Wint 89, p. 32.
1682. FARNSWORTH, Jared D.
"The Annesta-Myth." [YellowS] (30) Sum 89, p. 28.
"In the Worship of Flesh." [YellowS] (30) Sum 89, p. 28.
"The Mirror." [YellowS] (30) Sum 89, p. 28.
"Odysseus to Selena." [YellowS] (30) Sum 89, p. 29.
1683. FARQUHAR, Dion
"All the King's Men." [RedBass] (14) 89, p. 60.
"Clay Head." [Bound] (16:2/3) Wint-Spr 89, p. 309.
"Empire State." [Hawai'iR] (13:2, #26) Sum 89, p. 52-53.
"Fed Up." [Bound] (16:2/3) Wint-Spr 89, p. 305-308.
"Fifties." [Bound] (16:2/3) Wint-Spr 89, p. 310.

"Pink Slips." [CentralP] (16) Fall 89, p. 186-187.
"Queen City." [RedBass] (14) 89, p. 61-63.
1684. FARRAH, David
"A Pelican." [DenQ] (24:2) Fall 89, p. 45.
1685. FARRANT, M.A.C.
"The Early Plastic Shrine." [Rampike] (6:2) 88, p. 76.
1686. FARRAR, Gretchen E.
"New Year." [HangL] (54) 89, p. 55.
"RJ." [Footwork] 89, p. 50.
1687. FARRELL, John
"Koan." [Sequoia] (33:1) Sum 89, p. 64.
1688. FARRELL, Kate
"La Chambre sur la Cour." [AntigR] (76) Wint 89, p. 74.
"Girl with Bare Shoulders." [AntigR] (76) Wint 89, p. 73.
"Nude Girl." [AntigR] (76) Wint 89, p. 74.
"Room Facing East (Rue Terre Neuve)." [AntigR] (76) Wint 89, p. 73.
1689. FARRIS, Earl F.
"Footsteps." [EmeraldCR] (1989) c1988, p. 95.
"Wizard." [EmeraldCR] (1989) c1988, p. 95.
1690. FASCE, Maria de los Angeles
"Soneto de mi Agrestividad." [Mairena] (11:27) 89, p. 65.
1691. FASEL, Ida
"Hanging Wash." [CapeR] (24:1) Spr 89, p. 26-27.
"Playing the Parts." [ChrC] (106:31) O 25, 89, p. 956.
"Showrooms." [PoetL] (84:4) Wint 89-90, p. 17.
"Worshipfully." [ChrC] (106:11) Ap 5, 89, p. 350.
1692. FASS, Deborah
"Rachel." [HarvardA] (124:1) N 89, p. 7.
"The Shop." [HarvardA] (123:2) Ja 89, p. 12.
1693. FASULO, Anne
"Lines for Anne Pasternak." [Kaleid] (19) Sum-Fall 89, p. 81.
1694. FAUX, Gus
"Meeting Point." [Grain] (17:3) Fall 89, p. 50.
1695. FAVORITE, Malaika
"The Birthing Song." [Vis] (30) 89, p. 42.
"For Men Missing in the Mississippi." [Vis] (30) 89, p. 39-41.
1696. FAY, Julie
"Christmas Shopping in Venice." [Ploughs] (15:4) Wint 89-90, p. 72-74.
"It Etait une Fois." [Ploughs] (15:4) Wint 89-90, p. 69-71.
"The Lilac Age." [LaurelR] (23:1) Wint 89, p. 15-16.
"October." [Ploughs] (15:1) 89, p. 37-38.
"Sicilian Sestets at Etna" (for Laszlo). [Ploughs] (15:1) 89, p. 39-40.
"The Teachings of Lilacs" (for Kinereth Gensler). [LaurelR] (23:1) Wint 89, p.
16-17.
1697. FEATURE, Thomas Schaller. Special Translation
"Thirty Running Haikus" (for Allen Ginsberg, tr. of Christoph Derschau). [MidAR]
(9:1) 89, p. 1-23.
1698. FEDERMAN, Raymond
"Ceci N'Est Pas le Commencement: Excerpts from Double or Nothing" (tr. by the
author). [Rampike] (6:1) 87, p. 26-27.
"In the End." [MissR] (17:3, #51), p. 46.
"Jazz Solo Jazz." [Caliban] (7) 89, p. 124.
1699. FEDO, David
"An Exercise on Understanding Death." [KanQ] (21:1/2) Wint-Spr 89, p. 58.
"Lake Skatutakee" (for Lou and Helen Carey). [KanQ] (21:1/2) Wint-Spr 89, p. 57.
1700. FEELA, David J.
"Amnesty" (for Peggy Koehler). [OxfordM] (5:2) Fall-Wint 89, p. 63.
"Grandmother's Hiatus." [PassN] (10:1) Wint 89, p. 21.
"Interlude." [OxfordM] (5:2) Fall-Wint 89, p. 64.
1701. FEENY, Thomas
"Good Things Die." [CapeR] (24:2) Fall 89, p. 34.
1702. FEES, Sandy
"Among the Wreckage." [Footwork] 89, p. 14.
1703. FEIERSTEIN, Ricardo
"We, the Generation in the Wilderness" (Selections: 1, 7-11, 14, tr. by J. Kates and
Stephen A. Sadow). [Pig] (15) 88, p. 96.

1704. FEIN, Richard
    "The Champion Retires." [StoneC] (16:3/4) Spr-Sum 89, p. 41.
    "Live Free and Die." [Outbr] (20) 89, p. 28.
    "Morning Stroll." [Plain] (10:1) 89, p. 30.
1705. FEINSTEIN, Robert N.
    "Love and Taxes." [HolCrit] (26:3) Je 89, p. 20.
1706. FEINSTEIN, Sascha
    "Monk's Mood." [MissouriR] (12:1) 89, p. 30-31.
1707. FEIRSTEIN, Frederick
    "After the Revolution" (For Sam). [Salm] (84) Fall 89, p. 63.
    "A Day in Disney World." [CrossCur] (8:2) Ja 89, p. 77-81.
1708. FELDMAN, Alan
    "Anniversary." [MissR] (18:1, #52) 89, p. 72-73.
    "Another Visit from My Sister." [Iowa] (19:3) Fall 89, p. 55.
    "Guest." [BostonR] (14:5) O 89, p. 12.
    "Marini's *Man on a Horse*." [Iowa] (19:3) Fall 89, p. 55.
    "One of My Daughter's Drawings." [TarRP] (29:1) Fall 89, p. 55.
1709. FELDMAN, Irving
    "Ambition." [GrandS] (8:3) Spr 89, p. 235.
    "Arslan & Arpad: On the Question of Craft." [GrandS] (8:3) Spr 89, p. 235.
    "Immortality." [NewYorker] (64:46) 2 Ja 89, p. 32.
    "The Life and Letters." [NewYorker] (65:32) 25 S 89, p. 52.
    "Only Then." [GrandS] (9:1) Aut 89, p. 51-52.
    "West Street." [NewRep] (201:22) 27 N 89, p. 32.
1710. FELDMAN, Ruth
    "The Right Perspective." [SouthernR] (25:4) Aut 89, p. 945.
    "White Night." [Agni] (28) 89, p. 272-273.
1711. FELDSTEIN, Charles
    "Tennis: A Love Game." [Kalliope] (10:3) 88, p. 68.
1712. FELLMAN, Stanley A.
    "Checking the Medical Library for Mystery Show Television." [InterPR] (15:2) Fall
        89, p. 103.
    "Deftly Climbing Smoke." [Nimrod] (33:1) Fall-Wint 89, p. 80.
    "The Idle Subversives." [InterPR] (15:2) Fall 89, p. 104.
    "Joan." [InterPR] (15:2) Fall 89, p. 105.
    "To the End to the End." [Nimrod] (33:1) Fall-Wint 89, p. 78.
    "U.S.A. -- History's Dream When It Sleeps" (for Eric). [InterPR] (15:2) Fall 89, p.
        105.
    "What Bird Song Remains." [Amelia] (5:3, #14) 89, p. 106.
    "What Bird Song Remains." [InterPR] (15:2) Fall 89, p. 104.
    "What Bird Song Remains." [Nimrod] (33:1) Fall-Wint 89, p. 77.
    "Your Nearest Eye." [Nimrod] (33:1) Fall-Wint 89, p. 79.
FEMAT, Socorro Leon
    See LEON FEMAT, Socorro
FENYONG, Li
    See LI, Fenyong
1713. FERBER, Al
    "Cowboys and Indians." [PaintedB] (38) 89, p. 62.
1714. FERBEY, Orysia
    "The Firebird" (tr. of Yar Slavutych). [CanLit] (120) Spr 89, p. 90.
    "Poem: It was when you arrived in white" (tr. of Yar Slavutych). [CanLit] (120) Spr
        89, p. 115.
1715. FERGAR, Feyyaz
    "Division of Labor" (tr. of Feyyaz Kayacan). [Trans] (21) Spr 89, p. 233.
    "Lament of the Misled" (tr. of Feyyaz Kayacan). [Trans] (21) Spr 89, p. 232.
    "Mystery" (tr. of Hilmi Yavuz). [Trans] (21) Spr 89, p. 231.
1716. FERGUSON, Key Leigh
    "Back in the Kitchen." [GreensboroR] (46) Sum 89, p. 208.
1717. FERGUSON, Mark T.
    "Snow Country" (Selection: Parts I-II, tr. of Yasunari Kawabata). [Trans] (22) Fall
        89, p. 237-257.
1718. FERGUSON, Scott
    "The Romantic Age." [BrooklynR] (6) 89, p. 11.
1719. FERLINGHETTI, Lawrence
    "The Plow of Time" (for Vojo Sindolic 6/82, from forthcoming "European Poems,"
        1983). [AlphaBS] (6) Wint 89-90, p. 31.

"Poet as Fisherman." [Antaeus] (62) Spr 89, p. 75-76.
1720. FERNANDEZ, Pablo Armando
    "Parabola" (tr. by Pat Carrothers and Armando Romero). [Pig] (15) 88, p. 75.
1721. FERNANDEZ RETAMAR, Roberto
    "Last Letter" (tr. by Lourdes González). [Pig] (15) 88, p. 70-71.
1722. FERRARELLI, Rina
    "Emigrant/Immigrant." [WestB] (23) 89, p. 99.
    "Here" (tr. of Bartolo Cattafi). [InterPR] (15:2) Fall 89, p. 69.
    "The Imagined and the Real" (to my daughter). [Footwork] 89, p. 51.
    "Into Its Cold" (tr. of Bartolo Cattafi). [InterPR] (15:2) Fall 89, p. 69.
    "It's Here That God" (tr. of Bartolo Cattafi). [InterPR] (15:2) Fall 89, p. 71.
    "Missed Opportunity" (tr. of Bartolo Cattafi). [BlueBldgs] (11) 89, p. 41.
    "Missed Opportunity" (tr. of Bartolo Cattafi). [InterPR] (15:2) Fall 89, p. 73.
    "My Hometown." [Footwork] 89, p. 51.
    "A Needle Point Canvas." [BallSUF] (30:4) Aut 89, p. 23-24.
    "Path" (tr. of Bartolo Cattafi). [BlueBldgs] (11) 89, p. 40.
    "Path" (tr. of Bartolo Cattafi). [InterPR] (15:2) Fall 89, p. 69.
    "Pyracantha" (tr. of Bartolo Cattafi). [InterPR] (15:2) Fall 89, p. 73.
    "Spring Breezes" (tr. of Bartolo Cattafi). [InterPR] (15:2) Fall 89, p. 71.
    "To the Two of Us" (tr. of Bartolo Cattafi). [BlueBldgs] (11) 89, p. 42.
    "Wind Sculptures." [BallSUF] (30:4) Aut 89, p. 20.
    "Your Relief" (tr. of Bartolo Cattafi). [InterPR] (15:2) Fall 89, p. 71.
1723. FERRIS, Beth
    "Eight-Eyed Vision" (Honorable Mention). [Nimrod] (33:1) Fall-Wint 89, p. 36-37.
1724. FETZER, Glenn W.
    "Hands Smooth" (tr. of Jacques Dupin). [InterPR] (15:2) Fall 89, p. 79.
    "In This Oblivion" (tr. of Jacques Dupin). [InterPR] (15:2) Fall 89, p. 77.
    "Let the Words Take Hold in the Air" (tr. of Jacques Dupin). [InterPR] (15:2) Fall
        89, p. 81.
    "Now I Speak" (tr. of Jacques Dupin). [InterPR] (15:2) Fall 89, p. 77.
    "Plunging" (tr. of Jacques Dupin). [InterPR] (15:2) Fall 89, p. 79.
    "Raised Stones" (tr. of Jacques Dupin). [InterPR] (15:2) Fall 89, p. 79.
    "Story of the Traveler" (tr. of Jacques Dupin). [InterPR] (15:2) Fall 89, p. 77.
    "Torn Book" (tr. of Jacques Dupin). [InterPR] (15:2) Fall 89, p. 77.
    "Water Streams" (tr. of Jacques Dupin). [InterPR] (15:2) Fall 89, p. 77.
1725. FIAMENGO, Marya
    "Raspolozenje." [CanLit] (120) Spr 89, p. 64-66.
FICK, Marlon Ohnesorge
    See OHNESORGE-FICK, Marlon
1726. FICOCIELLO, John
    "Flatulence." [AntR] (47:1) Wint 89, p. 67.
1727. FICOWSKI, Jerzy
    "Ex-Jewish Things" (tr. by Stanislaw Baranczak and Clare Cavanagh). [SenR]
        (19:2) Fall 89, p. 25.
    "How to Spoil Cannibals' Fun" (tr. by Stanislaw Baranczak and Clare Cavanah).
        [Trans] (21) Spr 89, p. 44-45.
1728. FIELD, Edward
    "The Best Friend." [Witness] (2:1) Spr 88, p. 150-151.
    "The Dog Sitters." [WestHR] (43:3) Aut 89, p. 188-189.
1729. FIELDER, William
    "In the Home for the Aged" (tr. of Özcan Yalim, w. the author and Dionis Coffin
        Riggs). [StoneC] (16:3/4) Spr-Sum 89, p. 35.
1730. FIELDS, Robert
    "They Give It a Name." [InterPR] (15:2) Fall 89, p. 106-107.
1731. FIKE, Francis
    "Deor" (tr. from the anonymous Gaelic[?]). [CumbPR] (8:2) Spr 89, p. 87, 89.
    "Kisses" (after Catullus, V). [CumbPR] (8:2) Spr 89, p. 90.
1732. FILES, Meg
    "The Day Awake." [TampaR] (2) 89, p. 88-89.
    "The Lighthouse at Ponce Point." [Writer] (102:9) S 89, p. 21-22.
1733. FILIP, Raymond
    "Kucios." [Grain] (17:4) Wint 89, p. 48-49.
1734. FILIPOWSKA, Patricia
    "Flying Back Home to Iowa." [PoetC] (21:1) Fall 89, p. 28.
    "On Her Ninetieth Birthday." [PoetC] (21:1) Fall 89, p. 29.

1735. FILKINS, Peter
"Every Day" (tr. of Ingeborg Bachmann). [TriQ] (74) Wint 89, p. 214.
"No Delicacies" (tr. of Ingeborg Bachmann). [TriQ] (74) Wint 89, p. 215-216.
1736. FINALE, Frank
"The Return." [BrooklynR] (5) 88, p. 38.
1737. FINCH, Annie
"Goddess." [WeberS] (6:2) Fall 89, p. 39.
"Mother." [WeberS] (6:2) Fall 89, p. 41.
"Muse-Daughter." [WeberS] (6:2) Fall 89, p. 40.
"The Native American Birds." [KanQ] (21:1/2) Wint-Spr 89, p. 70.
"Separate Spheres." [WeberS] (6:2) Fall 89, p. 42.
"The Woman on the Beach." [WeberS] (6:2) Fall 89, p. 39.
1738. FINCH, Casey
"Egypt." [Ploughs] (15:4) Wint 89-90, p. 75-76.
1739. FINCH, Roger
"Apsara" (Fundukistan, 7th Century). [LaurelR] (23:2) Sum 89, p. 70.
"Evenings in Kashgar." [BelPoJ] (40:1) Fall 89, p. 21-22.
"In a Sari Shop." [BelPoJ] (40:1) Fall 89, p. 20-21.
"The Lacemaker." [WormR] (29:4, #116) 89, p. 100.
"Lady Standing at a Virginal." [WormR] (29:4, #116) 89, p. 101.
"The Love Letter." [WebR] (14:1) Spr 89, p. 79.
"The Sunflower." [WebR] (14:1) Spr 89, p. 78.
"The Wisteria That Strangled the House." [Event] (18:3) Fall 89, p. 50.
1740. FINCKE, Gary
"At Breakfast." [CapeR] (24:1) Spr 89, p. 6.
"At the Reception in Our Yard." [GettyR] (2:1) Wint 89, p. 174-175.
"Doing the All-White Puzzle." [BlueBldgs] (11) 89, p. 26.
"The Fiction of the Bypass." [AnotherCM] (19) 89, p. 67-68.
"The Flower Remedies." [PoetryNW] (30:2) Sum 89, p. 31-33.
"Fund Drive." [CapeR] (24:1) Spr 89, p. 7.
"Green." [WebR] (14:1) Spr 89, p. 65.
"History Bites." [BelPoJ] (40:2) Wint 89-90, p. 3-4.
"The Hollow Earth." [BelPoJ] (39:4) Sum 89, p. 25-26.
"Horses." [SoCoast] (6) Fall 88, p. 34.
"In Films, the Army Ants Are Always Intelligent." [PoetryNW] (30:3) Aut 89, p. 26-27.
"Iridology." [OxfordM] (5:2) Fall-Wint 89, p. 65-66.
"Ishi." [Journal] (12:2) Fall-Wint 88-89, p. 38.
"Learning Cursive." [PoetryNW] (30:3) Aut 89, p. 27-29.
"Liberty Bells." [PoetL] (84:3) Fall 89, p. 25-26.
"Opening the Locks." [BelPoJ] (39:4) Sum 89, p. 24-25.
"Remedies." [AnotherCM] (19) 89, p. 69-70.
"Scorecards." [NoAmR] (274:1) Mr 89, p. 57.
"The Skill of the Sunlight's Good." [GettyR] (2:1) Wint 89, p. 176.
"Tumblebug." [PoetL] (84:3) Fall 89, p. 27.
"Walking." [Poetry] (154:5) Ag 89, p. 266-268.
1741. FINK, Janie
"A Million Questions." [Antaeus] (62) Spr 89, p. 77.
1742. FINK, Robert A.
"I. C. U." [TriQ] (74) Wint 89, p. 203-204.
"In the Hospital Waiting Room." [Poetry] (154:4) Jl 89, p. 199.
1743. FINKE, Matt
"Whew! Does It Smell in Here." [Mildred] (3:1) Spr-Sum 89, p. 36.
1744. FINKEL, Donald
"Accomplices" (tr. of Bei Dao, w. Xueliang Chen). [LitR] (32:3) Spr 89, p. 340.
"At Roxy's Topless" (For Cinnamon). [KenR] (NS 11:1) Wint 89, p. 31.
"Campus Dogs." [KenR] (NS 11:1) Wint 89, p. 32.
"Elegy" (tr. of Bei Dao, w. Xueliang Chen). [LitR] (32:3) Spr 89, p. 342.
"Here." [RiverS] (30) [89], p. 27.
"The Host" (tr. of Bei Dao, w. Xueliang Chen). [LitR] (32:3) Spr 89, p. 343.
"I'm Forever a Stranger" (tr. of Bei Dao, w. Xueliang Chen). [LitR] (32:3) Spr 89, p. 340.
"The Incomparable Oates." [RiverS] (30) [89], p. 29-30.
"It's Time." [RiverS] (30) [89], p. 28.
"Justo the Painter and the Conquest of Lawrence" (Lawrence, Massachusetts 1987). [RiverS] (30) [89], p. 33.

"Memory" (tr. of Bei Dao, w. Xueliang Chen). [LitR] (32:3) Spr 89, p. 343.
"Night: Theme and Variations" (tr. of Bei Dao, w. Xueliang Chen). [LitR] (32:3)
    Spr 89, p. 341.
"No Tomorrow" (tr. of Bei Dao, w. Xueliang Chen). [LitR] (32:3) Spr 89, p. 339.
"Shore" (tr. of Bei Dao, w. Xueliang Chen). [LitR] (32:3) Spr 89, p. 342.
"So Long." [NewEngR] (11:4) Sum 89, p. 439.
"Toast" (tr. of Bei Dao, w. Xueliang Chen). [LitR] (32:3) Spr 89, p. 339.
1745. FINKELSTEIN, Norman
    "Have I loved the Torah more than God" (1st line. Title in Hebrew characters).
        [Talisman] (2) Spr 89, p. 55.
    "Odradek." [Salm] (81) Wint 89, p. 97-98.
    "The Weary Pleasure Seekers." [DenQ] (23:3/4) Wint-Spr 89, p. 96-97.
1746. FINLEY, C. Stephen
    "Amulet." [SouthernHR] (23:2) Spr 89, p. 135.
    "At Dawn." [Wind] (19:65) 89, p. 7-8.
    "In January." [Wind] (19:65) 89, p. 7.
    "Journey." [Wind] (19:65) 89, p. 7.
1747. FINLEY, Robert
    "Ago." [Grain] (17:1) Spr 89, p. 27.
1748. FINNEGAN, James
    "Beach Glass." [SoCaR] (21:2) Spr 89, p. 47.
    "The Crystallography of Cities." [Nimrod] (33:1) Fall-Wint 89, p. 84.
    "Lost Home." [PraS] (63:2) Sum 89, p. 88-89.
    "Ordinary Life." [Nimrod] (33:1) Fall-Wint 89, p. 82-83.
    "Whitman's Etceteras." [Nimrod] (33:1) Fall-Wint 89, p. 85-86.
1749. FINNELL, Dennis
    "Banzai." [Sequoia] (32:2) Wint-Spr 89, p. 12.
    "Belladonna." [TarRP] (28:2) Spr 89, p. 31-32.
    "The Fifth Season." [RiverC] (10:1) Fall 89, p. 72-73.
    "Oscar in a Tree." [ColEng] (51:2) F 89, p. 154.
    "Oscar, Just Not Himself." [ColEng] (51:2) F 89, p. 152.
    "Oscar, On Skin and Light." [ColEng] (51:2) F 89, p. 153.
    "Pass It On." [RiverC] (10:1) Fall 89, p. 70-71.
    "Red Cottage." [ColEng] (51:2) F 89, p. 151.
    "Third Island" (for W. S. Graham). [DenQ] (23:3/4) Wint-Spr 89, p. 98-99.
    "Triptych: A Joyful Noise" (for Kelly McFarland). [NewL] (55:3) Spr 89, p. 46-49.
1750. FINORA, Deborah
    "Back to School." [EmeraldCR] (1989) c1988, p. 114.
FIRMAT, Gustavo Pérez
    See PEREZ FIRMAT, Gustavo
1751. FIRMIN, Sarah
    "Hot Air Balloon." [Mildred] (3:1) Spr-Sum 89, p. 35.
1752. FISCHER, Aaron
    "Homage to Frank O'Hara." [PoetryE] (28) Fall 89, p. 165-166.
1753. FISCHER, Allen C. (See also FISHER, Allen)
    "By the Sun's Early Fat." [SenR] (19:1) 89, p. 61.
    "Life Among the Gadflies." [RiverS] (30) [89], p. 53.
    "A Will." [SenR] (19:1) 89, p. 62.
1754. FISCHEROVA, Sylva
    "Drinking Coffee" (tr. by Jarmila and Ian Milner). [Verse] (6:1) Mr 89, p. 37.
    "Not that we didn't expect it" (tr. by Jarmila and Ian Milner). [Verse] (6:1) Mr 89, p.
        36.
    "The Pripet Marshes" (tr. by Jarmila and Ian Milner). [Verse] (6:2) Je 89, p. 64.
1755. FISER, Karen
    "Just Before the Dove Begins to Call." [HangL] (55) 89, p. 16.
    "Night Shift." [HangL] (55) 89, p. 15.
1756. FISH, Karen
    "The Backroom" (for Emmy). [AmerPoR] (18:6) N-D 89, p. 43.
    "The Dreams." [ParisR] (31:112) Fall 89, p. 26-27.
    "Swans." [AmerPoR] (18:6) N-D 89, p. 45.
    "What Is Beyond Us" (For Tim). [AmerPoR] (18:6) N-D 89, p. 44.
    "Woods Hole: Cape Cod." [AmerPoR] (18:6) N-D 89, p. 44.
1757. FISHER, Allen (See also FISCHER, Allen C.)
    "Charley-Bop" (from Gravity as a Consequence of Shape). [Notus] (4:1) Spr 89, p.
        61-63.

1758. FISHER, David
"Nude." [YellowS] (32) Wint 89, p. 41.
1759. FISHER, Joan
"Pressed" (for JRB). [PaintedB] (37) 89, p. 59.
1760. FISHER, Steve
"Dysphoria." [Shen] (39:1) Spr 89, p. 100-101.
1761. FISHMAN, Charles
"Birthday Present." [NewL] (55:3) Spr 89, p. 19.
"Damnation" (tr. of Sarah Kirsch, w. Marina Roscher). [WebR] (14:1) Spr 89, p. 12.
"Gentle Hunt" (tr. of Sarah Kirsch, w. Marina Roscher). [WebR] (14:1) Spr 89, p. 15.
"Heartstone" (tr. of Sarah Kirsch, w. Marina Roscher). [WebR] (14:1) Spr 89, p. 14.
"Ravens" (tr. of Sarah Kirsch, w. Marina Roscher). [WebR] (14:1) Spr 89, p. 14.
"The Sleeper" (tr. of Sarah Kirsch, w. Marina Roscher). [WebR] (14:1) Spr 89, p. 13.
"The Trochel" (tr. of Sarah Kirsch, w. Marina Roscher). [WebR] (14:1) Spr 89, p. 15.
1762. FISKE, Ingrid
"Small Passing." [AmerPoR] (18:4) Jl-Ag 89, p. 35.
1763. FISTER, Mary
"Gabriel's Horn." [AnotherCM] (19) 89, p. 71.
"Kept in Stitches." [AnotherCM] (19) 89, p. 72-73.
1764. FITZGERALD, D. Marie
"Lack of Any Title." [Footwork] 89, p. 39.
1765. FITZGERALD, F. Scott
"The Way of Purgation." [PoetL] (84:4) Wint 89-90, p. 32.
1766. FITZHUGH, Gwen
"For Robert Frost." [EngJ] (78:2) F 89, p. 97.
1767. FIX, Charlene
"Cats Are Birds." [AntR] (47:4) Fall 89, p. 463.
"We Are the Clocks." [Wind] (19:64) 89, p. 14.
1768. FIXEL, Lawrence
"Among Other Things." [Notus] (4:1) Spr 89, p. 64-65.
"The Error Catastrophe." [HeavenB] (7) Wint 89, p. 46.
"In the Land of Un. In the Land of Dis." [Notus] (4:2) Fall 89, p. 82-84.
"The News from Dronesville." [Talisman] (3) Fall 89, p. 112-113.
"One Vote for the Vulture." [Notus] (4:1) Spr 89, p. 66.
"A Stone Taking Notes." [HeavenB] (7) Wint 89, p. 47.
"The Trial of Two Cities." [Caliban] (6) 89, p. 180.
1769. FLANDERS, Jane
"Family Ground." [NewYorker] (65:39) 13 N 89, p. 50.
"The Punches." [WestB] (25) 89, p. 108-109.
1770. FLANNERY, Matthew
"In the Mountains" (for J. E., tr. of Wei Wang). [StoneC] (17:1/2) Fall-Wint 89-90, p. 43.
1771. FLANZBAUM, Hilene
"Getting Some." [Pequod] (26/27) 89, p. 37-38.
1772. FLECK, Polly
"Dad's Secretary, 1945." [Dandel] (16:1) Spr-Sum 89, p. 45.
"Her New Husband Went Elaborately to Bed." [Dandel] (16:1) Spr-Sum 89, p. 46-47.
1773. FLECK, Richard
"An Overland Memory." [DeKalbLAJ] (22:1/4) 89, p. 54.
1774. FLEISHER, Bernice
"A Drift of Ashes." [Nimrod] (33:1) Fall-Wint 89, p. 64.
"The Leopard." [Nimrod] (33:1) Fall-Wint 89, p. 63.
1775. FLEMING, Deborah
"Bright Angel Trail." [Lactuca] (13) N 89, p. 65.
"House on Columbia Avenue in Steubenville." [Lactuca] (13) N 89, p. 66.
1776. FLEMING, Harold (Harold Lee)
"Ann Belfry, Dying." [MSS] (6:3) 89, p. 21.
"Ann Belfry's Nightsong." [MSS] (6:3) 89, p. 20.
"The Monday Wash." [Vis] (30) 89, p. 36.
"My Russian Lady." [NegC] (9:1) 89, p. 28.

"The Night, the Wind." [Wind] (19:64) 89, p. 16.
1777. FLEMING, Thomas
"Thanksgiving." [CrossCur] (8:2) Ja 89, p. 86.
1778. FLETCHER, Dorothy
"Man by Van Gogh." [KeyWR] (2:1/2) Fall-Wint 89, p. 117.
1779. FLETCHER, Luellen
"One Winter." [PassN] (10:1) Wint 89, p. 20.
1780. FLOCK, Miriam
"Baby's First Year." [NewL] (55:3) Spr 89, p. 88.
"Castles in Spain." [PoetryNW] (30:4) Wint 89-90, p. 28.
"The Dark Lady" (Selections: VIII, IX). [HampSPR] Wint 89, p. 52.
"Postcards from China." [PoetryNW] (30:4) Wint 89-90, p. 26-28.
1781. FLOOK, Maria
"A Seaside Moon." [IndR] (12:2) Spr 89, p. 113-114.
1782. FLOREA, Ted
"Untitled: My son's line winds impatiently." [Plain] (10:1) 89, p. 19.
1783. FLORES, Luis E.
"Al Hombre Triste Que Me Mira Cuando Paso y Que Además No Existe."
[Americas] (17:3/4) Fall-Wint 89, p. 54-55.
"Oda a la Mujer." [Americas] (17:3/4) Fall-Wint 89, p. 56-59.
"Una Tarde de Marzo, Educando a Luis." [Americas] (17:3/4) Fall-Wint 89, p.
60-62.
FLORIDO, Jorge J. Rodriguez
See RODRIGUEZ-FLORIDO, Jorge J.
1784. FLORY, Suzy
"Brian." [SlipS] (9) 89, p. 16-17.
"Mary Got Busted." [SlipS] (9) 89, p. 15-16.
"My Room at Mother's Ten Years Later." [PassN] (10:2) Sum 89, p. 26.
1785. FLYNN, Jim
"Alone." [Mildred] (3:1) Spr-Sum 89, p. 37.
1786. FLYNN, Richard
"The Last Resort." [WashR] (15:3) O-N 89, p. 19.
FOE, Mark de
See DeFOE, Mark
1787. FOERSTER, Richard
"At the Church of the Assumption" (Salz an der Saale). [SoCoast] (7) Spr-Fall 89, p.
26.
"Carousel." [SoCoast] (7) Spr-Fall 89, p. 27.
"Counterpoint" (11 October 1896). [SoCoast] (7) Spr-Fall 89, p. 24.
"The Day Stalin Died." [SouthwR] (74:2) Spr 89, p. 259.
"Horizon." [KeyWR] (2:1/2) Fall-Wint 89, p. 137.
"Shorebirds in October." [KeyWR] (2:1/2) Fall-Wint 89, p. 136.
"Strategy." [Poetry] (154:5) Ag 89, p. 274.
"The Trees at Mt. San Angelo" (Sweet Briar, Virginia). [SoCoast] (7) Spr-Fall 89,
p. 25.
1788. FOGDEN, Barry
"Machu Picchu" (the permanence of). [SpiritSH] (55) Fall-Wint 89 [90 on cover], p.
45.
1789. FOGEL, Aaron
"The Chessboard Is on Fire." [Boulevard] (4:2, #11) Fall 89, p. 165-169.
1790. FOGELMAN, Betsy
"A Man Speaks to His Woman." [TriQ] (74) Wint 89, p. 184.
"Remembrance by a Vase." [TriQ] (74) Wint 89, p. 182-183.
"Womanly." [TriQ] (74) Wint 89, p. 185.
1791. FOGG, Karen
"Travelling" (Prose Poem Winter, the First Short Grain Contest). [Grain] (17:3) Fall
89, p. 70.
1792. FOLAYAN, Ayofemi Stowe
"Dyslexia" (dedicated to Helen Irlen). [SinW] (39) Wint 89-90, p. 87-88.
1793. FOLEY, Michael
"The Hag of Bréhéc." [Stand] (30:3) Sum 89, p. 65.
"Homage to Life" (after Jules Supervielle). [Stand] (30:3) Sum 89, p. 64.
1794. FOLLIN-JONES, Elizabeth
"The Walker." [SingHM] (16) 89, p. 30.
1795. FONDANE, Benjamin
"From: Ulysses" (tr. by Leonard Schwartz and E. M. Cioran). [PartR] (56:1) Wint

89, p. 120-121.
"Mtasipol" (tr. by Leonard Schwartz). [Pequod] (28/29/30) 89, p. 188-194.
1796. FONT, María Cecilia
"El Desierto." [Mairena] (11:27) 89, p. 76.
1797. FOOTMAN, Jennifer
"After D.H. Lawrence." [Quarry] (38:1) Wint 89, p. 27.
1798. FORBES, John
"Colonial Aubade." [Verse] (6:1) Mr 89, p. 15.
1799. FORCE, Kathy
"Without a Proper Place." [Plain] (9:3) Spr 89, p. 6.
1800. FORD, Elizabeth
"A *New Yorker* Cover." [GreensboroR] (47) Wint 89-90, p. 51.
1801. FORD, William
"Doctor Doctorum" (In Memoriam D.D.G.). [Poetry] (154:6) S 89, p. 317-318.
1802. FORITANO, Jim
"Telling Time." [Plain] (9:3) Spr 89, p. 23.
1803. FORNOFF, Frederick H.
"Avila" (tr. of Guillermo Carnero). [AmerPoR] (18:2) Mr-Ap 89, p. 32.
"Dawn in Burgos" (Las Huelgas, tr. of Guillermo Carnero). [AmerPoR] (18:2)
Mr-Ap 89, p. 32.
"Embarking for Cythera" (tr. of Guillermo Carnero). [ChiR] (36:3/4) 89, p. 31-32.
1804. FORSSTRÖM, Tua
"A Body Is to Bear a Shrine" (from "Penelope," tr. by David McDuff). [Stand]
(30:3) Sum 89, p. 53.
"The Fieldmouse's Prayer" (tr. by David McDuff). [Stand] (30:3) Sum 89, p. 53.
"I See You in the Slow Night" (tr. by David McDuff). [Stand] (30:3) Sum 89, p. 53.
1805. FORSYTH, Sheila
"Rainy Day Shoppers." [Writer] (102:6) Je 89, p. 28.
1806. FORT, Charles
"Darvil and the 4th of July." [ColR] (NS 16:1) Spr-Sum 89, p. 43.
"Darvil Meets James Brown in Harlem and New Orleans." [Callaloo] (12:1, #38)
Wint 89, p. 152.
"Darvil Rides a Subway in New York City." [ColR] (NS 16:1) Spr-Sum 89, p. 41.
"Dog Tag Rag." [ColR] (NS 16:1) Spr-Sum 89, p. 42.
"The Maiden's Psalm." [ColR] (NS 16:1) Spr-Sum 89, p. 38.
"Old Christmas." [GreensboroR] (47) Wint 89-90, p. 133.
"Rite-of-Passage." [ColR] (NS 16:1) Spr-Sum 89, p. 40.
"Thieves in the Sanctuary of James Baldwin." [ColR] (NS 16:1) Spr-Sum 89, p. 39.
"To a Young Child Waking." [ColR] (NS 16:1) Spr-Sum 89, p. 37.
1807. FORTH, John
"An Awkward Age." [Verse] (6:3) Wint 89, p. 47.
"Cold War." [Verse] (6:2) Je 89, p. 43.
1808. FORTIN, Suzanne
"They Bit the Hand That Fed Them." [AlphaBS] (5) Jl 89, p. 66.
1809. FORTINI, Franco
"1944-1947" (tr. by W. S. Di Piero). [Poetry] (155:1/2) O-N 89, p. 37-38.
"Dalla Cina." [Poetry] (155:1/2) O-N 89, p. 36.
"One September Night" (tr. by W. S. Di Piero). [Poetry] (155:1/2) O-N 89, p. 40.
"Out of China" (tr. by W. S. Di Piero). [Poetry] (155:1/2) O-N 89, p. 36.
"The Trees" (tr. by W. S. Di Piero). [Poetry] (155:1/2) O-N 89, p. 39.
"You Look Out and See" (tr. by W. S. Di Piero). [Poetry] (155:1/2) O-N 89, p. 41.
1810. FORTNEY, Steven D.
"Nothing and the Sun." [HeavenB] (6) Wint-Spr 89, p. 29-31.
1811. FORTUNATO, Peter
"Cuban Rosa." [YellowS] (29) Spr 89, p. 20.
1812. FOSS, Phillip
"Th' Excess of Glory Obscured, As When the Sun New-Ris'n Looks Through the
Horizontal Misty Air Shorn of His Beams." [Conjunc] (13) 89, p. 176-178.
"The Manichean Apology" (Pages missing, indexed from Table of Contents).
[Temblor] (10) 89, p. 42-50.
"The Theater of Perfumes." [Sulfur] (9:1, #24) Spr 89, p. 155-163.
"Vinland" (Pages missing, indexed from Table of Contents). [Temblor] (10) 89, p.
42-50.
1813. FOSTER, Leslie (Leslie D.)
"Booking Space." [Lactuca] (13) N 89, p. 58.
"Lisa, the Widow, and Poetry." [GeoR] (43:3) Fall 89, p. 587.

1814. FOSTER, Linda Nemec
    "Untitled: In her dreams, it is always cancer." [BlueBldgs] (11) 89, p. 62.
1815. FOSTER, Sesshu
    "The Budget of the North American Housewife." [SlipS] (9) 89, p. 79-81.
    "The Corpse of a Forgetful Man Will Suddenly Sit Up and Look Around."
        [RedBass] (14) 89, p. 64-66.
    "Jeff told billy and me." [ChangingM] (20) Wint-Spr 89, p. 24.
1816. FOSTER, Thelma
    "Mrs. Elwyn." [Grain] (17:4) Wint 89, p. 57.
    "Tsawwassen Ferry." [Grain] (17:1) Spr 89, p. 57.
1817. FOURNIER, Laurie
    "Insomnia." [AntigR] (77/78) Spr-Sum 89, p. 114-115.
    "Keep Dancing." [AntigR] (77/78) Spr-Sum 89, p. 116.
FOUST, Michelle Mitchell
    See MITCHELL-FOUST, Michelle
FOWLER, Anne Carol
    See FOWLER, Anne Carroll
1818. FOWLER, Anne Carroll
    "How to Be the Other Woman." [CumbPR] (8:2) Spr 89, p. 82.
    "I Must Obey." [KanQ] (21:1/2) Wint-Spr 89, p. 130-131.
    "Mine Is No Ordinary." [CumbPR] (8:2) Spr 89, p. 79-80.
    "Tableau." [KanQ] (21:1/2) Wint-Spr 89, p. 131.
    "Weather" (in memory, the Reverend Richard Martin). [HayF] (5) Fall 89, p. 41.
    "What If." [CumbPR] (8:2) Spr 89, p. 81.
1819. FOWLER, Jay Bradford, Jr.
    "Van Gogh Threw His Shoes in the Yard This Morning." [WindO] (52) Wint 89-90,
        p. 28.
1820. FOWLER, Russell
    "The Old Man's Tools." [Interim] (8:1) Spr 89, p. 34.
    "Snag End." [Interim] (8:1) Spr 89, p. 35.
    "There Is Always a Dog." [KanQ] (21:3) Sum 89, p. 75.
1821. FOWLKES, Vernon, Jr.
    "A Gathering of Voices." [NegC] (9:2) 89, p. 44-45.
1822. FOX, Gail
    "Epiphany." [CanLit] (121) Sum 89, p. 85.
    "Fragments to Compose a Better World" (for M.A.). [MalR] (87) Sum 89, p. 36-42.
    "Prayer of Sorts." [AntigR] (77/78) Spr-Sum 89, p. 210.
    "The Terrorist: Reflections on Charles Ives's Concord Sonata" (for Margaret
        Laurence). [CrossC] (11:3) 89, p. 5.
1823. FOX, Hugh
    "Camille, Mimi, Etc." [SlipS] (9) 89, p. 72-73.
    "T.L." [SlipS] (9) 89, p. 71.
    "The Trouble with Harry." [SlipS] (9) 89, p. 71-72.
1824. FOX, Leonard
    "Between Night and Day" (tr. of Marie Under). [InterPR] (15:2) Fall 89, p. 15.
    "The Kiss" (tr. of Marie Under). [InterPR] (15:2) Fall 89, p. 11.
    "Lightward Movement" (tr. of Marie Under). [InterPR] (15:2) Fall 89, p. 13.
    "Shooting Star" (tr. of Marie Under). [InterPR] (15:2) Fall 89, p. 19.
    "The Time of Parting" (tr. of Marie Under). [InterPR] (15:2) Fall 89, p. 7.
    "The Tree of Birds" (tr. of Marie Under). [InterPR] (15:2) Fall 89, p. 9.
    "Vigil" (tr. of Marie Under). [InterPR] (15:2) Fall 89, p. 17, 19.
1825. FOX, Linda L.
    "Bald Head Island." [MalR] (87) Sum 89, p. 55.
    "Selling Traveler." [GreensboroR] (46) Sum 89, p. 139-141.
1826. FOX, Lucia
    "Outing." [Kalliope] (11:2) 89, p. 65.
1827. FOX, Margaret
    "The Difference." [EmeraldCR] (1989) c1988, p. 118.
    "On Fooling Around in Someone Else's Garden." [EmeraldCR] (1989) c1988, p.
        117-118.
FOX, Sandra Inskeep
    See INSKEEP-FOX, Sandra
1828. FOX, Susan
    "Teheran, January 1979." [Boulevard] (4:2, #11) Fall 89, p. 159.
1829. FOX, Suzanne
    "Adjustments." [PoetryNW] (30:1) Spr 89, p. 41.

1830. FOX, Valerie
"I stood my ground across the street." [MSS] (6:3) 89, p. 40.
"Runaway." [PaperAir] (4:2) 89, p. 112.
1831. FOY, John (John F.)
"The Cabinet." [AntigR] (76) Wint 89, p. 50.
"Dieppe." [AntigR] (76) Wint 89, p. 50-51.
"Horse (from Job)." [AntigR] (76) Wint 89, p. 51.
"Lauterbrunnen" (for Rosanna Warren). [GrahamHR] (12) Spr 89, p. 68.
"The Rue des Martyrs Sequence" (Selections: 9, 11, 13). [AntigR] (79) Aut 89, p.
40-41.
1832. FRANCES, Dianne
"Apparition in the Garden in August." [RiverS] (29) [89], p. 43.
1833. FRANCIS, Jim
"The Man in the Rumpled Overcoat Said." [Rampike] (6:1) 87, p. 61.
"The Vancouver Rorschach Conspiracy" (Selections: Rorschach #2, #4, #6).
[Rampike] (6:2) 88, p. 50-51.
1834. FRANCIS, Robert
"Pitcher." [YaleR] (78:3) Spr 89, p. 346.
1835. FRANCIS, Scott
"Day's End: A Foreigner Jogs into the Fields." [GrahamHR] (12) Spr 89, p. 20.
"Mongolian Frontier History" (tr. of Xuan Xi Li). [Sequoia] (33:1) Sum 89, p. 77.
"Mongolian Frontier: Many Good Meanings" (tr. of Xuan Xi Li). [Sequoia] (33:1)
Sum 89, p. 78-79.
1836. FRANCISCO, Edward
"Caveat to Vandals on Stealing My Grandmother's Gravestone." [CapeR] (24:1) Spr
89, p. 33.
"Elegy" (Written on July 4, 1988, for the Iranian Business Man Who Lost His
Family When a U. S. Navy Ship Shot Down a Civilian Jetliner). [CapeR]
(24:1) Spr 89, p. 32.
1837. FRANCO, Michael
"Meaning a Life." [Notus] (4:2) Fall 89, p. 66-67.
"The Swell." [Notus] (4:2) Fall 89, p. 68.
1838. FRANDSEN, Wendy Jean
"Girls." [Kalliope] (10:1/2) 88, p. 97-98.
1839. FRANK, Bernhard
"The Bright Stones move through the air" (From *Niemandsrose*, tr. of Paul Celan).
[AntigR] (76) Wint 89, p. 125.
"The Fifth Duino Elegy" (tr. of Rainer Maria Rilke). [WebR] (14:1) Spr 89, p. 5-7.
"Schneepart" (Selections: 6 poems, tr. of Paul Celan). [AntigR] (79) Aut 89, p.
130-135.
"The Way I wear the ring's shadow" (From *Zeitgehöff*, tr. of Paul Celan). [AntigR]
(76) Wint 89, p. 127.
"You Toss Gold after me" (From *Zeitgehöff*, tr. of Paul Celan). [AntigR] (76) Wint
89, p. 127.
1840. FRANKEL, Lillian
"Through the Mountains." [PoetL] (84:4) Wint 89-90, p. 18.
1841. FRANKLIN, Lurlynn
"Choice." [Calyx] (12:2) Wint 89-90, p. 14.
1842. FRANKLIN, Tom
"At Flood Time." [NegC] (9:2) 89, p. 46-47.
1843. FRANKLIN, Walt
"On Visiting the Buffalo Psychiatric Center." [SlipS] (9) 89, p. 31.
1844. FRANTA, MaryAnn
"Watching the Carpenter" (for Ewen McClellan). [FloridaR] (16:2/3) Fall-Wint 89,
p. 100.
1845. FRANZEN, Cola
"The Captive Woman and the Light II" (tr. of Marjorie Agosin). [Pig] (15) 88, p. 94.
"Disappeared Woman I" (tr. of Marjorie Agosin). [Pig] (15) 88, p. 94.
"Don't Jump" (tr. of Alicia Borinsky). [Pig] (15) 88, p. 93.
"Home" (tr. of Alicia Borinsky). [Pig] (15) 88, p. 91.
"Justification" (tr. of Alicia Borinsky). [AnotherCM] (19) 89, p. 11.
"Last More Than Round" (tr. of Marjorie Agosin). [NewAW] (5) Fall 89, p. 66-67.
"Letters" (tr. of Marjorie Agosin). [NewAW] (5) Fall 89, p. 65-66.
"Off to Nevernever Land" (tr. of Saúl Yurkievich). [PartR] (56:1) Wint 89, p.
118-119.
"Plaza Echaurren" (tr. of Juan Cameron). [Pig] (15) 88, p. 94.

"Purchase and Sale Agreement for the Marionette" (tr. of Alicia Borinsky).
    [AnotherCM] (19) 89, p. 13.
"Visits to the Doctor" (tr. of Alicia Borinsky). [Pig] (15) 88, p. 92.
1846. FRASER, Caroline
    "Immature Technology." [NewYorker] (65:32) 25 S 89, p. 60.
1847. FRASER, Grant
    "Auschwitz 2: Waiting for the Russians." [SpiritSH] (54) Spr-Sum 89, p. 10.
    "Guernica." [SpiritSH] (54) Spr-Sum 89, p. 7.
    "Holocaust 1: The Victims." [SpiritSH] (54) Spr-Sum 89, p. 8.
    "Holocaust 2." [SpiritSH] (54) Spr-Sum 89, p. 9.
    "Logging Trucks." [SpiritSH] (54) Spr-Sum 89, p. 10.
    "Mishima." [SpiritSH] (54) Spr-Sum 89, p. 11.
1848. FRASER, Kathleen
    "In Commemoration of the Visit of Foreign Commercial Representatives to Japan,
        1947" (for Bob Glück). [Temblor] (9) 89, p. 7-13.
1849. FRAZIER, Jan
    "The Legacy." [Kalliope] (11:2) 89, p. 52-53.
1850. FREDERICKSON, Todd
    "During Our Move from Minnesota to New York, We Stop in Saxon Harbor,
        Wisconsin, and Feel the Uncertainty of Everything." [SoDakR] (27:2) Sum
        89, p. 93-94.
    "Elegy for August Gordon." [SoDakR] (27:2) Sum 89, p. 91-92.
    "Seven Trees Against Sunset" (tr. of Pablo Antonio Cuadra, w. K. H. Anton).
        [AnotherCM] (19) 89, p. 31-49.
1851. FREED, Florence Wallach
    "The Triangle Factory Fire" (Washington Square, New York City, March 25, 1911).
        [SingHM] (16) 89, p. 59.
1852. FREELAND, Charles
    "Subjunctive." [BellR] (12:1, #25) Spr 89, p. 26-27.
1853. FREEMAN, Grace B.
    "Class Distinction in the Twenties." [Pembroke] (21) 89, p. 63-64.
1854. FREEMAN, Jessica
    "Southern Spectrums." [InterPR] (15:2) Fall 89, p. 108.
    "Unwashed Perimeter." [InterPR] (15:2) Fall 89, p. 109.
1855. FREER, Ulli
    "Rushlight 8." [PaperAir] (4:2) 89, p. 111-112.
1856. FREERICKS, Charles Avakian
    "Her Red Renault." [JINJPo] [11] 89, p. 11.
FREES, Madeline de
    See DeFREES, Madeline
1857. FRENCH, Catherine
    "At the Edge of a Continent, Releasing the Dreams." [PoetryNW] (30:1) Spr 89, p.
        21.
    "Gogol, Toward St. Petersburg." [RiverC] (10:1) Fall 89, p. 77.
    "Huntington's Disease." [PoetryNW] (30:1) Spr 89, p. 20.
    "Unmaking the Horse." [RiverC] (10:1) Fall 89, p. 76.
FRENCH, Dayv James
    See JAMES-FRENCH, Dayv
1858. FRID, Marcia
    "Frostbite" (Prose Poem Winter, the First Short Grain Contest). [Grain] (17:3) Fall
        89, p. 74.
1859. FRIEBERT, Stuart
    "And Everything Slips Easily Away" (tr. of Marin Sorescu, w. Adriana Varga and
        Gabriela Dragnea). [Timbuktu] (4) Sum-Fall 89, p. 25.
    "Between Stars" (tr. of Marin Sorescu, w. Adriana Varga and Gabriela Dragnea).
        [MalR] (88) Fall 89, p. 79.
    "But Names Will Never Hurt You." [MissouriR] (12:2) 89, p. 170.
    "Caesarean." [MissouriR] (12:2) 89, p. 169.
    "Chair" (tr. of Giovanni Raboni, w. Vinio Rossi). [NewL] (55:3) Spr 89, p. 21.
    "Codicils" (tr. of Giovanni Raboni, w. Vinio Rossi). [NewL] (55:3) Spr 89, p.
        20-21.
    "Coffee House, with Pigeons" (tr. of Judita Vaiciunaite, w. Viktoria Skrupskelis).
        [Field] (41) Fall 89, p. 71.
    "Confessions of a Cold Potato." [CinPR] (20) Fall 89, p. 17.
    "Damfoolskis." [CentR] (33:1) Wint 89, p. 54-55.
    "Dream" (tr. of Marin Sorescu, w. Adriana Varga and Gabriela Dragnea).

[Timbuktu] (4) Sum-Fall 89, p. 27.
"The End of Some Things" (tr. of Karl Krolow). [WestB] (24) 89, p. 26.
"Game" (tr. of Marin Sorescu, w. Adriana Varga and Gabriela Dragnea). [Timbuktu] (4) Sum-Fall 89, p. 29.
"Here Cossie, Cossie." [CinPR] (20) Fall 89, p. 16.
"Hide and Seek" (tr. of Marin Sorescu, w. Adriana Varga and Gabriela Dragnea). [Field] (40) Spr 89, p. 40.
"Horoscope" (tr. of Marin Sorescu, w. Adriana Varga and Gabriela Dragnea). [Timbuktu] (4) Sum-Fall 89, p. 35.
"The House" (tr. of Marin Sorescu, w. Adriana Varga and Gabriela Dragnea). [Timbuktu] (4) Sum-Fall 89, p. 31.
"Hyena" (tr. of Marin Sorescu, w. Adriana Varga and Gabriela Dragnea). [Field] (40) Spr 89, p. 42.
"In Between" (tr. of Karl Krolow). [Interim] (8:2) Fall 89, p. 22.
"In the Country" (tr. of Karl Krolow). [OhioR] (44) 89, p. 30.
"Laocoon" (tr. of Marin Sorescu, w. Adriana Varga and Gabriela Dragnea). [Timbuktu] (4) Sum-Fall 89, p. 29.
"Launching" (tr. of Marin Sorescu, w. Adriana Varga and Gabriela Dragnea). [MalR] (88) Fall 89, p. 83.
"Lightning Passed" (tr. of Marin Sorescu, w. Adriana Varga and Gabriela Dragnea). [Field] (40) Spr 89, p. 41.
"Little by Little." [MissouriR] (12:2) 89, p. 171.
"The Mountains" (tr. of Marin Sorescu, w. Adriana Varga). [Iowa] (19:2) Spr-Sum 89, p. 167-168.
"Much Safer Now." [PraS] (63:2) Sum 89, p. 29-31.
"The Murderer" (tr. of Karl Krolow). [Journal] (13:1) Spr-Sum 89, p. 56.
"News of Death" (tr. of Karl Krolow). [ColR] (NS 16:2) Fall 89-Wint 90, p. 84-85.
"Old People's Spring" (tr. of Karl Krolow). [OhioR] (44) 89, p. 29.
"On Heat and Cold." [NoAmR] (274:3) S 89, p. 30.
"Paintings" (tr. of Marin Sorescu, w. Adriana Varga and Gabriela Dragnea). [Field] (40) Spr 89, p. 38-39.
"Paper" (tr. of Marin Sorescu, w. Adriana Varga and Gabriela Dragnea). [MalR] (88) Fall 89, p. 80-81.
"Parade" (tr. of Karl Krolow). [ArtfulD] (16/17) Fall 89, p. 94.
"Passport" (tr. of Marin Sorescu, w. Adriana Varga and Gabriela Dragnea). [MalR] (88) Fall 89, p. 78.
"Perspective" (tr. of Marin Sorescu, w. Adriana Varga). [Os] (29) 89, p. 7.
"Pliers" (tr. of Marin Sorescu, w. Adriana Varga). [Os] (29) 89, p. 9.
"The Sacred Fire" (tr. of Marin Sorescu, w. Adriana Varga). [Iowa] (19:2) Spr-Sum 89, p. 166-167.
"The Shooting Needs to Stop." [NegC] (9:1) 89, p. 41.
"Someone" (tr. of Karl Krolow). [Interim] (8:2) Fall 89, p. 23.
"Spiral" (tr. of Marin Sorescu, w. Adriana Varga and Gabriela Dragnea). [MalR] (88) Fall 89, p. 82.
"Subjectivism" (tr. of Marin Sorescu, w. Adriana Varga and Gabriela Dragnea). [Timbuktu] (4) Sum-Fall 89, p. 33.
"These Old Men" (tr. of Karl Krolow). [Journal] (13:1) Spr-Sum 89, p. 55.
"Untitled: I have my father's years, I have his hands" (tr. of Giovanni Raboni, w. Vinio Rossi). [CentR] (33:1) Wint 89, p. 58-59.
"Untitled: I'll freeze, a column of salt" (tr. of Judita Vaiciunaite, w. Viktoria Skrupskelis). [Field] (41) Fall 89, p. 69.
"Vibrations" (tr. of Marin Sorescu, w. Adriana Varga and Gabriela Dragnea). [Timbuktu] (4) Sum-Fall 89, p. 33.
"Village Museum" (tr. of Marin Sorescu, w. Adriana Varga). [Iowa] (19:2) Spr-Sum 89, p. 165-166.
"Vision" (tr. of Marin Sorescu, w. Adriana Varga). [Vis] (30) 89, p. 5.
"Where Do You Suppose He'd Go Now?" [CrabCR] (6:2) Wint 89, p. 19.
"Whim" (tr. of Marin Sorescu, w. Adriana Varga). [Iowa] (19:2) Spr-Sum 89, p. 168.
"Wild Plum in Bloom" (tr. of Judita Vaiciunaite, w. Viktoria Skrupskelis). [Field] (41) Fall 89, p. 68.
"Winter II" (tr. of Judita Vaiciunaite, w. Viktoria Skrupskelis). [Field] (41) Fall 89, p. 70.
1860. FRIED, Erich
"Against Forgetting" (tr. by John Linthicum). [LitR] (33:1) Fall 89, p. 11.
"Breeding Stones" (tr. by John Linthicum). [LitR] (33:1) Fall 89, p. 10.

"A Call" (tr. by John Linthicum). [LitR] (33:1) Fall 89, p. 12.
"Once Again" (tr. by John Linthicum). [LitR] (33:1) Fall 89, p. 12.
"The Stillness" (tr. by John Linthicum). [LitR] (33:1) Fall 89, p. 13.
"What Don Quixote Left Unsaid" (tr. by John Linthicum). [LitR] (33:1) Fall 89, p. 9.
"Winter Garden" (tr. by John Linthicum). [LitR] (33:1) Fall 89, p. 14.
1861. FRIED, Philip
"God Contemplates My Grandmother Snoring." [NoDaQ] (57:1) Wint 89, p. 231.
1862. FRIEDLANDER, Benjamin
"25 Mar. '84, for George." [Screens] (1) 89, p. 74.
"Kristallnacht" (with photographs by Paul Batlan). [Acts] (10) 89, p. 49-60.
"On the Bicentennial of the Constitution." [Screens] (1) 89, p. 74.
1863. FRIEDMAN, Anne (Anne Laura)
"Elegy for the Beekeeper." [PoetryE] (28) Fall 89, p. 80.
"Keith Richards Sings Back-Up." [PaintedB] (37) 89, p. 20.
1864. FRIEDMAN, Dorothy
"Relentless Landlord, Time." [Writer] (102:12) D 89, p. 26.
1865. FRIEDSON, A. M.
"Dear Adolf." [Hawai'iR] (13:1, #25) Spr 89, p. 69-70.
1866. FRIEL, Raymond
"One Less." [Verse] (6:3) Wint 89, p. 46-47.
"The Working-Class Poet." [Verse] (6:3) Wint 89, p. 46.
1867. FRIES, Kenny
"Anesthesia." [FiveFR] (7) 89, p. 3.
1868. FRIGGIERI, Oliver
"Plants" (tr. of Mario Azzopardi). [Vis] (31) 89, p. 10.
"Somos Agua Viva" (tr. into Spanish by Alfred Cauchi). [Mairena] (11:27) 89, p. 91.
1869. FRIMAN, Alice
"Angel Jewell." [Poetry] (153:4) Ja 89, p. 200.
"The Bat." [PraS] (63:4) Wint 89, p. 52.
"Hiking around Jenny Lake" (Grand Teton National Park). [PraS] (63:4) Wint 89, p. 50-51.
"Inside Spring." [TexasR] (10:1/2) Spr-Sum 89, p. 105.
"Ophelia." [LaurelR] (23:2) Sum 89, p. 63-64.
"Snapshot." [TexasR] (10:1/2) Spr-Sum 89, p. 104.
"Stars." [Poetry] (155:3) D 89, p. 203.
1870. FRISARDI, Andrew
"Song for Jan." [Verse] (6:2) Je 89, p. 44.
1871. FRITCHIE, Barbara
"Bye-Bye Boyfriend." [SouthernPR] (29:2) Fall 89, p. 34.
1872. FROST, Carol
"Apple Rind." [PraS] (63:4) Wint 89, p. 48-49.
"Biology." [Journal] (12:2) Fall-Wint 88-89, p. 25.
"Child Frightened by a Monkey" (Tokugawa Period). [Journal] (12:2) Fall-Wint 88-89, p. 23-24.
"Dynasty, 1989." [NewEngR] (12:2) Wint 89, p. 170.
"Icarus in Winter." [GettyR] (2:4) Aut 89, p. 679.
"The King's First Soliloquy" (after the carving of the Tukulti Altar). [SenR] (19:2) Fall 89, p. 35-36.
"Mobile Home." [Journal] (12:2) Fall-Wint 88-89, p. 26.
"Nature Morte." [DenQ] (24:2) Fall 89, p. 46.
"Puppet Master." [Journal] (12:2) Fall-Wint 88-89, p. 22.
"Roadside Shrine, San Cristobal, Venezuela." [NewEngR] (12:2) Wint 89, p. 169.
"Root." [PraS] (63:4) Wint 89, p. 49.
"Skinny Dipping." [WilliamMR] (27) 89, p. 51.
1873. FROST, Celestine
"The Refusal." [WritersF] (15) Fall 89, p. 88.
1874. FROST, Elisabeth
"Casualty." [Jacaranda] (4:1) Spr-Sum 89, p. 33.
"Clair de Lune (Moonlight)" (tr. of Blaise Cendrars). [Jacaranda] (4:1) Spr-Sum 89, p. 58.
"Notes on Translation." [Jacaranda] (4:1) Spr-Sum 89, p. 34-35.
1875. FROST, Helen
"Wandering Around, Getting Nowhere." [MalR] (86) Spr 89, p. 45-46.

1876. FROST, Kenneth
    "Adam's Names." [Confr] (39/40) Fall 88-Wint 89, p. 226.
    "It collapsed, just like that." [NegC] (9:1) 89, p. 32.
    "My thoughts crawl around the surface of my brain." [ChamLR] (3:1, #5) Fall 89, p. 55.
    "Who is drumming on the concrete overhead?" [NegC] (9:1) 89, p. 33.
1877. FROST, Linda A.
    "A Story for Raoul." [CinPR] (19) Spr 89, p. 28.
1878. FROST, Richard
    "The Good Friend." [Interim] (8:1) Spr 89, p. 39.
    "My Father's Accounts." [Interim] (8:1) Spr 89, p. 37.
    "The Virgin." [Interim] (8:1) Spr 89, p. 38.
    "Words." [NegC] (9:1) 89, p. 58-59.
1879. FROST, Rob
    "Arapahoe Lost in St. Louis." [Farm] (6:2) Fall 89, p. 66.
1880. FROST, Robert
    "Design." [SoCaR] (22:1) Fall 89, p. 35.
1881. FRUMKIN, Gene
    "Dostoevsky & Other Nature Poems" (13 poems). [Manoa] (1:1/2) Fall 89, p. 86-94.
    "Maps." [Caliban] (6) 89, p. 49-50.
    "Walter Benjamin in Moscow." [AnotherCM] (19) 89, p. 74-79.
1882. FRY, Nan
    "Bearskin." [Kalliope] (11:1) 89, p. 51-52.
1883. FU, Chuan Y.
    "Grasses" (tr. of Po Chu-yi, w. Nick Otten). [RiverS] (30) [89], p. 79.
    "Premier of Shu" (tr. of Tu Fu, w. Nick Otten). [RiverS] (30) [89], p. 78.
FU, Du
    See DU ,Fu
FU, Tu
    See DU ,Fu
1884. FUJIWARA NO OKIKAZE (ca. 910)
    "How very much love I gave!" (tr. by Sam Hamill). [PoetryE] (28) Fall 89, p. 203.
1885. FUJIWARA NO SANEKATA (d. 998)
    "Weary clear to his feet" (tr. by Sam Hamill). [PoetryE] (28) Fall 89, p. 199.
FUKUYABU, Kiyowara (900-930)
    See KIYOWARA, Fukuyabu (900-930)
1886. FULKER, Tina
    "Pain." [Vis] (30) 89, p. 55.
1887. FULLER, Guy M.
    "Ars(e) Poet i ca." [Writer] (102:6) Je 89, p. 26.
1888. FULLER, Jane Ann Devol
    "Forsythia." [DenQ] (24:2) Fall 89, p. 47.
1889. FULLER, John
    "Lawn Games." [Pequod] (26/27) 89, p. 86.
    "Little Mouths, Little Ghosts." [Pequod] (26/27) 89, p. 85.
1890. FULLER, William
    "The Windowbox." [PaperAir] (4:2) 89, p. 84-85.
1891. FULTON, Alice
    "Cascade Experiment." [GrandS] (9:1) Aut 89, p. 167-168.
    "The Collected Carmen Lionhart." [Hudson] (42:3) Aut 89, p. 441-443.
    "Concerning Things That Can Be Doubted." [Epoch] (38:2) 89, p. 143-145.
    "Disorder Is a Measure of Warmth." [GettyR] (2:2) Spr 89, p. 211-212.
    "Everything to Go." [GrandS] (9:1) Aut 89, p. 166-167.
    "The Expense of Spirit." [Boulevard] (4:2, #11) Fall 89, p. 75.
    "The Orthodox Waltz." [NewRep] (200:11) 13 Mr 89, p. 35.
    "The Private Sector." [OntR] (31) Fall-Wint 89-90, p. 20-22.
    "Romance in the Dark." [Boulevard] (4:2, #11) Fall 89, p. 76-78.
1892. FULTON, Robin
    "Berceuse" (tr. of Tomas Tranströmer). [Verse] (6:3) Wint 89, p. 22.
    "Female Portrait, 19th Century" (tr. of Tomas Tranströmer). [Verse] (6:3) Wint 89, p. 23.
    "The Inheritance" (tr. of Tomas Tranströmer). [Verse] (6:3) Wint 89, p. 21.
    "Leaflet" (tr. of Tomas Tranströmer). [Verse] (6:3) Wint 89, p. 22.
    "Medieval Motif" (tr. of Tomas Tranströmer). [Verse] (6:3) Wint 89, p. 23.
    "Six Winters" (tr. of Tomas Tranströmer). [Verse] (6:3) Wint 89, p. 21-22.

1893. FULWYLIE, Christine B. J.
"Beyond the Barren Rock." [EmeraldCR] (1989) c1988, p. 112.
"The Debt Unpaid." [EmeraldCR] (1989) c1988, p. 111-112.
1894. FUNGE, Robert
"Father and Son." [Hawai'iR] (13:2, #26) Sum 89, p. 15.
"First Having Read." [CumbPR] (8:2) Spr 89, p. 92.
"The Last Act." [SoCoast] (6) Fall 88, p. 21.
"The Last Song (from John/Henry)." [SoDakR] (27:3) Aut 89, p. 128.
"Light's Dying" (from John/Henry). [Pembroke] (21) 89, p. 15-16.
"Loss." [SpoonRQ] (14:2) Spr 89, p. 14.
"Man of Hours." [BellR] (12:1, #25) Spr 89, p. 52.
1895. FUNKHOUSER, Erica
"Apple Tree." [Poetry] (154:2) My 89, p. 69.
"Grief." [Poetry] (154:2) My 89, p. 71.
"Tae Kwon Do." [Poetry] (154:2) My 89, p. 70.
1896. FUQUA, C. S.
"Waiting for the Post." [SlipS] (9) 89, p. 32-34.
1897. FURBISH, Dean
"We debated" (tr. of Vasily Fyodorov). [PoetryE] (28) Fall 89, p. 174.
1898. FURLAN, Luis Ricardo
"El Exiliado." [Mairena] (11:27) 89, p. 87.
1899. FUSEK, Serena
"Travelling Together." [SlipS] (9) 89, p. 34.
1900. FUTORANSKY, Luisa
"Crema Catalana." [LindLM] (8:3) Jl-S 89, p. 9.
1901. FYODOROV, Vasily
"We debated" (tr. by Dean Furbish). [PoetryE] (28) Fall 89, p. 174.
1902. GABOR, Al
"Uncle George's Lady Friend." [ChatR] (9:3) Spr 89, p. 50.
1903. GAGE, Carolyn
"On Singing Women's Praises." [SinW] (37) Spr 89, p. 7.
1904. GAGNON, Madeleine
"Rue Chabot, 30 Octobre 1987." [Os] (29) 89, p. 4.
"Rue Chabot, 31 Octobre 1987." [Os] (29) 89, p. 5.
1905. GALASSI, Jonathan
"Ex Abrupto" (tr. of Eugenio Montale). [Poetry] (155:1/2) O-N 89, p. 2.
"Hypotheses on Love" (Selections: 1, 2, 4, 9, 11, tr. of Annalisa Cima). [Poetry]
(155:1/2) O-N 89, p. 109-113.
"I Love Uncertain Gestures" (tr. of Valerio Magrelli). [Poetry] (155:1/2) O-N 89, p.
159.
"It's Only an Error" (tr. of Eugenio Montale). [Poetry] (155:1/2) O-N 89, p. 1.
"January 20 or Age 30" (tr. of Eugenio Montale). [Poetry] (155:1/2) O-N 89, p. 2.
"The Storm and Other Things" (Selections: 5 poems, tr. of Eugenio Montale).
[Poetry] (155:1/2) O-N 89, p. 5-13.
"There's Silence Between One Page and Another" (tr. of Valerio Magrelli). [Poetry]
(155:1/2) O-N 89, p. 160.
1906. GALE, Vi
"Vine Maple Country." [BallSUF] (30:4) Aut 89, p. 5.
"Words for a Friend's Old Cat." [BallSUF] (30:4) Aut 89, p. 78.
1907. GALLAGHER, Tess
"Crazy Menu." [Zyzzyva] (5:, #20) Wint 89, p. 51-52.
"Red Poppy." [NewYorker] (65:33) 2 O 89, p. 52.
1908. GALLER, David
"Above the Irish Sea, 1971." [TriQ] (77) Wint 89-90, p. 279.
"Business." [PraS] (63:4) Wint 89, p. 56-57.
"The Enemy." [PraS] (63:4) Wint 89, p. 53-55.
"The Hammer." [TriQ] (77) Wint 89-90, p. 276-278.
"Logorrhea." [PraS] (63:4) Wint 89, p. 57.
"Meditation on a Writer's Notebook." [SouthwR] (74:3) Sum 89, p. 389.
1909. GALLO, Guy
"Letter to Nebraska." [Bomb] (28) Sum 89, p. 54.
"Max's Notebook." [Bomb] (30) Wint 89-90, p. 80-85.
1910. GALVAN, Kyra
"My Flaws Among the Peach Blossoms" (tr. by T. Hoeksema). [Jacaranda] (4:1)
Spr-Sum 89, p. 65-66.
"Praise to the Snail" (tr. by Thomas Hoeksema). [RiverS] (28) 89, p. 50.

1911. GALVIN, Brendan
"Backtalk." [Poetry] (154:6) S 89, p. 331.
"Carrowkeel." [Poetry] (154:6) S 89, p. 319-320.
"Hearing Irish Spoken." [Poetry] (154:6) S 89, p. 330.
"Loranzo Newcomb's Fiddler Crab Letter to Mistress Mary Colby" (1718). [PraS]
(63:1) Spr 89, p. 85-87.
"Loranzo Newcomb's Weather Saws" (American, 18th Century). [Chelsea] (48) 89,
p. 138-140.
"A Man of Skill in These Colonies" (American, 18th Century). [PraS] (63:1) Spr 89,
p. 88-90.
"My Grandmother Steals Her Last Trout" (Donegal, 1884). [Poetry] (154:2) My 89,
p. 85-86.
"Sengekontacket" (for my father). [Chelsea] (48) 89, p. 140-141.
1912. GALVIN, James
"Cache La Poudre." [NewL] (56:2/3) Wint 89-Spr 90, p. 91.
"Homesteader." [NewL] (56:2/3) Wint 89-Spr 90, p. 89-90.
"Reading the Will." [NewL] (56:2/3) Wint 89-Spr 90, p. 92.
"To the Republic." [NewL] (56:2/3) Wint 89-Spr 90, p. 93.
1913. GALVIN, Martin
"Coming to Ground" (from *Wild Card*). [Bogg] (61) 89, p. 30-31.
"Emergency Room." [PoetC] (20:2) Wint 89, p. 17.
"Hack." [WashR] (14:6) Ap-My 89, p. 22.
"Prostitute in the Cancer Ward" (from *Wild Card*). [Bogg] (61) 89, p. 30.
1914. GANASSI, Ian
"Dolores." [BlackWR] (15:2) Spr 89, p. 43.
1915. GANDER, Forrest
"Final Testament." [Agni] (28) 89, p. 62.
"Land Surveyor." [Agni] (28) 89, p. 63.
"Life of Johnson Upside Your Head." [TriQ] (74) Wint 89, p. 232-246.
"Thin Lips." [FiveFR] (7) 89, p. 20.
"The Violence of the Egg." [Caliban] (6) 89, p. 176-177.
1916. GANGEMI, Kenneth (Ken)
"Excerpts from Her Letters" (for Jamie Frucht). [CentralP] (15) Spr 89, p. 170-171.
"Susie Falls Asleep." [CentralP] (15) Spr 89, p. 169.
"Tanks in Greenwich Village." [Rampike] (6:3) 88, p. 54.
1917. GANICK, Peter
"Remove a Concept" (from part thirty-one). [Screens] (1) 89, p. 80-83.
1918. GANSZ, David C. D.
"Per Missions" (Selections, in progress, from "Millennial Scriptions). [Temblor]
(10) 89, p. 51-53.
"The Sentencing" (anima christi, anima mundi. Part III of Millennial Scriptions).
[Temblor] (9) 89, p. 59-70.
1919. GAO, Fa-lin
"Flint" (tr. by Edward Morin, Dennis Ding and Dai Fang). [Pig] (15) 88, p. 6.
1920. GAO, Xiang
"Inscription on a Half-Hiddnen Landscape" (tr. by Carolyn Lau). [YellowS] (31)
Aut 89, p. 7.
1921. GARCIA, Albert
"The More You Think." [KanQ] (21:3) Sum 89, p. 122.
1922. GARCIA, Carlos Ernesto
"A Hundred and Fifty Thousand Degrees Below Zero" (tr. by Elizabeth Gamble
Miller). [MidAR] (9:2) 89, p. 168.
"The Summer of 80 and Five" (tr. by Elizabeth Gamble Miller). [MidAR] (9:2) 89,
p. 170.
"A Tribute" (tr. by Elizabeth Gamble Miller). [MidAR] (9:2) 89, p. 169.
GARCIA, Eloisa Marco
See MARCO GARCIA, Eloisa
1923. GARCIA, Enildo
"Black Woman" (tr. of Nancy Morejon, w. Daniela Gioseffi). [Contact] (9:50/51/52)
Fall-Wint 88-Spr 89, p. 44-45.
"The Boy Who Sells Greens" (tr. of Carilda Oliver Labra, w. Daniela Gioseffi).
[Contact] (9:50/51/52) Fall-Wint 88-Spr 89, p. 39.
"Declaration of Love" (1963, October Cuban Missile Crisis, tr. of Carilda Oliver
Labra, w. Daniela Gioseffi). [Contact] (9:50/51/52) Fall-Wint 88-Spr 89, p.
38.
"Dying in Sadness" (Camen Miranda in memoriam, tr. of Nancy Morejon, w.

Daniela Gioseffi). [Contact] (9:50/51/52) Fall-Wint 88-Spr 89, p. 43.
"The Last Conversation with Rolando Escardo" (tr. of Carilda Oliver Labra, w. Daniela Gioseffi). [Contact] (9:50/51/52) Fall-Wint 88-Spr 89, p. 41.
"Of the Word" (tr. of Carilda Oliver Labra, w. Daniela Gioseffi). [Contact] (9:50/51/52) Fall-Wint 88-Spr 89, p. 40.
"Polished Stone" (tr. of Nancy Morejon, w. Daniela Gioseffi). [Contact] (9:50/51/52) Fall-Wint 88-Spr 89, p. 43.
"Reportage from Viet Nam, Especially for International Woman's Day" (tr. of Minera Salado, w. Daniela Gioseffi). [Contact] (9:50/51/52) Fall-Wint 88-Spr 89, p. 46.
"To the Passing Days and Birthdays" (to Carilda Oliver Labra, tr. of Nancy Morejon, w. Daniela Gioseffi). [Contact] (9:50/51/52) Fall-Wint 88-Spr 89, p. 42.
"Today's Interview" (tr. of Minera Salado, w. Daniela Gioseffi). [Contact] (9:50/51/52) Fall-Wint 88-Spr 89, p. 47.
"When Papa" (tr. of Carilda Oliver Labra, w. Daniela Gioseffi). [Contact] (9:50/51/52) Fall-Wint 88-Spr 89, p. 40.
1924. GARCIA, José
"The Young Fisherman" (A wall painting, Akrotiri, Santorini, 1500 B.C.). [Jacaranda] (4:1) Spr-Sum 89, p. 154.
GARCIA, Luis Miguel Vicente
See VICENTE GARCIA, Luis Miguel
1925. GARCIA, Richard
"Los Danzantes." [Americas] (17:2) Sum 89, p. 43.
"The Flying Garcias." [Ploughs] (15:1) 89, p. 41-42.
"Holding Cell." [Americas] (17:2) Sum 89, p. 40.
"Visiting the Old Neighborhood." [Americas] (17:2) Sum 89, p. 41.
"Waking to the Radio." [Americas] (17:2) Sum 89, p. 42.
1926. GARCIA CASTELLON, Manuel
"Ghost Town (Canto de Mineros)." [Mairena] (11:27) 89, p. 77.
1927. GARCIA GOMEZ, Alejandro
"Sur." [Mairena] (11:27) 89, p. 89.
1928. GARCIA GOMEZ, Emilio
"To Abu Bakr ben Ammar Going to Silves" (tr. of Abu 'l-Kasim Mohammed Ibn-Abbad Al-Mutamid, retranslated into English by Christopher Middleton). [SouthwR] (74:2) Spr 89, p. 225-226.
1929. GARCIA LORCA, Federico
"The Arrest of Little Tony Camborio on the Seville Highway" (To Margarita Xirgu, tr. by Will Kirkland). [Sequoia] (32:2) Wint-Spr 89, p. 15-16.
"De Profundis" (tr. by Francis Golffing). [SpiritSH] (54) Spr-Sum 89, p. 35.
"The Death of Little Tony Camborio" (To José Antonio Rubio Sacristán, tr. by Will Kirkland). [Sequoia] (32:2) Wint-Spr 89, p. 19-20.
"Muerte de Antonito el Camborio" (a José Antonio Rubio Sacristán). [Sequoia] (32:2) Wint-Spr 89, p. 17-18.
"Night: Suite for Piano & Poet's Voice" (tr. by Jerome Rothenberg). [ParisR] (31:110) Spr 89, p. 20-24.
"Ode to Salvador Dalí" (tr. by Christopher Sawyer-Lauçanno). [AmerPoR] (18:3) My-Je 89, p. 5-6.
"The Poet Speaks with His Beloved on the Telephone" (tr. by J. K. Walsh and Francisco Aragon). [ChamLR] (3:1, #5) Fall 89, p. 76.
"The Poet Tells the Truth" (tr. by J. K. Walsh and Francisco Aragon). [ChamLR] (3:1, #5) Fall 89, p. 75.
"Prendimiento de Antonito el Camborio en el Camino de Sevilla" (a Margarita Xirgu). [Sequoia] (32:2) Wint-Spr 89, p. 13-14.
"Sonnet of the Sweet Complaint" (tr. by J. K. Walsh and Francisco Aragon). [ChamLR] (3:1, #5) Fall 89, p. 77.
1930. GARCIA MAFFLA, Jaime
"Ajena Ley." [LindLM] (8:2) Ap-Je 89, p. 4.
1931. GARCIA SAUCEDO, Jaime
"Balcon Rodante." [LindLM] (8:4) O-D 89, p. 23.
"Un Largo Viaje." [LindLM] (8:4) O-D 89, p. 23.
GARDEUR, Lili le
See LeGARDEUR, Lili
1932. GARDINIER, Suzanne
"1494." [Ploughs] (15:4) Wint 89-90, p. 77.
"1853." [Ploughs] (15:4) Wint 89-90, p. 80-81.
"1967." [Ploughs] (15:4) Wint 89-90, p. 78.

"1987." [Ploughs] (15:4) Wint 89-90, p. 79.
"Harmonica." [GrandS] (8:2) Wint 89, p. 32-33.
"The Stones." [NewYorker] (64:51) 6 F 89, p. 30.
"The West Point Museum." [GrandS] (8:4) Sum 89, p. 196-200.
1933. GARDNER, Geoffrey
"Heavy" (tr. of Jules Supervielle). [SenR] (19:2) Fall 89, p. 68.
"The Little Forest" (tr. of Jules Supervielle). [SenR] (19:2) Fall 89, p. 63.
"The Room Next Door" (tr. of Jules Supervielle). [SenR] (19:2) Fall 89, p. 65.
"The Sick Man" (tr. of Jules Supervielle). [SenR] (19:2) Fall 89, p. 64.
"Without God" (tr. of Jules Supervielle). [SenR] (19:2) Fall 89, p. 66-67.
1934. GARFINKEL, Patricia
"At the School Crossing." [SwampR] (1:4) Sum 89, p. 67.
"Chewing Thread." [SwampR] (1:4) Sum 89, p. 66.
1935. GARFITT, Roger
"Lower Lumb Mill" (For Ellie, and for the teachers and pupils of Nicholls Ardwick
    School, Manchester). [Stand] (30:2) Spr 89, p. 60-65.
1936. GARIN, Marita
"Altered Landscape." [TarRP] (29:1) Fall 89, p. 16-17.
"In Training." [TarRP] (29:1) Fall 89, p. 17-18.
1937. GARLAND, Max
"Requiem for a Boom Town." [PoetC] (20:3) Spr 89, p. 29.
1938. GARLICK, Raymond
"Explanatory Note." [NoDaQ] (57:2) Spr 89, insert p. 49.
"Gors Goch." [NoDaQ] (57:2) Spr 89, insert p. 51.
"Matters Arising." [NoDaQ] (57:2) Spr 89, insert p. 50.
1939. GARMON, John
"Andrew Marcum" (killed by a hit-and-run driver, 1958, on Highway 66, at the edge
    of Groom, Texas). [PassN] (10:2) Sum 89, p. 27.
"Supper, The Last." [Interim] (8:1) Spr 89, p. 15.
1940. GARNETT, Ruth M.
"You Want the World Flat Again." [Callaloo] (12:1, #38) Wint 89, p. 178.
1941. GARREN, Christine
"A Mother Speaks to Her Son" (Literary Wards: Honorable Mention).
    [GreensboroR] (47) Wint 89-90, p. 21.
"Waking." [GreensboroR] (47) Wint 89-90, p. 20.
1942. GARRETT, Daniel
"Forms." [BlackALF] (23:3) Fall 89, p. 476.
"The Wisdom" (for Marge). [ChangingM] (20) Wint-Spr 89, p. 24.
1943. GARRETT, E. Cortez
"Nightmare." [CreamCR] (13:2) Fall 89, p. 161.
1944. GARRETT, George
"A Dear John Letter" (for John Ciardi). [ThRiPo] (31/32) 88, p. 25-26.
1945. GARRETT, Nola
"Job, Too." [GeoR] (43:4) Wint 89, p. 691-692.
1946. GARRISON, David
"Another You" (tr. of Pedro Salinas). [InterPR] (15:2) Fall 89, p. 55.
"Juice" (tr. of Pedro Salinas). [InterPR] (15:2) Fall 89, p. 57.
"Lofty Solitudes" (tr. of José Bergamín). [LitR] (32:2) Wint 89, p. 162.
"Snow" (tr. of José Bergamín). [LitR] (32:2) Wint 89, p. 162.
"Time Crystal" (tr. of José Bergamín). [LitR] (32:2) Wint 89, p. 161.
"Vocation" (tr. of Pedro Salinas). [InterPR] (15:2) Fall 89, p. 59.
"Your Voice" (tr. of José Bergamín). [LitR] (32:2) Wint 89, p. 161.
1947. GARRISON, Mary
"Love Song to a Poet I've Yet to Meet (Or Maybe I Have)." [AlphaBS] (5) Jl 89, p.
    65.
"There Was a Point When I Was Homesick for Detroit." [AlphaBS] (5) Jl 89, p.
    63-64.
1948. GARRISON, Philip
"Metastasis." [NoAmR] (274:3) S 89, p. 62.
1949. GARSON, Karl
"Fishes of the Mekong." [SoCoast] (7) Spr-Fall 89, p. 20.
"Night Clearing." [SoCoast] (7) Spr-Fall 89, p. 38.
1950. GARTLAND, Joan
"Delivering the Flowers." [PassN] (10:2) Sum 89, p. 10.
1951. GASH, Sondra
"Housewife's Swansong." [Footwork] 89, p. 33.

"I See My Mother Years Before I Am Born." [Footwork] 89, p. 33.
"The Key." [Footwork] 89, p. 33.
"The Kosmos, Moscow, August 1987." [US1] (22/23) Spr 89, p. 15.
1952. GASTIGER, Joseph
"The Children of Mechanics." [TriQ] (76) Fall 89, p. 100-101.
1953. GATES, Bob
"Meaning." [Wind] (19:65) 89, p. 9.
"Moses." [NewRena] (7:3, #23) 89, p. 83.
"The Showing." [BrooklynR] (5) 88, p. 7.
"Spring Fever." [BrooklynR] (5) 88, p. 8.
1954. GATES, Edward
"The Fortune Teller." [AntigR] (76) Wint 89, p. 95-96.
"School." [AntigR] (76) Wint 89, p. 94.
1955. GATES, Rosemary
"White Ground." [SouthernR] (25:1) Wint 89, p. 166-167.
1956. GATTO, Alfonso
"A Dawn" (tr. by Philip Parisi). [Journal] (13:1) Spr-Sum 89, p. 54.
"For the Martyrs of Piazzale Loreto" (tr. by Philip Parisi). [Journal] (13:1) Spr-Sum
89, p. 52-53.
"Returning at Dawn through San Vittore" (tr. by Philip Parisi). [Journal] (13:1)
Spr-Sum 89, p. 51.
1957. GAVRONSKY, Serge
"A House in the Low Brush." [Boulevard] (4:1, #10) Spr 89, p. 176.
1958. GAWRON, James
"Girl in the Movie." [SlipS] (9) 89, p. 7-8.
"Winter Solstice." [HeavenB] (7) Wint 89, p. 41.
1959. GAY, Laura
"She Drives by Night." [AlphaBS] (5) Jl 89, p. 62.
1960. GAYLE, Elizabeth (Mary Elizabeth)
"Seated on Her Cedar Chest, Miss Lizzy Faces Adolescence: Easter, 1966."
[GreensboroR] (46) Sum 89, p. 205-206.
"Sky Music" (October 21, 1986). [Shen] (39:3) Fall 89, p. 20-21.
1961. GEARING, Jeff
"Dream in Exile" (tr. of Reiner Kunze, w. Thomas S. Edwards, Ken Letko, and
Thomas Schaller). [Nimrod] (33:1) Fall-Wint 89, p. 111.
"On the Danube in the Fog" (tr. of Reiner Kunze, w. Thomas S. Edwards, Ken
Letko, and Thomas Schaller). [Nimrod] (33:1) Fall-Wint 89, p. 111.
"The Silhouette of Lübeck" (tr. of Reiner Kunze, w. Thomas S. Edwards, Ken
Letko, and Thomas Schaller). [Nimrod] (33:1) Fall-Wint 89, p. 111.
1962. GEDDES, Gary
"Coming Up for Air." [CapilR] (1st series: 50) 89, p. 185-192.
1963. GEDEÃO, António
"Pedra Filosofal." [Ometeca] (1:1) 89, p. 18-20.
1964. GEHLHOFF-CLAES, Astrid
"Scene of the Crime" (tr. by John Linthicum). [LitR] (33:1) Fall 89, p. 73.
"Summer" (tr. by John Linthicum). [LitR] (33:1) Fall 89, p. 71.
"Toward Evening an Orange Tree" (tr. by John Linthicum). [LitR] (33:1) Fall 89, p.
72.
"Visit" (tr. by John Linthicum). [LitR] (33:1) Fall 89, p. 73.
1965. GEHMAN, E. A.
"The Duchess de Polignac at Large on the River of Heaven." [Timbuktu] (3)
Wint-Spr 89, p. 23-24.
"The History of Water in Los Angeles." [Timbuktu] (3) Wint-Spr 89, p. 17-22.
"Permutations." [GreensboroR] (47) Wint 89-90, p. 68-70.
"The Suicide's Daughters" (-- Berlin). [Timbuktu] (3) Wint-Spr 89, p. 26-29.
1966. GENEGA, Paul
"Cul-De-Sac." [Journal] (13:1) Spr-Sum 89, p. 12-13.
"Epic." [SouthwR] (74:3) Sum 89, p. 339.
"First Down." [Footwork] 89, p. 69.
"Good" (For Bill Daughton, 1949-1987). [LitR] (32:2) Wint 89, p. 193.
"History." [Journal] (13:1) Spr-Sum 89, p. 14-15.
"Mangrove." [Journal] (13:1) Spr-Sum 89, p. 10-11.
"Soldiers." [Footwork] 89, p. 69.
"That Fall." [Footwork] 89, p. 70.
1967. GENT, Andrew
"Sonnet: I am starting over with a rock." [BrooklynR] (5) 88, p. 56.

"Sonnet: I started reading three books." [BrooklynR] (5) 88, p. 55.
"Sonnet ('The Swimmer')." [WestHR] (43:4) Wint 89, p. 302.
"Sonnet ('Variations on a Poem by Li Po')." [WestHR] (43:4) Wint 89, p. 301.
1968. GENTRY, Jane
"The Garden." [HolCrit] (26:1) F 89, p. 19.
1969. GEORGE, Beth
"Brain Tumor." [WestB] (23) 89, p. 104-105.
1970. GEORGE, David
"Hope." [HeavenB] (7) Wint 89, p. 45.
"Owl-Call." [HeavenB] (7) Wint 89, p. 45.
"The Shape of Things." [HeavenB] (6) Wint-Spr 89, p. 42.
1971. GEORGE, Emery
"At Orly Airport" (tr. of Lajos Kassák). [WebR] (14:1) Spr 89, p. 24-25.
"The Clock Has Stopped" (tr. of Lajos Kassák). [WebR] (14:1) Spr 89, p. 27.
"Light Signals" (tr. of Lajos Kassák). [WebR] (14:1) Spr 89, p. 25.
"The Miracle of Twenty-Third Street." [KanQ] (21:1/2) Wint-Spr 89, p. 155.
"Moments" (tr. of Lajos Kassák). [WebR] (14:1) Spr 89, p. 27.
"Vision" (tr. of Lajos Kassák). [WebR] (14:1) Spr 89, p. 28.
"Windpaths" (tr. of Lajos Kassák). [WebR] (14:1) Spr 89, p. 26.
1972. GEORGE, Roberta
"June." [ApalQ] (32) 89, p. 88-91.
1973. GEORGE, Stefan
"Don't Dwell on Things That Can't Be Known" (tr. by Leonard Kress). [PaintedB]
    (37) 89, p. 31.
1974. GEORGE, Tom
"The Secretary." [ApalQ] (31) 89, p. 58.
1975. GERLACH, Lee
"In the First Week of December." [BostonR] (14:4) Ag 89, p. 11.
"Vacillations" (I & II, tr. of Han Yu). [LitR] (32:3) Spr 89, p. 387-388.
1976. GERMAN, Greg
"The Limestone Cowboy Sees God, and It's a Woman." [Hawai'iR] (13:2, #26)
    Sum 89, p. 28.
1977. GERMAN, Norman
"Facing North." [CrabCR] (6:1) 89, p. 17.
"Mowing the Snow." [StoneC] (16:3/4) Spr-Sum 89, p. 12-13.
"The Three Bears." [WritersF] (15) Fall 89, p. 118-119.
"Trying Again." [WritersF] (15) Fall 89, p. 118.
1978. GERMANACOS, N. C.
"Makers." [KenR] (NS 11:2) Spr 89, p. 57-58.
"Sanctity." [KenR] (NS 11:2) Spr 89, p. 58.
1979. GERRY, Carol
"Wake with Me." [Sequoia] (32:2) Wint-Spr 89, p. 75.
1980. GERSHATOR, Phyllis
"October." [Footwork] 89, p. 53-54.
1981. GERSTLER, Amy
"Early Hour" (for Benjamin Weissman). [ParisR] (31:112) Fall 89, p. 100-101.
"A Father at His Son's Baptism." [ParisR] (31:112) Fall 89, p. 98-99.
"How to Hypnotize." [Witness] (2:1) Spr 88, p. 11.
"The Ice Age." [ParisR] (31:112) Fall 89, p. 102-104.
"Losing Heart." [BrooklynR] (6) 89, p. 58.
"Lost in the Forest." [Witness] (2:1) Spr 88, p. 10.
"The Nature of Suffering." [Witness] (2:1) Spr 88, p. 9.
"That Calm Sunday That Rolls On and On." [BrooklynR] (6) 89, p. 59.
1982. GERVAIS, C. H.
"Scenes from the Present." [Quarry] (38:1) Wint 89, p. 31.
"Trophies at Piazza Maggiore." [Quarry] (38:1) Wint 89, p. 32.
"Le Zoo." [Quarry] (38:1) Wint 89, p. 30.
1983. GERVAIS, Marty
"The Way Heavenly Bodies Exist." [Rampike] (6:2) 88, p. 42.
1984. GERVASIO, Michael
"Crazy John, the Fisherman." [LitR] (32:2) Wint 89, p. 179.
1985. GERY, John
"Death in Various Parts." [SoDakR] (27:2) Sum 89, p. 58-62.
"Deep South." [CharR] (15:1) Spr 89, p. 52-53.
"Light Verse Against Darkness." [Outbr] (20) 89, p. 71.
"The Mosquito, or, Her Reply to Donne." [Outbr] (20) 89, p. 70.

"A Sleep and a Forgetting." [CrossCur] (8:2) Ja 89, p. 129.
"To a Friend's Wife." [SoDakR] (27:2) Sum 89, p. 63.
"To the Pedestrian Crossing Elysian Fields at Humanity in New Orleans." [RiverC]
    (9:1) Spr 89, p. 39.
"What Are Chores?" [CrossCur] (8:2) Ja 89, p. 130-131.
1986. GESSNER, Richard
    "The Spam of Vegas-Roit" (Excerpt). [Rampike] (6:2) 88, p. 43.
1987. GETSI, Lucia
    "Her Father's Touch" (for John). [PraS] (63:2) Sum 89, p. 41-42.
    "In This Story." [PraS] (63:2) Sum 89, p. 45-46.
    "Oradour-sur-Glane. Silence." [PraS] (63:2) Sum 89, p. 42-44.
1988. GETTLER, Andrew
    "Messiah of the Black Heart." [AlphaBS] (6) Wint 89-90, p. 10.
    "Spoils of War." [SlipS] (9) 89, p. 35.
    "Toi Com Biet" (Vietnamese: "I don't understand"). [Vis] (30) 89, p. 27.
1989. GEWANTER, David
    "Letter In My Desk." [Agni] (28) 89, p. 193-196.
    "Push Play." [Thrpny] (36) Wint 89, p. 15.
1990. GHANDOUR, Sabah
    "Beware of Our Death in the South" (tr. of Jawdat Fakhr al-Dine). [Jacaranda] (4:1)
        Spr-Sum 89, p. 60.
GHLINN, Aine Ni
    See Ni GHLINN, Aine
1991. GIBB, Robert
    "The Bed Frame." [CinPR] (19) Spr 89, p. 29.
    "Mercer's Pottery and Tile Works, Doylestown, Pennsylvania, 1964" (for Ron
        Bower). [CinPR] (19) Spr 89, p. 32-33.
    "Poem Against the Marketplace." [CinPR] (19) Spr 89, p. 30-31.
    "Portraits of the Artists." [StoneC] (17:1/2) Fall-Wint 89-90, p. 18-19.
    "Refusal to End the Year with a Poem of Grieving." [PoetryNW] (30:4) Wint 89-90,
        p. 40-41.
    "Shooting the Suburbs." [PoetryNW] (30:4) Wint 89-90, p. 41-42.
1992. GIBBONS, Reginald
    "Mekong Restaurant, 1988." [MissouriR] (12:1) 89, p. 32-33.
1993. GIBIAN, Ruth
    "Dancing at 'The Cherry Tree'" (for Marina). [Nimrod] (33:1) Fall-Wint 89, p.
        107-108.
1994. GIBSON, Michelle
    "First Frost." [Prima] (13) 89, p. 25.
1995. GIBSON, Morgan
    "Singing Image of a Whirling Ring of Fire" (tr. of Kukai, w. Hiroshi Murakami).
        [LitR] (32:3) Spr 89, p. 360.
    "Singing Image of an Echo" (tr. of Kukai, w. Hiroshi Murakami). [LitR] (32:3) Spr
        89, p. 360.
1996. GIBSON, Rubye
    "Hags Riding on His Back." [MinnR] (NS 33) Fall 89, p. 28.
1997. GIL, Lourdes
    "6 de Junio de 1982." [LindLM] (8:1) Ja-Mr 89, p. 15.
    "A Julia Fusco, Quien Perdio un Hijo en las Guerras de Centroamerica:
        Transfiguracion." [LindLM] (8:1) Ja-Mr 89, p. 15.
    "Transfiguracion" (A Julia Fusco, quien perdió un hijo en las guerras de
        Centroamérica). [CuadP] (7:19) S-D 89, p. 79-80.
1998. GILBERT, Christopher
    "Bad." [IndR] (13:1) Wint 89, p. 87-88.
    "On the Way Back Home." [IndR] (13:1) Wint 89, p. 89.
    "A Passage." [IndR] (13:1) Wint 89, p. 90.
1999. GILBERT, David
    "White Out." [Screens] (1) 89, p. 53-55.
2000. GILBERT, Gerry
    "Bursts of Friendliness." [CapilR] (1st series: 50) 89, p. 22.
    "Defective Story." [CapilR] (1st series: 50) 89, p. 23.
2001. GILBERT, Gregory W.
    "Border Line Crazy." [PacificR] (7) 89, p. 38.
2002. GILDNER, Gary
    "Coaching the Warsaw Baseball Team" (a poetic sequence. Selections: 3 poems).
        [RiverS] (29) [89], p. 67-70.

"The Day Before Thanksgiving, a Call Comes to Me Concerning Insulation."
  [NewL] (56:2/3) Wint 89-Spr 90, p. 96.
"A Field Mouse at My Fishing Hole." [NewL] (56:2/3) Wint 89-Spr 90, p. 94-95.
"Forty Dollars." [TampaR] (2) 89, p. 55-57.
"In a Warsaw Classroom Containing Chairs." [GrandS] (8:2) Wint 89, p. 157-159.
"Miedzryzecz." [NewL] (56:2/3) Wint 89-Spr 90, p. 98.
"A Mouse." [NewL] (56:2/3) Wint 89-Spr 90, p. 97.
"Primarily We Miss Ourselves As Children" (a Warsaw student, overheard).
  [RiverS] (29) [89], p. 66.
2003. GILES, Paulette
  "My Father and the Sea" (tr. of Du Wei Ping). [GrahamHR] (12) Spr 89, p. 40-41.
2004. GILGUN, John
  "Cock." [JamesWR] (6:3) Spr 89, p. 11.
  "Hot Springs." [Ploughs] (15:1) 89, p. 43.
2005. GILL, James
  "Child Left at the Roadside" (tr. of Jean Tardieu). [MissR] (17:3, #51), p. 86-87.
  "It Is True" (tr. of Jean Pierre Vallotton). [MissR] (17:3, #51), p. 88.
  "The Mask" (tr. of Jean Tardieu). [MissR] (17:3, #51), p. 83.
  "The Young Man and the Sea" (tr. of Jean Tardieu). [MissR] (17:3, #51), p. 84-85.
2006. GILL, Michael J.
  "Buying a Used Flute." [PoetL] (84:3) Fall 89, p. 9.
  "Love Poem." [HiramPoR] (46) Spr-Sum 89, p. 15-16.
  "Morning at My Desk." [HiramPoR] (46) Spr-Sum 89, p. 13-14.
2007. GILL-LONERGAN, Janet
  "Into the Urban Fold." [BellArk] (5:4) Jl-Ag 89, p. 1.
  "Saturday Morning." [BellArk] (5:1) Ja-F 89, p. 3.
  "Snowbound." [BellArk] (5:6) N-D 89, p. 1.
2008. GILLESPIE, Joseph
  "Masturbation." [Hawai'iR] (13:1, #25) Spr 89, p. 108.
2009. GILLILAND, Mary
  "Feral Gift." [SpoonRQ] (14:3) Sum 89, p. 62.
  "Flaming Stalks." [SpoonRQ] (14:3) Sum 89, p. 63.
  "The Great Bear in Winter." [StoneC] (16:3/4) Spr-Sum 89, p. 24.
  "Springs Great Bear." [StoneC] (16:3/4) Spr-Sum 89, p. 24.
  "You've Seen Them All." [SpoonRQ] (14:3) Sum 89, p. 61.
2010. GILMORE, Brian Guy
  "Angry Voices." [Obs] (3:3) Wint 88, p. 27-30.
  "Slave Ship Ride." [Obs] (3:3) Wint 88, p. 26-27.
2011. GILMORE, Christine
  "In the Tajo, Ronda." [Pequod] (26/27) 89, p. 174-175.
  "What Is to Come." [GrahamHR] (12) Spr 89, p. 96.
2012. GILMORE, Patricia
  "Salzburg Singing School." [PacificR] (7) 89, p. 91.
2013. GILSDORF, Gordon
  "Gospel Celebrities." [FourQ] (2d series 3:1) Spr 89, p. 29.
  "A Little Sonnet on Celibacy." [FourQ] (2d series 3:1) Spr 89, p. 30.
GINEBRA, Arminda Valdés
  See VALDÉS GINEBRA, Arminda
2014. GINSBERG, Allen
  "Cosmopolitan Greetings" (To Struga Festival Golden Wreath Laureates &
    International Bards 1986). [AlphaBS] (6) Wint 89-90, p. 36-37.
  "Graphic Winces" (Chain Poem by Allen Ginsberg with M.F.A. Classes and
    Friends, 10/4/87). [BrooklynR] (5) 88, p. 57-59.
  "Graphic Winces" (Excerpt, A chain poem written by the author in collaboration with
    his students). [Harp] (278:1667) Ap 89, p. 38.
  "Improvisation in Beijing" (Oct. 21, 1984, discourse at conference of Chinese
    Writers Association . . .). [AlphaBS] (6) Wint 89-90, p. 33-35.
  "Proclamation." [Vis] (30) 89, p. 5.
2015. GINTER, Laurel
  "Questions." [Confr] (39/40) Fall 88-Wint 89, p. 233.
2016. GIOIA, Dana
  "All Souls." [NewYorker] (65:34) 9 O 89, p. 46.
  "Each Photographed Face" (tr. of Valerio Magrelli). [Poetry] (155:1/2) O-N 89, p.
    158.
  "The Homecoming." [CrossCur] (8:2) Ja 89, p. 41-53.
  "Hunt" (tr. of Mario Luzi). [Poetry] (155:1/2) O-N 89, p. 26.

"I Have Often Imagined That Glances" (tr. of Valerio Magrelli). [Poetry] (155:1/2) O-N 89, p. 158.
"In the Mediterranean Stain" (tr. of Bartolo Cattafi). [Poetry] (155:1/2) O-N 89, p. 55.
"My Love, Don't Believe" (tr. of Bartolo Cattafi). [Poetry] (155:1/2) O-N 89, p. 53.
"Night Must Fall" (tr. of Nina Cassian). [WilliamMR] (27) 89, p. 49.
"On Approaching Forty" (tr. of Mario Luzi). [Poetry] (155:1/2) O-N 89, p. 25.
"These Little Birds" (tr. of Bartolo Cattafi). [Poetry] (155:1/2) O-N 89, p. 53.
"This Handwriting Wears Itself Away" (tr. of Valerio Magrelli). [Poetry] (155:1/2) O-N 89, p. 159.
"This Red Cup" (tr. of Valerio Magrelli). [Poetry] (155:1/2) O-N 89, p. 157.
2017. GIOSEFFI, Daniela
"Black Woman" (tr. of Nancy Morejon, w. Enildo Garcia). [Contact] (9:50/51/52) Fall-Wint 88-Spr 89, p. 44-45.
"The Boy Who Sells Greens" (tr. of Carilda Oliver Labra, w. Enildo Garcia). [Contact] (9:50/51/52) Fall-Wint 88-Spr 89, p. 39.
"Declaration of Love" (1963, October Cuban Missile Crisis, tr. of Carilda Oliver Labra, w. Enildo Garcia). [Contact] (9:50/51/52) Fall-Wint 88-Spr 89, p. 38.
"Dying in Sadness" (Camen Miranda in memoriam, tr. of Nancy Morejon, w. Enildo Garcia). [Contact] (9:50/51/52) Fall-Wint 88-Spr 89, p. 43.
"The Last Conversation with Rolando Escardo" (tr. of Carilda Oliver Labra, w. Enildo Garcia). [Contact] (9:50/51/52) Fall-Wint 88-Spr 89, p. 41.
"Of the Word" (tr. of Carilda Oliver Labra, w. Enildo Garcia). [Contact] (9:50/51/52) Fall-Wint 88-Spr 89, p. 40.
"Polished Stone" (tr. of Nancy Morejon, w. Enildo Garcia). [Contact] (9:50/51/52) Fall-Wint 88-Spr 89, p. 43.
"Reportage from Viet Nam, Especially for International Woman's Day" (tr. of Minera Salado, w. Enildo Garcia). [Contact] (9:50/51/52) Fall-Wint 88-Spr 89, p. 46.
"To the Passing Days and Birthdays" (to Carilda Oliver Labra, tr. of Nancy Morejon, w. Enildo Garcia). [Contact] (9:50/51/52) Fall-Wint 88-Spr 89, p. 42.
"Today's Interview" (tr. of Minera Salado, w. Enildo Garcia). [Contact] (9:50/51/52) Fall-Wint 88-Spr 89, p. 47.
"When Papa" (tr. of Carilda Oliver Labra, w. Enildo Garcia). [Contact] (9:50/51/52) Fall-Wint 88-Spr 89, p. 40.
2018. GIOVANNI, Nikki
"Crutches." [Kaleid] (19) Sum-Fall 89, p. 39.
2019. GIRRI, Alberto
"Asking Oneself, Every Once in a While" (tr. by Thorpe Running). [LitR] (32:4) Sum 89, p. 493-494.
"On Opening Your Eyes and Not Hearing" (tr. by Thorpe Running). [LitR] (32:4) Sum 89, p. 492-493.
"The Poem as Unstable" (tr. by Thorpe Running). [LitR] (32:4) Sum 89, p. 494-495.
"Simplistic, Convincing Version" (tr. by Thorpe Running). [LitR] (32:4) Sum 89, p. 491-492.
"The Sketch as Poem" (tr. by Patsy Boyer and Mary Crow). [LitR] (32:4) Sum 89, p. 495-496.
2020. GISCOMBE, C. S.
"Look Ahead -- Look South" (Excerpt). [Callaloo] (12:3, #40) Sum 89, p. 519-522.
2021. GITZEN, Julian
"A Brief History of One Corncrib." [CapeR] (24:1) Spr 89, p. 34.
"Watchfulness in Fountain County." [Interim] (8:1) Spr 89, p. 14.
2022. GIUDICI, Giovanni
"La Bovary C'Est Moi" (Poesie per una Voce. Selection: I). [Poetry] (155:1/2) O-N 89, p. 70.
"An Evening Like So Many Others" (tr. by Charles Wright). [Poetry] (155:1/2) O-N 89, p. 72-73.
"Madame Bovary C'Est Moi" (Poem for one voice. Selection: I, tr. by Charles Wright). [Poetry] (155:1/2) O-N 89, p. 71.
2023. GIZZI, Michael
"Saltines" (In Memoriam: Tony Gizzi). [Screens] (1) 89, p. 59.
2024. GIZZI, Peter
"About the Nursery" (for Trevor Winkfield). [Screens] (1) 89, p. 28.
"The Frontier." [Talisman] (3) Fall 89, p. 105.

2025. GJUZEL, Bogomil
"Survival" (tr. by Mary Crow and the Author). [ColR] (NS 16:1) Spr-Sum 89, p. 100.
2026. GLADDING, Jody
"Eight Difficult Situations." [PoetryNW] (30:1) Spr 89, p. 3-9.
2027. GLADE, Jon Forrest
"Ghost Stories." [Lactuca] (12) F 89, p. 46-47.
"Indian Payday" (Bernie's Bar, 1976). [Lactuca] (12) F 89, p. 48.
"Shitbirds." [Lactuca] (12) F 89, p. 47.
"Specialist Fletcher." [Lactuca] (12) F 89, p. 47.
"Viper" (Ashau Valley, 1969). [Bogg] (61) 89, p. 17.
2028. GLADING, Jan
"That Strange Fire." [Kaleid] (19) Sum-Fall 89, p. 51.
2029. GLAEFKE, Deborah S.
"Easter Brahman." [Plain] (9:3) Spr 89, p. 24.
2030. GLANCY, Diane
"Air for Flute Stop." [HighP] (4:3) Wint 89-90, p. 129.
"Assessment." [SwampR] (1:4) Sum 89, p. 70.
"Boarding School for Indian Women." [SenR] (19:2) Fall 89, p. 38-40.
"The Bowl of Judgments." [SwampR] (1:4) Sum 89, p. 71.
"Buying Buttons, Russellville, Arkansas." [SwampR] (1:4) Sum 89, p. 69.
"Death Cry for the Language." [Nimrod] (32:2) Spr-Sum 89, p. 103-112.
"The First Reader" (Santee Training School, 1873). [NegC] (9:2) 89, p. 50.
"First Snow." [CrabCR] (6:1) 89, p. 23.
"Neighbor." [Nimrod] (32:2) Spr-Sum 89, p. 101.
"Night Shift." [SpoonRQ] (14:2) Spr 89, p. 39-40.
"Oil Field Wife." [CimR] (87) Ap 89, p. 50.
"Portrait of the Disguise Artist." [AmerV] (14) Spr 89, p. 29.
"She Was Spinning in Space." [SenR] (19:2) Fall 89, p. 42.
"A Single Row of Pines." [SenR] (19:2) Fall 89, p. 41.
"Three Ducks in the Marias des Cygnes Wildlife Reserve" (Highway 69, Kansas 12/25/84). [Nimrod] (32:2) Spr-Sum 89, p. 102.
"Umberta." [LaurelR] (23:1) Wint 89, p. 79-80.
"Vici, Oklahoma." [CimR] (87) Ap 89, p. 51.
2031. GLANCY, Gabrielle
"The Way the World Appears." [ParisR] (31:113) Wint 89, p. 156.
2032. GLASER, Elton
"Bible Browsing." [SouthernHR] (23:2) Spr 89, p. 138.
"Color Photographs of the Ruins." [LaurelR] (23:1) Wint 89, p. 58-60.
"Dog Nights." [OxfordM] (5:1) Spr-Sum 89, p. 35.
"Forecasts." [NoDaQ] (57:3) Sum 89, p. 102.
"Freefall at Evening." [GeoR] (43:3) Fall 89, p. 475.
"Housebreaker." [NoDaQ] (57:3) Sum 89, p. 100.
"Mardi Gras Indians." [FloridaR] (16:2/3) Fall-Wint 89, p. 216.
"The Mineral Kingdom" (tr. of Jacques Dupin). [StoneC] (17:1/2) Fall-Wint 89-90, p. 67.
"Nothing of Ourselves." [SouthernHR] (23:2) Spr 89, p. 144.
"The Origin of Myth." [SouthernPR] (29:2) Fall 89, p. 38-39.
"The Prisoner" (tr. of Jacques Dupin). [StoneC] (17:1/2) Fall-Wint 89-90, p. 66.
"Proles Before Swans." [CinPR] (20) Fall 89, p. 58.
"Wings and a Prayer." [NoDaQ] (57:3) Sum 89, p. 101.
2033. GLASER, James K.
"In Spring." [ChrC] (106:10) Mr 22-29, 89, p. 301.
2034. GLASER, Michael S.
"Apples." [ChrC] (106:12) Ap 12, 89, p. 382.
"Pearls." [ChrC] (106:6) F 22, 89, p. 197.
"Tell Me Zucchini." [NewL] (55:3) Spr 89, p. 23.
"Thanksgiving Ritual." [ChrC] (106:35) N 22, 89, p. 1079.
2035. GLASS, Jesse
"Orpheus." [NewEngR] (11:4) Sum 89, p. 381-390.
2036. GLASS, Malcolm
"Faces." [SewanR] (97:1) Wint 89, p. 22-23.
"Hunchback." [SewanR] (97:1) Wint 89, p. 24-25.
"Reunion." [PoetC] (20:2) Wint 89, p. 41.
"The Rites of Owls." [HighP] (4:3) Wint 89-90, p. 19-20.
"The Skull of the Owl." [WebR] (14:1) Spr 89, p. 56.

"Snapshot." [WebR] (14:1) Spr 89, p. 57.
"Surviving the Workshop." [PoetC] (20:2) Wint 89, p. 42-43.
"The Truth About Polar Bears." [Poetry] (153:4) Ja 89, p. 228.
2037. GLASSER, Jane Ellen
"With Difficulty the Poet Dissolves His Love Affair with Prosody." [BelPoJ] (40:2)
Wint 89-90, p. 18-19.
2038. GLAZE, Andrew
"Goodbye Captain Rickenbacker." [Journal] (12:2) Fall-Wint 88-89, p. 86.
"A Journey." [Journal] (12:2) Fall-Wint 88-89, p. 85.
"Laocoon." [NegC] (9:2) 89, p. 11-12.
"Life of Luck." [NegC] (9:1) 89, p. 102.
"Nursing Home." [TriQ] (76) Fall 89, p. 93.
"There Used to Be Morning." [Journal] (12:2) Fall-Wint 88-89, p. 85-86.
2039. GLAZER, Michele
"Morning Glory." [DenQ] (24:1) Sum 89, p. 19-20.
"Pomegranate." [GeoR] (43:1) Spr 89, p. 92.
2040. GLAZIER, Loss Pequeño
"Its Prodigies Held in Time's Amber." [Os] (28) 89, p. 28.
2041. GLAZNER, Greg
"Trash Assemblage at Agua Fria." [Sonora] (17) Spr-Sum 89, p. 31-32.
2042. GLEASURE, James
"Claustrophobia" (tr. of Seán O Ríordáin). [Trans] (22) Fall 89, p. 47.
"Mary Hogan's Quatrains" (tr. of Máire Mhac an tSaoi). [Trans] (22) Fall 89, p.
59-61.
2043. GLEN, Emilie
"Voice." [Footwork] 89, p. 49.
2044. GLENN, Jerry
"They Followed" (tr. of Hans-Jürgen Heise). [NewOR] (16:4) Wint 89, p. 72.
2045. GLICKMAN, Susan
"Henry Moore's Sheep" (for Bronwen Wallace). [MalR] (86) Spr 89, p. 29-38.
"A House" (for Toan). [Event] (18:2) Sum 89, p. 56-59.
"Reading." [CanLit] (121) Sum 89, p. 25.
2046. GLOEGGLER, Tony
"New Year's Eve." [Bogg] (61) 89, p. 18.
"Window Shopping." [YellowS] (32) Wint 89, p. 36.
2047. GLOWNEY, John
"Downriver." [Northeast] (ser. 5:1) Wint 89-90, p. 24-25.
2048. GLÜCK, Louise
"Celestial Music." [NewL] (56:2/3) Wint 89-Spr 90, p. 104-105.
"Dedication to Hunger." [NewL] (56:2/3) Wint 89-Spr 90, p. 100-102.
"The Drowned Children." [NewL] (56:2/3) Wint 89-Spr 90, p. 99.
"Lullaby." [NewL] (56:2/3) Wint 89-Spr 90, p. 103.
2049. GLYNN, Daniel
"Convergences." [KanQ] (21:3) Sum 89, p. 96-97.
2050. GOBLE, Lisa
"Adjustment Disorder." [PacificR] (7) 89, p. 39.
2051. GODFREY, John
"Prolly Not" (for George V.). [Talisman] (3) Fall 89, p. 103.
2052. GODIN, Deborah
"2 P.M. MST <-- Flight of Birds --> 3 P.M. MDT." [Rampike] (6:2) 88, p. 75.
2053. GOEDICKE, Patricia
"Above the Birds." [ColR] (NS 16:2) Fall 89-Wint 90, p. 48-49.
"As the Years Get into Their Cars." [PraS] (63:4) Wint 89, p. 77-79.
"Each Day the Mind Rises." [SenR] (19:1) 89, p. 38-40.
"The Goldberg Variations." [Hudson] (42:3) Aut 89, p. 435-440.
"Letter to Jonathan from Missoula." [MassR] (30:2) Sum 89, p. 295-297.
"So With Death." [ColR] (NS 16:2) Fall 89-Wint 90, p. 50-51.
"Tell Me." [ColR] (NS 16:2) Fall 89-Wint 90, p. 45-47.
"The Wind That Swept Up Great Homer." [GettyR] (2:2) Spr 89, p. 354-355.
"The Wrong Thing." [SenR] (19:1) 89, p. 41-42.
2054. GOEL, Rashmi
"Juhu." [Grain] (17:2) Sum 89, p. 50-51.
GOGISGI
See ARNETT, Carroll
2055. GOLD, Arthur R.
"Paris in the Summer of 1988." [NewRep] (200:5) 30 Ja 89, p. 30.

2056. GOLDBARTH, Albert
  "After Seeing the Impressionist Group Exhibit in Kansas City, We Drive Back
      Through Flatness to Wichita." [Poetry] (155:3) D 89, p. 214.
  "Alien Tongue." [NowestR] (27:3) 89, p. 34-35.
  "The Aliens' Translation Machine." [GeoR] (43:4) Wint 89, p. 749.
  "Alone." [LaurelR] (23:2) Sum 89, p. 5-16.
  "Another Portrait." [RiverC] (10:1) Fall 89, p. 10-12.
  "As Response." [RiverC] (10:1) Fall 89, p. 8-9.
  "Blade." [TarRP] (28:2) Spr 89, p. 1-2.
  "The Book of Numbers." [PoetryNW] (30:3) Aut 89, p. 30-32.
  "Burnt Offering." [KenR] (N 11:4) Fall 89, p. 123-126.
  "Collecting: An Essay" (for Barbara & David Clewell). [Boulevard] (4:2, #11) Fall
      89, p. 170-174.
  "The Dazzle." [BelPoJ] (39:3) Spr 89, p. 16-18.
  "Desert Song." [NewRep] (200:4) 23 Ja 89, p. 34.
  "Domains." [ParisR] (31:112) Fall 89, p. 178-179.
  "The Earliest Punctuation." [Iowa] (19:2) Spr-Sum 89, p. 115-116.
  "Elegy." [Boulevard] (4:1, #10) Spr 89, p. 186.
  "Entropysong." [PoetryNW] (30:1) Spr 89, p. 38-39.
  "An Explanation." [Iowa] (19:2) Spr-Sum 89, p. 114.
  "The Gate." [Ploughs] (15:1) 89, p. 44-45.
  "Giverny." [NewRep] (200:4) 23 Ja 89, p. 34.
  "The History of Buttons." [Caliban] (6) 89, p. 199-202.
  "How Fast." [Iowa] (19:2) Spr-Sum 89, p. 113.
  "How the World Works: An Essay." [CimR] (89) O 89, p. 82-84.
  "In the Midst of Intrusive Richness." [Poetry] (153:6) Mr 89, p. 316-317.
  "A Letter." [Poetry] (153:6) Mr 89, p. 317-318.
  "Lithium Sonnet." [ParisR] (31:112) Fall 89, p. 177.
  "Little Burger Blues Song." [PoetryE] (28) Fall 89, p. 26-27.
  "The Locks." [PoetryE] (28) Fall 89, p. 25.
  "Messenger." [PoetryNW] (30:1) Spr 89, p. 39-40.
  "The Mystery Poem." [PoetryNW] (30:3) Aut 89, p. 32-33.
  "The Need for Private Space Is Here." [TarRP] (28:2) Spr 89, p. 2-4.
  "The Niggling Mystery." [OntR] (30) Spr-Sum 89, p. 32-34.
  "The Nile." [BelPoJ] (39:3) Spr 89, p. 10-15.
  "Of the Doubleness." [Ploughs] (15:4) Wint 89-90, p. 82-84.
  "A Paean to the Concept." [NowestR] (27:3) 89, p. 36-37.
  "A Partner." [PoetryE] (28) Fall 89, p. 21.
  "Poem with 2 Lines from a Catalogue." [NewRep] (200:4) 23 Ja 89, p. 34.
  "Radio Baseball." [KenR] (N 11:4) Fall 89, p. 128-131.
  "The Sciences Wing a Lullabye." [Iowa] (19:2) Spr-Sum 89, p. 114-115.
  "Sculpture Garden." [PoetryE] (28) Fall 89, p. 23-24.
  "Sensitivity." [BelPoJ] (39:3) Spr 89, p. 19-22.
  "Some Things." [PoetryE] (28) Fall 89, p. 22.
  "Steeplejacks." [RiverC] (10:1) Fall 89, p. 6-7.
  "A Tale." [PoetryNW] (30:1) Spr 89, p. 37-38.
  "The Talk Show." [Poetry] (155:3) D 89, p. 215-216.
  "Threshold." [NewEngR] (11:4) Sum 89, p. 351-380.
  "Tightly." [PoetryE] (28) Fall 89, p. 28.
  "Toil." [KenR] (N 11:4) Fall 89, p. 127-128.
  "Too Much." [GeoR] (43:4) Wint 89, p. 745-746.
  "Vigil." [Poetry] (155:3) D 89, p. 217-218.
  "Wind-Up Sushi" (with catalogues and instructions for assembly). [DenQ] (24:1)
      Sum 89, p. 21-42.
2057. GOLDBERG, Barbara
  "Abishag" (tr. of Moshe Dor). [WebR] (14:1) Spr 89, p. 34.
  "Alternate Possibilities" (tr. of Moshe Dor). [Trans] (21) Spr 89, p. 126-127.
  "Ballad of the Id." [NewEngR] (11:3) Spr 89, p. 336.
  "Coalman" (tr. of Moshe Dor). [Trans] (21) Spr 89, p. 128.
  "The Count of Monte Cristo" (tr. of Moshe Dor). [WebR] (14:1) Spr 89, p. 31-32.
  "Dream-Life" (tr. of Moshe Dor). [WebR] (14:1) Spr 89, p. 33.
  "Khamsin" (tr. of Moshe Dor). [WebR] (14:1) Spr 89, p. 34.
  "Night Watch." [Poetry] (153:5) F 89, p. 272.
  "Toward Evening" (tr. of Moshe Dor). [Trans] (21) Spr 89, p. 127.
  "What Is Served." [Poetry] (153:5) F 89, p. 273.
  "When You Are With Me" (tr. of Moshe Dor). [WebR] (14:1) Spr 89, p. 32.

2058. GOLDBERG, Beckian Fritz
"Bad Sleep." [HayF] (4) Spr 89, p. 124-125.
"Balconies." [PoetryNW] (30:1) Spr 89, p. 46.
"Black Fish Blues." [BlackWR] (16:1) Fall-Wint 89, p. 22-23.
"Desert Winter." [GettyR] (2:1) Wint 89, p. 77.
"First Crazy." [HayF] (4) Spr 89, p. 122-123.
"Holy Days." [PoetryNW] (30:1) Spr 89, p. 46-47.
"Revolution." [PoetryNW] (30:1) Spr 89, p. 43-44.
"She Comes to My Door." [GettyR] (2:1) Wint 89, p. 78-79.
"What We Do in the Evening." [PoetryNW] (30:1) Spr 89, p. 44-45.
"The Winged Eye." [BlackWR] (16:1) Fall-Wint 89, p. 24.
GOLDBERG, Caryn Mirriam
    See MIRRIAM-GOLDBERG, Caryn
2059. GOLDBERG, Janet
"Working in the Lingerie Department." [StoneC] (16:3/4) Spr-Sum 89, p. 42-43.
2060. GOLDBERG, Jason S.
"The Hundred-Thousand Russian Czars." [Footwork] 89, p. 58.
2061. GOLDBERG, Nancy
"Tina." [US1] (22/23) Spr 89, p. 16.
2062. GOLDEN, Virginia
"Widowhood." [Amelia] (5:3, #14) 89, p. 58.
2063. GOLDENHAR, Edith
"Because the Song Must Match." [Caliban] (7) 89, p. 61-62.
2064. GOLDMAN, Judy
"The End of Something Simple." [GettyR] (2:1) Wint 89, p. 92.
"For My Brother Who Has Ended Another Relationship." [KanQ] (21:1/2) Wint-Spr
    89, p. 250.
"Night Vision." [ThRiPo] (33/34) 89, p. 50-51.
"The Peace of the House." [GettyR] (2:1) Wint 89, p. 93.
"Sunday Night, Driving Home." [SouthernR] (25:2) Spr 89, p. 499-500.
"Widow." [SouthernR] (25:2) Spr 89, p. 500.
2065. GOLDSMITH, Ann S.
"Red Riding Hood: Her Story." [HeliconN] (20) 89, p. 35.
"Red Riding Hood: The Mother Speaks." [HeliconN] (20) 89, p. 34.
2066. GOLDSTEIN, Laurence
"Elderly Surfer." [Poetry] (154:5) Ag 89, p. 270.
"London." [SouthernR] (25:3) Sum 89, p. 611-612.
"Posies." [Poetry] (153:6) Mr 89, p. 329.
"The Turbulent Goldstein Problem." [OntR] (30) Spr-Sum 89, p. 103-104.
2067. GOLDSTEIN, Marion
"Puzzle." [Plain] (9:2) Wint 89, p. 9.
2068. GOLDSTEIN, Sanford
"Underground Ambiguities: A Tanka String." [ChamLR] (2:2, #4) Spr 89, p. 82-84.
2069. GOLDSWORTHY, Peter
"Mass for the Middle-Aged." [Verse] (6:1) Mr 89, p. 10-11.
2070. GOLFFING, Francis
"Coming Home" (tr. of Heinrich Heine). [SpiritSH] (55) Fall-Wint 89 [90 on
    cover], p. 30-31.
"De Profundis" (tr. of Federico Garcia Lorca). [SpiritSH] (54) Spr-Sum 89, p. 35.
"Man" (tr. of Blas de Otero). [SpiritSH] (54) Spr-Sum 89, p. 33.
"Ode" (tr. of Sappho). [SouthwR] (74:2) Spr 89, p. 213.
"To a Supine Lady" (tr. of Sappho). [SpiritSH] (55) Fall-Wint 89 [90 on cover], p.
    30.
"The Tomb of Edgar Poe" (tr. of Stephan Mallarmé). [SpiritSH] (54) Spr-Sum 89,
    p. 34.
2071. GOLLATA, James A.
"Jack." [MoodySI] (20/21) Spr 89, p. 7.
GOMEZ, Alejandro Garcia
    See GARCIA GOMEZ, Alejandro
GOMEZ, Emilio García
    See GARCIA GOMEZ, Emilio
2072. GOMEZ BARROSO, Pero
"Song About a Worsening World" (tr. by Richard Zenith). [SouthwR] (74:2) Spr
    89, p. 218-219.
2073. GOMEZ BERAS, Carlos Roberto
"Anticipo de la Paloma." [Mairena] (11:27) 89, p. 59.

2074. GOMEZ ROSA, Alexis
"1. El Espejo del Matrimonio." [CuadP] (6:17) Enero-Abril 89, p. 57-58.
"2. Cafe Sublime Verde y Negro." [CuadP] (6:17) Enero-Abril 89, p. 59-60.
"3. Carrusel de los Gordos Felices y Dichosos." [CuadP] (6:17) Enero-Abril 89, p. 60-61.
"4. Tematica de Mercado con Utensilios de Mercado." [CuadP] (6:17) Enero-Abril 89, p. 61-64.
"5. Escalofrio Analogo del Tren Numero Siete." [CuadP] (6:17) Enero-Abril 89, p. 64-66.
"6. Banquete de Familia II." [CuadP] (6:17) Enero-Abril 89, p. 66-68.
"7. Aprendiz de Dos Mundos." [CuadP] (6:17) Enero-Abril 89, p. 68-69.
"Haiku" (13 poems). [CuadP] (6:17) Enero-Abril 89, p. 69-71.
2075. GOMPERT, Chris
"Traumatic Amputation." [StoneC] (17:1/2) Fall-Wint 89-90, p. 22.
2076. GON, Sam, III
"Two Ho'okupu." [BambooR] (44) Fall 89, p. 10-11.
2077. GONZALEZ, Angel
"An Astonishing World" (tr. by Steven Ford Brown and Pedro Gutierrez Revuelta). [SenR] (19:2) Fall 89, p. 75.
"The Battlefield" (tr. by Steven Ford Brown and Pedro Gutierrez Revuelta). [NegC] (9:1) 89, p. 191, 193.
"Before I Could Call Myself Angel González" (10 Poems in Spanish & English, Translation Chapbook Series, tr. by Steven Ford Brown and Gutierrez Revuelta). [MidAR] (9:2) 89, p. 97-123.
"El Campo de Batalla." [NegC] (9:1) 89, p. 190, 192.
"Diatribe Against the Dead" (tr. by Steven Ford Brown and Pedro Gutierrez Revuelta). [SenR] (19:2) Fall 89, p. 73.
"Horoscope for a Forgotten Dictator" (tr. by Steven Ford Brown and Pedro Gutierrez Revuelta). [SenR] (19:2) Fall 89, p. 74.
"Sonata for Violin Solo" (Johann Sebastian Bach, tr. by Steven Ford Brown and Pedro Gutierrez Revuelta). [NegC] (9:1) 89, p. 189.
"Sonata para Violin Solo" (Juan Sebastian Bach). [NegC] (9:1) 89, p. 188.
"A Traveler's Notes" (tr. by Steven Ford Brown and Pedro Gutierrez Revuelta). [PoetL] (84:3) Fall 89, p. 47-49.
2078. GONZALEZ, Lourdes
"The Abduction of the Mulattoes" (Owing to Carlos Enríquez, tr. of César López). [Pig] (15) 88, p. 67.
"After the Drums and the Steps" (tr. of Soleida Ríos). [Pig] (15) 88, p. 72.
"Ancient" (tr. of Soleida Ríos). [Pig] (15) 88, p. 72.
"Another's Bolero" (tr. of Soleida Ríos). [Pig] (15) 88, p. 74.
"At the Designated Hour" (For Juan Antonio Bardem in flight Madrid-Prague, tr. of Luis Rogelio Nogueras). [Pig] (15) 88, p. 69.
"Aunt Pepilla Embroiders a Bouquet" (In the style of Manuel Justo de Rubalcava, tr. of César López). [Pig] (15) 88, p. 66.
"Bolero for Albino" (tr. of Soleida Ríos). [Pig] (15) 88, p. 73.
"Creation Sunday" (tr. of León de la Hoz). [Pig] (15) 88, p. 65.
"Dreaming" (tr. of Soleida Ríos). [Pig] (15) 88, p. 73.
"Give, Claudia, My Regards to Lenin" (tr. of Manuel Díaz-Martínez, w. Ofelia Martínez). [Pig] (15) 88, p. 68.
"Last Letter" (tr. of Roberto Fernández Retamar). [Pig] (15) 88, p. 70-71.
"Old Postcard" (To my friend Juan Villalobos, tr. of César López). [Pig] (15) 88, p. 66.
"Supper" (for my parents, tr. of Nancy Moréjon). [Pig] (15) 88, p. 65.
"Those Brief Goodbyes" (tr. of Manuel Díaz-Martínez, w. Ofelia Martínez). [Pig] (15) 88, p. 68.
"The Worm or Desire" (tr. of León de la Hoz). [Pig] (15) 88, p. 64.
2079. GONZALEZ, Ray
"Walking Across a College Campus in 1988, I Hear Jimi Hendrix Blasting Out of a Dorm Window." [CinPR] (19) Spr 89, p. 54.
"Watching the Snowfall on Thanksgiving, I Think About Bly's Poems About the Father." [CinPR] (19) Spr 89, p. 53.
"Years Later." [CinPR] (19) Spr 89, p. 52.
GONZALEZ, Salvador Lopez
See LOPEZ GONZALEZ, Salvador
2080. GONZALEZ DURAN, Laura
"Clear and fragile figure" (tr. by T. Hoeksema). [Jacaranda] (4:1) Spr-Sum 89, p.

67.
"Poem: Because I reflect" (tr. by Thomas Hoeksema). [RiverS] (28) 89, p. 53.
2081. GONZALEZ-GUERRERO, Francisco
"Adios a Alfonso Reyes" (En la estación de México, en 1913). [Mairena] (11:27) 89,
p. 95.
2082. GOOD, Ruth
"Drunkenness." [LitR] (32:2) Wint 89, p. 212.
2083. GOODELL, Larry
"Boogie on the Square." [Conjunc] (13) 89, p. 258.
"Kiss Hello." [Conjunc] (13) 89, p. 257.
"Stairway to the Stars." [Conjunc] (13) 89, p. 258.
"Unlocked" (for Lenore). [Conjunc] (13) 89, p. 257.
2084. GOODENOUGH, J. B.
"After Supper." [Journal] (12:2) Fall-Wint 88-89, p. 46.
"Belling." [Journal] (12:2) Fall-Wint 88-89, p. 47.
"Child." [Mildred] (3:1) Spr-Sum 89, p. 98.
"The Cistern." [BallSUF] (30:4) Aut 89, p. 19.
"Eating the Salt." [CinPR] (20) Fall 89, p. 34.
"Escaping the Shoe." [BallSUF] (30:4) Aut 89, p. 17.
"Feud." [ChiR] (36:3/4) 89, p. 24.
"The Good Wife." [FourQ] (2d series 3:1) Spr 89, p. 10.
"In for the Season." [FourQ] (2d series 3:1) Spr 89, p. 10.
"Lady Wife." [Mildred] (3:1) Spr-Sum 89, p. 98.
"The Little Stones." [ChiR] (36:3/4) 89, p. 23.
"Moon-Mending." [SoCoast] (6) Fall 88, p. 53.
"Sea-Wife." [CinPR] (20) Fall 89, p. 35.
"Solstice" (St. Michael's Bay). [Poem] (62) N 89, p. 66.
"A Way Out." [TarRP] (29:1) Fall 89, p. 55-56.
2085. GOODMAN, Dottie
"Space." [EngJ] (78:6) O 89, p. 92.
2086. GOODMAN, Judith
"Solstice." [CentR] (33:2) Spr 89, p. 136.
2087. GOODMAN, Michael
"First Date." [NegC] (9:2) 89, p. 48-49.
2088. GOODMAN, Miriam
"Father's Mirror." [Poetry] (154:3) Je 89, p. 150.
2089. GOODWIN, Douglas
"A Slice." [Bogg] (61) 89, p. 49.
2090. GOODWIN, June
"Homage to Two Poets." [FreeL] (3) Aut 89, p. 20.
"Trust." [FreeL] (3) Aut 89, p. 21.
2091. GOOSE, Bruce
"God's Daughter." [AlphaBS] (5) Jl 89, p. 12.
2092. GORCZYNSKI, Renata
"Sails" (tr. of Adam Zagajewski, w. Benjamin Ivry). [NewYorker] (65:36) 23 O 89,
p. 56.
2093. GORDON, Carol
"Daughter in the World." [Kalliope] (11:1) 89, p. 47.
"Locked Out." [PaintedB] (38) 89, p. 21.
"Tits." [Calyx] (12:1) Sum 89, p. 17.
2094. GORDON, David
"Crossing a Boat-Bridge to South Tower"" (tr. of Lu Yu). [LitR] (32:3) Spr 89, p.
384.
"For Wei Pa, in Quiet" (tr. of Tu Fu). [LitR] (32:3) Spr 89, p. 382.
"A Garden's Mixed Notes"" (tr. of Lu Yu). [LitR] (32:3) Spr 89, p. 385.
"Going Out in the Rain to Look Around I Wrote This"" (tr. of Lu Yu). [LitR] (32:3)
Spr 89, p. 385.
"In Answer" (tr. of Mu Tung). [LitR] (32:3) Spr 89, p. 383.
"Not Finding Yuan" (tr. of Meng Hao-jan). [LitR] (32:3) Spr 89, p. 383.
"Old Field" (tr. of Tu Fu). [LitR] (32:3) Spr 89, p. 381.
"War Wall South" (tr. of Li Po). [LitR] (32:3) Spr 89, p. 386.
2095. GORDON, Gerry
"Called Susan." [Sonora] (17) Spr-Sum 89, p. 115.
2096. GORDON, Kirpal
"Disappearance in Greece: A Cycle of Poems" (6 poems). [Bound] (16:2/3)
Wint-Spr 89, p. 161-167.

"Macchu Picchu by Foot." [HeavenB] (6) Wint-Spr 89, p. 37-38.
"Saturday in the Financial District." [SlipS] (9) 89, p. 56.
"The Wonder That Was India." [HeavenB] (7) Wint 89, p. 16.
2097. GORHAM, Sarah
"Acrostic After Lewis Carroll." [CrossCur] (8:2) Ja 89, p. 169.
"The Bridgeport / Port Jefferson Ferry." [CrossCur] (8:2) Ja 89, p. 11.
"Circles" (after Emerson). [PoetryNW] (30:1) Spr 89, p. 12-13.
"Dancing with the Empress." [Ploughs] (15:4) Wint 89-90, p. 88.
"The Empress Speaks to Buddha." [Ploughs] (15:4) Wint 89-90, p. 87.
"I Go Back." [PoetryNW] (30:1) Spr 89, p. 13.
"In the Empress's Palace." [Ploughs] (15:4) Wint 89-90, p. 85.
"Moon Cakes." [Ploughs] (15:4) Wint 89-90, p. 86.
"Snow Melt." [PoetryNW] (30:1) Spr 89, p. 10.
"Starfish." [PoetryNW] (30:1) Spr 89, p. 11.
2098. GORMAN, LeRoy
"Haiku: Border crossing." [CrossC] (11:1) 89, p. 27.
2099. GOROSTIZA, José
"Aquarium" (To Xavier Villaurrutia, tr. by Joe Bolton). [Pig] (15) 88, p. 77.
2100. GORST, Norma
"Artist's Lyric." [ChamLR] (2:2, #4) Spr 89, p. 77.
"Last Work" (for G.B.W.). [ChamLR] (3:1, #5) Fall 89, p. 93-94.
"Lotus Seed." [ChamLR] (2:2, #4) Spr 89, p. 78.
2101. GOTERA, Vince
"Dance of the Letters." [Ploughs] (15:1) 89, p. 46-47.
"A Visitor on Ash Wednesday." [Caliban] (7) 89, p. 69-70.
2102. GOTO, T. M.
"Rappelling." [ChamLR] (2:2, #4) Spr 89, p. 118.
"Yellow River" (for CKT). [BambooR] (41) Wint 89, p. 8.
2103. GOTT, George
"Hotel Brevoort." [Amelia] (5:3, #14) 89, p. 87.
"Winter." [MidwQ] (30:4) Sum 89, p. 445.
2104. GOTTESMAN, Carl (Carl A.)
"Balance." [HampSPR] Wint 89, p. 24.
"Keening the Sunrise." [HampSPR] Wint 89, p. 25.
"Lilies of the Valley." [StoneC] (17:1/2) Fall-Wint 89-90, p. 47.
"Thirty-Eighth Week." [HeavenB] (7) Wint 89, p. 42.
2105. GOULD, Kathleen
"The Heretic." [KanQ] (21:3) Sum 89, p. p175.
"In Time, Rhyme." [KanQ] (21:3) Sum 89, p. 174.
2106. GOUMAS, Yannis
"Loneliness." [Dandel] (16:1) Spr-Sum 89, p. 27.
2107. GOURLAY, Elizabeth
"Snapshot by Stieglitz." [Event] (18:2) Sum 89, p. 66-67.
2108. GOWIN, Wolf
"Sowieso." [Os] (29) 89, p. 33.
"Waldermarstrasse" (Für Dietrich Plewnia). [Os] (29) 89, p. 34-35.
2109. GRAFF, E. J.
"By the Waters of Babylon." [AmerV] (14) Spr 89, p. 4.
2110. GRAFF, Juliette
"Death's Shelter." [Lactuca] (13) N 89, p. 15-16.
"Grief's Shadow." [Lactuca] (13) N 89, p. 12.
"Old Moons." [Lactuca] (13) N 89, p. 18.
"Time's Choice." [Lactuca] (13) N 89, p. 14.
2111. GRAFTON, Grace
"Blessing." [BellArk] (5:5) S-O 89, p. 4.
"Into It!" (-- Kenneth Patchen). [BellArk] (5:1) Ja-F 89, p. 3.
2112. GRAHAM, David
"Effects of Twilight." [Pembroke] (21) 89, p. 121.
"Eleanor's House." [Pembroke] (21) 89, p. 119-120.
"Instructions for the Dream." [Pembroke] (21) 89, p. 121.
"The Iron Crib" (for Tyler Munro Graham). [OxfordM] (5:1) Spr-Sum 89, p. 73-74.
"The Love of Poverty Creek." [Pembroke] (21) 89, p. 120.
"The Names of Parents." [WillowS] (23) Wint 89, p. 58.
"The Word Hard." [Talisman] (2) Spr 89, p. 79.
2113. GRAHAM, Desmond
"Dr. Korczak's Lie" (tr. of Anna Kamienska, w. Tomasz P. Krzeszowski). [Stand]

(30:1) Wint 88-89, p. 40.
2114. GRAHAM, James
"Jubilant Poem" (Homage to a poem of Andre Breton, tr. of Roque Dalton).
[Contact] (9:50/51/52) Fall-Wint 88-Spr 89, p. 55-56.
"Seeing You Naked" (To Maria del Carmen, tr. of Roque Dalton). [Contact]
(9:50/51/52) Fall-Wint 88-Spr 89, p. 56.
"Vernacular Elegy for Francisco Sorto" (tr. of Roque Dalton). [Contact] (9:50/51/52)
Fall-Wint 88-Spr 89, p. 58-59.
2115. GRAHAM, Jorie
"Detail from the Creation of Man." [Boulevard] (4:1, #10) Spr 89, p. 32-34.
"Fission." [NewYorker] (65:40) 20 N 89, p. 50-51.
"The Hiding Place." [NewYorker] (65:14) 22 My 89, p. 38-39.
"Orpheus and Eurydice." [NewL] (56:2/3) Wint 89-Spr 90, p. 112-114.
"The Phase After History." [ParisR] (31:113) Wint 89, p. 53-60.
"Picnic." [Boulevard] (4:1, #10) Spr 89, p. 28-31.
"The Republic for Which We Stand" (LFW 1922-1988). [NewL] (56:2/3) Wint
89-Spr 90, p. 115-117.
"Salmon." [NewL] (56:2/3) Wint 89-Spr 90, p. 110-111.
"Scirocco." [NewL] (56:2/3) Wint 89-Spr 90, p. 106-109.
"Spring." [ParisR] (31:110) Spr 89, p. 25-28.
"The Tree of Knowledge." [NewYorker] (65:2) 27 F 89, p. 38-39.
"Ultrahigh Frequency." [GrandS] (8:2) Wint 89, p. 116-119.
2116. GRAHAM, Malu
"In the Ebb Tide Bar." [EmeraldCR] (1989) c1988, p. 131-132.
2117. GRAHAM, Matthew
"The Catskills." [IndR] (12:3) Sum 89, p. 5-6.
2118. GRAHAM, Neile
"My Grandmother's Photograph." [Dandel] (16:2) Fall-Wint 89, p. 8.
"So We Know It's Not Just Us." [CanLit] (121) Sum 89, p. 11.
2119. GRANT, Jamie
"Perfume." [Verse] (6:1) Mr 89, p. 7-8.
"Powerhouse." [Verse] (6:1) Mr 89, p. 9.
"Skywriting." [Verse] (6:1) Mr 89, p. 6-7.
2120. GRANT, Paul
"The Mother of Beauty." [SewanR] (97:3) Sum 89, p. 315-318.
"Rondeau for Stepdaughters." [RiverC] (9:1) Spr 89, p. 84.
2121. GRANT, R. W.
"Ode to Michael Milken" (From "Tom Smith and His Incredible Bread Machine").
[Harp] (279:1670) Jl 89, p. 25-26.
2122. GRASS, Günter
"I Dreamed I Would Have to Say Goodbye" (tr. by John Linthicum). [LitR] (33:1)
Fall 89, p. 140-142.
"Old Iron" (tr. by John Linthicum). [LitR] (33:1) Fall 89, p. 143.
"Scenic Madrigal" (tr. by John Linthicum). [LitR] (33:1) Fall 89, p. 143.
2123. GRAVES, Bob
"Confession." [EmeraldCR] (1989) c1988, p. 100.
"Normandy." [EmeraldCR] (1989) c1988, p. 99.
2124. GRAVES, Michael P.
"Death Wish." [ChrC] (106:31) O 25, 89, p. 948.
2125. GRAVES, Paul
"The Adoration of the Magi" (tr. of Aleksandr Kushner). [PartR] (56:1) Wint 89, p.
117-118.
"Untitled: In the morning, the drafts in the blinds and the curtains" (tr. of Aleksandr
Kushner). [PartR] (56:1) Wint 89, p. 115-116.
"Untitled: We don't get to choose our century" (tr. of Aleksandr Kushner). [PartR]
(56:1) Wint 89, p. 116-117.
2126. GRAVES, Steven
"Improvisation in White." [CumbPR] (9:1) Fall 89, p. 48.
"Lilacs." [WestHR] (43:4) Wint 89, p. 243-244.
"Mary O'Driscoll's." [CumbPR] (9:1) Fall 89, p. 49-50.
2127. GRAY, Frank E., III
"Reflections of Being." [HeavenB] (7) Wint 89, p. 29.
2128. GRAY, Janet
"100 Flowers" (Selections: LXXXVI, LXXXVII). [Colum] (14) 89, p. 186-187.
"Love's Labour's Lost." [BrooklynR] (6) 89, p. 40-43.
"Quinnipiac R." [Aerial] (5) 89, p. 132-134.

2129. GRAY, Kate
"To Write a Poem." [PoetryNW] (30:3) Aut 89, p. 18-19.
2130. GRAY, Martin
"Tom Thomson's 'The West Wind'." [CrossC] (11:1) 89, p. 10.
2131. GRAY, Pamela
"Pomegranate Seeds." [SinW] (37) Spr 89, p. 83-86.
2132. GRAY, Pat
"Bicycling." [Shen] (39:1) Spr 89, p. 97-98.
2133. GRAY, Patrick Worth
"Church-Going." [SlipS] (9) 89, p. 81-82.
"The Earthen Smell of Small Things." [Farm] (6:2) Fall 89, p. 71.
"Late at Night I Hear Them Rocking. . . ." [CapeR] (24:2) Fall 89, p. 15.
"May in Omaha." [Footwork] 89, p. 65.
"No Difference." [Footwork] 89, p. 65.
"Nui Ba Dinh" (Black Virgin Mountain). [ColEng] (51:4) Ap 89, p. 388.
"The Sabbath the Preacher and the Choir Director Ran Off." [PoetC] (21:1) Fall 89,
    p. 14.
"Uncle Christopher." [OxfordM] (5:2) Fall-Wint 89, p. 62.
2134. GRAYSON, Lisa
"A Bone in the Desert." [Prima] (13) 89, p. 63.
"Scratch." [Prima] (13) 89, p. 8-9.
GRAZIA, Emilio de
    See DeGRAZIA, Emilio
2135. GRAZIDE, Richard
"Those of pulvinated heart." [Notus] (4:1) Spr 89, p. 67.
"Venus Admonishing." [Notus] (4:1) Spr 89, p. 68.
GRECO, Robert del
    See Del GRECO, Robert
2136. GREEN, Anita
"We Be Signifying." [SinW] (37) Spr 89, p. 50.
2137. GREEN, Connie J.
"Winter Evenings." [CumbPR] (8:2) Spr 89, p. 67.
2138. GREEN, Coppie
"Selling Gold." [GreensboroR] (46) Sum 89, p. 155.
2139. GREEN, Jaki Shelton
"Warriors at Play" (Selections: 4 poems). [Obs] (3:2) Sum 88, p. 97-106.
2140. GREEN, Phyllisjean
"Sailing Was." [Plain] (9:2) Wint 89, p. 11.
2141. GREEN, W. H.
"Not Me." [MidAR] (9:2) 89, p. 152.
2142. GREENBAUM, Jessica
"Leaving Williamsburg." [Ploughs] (15:4) Wint 89-90, p. 91-92.
"Vassar's Orange Living Room" (to Vassar Miller). [Ploughs] (15:4) Wint 89-90, p.
    89-90.
"Where I Work." [SouthwR] (74:3) Sum 89, p. 360.
2143. GREENBERG, Alvin
"Freight Train, Freight Train." [GettyR] (2:3) Sum 89, p. 491.
2144. GREENE, Ben
"A Civil Man." [GreensboroR] (46) Sum 89, p. 184.
2145. GREENE, Jeffrey
"Arrivals." [RiverC] (10:1) Fall 89, p. 106-107.
"The Lie." [Crazy] (36) Spr 89, p. 48-49.
"Love of the Faithless." [PraS] (63:2) Sum 89, p. 117-118.
"The Separation." [PraS] (63:2) Sum 89, p. 116-117.
"The Sunken Cathedral." [Crazy] (36) Spr 89, p. 46-47.
2146. GREENE, Mary
"Glass in the Asphalt." [BrooklynR] (5) 88, p. 20.
"Lettuce and Tomatoes Are Free." [BrooklynR] (5) 88, p. 21.
2147. GREENE, Ruth
"A Language That Sounds Like Birds Flying Sideways." [BrooklynR] (6) 89, p. 10.
"Nuptial." [BrooklynR] (6) 89, p. 9.
2148. GREENE, W. Michael
"Mother and Son." [BelPoJ] (39:4) Sum 89, p. 34-35.
2149. GREENFIELD, Robert L.
"Poem to Los Angeles, California." [WormR] (29:1, #113) 89, p. 2.
"She Said." [WormR] (29:1, #113) 89, p. 2-3.

"To the Girls at the University, to the Soft Ones." [WormR] (29:1, #113) 89, p. 1.
2150. GREENING, John
"The Day I Found King Tut." [Verse] (6:3) Wint 89, p. 81.
2151. GREENWALD, Martha
"Pensione Cristallo: Festa del Redentore." [GrandS] (9:1) Aut 89, p. 147-149.
2152. GREENWALD, Robert
"The Silent Ringmaster." [Kaleid] (19) Sum-Fall 89, p. 19.
"Where I Stand." [Kaleid] (19) Sum-Fall 89, p. 18.
2153. GREENWAY, William
"Anyone." [PraS] (63:4) Wint 89, p. 25.
"Diminishing Returns." [SpoonRQ] (14:1) Wint 89, p. 14.
"Elementary." [SpoonRQ] (14:1) Wint 89, p. 15.
"Father Dreams" (vi, vii, viii). [CapeR] (24:1) Spr 89, p. 15-17.
"Happy." [LaurelR] (23:1) Wint 89, p. 104.
"Intensive Care." [Poetry] (155:3) D 89, p. 220-221.
"The Names of Things." [ChatR] (9:2) Wint 89, p. 37.
"On Finding the Future Closed." [PraS] (63:4) Wint 89, p. 23.
"Once More to the Lake." [NegC] (9:1) 89, p. 86-87.
"Theater." [SpoonRQ] (14:1) Wint 89, p. 13.
"Yards." [PraS] (63:4) Wint 89, p. 24.
2154. GREGER, Debora
"The Family Rilke." [DenQ] (24:2) Fall 89, p. 49-50.
"St. Jerome in an Italian Landscape." [DenQ] (24:2) Fall 89, p. 48.
2155. GREGG, Cindy
"As I Look at You." [SingHM] (16) 89, p. 91.
"Timing Is Everything." [SingHM] (16) 89, p. 90.
2156. GREGG, Linda
"Costa." [Pequod] (26/27) 89, p. 191.
"Dancer Holding Still." [Pequod] (26/27) 89, p. 193.
"Dancing." [Pequod] (26/27) 89, p. 194.
"The Earth Itself Is the Measure." [PoetryE] (28) Fall 89, p. 78.
"A Flower No More Than Itself." [PoetryE] (28) Fall 89, p. 76.
"The Gods in the Twilight." [Pequod] (26/27) 89, p. 190.
"The Last Night in Mithymna." [Atlantic] (263:4) Ap 89, p. 78.
"Night Standing Back from the World." [Pequod] (26/27) 89, p. 189.
"Nights in the Neighborhood." [PoetryE] (28) Fall 89, p. 79.
"Not Saying Much." [NewL] (56:2/3) Wint 89-Spr 90, p. 120.
"Resisting the Music." [Pequod] (26/27) 89, p. 192.
"A Stranger in the Wonderful Light." [NewL] (56:2/3) Wint 89-Spr 90, p. 122.
"The War." [NewL] (56:2/3) Wint 89-Spr 90, p. 121.
"What If the World Stays Always Far Off." [NewL] (56:2/3) Wint 89-Spr 90, p. 118-120.
"What Way Is Home." [PoetryE] (28) Fall 89, p. 77.
2157. GREGORY, Cynde
"To a Pregnant Doe, Dead on the Side of the Road." [Mildred] (3:2) 89, p. 12.
2158. GREGORY, Michael
"Cliché Pantoum." [WritersF] (15) Fall 89, p. 117-118.
2159. GREGORY, Robert
"1959." [RedBass] (14) 89, p. 48.
"The Angel Who Spoke From Inside a Weed." [RedBass] (14) 89, p. 49.
"Reddish Pre-Korean Sun." [Aerial] (5) 89, p. 93.
"Twin I-Beam Construction, or What It Was Like to Be Crazy in Germany in 1889." [Aerial] (5) 89, p. 94-96.
2160. GRENNAN, Eamon
"Aloft." [Nat] (249:13) 23 O 89, p. 468.
"Bite." [Vis] (29) 89, p. 48-49.
"Blood, Nest, Stars." [Nat] (248:18) 8 My 89, p. 638.
"Breaking Points." [KenR] (N 11:4) Fall 89, p. 44-45.
"Compass Reading." [NewYorker] (65:40) 20 N 89, p. 56.
"Deceptions." [KenR] (N 11:4) Fall 89, p. 43-44.
"Diagnosis." [KenR] (N 11:4) Fall 89, p. 41-42.
"Endangered Species." [Colum] (14) 89, p. 31.
"Moving." [NewYorker] (65:24) 31 Jl 89, p. 34.
"Night Visitor." [Vis] (29) 89, p. 50-51.
"Reports from the Front." [NewYorker] (65:1) 20 F 89, p. 44.
"Room and Sun." [NewYorker] (65:35) 16 O 89, p. 48.

"Sign Language." [Nat] (248:14) 10 Ap 89, p. 497.
"That Ocean." [NewYorker] (65:28) 28 Ag 89, p. 38.
"Unnatural Act." [Vis] (29) 89, p. 47-48.
"Words." [Vis] (30) 89, p. 38.
2161. GRESHAM, Geraldine
"As I walk through this Straight way." [EmeraldCR] (1989) c1988, p. 135.
2162. GREY, John
"The Call to Dinner." [SmPd] (26:2 #76) Spr 89, p. 16.
"The Cliché Can Warm You." [InterPR] (15:2) Fall 89, p. 112.
"Dawn Busters." [Lactuca] (13) N 89, p. 23.
"A Dialectic." [InterPR] (15:2) Fall 89, p. 111.
"Distant Cycle." [Interim] (8:1) Spr 89, p. 33.
"For the Explosion." [Lactuca] (13) N 89, p. 22.
"Holding On." [Os] (28) 89, p. 29.
"In the Slow." [Lactuca] (13) N 89, p. 23.
"Ladakhi." [InterPR] (15:2) Fall 89, p. 110.
"Loon of Memory." [StoneC] (16:3/4) Spr-Sum 89, p. 60-61.
"Night of the Magician." [Vis] (31) 89, p. 41.
"Origami." [Plain] (10:1) 89, p. 29.
"The Silk Fields." [Lactuca] (13) N 89, p. 24.
"You're Dating a Nazi." [CreamCR] (13:2) Fall 89, p. 193.
2163. GREY, Robert
"In Other Words." [WillowS] (23) Wint 89, p. 83.
"Winter Beach." [SouthernHR] (23:1) Wint 89, p. 36.
2164. GRIFFIN, Sheila
"Get Out of Dodge." [AmerPoR] (18:4) Jl-Ag 89, p. 32.
"A Good Woman." [DenQ] (24:2) Fall 89, p. 51.
"Your Widow." [PoetryNW] (30:1) Spr 89, p. 24.
2165. GRIFFIN, Walter
"After the Inner Sanctum and the Last Drink of Water, 1945." [CrabCR] (6:2) Wint
   89, p. 24-25.
"After the Inner Sanctum and the Last Drink of Water, 1945." [KanQ] (21:1/2)
   Wint-Spr 89, p. 146.
"After the Inner Sanctum and the Last Drink of Water, 1945." [NewEngR] (11:4)
   Sum 89, p. 420.
"Day of the Soft Mouth." [KanQ] (21:1/2) Wint-Spr 89, p. 146-147.
"Fish Leaves." [CrabCR] (6:2) Wint 89, p. 25-26.
"Mother's Day." [Poetry] (154:2) My 89, p. 97.
"Night Trains." [SouthernR] (25:1) Wint 89, p. 175.
"The Self Gardener." [CrabCR] (6:2) Wint 89, p. 26.
"The Trees Are Falling." [CrabCR] (6:2) Wint 89, p. 24.
"Vogelsang 5." [HolCrit] (26:1) F 89, p. 20.
"Wet Pavement." [CrabCR] (6:2) Wint 89, p. 24.
"Wet Pavement." [KanQ] (21:1/2) Wint-Spr 89, p. 148.
"Wet Pavement." [PacificR] (7) 89, p. 92.
2166. GRIFFITH, Kevin
"Hawk Over the Rutherford Funeral Home." [MidAR] (9:1) 89, p. 44.
"A Krakow Cemetery Shortcut." [MinnR] (NS 33) Fall 89, p. 18-19.
"The Pond Near Crematorium Four." [MinnR] (NS 33) Fall 89, p. 18.
"Wait." [Os] (29) 89, p. 10.
2167. GRIFFITH, Leon Odell
"Gentleman's Problem." [EmeraldCR] (1989) c1988, p. 12.
"To A. R." [EmeraldCR] (1989) c1988, p. 12.
"To Death." [EmeraldCR] (1989) c1988, p. 12-13.
2168. GRIFFITH, Phillip Hansford
"Funeral." [EmeraldCR] (1989) c1988, p. 129.
2169. GRIGORESCU, Irina
"Only the Blank Page" (tr. of Anghel Dumbraveanu, w. Adam J. Sorkin). [NewOR]
   (16:2) Sum 89, p. 92.
"Runes" (tr. of Anghel Dumbraveanu, w. Adam J. Sorkin). [NewOR] (16:2) Sum
   89, p. 96.
2170. GRIM, Jessica
"Dreaming of Bonzai." [Screens] (1) 89, p. 92-98.
2171. GRIMM, Reinhold
"Arrière-Pensée" (tr. of Hans Magnus Enzensberger). [LitR] (33:1) Fall 89, p. 23.
"The Divorce" (tr. of Hans Magnus Enzensberger, w. Felix Pollak). [LitR] (33:1)

Fall 89, p. 19.
"The Dresses" (tr. of Hans Magnus Enzensberger, w. Felix Pollak). [LitR] (33:1)
Fall 89, p. 22.
"Shit" (tr. of Hans Magnus Enzensberger, w. Felix Pollak). [LitR] (33:1) Fall 89, p.
21.
"Short History of the Bourgeoisie" (tr. of Hans Magnus Enzensberger, w. Felix
Pollak). [LitR] (33:1) Fall 89, p. 20.
2172. GRIMM, Susan
"At the Movies." [FloridaR] (16:2/3) Fall-Wint 89, p. 98-99.
"The Body Becomes a Kingdom." [FloridaR] (16:2/3) Fall-Wint 89, p. 94-95.
"Torch Dance with Drums." [FloridaR] (16:2/3) Fall-Wint 89, p. 96-97.
2173. GRINDLEY, Carl
"Before the Return." [Quarry] (38:4) Fall 89, p. 72-74.
2174. GRISWOLD, Jay
"Bloodlines." [SouthernPR] (29:2) Fall 89, p. 38.
"The Death of Vicente Aleixandre." [KanQ] (21:3) Sum 89, p. 15.
"Fieldworkers." [ColR] (NS 16:2) Fall 89-Wint 90, p. 28-29.
"Harvest." [WashR] (14:5) F-Mr 89, p. 16-17.
"The Lost Stars" (for Jim Tipton). [MidAR] (9:2) 89, p. 26.
"Memories of the Dispossessed." [MidAR] (9:2) 89, p. 27-29.
"Rio Las Animas." [WritersF] (15) Fall 89, p. 115-116.
"Steel." [ColR] (NS 16:2) Fall 89-Wint 90, p. 30.
"Wild Geese." [BallSUF] (30:4) Aut 89, p. 53.
2175. GRITZ, Ona
"Because the Child." [AmerV] (15) Sum 89, p. 8.
"In Rockaway." [AmerV] (16) Fall 89, p. 13.
2176. GROFF, David
"Mrs May Finally Gets Hold of Mr Greenleaf's Scrub Bull" (after Flannery
O'Connor). [ConnPR] (8:1) 89, p. 4.
"The Sense of Well-Being." [Poetry] (154:4) Jl 89, p. 232.
2177. GROSHOLZ, Emily
"Dark Tents and Fires." [Hudson] (42:3) Aut 89, p. 445-446.
"The Hawk" (from the French of Yves Bonnefoy). [Hudson] (42:3) Aut 89, p. 447.
"The Neolithic Revolution of 1956." [Pequod] (28/29/30) 89, p. 226-227.
"On Spadina Avenue." [Hudson] (42:3) Aut 89, p. 444-445.
"Pilgrims." [Pequod] (28/29/30) 89, p. 228-229.
"The Trees" (from the French of Yves Bonnefoy). [Hudson] (42:3) Aut 89, p. 448.
2178. GROSS, Pamela
"Summoning the Short-Eared Owl." [StoneC] (17:1/2) Fall-Wint 89-90, p. 57.
"White Iris." [AntR] (47:1) Wint 89, p. 76.
GROSS, Sonja Kravanja
See KRAVANJA-GROSS, Sonja
2179. GROSSMAN, Allen
"Dust" (Ars Poetica). [Agni] (28) 89, p. 46-47.
2180. GROSSMAN, Andrew J.
"Porcelain." [Pembroke] (21) 89, p. 127-128.
2181. GROSSMAN, Florence
"Sledding." [Nat] (248:13) 3 Ap 89, p. 464.
2182. GROSSMAN, K. Margaret
"Lizard Tales." [BlueBldgs] (11) 89, p. 58-59.
2183. GROTH, Lollie
"South to the Heart Place." [BellArk] (5:3) My-Je 89, p. 20.
2184. GROTH, Susan Charles
"Dolphins." [JINJPo] (11) 89, p. 12-13.
"Jael, the Tigress." [JINJPo] (11) 89, p. 14-15.
2185. GRUBE, John
"Boot Camp." [Rampike] (6:2) 88, p. 65.
2186. GRUE, Lee Meitzen
"The Biographer." [FreeL] (3) Aut 89, p. 4-5.
"Daisy the Signing Chimp Moves to the Bush." [FreeL] (3) Aut 89, p. 6.
"Quarantine in Room 202 at the Corinth Hotel in Mississippi." [SoCoast] (5) Spr 88,
p. 33.
2187. GU, Cheng
"In This Spacious and Bright World" (tr. by Dong Jiping). [Footwork] 89, p. 27.
"Law Case" (tr. by Dong Jiping). [Footwork] 89, p. 27.
"The Queen in a Coin" (tr. by Dong Jiping). [Footwork] 89, p. 28.

178

"Scene" (tr. by Jun Wang). [Vis] (31) 89, p. 10.
"Yesterday Was a Black Snake" (tr. by Dong Jiping). [Footwork] 89, p. 27.
2188. GUBMAN, G. D.
"When We Walk the Dog." [US1] (22/23) Spr 89, p. 4.
2189. GUEREÑA, Jacinto-Luis
"La parole, de très loin, s'ajuste aux marées du doute." [Os] (28) 89, p. 6-7.
"Tombe de l'Oubli." [Os] (29) 89, p. 13.
"Tombeau de Fené Char." [Os] (29) 89, p. 12.
2190. GUERIN, Christopher
"Point Lobos." [Wind] (19:65) 89, p. 10.
2191. GUERNSEY, Bruce
"The Hall of Fame." [IndR] (13:1) Wint 89, p. 27.
"The Search." [Poetry] (154:3) Je 89, p. 129-132.
2192. GUERNSEY, Julia
"Arm and Hammer." [PoetL] (84:2) Sum 89, p. 54.
GUERRERO, Francisco Gonzalez
See GONZALEZ-GUERRERO, Francisco
2193. GUEST, Barbara
"Expectation." [Conjunc] (14) 89, p. 48-50.
"Geese Blood." [Conjunc] (14) 89, p. 50-52.
"The Pleiades." [BrooklynR] (6) 89, p. 62-63.
"Psyche." [Conjunc] (14) 89, p. 52-53.
2194. GUEVARA, Maurice Kilwein
"Postmortem." [CreamCR] (13:2) Fall 89, p. 71.
2195. GUGLIELMI, Joseph
"Dawn" (Excerpt, tr. by Rosmarie Waldrop). [Notus] (4:2) Fall 89, p. 36-39.
2196. GUGLIELMINO, Griogio
"Che altro senso aggiunge un'ora di ghiaccio : which other sense adds hours of ice"
   (in Italian and English). [Os] (28) 89, p. 2.
2197. GUIDACCI, Margherita
"A Febo Oltre il Confine." [InterPR] (15:2) Fall 89, p. 74.
"In Morte di Febo Delfi." [InterPR] (15:2) Fall 89, p. 74.
"On the Death of Phoebus Delphi" (tr. by Renata Treitel). [InterPR] (15:2) Fall 89,
   p. 75.
"Over Your Absence Glides" (tr. by Carol Lettieri and Irene Marchegiani Jones).
   [MidAR] (9:1) 89, p. 43.
"To Phoebus Beyond the Border" (tr. by Renata Treitel). [InterPR] (15:2) Fall 89, p.
   75.
2198. GUIMOND, Daniel
"Limit's Eden." [Rampike] (6:2) 88, p. 71.
GUIN, Ursula K. le
See Le GUIN, Ursula K.
2199. GUINEY, Mike
"Gone Dry." [AntigR] (76) Wint 89, p. 86.
2200. GUITART, Jorge
"Modern Notes." [LindLM] (8:1) Ja-Mr 89, p. 9.
"Of the River." [LindLM] (8:4) O-D 89, p. 19.
"One More Rondo." [LindLM] (8:1) Ja-Mr 89, p. 9.
2201. GULLANS, Charles
"Points of Intersection." [MichQR] (28:3) Sum 89, p. 397-398.
2202. GULLETTE, David
"Disaffiliation." [DenQ] (24:2) Fall 89, p. 52.
2203. GUNDERSON, Joanna
"Journal Notes" (An Excerpt). [Rampike] (6:3) 88, p. 36-38.
2204. GUNDY, Jeff
"Inquiries into the Technology of Beauty" (after Apollinaire). [OhioR] (44) 89, p.
   102-103.
"Inquiry into Gifts, or the Indigo Bunting." [SpoonRQ] (14:1) Wint 89, p. 7.
"Inquiry into Lagniappe." [ArtfulD] (16/17) Fall 89, p. 4.
"Inquiry into Lightness" (after Italo Calvino). [Journal] (13:1) Spr-Sum 89, p. 29.
"Inquiry into Praises." [MidAR] (9:2) 89, p. 67-68.
"Inquiry into the Final Reading" (for Bill Greenway). [SpoonRQ] (14:3) Sum 89, p.
   6-7.
"Inquiry on Muscular Christianity." [OxfordM] (5:1) Spr-Sum 89, p. 71.
"Inquiry on the Analogical Perspective, or Why on This Day the Poet Will Enter No
   Complaints." [Journal] (13:1) Spr-Sum 89, p. 28.

179

GUNDY

"Inquiry on the Fire Sermon." [ArtfulD] (16/17) Fall 89, p. 3.
"On Dogs, Cars, Singing." [CinPR] (20) Fall 89, p. 56.
"Sticktights" (For Kellie). [NegC] (9:1) 89, p. 94-95.
2205. GUNN, Genni
"Departures." [Quarry] (38:2) Spr 89, p. 42-48.
2206. GUNN, Thom
"All Do Not All Things Well." [Thrpny] (36) Wint 89, p. 5.
"The Beautician." [Ploughs] (15:4) Wint 89-90, p. 93.
"A Blank." [Thrpny] (39) Fall 89, p. 6.
"Duncan." [Thrpny] (37) Spr 89, p. 9.
"The Man in the Helmet." [Ploughs] (15:4) Wint 89-90, p. 94-95.
2207. GUNSTROM, Nickie
"The Day Coyote Came to Ground." [CapeR] (24:1) Spr 89, p. 8.
2208. GUNTNER, Bobby Charles
"Photographs of a Bush Drama." [Pig] (15) 88, p. 49.
2209. GUO, Hong
"Sitting All Alone" (tr. by Dong Jiping). [Footwork] 89, p. 24.
2210. GURNEY, Ivor
"At the Time." [Stand] (30:3) Sum 89, p. 17, 19.
"Dawn Soon." [Stand] (30:3) Sum 89, p. 17.
"Joseph." [Stand] (30:3) Sum 89, p. 21.
"Picture of Two Veterans." [Stand] (30:3) Sum 89, p. 19.
"Portrait of a Coward." [Stand] (30:3) Sum 89, p. 19, 21.
"Untitled: How strange it was to hear under the guns." [Stand] (30:3) Sum 89, p. 17.
2211. GUSTAFSON, Ralph
"Tuscany to Venezia." [WestCR] (23:4) Spr 89, p. 5-13.
2212. GUSTAFSSON, Lars
"Elegy" (tr. by Philip Martin). [Field] (40) Spr 89, p. 69-70.
"Notes on the 1860s" (tr. by Christopher Middleton). [Field] (40) Spr 89, p. 70-71.
"Warm Rooms and Cold" (tr. by Yvonne Sandstroem). [Field] (40) Spr 89, p. 72.
2213. GUSTAVSON, Jeffrey
"Kimble Fugit." [Agni] (28) 89, p. 110-114.
GUT, Karen Alkalay
See ALKALAY-GUT, Karen
2214. GUTFREUND, Geraldine Marshall
"Artemis" (in memory of my mother). [Writer] (102:3) Mr 89, p. 23.
2215. GUTIERREZ REVUELTA, Pedro
"Ajenjo." [Americas] (17:2) Sum 89, p. 46-47.
"An Astonishing World" (tr. of Angel Gonzalez, w. Steven Ford Brown). [SenR] (19:2) Fall 89, p. 75.
"The Battlefield" (tr. of Angel Gonzalez, w. Steven Ford Brown). [NegC] (9:1) 89, p. 191, 193.
"Before I Could Call Myself Angel González" (10 Poems in Spanish & English, Translation Chapbook Series, tr. of Angel González, w. Steven Ford Brown). [MidAR] (9:2) 89, p. 97-123.
"Diatribe Against the Dead" (tr. of Angel Gonzalez, w. Steven Ford Brown). [SenR] (19:2) Fall 89, p. 73.
"Exorcismo." [Americas] (17:2) Sum 89, p. 48-49.
"Horoscope for a Forgotten Dictator" (tr. of Angel Gonzalez, w. Steven Ford Brown). [SenR] (19:2) Fall 89, p. 74.
"Sonata for Violin Solo" (Johann Sebastian Bach, tr. of Angel Gonzalez, w. Steven Ford Brown). [NegC] (9:1) 89, p. 189.
"A Traveler's Notes" (tr. of Angel Gonzalez, w. Steven Ford Brown). [PoetL] (84:3) Fall 89, p. 47-49.
"Visión de Angel González." [Americas] (17:2) Sum 89, p. 44-45.
GUTIRREZ REVUELTA, Pedro
See GUTIERREZ REVUELTA, Pedro
2216. GUZLOWSKI, John
"Joe's First Deer." [NegC] (9:1) 89, p. 68.
"No Sweet Land." [NegC] (9:1) 89, p. 67.
2217. GUZMAN, Graciela
"Generaciones en Comparsa." [InterPR] (15:2) Fall 89, p. 52.
"Generations in Masquerade" (tr. by Sandra Gail Teichmann). [InterPR] (15:2) Fall 89, p. 53.
"Pretext for Comfort from the Agony" (tr. by Sandra Gail Teichmann). [InterPR]

(15:2) Fall 89, p. 51.
"Pretexto para Solaz de la Agonía." [InterPR] (15:2) Fall 89, p. 50.
"Useless Offsprings of a Body" (tr. by Sandra Gail Teichmann). [InterPR] (15:2) Fall 89, p. 51.
"Vanas Descendencias de un Cuerpo." [InterPR] (15:2) Fall 89, p. 50.
GUZMAN, Maria de
   See DeGUZMAN, Maria
2218. GVOZDZIUS, Vidas
   "Fairy Tales." [WritersF] (15) Fall 89, p. 114-115.
2219. GWALA, Mafika
   "Getting Off the Ride." [AmerPoR] (18:4) Jl-Ag 89, p. 36-38.
2220. GWYNN, R. S.
   "A Letter from Biltmore." [KeyWR] (2:1/2) Fall-Wint 89, p. 59-60.
   "West Palm." [KeyWR] (2:1/2) Fall-Wint 89, p. 56-58.
2221. H., Wf.
   "Anchored to Blood." [MidAR] (9:2) 89, p. 149-151.
   "The Isolation." [MidAR] (9:2) 89, p. 148.
HA, Jin
   See JIN, Ha
2222. HABRA, Hedy
   "Waiting for Marie." [LindLM] (8:4) O-D 89, p. 19.
2223. HACKER, Marilyn
   "Celles" (for Julie Fay). [YaleR] (78:4) Sum 89, p. 579-580.
   "Days of 1987" (for K.J.). [YaleR] (78:4) Sum 89, p. 580-582.
   "Elevens." [GrandS] (9:1) Aut 89, p. 173-174.
   "Elevens." [NewL] (56:2/3) Wint 89-Spr 90, p. 128-129.
   "Nights of 1962: The River Merchant's Wife" (for Carol Lee Hane). [Vis] (30) 89, p. 49-52.
   "Separate Lives." [Boulevard] (4:2, #11) Fall 89, p. 12-15.
   "Taking Notice." [NewL] (56:2/3) Wint 89-Spr 90, p. 123-127.
   "Torch." [NewL] (56:2/3) Wint 89-Spr 90, p. 129.
   "Two Cities." [ParisR] (31:110) Spr 89, p. 152-156.
2224. HACKMAN, Martha
   "Monet's Grainstacks." [MalR] (87) Sum 89, p. 112.
2225. HADAS, Pamela White
   "Rara Avis." [ParisR] (31:110) Spr 89, p. 29-30.
2226. HADAS, Rachel
   "At a Distance." [WestHR] (43:3) Aut 89, p. 190.
   "The Cliff." [ColEng] (51:3) Mr 89, p. 282.
   "Cover-Ups." [Ploughs] (15:4) Wint 89-90, p. 96-98.
   "Elegy Variations I." [AmerS] (58:3) Sum 89, p. 406.
   "Expression." [Agni] (28) 89, p. 274-275.
   "Hortus Conclusus" (to Mark Rudman). [PraS] (63:1) Spr 89, p. 32-35.
   "In the Middle." [Thrpny] (39) Fall 89, p. 16.
   "Joining and Parting." [Boulevard] (4:1, #10) Spr 89, p. 120-122.
   "Moments of Summer." [CrossCur] (8:2) Ja 89, p. 13-14.
   "Nine Tiles: The Story of the Fire" (to Sylvia Benitez Stewart). [ColEng] (51:3) Mr 89, p. 283.
   "Sea, Sky, Mountain, Lantern." [PartR] (56:3) Sum 89, p. 449.
2227. HADERLAP, Maja
   "Arrivals II" (tr. by Tom Priestly). [ColR] (NS 16:1) Spr-Sum 89, p. 93.
2228. HAECK, Philippe
   "Autoportrait" (à J., in French). [Os] (28) 89, p. 12-13.
2229. HAGGERTY, Tabitha
   "Pittsburgh to Seattle." [SlipS] (9) 89, p. 45.
2230. HAGUE, Richard
   "Legends." [Journal] (12:2) Fall-Wint 88-89, p. 43.
   "Standing by the Garden, I Dream the Flash." [Journal] (12:2) Fall-Wint 88-89, p. 42.
2231. HAHN, Lauren
   "And the Beauty" (tr. of Paul Celan). [InterPR] (15:2) Fall 89, p. 83.
   "Breton Beach" (tr. of Paul Celan). [InterPR] (15:2) Fall 89, p. 85.
   "Evening of Words" (tr. of Paul Celan). [InterPR] (15:2) Fall 89, p. 85.
   "The Guest" (tr. of Paul Celan). [InterPR] (15:2) Fall 89, p. 83.
2232. HAHN, Robert
   "Desperado." [Iowa] (19:1) Wint 89, p. 82-83.

"The Interior at Petworth." [Iowa] (19:1) Wint 89, p. 83-84.
"Object in an Inventory." [GeoR] (43:1) Spr 89, p. 33-34.
"Wittgenstein Eats." [AntR] (47:3) Sum 89, p. 334-335.
2233. HAHN, Steven
"Love's Labour." [YellowS] (29) Spr 89, p. 12-13.
"Mustique Variations." [AmerPoR] (18:2) Mr-Ap 89, p. 46.
2234. HAHN, Susan
"Amphibians." [SouthernR] (25:3) Sum 89, p. 626-627.
"Flowers." [Poetry] (153:5) F 89, p. 296.
"Of Tulips and Trillium." [Shen] (39:2) Sum 89, p. 56.
"The Tonsure." [SouthernPR] (29:1) Spr 89, p. 8-9.
"Trichotillomania." [Shen] (39:2) Sum 89, p. 55-56.
2235. HAHN, Ulla
"Blessèd Are Those Who Wait" (tr. by John Linthicum). [LitR] (33:1) Fall 89, p.
90.
"Dead Love" (tr. by John Linthicum). [LitR] (33:1) Fall 89, p. 87.
"Error" (tr. by John Linthicum). [LitR] (33:1) Fall 89, p. 89.
"Everybody's Man" (tr. by John Linthicum). [LitR] (33:1) Fall 89, p. 89.
"Faithfulness" (tr. by John Linthicum). [LitR] (33:1) Fall 89, p. 88.
"Nothing But" (tr. by John Linthicum). [LitR] (33:1) Fall 89, p. 88.
"Sometimes There" (tr. by John Linthicum). [LitR] (33:1) Fall 89, p. 87.
"Through the Village" (tr. by John Linthicum). [LitR] (33:1) Fall 89, p. 91.
"Unanswered Closeness" (tr. by John Linthicum). [LitR] (33:1) Fall 89, p. 87.
2236. HAI-JEW, Shalin
"Kiss (for the Men)." [Kalliope] (11:3) 89, p. 11-12.
"Land of Mutational Artists" (Nanchang, Jiangxi Province, P.R.C. 1989). [Kalliope]
(11:3) 89, p. 9-10.
"To be a Parent Is That Bodily Prayer" (for Rodin Max). [Kalliope] (10:1/2) 88, p.
92-93.
2237. HAIGHT, Robert
"The Danger of Poetry." [PassN] (10:1) Wint 89, p. 13.
"Learning to Fly." [PassN] (10:2) Sum 89, p. 19.
2238. HAINES, Anne
"Arpilleras." [SinW] (37) Spr 89, p. 90-92.
2239. HAINES, John
"Days of Edward Hopper." [OhioR] (43) 89, p. 7-12.
HAIXIN, Xu
See XU, Haixin
2240. HAKES, Jana
"Manipulation." [Writer] (102:12) D 89, p. 24.
2241. HALE, Dori
"Chichicastenango." [BellR] (12:2, #26) Fall 89, p. 12.
2242. HALE, Terrel
"Four Covered Cricket Jars for Summer Use." [Screens] (1) 89, p. 33.
"Historical Meaning." [Screens] (1) 89, p. 34-35.
"The Noise of the Social Landscape." [Screens] (1) 89, p. 35-37.
2243. HALES, Corrinne
"Testimony." [KenR] (N 11:4) Fall 89, p. 4-5.
2244. HALEY, Vanessa
"Groundhogging with My Father." [SouthernPR] (29:2) Fall 89, p. 33.
2245. HALL, Dana Naone
"The House of Light." [Hawai'iR] (13:3) Fall 89, p. 2-3.
2246. HALL, Daniel
"Andrew's Jewelweed." [YaleR] (78:3) Spr 89, p. 484.
"The People's Hotel." [YaleR] (78:3) Spr 89, p. 484.
2247. HALL, Donald
"At the Wineshop." [Witness] (2:4) Wint 88, p. 55.
"Instructions to a Painter." [SouthernHR] (23:1) Wint 89, p. 38.
"Material." [Atlantic] (264:2) Ag 89, p. 68.
"Moon Clock." [NewYorker] (65:1) 20 F 89, p. 98.
"The Other Game." [Witness] (2:4) Wint 88, p. 54.
"Praise for Death." [GettyR] (2:2) Spr 89, p. 191-198.
"Praise for Death." [Verse] (6:3) Wint 89, p. 15-20.
"Six Naps in One Day." [NewYorker] (65:40) 20 N 89, p. 72.
2248. HALL, H. Gaston
"Four Sonnets" (tr. of Garcilaso de la Vega). [BallSUF] (30:3) Sum 89, p. 28-30.

2249. HALL, Jim
"Women." [AmerS] (58:4) Aut 89, p. 511-512.
2250. HALL, Judith
"Robes." [WestHR] (43:4) Wint 89, p. 288-289.
"A Wild Plum Is for Independence." [WestHR] (43:4) Wint 89, p. 290-292.
2251. HALL, Kathryn
"Alley." [NegC] (9:2) 89, p. 51.
2252. HALL, Phil
"Jericho Beach Hostel, Vancouver 1979." [Event] (18:3) Fall 89, p. 48-49.
2253. HALL, Stephen H.
"Inkstains." [EmeraldCR] (1989) c1988, p. 104.
"One Mistake." [EmeraldCR] (1989) c1988, p. 105.
2254. HALL, William Keith
"Elam." [SouthernPR] (29:2) Fall 89, p. 10-11.
2255. HALLERMAN, Victoria
"Nothing to Say." [NoDaQ] (57:4) Fall 89, p. 137.
"The Work of the Water." [NoDaQ] (57:4) Fall 89, p. 138.
2256. HALLIDAY, Mark
"American Reformation." [Crazy] (36) Spr 89, p. 28-29.
"Business." [DenQ] (23:3/4) Wint-Spr 89, p. 100-101.
"Chekhov." [MissR] (18:1, #52) 89, p. 70-71.
"February Lake." [DenQ] (23:3/4) Wint-Spr 89, p. 103.
"Fine World." [VirQR] (65:1) Wint 89, p. 72-73.
"Fox Point Health Clinic, 1974." [VirQR] (65:1) Wint 89, p. 70-71.
"Julie at the Reading." [Crazy] (37) Wint 89, p. 37.
"A Kind of Reply." [Poetry] (154:6) S 89, p. 314-315.
"Lingo Bistro." [IndR] (12:3) Sum 89, p. 15-16.
"Modern Consciousness." [VirQR] (65:1) Wint 89, p. 73.
"Parked Cars in New Brunswick." [DenQ] (23:3/4) Wint-Spr 89, p. 102.
"Polack Reverie." [Crazy] (37) Wint 89, p. 35-36.
"Reality U.S.A." [Crazy] (36) Spr 89, p. 21-23.
"Repetition Rider." [TarRP] (29:1) Fall 89, p. 22-23.
"Sad News." [NewEngR] (12:2) Wint 89, p. 140.
"Seventh Avenue." [Crazy] (36) Spr 89, p. 24-25.
"Shunk Street." [OhioR] (44) 89, p. 134.
"The Truth." [GettyR] (2:2) Spr 89, p. 266-267.
"U-2." [OhioR] (44) 89, p. 135.
"What to Do." [Agni] (28) 89, p. 288-290.
2257. HALLISSEY, Veronica
"The Homecoming." [PassN] (10:1) Wint 89, p. 19.
2258. HALLOCK, Maureen Miller
"Or Autumn in the Oaks." [GreensboroR] (46) Sum 89, p. 209.
2259. HALME, Kathleen
"The Second Sunday of Easter." [LaurelR] (23:1) Wint 89, p. 61-62.
"What We Ask of Azure." [OxfordM] (5:1) Spr-Sum 89, p. 40.
2260. HALPERIN, Mark
"November." [PraS] (63:1) Spr 89, p. 59.
"Silences." [PraS] (63:1) Spr 89, p. 58.
2261. HALPERN, Daniel
"Bell & Capitol." [OntR] (31) Fall-Wint 89-90, p. 88.
"Candles for Bessie." [OntR] (31) Fall-Wint 89-90, p. 89.
2262. HALPERN, Moyshe-Leyb
"Isaac Leybush Peretz." [Agni] (28) 89, p. 77-79.
2263. HALPERN, Sal
"Survivors." [WillowS] (23) Wint 89, p. 41.
2264. HALSTEAD, Gertrude
"The Palmreader." [US1] (22/23) Spr 89, p. 25.
2265. HAMBURGER, Michael
"Babel's Death" (tr. of Thomas Brasch). [Stand] (30:2) Spr 89, p. 18.
"Elegy" (tr. of Bernd Jentzsch). [Stand] (30:2) Spr 89, p. 19.
"End of Quotation" (tr. of Kurt Bartsch). [Stand] (30:2) Spr 89, p. 17.
"The Passport" (tr. of Kurt Bartsch). [Stand] (30:2) Spr 89, p. 14-17.
"Prayer in Extremis" (tr. of Bernd Jentzsch). [Stand] (30:2) Spr 89, p. 19.
2266. HAMBY, Barbara
"The Poodles of Desire." [SpoonRQ] (14:1) Wint 89, p. 33-35.
"Your Enemies Are Everywhere." [SpoonRQ] (14:1) Wint 89, p. 36.

2267. HAMILL, Sam
"Across Kasuga Moor" (tr. of Otoma no Katami (ca. 750)). [PoetryE] (28) Fall 89,
p. 201.
"All alone" (tr. of Yosano Akiko (ca. 1900)). [PoetryE] (28) Fall 89, p. 204.
"All this summer night" (tr. of Tsurayuki (883-946)). [PoetryE] (28) Fall 89, p. 199.
"Alone" (tr. of Li Po). [LitR] (32:3) Spr 89, p. 348.
"Alone by the Autumn River" (tr. of Li Shang-yin). [LitR] (32:3) Spr 89, p. 351.
"Angry river winds" (tr. of Tsurayuki (883-946)). [PoetryE] (28) Fall 89, p. 202.
"A Country Road" (tr. of Li Po). [LitR] (32:3) Spr 89, p. 350.
"Early morning glows" (Kokinshu 637, tr. of anonymous poem). [PoetryE] (28)
Fall 89, p. 200.
"Even when we wandered together" (tr. of Princess Oku (7th c.)). [PoetryE] (28)
Fall 89, p. 200.
"The fall moon still shines" (tr. of Kakinomoto no Hitomaro (ca. 692)). [PoetryE]
(28) Fall 89, p. 204.
"How very much love I gave!" (tr. of Fujiwara no Okikaze (ca. 910)). [PoetryE]
(28) Fall 89, p. 203.
"In a Village by the River" (tr. of Li Po). [LitR] (32:3) Spr 89, p. 349.
"In the autumn sea" (tr. of Kiyowara Fukuyabu (900-930)). [PoetryE] (28) Fall 89,
p. 201.
"In the dark godless month" (tr. of the monk Sosei (ca. 890)). [PoetryE] (28) Fall
89, p. 200.
"Late evening finally comes" (tr. of Yakamochi (718-785)). [PoetryE] (28) Fall 89,
p. 199.
"Light snow silently sweeps" (tr. of Yakamochi (718-785)). [PoetryE] (28) Fall 89,
p. 202.
"Like a tall ship" (tr. of Prince Yuke (7th c.)). [PoetryE] (28) Fall 89, p. 201.
"Like an old love-letter" (tr. of Tsumori Kunimoto (1023-1103)). [PoetryE] (28) Fall
89, p. 203.
"Little nightingale"" (tr. of Nakatsukasa (ca. 900)). [PoetryE] (28) Fall 89, p. 202.
"Men love to gossip" (tr. of Princess Tajima (ca. 687)). [PoetryE] (28) Fall 89, p.
204.
"My love grows" (tr. of Ono no Yoshiki (d. 902)). [PoetryE] (28) Fall 89, p. 203.
"Old Dust" (tr. of Li Po). [LitR] (32:3) Spr 89, p. 349.
"River fog rises" (tr. of Kiyowara Fukuyabu (900-930)). [PoetryE] (28) Fall 89, p.
200.
"Silent at Her Window" (tr. of Wang Ch'ang-ling). [LitR] (32:3) Spr 89, p. 350.
"Spending the whole night" (tr. of Ariwara no Narihira (825-880)). [PoetryE] (28)
Fall 89, p. 202.
"Traveling Song" (tr. of Li Po). [LitR] (32:3) Spr 89, p. 349.
"Under the sky's broad reaches" (Kokinshu 542, tr. of anonymous poem).
[PoetryE] (28) Fall 89, p. 201.
"Weary clear to his feet" (tr. of Fujiwara no Sanekata (d. 998)). [PoetryE] (28) Fall
89, p. 199.
"Where is the dark seed" (tr. of the monk Sosei (ca. 890)). [PoetryE] (28) Fall 89, p.
203.
"Yen-Chou City Wall Tower" (tr. of Tu Fu). [LitR] (32:3) Spr 89, p. 351.
2268. HAMILTON, Alfred Starr
"The Man with the Hoe." [WormR] (29:4, #116) 89, p. 98-99.
"North Atlantic Bracelets." [WormR] (29:4, #116) 89, p. 99.
"Of the Death of a Rhinoceros." [WormR] (29:4, #116) 89, p. 99.
"A Pebble." [Footwork] 89, p. 40.
"Resurgence." [Footwork] 89, p. 40.
"Sky and Purposes." [WormR] (29:4, #116) 89, p. 100.
2269. HAMILTON, Candy
"South and West." [KanQ] (21:1/2) Wint-Spr 89, p. 167.
2270. HAMILTON, Carol
"Lasting Links." [ChrC] (106:36) N 29, 89, p. 1109.
"Observatory at Dawn." [PoetL] (84:3) Fall 89, p. 18.
"This December afternoon." [StoneC] (17:1/2) Fall-Wint 89-90, p. 21.
2271. HAMILTON, Fritz
"All Written!" [KanQ] (21:3) Sum 89, p. 146.
"Automobiles!" [KanQ] (21:4) Fall 89, p. 4.
"Chuck." [SmPd] (26:2 #76) Spr 89, p. 28.
"Gav!" [HolCrit] (26:4) O 89, p. 16-17.
"Incensed" (for Phoebe). [AntigR] (79) Aut 89, p. 54.

"It's Me!" [SmPd] (26:2 #76) Spr 89, p. 29.
"Mock & Shame." [CapeR] (24:2) Fall 89, p. 48.
"Pigeon Amazement." [Kaleid] (19) Sum-Fall 89, p. 53.
"So What?" [SmPd] (26:3 #77) Fall 89, p. 40.
"Spiritual Matrix." [Footwork] 89, p. 54.
"Texas Flower" (for Cathy). [SmPd] (26:2 #76) Spr 89, p. 30.
"When It's Raining Dogs & . . ." [Hawai'iR] (13:2, #26) Sum 89, p. 92-93.
2272. HAMILTON, Horace
"Black Dragon River" (known as the Amur). [LitR] (32:2) Wint 89, p. 174.
2273. HAMILTON, Jeff
"Design." [RiverS] (28) 89, p. 39.
"Lucky Miracles in Paradise." [RiverS] (28) 89, p. 37-38.
2274. HAMILTON, Saskia
"Mapping Distances" (1989 National Collegiate Poetry Fellowship Competition).
[IndR] (12:3) Sum 89, p. 95-97.
"Notes After We Walked from the Fen" (1989 National Collegiate Poetry Fellowship
Competition). [IndR] (12:3) Sum 89, p. 98-100.
2275. HAMMOND, Karla M.
"First Caress (1891)" (after Mary Cassatt). [Footwork] 89, p. 44.
"From Grief to Grace." [Footwork] 89, p. 44.
"The Lions at the Gate." [Footwork] 89, p. 44.
2276. HAMMOND, Mary Stewart
"Paying Respect." [NewYorker] (65:31) 18 S 89, p. 44.
"Saving Memory." [Atlantic] (263:2) F 89, p. 50.
"Small Talk." [NewYorker] (65:19) 26 Je 89, p. 34.
2277. HAMMOND, Ralph
"Turtle Talk." [NegC] (9:1) 89, p. 96-97.
2278. HAN, Dong
"Someone Brings Flowers Today" (tr. by Dong Jiping). [Footwork] 89, p. 29.
"To Dusk, or Grief" (tr. by Dong Jiping). [Footwork] 89, p. 29.
2279. HAN, Shan
"Some Critic Tried to Put Me Down" (tr. by Gary Snyder). [LitR] (32:3) Spr 89, p.
443.
"When Men See Han-Shan" (tr. by Gary Snyder). [LitR] (32:3) Spr 89, p. 443.
2280. HAN, Yu
"At the Pass" (tr. by Kenneth O. Hanson). [LitR] (32:3) Spr 89, p. 332.
"Early Spring: Two Poems Presented to Secretary Chang in the Ministry of Waters"
(tr. by Kenneth O. Hanson). [LitR] (32:3) Spr 89, p. 333.
"Poem Written After Drinking Too Much" (tr. by Kenneth O. Hanson). [LitR] (32:3)
Spr 89, p. 331.
"Riding into Exile I Read This Poem to Han Hsiang, My Brother's Grandson" (tr.
by Kenneth O. Hanson). [LitR] (32:3) Spr 89, p. 334.
"Vacillations" (I & II, tr. by Lee Gerlach). [LitR] (32:3) Spr 89, p. 387-388.
"The Wild Tiger's Personal Story" (tr. by Kenneth O. Hanson). [LitR] (32:3) Spr
89, p. 335-336.
2281. HAND, Kathy
"Come Live with Me and Be My Love." [WormR] (29:4, #116) 89, p. 107-108.
"Norma Jeane." [WormR] (29:4, #116) 89, p. 107.
"Two Scientifically Proven Facts." [WormR] (29:4, #116) 89, p. 108.
2282. HANDLER, Joan (Joan Cusack)
"Everyone Would Say It Was Foolish." [Footwork] 89, p. 12.
"A Sister's Secret." [US1] (22/23) Spr 89, p. 38.
"Why Women Love Women." [Footwork] 89, p. 12-13.
2283. HANDLIN, Jim
"Burying My Father." [Footwork] 89, p. 50.
"Flights." [Footwork] 89, p. 51.
"Miyaki." [Footwork] 89, p. 50-51.
"Trains." [Footwork] 89, p. 50.
2284. HANDY, Nixeon Civille
"No Name Bar" (-- Rick Anderson, *Seattle Times*). [Wind] (19:65) 89, p. 41.
2285. HANFORD, Mary
"Change." [SwampR] (1:4) Sum 89, p. 50.
"Deadly Calm." [SwampR] (1:4) Sum 89, p. 47.
"Discovery." [SwampR] (1:4) Sum 89, p. 45.
"Flight." [SwampR] (1:4) Sum 89, p. 46.
"Kinship." [SwampR] (1:4) Sum 89, p. 53.

"Lesson." [SwampR] (1:4) Sum 89, p. 51.
"Prophecy." [SwampR] (1:4) Sum 89, p. 48.
"Restoration." [SwampR] (1:4) Sum 89, p. 55.
"Reverie." [SwampR] (1:4) Sum 89, p. 52.
"Snakes on Ash Wednesday." [SwampR] (1:4) Sum 89, p. 54.
2286. HANLEY, Aedan (Aedan Alexander)
"Ghetto Spring." [BlackALF] (23:3) Fall 89, p. 501.
"Kansas, Hwy. 67." [KanQ] (21:3) Sum 89, p. 112.
"Louanne and the Pack of Kents." [Iowa] (19:2) Spr-Sum 89, p. 163-164.
"Mrs. Miller." [FloridaR] (16:2/3) Fall-Wint 89, p. 176-177.
"A Woman by the Mississippi." [Iowa] (19:2) Spr-Sum 89, p. 164.
2287. HANNON, Michael
"Slender Means." [Manoa] (1:1/2) Fall 89, p. 28-30.
2288. HANSEN, Paul
"Drifing on the Lake I Reach the Eastern Ching River" (tr. of Lu Yu). [LitR] (32:3)
     Spr 89, p. 355.
"Leaving a Mountain Post Station at Dawn" (tr. of Kao Ch'i). [LitR] (32:3) Spr 89,
     p. 354.
"Outside the Dust" (tr. of Chu Chi-fang). [LitR] (32:3) Spr 89, p. 355.
"Roaming in the Clouds I Come Back Alone" (tr. of Hsü Yün). [LitR] (32:3) Spr 89,
     p. 354.
"Sending Off Ssz Tuan to Return East" (tr. of Hsi Chou). [LitR] (32:3) Spr 89, p.
     353.
"Sent to Huai Ku" (tr. of Hsi Chou). [LitR] (32:3) Spr 89, p. 352.
2289. HANSEN, Tom
"Ancient Japanese Drawing." [LitR] (32:2) Wint 89, p. 175.
"Dead Ringer." [WebR] (14:1) Spr 89, p. 81.
"In the Middle of the Journey of Our Life." [AmerS] (58:4) Aut 89, p. 564-566.
"Nomads." [WebR] (14:1) Spr 89, p. 82.
"Reasons for Refusing to Comply." [TarRP] (29:1) Fall 89, p. 36-37.
2290. HANSEN, Twyla
"1964." [MidwQ] (30:2) Wint 89, p. 197.
"Gravy." [LaurelR] (23:1) Wint 89, p. 99.
"Highway." [SwampR] (1:4) Sum 89, p. 64.
"Making Lard." [MidwQ] (30:2) Wint 89, p. 199.
"The Other Woman." [KanQ] (21:1/2) Wint-Spr 89, p. 228-229.
2291. HANSON, Julie Jordan
"Patience." [SoDakR] (27:3) Aut 89, p. 28-30.
2292. HANSON, Kenneth O.
"At the Pass" (tr. of Han Yu). [LitR] (32:3) Spr 89, p. 332.
"The Divide" (tr. of Lin Ho-ching). [LitR] (32:3) Spr 89, p. 327.
"Drunk I Fell, Sober They Bring Me Wine" (After Tu Fu). [LitR] (32:3) Spr 89, p.
     329-330.
"Early Spring: Two Poems Presented to Secretary Chang in the Ministry of Waters"
     (tr. of Han Yu). [LitR] (32:3) Spr 89, p. 333.
"Poem Written After Drinking Too Much" (tr. of Han Yu). [LitR] (32:3) Spr 89, p.
     331.
"Rice Field" (tr. of Lin Ho-ching). [LitR] (32:3) Spr 89, p. 327.
"Riding into Exile I Read This Poem to Han Hsiang, My Brother's Grandson" (tr. of
     Han Yu). [LitR] (32:3) Spr 89, p. 334.
"Spring" (tr. of Lin Ho-ching). [LitR] (32:3) Spr 89, p. 328.
"Traveler's Song" (after Yen T'iao-yu). [LitR] (32:3) Spr 89, p. 328.
"The Wild Tiger's Personal Story" (tr. of Han Yu). [LitR] (32:3) Spr 89, p.
     335-336.
2293. HANZIMANOLIS, Margaret
"To an American Abroad in America." [BelPoJ] (39:3) Spr 89, p. 2.
2294. HANZLICEK, C. G.
"Primitive Sand." [KenR] (N 11:4) Fall 89, p. 27.
2295. HANZLIK, Josef
"Air Show" (tr. by Jarmila and Ian Milner). [Stand] (30:1) Wint 88-89, p. 52-55.
HAO-JAN, Meng
     See MENG, Hao-jan
2296. HARA, Mavis
"Thinking of an Octopus." [BambooR] (41) Wint 89, p. 14-15.
"This Is America." [BambooR] (41) Wint 89, p. 11-13.
"Visiting Hickam Air Force Base, 1956." [BambooR] (41) Wint 89, p. 9-10.

2297. HARD, Rock
"Apparition in Search of the Ideal." [EmeraldCR] (1989) c1988, p. 143-144.
2298. HARDIN, Jeff
"Valedictorian Explaining the Failure of His Life." [CapeR] (24:2) Fall 89, p. 37.
2299. HARDING, Deborah
"The Drill." [KanQ] (21:3) Sum 89, p. 132.
2300. HARDING-RUSSELL, Gillian
"Late Night News and After: Following the Armenian Earthquake and the British
Railway Disaster December 12, 1988." [CapilR] (1st series: 50) 89, p.
169-173.
2301. HARDY, Jan
"Submitting Poems to a Straight Magazine." [SinW] (37) Spr 89, p. 82.
2302. HARER, Katharine
"Frida." [FiveFR] (7) 89, p. 24.
"Frida Kahlo & Diego Rivera." [FiveFR] (7) 89, p. 23.
"Georgia O'Keeffe & Stieglitz." [FiveFR] (7) 89, p. 22.
2303. HARGITAI, Peter
"The Art of Taxidermi." [ColEng] (51:8) D 89, p. 833.
"Doctor." [ColEng] (51:8) D 89, p. 834.
2304. HARGRAVES, Joseph
"Degrees." [WormR] (29:1, #113) 89, p. 11.
"It Takes One to Know One." [WormR] (29:1, #113) 89, p. 10.
"Robert Frost." [WormR] (29:1, #113) 89, p. 10.
2305. HARJO, Joy
"Death Is a Woman." [Nimrod] (32:2) Spr-Sum 89, p. 57.
"Deer Dancer." [Ploughs] (15:4) Wint 89-90, p. 101-102.
"Desire." [Ploughs] (15:4) Wint 89-90, p. 99.
"Equinox." [Sonora] (17) Spr-Sum 89, p. 59-60.
"For Anna Mae Aquash Whose Spirit Is Present Here and in the Dappled Stars."
[Nimrod] (32:2) Spr-Sum 89, p. 60-61.
"For Anna Mae Aquash, Whose Spirit Is Present Here and in the Dappled Stars"
(For we remember the story and must tell it again so we may all live).
[RedBass] (14) 89, p. 15.
"If I Think About You Again It Will be the Fifty Third Monday of Next Year."
[Nimrod] (32:2) Spr-Sum 89, p. 58.
"Legacy." [RedBass] (14) 89, p. 37.
"Northern Lights" (an essay in verse). [AmerV] (17) Wint 89, p. 45-47.
"Original Memory." [Nimrod] (32:2) Spr-Sum 89, p. 55-56.
"Santa Fe." [Ploughs] (15:4) Wint 89-90, p. 100.
"September Moon." [Cond] (16) 89, p. 83.
"Sonata for the Invisibly Present" (for my son). [Sonora] (17) Spr-Sum 89, p. 58.
"Trickster." [Nimrod] (32:2) Spr-Sum 89, p. 54.
"War Dog." [Cond] (16) 89, p. 160-161.
2306. HARKINS, Patricia
"Song for My Daughter." [NegC] (9:1) 89, p. 62.
2307. HARLOW, Robert
"Some Nights." [Mildred] (3:1) Spr-Sum 89, p. 85.
2308. HARMON, Lindsey
"Dog Days Waning." [KeyWR] (2:1/2) Fall-Wint 89, p. 101.
2309. HARMS, James
"Fragile Bridges." [IndR] (13:1) Wint 89, p. 71-72.
"Inherit the Earth." [IndR] (13:1) Wint 89, p. 70.
"My Androgynous Years." [Crazy] (36) Spr 89, p. 19-20.
"See How We Are." [Ploughs] (15:1) 89, p. 48-49.
"The Sequel." [Crazy] (36) Spr 89, p. 17-18.
"Versions of Transport." [IndR] (13:1) Wint 89, p. 68-69.
2310. HARNACK, Curtis
"Earth Ice." [CreamCR] (13:2) Fall 89, p. 31.
2311. HARP, Jerry
"Paul Years Later." [OxfordM] (5:2) Fall-Wint 89, p. 12-13.
2312. HARPER, Michael S.
"Br'er Sterling and the Rocker." [BlackALF] (23:1) Spr 89, p. 112.
"Br'er Sterling and the Rocker" (for Sterling A. and Daisy T. Brown, 16 June 1973,
in memoriam Sterling A. Brown, 1901-1989). [IndR] (12:2) Spr 89, p. 14.
2313. HARPER, Nanette
"Trader." [EmeraldCR] (1989) c1988, p. 122.

"Untitled: I do not want to shriek my sorrows." [EmeraldCR] (1989) c1988, p. 123.
"Untitled: Young Eagle plays his love-flute tenderly." [EmeraldCR] (1989) c1988, p. 123.
2314. HARR, Barbara
"The Meditation of Sarah." [ChrC] (106:34) N 15, 89, p. 1036.
2315. HARRINGTON, Margaret
"Memories Rerun." [AnthNEW] (1) 89, p. 10.
2316. HARRINGTON, S. G.
"Tabasco's Bar." [Amelia] (5:3, #14) 89, p. 111.
2317. HARRIS, Jana
"The Sourlands" (Selections: 2 poems). [OntR] (30) Spr-Sum 89, p. 28-31.
2318. HARRIS, Lisa
"Arrival." [SlipS] (9) 89, p. 27.
"Labor." [SlipS] (9) 89, p. 27.
"My Mother's Death." [SlipS] (9) 89, p. 28-30.
"Waiting." [SlipS] (9) 89, p. 26.
2319. HARRIS, Lynn Farmer
"Pignati." [EngJ] (78:2) F 89, p. 96.
2320. HARRIS, Marie
"Lo!" [HangL] (55) 89, p. 18.
"Tourist/Home: Prince Edward Island." [HangL] (55) 89, p. 17.
"Vintage." [HangL] (55) 89, p. 19.
2321. HARRIS, Maureen
"Crossing the Bar" (for Jane Urquhart). [MalR] (87) Sum 89, p. 73-74.
"The Particulars." [Grain] (17:4) Wint 89, p. 44.
2322. HARRIS, Melanie (Melanie Gause)
"In Yellowstone Park, Fires Burn Out of Control." [SoCaR] (22:1) Fall 89, p. 22.
"When I Am Away." [Kalliope] (11:1) 89, p. 53.
2323. HARRIS, Nathaniel
"Hoboken." [Boulevard] (4:1, #10) Spr 89, p. 95.
HARRIS, Robert Dassanowsky
   See DASSANOWSKY-HARRIS, Robert
2324. HARRISON, Devin
"30 Years Later." [Plain] (9:3) Spr 89, p. 26.
"Flowers for Father." [WindO] (52) Wint 89-90, p. 11.
2325. HARRISON, Jeffrey
"Early Frost and Late Snow." [Hudson] (42:1) Spr 89, p. 100.
"Night Visitors." [MissouriR] (12:1) 89, p. 153.
"Summer Memory ." [MissouriR] (12:1) 89, p. 152.
2326. HARRISON, Jim
"The Davenport Lunar Eclipse, August 16, 1989." [Caliban] (7) 89, p. 22-23.
2327. HARRISON, Joseph
"Vanysshynge." [MissouriR] (12:2) 89, p. 53.
2328. HARROD, Lois Marie
"Ontogeny Repeats Phylogeny." [Footwork] 89, p. 40.
2329. HARSHMAN, Marc
"Milbert's Tortoiseshell." [SouthernHR] (23:1) Wint 89, p. 66.
2330. HART, Bobby Sidna
"Tourniquet." [Pembroke] (21) 89, p. 115.
2331. HART, C. M.
"Dustcovers." [Grain] (17:4) Wint 89, p. 56.
2332. HART, Henry
"Janet Morgan and the Moon Shot." [MichQR] (28:3) Sum 89, p. 326-327.
2333. HART, Howard
"Thelonius Monk." [Caliban] (7) 89, p. 125-126.
2334. HART, Jack
"An Office Overlooking the Green." [FourQ] (2d series 3:1) Spr 89, p. 38.
"Quiveys' Spring." [Vis] (31) 89, p. 15.
2335. HART, John
"Evening News." [Interim] (8:1) Spr 89, p. 4.
"Mount Saint Helens." [Interim] (8:1) Spr 89, p. 5.
"Night Rappel." [Interim] (8:1) Spr 89, p. 3.
2336. HART, John W., III
"Howls" (From "The Found Poetry of Lt. Col. Oliver L. North," compiled by John W. Hart III). [Harp] (279:1673) O 89, p. 30.

2337. HART, Kevin
"The Gift." [Descant] (20:3/4, #66/67) Fall-Wint 89, p. 192.
"The Pleasure of Falling Out of Trees" (for Emily Kratzmann). [Descant] (20:3/4,
#66/67) Fall-Wint 89, p. 193.
"The Ship." [Verse] (6:3) Wint 89, p. 9.
"The Story." [Verse] (6:3) Wint 89, p. 10.
"Winter Rain" (In memory of Vincent Buckley). [Verse] (6:2) Je 89, p. 6.
2338. HARTER, Penny
"Black Deer." [Footwork] 89, p. 57.
"For Flight 103." [Footwork] 89, p. 57-58.
2339. HARTLEY, Dean W. (Dean Wilson)
"The Dream Life of Rita McCrosky." [SoCoast] (5) Spr 88, p. 31.
"Winter Resort in Indiana." [Farm] (6:1) Wint-Spr 88-89, p. 81-87.
2340. HARTLEY, Kathryn
"Poem on the Bank of a Greyhound Ticket." [Grain] (17:2) Sum 89, p. 16.
"The Secret." [Grain] (17:2) Sum 89, p. 15.
2341. HARTMANN, David
"Young in the Wheat" (for my brother). [Plain] (9:3) Spr 89, p. 9.
2342. HARTNETT, Michael
"Feeding a Child" (tr. of Nuala Ni Dhomhnaill). [Trans] (22) Fall 89, p. 141-142.
"The Gaeltacht Face" (tr. by the author). [Trans] (22) Fall 89, p. 94.
"Kiss" (tr. of Nuala Ni DHOMHNAILL). [YellowS] (30) Sum 89, p. 49.
"Love Song for Vietnam" (tr. of Caitlín Maude). [Trans] (22) Fall 89, p. 98-99.
"The Mermaid" (tr. of Nuala Ni Dhomhnaill). [Trans] (22) Fall 89, p. 139-140.
"Miscarriage Abroad" (tr. of Nuala Ni Dhomhnaill). [Trans] (22) Fall 89, p. 138.
"The Naked Surgeon" (tr. by the author). [Trans] (22) Fall 89, p. 84-93.
"Poem for Lara, 10" (tr. by the author). [Trans] (22) Fall 89, p. 95.
"Poem for Melissa" (tr. of Nuala Ni Dhomhnaill). [Trans] (22) Fall 89, p. 143.
"The Race" (tr. of Nuala Ni Dhomhnaill). [Trans] (22) Fall 89, p. 144-145.
"The Retreat of Ita Cagney" (Selections: 1-2, for Liam Brady, tr. by the author).
[Trans] (22) Fall 89, p. 96-97.
"Rust and Rampart of Rushes" (for Máire, tr. of Michael Davitt, w. Gabriel
Rosenstock). [Trans] (22) Fall 89, p. 126-127.
"The Shannon Estuary Welcoming the Fish" (tr. of Nuala Ni DHOMHNAILL).
[YellowS] (30) Sum 89, p. 49.
"The Visitor" (tr. of Nuala Ni Dhomhnaill). [Trans] (22) Fall 89, p. 137.
2343. HARTWIG, Julia
"Above Us" (tr. by Stanislaw Baranczak and Clare Cavanagh). [PartR] (56:2) Spr
89, p. 282.
"What Can They" (tr. by Stanislaw Baranczak and Clare Cavanagh). [PartR] (56:2)
Spr 89, p. 283.
"Who Says" (tr. by Stanislaw Baranczak and Clare Cavanah). [Trans] (21) Spr 89,
p. 35.
2344. HARTY, William
"Holiday Fever." [Verse] (6:3) Wint 89, p. 78.
"Smashing Heart." [Verse] (6:1) Mr 89, p. 59.
2345. HARVEY, Gayle Elen
"After Failing to Write a Rumage." [StoneC] (17:1/2) Fall-Wint 89-90, p. 64.
"Enter the Wind-Chill Factor." [Prima] (13) 89, p. 24.
2346. HARVEY, Kenneth J.
"Things Went On Forever." [AntigR] (76) Wint 89, p. 64.
2347. HARVILCHUCK, Lucia
"Sonnet 15." [EmeraldCR] (1989) c1988, p. 79.
2348. HARVOR, Elisabeth
"At the Horse Pavilion." [MalR] (87) Sum 89, p. 51-52.
"The Favourite Flies Home." [MalR] (89) Wint 89, p. 70-73.
"Four O'Clock, New Year's Morning, New River Beach." [MalR] (87) Sum 89, p.
53-54.
"Letter to a Younger Man in Another Country." [AntigR] (77/78) Spr-Sum 89, p.
37.
"One of the Lovesick Women of History." [AntigR] (77/78) Spr-Sum 89, p. 44-45.
"The Other Woman." [AntigR] (77/78) Spr-Sum 89, p. 35-36.
"The Radiologist's Daughter." [AntigR] (77/78) Spr-Sum 89, p. 40-43.
"The Sky or the Forest or the Cupboard." [AntigR] (77/78) Spr-Sum 89, p. 38-39.
2349. HASAN, Rabiul
"Insomnia." [Plain] (10:1) 89, p. 12.

2350. HASHIMOTO, Sharon
"Sahei Hashimoto Apologizes to His Wife for Dying." [KanQ] (21:3) Sum 89, p. 95.
"Tribe." [ThRiPo] (31/32) 88, p. 27.
2351. HASHMI, Alamgir
"Ode to Föhn." [Pig] (15) 88, p. 29.
2352. HASKINS, Lola
"A Confluence." [SouthernPR] (29:1) Spr 89, p. 72.
"Django." [MissouriR] (12:2) 89, p. 176.
"Of the Pleasures Which May be Discovered in Books, 1902." [MissouriR] (12:2) 89, p. 177.
"Scaling Bacalao" (for Hernan). [BelPoJ] (39:3) Spr 89, p. 23.
"Spelunking." [BelPoJ] (39:3) Spr 89, p. 23.
2353. HASS, Robert
"Fragments of Summers." [Antaeus] (62) Spr 89, p. 89-94.
"Incarnated" (tr. of Czeslaw Milosz, w. the author). [NewYorker] (65:44) 18 D 89, p. 40.
"The Thistle, the Nettle" (tr. of Czeslaw Milosz, w. the author). [NewYorker] (65:41) 27 N 89, p. 46.
2354. HASSELSTROM, Linda M.
"The Poet Falls in Love with a Cowboy." [SwampR] (1:4) Sum 89, p. 58-59.
"Staying in One Place." [SoDakR] (27:1) Spr 89, p. 123.
"Staying in One Place." [SwampR] (1:4) Sum 89, p. 57-58.
2355. HATHAWAY, Jeanine
"Fido" (Honorable Mention Poem, 1988/1989). [KanQ] (21:1/2) Wint-Spr 89, p. 28.
2356. HATHAWAY, William
"Grief in Early Spring." [KanQ] (21:1/2) Wint-Spr 89, p. 49.
"Inflation." [KanQ] (21:1/2) Wint-Spr 89, p. 48.
"Mirth." [GettyR] (2:1) Wint 89, p. 123.
"A Poem in Response to Doom." [Crazy] (37) Wint 89, p. 61-63.
"You See I Hear." [LaurelR] (23:1) Wint 89, p. 98.
2357. HAUFS, Rolf
"Generation" (tr. by John Linthicum). [LitR] (33:1) Fall 89, p. 35.
"The Left Side" (tr. by John Linthicum). [LitR] (33:1) Fall 89, p. 37.
"Like Something from a Story" (tr. by John Linthicum). [LitR] (33:1) Fall 89, p. 35.
"Silent Stars" (tr. by John Linthicum). [LitR] (33:1) Fall 89, p. 37.
"Suddenly" (tr. by John Linthicum). [LitR] (33:1) Fall 89, p. 36.
"The World Again" (tr. by John Linthicum). [LitR] (33:1) Fall 89, p. 36.
2358. HAUG, James
"Cloud Rises Seven Miles from Observers." [MassR] (30:1) Spr 89, p. 13.
"Walk-Up off Sixth Avenue." [MassR] (30:1) Spr 89, p. 12.
2359. HAUGE, Olav
"An Old-World Norseman" (tr. by Anne Born). [Verse] (6:1) Mr 89, p. 46.
"Pigs" (tr. by Anne Born). [Verse] (6:1) Mr 89, p. 45.
2360. HAUPTMAN, Terry
"Crouched in the Healing Rite." [CrossCur] (8:3) Apr 89, p. 133-134.
"A Force to be Reckoned With for B.C." [HighP] (4:1) Spr 89, p. 92-93.
"The Salt Sweat of Mint." [Caliban] (7) 89, p. 77.
"Sidestepping." [Caliban] (7) 89, p. 75-76.
"The Singed Wings of Ravished Alphabets" (for Jane Bowles). [Caliban] (7) 89, p. 72-74.
2361. HAUSEMER, Georges
"Don't Tell Me" (tr. by Karen Subach). [Vis] (31) 89, p. 41.
2362. HAUSER, Frank
"In Memoriam Harold Lang." [GrandS] (8:2) Wint 89, p. 192-197.
2363. HAUSER, Susan
"The Nest." [LakeSR] (23) 89, p. 30.
2364. HAVEN, Richard
"Noises Off: Catullus on Stage." [MassR] (30:4) Wint 89, p. 571-572.
2365. HAVEN, Stephen
"Ecclesiastes." [Crazy] (37) Wint 89, p. 26-27.
"Twinning." [Crazy] (37) Wint 89, p. 28-29.
2366. HAVIARAS, Stratis
"Farm Woman" (tr. of Yannis Ritsos). [Trans] (22) Fall 89, p. 260-261.

2367. HAWKINS, Tom
"When Navy Blue Fatigue." [GreensboroR] (46) Sum 89, p. 120.
2368. HAWKSWORTH, Marjorie
"Flashback." [ConnPR] (8:1) 89, p. 3.
2369. HAWLEY, Beatrice
"Advice." [AmerPoR] (18:1) Ja-F 89, p. 21.
"Agriculture." [Kalliope] (11:2) 89, p. 14.
"Aquileia." [AmerPoR] (18:1) Ja-F 89, p. 21.
"Arrival" (after Apollinaire). [AmerPoR] (18:1) Ja-F 89, p. 22.
"The Book of Maps." [AmerPoR] (18:1) Ja-F 89, p. 22.
"Homecoming." [Kalliope] (11:2) 89, p. 15.
"Muse." [AmerPoR] (18:1) Ja-F 89, p. 21.
"On Losing the Miracle in China." [SenR] (19:1) 89, p. 71-72.
"Pastoral." [Kalliope] (11:2) 89, p. 14.
"Ravioli Fiorentini." [Iowa] (19:3) Fall 89, p. 109.
"Recovery." [Kalliope] (11:2) 89, p. 15.
"The Swing." [MidAR] (9:2) 89, p. 132.
"To a Friend." [AmerPoR] (18:1) Ja-F 89, p. 21.
2370. HAXTON, Brooks
"Dithyramb." [GrahamHR] (12) Spr 89, p. 71-73.
"For the Returning and Remaining Absent." [AmerPoR] (18:2) Mr-Ap 89, p. 18.
"Lasting Wood, Though Soft, Though Broken." [AmerPoR] (18:2) Mr-Ap 89, p. 18.
"My Neighbor." [SouthernR] (25:2) Spr 89, p. 490.
"The Stars at Moonrise, Adams County." [SouthernR] (25:2) Spr 89, p. 489.
2371. HAYDEN, Robert
"The Diver." [WorldO] (22:1/2) Fall-Wint 87-88, c90, p. 12.
2372. HAYDON, Rich
"Hungry Mountains." [WindO] (51) Spr 89, p. 20.
"Marking Passage." [SoCoast] (6) Fall 88, p. 45.
2373. HAYES, Elliott
"Block." [AntigR] (77/78) Spr-Sum 89, p. 127.
"Collage." [AntigR] (77/78) Spr-Sum 89, p. 125.
"Terpsichore." [AntigR] (77/78) Spr-Sum 89, p. 126.
2374. HAYES, Glenn
"Destroying Angel." [Quarry] (38:1) Wint 89, p. 20.
2375. HAYES, Jack
"The Birds of God." [SouthernPR] (29:2) Fall 89, p. 71-72.
2376. HAYES, Noreen
"For Our Rowan Tree, Down in a Storm." [SpiritSH] (55) Fall-Wint 89 [90 on cover], p. 13.
"For Susan and Suffolk." [SpiritSH] (55) Fall-Wint 89 [90 on cover], p. 15.
"Loveletter." [SpiritSH] (55) Fall-Wint 89 [90 on cover], p. 14.
2377. HAYMON, Ava Leavell
"The Child Born." [Mildred] (3:1) Spr-Sum 89, p. 64.
"Denmother's Conversation." [ApalQ] (31) 89, p. 46.
2378. HAYNES, Robert E.
"The Last Witch." [PoetL] (84:4) Wint 89-90, p. 8.
2379. HAYWARD, Amber
"Letter from Greece and Letter to Greece (Returned)." [Dandel] (16:2) Fall-Wint 89, p. 20.
"Lost Doll." [Quarry] (38:2) Spr 89, p. 18.
2380. HAYWARD, Camille
"My Great-Grandmother's Foxgloves." [BellArk] (5:2) Mr-Ap 89, p. 12.
"Pears." [BellArk] (5:2) Mr-Ap 89, p. 13.
"The week that Margaret put herself to bed." [BellArk] (5:2) Mr-Ap 89, p. 14.
2381. HAYWARD, Steve
"Variations on Impressions of Children's Play." [SoCoast] (5) Spr 88, p. 6.
2382. HAZAK, Tama
"The Kingdom of Locust Eaters." [BlueBldgs] (11) 89, p. 13.
2383. HAZARD, John
"My Son's Sleep." [PassN] (10:1) Wint 89, p. 20.
2384. HAZELTON, Jonathan
"The Young Hunter Who Shot Himself." [CreamCR] (13:2) Fall 89, p. 125-126.
2385. HAZEN, James
"Distant Poppies." [CapeR] (24:1) Spr 89, p. 2.

"The Helicopter." [CapeR] (24:1) Spr 89, p. 4.
"Let Me Know How You Feel." [PaintedB] (37) 89, p. 28.
"A Strong One." [CapeR] (24:1) Spr 89, p. 3.
2386. HAZO, Samuel
"At Midnight There Are No Horizons." [PaintedB] (39) 89, p. 26-28.
"The Courage Not to Talk." [Talisman] (2) Spr 89, p. 60-61.
2387. HAZOUMÉ, Roger Aralamon
"Ry th ming" (tr. by Dorothy Aspinwall). [WebR] (14:1) Spr 89, p. 20.
2388. HAZUKA, Tom
"Becoming Cloud" (for Gertrude Clark). [SlipS] (9) 89, p. 59.
HE, Li
   See LI, He
2389. HEAD, Linda Weasel
"Grandma Moon Is Watching." [HighP] (4:3) Wint 89-90, p. 120-123.
"Smoked Hides and Meat." [HighP] (4:3) Wint 89-90, p. 118-119.
2390. HEAD, Robert
"I hav crost the continental divide." [Bogg] (61) 89, p. 22.
2391. HEANEY, Seamus
"Crossings." [NewYorker] (65:9) 17 Ap 89, p. 35.
"The Golden Bough" (Aeneid Book VI, tr. of Vergil, in memory of Jack and Máire
   Sweeney). [Trans] (22) Fall 89, p. 197-201.
2392. HEAP, Chad
"Another Letter, Long Overdue." [HarvardA] (124:1) N 89, p. 13.
"Freak Shift of Winter." [HarvardA] (123:3) Mr 89, p. 27.
2393. HEARD, Georgia
"Play It Slower." [Ploughs] (15:4) Wint 89-90, p. 106.
"This We'll Defend." [Ploughs] (15:4) Wint 89-90, p. 103-105.
2394. HEARLE, Kevin (Kevin J.)
"Each Thing We Know Is Changed Because We Know It." [YaleR] (78:3) Spr 89,
   p. 414.
"Two Composers in Search of One Los Angeles." [GeoR] (43:1) Spr 89, p.
   117-119.
2395. HEARN, Amanda
"The Storm" (Mainstreet Elementary Poetry Contest, 7th Grade, 2nd Place).
   [DeKalbLAJ] (22:1/4) 89, p. 107.
2396. HEATH, Caroline
"The Swallow." [Grain] (17:2) Sum 89, p. 1.
2397. HEATH-STUBBS, John
"At the Moscow Zoo" (tr. of Eugene Dubnov, w. the author). [HolCrit] (26:2) Ap
   89, p. 20.
2398. HEBERT, Arlene
"Reflection." [BellArk] (5:4) Jl-Ag 89, p. 6.
"Witch's Wheel." [BellArk] (5:1) Ja-F 89, p. 10.
2399. HEBRON, Elizabeth Mackenzie
"Aunt Mary." [BellArk] (5:3) My-Je 89, p. 6.
2400. HECHT, Anthony
"Eclogue of the Shepherd and the Townie." [SewanR] (97:3) Sum 89, p. 428-430.
"Naming the Animals." [NewYRB] (36:13) 17 Ag 89, p. 8.
2401. HECHT, Susan
"The Woman Who Grows Poems." [Kalliope] (10:1/2) 88, p. 49.
2402. HEDGES, David
"The Rose to St. Louis" (Aboard the Portland Rose, June 1, 1948). [BellArk] (5:1)
   Ja-F 89, p. 6-8.
2403. HEDIN, Laura
"Courtship." [Kalliope] (11:1) 89, p. 62.
2404. HEDIN, Robert
"Haydn" (tr. of Rolf Jacobsen). [MidAR] (9:2) 89, p. 131.
"In the Great Parks" (tr. of Rolf Jacobsen). [MidAR] (9:2) 89, p. 130.
"A Play with Shadows" (tr. of Rolf Jacobsen). [Vis] (31) 89, p. 11.
"Tanners' Creek." [CarolQ] (42:1) Fall 89, p. 15.
2405. HEFFERNAN, Michael
"The Catch." [LaurelR] (23:1) Wint 89, p. 23-24.
"The Dream of the Great Poem." [PoetryNW] (30:2) Sum 89, p. 36.
"Jack Tierney Mutters Home from Condon's Bar." [LaurelR] (23:1) Wint 89, p. 23.
"A Light in the House." [Iowa] (19:3) Fall 89, p. 54.
"Old Neighborhood." [PoetryNW] (30:2) Sum 89, p. 37.

"A Phantom of Delight." [Iowa] (19:3) Fall 89, p. 53.
"This Life." [PoetryNW] (30:2) Sum 89, p. 37.
2406. HEIGHTON, Steven
"Another View of Mt Fuji" (Nagai). [PraF] (10:4, #49) Wint 89-90, p. 15.
"Border Crossing, Mae Sai." [PraF] (10:4, #49) Wint 89-90, p. 18.
"Borderlands." [PraF] (10:4, #49) Wint 89-90, p. 19.
"Chinatown." [AntigR] (76) Wint 89, p. 36.
"(From a Journal: September 18)." [AntigR] (76) Wint 89, p. 37.
"Sakura No Hana To Koto" (Nijo Castle, Kyoto). [PraF] (10:4, #49) Wint 89-90, p. 17.
"Views of a Summer War" (Osaka Castle). [PraF] (10:4, #49) Wint 89-90, p. 16.
2407. HEIM, Scott
"China." [SmPd] (26:3 #77) Fall 89, p. 8.
2408. HEINE, Heinrich
"Coming Home" (tr. by Francis Golffing). [SpiritSH] (55) Fall-Wint 89 [90 on cover], p. 30-31.
"Katharina" (in German). [CumbPR] (9:1) Fall 89, p. 56.
"Katharina" (tr. by Aaron Kramer). [CumbPR] (9:1) Fall 89, p. 57.
"Die Unbekannte." [CumbPR] (9:1) Fall 89, p. 58-59.
"The Unknown One" (tr. by Aaron Kramer). [CumbPR] (9:1) Fall 89, p. 60-61.
2409. HEINLEIN, David A.
"Ty Heineken's." [US1] (22/23) Spr 89, p. 26-27.
"Zen and Some." [US1] (22/23) Spr 89, p. 27.
2410. HEINY, Katherine
"The Bus Driver." [HangL] (55) 89, p. 20.
2411. HEISE, Hans-Jürgen
"They Followed" (tr. by Jerry Glenn). [NewOR] (16:4) Wint 89, p. 72.
2412. HEISS, Karl
"A Distant Wave" (Platonic Poetry: The Dodecahedron). [HeavenB] (7) Wint 89, p. 44.
2413. HEISSENBÜTTEL, Helmut
"Doubled Doris" (tr. by John Linthicum). [LitR] (33:1) Fall 89, p. 123.
"Island Whodunit" (tr. by John Linthicum). [LitR] (33:1) Fall 89, p. 124.
"The Material the Imagination Has Made Up" (tr. by John Linthicum). [LitR] (33:1) Fall 89, p. 125.
2414. HEJINIAN, Lyn
"The Cell" (Excerpts). [Screens] (1) 89, p. 164-169.
"The Cell" (Excerpts). [Sonora] (17) Spr-Sum 89, p. 23-26.
"The Cell" (for Kit Robinson, selections: 22 poems). [PaperAir] (4:2) 89, p. 41-62.
"The Flying Statue" (for Ray Di Palma). [NewAW] (5) Fall 89, p. 73-81.
"Observation of a Fallen Leaf as the 'Ultimate Basis' of Landscape" (a reading, tr. of Arkadii Dragomoshchenko, w. Elena Balashova). [PaperAir] (4:2) 89, p. 63-66.
"Opsis" (from "Syn tax," tr. of Arkadii Dragomoshchenko, w. Elena Balashova). [MichQR] (28:4) Fall 89, p. 734-736.
2415. HEJMADI, Padma
"Two Woman Talk: Sokhom Means 'a Little Safety'." [RiverS] (28) 89, p. 49.
2416. HELLER, Ben A.
"Hermit Thrush at Summer's End / An Outline of the Poem" (tr. of Raúl Barrientos). [SenR] (19:1) 89, p. 54.
"The Joke." [MissouriR] (12:2) 89, p. 173.
"Orchids, Etc." [MissouriR] (12:2) 89, p. 172.
"Stephanie" (tr. of Raúl Barrientos). [SenR] (19:1) 89, p. 51-52.
"They Will Scatter Salt Over Us" (tr. of Raúl Barrientos). [SenR] (19:1) 89, p. 53.
"Triptych" (tr. of Raúl Barrientos). [SenR] (19:1) 89, p. 55-56.
2417. HELLER, Michael
"Mythos of Logos." [Talisman] (2) Spr 89, p. 66.
2418. HELWIG, Maggie
"Translation." [Rampike] (6:2) 88, p. 63.
2419. HEMPEL, Amy
"In the Animal Shelter." [TampaR] (2) 89, p. 41.
2420. HEMPEL, Elise
"Cicadas." [SpoonRQ] (14:3) Sum 89, p. 64.
"The Field." [Farm] (6:1) Wint-Spr 88-89, p. 37.
2421. HEMPHILL, Essex
"Album." [Callaloo] (12:3, #40) Sum 89, p. 471-472.

"I Want to Talk About You." [Callaloo] (12:3, #40) Sum 89, p. 473.
2422. HEMSCHEMEYER, Judith
"Balancing." [ColR] (NS 16:2) Fall 89-Wint 90, p. 53.
"Russian History Lesson." [ColR] (NS 16:2) Fall 89-Wint 90, p. 52.
"What I Want" (8 poems). [Hudson] (42:1) Spr 89, p. 70-76.
2423. HENDERSON, Archibald
"Dear Abby." [NegC] (9:1) 89, p. 69.
2424. HENDERSON, David
"Father and I Visit Mother in the Sanitorium." [ThRiPo] (33/34) 89, p. 43-44.
"Prosthesis." [NewAW] (5) Fall 89, p. 120.
2425. HENDERSON, Shaun O.
"How Africa Was One/Won" (from *Give me Till Tomorrow*). [Obs] (3:2) Sum 88,
p. 89-90.
2426. HENDRICK, Beckie
"Dalila." [Farm] (6:1) Wint-Spr 88-89, p. 62-63.
2427. HENDRICKS, Brent
"In His Sleep, My Father Inspects the Work of the Army Corps of Engineers."
[Poetry] (154:3) Je 89, p. 147.
2428. HENDRYSON, Barbara
"Photograph of My Father." [Kalliope] (11:1) 89, p. 27.
"The Wedding." [Kalliope] (11:1) 89, p. 26-27.
2429. HENJO, Bishop
"Maiden Flower" (From the First Imperial Anthology, Kokinwakashu, of 905, tr. by
Graeme Wilson). [Jacaranda] (4:1) Spr-Sum 89, p. 72.
2430. HENKE, Mark
"Roosting." [CapeR] (24:2) Fall 89, p. 24-25.
2431. HENKEL, Vera
"After the Dark Night" (tr. by John Linthicum). [LitR] (33:1) Fall 89, p. 98.
"The Sadness Has Arrived" (tr. by John Linthicum). [LitR] (33:1) Fall 89, p. 97.
"When You Left Me So Suddenly" (tr. by John Linthicum). [LitR] (33:1) Fall 89, p.
98.
"Why Are You Telling Me" (tr. by John Linthicum). [LitR] (33:1) Fall 89, p. 97.
2432. HENN, Mary Ann
"From My Envelope of Excuses." [FreeL] (3) Aut 89, p. 23.
"Give a Litte . . . Laugh." [FreeL] (3) Aut 89, p. 23.
2433. HENNING, Barbara
"Rooftops & Dreams." [PaintedB] (38) 89, p. 69-70.
2434. HENNING, Dianna
"At Louisa Pardini's." [SpoonRQ] (14:3) Sum 89, p. 47.
"Sister Has Planted Ivy in the Pot We Used to Pee In." [SpoonRQ] (14:3) Sum 89,
p. 45-46.
"Washday." [OxfordM] (5:1) Spr-Sum 89, p. 42.
2435. HENRIE, Carol
"In My Father's House." [PoetryNW] (30:4) Wint 89-90, p. 20-22.
"The Snake." [PraS] (63:2) Sum 89, p. 73-74.
"Summer." [PraS] (63:2) Sum 89, p. 75-76.
2436. HENRY, Gerrit
"Pfitzner's 'Palestrina'" (for John Ash). [Colum] (14) 89, p. 188-189.
"The Watchers." [ParisR] (31:113) Wint 89, p. 117-119.
2437. HENSCHEL, Sandi
"At Beadle's Slaughterhouse." [SlipS] (9) 89, p. 46.
2438. HENSON, Lance
"Bounty Hunters." [Nimrod] (32:2) Spr-Sum 89, p. 94.
"Coyote" (Selections: poems two and three). [Nimrod] (32:2) Spr-Sum 89, p. 89.
"Four Poems from the Crow." [Nimrod] (32:2) Spr-Sum 89, p. 90-91.
"Just After Noon V A Alcohol Recovery Ward Oklahoma City." [Nimrod] (32:2)
Spr-Sum 89, p. 93.
2439. HENSON, Sandy Meek
"The Dream Web." [BlueBldgs] (11) 89, p. 49-52.
"Journal of a Lie." [SouthernPR] (29:2) Fall 89, p. 52-53.
2440. HENTZ, Robert R.
"Morning Talk Show." [Poem] (62) N 89, p. 59.
"Romance and Reason." [Poem] (62) N 89, p. 58.
2441. HERBECK, Ernst
"The Sword" (tr. by Melissa Monroe). [PartR] (56:1) Wint 89, p. 115.

2442. HERBERT, W. N.
"Cleanliness." [Verse] (6:1) Mr 89, p. 21.
"The Dominie." [Verse] (6:3) Wint 89, p. 44.
"Morn-Come-Never" (for Debbie). [Verse] (6:3) Wint 89, p. 44-45.
"Slowdive." [Verse] (6:3) Wint 89, p. 43.

2443. HERBERT, Zbigniew
"Landscape" (tr. by Bogdana and John Carpenter). [PartR] (56:1) Wint 89, p. 113.
"Mr. Cogito Meditates on Redemption" (tr. by Ioanna-Veronika). [Jacaranda] (4:1)
    Spr-Sum 89, p. 55.
"The Nepenthe Family" (tr. by Bogdana and John Carpenter). [PartR] (56:1) Wint
    89, p. 113-114.
"Nike Hesitates" (tr. by Ioanna-Veronika). [Jacaranda] (4:1) Spr-Sum 89, p. 50-51.
"Revelation" (tr. by Ioanna-Veronika). [Jacaranda] (4:1) Spr-Sum 89, p. 51-52.
"A Sign" (tr. by Ioanna-Veronika). [Jacaranda] (4:1) Spr-Sum 89, p. 57.
"A Stool" (tr. by Ioanna-Veronika). [Jacaranda] (4:1) Spr-Sum 89, p. 56.
"A Suicide" (tr. by Marek Labinski). [WillowS] (23) Wint 89, p. 59.
"The Voice" (tr. by Ioanna-Veronika). [Jacaranda] (4:1) Spr-Sum 89, p. 53-54.

2444. HERBST, Nikki
"Verdant" (Paul Gauguin: Les Baigneuses, 1885, Women Bathing). [Kalliope]
    (11:2) 89, p. 51.

2445. HERMAN, Peter
"Ancestor." [AntigR] (77/78) Spr-Sum 89, p. 96.

2446. HERMANN, Phillip D.
"Nature Notorious." [Writer] (102:6) Je 89, p. 29.

2447. HERNANDEZ, Miguel
"25. Don't spy at the window" (tr. by Tony Barnstone). [InterPR] (15:2) Fall 89, p.
    47.
"25. No te asomes a la ventana." [InterPR] (15:2) Fall 89, p. 46.
"30. Tú de blanco, yo de negro." [InterPR] (15:2) Fall 89, p. 46.
"30. You in white, I in black" (tr. by Tony Barnstone). [InterPR] (15:2) Fall 89, p.
    47.
"31. La Luciérnaga en celo." [InterPR] (15:2) Fall 89, p. 46.
"31. The ardent firefly" (tr. by Tony Barnstone). [InterPR] (15:2) Fall 89, p. 47.
"32. I can't forget" (tr. by Tony Barnstone). [InterPR] (15:2) Fall 89, p. 49.
"32. No puedo olvidar." [InterPR] (15:2) Fall 89, p. 48.
"38. Enciende las dos puertas." [InterPR] (15:2) Fall 89, p. 48.
"38. The two doors catch fire" (tr. by Tony Barnstone). [InterPR] (15:2) Fall 89, p.
    49.
"71. El cementerio está cerca." [InterPR] (15:2) Fall 89, p. 48.
"71. The cemetery is near" (tr. by Tony Barnstone). [InterPR] (15:2) Fall 89, p. 49.

2448. HERNANDEZ, Orlando José
"Insomnio" (tr. of Elizabeth Bishop). [Lyra] (2:1/2) 88, c89, p. 2.
"Paisaje Marino" (tr. of Elizabeth Bishop). [Lyra] (2:1/2) 88, c89, p. 4.

2449. HERNANDEZ, Pablo Fernando
"In a Permanent Place" (tr. by John Brotherson). [PoetryE] (28) Fall 89, p. 190.
"Learning to Die" (tr. by John Brotherson). [PoetryE] (28) Fall 89, p. 187-188.
"Parable" (tr. by John Brotherson). [PoetryE] (28) Fall 89, p. 185-186.
"What I Know" (tr. by John Brotherson). [PoetryE] (28) Fall 89, p. 189.

2450. HERNANDEZ AQUINO, Luis
"Elegia del Cafetal: III. El Hombre." [Mairena] (11:27) 89, p. 79.

2451. HERRERA, Georgina
"A Small Elegy for Myself" (tr. by Brucette Ohe). [Pig] (15) 88, p. 63.

2452. HERRERA, Juan Felipe
"AIDS Hearing in the Metropolis." [BostonR] (14:5) O 89, p. 6.
"Mexican World Mural 5 x 25" (In memory of Ramon Medina Silva). [BostonR]
    (14:5) O 89, p. 6.

2453. HERRICK, Kathleen
"Cowboys Never Tango." [PacificR] (7) 89, p. 5.

2454. HERRSTROM, David Sten
"Obsidian Considered as an Object of Affection." [US1] (22/23) Spr 89, p. 6-7.

2455. HERSCH, Greer
"Ask Dawn About It." [HarvardA] (124:1) N 89, p. 27.
"Two Causes for Murder." [HarvardA] (123:3) Mr 89, p. 14.
"Very Small." [HarvardA] (124:1) N 89, p. 10.
"What I Have Got to Say Keeps Getting Louder." [HarvardA] (123:2) Ja 89, p. 20.

2456. HERSHEY, Christopher
"While We Waited in the Free World." [JamesWR] (7:1) Fall 89, p. 10.
2457. HERSHON, Robert
"Bleecker and Carmine: Walk to Work." [PoetryNW] (30:4) Wint 89-90, p. 10-12.
"Dead Steve McQueen." [PoetryNW] (30:1) Spr 89, p. 15.
"January 18th: Bedford and Carmine." [PoetryNW] (30:4) Wint 89-90, p. 12.
"Myrna Loy in Real Life." [PoetryNW] (30:1) Spr 89, p. 16.
"A Nature Poem." [PoetryNW] (30:4) Wint 89-90, p. 13.
"Or Is She in the Pay of a Foreign Power." [PoetryNW] (30:1) Spr 89, p. 16.
"Trades." [PoetryNW] (30:1) Spr 89, p. 16-17.
2458. HESKETH, Phoebe
"Words." [Stand] (30:2) Spr 89, p. 47.
2459. HESS, Errol
"Driving." [Lactuca] (12) F 89, p. 53.
2460. HESS, Sonya
"A Breath of Shadow." [WestB] (24) 89, p. 100-101.
2461. HETRICK, Lawrence
"Riverbottom Dream" (To Andrew Hetrick, my sometime partner on the Suwannee,
St. Mary's, Alapaha). [ChatR] (10:1) Fall 89, p. 61.
"To My Young Son in a Distant Town" (Creative Writing Club Contest, 1st Place).
[DeKalbLAJ] (22:1/4) 89, p. 77.
HEUREUX, Maurice l'
See L'HEUREUX, Maurice
2462. HEWITT, Geof
"In Sadness." [NegC] (9:1) 89, p. 70.
"Wealth." [NegC] (9:1) 89, p. 71-73.
2463. HEYEN, William
"Americans." [PoetL] (84:1) Spr 89, p. 36.
"Before Sleep." [ColR] (NS 16:2) Fall 89-Wint 90, p. 40.
"Children's Poem: This Village." [ColR] (NS 16:2) Fall 89-Wint 90, p. 39.
"Matrix." [ColR] (NS 16:2) Fall 89-Wint 90, p. 43-44.
"Stiletto." [PoetL] (84:1) Spr 89, p. 33-35.
"The Swamp." [ColR] (NS 16:2) Fall 89-Wint 90, p. 41-42.
"Trees." [OhioR] (43) 89, p. 48.
"Waterhook" (Richard Purdum, d. 1968). [NewEngR] (12:2) Wint 89, p. 136.
"Wildflower." [PaintedB] (39) 89, p. 83.
2464. HEYNEN, Jim
"Tourist Guide: How You Can Tell for Sure You're in South Dakota." [SoDakR]
(27:1) Spr 89, p. 125.
HIAGIWARA, Sakutaro
See SAKUTARO, Hiagiwara
2465. HICKNEY, Danielle
"Esteli." [MinnR] (NS 32) Spr 89, p. 74.
"Los Perros." [MinnR] (NS 32) Spr 89, p. 75-76.
2466. HIESTAND, Emily
"Holly Comes from a Cold Heaven." [Nat] (248:2) 9-16 Ja 89, p. 66.
"Idée du Jour." [Salm] (84) Fall 89, p. 59-60.
"Life." [Nat] (248:1) 2 Ja 89, p. 30.
"Slippery Elm." [Nat] (248:7) 20 F 89, p. 244.
"The Witch Hazel Wood." [Nat] (248:6) 13 F 89, p. 212.
2467. HIGGINS, Rita Ann
"I Went to School With You." [Vis] (29) 89, p. 23-24.
2468. HIGH, John
"And Schubert on the water, and Pushkin living on rations" (tr. of Aleksandr
Eremenko, w. Katya Olmsted). [FiveFR] (7) 89, p. 97.
"But already sensing terror" (tr. of Ivan Zhdanov). [FiveFR] (7) 89, p. 73.
"Falling, a tree's shadow carries some of the leaves along" (tr. of Ivan Zhdanov).
[FiveFR] (7) 89, p. 72.
"I look at you from such deep graves" (To Hieronymus Bosch, inventor of the
projector, tr. of Aleksandr Eremenko). [FiveFR] (7) 89, p. 98-101.
"I'm not the branch, only the prebranchness" (tr. of Ivan Zhdanov). [FiveFR] (7)
89, p. 71.
"In the savage bathroom, a razor blade glitters" (tr. of Aleksei Parshchikov).
[FiveFR] (7) 89, p. 29.
"An Overture Spoken to the Work Tools" (tr. of Aleksei Parshchikov). [MichQR]
(28:4) Fall 89, p. 724-726.

"Philological Verse" (tr. of Aleksandr Eremenko). [MichQR] (28:4) Fall 89, p. 722-723.
"Portrait" (tr. of Ivan Zhdanov, w. Katya Olmsted). [FiveFR] (7) 89, p. 74.
"Prelude, Spoken to My Work Tools" (tr. of Aleksei Parshchikov). [FiveFR] (7) 89, p. 30-31.
"Still-Life" (tr. of Nina Iskrenko, w. Katya Olmsted). [FiveFR] (7) 89, p. 54.
"Talking to my crested hen" (tr. of Nina Iskrenko, w. Katya Olmsted). [FiveFR] (7) 89, p. 55.
"To Beat or Not to Beat" (tr. of Nina Iskrenko, w. Katya Olmsted). [FiveFR] (7) 89, p. 56-57.
"To talk with you is like burning in the marsh" (tr. of Nina Iskrenko, w. Katya Olmsted). [FiveFR] (7) 89, p. 53.
"Two Women Make-Up Artists" (A variation on Michael Lermontov's poem, "In noon's heat . . .", tr. of Aleksei Parshchikov). [FiveFR] (7) 89, p. 32.
2469. HIGH, Maura
"The Etiquette of Grief." [KenR] (N 11:4) Fall 89, p. 61.
"A Kind of Aubade." [KenR] (N 11:4) Fall 89, p. 62.
"To the Tune of 'Danny Boy'." [KenR] (N 11:4) Fall 89, p. 63.
2470. HIKMET, Nazim
"9-10 P.M. Poems" (tr. by Randy Blasing and Mutlu Konuk Blasing). [PoetryE] (27) Spr 89, p. 31-46.
"Istanbul House of Detention" (tr. by Randy Blasing and Mutlu Konuk Blasing). [PoetryE] (27) Spr 89, p. 17-20.
"A Letter from Prison" (tr. by Agha Shahid Ali of Faiz Ahmed Faiz's Urdu version). [PoetryE] (27) Spr 89, p. 101.
"Letters from Chankiri Prison" (tr. by Randy Blasing and Mutlu Konuk Blasing). [PoetryE] (27) Spr 89, p. 24-30.
"One Night of Knee-Deep Snow" (tr. by Randy Blasing and Mutlu Konuk Blasing). [PoetryE] (27) Spr 89, p. 14-16.
"Since I Was Thrown Inside" (tr. by Randy Blasing and Mutlu Konuk Blasing). [PoetryE] (27) Spr 89, p. 21-23.
"Some Advice to Those Who Will Serve Time in Prison" (tr. by Randy Blasing and Mutlu Konuk Blasing). [PoetryE] (27) Spr 89, p. 12-13.
2471. HILBERRY, Conrad
"The Messenger" (for John Spencer). [Shen] (39:1) Spr 89, p. 63-64.
"North and South." [Shen] (39:1) Spr 89, p. 60.
"On Hearing a Guide Explain That the Delphic Oracle Was a Hoax from the Beginning." [Shen] (39:1) Spr 89, p. 61.
"Rock Video: All Night on the Road." [Shen] (39:1) Spr 89, p. 62.
"The Spit." [PoetryNW] (30:1) Spr 89, p. 23.
2472. HILBERT, Donna
"From a Rhizome." [PassN] (10:1) Wint 89, p. 19.
2473. HILDRETH, Lee
"Dyâli" (For Léopold Sédar Senghor, tr. of Aimé Césaire). [Callaloo] (12:1, #38) Wint 89, p. 53, 55.
"It Is the Necessary Passage" (tr. of Aimé Césaire). [Callaloo] (12:1, #38) Wint 89, p. 73.
"References" (tr. of Aimé Césaire). [Callaloo] (12:1, #38) Wint 89, p. 69.
"Supreme Mask" (tr. of Aimé Césaire). [Callaloo] (12:1, #38) Wint 89, p. 71.
2474. HILL, Daniel
"A Reminder." [Interim] (8:2) Fall 89, p. 24.
2475. HILL, Gerald
"A Good Nude Model, Four Poses." [Grain] (17:4) Wint 89, p. 15-17.
"Mad River." [PraF] (10:4, #49) Wint 89-90, p. 45.
"A Poetic." [Grain] (17:4) Wint 89, p. 18-19.
2476. HILL, Hyacinthe
"Knight's Move." [CreamCR] (13:2) Fall 89, p. 26.
2477. HILL, John Meredith
"Penmanship." [MSS] (6:3) 89, p. 112.
2478. HILL, Laban Carrick
"Meanwhile, Aubade." [DenQ] (24:2) Fall 89, p. 53-54.
2479. HILL, Larry
"The City Beneath the Sea" (1989 National Collegiate Poetry Fellowship Competition). [IndR] (12:3) Sum 89, p. 101-102.
2480. HILL, Pamela Steed
"The Swan Boats" (for Anne Sexton -- who was thirty that November). [CapeR]

(24:1) Spr 89, p. 23.
"The Swan Boats" (for Anne Sexton, who was thirty that November). [BlueBldgs]
(11) 89, p. 27.
2481. HILL, Sarah
"A Summer's Tale." [SouthernR] (25:2) Spr 89, p. 494-495.
2482. HILL, Selima
"Sweet Williams." [Pequod] (26/27) 89, p. 89.
"Topsy." [Pequod] (26/27) 89, p. 88.
"Visiting the Zoo." [Pequod] (26/27) 89, p. 87.
2483. HILL, Steven
"Monopoly Capital Sexuality." [MinnR] (NS 32) Spr 89, p. 62.
2484. HILL, Virginia Reid
"Grace in Pure Objects." [Wind] (19:65) 89, p. 11.
2485. HILLER, Tobey
"City." [Caliban] (6) 89, p. 110-111.
2486. HILLES, Robert
"Forgetting the Smells." [AntigR] (79) Aut 89, p. 110-111.
"Letter 2." [PraF] (10:1, #46) Spr 89, p. 41.
"Progress." [AntigR] (79) Aut 89, p. 112-113.
2487. HILLIARD, Garrison L.
"Brief visit to woman." [SmPd] (26:2 #76) Spr 89, p. 19.
2488. HILLINGA, Helena M.
"The Breath of Lands" (Selections: 5 poems). [BellArk] (5:2) Mr-Ap 89, p. 1.
2489. HILLMAN, Brenda
"Food." [Thrpny] (36) Wint 89, p. 12.
2490. HILLMAN, Grady
"Election Day." [HighP] (4:1) Spr 89, p. 84-85.
2491. HILLRINGHOUSE, Mark
"Dizzy Gillespie." [Talisman] (3) Fall 89, p. 116.
2492. HILLS, Ellen
"Four on the Rocks." [AnthNEW] (1) 89, p. 11.
"Ice Age." [AnthNEW] (1) 89, p. 12.
"Three Beach Pebbles." [AnthNEW] (1) 89, p. 11.
2493. HINES, Debra
"The Parrot." [CarolQ] (42:1) Fall 89, p. 51.
"Ursula's Chef Soubrette." [CarolQ] (42:1) Fall 89, p. 50.
2494. HINOJOSA, Francisco
"Robinson Perseguido" (Selection: III). [Nimrod] (33:1) Fall-Wint 89, p. 128, 130.
"Robinson Pursued" (tr. by Thomas Hoeksema and Romelia Enríquez). [Nimrod]
(33:1) Fall-Wint 89, p. 129, 131.
2495. HINRICHSEN, Dennis
"Burying a Child" (for Joseph Lyle Huhn). [NewEngR] (12:1) Aut 89, p. 66.
"The End of Mercy." [RiverC] (9:1) Spr 89, p. 11.
"Free Throws." [TarRP] (28:2) Spr 89, p. 10.
"The Hellfighters." [IndR] (13:1) Wint 89, p. 79-80.
"Late Shift." [PoetryNW] (30:2) Sum 89, p. 25.
"Players" (for Owens, Pijewski, Ripple). [IndR] (13:1) Wint 89, p. 77-78.
"Reading Dante by Electric Light." [NewEngR] (12:1) Aut 89, p. 67-68.
"Spectrum." [TarRP] (28:2) Spr 89, p. 9.
"Stillborn" (for Steve and Pat Huhn). [RiverC] (9:1) Spr 89, p. 10.
2496. HINTON, David
"Jade-Blossom Palace" (tr. of Tu Fu). [LitR] (32:3) Spr 89, p. 423.
"Leaving Kung-An at Dawn" (tr. of Tu Fu). [LitR] (32:3) Spr 89, p. 424.
"Moonlit Night Thinking of My Brothers" (tr. of Tu Fu). [LitR] (32:3) Spr 89, p.
426.
"The New Moon" (tr. of Tu Fu). [LitR] (32:3) Spr 89, p. 423.
"Returning Late" (tr. of Tu Fu). [LitR] (32:3) Spr 89, p. 424.
"Song at Year's End" (tr. of Tu Fu). [LitR] (32:3) Spr 89, p. 425.
"Song for Silkworms and Grain" (tr. of Tu Fu). [LitR] (32:3) Spr 89, p. 426.
"A Traveler From " (tr. of Tu Fu). [LitR] (32:3) Spr 89, p. 425.
HIROSHI, Murakami
See MURAKAMI, Hiroshi
2497. HIRSCH, Edward
"Art Pepper." [ParisR] (31:113) Wint 89, p. 148-149.
"The Blue Rider." [WestHR] (43:2) Sum 89, p. 118.
"The Brightness." [WestHR] (43:2) Sum 89, p. 117.

"Memorandums." [NewYorker] (64:52) 13 F 89, p. 36.
"The Motor." [CinPR] (19) Spr 89, p. 7.
"The Romance of American Communism." [NewRep] (201:21) 20 N 89, p. 36.
2498. HIRSCH, Steven
"Climbing the Stair" (for Jon Anderson). [HeavenB] (7) Wint 89, p. 6.
"Firmament." [HeavenB] (6) Wint-Spr 89, p. 14-15.
2499. HIRSCHMAN, Jack
"Glyph." [Sonora] (17) Spr-Sum 89, p. 6-8.
"Running Poem." [AnotherCM] (19) 89, p. 105.
HITOMARO, Kakinomoto no (ca. 692)
   See KAKINOMOTO NO HITOMARO (CA. 692)
2500. HIX, H. L.
"Recumbent Lover, Seated Lover." [StoneC] (17:1/2) Fall-Wint 89-90, p. 19.
HO-CHING, Lin
   See LIN, Ho-ching
2501. HOAD, Patricia Joan
"Bad Dreams." [US1] (22/23) Spr 89, p. 45.
2502. HOAGLAND, Bill
"Paul Gauguin." [SoCoast] (7) Spr-Fall 89, p. 41.
"Teen Blizzard." [SoCoast] (7) Spr-Fall 89, p. 40.
2503. HOAGLAND, Tony
"My Country." [AmerPoR] (18:2) Mr-Ap 89, p. 15.
2504. HOBEN, Sandra
"Three Dresses." [SoCoast] (7) Spr-Fall 89, p. 12.
2505. HOBROCK, P. J. M.
"A Gently Humorous Sonnet for Dr. Schwarz and Dr. Green" (creators of the
   Superstring Theory of the Universe). [Plain] (9:2) Wint 89, p. 33.
2506. HOCHHEISER, Marilyn
"Angie Wood Is a Stuck-Up Rag." [CrossCur] (8:3) Apr 89, p. 13.
2507. HOCHMAN, Will
"Seventeen." [SwampR] (1:4) Sum 89, p. 65.
2508. HODGE, Marion
"Shrieks in the Afternoon." [ColEng] (51:4) Ap 89, p. 391.
2509. HODGEN, John
"Bodywash." [MassR] (30:2) Sum 89, p. 319.
"News." [MassR] (30:2) Sum 89, p. 320.
2510. HODGES, Gregg
"An Anchorite's Lament." [NewRep] (200:9) 27 F 89, p. 35.
"A Music." [NewRep] (201:9) 28 Ag 89, p. 38.
"The Two Cities." [NewRep] (200:22) 29 My 89, p. 34.
2511. HODGES, Janice
"Intimate Times." [Obs] (4:2) Sum 89, p. 58-59.
2512. HODOR, Timothy
"The Three Figures in Resselpark." [NegC] (9:1) 89, p. 92.
2513. HOEBER, Ditta Baron
"No / Only for a Moment / Nothing Stuck: Three Poems." [OhioR] (44) 89, p.
   131-133.
2514. HOEKSEMA, Thomas
"Clear and fragile figure" (tr. of Laura Gonzalez Duran). [Jacaranda] (4:1) Spr-Sum
   89, p. 67.
"Fragments flee" (tr. of Adriana Yañez). [RiverS] (28) 89, p. 52.
"Gray emptiness" (tr. of Adriana Yanez, w. R. Enriquez). [Jacaranda] (4:1)
   Spr-Sum 89, p. 63.
"In a Delicate Mimicry of Rain" (9 Poems, Translation Chapbook Series, tr. of Coral
   Bracho, w. Romelia Enríquez). [MidAR] (9:1) 89, p. 81-115.
"My Flaws Among the Peach Blossoms" (tr. of Kyra Galvan). [Jacaranda] (4:1)
   Spr-Sum 89, p. 65-66.
"Poem: Because I reflect" (tr. of Laura Gonzalez Duran). [RiverS] (28) 89, p. 53.
"Poem: Heavy burden of thoughts" (tr. of Socorro Leon Femat). [RiverS] (28) 89,
   p. 51.
"Praise to the Snail" (tr. of Kyra Galvan). [RiverS] (28) 89, p. 50.
"Robinson Pursued" (tr. of Francisco Hinojosa, w. Romelia Enríquez). [Nimrod]
   (33:1) Fall-Wint 89, p. 129, 131.
"Transparent bodies emerge" (tr. of Socorro Leon Femat). [Jacaranda] (4:1)
   Spr-Sum 89, p. 64.

2515. HOEPPNER, Edward Haworth
    "The Kabbalistics of This Board Game." [OhioR] (43) 89, p. 75-76.
    "Red Shoulders." [SpoonRQ] (14:3) Sum 89, p. 54-55.
    "Tontine." [SpoonRQ] (14:3) Sum 89, p. 53.
    "What These Dwellers Loved." [OhioR] (43) 89, p. 77.
HOEY, Alan
    See HOEY, Allen
2516. HOEY, Allen
    "Between Seasons." [SouthernHR] (23:2) Spr 89, p. 137.
    "Dividing the Firmament Hourly in Rome." [Poetry] (154:5) Ag 89, p. 258-261.
    "In Florence." [NoDaQ] (57:3) Sum 89, p. 219-220.
    "Plein Air" (Monet at Giverny, 1917). [CumbPR] (8:2) Spr 89, p. 3-6.
    "She Goes Nowhere Fast." [PoetryNW] (30:4) Wint 89-90, p. 39-40.
2517. HOEY, Gertrude
    "The Song of That Bird." [AnthNEW] (1) 89, p. 13.
2518. HOFFMAN, Daniel
    "Dr. Kilmer." [Boulevard] (4:2, #11) Fall 89, p. 111.
    "Evidence." [YaleR] (78:4) Sum 89, p. 626-627.
2519. HOFFMAN, Jill
    "Puffy's." [HeliconN] (20) 89, p. 87.
    "Sorry. I Think You Have the Wrong Number." [HeliconN] (20) 89, p. 87.
2520. HOFFMAN, L. K.
    "Can't Walk." [CapeR] (24:1) Spr 89, p. 11.
2521. HOFFMAN, Peggy
    "Michael." [AntigR] (79) Aut 89, p. 74.
    "Roasting Winter Fruit." [AntigR] (79) Aut 89, p. 75.
HOFFMAN, Roald
    See HOFFMANN, Roald
2522. HOFFMANN, Roald
    "From Lake Louise." [NewRena] (7:3, #23) 89, p. 30.
    "Hitchhiking." [PraS] (63:2) Sum 89, p. 26-27.
    "Survival Techniques." [PraS] (63:2) Sum 89, p. 27-29.
    "What We Have Learned About the Pineal." [Jacaranda] (4:1) Spr-Sum 89, p.
        153-154.
2523. HOFMANN, Michael
    "Sally." [Colum] (14) 89, p. 89.
2524. HOGAN, Linda
    "The Direction of Light." [Nimrod] (32:2) Spr-Sum 89, p. 32-33.
    "Harbor." [Nimrod] (32:2) Spr-Sum 89, p. 34-35.
2525. HOGARTH, Margaret
    "Marriage, an Economic Arrangement." [PacificR] (7) 89, p. 93.
2526. HOGGARD, James
    "Baroque Body" (tr. of Julio Ortega). [StoneC] (16:3/4) Spr-Sum 89, p. 23.
    "Joseph and Child" (Piazza della Republica, Rome). [TexasR] (10:3/4) Fall-Wint 89,
        p. 71.
    "Winter Refrain." [StoneC] (16:3/4) Spr-Sum 89, p. 21.
2527. HOGUE, Cynthia
    "Little Nothings." [Sequoia] (32:2) Wint-Spr 89, p. 2.
    "Meditation." [Sequoia] (32:2) Wint-Spr 89, p. 3.
    "Voodoo (Economics)." [CentralP] (16) Fall 89, p. 95-97.
    "The Woman in Red." [AmerPoR] (18:4) Jl-Ag 89, p. 4.
2528. HOHEISEL, Peter
    "At Bessemer Cemetery" (for Diane, Honorable Mention, 1989 Poetry Competition).
        [PassN] (10:2) Sum 89, p. 9.
2529. HOHN, Donovan
    "Head Start" (for my brother, August, 1988). [HangL] (55) 89, p. 59.
    "The Ocean in the Shell." [HangL] (55) 89, p. 60.
    "Tadpoles in the Gutter." [HangL] (55) 89, p. 61.
2530. HOLAN, Vladimír
    "Evening" (tr. by Jarmila and Ian Milner). [Verse] (6:2) Je 89, p. 62.
    "To Whom?" (tr. by Jarmila and Ian Milner). [Verse] (6:2) Je 89, p. 62.
2531. HOLDEN, Jonathan
    "American Gothic." [PoetC] (21:1) Fall 89, p. 7-8.
    "April 15." [Journal] (13:1) Spr-Sum 89, p. 8-9.
    "First Day of School." [KenR] (N 11:4) Fall 89, p. 79.
    "A Fixed Form." [PoetC] (21:1) Fall 89, p. 10.

"Pope's House." [KenR] (N 11:4) Fall 89, p. 80.
"Summer School." [CimR] (89) O 89, p. 102-103.
"Teaching My Son to Drive." [PoetC] (21:1) Fall 89, p. 9.
"Tumbleweed." [CimR] (89) O 89, p. 101.
"The Wisdom Tooth" (for Bill Strutz). [Journal] (13:1) Spr-Sum 89, p. 6-7.
2532. HÖLDERLIN, Friedrich
"Age" (tr. of Pindar, w. David Rattray). [Temblor] (10) 89, p. 198.
"The Asylums" (tr. of Pindar, w. David Rattray). [Temblor] (10) 89, p. 198.
"The Enlivener" (tr. of Pindar, w. David Rattray). [Temblor] (10) 89, p. 199.
"The Faithlessness of Wisdom" (tr. of Pindar, w. David Rattray). [Temblor] (10)
89, p. 196.
"The Infinite" (tr. of Pindar, w. David Rattray). [Temblor] (10) 89, p. 198.
"Of Peace" (tr. of Pindar, w. David Rattray). [Temblor] (10) 89, p. 196.
"Of the Dolphin" (tr. of Pindar, w. David Rattray). [Temblor] (10) 89, p. 197.
"Of Truth" (tr. of Pindar, w. David Rattray). [Temblor] (10) 89, p. 196.
"The Supreme" (tr. of Pindar, w. David Rattray). [Temblor] (10) 89, p. 197.
2533. HOLDSTOCK, P. J.
"Canticle." [Rampike] (6:2) 88, p. 74.
2534. HOLDT, David
"Deer Crossing." [Blueline] (10:1/2) 89, p. 33-34.
2535. HOLIHEN, J. Markham
"Thoughts at Fleming Fountain on a July Day." [EmeraldCR] (1989) c1988, p. 109.
2536. HOLINGER, Richard
"August Skies" (Inspired by "The August Almanac" in the August 1987 *Atlantic*).
[Farm] (6:2) Fall 89, p. 45-51.
"Late Arrivals, Early Beginnings." [BallSUF] (30:4) Aut 89, p. 68.
"Screaming Beneath the Ruins." [HampSPR] Wint 89, p. 45.
"There and Back." [HampSPR] Wint 89, p. 43-45.
2537. HOLLADAY, Hilary
"The Fur Man of Gordonsville." [Verse] (6:1) Mr 89, p. 57.
"The Reply." [TarRP] (29:1) Fall 89, p. 20.
"What Summer Was." [WestB] (23) 89, p. 13.
2538. HOLLAHAN, Eugene
"Eat Your Veggies." [DeKalbLAJ] (22:1/4) 89, p. 55.
"Gramma." [ColR] (NS 16:1) Spr-Sum 89, p. 53.
"Maybe Möbius?" [DeKalbLAJ] (22:1/4) 89, p. 55.
2539. HOLLAND, Larry
"Curly." [Plain] (9:2) Wint 89, p. 22.
"Mid-January Thaw." [WestB] (25) 89, p. 107.
"Scotsmen Do Have an Edge When It Matters." [Plain] (9:3) Spr 89, p. 8.
2540. HOLLAND, Michelle
"I Knew of Caged Birds Freed." [Footwork] 89, p. 42.
2541. HOLLANDER, Jean
"The Dignity of Unmolested Modern Statues." [US1] (22/23) Spr 89, p. 22.
"Flying from the Sun." [Footwork] 89, p. 55.
"H. Brooks: A Simple Officer." [US1] (22/23) Spr 89, p. 23.
"Trees, Like Children." [Footwork] 89, p. 55.
"Ways to Die." [US1] (22/23) Spr 89, p. 22.
2542. HOLLANDER, John
"About the Canzone." [Poetry] (153:6) Mr 89, p. 347-348.
"Air for the Musette." [Salm] (84) Fall 89, p. 51.
"Any Other Names." [Pequod] (28/29/30) 89, p. 45.
"From Out of the Black." [Nat] (248:16) 24 Ap 89, p. 568.
"Ghazals." [Nat] (249:2) 10 Jl 89, p. 68.
"Into the Black." [Nat] (248:16) 24 Ap 89, p. 568.
"An Old Counting-Game." [NewYRB] (36:1) 1 F 89, p. 4.
"An Old-Fashioned Song" ("Nous n'irons plus au bois"). [NewRep] (200:13) 27 Mr
89, p. 30.
"Perseus Holds Medusa's Head Aloft." [Salm] (84) Fall 89, p. 50.
"Summer Day." [NewYorker] (65:26) 14 Ag 89, p. 28.
"With a Book of Verses." [Pequod] (28/29/30) 89, p. 47.
"With a Copy of *The Figure of Echo*" (to A. B. Giamatti). [Pequod] (28/29/30) 89,
p. 48.
"With a Copy of the Loeb Edition of Aristotle's *Poetics* and Longinus *On the
Sublime*." [Pequod] (28/29/30) 89, p. 46.
"With My Old Copy of *Death's Jest-Book*" (to Larry Day). [Pequod] (28/29/30) 89,

p. 49.
2543. HOLLANDER, Martha
"Accidents." [SouthwR] (74:4) Aut 89, p. 546-547.
"Pillar of Salt." [YaleR] (79:1) Aut 89, p. 124.
"When We Ride Off." [ParisR] (31:113) Wint 89, p. 90-91.
2544. HOLLEY, Margaret
"Pumpkin Face." [SoCoast] (7) Spr-Fall 89, p. 10.
2545. HOLLINSON, Jayne
"After Babel." [Stand] (30:4) Aut 89, p. 60-61.
2546. HOLLO, Anselm
"Arcana Gardens." [NewAW] (5) Fall 89, p. 91-97.
"The conditions for life to begin" (tr. of Pentti Saarikoski). [PoetryE] (27) Spr 89, p.
156.
"A free enterprise economy and the right to say" (tr. of Pentti Saarikoski). [PoetryE]
(27) Spr 89, p. 159.
"Had my last cup of tea" (tr. of Pentti Saarikoski). [PoetryE] (27) Spr 89, p. 154.
"High poetry, the sun sets, the sun rises" (tr. of Pentti Saarikoski). [PoetryE] (27)
Spr 89, p. 148.
"I live in Helsinki" (tr. of Pentti Saarikoski). [PoetryE] (27) Spr 89, p. 146.
"The new suburbs surrounded by woods" (tr. of Pentti Saarikoski). [PoetryE] (27)
Spr 89, p. 158.
"No need to decide" (tr. of Pentti Saarikoski). [PoetryE] (27) Spr 89, p. 152-153.
"Not sure" (tr. of Pentti Saarikoski). [PoetryE] (27) Spr 89, p. 160.
"Out Loud" (tr. of Pentti Saarikoski). [PoetryE] (27) Spr 89, p. 144-145.
"Parliament has been dissolved" (tr. of Pentti Saarikoski). [PoetryE] (27) Spr 89, p.
155.
"Psalm 4" (tr. of Mahmoud Darwish, w. Lena Jayyusi). [PoetryE] (27) Spr 89, p.
73.
"Psalm 5" (tr. of Mahmoud Darwish, w. Lena Jayyusi). [PoetryE] (27) Spr 89, p.
74.
"Psalm 7" (tr. of Mahmoud Darwish, w. Lena Jayyusi). [PoetryE] (27) Spr 89, p.
75-76.
"Psalm 8" (tr. of Mahmoud Darwish, w. Lena Jayyusi). [PoetryE] (27) Spr 89, p.
77.
"Psalm 13" (tr. of Mahmoud Darwish, w. Lena Jayyusi). [PoetryE] (27) Spr 89, p.
79.
"Sales Figures are Up!" (for B.G.). [Screens] (1) 89, p. 155.
"Sun, hot through the window" (tr. of Pentti Saarikoski). [PoetryE] (27) Spr 89, p.
149-151.
"This started two years before the wars" (tr. of Pentti Saarikoski). [PoetryE] (27)
Spr 89, p. 147.
"The Tiarnia Trilogy" (Selections: XLIII, XVIV, XLVIII, LII, tr. of Pentti
Saarikoski). [PoetryE] (27) Spr 89, p. 161-166.
"Untitled: Peace to the people of this earth" (tr. of Tomaz Salamun, w. the author).
[Field] (40) Spr 89, p. 74-75.
"Vacation Time" (tr. of Tomaz Salamun, w. the author). [ColR] (NS 16:1) Spr-Sum
89, p. 103.
"What are they talking about" (tr. of Pentti Saarikoski). [PoetryE] (27) Spr 89, p.
157.
2547. HOLMES, Bobby
"The Walls." [NegC] (9:1) 89, p. 10.
2548. HOLMES, Elizabeth
"Even Your Faults Were Charming Then." [MichQR] (28:2) Spr 89, p. 235.
"A Woman and Two Rugs." [MichQR] (28:2) Spr 89, p. 236.
2549. HOLMES, Janet
"Seven Lyrics of Autumn." [PraS] (63:2) Sum 89, p. 82-84.
2550. HOLMES, Maire C.
"Touch." [Vis] (29) 89, p. 16.
2551. HOLMES, Olivia
"Not Cervantes." [NegC] (9:2) 89, p. 52.
2552. HOLMES, Thomas Alan
"Strength." [FloridaR] (16:2/3) Fall-Wint 89, p. 200.
2553. HOLSTEIN, Michael
"Ewer Tiger in Yellowed Green Glaze" (E. Jin period, 317-420 A.D.). [Pig] (15)
88, p. 7.
"Plum Blossoms and Rock: Three Poems." [Pig] (15) 88, p. 7.

2554. HOLT, John Dominis
"Joe Kekela." [BambooR] (44) Fall 89, p. 12-14.
"Ka'ili Pau." [Hawai'iR] (13:3) Fall 89, p. 64-65.
2555. HOLT, Rochelle Lynn
"A Thank You Sonnet for Gwendolyn Brooks" (who read at Union College in
Cranford, NJ, on 10/15/85). [ColR] (NS 16:1) Spr-Sum 89, p. 61.
2556. HOLTAN, Peder
"Itinerary." [HampSPR] Wint 89, p. 49.
"Orchestra." [HampSPR] Wint 89, p. 48.
2557. HOLTZMAN, Clark
"The Walking." [SmPd] (26:3 #77) Fall 89, p. 22.
2558. HOLZER, Ryszard
"Bedziemy Oddychac Cicho." [AnotherCM] (19) 89, p. 112.
"Breath" (tr. by Daniel Bourne). [AnotherCM] (19) 89, p. 111.
"Cat Hunters #1" (tr. by Daniel Bourne). [AnotherCM] (19) 89, p. 107.
"Cat Hunters #2" (tr. by Daniel Bourne). [AnotherCM] (19) 89, p. 109.
"Drugi Wiersz Na Ten Sam Temat (Lowcy Kotów)." [AnotherCM] (19) 89, p. 108.
"Lowcy Kotów." [AnotherCM] (19) 89, p. 106.
"Oddech." [AnotherCM] (19) 89, p. 110.
"Postcard from Martial Law" (to Edward Nowak, the Lenin Steelmills, tr. by Daniel
Bourne). [Pequod] (26/27) 89, p. 14.
"We'll Breathe Quietly" (tr. by Daniel Bourne). [AnotherCM] (19) 89, p. 113.
2559. HOMER
"Hector Returns to Troy: The *Iliad*, Book VI" (tr. by Robert Fagles). [TriQ] (77)
Wint 89-90, p. 302-319.
"Odyssey" (Book VI, tr. by Harvey Bialy). [Notus] (4:1) Spr 89, p. 29-38.
"The Shield of Achilles" *(The Iliad*, Book XVIII, tr. by Robert Fagles). [GrandS]
(8:3) Spr 89, p. 147-165.
2560. HOMER, Art
"Cottonwood Blue." [Poetry] (154:5) Ag 89, p. 262-263.
"Late Portrait of Robert." [SouthernPR] (29:1) Spr 89, p. 70-71.
"Mary Cassatt: The Bath." [TarRP] (29:1) Fall 89, p. 5-6.
"Nocturne Moderne." [Poetry] (154:5) Ag 89, p. 262.
"Pawnshops." [SouthernPR] (29:2) Fall 89, p. 29-30.
HONG, Guo
See GUO, Hong
2561. HONIG, Edwin
"Buildings and Tombs" (London last summer). [Witness] (2:1) Spr 88, p. 44-45.
"A Late Visit to Robert Graves" (for Elaine Kerrigan). [Agni] (28) 89, p. 241-242.
"Sown Seeds." [ConnPR] (8:1) 89, p. 23-24.
2562. HOOD, Mary
"Erosion." [EmeraldCR] (1989) c1988, p. 100-101.
"Old Friend." [EmeraldCR] (1989) c1988, p. 101-102.
2563. HOOGLAND, Cornelia
"Frog Prince." [MassR] (30:1) Spr 89, p. 84.
"Hoard." [AntigR] (76) Wint 89, p. 116.
"Photograph of a Split-Fern." [MalR] (86) Spr 89, p. 101.
"What I Know of Her." [AntigR] (76) Wint 89, p. 117.
"White Bread and Cake." [MassR] (30:1) Spr 89, p. 83.
2564. HOOPER, Patricia
"There." [PassN] (10:1) Wint 89, p. 20.
2565. HOOPER, Virginia
"Argument for Resurrection." [Sulfur] (9:1, #24) Spr 89, p. 73-75.
"The Book of Dreams." [Sulfur] (9:1, #24) Spr 89, p. 71-73.
"Climbing Out of the Cage." [DenQ] (24:2) Fall 89, p. 55-57.
"The Decision Making Stage." [NewAW] (5) Fall 89, p. 99.
"Deep Season." [SouthwR] (74:1) Wint 89, p. 75.
"False Laughter [Response to Clamor]." [NewAW] (5) Fall 89, p. 98.
"Flight into Idleness." [Epoch] (38:1) 89, p. 14-20.
"Post Cards." [SouthwR] (74:1) Wint 89, p. 75-76.
HOOSE, Susanna van
See Van HOOSE, Susanna
2566. HOOVER, Paul
"The Artist." [AnotherCM] (20) 89, p. 77.
"The Novel." [MissR] (18:1, #52) 89, p. 62-66.
"White Noise." [AnotherCM] (20) 89, p. 78.

2567. HOPE, Akua Lezli
"For Bob Thompson." [Contact] (9:53/54/55) Sum-Fall 89, p. 14.
"For the Homeless" (MLK Day 1987). [Obs] (3:3) Wint 88, p. 23.
"Interpenetration Side Two" (For Thrill). [Obs] (3:3) Wint 88, p. 22.
"New Alchemy" (for Wilfredo Lam). [Contact] (9:53/54/55) Sum-Fall 89, p. 15.
"Report on Training Assignment One." [Contact] (9:53/54/55) Sum-Fall 89, p. 16.
"A Valentine." [Obs] (3:3) Wint 88, p. 21-22.
"When the Horn Fits, Blow It." [Contact] (9:53/54/55) Sum-Fall 89, p. 16.
2568. HOPES, David Brendan
"Mountain Moving Day." [SouthernPR] (29:2) Fall 89, p. 51.
2569. HOPKINS, Els T. Cecile
"For Tibetan Gyume Monks Who Celebrate Sangwadupa Communion . . ." (In
Memoriam, David M. Heinlein). [US1] (22/23) Spr 89, p. 33.
2570. HOPPER, Robert
"Confessions." [Mildred] (3:1) Spr-Sum 89, p. 90.
"Didya Hear the One?" [Mildred] (3:1) Spr-Sum 89, p. 91.
2571. HORACE
"Third Poem, Odes Book I" (tr. by Michael Taylor). [Zyzzyva] (5:3, #19) Fall 89, p.
121-122.
2572. HORD, Fred Lee
"Our Love Ain't Evol." [Obs] (2:1) Spr 87, p. 52-56.
"Words." [Obs] (2:1) Spr 87, p. 51-52.
2573. HORNE, Lewis
"The Big Sadness." [SouthernR] (25:1) Wint 89, p. 168-169.
"Under a Morning Sky in Winter." [SouthernR] (25:1) Wint 89, p. 169-170.
2574. HORNOSTY, Cornelia (Cornelia C.)
"Bag Man." [Event] (18:2) Sum 89, p. 70-71.
"Widow Gazing at Lake Michigan." [CanLit] (121) Sum 89, p. 84-85.
2575. HOROWITZ, Mikhail
"The 12." [HeavenB] (7) Wint 89, p. 38.
"What I'm Doing at This Very Moment in 12 Parallel Universes." [HeavenB] (7)
Wint 89, p. 39.
2576. HORSTING, Eric
"1945: Oma in Amsterdam as the War Ends." [CumbPR] (8:2) Spr 89, p. 84.
"At Perry Lake, in Kansas." [BellR] (12:2, #26) Fall 89, p. 8.
"Blizzard." [ConnPR] (8:1) 89, p. 35.
2577. HORTON, Barbara
"A Bridge Begins in the Trees" (Commended). [StoneC] (17:1/2) Fall-Wint 89-90,
p. prelim. p. 7.
2578. HORVATH, Brooke
"Abrasion." [DenQ] (23:3/4) Wint-Spr 89, p. 15.
"Academia: Florence." [Poetry] (153:6) Mr 89, p. 313-314.
"Christmas Eve." [DenQ] (23:3/4) Wint-Spr 89, p. 16.
"Christmas Morning." [DenQ] (23:3/4) Wint-Spr 89, p. 17.
"Elegy." [ChiR] (36:3/4) 89, p. 35-36.
"My Grandparents' House." [DenQ] (23:3/4) Wint-Spr 89, p. 18.
2579. HOSPITAL, Caroline
"Bedtime Story." [Americas] (17:1) Spr 89, p. 50.
"Dear Tía." [Americas] (17:1) Spr 89, p. 48.
"Lovers." [Americas] (17:1) Spr 89, p. 51.
"Papa." [Americas] (17:1) Spr 89, p. 49.
"Salvation Part II." [Americas] (17:1) Spr 89, p. 52.
2580. HOTCH, Phyllis
"Camille Claudel" (a great sculptress, she was Rodin's pupil and then his mistress).
[Vis] (30) 89, p. 16-18.
2581. HOUCHIN, Ron
"Apple Time." [CinPR] (20) Fall 89, p. 25.
"Death Notice." [MSS] (6:3) 89, p. 206.
"The Long Knife." [PoetL] (84:3) Fall 89, p. 56.
"The Red Jeep." [PaintedB] (38) 89, p. 66.
"The Thing Is, I Am Bread." [PaintedB] (38) 89, p. 65.
2582. HOUGEN, Judith
"This Town That Takes the Series." [IndR] (13:1) Wint 89, p. 28.
2583. HOUGHTELING, Marla Key
"A Woman's Life Through Trees." [PassN] (10:2) Sum 89, p. 17.

2584. HOUGHTON, Timothy
"Below Two Skies." [DenQ] (24:2) Fall 89, p. 58-59.
2585. HOUSE, Tom
"The Welder." [SlipS] (9) 89, p. 5.
2586. HOUSTON, Beth
"Falling in Love." [Outbr] (20) 89, p. 76.
"Grandmother's Garden." [Kalliope] (11:2) 89, p. 35-36.
"The Jungle of My Body." [SinW] (38) Sum-Fall 89, p. 79-80.
"The News." [Comm] (116:2) Ja 27, 89, p. 46.
2587. HOUSTON, Lee
"Break Time at City Lights." [Obs] (2:3) Wint 87, p. 42.
HOUTEN, Lois van
See Van HOUTEN, Lois
HOVANESSIAN, Diana Der
See DER-HOVANESSIAN, Diana
2588. HOVELL, Laurie
"Ambedkar, 79" (tr. of Namdeo Dhasal, w. Asha Mundlay and Jayant Karve).
[Trans] (21) Spr 89, p. 234-235.
"Just a Bit More Time" (tr. of Namdeo Dhasal, w. Jayant Karve). [Trans] (21) Spr
89, p. 235.
2589. HOWARD, Ben
"For the Calvinists." [Poetry] (154:4) Jl 89, p. 215.
"In the Regions of Belief." [Poetry] (153:6) Mr 89, p. 332.
"Lute Music." [Poetry] (153:6) Mr 89, p. 332-334.
"Sabula." [Poetry] (154:4) Jl 89, p. 214.
2590. HOWARD, David
"Care of the Commanding Officer." [Descant] (20:3/4, #66/67) Fall-Wint 89, p. 208.
"The Portrait Gallery." [Descant] (20:3/4, #66/67) Fall-Wint 89, p. 209-212.
2591. HOWARD, Ginnah
"Winter Cache." [Vis] (31) 89, p. 26.
2592. HOWARD, Richard
"Et Dona Ferentes" (For Eleanor Cook). [Raritan] (8:4) Spr 89, p. 30-33.
"For Robert Phelps, Dead at 66." [NewRep] (201:19) 6 N 89, p. 107.
"Poem Beginning with a Line by Isadora Duncan." [PartR] (56:3) Sum 89, p.
442-444.
"La Voix" (tr. of Pierre Charles Baudelaire). [SouthwR] (74:2) Spr 89, p. 152-153.
2593. HOWE, Fanny
"Definitions of a Soul." [Screens] (1) 89, p. 138.
"The End of Advent." [Screens] (1) 89, p. 136-137.
2594. HOWE, Susan
"A Bibliography of the King's Book, or, Eikon Basilike" (Part Two, Selections).
[Temblor] (9) 89, p. 31-58.
"The Big Tradition." [Shen] (39:2) Sum 89, p. 53-54.
2595. HOWELL, Bill
"Descousse, Isle Madame" (for Lulu and Silver Don). [AntigR] (77/78) Spr-Sum 89,
p. 146.
"Slitting the Deadman's Throat" (for Marc Patrick Terrio, Champion of Isle Madame,
Cape Breton). [AntigR] (77/78) Spr-Sum 89, p. 148.
"What the Fiddles Never Forget." [AntigR] (77/78) Spr-Sum 89, p. 147.
2596. HOWELL, Christopher
"The Blue Flight Back: Adam's Song." [MissR] (17:3, #51), p. 30-31.
"Contemporary Theory." [GettyR] (2:2) Spr 89, p. 226.
"Exclusivity." [MissR] (17:3, #51), p. 34-35.
"Streets." [MissR] (17:3, #51), p. 32-33.
2597. HOWELL, John D.
"The 4A Shuffle." [MissouriR] (12:3) 89, p. 170-191.
"I'm Not Confessing Anything." [MissouriR] (12:3) 89, p. 169-170.
2598. HOWES, Mary
"Cutoff." [Dandel] (16:2) Fall-Wint 89, p. 27.
"Easy Street." [Dandel] (16:2) Fall-Wint 89, p. 29.
"Fuzzy." [Dandel] (16:2) Fall-Wint 89, p. 28.
2599. HOWLAND, Ted
"I Watched My Father." [CimR] (87) Ap 89, p. 63.
2600. HOZ, León de la
"Creation Sunday" (tr. by Lourdes González). [Pig] (15) 88, p. 65.
"The Worm or Desire" (tr. by Lourdes González). [Pig] (15) 88, p. 64.

2601. HSI, Chou
"Sending Off Ssz Tuan to Return East" (tr. by Paul Hansen). [LitR] (32:3) Spr 89,
p. 353.
"Sent to Huai Ku" (tr. by Paul Hansen). [LitR] (32:3) Spr 89, p. 352.
2602. HSIANG, Yü
"Frontier Song" (tr. by Eric Sackheim). [LitR] (32:3) Spr 89, p. 420.
2603. HSU, Tsai-ssu
"Party Ending" (tr. by Graeme Wilson). [DenQ] (24:1) Sum 89, p. 86.
2604. HSÜ, Wei
"Bamboo and Rock" (tr. by James M. Cryer). [LitR] (32:3) Spr 89, p. 412.
"Butterflies on a Fan" (tr. by James M. Cryer). [LitR] (32:3) Spr 89, p. 411.
"Cloud Gate Temple: Painting Plum Trees" (tr. by James M. Cryer). [LitR] (32:3)
Spr 89, p. 409.
"Crabs" (tr. by James M. Cryer). [LitR] (32:3) Spr 89, p. 411.
"Dark Stream: Album Leaf" (tr. by James M. Cryer). [LitR] (32:3) Spr 89, p. 410.
"Painting Bamboo" (tr. by James M. Cryer). [LitR] (32:3) Spr 89, p. 410.
"Pear Blossoms" (tr. by James M. Cryer). [LitR] (32:3) Spr 89, p. 409.
"Two Locusts" (tr. by James M. Cryer). [LitR] (32:3) Spr 89, p. 412.
2605. HSÜ, Yün
"Roaming in the Clouds I Come Back Alone" (tr. by Paul Hansen). [LitR] (32:3) Spr
89, p. 354.
2606. HSÜEH, T'ao
"Poem in Response to Commissioner Wu" (tr. by Jeanne Larsen). [LitR] (32:3) Spr
89, p. 399.
"Spring-Gazing Song" (tr. by Carolyn Kizer). [LitR] (32:3) Spr 89, p. 326.
"Spring-Gazing Song II" (tr. by Carolyn Kizer). [LitR] (32:3) Spr 89, p. 326.
"To General Gao, Who Smashed the Rebellion for the Son of Heaven" (tr. by Jeanne
Larsen). [LitR] (32:3) Spr 89, p. 399.
"Weaving Love-knots" (tr. by Carolyn Kizer). [LitR] (32:3) Spr 89, p. 326.
"Weaving Love-knots #13" (tr. by Carolyn Kizer). [LitR] (32:3) Spr 89, p. 326.
HUA, Bai
See BAI, Hua
2607. HUACO, Enrique
"And If in the History of Man" (tr. by Joe Bolton). [Pig] (15) 88, p. 92.
"Justification of a War" (tr. by Joe Bolton). [Pig] (15) 88, p. 91.
2608. HUANG, Shen
"When cherries are red and elm pods naked" (tr. by Carolyn Lau). [YellowS] (31)
Aut 89, p. 5.
2609. HUANG, Yong-yu
"The Girl I Knew Is Dead" (tr. by Edward Morin and Dennis Ding). [Pig] (15) 88,
p. 6.
2610. HUBER, Carol Wadleigh
"The Parable of the Wise and Foolish Weavers." [PoetryNW] (30:2) Sum 89, p.
33-34.
2611. HUBER, J. Argus
"Life at the Semiconductor Plant, 1981." [SlipS] (9) 89, p. 84.
2612. HUDGINS, Andrew
"After the Prom." [Ploughs] (15:4) Wint 89-90, p. 107.
"The Air." [SouthernR] (25:1) Wint 89, p. 144.
"As a Child in the Temple." [ParisR] (31:113) Wint 89, p. 224.
"Castrating Bulls with My Grandpa." [ParisR] (31:113) Wint 89, p. 225.
"Hot August Nights." [IndR] (13:1) Wint 89, p. 24-25.
"A Mystery." [GeoR] (43:1) Spr 89, p. 120.
"An Old Joke: Christ and the Woman Take in Adultery." [NewRep] (201:10) 4 S 89,
p. 38.
"Thus." [Atlantic] (263:1) Ja 89, p. 39.
"Web." [SouthernR] (25:1) Wint 89, p. 143.
2613. HUDSON, Marc
"Orkney Diptych." [NewRena] (7:3, #23) 89, p. 118-121.
2614. HUDZIK, Robert
"Eating Chinese" (for Jim Cummins). [CinPR] (19) Spr 89, p. 55.
2615. HUECKSTEDT, Robert A.
"To Father Gone to Heaven" (tr. of Sarveshvar Dayal Saxena). [Pig] (15) 88, p. 15.
2616. HUESGEN, Jan
"Living with What Belongs to Us." [SoDakR] (27:3) Aut 89, p. 50-51.
"Unfamiliar Waters." [SoDakR] (27:3) Aut 89, p. 52-53.

2617. HUFF, Robert
"A." [Margin] (8) 89, p. 30.
"Bittern." [Margin] (8) 89, p. 30.
"Red Phalaropes." [Margin] (8) 89, p. 46.
2618. HUFFSTICKLER, Albert
"My Father's Pipes." [Lactuca] (13) N 89, p. 69.
"Political Refugee." [Lactuca] (13) N 89, p. 68.
"Still Trying to Get the Last Word In." [Lactuca] (13) N 89, p. 70.
"Ten-Thirty at Night on Carol's Forty-First Birthday." [SlipS] (9) 89, p. 6.
"Where I Was." [Lactuca] (13) N 89, p. 67-68.
2619. HUGGINS, Peter
"The Dare Stones." [NegC] (9:1) 89, p. 44.
"The Underwater Archangel." [NegC] (9:1) 89, p. 45.
"Webster's Bar." [ApalQ] (31) 89, p. 48.
"Who Can Tell a Man?" [NegC] (9:2) 89, p. 53-54.
2620. HUGHES, C. G. (Charlie G., Charles G.)
"From the Doldrums." [CumbPR] (9:1) Fall 89, p. 31.
"Sheep Song." [CinPR] (20) Fall 89, p. 18.
2621. HUGHES, Henry J.
"Gettysburg." [CapeR] (24:1) Spr 89, p. 21.
"Men Holding Eggs." [CapeR] (24:1) Spr 89, p. 20.
"Working on the Cable Team, New York, 1987." [CarolQ] (41:3) Spr 89, p. 27.
2622. HUGHES, Ingrid
"Crazy Baby." [MassR] (30:3) Aut 89, p. 485-486.
"Having It All." [NegC] (9:1) 89, p. 101.
2623. HUGHES, Pamela
"Fires." [BrooklynR] (6) 89, p. 53.
"A Stranger in Paradise." [BrooklynR] (6) 89, p. 54-55.
2624. HUGHES, Peter
"The Eve of St. Cecilia." [Pequod] (26/27) 89, p. 91.
"Premonition." [Pequod] (26/27) 89, p. 90.
2625. HUGHES, Sophie
"Cow Judging at the Topsham Fair" (a poem for two voices and a chorus).
        [SingHM] (16) 89, p. 56-57.
"The Offering Stance." [Confr] (39/40) Fall 88-Wint 89, p. 184.
"Seattle Museum" (Standing Buddha, China, from Hebei Province Northern Qi
        Dynasty, 550-557. White marble). [HeavenB] (7) Wint 89, p. 5.
2626. HUGHES, Ted
"For the Duration." [Vis] (30) 89, p. 25-26.
"On the Reservations" (for Jack Brown). [Vis] (30) 89, p. 20-24.
2627. HUGS, Diane
"Who Needs a Perfect Body?" [SinW] (39) Wint 89-90, p. 34.
2628. HULL, Lynda
"The Crossing, 1927." [QW] (28) Wint-Spr 89, p. 78-80.
"Fairy Tales: Steel Engravings." [DenQ] (23:3/4) Wint-Spr 89, p. 104-105.
"Hospice." [Ploughs] (15:1) 89, p. 52-54.
"The Star Ledger." [Ploughs] (15:1) 89, p. 50-51.
"Utsuroi." [QW] (28) Wint-Spr 89, p. 81-82.
2629. HULL, Robert
"Camera." [CumbPR] (8:2) Spr 89, p. 47-49.
"Encouraging Shakespeare." [CumbPR] (8:2) Spr 89, p. 35-37.
"Frogs." [CumbPR] (8:2) Spr 89, p. 44-46.
"Gnome." [CumbPR] (8:2) Spr 89, p. 38-40.
"Wishing Well — £37-50." [CumbPR] (8:2) Spr 89, p. 41-43.
2630. HULSE, Michael
"An Aluminium Casket Would Be a Good Idea." [Stand] (30:1) Wint 88-89, p.
        60-62.
2631. HUMES, Harry
"357 Ash Alley." [WestB] (23) 89, p. 55-56.
"The Blue Heron on Assoteague." [CinPR] (19) Spr 89, p. 16.
"The Catfish." [WestB] (23) 89, p. 56.
"Certain Mornings Are Different." [Journal] (13:1) Spr-Sum 89, p. 36.
"The Fan House Tunnel." [PoetryNW] (30:2) Sum 89, p. 35-36.
"The Glacier with My Family's Name." [PoetryNW] (30:2) Sum 89, p. 34-35.
"The Journalist." [CinPR] (19) Spr 89, p. 14-15.
"A Map of White Weather." [Journal] (13:1) Spr-Sum 89, p. 39.

"My Father Planted Tomatoes in Coal Ash." [Poetry] (154:3) Je 89, p. 133.
"The Note on the Counter." [WestB] (23) 89, p. 57.
"The Pigeon Father." [Journal] (13:1) Spr-Sum 89, p. 37-38.
2632. HUMMER, T. R.
"Austerity in Vermont." [GettyR] (2:2) Spr 89, p. 341-342.
"Slow Train Through Georgia." [GettyR] (2:3) Sum 89, p. 413.
2633. HUMPHREYS, Helen
"Night Vocabulary." [Grain] (17:3) Fall 89, p. 16.
2634. HUMPHRIES, Jefferson
"Mardi Gras." [SoCoast] (5) Spr 88, p. 3.
HUNG-TAO, Yüan
   See YÜAN, Hung-tao
2635. HUNT, Holly
"Joseph's Cousin." [Nimrod] (33:1) Fall-Wint 89, p. 81.
2636. HUNT, Leigh
"An Analysis of Greatness." [Amelia] (5:3, #14) 89, p. 102.
"Morning Concert." [Amelia] (5:3, #14) 89, p. 103.
2637. HUNT, Tim
"Poem for My Uncle." [SoCoast] (5) Spr 88, p. 37.
"Shopping with the Poet" (for Bill Matthews). [SoCoast] (5) Spr 88, p. 30.
2638. HUNTER, Donnell
"A Few Words of Advice for Emma Bovary." [HayF] (4) Spr 89, p. 46.
"For Every New Star My Life Turns a Little Crazy." [Interim] (8:2) Fall 89, p. 42.
"For the McDonalds Poet in Missoula." [Interim] (8:2) Fall 89, p. 41.
2639. HUNTER, Paul C.
"Highwire." [BelPoJ] (39:4) Sum 89, p. 2-4.
"Hotwire." [Farm] (6:2) Fall 89, p. 42-44.
2640. HUNTINGTON, Cynthia
"Bill the Landlord Learns to Fly." [KenR] (NS 11:3) Sum 89, p. 21-22.
"Breaking." [KenR] (NS 11:3) Sum 89, p. 23-24.
"Passing Through Hometown." [KenR] (NS 11:3) Sum 89, p. 22-23.
2641. HURLEY, Maureen
"Barking Up the Wrong Tree." [Outbr] (20) 89, p. 64.
"Blueberries" (for Boschka Layton). [Outbr] (20) 89, p. 65.
"Letter to 'Crappa'" (For Roger Kent 1910-1982). [ChamLR] (3:1, #5) Fall 89, p.
      155-156.
"Merwin's Inlet." [ChamLR] (3:1, #5) Fall 89, p. 157.
"On Hearing John Handy Play Jazz After Midnight, New Year's Eve." [Outbr] (20)
      89, p. 63.
"On the Anniversary of James Wright's Death." [ChamLR] (3:1, #5) Fall 89, p. 158.
2642. HURLOW, Marcia L.
"For the Linguist Doing Field Work." [Poetry] (155:3) D 89, p. 212.
"The Sisterhood" (Shakertown at Pleasant Hill, Kentucky). [Poetry] (153:5) F 89, p.
      299-300.
2643. HURTADO, Rogelio Fabio
"Cita Aplazada." [LindLM] (8:4) O-D 89, p. 21.
"Parque Manila" (A Juan Miguel Espino, amigo). [LindLM] (8:4) O-D 89, p. 21.
"Soledad A.M." [LindLM] (8:4) O-D 89, p. 21.
2644. HUSSEY, Charlotte
"After the Andrew Wyeth Painting, Alvaro and Christina." [AntigR] (77/78)
      Spr-Sum 89, p. 201.
"Holiday Inn Snapshot." [AntigR] (77/78) Spr-Sum 89, p. 202.
2645. HUTCHINGS, Pat
"Dreams After Planting." [ClockR] (5:2) 89, p. 31.
2646. HUTCHISON, Joseph
"Lethe." [MissR] (17:3, #51), p. 68-69.
"Out of the Shadow River." [CharR] (15:1) Spr 89, p. 63.
"Recalling the Solstice." [MissR] (17:3, #51), p. 74.
"Robert Emmitt." [WritersF] (15) Fall 89, p. 24-25.
"The Shadow in the Well." [MissR] (17:3, #51), p. 70-73.
"The Stone Forest." [WritersF] (15) Fall 89, p. 25.
"The Trembling." [Hudson] (42:1) Spr 89, p. 99.
"Vacation." [WestB] (23) 89, p. 63.
2647. HUTH, Geof (Geof A.)
"At." [HampSPR] Wint 89, p. 18.
"Carl Becomes Cook." [FreeL] (2) Sum 89, p. 29.

"Carl's Soliloquy." [FreeL] (2) Sum 89, p. 30.
"Conversations with a Mind." [Mildred] (3:1) Spr-Sum 89, p. 100-101.
"Erin's Eyes of October." [Mildred] (3:1) Spr-Sum 89, p. 99.
"Kiss." [Mildred] (3:1) Spr-Sum 89, p. 99.
"Lip." [HampSPR] Wint 89, p. 17.
"Neglect." [AmerPoR] (18:2) Mr-Ap 89, p. 22.
"Sentence." [AmerPoR] (18:2) Mr-Ap 89, p. 22.
"To Hunt, There's Nothing Else, to Hunt." [Journal] (12:2) Fall-Wint 88-89, p. 17.
"La Vida Significa Nada." [CentR] (33:2) Spr 89, p. 139-140.
2648. HWANG, Byong Ha
"La Canción de un Mojado, el Limpiador José." [Mester] (18:1) Spr 89, p. 52.
HYE, Yung Park
See PARK, Hye Yung
2649. HYETT, Barbara Helfgott
"At the Zoo When It Rains." [Kalliope] (10:1/2) 88, p. 80-81.
"Poem for a Son Leaving Home." [Kalliope] (10:1/2) 88, p. 91.
2650. HYLEN, Susan K.
"Midwinter in New Hampshire, 1967." [StoneC] (16:3/4) Spr-Sum 89, p. 45.
2651. HYMAS, June Hopper
"All Those Little Girls." [Mildred] (3:1) Spr-Sum 89, p. 78-79.
"Windows Overlooking a Ravine." [NegC] (9:1) 89, p. 81.
2652. IAMMARTINO, Dave
"Pancho and Lefty." [HangL] (55) 89, p. 62.
2653. IBUR, Jane Ellen
"Eight Riddles." [WebR] (14:1) Spr 89, p. 108-109.
2654. IBYKOS
"Eros" (in Greek & English, tr. by Michael L. Johnson). [BallSUF] (30:4) Aut 89,
    p. 36.
2655. ICHIDA, Karl K.
"An Early Dinner." [BambooR] (44) Fall 89, p. 15-16.
2656. ICHIGEN
"Joshu Exclaimed, 'Dog's No Buddha'" (tr. by Lucien Stryk). [LitR] (32:3) Spr 89,
    p. 359.
2657. IDDINGS, Kathleen
"I Hadn't Been Home in Years." [Footwork] 89, p. 47.
2658. IGNATOW, David
"Adolescence." [TampaR] (2) 89, p. 11-12.
"Autumnal Journey" (tr. of Johannes Edfelt, w. Leif Sjöberg). [Pequod] (26/27) 89,
    p. 26.
"Denied." [VirQR] (65:3) Sum 89, p. 442-444.
"Questioning." [OxfordM] (5:1) Spr-Sum 89, p. 10.
"Quit." [OxfordM] (5:1) Spr-Sum 89, p. 11.
"This Is You" (tr. of Johannes Edfelt, w. Leif Sjöberg). [Pequod] (26/27) 89, p. 26.
2659. IKACH, Lynne
"Poetry in Yiddish" (tr. of Aleksandar Petrov). [ColR] (NS 16:1) Spr-Sum 89, p.
    99.
2660. IKKYU
"About the Hall at Ryusho-Ji" (tr. by Jim Sanford). [LitR] (32:3) Spr 89, p. 358.
"Beneath the Trees, Among the Boulders, a Rustic Hut" (tr. by Jim Sanford). [LitR]
    (32:3) Spr 89, p. 358.
"A Natural Way" (tr. by Jim Sanford). [LitR] (32:3) Spr 89, p. 358.
2661. ILLYÉS, Gyula
"Ebb Tide" (tr. by Bruce Berlind, w. Maria Korosy). [Colum] (14) 89, p. 125.
"Elegy" (tr. by Nicholas Kolumban). [NowestR] (27:2) 89, p. 19-20.
"Evening Song" (tr. by Bruce Berlind, w. Maria Korosy). [Colum] (14) 89, p. 124.
"Ode to Bartok" (tr. by Margaret Avison and Ilonn Duczynska). [CanLit] (120) Spr
    89, p. 46-49.
2662. IMLAH, Mick
"Goldilocks." [Pequod] (26/27) 89, p. 92-95.
2663. INADA, Lawson Fusao
"What Can I Say?" (For Kathryn VanSpanckeren, who asked, and for Diana Savas,
    who told). [TampaR] (2) 89, p. 82-86.
2664. INEZ, Colette
"Flightsong." [Kalliope] (10:1/2) 88, p. 25.
"Foster Mother Dee's Departure." [WestB] (23) 89, p. 78-79.
"Marthe's Almanac." [AntR] (47:3) Sum 89, p. 322-323.

"Reverie, Holy Cross Cemetery." [WestB] (23) 89, p. 77.
"Ruby Scenes of Autumn Losses." [WestB] (23) 89, p. 79.
"Seeing Music in Winter." [DenQ] (24:2) Fall 89, p. 60-61.
"To Invoke the Great Nebulous Crab." [GrahamHR] (12) Spr 89, p. 39.
"Waves of Lakeside." [WestB] (23) 89, p. 80.
2665. ING, Mahealani
"Keauhou (Song of Renewal." [Hawai'iR] (13:3) Fall 89, p. 1.
"Kid Standing Outside Beretania Follies." [Hawai'iR] (13:1, #25) Spr 89, p. 39-40.
2666. INGEBRETSEN, Mark
"The Second Coming." [Plain] (10:1) 89, p. 32.
2667. INGERSON, Martin I.
"Blue Venus by the Water." [BellArk] (5:2) Mr-Ap 89, p. 9.
"Early Autumn" (for Ingrid). [BellArk] (5:6) N-D 89, p. 1.
"The Face Changers." [BellArk] (5:2) Mr-Ap 89, p. 8-9.
"Perspectives: Away to a New Day." [BellArk] (5:5) S-O 89, p. 7.
"Prelude: For Ingrid." [BellArk] (5:1) Ja-F 89, p. 5.
"Red Blonde, You, Early Spring." [BellArk] (5:2) Mr-Ap 89, p. 9.
"The Snow Leopards." [BellArk] (5:2) Mr-Ap 89, p. 10.
"This Also May Be True." [BellArk] (5:2) Mr-Ap 89, p. 10.
2668. INGRAM, A. M.
"The Birdcage." [SmPd] (26:1, #75) Wint 89, p. 13-14.
2669. INNIS, Wendy
"Maida / Grandmother." [Pig] (15) 88, p. 27.
2670. INSKEEP-FOX, Sandra
"Have You Heard the One About the Voluptuous Poet?" [CentR] (33:3) Sum 89, p.
246-247.
2671. IOANNA-VERONIKA
"Baudelaire in the Sierras." [TarRP] (28:2) Spr 89, p. 39-41.
"Bighorn Sheep." [TarRP] (28:2) Spr 89, p. 37-39.
"Factories in Lodz." [Interim] (8:1) Spr 89, p. 45.
"Knowing the Way." [Interim] (8:1) Spr 89, p. 44-45.
"Mr. Cogito Meditates on Redemption" (tr. of Zbigniew Herbert). [Jacaranda] (4:1)
Spr-Sum 89, p. 55.
"Nike Hesitates" (tr. of Zbigniew Herbert). [Jacaranda] (4:1) Spr-Sum 89, p. 50-51.
"Revelation" (tr. of Zbigniew Herbert). [Jacaranda] (4:1) Spr-Sum 89, p. 51-52.
"A Sign" (tr. of Zbigniew Herbert). [Jacaranda] (4:1) Spr-Sum 89, p. 57.
"A Stool" (tr. of Zbigniew Herbert). [Jacaranda] (4:1) Spr-Sum 89, p. 56.
"The Voice" (tr. of Zbigniew Herbert). [Jacaranda] (4:1) Spr-Sum 89, p. 53-54.
"Wheat" (for the people of the village of Ponikla). [TarRP] (28:2) Spr 89, p. 36.
2672. IOANNOU, Susan
"Kathleen Marshall." [AntigR] (79) Aut 89, p. 69.
2673. IREMONGER, Valentin
"Aran 1947" (tr. of Máirtín O Direáin). [Trans] (22) Fall 89, p. 36.
"Frozen" (tr. of Seán O Ríordáin). [Trans] (22) Fall 89, p. 40.
"I Remember a Room on the Seaward Side" (tr. of Máire Mhac an tSaoi). [Trans]
(22) Fall 89, p. 58.
"My Mother's Burying" (tr. of Seán O Ríordáin). [Trans] (22) Fall 89, p. 38-40.
2674. IRWIN, Mark
"Gorge." [WestHR] (43:1) Spr 89, p. 65.
2675. ISAACSON, Lisa
"Biopsy." [PassN] (10:2) Sum 89, p. 18.
2676. ISBELL, Camelia
"Speedwell." [RiverS] (29) [89], p. 46-47.
2677. ISKRENKO, Nina
"Still-Life" (tr. by John High and Katya Olmsted). [FiveFR] (7) 89, p. 54.
"Talking to my crested hen" (tr. by John High and Katya Olmsted). [FiveFR] (7) 89,
p. 55.
"To Beat or Not to Beat" (tr. by John High and Katya Olmsted). [FiveFR] (7) 89, p.
56-57.
"To talk with you is like burning in the marsh" (tr. by John High and Katya
Olmsted). [FiveFR] (7) 89, p. 53.
2678. ISLAS, Maya
"Sigo en ti." [LindLM] (8:1) Ja-Mr 89, p. 10.
"Ven a ver mi párpado." [LindLM] (8:1) Ja-Mr 89, p. 10.
2679. ISMAILI, Rashidah
"Appearance-1." [Bomb] (28) Sum 89, p. 84.

"Appeared-2." [Bomb] (28) Sum 89, p. 85.
"Detained." [Bomb] (28) Sum 89, p. 85.
"Missing in Action." [Obs] (2:3) Wint 87, p. 12-13.
"Missing in Action and Presumed Dead." [Obs] (2:3) Wint 87, p. 11-12.
"Missing Person-1." [Obs] (2:3) Wint 87, p. 14.
"Tell the Heroes to Wait." [Obs] (2:3) Wint 87, p. 17-18.
"The Wanderers-1." [Obs] (2:3) Wint 87, p. 15-17.
2680. ISOM, Joan Shaddox
"Icebound." [Nimrod] (32:2) Spr-Sum 89, p. 95.
"Metamorphosis: At the Van Gogh Museum." [Nimrod] (32:2) Spr-Sum 89, p. 96.
"To the Audience at a Poetry Reading." [Nimrod] (32:2) Spr-Sum 89, p. 98.
"Vigil." [Nimrod] (32:2) Spr-Sum 89, p. 97.
2681. ISRAEL, Inge
"Kyokusui-no-utage" (Kyoto, 1988). [Grain] (17:1) Spr 89, p. 20.
2682. ITALLIE, Jean-Claude van
"Struck Dumb" (w. Joseph Chaikin). [Kaleid] (19) Sum-Fall 89, p. 10-18.
2683. ITO, Sally
"Al's Inside His Sax and Won't Come Out" (tr. of Kazuko Shiraishi). [Rampike]
(6:2) 88, p. 67.
"March" (tr. of Kazuko Shiraishi). [Rampike] (6:2) 88, p. 67.
"Zero." [AntigR] (76) Wint 89, p. 92-93.
2684. IVES, Rich
"Old Friends." [MissR] (17:3, #51), p. 91-93.
"One of those Important Brief Moments." [MissR] (17:3, #51), p. 94-95.
2685. IVRY, Benjamin
"Captions to Certain Slide Lectures." [NewRep] (200:8) 20 F 89, p. 42.
"Sails" (tr. of Adam Zagajewski, w. Renata Gorczynski). [NewYorker] (65:36) 23
O 89, p. 56.
J-SON, Wooi-chin
See WOOI-CHIN, J-son
JABER, Diana Abu
See ABU-JABER, Diana
2686. JABES, Edmond
"The Book of Resemblances" (Selections, tr. by Rosmarie Waldrop). [Temblor] (10)
89, p. 182-191.
"To Answer to, To Answer for." [Acts] (10) 89, p. 28-30.
2687. JACK, Beth Ellen
"Copper Penny Eyes" (For Turtle). [Writer] (102:3) Mr 89, p. 24.
2688. JACKMAN, Vernon L.
"Brown Girl in the Ring." [BlackALF] (23:3) Fall 89, p. 496-497.
2689. JACKSON, Diana Whitaker
"Pulling Poems." [EngJ] (78:8) D 89, p. 90.
2690. JACKSON, Fleda Brown
"Dock." [StoneC] (17:1/2) Fall-Wint 89-90, p. 39.
"Edna St. Vincent Millay Learns Her Lines." [NegC] (9:1) 89, p. 34-35.
"For Michelle." [Iowa] (19:3) Fall 89, p. 27.
"The Location of Fleda Phillips Brown." [BelPoJ] (40:1) Fall 89, p. 19.
"A Long and Happy Life." [GeoR] (43:3) Fall 89, p. 460.
"Mississippi River, Near Cape Girardeau, Mo." [Iowa] (19:3) Fall 89, p. 28.
"Next-Door Neighbors." [StoneC] (17:1/2) Fall-Wint 89-90, p. 38.
2691. JACKSON, Gale
"Maryland, Africa." [Ploughs] (15:4) Wint 89-90, p. 108.
"Mozambique." [Ploughs] (15:4) Wint 89-90, p. 109.
2692. JACKSON, Haywood
"The Trouble the Bees Go Through." [StoneC] (17:1/2) Fall-Wint 89-90, p. 27.
2693. JACKSON, Leslie M.
"Up the Hill." [Grain] (17:2) Sum 89, p. 64.
2694. JACKSON, Loretta Sallman
"Drifting Away." [KanQ] (21:3) Sum 89, p. 74.
2695. JACKSON, Lorri (Lorrie)
"Judy Jetson (on Her Back, Tattooed)." [PaintedB] (38) 89, p. 67.
"Still Life: Boy on Couch." [NewAW] (5) Fall 89, p. 123.
"Two." [NewAW] (5) Fall 89, p. 121-122.
2696. JACKSON, Mary Hale
"Letters to a Penitentiary." [BambooR] (44) Fall 89, p. 17.

2697. JACKSON, Reuben M.
"Changing Antifreeze." [IndR] (12:2) Spr 89, p. 41.
"Clara." [WashR] (14:5) F-Mr 89, p. 17.
"Donald in Love." [IndR] (12:2) Spr 89, p. 40.
"From Augusta, Georgia to Washington, D.C." [WashR] (14:5) F-Mr 89, p. 16.
"Saturday Night." [IndR] (12:2) Spr 89, p. 42.
"Ten Years After." [IndR] (12:2) Spr 89, p. 39.
2698. JACKSON, Richard (Richard P.)
"The Angels of 1912 and 1972." [IndR] (12:2) Spr 89, p. 115-116.
"Brevity" (after Hölderlin). [SpoonRQ] (14:1) Wint 89, p. 9.
"Everything's Coming My Way." [SpoonRQ] (14:1) Wint 89, p. 10.
"Footnote #2, Page 3, 'They'." [RiverC] (10:1) Fall 89, p. 4-5.
"History." [LaurelR] (23:2) Sum 89, p. 38-39.
"The Real World." [LaurelR] (23:2) Sum 89, p. 39-40.
"Shadows." [Crazy] (36) Spr 89, p. 53-57.
"Stones." [IndR] (12:2) Spr 89, p. 117-118.
"Stones." [SpoonRQ] (14:1) Wint 89, p. 8.
"The Words." [SpoonRQ] (14:1) Wint 89, p. 9.
2699. JACKSON, Stephen Joseph
"Black Dust." [HayF] (5) Fall 89, p. 62.
"This." [HayF] (5) Fall 89, p. 63.
2700. JACOB, Max
"Agonies and More" (tr. by Rosanna Warren). [SenR] (19:2) Fall 89, p. 72.
"Christ at the Movies" (tr. by Rosanna Warren). [SenR] (19:2) Fall 89, p. 123-125.
"In the Brouhaha of the Fair" (tr. by Rosanna Warren). [SenR] (19:2) Fall 89, p. 71.
"Infernal Vision in the Form of a Madrigal" (tr. by Rosanna Warren). [SenR] (19:2)
Fall 89, p. 69-70.
2701. JACOBIK, Gray
"Bulgaria" (for Shirley and Mary Ann). [LaurelR] (23:1) Wint 89, p. 70.
"In Medius Res." [OxfordM] (5:2) Fall-Wint 89, p. 67.
"Pink Tulips: Georgia O'Keeffe." [SoDakR] (27:4) Wint 89, p. 65.
"Portions." [Blueline] (10:1/2) 89, p. 13.
2702. JACOBITZ, Regina H.
"The Queen Bee." [Plain] (9:3) Spr 89, p. 30.
2703. JACOBOWITZ, Judah
"Spudyick." [RiverC] (9:1) Spr 89, p. 86-87.
"Surprised." [RiverC] (9:1) Spr 89, p. 85.
2704. JACOBS, Helen
"The Cake Stand Is Quite Explicit." [Descant] (20:3/4, #66/67) Fall-Wint 89, p. 166.
"Stating It." [Descant] (20:3/4, #66/67) Fall-Wint 89, p. 167-168.
"Systems Discards -- Qualified Political." [Descant] (20:3/4, #66/67) Fall-Wint 89,
p. 170.
"Walnut Brown." [Descant] (20:3/4, #66/67) Fall-Wint 89, p. 169.
2705. JACOBSEN, Josephine
"The Birthday Party." [TriQ] (74) Wint 89, p. 205-206.
"The Dogs." [TriQ] (74) Wint 89, p. 207.
"Here" (for Roy and Bee). [Talisman] (2) Spr 89, p. 7.
"Loss of Sounds." [TriQ] (74) Wint 89, p. 208.
"Next Summer." [NewYorker] (65:2) 27 F 89, p. 65.
"Of Pairs." [Ploughs] (15:4) Wint 89-90, p. 110.
"Only Alice." [Atlantic] (263:5) My 89, p. 51.
"Reading on the Beach." [NewYorker] (65:26) 14 Ag 89, p. 36.
"The Shrivers." [GrandS] (8:3) Spr 89, p. 205-206.
"The Woods." [Ploughs] (15:4) Wint 89-90, p. 111-112.
2706. JACOBSEN, Rolf
"Haydn" (tr. by Robert Hedin). [MidAR] (9:2) 89, p. 131.
"In the Great Parks" (tr. by Robert Hedin). [MidAR] (9:2) 89, p. 130.
"A Play with Shadows" (tr. by Robert Hedin). [Vis] (31) 89, p. 11.
2707. JACOBWITZ, Judah
"Alien." [SmPd] (26:3 #77) Fall 89, p. 23.
2708. JACQMIN, Francois
"Summer Morning" (tr. by David Siefkin). [Vis] (31) 89, p. 30.
2709. JAEGER, Lowell
"Constantin Brancusi's 'Sleeping Muse'." [SoCoast] (6) Fall 88, p. 52.
"Disconnecting." [StoneC] (16:3/4) Spr-Sum 89, p. 73.
"Goose Pantoum." [SoCoast] (5) Spr 88, p. 47.

"Hope Against Hope." [PoetryNW] (30:2) Sum 89, p. 30-31.
"The Lion's Tooth." [CreamCR] (13:2) Fall 89, p. 251.
"Lust." [Pig] (15) 88, p. 14.
"The Roots of Trees." [PoetryNW] (30:2) Sum 89, p. 29-30.
"Splash." [OxfordM] (5:1) Spr-Sum 89, p. 36.
"Steaming After Gaddafi." [Pig] (15) 88, p. 37.
"Thistles, 1983." [RiverS] (29) [89], p. 44-45.

2710. JAFFE, Caroline
"Donna." [CinPR] (20) Fall 89, p. 61.

2711. JAFFE, Dan
"Figure Found in a Group Photograph of the Missouri Historical Society." [NewL]
(56:2/3) Wint 89-Spr 90, p. 132.
"In a Sidewalk Cafe 89 Miles from Downtown Damascus" (for Natan Zach).
[NewL] (56:2/3) Wint 89-Spr 90, p. 134.
"Last Call" (for John Ciardi). [NewL] (56:2/3) Wint 89-Spr 90, p. 133.
"Play On." [NewL] (56:2/3) Wint 89-Spr 90, p. 130-131.

2712. JAFFE, Maggie
"Teufel." [Vis] (31) 89, p. 21.

2713. JAIDE, Tanure O
"Orphans of Hope." [Obs] (3:1) Spr 88, p. 51.

2714. JAKELSKI, Lisa
"Sailing On" (Mainstreet Elementary Poetry Contest, 5th Grade, 3rd Place).
[DeKalbLAJ] (22:1/4) 89, p. 105.

2715. JAMES, David
"After the Harvest." [CapeR] (24:1) Spr 89, p. 14.
"Light on Light." [PassN] (10:1) Wint 89, p. 19.
"The Music of an Idiot." [Caliban] (6) 89, p. 175.
"The Nightmare of an Idiot." [Caliban] (6) 89, p. 174.
"Out of the Despair of Day." [CapeR] (24:2) Fall 89, p. 45.
"Reign of Tulips." [CentR] (33:2) Spr 89, p. 134.
"Slow Night in Saline." [CapeR] (24:2) Fall 89, p. 46.

2716. JAMES, John
"For the Safety of Lovers." [Pequod] (26/27) 89, p. 96.

2717. JAMES, Kathi
"The Four Seasons Reflected in Water." [Mildred] (3:2) 89, p. 116.
"Homeward Bound." [Blueline] (10:1/2) 89, p. 77.

2718. JAMES, Stewart
"A Few Words." [DenQ] (24:1) Sum 89, p. 43.
"Packing Her Scarves." [DenQ] (24:1) Sum 89, p. 44.
"Termination of a Disorder, Burghölzli, 1900." [GrandS] (9:1) Aut 89, p. 131-132.

2719. JAMES-FRENCH, Dayv
"Estrangement." [Quarry] (38:1) Wint 89, p. 48.
"The Game of Father and Son." [Grain] (17:2) Sum 89, p. 74.
"Student Loan." [Quarry] (38:1) Wint 89, p. 47.
"Voyager, Three Years Old." [Dandel] (16:2) Fall-Wint 89, p. 19.

2720. JAMIE, Kathleen
"Child with Pillar Box and Bin Bags." [Pequod] (26/27) 89, p. 99.
"Hagen and the Owls at Glencoe." [Pequod] (26/27) 89, p. 97.
"The Horse-Drawn Sun." [Pequod] (26/27) 89, p. 98.

2721. JAMISON, Mark
"Station." [EvergreenC] (4:3) Spr 89, p. 8-11.

2722. JAMMES, Francis
"The house would be replete with roses and with wasps" (tr. by Joyce Oliver
Lowrie). [AmerPoR] (18:2) Mr-Ap 89, p. 49.
"One of these Sunday afternoons when it is hot" (tr. by Joyce Oliver Lowrie).
[AmerPoR] (18:2) Mr-Ap 89, p. 49.
"A Prayer to Go to Paradise with the Donkeys" (tr. by Richard Wilbur, to Máire and
Jack). [Trans] (22) Fall 89, p. 258-259.
"Upon my death, you with blue eyes" (tr. by Joyce Oliver Lowrie). [AmerPoR]
(18:2) Mr-Ap 89, p. 49.

2723. JAMPOLE, Marc
"Fat Women." [OxfordM] (5:2) Fall-Wint 89, p. 43.
"July 4th." [OxfordM] (5:1) Spr-Sum 89, p. 34.

2724. JANECEK, Gerald
"Forty-Fifth Alphabet Poem (tsa-tsa)" (Moscow, 1985, tr. of Dmitrii Prigov).
[MichQR] (28:4) Fall 89, p. 728-730.

"From Thursday to Friday" (Excerpt, tr. of Lev Rubinshtein). [MichQR] (28:4) Fall 89, p. 741-742.
"I live and see" (tr. of Vsevolod Nekrasov). [MichQR] (28:4) Fall 89, p. 731.
"That's who is guilty" (tr. of Vsevolod Nekrasov). [MichQR] (28:4) Fall 89, p. 732.
2725. JANIK, Phyllis
"Fuse" (Selections: 5 poems). [MidwQ] (30:3) Spr 89, p. 325-345.
"Squirrelhouse Blues." [NewL] (55:3) Spr 89, p. 25.
2726. JANOWITZ, Phyllis
"Memory and the Blue-Eyed Man." [OhioR] (44) 89, p. 104-105.
2727. JANUS, Gustav
"The Classless Society" (tr. by Michael Biggins). [NewEngR] (11:3) Spr 89, p. 236-237.
2728. JANZEN, Jean
"After the Pruning." [GettyR] (2:2) Spr 89, p. 280.
"January Happiness." [AntR] (47:1) Wint 89, p. 66.
"Plain Wedding." [GettyR] (2:2) Spr 89, p. 279.
"This Earth." [PoetL] (84:3) Fall 89, p. 30.
"Vermeer Had It Right." [PoetL] (84:3) Fall 89, p. 31.
2729. JARAMILLO AGUDELO, Dario
"Miguel a Osorio." [LindLM] (8:2) Ap-Je 89, p. 4.
2730. JARAMILLO LEVI, Enrique
"Monologo al Pie de las Montañas." [LindLM] (8:3) Jl-S 89, p. 20.
"Paso a la Imaginacion." [LindLM] (8:3) Jl-S 89, p. 20.
"Solo el Amor." [Mairena] (11:27) 89, p. 86.
2731. JARMAN, Mark
"The Black Riviera." [BostonR] (14:4) Ag 89, p. 8.
"Cavafy in Redondo." [BostonR] (14:4) Ag 89, p. 8.
"The Double Bow." [Hudson] (42:2) Sum 89, p. 269-270.
"Dressing My Daughters." [Hudson] (42:2) Sum 89, p. 268-269.
"The Elephant Graveyard." [CrossCur] (8:2) Ja 89, p. 63.
"An Ivory Gate and a Gate of Horn." [PoetryNW] (30:1) Spr 89, p. 29-30.
"A One-Ring Circus." [CrossCur] (8:2) Ja 89, p. 61-62.
"Sea-Fig." [PraS] (63:1) Spr 89, p. 59-62.
"Suite." [Crazy] (37) Wint 89, p. 7-12.
"The Supremes." [BostonR] (14:4) Ag 89, p. 8.
"To Zoë, Beginning Winter." [PoetryNW] (30:1) Spr 89, p. 31.
"Wave." [NewEngR] (11:3) Spr 89, p. 337.
"Waves." [PoetryNW] (30:1) Spr 89, p. 32.
2732. JARNIEWICZ, Jerzy
"A Fairy Tale" (tr. by the author). [ParisR] (31:113) Wint 89, p. 98.
"In Australia" (tr. by the author). [ParisR] (31:113) Wint 89, p. 97.
"The King and the Poet" (tr. of Andrzej Strak). [TampaR] (2) 89, p. 69.
"A Letter from Verona" (tr. of Edward Kolbus). [TampaR] (2) 89, p. 67.
"My Last Will" (tr. of Zdzislaw Jaskula). [TampaR] (2) 89, p. 68.
"A Stone" (tr. by the author). [TampaR] (2) 89, p. 66.
2733. JARNOT, Lisa
"Dear." [Screens] (1) 89, p. 51.
"Dear Dad." [Screens] (1) 89, p. 51.
"Dear Jack." [Screens] (1) 89, p. 52.
2734. JASKULA, Zdzislaw
"My Last Will" (tr. by Jerzy Jarniewicz). [TampaR] (2) 89, p. 68.
2735. JASON, Kathrine
"Barberino Val d'Elsa" (For James Wright, 1927-1980). [SoCoast] (6) Fall 88, p. 46-47.
"Climb." [Kalliope] (11:3) 89, p. 38-39.
2736. JASPER, Pat
"The Girls of Summer." [CrossC] (11:2) 89, p. 14.
"May Day, Salisbury" (for my mother). [Dandel] (16:1) Spr-Sum 89, p. 25.
"Saturday Morning." [AntigR] (77/78) Spr-Sum 89, p. 121-122.
2737. JASTRUN, Mieczyslaw
"Mantegna's Christ" (tr. by Stanislaw Baranczak and Clare Cavanah). [Trans] (21) Spr 89, p. 17.
2738. JASTRUN, Tomasz
"A Bird Gets the Death Sentence" (tr. by Daniel Bourne). [OhioR] (44) 89, p. 27.
"A Call for Peace" (tr. by Daniel Bourne). [MinnR] (NS 32) Spr 89, p. 80.
"Each Night" (tr. by Daniel Bourne). [ColR] (NS 16:2) Fall 89-Wint 90, p. 87.

"Eyes" (tr. by Daniel Bourne). [Chelsea] (48) 89, p. 22.
"Fatherland" (tr. by Daniel Bourne). [LitR] (32:2) Wint 89, p. 167.
"Fire" (tr. by Daniel Bourne). [LitR] (32:2) Wint 89, p. 167.
"Five Before Twelve" (tr. by Daniel Bourne). [AntigR] (79) Aut 89, p. 8.
"The Flip Side of the Medal" (tr. by Daniel Bourne). [GrahamHR] (12) Spr 89, p. 59.
"Fruitless" (tr. by Daniel Bourne). [Chelsea] (48) 89, p. 20.
"The Great Emigration" (tr. by Daniel Bourne). [OhioR] (44) 89, p. 27.
"Ground Cover" (tr. by Daniel Bourne). [AntigR] (79) Aut 89, p. 9.
"Guardian Angel" (tr. by Daniel Bourne). [BelPoJ] (39:3) Spr 89, p. 30.
"In a Cage" (tr. by Daniel Bourne). [CumbPR] (9:1) Fall 89, p. 26.
"The Last Days of My Guardian Angel" (tr. by Daniel Bourne). [BelPoJ] (39:3) Spr 89, p. 31.
"A Letter from Prison" (tr. by Daniel Bourne). [Shen] (39:2) Sum 89, p. 54.
"Lights" (tr. by Daniel Bourne). [Chelsea] (48) 89, p. 21.
"Nothing" (tr. by Daniel Bourne). [Chelsea] (48) 89, p. 19.
"Our Table of Desire" (tr. by Daniel Bourne). [ConnPR] (8:1) 89, p. 17.
"Peasant Farmer" (tr. by Daniel Bourne). [ConnPR] (8:1) 89, p. 18.
"Possessed" (tr. by Daniel Bourne). [SoCaR] (21:2) Spr 89, p. 73.
"Power" (tr. by Daniel Bourne). [LitR] (32:2) Wint 89, p. 166.
"The Retreat of the Home Army" (tr. by Daniel Bourne). [GrahamHR] (12) Spr 89, p. 58.
"Silence" (tr. by Daniel Bourne). [LitR] (32:2) Wint 89, p. 166.
"A Single Drop" (tr. by Daniel Bourne). [LitR] (32:2) Wint 89, p. 167.
"Smoke" (tr. by Stanislaw Baranczak and Clare Cavanah). [Trans] (21) Spr 89, p. 80.
"Straw" (tr. by Daniel Bourne). [ColR] (NS 16:2) Fall 89-Wint 90, p. 86.
"W Klatce" (in Polish). [CumbPR] (9:1) Fall 89, p. 26.
"Wall" (tr. by Daniel Bourne). [AntigR] (79) Aut 89, p. 11.
"Yet Another Time" (tr. by Daniel Bourne). [AntigR] (79) Aut 89, p. 10.
"Zomo" (in Polish). [CumbPR] (9:1) Fall 89, p. 25.
"Zomo" (tr. by Daniel Bourne). [CumbPR] (9:1) Fall 89, p. 25.

2739. JAUNZEMS, Andy
"My Father." [AntigR] (77/78) Spr-Sum 89, p. 187.
"Rainmaker." [SmPd] (26:1, #75) Wint 89, p. 20.
"They Were All Angels, the Girls." [AntigR] (77/78) Spr-Sum 89, p. 186.

2740. JAUSS, David
"The Border." [Shen] (39:3) Fall 89, p. 41-42.
"The Door." [CarolQ] (41:3) Spr 89, p. 28.
"Here" (for Judy). [Shen] (39:3) Fall 89, p. 43.
"Jeanne." [Ploughs] (15:1) 89, p. 55.
"The Logic of a Hurt Animal." [DenQ] (24:2) Fall 89, p. 62.
"The Moment After." [PoetryE] (28) Fall 89, p. 75.
"The Morning After the Quarrel." [ChatR] (9:3) Spr 89, p. 39.
"Vietnam Veterans Memorial" (for Andrea and Susanne Dunn). [Shen] (39:3) Fall 89, p. 44-45.

2741. JAYYUSI, Lena
"Athens Airport" (tr. of Mahmoud Darwish, w. Anne Waldman). [PoetryE] (27) Spr 89, p. 80.
"Contemplating an Absent Scene" (tr. of Mahmoud Darwish, w. W. S. Merwin). [PoetryE] (27) Spr 89, p. 88-89.
"Guests on the Sea" (tr. of Mahmoud Darwish, w. W. S. Merwin). [PoetryE] (27) Spr 89, p. 81-83.
"Homing Pigeons" (Excerpt, tr. of Mahmoud Darwish, w. W. S. Merwin). [PoetryE] (27) Spr 89, p. 94.
"Horses Neighing on the Slope" (tr. of Mahmoud Darwish, w. Anne Waldman). [PoetryE] (27) Spr 89, p. 84.
"I Am from There" (tr. of Mahmoud Darwish, w. Jeremy Reed). [PoetryE] (27) Spr 89, p. 72.
"I Am the Ill-Fated Lover" (tr. of Mahmoud Darwish, w. W. S. Merwin). [PoetryE] (27) Spr 89, p. 85-87.
"Psalm 4" (tr. of Mahmoud Darwish, w. Anselm Hollo). [PoetryE] (27) Spr 89, p. 73.
"Psalm 5" (tr. of Mahmoud Darwish, w. Anselm Hollo). [PoetryE] (27) Spr 89, p. 74.
"Psalm 7" (tr. of Mahmoud Darwish, w. Anselm Hollo). [PoetryE] (27) Spr 89, p.

75-76.
"Psalm 8" (tr. of Mahmoud Darwish, w. Anselm Hollo). [PoetryE] (27) Spr 89, p. 77.
"Psalm 9" (tr. of Mahmoud Darwish, w. Christopher Middleton). [PoetryE] (27) Spr 89, p. 78.
"Psalm 13" (tr. of Mahmoud Darwish, w. Anselm Hollo). [PoetryE] (27) Spr 89, p. 79.
"There Is a Night" (tr. of Mahmoud Darwish, w. Jeremy Reed). [PoetryE] (27) Spr 89, p. 93.
"You Will Carry the Butterfly's Burden" (tr. of Mahmoud Darwish, w. W. S. Merwin). [PoetryE] (27) Spr 89, p. 90-92.
2742. JEANMARIE, Redvers
"Sonata" (for Anne Jeanmarie, in memoriam). [ChangingM] (20) Wint-Spr 89, p. 20.
2743. JECH, Jon
"The World's Largest Elephant in Captivity" (Selections: 3 poems). [BellArk] (5:2) Mr-Ap 89, p. 15-16.
2744. JEFFERS, Robinson
"Hooded Night." [NoDaQ] (57:2) Spr 89, p. 31.
"October Week-End." [NoDaQ] (57:2) Spr 89, p. 32.
2745. JEFFERSON, Bonnie
"Signals" (tr. of Reina María Rodríguez). [Pig] (15) 88, p. 75.
"The Temporary Madness of Quixote" (tr. of Cira Andrés). [Pig] (15) 88, p. 64.
JELLOUN, Tahar Ben
See Ben JELLOUN, Tahar
2746. JENKINS, Alan
"Caravaggio: Self-Portrait with Severed Head." [Pequod] (26/27) 89, p. 102-103.
"Triptych." [Pequod] (26/27) 89, p. 100-101.
2747. JENKINS, Louis
"Basketball." [BostonR] (14:2) Ap 89, p. 17.
"Confessional Poem." [BostonR] (14:2) Ap 89, p. 17.
"Fishing Below the Dam." [BostonR] (14:2) Ap 89, p. 17.
"In the Streets." [BostonR] (14:2) Ap 89, p. 17.
"Intermission." [BostonR] (14:2) Ap 89, p. 17.
"Invisible." [BostonR] (14:2) Ap 89, p. 17.
"A Portrait of the Master." [Agni] (28) 89, p. 247.
"Twins." [BostonR] (14:2) Ap 89, p. 17.
"The Ukrainian Easter Egg." [BostonR] (14:2) Ap 89, p. 17.
"Unfortunate Location." [BostonR] (14:2) Ap 89, p. 17.
"Vibration." [BostonR] (14:2) Ap 89, p. 17.
2748. JENKINS, Mike
"Chartist Meeting" (Heolgerrig, 1842). [NoDaQ] (57:2) Spr 89, insert p. 72-73.
"Survivor." [NoDaQ] (57:2) Spr 89, insert p. 74.
2749. JENKINSON, Biddy
"Birthday" (tr. by the author). [Vis] (29) 89, p. 38.
"An Ecologist" (tr. by Seán O Tuama). [Trans] (22) Fall 89, p. 114.
"One Day Old" (tr. by Alex Osborne). [Trans] (22) Fall 89, p. 115.
"Spray" (tr. by Alex Osborne). [Trans] (22) Fall 89, p. 116.
"Woodful" (tr. by Jerry Stritch). [Trans] (22) Fall 89, p. 117.
2750. JENNER, Ted
"Chorus Girls, 2: A Brief History of the Muses." [Sulfur] (9:1, #24) Spr 89, p. 126-129.
2751. JENNINGS, Kate
"Hard Moon." [FourQ] (2d series 3:1) Spr 89, p. 51.
2752. JENNINGS, Michael
"The Road Home, November." [SouthernR] (25:2) Spr 89, p. 496.
2753. JENSEN, Jeffry
"The Routine." [SoCoast] (5) Spr 88, p. 34.
2754. JENSEN, Laura
"After Walking." [AmerPoR] (18:2) Mr-Ap 89, p. 16.
"All Saints." [NewL] (56:2/3) Wint 89-Spr 90, p. 138-140.
"Amusing." [NewL] (56:2/3) Wint 89-Spr 90, p. 140-141.
"Hot Gravel." [NewL] (56:2/3) Wint 89-Spr 90, p. 137.
"Lipstick." [NewL] (56:2/3) Wint 89-Spr 90, p. 135-136.
"What Can We Wish for and Believe We Can Have?" [AmerPoR] (18:2) Mr-Ap 89, p. 16-17.

2755. JENTZSCH, Bernd
"Elegy" (tr. by Michael Hamburger). [Stand] (30:2) Spr 89, p. 19.
"Prayer in Extremis" (tr. by Michael Hamburger). [Stand] (30:2) Spr 89, p. 19.
2756. JEROME, Judson
"Confrontation: Road Town Harbour." [WorldO] (22:1/2) Fall-Wint 87-88, c90, p. 18.
"Paying Attention." [NegC] (9:2) 89, p. 13-14.
2757. JEROZAL, Gregory
"After the Bombing in the Capitol Building." [WindO] (51) Spr 89, p. 24.
"After the Bombing in the Capitol Building" (To Justine Wimsatt). [HampSPR] Wint 89, p. 38.
"Borges." [SmPd] (26:2 #76) Spr 89, p. 7.
2758. JESIH, Milan
"At Evening the Nomads" (tr. by Michael Biggins). [NewEngR] (11:3) Spr 89, p. 238.
"A Tiny Poem" (tr. by Michael Biggins). [NewEngR] (11:3) Spr 89, p. 238.
JEW, Shalin Hai
See HAI-JEW, Shalin
2759. JEWELL, Terri (Terri L.)
"Basketeer." [SinW] (38) Sum-Fall 89, p. 10.
"Covenant." [Obs] (2:1) Spr 87, p. 16.
"Face of Africa." [SinW] (38) Sum-Fall 89, p. 8.
"Fragile Flower." [Obs] (3:3) Wint 88, p. 120.
"Marking Time." [Obs] (3:3) Wint 88, p. 120-121.
"One Night Reunion." [EvergreenC] (4:3) Spr 89, p. 13.
"She Who Bears the Thorn." [AmerV] (15) Sum 89, p. 68.
"She Who Bears the Thorn." [BlackALF] (23:3) Fall 89, p. 462.
"A Sister Gives Warning." [Obs] (2:1) Spr 87, p. 17.
"Terms with Past Things." [Obs] (2:1) Spr 87, p. 18.
"The Want." [Kalliope] (11:2) 89, p. 23.
"Woman Without Melody." [Obs] (2:1) Spr 87, p. 17-18.
JI, Zhang
See ZHANG, Ji
JIANPU, Peng
See PENG, Jianpu
JIAXIN, Wang
See WANG, Jiaxin
2760. JILES, Paulette
"Song to the Rising Sun." [MalR] (86) Spr 89, p. 71-83.
2761. JIMÉNEZ, Juan Ramón
"Dream" (tr. by Mary Rae). [NewRena] (7:3, #23) 89, p. 69.
"Sueño." [NewRena] (7:3, #23) 89, p. 68.
2762. JIN, Ha
"A Battalion Commander Complains to His Secretary." [Agni] (28) 89, p. 176-177.
"A Brother's Advice." [Agni] (28) 89, p. 179.
"Marching Towards Martyrdom." [Agni] (28) 89, p. 175.
"My Knowledge of the Russian Language." [Agni] (28) 89, p. 180.
"On the 20th National Anniversary." [Agni] (28) 89, p. 172.
"A Page from a Schoolboy's Diary." [Agni] (28) 89, p. 170.
"Promise." [Agni] (28) 89, p. 173-174.
"A Thirteen-Year-Old Accuses His Teacher." [Agni] (28) 89, p. 171.
"A Young Worker's Lament to His Former Girlfriend." [Agni] (28) 89, p. 178.
2763. JIN-OCK
"Iron, We Were Told" (Three Poems by Kisang, tr. by Constantine Contogenis and Wolhee Choe). [BelPoJ] (39:4) Sum 89, p. 32.
JING, An
See AN, Jing
JINGYA, Xu
See XU, Jingya
JIPING, Dong
See DONG, Jiping
2764. JIRGENS, Karl E.
"Editorial: Ontologie! / Ontology!" [Rampike] (6:1) 87, p. 3.
"Editorial: Reality is constituted where two discourses / two codes inter-sect." [Rampike] (6:3) 88, p. 3.

2765. JOENS, Harley
 "The City." [Northeast] (ser. 5:1) Wint 89-90, p. 20.
2766. JOHANNES, Joan
 "A Dragon of Tremendous Size." [WindO] (52) Wint 89-90, p. 26.
2767. JOHANSSEN, Kerry
 "Caterwaul" (Runner Up, Poetry Award). [NewL] (56:1) Fall 89, p. 67-70.
 "The Geometry of Memory" (Runner Up, Poetry Award). [NewL] (56:1) Fall 89, p.
 59-61.
 "Not Talking with a Split Tongue" (Runner Up, Poetry Award). [NewL] (56:1) Fall
 89, p. 62-64.
 "Partial Eclipse" (Runner Up, Poetry Award). [NewL] (56:1) Fall 89, p. 66.
 "Through the Eye of Our Four-Headed Beast" (Runner Up, Poetry Award). [NewL]
 (56:1) Fall 89, p. 70-72.
 "Tracking Device" (Runner Up, Poetry Award). [NewL] (56:1) Fall 89, p. 64-65.
2768. JOHN, Elizabeth Mische
 "Earth Science." [PassN] (10:1) Wint 89, p. 11.
 "Paul's Song." [PassN] (10:2) Sum 89, p. 22.
2769. JOHNSEN, Gretchen
 "Interval." [PaperAir] (4:2) 89, p. 101.
2770. JOHNSON, Dan
 "The Changelings." [CumbPR] (8:2) Spr 89, p. 73.
 "In Plague Years." [CumbPR] (8:2) Spr 89, p. 74.
2771. JOHNSON, David
 "Driving North and Knowing What Hunger Can Be." [DenQ] (24:1) Sum 89, p. 45.
2772. JOHNSON, Don
 "Polly Hyder Waits to Be Moved." [SouthernHR] (23:2) Spr 89, p. 121.
2773. JOHNSON, Floyd
 "Ghetto Sound." [FiveFR] (7) 89, p. 45-46.
2774. JOHNSON, Frank
 "Maybe Now You Know." [BelPoJ] (40:2) Wint 89-90, p. 13.
2775. JOHNSON, Greg
 "Last Words." [GeoR] (43:2) Sum 89, p. 383-384.
2776. JOHNSON, Jacqueline
 "Moseka's Way." [Obs] (3:1) Spr 88, p. 66.
 "Pearls." [Obs] (3:3) Wint 88, p. 24-25.
2777. JOHNSON, Judith E. (Judith Emlyn)
 "As If I Watched Late Last Night with Baudelaire." [VirQR] (65:4) Aut 89, p.
 647-649.
 "For Margaret, Dead by Suicide." [Chelsea] (48) 89, p. 143-145.
 "Under the Lights." [Ploughs] (15:4) Wint 89-90, p. 113-114.
2778. JOHNSON, Kate (Kate Knapp)
 "Breaking from Darkness." [NewL] (56:2/3) Wint 89-Spr 90, p. 142-143.
 "For the Dogwood." [NewL] (56:2/3) Wint 89-Spr 90, p. 144.
 "Michael." [NewL] (56:2/3) Wint 89-Spr 90, p. 146-147.
 "POEM (Perfect Life)." [NewL] (56:2/3) Wint 89-Spr 90, p. 145-146.
2779. JOHNSON, Kathleen
 "Farm Wife." [MidwQ] (30:2) Wint 89, p. 184-185.
2780. JOHNSON, Larry
 "Beginning." [KanQ] (21:1/2) Wint-Spr 89, p. 132.
 "Red Skeletons of Herculaneum." [NewOR] (16:3) Fall 89, p. 42.
 "When I Die." [KanQ] (21:1/2) Wint-Spr 89, p. 133.
2781. JOHNSON, Lemuel
 "Summer Before the Fall, 1982" (for George, in Beirut). [WorldO] (22:1/2)
 Fall-Wint 87-88, c90, p. 20-21.
2782. JOHNSON, Linnea
 "Evensong." [PraS] (63:1) Spr 89, p. 90-91.
 "Knowing I Need to Know." [PraS] (63:1) Spr 89, p. 92-93.
 "Lives." [SpoonRQ] (14:1) Wint 89, p. 21-22.
 "Lost." [PraS] (63:1) Spr 89, p. 91-92.
 "Vincent from the Old Neighborhood." [SpoonRQ] (14:1) Wint 89, p. 23-26.
2783. JOHNSON, Marael
 "Collared and Cuffed." [SoCoast] (7) Spr-Fall 89, p. 53.
2784. JOHNSON, Mark Allan
 "Fires." [BellArk] (5:6) N-D 89, p. 7.
 "The Greenhouse Effect." [BellArk] (5:1) Ja-F 89, p. 17.
 "Laughter at a Wake" (Selections: 4 poems). [BellArk] (5:2) Mr-Ap 89, p. 10-11.

"Mr. D'Eath and the Dance of Life." [BellArk] (5:1) Ja-F 89, p. 5.
"The Red Radio." [BellArk] (5:4) Jl-Ag 89, p. 3.
"Viewing the Crescent Moon Through a Telescope." [BellArk] (5:5) S-O 89, p. 4.
"Wash in an Unfinished Room." [BellArk] (5:4) Jl-Ag 89, p. 7.
"Wild Heart." [BellArk] (5:5) S-O 89, p. 1.
2785. JOHNSON, Meryl
"At This Moment." [BallSUF] (30:4) Aut 89, p. 20.
"Vaccinia" (Translated from the Scientific Jargon). [BallSUF] (30:4) Aut 89, p. 40.
2786. JOHNSON, Michael L.
"Age." [PoetC] (20:3) Spr 89, p. 35.
"AIDS." [Amelia] (5:3, #14) 89, p. 13.
"Aye-Aye." [CreamCR] (13:2) Fall 89, p. 191.
"Backed-Up Sink." [SoCoast] (6) Fall 88, p. 50.
"Black Hole." [Mildred] (3:2) 89, p. 14.
"Captiva." [PoetC] (20:3) Spr 89, p. 34.
"Eros" (tr. of Ibykos). [BallSUF] (30:4) Aut 89, p. 36.
"The Fallow Deer" (tr. of Severo Sarduy). [Mildred] (3:2) 89, p. 13.
"Family Reunion." [SoCoast] (6) Fall 88, p. 26-27.
"The Older I Get." [KanQ] (21:3) Sum 89, p. 35.
"Poem of Inevitable Love" (tr. of Jorge Debravo). [BlueBldgs] (11) 89, p. 10.
"A Poem Using Only the Nine Most Used Words in English." [SoCoast] (5) Spr 88,
        p. 28.
2787. JOHNSON, Nancy
"Audience." [CarolQ] (41:2) Wint 89, p. 17.
"The Bingo Bus" (1960, Bethlehem, Pennsylvania). [HayF] (5) Fall 89, p. 48.
2788. JOHNSON, Quirana
"My Teacher" (Mainstreet Elementary Poetry Contest, 7th Grade, 3rd Place).
        [DeKalbLAJ] (22:1/4) 89, p. 108.
2789. JOHNSON, Rick
"Signs." [Descant] (20:3/4, #66/67) Fall-Wint 89, p. 63.
"Two Birth Poems" (1. "A Shift of Emphasis," 2. "Zero Population Grwoth").
        [Descant] (20:3/4, #66/67) Fall-Wint 89, p. 58-60.
"Wellington Letter: VIII." [Descant] (20:3/4, #66/67) Fall-Wint 89, p. 62-63.
2790. JOHNSON, Robert K.
"Fear Is the Spur." [Wind] (19:65) 89, p. 12.
"To Readers of My Poems." [Wind] (19:65) 89, p. 12-13.
2791. JOHNSON, Robyn
"Ancestral Tongue." [Calyx] (12:1) Sum 89, p. 14.
"Peeling an Onion." [Calyx] (12:1) Sum 89, p. 15.
2792. JOHNSON, Ronald
"Eyes & Objects" (Selections: 10 poems). [Screens] (1) 89, p. 4-13.
2793. JOHNSON, S. Paul
"Aquarium Street." [Colum] (14) 89, p. 183-184.
"Steps to Reach Home." [Colum] (14) 89, p. 185.
2794. JOHNSON, Sarah Jane
"To Gloria Steinem" (After Her Lecture at Michigan Technological University).
        [PassN] (10:2) Sum 89, p. 15.
2795. JOHNSON, Sheila Golburgh
"Extend Hands, Not Arms." [SingHM] (16) 89, p. 96.
"In the Beginning." [PoetryE] (28) Fall 89, p. 61-62.
"Something Small." [PoetryE] (28) Fall 89, p. 64-65.
"You're Eating Me Up." [PoetryE] (28) Fall 89, p. 63.
2796. JOHNSON, Stacey (Stacey L.)
"Distractions, As Persians." [SpoonRQ] (14:2) Spr 89, p. 8-9.
"Tapestries." [Farm] (6:2) Fall 89, p. 97-98.
2797. JOHNSON, Susan Matthis
"Gathering." [LaurelR] (23:1) Wint 89, p. 25.
"Modeling for de Kooning." [LaurelR] (23:1) Wint 89, p. 26.
2798. JOHNSON, Tom
"Mystery Story." [Poetry] (154:4) Jl 89, p. 202-203.
2799. JOHNSON, W. R.
"Caedmon." [Poem] (62) N 89, p. 28.
"Fridays at Dusk." [Poem] (62) N 89, p. 27.
"Kleist in Paris." [Poem] (62) N 89, p. 29.
"Rosa's Garden." [Poem] (62) N 89, p. 30.

2800. JOHNSON, William
"At the Wilderness Boundary." [TexasR] (10:1/2) Spr-Sum 89, p. 89.
2801. JOHNSTON, Allan
"Heuristics." [WeberS] (6:2) Fall 89, p. 75.
"Long Rivers." [WeberS] (6:2) Fall 89, p. 72-73.
"The Moon at the Tail of the Train." [WeberS] (6:2) Fall 89, p. 71.
"L'Orfeo." [WeberS] (6:2) Fall 89, p. 73.
"Voice." [WeberS] (6:2) Fall 89, p. 74.
2802. JOHNSTON, Arnie (Arnold)
"Canzone: The Tree in Our Bed." [MalR] (87) Sum 89, p. 57-59.
"Contract Language." [MalR] (87) Sum 89, p. 56.
"For Kristin: Old Debts." [StoneC] (17:1/2) Fall-Wint 89-90, p. 60-61.
"Late Summer, Lake Michigan." [CumbPR] (8:2) Spr 89, p. 50.
"Syzygy in Center Field" (Third Prize, 1989 Poetry Competition). [PassN] (10:2)
         Sum 89, p. 4.
2803. JOHNSTON, Bob
"Redefinition." [KanQ] (21:1/2) Wint-Spr 89, p. 54.
2804. JOHNSTON, Fred
"The Boatmakers" (for Gregory Brown, at Maine). [PoetC] (20:3) Spr 89, p. 24-25.
"By You I Am Blessed" (for Suzanne Ahearne). [NewL] (55:3) Spr 89, p. 87.
"The Conquest of the Island" (for Joaquin Roncero del Pino). [NoDaQ] (57:1) Wint
         89, p. 85-86.
"Crannóg." [NoDaQ] (57:1) Wint 89, p. 86.
"Droit de Seigneur." [NoDaQ] (57:1) Wint 89, p. 88.
"Ebb and Flow." [Vis] (29) 89, p. 28.
"The Florentines" (for John Hogan). [NoDaQ] (57:1) Wint 89, p. 87.
"Lines to an Old Friend." [Vis] (29) 89, p. 28.
2805. JOHNSTON, George
"Pity." [MalR] (89) Wint 89, p. 49.
2806. JOHNSTON, Mark
"Cat Yawning." [BlueBldgs] (11) 89, p. 31.
"The Difficulty of Revision." [CumbPR] (8:2) Spr 89, p. 31-32.
"Disaster Footage, with Commercials." [ColEng] (51:5) S 89, p. 482-483.
"Ecdysiast." [PoetL] (84:3) Fall 89, p. 42.
"The Girl in the Left Hand Corner." [BallSUF] (30:4) Aut 89, p. 56.
"Grandfather Courts the Hardware Lady." [SoCoast] (5) Spr 88, p. 19.
"Short Periods of Lucidity." [SoCoast] (5) Spr 88, p. 17.
"Small Icon from a Painting by Bosch." [BallSUF] (30:4) Aut 89, p. 18.
"Spirits of the Closet." [CumbPR] (8:2) Spr 89, p. 33.
"Utopia." [SoCoast] (5) Spr 88, p. 18.
"Vermeer: Girl Asleep." [Kalliope] (10:3) 88, p. 26.
"Zeno Asleep." [Colum] (14) 89, p. 126.
2807. JONAS, Ann Rae
"Everything Moves." [RiverC] (9:1) Spr 89, p. 80.
"Phantom Light." [CrossCur] (8:3) Apr 89, p. 99.
"Time Dilation." [RiverC] (9:1) Spr 89, p. 81.
2808. JONES
"The Edge." [AlphaBS] (6) Wint 89-90, p. 24.
2809. JONES, Arlene
"The Cabbage Sphere." [KanQ] (21:1/2) Wint-Spr 89, p. 114.
JONES, Elizabeth Follin
     See FOLLIN-JONES, Elizabeth
2810. JONES, Glyn
"The Common Path." [NoDaQ] (57:2) Spr 89, insert p. 17-18.
"Swifts." [NoDaQ] (57:2) Spr 89, insert p. 20.
"You, Taliesin." [NoDaQ] (57:2) Spr 89, insert p. 18-19.
2811. JONES, Gretchen
"Where Do Monsters Go to Cry?" (Mainstreet Elementary Poetry Contest, 6th
         Grade, 1st Place). [DeKalbLAJ] (22:1/4) 89, p. 107.
2812. JONES, Irene Marchegiani
"Over Your Absence Glides" (tr. of Margherita Guidacci, w. Carol Lettieri).
         [MidAR] (9:1) 89, p. 43.
2813. JONES, Jacquie
"Alison." [Obs] (2:3) Wint 87, p. 21-22.
"Cooking." [Obs] (2:3) Wint 87, p. 22.
"Franco." [Obs] (2:3) Wint 87, p. 19-20.

"Migori." [Obs] (2:3) Wint 87, p. 20-21.
"Paul Chacha." [Obs] (2:3) Wint 87, p. 23-24.
2814. JONES, Jamie
"To Susan Sherrill / to Us All." [EmeraldCR] (1989) c1988, p. 141-142.
2815. JONES, Jill
"I Didn't Know (It Would Be Like This)." [AntigR] (77/78) Spr-Sum 89, p. 124.
"Letter to a Friend on Mars." [AntigR] (77/78) Spr-Sum 89, p. 123.
2816. JONES, John
"Black Study: Paranoia Poem No. 4." [HangL] (54) 89, p. 11.
"For Jack Spicer." [HangL] (54) 89, p. 12.
2817. JONES, Monty
"Texture of Gray and Yellow." [CumbPR] (8:2) Spr 89, p. 59.
2818. JONES, Patricia Jane
"Daughter Of." [Nimrod] (32:2) Spr-Sum 89, p. 99-100.
2819. JONES, Paula
"Pescadero Marsh." [ThRiPo] (33/34) 89, p. 33.
"Search By the River." [ThRiPo] (33/34) 89, p. 31-32.
2820. JONES, Richard
"The Color of Grief." [GrahamHR] (12) Spr 89, p. 97.
2821. JONES, Rodney
"A Blasphemy." [KenR] (NS 11:3) Sum 89, p. 79.
"Burnt Oil and Hawk." [NegC] (9:1) 89, p. 18-20.
"Carpe Diem." [Poetry] (153:4) Ja 89, p. 215-216.
"Dangers." [KenR] (NS 11:3) Sum 89, p. 80-81.
"An Explanation of the Exhibit." [Poetry] (153:4) Ja 89, p. 214-215.
"In Manufacturing." [Atlantic] (263:3) Mr 89, p. 64.
"Meditation at Home." [KenR] (NS 11:3) Sum 89, p. 83-84.
"Meeting Bobby." [KenR] (NS 11:3) Sum 89, p. 84-85.
"Pastoral for Derrida." [AmerPoR] (18:2) Mr-Ap 89, p. 36.
"Serious Partying." [KenR] (NS 11:3) Sum 89, p. 81-82.
2822. JONES, Roger
"The Dead Miners." [PoetL] (84:2) Sum 89, p. 41.
"Family History." [TexasR] (10:3/4) Fall-Wint 89, p. 102.
"Infestation." [Wind] (19:64) 89, p. 38.
"Revelations, the First Time." [TexasR] (10:1/2) Spr-Sum 89, p. 100.
"Sleeping on a Pallet." [TexasR] (10:1/2) Spr-Sum 89, p. 101.
"A West Texas Oilfield." [TexasR] (10:3/4) Fall-Wint 89, p. 103.
"Wild Oats." [TexasR] (10:3/4) Fall-Wint 89, p. 104.
2823. JONES, Sally Roberts
"Ann Griffiths." [NoDaQ] (57:2) Spr 89, insert p. 59.
"Tryweryn." [NoDaQ] (57:2) Spr 89, insert p. 58.
JONES, Teruko Anderson
See ANDERSON-JONES, Teruko
2824. JONES, Tom
"Sister Escaline." [PoetL] (84:4) Wint 89-90, p. 19-20.
2825. JONES, Tom O.
"Hair Worshippers." [RagMag] (7:1) 89, p. 18-19.
"The Ma 'n Pa Store." [DeKalbLAJ] (22:1/4) 89, p. 56.
"Speculation Books." [WindO] (51) Spr 89, p. 13.
2826. JONES, Tony
"Mango Baseball." [BambooR] (44) Fall 89, p. 18.
2827. JONES, Tyrone
"If by Chance" (To Nikki Giovanni). [BlackALF] (23:3) Fall 89, p. 454.
2828. JORDAN, Barbara
"Branching." [Sulfur] (9:1, #24) Spr 89, p. 153-154.
"A Skull Enwalled Garden" (from *Visions of the Fathers of Lascaux* by Clayton
    Eshleman). [ParisR] (31:113) Wint 89, p. 222-223.
"The Tutelaries." [Notus] (4:2) Fall 89, p. 76-78.
2829. JORDAN, Jim
"What are you suffering?" [WindO] (51) Spr 89, p. 3.
2830. JORDAN, Johanna
"Valentine." [BellArk] (5:4) Jl-Ag 89, p. 1.
2831. JORDAN, Lewis
"Do You Have Anything to Say?" [Sequoia] (32:2) Wint-Spr 89, p. 1.
2832. JORIS, Pierre
"Lemur Mornings" (Selections: First and Second Lemur Morning). [Notus] (4:2)

Fall 89, p. 74-75.
"Turbulence" (Excerpts). [Screens] (1) 89, p. 111-113.
2833. JORON, Andrew
"I Am Joe's Brain." [Caliban] (6) 89, p. 94.
2834. JOSEPH, Allison
"Bronx Bombers." [Ploughs] (15:1) 89, p. 70-71.
"Habitat: Northeast Bronx." [PassN] (10:1) Wint 89, p. 22.
"Laundry." [PoetC] (20:3) Spr 89, p. 5-6.
2835. JOSEPH, Lawrence
"Lamentation." [Witness] (3:1) Spr 89, p. 62-63.
2836. JOUBERT, Jean
"Interior" (after Bonnard, tr. by Hilary Davies). [Verse] (6:2) Je 89, p. 17.
2837. JOYCE, Jane Wilson
"A Single Woman Experiences Failure in the Kitchen" (Ten Songs). [AmerV] (15)
        Sum 89, p. 14-23.
2838. JUANITA, Judy
"Modulation." [Footwork] 89, p. 60.
"We Left Him Behind." [Footwork] 89, p. 60.
2839. JUARROZ, Roberto
"Vertical Poetry" (six poems from "Novena poesía vertical," tr. by Mary Crow).
        [LitR] (32:4) Sum 89, p. 508-511.
2840. JUDGE, Joseph M.
"Watching the Hurrican Arrive." [StoneC] (16:3/4) Spr-Sum 89, p. 46.
"What Any Child Can Do." [Vis] (31) 89, p. 31.
2841. JUDSON, John
"Ant Tale." [LaurelR] (23:1) Wint 89, p. 87.
"In Which the Poet Who Has Never Heard Gabriel Sings of Two Who Have Truly
        Blown." [KanQ] (21:1/2) Wint-Spr 89, p. 98.
"It's a Tough Day to Face the Fall" (for Irene Ware & Bela Fowler). [ThRiPo]
        (33/34) 89, p. 40.
"On the Importance of Style." [KanQ] (21:1/2) Wint-Spr 89, p. 99.
2842. JULAVITS, Virginia (Virginia Webb)
"Carson McCullers Can You Hear Me?" [KanQ] (21:3) Sum 89, p. 121.
"Don't Look in the Garden." [SouthernR] (25:3) Sum 89, p. 606-607.
"Hybrid." [SouthernR] (25:2) Spr 89, p. 487.
"My Karl Shapiro Doll." [NegC] (9:1) 89, p. 37.
"Okeechobee Chicken Pen." [SouthernR] (25:2) Spr 89, p. 488.
"They Met on the Ferry from Calais to Dover." [SoCoast] (5) Spr 88, p. 16.
"Virginia Woolf's Shopping List." [NegC] (9:1) 89, p. 199.
2843. JULIANUS OF EGYPT
"I sang it often, and I'll go on" (tr. by James Michie). [GrandS] (8:4) Sum 89, p.
        84.
"To a Skeptic Philosopher" (tr. by James Michie). [GrandS] (8:4) Sum 89, p. 84.
JUN, Wang
        See WANG, Jun
2844. JUNKINS, Donald
"After Trout Fishing in the Rio Frio, Spain, Late June." [Field] (40) Spr 89, p. 18.
"Every Day We Know More Exactly." [Salm] (84) Fall 89, p. 52-53.
"The Late June Church VBells Ring in Mijas, Spain." [Salm] (84) Fall 89, p. 53.
"The Night Wind: Swan's Island, October." [Field] (40) Spr 89, p. 16.
"October: Lines Begun Near the Shore in a High Wind." [Field] (40) Spr 89, p. 13.
"Painting the Front Bow Window in October." [Field] (40) Spr 89, p. 14-15.
"Perugia, Late July." [CinPR] (20) Fall 89, p. 44-46.
2845. JUSTICE, Donald
"Incident in a Rose Garden." [ChatR] (9:4) Sum 89, p. 95-96.
"Young Girls Growing Up." [ChatR] (9:4) Sum 89, p. 77-78.
2846. JUSTICE, Jack
"It Is a Geography." [HampSPR] Wint 89, p. 15.
2847. JUSTICZ, Julie
"Look Twice Now." [SinW] (37) Spr 89, p. 56.
JUYI, Bai
        See BAI, Juyi
2848. KABIR
"Take a pitcher full of water and set it down on the water" (tr. by Robert Bly).
        [Mildred] (3:2) 89, p. 132.

2849. KAE-JU
"Let My Cassia Boat" (Three Poems by Kisang, tr. by Constantine Contogenis and Wolhee Choe). [BelPoJ] (39:4) Sum 89, p. 33.
2850. KAFATOU, Sarah
"A Flier" (for my father). [Ploughs] (15:1) 89, p. 72-73.
2851. KAFKA, Paul
"At Home with Marcel." [ConnPR] (8:1) 89, p. 1-2.
2852. KAHAKALAU, Ku
"'O Kaho'olawe I Ka Malie." [Hawai'iR] (13:3) Fall 89, p. 38.
"Peaceful Kaho'olawe." [Hawai'iR] (13:3) Fall 89, p. 39.
2853. KAI, Nubia
"W. E. B. Du Bois." [BlackALF] (23:3) Fall 89, p. 502-503.
2854. KAIKOWSKA, Catherine
"This Story Is Mine. I Want to." [CentR] (33:2) Spr 89, p. 131-132.
2855. KAKINOMOTO NO HITOMARO (ca. 692)
"The fall moon still shines" (tr. by Sam Hamill). [PoetryE] (28) Fall 89, p. 204.
2856. KALAHELE, 'Imaikalani
"From the Source." [Hawai'iR] (13:3) Fall 89, p. 70.
"I Have a Need." [Hawai'iR] (13:3) Fall 89, p. 68.
2857. KALAMARAS, George
"At Night." [BlackWR] (16:1) Fall-Wint 89, p. 80.
"The Distance." [YellowS] (31) Aut 89, p. 38.
"Evening." [Caliban] (7) 89, p. 139.
"Father & Son, Mother & Daughter, etc." [Caliban] (7) 89, p. 135-136.
"For Sophia." [SenR] (19:1) 89, p. 34-35.
"In Absence." [Caliban] (7) 89, p. 138.
"Steps." [Caliban] (7) 89, p. 137.
"Tonight, the Wind." [BlackWR] (16:1) Fall-Wint 89, p. 81.
"Why I Fly" (a letter from Bruno to Roberto Zingarello, Italy, 1939). [Sulfur] (9:2, #25) Fall 89, p. 126-130.
"Your Letter, with Its Wild Scent" (for John Bradley). [YellowS] (31) Aut 89, p. 10.
2858. KALE, Bonita
"Artist Looking Forward." [Plain] (9:3) Spr 89, p. 18.
2859. KALLMAN, Chester
"The Faun and the Shepherdess" (tr. of Aleksander Pushkin). [SouthwR] (74:2) Spr 89, p. 214-217.
2860. KALOGERIS, George
"Agganis." [Agni] (28) 89, p. 206.
KAMAIKE, Susumu
See SUSUMU, Kamaike
2861. KAMAL, Daud
"Endurance." [Vis] (30) 89, p. 55.
"Seawolf." [Vis] (31) 89, p. 20.
"Still Alive." [Vis] (30) 89, p. 55.
2862. KAMEEN, Paul
"Morning Song, 1." [WestB] (24) 89, p. 122.
"Morning Song, 4." [WestB] (24) 89, p. 123.
2863. KAMENETZ, Rodger
"Commuting to Thebes." [WestHR] (43:2) Sum 89, p. 122.
"For Primo Levi." [SouthernR] (25:4) Aut 89, p. 946-947.
"Homemade Voodoo." [GrandS] (8:3) Spr 89, p. 106-107.
"Lover by Lover." [GrandS] (8:3) Spr 89, p. 105-106.
"Slow Dissolve." [MissR] (17:3, #51), p. 89-90.
"The Unfortunate Traveler" (for D.W.). [WestHR] (43:2) Sum 89, p. 123.
2864. KAMENSZAIN, Tamara
"La Casa Grande" (eleven poems, tr. by Carlos and Monique Altschul). [LitR] (32:4) Sum 89, p. 512-517.
2865. KAMIENSKA, Anna
"Dr. Korczak's Lie" (tr. by Tomasz P. Krzeszowski and Desmond Graham). [Stand] (30:1) Wint 88-89, p. 40.
"Funny" (tr. by Stanislaw Baranczak and Clare Cavanah). [Trans] (21) Spr 89, p. 20.
2866. KANE, Jean
"Is It a Watch, Is It a Warning." [PraS] (63:2) Sum 89, p. 97-98.
"One Girl's Last Green Summer." [PraS] (63:2) Sum 89, p. 99-100.

2867. KANGAS, J. R.
"The Produce Emporium." [EvergreenC] (5:1) Fall 89, p. 23.
"Quaking Aspen." [Bogg] (61) 89, p. 54.
2868. KANTCHEV, Nikolai
"Night Watchman of the Dawn" (tr. by Bradley R. Strahan, w. Pamela Perry). [Vis] (30) 89, p. 4.
2869. KAO, Ch'i
"Leaving a Mountain Post Station at Dawn" (tr. by Paul Hansen). [LitR] (32:3) Spr 89, p. 354.
2870. KAPLAN, Howard
"Farmer's Market." [AmerV] (16) Fall 89, p. 3.
"Young Poet, Reading" (for J.O.G.). [MSS] (6:3) 89, p. 67.
2871. KAPLAN, Robert
"Howard Beach." [MinnR] (NS 33) Fall 89, p. 23-25.
2872. KAPOOR, Suman K.
"The Attic." [BallSUF] (30:4) Aut 89, p. 12-13.
"Dregs of Light." [Verse] (6:3) Wint 89, p. 79.
2873. KARANDIKAR, Vinda (Karandikar, Govind Vinayak)
"The Knot" (tr. by Vinay Dharwadker). [TriQ] (77) Wint 89-90, p. 187-190.
2874. KARP, Vickie
"Stars." [NewYorker] (65:4) 13 Mr 89, p. 40.
2875. KARR, Mary
"All This and More." [IndR] (13:1) Wint 89, p. 73-74.
"Mass Eye and Ear: The Ward" (for my mother). [IndR] (13:1) Wint 89, p. 75.
"Post-Larkin Triste." [TriQ] (76) Fall 89, p. 98-99.
"Small But Urgent Request to the Unknowable" (for Jean Kilbourne and Thomas Lux). [IndR] (13:1) Wint 89, p. 76.
2876. KARVE, Jayant
"Ambedkar, 79" (tr. of Namdeo Dhasal, w. Laurie Hovell and Asha Mundlay). [Trans] (21) Spr 89, p. 234-235.
"Just a Bit More Time" (tr. of Namdeo Dhasal, w. Laurie Hovell). [Trans] (21) Spr 89, p. 235.
2877. KASDORF, Julia
"Mennonites." [WestB] (24) 89, p. 89-90.
"The Only Photograph of My Father As a Boy." [WestB] (24) 89, p. 90.
2878. KASISCHKE, Laura K.
"At the Last Trumpet" (after Clifford Brown). [Vis] (31) 89, p. 45.
"Iguana." [PoetL] (84:3) Fall 89, p. 14-16.
2879. KASSAK, Lajos
"At Orly Airport" (tr. by Emery George). [WebR] (14:1) Spr 89, p. 24-25.
"The Clock Has Stopped" (tr. by Emery George). [WebR] (14:1) Spr 89, p. 27.
"Light Signals" (tr. by Emery George). [WebR] (14:1) Spr 89, p. 25.
"Moments" (tr. by Emery George). [WebR] (14:1) Spr 89, p. 27.
"Vision" (tr. by Emery George). [WebR] (14:1) Spr 89, p. 28.
"Windpaths" (tr. by Emery George). [WebR] (14:1) Spr 89, p. 26.
2880. KASSELMANN, Barbara
"Love Poem." [Kalliope] (11:1) 89, p. 15-17.
KATAMI, Otoma no (ca. 750)
See OTOMA NO KATAMI (CA. 750)
2881. KATES, J.
"At Twenty-Four" (for Sandy Perpignani). [ConnPR] (8:1) 89, p. 38.
"Certainty" (tr. of Alioune (David) Diop). [StoneC] (17:1/2) Fall-Wint 89-90, p. 25.
"Imagining the Worst" (An NPR Special Report). [FloridaR] (16:2/3) Fall-Wint 89, p. 60-61.
"Motif." [FloridaR] (16:2/3) Fall-Wint 89, p. 59.
"Riddle." [FloridaR] (16:2/3) Fall-Wint 89, p. 58.
"The Thousandth Anniversary of the Christianization of Rus" (tr. of Tat'iana Shcherbina). [MichQR] (28:4) Fall 89, p. 737.
"We, the Generation in the Wilderness" (Selections: 1, 7-11, 14, tr. of Ricardo Feierstein, w. Stephen A. Sadow). [Pig] (15) 88, p. 96.
"What I Can Take" (for Sarah Hawes). [OxfordM] (5:2) Fall-Wint 89, p. 30.
2882. KATROVAS, Richard
"After Reading Several Pages of Panofsky over a Cup of Coffee in La Marquise." [MissouriR] (12:1) 89, p. 176-177.
"Glory's Punk." [IndR] (12:2) Spr 89, p. 106-108.
"This Tenderness." [SouthernPR] (29:1) Spr 89, p. 60.

2883. KATYAL, Anjum
"Absence I." [SouthernR] (25:4) Aut 89, p. 916.
"Absence II." [SouthernR] (25:4) Aut 89, p. 917.
"Kite." [SouthernR] (25:4) Aut 89, p. 917.
2884. KATZ, Steve
"Journalism" (Selections: Two Poems). [NewAW] (5) Fall 89, p. 109.
2885. KATZ-LEVINE, Judy
"Clownshine." [US1] (22/23) Spr 89, p. 24.
2886. KAUCHER, Candy
"F.F." [PaintedB] (38) 89, p. 18.
"I Was So Stupid." [PaintedB] (38) 89, p. 19.
"Peace Hole." [PaintedB] (38) 89, p. 17.
"Propelled Backwards." [PaintedB] (38) 89, p. 20.
2887. KAUFFMAN, Janet
"The Blue Door of Detroit." [Caliban] (6) 89, p. 26.
"Cultivated places -- don't name names." [DenQ] (24:2) Fall 89, p. 63.
"I cannot say weather does this damage, and more." [DenQ] (24:2) Fall 89, p. 64.
"Now it is calm." [DenQ] (24:2) Fall 89, p. 63-64.
2888. KAUFMAN, Andrew
"Getting There." [BrooklynR] (5) 88, p. 39.
"November Coldspell in New York City." [MinnR] (NS 32) Spr 89, p. 69.
"Outside." [CarolQ] (41:3) Spr 89, p. 29.
2889. KAUFMAN, Bob
"Suicide." [AlphaBS] (5) Jl 89, p. 13.
2890. KAUFMAN, Debra
"On Highway 421 Going Away from You I Learn." [GreensboroR] (47) Wint
89-90, p. 122.
2891. KAUFMAN, Ellen
"Giraffes." [SenR] (19:1) 89, p. 74.
"Lethe." [BelPoJ] (39:4) Sum 89, p. 27.
"Sonatina." [CarolQ] (42:1) Fall 89, p. 25-26.
2892. KAUFMAN, Margaret
"Old Quilts." [PassN] (10:1) Wint 89, p. 16.
2893. KAUFMAN, Shirley
"Lake." [WestHR] (43:2) Sum 89, p. 130.
"Leftovers." [Thrpny] (39) Fall 89, p. 24.
"Riding the Longest Tramway in the World at Albuquerque." [WestHR] (43:2) Sum
89, p. 131.
"The Status Quo" (Jerusalem, 1988). [NewRep] (201:1) 3 Jl 89, p. 32.
2894. KAUNE, Gayle Rogers
"Family Inheritance." [PoetC] (21:1) Fall 89, p. 22-23.
"Monday Morning in October." [CrabCR] (6:2) Wint 89, p. 23.
"Receiving Your Call." [CrabCR] (6:2) Wint 89, p. 23.
2895. KAUSHANSKY, Lauren
"Viewing Turtles with Alexis Lee." [BellArk] (5:3) My-Je 89, p. 5.
2896. KAWABATA, Yasunari
"Snow Country" (Selection: Parts I-II, tr. by Mark T. Ferguson). [Trans] (22) Fall
89, p. 237-257.
2897. KAYACAN, Feyyaz
"Division of Labor" (tr. by Feyyaz Fergar). [Trans] (21) Spr 89, p. 233.
"Lament of the Misled" (tr. by Feyyaz Fergar). [Trans] (21) Spr 89, p. 232.
2898. KAZANTZIS, Judith
"Dusk and a Portuguese Man o' War." [KeyWR] (2:1/2) Fall-Wint 89, p. 38.
"Feudal" (*Lancelot du Lac*, by Bresson: mediaeval France). [Stand] (30:4) Aut 89, p.
29-30.
"Sisyphus-Who-Was-Prometheus." [Stand] (30:4) Aut 89, p. 28-29.
"With Love, January." [Verse] (6:1) Mr 89, p. 52.
2899. KAZEMEK, Francis E.
"Kinds of Reading." [EngJ] (78:3) Mr 89, p. 89.
KAZUKO, Shiraishi
See SHIRAISHI, Kazuko
2900. KEARNEY, Doris
"Mothers of the Beirut Massacre." [AnthNEW] (1) 89, p. 14.
2901. KEARNEY, Larry
"Sleepwalk" (Selections: 1-49). [Temblor] (10) 89, p. 139-152.

2902. KEBE, Mbaya Gana
"Game" (tr. by Jan Pallister). [Pig] (15) 88, p. 50.
"The Little Signare" (tr. by Jan Pallister). [Pig] (15) 88, p. 50.
"Words" (tr. by Jan Pallister). [Pig] (15) 88, p. 50.
2903. KEEFER, Janice Kulyk
"Fields." [Event] (18:3) Fall 89, p. 28-37.
2904. KEEGAN, Marilyn
"Somewhere Through the Tumbling Night." [AmerPoR] (18:4) Jl-Ag 89, p. 33.
2905. KEELE, Alan
"Sonnets to Orpheus" (Selections: I: 15, 26, II: 3, 19, tr. of Rainer Maria Rilke, w.
Leslie Norris). [QW] (28) Wint-Spr 89, p. 93-96.
2906. KEELER, Wally
"Biography -- 1981" (tr. of Brigitta Bali). [Rampike] (6:2) 88, p. 66.
"Replacement" (tr. of Brigitta Bali). [Rampike] (6:2) 88, p. 66-67.
2907. KEELEY, Edmund
"Accented-Unaccented" (tr. of Yannis Ritsos). [PoetryE] (27) Spr 89, p. 54.
"Death Portrait" (tr. of Yannis Ritsos). [Caliban] (6) 89, p. 151.
"Description" (tr. of Yannis Ritsos). [Caliban] (6) 89, p. 150.
"Freedom" (tr. of Yannis Ritsos). [PoetryE] (27) Spr 89, p. 57.
"Healing" (tr. of Yannis Ritsos). [PoetryE] (27) Spr 89, p. 58.
"Insomnia" (tr. of Yannis Ritsos). [PoetryE] (27) Spr 89, p. 51.
"The Meaning of Simplicity" (tr. of Yannis Ritsos). [PoetryE] (27) Spr 89, p. 55.
"Mode of Acquisition" (tr. of Yannis Ritsos). [PoetryE] (27) Spr 89, p. 56.
"Second Coming" (tr. of Yannis Ritsos). [Caliban] (6) 89, p. 151.
"Sketch" (tr. of Yannis Ritsos). [PoetryE] (27) Spr 89, p. 53.
"Slowly" (tr. of Yannis Ritsos). [PoetryE] (27) Spr 89, p. 52.
"Toward Saturday" (tr. of Yannis Ritsos). [PoetryE] (27) Spr 89, p. 50.
"Variation" (tr. of Yannis Ritsos). [Caliban] (6) 89, p. 150.
"We Wait" (tr. of Yannis Ritsos). [PoetryE] (27) Spr 89, p. 48.
"Women" (tr. of Yannis Ritsos). [PoetryE] (27) Spr 89, p. 49.
2908. KEENAN, Deborah
"The City." [Caliban] (6) 89, p. 192-193.
"Lilacs and Hail." [Shen] (39:2) Sum 89, p. 30-31.
"What Drives Us." [Shen] (39:2) Sum 89, p. 31.
2909. KEENER, Earl R.
"Contemplating the Furies." [WestB] (23) 89, p. 101.
2910. KEERY, James
"August Nights." [Bogg] (61) 89, p. 48.
2911. KEILEY, Lizbeth
"Baby Shower." [BrooklynR] (5) 88, p. 36.
"Child of an Eye So Seldom Seen." [CinPR] (20) Fall 89, p. 67.
"The Steaming Paint of Sky." [BrooklynR] (6) 89, p. 6.
"Tears Are Invisible." [BrooklynR] (5) 88, p. 37.
2912. KEILLOR, Garrison
"The Beluga Whales at the Minnesota Zoo." [LakeSR] (23) 89, p. 7.
"To a St. Paul Columnist." [LakeSR] (23) 89, p. 8.
2913. KEITGES, Julie
"Random Return." [Kalliope] (11:3) 89, p. 30.
"Vectors." [Kalliope] (11:3) 89, p. 31.
"What Death?" [Kalliope] (11:3) 89, p. 31.
2914. KEITH, W. J.
"End Papers." [AntigR] (79) Aut 89, p. 57.
"First, There Are Words." [AntigR] (79) Aut 89, p. 55.
"Nobody Has Written." [AntigR] (79) Aut 89, p. 56.
2915. KEITHLEY, George
"Black Water." [ColR] (NS 16:2) Fall 89-Wint 90, p. 34.
"Did I Tell You?" [ColR] (NS 16:2) Fall 89-Wint 90, p. 33.
"Mount St. Helens, May 1980." [ColR] (NS 16:2) Fall 89-Wint 90, p. 35-36.
2916. KELLER, David
"After the First Death." [SouthernPR] (29:2) Fall 89, p. 16.
"The Animals' Return." [HighP] (4:3) Wint 89-90, p. 77-78.
"Dancing in the Dark." [ThRiPo] (31/32) 88, p. 28.
"The Man Who Knew the Words to 'Louie, Louie'." [OhioR] (44) 89, p. 82-83.
"Middle-Aged Man with Crayons." [HighP] (4:3) Wint 89-90, p. 75-76.
"The Mystery at the Old Radio Station." [ThRiPo] (31/32) 88, p. 29.
"Sculpture, Voices from Memory" (for Jim Colavita). [US1] (22/23) Spr 89, p.

39-41.
"Sunrise." [MissouriR] (12:2) 89, p. 29.
2917. KELLER, Tsipi
"The Art of Minimalism" (tr. of Dan Pagis). [PoetryE] (28) Fall 89, p. 178.
2918. KELLEY, Karen
"Anonymous Woman" (Selections: VII, VIII). [Sulfur] (9:2, #25) Fall 89, p. 51-52.
"Anonymous Woman III." [CentralP] (16) Fall 89, p. 172-173.
"Anonymous Woman IV." [CentralP] (16) Fall 89, p. 174-175.
"Comfort." [BrooklynR] (5) 88, p. 17-19.
2919. KELLMAN, Anthony
"Tropical Graveyard." [Callaloo] (12:3, #40) Sum 89, p. 525-526.
"Watercourse." [Obs] (3:3) Wint 88, p. 122-125.
2920. KELLOGG, David
"Cow Sonnets." [CreamCR] (13:2) Fall 89, p. 158-159.
"Outside the Office, the Dead." [AntR] (47:3) Sum 89, p. 336-337.
2921. KELLY, Angela
"After the Wedding Rehearsal." [Vis] (31) 89, p. 42.
"Hating Sugar." [SwampR] (1:4) Sum 89, p. 68.
2922. KELLY, Anne M.
"Black Cat Ghazal." [PraF] (10:1, #46) Spr 89, p. 38.
"A Conspiracy of Angels." [PraF] (10:1, #46) Spr 89, p. 37.
"Glossolalia." [CanLit] (122/123) Aut-Wint 89, p. 38-41.
"Mobile Over Hecate Strait." [CanLit] (122/123) Aut-Wint 89, p. 123.
2923. KELLY, Carol E.
"English Soldiers." [Vis] (29) 89, p. 10.
2924. KELLY, John
"Rooks on a Spring Morning." [NoDaQ] (57:1) Wint 89, p. 89.
2925. KELLY, Joseph J.
"First Girlfriend." [Vis] (31) 89, p. 14.
2926. KELLY, Robert
"A Book of Emblems" (Selections: First-Fifth Emblems). [Notus] (4:1) Spr 89, p.
16-22.
"London Sonnets." [GrandS] (8:4) Sum 89, p. 104-105.
"Natural Histories." [Notus] (4:1) Spr 89, p. 14-15.
"Niagara Frontier, Song Scattered Among Friends." [Notus] (4:2) Fall 89, p. 22-23.
2927. KELLY, Robert A.
"The Prophecy." [AntigR] (76) Wint 89, p. 18.
2928. KELPFISZ, Irena
"The Monkey House and Other Cages" (Selections: 1-9. The voice is that of a female
monkey born and raised in a zoo.). [Cond] (16) 89, p. 2-5.
KELVER, Sue de
See DeKELVER, Sue
2929. KEMP, Carolyn
"Peduncle" (Excerpt). [Screens] (1) 89, p. 14-15.
2930. KEMPA, Rick
"Because I Am Tactful and Lewd" (X Ranch, Idaho). [YellowS] (29) Spr 89, p. 6.
"Ode to Paperclips." [EngJ] (78:3) Mr 89, p. 90.
2931. KEMPHER, Ruth Moon
"As for If." [BlueBldgs] (11) 89, p. 63.
"Hilda Halfheart's Notes to the Milkman, #76." [WindO] (52) Wint 89-90, p. 32.
"O no -- this is not the last Rain Poem." [Bogg] (61) 89, p. 53.
"Presuming on Emily's #341." [HiramPoR] (46) Spr-Sum 89, p. 17.
"Sylvia Savage Interviews D.H. Lawrence Not Either in Heaven or in Hell, But."
[Kalliope] (11:3) 89, p. 49.
"The Three Little Pigs and Their Diets." [WindO] (52) Wint 89-90, p. 31.
"Yam Plant Variations." [Kalliope] (10:1/2) 88, p. 120.
2932. KEMPTON, Amy
"Moments from the Votary." [SmPd] (26:3 #77) Fall 89, p. 24.
2933. KENDIG, Diane
"Ceferino, the Peasant" (tr. of Grethel Cruz). [Pig] (15) 88, p. 88.
"Last Night" (tr. of Porfirio Salgado). [Pig] (15) 88, p. 88.
2934. KENDRICK, Dolores
"Fast Food." [IndR] (12:2) Spr 89, p. 58-60.
"Rose Lane at Ninety." [IndR] (12:2) Spr 89, p. 56-57.
2935. KENNEDY, Chris
"The Criminal." [Thrpny] (38) Sum 89, p. 33.

2936. KENNEDY, Monique M.
"White Fever" (Selection: "Seen (Set)," tr. of Pia Tafdrup, w. Thomas E. Kennedy).
[Pequod] (26/27) 89, p. 195.
2937. KENNEDY, Thomas E.
"To Sappho." [HolCrit] (26:2) Ap 89, p. 18-19.
"White Fever" (Selection: "Seen (Set)," tr. of Pia Tafdrup, w. Monique M.
Kennedy). [Pequod] (26/27) 89, p. 195.
2938. KENNEDY, X. J.
"Invitation to Dance." [NegC] (9:1) 89, p. 15-17.
"Long Distance." [TarRP] (29:1) Fall 89, p. 56.
"Sisyphus" (a parable of the writer's lot, for Robert Watson). [GreensboroR] (46)
Sum 89, p. 92.
2939. KENNEY, Paige
"The Model Child." [CreamCR] (13:2) Fall 89, p. 160.
2940. KENNY, Adele
"Mussolini's Riding Academy." [Footwork] 89, p. 63-64.
"Snow Agnels." [Footwork] 89, p. 63.
2941. KENT, Rolly
"Gilgamesh's Flower." [PraS] (63:1) Spr 89, p. 93-95.
2942. KENTER, Robert
"I. Montreal Winter Hotel." [Grain] (17:1) Spr 89, p. 56.
"II. We Have Been Given a House." [Grain] (17:1) Spr 89, p. 56.
"Letters." [Rampike] (6:2) 88, p. 77.
2943. KENYON, Jane
"At the Dime Store." [Atlantic] (264:4) O 89, p. 76.
"At the IGA: Franklin, New Hampshire." [OntR] (31) Fall-Wint 89-90, p. 87.
"At the Public Market Museum: Charleston, South Carolina." [NewYorker] (65:26)
14 Ag 89, p. 73.
"A Boy Goes into the World." [Iowa] (19:1) Wint 89, p. 90-91.
"Cultural Exchange." [Iowa] (19:1) Wint 89, p. 89-90.
"Geranium." [Nat] (248:11) 20 Mr 89, p. 388.
"Ice Out." [Iowa] (19:1) Wint 89, p. 89.
"Insomnia." [NewL] (56:2/3) Wint 89-Spr 90, p. 150.
"Summer 1890: Near the Gulf." [NewL] (56:2/3) Wint 89-Spr 90, p. 148.
"Three Crows." [NewL] (56:2/3) Wint 89-Spr 90, p. 149.
"We Let the Boat Drift." [KenR] (NS 11:2) Spr 89, p. 14.
"What Came to Me." [NewL] (56:2/3) Wint 89-Spr 90, p. 149.
2944. KEON, W.
"Big Steve." [Dandel] (16:2) Fall-Wint 89, p. 16.
"Down on the Yucatan." [Dandel] (16:2) Fall-Wint 89, p. 12-15.
"Howlin at the Moon." [Dandel] (16:2) Fall-Wint 89, p. 17-18.
"Spirit Spinnin." [Dandel] (16:2) Fall-Wint 89, p. 11.
2945. KERCHEVAL, Jesse Lee
"Falling to the Sound of My Mother's Voice." [Amelia] (5:3, #14) 89, p. 133.
"Goodbye at the Gare." [Amelia] (5:3, #14) 89, p. 132-133.
"Why I Work." [Amelia] (5:3, #14) 89, p. 132.
2946. KERN, Gary
"Untitled: The daring dreams of willful admissions" (tr. of Pavel Peppershtein).
[MichQR] (28:4) Fall 89, p. 733.
2947. KEROUAC, Jack
"Clown Hero" (1956). [AlphaBS] (6) Wint 89-90, p. 32.
"I Get a Kick" (cca. early 50's). [AlphaBS] (6) Wint 89-90, p. 32.
2948. KERR, Colin
"Passages." [MalR] (86) Spr 89, p. 99.
2949. KERR, Nora F.
"Andromeda." [RagMag] (7:1) 89, p. 20.
"In the Bee-Loud Glade." [RagMag] (7:1) 89, p. 21.
2950. KERRIGAN, Anthony
"Hard Times" (tr. of Heberto Padilla). [Salm] (82/83) Spr-Sum 89, p. 321.
"The Old Bards Say" (tr. of Heberto Padilla, w. Jeanne Cook). [Salm] (82/83)
Spr-Sum 89, p. 320.
"A Swim Off Havana" (tr. of Heberto Padilla, w. Jeanne Cook). [Salm] (82/83)
Spr-Sum 89, p. 320.
2951. KERSHNER, Brandon
"The Adult Child of the Alcoholic." [Kalliope] (10:3) 88, p. 15-16.
"Superossification." [Kalliope] (10:3) 88, p. 17.

2952. KERSHNER, Ivan
"Funeral." [Plain] (9:3) Spr 89, p. 11.
2953. KESSLER, Jascha
"The Bees' Calendar" (tr. of Nicolai Kunchev). [Confr] (39/40) Fall 88-Wint 89, p. 143.
"A Blade of Grass" (tr. of Ottó Orbán). [Jacaranda] (4:1) Spr-Sum 89, p. 48.
"March Fires" (tr. of Kirsti Simonsuuri). [MidAR] (9:1) 89, p. 161.
"A Nice Little War" (tr. of Ottó Orbán). [Jacaranda] (4:1) Spr-Sum 89, p. 47.
"Photograph" (tr. of Ottó Orbán). [Jacaranda] (4:1) Spr-Sum 89, p. 49.
"Poverty" (tr. of Ottó Orbán, w. Maria Körösy). [Margin] (9) 89, p. 36.
2954. KESSLER, Milton
"Untitled: I am writing quickly this morning of April 24th, 1989." [PaintedB] (39) 89, p. 81-82.
2955. KESSLER, Sydney
"Toward Harvest." [LitR] (32:2) Wint 89, p. 196.
2956. KETTNER, M.
"Too Many Steaks and Cigarettes." [Rampike] (6:2) 88, p. 75.
2957. KETZER, Steve, Jr.
"Pumpkin and the Praxis 48." [BallSUF] (30:4) Aut 89, p. 61.
2958. KEYES, Robert Lord
"Old German Wives' Tales." [BelPoJ] (39:3) Spr 89, p. 9.
2959. KEYISHIAN, Marge
"Byways." [Footwork] 89, p. 59.
"Prayer." [Footwork] 89, p. 60.
"Slow Runner." [Footwork] 89, p. 59.
2960. KEYWORTH, Suzanne
"A Fairy Tale of Sorts." [Shen] (39:4) Wint 89, p. 82-83.
"For My Sister, Charlene." [Shen] (39:4) Wint 89, p. 85.
"Kingdom." [Shen] (39:4) Wint 89, p. 84.
"Walkways." [Shen] (39:4) Wint 89, p. 85-86.
2961. KHA, Tran
"The Final Freedom" (tr. by Nguyen Ngoc Bich). [Vis] (31) 89, p. 21.
2962. KHOSLA, Maya
"Tao of the Running Child." [SmPd] (26:1, #75) Wint 89, p. 21.
2963. KIDMAN, Fiona
"Carole Something Like a Lombard" (Carole Lombard died in a plane crash over the Atlantic in 1942). [Descant] (20:3/4, #66/67) Fall-Wint 89, p. 177-179.
"The Man Who Loved Violets." [Descant] (20:3/4, #66/67) Fall-Wint 89, p. 175.
"The Presence of M. at a School Reunion." [Descant] (20:3/4, #66/67) Fall-Wint 89, p. 176.
2964. KIEFER, Rita
"Campfire." [ColR] (NS 16:2) Fall 89-Wint 90, p. 32.
"The Day I Found Out from the Dictionary How the Local Rotarians Do It." [ColR] (NS 16:2) Fall 89-Wint 90, p. 31.
"In the Uneven Yellow." [HighP] (4:2) Fall 89, p. 44-45.
2965. KIERNAN, Phyllis
"Walking in the Desert." [CinPR] (20) Fall 89, p. 26-27.
2966. KIKEL, Rudy
"You, Me, and Mootsie." [Tribe] (1:1) Wint 89, p. 75-85.
2967. KIKUCHI, Carl
"The Cicadas." [OxfordM] (5:2) Fall-Wint 89, p. 51-52.
"Imagination" (for Engman). [OxfordM] (5:2) Fall-Wint 89, p. 52.
"Telepathy: 17 Poems for My Sister" (Selections: 8 poems). [WashR] (15:1) Je-Jl 89, p. 16-17.
2968. KILDARE, D.
"Sweet Boys." [SoCaR] (21:2) Spr 89, p. 24.
2969. KILLEEN, Ger
"The Catch." [Sparrow] (56) 89, p. 19.
"Les Fleurs de Nuit." [Sparrow] (56) 89, p. 22.
"The Holy Well." [Sparrow] (56) 89, p. 24-25.
"Home Sickness." [Sparrow] (56) 89, p. 23.
"Jealousy." [Sparrow] (56) 89, p. 17.
"My Father Shaving." [Sparrow] (56) 89, p. 18.
"Scrimshaw." [Sparrow] (56) 89, p. 16.
"Vincent: Cafe Terrace at Night." [Sparrow] (56) 89, p. 20-21.

229

2970. KILLGORE, Edward H., Jr.
"Feet Quite Bare." [EmeraldCR] (1989) c1988, p. 92.
2971. KILLIAN, Dorothy Jean
"Appointment at 1:00 P.M." (from *October's Child*). [Obs] (3:2) Sum 88, p. 96.
2972. KILLIAN, Sean
"Blindfold, Wooly Cape and Shoes of Lead." [Sulfur] (9:1, #24) Spr 89, p.
135-136.
"Epilogues." [PaintedB] (37) 89, p. 78.
"Juices of Rubato (Stolen Time)." [Sulfur] (9:1, #24) Spr 89, p. 136-138.
"You're (History)." [Sulfur] (9:1, #24) Spr 89, p. 139.
2973. KIM, Chun-Soo
"Insect Eyes" (tr. by Chang Soo Ko). [Vis] (31) 89, p. 36.
"The Painter As I Saw Him" (tr. by Chang Soo Ko). [Vis] (31) 89, p. 37.
2974. KIM, Myung Mi
"I Cannot Heave My Heart into My Mouth" (Cordelia, *King Lear*). [Sulfur] (9:2,
#25) Fall 89, p. 64-65.
"Under Flag." [Sulfur] (9:2, #25) Fall 89, p. 60-63.
2975. KIM, Willyce
"Makai / First Light." [Cond] (16) 89, p. 154.
2976. KIM, Yong U.
"Learning Our Old Address." [IndR] (13:1) Wint 89, p. 26.
2977. KIMMELMAN, Burt (Burt J.)
"5.2.87 Waiting for Diane at the Klee Show, Museum of Modern Art." [Talisman]
(2) Spr 89, p. 6.
"8/6/86 Tate Gallery, Gaudier-Brzeska's Pound, *The Hieratic Head*." [Pequod]
(28/29/30) 89, p. 36.
2978. KINCAID, Joan Payne
"Being the Other." [HampSPR] Wint 89, p. 19.
"The Party." [Bogg] (61) 89, p. 12.
2979. KING, David W.
"I love you like an orange pump." [Poem] (61) My 89, p. 21.
"My noise is a noise." [Poem] (61) My 89, p. 17.
"A Poem to My Wife." [Poem] (61) My 89, p. 20.
"Sand Incident." [Poem] (61) My 89, p. 18-19.
"Virginia Churches." [Poem] (61) My 89, p. 13-16.
2980. KING, Gloria
"Between No Rain and Rain." [Interim] (8:2) Fall 89, p. 40.
2981. KING, Jon
"After Visiting the Museum." [HangL] (54) 89, p. 56.
"Before the Rapture." [HangL] (54) 89, p. 57.
"Two Hours Later." [HangL] (54) 89, p. 58.
2982. KING, Kenneth
"The Fleas." [ColEng] (51:8) D 89, p. 833.
"Intellect." [ColEng] (51:8) D 89, p. 832.
2983. KING, Lyn
"Canoeing." [MalR] (87) Sum 89, p. 91.
"Direction." [MalR] (87) Sum 89, p. 89.
"Freedom." [MalR] (87) Sum 89, p. 90.
2984. KING, R. D.
"At the Not My (Big, Rendered Picture)." [NowestR] (27:3) 89, p. 39.
"Christian Fowl Rhapsody." [NowestR] (27:3) 89, p. 38.
2985. KING, Robert
"Eating Vegetables." [BellArk] (5:2) Mr-Ap 89, p. 26.
"Fire Control." [BellArk] (5:2) Mr-Ap 89, p. 26.
"First Hail." [BellArk] (5:2) Mr-Ap 89, p. 26.
"Flashes." [BellArk] (5:2) Mr-Ap 89, p. 26.
"Thanks for the Memories Herb N Marilyn" (-- words on a sign that replace the sale
price of lean ground beef). [BellArk] (5:1) Ja-F 89, p. 17.
2986. KING, Sharon
"A Sonnet in Dialogue" (tr. of Francisco de Quevedo). [Jacaranda] (4:1) Spr-Sum
89, p. 59.
2987. KING, Susan Deborah
"Evening." [SpoonRQ] (14:1) Wint 89, p. 11.
2988. KINGSTON, Katie
"Between Two Towns." [Plain] (10:1) 89, p. 19.

2989. KINKEAD, Mary Ellen
"The words on yellow paper." [EngJ] (78:5) S 89, p. 97.
2990. KINLOCH, David
"Mounsey in le Pensionnat D'Humming-Bird Garden." [Verse] (6:3) Wint 89, p. 34.
"Now you will see everything is going to happen very slowly" (tr. of Michel
Deguy). [Verse] (6:2) Je 89, p. 16.
"Quasimodo." [Verse] (6:3) Wint 89, p. 33.
2991. KINNELL, Galway
"I Explain a Few Things" (tr. of Pablo Neruda). [Trans] (22) Fall 89, p. 177-179.
2992. KINSELLA, Thomas
"The Furnace." [NoDaQ] (57:1) Wint 89, p. 93.
"Harmonies." [NoDaQ] (57:1) Wint 89, p. 92.
"Native Wisdom." [NoDaQ] (57:1) Wint 89, p. 90-91.
2993. KINSLEY, Robert
"Grasshoppers." [MidAR] (9:2) 89, p. 171-172.
2994. KINSOLVING, Susan
"Half Note." [WestHR] (43:1) Spr 89, p. 46.
"Sotto Voce." [WestHR] (43:1) Spr 89, p. 47.
2995. KINZIE, Mary
"Bye Bye Blackbird." [TriQ] (74) Wint 89, p. 190-192.
"The Chanticleer." [AmerPoR] (18:4) Jl-Ag 89, p. 40.
"The Charm." [Salm] (81) Wint 89, p. 76-80.
"L'Estate." [Salm] (81) Wint 89, p. 85-89.
"Half Rations." [Poetry] (154:4) Jl 89, p. 219.
"Looking into Life." [Thrpny] (36) Wint 89, p. 28.
"Lunar Frost." [NewYorker] (64:51) 6 F 89, p. 34-35.
"The Palace of Defectives." [Salm] (81) Wint 89, p. 81-82.
"The Shed." [NewRep] (200:23) 5 Je 89, p. 32.
"Small Birthday Poem." [AmerS] (58:2) Spr 89, p. 270.
"Sparrows." [SouthwR] (74:1) Wint 89, p. 40.
"Summer Globe." [Salm] (81) Wint 89, p. 82-85.
2996. KIPP, Karen
"Ditches" (For Sheila Griffin). [AmerPoR] (18:4) Jl-Ag 89, p. 30.
"I'm Sending You Saint Francis Preaching to the Birds." [AmerPoR] (18:4) Jl-Ag
89, p. 31.
"The Rat." [AmerPoR] (18:4) Jl-Ag 89, p. 30.
2997. KIRBY, Barney
"Manchuria." [AntR] (47:2) Spr 89, p. 194-195.
2998. KIRBY, David
"The Gigolo in the Gazebo." [ChatR] (9:3) Spr 89, p. 51.
"Money Won't Change You (But Time Will Take You Out)" (title of a song by James
Brown). [CarolQ] (42:1) Fall 89, p. 60-61.
2999. KIRCHWEY, Karl
"Ambulance." [Pequod] (26/27) 89, p. 41-42.
"Avalanche Barriers, Erstfeld." [AntR] (47:2) Spr 89, p. 208.
"Drayton Gardens, S.W. 10." [Pequod] (26/27) 89, p. 39-40.
"German Nudists, Kalamaki, Crete." [NewYorker] (65:29) 4 S 89, p. 38.
"In Passing." [Nat] (248:3) 23 Ja 89, p. 103.
"Medon on Lemnos." [GrandS] (9:1) Aut 89, p. 210-211.
3000. KIRK, James
"Morning Watch." [Footwork] 89, p. 58.
3001. KIRK, Laurie
"Accomplices." [PoetryE] (28) Fall 89, p. 152-153.
"A Perfect Imbalance." [PoetryE] (28) Fall 89, p. 150-151.
"Rehearsals." [Footwork] 89, p. 12.
3002. KIRKLAND, Leigh
"The World Ends at Fairfax High School." [HayF] (4) Spr 89, p. 44.
3003. KIRKLAND, Will
"The Arrest of Little Tony Camborio on the Seville Highway" (To Margarita Xirgu,
tr. of Federico Garcia Lorca). [Sequoia] (32:2) Wint-Spr 89, p. 15-16.
"The Death of Little Tony Camborio" (To José Antonio Rubio Sacristán, tr. of
Federico Garcia Lorca). [Sequoia] (32:2) Wint-Spr 89, p. 19-20.
3004. KIRSCH, Sarah
"Cat's Lives" (tr. by John Linthicum). [LitR] (33:1) Fall 89, p. 64.
"Damnation" (tr. by Charles Fishman and Marina Roscher). [WebR] (14:1) Spr 89,
p. 12.

"Damnation" (tr. by John Linthicum). [LitR] (33:1) Fall 89, p. 65.
"The Day's Beginning" (tr. by John Linthicum). [LitR] (33:1) Fall 89, p. 64.
"Gentle Hunt" (tr. by Charles Fishman and Marina Roscher). [WebR] (14:1) Spr 89, p. 15.
"Heartstone" (tr. by Charles Fishman and Marina Roscher). [WebR] (14:1) Spr 89, p. 14.
"Ravens" (tr. by Charles Fishman and Marina Roscher). [WebR] (14:1) Spr 89, p. 14.
"The Sleeper" (tr. by Charles Fishman and Marina Roscher). [WebR] (14:1) Spr 89, p. 13.
"Snow" (tr. by John Linthicum). [LitR] (33:1) Fall 89, p. 63.
"The Trochel" (tr. by Charles Fishman and Marina Roscher). [WebR] (14:1) Spr 89, p. 15.
"When the Ice Goes" (tr. by John Linthicum). [LitR] (33:1) Fall 89, p. 63.
3005. KIRSCHENBAUM, Sara
"Soundings: The Barb Papers" (#8, day 23). [Kalliope] (11:2) 89, p. 5.
3006. KIRSCHNER, Elizabeth
"The Blueness of Stars." [ThRiPo] (33/34) 89, p. 36-37.
"Not Far From Here." [OhioR] (43) 89, p. 113-114.
"This Dusk." [ThRiPo] (33/34) 89, p. 35.
3007. KIRSTEIN, Lincoln
"Idiot Savant." [Raritan] (9:2) Fall 89, p. 26-28.
3008. KISIEL, Caroline M.
"Woman Song" (tr. of Rosa Marta Zárate Macías). [ChrC] (106:18) My 24-31, 89, p. 561.
3009. KISNER, S. J.
"Leatherback." [Outbr] (20) 89, p. 73-74.
3010. KITTO, William
"The Clock." [AnthNEW] (1) 89, p. 15.
3011. KIYOWARA, Fukuyabu (900-930)
"In the autumn sea" (tr. by Sam Hamill). [PoetryE] (28) Fall 89, p. 201.
"River fog rises" (tr. by Sam Hamill). [PoetryE] (28) Fall 89, p. 200.
3012. KIZER, Carolyn
"Adviser to the Court" (tr. of Tu Fu). [LitR] (32:3) Spr 89, p. 325.
"Dejeuner sur l'Herbe" (tr. of Tu Fu). [LitR] (32:3) Spr 89, p. 323.
"I Go Too" (tr. of Tu Fu). [LitR] (32:3) Spr 89, p. 321.
"A Muse of Water." [DenQ] (23:3/4) Wint-Spr 89, p. 23-25.
"On the Way Out" (tr. of Tu Fu). [LitR] (32:3) Spr 89, p. 322.
"Perhaps" (for the loneliness of an author, tr. of Shu Ting). [LitR] (32:3) Spr 89, p. 320.
"Reply to a Friend's Advice" (tr. of Tu Fu). [LitR] (32:3) Spr 89, p. 322.
"The Singing Flower" (7 selections: I, II, IV, V, VIII, X, XVI, tr. of Shu Ting). [LitR] (32:3) Spr 89, p. 318-320.
"Spring-Gazing Song" (tr. of Hsüeh T'ao). [LitR] (32:3) Spr 89, p. 326.
"Spring-Gazing Song II" (tr. of Hsüeh T'ao). [LitR] (32:3) Spr 89, p. 326.
"Spring Goes" (tr. of Tu Fu). [LitR] (32:3) Spr 89, p. 321.
"Thwarted" (tr. of Tu Fu). [LitR] (32:3) Spr 89, p. 324.
"Weaving Love-knots" (tr. of Hsüeh T'ao). [LitR] (32:3) Spr 89, p. 326.
"Weaving Love-knots #13" (tr. of Hsüeh T'ao). [LitR] (32:3) Spr 89, p. 326.
3013. KLANDER, Sharon
"Visitation." [WestHR] (43:2) Sum 89, p. 119.
3014. KLARE, Judy
"Midwestern Town." [KanQ] (21:1/2) Wint-Spr 89, p. 97.
3015. KLASS, Stephen
"Aniara" (Selections: V, XXIX, tr. of Harry Martinson, w. Leif Sjöberg). [Pequod] (26/27) 89, p. 35-36.
3016. KLASSEN, Sarah
"All Along" (Prose Poem Winter, the First Short Grain Contest). [Grain] (17:3) Fall 89, p. 66-67.
"Beautiful Girls of Souzhou." [PraF] (10:1, #46) Spr 89, p. 38-39.
"Year of the Pig" (Guangzhou, 1987). [PraF] (10:1, #46) Spr 89, p. 40.
3017. KLAVAN, Andrew
"The Pond." [NegC] (9:2) 89, p. 55.
3018. KLAWITTER, George
"Discoveries: Anatomy 121." [CumbPR] (8:2) Spr 89, p. 25.

3019. KLEIN, Michael
"Chamber Music." [Crazy] (37) Wint 89, p. 24-25.
"The Echo: Heart" (for J.D.). [CimR] (89) O 89, p. 93-94.
"The Guff." [Pequod] (26/27) 89, p. 171-172.
"How Everyone Is the First One to Notice Fire" (for RHC). [Sonora] (17) Spr-Sum
89, p. 16-18.
"More Light" (for Brian). [BlackWR] (15:2) Spr 89, p. 34-35.
"Spectacular Bid." [Crazy] (37) Wint 89, p. 22-23.
"Straw." [CimR] (89) O 89, p. 95-96.
3020. KLEIN, P. H.
"Hauptmann Reconsidered." [ChiR] (36:3/4) 89, p. 41-42.
3021. KLEINSCHMIDT, Edward
"Anesthetic." [AmerPoR] (18:5) S-O 89, p. 38.
"Boustrophedon." [PoetryNW] (30:3) Aut 89, p. 17.
"Cicatrix." [Zyzzyva] (5:3, #19) Fall 89, p. 91-92.
"Counting Down." [NoDaQ] (57:4) Fall 89, p. 11.
"Down River" (for John Ashbery, Edward Haworth Hoeppner, Eugene D. Richie).
[DenQ] (23:3/4) Wint-Spr 89, p. 106-107.
"Echolalia." [ColEng] (51:5) S 89, p. 480.
"Gangue." [GettyR] (2:1) Wint 89, p. 80.
"Infantry." [AmerPoR] (18:5) S-O 89, p. 38.
"Like Tulipomania." [NoDaQ] (57:4) Fall 89, p. 9-10.
"Manufacture." [NewAW] (5) Fall 89, p. 111.
"More or Less." [Confr] (39/40) Fall 88-Wint 89, p. 104-105.
"Orchestrion." [NewYorker] (65:38) 6 N 89, p. 54.
"Questionnaire." [CentR] (33:2) Spr 89, p. 132-133.
"Speech-Thought." [RiverS] (28) 89, p. 64.
"Tabula Rasa." [MassR] (30:2) Sum 89, p. 238.
"The Use and the matter." [Sequoia] (32:2) Wint-Spr 89, p. 52.
"Watch." [Sequoia] (32:2) Wint-Spr 89, p. 53.
3022. KLEINZAHLER, August
"Afternoons." [Epoch] (38:1) 89, p. 8-9.
"A Birthday Bash for Thomas Nashe." [Epoch] (38:1) 89, p. 10.
"On the Occasion of Thom Gunn's 60th Birthday" (after Catullus). [Zyzzyva] (5:3,
#19) Fall 89, p. 95-96.
"Sunday in November." [NewYorker] (65:11) 1 My 89, p. 74.
3023. KLEPFISZ, Irena
"East Jerusalem, 1987: *Bet Shalom* (House of Peace)" (To a Palestinian woman
whom I am afraid to name). [NewL] (56:2/3) Wint 89-Spr 90, p. 161-163.
"Fradel Schtok" (Yiddish writer, B. 1890 in Skale, Galicia. Emigrated to New York
in 1907 . . .). [NewL] (56:2/3) Wint 89-Spr 90, p. 159-160.
"Royal Pearl." [NewL] (56:2/3) Wint 89-Spr 90, p. 158.
"Solitary Acts" (for my aunt Gina Klepfisz, 1908?-1942). [NewL] (56:2/3) Wint
89-Spr 90, p. 151-157.
3024. KLIEWER, Warren
"A Story About Beginning." [CinPR] (20) Fall 89, p. 51.
3025. KLINE, Wayne
"Joy in a Yellow Cantina." [Aerial] (5) 89, p. 98.
"Modern Japanese Autobody Versus the Audience Cult, A Transition." [Screens] (1)
89, p. 125.
"Ode to a Left Margin." [Aerial] (5) 89, p. 97.
3026. KLINGER, Adria
"The captive cow." [KeyWR] (2:1/2) Fall-Wint 89, p. 141.
"Meditation." [KeyWR] (2:1/2) Fall-Wint 89, p. 140.
3027. KLOEFKORN, William
"Abandoned Farmhouse." [SoDakR] (27:4) Wint 89, p. 13-14.
"Biting the Dust." [Journal] (13:1) Spr-Sum 89, p. 76.
"Burning the Hymnal." [Journal] (13:1) Spr-Sum 89, p. 72-73.
"Dancing in the Cornfield." [WestB] (23) 89, p. 5-6.
"Drifting." [SoDakR] (27:4) Wint 89, p. 15-16.
"Epiphany." [CapeR] (24:1) Spr 89, p. 40.
"Fastpitch Finals, 1954." [Journal] (13:1) Spr-Sum 89, p. 77-78.
"Full Moon Rising over the Lumberyard." [PraS] (63:2) Sum 89, p. 96-97.
"George Eat Old Gray Rat at Pappy's House Yesterday" (for David Lee). [PraS]
(63:2) Sum 89, p. 94-95.
"Legend." [WeberS] (6:2) Fall 89, p. 26-27.

"Moving Full Throttle on a Limited Sea." [WestB] (23) 89, p. 6-7.
"The Night Joe Louis Went 21-0 by Dropping Tami Mauriello." [MissouriR] (12:1) 89, p. 24-25.
"Paper Route, 2 August 1945." [Journal] (13:1) Spr-Sum 89, p. 75.
"Physical." [Journal] (13:1) Spr-Sum 89, p. 79.
"Selling the Shotgun." [OxfordM] (5:1) Spr-Sum 89, p. 38-39.
"Stopping the Tractor with the Plowing Almost Done to Chase a Rabbit." [WeberS] (6:2) Fall 89, p. 25-26.
"Swamping *Our Lady of the Loup*." [Journal] (13:1) Spr-Sum 89, p. 74.
"Visiting the Graves of Friends." [WestB] (23) 89, p. 7-8.
3028. KLOKKER, Jay
"Adjusting the Vertical." [BelPoJ] (40:1) Fall 89, p. 9.
"A Classical Education" (in answer to Hirsch, Bloom & Co.). [BelPoJ] (40:1) Fall 89, p. 8.
3029. KLOSE, Robert T.
"Cotillion." [NewOR] (16:1) Spr 89, p. 33.
3030. KNE, Majda
"Noonday Bells in Trnovo" (tr. by Michael Biggins). [NewEngR] (11:3) Spr 89, p. 239.
3031. KNIGHT, Arthur Winfield
"Bat Masterson: The News." [InterPR] (15:2) Fall 89, p. 116.
"Emmett Dalton: Coffeyville." [InterPR] (15:2) Fall 89, p. 115.
"The Men on the Moon." [PaintedB] (37) 89, p. 29.
"Saying Goodbye." [InterPR] (15:2) Fall 89, p. 117.
"Wyatt Earp: Legends." [InterPR] (15:2) Fall 89, p. 113-114.
3032. KNIGHT, Denis
"The Dancing Man." [Stand] (30:3) Sum 89, p. 35.
"Nora in Occitania." [Stand] (30:3) Sum 89, p. 54.
"Olivia's Watersnake." [Stand] (30:3) Sum 89, p. 55.
"Where the Windmill Was." [Stand] (30:3) Sum 89, p. 54.
3033. KNIGHT, Kit
"Jacking Off the Rhino." [PaintedB] (37) 89, p. 87.
3034. KNIGHT, Sondra
"Sable." [SinW] (38) Sum-Fall 89, p. 108.
3035. KNIGHTS, Maudeen
"Scenes: West Seattle." [BellArk] (5:6) N-D 89, p. 8.
3036. KNOEPFLE, John
"East in McLean County." [PraS] (63:4) Wint 89, p. 127.
"Edwardsville Before Sunrise." [PraS] (63:4) Wint 89, p. 123.
"For a Child Who Lived Six Hours." [PraS] (63:4) Wint 89, p. 125.
"Looking Out in the Evening from East of Sizhou City." [PraS] (63:4) Wint 89, p. 123.
"Mary Louise." [PraS] (63:4) Wint 89, p. 124.
"Moonscapes from the Book of Job." [CharR] (15:1) Spr 89, p. 50.
"North Carolina Outer Banks." [ClockR] (5:2) 89, p. 43.
"Peoria-Miami Free Form." [Nimrod] (32:2) Spr-Sum 89, p. 122-143.
"Poet in a Small Place." [Farm] (6:1) Wint-Spr 88-89, p. 19.
"San Antonio Rose." [CharR] (15:1) Spr 89, p. 51.
"Searching for Makonza." [CharR] (15:1) Spr 89, p. 49.
"St. Louise Midnight." [PraS] (63:4) Wint 89, p. 124.
3037. KNOPP, Lisa
"Eulogy for a Great Aunt." [Plain] (9:2) Wint 89, p. 29.
3038. KNOTT, Kip
"Cave-In at Scratch Back Mine." [MidAR] (9:1) 89, p. 167.
"River Watch." [MidAR] (9:1) 89, p. 166.
"Unveiling the Stealth Bomber." [MidwQ] (31:1) Aut 89, p. 50.
"Working in the Zoology Storeroom" (a title suggested by my father). [Journal] (13:1) Spr-Sum 89, p. 57.
3039. KNOWLTON, Lindsay
"Guilty." [WillowS] (23) Wint 89, p. 37-38.
3040. KNOX, Ann B.
"The Brown Pelican: 2:30 PM" (Note found on his calendar). [PoetL] (84:3) Fall 89, p. 13.
3041. KNOX, Caroline
"Booz Endormi." [ApalQ] (31) 89, p. 61.
"Citizen." [WestHR] (43:3) Aut 89, p. 205.

"Exploring Unknown Territory." [ApalQ] (32) 89, p. 27-32.
"Names for the Sun." [WestHR] (43:3) Aut 89, p. 206.
3042. KO, Chang Soo
"Insect Eyes" (tr. of Chun-Soo Kim). [Vis] (31) 89, p. 36.
"The Painter As I Saw Him" (tr. of Chun-Soo Kim). [Vis] (31) 89, p. 37.
KOBO, Dashi
See KUKAI
3043. KOCBEK, Edvard
"Hands" (tr. by Michael Biggins). [NewEngR] (11:3) Spr 89, p. 240.
"Lipizzaners" (tr. by Michael Scammell and Veno Taufer). [ColR] (NS 16:1)
Spr-Sum 89, p. 95-97.
"Moon Shining onto Fenced Pastures" (tr. by Michael Biggins). [NewEngR] (11:3)
Spr 89, p. 240.
3044. KOCH, Claude
"Palimpsest" (Tulagi Harbor, British Solomon Islands, 1942-1987). [SewanR]
(97:1) Wint 89, p. 26.
3045. KOERNER, Edgar
"For Dylan Thomas." [PoetryE] (28) Fall 89, p. 149.
"The Night That He Tried." [PoetryE] (28) Fall 89, p. 146-147.
"Two Minutes." [PoetryE] (28) Fall 89, p. 148.
3046. KOESTENBAUM, Wayne
"The Debut" (from "Ode to Anna Moffo"). [WestHR] (43:4) Wint 89, p. 235-242.
"Fantasia on My Father's Gift" (Prizewinning Poets -- 1989). [Nat] (248:20) 22 My
89, p. 706-707.
"A History of Private Life." [ParisR] (31:112) Fall 89, p. 92-95.
"Teachers of Obscure Subjects." [Jacaranda] (4:1) Spr-Sum 89, p. 22-24.
3047. KOETHE, John
"The Constructor." [GettyR] (2:1) Wint 89, p. 124-129.
"A Pathetic Landscape." [SouthwR] (74:3) Sum 89, p. 309.
"The Waiting Game." [SouthwR] (74:3) Sum 89, p. 310-311.
3048. KOKOT, Andrej
"The Crow's Song" (tr. by Michael Biggins). [NewEngR] (11:3) Spr 89, p. 241.
3049. KOLATKAR, Arun
"The Alphabet" (in Marathi). [TriQ] (77) Wint 89-90, p. 185.
"The Alphabet" (tr. by Vinay Dharwadker). [TriQ] (77) Wint 89-90, p. 184.
"Bread" (tr. by Vinay Dharwadker). [TriQ] (77) Wint 89-90, p. 182.
"Buildings" (in Marathi). [TriQ] (77) Wint 89-90, p. 181.
"Buildings" (tr. by Vinay Dharwadker). [TriQ] (77) Wint 89-90, p. 180.
"Licked Clean" (tr. by Vinay Dharwadker). [TriQ] (77) Wint 89-90, p. 183.
3050. KOLBUS, Edward
"A Letter from Verona" (tr. by Jerzy Jarniewicz). [TampaR] (2) 89, p. 67.
3051. KOLODNY, Susan
"Shoreline." [SoCoast] (7) Spr-Fall 89, p. 32.
3052. KOLUMBAN, Nicholas
"Again and Again" (tr. of Katalin Mezey). [ArtfulD] (16/17) Fall 89, p. 74.
"An American Indian on the Hungarian Radio" (For the poet Willima Least Heat
Moon, tr. of Géza Szöcs). [NoDaQ] (57:4) Fall 89, p. 12-13.
"Dawn." [ArtfulD] (16/17) Fall 89, p. 69.
"Elegy" (tr. of Gyula Illyés). [NowestR] (27:2) 89, p. 19-20.
"Elegy for My Wife's Father, John Meilinger." [ArtfulD] (16/17) Fall 89, p. 70.
"Ergo I'm Getting Warm. I May Even Eat Supper, . . ." (tr. of Tibor Zalan).
[ArtfulD] (16/17) Fall 89, p. 73.
"Evenings When Silence Arrives in My Apartment with a Boom, . . ." (tr. of Tibor
Zalan). [ArtfulD] (16/17) Fall 89, p. 72.
"Fear of 14-Year Olds." [Footwork] 89, p. 54.
"How to Make Hungarian Goulash." [ArtfulD] (16/17) Fall 89, p. 71.
"May Dog Dundas" (tr. of János Olah). [Hawai'iR] (13:1, #25) Spr 89, p. 53.
"The Night Song of the Peeping Tom" (tr. of Gyösrgy Petri). [ArtfulD] (16/17) Fall
89, p. 75.
"On a January Morning" (from Romania, tr. of Géza Szöcs). [PoetryE] (28) Fall 89,
p. 180-181.
"A Report on Myself." [ArtfulD] (16/17) Fall 89, p. 67.
"Solar Eclipse" (tr. of Irén Négyesy, w. Daniel Bourne). [ArtfulD] (16/17) Fall 89,
p. 76.
"They Say It's Delicious." [ArtfulD] (16/17) Fall 89, p. 68.
"You Are Asking Me" (tr. of Imre Oravecz). [PoetryE] (28) Fall 89, p. 179.

3053. KOMLOSI, László
"Elegy on the Death of Gyula Juhász" (tr. of Miklós Radnóti, w. Len Roberts).
[IndR] (12:2) Spr 89, p. 97.
3054. KOMUNYAKAA, Yusef
"Believing in Iron." [GeoR] (43:3) Fall 89, p. 588.
"Blackberries." [Ploughs] (15:1) 89, p. 76.
"Cousins." [Ploughs] (15:4) Wint 89-90, p. 117.
"Holloween, the Fifties." [Ploughs] (15:1) 89, p. 74-75.
"Mismatched Shoes." [Ploughs] (15:4) Wint 89-90, p. 115-116.
"Poetics of Paperwood." [RiverS] (28) 89, p. 1.
"A Quality of Light." [WillowS] (23) Wint 89, p. 42.
"The Soft Touch." [RiverS] (28) 89, p. 3.
"Temples of Smoke." [Ploughs] (15:1) 89, p. 77.
"The Thirteenth." [RiverS] (28) 89, p. 2.
3055. KONO, Juliet (Juliet S.)
"Drowning." [ChamLR] (3:1, #5) Fall 89, p. 113.
"The First Time." [ChamLR] (3:1, #5) Fall 89, p. 111-112.
"This Rocking Chair." [BambooR] (41) Wint 89, p. 16-18.
"The Vegetable Peddler." [ChamLR] (3:1, #5) Fall 89, p. 114.
3056. KONOPKA, Amy
"The Flower" (Mainstreet Elementary Poetry Contest, 7th Grade, 3rd Place).
[DeKalbLAJ] (22:1/4) 89, p. 108.
KOON, Woon
See WOON, Koon
3057. KOOSER, Ted
"Across the Pond." [LaurelR] (23:2) Sum 89, p. 48.
"Cleaning a Bass." [SwampR] (1:4) Sum 89, p. 59.
"Elegy for Helene Mierkalns." [SwampR] (1:4) Sum 89, p. 73.
"A Ghost Story." [CreamCR] (13:2) Fall 89, p. 25.
"The Giant Slide." [SwampR] (1:4) Sum 89, p. 59.
"In a Kitchen Garden." [SwampR] (1:4) Sum 89, p. 74.
"In Late Spring." [PraS] (63:2) Sum 89, p. 78-79.
"A Letter in October." [CreamCR] (13:2) Fall 89, p. 24.
"The Little Hats." [PraS] (63:2) Sum 89, p. 77.
"The Man Who Measures Himself against Money." [PraS] (63:2) Sum 89, p. 76-77.
"A November Dawn." [PraS] (63:2) Sum 89, p. 79.
"The Snake." [LaurelR] (23:2) Sum 89, p. 48.
"Spider Eggs." [SouthernPR] (29:1) Spr 89, p. 73.
"The Sweeper." [CreamCR] (13:2) Fall 89, p. 23.
"Yard Light." [SwampR] (1:4) Sum 89, p. 75.
3058. KOOSMAN, Toby
"Hen." [BlueBldgs] (11) 89, p. 60-61.
3059. KOOTZ, Haven
"Woodsmoke on My Hands." [YellowS] (29) Spr 89, p. 40-41.
3060. KOPELKE, Kendra
"The Nexell Factory." [FreeL] (3) Aut 89, p. 30-31.
"Smoke." [FreeL] (3) Aut 89, p. 28-29.
3061. KORBUL, John
"Rain Revisited." [Footwork] 89, p. 56.
3062. KORELITZ, Jean Hanff
"Munich." [Pequod] (26/27) 89, p. 20.
"Smoke." [Pequod] (26/27) 89, p. 21.
3063. KORETZ, Willa
"Fire Fruit." [Mildred] (3:2) 89, p. 20.
3064. KORN, Rohel
"An Evening in the Old People's Home" (tr. by Miriam Waddington). [CanLit] (120)
Spr 89, p. 20.
3065. KORNHAUSER, Julian
"Barricade" (tr. by Stanislaw Baranczak and Clare Cavanah). [Trans] (21) Spr 89, p.
78.
3066. KÖRÖSY, Mária
"After We Broke Up" (tr. of Imre Oravecz, w. Bruce Berlind). [TriQ] (77) Wint
89-90, p. 296.
"Autumn in the Midwest" (tr. of Imre Oravecz, w. Bruce Berlind). [ArtfulD] (16/17)
Fall 89, p. 66.
"Ebb Tide" (tr. of Gyula Illyes, w. Bruce Berlind). [Colum] (14) 89, p. 125.

"Evening Song" (tr. of Gyula Illyes, w. Bruce Berlind). [Colum] (14) 89, p. 124.
"It Was Still Summer" (tr. of Imre Oravecz, w. Bruce Berlind). [TriQ] (77) Wint
 89-90, p. 297.
"Poverty" (tr. of Ottó Orbán, w. Jascha Kessler). [Margin] (9) 89, p. 36.
"When Now and Then We Run Into Each Other" (tr. of Imre Oravecz, w. Bruce
 Berlind). [TriQ] (77) Wint 89-90, p. 295.
3067. KORUSIEWICZ, Maria
"III. I have this poor sick head again" (tr. by Alexandra Olejniszym). [Verse] (6:1)
 Mr 89, p. 40.
3068. KOSTELANETZ, Richard
"Milestones in a Life." [BostonR] (14:2) Ap 89, p. 4.
"Minimal Audio Plays (1989)" (Excerpt). [CentralP] (15) Spr 89, p. 17-19.
"More Openings & Closings." [Caliban] (7) 89, p. 103-108.
"Partitions." [AnotherCM] (19) 89, p. 119-123.
"Partitions" (Excerpts). [FreeL] (2) Sum 89, p. 10.
3069. KOTARY, Judith
"To Any Woman Dying of February." [BelPoJ] (40:1) Fall 89, p. 23.
3070. KOTESKEY, Fred
"The Golden Eagle King." [EmeraldCR] (1989) c1988, p. 134.
3071. KOTTLER, Dorian Brooks
"Toad Tunnels." [LakeSR] (23) 89, p. 3.
"Walden Forever Wild." [LakeSR] (23) 89, p. 4.
3072. KOVACIK, Karen
"The Spiders Electric." [BelPoJ] (40:2) Wint 89-90, p. 33-34.
"Wedding Song." [BelPoJ] (40:2) Wint 89-90, p. 32-33.
3073. KOVACS, Edna
"Pumpkin Season." [BellArk] (5:1) Ja-F 89, p. 3.
3074. KOVANDA, William James
"The Thin Grey Line." [Wind] (19:65) 89, p. 14.
3075. KOVIC, Kajetan
"Buffaloes" (tr. by Michael Biggins). [NewEngR] (11:3) Spr 89, p. 242.
3076. KOWALSKI, Beth Ann
"Knots." [SoCoast] (7) Spr-Fall 89, p. 42-43.
3077. KOZIELSKI, Dolores
"A Found Sonnet" (A Taking from Iambic Pentameter). [SingHM] (16) 89, p. 13.
"Lines." [SingHM] (16) 89, p. 13.
3078. KOZMA, Lynn
"Montauk." [SmPd] (26:3 #77) Fall 89, p. 25.
3079. KRAFT, Eugene
"As I Step Down from the Train." [ChrC] (106:30) O 18, 89, p. 932.
"Blakat Blues." [Obs] (4:3) Wint 89, p. 67-68.
"Parsing, 1933." [Obs] (4:3) Wint 89, p. 66.
"The Rattlesnake's Goodness." [CimR] (87) Ap 89, p. 36-37.
"Red Sun at Morning." [Obs] (4:3) Wint 89, p. 67.
3080. KRAMER, Aaron
"The Door." [Wind] (19:65) 89, p. 15.
"Going In." [Wind] (19:65) 89, p. 15-16.
"Katharina" (tr. of Heinrich Heine). [CumbPR] (9:1) Fall 89, p. 57.
"New Decade." [NewEngR] (11:4) Sum 89, p. 438.
"The Unknown One" (tr. of Heinrich Heine). [CumbPR] (9:1) Fall 89, p. 60-61.
3081. KRATT, Mary
"Elizabeth Takes an Evening Walk." [TexasR] (10:1/2) Spr-Sum 89, p. 92.
"Eva's Travels." [SpoonRQ] (14:1) Wint 89, p. 20.
"The Need to Name." [SpoonRQ] (14:1) Wint 89, p. 16-17.
"The Rider." [SpoonRQ] (14:1) Wint 89, p. 18.
"To a Friend Who Loaned Us His House in the Mountains." [SpoonRQ] (14:1) Wint
 89, p. 19.
3082. KRAUS, Jim
"Shadow Poem." [Wind] (19:65) 89, p. 16.
3083. KRAUS, Sharon
"After Visiting the Berkshires Nature Preserve and Finding the Gray's Sedge in
 Bloom." [Colum] (14) 89, p. 30.
"What the Door Gives Onto." [Colum] (14) 89, p. 28-29.
3084. KRAUSE, Judith
"Scare" (Prose Poem Winter, the First Short Grain Contest). [Grain] (17:3) Fall 89,
 p. 72.

3085. KRAUSE, Rudiger
 "Aurora Borealis." [CanLit] (120) Spr 89, p. 11.
 "This Land (Canadata)." [CanLit] (120) Spr 89, p. 142-143.
3086. KRAUSHAAR, Mark
 "Express." [PoetryNW] (30:3) Aut 89, p. 16-17.
 "House of Chong." [PoetryNW] (30:2) Sum 89, p. 24.
 "WW II Plane Found on Moon" (Headline from *World News*). [PoetryNW] (30:3)
 Aut 89, p. 15.
3087. KRAVANJA-GROSS, Sonja
 "Shepherd" (tr. of Tomaz Salamun, w. Charles Simic). [WestHR] (43:1) Spr 89, p.
 64.
 "The Tree of Life" (tr. of Tomaz Salamun). [Field] (40) Spr 89, p. 75-76.
3088. KREITER-KURYLO, Carolyn
 "The Woman of Innsbruck." [Vis] (30) 89, p. 15.
3089. KRESH, David
 "Buffalo Grass." [Bound] (16:2/3) Wint-Spr 89, p. 247-249.
 "I Remembered Clifford" (for Mitch Freedman). [Caliban] (6) 89, p. 181-182.
3090. KRESS, Leonard
 "After the War." [ArtfulD] (16/17) Fall 89, p. 99.
 "Burning the Bride's Hair." [ArtfulD] (16/17) Fall 89, p. 100.
 "Don't Dwell on Things That Can't be Known" (tr. of Stefan George). [PaintedB]
 (37) 89, p. 31.
 "Looms." [WestB] (24) 89, p. 66-67.
 "The Manichean Heresey." [AmerPoR] (18:3) My-Je 89, p. 42.
 "Poppy Seeds." [MissouriR] (12:2) 89, p. 178.
 "Two Cemeteries in a Town in the Kurpie Forest." [PaintedB] (37) 89, p. 30.
3091. KRETZ, Thomas
 "Almost." [HolCrit] (26:3) Je 89, p. 13.Stryk, Dan "Cave Bull." [HolCrit] (26:3) Je
 89, p. 18.
 "The Letters That I Write to You, Michele." [InterPR] (15:2) Fall 89, p. 118.
3092. KRICORIAN, Nancy
 "Armenia" (for M.K.K., 1904?-1985). [Witness] (2:1) Spr 88, p. 37-39.
 "The Red Armenian Slippers." [LitR] (32:2) Wint 89, p. 232.
 "Your Face." [StoneC] (17:1/2) Fall-Wint 89-90, p. 41.
3093. KRIESEL, Michael
 "Birthday Card." [Bogg] (61) 89, p. 18.
3094. KRIM, Nancy
 "Letter of Recommendation." [EngJ] (78:5) S 89, p. 97.
3095. KRIVULIN, Viktor
 "Poems on Maps" (Excerpt, tr. by Michael Molnar). [MichQR] (28:4) Fall 89, p.
 738.
3096. KROCKE, Mary K.
 "Drei Stucke." [NegC] (9:2) 89, p. 56-57.
3097. KROLL, Ernest
 "Ball Field." [KanQ] (21:1/2) Wint-Spr 89, p. 230.
 "Destructive Elements." [KanQ] (21:1/2) Wint-Spr 89, p. 229.
 "Flight into Italy." [PoetC] (21:1) Fall 89, p. 37.
 "In a Grove of Sugar Pines" (Sierra Nevada). [Bound] (16:2/3) Wint-Spr 89, p.
 168.
 "The Missouri." [Bound] (16:2/3) Wint-Spr 89, p. 169.
 "Pressure Under Grace" (Oak Park, Ill.). [FourQ] (2d series 3:1) Spr 89, p. 38.
3098. KROLL, Judith
 "At the Centrepoint" (for E.D.). [KeyWR] (2:1/2) Fall-Wint 89, p. 96-97.
3099. KROLOW, Karl
 "The End of Some Things" (tr. by Stuart Friebert). [WestB] (24) 89, p. 26.
 "In Between" (tr. by Stuart Friebert). [Interim] (8:2) Fall 89, p. 22.
 "In the Country" (tr. by Stuart Friebert). [OhioR] (44) 89, p. 30.
 "In the Eighties" (tr. by John Linthicum). [LitR] (33:1) Fall 89, p. 95.
 "The Long Journey" (tr. by John Linthicum). [LitR] (33:1) Fall 89, p. 92.
 "Maybe a Sort Will Turn Up" (tr. by John Linthicum). [LitR] (33:1) Fall 89, p. 94.
 "Moment" (tr. by John Linthicum). [LitR] (33:1) Fall 89, p. 92.
 "The Murderer" (tr. by Stuart Friebert). [Journal] (13:1) Spr-Sum 89, p. 56.
 "News of Death" (tr. by Stuart Friebert). [ColR] (NS 16:2) Fall 89-Wint 90, p.
 84-85.
 "Next Door" (tr. by John Linthicum). [LitR] (33:1) Fall 89, p. 94.
 "Old People's Spring" (tr. by Stuart Friebert). [OhioR] (44) 89, p. 29.

"Parade" (tr. by Stuart Friebert). [ArtfulD] (16/17) Fall 89, p. 94.
"Some Countries" (tr. by John Linthicum). [LitR] (33:1) Fall 89, p. 96.
"Someone" (tr. by Stuart Friebert). [Interim] (8:2) Fall 89, p. 23.
"These Old Men" (tr. by Stuart Friebert). [Journal] (13:1) Spr-Sum 89, p. 55.
"Walking" (tr. by John Linthicum). [LitR] (33:1) Fall 89, p. 93.
3100. KRON, Paul
"What the Potter Said." [Quarry] (38:4) Fall 89, p. 19.
"White Truck." [Quarry] (38:4) Fall 89, p. 20.
3101. KRONEN, Steve
"For L, Born August 6, 1945." [Thrpny] (38) Sum 89, p. 19.
"An Incident at Andersonville -- From the Recollections of Private Charles
     Hopkins." [RiverS] (30) [89], p. 34.
"Natural History" (for Ellie). [PraS] (63:3) Fall 89, p. 110-111.
"This Afternoon." [PraS] (63:3) Fall 89, p. 112.
3102. KRONENFELD, Judy
"Service." [MSS] (6:3) 89, p. 22-23.
3103. KRÜGER, Michael
"A Conversation During Rain" (tr. by John Linthicum). [LitR] (33:1) Fall 89, p.
     111.
"A Letter from Rome" (tr. by John Linthicum). [LitR] (33:1) Fall 89, p. 112.
"A Painting Comes into Being" (tr. by John Linthicum). [LitR] (33:1) Fall 89, p.
     110.
3104. KRUKOWSKI, Damon
"In exaggeration of modesty I was unable to enter the house." [Caliban] (6) 89, p.
     205.
"Let's unmake the bed, and imagine the middles ages." [Caliban] (6) 89, p. 205.
"Listening to your unconscious." [Caliban] (6) 89, p. 205.
3105. KRUSOE, James (Jim)
"The Dictator." [BrooklynR] (6) 89, p. 5.
"Dolphins." [QW] (28) Wint-Spr 89, p. 97.
"Elvis." [BrooklynR] (6) 89, p. 4.
"Flamingos." [AntR] (47:3) Sum 89, p. 326.
"Pieta" (for Lazlo Toth). [Witness] (3:1) Spr 89, p. 21.
"Snow White." [Witness] (3:1) Spr 89, p. 22.
"A Window" (in memory of Eugene Marais). [Witness] (3:1) Spr 89, p. 20.
3106. KRYGOWSKI, Nancy
"Arm." [Thrpny] (37) Spr 89, p. 17.
"Everything." [WestB] (24) 89, p. 21.
"I Want to Talk About Life and Love." [WestB] (24) 89, p. 20.
"My Story (or Spring)." [FloridaR] (16:2/3) Fall-Wint 89, p. 173.
"Potato Garlic Soup." [WestB] (24) 89, p. 22.
3107. KRYNICKI, Ryszard
"Facing the Wall" (tr. by Stanislaw Baranczak and Clare Cavanagh). [PartR] (56:2)
     Spr 89, p. 288.
"A New Day" (tr. by Stanislaw Baranczak and Clare Cavanah). [Trans] (21) Spr 89,
     p. 67.
"Socialist Realism" (tr. by Stanislaw Baranczak and Clare Cavanagh). [PartR] (56:2)
     Spr 89, p. 287.
"A Stop" (tr. by Stanislaw Baranczak and Clare Cavanagh). [PartR] (56:2) Spr 89,
     p. 287.
"You're Free" (tr. by Stanislaw Baranczak and Clare Cavanagh). [PartR] (56:2) Spr
     89, p. 287.
3108. KRYNOCK, Kim
"My Father Is Made of Smoke." [SoCoast] (7) Spr-Fall 89, p. 44-45.
3109. KRYSL, Marilyn
"Are You the Malthus Ma or the Marxist Ma?" [CinPR] (19) Spr 89, p. 64-65.
"Sea Legs." [CinPR] (19) Spr 89, p. 62-63.
"Sestina for Bright Cloud, Singing (But Not the Blues)." [Cond] (16) 89, p. 36-37.
3110. KRZESZOWSKI, Tomasz P.
"Dr. Korczak's Lie" (tr. of Anna Kamienska, w. Desmond Graham). [Stand] (30:1)
     Wint 88-89, p. 40.
KUAN, Ch'in
     See CH'IN, Kuan
3111. KUBICEK, J. L.
"The Colors That Never Fade." [NewRena] (7:3, #23) 89, p. 82.

3112. KUCHARSKI, Lisa
"For a Man in a Gallery." [Lactuca] (12) F 89, p. 52.
"Juliet." [Lactuca] (12) F 89, p. 52.
"No Crutch for the Weak." [Lactuca] (12) F 89, p. 52.
"No Name / No Moral." [Lactuca] (12) F 89, p. 51.
3113. KUENZI, David
"The Mantis' Prayer." [Nat] (248:4) 30 Ja 89, p. 138.
3114. KUFFEL, Frances
"Waiting Room" (for Michael Marks." [BellR] (12:2, #26) Fall 89, p. 44-45.
3115. KUKAI
"Singing Image of a Whirling Ring of Fire" (tr. by Morgan Gibson and Hiroshi
Murakami). [LitR] (32:3) Spr 89, p. 360.
"Singing Image of an Echo" (tr. by Morgan Gibson and Hiroshi Murakami). [LitR]
(32:3) Spr 89, p. 360.
3116. KUMIN, Maxine
"Looking for Luck in Bangkok." [NewYorker] (65:17) 12 Je 89, p. 42.
"Taking the Lambs to Market." [TriQ] (77) Wint 89-90, p. 285.
"Waking to Moonlight." [CrabCR] (6:1) 89, p. 11.
3117. KUNCHEV, Nicolai
"The Bees' Calendar" (tr. by Jascha Kessler). [Confr] (39/40) Fall 88-Wint 89, p.
143.
3118. KUNERT, Günter
"Commemoration Day in May" (tr. by John Linthicum). [LitR] (33:1) Fall 89, p. 58.
"Elegy" (tr. by John Linthicum). [LitR] (33:1) Fall 89, p. 57.
"In the Border Zone" (tr. by John Linthicum). [LitR] (33:1) Fall 89, p. 56.
"The Jewish Cemetery in Weissensee" (tr. by John Linthicum). [LitR] (33:1) Fall
89, p. 56.
"Observation" (tr. by John Linthicum). [LitR] (33:1) Fall 89, p. 58.
"On Crete" (tr. by John Linthicum). [LitR] (33:1) Fall 89, p. 59.
"Perspective" (tr. by John Linthicum). [LitR] (33:1) Fall 89, p. 59.
KUNIMOTO, Tsumori (1023-1103)
See TSUMORI, Kunimoto (1023-1103)
3119. KUNZE, Reiner
"An der Donau im Hebel." [Nimrod] (33:1) Fall-Wint 89, p. 110.
"Dream in Exile" (tr. by Thomas S. Edwards, Ken Letko, Thomas Schaller, and Jeff
Gearing). [Nimrod] (33:1) Fall-Wint 89, p. 111.
"Early Spring" (tr. by John Linthicum). [LitR] (33:1) Fall 89, p. 75.
"Easter" (tr. by John Linthicum). [LitR] (33:1) Fall 89, p. 76.
"Edvard Munch: Rouge et Noir, Colored Woodcut, 1898" (tr. by John Linthicum).
[LitR] (33:1) Fall 89, p. 74.
"Foehn" (tr. by John Linthicum). [LitR] (33:1) Fall 89, p. 77.
"Meditation on a Torso" (tr. by John Linthicum). [LitR] (33:1) Fall 89, p. 74.
"My Father, Much Aged" (tr. by John Linthicum). [LitR] (33:1) Fall 89, p. 75.
"Old Metropolitan Cemetery" (tr. by John Linthicum). [LitR] (33:1) Fall 89, p. 75.
"On the Danube in the Fog" (tr. by Thomas S. Edwards, Ken Letko, Thomas
Schaller, and Jeff Gearing). [Nimrod] (33:1) Fall-Wint 89, p. 111.
"Overdose" (in memoriam: Jean Améry, tr. by John Linthicum). [LitR] (33:1) Fall
89, p. 77.
"The Silhouette of Lübeck" (tr. by Thomas S. Edwards, Ken Letko, Thomas
Schaller, and Jeff Gearing). [Nimrod] (33:1) Fall-Wint 89, p. 111.
"Die Silhouette von Lübeck." [Nimrod] (33:1) Fall-Wint 89, p. 110.
"Traum im Exil." [Nimrod] (33:1) Fall-Wint 89, p. 110.
"Young Motorcyclists" (tr. by John Linthicum). [LitR] (33:1) Fall 89, p. 76.
3120. KUPELE, David M.
"The Larry Ching Swing" (dedicated to Larry F. C. Ching, businessman, historian
and first President of the Hawaii Chinese History Center). [Hawai'iR] (13:3)
Fall 89, p. 67.
3121. KUPPNER, Frank
"Eclipsing Binaries." [Verse] (6:2) Je 89, p. 52-55.
"A Real Drumchapel Pastoral." [Verse] (6:1) Mr 89, p. 16-17.
3122. KURDI, Mária
"Fog, I Hear the Crack of Bullets" (tr. of Zsuzsa Takács, w. Len Roberts). [IndR]
(12:2) Spr 89, p. 98-99.
3123. KUSANO, Shimpei
"A Batch of Late Poems" (9 poems, tr. by Cid Corman and Kamaike Susumu).
[Sulfur] (9:1, #24) Spr 89, p. 60-69.

3124. KUSCH, Robert
"Prague." [WashR] (14:5) F-Mr 89, p. 17.
3125. KUSHNER, Aleksandr
"The Adoration of the Magi" (tr. by Paul Graves). [PartR] (56:1) Wint 89, p.
117-118.
"Untitled: In the morning, the drafts in the blinds and the curtains" (tr. by Paul
Graves). [PartR] (56:1) Wint 89, p. 115-116.
"Untitled: We don't get to choose our century" (tr. by Paul Graves). [PartR] (56:1)
Wint 89, p. 116-117.
3126. KUSHNER, Dale
"Caduceus." [Crazy] (37) Wint 89, p. 43.
"Post Modern." [Crazy] (37) Wint 89, p. 44.
3127. KUSZ, Natalie
"Masseuse." [LakeSR] (23) 89, p. 21.
3128. KUUSISTO, Stephen
"At the Summer House." [MissR] (17:3, #51), p. 44-45.
"Lying Still." [SenR] (19:1) 89, p. 64.
"Still." [SenR] (19:1) 89, p. 65.
"Summer at North Farm" (Finnish rural life, ca. 1910). [Poetry] (154:5) Ag 89, p.
273.
3129. KUZMA, Greg
"Dog Stories." [DenQ] (24:2) Fall 89, p. 65-66.
"Fathers and Sons." [CharR] (15:2) Fall 89, p. 53.
"For the Reader." [SpoonRQ] (14:2) Spr 89, p. 15-17.
"Forty-Three." [MidwQ] (31:1) Aut 89, p. 51-52.
"The Hemlock Tree." [PoetC] (20:2) Wint 89, p. 44.
"I Had Forgot the Dandelions." [NoDaQ] (57:4) Fall 89, p. 37-38.
"I Wept and Then." [Plain] (9:2) Wint 89, p. 21.
"Snow." [MidwQ] (31:1) Aut 89, p. 53.
"Summer." [MidwQ] (31:1) Aut 89, p. 54.
"The Traffic Dog." [PoetC] (20:2) Wint 89, p. 45-46.
"The Truck." [GreensboroR] (47) Wint 89-90, p. 121.
"Work." [NoDaQ] (57:4) Fall 89, p. 38-39.
"Worlds." [WillowS] (23) Wint 89, p. 50-51.
3130. KYGER, Joanne
"Winter Sequence at Jon's House." [Temblor] (10) 89, p. 134-138.
La . . .
See also names beginning with "La" without the following space, filed below in their
alphabetic positions, e.g., LaSALLE.
3131. La CHARITY, Ralph
"Invention of Espionage." [Rampike] (6:3) 88, p. 68.
La HOZ, León de
See HOZ, León de la
3132. La ROSA, Pablo
"The Tooth Fairy Wears Dentures." [KanQ] (21:1/2) Wint-Spr 89, p. 193.
La VEGA, Garcilaso de
See VEGA, Garcilaso de la
3133. LAABI, Abdellatif
"The Smile" (tr. by Victor Reinking). [Vis] (31) 89, p. 45.
3134. LABINSKI, Marek
"Evenings" (tr. of Halina Poswiatowska). [WillowS] (23) Wint 89, p. 60.
"In My Barbaric Language" (tr. of Halina Poswiatowska). [PoetryE] (28) Fall 89, p.
175.
"A Suicide" (tr. of Zbigniew Herbert). [WillowS] (23) Wint 89, p. 59.
"These Words Have Always Been" (tr. of Halina Poswiatowska). [PoetryE] (28)
Fall 89, p. 176.
LABRA, Carilda Oliver
See OLIVER LABRA, Carilda
3135. LaBRUNO, Michael
"Dead-Sea Dead." [Footwork] 89, p. 74.
"My Best Friend Thinks." [Footwork] 89, p. 74.
"Open Letter to Talk Show Host After First Radio Poetry Reading, Thank You
Louise." [Footwork] 89, p. 75.
3136. LACERDA, Alberto de
"Lake Nyasa" (tr. by Jean R. Longland). [Pig] (15) 88, p. 40.

241

3137. LAGIER, Jennifer
"Eating It: The Compulsory Feast." [SlipS] (9) 89, p. 85.
"Let Us Sing to the Tune of a City Perverted." [SlipS] (9) 89, p. 86-87.
"Swimming in Circles." [SlipS] (9) 89, p. 86.
3138. LAGO, David
"Hurra!" (Madrid 1989, 1 de mayo). [LindLM] (8:3) Jl-S 89, p. 13.
3139. LAI, Dao
"September." [Amelia] (5:3, #14) 89, p. 30.
3140. LAKE, Paul
"The Century Killer." [ParisR] (31:113) Wint 89, p. 152-155.
"A Grain of Salt." [CarolQ] (41:2) Wint 89, p. 62.
"Revised Standard Version." [CarolQ] (41:2) Wint 89, p. 61.
"Thorn." [Boulevard] (4:1, #10) Spr 89, p. 133-134.
"Two Hitchhikers." [CrossCur] (8:2) Ja 89, p. 112-115.
3141. LAMANTIA, Philip
"No Closure" (Excerpt). [Caliban] (7) 89, p. 19-21.
3142. LAMAZARES, Ivonne
"At Thirty" (LLM English Language Poetry Prize). [LindLM] (8:4) O-D 89, p. 8.
"Fable" (LLM English Language Poetry Prize). [LindLM] (8:4) O-D 89, p. 8.
"Frida Kahlo." [LindLM] (8:2) Ap-Je 89, p. 9.
"My Father's Dictionary" (LLM English Language Poetry Prize). [LindLM] (8:4)
O-D 89, p. 8.
3143. LAMB, Joe
"Reuniting Gondwanaland." [FiveFR] (7) 89, p. 118.
"Cherries." [FiveFR] (7) 89, p. 116.
"The Smell of Sage." [FiveFR] (7) 89, p. 117.
"What We're Taught to Forget." [FiveFR] (7) 89, p. 115.
3144. LAMON, Laurie
"Between Us." [Nimrod] (33:1) Fall-Wint 89, p. 137.
"In Your Quiet Neighborhood." [Nimrod] (33:1) Fall-Wint 89, p. 138.
3145. LAND, Thomas Grover
"Disaffected Monsters." [Plain] (9:2) Wint 89, p. 22.
3146. LANDAU, Julie
"Ju Meng Ling" (tr. of Li Ch'ing-chao). [Trans] (21) Spr 89, p. 218.
"Lin Chiang Hsien" (tr. of Li Ch'ing-chao). [Trans] (21) Spr 89, p. 217.
"Mid Autumn Festival" (tr. of Su Shin). [MSS] (6:3) 89, p. 71.
"Tsui Hua Yin" (tr. of Li Ch'ing-chao). [Trans] (21) Spr 89, p. 218.
"Wan Hsi Sha" (tr. of Li Ch'ing-chao). [Trans] (21) Spr 89, p. 218.
3147. LANDGRAF, Susan
"The Grasses." [SpoonRQ] (14:3) Sum 89, p. 52.
"In Praise of Extravagance." [SpoonRQ] (14:3) Sum 89, p. 49.
"Near the Family Truth." [SpoonRQ] (14:3) Sum 89, p. 50-51.
"Old Is This Road and Foxes." [Calyx] (12:2) Wint 89-90, p. 9.
"There Are Other Moons But This Is the One We See." [Calyx] (12:2) Wint 89-90,
p. 8.
"Written Affair." [SpoonRQ] (14:3) Sum 89, p. 48.
3148. LANE, Dixie
"The City Speaks." [KenR] (NS 11:3) Sum 89, p. 70-72.
"Doll Hospital." [MissouriR] (12:2) 89, p. 140-141.
"Hotel Fresno." [AntR] (47:2) Spr 89, p. 196-197.
"Snake in the Piano." [MissouriR] (12:2) 89, p. 142-143.
3149. LANE, Donna M.
"Naming Plants." [SwampR] (1:4) Sum 89, p. 28.
3150. LANE, M. Travis
"Cliff Head." [Quarry] (38:1) Wint 89, p. 63.
"Prospero on Setebos." [AntigR] (77/78) Spr-Sum 89, p. 8.
"Whale Watching." [AntigR] (77/78) Spr-Sum 89, p. 7.
"You Go On." [Quarry] (38:1) Wint 89, p. 62.
3151. LANE, Mervin
"Interview." [Kalliope] (10:3) 88, p. 33.
3152. LANE, Patrick
"The Witnesses." [CanLit] (122/123) Aut-Wint 89, p. 57-58.
3153. LANE, Pinkie Gordon
"Lyric: I Am Looking at Music" (for Madge Sinclair, actress). [BlackALF] (23:3)
Fall 89, p. 452-453.
"Photograph." [BlackALF] (23:3) Fall 89, p. 451.

"Prose Poem Portrait." [BlackALF] (23:3) Fall 89, p. 453.
"Song for an Eagle." [BlackALF] (23:3) Fall 89, p. 452.
3154. LANE, S. Susan (Sigrun Susan)
"The Grey Wolf." [BellR] (12:2, #26) Fall 89, p. 31.
"Umma." [BellArk] (5:6) N-D 89, p. 5.
3155. LANEY, Marion L.
"So Far" (Selections: 2 poems). [Obs] (3:2) Sum 88, p. 118-119.
3156. LANG, J. Stephen
"An Eavesdropper in Jackson Square, New Orleans." [Outbr] (20) 89, p. 78-79.
"Incense in Maytime." [Poem] (61) My 89, p. 71.
"Key Lime Pie, and the Galleries." [Poem] (61) My 89, p. 70.
"A Lover in Neon." [Poem] (61) My 89, p. 69.
"Sailing on Front Street." [Outbr] (20) 89, p. 77.
"The Window Rattled in the Wind All Night Long." [Outbr] (20) 89, p. 80.
3157. LANG, Leonard
"California Vacation, February." [RagMag] (7:1) 89, p. 22.
"Clearing Snow in a Blizzard." [RagMag] (7:1) 89, p. 23.
"Night Angel." [CentR] (33:3) Sum 89, p. 243-244.
"The Return." [MidwQ] (30:4) Sum 89, p. 446.
"The Water in Which All Women Walk." [RagMag] (7:1) 89, p. 23.
LANG, Meng
See MENG, Lang
3158. LANG, Stephen
"With M. C. on the Balcony." [KanQ] (21:1/2) Wint-Spr 89, p. 132.
3159. LANGE, Dan
"Aleutian Outpost." [Writer] (102:3) Mr 89, p. 26.
3160. LANGE, Jennifer
"Degas Degas Degas." [PoetL] (84:4) Wint 89-90, p. 23-24.
"The Lady, Thinking of Sending Her Hat Into Eternity." [CreamCR] (13:2) Fall 89,
p. 27.
"This Morning." [PoetL] (84:4) Wint 89-90, p. 25.
3161. LANGE, Sophie
"Girl Child." [CrossCur] (8:3) Apr 89, p. 148-149.
3162. LANGHORNE, Henry
"Cottonwood Creek." [CapeR] (24:2) Fall 89, p. 33.
"The Gold Coast." [EmeraldCR] (1989) c1988, p. 93.
3163. LANGLAS, James
"Barefoot." [Plain] (9:3) Spr 89, p. 35.
"Ice." [Plain] (9:2) Wint 89, p. 23.
"Winter Winds." [Farm] (6:1) Wint-Spr 88-89, p. 80.
3164. LANGMAN, Peter
"A Hawk Sprawled on the Sidewalk." [CrossCur] (8:3) Apr 89, p. 147.
3165. LANGTON, Daniel J.
"Funerals." [StoneC] (17:1/2) Fall-Wint 89-90, p. 47.
"Slow Poem." [CharR] (15:1) Spr 89, p. 59.
3166. LANHAM, Michael C.
"The Dare." [JamesWR] (6:3) Spr 89, p. 11.
3167. LANIER, David
"My Mother, Trimming Hedges" (Runner-Up, 1989 Ratner-Ferber-Poet Lore
Competition). [PoetL] (84:2) Sum 89, p. 8-9.
3168. LANSDOWN, Andrew
"Four Men." [Verse] (6:3) Wint 89, p. 7-8.
"Removing a Cap." [Verse] (6:3) Wint 89, p. 7.
"Windmill." [Verse] (6:1) Mr 89, p. 56.
3169. LAO, Tzu
"Tao Te Ching" (6 selections, tr. by Ursula K. Le Guin). [LitR] (32:3) Spr 89, p.
364-367.
LARA, Fernando Charry
See CHARRY LARA, Fernando
3170. LARDAS, Konstantinos
"Where I May Stand." [HolCrit] (26:1) F 89, p. 18.
3171. LaRIVIERE, Gladys M.
"Cor Sacrum." [ChamLR] (2:2, #4) Spr 89, p. 11-12.
3172. LARKIN, Joan
"Brooklyn Morning" (for David Trinidad). [BrooklynR] (6) 89, p. 60-61.

3173. LARNER, Jeremy
"Off My Foot." [Thrpny] (37) Spr 89, p. 16.
3174. LAROCCHI, Marica
"Don't Jump Out of Your Skin" (tr. by Beverly Allen). [Poetry] (155:1/2) O-N 89,
p. 116.
"In Questa Forma" (Selection: VI). [Poetry] (155:1/2) O-N 89, p. 114.
"In This Way" (Selection: VI, tr. by Beverly Allen). [Poetry] (155:1/2) O-N 89, p.
115.
"Sailing to Aphinar" (For Stefano Agosti, tr. by Beverly Allen). [Poetry] (155:1/2)
O-N 89, p. 117.
LaROSA, Pablo
See La ROSA, Pablo
3175. LARSEN, Deborah
"Disappearances." [GettyR] (2:3) Sum 89, p. 414-415.
"Forensics." [OxfordM] (5:2) Fall-Wint 89, p. 10.
"Slant Shape." [YaleR] (78:4) Sum 89, p. 654.
3176. LARSEN, Jeanne
"Poem in Response to Commissioner Wu" (tr. of Xue Tao). [LitR] (32:3) Spr 89, p.
399.
"To General Gao, Who Smashed the Rebellion for the Son of Heaven" (tr. of Xue
Tao). [LitR] (32:3) Spr 89, p. 399.
3177. LARSON, Rustin
"At the Break of Day on My Wooden Porch." [Bound] (16:2/3) Wint-Spr 89, p.
172-173.
"Having Arrived in Washington, D.C., I Seek Employment." [Bound] (16:2/3)
Wint-Spr 89, p. 170.
"Leaning into a Mirror I Address My Image." [Bound] (16:2/3) Wint-Spr 89, p. 171.
3178. LaSALLE, Peter
"The Mysteries of Paris." [ColEng] (51:7) N 89, p. 704.
"Paternale." [KeyWR] (2:1/2) Fall-Wint 89, p. 54.
"Triad." [KeyWR] (2:1/2) Fall-Wint 89, p. 55.
3179. LASDUN, James
"Edenesque." [YaleR] (79:1) Aut 89, p. 125-126.
"Powder Compact." [NewYorker] (65:5) 20 Mr 89, p. 40.
3180. LASHER, Susan
"The Zionist." [Verse] (6:2) Je 89, p. 30.
3181. LASKIN, Pamela L.
"Silence." [Vis] (31) 89, p. 28.
3182. LASSELL, Michael
"A Modest Proposal, Overtly Political" (For Jim Pickett). [CentralP] (16) Fall 89, p.
37-40.
"Surviving." [JamesWR] (7:1) Fall 89, p. 10.
3183. LAU, Barbara
"After Bathing." [FreeL] (2) Sum 89, p. 25.
"Splitting in Two." [FreeL] (2) Sum 89, p. 24.
3184. LAU, Carolyn
"Inscription on a Half-Hiddnen Landscape" (tr. of Gao Xiang). [YellowS] (31) Aut
89, p. 7.
"Liu 2." [YellowS] (31) Aut 89, p. 37.
"Painting the Plum Flowers" (tr. of Li Fenyong). [YellowS] (31) Aut 89, p. 9.
"A Play Called 'Go'" (for Xu Tao). [YellowS] (30) Sum 89, p. 17-25.
"When cherries are red and elm pods naked" (tr. of Huang Shen). [YellowS] (31)
Aut 89, p. 5.
LAUÇANNO, Christopher Sawyer
See SAWYER-LAUÇANNO, Christopher
3185. LAUGHLIN, J. (James)
"The Hand Trick." [Chelsea] (48) 89, p. 134.
"The Inn at Kirchstetten" (Notes penciled in the margins of a book of the Dichtungen
of Georg Trakl). [Antaeus] (62) Spr 89, p. 95-97.
"The Long Night." [Chelsea] (48) 89, p. 132-133.
"Self-Control." [NewAW] (5) Fall 89, p. 64.
"The Smallest Blessing." [Talisman] (2) Spr 89, p. 78.
"Then and Now." [Poetry] (153:6) Mr 89, p. 325.
"To Love Is to Hold Dear." [Chelsea] (48) 89, p. 134.
3186. LAURANS, Penelope
"1986" (World Series, Game 6, Inning 10, Bill Buckner). [TampaR] (2) 89, p. 54.

3187. LAUTER, Elva
"Sitting in the Dining Room." [EngJ] (78:7) N 89, p. 93.
3188. LAUTERBACH, Ann
"Boy Sleeping" (for Richard Robbins). [Pequod] (28/29/30) 89, p. 242-243.
"Chase" (Selections: 4-5, 7). [Ploughs] (15:4) Wint 89-90, p. 118-119.
"How Things Bear Their Telling." [Conjunc] (13) 89, p. 67-69.
"Report." [Colum] (14) 89, p. 32-33.
"Thin." [Colum] (14) 89, p. 33.
3189. LAUTERMILCH, Steven
"Dark one, you say you are from outer space." [Pembroke] (21) 89, p. 153.
"A rice-paper rubbing from the wall of a shrine in India." [Pembroke] (21) 89, p. 153.
3190. LAUX, Dorianne
"On the River." [Zyzzyva] (5:, #20) Wint 89, p. 97.
3191. LAW, Tim H.
"Route 78." [MidwQ] (31:1) Aut 89, p. 55.
3192. LAWDER, Donald
"Tracks in the Snow." [Journal] (12:2) Fall-Wint 88-89, p. 36-37.
3193. LAWRENCE, Catherine
"The Daughters of Love." [Writer] (102:3) Mr 89, p. 25-26.
3194. LAWRENCE, Sean A.
"Death's Prairie." [Plain] (9:3) Spr 89, p. 18.
3195. LAWSON, D. S.
"Fidel Castro's Mistress." [WindO] (51) Spr 89, p. 47.
3196. LAWTHER, Marcia
"Driving the San Joaquin Valley." [SoCoast] (7) Spr-Fall 89, p. 50-51.
"Up Here." [Blueline] (10:1/2) 89, p. 66.
3197. LAYMAN, Richard
"Leftovers." [EmeraldCR] (1989) c1988, p. 132.
"Where We Sit." [EmeraldCR] (1989) c1988, p. 132-133.
3198. LAYTON, Irving
"Attending Suzanne's Funeral." [CanLit] (120) Spr 89, p. 63.
3199. LAZER, Hank
"Compositions 2." [Temblor] (10) 89, p. 158.
"Compositions 10." [Screens] (1) 89, p. 38.
"Compositions 18." [Temblor] (10) 89, p. 158-159.
"Five Small Stories Beginning with Today." [SouthernR] (25:2) Spr 89, p. 491-493.
"Law-Poems 5: Be So Determined." [CentralP] (16) Fall 89, p. 107-110.
"Law-Poems, 7: Catch of the Day." [Aerial] (5) 89, p. 86-90.
"Negation, 9." [CentralP] (15) Spr 89, p. 56-58.
"Not My Own Life." [VirQR] (65:3) Sum 89, p. 446-449.
"Patterns, 3." [Sequoia] (33:1) Sum 89, p. 16.
"Placements, 5." [Sequoia] (33:1) Sum 89, p. 17.
3200. LAZIC, Radmila
"The Good Waters of Old Tales" (tr. by Krinka Petrov). [ColR] (NS 16:1) Spr-Sum 89, p. 98.
Le . . .
See also names beginning with "Le" without the following space, filed below in their alphabetic positions, e.g., LeFEVRE.
3201. Le GUIN, Ursula K.
"Riding Shotgun" (From a diary written in the right front seat of a diesel VW . . .). [Antaeus] (61) Aut 88, p. 251-258.
"Tao Te Ching" (6 selections, tr. of Lao Tzu). [LitR] (32:3) Spr 89, p. 364-367.
3202. LEA, Sydney
"Amputee" (Good Friday, Caledonia County). [Verse] (6:3) Wint 89, p. 61-62.
"Black Bear Cuffing for Food." [TarRP] (28:2) Spr 89, p. 19-20.
"D Day Ode for Dean." [Verse] (6:3) Wint 89, p. 63-64.
"For Faith." [Antaeus] (62) Spr 89, p. 98-99.
"Late Season." [PraS] (63:1) Spr 89, p. 98-100.
"Museum" (recalling George MacArthur and Donald Chambers). [GeoR] (43:3) Fall 89, p. 490-492.
"Pietà." [PraS] (63:1) Spr 89, p. 96-98.
"Private Boys' School, 3rd Grade." [Crazy] (37) Wint 89, p. 33-34.
"Revision: Early December." [TarRP] (28:2) Spr 89, p. 18-19.
"Roadside, February." [GettyR] (2:1) Wint 89, p. 25-26.
"Six Sundays toward a Seventh" (21 February-3 April, 1988). [KenR] (N 11:4) Fall

89, p. 107-115.
"Spite: Her Tale." [KenR] (NS 11:1) Wint 89, p. 86-90.
"Sun, Rising." [MissouriR] (12:1) 89, p. 156-157.
3203. LEALE, B. C.
"Bone Thrower." [Bogg] (61) 89, p. 44.
"The Hands of My Fabergé Watch" (For John Digby). [Margin] (8) 89, p. 58.
3204. LEASE, Joseph
"A Black Mark." [Caliban] (7) 89, p. 166-167.
"But You." [BostonR] (14:1) F 89, p. 8.
"Comic Book." [BostonR] (14:1) F 89, p. 8.
"Crystal Rock." [ParisR] (31:113) Wint 89, p. 113-116.
"Green Cold Water." [Temblor] (10) 89, p. 57-58.
"Hard, Oiled Wood." [Notus] (4:2) Fall 89, p. 26.
"I Can Burst." [BostonR] (14:1) F 89, p. 8.
"I Can Burst." [Notus] (4:2) Fall 89, p. 31.
"I Can No Longer Live by Thinking." [BostonR] (14:1) F 89, p. 8.
"I Can No Longer Live by Thinking." [Notus] (4:2) Fall 89, p. 30.
"I Can't Give You Anything." [Notus] (4:2) Fall 89, p. 25.
"Nerves Torn to Shreds." [BostonR] (14:1) F 89, p. 8.
"Nerves Torn to Shreds." [Notus] (4:2) Fall 89, p. 27.
"The Night I Met Sue She Told Me This." [BostonR] (14:1) F 89, p. 8.
"The Night I Met Sue She Told Me This." [Notus] (4:2) Fall 89, p. 28.
"We Layer Folded Heat." [BostonR] (14:1) F 89, p. 8.
"We Layer Folded Heat." [Notus] (4:2) Fall 89, p. 24.
"You Brush Me Over and Over." [Notus] (4:2) Fall 89, p. 29.
3205. LeBOUTILLIER, Michelle
"Waters of the Mother." [Rampike] (6:2) 88, p. 62.
3206. LeCLAIR, Mary Ellen
"Crystal Bowl" (For Ellen Casey Weir). [Vis] (29) 89, p. 39-41.
3207. LECLERC, Félix
"Le Crois-Tu?" (From Rêves à Vendre). [AntigR] (77/78) Spr-Sum 89, p. 90.
"The Villon Legacy" (tr. by Philip Stratford). [CanLit] (121) Sum 89, p. 107-114.
"Would You Believe It?" (From Rêves à Vendre, tr. by John Palander). [AntigR] (77/78) Spr-Sum 89, p. 91.
3208. LEDBETTER, J. T.
"First Time." [Vis] (31) 89, p. 24.
"What They Told Her." [SenR] (19:1) 89, p. 69-70.
3209. LEDDY, Phillipa
"E. T." (tr. of Pablo Antonio Cuadra). [KeyWR] (2:1/2) Fall-Wint 89, p. 142.
"The New Time" (tr. of Pablo Antonio Cuadra). [KeyWR] (2:1/2) Fall-Wint 89, p. 143.
3210. LEDUC, Daniel
"El caminante siembra sus pasos" (tr. into Spanish by María S. Molina-López). [Mairena] (11:27) 89, p. 77.
3211. LEDWON, Lenora
"Antigone" (fragment in remembrance of the Hungarian workers, students and soldiers, 1949, tr. of Czeslaw Milosz). [TriQ] (74) Wint 89, p. 217-220.
3212. LEE, Ann
"Friend." [HolCrit] (26:1) F 89, p. 18.
"Houdini at the Supper Club." [HolCrit] (26:5) D 89, p. 15.
3213. LEE, Cherylene
"Last Shrimp." [BambooR] (44) Fall 89, p. 19-22.
3214. LEE, David
"Broken Leg." [HayF] (5) Fall 89, p. 58-60.
"Deaf." [HayF] (5) Fall 89, p. 61.
3215. LEE, John B.
"Driving the Drumlin Road by Jocelyn's at Dusk." [CrossC] (11:3) 89, p. 10.
"To Find and Forgive." [Quarry] (38:4) Fall 89, p. 43.
"Why Some People Retire" (for Roger). [CrossC] (11:3) 89, p. 10.
3216. LEE, Li-Young
"Autumn and a Woman's Room" (tr. of Li Yu, w. Anthony Piccione and Carol Zhigong Chang). [LitR] (32:3) Spr 89, p. 390.
"The Cleaving." [TriQ] (77) Wint 89-90, p. 258-266.
"Past Thoughts" (tr. of Li Yu, w. Anthony Piccione and Carol Zhigong Chang). [LitR] (32:3) Spr 89, p. 390.
"Rising Late" (tr. of Meng Hao-jan, w. Anthony Piccione and Carol Zhigong

Chang). [LitR] (32:3) Spr 89, p. 389.
"Separation" (tr. of Su Shih, w. Anthony Piccione and Carol Zhigong Chang).
    [LitR] (32:3) Spr 89, p. 389.
"A Story." [AmerV] (16) Fall 89, p. 57.
"The Waiting." [TriQ] (77) Wint 89-90, p. 254-257.
3217. LEE, Rebecca
    "45 in a Dry Season." [Hawai'iR] (13:1, #25) Spr 89, p. 56.
3218. LEEDAHL, Shelley A.
    "Blanca." [AntigR] (79) Aut 89, p. 96.
    "Dog Is *Perro*, in Spanish." [Grain] (17:4) Wint 89, p. 20.
    "La Muñeca." [Grain] (17:4) Wint 89, p. 21.
3219. LEEDS, Charlie
    "To Hell with This Cock-Eyed World!" (Prologue, from "Tillie's Punctured
        Romance . . .," 1970). [AlphaBS] (5) Jl 89, p. 54-55.
3220. LEET, Judith
    "Singleminded." [OntR] (31) Fall-Wint 89-90, p. 53-54.
3221. LEFCOWITZ, Barbara F.
    "Dryer." [BrooklynR] (5) 88, p. 16.
    "Spa." [Confr] (39/40) Fall 88-Wint 89, p. 126.
3222. LEFEBURE, Stephen
    "The Angel of the Apocalypse." [LitR] (32:2) Wint 89, p. 230.
3223. LEFKOWITZ, Larry
    "Recollected Moment." [Pig] (15) 88, p. 35.
3224. LEFTWICH, Jim
    "Looking Back at the Landscape of Solitude." [FiveFR] (7) 89, p. 94.
3225. LeGARDEUR, Lili
    "Let's." [Colum] (14) 89, p. 90-91.
3226. LEGGO, Carl
    "The Concrete Boat." [Grain] (17:1) Spr 89, p. 41.
    "Nietzsche, F. Scott Fitzgerald, Pascal, Charlie Brown and I." [Grain] (17:1) Spr
        89, p. 42-43.
3227. LEGGOTT, Michele
    "Deluge in a Paper Cup." [Descant] (20:3/4, #66/67) Fall-Wint 89, p. 204-205.
    "Learning to Swim." [Descant] (20:3/4, #66/67) Fall-Wint 89, p. 206-207.
3228. LEHBERT, Margitt
    "Dreamlike Excursion with Rosa L." (tr. of Steffen Mensching). [AmerPoR] (18:6)
        N-D 89, p. 33.
    "In Late Summer" (tr. of Steffen Mensching). [AmerPoR] (18:6) N-D 89, p. 33.
3229. LEHMAN, David
    "1967." [NewAW] (5) Fall 89, p. 107-108.
    "The Desire for Strange Cities." [PartR] (56:3) Sum 89, p. 451-452.
    "Henry James: The Movie." [ParisR] (31:112) Fall 89, p. 181-182.
    "Literal Lives." [NewRep] (201:25) 18 D 89, p. 32.
    "Museum, 1980." [Pequod] (28/29/30) 89, p. 111-113.
    "One Size Fits All: A Critical Essay." [NewYRB] (36:12) 20 Jl 89, p. 19.
    "Pascal's Wager." [GettyR] (2:2) Spr 89, p. 238-241.
    "Perfidia." [ParisR] (31:112) Fall 89, p. 180.
    "The Private Sector." [OntR] (30) Spr-Sum 89, p. 78-79.
    "The Public Sector." [GettyR] (2:3) Sum 89, p. 535-538.
    "With Tenure." [NewYRB] (36:2) 16 F 89, p. 23.
3230. LEIPER, Esther M.
    "The Wars of Faery" (Book 1, Canto XI-XII). [Amelia] (5:3, #14) 89, p. p. 68-78.
3231. LEITHAUSER, Brad
    "Rain & Snow" (Kyoto, Japan). [NewYorker] (65:39) 13 N 89, p. 146.
    "Your Natural History." [Atlantic] (264:5) N 89, p. 78.
3232. LELAND, Blake
    "*Chora* in Hell, 2." [Epoch] (38:3) 89, p. 224.
    "*Chora* in Hell: Nine Days Old." [Epoch] (38:3) 89, p. 223.
3233. LEMAIRE, Jean-Pierre
    "Brother of the Prodigal Son" (tr. by Dorothy Aspinwall). [WebR] (14:1) Spr 89, p.
        19.
3234. LENDENNIE, Jessie
    "Gratton Strand." [Vis] (29) 89, p. 12.
    "Oklahoma Patchwork" (for Nuala). [Vis] (29) 89, p. 12.
3235. LENHART, Gary
    "Chemists." [HangL] (54) 89, p. 13.

"The Cumbrous World of Wheels." [HangL] (54) 89, p. 16-17.
"Larry." [HangL] (54) 89, p. 13.
"Michigan." [HangL] (54) 89, p. 14-15.
3236. LENIHAN, Dan
"Ruth and Ellis Watch a Little T.V." [Bogg] (61) 89, p. 26-27.
"The Weaning of Baby Roy" (A Wormwood Chapbook). [WormR] (29:2/3,
#114-115) 89, p. 49-96.
3237. LENIHAN, Edmund
"Trees of Ireland." [KanQ] (21:1/2) Wint-Spr 89, p. 145.
3238. LENNON, Frank
"Between Religions." [RagMag] (7:1) 89, p. 24.
3239. LENSE, Edward
"Ben Bulben." [Journal] (13:1) Spr-Sum 89, p. 66-67.
"Monster." [Journal] (13:1) Spr-Sum 89, p. 64-65.
3240. LENSON, David
"Herodiade" (tr. of Stephane Mallarmé). [MassR] (30:4) Wint 89, p. 573-588.
3241. LEON FEMAT, Socorro
"Poem: Heavy burden of thoughts" (tr. by Thomas Hoeksema). [RiverS] (28) 89, p.
51.
"Transparent bodies emerge" (tr. by T. Hoeksema). [Jacaranda] (4:1) Spr-Sum 89,
p. 64.
3242. LEONARD, Gregory
"The House of the Hanged Man." [BlueBldgs] (11) 89, p. 57.
3243. LEONIDAS OF TARENTUM
"Now like a vine supported on a stake" (tr. by James Michie). [GrandS] (8:4) Sum
89, p. 80.
3244. LEOPOLD, Nikia
"Cutting Board." [PoetL] (84:3) Fall 89, p. 29.
"October." [PoetL] (84:3) Fall 89, p. 28.
3245. LEPKOWSKI, Frank
"Hard Labor." [KanQ] (21:1/2) Wint-Spr 89, p. 247.
"Springtime in the Unconscious." [KanQ] (21:1/2) Wint-Spr 89, p. 242.
3246. LEPOVETSKY, Lisa
"A Glass of Darkness." [Interim] (8:2) Fall 89, p. 17.
"Making Gazpacho." [Interim] (8:2) Fall 89, p. 18.
3247. LERNER, Elizabeth (Betsy)
"Breaking Points." [FloridaR] (16:2/3) Fall-Wint 89, p. 101.
"Circumference." [AntR] (47:4) Fall 89, p. 457.
"Lithium for Medea." [FloridaR] (16:2/3) Fall-Wint 89, p. 102-103.
3248. LesCARBEAU, Mitchell
"Joseph." [PoetL] (84:4) Wint 89-90, p. 33-34.
"On Looking at an X-Ray of My Daughter's Skull." [Hawai'iR] (13:1, #25) Spr 89,
p. 112-113.
3249. LESLIE, Naton
"Circulation." [CinPR] (19) Spr 89, p. 42.
"Sing." [StoneC] (17:1/2) Fall-Wint 89-90, p. 52.
"Stay the Night." [PraS] (63:2) Sum 89, p. 91-92.
"Where Goes the North Sea." [PraS] (63:2) Sum 89, p. 93-94.
3250. LESSER, Rika
"Aby, Öland, 1982" (tr. of Göran Sonnevi). [SouthwR] (74:2) Spr 89, p. 227-229.
"Escape Attempt." [Pequod] (28/29/30) 89, p. 195-196.
3251. LESSING, Karin
"A Winter's Dream Journal II." [Sulfur] (9:1, #24) Spr 89, p. 36-40.
3252. LeSUEUR, Meridel
"Earthshe." [SingHM] (16) 89, p. 103-109.
3253. LETKO, Ken
"Dream in Exile" (tr. of Reiner Kunze, w. Thomas S. Edwards, Thomas Schaller,
and Jeff Gearing). [Nimrod] (33:1) Fall-Wint 89, p. 111.
"Fewer Words." [WorldO] (22:1/2) Fall-Wint 87-88, c90, p. 19.
"On the Danube in the Fog" (tr. of Reiner Kunze, w. Thomas S. Edwards, Thomas
Schaller, and Jeff Gearing). [Nimrod] (33:1) Fall-Wint 89, p. 111.
"The Silhouette of Lübeck" (tr. of Reiner Kunze, w. Thomas S. Edwards, Thomas
Schaller, and Jeff Gearing). [Nimrod] (33:1) Fall-Wint 89, p. 111.
3254. LETTIERI, Carol
"Over Your Absence Glides" (tr. of Margherita Guidacci, w. Irene Marchegiani
Jones). [MidAR] (9:1) 89, p. 43.

LEV, Dina Ben
        See BEN-LEV, Dina
3255. LEV, Donald
        "Aria." [Contact] (9:50/51/52) Fall-Wint 88-Spr 89, p. 17.
        "Centering." [Contact] (9:50/51/52) Fall-Wint 88-Spr 89, p. 17.
        "Don't Take My Love Like a Joke" (title overheard in a young man's telephone
                conversation). [NegC] (9:2) 89, p. 58.
3256. LEVANT, Jonathan
        "And the House Would Creek Ever Windward." [Footwork] 89, p. 35.
        "But Her Keeper, of Course, in Little." [SpoonRQ] (14:1) Wint 89, p. 63.
        "Editor to Emily D." [ChatR] (9:2) Wint 89, p. 38.
        "Hubrisolipsistic Tie Ins Yes Sir." [WindO] (52) Wint 89-90, p. 21.
        "Janitor to Jerk." [InterPR] (15:2) Fall 89, p. 119.
        "Oiled Feet Smoothing Certain Now Old Waves." [Footwork] 89, p. 35.
        "Orpheus to Sonnets." [WindO] (52) Wint 89-90, p. 22.
        "Outside of Time." [InterPR] (15:2) Fall 89, p. 119.
3257. LeVASSEUR, Jeanne
        "Fourteen." [SmPd] (26:1, #75) Wint 89, p. 11.
        "Hurricane Harry." [StoneC] (17:1/2) Fall-Wint 89-90, p. 45.
        "There Is a Different Weakness." [SoCoast] (5) Spr 88, p. 52.
3258. LEVENSON, Christopher
        "Animal Sketches." [Grain] (17:2) Sum 89, p. 24.
        "Composition" (for Christopher Pratt). [CanLit] (121) Sum 89, p. 125.
        "Dog." [Dandel] (16:2) Fall-Wint 89, p. 30.
        "Frontiers." [Dandel] (16:2) Fall-Wint 89, p. 31.
        "Rickshaw Wallah." [Quarry] (38:4) Fall 89, p. 38.
        "Shots." [Quarry] (38:4) Fall 89, p. 35-36.
        "Temples." [Quarry] (38:4) Fall 89, p. 37.
3259. LEVERTOV, Denise
        "An Early Love." [TampaR] (2) 89, p. 26.
        "Entering Another Chapter." [SoCoast] (7) Spr-Fall 89, p. 3.
        "Flickering Mind." [AmerPoR] (18:4) Jl-Ag 89, p. 24.
        "Ikon: The Harrowing of Hell." [AmerPoR] (18:4) Jl-Ag 89, p. 23.
        "Link." [SenR] (19:2) Fall 89, p. 30-31.
        "Midnight Gladness." [AmerPoR] (18:4) Jl-Ag 89, p. 23.
        "The Past." [AmerPoR] (18:4) Jl-Ag 89, p. 25.
        "Praise of a Palmtree." [AmerPoR] (18:4) Jl-Ag 89, p. 23.
        "Rearrangement." [TampaR] (2) 89, p. 27.
        "The Sculptor" (Homage to Chillida). [SoCoast] (7) Spr-Fall 89, p. 4.
        "To R.D., March 4th 1988." [AmerPoR] (18:4) Jl-Ag 89, p. 24.
        "Two Mountains." [SoCoast] (7) Spr-Fall 89, p. 5.
        "Variation on a Theme by Rilke" (Book of Hours, Book I, #15). [AmerPoR] (18:4)
                Jl-Ag 89, p. 24.
        "Variation on a Theme by Rilke" (Book of Hours, Poem 8). [AmerPoR] (18:4) Jl-Ag
                89, p. 25.
        "Wings in the Pedlar's Pack." [AmerPoR] (18:4) Jl-Ag 89, p. 25.
3260. LEVET, Henry J. M.
        "Homewards" (to M. P. Bons d'Anty, tr. by Kirby Olson). [PartR] (56:1) Wint 89,
                p. 122.
        "Outwards" (to Francis Jammes, tr. by Kirby Olson). [PartR] (56:1) Wint 89, p.
                121-122.
LEVI, Enrique Jaramillo
        See JARAMILLO LEVI, Enrique
3261. LEVI, Helen
        "End of June" (Prose Poem Winter, the First Short Grain Contest). [Grain] (17:3)
                Fall 89, p. 73.
3262. LEVI, Jan Heller
        "Conversation." [PoetryE] (28) Fall 89, p. 141-144.
        "In Trouble." [Ploughs] (15:4) Wint 89-90, p. 121-123.
3263. LEVI, Toni Mergentime
        "Thoughts on the Death of N." [CrossCur] (8:3) Apr 89, p. 130-131.
3264. LEVIN, John
        "Another Filthy Lie." [WormR] (29:1, #113) 89, p. 40-41.
        "Going Back Seven." [WormR] (29:1, #113) 89, p. 41.
        "No Way of Knowing." [WormR] (29:1, #113) 89, p. 40.
        "Pretty -- Pretty." [WormR] (29:1, #113) 89, p. 40.

"Sometimes It Takes 5 Years." [WormR] (29:1, #113) 89, p. 39.
"This Editor." [WormR] (29:1, #113) 89, p. 41.
3265. LEVIN, Julie
"The Garden." [Jacaranda] (4:1) Spr-Sum 89, p. 27.
3266. LEVIN, Phillis
"Sabbath" (for Tomaz Salamun). [CrossCur] (8:2) Ja 89, p. 29.
3267. LEVINE, Anne-Marie
"A Nice Jewish Man" (from *Ghosts*). [Pequod] (28/29/30) 89, p. 252-253.
LEVINE, Judy Katz
See KATZ-LEVINE, Judy
3268. LEVINE, Julia
"Penis Envy." [FiveFR] (7) 89, p. 90.
3269. LEVINE, Nancy
"Greek Myths" (with apologies to Robert Graves). [KeyWR] (2:1/2) Fall-Wint 89,
p. 51-53.
3270. LEVINE, Philip
"Agnus Dei." [KenR] (N 11:4) Fall 89, p. 1.
"Fire." [NewYorker] (65:22) 17 Jl 89, p. 32.
"First Poems" (for Donald Justice). [Zyzzyva] (5:3, #19) Fall 89, p. 105.
"Innocence." [KenR] (N 11:4) Fall 89, p. 2-3.
"M. Degas Teaches Art & Science at Durfee Intermediate School" (Detroit, 1942).
[NewYorker] (65:9) 17 Ap 89, p. 42.
"My Grave." [MichQR] (28:2) Spr 89, p. 267-269.
"Overtime." [NewYorker] (65:5) 20 Mr 89, p. 46.
"Perennials." [NewYorker] (64:48) 16 Ja 89, p. 38.
"Scouting." [WestHR] (43:1) Spr 89, p. 27-28.
"Snails." [NewYorker] (65:42) 4 D 89, p. 54.
"Those Perfect Summer Nights." [GettyR] (2:3) Sum 89, p. 394-395.
3271. LEVINSON, Jim
"For Georgia O'Keefe." [SmPd] (26:3 #77) Fall 89, p. 7.
3272. LEVIS, Larry
"The Perfection of Solitude, Oaxaca, 1983." [AmerPoR] (18:4) Jl-Ag 89, p. 26-27.
"Sleeping Lioness." [GettyR] (2:3) Sum 89, p. 443-446.
"The Widening Spell of the Leaves" (The Carpathian Frontier, October 1968).
[AmerPoR] (18:4) Jl-Ag 89, p. 28-29.
3273. LEVITIN, Alexis
"Beauty" (tr. of Eugenio de Andrade). [HampSPR] Wint 89, p. 47.
"Boulevard Delessert" (tr. of Eugenio de Andrade). [HampSPR] Wint 89, p. 46.
"Call" (tr. of Eugenio de Andrade). [CentralP] (15) Spr 89, p. 176.
"Childhood" (tr. of Eugenio de Andrade). [Trans] (22) Fall 89, p. 234.
"Confidence" (tr. of Eugenio de Andrade). [Trans] (22) Fall 89, p. 234.
"The day clean as a deserted churchyard" (tr. of Eugenio de Andrade). [AmerPoR]
(18:6) N-D 89, p. 48.
"The Flower of Thessaly" (tr. of Eugenio de Andrade). [OxfordM] (5:1) Spr-Sum
89, p. 52.
"The Flute" (tr. of Eugenio de Andrade). [Chelsea] (48) 89, p. 26-27.
"I No Longer Know" (tr. of Eugenio de Andrade). [CreamCR] (13:2) Fall 89, p.
162.
"If the Wind Comes" (tr. of Eugenio de Andrade). [CentralP] (15) Spr 89, p. 176.
"It is within that the mouth is luminous" (tr. of Eugenio de Andrade). [AmerPoR]
(18:6) N-D 89, p. 48.
"Melancholy" (tr. of Eugenio de Andrade). [Chelsea] (48) 89, p. 26.
"Night had brought him round" (tr. of Eugenio de Andrade). [AmerPoR] (18:6) N-D
89, p. 48.
"Old Music" (tr. of Eugenio de Andrade). [Trans] (22) Fall 89, p. 234.
"On Japanese Poetry" (tr. of Eugenio de Andrade). [BlackWR] (15:2) Spr 89, p.
105.
"The open book forgotten in the grass" (tr. of Eugenio de Andrade). [AmerPoR]
(18:6) N-D 89, p. 48.
"Porto" (tr. of Eugenio de Andrade). [BlackWR] (15:2) Spr 89, p. 107.
"Praca da Alegria" (tr. of Eugenio de Andrade). [HampSPR] Wint 89, p. 46.
"Solar Matter" (Selections: 20-22, tr. of Eugenio de Andrade). [NowestR] (27:1) 89,
p. 37-39.
"Solar Matter" (tr. of Eugenio de Andrade). [OxfordM] (5:2) Fall-Wint 89, p. 50.
"That Sheet" (tr. of Eugenio de Andrade). [Trans] (22) Fall 89, p. 233.
"There must be somewhere where one arm" (tr. of Eugenio de Andrade). [AmerPoR]

(18:6) N-D 89, p. 48.
"Winter's Tale" (tr. of Eugenio de Andrade). [StoneC] (17:1/2) Fall-Wint 89-90, p. 20.
"A Working Hypothesis" (tr. of Eugenio de Andrade). [Chelsea] (48) 89, p. 27.
"You can almost see it from here, the summer" (tr. of Eugenio de Andrade). [AmerPoR] (18:6) N-D 89, p. 48.
3274. LEVY, Andrew
"Memory Li(n)es." [Screens] (1) 89, p. 39-44.
"RUMI Improvisations." [Aerial] (5) 89, p. 113-119.
3275. LEVY, Emily
"The Swooner (the Bedder)." [SinW] (39) Wint 89-90, p. 103.
3276. LEVY, Robert
"Biology." [Pequod] (26/27) 89, p. 143-144.
"Six O'Clock News: Watching the Bereaved." [Pequod] (26/27) 89, p. 141-142.
3277. LEVY, Robert J.
"The Good Men." [DenQ] (23:3/4) Wint-Spr 89, p. 108.
3278. LEVY, Ronna
"Mirror." [BrooklynR] (6) 89, p. 15.
3279. LEWANDOWSKI, S.
"Chanterelles." [Blueline] (10:1/2) 89, p. 84.
3280. LEWIS, Diane Q. (Diane Quintrall)
"Eclipse." [Mildred] (3:1) Spr-Sum 89, p. 79.
"Fish." [SmPd] (26:1, #75) Wint 89, p. 19.
"I Love Those Big Dead Fish." [SmPd] (26:1, #75) Wint 89, p. 17-18.
3281. LEWIS, Georgeanna I.
"One System" (3rd Prize, 3rd Annual Contest). [SoCoast] (6) Fall 88, p. 51.
3282. LEWIS, J. Patrick
"Crazy Love on the North Thompson." [SouthernHR] (23:3) Sum 89, p. 253.
"Tolstoy's Hands." [WestB] (23) 89, p. 10.
3283. LEWIS, Joel
"The Audible Suburbs." [NewAW] (5) Fall 89, p. 112.
"Journal Square." [NewAW] (5) Fall 89, p. 113.
3284. LEWIS, Lisa
"Night Ride." [RiverS] (29) [89], p. 3-5.
"That Lie" (For Boon T. Lim). [RiverS] (29) [89], p. 2.
3285. LEWIS, Melvin E.
"Cypress." [Obs] (4:1) Spr 89, p. 57-58.
"Sandhills." [Obs] (4:1) Spr 89, p. 55-56.
"Sea." [Obs] (4:1) Spr 89, p. 56-57.
"Winslow" (For Patricia). [Obs] (4:1) Spr 89, p. 58-59.
3286. LEWIS, Steven
"Hallelujah" (for my daughter Nancy). [Confr] (39/40) Fall 88-Wint 89, p. 40.
3287. LEYNER, Mark
"The Aspen Sunflower Produces a Nectar That Ants Adore." [Rampike] (6:3) 88, p. 57.
3288. L'HEUREUX, Maurice
"TV." [SmPd] (26:3 #77) Fall 89, p. 39.
LI, Bai
    See LI, Po
3289. LI, Ch'ing-chao
"Ju Meng Ling" (tr. by Julie Landau). [Trans] (21) Spr 89, p. 218.
"Lin Chiang Hsien" (tr. by Julie Landau). [Trans] (21) Spr 89, p. 217.
"Tsui Hua Yin" (tr. by Julie Landau). [Trans] (21) Spr 89, p. 218.
"Wan Hsi Sha" (tr. by Julie Landau). [Trans] (21) Spr 89, p. 218.
3290. LI, Chung
"Thinking of Our Spring Excursions in Kouyang and and Moved by Memories of Times Long Past . . ." (tr. by Maureen Robertson). [LitR] (32:3) Spr 89, p. 393.
"Waking Up Sober" (tr. by Maureen Robertson). [LitR] (32:3) Spr 89, p. 393.
3291. LI, Fenyong
"Painting the Plum Flowers" (tr. by Carolyn Lau). [YellowS] (31) Aut 89, p. 9.
3292. LI, He
"Moved to Protest" (tr. by Maureen Robertson). [LitR] (32:3) Spr 89, p. 394.
3293. LI, Po
"Alone" (tr. by Sam Hamill). [LitR] (32:3) Spr 89, p. 348.
"A Country Road" (tr. by Sam Hamill). [LitR] (32:3) Spr 89, p. 350.

"In a Village by the River" (tr. by Sam Hamill). [LitR] (32:3) Spr 89, p. 349.
"The Jewel Stairs' Grievance" (tr. by Ezra Pound). [LitR] (32:3) Spr 89, p. 301.
"Old Dust" (tr. by Sam Hamill). [LitR] (32:3) Spr 89, p. 349.
"The Past at Yüeh" (tr. by Cid Corman). [LitR] (32:3) Spr 89, p. 376.
"The River-Merchant's Wife: A Letter" (tr. by Ezra Pound). [LitR] (32:3) Spr 89, p. 302.
"Set Piece" (tr. by Cid Corman). [LitR] (32:3) Spr 89, p. 376.
"Traveling Song" (tr. by Sam Hamill). [LitR] (32:3) Spr 89, p. 349.
"War Wall South" (tr. by David Gordon). [LitR] (32:3) Spr 89, p. 386.
"We Drink" (tr. by Cid Corman). [LitR] (32:3) Spr 89, p. 377.
"Young Strong and Willing" (tr. by Cid Corman). [LitR] (32:3) Spr 89, p. 376.
3294. LI, Shang-yin
"Alone by the Autumn River" (tr. by Sam Hamill). [LitR] (32:3) Spr 89, p. 351.
"Night Rain Poem" (tr. by James F. Maybury). [NewOR] (16:3) Fall 89, p. 45.
"Untitled Love Poem I" (tr. by David Young). [Field] (41) Fall 89, p. 90.
"Untitled Love Poem II" (tr. by David Young). [Field] (41) Fall 89, p. 91.
"Untitled Love Poem III" (tr. by David Young). [Field] (41) Fall 89, p. 92.
"Untitled Love Poem IV" (tr. by David Young). [Field] (41) Fall 89, p. 93.
"Untitled Love Poem V" (tr. by David Young). [Field] (41) Fall 89, p. 94.
LI, T'ai-po
See LI, Po
3295. LI, Te-Ho
"Waterlilies" (tr. by Anne A. Cheng). [Jacaranda] (4:1) Spr-Sum 89, p. 71.
3296. LI, Xijian
"The Queen of the Farm Courtyard" (tr. of Liu Xiaofang, w. Gordon Osing). [BelPoJ] (40:2) Wint 89-90, p. 14-15.
"Smoke from the Kitchen Chimneys in My Hometown" (tr. of Yang Mu, w. Gordon Osing). [BelPoJ] (40:2) Wint 89-90, p. 16-17.
3297. LI, Xuan Xi
"Mongolian Frontier History" (tr. by Scott Francis). [Sequoia] (33:1) Sum 89, p. 77.
"Mongolian Frontier: Many Good Meanings" (tr. by Scott Francis). [Sequoia] (33:1) Sum 89, p. 78-79.
3298. LI, Yeh
"Parting on a Moonlit Night" (tr. by Maureen Robertson). [LitR] (32:3) Spr 89, p. 395.
3299. LI, Yu
"Autumn and a Woman's Room" (tr. by Anthony Piccione, Li Young Lee, and Carol Zhigong Chang). [LitR] (32:3) Spr 89, p. 390.
"Past Thoughts" (tr. by Anthony Piccione, Li Young Lee, and Carol Zhigong Chang). [LitR] (32:3) Spr 89, p. 390.
"Thinking of You: To the tune of 'Grateful for New Favors, II'" (tr. by Susan Dolling). [LitR] (32:3) Spr 89, p. 347.
"To Be Delivered to My Twelfth Brother, the Lord of Zheng . . ." (tr. by Susan Dolling). [LitR] (32:3) Spr 89, p. 347.
"To the Tune of 'Gathering Mulberries'" (tr. by Susan Dolling). [LitR] (32:3) Spr 89, p. 346.
"To the Tune of 'Song of Sand-Sifting Waves'" (tr. by Susan Dolling). [LitR] (32:3) Spr 89, p. 346.
LI-HONG, Zhao
See ZHAO, Li-hong
3300. LIATSOS, Sandra
"Christmas Conjuring." [CapeR] (24:2) Fall 89, p. 47.
"The Iris" (after seeing the painting by Georgia O'Keefe). [Mildred] (3:2) 89, p. 122.
"New England Landscape." [Mildred] (3:2) 89, p. 121.
"To Cure My Brother." [DeKalbLAJ] (22:1/4) 89, p. 57.
"To My Husband, the Cynic." [DeKalbLAJ] (22:1/4) 89, p. 57.
3301. LIBBEY, Elizabeth
"The Exchange." [PoetryNW] (30:1) Spr 89, p. 14-15.
3302. LIBBY, Anthony
"The Lost Boys." [Journal] (13:1) Spr-Sum 89, p. 34-35.
"'Le Moulin de la Galette,' Picasso, 1900." [Journal] (13:1) Spr-Sum 89, p. 33.
"Turner's Cat, 1842." [Journal] (13:1) Spr-Sum 89, p. 32.
"Various Vivaldis." [AntR] (47:2) Spr 89, p. 206-207.

3303. LIBERA, Sharon
     "Second Child." [Poetry] (153:4) Ja 89, p. 193.
3304. LICHTIG, Denise
     "Film Seen in an Easter Confection." [HayF] (5) Fall 89, p. 81.
     "The Split Bow." [HayF] (5) Fall 89, p. 82-83.
3305. LIEBERMAN, Laurence
     "Courtship of the Jersey Lineman." [Hudson] (42:1) Spr 89, p. 56-60.
3306. LIES, Betty
     "Grandmothers." [Footwork] 89, p. 47-48.
3307. LIEU, Jocelyn
     "Tooth of the Ghost." [AntR] (47:4) Fall 89, p. 456.
3308. LIFSHIN, Lyn
     "7-Year-Old Finds Her Murdered Mother's Naked Body." [SlipS] (9) 89, p. 76.
     "Actress Madonna." [WormR] (29:1, #113) 89, p. 7.
     "After the Black Rain, Hiroshima." [Farm] (6:2) Fall 89, p. 36.
     "After the First Snow." [Footwork] 89, p. 68.
     "After the War." [Hawai'iR] (13:2, #26) Sum 89, p. 70.
     "Afternoons in the Blue Rain, Ravena." [Hawai'iR] (13:1, #25) Spr 89, p. 106.
     "Afterward It." [Contact] (9:53/54/55) Sum-Fall 89, p. 17.
     "Airport Madonna." [SwampR] (1:4) Sum 89, p. 34.
     "The Aquarium." [DeKalbLAJ] (22:1/4) 89, p. 58.
     "Aquarium." [Interim] (8:1) Spr 89, p. 17.
     "Bat Madonna." [WormR] (29:1, #113) 89, p. 7.
     "Beige Madonna." [WormR] (29:1, #113) 89, p. 7.
     "Bill Schroeder Dies." [ChamLR] (2:2, #4) Spr 89, p. 45.
     "Birch Madonna." [SwampR] (1:4) Sum 89, p. 38.
     "Blackberry Madonna." [SwampR] (1:4) Sum 89, p. 39.
     "Blue Lace Down There." [Plain] (9:2) Wint 89, p. 8.
     "Bringing the First Tomatoes In." [SwampR] (1:4) Sum 89, p. 24-25.
     "Burn Out Madonna." [WormR] (29:1, #113) 89, p. 7.
     "Call Girl Madonna." [WormR] (29:1, #113) 89, p. 6.
     "Cars and Men." [Event] (18:2) Sum 89, p. 60.
     "Catholic School Madonna." [WormR] (29:1, #113) 89, p. 6.
     "The Chinese Restaurant." [FreeL] (1) 89, p. 29.
     "The Class Like a Bad Date." [RagMag] (7:1) 89, p. 33.
     "Common Plantain Madonna." [WormR] (29:1, #113) 89, p. 5.
     "Depression." [Interim] (8:1) Spr 89, p. 16.
     "Facing Away from Where You're Going." [Farm] (6:2) Fall 89, p. 37.
     "Fallen Leaf Madonna." [SwampR] (1:4) Sum 89, p. 37.
     "First I go after the grapes." [Cond] (16) 89, p. 38-39.
     "Gary Hart's Madonna, 2." [WormR] (29:1, #113) 89, p. 6.
     "Gary Hart's Madonna, 3." [WormR] (29:1, #113) 89, p. 6.
     "Gary Hart's Madonna, 4." [WormR] (29:1, #113) 89, p. 6.
     "Going to Sleep in the Glow Of It." [Footwork] 89, p. 68.
     "He Said I Wanted to Capture This Kid Henry." [Contact] (9:53/54/55) Sum-Fall 89,
          p. 19.
     "He Said It Was Ok." [Contact] (9:53/54/55) Sum-Fall 89, p. 18.
     "He Said That Was Smart, Not to Touch Me Never." [RagMag] (7:1) 89, p. 32.
     "He Shoves Everyone Away." [Grain] (17:4) Wint 89, p. 37.
     "He'd Rather Have a Paper Doll She Said." [Hawai'iR] (13:2, #26) Sum 89, p.
          54-55.
     "I Had a Feeling He Said The Blood Sun Falling." [Contact] (9:53/54/55) Sum-Fall
          89, p. 19.
     "In a Wreathe of Glass on 20." [Pembroke] (21) 89, p. 128.
     "Indian Summer." [SwampR] (1:4) Sum 89, p. 26.
     "It Was Like." [ConnPR] (8:1) 89, p. 15.
     "Jealous Madonna." [SwampR] (1:4) Sum 89, p. 39.
     "Just As the Woman Being Turned Over to Soothe Her Chafed Skin." [PaintedB]
          (38) 89, p. 63.
     "Leather Madonna." [WormR] (29:1, #113) 89, p. 7.
     "M and M Madonna." [WormR] (29:1, #113) 89, p. 7.
     "The Mad Girl Cringes from Students." [DeKalbLAJ] (22:1/4) 89, p. 58-59.
     "The Mad Girl Goes Back, Thinks of All the Men She Thought of as Heart
          Breaking." [Farm] (6:1) Wint-Spr 88-89, p. 64.
     "The Mad Girl Hates 800 Numbers." [AnotherCM] (19) 89, p. 124.
     "The Mad Girl Is Flip, Uses Words." [SwampR] (1:4) Sum 89, p. 37.

"The Mad Girl Is Reminded G.E. Wives Should Have Babies, Go to Library School
　　But Never Be Too Creative." [Plain] (10:1) 89, p. 37.
"The Mad Girl Sees Flaws in Herself and Her House." [AnotherCM] (19) 89, p.
　　125.
"The Mad Girl's Life Seems a Lost Radio Station." [DeKalbLAJ] (22:1/4) 89, p. 59.
"Madonna Burned by Irish Men from Boston." [WormR] (29:1, #113) 89, p. 5.
"Madonna in Love." [WormR] (29:1, #113) 89, p. 7.
"Madonna of the Ambivalences." [WormR] (29:1, #113) 89, p. 6.
"Madonna of the Bonsai Man." [Plain] (10:1) 89, p. 17.
"Madonna of the Perfectionist." [WormR] (29:1, #113) 89, p. 6.
"Madonna on the Economy." [WormR] (29:1, #113) 89, p. 7.
"Madonna to Her Ride." [WormR] (29:1, #113) 89, p. 6.
"Madonna Who Has Trouble Getting Enough Action in Her Novels." [WormR]
　　(29:1, #113) 89, p. 7.
"Madonna Who You Get Giggling." [WormR] (29:1, #113) 89, p. 7.
"Madonna's SOS." [WormR] (29:1, #113) 89, p. 6.
"Memorial Day Week." [ConnPR] (8:1) 89, p. 12.
"Menage A Tois." [Footwork] 89, p. 68.
"My Mother Who Could Always See a Smudge of Grit on the Scrubbed Bathtub."
　　[ChamLR] (3:1, #5) Fall 89, p. 10-11.
"My Mother's Address Book." [AntigR] (76) Wint 89, p. 49.
"Nuclear Power Madonna." [SwampR] (1:4) Sum 89, p. 39.
"Oh Yes He Wants to Feel Happier Help People." [BlackWR] (15:2) Spr 89, p. 44.
"Onion Ring Madonna." [WormR] (29:1, #113) 89, p. 7.
"Oral Madonna." [SwampR] (1:4) Sum 89, p. 37.
"The Phone Belches." [PaintedB] (38) 89, p. 64.
"Pleasing Madonna." [WormR] (29:1, #113) 89, p. 6.
"Roofless Madonna, 1." [WormR] (29:1, #113) 89, p. 6.
"Scarlet O'Hara Madonna." [SwampR] (1:4) Sum 89, p. 39.
"Snow Madonna." [SwampR] (1:4) Sum 89, p. 38-39.
"Sonny Terry Is Dead." [FreeL] (2) Sum 89, p. 28.
"Super Highway Madonna." [SwampR] (1:4) Sum 89, p. 39.
"There's Nobody She." [ChamLR] (3:1, #5) Fall 89, p. 8-9.
"This Maple Tree, This July Morning." [Farm] (6:1) Wint-Spr 88-89, p. 65.
"The Visit." [Footwork] 89, p. 68.
"We Never Got Inside It." [Grain] (17:4) Wint 89, p. 36.
"Yarrow Madonna." [SwampR] (1:4) Sum 89, p. 38.
3309. LIFSHITZ, Mendel
　　"The Air Cries Out" (tr. by Harold Black). [Vis] (31) 89, p. 22.
3310. LIFSON, Martha (Martha Ronk)
　　"Alibi" (3 poems). [Temblor] (9) 89, p. 137.
　　"Corot." [DenQ] (24:1) Sum 89, p. 46.
　　"Duchamps in the Garden." [Sulfur] (9:2, #25) Fall 89, p. 132-133.
　　"Lady Emma Hamilton as *La Baccante*." [DenQ] (24:1) Sum 89, p. 47-48.
　　"Misled by the Specificity of Prose." [Temblor] (9) 89, p. 135-136.
　　"The Oject of Desire." [Sulfur] (9:2, #25) Fall 89, p. 131-132.
　　"Still Life: to Name, to Want." [DenQ] (24:1) Sum 89, p. 49.
3311. LIGHTFOOT, Judy
　　"Incident." [PoetryNW] (30:4) Wint 89-90, p. 34.
　　"Taking in the Wild." [PoetryNW] (30:4) Wint 89-90, p. 35.
3312. LIGNELL, Kathleen
　　"Cows on the Road to Freedom, Maine." [StoneC] (16:3/4) Spr-Sum 89, p. 81.
　　"The Horse Painter." [StoneC] (16:3/4) Spr-Sum 89, p. 80.
3313. LIHN, Enrique
　　"Animita de Éxito." [LindLM] (8:3) Jl-S 89, p. 6.
　　"Hay Sólo Dos Paises." [LindLM] (8:3) Jl-S 89, p. 6.
　　"El Número de los Muertos." [LindLM] (8:3) Jl-S 89, p. 6.
　　"Recuerdos de un Cirujano." [LindLM] (8:3) Jl-S 89, p. 6.
3314. LILBURN, Tim
　　"Hawk." [Quarry] (38:2) Spr 89, p. 19-20.
　　"In the Earlier Lives of Crows." [Quarry] (38:2) Spr 89, p. 23.
　　"Newton, the Alchemist." [Quarry] (38:2) Spr 89, p. 21-22.
3315. LILBURNE, Geoffrey R.
　　"Neighbor." [ChrC] (106:7) Mr 1, 89, p. 230.
3316. LILLARD, Charles
　　"Avant-Propos." [PraF] (10:1, #46) Spr 89, p. 19.

254

"Frontier with Figures." [PraF] (10:1, #46) Spr 89, p. 18.
3317. LILLIE, Mary Prentice
      "Selections from Ancient Middle-American Poetry Inscribed on Walls of the
            Anthropological Museum in Mexico City" (tr. of anonymous works).
            [InterPR] (15:2) Fall 89, p. 27-29.
3318. LILLYWHITE, Harvey
      "After the Game." [AntR] (47:1) Wint 89, p. 68.
      "Flying Over the Quarries Outside O'Hare." [PoetryE] (28) Fall 89, p. 55.
      "The Garden" (for Jacob and Eileen). [CreamCR] (13:2) Fall 89, p. 124.
3319. LIM, Robin
      "Something of Ours." [BambooR] (44) Fall 89, p. 23.
3320. LIM, Shirley Geok-lin
      "Dandelions." [Contact] (9:53/54/55) Sum-Fall 89, p. 50.
      "How Does a Building Collapse?" (New World Hotel, Singapore, 1986). [Contact]
            (9:53/54/55) Sum-Fall 89, p. 48.
      "Myopia." [Contact] (9:53/54/55) Sum-Fall 89, p. 50.
      "Poetry and Criticism." [Contact] (9:53/54/55) Sum-Fall 89, p. 49.
      "The Tent." [Confr] (39/40) Fall 88-Wint 89, p. 24.
      "Too Late." [Contact] (9:53/54/55) Sum-Fall 89, p. 47.
      "Why a Poetry Reading?" [Contact] (9:53/54/55) Sum-Fall 89, p. 49.
3321. LIMA, Robert
      "Angularity." [Ometeca] (1:1) 89, p. 23.
      "Azimuth." [Ometeca] (1:1) 89, p. 22.
      "Black Hole." [Ometeca] (1:1) 89, p. 21.
      "Goddesses." [Lyra] (2:1/2) 88, c89, p. 17.
      "Sabbat." [Lyra] (2:1/2) 88, c89, p. 17.
3322. LIMAN, Claude
      "Dome Car Scavenger Hunt" (For Richard Hugo). [BellR] (12:1, #25) Spr 89, p.
            21.
3323. LIN, Ho-ching
      "The Divide" (tr. by Kenneth O. Hanson). [LitR] (32:3) Spr 89, p. 327.
      "Rice Field" (tr. by Kenneth O. Hanson). [LitR] (32:3) Spr 89, p. 327.
      "Spring" (tr. by Kenneth O. Hanson). [LitR] (32:3) Spr 89, p. 328.
3324. LINCOLN, Jenny
      "The Power of Everything to Make You Sane." [DeKalbLAJ] (22:1/4) 89, p. 60.
3325. LINDEMAN, Jack
      "One Head to Another." [KanQ] (21:1/2) Wint-Spr 89, p. 116.
      "Overseas." [HighP] (4:1) Spr 89, p. 20.
      "Sam Bradley." [KanQ] (21:1/2) Wint-Spr 89, p. 115.
3326. LINDHOLDT, Paul
      "Inscription." [SewanR] (97:4) Fall 89, p. 508.
      "Kit Gardiner, Banished." [SewanR] (97:4) Fall 89, p. 506-507.
      "Promoter of the Colonies." [SewanR] (97:4) Fall 89, p. 509.
3327. LINDNER, Carl
      "Hang Gliding." [GreensboroR] (47) Wint 89-90, p. 22.
      "Leopard." [LitR] (32:2) Wint 89, p. 227.
      "Night Fishing." [SoCaR] (22:1) Fall 89, p. 52.
      "Optometrist." [SouthernPR] (29:2) Fall 89, p. 21-22.
      "Starting a Garden." [KanQ] (21:1/2) Wint-Spr 89, p. 216-217.
      "Window." [KanQ] (21:3) Sum 89, p. 177.
3328. LINDSAY, Frances (Frannie)
      "Red Efts." [BelPoJ] (40:1) Fall 89, p. 32-33.
      "An Iris from Purgatory." [YaleR] (78:3) Spr 89, p. 480-481.
      "The Shape of the Story." [NewEngR] (11:4) Sum 89, p. 440-441.
3329. LINER, Tom
      "The Wheel within a Wheel." [EngJ] (78:6) O 89, p. 93.
3330. LINES, Virginia
      "Heliotropic Sequence." [OhioR] (44) 89, p. 19-24.
3331. LINETT, Deena
      "In Memory of the Nine Teenagers Killed at a Railroad Crossing" (March 1982).
            [Kalliope] (11:3) 89, p. 58-59.
3332. LINTHICUM, John
      "Abel Stand Up" (tr. of Hilde Domin). [LitR] (33:1) Fall 89, p. 30-31.
      "After the Dark Night" (tr. of Vera Henkel). [LitR] (33:1) Fall 89, p. 98.
      "Against Forgetting" (tr. of Erich Fried). [LitR] (33:1) Fall 89, p. 11.
      "Age of the Ants" (Two Passages, tr. of Rolfrafael Schröer). [LitR] (33:1) Fall 89,

p. 136-137.
"Alone in Your House of Skin" (tr. of Käte Reiter). [LitR] (33:1) Fall 89, p. 78.
"Alterer's" (tr. of Ralf Thenior). [LitR] (33:1) Fall 89, p. 132.
"The Angel" (tr. of Käte Reiter). [LitR] (33:1) Fall 89, p. 78.
"Apple" (tr. of Wolf Biermann). [LitR] (33:1) Fall 89, p. 32.
"Back Then I Owned an Ocean" (tr. of Johannes Poethen). [LitR] (33:1) Fall 89, p.
      70.
"Before the Crisis" (tr. of Jürgen Becker). [LitR] (33:1) Fall 89, p. 122.
"Bengali, 12/31" (tr. of Karl Corino). [LitR] (33:1) Fall 89, p. 42.
"Blessèd Are Those Who Wait" (tr. of Ulla Hahn). [LitR] (33:1) Fall 89, p. 90.
"Breath" (tr. of André Michael Bolten). [LitR] (33:1) Fall 89, p. 66.
"Breeding Stones" (tr. of Erich Fried). [LitR] (33:1) Fall 89, p. 10.
"A Call" (tr. of Erich Fried). [LitR] (33:1) Fall 89, p. 12.
"Catching Breath" (tr. of Johann P. Tammen). [LitR] (33:1) Fall 89, p. 44.
"Cat's Lives" (tr. of Sarah Kirsch). [LitR] (33:1) Fall 89, p. 64.
"The Child Has Gray Eyes" (tr. of Käte Reiter). [LitR] (33:1) Fall 89, p. 79.
"Chorus of the Hunters" (tr. of Jürgen Theobaldy). [LitR] (33:1) Fall 89, p. 24.
"Commemoration Day in May" (tr. of Günter Kunert). [LitR] (33:1) Fall 89, p. 58.
"A Conversation During Rain" (tr. of Michael Krüger). [LitR] (33:1) Fall 89, p. 111.
"Crossing" (tr. of Hilde Domin). [LitR] (33:1) Fall 89, p. 29.
"Crossing" (tr. of Wolf Biermann). [LitR] (33:1) Fall 89, p. 32.
"The Cry of the Owl" (tr. of Guntram Vesper). [LitR] (33:1) Fall 89, p. 62.
"Damnation" (tr. of Sarah Kirsch). [LitR] (33:1) Fall 89, p. 65.
"The Day's Beginning" (tr. of Sarah Kirsch). [LitR] (33:1) Fall 89, p. 64.
"Dead Love" (tr. of Ulla Hahn). [LitR] (33:1) Fall 89, p. 87.
"The Divorcée" (tr. of Karl Corino). [LitR] (33:1) Fall 89, p. 42.
"Doubled Doris" (tr. of Helmut Heissenbüttel). [LitR] (33:1) Fall 89, p. 123.
"Early Spring" (tr. of Reiner Kunze). [LitR] (33:1) Fall 89, p. 75.
"Easter" (tr. of Reiner Kunze). [LitR] (33:1) Fall 89, p. 76.
"Edvard Munch: Rouge et Noir, Colored Woodcut, 1898" (tr. of Reiner Kunze).
      [LitR] (33:1) Fall 89, p. 74.
"Elegy" (tr. of Günter Kunert). [LitR] (33:1) Fall 89, p. 57.
"End" (tr. of Ludwig Soumagne). [LitR] (33:1) Fall 89, p. 131.
"Envious" (tr. of Ludwig Soumagne). [LitR] (33:1) Fall 89, p. 131.
"Error" (tr. of Ulla Hahn). [LitR] (33:1) Fall 89, p. 89.
"Eternal Peace" (tr. of Wolf Biermann). [LitR] (33:1) Fall 89, p. 33.
"Everybody's Man" (tr. of Ulla Hahn). [LitR] (33:1) Fall 89, p. 89.
"The Face in the Water" (tr. of Johannes Poethen). [LitR] (33:1) Fall 89, p. 68-69.
"Faithfulness" (tr. of Ulla Hahn). [LitR] (33:1) Fall 89, p. 88.
"Far and Near" (tr. of Jürgen Becker). [LitR] (33:1) Fall 89, p. 121.
"Foehn" (tr. of Reiner Kunze). [LitR] (33:1) Fall 89, p. 77.
"The Following Dream" (tr. of Wolfgang Schiffer). [LitR] (33:1) Fall 89, p. 39.
"Generation" (tr. of Rolf Haufs). [LitR] (33:1) Fall 89, p. 35.
"German Song" (tr. of Jürgen Theobaldy). [LitR] (33:1) Fall 89, p. 24-25.
"Grape and Olive" (tr. of Karl Corino). [LitR] (33:1) Fall 89, p. 41.
"Guarded Hope" (tr. of Hilde Domin). [LitR] (33:1) Fall 89, p. 27.
"Head Start" (tr. of Gabriele Wohmann). [LitR] (33:1) Fall 89, p. 103.
"High Water in Paris" (tr. of Wolf Biermann). [LitR] (33:1) Fall 89, p. 34.
"I Don't Want to Die in the Evening" (tr. of Gabriele Wohmann). [LitR] (33:1) Fall
      89, p. 104.
"I Dreamed I Would Have to Say Goodbye" (tr. of Günter Grass). [LitR] (33:1) Fall
      89, p. 140-142.
"I Want to Know" (tr. of André Michael Bolten). [LitR] (33:1) Fall 89, p. 66.
"In the Border Zone" (tr. of Günter Kunert). [LitR] (33:1) Fall 89, p. 56.
"In the Eighties" (tr. of Karl Krolow). [LitR] (33:1) Fall 89, p. 95.
"In the South" (tr. of Karl Corino). [LitR] (33:1) Fall 89, p. 41.
"In the Vicinity" (tr. of Jürgen Becker). [LitR] (33:1) Fall 89, p. 122.
"The Invaders" (tr. of Ralf Thenior). [LitR] (33:1) Fall 89, p. 135.
"Is There More Wood" (tr. of Käte Reiter). [LitR] (33:1) Fall 89, p. 79.
"Island Whodunit" (tr. of Helmut Heissenbüttel). [LitR] (33:1) Fall 89, p. 124.
"Jasnando's Nightsong" (Selections: 7 poems, tr. of Christoph Meckel). [LitR]
      (33:1) Fall 89, p. 106-109.
"The Jewish Cemetery in Weissensee" (tr. of Günter Kunert). [LitR] (33:1) Fall 89,
      p. 56.
"Knife Beneath the Fig Tree" (tr. of Johannes Schenk). [LitR] (33:1) Fall 89, p.
      99-100.

"Landscape with Angels" (tr. of Peter Maiwald). [LitR] (33:1) Fall 89, p. 16.
"Lapsed" (tr. of Karl Corino). [LitR] (33:1) Fall 89, p. 43.
"The Last Circus" (tr. of Rolfrafael Schröer). [LitR] (33:1) Fall 89, p. 138.
"Last Report" (tr. of Johann P. Tammen). [LitR] (33:1) Fall 89, p. 44-45.
"Latest Report" (tr. of Ludwig Soumagne). [LitR] (33:1) Fall 89, p. 130.
"The Left Side" (tr. of Rolf Haufs). [LitR] (33:1) Fall 89, p. 37.
"Legends" (tr. of Jürgen Becker). [LitR] (33:1) Fall 89, p. 118.
"A Letter from Rome" (tr. of Michael Krüger). [LitR] (33:1) Fall 89, p. 112.
"Like Something from a Story" (tr. of Rolf Haufs). [LitR] (33:1) Fall 89, p. 35.
"The Lily-Eater" (tr. of Johannes Schenk). [LitR] (33:1) Fall 89, p. 100-102.
"Litany" (tr. of Ludwig Soumagne). [LitR] (33:1) Fall 89, p. 129.
"Living" (tr. of Wolfgang Schiffer). [LitR] (33:1) Fall 89, p. 38.
"The Long Journey" (tr. of Karl Krolow). [LitR] (33:1) Fall 89, p. 92.
"The Lovers" (tr. of Peter Maiwald). [LitR] (33:1) Fall 89, p. 18.
"Many" (tr. of Hilde Domin). [LitR] (33:1) Fall 89, p. 30.
"The Material the Imagination Has Made Up" (tr. of Helmut Heissenbüttel). [LitR]
        (33:1) Fall 89, p. 125.
"Maybe a Sort Will Turn Up" (tr. of Karl Krolow). [LitR] (33:1) Fall 89, p. 94.
"Meditation on a Torso" (tr. of Reiner Kunze). [LitR] (33:1) Fall 89, p. 74.
"A Modest Request That the Weathercock Be Released" (tr. of Johann P. Tammen).
        [LitR] (33:1) Fall 89, p. 45.
"Moment" (tr. of Karl Krolow). [LitR] (33:1) Fall 89, p. 92.
"My Father, Much Aged" (tr. of Reiner Kunze). [LitR] (33:1) Fall 89, p. 75.
"My Son" (tr. of Wolfgang Schiffer). [LitR] (33:1) Fall 89, p. 38.
"Next Door" (tr. of Karl Krolow). [LitR] (33:1) Fall 89, p. 94.
"No More Songs" (tr. of Johann P. Tammen). [LitR] (33:1) Fall 89, p. 47.
"Nothing But" (tr. of Ulla Hahn). [LitR] (33:1) Fall 89, p. 88.
"Observation" (tr. of Günter Kunert). [LitR] (33:1) Fall 89, p. 58.
"Occasional Poem" (tr. of Jürgen Theobaldy). [LitR] (33:1) Fall 89, p. 25.
"Old Comrade" (tr. of Guntram Vesper). [LitR] (33:1) Fall 89, p. 60.
"Old Iron" (tr. of Günter Grass). [LitR] (33:1) Fall 89, p. 143.
"Old Metropolitan Cemetery" (tr. of Reiner Kunze). [LitR] (33:1) Fall 89, p. 75.
"On a Bright Afternoon Occasionally" (tr. of Johannes Poethen). [LitR] (33:1) Fall
        89, p. 70.
"On Crete" (tr. of Günter Kunert). [LitR] (33:1) Fall 89, p. 59.
"On My Sleep" (tr. of Oskar Pastior). [LitR] (33:1) Fall 89, p. 126.
"Once Again" (tr. of Erich Fried). [LitR] (33:1) Fall 89, p. 12.
"Overdose" (in memoriam: Jean Améry, tr. of Reiner Kunze). [LitR] (33:1) Fall 89,
        p. 77.
"A Painting Comes into Being" (tr. of Michael Krüger). [LitR] (33:1) Fall 89, p.
        110.
"Perspective" (tr. of Günter Kunert). [LitR] (33:1) Fall 89, p. 59.
"Poetry" (tr. of André Michael Bolten). [LitR] (33:1) Fall 89, p. 67.
"Portrait" (tr. of Ralf Thenior). [LitR] (33:1) Fall 89, p. 132.
"Reading with Desert Plinth Desert" (Selection: 2, tr. of Oskar Pastior). [LitR] (33:1)
        Fall 89, p. 127.
"Reading with Distorter" (Selection: 13, tr. of Oskar Pastior). [LitR] (33:1) Fall 89,
        p. 128.
"The Sadness Has Arrived" (tr. of Vera Henkel). [LitR] (33:1) Fall 89, p. 97.
"Scene of the Crime" (tr. of Astrid Gehlhoff-Claes). [LitR] (33:1) Fall 89, p. 73.
"Scenic Madrigal" (tr. of Günter Grass). [LitR] (33:1) Fall 89, p. 143.
"Season" (tr. of Jürgen Becker). [LitR] (33:1) Fall 89, p. 119.
"The Self Made of Words" (tr. of Johannes Poethen). [LitR] (33:1) Fall 89, p. 69.
"Silent Stars" (tr. of Rolf Haufs). [LitR] (33:1) Fall 89, p. 37.
"Simple Things" (tr. of Ralf Thenior). [LitR] (33:1) Fall 89, p. 134.
"Snow" (tr. of Ralf Thenior). [LitR] (33:1) Fall 89, p. 134.
"Snow" (tr. of Sarah Kirsch). [LitR] (33:1) Fall 89, p. 63.
"Some Countries" (tr. of Karl Krolow). [LitR] (33:1) Fall 89, p. 96.
"Sometimes There" (tr. of Ulla Hahn). [LitR] (33:1) Fall 89, p. 87.
"Songsong" (tr. of Rolfrafael Schröer). [LitR] (33:1) Fall 89, p. 139.
"Sorting Walls" (tr. of Hilde Domin). [LitR] (33:1) Fall 89, p. 26.
"The Stillness" (tr. of Erich Fried). [LitR] (33:1) Fall 89, p. 13.
"Strong As Death" (tr. of Guntram Vesper). [LitR] (33:1) Fall 89, p. 61.
"Suddenly" (tr. of Rolf Haufs). [LitR] (33:1) Fall 89, p. 36.
"Summer" (tr. of Astrid Gehlhoff-Claes). [LitR] (33:1) Fall 89, p. 71.
"Summer Evening" (tr. of Peter Maiwald). [LitR] (33:1) Fall 89, p. 15-16.

"The Sun" (tr. of Käte Reiter). [LitR] (33:1) Fall 89, p. 79.
"Taking the Things" (tr. of Wolfgang Schiffer). [LitR] (33:1) Fall 89, p. 40.
"Talent" (tr. of Ludwig Soumagne). [LitR] (33:1) Fall 89, p. 131.
"Tell Me Everything" (tr. of Ludwig Soumagne). [LitR] (33:1) Fall 89, p. 129.
"That's Not It" (tr. of Hilde Domin). [LitR] (33:1) Fall 89, p. 28-29.
"They Listen to Me" (tr. of Peter Maiwald). [LitR] (33:1) Fall 89, p. 17.
"Thirty" (tr. of Peter Maiwald). [LitR] (33:1) Fall 89, p. 17.
"Through the Village" (tr. of Ulla Hahn). [LitR] (33:1) Fall 89, p. 91.
"Time for the Good Things" (tr. of Gabriele Wohmann). [LitR] (33:1) Fall 89, p. 105.
"The Tomcat" (tr. of André Michael Bolten). [LitR] (33:1) Fall 89, p. 67.
"Toward Evening an Orange Tree" (tr. of Astrid Gehlhoff-Claes). [LitR] (33:1) Fall 89, p. 72.
"Transplantation" (tr. of Ludwig Soumagne). [LitR] (33:1) Fall 89, p. 130.
"Two Nights" (tr. of Jürgen Becker). [LitR] (33:1) Fall 89, p. 118.
"Two Windows" (tr. of Jürgen Becker). [LitR] (33:1) Fall 89, p. 119.
"Unanswered Closeness" (tr. of Ulla Hahn). [LitR] (33:1) Fall 89, p. 87.
"The Unexpected" (tr. of Karl Corino). [LitR] (33:1) Fall 89, p. 43.
"Visit" (tr. of Astrid Gehlhoff-Claes). [LitR] (33:1) Fall 89, p. 73.
"Wahner Heath" (tr. of Jürgen Becker). [LitR] (33:1) Fall 89, p. 120.
"Wait, My Friend?" (tr. of Wolfgang Schiffer). [LitR] (33:1) Fall 89, p. 39.
"Walking" (tr. of Karl Krolow). [LitR] (33:1) Fall 89, p. 93.
"Weekend" (tr. of Jürgen Becker). [LitR] (33:1) Fall 89, p. 120.
"What Don Quixote Left Unsaid" (tr. of Erich Fried). [LitR] (33:1) Fall 89, p. 9.
"When Nothing Else Is Left" (for Miroslav Holub, tr. of Johann P. Tammen). [LitR] (33:1) Fall 89, p. 46.
"When the Ice Goes" (tr. of Sarah Kirsch). [LitR] (33:1) Fall 89, p. 63.
"When You Left Me So Suddenly" (tr. of Vera Henkel). [LitR] (33:1) Fall 89, p. 98.
"Why Are You Telling Me" (tr. of Vera Henkel). [LitR] (33:1) Fall 89, p. 97.
"Winter Garden" (tr. of Erich Fried). [LitR] (33:1) Fall 89, p. 14.
"The Woman" (tr. of Peter Maiwald). [LitR] (33:1) Fall 89, p. 15.
"The World Again" (tr. of Rolf Haufs). [LitR] (33:1) Fall 89, p. 36.
"Yellow-lit Crosswalk Stripes" (tr. of Ralf Thenior). [LitR] (33:1) Fall 89, p. 133.
"Yes, Your Honors" (tr. of Wolfgang Schiffer). [LitR] (33:1) Fall 89, p. 40.
"Young Motorcyclists" (tr. of Reiner Kunze). [LitR] (33:1) Fall 89, p. 76.
3333. LINTON, David
"Out to Breakfast with Florence, You and I." [Poem] (61) My 89, p. 63.
3334. LIOTTA, Peter
"Chronicle" (tr. of Branko Miljkovic). [ColR] (NS 16:1) Spr-Sum 89, p. 88.
3335. LIPSITZ, Lou
"The Ideal Robert Frost." [SouthernPR] (29:1) Spr 89, p. 68-69.
"Middle-Aged Man Experiences Spring." [SouthernPR] (29:2) Fall 89, p. 63.
"On the Declaration of Martial Law in Poland, December 18, 1981" (for Annie, Jon, Ela and Peter). [SouthernPR] (29:1) Spr 89, p. 65-68.
"Why the Dodgers Never Left Brooklyn." [NowestR] (27:3) 89, p. 55-56.
3336. LIPSKA, Ewa
"From the Gulf Stream of Sleep" (tr. by Stanislaw Baranczak and Clare Cavanah). [Trans] (21) Spr 89, p. 77.
3337. LIPSON, Susan L.
"Delight in the Order of 'Delight in Disorder' (Robert Herrick 1648)." [Writer] (102:9) S 89, p. 23.
3338. LISELLA, Julia
"The Language of Silence." [WestB] (25) 89, p. 109.
3339. LISHAN, Stuart
"On the Origins of Rainbows: Moonlight Gives an Interview." [MissouriR] (12:1) 89, p. 150.
3340. LISK, Thomas
"Order Blank." [OxfordM] (5:2) Fall-Wint 89, p. 40.
"The Secret of Life." [SoCoast] (7) Spr-Fall 89, p. 57.
3341. LISOWSKI, Joseph
"Deer Park" (tr. of P'ei Ti and Wang Wei). [LitR] (32:3) Spr 89, p. 422.
"Frost Bamboo Ranges" (tr. of P'ei Ti and Wang Wei). [LitR] (32:3) Spr 89, p. 421.
"Lakeside Pavilion" (tr. of P'ei Ti). [KanQ] (21:3) Sum 89, p. 72.
"Lakeside Pavilion" (tr. of Wang Wei). [KanQ] (21:3) Sum 89, p. 73.
"Magnolia Enclosure" (tr. of P'ei Ti and Wang Wei). [LitR] (32:3) Spr 89, p. 422.

"Meng Wall Cove" (tr. of P'ei Ti and Wang Wei). [LitR] (32:3) Spr 89, p. 421.
3342. LITT, Iris
"Fable." [StoneC] (16:3/4) Spr-Sum 89, p. 77.
3343. LITTLE, Carl
"Running Out of Ideas One Day." [ParisR] (31:110) Spr 89, p. 88.
3344. LITTLE, Geraldine C.
"Jinrikisha Boy: Johannesburg, South Africa." [Confr] (39/40) Fall 88-Wint 89, p. 39.
"Triptych: Three Mothers" (Second Prize). [Nimrod] (33:1) Fall-Wint 89, p. 26-29.
3345. LITTLEFIELD, Susan
"In Thomas Street Park." [BellArk] (5:3) My-Je 89, p. 10.
"October 22nd, Blue Funk." [BellArk] (5:3) My-Je 89, p. 20.
"To an Addict." [BellArk] (5:3) My-Je 89, p. 4.
3346. LIU, Timothy
"Martial Art." [Jacaranda] (4:1) Spr-Sum 89, p. 145.
"Variations on Death." [Jacaranda] (4:1) Spr-Sum 89, p. 146-147.
3347. LIU, Tsung-yüan
"River Show" (tr. by Gary Snyder). [LitR] (32:3) Spr 89, p. 445.
3348. LIU, Xiaofang
"The Queen of the Farm Courtyard" (tr. by Li Xijian and Gordon Osing). [BelPoJ] (40:2) Wint 89-90, p. 14-15.
3349. LIU, Yin
"Vast the World and Its Forge of Time" (tr. by J. I. Crump). [LitR] (32:3) Spr 89, p. 419.
3350. LIVINGSTONE, William
"A Message to the Bard" (tr. by Iain Crichton Smith). [Stand] (30:1) Wint 88-89, p. 12-14.
3351. LLEWELLYN, Chris
"Hiawatha in South Africa" (For Dennis Brutus, whose mother recited Longfellow's poems). [Ploughs] (15:4) Wint 89-90, p. 125.
"Portrait of a Packer" (for Gale S.). [Ploughs] (15:4) Wint 89-90, p. 124.
LLOSA, Ricardo Pau
    See PAU-LLOSA, Ricardo
3352. LLOYD, Margaret
"Aberystwyth." [Poem] (61) My 89, p. 31.
"A Bird." [PassN] (10:1) Wint 89, p. 8.
"Evelyn." [Poem] (61) My 89, p. 33.
"Presence" (for my father, 1910-1968). [Poem] (61) My 89, p. 34.
"The Rings." [Poem] (61) My 89, p. 32.
3353. LOCHHEAD, Douglas
"From A & E (22/3/80)." [AntigR] (76) Wint 89, p. 156-157.
"Open Wide a Wilderness." [AntigR] (76) Wint 89, p. 151-156.
3354. LOCKE, Duane
"Childhood Impression, Tampa." [AmerPoR] (18:2) Mr-Ap 89, p. 38.
"Post Office." [AmerPoR] (18:2) Mr-Ap 89, p. 40.
"Roman Summer." [AmerPoR] (18:2) Mr-Ap 89, p. 39.
"Trestle." [AmerPoR] (18:2) Mr-Ap 89, p. 38.
"White Tree by the Gulf." [AmerPoR] (18:2) Mr-Ap 89, p. 40.
3355. LOCKE, Edward
"Bell Rings" (for Alice Walton, age 91). [WebR] (14:1) Spr 89, p. 73.
"The Dark Zodiac of the Unicorn." [ChatR] (10:1) Fall 89, p. 65.
"Dylan Thomas." [ChatR] (10:1) Fall 89, p. 64.
"From Michael Straight's Autobiography." [BelPoJ] (39:3) Spr 89, p. 25.
"Mediterranean Tour." [BelPoJ] (39:3) Spr 89, p. 25.
"Rapid Fire." [GeoR] (43:3) Fall 89, p. 546-547.
"Think Now of the World." [WebR] (14:1) Spr 89, p. 74.
3356. LOCKE, Sharese
"And the Rain Came." [BlackALF] (23:3) Fall 89, p. 460-461.
3357. LOCKLIN, Gerald
"Arming for Peace." [SlipS] (9) 89, p. 89.
"A Door Can Be Beaten Down from Either Side." [WormR] (29:1, #113) 89, p. 42.
"The Henny Youngman of Creative Writing." [WormR] (29:1, #113) 89, p. 42.
"Monet: Impression, Sunrise." [FreeL] (2) Sum 89, p. 27.
"Reality Therapy." [SlipS] (9) 89, p. 88.
"Renoir: Alphonsine Fournaise." [FreeL] (2) Sum 89, p. 26.
"Surprise Party." [WormR] (29:1, #113) 89, p. 43.

"The Valley." [FreeL] (2) Sum 89, p. 21.
"Winslow Homer: *Children on a Fence 1874.*" [FreeL] (2) Sum 89, p. 26.
3358. LOCKWOOD, Virginia
"For Issac Newton." [US1] (22/23) Spr 89, p. 34.
"Remembering." [US1] (22/23) Spr 89, p. 34.
"Vacuum." [US1] (22/23) Spr 89, p. 34.
3359. LODEN, Rachel
"The House and Its Wife." [PoetC] (20:3) Spr 89, p. 39.
"How to Give Up Everything." [BelPoJ] (40:1) Fall 89, p. 31.
"Ice Age." [MidwQ] (30:4) Sum 89, p. 447.
3360. LOGAN, Char
"Expecting." [SingHM] (16) 89, p. 76-77.
3361. LOGAN, John
"The Avocado." [PaintedB] (39) 89, p. 46.
"Twilight Land" (after Georg Trakl). [PaintedB] (39) 89, p. 64-65.
"Twilight Land" (tr. of Georg Trakl). [PaintedB] (39) 89, p. 64-65.
3362. LOGAN, William
"The Early Summers." [WestHR] (43:4) Wint 89, p. 264.
"The English out of England." [WestHR] (43:4) Wint 89, p. 263.
"Florida Pest Control." [ParisR] (31:113) Wint 89, p. 112.
"Nativity." [Boulevard] (4:2, #11) Fall 89, p. 45.
"NE Seventh Street As the Pequod." [Thrpny] (38) Sum 89, p. 33.
"New Year's at the Methodists." [Nat] (248:23) 12 Je 89, p. 826.
"The Rule of the Rule of Law." [YaleR] (78:4) Sum 89, p. 627-628.
"The Shadow-Line." [NewYorker] (64:51) 6 F 89, p. 30.
3363. LOHMANN, Jeanne
"The Accident." [PassN] (10:1) Wint 89, p. 6.
"As a Little Child." [PoetryNW] (30:2) Sum 89, p. 27-28.
"Festival: *Bon-Odori.*" [PoetryNW] (30:2) Sum 89, p. 28.
"Regardless." [PoetryNW] (30:2) Sum 89, p. 26-27.
"Winter Poem." [CentR] (33:1) Wint 89, p. 52.
3364. LOMBARDO, Stanley
"Altar" (tr. of x Dodiadas). [Temblor] (10) 89, p. 203.
"Axe" (tr. of Simmias of Rhodes). [Temblor] (10) 89, p. 201.
"Egg" (tr. of Simmias of Rhodes). [Temblor] (10) 89, p. 202.
"Syrinx" (tr. of Theocritus). [Temblor] (10) 89, p. 203.
"Wings" (tr. of Simmias of Rhodes). [Temblor] (10) 89, p. 200.
3365. LONDON, Jonathan
"The Black Feather" (for Jim Montrose, poet 1923-1984). [Wind] (19:64) 89, p. 28.
"Lizzy." [SlipS] (9) 89, p. 19-20.
"Starting from an Actual Place." [FiveFR] (7) 89, p. 42.
"The Way the Green Takes the Light." [SwampR] (1:4) Sum 89, p. 29.
LONERGAN, Janet Gill
See GILL-LONERGAN, Janet
3366. LONG, A. E.
"Last Month's *Geographic.*" [EmeraldCR] (1989) c1988, p. 98-99.
3367. LONG, Doughtry ("Doc")
"At Cinaminson Alternate School." [Obs] (4:1) Spr 89, p. 75-75.
"At Fitz's Place." [Obs] (4:1) Spr 89, p. 74-75.
"Blues Walk I." [Obs] (4:1) Spr 89, p. 76.
"Blues Walk I." [PaintedB] (38) 89, p. 75.
"The Capitalist." [Obs] (4:1) Spr 89, p. 72-73.
"Fourth-Period." [Obs] (4:1) Spr 89, p. 75.
"Introduction to Dream Cycle I." [Obs] (4:1) Spr 89, p. 77.
"On Lebanon Lake." [Obs] (4:1) Spr 89, p. 73-74.
"Progeni." [Obs] (4:1) Spr 89, p. 76.
"Sometimes the Way It Is In This World." [Obs] (4:1) Spr 89, p. 72.
3368. LONG, Joel
"To Follow Wing Prints." [Sonora] (17) Spr-Sum 89, p. 9.
3369. LONG, Judy
"Distance." [RagMag] (7:1) 89, p. 37.
"Words." [RagMag] (7:1) 89, p. 36.
3370. LONG, Richard
"A Number with the Zeroes of a Light Year." [NegC] (9:2) 89, p. 18.
"Taking the Comfort with Us." [CreamCR] (13:2) Fall 89, p. 217.

3371. LONG, Robert Hill
"Effigies" (8 selections). [KenR] (NS 11:3) Sum 89, p. 115-123.
"The Milkweed Wife." [SenR] (19:2) Fall 89, p. 78-79.
"The Third River." [Poetry] (154:3) Je 89, p. 144-146.
"Yellow Stars." [NewEngR] (12:1) Aut 89, p. 35.
3372. LONGLAND, Jean R.
"Children" (tr. of Jorge Barbosa). [Pig] (15) 88, p. 52.
"Island" (tr. of Jorge Barbosa). [Pig] (15) 88, p. 51.
"Lake Nyasa" (tr. of Alberto de Lacerda). [Pig] (15) 88, p. 40.
"Lullaby" (tr. of Jorge Barbosa). [Pig] (15) 88, p. 51.
3373. LONGLEY, Judy
"Late Afternoon in the Antique Store" (for Marilyn 1941-1988). [PassN] (10:2) Sum
89, p. 10.
"Triptych of My Father." [NegC] (9:2) 89, p. 59-61.
3374. LONGLEY, Michael
"An Amish Rug." [NoDaQ] (57:1) Wint 89, p. 94.
"Aubade" (tr. of Nuala Ni Dhomhnaill). [Trans] (22) Fall 89, p. 147.
"Detour." [NoDaQ] (57:1) Wint 89, p. 95.
3375. LOO, Jeff
"The Power." [Mildred] (3:2) 89, p. 65.
3376. LOONEY, George
"Flesh Made Words." [ApalQ] (32) 89, p. 67-80.
"For the Workers of Machinists Union, Local 765." [PoetryE] (28) Fall 89, p.
100-103.
"A Geography of the Ohio" (for James Wright). [TarRP] (28:2) Spr 89, p. 16-17.
"Letter to Smith from Chicago" (in memory of Richard Hugo). [PoetryE] (28) Fall
89, p. 98-99.
"No Matter the Weather." [KenR] (NS 11:2) Spr 89, p. 45-46.
"Songs I Know by Heart and Love." [BlackWR] (15:2) Spr 89, p. 129-135.
"Trusting Your Way Home." [GettyR] (2:3) Sum 89, p. 492-494.
3377. LOOTS, Barbara
"Cross Country." [SoCoast] (6) Fall 88, p. 37.
3378. LOPEZ, Adelaida
"Angela." [LindLM] (8:2) Ap-Je 89, p. 6.
"Emilia." [LindLM] (8:2) Ap-Je 89, p. 6.
"El Volcan." [LindLM] (8:2) Ap-Je 89, p. 6.
3379. LOPEZ, César
"The Abduction of the Mulattoes" (Owing to Carlos Enríquez, tr. by Lourdes
González). [Pig] (15) 88, p. 67.
"Aunt Pepilla Embroiders a Bouquet" (In the style of Manuel Justo de Rubalcava, tr.
by Lourdes González). [Pig] (15) 88, p. 66.
"Old Postcard" (To my friend Juan Villalobos, tr. by Lourdes González). [Pig] (15)
88, p. 66.
LOPEZ, María S. Molina
See MOLINA LOPEZ, María S.
3380. LOPEZ GONZALEZ, Salvador
"Felipe." [Mairena] (11:27) 89, p. 74.
3381. LOPO
"Song of a Restless Heart (Cantiga d'Amigo)" (tr. by Richard Zenith). [PoetryE]
(28) Fall 89, p. 198.
3382. LORBERER, Eric
"A Little Night Music: Armistice Day, 1987." [DenQ] (23:3/4) Wint-Spr 89, p. 109.
LORCA, Federico García
See GARCIA LORCA, Federico
3383. LORD, Phoebe
"Pantoum of Bruises." [Ploughs] (15:4) Wint 89-90, p. 126-128.
3384. LORD, Ted
"Five Accounts, Like Hands Passing Through Tea Steam." [BlueBldgs] (11) 89, p.
22-24.
"Lake George, August 22nd." [CarolQ] (41:3) Spr 89, p. 71.
3385. LORTS, Jack E.
"When the snow drifts knee-deep." [EngJ] (78:7) N 89, p. 93.
3386. LOTHMANN, Jeanne
"Saint Patrick's." [Shen] (39:2) Sum 89, p. 94-95.
3387. LOTT, Rick
"The Children of Tela." [PraS] (63:4) Wint 89, p. 84-85.

"Coming Home from Arkansas." [CarolQ] (41:2) Wint 89, p. 64.
"The Patience of Horses." [CarolQ] (41:2) Wint 89, p. 63.
"Sunday, Devouring Fire." [PraS] (63:4) Wint 89, p. 85-86.
3388. LOUIS, Adrian (Adrian C.)
"Drinking Beer at Wounded Knee." [SmPd] (26:2 #76) Spr 89, p. 11.
"Farewell to Synthesis." [KenR] (NS 11:2) Spr 89, p. 124.
"Fire Water World" (Selections: 3 poems). [Mildred] (3:1) Spr-Sum 89, p. 123-125.
"Pine Ridge Lullaby." [SmPd] (26:2 #76) Spr 89, p. 10.
3389. LOVE, B. D.
"The Dance." [LaurelR] (23:2) Sum 89, p. 41-42.
"Driving." [LaurelR] (23:2) Sum 89, p. 41.
3390. LOVELOCK, Yann
"Not Locus If You Will But Envelope." [Os] (28) 89, p. 22-23.
3391. LOVESEY, Oliver
"Omphalos." [Grain] (17:4) Wint 89, p. 31.
3392. LOVITT, Robert
"The entire north american continent." [MoodySI] (20/21) Spr 89, p. 41.
3393. LOW, Denise
"Body Memory." [CinPR] (19) Spr 89, p. 51.
"Lacuna: Ogallala Aquifer." [KanQ] (21:3) Sum 89, p. 88.
"Mornings I Never Leave You." [HeliconN] (20) 89, p. 30.
LOW, Jackson Mac
   See Mac LOW, Jackson
3394. LOWE, Janice
"Between Acts." [Callaloo] (12:2, #39) Spr 89, p. 292-293.
3395. LOWENSTEIN, Robert
"Res Gestae." [StoneC] (17:1/2) Fall-Wint 89-90, p. 35.
3396. LOWERY, Janet
"The Bad Parts." [MSS] (6:3) 89, p. 113.
"Failed Angel." [MSS] (6:3) 89, p. 115.
"Resolution." [MSS] (6:3) 89, p. 114.
"That." [MSS] (6:3) 89, p. 116.
3397. LOWERY, Joanne
"Death of Zaira J." [WestB] (23) 89, p. 58-59.
"The Experiment." [HampSPR] Wint 89, p. 34.
"The First Little Pig." [CrabCR] (6:1) 89, p. 27.
"Girls." [HampSPR] Wint 89, p. 33.
"Medusa Is Just Another Way to Say I Love You." [GrahamHR] (12) Spr 89, p.
   28-29.
"The Park." [BallSUF] (30:4) Aut 89, p. 33.
3398. LOWEY, Mark
"The Ashtray My Uncle Stole." [PraF] (10:4, #49) Wint 89-90, p. 43.
"February I Ching." [Dandel] (16:1) Spr-Sum 89, p. 43.
3399. LOWITZ, Leza
"The Aftermath." [FiveFR] (7) 89, p. 92-93.
"Feeding Flowers." [FiveFR] (7) 89, p. 91.
3400. LOWRIE, Joyce Oliver
"The house would be replete with roses and with wasps" (tr. of Francis Jammes).
   [AmerPoR] (18:2) Mr-Ap 89, p. 49.
"One of these Sunday afternoons when it is hot" (tr. of Francis Jammes).
   [AmerPoR] (18:2) Mr-Ap 89, p. 49.
"Upon my death, you with blue eyes" (tr. of Francis Jammes). [AmerPoR] (18:2)
   Mr-Ap 89, p. 49.
3401. LOWRY, Malcolm
"I met a man who had got drunk with Christ." [CanLit] (121) Sum 89, p. 58.
"Midnight denies poursuivant of the dawn." [CanLit] (121) Sum 89, p. 57.
"Sun, Aeroplane, Lovers." [CanLit] (121) Sum 89, p. 58.
3402. LU, Lu
"Byzantium, Byzantium" (tr. by Dong Jiping). [Footwork] 89, p. 26.
"Matisse, the Wild Beast" (tr. by Dong Jiping). [Footwork] 89, p. 26.
"Old Song" (tr. by Dong Jiping). [Footwork] 89, p. 26-27.
3403. LU, Yu
"Crossing a Boat-Bridge to South Tower"" (tr. by David Gordon). [LitR] (32:3) Spr
   89, p. 384.
"Drifing on the Lake I Reach the Eastern Ching River" (tr. by Paul Hansen). [LitR]
   (32:3) Spr 89, p. 355.

"A Garden's Mixed Notes"" (tr. by David Gordon). [LitR] (32:3) Spr 89, p. 385.
"Going Out in the Rain to Look Around I Wrote This"" (tr. by David Gordon).
    [LitR] (32:3) Spr 89, p. 385.
LU LU
    See LU, Lu
LUCA, Geraldine de
    See DeLUCA, Geraldine
3404. LUCAS, Barbara
    "House of Rain." [WindO] (51) Spr 89, p. 12.
3405. LUCAS, Carolyn
    "Wild Rests." [PaintedB] (37) 89, p. 24.
3406. LUCAS, Marie B.
    "Health Unit." [Pembroke] (21) 89, p. 127.
3407. LUCIA, Joseph
    "Hill Music." [Poem] (62) N 89, p. 24.
    "Rush Hour." [Poem] (62) N 89, p. 26.
    "Storm After Climbing." [Poem] (62) N 89, p. 25.
3408. LUCINA, Mary
    "Pages." [WebR] (14:1) Spr 89, p. 70.
    "Reading Wood." [Nimrod] (33:1) Fall-Wint 89, p. 90.
3409. LUDVIGSON, Susan
    "Au Premier Coup." [Nat] (248:19) 15 My 89, p. 676.
    "Dreaming the Summer Nights: Scandinavian Paintings from the Turn of the
        Century." [TarRP] (29:1) Fall 89, p. 1-4.
    "The Gold She Finds" (On the Life of Camille Claudel, Sculptor). [SouthernR]
        (25:4) Aut 89, p. 877-899.
    "New Physics." [SouthernPR] (29:1) Spr 89, p. 41.
    "Paris Aubade." [GeoR] (43:2) Sum 89, p. 298.
    "There Are Reasons." [Nat] (248:10) 13 Mr 89, p. 353.
3410. LUDWIG, Leslaw
    "Music As It Is" (tr. of Miroslaw Stecewicz). [BelPoJ] (40:2) Wint 89-90, p. 22-31.
LUIS, Sara Bellini
    See BELLINI LUIS, Sara
3411. LUM, Wing Tek
    "Chinese Hot Pot." [BambooR] (42/43) Spr-Sum 89, p. 147.
    "Filial Thoughts." [BambooR] (44) Fall 89, p. 26.
    "An Image of the Good Times." [BambooR] (44) Fall 89, p. 24-25.
    "Juk." [BambooR] (42/43) Spr-Sum 89, p. 151-152.
    "Kindergarten." [BambooR] (42/43) Spr-Sum 89, p. 155-156.
    "The Poet Imagines His Grandfather's Thoughts on the Day He Died." [BambooR]
        (42/43) Spr-Sum 89, p. 148.
    "Poetic License." [BambooR] (41) Wint 89, p. 19.
    "Poetic License." [BambooR] (42/43) Spr-Sum 89, p. 157.
    "T-Bone Steak." [BambooR] (42/43) Spr-Sum 89, p. 153-154.
    "Taking Her to the Open Market." [BambooR] (42/43) Spr-Sum 89, p. 149-150.
3412. LUMMIS, Suzanne
    "Why Her Name and Face Are Everywhere." [AntR] (47:1) Wint 89, p. 64-65.
LUNA, Hernando Cardozo
    See CARDOZO LUNA, Hernando
3413. LUND, Orval
    "Bird, Cat, Man, Fish." [KanQ] (21:3) Sum 89, p. 98.
    "For John, Who Did Not Choose Baseball." [PassN] (10:1) Wint 89, p. 13.
    "In the Chiropractor's Office." [NoDaQ] (57:3) Sum 89, p. 202.
    "Moofer." [NoDaQ] (57:3) Sum 89, p. 201-202.
    "Sophie's Breasts." [SpoonRQ] (14:3) Sum 89, p. 10-11.
    "Uncle Ed Lacked a Finger." [SpoonRQ] (14:3) Sum 89, p. 8-9.
3414. LUNDAY, Robert
    "Bad." [PraS] (63:4) Wint 89, p. 80.
    "Deep in the Heart of Texas, 1940." [GrahamHR] (12) Spr 89, p. 30.
    "Fifteen Captions." [AnotherCM] (19) 89, p. 142.
    "Gemara." [ChatR] (9:2) Wint 89, p. 43.
    "Georgia Lamb." [SouthernPR] (29:2) Fall 89, p. 64-67.
    "The Nautilus." [SouthernPR] (29:1) Spr 89, p. 62.
3415. LUNDE, David
    "Morganlieder." [Confr] (39/40) Fall 88-Wint 89, p. 62.

3416. LUNDQUIST, Kaye
"Birth" (for Aubrielle). [BellArk] (5:1) Ja-F 89, p. 20.
"Tiger Lilies Remember." [BellArk] (5:1) Ja-F 89, p. 10.
3417. LUNN, Jean
"Provincetown, September 1987." [StoneC] (16:3/4) Spr-Sum 89, p. 74.
3418. LUPAN, Radu
"Din Noaptea" (tr. of Mihai Eminescu, w. W. D. Snodgrass and Dona Rosu).
[AmerPoR] (18:6) N-D 89, p. 32.
"Sonnets" (I, II, III, tr. of Mihai Eminescu, w. W. D. Snodgrass and Dona Rosu).
[AmerPoR] (18:6) N-D 89, p. 32.
3419. LUSK, Daniel
"Church." [PaintedB] (37) 89, p. 38.
"The Guest." [PaintedB] (37) 89, p. 43.
"Hope" (for my brother, John). [PaintedB] (37) 89, p. 44-46.
"House of Paper Light." [PaintedB] (37) 89, p. 39-40.
"Lift." [PaintedB] (37) 89, p. 47.
"Solstice." [PaintedB] (37) 89, p. 35.
"Surfacing." [PaintedB] (37) 89, p. 41-42.
"Wings Folding Up." [PaintedB] (37) 89, p. 36-37.
3420. LUTHER, Susan M.
"Sheaves" (A Virginal). [YellowS] (30) Sum 89, p. 10.
3421. LUX, Thomas
"All That's Left." [GettyR] (2:2) Spr 89, p. 316.
"At Least Let Me Explain." [GettyR] (2:2) Spr 89, p. 314-315.
"Backyard Swing Set." [Poetry] (153:4) Ja 89, p. 210.
"Benighted (With Connotations of Bad Luck)." [AmerPoR] (18:5) S-O 89, p. 26.
"Black Road Over Which Green Trees Grow." [NewL] (56:2/3) Wint 89-Spr 90, p.
167.
"Children in School During Heavy Snowfall." [AmerPoR] (18:5) S-O 89, p. 24.
"The Creature Has a Purpose." [AmerPoR] (18:5) S-O 89, p. 24.
"Dr. Goebbel's Novels." [StoneC] (16:3/4) Spr-Sum 89, p. 7.
"Elegy for Frank Stanford, 1949-1978." [NewL] (56:2/3) Wint 89-Spr 90, p.
164-165.
"Falling Through the Leaves." [AmerPoR] (18:5) S-O 89, p. 23.
"Floating Baby Paintings." [NewL] (56:2/3) Wint 89-Spr 90, p. 169.
"For My Daughter When She Can Read." [AmerPoR] (18:5) S-O 89, p. 25.
"Gold on Mule." [NewL] (56:2/3) Wint 89-Spr 90, p. 166.
"Great Advances in Vanity." [AmerPoR] (18:5) S-O 89, p. 26.
"Irreconcilibilia." [StoneC] (16:3/4) Spr-Sum 89, p. 9-10.
"A Little Tooth." [AmerPoR] (18:5) S-O 89, p. 25.
"Reluctant." [AmerPoR] (18:5) S-O 89, p. 26.
"Thrombosis Trombone." [AmerPoR] (18:5) S-O 89, p. 23.
"Time." [AmerPoR] (18:5) S-O 89, p. 24.
"Uncle Joe." [DenQ] (23:3/4) Wint-Spr 89, p. 29.
"Walt Whitman's Brain Dropped on Laboratory Floor." [NewL] (56:2/3) Wint
89-Spr 90, p. 168.
"Walt Whitman's Brain Dropped on Laboratory Floor." [StoneC] (16:3/4) Spr-Sum
89, p. 11.
"The Wordworths: William and Dorothy." [AmerPoR] (18:5) S-O 89, p. 23.
3422. LUZI, Mario
"Hunt" (tr. by Dana Gioia). [Poetry] (155:1/2) O-N 89, p. 26.
"If Only" (tr. by Ned Condini). [Trans] (21) Spr 89, p. 186.
"Mother and Son" (tr. by Ned Condini). [Trans] (21) Spr 89, p. 187.
"Nell'Imminenza dei Quarant'Anni." [Poetry] (155:1/2) O-N 89, p. 24.
"On Approaching Forty" (tr. by Dana Gioia). [Poetry] (155:1/2) O-N 89, p. 25.
"Tutto Perso, Tutto Parificato? (All Lost, All Made Equal?)" (Selections: 4 poems, tr.
by Stephen Sartarelli). [Poetry] (155:1/2) O-N 89, p. 27-29.
3423. LUZZARO, Susan
"Fin de Siècle." [MalR] (86) Spr 89, p. 48-49.
"Side to Side." [MalR] (86) Spr 89, p. 47.
3424. LUZZI, Joyce K.
"Daughter Coming Home in August." [BallSUF] (30:4) Aut 89, p. 9.
"Goodbye Christmas." [WindO] (51) Spr 89, p. 21.
"Innocents." [Poem] (62) N 89, p. 65.
"It's Just a Movie, Man." [LaurelR] (23:2) Sum 89, p. 43.
"Not Alone in My Body." [WindO] (51) Spr 89, p. 22.

"Too Late for Garlands." [Poem] (62) N 89, p. 63.
"Under the Fog." [Poem] (62) N 89, p. 64.
3425. LYDEN, Eileen
"Brian." [Kaleid] (18) Wint-Spr 89, p. 29.
"Stained Glass." [Kaleid] (18) Wint-Spr 89, p. 29.
3426. LYNCH, Annette
"Hand to Mouth in 1981." [Poem] (62) N 89, p. 48.
"Mother Died on Halloween." [Poem] (62) N 89, p. 50.
"Shame After Conscious or Unconscious Shame, We Play the Sympathetic Magic
Game." [Poem] (62) N 89, p. 51.
"Tour Stop, 1981." [Poem] (62) N 89, p. 49.
3427. LYNCH, Doris
"By the Levee." [SwampR] (1:4) Sum 89, p. 30.
"Dusk in a Green Dress, Sing-Sing" (Ethel Rosenberg, 1915-1953). [Prima] (13)
89, p. 21-22.
"On Forty-First Street." [SwampR] (1:4) Sum 89, p. 31.
"Visitation Rights." [SwampR] (1:4) Sum 89, p. 32.
"Walking in the Quaker Wood." [Prima] (13) 89, p. 23.
3428. LYNCH, Janice
"Mammogram." [BellR] (12:2, #26) Fall 89, p. 22.
"Only Bodies." [PassN] (10:2) Sum 89, p. 23.
3429. LYNCH, Thomas (Tom)
"Aisling." [Witness] (2:4) Wint 88, p. 103-104.
"Argyle's Ejaculations." [Witness] (2:4) Wint 88, p. 106.
"August." [Witness] (2:4) Wint 88, p. 107.
"How It's Done Here." [VirQR] (65:1) Wint 89, p. 80.
"Rhododendrons." [VirQR] (65:1) Wint 89, p. 78.
"These Things Happen in the Lives of Women." [VirQR] (65:1) Wint 89, p. 79-80.
"Tommy." [VirQR] (65:1) Wint 89, p. 78-79.
"Unnatural Act." [Witness] (2:4) Wint 88, p. 105.
"What Never Happened." [Witness] (2:4) Wint 88, p. 104.
3430. LYNES, Thomas
"After Rain in Late Fall." [FiveFR] (7) 89, p. 21.
LYNN, Elizabeth Cook
See COOK-LYNN, Elizabeth
3431. LYNSKEY, Edward (Ed C., Edward C.)
"At the Moon's Inn." [SouthernHR] (23:2) Spr 89, p. 143.
"Caution Lights." [YellowS] (29) Spr 89, p. 21.
"Getting Mad and Even." [Wind] (19:65) 89, p. 17.
"How Peter Lorre Could Have Saved My Life." [FloridaR] (16:2/3) Fall-Wint 89, p.
174.
"The Hyacinth Girl." [YellowS] (31) Aut 89, p. 28.
"If He Hollers, Let Him Go." [Wind] (19:65) 89, p. 17-18.
"Mrs. Lincoln Enters Bellevue Place." [ApalQ] (31) 89, p. 57.
"Portrait of the Outlaw." [WindO] (51) Spr 89, p. 26.
"Southern Cross." [FloridaR] (16:2/3) Fall-Wint 89, p. 175.
"Southern Cross." [YellowS] (32) Wint 89, p. 9.
"Trout Fishing in America." [Mildred] (3:2) 89, p. 16.
"Waifs." [WilliamMR] (27) 89, p. 86.
"The Whores' Coo." [WindO] (52) Wint 89-90, p. 27.
"The Whores' Coo." [YellowS] (32) Wint 89, p. 8.
3432. LYON, Hillary
"Dragon Winter." [Poem] (62) N 89, p. 67.
"The Red Tent." [Poem] (62) N 89, p. 68.
3433. LYON, Rick
"Almost Autumn" (Prizewinning Poets -- 1989). [Nat] (248:20) 22 My 89, p. 708.
"The Deer." [TarRP] (28:2) Spr 89, p. 32.
"Flocks." [TarRP] (28:2) Spr 89, p. 33.
"The Island" (Prizewinning Poets -- 1989). [Nat] (248:20) 22 My 89, p. 708.
3434. LYSAGHT, Sean
"The Village Tailor." [NoDaQ] (57:1) Wint 89, p. 96.
3435. LYTLE, L.
"The Death of Leaves." [CarolQ] (42:1) Fall 89, p. 17.
3436. MA, Chih-yüan
"You Left" (tr. by J. I. Crump). [LitR] (32:3) Spr 89, p. 417.

3437. MAAS, Peter E.
"Christmas Wrappings." [Footwork] 89, p. 36.
Mac . . .
    See also names beginning with Mc . . .
3438. Mac CORMACK, Karen
"The Appalachians Are Far From Self-Congratulatory" (from: Quill Driver). [Notus]
    (4:2) Fall 89, p. 32-33.
"/Error." [Rampike] (6:3) 88, p. 49.
"One No Trump." [Screens] (1) 89, p. 21.
"Refractions Breed Proof." [Screens] (1) 89, p. 20.
3439. Mac LOW, Jackson
"9th Merzgedicht *in Memoriam* Kurt Schwitters." [Conjunc] (13) 89, p. 90-114.
"12th Merzgedicht *in Memoriam* Kurt Schwitters." [NoDaQ] (57:3) Sum 89, p.
    215-217.
"27th Mersgedicht *in Memoriam* Kurt Schwitters." [Screens] (1) 89, p. 103-104.
"30th Mersgedicht *in Memoriam* Kurt Schwitters." [Screens] (1) 89, p. 102.
"35th Merzgedicht *in Memoriam* Kurt Schwitters." [Aerial] (5) 89, p. 54-55.
"37th Merzgedicht *in Memoriam* Kurt Schwitters." [Aerial] (5) 89, p. 56-57.
"60th Light Poem" (In Memoriam Robert Duncan 8-9 October 1988). [Sulfur] (9:1,
    #24) Spr 89, p. 7-8.
"Oners n Tenners 3" (from *Descriptive Mentality from the Head, Face and Hand* by
    Holmes W. Merton, 1899). [Sulfur] (9:1, #24) Spr 89, p. 140-150.
3440. MACAULAY, Liz
"Ordinary Moments" (for Mom). [SingHM] (16) 89, p. 73.
3441. MacBETH, George
"A Sense of Presence." [Stand] (30:3) Sum 89, p. 38.
MacCORMACK, Karen
    See Mac CORMACK, Karen
3442. MACDONALD, Cynthia
"The Precise Shape of a Wave." [Antaeus] (62) Spr 89, p. 100-101.
3443. MacDONALD, Kathryn
"Cat Craven Attempts to Explain the Theory of Everything to Ralph and Wanda."
    [SoCoast] (7) Spr-Fall 89, p. 46.
3444. MacDONALD, Ranald
"Husbands." [Verse] (6:3) Wint 89, p. 41.
"A Translation from the Hungarian." [Verse] (6:3) Wint 89, p. 41.
3445. MacDOUGALL, Joan
"The Albino Boy." [AntigR] (76) Wint 89, p. 118.
3446. MACFIE, Jenny
"Evening Song." [HeliconN] (20) 89, p. 31.
"In America." [HeliconN] (20) 89, p. 31.
3447. MacGLOIN, Thomas
"Music -- Ancient and Modern." [NoDaQ] (57:1) Wint 89, p. 97-98.
MACIAS, Rosa Marta Zarate
    See ZARATE MACIAS, Rosa Marta
3448. MACIOCI, R. Nikolas (R. Nicholas)
"Early Morning Basketball." [WindO] (52) Wint 89-90, p. 14.
"The New Thanksgiving" (Commended). [StoneC] (17:1/2) Fall-Wint 89-90, p.
    prelim. p. 8.
"The Okinawa Nudes." [NegC] (9:1) 89, p. 42.
"Redemption in a Hotel Room" (for Jean Rhys). [PaintedB] (38) 89, p. 73.
"Snow Talk." [PaintedB] (38) 89, p. 74.
3449. MACKENZIE, Bruce
"No Signs of A Watery Evolution." [SmPd] (26:3 #77) Fall 89, p. 17.
3450. MACKENZIE, Nancy
"I have heard what happens when you step too far." [PraF] (10:4, #49) Wint 89-90,
    p. 41.
3451. MACKEY, Mary
"Don't Start Something You Can't Finish." [YellowS] (30) Sum 89, p. 4.
3452. MACKEY, Nathaniel
"Each thing its due the ostensible end." [Screens] (1) 89, p. 31.
"Sweet Mystic Beast" (for Johnn Dyani, Abdullah Ibrahim, Joe Malinga, Dudu
    Pukwana . . .). [Epoch] (38:3) 89, p. 225-228.
"Synchronous flavor." [Screens] (1) 89, p. 32.
"Where the would-be City squeezes blood." [Screens] (1) 89, p. 30.

266

3453. MACKLIN, Elizabeth
"At the Creek Edge." [NewYorker] (65:43) 11 D 89, p. 52.
"I Imagine Back." [NewYorker] (65:29) 4 S 89, p. 70.
"In Tompkins Square Park" (1984). [SouthwR] (74:1) Wint 89, p. 86.
"Instruction: Early Epiphanies." [NewYorker] (65:17) 12 Je 89, p. 48.
"Looking to Console the Maker." [NewYorker] (65:4) 13 Mr 89, p. 101.
"The Only Child Sends a Gift to Her Mother." [NewYorker] (65:43) 11 D 89, p. 52.
"Our Fall." [NewYorker] (65:36) 23 O 89, p. 66.
"Reassurance in a Hot Summer." [NewYorker] (65:23) 24 Jl 89, p. 34.
"Surface Tension." [NewYorker] (64:50) 30 Ja 89, p. 36.
"A Translation of Love in Public." [Lyra] (2:1/2) 88, c89, p. 26-27.
3454. MacLEOD, Colin
"Russians." [RedBass] (14) 89, p. 63.
"To an Activist." [RedBass] (14) 89, p. 36.
3455. MacLEOD, Norman
"A Mad Micturator Way of Looking at Things." [Pembroke] (21) 89, p. 170-171.
"No, We Have Some Bananas, Yes!" [Pembroke] (21) 89, p. 169-170.
MacLOW, Jackson
See Mac LOW, Jackson
3456. MacMANUS, Mariquita
"In Yeats Country." [Vis] (29) 89, p. 15.
3457. MacMURRAY, Rose
"The Swedish Pot." [Vis] (29) 89, p. 29.
"Taking Off." [Vis] (29) 89, p. 30.
3458. MacNEIL, Maura
"Summer Garden: Leningrad 1942." [Crazy] (36) Spr 89, p. 50-52.
3459. MacNEIL, Rodney
"Mirrors in the Room." [Obs] (2:1) Spr 87, p. 14-15.
3460. MacNIDER, Keith
"Memories." [AntigR] (77/78) Spr-Sum 89, p. 111.
3461. MacPHERSON, Jennifer B.
"Table for Two." [CapeR] (24:1) Spr 89, p. 30.
3462. MacPHERSON, Mary
"When I Was Young" (tr. by Iain Crichton Smith). [Stand] (30:1) Wint 88-89, p.
      14-15.
3463. MACSIOMOIN, Tomás
"Berkeley" (tr. of Máirtín O Direáin, w. Douglas Sealy). [Trans] (22) Fall 89, p. 35.
"Grief's Dignity" (tr. of Máirtín O Direáin, w. Douglas Sealy). [Trans] (22) Fall 89,
      p. 32.
"Invitation to the Virgin" (tr. of Máirtín O Direáin, w. Douglas Sealy). [Trans] (22)
      Fall 89, p. 31.
"Spring in the West" (tr. of Máirtín O Direáin, w. Douglas Sealy). [Trans] (22) Fall
      89, p. 33.
"Stout Oars" (tr. of Máirtín O Direáin, w. Douglas Sealy). [Trans] (22) Fall 89, p.
      34.
3464. MacSWEEN, R. J.
"The Call." [AntigR] (79) Aut 89, p. 58-59.
"The Stars and Comets." [AntigR] (76) Wint 89, p. 7.
3465. MADARIAGA, Francisco
"Songs for D.H. Lawrence" (To Teresa Parodi, tr. by Mary Crow). [LitR] (32:4)
      Sum 89, p. 526-527.
3466. MADDOX, Marjorie
"Cartography." [Poetry] (154:4) Jl 89, p. 197-198.
"Chimera." [Poetry] (154:4) Jl 89, p. 198.
"City to City, Town to Town." [BellR] (12:2, #26) Fall 89, p. 6-7.
3467. MADER, Beth
"Mrs. Johnson." [EmeraldCR] (1989) c1988, p. 121-122.
3468. MADIGAN, Rick
"Little Elegy for Gay." [Ploughs] (15:1) 89, p. 78-79.
3469. MADOFF, Mark
"Listen to the Summer Boarder." [MalR] (89) Wint 89, p. 90-91.
"Oarsman." [MalR] (89) Wint 89, p. 88-89.
"The Rowing Ends." [MalR] (89) Wint 89, p. 94-95.
"Wolf Whiskers." [MalR] (89) Wint 89, p. 92-93.
3470. MAE-WHA
"Old Plum Trees" (tr. by Constantine Contogenis and Wolhee Choe). [ChiR]

(36:3/4) 89, p. 19.
"What Blight" (Three Poems by Kisang, tr. by Constantine Contogenis and Wolhee
Choe). [BelPoJ] (39:4) Sum 89, p. 32.
MAFFLA, Jaime Garcia
See GARCIA MAFFLA, Jaime
3471. MAGEE, Michael
"Parable of the Leaves." [CrabCR] (6:1) 89, p. 10.
3472. MAGGIO, Mike
"Frouzanda Mahrad" (tr. of Lamia Abbas Amara). [Pig] (15) 88, p. 28.
3473. MAGGIORE, Mary Ann
"The Clothesline." [FourQ] (2d series 3:1) Spr 89, p. 52.
MAGHUT, Muhammad al-
See Al-MAGHUT, Muhammad
3474. MAGINNES, Al
"My Father's Tattoo." [AntR] (47:1) Wint 89, p. 70.
3475. MAGOWAN, Robin
"The Aviary" (tr. of Saint Pol Roux). [Margin] (8) 89, p. 93.
"Birds" (tr. of Saint Pol Roux). [Margin] (8) 89, p. 94.
3476. MAGRELLI, Valerio
"Each Photographed Face" (tr. by Dana Gioia). [Poetry] (155:1/2) O-N 89, p. 158.
"I Have Often Imagined That Glances" (tr. by Dana Gioia). [Poetry] (155:1/2) O-N
89, p. 158.
"I Love Uncertain Gestures" (tr. by Jonathan Galassi). [Poetry] (155:1/2) O-N 89,
p. 159.
"Ricevo da Te Questa Tazza." [Poetry] (155:1/2) O-N 89, p. 156.
"There's Silence Between One Page and Another" (tr. by Jonathan Galassi). [Poetry]
(155:1/2) O-N 89, p. 160.
"This Handwriting Wears Itself Away" (tr. by Dana Gioia). [Poetry] (155:1/2) O-N
89, p. 159.
"This Red Cup" (tr. by Dana Gioia). [Poetry] (155:1/2) O-N 89, p. 157.
3477. MAGUIRE, Sarah
"Liminal." [Verse] (6:3) Wint 89, p. 32.
"Uisce Beatha." [Verse] (6:3) Wint 89, p. 32.
3478. MAHAPATRA, Anuradha
"Engraving" (in Bengali and English, tr. by Paramita Banerjee and Carolyn Wright,
w. the author). [BlackWR] (15:2) Spr 89, p. 86-87.
"Living in Disguise" (tr. by Paramita Banerjee and Carolyne Wright). [Iowa] (19:2)
Spr-Sum 89, p. 119.
"The Peacock" (tr. by Paramita Banerjee and Carolyne Wright). [Iowa] (19:2)
Spr-Sum 89, p. 118.
"Undesired" (tr. by Jyotirmoy Datta and Carolyne Wright). [NewEngR] (11:4) Sum
89, p. 457.
"Village Nocturne" (tr. by Paramita Banerjee and Carolyne Wright). [Iowa] (19:2)
Spr-Sum 89, p. 117.
"You" (in Bengali and English, tr. by Paramita Banerjee and Carolyn Wright, w. the
author). [BlackWR] (15:2) Spr 89, p. 88-89.
3479. MAHON, Derek
"Night Drive" (St. Petersburg, 1901, tr. of Rainer Maria Rilke). [Trans] (22) Fall
89, p. 180.
3480. MAHON, Jeanne
"Jared." [StoneC] (16:3/4) Spr-Sum 89, p. 20-21.
3481. MAHONEY, Dorothy
"In the Snow." [Quarry] (38:2) Spr 89, p. 61.
3482. MAHONY, Phillip
"A Detective's Daydream." [BrooklynR] (5) 88, p. 1-2.
3483. MAIDEN, Cullen
"Prodigal." [Callaloo] (12:3, #40) Sum 89, p. 523-524.
3484. MAIERS, Joan
"Putting in Iris During Hanukkah." [BellR] (12:2, #26) Fall 89, p. 9.
3485. MAINO, Jeannette
"Sonnet Not on Love." [KanQ] (21:1/2) Wint-Spr 89, p. 129.
"Young Man on Pearl Beach." [KanQ] (21:1/2) Wint-Spr 89, p. 129.
3486. MAIO, Samuel (Sam)
"The Burning of Los Angeles." [CharR] (15:2) Fall 89, p. 91.
"The Film Maker's Wife." [CharR] (15:2) Fall 89, p. 90.
"Gathering *Funghi*." [CimR] (87) Ap 89, p. 98.

"I Remember." [HighP] (4:3) Wint 89-90, p. 131-132.
"Vague Scene." [AntR] (47:3) Sum 89, p. 319.
3487. MAIR, Thomas
"Inside Passage" (Chapbook: 6 pieces). [OhioR] (44) 89, p. 65-76.
3488. MAIWALD, Peter
"Landscape with Angels" (tr. by John Linthicum). [LitR] (33:1) Fall 89, p. 16.
"The Lovers" (tr. by John Linthicum). [LitR] (33:1) Fall 89, p. 18.
"Summer Evening" (tr. by John Linthicum). [LitR] (33:1) Fall 89, p. 15-16.
"They Listen to Me" (tr. by John Linthicum). [LitR] (33:1) Fall 89, p. 17.
"Thirty" (tr. by John Linthicum). [LitR] (33:1) Fall 89, p. 17.
"The Woman" (tr. by John Linthicum). [LitR] (33:1) Fall 89, p. 15.
3489. MAJ, Bronislaw
"All Souls" (tr. by Daniel Bourne). [Hawai'iR] (13:1, #25) Spr 89, p. 128.
"Beyond the window there is rain, a glass of tea on the table" (tr. by Donald Pirie).
    [Verse] (6:1) Mr 89, p. 34.
"It Takes Just a Few Minutes" (tr. by Stanislaw Baranczak and Clare Cavanah).
    [Trans] (21) Spr 89, p. 82.
"It was all rather different to the way they later said it was" (tr. by Donald Pirie).
    [Verse] (6:1) Mr 89, p. 35.
"Nadal." [Hawai'iR] (13:1, #25) Spr 89, p. 127.
"No one has claimed it: homeless and untouched" (tr. by Donald Pirie). [Verse] (6:1)
    Mr 89, p. 34.
"This city died. Blue streetcars moan" (tr. by Stanislaw Baranczak and Clare
    Cavanagh). [PartR] (56:2) Spr 89, p. 291.
"Who will bear witness to these times?" (tr. by Donald Pirie). [Verse] (6:1) Mr 89,
    p. 35.
"Who will bear witness to these times?" (tr. by Stanislaw Baranczak and Clare
    Cavanagh). [PartR] (56:2) Spr 89, p. 290.
3490. MAJOR, Alice
"Calf-love." [Event] (18:3) Fall 89, p. 73.
3491. MAJOR, Clarence
"Coming into Existence." [BlackALF] (23:3) Fall 89, p. 478-479.
"Get Along Cindy." [BlackALF] (23:3) Fall 89, p. 477.
"The Swine Who's Eclipsed Me." [BlackALF] (23:3) Fall 89, p. 477-478.
3492. MAKAROVIC, Svetlana
"The Lighthouse" (tr. by Michael Biggins). [NewEngR] (11:3) Spr 89, p. 243.
3493. MAKELA, Joanne
"Warner's Pool." [RagMag] (7:1) 89, p. 35.
3494. MAKOFSKE, Mary
"Legacy." [PassN] (10:2) Sum 89, p. 22.
"Room for Song." [BellR] (12:1, #25) Spr 89, p. 28.
3495. MAKUCK, Peter
"Answering Voices." [Shen] (39:1) Spr 89, p. 48.
"Big Eddy, Upstream of the Grimesland Bridge." [PoetC] (20:3) Spr 89, p. 32.
"East of Cape Fear." [PoetryNW] (30:1) Spr 89, p. 22.
"From the Dark." [Shen] (39:1) Spr 89, p. 46-47.
"Hole in the Wall." [DenQ] (23:3/4) Wint-Spr 89, p. 110-111.
"Hometown Correspondence." [PoetC] (20:3) Spr 89, p. 30-31.
"Part of a Story." [Journal] (13:1) Spr-Sum 89, p. 71.
"Passage." [RiverC] (10:1) Fall 89, p. 74-75.
"Raven, Mountain, Snow." [GettyR] (2:4) Aut 89, p. 632.
"Skunk Flag." [GettyR] (2:4) Aut 89, p. 630-631.
"Tar River Again." [Journal] (13:1) Spr-Sum 89, p. 70.
3496. MALANGA, Gerard
"Ray Dean Brock 1929-1979." [RedBass] (14) 89, p. 24-31.
"Suddenly Next Summer" (In reply to a poem by John Logan, "Happening on
    Aegina"). [PaintedB] (39) 89, p. 54-55.
3497. MALEN, Lola
"City Traffic" (from *Vignettes From Guatemala*). [Quarry] (38:4) Fall 89, p. 67.
3498. MALLARMÉ, Stéphane
"The Clown Reproved (Tournan, 1864, Le Pitre Chatié)" (tr. by Daisy Aldan).
    [AmerPoR] (18:2) Mr-Ap 89, p. 14.
"Herodiade" (tr. by David Lenson). [MassR] (30:4) Wint 89, p. 573-588.
"Sea Breeze (Brise Marine)" (Tournan, May 1865, tr. by Daisy Aldan). [AmerPoR]
    (18:2) Mr-Ap 89, p. 14.
"The Tomb of Edgar Poe" (tr. by Francis Golffing). [SpiritSH] (54) Spr-Sum 89, p.

34.
        "Windows (Les Fenêtres)" (London, 1863, tr. by Daisy Aldan). [AmerPoR] (18:2)
            Mr-Ap 89, p. 14.
3499. MALLIN, Rupert
        "Pink Man." [Bogg] (61) 89, p. 45.
3500. MALTMAN, Kim
        "Installation #51 (The Rio Grande)." [Dandel] (16:1) Spr-Sum 89, p. 21.
        "Installation #57." [Dandel] (16:1) Spr-Sum 89, p. 22-23.
        "Installation #62." [Dandel] (16:1) Spr-Sum 89, p. 24.
        "The Technology of Inertia." [MalR] (87) Sum 89, p. 27-29.
MALTZAHN, Nicholas von
        See Von MALTZAHN, Nicholas
3501. MALYON, Carol
        "Nude and Dummy" (from the painting by Alex Colville). [CrossC] (11:1) 89, p. 4.
3502. MAMO, Catherine
        "The Lover." [Grain] (17:3) Fall 89, p. 23.
        "Sleep." [Grain] (17:3) Fall 89, p. 22.
3503. MANDEL, Charlotte
        "Keeping Him Alive." [WestB] (23) 89, p. 64.
        "The Life of Mary" (a poem-novella, selection: VII). [StoneC] (16:3/4) Spr-Sum 89,
            p. 26-27.
3504. MANDEL, Tom
        "The Contents of the Cube." [Screens] (1) 89, p. 22-25.
        "Good Song." [CentralP] (15) Spr 89, p. 188-190.
        "A Gram in the Scale." [Conjunc] (13) 89, p. 167-169.
        "The Life of Emile Novis." [Notus] (4:2) Fall 89, p. 47-56.
        "Ramah." [Temblor] (9) 89, p. 107-117.
        "Say 'Ja'." [NewAW] (5) Fall 89, p. 89-90.
        "Square Core of Stealth in the Tracery." [Caliban] (6) 89, p. 168-171.
3505. MANDELL, Arlene
        "Supermarket '88." [AlphaBS] (6) Wint 89-90, p. 23-24.
3506. MANESIOTIS, Joy
        "Voodoo." [AntR] (47:4) Fall 89, p. 455.
3507. MANEY, Jill Marion
        "Lesson." [Poetry] (154:6) S 89, p. 338-339.
3508. MANFRED, Freya
        "Bearer of Gifts." [OxfordM] (5:2) Fall-Wint 89, p. 29.
3509. MANGAN, Kathy
        "Above the Tree Line." [Shen] (39:2) Sum 89, p. 70.
        "The Saviors." [Shen] (39:2) Sum 89, p. 71-72.
3510. MANGAN, Margaret
        "The Poor." [Comm] (116:15) S 8, 89, p. 461.
3511. MANGOLD, Christoph
        "Harmonie" (in German). [StoneC] (17:1/2) Fall-Wint 89-90, p. 51.
        "Harmony" (tr. by Gary Sea). [StoneC] (17:1/2) Fall-Wint 89-90, p. 51.
        "Suite No. 6" (tr. by Gary Sea). [StoneC] (17:1/2) Fall-Wint 89-90, p. 50-51.
        "Suite Nr. 6" (in German). [StoneC] (17:1/2) Fall-Wint 89-90, p. 50.
3512. MANGUM, Donald
        "Casting." [EmeraldCR] (1989) c1988, p. 120-121.
3513. MANLEY, C. R.
        "Charlotte in the Slough." [SoDakR] (27:3) Aut 89, p. 106.
        "Elisabeth's Dream." [Farm] (6:1) Wint-Spr 88-89, p. 119.
3514. MANN, Barbara
        "Noah." [Agni] (28) 89, p. 284.
3515. MANN, Charles
        "Roger's Goodbye." [Thrpny] (37) Spr 89, p. 17.
3516. MANN, Chris Zithulele
        "Mr. Morgangeld and Two Women." [AmerPoR] (18:4) Jl-Ag 89, p. 33.
3517. MANN, John
        "After the Ice Storm." [ArtfulD] (16/17) Fall 89, p. 8.
        "The Drowning of the Animals." [ArtfulD] (16/17) Fall 89, p. 5.
        "The Ladder of Nature." [ArtfulD] (16/17) Fall 89, p. 6-7.
3518. MANN, Marilyn M.
        "Water into Memory." [KanQ] (21:3) Sum 89, p. 74.
3519. MANNEJC, Georg
        "The Dreams of Order" (Excerpt). [Verse] (6:3) Wint 89, p. 58.

"The Man in the Red Crowned Hat" (for G.B.M.). [Verse] (6:3) Wint 89, p. 58-59.
"Recurrent Nightmare." [Verse] (6:3) Wint 89, p. 59-60.
"Scientific Animals." [Verse] (6:3) Wint 89, p. 60-61.
3520. MANNER, George
"Patterns." [Sequoia] (33:1) Sum 89, p. 45.
3521. MANRIQUE, Jaime
"Recuerdos." [LindLM] (8:2) Ap-Je 89, p. 12.
3522. MANROE, Candace Ord
"A Familiar Place." [TexasR] (10:1/2) Spr-Sum 89, p. 76-77.
3523. MANSELL, Chris
"Black." [AntigR] (77/78) Spr-Sum 89, p. 208.
"Numbered." [AntigR] (77/78) Spr-Sum 89, p. 209.
"Two." [AntigR] (77/78) Spr-Sum 89, p. 207.
"With." [AntigR] (77/78) Spr-Sum 89, p. 206.
3524. MANYE i MARTI, Lourdes
"So Solemn" (tr. of Miquel Martí i Pol, w. Wayne Cox). [Shen] (39:3) Fall 89, p. 46.
"Things" (tr. of Miquel Martí i Pol, w. Wayne Cox). [Shen] (39:3) Fall 89, p. 46.
3525. MANYOKY-NEMETH, Charles
"Silence Grates." [CanLit] (120) Spr 89, p. 82.
3526. MAPP, Erica
"The Garden of St. Paul's Hospital in Arles" (Vincent van Gogh, October, 1889). [Comm] (116:18) O 20, 89, p. 564.
"Mountains at St. Remy" (Vincent van Gogh, July 1889). [Comm] (116:18) O 20, 89, p. 564.
"Tarascon Diligence" (Vincent van Gogh, October 1888, Arles). [Comm] (116:18) O 20, 89, p. 564.
3527. MAR, Richard DeLos
"His Photograph." [InterPR] (15:2) Fall 89, p. 120.
3528. MARCANO MONTAÑEZ, Jaime
"Siempre en tus ojos bañaré en el río." [Mairena] (11:27) 89, p. 83.
3529. MARCH, Andrew Lee
"A Pitch for Meditation." [KanQ] (21:3) Sum 89, p. 36.
3530. MARCHAMPS, Guy
"Cape Dorset Blues" (à Jimmy Manning, in French). [Os] (29) 89, p. 11.
3531. MARCHAND, Blaine
"Disparate Things." [CrossC] (11:2) 89, p. 14.
3532. MARCHANT, Fred (Frederick J.)
"Letter to a Young Poet: Rimbaud in Abyssinie." [WormR] (29:4, #116) 89, p. 97-98.
"Minotaur." [PoetryNW] (30:3) Aut 89, p. 5-6.
"Whiskey." [Agni] (28) 89, p. 205.
3533. MARCO GARCIA, Eloisa
"En el Espejo." [Mairena] (11:27) 89, p. 67.
3534. MARCONI, Catherine
"The Dowser." [SpoonRQ] (14:2) Spr 89, p. 58-59.
"To the Bull's Tooth." [Plain] (9:3) Spr 89, p. 24.
"Woody Tongue." [SpoonRQ] (14:2) Spr 89, p. 60-61.
3535. MARCUS, David
"Turnabout" (tr. of Seán O Ríordáin). [Trans] (22) Fall 89, p. 42.
"The Women's Christmas Night" (tr. of Seán O Ríordáin). [Trans] (22) Fall 89, p. 41.
3536. MARCUS, Mordecai
"Commitments." [Plain] (10:1) 89, p. 7.
"Encirclements." [BallSUF] (30:4) Aut 89, p. 34.
"Friction Song." [PoetC] (20:3) Spr 89, p. 36.
"Georgia Boy." [TarRP] (28:2) Spr 89, p. 25-26.
"In Spearfish Canyon." [SoDakR] (27:3) Aut 89, p. 89.
"It Is Only July." [TexasR] (10:1/2) Spr-Sum 89, p. 102-103.
"Taking Heed." [SoDakR] (27:3) Aut 89, p. 88.
3537. MARCUS, Stanley
"Self-Study in Wood (The Minor Artist)." [DenQ] (24:1) Sum 89, p. 50-51.
"To a Poet (Such As Myself) Writing a Poem on a Painting." [HampSPR] Wint 89, p. 30-31.
3538. MARDHEKAR, B. S. (Bal Sitaram)
"The Forest of Yellow Bamboo Trees" (tr. by Vinay Dharwadker). [TriQ] (77) Wint

89-90, p. 202.
"The Rats Died in a Wet Barrel" (tr. by Vinay Dharwadker). [TriQ] (77) Wint 89-90,
p. 200.
3539. MARGOSHES, Dave
"Not Born Cyd." [CanLit] (120) Spr 89, p. 98-99.
"Wore Dresses." [CanLit] (120) Spr 89, p. 97-98.
3540. MARGULIES, Stephen
"After the Next Deluge." [Timbuktu] (4) Sum-Fall 89, p. 50.
"Lips in Jail." [Timbuktu] (4) Sum-Fall 89, p. 48.
"Over the Bridge or, How to Change Trains." [Timbuktu] (4) Sum-Fall 89, p. 49.
"The Writer's Eye." [Timbuktu] (3) Wint-Spr 89, p. 30-31.
3541. MARIANI, Paul
"A&P Nightshift: January 1959" (for Phil Levine). [TriQ] (74) Wint 89, p. 193-195.
"Journey Westward." [GettyR] (2:3) Sum 89, p. 511-513.
"Photograph of Oldest Son, Postulant in the Society of Mary, Taken with Proud
Parents at Beacon, New York." [KenR] (N 11:4) Fall 89, p. 22-23.
"Road Kills." [KenR] (N 11:4) Fall 89, p. 23-24.
3542. MARIELS, Raymond
"Living in Elk Heart, Montana (Pop. 27): Laura." [Blueline] (10:1/2) 89, p. 14.
"Memories of an Old Fighter" (June 15, 1987). [SoCoast] (5) Spr 88, p. 48.
3543. MARINELLI, J. (Joanne)
"The Clash by Night." [SoCoast] (6) Fall 88, p. 22-23.
"The Grecian Way." [Aerial] (5) 89, p. 120-121.
"Hot Night at Hostoc's." [DeKalbLAJ] (22:1/4) 89, p. 61-62.
3544. MARINO, Gigi
"David's Aunt Aurelia" (for those who still pray). [Poem] (61) My 89, p. 38.
"Rider in the Canyon." [Poem] (61) My 89, p. 37.
"Stranger Contact." [Poem] (61) My 89, p. 39.
3545. MARION, Elizabeth
"My Muse and I." [HolCrit] (26:1) F 89, p. 15.
3546. MARION, Jeff Daniel
"Morning Poem." [SouthernPR] (29:1) Spr 89, p. 58.
MARIS, Ron de
See De MARIS, Ron
3547. MARKHAM, E. A.
"Looking Back, Ah, Looking Back." [Verse] (6:3) Wint 89, p. 77.
"The Thing Not Said." [Verse] (6:3) Wint 89, p. 77.
3548. MARKHAM, Jacquelyn
"Phantoms." [SingHM] (16) 89, p. 60.
3549. MARKOTIC, Nicole
"Foretold." [PraF] (10:1, #46) Spr 89, p. 52.
"Hands." [PraF] (10:1, #46) Spr 89, p. 53.
3550. MARKS, Gigi
"A Dog's Life." [RiverC] (9:1) Spr 89, p. 91.
"Domestic Weight." [NowestR] (27:1) 89, p. 32.
3551. MARKS, S. J.
"Nothing More." [PaintedB] (38) 89, p. 8.
3552. MARLATT, Daphne
"Compliments (of the Camera)." [CapilR] (1st series: 50) 89, p. 76.
"Unpaid Work." [CapilR] (1st series: 50) 89, p. 75.
3553. MARLIS, Stefanie
"The Same Orbit" (for W.P.). [BellR] (12:2, #26) Fall 89, p. 24.
"Squaw Valley Without You." [BellR] (12:2, #26) Fall 89, p. 23.
"Temple." [FiveFR] (7) 89, p. 6.
3554. MARMOR, Rachelle
"Contour Drawing." [MidwQ] (30:4) Sum 89, p. 448.
3555. MARPLE, Vivian
"Entrance." [AntigR] (76) Wint 89, p. 15.
"Winter Wheat." [AntigR] (76) Wint 89, p. 16-17.
3556. MARQUARDT, Randall
"Pheasant Hunt." [Plain] (9:3) Spr 89, p. 15.
3557. MARQUARDT, Stephen
"Extreme Birds." [Margin] (8) 89, p. 90.
3558. MARRIOTT, Anne
"A Grim Tale." [CanLit] (122/123) Aut-Wint 89, p. 124.

3559. MARRIOTT, David
"She is overt, & takes him by the hand." [Screens] (1) 89, p. 117-118.
3560. MARRON, Thomas
"A Cemetery." [SpiritSH] (55) Fall-Wint 89 [90 on cover], p. 42.
"A Language for Steve." [SpiritSH] (55) Fall-Wint 89 [90 on cover], p. 42.
MARS, Douglas de
    See DeMARS, Douglas
3561. MARSH, Donald
"Old Men with Penknives." [CrabCR] (6:2) Wint 89, p. 19.
3562. MARSH, Richard
"The Race." [Wind] (19:64) 89, p. 25.
3563. MARSHALL, Ernest
"Whatever Happened To." [Vis] (31) 89, p. 24.
3564. MARSHALL, Jack
"Coiled Springs." [Zyzzyva] (5:1, #17) Spr 89, p. 49-51.
"Gravesend." [Manoa] (1:1/2) Fall 89, p. 51-53.
"Green." [Manoa] (1:1/2) Fall 89, p. 53-54.
"Post-Humoresque." [AmerPoR] (18:3) My-Je 89, p. 48.
3565. MARSHALL, Peter
"Needles, Arizona." [Bogg] (61) 89, p. 25.
3566. MARSHALL, Tom
"The Eventual Poem for Gwendolyn" (December 1, 1987). [Quarry] (38:1) Wint 89,
        p. 82-83.
3567. MARSHBURN, Sandra
"After a False Start to Spring." [WestB] (24) 89, p. 120.
"Flea Market Blues." [WestB] (24) 89, p. 121.
"Native Woman." [ChatR] (9:4) Sum 89, p. 66.
"Plane Crash Kills Two." [PassN] (10:1) Wint 89, p. 11.
"Some Magic." [CentR] (33:1) Wint 89, p. 57.
3568. MARSTON, Missy
"I Don't Know About Men." [Grain] (17:4) Wint 89, p. 56.
3569. MARTEL, Richard
"Rhapsodie en Rouge" (Texte de la performance, soirée le 9 Avril CEGEP Garneau,
        Quebec 1987). [Rampike] (6:1) 87, p. 45-48.
MARTHA CHRISTINA
    See CHRISTINA, Martha
MARTHA ELIZABETH
    See ELIZABETH, Martha
MARTI, Lourdes Manye i
    See MANYE i MARTI, Lourdes
3570. MARTI i POL, Miquel
"So Solemn" (tr. by Lourdes Manye i Martí and Wayne Cox). [Shen] (39:3) Fall 89,
        p. 46.
"Things" (tr. by Lourdes Manye i Martí and Wayne Cox). [Shen] (39:3) Fall 89, p.
        46.
3571. MARTIAL
"Epigrams" (4 epigrams, tr. by Richard O'Connell). [ApalQ] (31) 89, p. 47.
"The Epigrams of Martial" (Selections in Latin and English, tr. by Joseph S.
        Selemi). [CumbPR] (9:1) Fall 89, p. 11-12.
"II.vii. You'll tackle anything" (tr. by Laurie Duggan). [TriQ] (74) Wint 89, p. 221.
"II.xii. Your sweet breath tells me" (tr. by Laurie Duggan). [TriQ] (74) Wint 89, p.
        221.
"III.75. For a long time now, Lupercus" (tr. by Joseph S. Salemi). [ArtfulD] (16/17)
        Fall 89, p. 10.
"III.xii. The perfumed anorexics of L.A." (tr. by Laurie Duggan). [TriQ] (74) Wint
        89, p. 222.
"VI.26. Our friend Sotades is in peril of his head" (tr. by Joseph S. Salemi).
        [ArtfulD] (16/17) Fall 89, p. 10.
"VIII.iii. Sixty epigrams are too many" (tr. by Laurie Duggan). [TriQ] (74) Wint 89,
        p. 222.
"XI.104. Wifey dear" (tr. by Joseph S. Salemi). [ArtfulD] (16/17) Fall 89, p. 11.
3572. MARTIN, Brent
"Once, with a Girl Who Had Epilepsy." [ChatR] (9:3) Spr 89, p. 40-41.
3573. MARTIN, Carlos
"Un Pajaro en el Hombro." [LindLM] (8:2) Ap-Je 89, p. 3.

3574. MARTIN, Charles
"Metaphor of Grass in California." [SouthwR] (74:4) Aut 89, p. 524.
"Snow" (9 August 1974). [CrossCur] (8:2) Ja 89, p. 109-111.
3575. MARTIN, David
"Blue Fish, Daniel." [Amelia] (5:3, #14) 89, p. 16.
"Milkweed Summer." [Amelia] (5:3, #14) 89, p. 15.
"That Year." [Amelia] (5:3, #14) 89, p. 17.
3576. MARTIN, E. S. A.
"Knowing You." [WorldO] (22:1/2) Fall-Wint 87-88, c90, p. 22.
3577. MARTIN, Harry
"The Angry Man." [Caliban] (7) 89, p. 71.
3578. MARTIN, Herbert Woodward
"Dark Pronouncements." [OxfordM] (5:2) Fall-Wint 89, p. 44.
"The Last Days of William Short" (Dishwasher, PWA, Houston. Selections: XI,
    XII, XV, XVII). [Ploughs] (15:4) Wint 89-90, p. 129-130.
"XV. Sacrifice is the mother of superstition." [BlackALF] (23:3) Fall 89, p. 470.
"XVI. A generation of Adams have fathered their seed in fertile earth." [BlackALF]
    (23:3) Fall 89, p. 470.
"XVII. This is my spring intent, to say this desolate prayer." [BlackALF] (23:3) Fall
    89, p. 470.
3579. MARTIN, Jeffrey
"Marble Shadow." [Footwork] 89, p. 42.
"Winter." [Footwork] 89, p. 42.
3580. MARTIN, Paul
"The Chickadee." [KanQ] (21:3) Sum 89, p. 145.
3581. MARTIN, Philip
"Elegy" (tr. of Lars Gustafsson). [Field] (40) Spr 89, p. 69-70.
3582. MARTIN, Sharon
"Kept by My Father from Drowning." [SoCoast] (6) Fall 88, p. 20.
3583. MARTIN, Sharon E.
"Bird's Eye View." [Amelia] (5:3, #14) 89, p. 10.
3584. MARTIN, Stephen-Paul
"Uroboric Soup." [HeavenB] (6) Wint-Spr 89, p. 6.
3585. MARTINDALE, Sheila
"You Brought Me Roses." [Bogg] (61) 89, p. 19.
3586. MARTINEZ, Dionisio (Dionisio D.)
"A Catholic Education." [Iowa] (19:1) Wint 89, p. 95.
"The Children of Suicides." [FloridaR] (16:2/3) Fall-Wint 89, p. 54-55.
"Dancing at the Chelsea." [Iowa] (19:1) Wint 89, p. 92-95.
"The Death of Isadora Duncan." [Caliban] (7) 89, p. 94-95.
"Doing What You Can with What You Have." [FloridaR] (16:2/3) Fall-Wint 89, p.
    56-57.
"Gulag para Turistas." [Inti] (29/30) Primavera-Otoño 89, p. 263.
"History As a Second Language." [AmerPoR] (18:1) Ja-F 89, p. 35.
"Home Is Where the Heart Aches." [SouthernPR] (29:2) Fall 89, p. 27.
"Intimate Distances." [TampaR] (2) 89, p. 51.
"Laura Desnuda." [Inti] (29/30) Primavera-Otoño 89, p. 264-265.
"The Law of Gravity: First Variation." [Caliban] (6) 89, p. 78.
"The Law of Gravity: Second Variation." [Caliban] (6) 89, p. 79.
"Playing Dvořák to Make the Rains Come" (For Rosana). [TampaR] (2) 89, p.
    49-50.
"Shelter." [TampaR] (2) 89, p. 52.
"Las Tías de Laura." [Inti] (29/30) Primavera-Otoño 89, p. 263-264.
"Tonight I Am Humming." [RiverC] (9:1) Spr 89, p. 14-15.
"La Trayectoria de la Parabola." [LindLM] (8:2) Ap-Je 89, p. 14.
MARTINEZ, Manuel Díaz
See DIAZ-MARTINEZ, Manuel
3587. MARTINEZ, Ofelia
"Give, Claudia, My Regards to Lenin" (tr. of Manuel Díaz-Martínez, w. Lourdes
    González). [Pig] (15) 88, p. 68.
"Those Brief Goodbyes" (tr. of Manuel Díaz-Martínez, w. Lourdes González). [Pig]
    (15) 88, p. 68.
3588. MARTINEZ-FALERO, Luis
"Del Conocimiento Sensible." [Mairena] (11:27) 89, p. 82.
3589. MARTINS, Max
"Mar-ahu" (in Portuguese). [RiverS] (30) [89], p. 76.

"Mar-ahu" (tr. by James Bogan). [RiverS] (30) [89], p. 77.
"Tempo" (para Dina Oliveira). [RiverS] (30) [89], p. 74.
"Time" (tr. by James Bogan). [RiverS] (30) [89], p. 75.
3590. MARTINSON, Harry
"Aniara" (Selections: V, XXIX, tr. by Stephen Klass and Leif Sjöberg). [Pequod]
(26/27) 89, p. 35-36.
3591. MARTONE, John
"After Meaning a Life." [AnotherCM] (19) 89, p. 143-144.
"Hiroshima Yesterday." [CentralP] (15) Spr 89, p. 107.
"'Out of' Two's, Paula E.-G., Emigrée." [CentralP] (15) Spr 89, p. 108-109.
"Some Groceries." [BrooklynR] (6) 89, p. 14.
3592. MARTOS, Laura Helena
"Deus ex Machina." [CuadP] (7:19) S-D 89, p. 75.
"El Enigma." [CuadP] (7:19) S-D 89, p. 76-77.
"La Rueda de la Vida." [CuadP] (7:19) S-D 89, p. 75-76.
3593. MARTOS, Marco
"The Four Seasons" (tr. by Mary Crow). [NewOR] (16:3) Fall 89, p. 39.
3594. MASARIK, Al
"Boarded Up." [PaintedB] (37) 89, p. 52.
"One Night Stand." [PaintedB] (37) 89, p. 53-54.
3595. MASINI, Donna
"Claim." [HighP] (4:2) Fall 89, p. 70-71.
"Giants in the Earth." [HighP] (4:2) Fall 89, p. 67-69.
"Moving In and Moving Up." [Pequod] (26/27) 89, p. 168-170.
3596. MASON, David
"Blackened Peaches." [CrossCur] (8:2) Ja 89, p. 19-24.
"The Day When Night Stays On." [CumbPR] (8:2) Spr 89, p. 69-72.
"Journal and Prayer." [PoetL] (84:3) Fall 89, p. 45-46.
"Small Elegies." [LitR] (32:2) Wint 89, p. 216.
"Triptych" (for Lane Hall). [LitR] (32:2) Wint 89, p. 217.
3597. MASON, Gordon
"To the Fair." [Stand] (30:1) Wint 88-89, p. 28.
3598. MASON, Julian
"An Apple for A. R. Ammons." [Pembroke] (21) 89, p. 102.
"Rehearsal." [Pembroke] (21) 89, p. 64.
3599. MASON, Julie A.
"Cordoba Front" (Based on photograph of a soldier by Robert Capa). [SoCoast] (7)
Spr-Fall 89, p. 49.
3600. MASON, Kathryn E.
"Speed Reading." [EmeraldCR] (1989) c1988, p. 108-109.
3601. MASON, Kenneth C.
"The Power of Seed" (a Plainsongs Award Poem). [Plain] (10:1) 89, p. 20-21.
3602. MASON, Lucinda
"Check." [SmPd] (26:2 #76) Spr 89, p. 27.
"Jade." [PoetryE] (28) Fall 89, p. 172.
"Steven." [ChatR] (9:3) Spr 89, p. 42.
3603. MASTERSON, Dan
"The List." [PraS] (63:4) Wint 89, p. 20-22.
"Snack." [PraS] (63:4) Wint 89, p. 17-18.
"Starting Over." [PraS] (63:4) Wint 89, p. 19-20.
3604. MATAS, Julio
"Estrambóticos" (5 poems). [LindLM] (8:3) Jl-S 89, p. 3.
3605. MATHEWS, Harry
"Three Epithalamia" (tr. of Georges Perec). [ParisR] (31:112) Fall 89, p. 68-77.
3606. MATHIAS, Roland
"Brechfa Chapel." [NoDaQ] (57:2) Spr 89, insert p. 26-27.
"Laus Deo" (No. X of the sequence "Tide-Reach"). [NoDaQ] (57:2) Spr 89, insert
p. 28.
"Porth Cwyfan." [NoDaQ] (57:2) Spr 89, insert p. 25-26.
3607. MATOS PAOLI, Francisco
"Invocacion a Luis Hernandez Aquino." [Mairena] (11:27) 89, p. 78.
3608. MATSAKIS, Cynthia
"A Winter Landscape." [StoneC] (16:3/4) Spr-Sum 89, p. 29.
3609. MATSON, Suzanne
"Elegy for Neil." [SouthernPR] (29:2) Fall 89, p. 23.
"Like." [BostonR] (14:6) D 89, p. 25.

3610. MATSUEDA, Pat
"The Flooding of the Amazon." [ChamLR] (3:1, #5) Fall 89, p. 33-34.
"The People Were Stories" (Selections: "Two," "All," "Three"). [Manoa] (1:1/2) Fall
89, p. 176-178.
"Two Exiles." [ChamLR] (3:1, #5) Fall 89, p. 31-32.
"Watching His Hands Drive." [ChamLR] (3:1, #5) Fall 89, p. 29-30.
3611. MATTAWA, Khaled
"The Glorious Yemen Restaurant." [IndR] (13:1) Wint 89, p. 37-38.
"History of My Face." [Iowa] (19:3) Fall 89, p. 30.
"Saniya's Dreams." [Iowa] (19:3) Fall 89, p. 29.
3612. MATTFIELD, Mary
"Across Bucarest After Rain" (tr. of Maria Banus). [GrahamHR] (12) Spr 89, p. 45.
"Gemütlich" (tr. of Maria Banus). [GrahamHR] (12) Spr 89, p. 42-43.
"In the Forest" (tr. of Maria Banus). [GrahamHR] (12) Spr 89, p. 47.
"Letter" (tr. of Maria Banus). [GrahamHR] (12) Spr 89, p. 44.
"Song Beneath Tanks" (tr. of Maria Banus). [GrahamHR] (12) Spr 89, p. 46.
3613. MATTHEWS, David
"Emily." [Vis] (30) 89, p. 18.
3614. MATTHEWS, William
"39,000 Feet." [Antaeus] (62) Spr 89, p. 102-103.
"The Blues." [Atlantic] (264:3) S 89, p. 60.
"It Don't Mean a Thing If It Ain't Got That Swing." [OhioR] (44) 89, p. 78-81.
"Mood Indigo." [NewYorker] (65:21) 10 Jl 89, p. 40.
"Nabokov's Blues." [Poetry] (154:5) Ag 89, p. 250-252.
"Onions." [Poetry] (154:5) Ag 89, p. 252-253.
"Otego to Roscoe to Manhattan." [Colum] (14) 89, p. 122-123.
"The Scalpel." [Poetry] (154:5) Ag 89, p. 254.
"Short Farewells." [Poetry] (154:5) Ag 89, p. 255.
"Smoke." [CreamCR] (13:2) Fall 89, p. 192.
"The Socratic Method." [SenR] (19:1) 89, p. 16-17.
"Spent Breath." [SenR] (19:1) 89, p. 18.
"What a Little Moonlight Can Do." [Poetry] (154:5) Ag 89, p. 249-250.
3615. MATTHIAS, John
"A Compostella Diptych" (Selection: Part I: France: The Ways). [TriQ] (76) Fall 89,
p. 113-122.
3616. MAUDE, Caitlín
"Love Song for Vietnam" (tr. by Michael Hartnett). [Trans] (22) Fall 89, p. 98-99.
3617. MAUNICK, Edouard
"4. My island is a ghetto" (from *Paroles pour solder la mer*, tr. by Elizabeth (Betty)
Wilson). [Callaloo] (12:3, #40) Sum 89, p. 504.
"Beirut, Lebanon" (for Adonis, from *Paroles pour solder la mer*, tr. by Elizabeth
(Betty) Wilson). [Callaloo] (12:3, #40) Sum 89, p. 501.
"Lvov, Ukraine" (for the Ivan Franko faithful, from *Paroles pour solder la mer*, tr.
by Elizabeth (Betty) Wilson). [Callaloo] (12:3, #40) Sum 89, p. 502-503.
"Milan in Lombardy" (for Maretta Campi, from *Paroles pour solder la mer*, tr. by
Elizabeth (Betty) Wilson). [Callaloo] (12:3, #40) Sum 89, p. 503.
"Parole 47" (from *Ensoleillé vif*, tr. by Elizabeth (Betty) Wilson). [Callaloo] (12:3,
#40) Sum 89, p. 505.
"Rome, Piazza Navona" (for Claude Couffon, from *Paroles pour solder la mer*, tr.
by Elizabeth (Betty) Wilson). [Callaloo] (12:3, #40) Sum 89, p. 502.
3618. MAVIGLIA, Joseph
"Evolution." [Quarry] (38:2) Spr 89, p. 60.
3619. MAXMIN, Jody
"92nd Street Y" (for Stephen and Mark). [PraS] (63:1) Spr 89, p. 108.
3620. MAXSON, Gloria
"Credo." [ChrC] (106:32) N 1, 89, p. 983.
3621. MAXWELL, Glyn
"Did I Image That." [Verse] (6:3) Wint 89, p. 24.
"Dominion." [Verse] (6:1) Mr 89, p. 50-51.
"The End of the Weekend." [Verse] (6:1) Mr 89, p. 48-50.
"Five-to-Four." [Verse] (6:3) Wint 89, p. 80.
"Prospectors on Cherry Mountain." [BelPoJ] (39:3) Spr 89, p. 4-5.
"True That I Lie." [BelPoJ] (39:3) Spr 89, p. 3.
3622. MAXWELL, Richard
"For John: Another Writers' Conference" (at the Foothill Writer's Conference, June
1976). [PaintedB] (39) 89, p. 50-51.

3623. MAY, Doug
"When Does the Frost Come In?" [CreamCR] (13:2) Fall 89, p. 225.
3624. MAY, Kathy
"Looking for Emily." [MissR] (17:3, #51), p. 63-65.
"Varicose." [AmerV] (15) Sum 89, p. 53.
3625. MAY, Michael
"Fiesta." [Bogg] (61) 89, p. 54.
3626. MAYBURY, James F.
"Night Rain Poem" (tr. of Li Shangyin). [NewOR] (16:3) Fall 89, p. 45.
"Poem: The bluebird bites a grape" (tr. of Peng Jianpu). [NewOR] (16:3) Fall 89, p. 28.
3627. MAYER, Bernadette
"Strawberry Chief Crunchie" (Excerpt, to H. P. LA and S. & M & M). [Screens] (1) 89, p. 153-154.
3628. MAYES, Frances
"Denouement." [NoAmR] (274:4) D 89, p. 45.
"Etruscan Head." [GettyR] (2:4) Aut 89, p. 608-609.
"The Long Bony Cats of Montecatini." [GettyR] (2:4) Aut 89, p. 610-611.
"The Untying of a Knot." [Poetry] (153:5) F 89, p. 290-291.
3629. MAYHALL, Jane
"He Copies." [ConnPR] (8:1) 89, p. 10.
"My Uncle's Canary." [AmerS] (58:1) Wint 89, p. 18.
3630. MAYHEW, Deborah
"A Certain View." [Footwork] 89, p. 54.
3631. MAYHEW, Lenore
"The Butterfly Loves Flowers: I remember being here before" (tr. of Nalan Singde, w. William McNaughton). [LitR] (32:3) Spr 89, p. 370.
"The Butterfly Loves Flowers: In the high trees" (tr. of Nalan Singde, w. William McNaughton). [LitR] (32:3) Spr 89, p. 371.
"I Remember the Beauty" (tr. of Nalan Singde, w. William McNaughton). [LitR] (32:3) Spr 89, p. 368.
"I Think of the Beauty" (tr. of Nalan Singde, w. William McNaughton). [LitR] (32:3) Spr 89, p. 370.
"The Moon Climbs the Cherry-Apple" (tr. of Nalan Singde, w. William McNaughton). [LitR] (32:3) Spr 89, p. 369.
"South Country" (tr. of Nalan Singde, w. William McNaughton). [LitR] (32:3) Spr 89, p. 369.
3632. MAYHOOD, Clif
"The Long Afternoon." [JamesWR] (6:4) Sum 89, p. 10.
"Self-Destruction" (for Bob Larsen). [JamesWR] (6:4) Sum 89, p. 10.
3633. MAYNE, Seymour
"Covenant." [CanLit] (120) Spr 89, p. 81.
"Last Chance." [CanLit] (120) Spr 89, p. 82.
3634. MAZZOCCO, Robert
"1815." [NewYorker] (65:23) 24 Jl 89, p. 28.
"Aubade." [NewYorker] (65:7) 3 Ap 89, p. 44.
"Loneliness in the City." [NewYorker] (65:13) 15 My 89, p. 56.
"Rimbaud." [NewYorker] (65:33) 2 O 89, p. 46.
3635. MBUTHIA, Waithira
"Dear Death." [Bomb] (28) Sum 89, p. 88.
"Determination." [Bomb] (28) Sum 89, p. 88.
"An Ode to Queen Mumbi." [Bomb] (28) Sum 89, p. 88.
"Tell 'Em I Ain't Home." [Bomb] (28) Sum 89, p. 88.
Mc . . .
See also names beginning with Mac . . .
3636. McADAM, Rhona
"Animal Kingdom." [Quarry] (38:4) Fall 89, p. 22.
"The Artisan." [Pig] (15) 88, p. 39.
"Beirut Spring" (The Capture of John McCarthy). [Quarry] (38:4) Fall 89, p. 21-22.
"Driven." [Quarry] (38:4) Fall 89, p. 23.
"Phases of Silver." [Quarry] (38:4) Fall 89, p. 24-25.
"Tanzanian Basket / Lost in Translation." [Pig] (15) 88, p. 39.
"Waiting for the End of the World." [Dandel] (16:1) Spr-Sum 89, p. 58-59.
3637. McADAMS, Janet
"A Disturbance in Memory" (For Michael Dinoff, 1933-1982). [NegC] (9:2) 89, p. 19-23.

"Flood." [Poetry] (154:5) Ag 89, p. 265.
3638. McALEAVEY, David
"Glimpse of the Garden." [Poem] (61) My 89, p. 40.
"Lascaux." [PoetC] (20:3) Spr 89, p. 18-19.
"Speaking with Others." [PoetL] (84:3) Fall 89, p. 5-7.
"Troy." [Poem] (61) My 89, p. 41.
3639. McALPINE, Katherine
"Estrogen and English II." [AntigR] (77/78) Spr-Sum 89, p. 172-173.
3640. McAULIFFE, Brian
"Halftime." [EngJ] (78:1) Ja 89, p. 93.
3641. McBREEN, Joan
"This Moon, These Stars." [Vis] (29) 89, p. 26-27.
"The Wind Beyond the Wall." [Vis] (29) 89, p. 27.
3642. McBRIDE, Mark
"3 a.m. Goodbye." [Wind] (19:64) 89, p. 15-16.
3643. McBRIDE, Regina
"The Dressmaker." [HighP] (4:3) Wint 89-90, p. 79-81.
"The Red Eyed Woods." [Pequod] (26/27) 89, p. 33-34.
3644. McBRIDE, Timothy Patrick
"Bonsai." [GreensboroR] (47) Wint 89-90, p. 50.
"Conn." [CumbPR] (9:1) Fall 89, p. 14.
3645. McBRIDE, Tom
"My Son Sleeps." [Wind] (19:64) 89, p. 17.
"Squirrels." [Farm] (6:1) Wint-Spr 88-89, p. 123.
3646. McCABE, Brian
"Story of the Thousand Forced to Flee." [MalR] (87) Sum 89, p. 78-79.
3647. McCABE, Victoria
"November Morning." [LitR] (32:2) Wint 89, p. 220.
3648. McCAFFERTY, Ed
"In Her Place." [PoetL] (84:4) Wint 89-90, p. 41-42.
3649. McCAFFERY, Steve
"Organized Happiness" (Excerpt). [Notus] (4:2) Fall 89, p. 34-35.
3650. McCANN, Janet
"The Builders." [JINJPo] [11] 89, p. 18.
"The Cat at the End of the Poetry Anthology." [CumbPR] (8:2) Spr 89, p. 24.
"Money." [Kalliope] (11:3) 89, p. 54.
"Mother's Day." [ArtfulD] (16/17) Fall 89, p. 9.
"The Root Canal Poem." [RiverC] (10:1) Fall 89, p. 118.
"Sestina Is." [Plain] (9:2) Wint 89, p. 14-15.
"Sister Rat." [JINJPo] [11] 89, p. 17.
"Texas Saturday." [JINJPo] [11] 89, p. 16.
3651. McCANN, Richard
"Gladiolas." [PraS] (63:3) Fall 89, p. 33-34.
"Jardin Zoologique." [PraS] (63:3) Fall 89, p. 32-33.
3652. McCARTHY, Fabian, Jr.
"Harvest Doubts." [Lactuca] (13) N 89, p. 41.
"The Sleeping Man." [Lactuca] (13) N 89, p. 40-41.
3653. McCARTHY, Julia
"The Perfect Plot." [AntigR] (76) Wint 89, p. 84.
"You Wore Black." [AntigR] (76) Wint 89, p. 85.
3654. McCARTHY, Ted
"Shane's Eyes." [Vis] (31) 89, p. 34.
3655. McCARTHY, Thomas
"Seasons" (tr. of Cathal O Searcaigh). [Trans] (22) Fall 89, p. 152.
"Words of a Brother" (tr. of Cathal O Searcaigh). [Trans] (22) Fall 89, p. 152.
3656. McCARTIN, Jim
"I Want to Die, She Said." [Footwork] 89, p. 41-42.
"Rothko's Suicide." [Footwork] 89, p. 41.
"The Wrong Thing." [Footwork] 89, p. 41.
3657. McCARTY, Jesse
"Aswimsleep." [HiramPoR] (46) Spr-Sum 89, p. 18.
"The Renaissance Whales." [Hawai'iR] (13:1, #25) Spr 89, p. 30-32.
3658. McCASLIN, Susan
"Apology for the Soul." [BellArk] (5:1) Ja-F 89, p. 9.
"A Canticle for Mary and Martha" (22 poems). [BellArk] (5:2) Mr-Ap 89, p. 30-32.

3659. McCAUGHEY, Kevin
"For Harpo." [CapeR] (24:2) Fall 89, p. 17.
3660. McCLATCHY, J. D.
"An Alphabet of Anger." [ParisR] (31:111) Sum 89, p. 83-85.
"City from Above" (tr. of Giovanni Raboni, w. David Stivender). [Poetry] (155:1/2)
O-N 89, p. 89.
"Cysts." [Ploughs] (15:4) Wint 89-90, p. 131-135.
"The Fan" (tr. of Pier Paolo Pasolini, w. David Stivender). [Poetry] (155:1/2) O-N
89, p. 50.
"Figures in the Park" (tr. of Giovanni Raboni, w. David Stivender). [Poetry]
(155:1/2) O-N 89, p. 90.
"Flesh and Sky" (tr. of Pier Paolo Pasolini, w. David Stivender). [Poetry] (155:1/2)
O-N 89, p. 51.
"Heads" (Jerusalem, November 1987). [NewYorker] (64:50) 30 Ja 89, p. 30.
"Il Pianto della Scavatrice (The Lament of the Excavator)" (Selection: V., tr. of Pier
Paolo Pasolini, w. David Stivender). [Poetry] (155:1/2) O-N 89, p. 48-49.
"*Medea* in Tokyo." [NewRep] (200:2/3) 9-16 Ja 89, p. 40.
"My Daughter's Birthday" (tr. of Giovanni Raboni, w. David Stivender). [Poetry]
(155:1/2) O-N 89, p. 91.
"Night Piece." [NewYorker] (65:39) 13 N 89, p. 56.
"Part of a Letter to the Codignola Boy" (tr. of Pier Paolo Pasolini, w. David
Stivender). [Poetry] (155:1/2) O-N 89, p. 47.
"The Rented House." [ParisR] (31:111) Sum 89, p. 80-82.
"Spencer's Tower" (Kilcolman, Co. Cork). [Nat] (248:17) 1 My 89, p. 601.
"Weeds." [NewRep] (201:14) 2 O 89, p. 34.
3661. McCLAURIN, Irma
"Black Phoenix" (after Elvyn). [Obs] (2:1) Spr 87, p. 1.
3662. McCLELLAN, Michael W.
"A Prime Time Guide." [FreeL] (3) Aut 89, p. 32.
3663. McCLELLAND, Bruce
"Given over to love the way a whirling column of finches" (for Suzanne). [Epoch]
(38:1) 89, p. 6-7.
"The Grotto" (Good Friday, 1989). [Notus] (4:2) Fall 89, p. 15.
"Hansel & Gretel in the Underworld." [Epoch] (38:1) 89, p. 5.
"The Law & the Fissure." [Notus] (4:2) Fall 89, p. 13-14.
"An Odd Ruse." [Notus] (4:2) Fall 89, p. 11-12.
"Web." [Notus] (4:2) Fall 89, p. 16.
"Who's on Dendron Tree." [Notus] (4:2) Fall 89, p. 17-18.
3664. McCLINTOCK, Wayne
"Dream Cattle." [CreamCR] (13:2) Fall 89, p. 163.
3665. McCLOSKEY, Mark
"Birthday Dog." [PoetryNW] (30:4) Wint 89-90, p. 37.
3666. McCLURE, Michael
"High Heels." [AnotherCM] (19) 89, p. 229-231.
"Politics of the Soul." [Caliban] (6) 89, p. 121.
"The Red the black the blue the white the yellow" (For Joanna, cca mid 80's).
[AlphaBS] (6) Wint 89-90, p. 41-42.
"Sure! Arrest old ladies kneeling on their knees . . ." (For those arrested . . ., cca
mid 80's). [AlphaBS] (6) Wint 89-90, p. 43.
"Wildflower from Imagination's Green and Golden Land" (Reading to the mob at the
rock concert). [AlphaBS] (6) Wint 89-90, p. 44.
3667. McCOMBS, Judith
"Translation." [SouthernPR] (29:2) Fall 89, p. 60-61.
3668. McCORKLE, Emily
"What Is Orange?" (Mainstreet Elementary Poetry Contest, 4th Grade, 2nd Place).
[DeKalbLAJ] (22:1/4) 89, p. 105.
3669. McCORKLE, J. (James)
"After the Cold Spring." [Boulevard] (4:2, #11) Fall 89, p. 73-74.
"With You, I Do My Best Free Associations." [DenQ] (24:2) Fall 89, p. 67-68.
3670. McCORMACK, James E.
"Fragments." [AntigR] (77/78) Spr-Sum 89, p. 200.
"Gardener." [AntigR] (77/78) Spr-Sum 89, p. 198.
"Jazz on a Saturday Afternoon" (Studio One, Glasgow). [AntigR] (77/78) Spr-Sum
89, p. 197.
"Old Woman." [AntigR] (77/78) Spr-Sum 89, p. 199.

3671. McCORMACK, P. G.
"The Dublin Jogger." [Vis] (29) 89, p. 22.
"Raindrops." [Vis] (31) 89, p. 30.
3672. McCORMICK, Don
"Christ." [Plain] (10:1) 89, p. 36.
3673. McCUE, Frances
"Etiquette." [PoetryNW] (30:1) Spr 89, p. 32-33.
3674. McCURDY, Harold
"The Fountain." [ChrC] (106:13) Ap 19, 89, p. 414.
"Gethsemane." [ChrC] (106:10) Mr 22-29, 89, p. 317.
3675. McCURRY, Jim
"Memo." [Farm] (6:2) Fall 89, p. 38.
"El Norte" (For John Coltrane, July 17, 1987). [Farm] (6:1) Wint-Spr 88-89, p. 99.
"On the Block." [Farm] (6:1) Wint-Spr 88-89, p. 100-101.
3676. McDADE, Thomas Michael
"Time Song." [SmPd] (26:2 #76) Spr 89, p. 9.
3677. McDANIEL, Wilma Elizabeth
"April 17, 1987." [HangL] (54) 89, p. 18.
"Bakersfield Theology." [HangL] (54) 89, p. 19.
"Subject Matter." [HangL] (54) 89, p. 20.
3678. McDONALD, Thomas
"GS3 Step 6" (from *Notes on the New Day Plantation*). [Obs] (3:2) Sum 88, p. 91.
3679. McDONALD, Walter
"After the Rains of Saigon." [Pequod] (26/27) 89, p. 28.
"Building on Hardscrabble." [Outbr] (20) 89, p. 9.
"Colonel Mackenzie Maps the Llano Estacado." [TexasR] (10:1/2) Spr-Sum 89, p.
55.
"A Cousin No Ones Claims." [SouthernPR] (29:1) Spr 89, p. 46.
"Digging in a Footlocker." [NewYRB] (36:15) 12 O 89, p. 19.
"Hawks in a Bitter Blizzard." [Atlantic] (264:3) S 89, p. 82.
"The Last Good Saddles." [CinPR] (20) Fall 89, p. 28-29.
"The Last Still Days in a Bunker." [Pequod] (26/27) 89, p. 30.
"The Laws of Hollow Wings." [CinPR] (20) Fall 89, p. 30.
"Living on Open Plains." [CrabCR] (6:1) 89, p. 16.
"Lullaby at Aspen." [KeyWR] (2:1/2) Fall-Wint 89, p. 43.
"Making Book on the Aquifer." [SewanR] (97:1) Wint 89, p. 28.
"The Meaning of Flat Fields." [Pequod] (26/27) 89, p. 29.
"Melanoma." [TexasR] (10:1/2) Spr-Sum 89, p. 54.
"The Middle Years." [Shen] (39:2) Sum 89, p. 72.
"Night Casting at Lake Raven." [HampSPR] Wint 89, p. 13.
"Night on Bald Mountain." [CrabCR] (6:1) 89, p. 16-17.
"Old Men Fishing at Brownwood." [PoetL] (84:4) Wint 89-90, p. 29.
"The Pee Wee Coach." [FloridaR] (16:2/3) Fall-Wint 89, p. 198-199.
"Settling the Plains." [SewanR] (97:1) Wint 89, p. 29.
"Sleeping with Strangers." [SewanR] (97:1) Wint 89, p. 27.
"Stars and the Laws of Motion." [TarRP] (29:1) Fall 89, p. 40.
"Summer Off." [Amelia] (5:3, #14) 89, p. 26.
"Sweet Nothings." [MichQR] (28:2) Spr 89, p. 179.
"With My Father in Winter." [HampSPR] Wint 89, p. 12.
3680. McDOUGALL, Jo
"Four P.M." [MidwQ] (30:2) Wint 89, p. 193.
3681. McDOWELL, Robert
"The Eighties." [CrossCur] (8:2) Ja 89, p. 155-166.
3682. McDUFF, David
"A Body Is to Bear a Shrine" (from "Penelope," tr. of Tua Forsström). [Stand]
(30:3) Sum 89, p. 53.
"The Fieldmouse's Prayer" (tr. of Tua Forsström). [Stand] (30:3) Sum 89, p. 53.
"I See You in the Slow Night" (tr. of Tua Forsström). [Stand] (30:3) Sum 89, p. 53.
3683. McELHONE, Jeff
"Carnate." [HeavenB] (7) Wint 89, p. 42.
"Lynn Trance." [HeavenB] (6) Wint-Spr 89, p. 5.
3684. McELROY, Colleen
"Bo Jangles Visits the Studio." [Ploughs] (15:4) Wint 89-90, p. 137-138.
"Sprung Sonnet For Dorothy Dandridge." [Ploughs] (15:4) Wint 89-90, p. 136.
3685. McEWEN, R. F.
"For Silky Sullivan: Three More Blocks to Crack." [Plain] (9:2) Wint 89, p. 37.

3686. McFADDEN, David
"Damsels in Distress." [MalR] (88) Fall 89, p. 93.
"A Date with bpNichol." [CapilR] (1st series: 50) 89, p. 77.
"Earthquake and Drought." [CapilR] (1st series: 50) 89, p. 78.
"Featherstone Point" (For M.O.). [CapilR] (1st series: 50) 89, p. 82.
"For My Brother Irving." [CapilR] (1st series: 50) 89, p. 80.
"Green Shadows." [MalR] (88) Fall 89, p. 94.
"Lord Vishnu." [MalR] (88) Fall 89, p. 95.
"Perfect and Sad." [CapilR] (1st series: 50) 89, p. 86.
"Portrait of You As a Little Girl." [CapilR] (1st series: 50) 89, p. 81.
"Shivering on the Doorstep" (For D.H.). [CapilR] (1st series: 50) 89, p. 79.
"Silent Shadows." [MalR] (88) Fall 89, p. 96-97.
"Ten Years Ago" (For Bonnie Ericson). [CapilR] (1st series: 50) 89, p. 83-85.
3687. McFALL, Gardner
"Moves" (Prizewinning Poets -- 1989). [Nat] (248:20) 22 My 89, p. 707.
3688. McFARLAND, Ron
"Apple Elegy." [WindO] (51) Spr 89, p. 8.
3689. McFEE, Michael
"Ever After." [Poetry] (153:4) Ja 89, p. 209.
"Floor Furnace." [Hudson] (42:2) Sum 89, p. 278.
"Kick the Can." [SouthernPR] (29:1) Spr 89, p. 12.
"The Picture." [Hudson] (42:2) Sum 89, p. 277.
"Reading in the Tulip Tree." [Hudson] (42:2) Sum 89, p. 279.
"Sad Girl Sitting on a Running Board." [Poetry] (154:4) Jl 89, p. 207.
"Stamp Album." [Hudson] (42:2) Sum 89, p. 280.
"Thomas Wolfe Aloft." [SewanR] (97:2) Spr 89, p. 276-277.
"World Without Men." [ThRiPo] (33/34) 89, p. 47-49.
3690. McFERREN, Martha
"How to Get Published." [HeliconN] (20) 89, p. 90-91.
"Weird Doctors." [Shen] (39:4) Wint 89, p. 75-76.
"Women in Cars." [Shen] (39:4) Wint 89, p. 73-74.
3691. McFERRIN, Linda
"Mysteries." [SoCoast] (5) Spr 88, p. 24-25.
3692. McGAHEY, Jeanne
"Homecoming with Reflections: Collected Poems" (46 poems). [QRL] (9:28-29) 89,
70 p.
3693. McGARTLAND, Nancy
"My Breasts." [Calyx] (12:1) Sum 89, p. 16.
3694. McGIMPSEY, David
"The Alligator Expert Prepares Tourists for the Hunt." [Event] (18:3) Fall 89, p.
90-93.
3695. McGINTY, S.
"I Have Even Heard." [SpiritSH] (54) Spr-Sum 89, p. 29.
"Untitled: It isn't anything." [SpiritSH] (54) Spr-Sum 89, p. 31.
"Yellow." [SpiritSH] (54) Spr-Sum 89, p. 30.
3696. McGOVERN, Martin
"Chanteuse with Dog, Walking." [WestHR] (43:3) Aut 89, p. 193.
"Hospital Corner." [WestHR] (43:3) Aut 89, p. 191-192.
"Processionalia." [Poetry] (154:2) My 89, p. 72-73.
"Summer Indians." [Poetry] (154:6) S 89, p. 320-322.
3697. McGOVERN, Robert
"Elegy for a Dead Confederate." [BallSUF] (30:1) Wint 89, p. 73.
3698. McGRADY, Nell
"Blessed Erratum." [CumbPR] (9:1) Fall 89, p. 42.
"Prelude: Daughter at Eleven." [CumbPR] (9:1) Fall 89, p. 43.
3699. McGRATH, Beth
"For My Father, on My Sister's Wedding Day." [Shen] (39:4) Wint 89, p. 34.
"Uncle John." [Hudson] (42:1) Spr 89, p. 98.
3700. McGRATH, Campbell
"Capitalist Poem #22." [Caliban] (6) 89, p. 188-189.
"The Genius of Industry." [Witness] (2:4) Wint 88, p. 56-61.
"What They Ate." [NewYorker] (65:41) 27 N 89, p. 50.
"What They Drank." [NewYorker] (65:41) 27 N 89, p. 50.
3701. McGRATH, Connell
"Improvisations on a Sound by Spicer." [Caliban] (7) 89, p. 43.

3702. McGRATH, Thomas (Tom)
    "Advertisements." [AmerPoR] (18:3) My-Je 89, p. 25.
    "Afternoon of a McGrath" (For my son Tomasito McGrath after a visit to McGrath,
        MN). [Nat] (249:15) 6 N 89, p. 535-536.
    "End of a Season" (--song from a play). [AmerPoR] (18:3) My-Je 89, p. 25.
    "A Fable for Poets." [NoDaQ] (57:3) Sum 89, p. 99.
    "Graveyard Shift." [PaperAir] (4:2) 89, p. 17.
    "Half Measures." [AmerPoR] (18:3) My-Je 89, p. 25.
    "The Language of the Dead." [AmerPoR] (18:3) My-Je 89, p. 25.
    "Longing." [AmerPoR] (18:3) My-Je 89, p. 24.
    "Mediterranean." [Nat] (249:15) 6 N 89, p. 536.
    "Night Meeting." [AmerPoR] (18:3) My-Je 89, p. 23.
    "A Promise." [PaperAir] (4:2) 89, p. 16.
    "Reading by Mechanic Light." [AmerPoR] (18:3) My-Je 89, p. 25.
    "Than Never." [PaperAir] (4:2) 89, p. 16.
    "Up the Dark Valley." [Nat] (249:15) 6 N 89, p. 535.
    "A Visit to the House of the Poet -- Nicaragua, 1987, Homage to Rubén Darío on
        His Birthday." [AmerPoR] (18:3) My-Je 89, p. 24.
    "Working in Darkness." [AmerPoR] (18:3) My-Je 89, p. 24.
McGUCKIAN, Mebdh
    See McGUCKIAN, Medbh
3703. McGUCKIAN, Medbh
    "Adonis Dark." [Vis] (29) 89, p. 34.
    "The Boathouse." [FourQ] (2d series 3:2) Fall 89, p. 10.
    "The Cloth Mother." [Pequod] (26/27) 89, p. 104.
    "A Dream of Stone." [Stand] (30:3) Sum 89, p. 13.
    "Garbo at the Gaumont." [Pequod] (26/27) 89, p. 105.
    "Girl-Mother and Child." [Pequod] (26/27) 89, p. 108.
    "The Invalid's Echo." [Vis] (29) 89, p. 31-33.
    "Postlude." [Colum] (14) 89, p. 211-212.
    "The Sea-House." [NoDaQ] (57:1) Wint 89, p. 99.
    "Shifting Flats." [CimR] (86) Ja 89, p. 30.
    "Springwater." [Pequod] (26/27) 89, p. 106-107.
    "Tiled Bathroom." [CimR] (86) Ja 89, p. 31.
    "Tiled Bathroom." [NoDaQ] (57:1) Wint 89, p. 99.
    "View Without a Room." [Stand] (30:3) Sum 89, p. 12.
3704. McGUINN, Rex A.
    "To Be Sent to the Shadow of the Sun" (tr. of Yu Ping Ding, w. An Jing). [LitR]
        (32:2) Wint 89, p. 168.
3705. McGUIRE, Catherine
    "Old Love." [CapeR] (24:2) Fall 89, p. 40.
3706. McGUIRE, Jamie
    "Haiti." [HeavenB] (6) Wint-Spr 89, p. 8-9.
3707. McHUGH, Heather
    "Big Ideas Among Earthlings." [NewL] (56:2/3) Wint 89-Spr 90, p. 172-173.
    "Breath." [NewL] (56:2/3) Wint 89-Spr 90, p. 170-171.
    "For a Man." [NewL] (56:2/3) Wint 89-Spr 90, p. 173.
    "ID." [WestHR] (43:2) Sum 89, p. 77.
    "Like." [NewL] (56:2/3) Wint 89-Spr 90, p. 171.
    "Nothing I Foresaw." [NewL] (56:2/3) Wint 89-Spr 90, p. 174-175.
3708. McINNIS, Nadine
    "Model Home 3." [Dandel] (16:1) Spr-Sum 89, p. 12.
    "Model Home 4." [Dandel] (16:1) Spr-Sum 89, p. 13.
3709. McINTOSH, Joan
    "The Beginning." [SoDakR] (27:3) Aut 89, p. 114.
    "Jade Silk." [SoDakR] (27:3) Aut 89, p. 115.
3710. McINTOSH, Michael
    "Mama's Stigmata." [CumbPR] (8:2) Spr 89, p. 30.
3711. McINTOSH, Molly
    "The Direction of Women." [Poem] (61) My 89, p. 53.
    "Poem for an Auditor." [Poem] (61) My 89, p. 54.
3712. McKAIN, David
    "Bus Stop in Soviet Georgia." [Shen] (39:1) Spr 89, p. 49-50.
    "Cremation." [SouthwR] (74:2) Spr 89, p. 260-261.
    "Homing Pigeons." [LaurelR] (23:1) Wint 89, p. 64-65.
    "Kinzua Dam." [MidAR] (9:1) 89, p. 38-39.

"Marching Against the Klan in Scotland, Connecticut." [AntR] (47:2) Spr 89, p. 202-203.
"Picking Bottles." [MidAR] (9:1) 89, p. 37.
"The Tanner's Pride." [LaurelR] (23:1) Wint 89, p. 63.
3713. McKAY, Leo, Jr.
"I Dissolve." [Grain] (17:2) Sum 89, p. 14.
3714. McKAY, Linda Back
"Nemesis." [Farm] (6:1) Wint-Spr 88-89, p. 60.
"Splits." [Farm] (6:1) Wint-Spr 88-89, p. 61.
3715. McKEAN, James
"Dead Reckoning." [PoetryNW] (30:3) Aut 89, p. 39-40.
"Reunion, Cannon Beach." [PoetryNW] (30:3) Aut 89, p. 38-39.
3716. McKEE, Louis
"The Buck Dancer on Chestnut Street." [Vis] (30) 89, p. 43.
"A Chaser" (in memory of John Logan). [PaintedB] (39) 89, p. 91.
"The Heat." [Footwork] 89, p. 53.
"Modern Times." [FreeL] (3) Aut 89, p. 9.
"My Brattleboro Memory" (after a poem by Irene McKinney). [SwampR] (1:4) Sum 89, p. 17.
"Something Large." [DeKalbLAJ] (22:1/4) 89, p. 62.
"Thoughts of Chile." [SlipS] (9) 89, p. 89-90.
"To My Son." [AmerPoR] (18:4) Jl-Ag 89, p. 29.
"Yardwork." [CapeR] (24:2) Fall 89, p. 35.
3717. McKENNA, J. J.
"Charles Darwin." [CapeR] (24:2) Fall 89, p. 11.
3718. McKENZIE-PORTER, Patricia
"The Path to the Shore." [CrossC] (11:1) 89, p. 4.
3719. McKERNAN, John
"Believable Dreams." [Kalliope] (10:3) 88, p. 50-52.
"I Have Always Wondered Whether Plants Have Orgasm." [KeyWR] (2:1/2) Fall-Wint 89, p. 82.
"The Ship of Sex." [Kalliope] (10:3) 88, p. 53-54.
"We Heard Schopenhauer Masturbating." [KeyWR] (2:1/2) Fall-Wint 89, p. 83.
3720. McKERNAN, Llewellyn
"For Billie Holiday: Lady Day." [Kalliope] (11:1) 89, p. 54-55.
3721. McKINNEY, Irene
"Preliminary Invocation." [HiramPoR] (46) Spr-Sum 89, p. 42-43.
"Visiting My Gravesite: Talbott Churchyard, West Virginia." [HiramPoR] (46) Spr-Sum 89, p. 48-49.
3722. McKINNEY, Joshua
"First Coon Hunt." [PassN] (10:1) Wint 89, p. 17.
3723. McKINNON, Barry
"Pulp Log" (Excerpt, work in progress). [CapilR] (1st series: 50) 89, p. 16-21.
3724. McKNIGHT, Lee
"Vision." [EmeraldCR] (1989) c1988, p. 130-131.
3725. McLAUGHLIN, Dorothy
"Closets." [StoneC] (17:1/2) Fall-Wint 89-90, p. 65.
"To Emily Bronte." [CapeR] (24:2) Fall 89, p. 14.
3726. McLAUGHLIN, Joe-Anne
"Companion Pieces." [GeoR] (43:2) Sum 89, p. 244-246.
3727. McLAUGHLIN, Rosemary
"Some Places Get Into Your Bones." [Footwork] 89, p. 43.
3728. McLAURIN, Ken
"Coming of Age." [PoetL] (84:1) Spr 89, p. 29.
"Connecting Light." [Vis] (31) 89, p. 17.
3729. McLEAN, Sammy
"Isolated House" (for Günter Eich, tr. of Hans Magnus Enzensberger). [AnotherCM] (19) 89, p. 66.
"Pill" (tr. of Helga M. Novak). [MissR] (18:1, #52) 89, p. 105-106.
"Ready" (tr. of Helga M. Novak). [MidAR] (9:1) 89, p. 42.
3730. McLEAVEY, David
"All the Senses." [WashR] (14:5) F-Mr 89, p. 16-17.
3731. McLEOD, Donald
"Primal Concern." [SlipS] (9) 89, p. 41-45.
"Urban Haiku." [SlipS] (9) 89, p. 40.

3732. McLEOD, Milt
"Plymouth Thanksgiving, 1983" (to Dennis Banks). [PacificR] (7) 89, p. 94.
"Small Boy with a Shovel" (Caldarin, Eastern Turkey, 1976). [CumbPR] (8:2) Spr
89, p. 29.
"A Theory of Compassion." [PacificR] (7) 89, p. 95.
3733. McLEOD, Ruth F.
"Nature Walk." [EmeraldCR] (1989) c1988, p. 139.
3734. McLEOD, Stephen
"The Broken Gull" (for Lucie Brock-Broido). [Agni] (28) 89, p. 245-246.
3735. McMAHON, Lynne
"Ann Lee" (founder of the First Church of the Millennium (Shakers))." [AmerPoR]
(18:3) My-Je 89, p. 41.
"Barbie's Ferrari." [AmerPoR] (18:3) My-Je 89, p. 40.
"Cheap Sunglasses." [IndR] (12:3) Sum 89, p. 18.
"Convalescence." [AmerPoR] (18:3) My-Je 89, p. 41.
"Dove Cottage." [IndR] (12:3) Sum 89, p. 19.
"Hopkins and Whitman." [KenR] (NS 11:3) Sum 89, p. 66-67.
"Little Elegy for the Age." [Crazy] (36) Spr 89, p. 26-27.
"Personal History." [KenR] (NS 11:3) Sum 89, p. 68-69.
"A Posthumous or Future Arrangement." [IndR] (12:3) Sum 89, p. 17.
"Rural Route." [DenQ] (24:1) Sum 89, p. 52.
"Swingset." [KenR] (NS 11:3) Sum 89, p. 67-68.
"Utopian Turtletop." [IndR] (12:3) Sum 89, p. 20-21.
"Wuthering Heights." [AmerPoR] (18:3) My-Je 89, p. 40.
3736. McMAHON, Michael
"Down in the Well." [Farm] (6:1) Wint-Spr 88-89, p. 24-26.
"Mutt." [Farm] (6:1) Wint-Spr 88-89, p. 20-23.
"Old Flames." [WindO] (51) Spr 89, p. 14.
"Shit." [Farm] (6:1) Wint-Spr 88-89, p. 27-32.
3737. McMANUS, James
"Smash and Scatteration: Performance." [NewAW] (5) Fall 89, p. 47-53.
3738. McNAIR, Wesley
"Happiness." [BostonR] (14:3) Je 89, p. 11.
"The Last Time Shorty Towers Fetched the Cows." [BostonR] (14:3) Je 89, p. 11.
"The Man with the Radios." [BostonR] (14:3) Je 89, p. 11.
"Mina Bell's Cows." [BostonR] (14:3) Je 89, p. 11.
"The Name." [BostonR] (14:3) Je 89, p. 11.
"The Traveler's Advisory." [BostonR] (14:3) Je 89, p. 11.
3739. McNALLY, Stephen
"Heavenly." [BlackWR] (15:2) Spr 89, p. 103.
"The Little Girl on the Bridge." [AmerPoR] (18:4) Jl-Ag 89, p. 6.
"Moon." [AmerPoR] (18:4) Jl-Ag 89, p. 5.
"Out by the Side of the House Where the Wild Flowers." [AmerPoR] (18:4) Jl-Ag
89, p. 5.
"Poem with Two Swans and a Pair of Glasses." [AmerPoR] (18:4) Jl-Ag 89, p. 5.
"Sick Child." [AmerPoR] (18:4) Jl-Ag 89, p. 6.
3740. McNAMARA, Blanche
"Down from the Mountain." [Writer] (102:3) Mr 89, p. 25.
3741. McNAMARA, Mary Colgan
"Myself, Comparing Religions." [Kalliope] (11:3) 89, p. 13.
3742. McNAMARA, Peter L.
"Edward Hopper." [Wind] (19:65) 89, p. 30.
3743. McNAMARA, Robert
"Absences." [Agni] (28) 89, p. 268-269.
"As You Stand Peeling an Orange." [MissouriR] (12:2) 89, p. 54-55.
"Teanaway River, Two Passes." [OhioR] (44) 89, p. 128-130.
"What Anyone Really Wanted." [Agni] (28) 89, p. 270-271.
3744. McNARIE, Alan Decker
"Berries for Pele." [BambooR] (41) Wint 89, p. 20-22.
3745. McNAUGHTON, Duncan
"The Black Bull." [CapilR] (1st series: 50) 89, p. 64-66.
"Clear Spot." [Temblor] (10) 89, p. 228.
"The Oak Grove." [Acts] (10) 89, p. 133-134.
"The White Antibes, the Canaries." [CapilR] (1st series: 50) 89, p. 62-63.
3746. McNAUGHTON, William
"Another to the Tune 'All the Garden's Fragrance'" (tr. of Ch'in Kuan, w. David

Young). [LitR] (32:3) Spr 89, p. 374.
"The Butterfly Loves Flowers: I remember being here before" (tr. of Nalan Singde, w. Lenore Mayhew). [LitR] (32:3) Spr 89, p. 370.
"The Butterfly Loves Flowers: In the high trees" (tr. of Nalan Singde, w. Lenore Mayhew). [LitR] (32:3) Spr 89, p. 371.
"I Remember the Beauty" (tr. of Nalan Singde, w. Lenore Mayhew). [LitR] (32:3) Spr 89, p. 368.
"I Think of the Beauty" (tr. of Nalan Singde, w. Lenore Mayhew). [LitR] (32:3) Spr 89, p. 370.
"The Moon Climbs the Cherry-Apple" (tr. of Nalan Singde, w. Lenore Mayhew). [LitR] (32:3) Spr 89, p. 369.
"South Country" (tr. of Nalan Singde, w. Lenore Mayhew). [LitR] (32:3) Spr 89, p. 369.
"A Third to the Tune 'As Though Dreaming'" (tr. of Ch'in Kuan, w. David Young). [LitR] (32:3) Spr 89, p. 373.
"To the Tune 'As Though Dreaming'" (tr. of Ch'in Kuan, w. David Young). [LitR] (32:3) Spr 89, p. 372.
"To the Tune 'Welcome Spring Music'" (tr. of Ch'in Kuan, w. David Young). [LitR] (32:3) Spr 89, p. 373.

3747. McNEIL, Elizabeth
"Pleasure." [ChamLR] (2:2, #4) Spr 89, p. 46.

3748. McNERNEY, Joan
"Accident." [Footwork] 89, p. 13.

3749. McNULTY, Tim
"Geese and Reeds" (Yuan Dynasty, Artist Unknown). [Contact] (9:50/51/52) Fall-Wint 88-Spr 89, p. 27.
"The Wind in Lost Basin." [Contact] (9:50/51/52) Fall-Wint 88-Spr 89, p. 27.

3750. McPHERSON, Michael
"The Green Flash." [Hawai'iR] (13:3) Fall 89, p. 73.
"Life Estate." [Manoa] (1:1/2) Fall 89, p. 117.
"To My Brother in San Juan." [Hawai'iR] (13:3) Fall 89, p. 72.

3751. McPHERSON, Sandra
"Bad Mother Blues." [AmerPoR] (18:3) My-Je 89, p. 3.
"Dancer to J.J. Malone and the Texas Twisters, Caspar, California." [AmerPoR] (18:3) My-Je 89, p. 4.
"Designating Duet." [Field] (41) Fall 89, p. 72-74.
"Diary: Day of Rest." [TriQ] (74) Wint 89, p. 180-181.
"For St. James, Who Said He Was on Tour with the Emotions" (with help from Percy Mayfield). [AmerPoR] (18:3) My-Je 89, p. 4.
"Holy Woman: Pecolia Warner." [Field] (41) Fall 89, p. 75.
"Mysterious-Shape Quilt Top, Anonymous, Oklahoma." [TriQ] (76) Fall 89, p. 90-92.
"Notes on a Missouri Quilt Top Pieced on a Western Auto Catalog and on Newspaper Dated December 22, 1956." [Field] (41) Fall 89, p. 76.
"Two Private Sermons from the Reverend Dr. Small . . . ." [Field] (41) Fall 89, p. 77-78.
"We Were Waking." [AmerPoR] (18:3) My-Je 89, p. 3.

3752. McQUILKIN, Rennie
"It's Been a Long Long Time." [MalR] (89) Wint 89, p. 76-78.
"Locksmith." [MalR] (89) Wint 89, p. 74-75.
"Riding the Tire." [Hudson] (42:1) Spr 89, p. 95-96.

3753. McRAY, Paul
"The Oblivion Festival." [BrooklynR] (5) 88, p. 29.
"A Part of You Is There." [SouthernPR] (29:1) Spr 89, p. 46-47.
"Several Ways to Poison Yourself." [PoetryNW] (30:1) Spr 89, p. 34-35.

3754. McROBERTS, Robert
"Jul 78." [KanQ] (21:1/2) Wint-Spr 89, p. 169.
"Shingle." [KanQ] (21:1/2) Wint-Spr 89, p. 168.

3755. McSEVENEY, Angela
"Janice." [Verse] (6:3) Wint 89, p. 45.

3756. McSWEEN, Harold B.
"Box Cakes and Ale." [HampSPR] Wint 89, p. 8.

3757. McVEAY, J. D.
"Camera World." [EmeraldCR] (1989) c1988, p. 133-134.

3758. MEAD, Jane
"Concerning That Prayer I Cannot Make." [VirQR] (65:2) Spr 89, p. 256-258.

"The Memory." [VirQR] (65:2) Spr 89, p. 259-261.
"My Father's Flesh." [VirQR] (65:2) Spr 89, p. 258-259.
3759. MEAD, Philip
"The Material Base." [Descant] (20:3/4, #66/67) Fall-Wint 89, p. 190-191.
3760. MEAD, S. E.
"Noah As a Musician." [BellArk] (5:4) Jl-Ag 89, p. 1.
3761. MEADE, Mary Ann
"The Day Room of Ward 72." [PoetC] (20:2) Wint 89, p. 16.
"Migration." [BallSUF] (30:4) Aut 89, p. 77.
"Working on a Back Ward." [PoetC] (20:2) Wint 89, p. 15.
3762. MEADOWS, Deborah
"Building a World" (Excerpt). [Os] (29) 89, p. 36.
"Why Carlos Hates Visitors." [BrooklynR] (6) 89, p. 47.
3763. MEANS, David
"Learning to Breathe" (for Geneve). [ChangingM] (20) Wint-Spr 89, p. 21.
3764. MEATS, Stephen
"Seeing My Father Again." [LaurelR] (23:2) Sum 89, p. 86.
3765. MECKEL, Christoph
"Hay Barge, in Summer Current, Touched" (tr. by Carol Bedwell). [MidAR] (9:1)
    89, p. 162.
"Jasnando's Nightsong" (Selections: 7 poems, tr. by John Linthicum). [LitR] (33:1)
    Fall 89, p. 106-109.
3766. MEDINA, Pablo
"Ana in Miami." [Footwork] 89, p. 67.
"The Apostate." [Americas] (17:2) Sum 89, p. 36.
"The Beginning." [Americas] (17:2) Sum 89, p. 37.
"The Daughter of Memory." [Americas] (17:2) Sum 89, p. 39.
"The Future." [US1] (22/23) Spr 89, p. 4.
"Giotto's Gift." [Footwork] 89, p. 66.
"Madame America." [Americas] (17:2) Sum 89, p. 33-35.
"Self-Portrait Brushing Teeth." [Footwork] 89, p. 67.
"True History." [US1] (22/23) Spr 89, p. 3.
"Why I Look Out Windows." [Americas] (17:2) Sum 89, p. 38.
"Woman Sleeping in the Morning." [Footwork] 89, p. 66.
3767. MEDLIN, John
"Dreaming of Rainstorms." [ChatR] (9:3) Spr 89, p. 46.
3768. MEHRHOFF, Charles (Charlie)
"(Awake and Shining)." [WindO] (52) Wint 89-90, p. 6.
"Blood from the Forest." [SmPd] (26:1, #75) Wint 89, p. 9.
"(Christmas Tree)." [WindO] (52) Wint 89-90, p. 6.
"Driving." [Mildred] (3:2) 89, p. 121.
"(From Salina)." [WindO] (52) Wint 89-90, p. 7.
"(Ghost Shirt)." [WindO] (52) Wint 89-90, p. 6.
"(Merton)." [WindO] (52) Wint 89-90, p. 7.
"No Buffalo." [SmPd] (26:1, #75) Wint 89, p. 8.
MEI, Yüan
    See YÜAN, Mei
3769. MEIER, Kay
"My Inheritance." [EngJ] (78:1) Ja 89, p. 92.
3770. MEIJI, Emperor
"Japanese Garden" (tr. by Graeme Wilson). [ConnPR] (8:1) 89, p. 19.
3771. MEINHOFF, Michael
"Ghost of the Spider World." [ChamLR] (3:1, #5) Fall 89, p. 52.
3772. MEINKE, Peter
"Dreaming Secretary." [Kalliope] (10:3) 88, p. 13.
"Fire in Fiesole." [GreensboroR] (47) Wint 89-90, p. 135-136.
"Greenhouse Statistics." [TampaR] (2) 89, p. 91-92.
"Happy Hour." [ApalQ] (31) 89, p. 42-43.
"The Housekeeper in London." [Kalliope] (10:3) 88, p. 12.
"Largo, Maestoso." [Kalliope] (10:3) 88, p. 14.
3773. MEISKEY, Elinor
"Snow." [DeKalbLAJ] (22:1/4) 89, p. 62.
3774. MELCHER, Michael
"I Am." [Contact] (9:53/54/55) Sum-Fall 89, p. 22.
"Surfaces." [Contact] (9:53/54/55) Sum-Fall 89, p. 21.
"The Young One." [Contact] (9:53/54/55) Sum-Fall 89, p. 20.

3775. MELDIU, Lazara
"Gentleman" (tr. by Beth Miller). [Jacaranda] (4:1) Spr-Sum 89, p. 70.
3776. MELEAGER
"Bored with the first hours of the day" (tr. by James Michie). [GrandS] (8:4) Sum
89, p. 80.
"I, goat-foot Pan" (tr. by James Michie). [GrandS] (8:4) Sum 89, p. 80.
3777. MELHEM, D. H.
"Gwendolyn Brooks." [ColR] (NS 16:1) Spr-Sum 89, p. 36.
3778. MELICK, Linda
"A Cry for Immortality." [HeavenB] (7) Wint 89, p. 3.
"Marlene's Collage." [HeavenB] (7) Wint 89, p. 3.
3779. MELNICK, David
"Men in Aïda" (Book II: Excerpt). [Screens] (1) 89, p. 181-183.
3780. MELNYCZUK, Askold
"De Tocqueville in Newark." [AntR] (47:4) Fall 89, p. 454.
"Goya's *Winter*" (for Beatra). [Pequod] (28/29/30) 89, p. 27-28.
"The Other Lives." [DenQ] (24:1) Sum 89, p. 53-54.
3781. MELTZER, David
"22 xii 81." [Talisman] (3) Fall 89, p. 80.
3782. MEMMOTT, David
"Intimations of the Subtle Body." [HeavenB] (6) Wint-Spr 89, p. 10.
"The Low Sun" (after a painting by Don Gray). [HeavenB] (6) Wint-Spr 89, p. 24.
"Slurring the Meaning of Praise." [Rampike] (6:2) 88, p. 55.
3783. MENARD-WARWICK, Julia
"The Knife of Not Knowing: Guatemala 1985." [Calyx] (12:1) Sum 89, p. 12-13.
3784. MENASHE, Samuel
"Awakening." [PartR] (56:3) Sum 89, p. 445.
"Forever and a Day." [PartR] (56:3) Sum 89, p. 446.
"Transplant." [PartR] (56:3) Sum 89, p. 445.
MÉNDEZ, Nilda Soto
See SOTO MÉNDEZ, Nilda
3785. MENDONSA, Michael
"Cloudy Sunday." [CarolQ] (41:2) Wint 89, p. 49.
"Ideogram in Alexandria." [AntR] (47:3) Sum 89, p. 332-333.
3786. MENDOZA, Walter
"Post Romantic." [AnthNEW] (1) 89, p. 17.
"Rebuff Rescue." [AnthNEW] (1) 89, p. 16.
"Sometimes I Pray." [AnthNEW] (1) 89, p. 16.
3787. MENEBROKER, Ann
"Sketching." [Bogg] (61) 89, p. 39.
3788. MENEFEE, Sarah
"The Blood about the Heart." [Acts] (10) 89, p. 1-11.
3789. MENG, Hao-jan
"Early Autumn" (tr. by Daniel Bryant). [LitR] (32:3) Spr 89, p. 398.
"I Am Not in Time to Say Farewell to Hsin Chih-o" (tr. by Daniel Bryant). [LitR]
(32:3) Spr 89, p. 398.
"Not Finding Yuan" (tr. by David Gordon). [LitR] (32:3) Spr 89, p. 383.
"On Reaching Ying on My Return Trip" (tr. by Daniel Bryant). [LitR] (32:3) Spr 89,
p. 398.
"Rising Late" (tr. by Anthony Piccione, Li Young Lee, and Carol Zhigong Chang).
[LitR] (32:3) Spr 89, p. 389.
3790. MENG, Lang
"Being Missing" (tr. by Dong Jiping). [Footwork] 89, p. 25.
3791. MENGHAM, Rod
"Neutrinos." [Pequod] (26/27) 89, p. 109-111.
MENOZZI, Wallis Wilde
See WILDE-MENOZZI, Wallis
3792. MENSCHING, Steffen
"Dreamlike Excursion with Rosa L." (tr. by Margitt Lehbert). [AmerPoR] (18:6)
N-D 89, p. 33.
"In Late Summer" (tr. by Margitt Lehbert). [AmerPoR] (18:6) N-D 89, p. 33.
3793. MENZIES, Ian
"Joe Snake." [AntigR] (77/78) Spr-Sum 89, p. 176.
"Through the Fan." [AntigR] (77/78) Spr-Sum 89, p. 175.
"To C.Z." [AntigR] (77/78) Spr-Sum 89, p. 174.

3794. MEREDITH, Joseph
"Teaching Goldfish." [Thrpny] (36) Wint 89, p. 24.
3795. MERRIAM, Eve
"Knowledge." [NewL] (55:3) Spr 89, p. 86-87.
3796. MERRILL, Christopher
"Breath" (for Stephen Dunn). [MissR] (18:1, #52) 89, p. 101-102.
"Country Inn." [Sonora] (17) Spr-Sum 89, p. 100.
"Early Poems" (variation on a theme by Donald Justice). [Chelsea] (48) 89, p. 135.
"Morning Song" (for Lisa). [QW] (28) Wint-Spr 89, p. 90.
"Signals." [MissR] (18:1, #52) 89, p. 103-104.
"Winterings" (for James Galvin). [QW] (28) Wint-Spr 89, p. 89.
3797. MERRILL, James
"Chinese Poem." [Antaeus] (62) Spr 89, p. 104.
"Introduction to the Media." [Margin] (9) 89, p. 13.
"Overdue Pilgrimage to Nova Scotia." [NewYorker] (65:36) 23 O 89, p. 50.
"Press Release." [GrandS] (9:1) Aut 89, p. 77-79.
"Quatrains for Pegasus." [Nat] (248:17) 1 My 89, p. 601.
3798. MERRILL, Karen
"Qingping Market, Guangzhou." [AntR] (47:1) Wint 89, p. 62.
3799. MERRILL, Stuart
"Days of Days." [Confr] (39/40) Fall 88-Wint 89, p. 41-42.
"The Demented King." [Confr] (39/40) Fall 88-Wint 89, p. 43-44.
"The Drowned." [Confr] (39/40) Fall 88-Wint 89, p. 42.
"The Lamentation of a King." [Confr] (39/40) Fall 88-Wint 89, p. 42.
"My Pain." [Confr] (39/40) Fall 88-Wint 89, p. 43.
3800. MERRITT, James W.
"The Suddenness of Symptoms." [JamesWR] (6:4) Sum 89, p. 11.
3801. MERSMAN, James
"Chilton County Woods: Revisiting the Garden in Ruins." [SouthernPR] (29:1) Spr
89, p. 45.
3802. MERWIN, W. S.
"The Black Jewel." [Field] (40) Spr 89, p. 84-85.
"Cinchona." [GrandS] (8:4) Sum 89, p. 60-65.
"Contemplating an Absent Scene" (tr. of Mahmoud Darwish, w. Lena Jayyusi).
[PoetryE] (27) Spr 89, p. 88-89.
"Exercise." [Field] (40) Spr 89, p. 82-83.
"Finally." [Field] (40) Spr 89, p. 81-82.
"Guests on the Sea" (tr. of Mahmoud Darwish, w. Lena Jayyusi). [PoetryE] (27)
Spr 89, p. 81-83.
"Homing Pigeons" (Excerpt, tr. of Mahmoud Darwish, w. Lena Jayyusi). [PoetryE]
(27) Spr 89, p. 94.
"I Am the Ill-Fated Lover" (tr. of Mahmoud Darwish, w. Lena Jayyusi). [PoetryE]
(27) Spr 89, p. 85-87.
"Inheritance." [GrandS] (8:4) Sum 89, p. 66-69.
"Manini." [Antaeus] (62) Spr 89, p. 105-107.
"The Morning Train." [NewYorker] (65:27) 21 Ag 89, p. 32.
"Mushrooms." [Atlantic] (264:1) Jl 89, p. 61.
"One Story." [Nat] (248:24) 19 Je 89, p. 859.
"Rimbaud's Piano." [GrandS] (9:1) Aut 89, p. 14-18.
"Touching the Tree." [OntR] (30) Spr-Sum 89, p. 67.
"You Will Carry the Butterfly's Burden" (tr. of Mahmoud Darwish, w. Lena
Jayyusi). [PoetryE] (27) Spr 89, p. 90-92.
3803. MERZLAK, Regina
"Phases." [SpiritSH] (54) Spr-Sum 89, p. 2.
3804. MESA, Lauren
"After Lovemaking." [PoetC] (21:1) Fall 89, p. 18-19.
"Camillia" (after Camille Corot's Little Reader, 1st Prize, 3rd Annual Contest).
[SoCoast] (6) Fall 88, p. 28-29.
"Cows." [Amelia] (5:3, #14) 89, p. 25-26.
"Crossroads." [SilverFR] (16) Spr 89, p. 7.
"The Dwelling Places of Grey" (for Sarah Christensen). [PoetC] (20:3) Spr 89, p.
10.
"The Hands of Old Men." [SoCoast] (6) Fall 88, p. 33.
"Honeymoon." [Amelia] (5:3, #14) 89, p. 24.
"Hunchback." [Amelia] (5:3, #14) 89, p. 25.
"Picking Blueberries." [SoCoast] (6) Fall 88, p. 54.

"Redwing Blackbird." [SoCoast] (7) Spr-Fall 89, p. 56.
"Sonora." [PoetC] (21:1) Fall 89, p. 16-17.
"What We Do with Sorrow." [SilverFR] (16) Spr 89, p. 6.
"Working Nights." [PoetC] (20:3) Spr 89, p. 9.
3805. MESMER, Sharon
"Fata Morgana." [NewAW] (5) Fall 89, p. 124.
3806. MESSBARGER, Rebecca
"Donne" (tr. of Carlo Villa). [Poetry] (155:1/2) O-N 89, p. 82.
"One Hundred of These Pages" (tr. of Carlo Villa). [Poetry] (155:1/2) O-N 89, p. 81.
"Overlappings" (tr. of Giampiero Neri). [Poetry] (155:1/2) O-N 89, p. 75, 77.
"Women" (tr. of Carlo Villa). [Poetry] (155:1/2) O-N 89, p. 83.
3807. MESSERLI, Douglas
"Along Without" (Selections: 2 poems). [Screens] (1) 89, p. 16-17.
"Mirror of Actual Notice." [Temblor] (9) 89, p. 131.
"Nones." [Talisman] (3) Fall 89, p. 54.
"Rather Than Exact." [Temblor] (9) 89, p. 132.
"Tour of Duty." [Conjunc] (13) 89, p. 240-241.
"Twas the Night." [Temblor] (9) 89, p. 131.
"What Saw Did Fell the Tree." [Conjunc] (13) 89, p. 239-240.
3808. MESTRE, Ramon A.
"After Antonin Artaud's Ce Matin" (For Gina Montaner). [LindLM] (8:2) Ap-Je 89, p. 22.
"After Ivan Goll's Je Porte Comme un Tatouage." [LindLM] (8:2) Ap-Je 89, p. 22.
"Self Portrait" (After Lucien Freud). [LindLM] (8:2) Ap-Je 89, p. 22.
3809. METRAS, Gary
"Concerto for Love: A Night Piece." [StoneC] (17:1/2) Fall-Wint 89-90, p. 26.
"A Sort of Plea." [PoetryE] (28) Fall 89, p. 73.
"Summer Morning." [PoetryE] (28) Fall 89, p. 74.
3810. MEYER, Douglas
"Awake." [JamesWR] (6:4) Sum 89, p. 1.
"The Test." [JamesWR] (6:4) Sum 89, p. 1.
3811. MEYER, William, Jr.
"On the Indian Nations Turnpike." [KanQ] (21:4) Fall 89, p. 75.
3812. MEZEY, Katalin
"Again and Again" (tr. by Nicholas Kolumban). [ArtfulD] (16/17) Fall 89, p. 74.
3813. Mhac an tSAOI, Máire
"The Hero's Sleep" (tr. by the author). [Trans] (22) Fall 89, p. 62-63.
"I Remember a Room on the Seaward Side" (tr. by Valentin Iremonger). [Trans] (22) Fall 89, p. 58.
"Mary Hogan's Quatrains" (tr. by James Gleasure). [Trans] (22) Fall 89, p. 59-61.
3814. MICHAEL, Christine
"Upon Leaving Ireland." [Vis] (29) 89, p. 18.
3815. MICHAELSON, Caren Lee
"Damn Near." [PaintedB] (37) 89, p. 21.
3816. MICHAUX, Henri
"Les Ravagés" (Selections: 2, 4, 7, 12, 21, tr. by David Ball). [MassR] (30:3) Aut 89, p. 396-398.
3817. MICHEAELS, Cathleen
"Water and Light, a Baptism." [SouthernPR] (29:1) Spr 89, p. 55.
MICHELE, Mary di
See Di MICHELE, Mary
3818. MICHELINE, Jack
"Prisoners Song" (New York City, 1956). [AlphaBS] (6) Wint 89-90, p. 22.
3819. MICHELSON, Peter
"Mixed Frequencies in the Golden West Saloon." [CinPR] (19) Spr 89, p. 43.
3820. MICHELSON, Richard
"I Wish He Had Died Then, His Body." [NegC] (9:2) 89, p. 62.
3821. MICHIE, James
"Androtion built me to give room" (tr. from the anonymous Greek). [GrandS] (8:4) Sum 89, p. 83.
"Armed against Love, reason my shield" (tr. of Rufinus). [GrandS] (8:4) Sum 89, p. 84.
"Aster" (tr. of Plato). [GrandS] (8:4) Sum 89, p. 79.
"Aster, my star, you raise" (tr. of Plato). [GrandS] (8:4) Sum 89, p. 79.
"Bored with the first hours of the day" (tr. of Meleager). [GrandS] (8:4) Sum 89, p.

80.
"Daphnis, the boy with the fair skin" (tr. of Theocritus). [GrandS] (8:4) Sum 89, p. 80.
"Everywhere the sea is the sea" (tr. of Antipater of Thessalonica). [GrandS] (8:4) Sum 89, p. 81.
"For the Spartan Dead at Thermopylae" (tr. of Simonides). [GrandS] (8:4) Sum 89, p. 79.
"Fortune and Hope, a long goodbye" (tr. from the anonymous Greek). [GrandS] (8:4) Sum 89, p. 85.
"Here, a small Priapus, I stand" (tr. of Archias). [GrandS] (8:4) Sum 89, p. 82.
"I, goat-foot Pan" (tr. of Meleager). [GrandS] (8:4) Sum 89, p. 80.
"I, Lais, whose proud beauty" (tr. from the anonymous Greek). [GrandS] (8:4) Sum 89, p. 81.
"I sang it often, and I'll go on" (tr. of Julianus of Egypt). [GrandS] (8:4) Sum 89, p. 84.
"If you who use this path catch sight" (tr. from the anonymous Greek). [GrandS] (8:4) Sum 89, p. 83.
"In Arcadia once, in a three-mile race" (tr. of Nicarchus). [GrandS] (8:4) Sum 89, p. 83.
"Like a heard of swine, we're all fed under guard" (tr. of Palladas). [GrandS] (8:4) Sum 89, p. 83.
"My name is -- Who cares? -- My birthplace" (tr. of Paulus Silentiarius). [GrandS] (8:4) Sum 89, p. 85.
"Now like a vine supported on a stake" (tr. of Leonidas of Tarentum). [GrandS] (8:4) Sum 89, p. 80.
"O greedy boatman of the Styx" (tr. of Bianor). [GrandS] (8:4) Sum 89, p. 81.
"Rose with the roses, tell me, what do you sell?" (tr. of Dionysius). [GrandS] (8:4) Sum 89, p. 81.
"So, bee-eating swallow with the chattering tongue" (tr. of Euenus). [GrandS] (8:4) Sum 89, p. 82.
"Three times, dear lamp, she swore here by your fire" (tr. of Asclepiades). [GrandS] (8:4) Sum 89, p. 79.
"To a Skeptic Philosopher" (tr. of Julianus of Egypt). [GrandS] (8:4) Sum 89, p. 84.
"To a Worthless Magistrate" (tr. from the anonymous Greek). [GrandS] (8:4) Sum 89, p. 84.
"To you, Bacchus, Xenophon the sot" (tr. of Eratosthenes). [GrandS] (8:4) Sum 89, p. 85.
"The Vine Speaks" (tr. of Euenus). [GrandS] (8:4) Sum 89, p. 82.
3822. MIDDLETON, Christopher
"Notes on the 1860s" (tr. of Lars Gustafsson). [Field] (40) Spr 89, p. 70-71.
"Psalm 9" (tr. of Mahmoud Darwish, w. Lena Jayyusi). [PoetryE] (27) Spr 89, p. 78.
"To Abu Bakr ben Ammar Going to Silves" (tr. of Abu 'l-Kasim Mohammed Ibn-Abbad Al-Mutamid, based on Emilio Garcfa Gómez's Spanish version). [SouthwR] (74:2) Spr 89, p. 225-226.
3823. MIDDLETON, Peter
"Justification." [Aerial] (5) 89, p. 128-129.
"Typical." [Aerial] (5) 89, p. 130-131.
3824. MIDDLETON, Stephen
"Target." [Bogg] (61) 89, p. 14.
3825. MIEDZYRZECKI, Artur
"Fate the Clerk Lays Down a New Set of By-Laws" (tr. by Stanislaw Baranczak and Clare Cavanagh). [PartR] (56:2) Spr 89, p. 281.
"The Reason of Existence" (tr. by Stanislaw Baranczak and Clare Cavanah). [Trans] (21) Spr 89, p. 40-41.
"The War of Nerves" (tr. by Stanislaw Baranczak and Clare Cavanagh). [PartR] (56:2) Spr 89, p. 282.
3826. MIELE, Frank
"A Ghost Among the Shadows." [Plain] (10:1) 89, p. 16-17.
"Running Away from the Circus." [HampSPR] Wint 89, p. 35.
MIELES, Edgardo Nieves
See NIEVES MIELES, Edgardo
3827. MIGONE, Christof
"23 Theories of One Second." [Rampike] (6:3) 88, p. 70.

3828. MIKITA, Nancy
"Proper Conditions for the Practice of Adultery." [HampSPR] Wint 89, p. 36-37.
3829. MIKKELSEN, Robert S.
"Agnostic at Sixty." [WeberS] (6:1) Spr 89, p. 30-32.
"Sunward." [WeberS] (6:1) Spr 89, p. 30.
"Virgin Stallion." [WeberS] (6:1) Spr 89, p. 32-34.
MILANÉS, Cecilia Rodriguez
See RODRIGUEZ MILANÉS, Cecilia
3830. MILBY, June
"Affirmation." [Pembroke] (21) 89, p. 137.
"Hunting the Wild Fish" (a morel mushroom which grows two weeks in April in
Kentucky and Indiana). [Pembroke] (21) 89, p. 135-136.
"Juggler." [Pembroke] (21) 89, p. 136-137.
3831. MILES, Jeff
"Bicorneal Transplant." [SouthernPR] (29:1) Spr 89, p. 64-65.
"Isabel." [GreensboroR] (46) Sum 89, p. 207.
3832. MILES, Judi Kiefer
"Life Is." [CapeR] (24:2) Fall 89, p. 22.
3833. MILES, Marti
"Breaking Wishbones with Myself." [SouthernPR] (29:1) Spr 89, p. 35.
3834. MILEY, James D.
"Killing the Pig." [MidwQ] (30:2) Wint 89, p. 194-195.
3835. MILIAUSKAITE, Nijole
"Children's Taste" (tr. by Jonas Zdanys). [Field] (40) Spr 89, p. 22.
"A cold evening, swollen painful" (tr. by Jonas Zdanys). [Field] (40) Spr 89, p. 20.
"Every spring as the meadows blossom" (tr. by Jonas Zdanys). [Field] (40) Spr 89,
p. 21.
"In the damp places" (tr. by Jonas Zdanys). [Field] (40) Spr 89, p. 22-23.
"Look, then: how big this bag is on my back" (tr. by Jonas Zdanys). [Field] (40) Spr
89, p. 20-21.
"On winter nights, when my grandmother went to work" (tr. by Jonas Zdanys).
[Field] (40) Spr 89, p. 21.
"These are lilacs" (tr. by Jonas Zdanys). [Field] (40) Spr 89, p. 19.
"You who led the way into the forest's cool shadows" (tr. by Jonas Zdanys). [Field]
(40) Spr 89, p. 19.
3836. MILJKOVIC, Branko
"Chronicle" (tr. by Peter Liotta). [ColR] (NS 16:1) Spr-Sum 89, p. 88.
3837. MILLER, A. McA.
"Dream Session 64: the Home Place." [SouthernPR] (29:1) Spr 89, p. 43-44.
3838. MILLER, Aine
"Basement Mother." [Vis] (29) 89, p. 20.
"Kitchening Christmas." [Vis] (29) 89, p. 20.
3839. MILLER, B. J.
"Dear Ron." [EmeraldCR] (1989) c1988, inside front cover.
"The Widow." [EmeraldCR] (1989) c1988, p. 120.
3840. MILLER, Beth
"Gentleman" (tr. of Lazara Meldiu). [Jacaranda] (4:1) Spr-Sum 89, p. 70.
"Self-Portrait" (tr. of Rosario Castellanos). [Jacaranda] (4:1) Spr-Sum 89, p. 68-69.
3841. MILLER, Derek
"#237." [HangL] (54) 89, p. 23-25.
"#239." [HangL] (54) 89, p. 26-27.
"Cherry Street." [HangL] (54) 89, p. 22.
"The Hands." [HangL] (54) 89, p. 21.
3842. MILLER, E. Ethelbert
"1962: My Brother Richard Enters the Monastery." [Callaloo] (12:4, #41) Fall 89, p.
623.
"Faith: My Brother Richard Returns Home from the Monastery." [Callaloo] (12:4,
#41) Fall 89, p. 624.
3843. MILLER, Elizabeth Gamble
"A Hundred and Fifty Thousand Degrees Below Zero" (tr. of Carlos Ernesto
Garcia). [MidAR] (9:2) 89, p. 168.
"The Summer of 80 and Five" (tr. of Carlos Ernesto Garcia). [MidAR] (9:2) 89, p.
170.
"A Tribute" (tr. of Carlos Ernesto Garcia). [MidAR] (9:2) 89, p. 169.
3844. MILLER, Errol
"The Assemblying." [RiverC] (9:1) Spr 89, p. 83.

"The Astounded Sister" (for Sylvia Plath, a Plainsongs Award Poem). [Plain] (9:2)
    Wint 89, p. 4.
"Downstream." [Plain] (9:3) Spr 89, p. 14-15.
"The Fool in the Forest." [Caliban] (6) 89, p. 106-109.
"Hot Springs, 1973." [RagMag] (7:1) 89, p. 39.
"The Man with the Paper Heart." [CapeR] (24:2) Fall 89, p. 43.
"Sanduskin." [Lactuca] (13) N 89, p. 19.
"Sonavax." [Lactuca] (13) N 89, p. 19.
"The Texas Waltz." [WritersF] (15) Fall 89, p. 113-114.
"Things in Their Places." [Interim] (8:2) Fall 89, p. 14.
"West Monroe, Louisiana, 1972." [RagMag] (7:1) 89, p. 38.
3845. MILLER, Frank
    "3 A.M." [Lactuca] (13) N 89, p. 39.
3846. MILLER, Greg
    "The Harrow." [Thrpny] (36) Wint 89, p. 18.
3847. MILLER, Heather Ross
    "Antigone, Miss World!" [SouthernPR] (29:2) Fall 89, p. 19-20.
    "Dracula's Bride." [LaurelR] (23:2) Sum 89, p. 98.
    "In Danger." [LaurelR] (23:2) Sum 89, p. 95.
    "The Park." [GreensboroR] (46) Sum 89, p. 119.
    "Playing Dress-Up." [LaurelR] (23:2) Sum 89, p. 95-96.
    "Pregnant." [Shen] (39:2) Sum 89, p. 92-93.
    "Total Eclipse." [GreensboroR] (46) Sum 89, p. 117-118.
    "Twila Jo and the Wrestler." [LaurelR] (23:2) Sum 89, p. 97.
3848. MILLER, Hugh
    "Post-Independence-Day Theology, 4 July 1982" (for Marilyn & Nori). [AntigR]
        (77/78) Spr-Sum 89, p. 142-143.
3849. MILLER, James A.
    "For a Celebration" (18 June 1988). [BellArk] (5:1) Ja-F 89, p. 5.
    "This Life, Grandfather, Resurrection." [BellArk] (5:1) Ja-F 89, p. 20.
3850. MILLER, Jane
    "The Butane Egg." [WillowS] (23) Wint 89, p. 77-78.
    "Cast from Heaven." [NewL] (56:2/3) Wint 89-Spr 90, p. 181-182.
    "Figure." [DenQ] (23:3/4) Wint-Spr 89, p. 30-31.
    "Foundered Star." [PoetryE] (28) Fall 89, p. 139-140.
    "Fragments for My Voyeuristic Biographer." [NewL] (56:2/3) Wint 89-Spr 90, p.
        177.
    "Lucky Pierre's." [WillowS] (23) Wint 89, p. 75-76.
    "New Body" (Poetry Chapbook: 9 poems). [BlackWR] (15:2) Spr 89, p. 49-64.
    "Sycamore Mall." [NewL] (56:2/3) Wint 89-Spr 90, p. 179-181.
    "Troika for Lovers." [NewL] (56:2/3) Wint 89-Spr 90, p. 178-179.
    "Venus de Milo." [BlackWR] (15:2) Spr 89, p. 146-147.
3851. MILLER, Julie
    "Number Nine Road." [PoetryNW] (30:4) Wint 89-90, p. 19-20.
3852. MILLER, Kevin
    "Ribbons." [CrabCR] (6:1) 89, p. 10.
3853. MILLER, Leslie A. (Leslie Adrienne)
    "Sick." [HeliconN] (20) 89, p. 29.
    "Sleeping on the Edge of the Bed." [SouthernPR] (29:2) Fall 89, p. 61-62.
    "What I Know About Music." [MissouriR] (12:1) 89, p. 220-221.
3854. MILLER, Mark
    "9 Notions of Night." [AntigR] (77/78) Spr-Sum 89, p. 188-189.
    "Leaves." [AntigR] (77/78) Spr-Sum 89, p. 190.
3855. MILLER, Marlene
    "Empty Places." [FreeL] (2) Sum 89, p. 32.
    "Heat Lightning." [OxfordM] (5:1) Spr-Sum 89, p. 18.
    "Quail Eggs." [FreeL] (2) Sum 89, p. 31.
3856. MILLER, Michael
    "The Return of Song." [SouthernPR] (29:1) Spr 89, p. 71.
3857. MILLER, O. Victor, Jr.,
    "Crow on Rye." [DeKalbLAJ] (22:1/4) 89, p. 63.
3858. MILLER, Patricia
    "Dead End Street." [Thrpny] (36) Wint 89, p. 32.
3859. MILLER, Patricia Cleary
    "Marcia." [HeliconN] (20) 89, p. 86.

3860. MILLER, Philip
"After the Fall." [StoneC] (17:1/2) Fall-Wint 89-90, p. 54.
"A Bargain Struck." [Poem] (62) N 89, p. 20.
"The Dark" (for Nancy). [KanQ] (21:3) Sum 89, p. 39.
"The Flood of '51." [Wind] (19:65) 89, p. 19.
"Gritting" (a Plainsongs Award Poem). [Plain] (9:2) Wint 89, p. 18.
"How Things Are" (a Plainsongs Award Poem). [Plain] (9:2) Wint 89, p. 18.
"If Endings Were Beginnings." [Poem] (62) N 89, p. 19.
"Leda at the Bar." [KanQ] (21:3) Sum 89, p. 38.
"Only Autumn." [Poem] (62) N 89, p. 18.
"Ore." [Plain] (9:3) Spr 89, p. 31.
"Skin." [SmPd] (26:2 #76) Spr 89, p. 23.
3861. MILLER, Raeburn
"Detente." [GrahamHR] (12) Spr 89, p. 70.
"Out of Mind." [NoDaQ] (57:4) Fall 89, p. 90.
"Word Afterward." [Nimrod] (33:1) Fall-Wint 89, p. 92.
3862. MILLER, Robert D.
"Public Showers." [Amelia] (5:3, #14) 89, p. 20.
3863. MILLER, Theresa W.
"Moving." [GreensboroR] (46) Sum 89, p. 154.
3864. MILLER, Tyrus
"Charmed." [Sequoia] (32:2) Wint-Spr 89, p. 54.
"Earthworks" (Selections: 3 poems). [Screens] (1) 89, p. 139-140.
"Earthworks: Mirror Displacement Series" (Selections: 2 poems). [Screens] (1) 89,
p. 141-142.
3865. MILLER, William
"Black Communists in Alabama, 1933." [Verse] (6:3) Wint 89, p. 65.
"Elpenor." [LaurelR] (23:1) Wint 89, p. 93-94.
"Grammar School Photo, 1965." [PoetC] (20:3) Spr 89, p. 27-28.
"The Moment." [SouthernPR] (29:2) Fall 89, p. 8.
"Noah's Wife." [HolCrit] (26:2) Ap 89, p. 14.
"Old Maps." [Poem] (62) N 89, p. 14-15.
"Rabbit Tobacco." [Poem] (62) N 89, p. 13.
"Sitting Up with the Dead." [LaurelR] (23:1) Wint 89, p. 92-93.
"Third Shift." [FloridaR] (16:2/3) Fall-Wint 89, p. 214-215.
"The Torturer's House." [HampSPR] Wint 89, p. 16.
3866. MILLER-DUGGAN, Devon
"Chivalry." [YellowS] (29) Spr 89, p. 29.
"Our Lady of the Snows." [YellowS] (29) Spr 89, p. 37.
3867. MILLETT, John
"The Gospel According to Seaton Callaghan." [Vis] (29) 89, p. 43-46.
"Martha Aging." [Vis] (30) 89, p. 54.
"Young Donald and a Ball of Dough." [Vis] (30) 89, p. 53-54.
3868. MILLIGAN, Bryce
"Looking at Life with Every Eye." [HighP] (4:2) Fall 89, p. 76-77.
3869. MILLIS, Christopher
"Insomnia on a Summer Night" (tr. of Umberto Saba). [MissouriR] (12:1) 89, p.
53.
"Sapling" (tr. of Umberto Saba). [MissouriR] (12:1) 89, p. 54.
"Trieste" (tr. of Umberto Saba). [MissouriR] (12:1) 89, p. 55.
3870. MILLS, George
"By the Cemetery" (Second Prize). [StoneC] (17:1/2) Fall-Wint 89-90, p. prelim. p.
2.
"First Love." [StoneC] (16:3/4) Spr-Sum 89, p. 56.
"Gandhi Blesses His Assassin." [StoneC] (16:3/4) Spr-Sum 89, p. 67.
"The Recognizable." [StoneC] (16:3/4) Spr-Sum 89, p. 57.
3871. MILLS, Joe
"Tom's Fence and These Two Trees." [Plain] (9:2) Wint 89, p. 24.
3872. MILLS, Maureen W.
"The Baths of Herculaneum" (August 25, A. D. 79). [BallSUF] (30:4) Aut 89, p.
37.
"Fragment" (after reading the *Carmina Archilochi*). [BallSUF] (30:4) Aut 89, p. 35.
3873. MILLS, Ralph J., Jr.
"Sky Of." [Northeast] (ser. 5:1) Wint 89-90, p. 22.
3874. MILLS, Sparling
"Death in Windsor." [Quarry] (38:1) Wint 89, p. 51.

"Drinking *Bell's*." [Quarry] (38:1) Wint 89, p. 50.
"Goldilocks." [Quarry] (38:1) Wint 89, p. 49.
"Ken." [AntigR] (77/78) Spr-Sum 89, p. 56.
"Rock-a-Bye." [AntigR] (77/78) Spr-Sum 89, p. 56.
3875. MILNER, Ian
"Air Show" (tr. of Josef Hanzlik, w. Jarmila Milner). [Stand] (30:1) Wint 88-89, p. 52-55.
"Circus" (tr. of Jana Stroblová, w. Jarmila Milner). [Verse] (6:2) Je 89, p. 60.
"Drinking Coffee" (tr. of Sylva Fischerová, w. Jarmila Milner). [Verse] (6:1) Mr 89, p. 37.
"Evening" (tr. of Vladimír Holan, w. Jarmila Milner). [Verse] (6:2) Je 89, p. 62.
"High-Flats and TV Screens" (tr. of Josef Simon, w. Jarmila Milner). [Verse] (6:2) Je 89, p. 63.
"Hour of the Wolf" (tr. of Ivo Smoldas, w. Jarmila Milner). [Verse] (6:2) Je 89, p. 63.
"Not that we didn't expect it" (tr. of Sylva Fischerová, w. Jarmila Milner). [Verse] (6:1) Mr 89, p. 36.
"The Pripet Marshes" (tr. of Sylva Fischerová, w. Jarmila Milner). [Verse] (6:2) Je 89, p. 64.
"The Slaughterhouse" (tr. of Jana Stroblová, w. Jarmila Milner). [Verse] (6:2) Je 89, p. 61.
"To Whom?" (tr. of Vladimír Holan, w. Jarmila Milner). [Verse] (6:2) Je 89, p. 62.
3876. MILNER, Jarmila
"Air Show" (tr. of Josef Hanzlik, w. Ian Milner). [Stand] (30:1) Wint 88-89, p. 52-55.
"Circus" (tr. of Jana Stroblová, w. Ian Milner). [Verse] (6:2) Je 89, p. 60.
"Drinking Coffee" (tr. of Sylva Fischerová, w. Ian Milner). [Verse] (6:1) Mr 89, p. 37.
"Evening" (tr. of Vladimír Holan, w. Ian Milner). [Verse] (6:2) Je 89, p. 62.
"High-Flats and TV Screens" (tr. of Josef Simon, w. Ian Milner). [Verse] (6:2) Je 89, p. 63.
"Hour of the Wolf" (tr. of Ivo Smoldas, w. Ian Milner). [Verse] (6:2) Je 89, p. 63.
"Not that we didn't expect it" (tr. of Sylva Fischerová, w. Ian Milner). [Verse] (6:1) Mr 89, p. 36.
"The Pripet Marshes" (tr. of Sylva Fischerová, w. Ian Milner). [Verse] (6:2) Je 89, p. 64.
"The Slaughterhouse" (tr. of Jana Stroblová, w. Ian Milner). [Verse] (6:2) Je 89, p. 61.
"To Whom?" (tr. of Vladimír Holan, w. Ian Milner). [Verse] (6:2) Je 89, p. 62.
3877. MILOSZ, Czeslaw
"Antigone" (fragment in remembrance of the Hungarian workers, students and soldiers, 1949, tr. by Lenora Ledwon). [TriQ] (74) Wint 89, p. 217-220.
"Incarnated" (tr. by the author and Robert Hass). [NewYorker] (65:44) 18 D 89, p. 40.
"Poems on My Father and My Mother" (15 poems, tr. of Anna Swir, w. Leonard Nathan). [AmerPoR] (18:1) Ja-F 89, p. 23-25.
"Song on Porcelain." [TriQ] (76) Fall 89, p. 197-198.
"The Thistle, the Nettle" (tr. by the author and Robert Hass). [NewYorker] (65:41) 27 N 89, p. 46.
3878. MINCZESKI, John
"Drunk at the Tennis Court." [AnotherCM] (19) 89, p. 145-146.
3879. MINER, Judy
"I am homesick" (tr. of Bronislava Volkova, w. the author). [InterPR] (15:2) Fall 89, p. 21.
3880. MINER, Ken
"Television." [KanQ] (21:1/2) Wint-Spr 89, p. 231.
3881. MINHINNICK, Robert
"The Coast." [NoDaQ] (57:2) Spr 89, insert p. 71.
"Eelers." [NoDaQ] (57:2) Spr 89, insert p. 70.
3882. MINISH, Geoffrey
"Elegy." [Verse] (6:3) Wint 89, p. 892.
3883. MINTON, Helena
"For the Motorcycle Riders." [WestB] (25) 89, p. 81-82.
"The Topaz." [BelPoJ] (39:4) Sum 89, p. 8-9.
"What Saltpeter Meant." [BelPoJ] (39:4) Sum 89, p. 6-7.

3884. MIRON, Gaston
"Felicite" (tr. by Dennis Egan). [Vis] (30) 89, p. 19.
3885. MIRRIAM-GOLDBERG, Caryn
"Between Air and Water." [Nimrod] (33:1) Fall-Wint 89, p. 87-88.
"Hagar on the Mountain." [SoDakR] (27:3) Aut 89, p. 105.
"The Road Behind My Body." [Nimrod] (33:1) Fall-Wint 89, p. 89.
3886. MIRSKIN, Jerry
"Adam & Eve." [Ascent] (14:3) 89, p. 14.
"Thirty." [MSS] (6:3) 89, p. 41.
"The Tree." [Ascent] (14:3) 89, p. 15.
3887. MIRZE, Esra
"To Hell with Saul's Soul" (tr. of Can Yücel). [Talisman] (3) Fall 89, p. 114-115.
3888. MISANCHUK, Melanie
"Crayons." [AntigR] (77/78) Spr-Sum 89, p. 171.
MISHA
     See CHOCHOLAK, Misha
3889. MISKOWSKI, Mike
"The Counterclockwise." [CentralP] (15) Spr 89, p. 143.
3890. MISTRAL, Gabriela
"Palabras Serenas." [Mairena] (11:27) 89, p. 93.
3891. MITCHELL, Hugh
"Praise." [StoneC] (16:3/4) Spr-Sum 89, p. 32.
3892. MITCHELL, Karen L.
"For John T. Allen, or, When a Man Can't Get to the Next Corner." [Ploughs]
     (15:4) Wint 89-90, p. 141-142.
"On the Anniversary of Your Death." [Ploughs] (15:4) Wint 89-90, p. 139-140.
3893. MITCHELL, Mary M.
"To the Poet." [EngJ] (78:8) D 89, p. 90.
3894. MITCHELL, Roger
"Adam Writing Home." [AmerPoR] (18:2) Mr-Ap 89, p. 8.
"At the Wayne County Courthouse." [Ploughs] (15:1) 89, p. 82.
"Birth." [AmerPoR] (18:2) Mr-Ap 89, p. 8.
"Desert." [PoetryNW] (30:2) Sum 89, p. 8-9.
"It Does It." [AmerPoR] (18:2) Mr-Ap 89, p. 8.
"Like a Sign." [AmerPoR] (18:2) Mr-Ap 89, p. 8.
"Listening." [Ploughs] (15:1) 89, p. 80-81.
"Loon." [OhioR] (43) 89, p. 38-39.
"My Dog, My Heart." [PoetryNW] (30:2) Sum 89, p. 10.
"No Water." [AmerPoR] (18:2) Mr-Ap 89, p. 8.
"Right There in the Parking Lot." [AmerPoR] (18:2) Mr-Ap 89, p. 8.
"Sky." [PoetryNW] (30:2) Sum 89, p. 7-8.
"Truth of the Matter." [PoetryNW] (30:2) Sum 89, p. 9-10.
"The Word for Everything." [AntR] (47:1) Wint 89, p. 73.
3895. MITCHELL, Stephen
"The Fishmonger's Stall" (Naples, tr. of Rainer Maria Rilke). [GrandS] (9:1) Aut
     89, p. 116-117.
"For Veronika Erdmann" (tr. of Rainer Maria Rilke). [ParisR] (31:111) Sum 89, p.
     270.
"Huang-Po" (from "Parables and Portraits"). [Zyzzyva] (5:3, #19) Fall 89, p. 60.
"Ein Leben" (tr. of Dan Pagis). [NewYorker] (65:7) 3 Ap 89, p. 85.
"Little Tear-Vase" (tr. of Rainer Maria Rilke). [ParisR] (31:111) Sum 89, p. 253.
"A Moment at the Louvre" (tr. of Dan Pagis). [NewYorker] (65:13) 15 My 89, p.
     42.
"Spinoza." [NewYorker] (65:25) 7 Ag 89, p. 36.
"Tao-Chi." [Nat] (249:17) 20 N 89, p. 608.
3896. MITCHELL, Susan
"Big Red Fish." [Ploughs] (15:1) 89, p. 83-85.
"Havana Birth." [Ploughs] (15:1) 89, p. 86-88.
3897. MITCHELL-FOUST, Michelle
"Summer, Under the Pavilion." [AntR] (47:4) Fall 89, p. 462.
3898. MITCHNER, Gary
"Benedick's Complaints: *Much Ado About Nothing*." [WestHR] (43:4) Wint 89, p.
     303.
3899. MITRA, Premendra
"The Touch" (tr. by Monish R. Chatterjee). [InterPR] (15:2) Fall 89, p. 87.

3900. MITRA, Swapna
"The Diamond of Character" (tr. of Kabita Sinha, w. Carolyne Wright). [Trans] (21)
Spr 89, p. 153.
"The Last Door's Name Is Sorrow" (tr. of Kabita Sinha, w. Carolyne Wright).
[Trans] (21) Spr 89, p. 151-152.
3901. MIZER, Ray
"Confessions, Tourist Class." [BellArk] (5:1) Ja-F 89, p. 5.
"Preservation Hall: On the Road." [BellArk] (5:4) Jl-Ag 89, p. 4.
"Test Question." [BellArk] (5:4) Jl-Ag 89, p. 7.
"There Is no Frigate" (-- Emily Dickinson). [BellArk] (5:5) S-O 89, p. 5.
"Windfall." [BellArk] (5:4) Jl-Ag 89, p. 10.
3902. MIZUMOTO, Gary
"Journeys." [SoCoast] (7) Spr-Fall 89, p. 6-7.
"Winter Garden" (To Lynne). [SoCoast] (7) Spr-Fall 89, p. 8.
3903. MOBILIO, Albert
"Repeated Talk." [Talisman] (3) Fall 89, p. 81.
3904. MOCARSKI, Tim
"Man Wearing a Baseball Hat." [EngJ] (78:7) N 89, p. 92.
3905. MOCZULSKI, Leszek A.
"Report" (tr. by Stanislaw Baranczak and Clare Cavanah). [Trans] (21) Spr 89, p.
66.
3906. MOE, H. D.
"Glass Pumpkins." [Sequoia] (33:1) Sum 89, p. 39.
3907. MOELLER, Eileen
"St. Vitus' Disease: Effie's Story." [Footwork] 89, p. 49.
3908. MOEN, Irvin
"Beginnings." [SoCoast] (6) Fall 88, p. 4-5.
"Men." [SoCoast] (6) Fall 88, p. 25.
"Night." [WestB] (24) 89, p. 47.
"Stone Road." [SoCoast] (6) Fall 88, p. 41.
MOEN, Irving
See MOEN, Irvin
3909. MOFFET, Penelope
"Gravitations" (for Janet Keller). [MissouriR] (12:1) 89, p. 154-155.
"In the Field." [FreeL] (2) Sum 89, p. 18.
3910. MOHR, Bill
"Elegy for Roy Orbison." [Sonora] (17) Spr-Sum 89, p. 21.
"Uncertainty." [Sonora] (17) Spr-Sum 89, p. 22.
3911. MOLDAW, Carol
"The Call." [Agni] (28) 89, p. 243.
"The Crossroads" (for Julie). [Agni] (28) 89, p. 244.
MOLEN, Robert vander
See VanderMOLEN, Robert
3912. MOLINA LOPEZ, María S.
"El caminante siembra sus pasos" (tr. of Daniel Leduc). [Mairena] (11:27) 89, p. 77.
3913. MOLINARO, Ursule
"The Desert Poem." [Hawai'iR] (13:1, #25) Spr 89, p. 1.
3914. MOLLOHAN, Terrie
"Men's Wiles: What We Teach Each Ohter." [SlipS] (9) 89, p. 47-48.
"Night People." [SlipS] (9) 89, p. 47.
3915. MOLNAR, Michael
"Momma Washed the Floor" (Excerpt, tr. of Lev Rubinshtein). [MichQR] (28:4) Fall
89, p. 739-740.
"Mudflats" (tr. of Aleksei Parshchikov). [MichQR] (28:4) Fall 89, p. 727.
"Poems on Maps" (Excerpt, tr. of Viktor Krivulin). [MichQR] (28:4) Fall 89, p.
738.
3916. MOLTON, Warren Lane
"First Calling." [ChrC] (106:18) My 24-31, 89, p. 551.
3917. MONAGHAN, Patricia
"Garland Sunday." [Vis] (29) 89, p. 25.
3918. MONROE, Melissa
"The Sword" (tr. of Ernst Herbeck). [PartR] (56:1) Wint 89, p. 115.
3919. MONTAGUE, John
"A Ballad for Berryman." [NoDaQ] (57:1) Wint 89, p. 112.
"The Broken Doll" (tr. of Nuala Ni Dhomhnaill). [Trans] (22) Fall 89, p. 146.
"Mount Eagle" (Selections: 4 poems). [OntR] (30) Spr-Sum 89, p. 57-63.

3920. MONTALE, Eugenio
"20 Gennaio o 30 Anni." [Poetry] (155:1/2) O-N 89, p. 2.
"At This Point" (tr. by William Arrowsmith). [AmerPoR] (18:4) Jl-Ag 89, p. 3.
"La Bufera e Altro" (Selections: 2 poems). [Poetry] (155:1/2) O-N 89, p. 4.-8.
"Changing Color" (tr. by William Arrowsmith). [AmerPoR] (18:4) Jl-Ag 89, p. 4.
"The Diver" (tr. by William Arrowsmith). [AmerPoR] (18:4) Jl-Ag 89, p. 3.
"E Solo un Vizio." [Poetry] (155:1/2) O-N 89, p. 1.
"Ex Abrupto" (in Italian). [Poetry] (155:1/2) O-N 89, p. 2.
"Ex Abrupto" (tr. by Jonathan Galassi). [Poetry] (155:1/2) O-N 89, p. 2.
"Hiding Places" (tr. by William Arrowsmith). [AmerPoR] (18:4) Jl-Ag 89, p. 3.
"Imitation of Thunder" (tr. by William Arrowsmith). [AmerPoR] (18:4) Jl-Ag 89, p. 4.
"The Imponderable" (tr. by William Arrowsmith). [AmerPoR] (18:4) Jl-Ag 89, p. 3.
"It's Only an Error" (tr. by Jonathan Galassi). [Poetry] (155:1/2) O-N 89, p. 1.
"January 20 or Age 30" (tr. by Jonathan Galassi). [Poetry] (155:1/2) O-N 89, p. 2.
"The Storm and Other Things" (Selections: 5 poems, tr. by Jonathan Galassi). [Poetry] (155:1/2) O-N 89, p. 5-13.
MONTAÑEZ, Jaime Marcano
See MARCANO MONTAÑEZ, Jaime
3921. MONTGOMERY, George
"Leo, Abe, and Louie" (January 19, 1987). [MoodySI] (20/21) Spr 89, p. 43.
3922. MOODIE, Scott
"The Stained Glass Window." [Rampike] (6:2) 88, p. 73.
3923. MOODY, Rodger
"Duty" (Johnston Atoll, 1970). [WindO] (52) Wint 89-90, p. 18.
"Unbending Intent." [SouthernPR] (29:2) Fall 89, p. 68-69.
"Winter in Indiana." [WindO] (52) Wint 89-90, p. 17.
3924. MOOLTEN, David
"At the Marine Corps War Memorial." [Shen] (39:3) Fall 89, p. 21-22.
"Nostalgia." [RiverC] (9:1) Spr 89, p. 12-13.
3925. MOON, Joe
"Nocturne." [CapeR] (24:2) Fall 89, p. 21.
3926. MOONFLOWER, Krystal
"The Shanti Shanti Bop" (Editorial). [Timbuktu] (3) Wint-Spr 89, p. 62.
3927. MOORE, Alice F.
"Rembrandt Wrestling the Angel." [CumbPR] (8:2) Spr 89, p. 1.
3928. MOORE, Barbara
"Evening Enjambed with Sparrows." [TarRP] (28:2) Spr 89, p. 27.
"In a Corner of Toulouse Lautrec." [TarRP] (28:2) Spr 89, p. 28.
3929. MOORE, David
"Labor Day, Racine, West Virginia." [KeyWR] (2:1/2) Fall-Wint 89, p. 118.
"Tangy Taste in the Bramble Bush." [KeyWR] (2:1/2) Fall-Wint 89, p. 119.
3930. MOORE, Honor
"Courtly Love." [Ploughs] (15:4) Wint 89-90, p. 143-144.
"Hotel Breakfast." [YellowS] (32) Wint 89, p. 37.
"Premonition." [YellowS] (31) Aut 89, p. 25.
3931. MOORE, Jacqueline
"Nighthawks" (after a painting by Edward Hopper). [Vis] (30) 89, p. 32.
"North Country." [Kalliope] (11:3) 89, p. 67.
"The Pollen Path." [Kalliope] (11:3) 89, p. 64-67.
"Room 277." [Vis] (30) 89, p. 30-31.
3932. MOORE, Janice Townley
"As Seen Through a Half-Opened Door." [StoneC] (16:3/4) Spr-Sum 89, p. 69.
"Honeymoon." [SwampR] (1:4) Sum 89, p. 63.
3933. MOORE, Lenard D.
"Running on Thin Air." [Obs] (4:2) Sum 89, p. 60.
"Vietnam." [Vis] (30) 89, p. 26.
"While in the Sun." [Obs] (2:3) Wint 87, p. 45.
3934. MOORE, Miles David
"Lucifer Recalls a Victorian Scandal." [PoetL] (84:2) Sum 89, p. 17-18.
3935. MOORE, Opal J.
"Freeing Ourselves of History: The Slave Closet." [Obs] (3:1) Spr 88, p. 68-70.
"A Poem: For Free." [Obs] (3:1) Spr 88, p. 71-75.
3936. MOORE, Richard
"The Nail." [Salm] (84) Fall 89, p. 58.
"The Pond." [PoetryE] (28) Fall 89, p. 130.

"Toaist and Confucian." [NegC] (9:1) 89, p. 14.
"Tristram's New Year." [CumbPR] (9:1) Fall 89, p. 13.
"Variations on a Dog." [Salm] (84) Fall 89, p. 54-57.
3937. MOORE, Todd
"Found." [Bogg] (61) 89, p. 42.
3938. MOORHEAD, Andrea
"The Light Final." [Os] (29) 89, p. 23.
"Niagara Calls." [Os] (29) 89, p. 22.
"North African Night." [Os] (29) 89, p. 21.
"Winter Planting." [DeKalbLAJ] (22:1/4) 89, p. 63.
3939. MOORHEAD, Andrew
"Always at Aachen." [Os] (28) 89, p. 10.
"The Land I Saw Was Ringed in Fire." [Os] (28) 89, p. 11.
"March Wind." [Os] (28) 89, p. 17.
3940. MORAFF, Barbara
"Aries." [Contact] (9:53/54/55) Sum-Fall 89, p. 42.
"Autumn Song." [Contact] (9:53/54/55) Sum-Fall 89, p. 42.
"Calligrapher's Moon" (for Jon Appleton, his music). [Contact] (9:53/54/55)
        Sum-Fall 89, p. 43.
"Choiceless Pledge." [Contact] (9:53/54/55) Sum-Fall 89, p. 46.
"Dawn Spider." [Contact] (9:53/54/55) Sum-Fall 89, p. 44.
"Dream." [Contact] (9:53/54/55) Sum-Fall 89, p. 46.
"Found Poem #28." [Contact] (9:53/54/55) Sum-Fall 89, p. 46.
"Functional Talking." [Contact] (9:53/54/55) Sum-Fall 89, p. 40-41.
"Going Along I Speak to My Mother" (a song of Thanksgiving). [Contact]
        (9:53/54/55) Sum-Fall 89, p. 45.
"Hawk Lifting." [Contact] (9:53/54/55) Sum-Fall 89, p. 44.
"Making the Word Flesh." [AlphaBS] (6) Wint 89-90, p. 11.
"Transparency." [Contact] (9:53/54/55) Sum-Fall 89, p. 42.
"Winter" (for Bob Arnold). [Contact] (9:53/54/55) Sum-Fall 89, p. 39.
3941. MORAN, Duncan
"Evening Walk with Dog and Cat." [MidwQ] (30:2) Wint 89, p. 204.
"Wings." [CumbPR] (8:2) Spr 89, p. 15.
3942. MORAN, Ronald
"I Think I Do." [ConnPR] (8:1) 89, p. 22.
3943. MORDECAI, Pamela
"The House of Cards." [Callaloo] (12:2, #39) Spr 89, p. 352-354.
3944. MORDENSKIS, Jan
"At Lake Erie." [CumbPR] (8:2) Spr 89, p. 61-62.
"Dreaming." [CumbPR] (8:2) Spr 89, p. 60.
MORE, René Palacios
        See PALACIOS MORE, René
3945. MOREHEAD, Maureen
"At First, Mary Cassatt." [PoetC] (20:3) Spr 89, p. 11.
"Emily Dickinson Talks to T. W. Higginson." [Iowa] (19:1) Wint 89, p. 78.
"The Flying Geese Quilt You'd Brought from Home" (for Priscilla Beaulieu
        Presley). [Iowa] (19:1) Wint 89, p. 77.
"No Room for That" (for Mary Cassatt). [AmerV] (14) Spr 89, p. 49-50.
"Plans." [SouthernPR] (29:2) Fall 89, p. 69.
3946. MORÉJON, Nancy
"Black Woman" (tr. by Daniela Gioseffi, w. Enildo Garcia). [Contact] (9:50/51/52)
        Fall-Wint 88-Spr 89, p. 44-45.
"Dying in Sadness" (Camen Miranda in memoriam, tr. by Daniela Gioseffi, w.
        Enildo Garcia). [Contact] (9:50/51/52) Fall-Wint 88-Spr 89, p. 43.
"Polished Stone" (tr. by Daniela Gioseffi, w. Enildo Garcia). [Contact] (9:50/51/52)
        Fall-Wint 88-Spr 89, p. 43.
"Supper" (for my parents, tr. by Lourdes González). [Pig] (15) 88, p. 65.
"To the Passing Days and Birthdays" (to Carilda Oliver Labra, tr. by Daniela
        Gioseffi, w. Enildo Garcia). [Contact] (9:50/51/52) Fall-Wint 88-Spr 89, p.
        42.
3947. MORELLI, John
"The sky is dark." [Mildred] (3:1) Spr-Sum 89, p. 37.
3948. MORGAN, Dale
"The Smell of Chicken" (for Daniel). [OhioR] (43) 89, p. 111-112.
3949. MORGAN, Diane
"Bison of Lascaux." [CapeR] (24:1) Spr 89, p. 45.

3950. MORGAN, Edwin
"The Colonnade of Teeth" (tr. of Sándor Weöres). [Field] (40) Spr 89, p. 62-63.
"Moon and Farmstead" (tr. of Sándor Weöres). [Field] (40) Spr 89, p. 66.
"Renaissance" (tr. of Sándor Weöres). [Field] (40) Spr 89, p. 67-68.
"Signs" (tr. of Sándor Weöres). [Field] (40) Spr 89, p. 64-65.
3951. MORGAN, Joey
"Only Make Believe" (shooting script, introduction to a work in progress,
    September, 1989). [CapilR] (2d series: 1) Fall 89, p. 57-80.
3952. MORGAN, John
"The Wreck." [DenQ] (23:3/4) Wint-Spr 89, p. 112-113.
3953. MORGAN, Robert
"Audubon's Flute." [KenR] (NS 11:3) Sum 89, p. 41.
"Buzzard." [SouthernHR] (23:1) Wint 89, p. 67.
"A Dissemblance." [Rampike] (6:3) 88, p. 66-67.
"Dung Frolic." [NewEngR] (11:3) Spr 89, p. 282.
"Eagle Bed." [SouthernHR] (23:1) Wint 89, p. 54.
"High Wallow." [GreensboroR] (46) Sum 89, p. 116.
"The Howl." [Blueline] (10:1/2) 89, p. 8.
"Land Suture." [KenR] (NS 11:3) Sum 89, p. 43.
"Navel." [Blueline] (10:1/2) 89, p. 5.
"Old Christmas." [NewEngR] (11:3) Spr 89, p. 281.
"Podington Air Field." [KenR] (NS 11:3) Sum 89, p. 44.
"Radiation Pressure." [GreensboroR] (46) Sum 89, p. 115.
"Revolution." [NewEngR] (11:3) Spr 89, p. 284.
"Ridgelines." [Blueline] (10:1/2) 89, p. 6.
"Shadow Matter." [KenR] (NS 11:3) Sum 89, p. 42.
"She-Rain." [Blueline] (10:1/2) 89, p. 4.
"Time's Feast." [Blueline] (10:1/2) 89, p. 7.
"Whiskey Tree." [NewEngR] (11:3) Spr 89, p. 283.
3954. MORGAN, Robin
"Arbitrary Bread." [AmerV] (14) Spr 89, p. 68-72.
3955. MORGENSTERN, Christian
"The Indoor Air." [SouthernR] (25:2) Spr 89, p. 268-269.
3956. MORI, Kyoko
"Dreaming of Hair: For Andrea Musher." [Footwork] 89, p. 6-7.
"Running Away: For Anne Hubbard." [Footwork] 89, p. 7.
"Speaking Through White: For My Mother." [Footwork] 89, p. 5-6.
3957. MORIARTY, Laura
"Before the War." [Temblor] (9) 89, p. 77-82.
"La Malinche." [Temblor] (9) 89, p. 73-76.
3958. MORIN, Edward
"The Circular Expressway and Straight Lines of the Ancient City" (tr. of Ye
    Yan-bing, w. Dennis Ding and Dai Fang). [Pig] (15) 88, p. 6.
"Flint" (tr. of Gao Fa-lin, w. Dennis Ding and Dai Fang). [Pig] (15) 88, p. 6.
"The Girl I Knew Is Dead" (tr. of Huang Yong-yu, w. Dennis Ding). [Pig] (15) 88,
    p. 6.
"The Han River Under Fog" (tr. of Cai Qi-jiao, w. Dai Fang). [MichQR] (28:3) Sum
    89, p. 399.
"Homo Faber." [Amelia] (5:3, #14) 89, p. 49.
"I'll Always Remember" (tr. of Yan-Xiang Shao, w. Dennis Ding). [DenQ] (24:2)
    Fall 89, p. 69.
"The Pledge" (tr. of Li-hong Zhao, w. Dai Fang). [CharR] (15:2) Fall 89, p. 60.
"Reverie on a Theme in PL/1" (For Camille). [Amelia] (5:3, #14) 89, p. 49.
"Seagull" (tr. of Cai Qi-jiao, w. Dai Fang). [MichQR] (28:3) Sum 89, p. 399.
"The Trolley Car Goes On" (tr. of Yan Yi, w. Dennis Ding). [MinnR] (NS 32) Spr
    89, p. 79.
3959. MORITZ, A. F.
"Big Weather." [WestHR] (43:3) Aut 89, p. 207.
"The Five-Foot Shelf." [GeoR] (43:3) Fall 89, p. 506-507.
"Home Again Home Again." [WestHR] (43:3) Aut 89, p. 208-209.
"Indifference." [GeoR] (43:2) Sum 89, p. 363-364.
3960. MORITZ, Yunna
"The Muscle of Water" (tr. by Thomas P. Whitney). [WestB] (24) 89, p. 45.
3961. MORPHEW, Lisa
"The Moth" (For Marilyn). [SinW] (38) Sum-Fall 89, p. 58.

3962. MORPHEW, Melissa
"The Density of Nothing." [KanQ] (21:3) Sum 89, p. 174.
"Dusk at the 25th Annual First Baptist Picnic." [Poem] (62) N 89, p. 16.
"Many Miles from Eden." [NegC] (9:1) 89, p. 76-77.
"Sunday Morning Services." [SoCoast] (5) Spr 88, p. 12.
"You Shall Eat Dust All the Days of Your Life." [Poem] (62) N 89, p. 17.
3963. MORRIS, Herbert
"Burlesque" (Gypsy Rose Lee and Her Girls, 1950: A photograph by Ralph
Steiner). [DenQ] (24:2) Fall 89, p. 70-80.
"Lausanne, Vevey, Montreux" (In memory of Charles Chaplin). [DenQ] (24:1) Sum
89, p. 55-64.
"The Map to Freud's House." [Poetry] (154:4) Jl 89, p. 193-196.
"Olana, Summer, 1872." [MassR] (30:2) Sum 89, p. 226-237.
"Spanish" (for Ashley Baquero). [Crazy] (36) Spr 89, p. 58-66.
3964. MORRIS, Kathryn
"Children" (from Pool Hall Poems). [Quarry] (38:4) Fall 89, p. 64.
"Manners" (from Pool Hall Poems). [Quarry] (38:4) Fall 89, p. 66.
"Wondering About the Taste of Beer" (from Pool Hall Poems). [Quarry] (38:4) Fall
89, p. 65.
3965. MORRIS, Peter
"Dead End." [PoetryE] (28) Fall 89, p. 49.
"My Fun-Loving Friends." [PoetryE] (28) Fall 89, p. 50.
"Scars." [PoetryE] (28) Fall 89, p. 51.
"Sounds." [PoetryE] (28) Fall 89, p. 52.
3966. MORRISON, John C.
"The Eighth Hole with My Father." [PoetryE] (28) Fall 89, p. 53-54.
3967. MORRISON, Lillian
"High Lights." [StoneC] (16:3/4) Spr-Sum 89, p. 46.
"Ode to a Shirt." [Kalliope] (11:2) 89, p. 45.
"Unauthorized Printout." [NewRena] (7:3, #23) 89, p. 117.
3968. MORRO, Henry J.
"Eruptions." [BlueBldgs] (11) 89, p. 53.
"The Ice Years." [BlueBldgs] (11) 89, p. 54.
3969. MORROW, Bradford
"A Bestiary" (Selections: "Earthworm," "Elephant"). [Screens] (1) 89, p. 18-19.
3970. MORSE, Michael
"Letter from Lewisburg." [WestB] (25) 89, p. 46.
"Purgatory." [WestB] (25) 89, p. 47.
3971. MORT, Graham
"Blonde Man, Horse, Woman." [Wind] (19:64) 89, p. 19-20.
"Into the Ashes." [Wind] (19:64) 89, p. 18-19.
3972. MORTON, Bridget Balthrop
"Family Practice." [Lactuca] (12) F 89, p. 63-64.
"Internal Combustion" (for Daniel). [Vis] (31) 89, p. 32.
3973. MORTON, Colin
"Diaspora" (Prose Poem Winter, the First Short Grain Contest). [Grain] (17:3) Fall
89, p. 68.
3974. MORTON, Grace
"Caedmon." [AnthNEW] (1) 89, p. 18.
3975. MORTUS, Cindy
"Breaking Bread." [Poem] (62) N 89, p. 5.
"Passage." [Poem] (62) N 89, p. 6.
"Shop Talk" (in memory of Jack). [Poem] (62) N 89, p. 4.
3976. MOSELEY, Jim
"Cykle." [AmerPoR] (18:1) Ja-F 89, p. 8.
"The Glittering Commotion of White Butterflies on a Magnum Blue Day."
[AmerPoR] (18:1) Ja-F 89, p. 8.
"In Memory of H.D." [AmerPoR] (18:1) Ja-F 89, p. 7.
"Indianapolis." [AmerPoR] (18:1) Ja-F 89, p. 8.
"The Tide." [AmerPoR] (18:1) Ja-F 89, p. 7.
3977. MOSES, W. R.
"Bee Wings." [Northeast] (ser. 5:1) Wint 89-90, p. 5.
"Deposit." [Northeast] (ser. 5:1) Wint 89-90, p. 6.
"A Dream for George." [Northeast] (ser. 5:1) Wint 89-90, p. 6.
"Of Death and Beauty." [SouthernPR] (29:1) Spr 89, p. 53-54.

3978. MOSHER, Mark L.
"Magnifier." [SmPd] (26:3 #77) Fall 89, p. 18.
3979. MOSLER, Charlie
"Doors." [US1] (22/23) Spr 89, p. 17.
3980. MOSS, Jennifer
"Coming of Age." [PoetryNW] (30:3) Aut 89, p. 10-11.
3981. MOSS, Stanley
"Krill." [GrahamHR] (12) Spr 89, p. 89.
"The Poor of Venice." [GrahamHR] (12) Spr 89, p. 88.
"Rainbows and Circumcision." [GrahamHR] (12) Spr 89, p. 86-87.
"Song of Alphabets." [GrahamHR] (12) Spr 89, p. 84-85.
3982. MOSS, Sylvia
"1913." [NewL] (56:2/3) Wint 89-Spr 90, p. 184.
"The Daughters of Edward Boit" (after Sargent). [NewL] (56:2/3) Wint 89-Spr 90,
p. 183-184.
"Partisan." [NewL] (56:2/3) Wint 89-Spr 90, p. 185.
"Stranger at the Harbor." [NewL] (56:2/3) Wint 89-Spr 90, p. 185.
3983. MOSS, Thylias
"Fullness." [Iowa] (19:1) Wint 89, p. 20.
"A Godiva." [Field] (40) Spr 89, p. 54-55.
"The Lynching." [Ploughs] (15:4) Wint 89-90, p. 146-147.
"November and Aunt Jemima." [GrahamHR] (12) Spr 89, p. 38.
"Redbones As Nothing Special." [Iowa] (19:1) Wint 89, p. 21.
"The Root of the Road." [Callaloo] (12:2, #39) Spr 89, p. 271.
"She Did My Hair Outside, the Wash a Tent Around Us." [Ploughs] (15:4) Wint
89-90, p. 145.
"She's Florida Missouri But She Was Born in Valhermosa and Lives in Ohio."
[Iowa] (19:1) Wint 89, p. 20.
"To Buckwheat and Other Pickaninnies." [Callaloo] (12:2, #39) Spr 89, p. 272-273.
3984. MOTION, Andrew
"Bad Dreams." [GrahamHR] (12) Spr 89, p. 82-83.
"One Who Disappeared." [GrahamHR] (12) Spr 89, p. 79-81.
"Somebody's Wife." [Pequod] (26/27) 89, p. 112-115.
3985. MOTT, Elaine
"The Deer." [PoetL] (84:2) Sum 89, p. 53.
3986. MOTT, Michael
"Carnival in Time of Plague." [SewanR] (97:3) Sum 89, p. 402.
"Letter to Thomas Hariot." [SewanR] (97:3) Sum 89, p. 399-400.
"Lines for Queen Gertrude." [TarRP] (29:1) Fall 89, p. 38-39.
"Motto." [TarRP] (29:1) Fall 89, p. 39.
"Quaker Ellwood." [SewanR] (97:3) Sum 89, p. 403.
"Wolsey." [SewanR] (97:3) Sum 89, p. 401.
3987. MOULTON-BARRETT, Donalee
"Brick Layers." [AntigR] (76) Wint 89, p. 103.
3988. MOURÉ, Erin
"Carolina." [CapilR] (1st series: 50) 89, p. 153.
"Grace." [CapilR] (1st series: 50) 89, p. 152.
"Gravity." [CapilR] (1st series: 50) 89, p. 150.
"Light." [CapilR] (1st series: 50) 89, p. 151.
"Lineal Answer." [CapilR] (1st series: 50) 89, p. 156.
"Magdalenic Answer." [CapilR] (1st series: 50) 89, p. 155.
"Sheepish Love." [CapilR] (1st series: 50) 89, p. 157-158.
"Vegetal Answer." [CapilR] (1st series: 50) 89, p. 154.
3989. MU, Tung
"In Answer" (tr. by David Gordon). [LitR] (32:3) Spr 89, p. 383.
MU, Yang
See YANG, Mu
3990. MUEGGE, Richard
"DogThought." [EngJ] (78:3) Mr 89, p. 90.
3991. MUELLER, John
"Omens and Remedies." [AnotherCM] (19) 89, p. 160.
3992. MUELLER, Lisel
"Aphasia." [NewL] (56:2/3) Wint 89-Spr 90, p. 191.
"The Escape." [NewL] (56:2/3) Wint 89-Spr 90, p. 186-187.
"Joy." [NewL] (56:2/3) Wint 89-Spr 90, p. 189.
"Mary." [NewL] (56:2/3) Wint 89-Spr 90, p. 188.

"Mary." [TriQ] (76) Fall 89, p. 107.
"Missing the Dead." [NewL] (56:2/3) Wint 89-Spr 90, p. 190.
"Oral History." [TriQ] (76) Fall 89, p. 108.
"Poem for My Birthday." [NewL] (56:2/3) Wint 89-Spr 90, p. 190-191.
"Poppy." [NewL] (56:2/3) Wint 89-Spr 90, p. 187.
3993. MUELLER, Paul Kennedy
"The Girl in the Mind of the Grenade." [PoetL] (84:2) Sum 89, p. 56.
"The Invisible Bear." [PoetL] (84:2) Sum 89, p. 57.
"Orchards of the Moon." [PoetL] (84:2) Sum 89, p. 58.
"Turrialba." [PoetL] (84:2) Sum 89, p. 55.
MUIRTHILE, Liam O
See O MUIRTHILE, Liam
3994. MUKHOPADHYAY, Vijaya
"To Be Worthy" (tr. by Sunil B. Ray and Carolyne Wright, w. the author).
[NewEngR] (11:4) Sum 89, p. 458.
3995. MUKTIBODH, G. M. (Gajanan Madhav)
"Distance" (tr. by Vinay Dharwadker). [TriQ] (77) Wint 89-90, p. 166-167.
"The Void" (tr. by Vinay Dharwadker). [TriQ] (77) Wint 89-90, p. 163-164.
3996. MULDOON, Paul
"August" (tr. of Michael Davitt). [Trans] (22) Fall 89, p. 121.
"The Mirror" (in memory of my father, tr. of Michael Davitt). [Trans] (22) Fall 89,
p. 124-125.
"To Pound, from God" (tr. of Michael Davitt). [Trans] (22) Fall 89, p. 122-123.
3997. MULFORD, Wendy
"Goodbye to the Bay of Naples." [Pequod] (26/27) 89, p. 117.
"In the Public Garden." [Pequod] (26/27) 89, p. 116.
"Interior with Figures." [Pequod] (26/27) 89, p. 118.
3998. MULHOLLAND, Mary Jane
"January." [PassN] (10:1) Wint 89, p. 10.
3999. MULHOLLAND, Megeen R.
"A July." [MSS] (6:3) 89, p. 108.
"Stems kicking, petals." [MSS] (6:3) 89, p. 108.
4000. MULLEN, Laura
"The Lease." [DenQ] (24:1) Sum 89, p. 65-66.
"The Self." [Notus] (4:1) Spr 89, p. 28.
"They." [Thrpny] (38) Sum 89, p. 26.
"Winter." [Notus] (4:1) Spr 89, p. 27.
4001. MULLENIX, Pamela L.
"Lamantha Woman." [Amelia] (5:3, #14) 89, p. 57.
4002. MULLIGAN, J. B.
"A Mining Town." [Wind] (19:65) 89, p. 20.
"The Tapestries of Appetite." [HeavenB] (6) Wint-Spr 89, p. 47.
"The Wheel." [HeavenB] (6) Wint-Spr 89, p. 4.
4003. MULLIN, Bob
"The Ride." [WorldO] (22:1/2) Fall-Wint 87-88, c90, p. 32-33.
"Sand." [WorldO] (21:3/4) Spr-Sum 87, c89, p. 23.
4004. MULLIN, Christine
"Falling." [Pequod] (26/27) 89, p. 24-25.
4005. MULRANE, Scott H.
"All Roads Lead to Rome." [StoneC] (17:1/2) Fall-Wint 89-90, p. 16.
"Antitoxin." [Interim] (8:2) Fall 89, p. 43.
"Taking the Cure." [Interim] (8:2) Fall 89, p. 44.
"Terns." [StoneC] (17:1/2) Fall-Wint 89-90, p. 16.
4006. MUMBULLA, Percy
"Uncle Abraham Whose Blackfeller's Name Was Minah" (Aboriginal narrative of
New South Wales, collected by Roland Robinson, related by Percy Mumbulla,
Wallaga Lake). [PraS] (63:3) Fall 89, p. 78-82.
4007. MUMFORD, Marilyn R,.
"Anniversary Poem." [SinW] (38) Sum-Fall 89, p. 81-82.
4008. MUNDLAY, Asha
"Ambedkar, 79" (tr. of Namdeo Dhasal, w. Laurie Hovell and Jayant Karve).
[Trans] (21) Spr 89, p. 234-235.
4009. MURA, David
"From the Pages of Corriere Della Sera (Oct. 29, 1975): A Lutheran Letter" (-- Pier
Paolo Pasolini). [NewRep] (200:19) 8 My 89, p. 32.
"Grandfather-In-Law." [AmerPoR] (18:5) S-O 89, p. 36.

"Listening." [Crazy] (36) Spr 89, p. 42-43.
"To H. N." [Crazy] (36) Spr 89, p. 40-41.
4010. MURAKAMI, Hiroshi
"Singing Image of a Whirling Ring of Fire" (tr. of Kukai, w. Morgan Gibson).
[LitR] (32:3) Spr 89, p. 360.
"Singing Image of an Echo" (tr. of Kukai, w. Morgan Gibson). [LitR] (32:3) Spr
89, p. 360.
4011. MURATORI, Fred
"Adam's Contract." [BrooklynR] (5) 88, p. 23.
"Erosion." [NoDaQ] (57:4) Fall 89, p. 139.
"The Obvious." [BrooklynR] (5) 88, p. 22.
"Sartre's Gift." [Talisman] (3) Fall 89, p. 106.
4012. MURAWSKI, Elisabeth
"Beautiful Ending." [CumbPR] (8:2) Spr 89, p. 53-54.
"Becoming." [CrabCR] (6:1) 89, p. 19.
"Break." [CrabCR] (6:1) 89, p. 19.
"Hatteras, Late." [CrabCR] (6:1) 89, p. 18.
"One Hour Wide." [CrabCR] (6:1) 89, p. 18.
"Star-Crossed." [CumbPR] (9:1) Fall 89, p. 32-33.
4013. MURDOCK, Suzanne
"Shiva." [DeKalbLAJ] (22:1/4) 89, p. 64-65.
4014. MURO, Saisei
"Railway Train" (tr. by Graeme Wilson). [ConnPR] (8:1) 89, p. 21.
4015. MURPHY, Barbara
"Balance." [Thrpny] (38) Sum 89, p. 35.
4016. MURPHY, Bruce
"Patience." [Pequod] (28/29/30) 89, p. 244.
4017. MURPHY, Carol
"Maid's Eye View." [Poem] (61) My 89, p. 62.
"Matinee." [Poem] (61) My 89, p. 64-65.
"René and Georgette Magritte." [Poem] (61) My 89, p. 60-61.
4018. MURPHY, Kevin
"Aces and Eights" (for by brother, 1940-1976). [SenR] (19:1) 89, p. 36-37.
4019. MURPHY, Peter E.
"The Narrows" (for my Mother). [US1] (22/23) Spr 89, p. 8.
4020. MURPHY, Richard
"The Mirror Wall" (poems based on songs written in Old Sinhalese, 8-10th
centuries, Sri Lanka). [GrandS] (8:3) Spr 89, p. 18-25.
4021. MURPHY, Sharman
"David Died in the Hour of the Wolf" (for David Valadon, 1945-1973). [FiveFR] (7)
89, p. 75.
4022. MURPHY, Sheila (Sheila E.)
"6 x 6" (w. Beverly Carver). [CentralP] (15) Spr 89, p. 152-158.
"Ann Arbor." [StoneC] (16:3/4) Spr-Sum 89, p. 25.
"Baptism." [Sequoia] (33:1) Sum 89, p. 62.
"Elementary." [WindO] (51) Spr 89, p. 30.
"Feast on How the Days Go By and Cannot Hurt Me." [Aerial] (5) 89, p. 155.
"Friday" (From "Days of the Week"). [FreeL] (2) Sum 89, p. 16.
"I'm Best at Playing the Game When I'm Not Playing the Game." [PaperAir] (4:2)
89, p. 82.
"A Portrait of Beverly C." [FreeL] (2) Sum 89, p. 17.
"The Question Following the Statement." [PaperAir] (4:2) 89, p. 83.
"Reading the Directions." [WindO] (51) Spr 89, p. 29.
"Songster Thought." [HeavenB] (6) Wint-Spr 89, p. 43.
"Spiritual." [Aerial] (5) 89, p. 154.
"Sunflower." [HayF] (4) Spr 89, p. 74.
"Therapy in the Fast Lane." [SlipS] (9) 89, p. 77-78.
4023. MURRAY, Dan
"The End of the Road" (for John Logan). [PaintedB] (39) 89, p. 80.
4024. MURRAY, Donald M.
"Waiting for a Poem." [Poetry] (153:6) Mr 89, p. 331.
4025. MURRAY, G. E.
"At the Station Bar." [AnotherCM] (19) 89, p. 161.
"The Body and Its Borders." [GrahamHR] (12) Spr 89, p. 21-22.
"Crossings: November 21-22" (for Dana Gioia). [Journal] (12:2) Fall-Wint 88-89,
p. 32-35.

"Four Themes on a Variation." [AnotherCM] (19) 89, p. 162.
"Walking the Blind Dog." [SewanR] (97:2) Spr 89, p. 183-188.
4026. MURRAY, Les A.
"Accordion Music." [Descant] (20:3/4, #66/67) Fall-Wint 89, p. 223.
"Ariel." [Verse] (6:3) Wint 89, p. 5.
"The Assimilation of Background." [NewRep] (200:6) 6 F 89, p. 26.
"An Australian History of the Practical Man." [Descant] (20:3/4, #66/67) Fall-Wint
    89, p. 221-222.
"Cave Divers Near Mount Gambier." [ParisR] (31:112) Fall 89, p. 187.
"The Cows on Killing Day." [ParisR] (31:112) Fall 89, p. 183-184.
"The Emerald Dove." [ParisR] (31:112) Fall 89, p. 188-189.
"Experiential." [Descant] (20:3/4, #66/67) Fall-Wint 89, p. 226.
"Gun-E-Darr." [ParisR] (31:112) Fall 89, p. 185.
"Hastings River Cruise" (i.m. Ruth and Harry Liston, d. Port Macquarie 1826).
    [Verse] (6:1) Mr 89, p. 3.
"High Sugar." [Verse] (6:1) Mr 89, p. 4.
"In Murray's Dictionary." [Verse] (6:3) Wint 89, p. 5.
"The Inverse Transports." [Descant] (20:3/4, #66/67) Fall-Wint 89, p. 224-225.
"Politics and Art." [Verse] (6:3) Wint 89, p. 6.
"Slip." [Verse] (6:3) Wint 89, p. 6.
"The Tube" (for Ann Moyal and Rob Crawford). [ParisR] (31:112) Fall 89, p. 186.
4027. MURRAY, Thomas A.
"The Garden of Wa Ta Si, Beijing." [CinPR] (19) Spr 89, p. 66-67.
4028. MUSGRAVE, Susan
"Desireless: Tom York (1940-1987)." [NegC] (9:1) 89, p. 131.
"Love Wasn't Always." [CrossC] (11:2) 89, p. 10.
"My Father Came Back for the Furniture." [CrossC] (11:2) 89, p. 10.
4029. MUSKA, Nick
"Hommage de l'Auteur: Mon Nom." [Pig] (15) 88, p. 60.
4030. MUSKAT, Timothy
"Before Knowing." [Poem] (61) My 89, p. 24-25.
"I Say." [Poem] (61) My 89, p. 26-27.
MUTAMID, Abu 'l-Kasim Mohammed Ibn-Abbad al-
    See Al-MUTAMID, Abu 'l-Kasim Mohammed Ibn-Abbad
4031. MUTH, Parke
"We Call You Our Child: Ty Cobb." [Hawai'iR] (13:1, #25) Spr 89, p. 96.
4032. MUTIS, Alvaro
"El Regreso de Leo Le Gris" (Para Otto de Greiff). [LindLM] (8:2) Ap-Je 89, p. 3.
4033. MUTTON, Paul
"Hyperion's Glass Envelope." [AlphaBS] (5) Jl 89, p. 52-53.
4034. MYCUE, Edward
"Although Summer Is Over." [MidwQ] (30:4) Sum 89, p. 449.
"Diffidence vs / at Poles from Zeal." [JamesWR] (5:2 [i.e. 6:2]) Wint 89, p. 15.
"Far Enough (Beyond Provocative)." [Caliban] (6) 89, p. 8.
"Poison Rose." [JamesWR] (6:3) Spr 89, p. 12.
"A Short Message for a Long Life." [JamesWR] (5:2 [i.e. 6:2]) Wint 89, p. 15.
4035. MYERS, Douglas
"In the Ruins of Fort Abraham Lincoln." [HayF] (5) Fall 89, p. 79.
4036. MYERS, George, Jr.
"1918 Manifestoes." [Rampike] (6:2) 88, p. 71.
4037. MYERS, Jack
"The Experts." [AmerPoR] (18:4) Jl-Ag 89, p. 48.
"Have a Nice Day." [NoAmR] (274:4) D 89, p. 21.
"I Don't Know, You Probably Know Everything I Know" (for Walter Wetherell's
    bad back). [MissouriR] (12:2) 89, p. 148.
"Washed Up." [Crazy] (37) Wint 89, p. 18-21.
"Why Don't You Ask Your Father? Fugue." [MissouriR] (12:2) 89, p. 146-147.
4038. MYERS, Joan Rohr
"Blue Plates." [Comm] (116:11) Je 2, 89, p. 348.
"Interiors." [Comm] (116:4) F 24, 89, p. 118.
"Offertory." [Comm] (116:4) F 24, 89, p. 118.
"What We Wear." [Comm] (116:4) F 24, 89, p. 118.
4039. MYERS, Neil
"Homage to the Tao Te Ching." [CharR] (15:2) Fall 89, p. 22-23.
4040. MYERS, Sandra J.
"Dreaming Brazil." [BellR] (12:1, #25) Spr 89, p. 29.

4041. MYERS, Teresa
  "My Worst Fears" (Excerpt). [SinW] (39) Wint 89-90, p. 45.
4042. MYLES, Eileen
  "Holes." [BrooklynR] (6) 89, p. 1-3.
  "Immanence." [Ploughs] (15:4) Wint 89-90, p. 148.
  "Peanut Butter." [Ploughs] (15:4) Wint 89-90, p. 149-152.
4043. MYLES, Naomi
  "Tea Ceremony." [StoneC] (16:3/4) Spr-Sum 89, p. 71.
4044. NAAS, Ron
  "Circles of Wonder." [BellArk] (5:6) N-D 89, p. 7.
  "Grandma Jones." [BellArk] (5:4) Jl-Ag 89, p. 5.
4045. NACEY, Robert
  "Dancing with My Angel." [Timbuktu] (4) Sum-Fall 89, p. 65.
  "I Told Her I'd Be Home When the Bars Close." [Timbuktu] (4) Sum-Fall 89, p.
    65.
4046. NADELMAN, Cynthia
  "I Bought a Camera." [ParisR] (31:112) Fall 89, p. 66-67.
  "My Berlin." [Pequod] (28/29/30) 89, p. 137-138.
4047. NADIAN, Manuel
  "Now" (tr. by Kevin Orth). [Vis] (31) 89, p. 15.
4048. NAFFZIGER, Audrey
  "Birth of a Non-Denominationalist." [Pig] (15) 88, p. 40.
4049. NAJARIAN, James
  "The Bodies of Men." [Jacaranda] (4:1) Spr-Sum 89, p. 16.
  "Taking the Train to Reading, PA." [Jacaranda] (4:1) Spr-Sum 89, p. 14-15.
4050. NAJERA, Francisco
  "Niños en el Palacio de Hielo." [Inti] (29/30) Primavera-Otoño 89, p. 249-251.
  "Oh Sefiroth de Mis Deseos." [LindLM] (8:1) Ja-Mr 89, p. 19.
  "Progresion." [LindLM] (8:1) Ja-Mr 89, p. 19.
4051. NAKATSUKASA (ca. 900)
  "Little nightingale"" (tr. by Sam Hamill). [PoetryE] (28) Fall 89, p. 202.
4052. NALAN SINGDE
  "The Butterfly Loves Flowers: I remember being here before" (tr. by Lenore
    Mayhew and William McNaughton). [LitR] (32:3) Spr 89, p. 370.
  "The Butterfly Loves Flowers: In the high trees" (tr. by Lenore Mayhew and William
    McNaughton). [LitR] (32:3) Spr 89, p. 371.
  "I Remember the Beauty" (tr. by Lenore Mayhew and William McNaughton). [LitR]
    (32:3) Spr 89, p. 368.
  "I Think of the Beauty" (tr. by Lenore Mayhew and William McNaughton). [LitR]
    (32:3) Spr 89, p. 370.
  "The Moon Climbs the Cherry-Apple" (tr. by Lenore Mayhew and William
    McNaughton). [LitR] (32:3) Spr 89, p. 369.
  "South Country" (tr. by Lenore Mayhew and William McNaughton). [LitR] (32:3)
    Spr 89, p. 369.
4053. NAMEROFF, Rochelle
  "Finding the Way Home." [LaurelR] (23:1) Wint 89, p. 88-89.
  "The Invitation." [LaurelR] (23:1) Wint 89, p. 89-90.
  "The Marriage Window." [RiverS] (30) [89], p. 55.
  "Second Love Poem." [RiverS] (30) [89], p. 54.
4054. NANI, Christel
  "In the Emergency Room." [Grain] (17:3) Fall 89, p. 47.
  "When Your Mother Dies." [Grain] (17:3) Fall 89, p. 46.
4055. NAPIER, Alan
  "Becoming Unborn." [ColR] (NS 16:2) Fall 89-Wint 90, p. 66.
  "Chameleon." [StoneC] (17:1/2) Fall-Wint 89-90, p. 44.
  "Donatien Alphonse Addresses the Ills of the World." [Chelsea] (48) 89, p.
    117-119.
  "The Dry Heart" (Brimfield / night 1976). [KeyWR] (2:1/2) Fall-Wint 89, p. 123.
  "Night of the Storm." [HiramPoR] (46) Spr-Sum 89, p. 19.
  "Ode to a Deep Deception" (Florida / early morning 1963). [KeyWR] (2:1/2)
    Fall-Wint 89, p. 122.
  "Olmsby Drive." [HiramPoR] (46) Spr-Sum 89, p. 20.
  "One of the Grass-People." [Nimrod] (32:2) Spr-Sum 89, p. 80.
4056. NARAYAN, Kunwar
  "Towards Delhi" (tr. by Vinay Dharwadker). [TriQ] (77) Wint 89-90, p. 153.
  "An Unusual Day" (tr. by Vinay Dharwadker). [TriQ] (77) Wint 89-90, p. 154.

NARIHIRA, Ariwara no (825-880)
   See ARIWARA NO NARIHIRA (825-880)
4057. NASH, Roger
   "Abstract Art." [Dandel] (16:2) Fall-Wint 89, p. 23.
   "Ageing Gracefully." [AntigR] (79) Aut 89, p. 93.
   "Betting on History." [Dandel] (16:2) Fall-Wint 89, p. 21-22.
   "A Creation Story." [AntigR] (79) Aut 89, p. 92.
   "I Couldn't Count the Ways." [Quarry] (38:1) Wint 89, p. 29.
   "Night Thoughts." [MalR] (86) Spr 89, p. 91.
   "The Ruin" (tr. of Anonymous Anglo-Saxon poem). [AntigR] (79) Aut 89, p. 95.
   "The Seafarer" (tr. of Anonymous Anglo-Saxon poem). [AntigR] (79) Aut 89, p.
      94.
   "The Street of Gold." [Dandel] (16:2) Fall-Wint 89, p. 24.
   "We Are All of Us Amazing to Be Here." [Quarry] (38:1) Wint 89, p. 28.
4058. NASH, Susan Smith
   "Abu Dhabi Promise." [PaperAir] (4:2) 89, p. 69-71.
   "The Factory." [Aerial] (5) 89, p. 20-21.
   "Michelangelo in Frontier." [Screens] (1) 89, p. 110.
   "Naked Breakfast." [PaperAir] (4:2) 89, p. 67-68.
NATALE, Nanci Roth
   See ROTH-NATALE, Nanci
4059. NATHAN, Leonard
   "Black Bull." [Witness] (2:4) Wint 88, p. 16.
   "Fools." [PoetL] (84:3) Fall 89, p. 19-20.
   "Homecoming." [PraS] (63:3) Fall 89, p. 18.
   "March Slav." [Witness] (2:4) Wint 88, p. 27.
   "The Nest." [PraS] (63:3) Fall 89, p. 17.
   "Poems on My Father and My Mother" (15 poems, tr. of Anna Swir, w. Czeslaw
      Milosz). [AmerPoR] (18:1) Ja-F 89, p. 23-25.
4060. NATHAN, Norman
   "Dedication." [ChamLR] (2:2, #4) Spr 89, p. 105.
   "HIS." [ChamLR] (2:2, #4) Spr 89, p. 106.
   "Lethargy." [SpiritSH] (54) Spr-Sum 89, p. 36.
   "Mood (While Reading)." [SpiritSH] (54) Spr-Sum 89, p. 35.
4061. NATT, Gregory
   "Cold Morning" (after Lajos Kassak). [Vis] (31) 89, p. 43.
4062. NATT, Rochelle
   "Four Paintings by Paul Gauguin Viewed by His Wife, Mette." [NegC] (9:2) 89, p.
      66-67.
4063. NAWROCKI, Sarah
   "New Hampshire with Brian." [GreensboroR] (47) Wint 89-90, p. 36-37.
4064. NDLORU, Duma
   "Kunyenyeza Ezikhotheni" (Voices in the Wilderness). [Bomb] (28) Sum 89, p. 86.
4065. NEALON, Mary Jane
   "Warrensburg, Missouri." [MidAR] (9:2) 89, p. 24-25.
4066. NEELD, Judith
   "The Climb at Hound Tor." [MassR] (30:1) Spr 89, p. 14.
   "A Genealogy in Cheshire, England." [CinPR] (19) Spr 89, p. 19.
   "On the Cliffs, Dieppe" (Claude Monet, 1897). [TexasR] (10:1/2) Spr-Sum 89, p.
      88.
4067. NEELON, Ann
   "Argument from the Heart." [Sequoia] (33:1) Sum 89, p. 63.
4068. NÉGYESY, Irén
   "Solar Eclipse" (tr. by Nicholas Kolumban and Daniel Bourne). [ArtfulD] (16/17)
      Fall 89, p. 76.
4069. NEHEMIAH, Marcia
   "Childless." [JINJPo] [11] 89, p. 20.
   "The Mask." [JINJPo] [11] 89, p. 19.
4070. NEIDERBACH, Shelley
   "Women Writers' Workshop: Pine Lake" (pour toutes les femmes). [StoneC]
      (16:3/4) Spr-Sum 89, p. 76.
4071. NEIL, Pagan
   "Coyote" (Selection: Second Breath). [Sequoia] (33:1) Sum 89, p. 52-53.
4072. NEIPRIS, Jeff
   "Grist." [MoodySI] (20/21) Spr 89, p. 19.

4073. NEKRASOV, Vsevolod
"I live and see" (tr. by Gerald Janecek). [MichQR] (28:4) Fall 89, p. 731.
"That's who is guilty" (tr. by Gerald Janecek). [MichQR] (28:4) Fall 89, p. 732.
4074. NELSON, Eric
"Everywhere Pregnant Women Appear." [ThRiPo] (33/34) 89, p. 34.
"Safe House." [PoetryNW] (30:4) Wint 89-90, p. 45.
"The Scene." [MissouriR] (12:2) 89, p. 144-145.
4075. NELSON, Gale
"Mandala" (Excerpt). [CentralP] (15) Spr 89, p. 47.
4076. NELSON, Greg
"Assassination Dream." [PoetL] (84:3) Fall 89, p. 50.
4077. NELSON, Howard
"The Boy with Breasts." [Mildred] (3:1) Spr-Sum 89, p. 92.
"The Rock." [Mildred] (3:1) Spr-Sum 89, p. 94.
"The Rules." [Mildred] (3:1) Spr-Sum 89, p. 95.
"Small Girl Waving." [Mildred] (3:1) Spr-Sum 89, p. 93.
4078. NELSON, Kristofer
"I'll Wait." [CimR] (86) Ja 89, p. 81.
4079. NELSON, Leslie
"Ironing." [SouthernHR] (23:1) Wint 89, p. 64-65.
4080. NELSON, Sandra
"Always in the Dark." [PoetryE] (28) Fall 89, p. 68.
"Bone Lake." [KanQ] (21:3) Sum 89, p. 111.
"Closures." [PoetryE] (28) Fall 89, p. 67.
"East Grandville School." [Iowa] (19:1) Wint 89, p. 85-86.
"Hillside Fish Market." [Iowa] (19:1) Wint 89, p. 87.
"Lagoon." [Iowa] (19:1) Wint 89, p. 88.
"Portrait of a Girl Holding a Rat." [TarRP] (29:1) Fall 89, p. 9-10.
"Saturday in America." [Mildred] (3:1) Spr-Sum 89, p. 107.
"Six Leggers." [PoetryE] (28) Fall 89, p. 66.
"Toulouse at the Circus." [CinPR] (19) Spr 89, p. 69.
4081. NELSON, W. Dale
"The Embarkation for Cythera from the South Lawn of the White House." [KanQ]
        (21:1/2) Wint-Spr 89, p. 118.
4082. NEMEROV, Howard
"Analogies" (in Memory of William Empson). [PraS] (63:1) Spr 89, p. 7.
"Fish Swimming Amid Falling Flowers." [RiverS] (28) 89, p. 67-68.
"Landscape with Self-Portrait." [RiverS] (28) 89, p. 71.
"Larkin." [PraS] (63:1) Spr 89, p. 6-7.
"Literature." [RiverS] (28) 89, p. 66.
"The Makers." [RiverS] (28) 89, p. 73.
NEMETH, Charles Manyoky
See MANYOKY-NEMETH, Charles
4083. NEMETH, Peg
"Natural Selection." [CreamCR] (13:2) Fall 89, p. 156.
4084. NERI, Giampiero
"Overlappings" (tr. by Rebecca Messbarger). [Poetry] (155:1/2) O-N 89, p. 75, 77.
"Sovrapposizioni." [Poetry] (155:1/2) O-N 89, p. 74, 76.
4085. NERI, Judy
"The Why of It All." [PoetL] (84:1) Spr 89, p. 41.
4086. NERUDA, Pablo
"I Explain a Few Things" (tr. by Galway Kinnell). [Trans] (22) Fall 89, p. 177-179.
"Melancholy inside Families" (tr. by Robert Bly and James Wright). [Quarry] (38:2)
        Spr 89, p. 76-77.
"Ode to a Pantheress" (tr. by Margaret Sayers Peden). [NewOR] (16:2) Sum 89, p.
        62-63.
"Ode to a Ship in a Bottle" (tr. by Margaret Sayers Peden). [NewOR] (16:2) Sum
        89, p. 86-87.
"The Sea and the Bells" (Selections: 5 poems, tr. by William O'Daly). [PoetryE] (27)
        Spr 89, p. 134-138.
"The Separate Rose" (Selections: IV, VII, XII, tr. by William O'Daly). [PoetryE]
        (27) Spr 89, p. 124-126.
"Still Another Day" (Selections: I, V, XVII, tr. by William O'Daly). [PoetryE] (27)
        Spr 89, p. 127-129.
"The United Fruit Company" (tr. by Robert Bly). [PoetryE] (27) Spr 89, p.
        119-120.

"The Winter Garden" (Selections: 3 poems, tr. by William O'Daly). [PoetryE] (27)
Spr 89, p. 130-133.
4087. NESANOVICH, Stella
"A Dream: To Her Lover." [PoetL] (84:1) Spr 89, p. 46.
4088. NESBITT, R. J.
"Eight Ways to Look at an Orange." [AntigR] (79) Aut 89, p. 123-124.
4089. NESTOR, Jack
"Jealous of the Rain." [StoneC] (16:3/4) Spr-Sum 89, p. 33.
4090. NEUFELDT, Leonard
"Sunday Services." [MalR] (87) Sum 89, p. 109.
"The Women of Yarrow" (for Lora and Carol). [MalR] (87) Sum 89, p. 108.
4091. NEUMAN, Scott
"Breakfast with W.C.W. the Morning After the Famous Plum Ingestion." [WindO]
(52) Wint 89-90, p. 29.
"A Professor of Chemistry." [WindO] (52) Wint 89-90, p. 30.
4092. NEVAQUAYA, Joe Dale Tate
"Flecks." [Nimrod] (32:2) Spr-Sum 89, p. 31.
"Nightline." [Nimrod] (32:2) Spr-Sum 89, p. 30.
4093. NEVILLE, Tam Lin
"A Plain Story." [Crazy] (36) Spr 89, p. 44-45.
"Street." [MassR] (30:1) Spr 89, p. 15.
4094. NEWCOMB, P. F.
"Chrysanthemums." [CapeR] (24:2) Fall 89, p. 18.
"Fallen Bodies." [Plain] (10:1) 89, p. 33.
4095. NEWCOMB, Richard
"Avocado Sestina." [RiverC] (9:1) Spr 89, p. 20-21.
"This Is a Poem for Those." [RiverC] (9:1) Spr 89, p. 18-19.
4096. NEWKIRK, Peg
"To Heather -- At Sixteen." [Kalliope] (11:2) 89, p. 16-17.
4097. NEWLOVE, John
"God Bless the Bear." [MalR] (86) Spr 89, p. 94.
"Telephone Book." [MalR] (86) Spr 89, p. 95.
4098. NEWMAN, Amy
"The Next Town." [DenQ] (24:2) Fall 89, p. 81.
4099. NEWMAN, Michael
"Middle Age." [Bogg] (61) 89, p. 28-29.
4100. NEWMAN, P. B.
"Aquarius." [TarRP] (29:1) Fall 89, p. 42.
"Christmas." [KanQ] (21:3) Sum 89, p. 61.
"The Death of Henry James." [GeoR] (43:3) Fall 89, p. 476.
"Letter to a Woman on the Landscape." [KanQ] (21:1/2) Wint-Spr 89, p. 27.
"Of Time and the River." [Wind] (19:64) 89, p. 21-22.
"Ward's Pond." [Wind] (19:64) 89, p. 21.
4101. NEWMAN, Wade
"Business and Poetry." [CrossCur] (8:2) Ja 89, p. 39.
4102. NEWMARK-SHPANCER, Brittany
"The Wild Flowers of Belgrade." [SenR] (19:1) 89, p. 32-33.
NGUYEN, Ngoc Bich
See BICH, Nguyen Ngoc
4103. Ni CHUILLEANAIN, Eileán
"A Voice." [FourQ] (2d series 3:2) Fall 89, p. 9.
4104. Ni DHOMHNAILL, Nuala
"Aubade" (tr. by Michael Longley). [Trans] (22) Fall 89, p. 147.
"The Broken Doll" (tr. by John Montague). [Trans] (22) Fall 89, p. 146.
"Feeding a Child" (tr. by Michael Hartnett). [Trans] (22) Fall 89, p. 141-142.
"The Green Eyes" (tr. by the author). [Trans] (22) Fall 89, p. 130-131.
"In Baile an tSléibhe" (tr. by the author). [Trans] (22) Fall 89, p. 134-135.
"Kiss" (tr. by Michael Hartnett). [YellowS] (30) Sum 89, p. 49.
"Labysheedy (The Silken Bed)" (tr. by the author). [Trans] (22) Fall 89, p. 132-133.
"The Mermaid" (tr. by Michael Hartnett). [Trans] (22) Fall 89, p. 139-140.
"Miscarriage Abroad" (tr. by Michael Hartnett). [Trans] (22) Fall 89, p. 138.
"Poem for Melissa" (tr. by Michael Hartnett). [Trans] (22) Fall 89, p. 143.
"The Race" (tr. by Michael Hartnett). [Trans] (22) Fall 89, p. 144-145.
"The Shannon Estuary Welcoming the Fish" (tr. by Michael Hartnett). [YellowS]
(30) Sum 89, p. 49.
"The Shannon Estuary Welcoming the Fish" (tr. by the author). [Trans] (22) Fall 89,

308

p. 136.
"They Have Painted the Walls White" (tr. of Aine Ni Ghlinn). [Trans] (22) Fall 89, p. 150-151.
"The Visitor" (tr. by Michael Hartnett). [Trans] (22) Fall 89, p. 137.
4105. Ni GHLINN, Aine
"The Broken Step" (tr. by the author). [Trans] (22) Fall 89, p. 148-149.
"They Have Painted the Walls White" (tr. by Nuala Ni-Dhomhnaill). [Trans] (22) Fall 89, p. 150-151.
4106. NI LOINN, E.
"The Moths" (tr. of Seán O Ríordáin). [Trans] (22) Fall 89, p. 48.
4107. NIATUM, Duane
"Landscape of the Whirling Dust." [NoDaQ] (57:2) Spr 89, p. 103.
4108. NICARCHUS
"In Arcadia once, in a three-mile race" (tr. by James Michie). [GrandS] (8:4) Sum 89, p. 83.
4109. NICEWONGER, Kirk
"Limbo." [AmerPoR] (18:6) N-D 89, p. 34.
"Mare Nostrum." [LitR] (32:2) Wint 89, p. 228.
"The Sleepless Man Dreams." [AmerPoR] (18:6) N-D 89, p. 34.
"Waiting" (From *I Ching*, Hexagram 5). [AmerPoR] (18:6) N-D 89, p. 34.
4110. NICHOL, B. P.
"Love Song 2" (from *Zygal*). [Rampike] (6:2) 88, p. 3.
"St. Anzas IX." [CapilR] (1st series: 50) 89, p. 67-70.
4111. NICHOLAS, Leland A.
"Emma." [AntigR] (77/78) Spr-Sum 89, p. 170.
4112. NICHOLLS, Sandra
"Sleeping Under Glass." [Dandel] (16:1) Spr-Sum 89, p. 10-11.
"Small Cracks." [Grain] (17:1) Spr 89, p. 16.
"Wild, Blue-eyed Woman" (for Dorothy Livesay). [Grain] (17:1) Spr 89, inside back cover.
4113. NICHOLS, Martha
"The Hidden Country." [FiveFR] (7) 89, p. 2.
4114. NICHOLS, Sonja
"Afternoon Feast." [EmeraldCR] (1989) c1988, p. 89.
4115. NICHOLS-ORIANS, Judith
"Along the Sarapiqui." [PoetL] (84:1) Spr 89, p. 24.
"Market." [PoetL] (84:1) Spr 89, p. 23.
"Stopping at the Spice Farm" (Costa Rica). [PoetL] (84:1) Spr 89, p. 25.
4116. NICKLAS, Deborah (Deborah Pierce)
"Daddy-Long-Legs." [SouthernPR] (29:1) Spr 89, p. 61.
"Doubts." [CumbPR] (8:2) Spr 89, p. 26.
"The Dutch Elm Disease Hits New England." [Nimrod] (33:1) Fall-Wint 89, p. 96.
"Indian Summer Day." [Nimrod] (33:1) Fall-Wint 89, p. 97.
4117. NICOL, Mike
"A Winter's Tale." [AmerPoR] (18:4) Jl-Ag 89, p. 38.
4118. NIDITCH, B. Z.
"Akhmatova at Tsarskoye Selo." [DenQ] (24:2) Fall 89, p. 82.
"Anna Akhmatova." [Sequoia] (32:2) Wint-Spr 89, p. 59.
"Berlin Diary, 1939." [DenQ] (24:2) Fall 89, p. 83.
"A Bird of Repentance." [SpiritSH] (55) Fall-Wint 89 [90 on cover], p. 22.
"Boston's First Storm." [SpiritSH] (54) Spr-Sum 89, p. 18.
"Budapest, 1956." [SpiritSH] (55) Fall-Wint 89 [90 on cover], p. 24.
"Budapest, 1988." [FreeL] (2) Sum 89, p. 22.
"Conrad Aiken." [Amelia] (5:3, #14) 89, p. 120.
"Day of Robert Lowell's Funeral." [InterPR] (15:2) Fall 89, p. 124-125.
"Dought, 1988." [Sequoia] (32:2) Wint-Spr 89, p. 60.
"Even When You Arrived." [Confr] (39/40) Fall 88-Wint 89, p. 74.
"A Four-Letter Word." [Footwork] 89, p. 43.
"French Diary, 1940." [SpiritSH] (54) Spr-Sum 89, p. 16.
"Georgian Wings." [SpiritSH] (55) Fall-Wint 89 [90 on cover], p. 23.
"Harmonies." [SpiritSH] (55) Fall-Wint 89 [90 on cover], p. 20.
"January 5, 1966" (tr. of Yuli Daniel). [StoneC] (17:1/2) Fall-Wint 89-90, p. 24.
"January 16, 1966" (tr. of Yuli Daniel). [StoneC] (17:1/2) Fall-Wint 89-90, p. 24.
"The Nineties Again." [SpiritSH] (54) Spr-Sum 89, p. 15.
"Nobody Lands." [Interim] (8:1) Spr 89, p. 7.
"Nobody Lands." [Plain] (9:2) Wint 89, p. 25.

"Portrait." [SpiritSH] (55) Fall-Wint 89 [90 on cover], p. 29.
"Preoccupation." [Sequoia] (32:2) Wint-Spr 89, p. 58.
"Return to Budapest." [SpiritSH] (55) Fall-Wint 89 [90 on cover], p. 28-29.
"Returning Home." [Interim] (8:1) Spr 89, p. 6.
"Russian Return." [InterPR] (15:2) Fall 89, p. 123.
"Siege of Stalingrad." [InterPR] (15:2) Fall 89, p. 123-124.
"The Somatic Poet." [SpiritSH] (55) Fall-Wint 89 [90 on cover], p. 25-27.
"Sorry, No Gilded Image for Me." [SpiritSH] (55) Fall-Wint 89 [90 on cover], p. 20.
"The Town Fool." [Sequoia] (32:2) Wint-Spr 89, p. 61.
"Vagankovskoye Cemetery at the Funeral of Yuli M. Daniel" (January 2, 1989). [StoneC] (17:1/2) Fall-Wint 89-90, p. 40.
"Valley Grove, Milton" (For David Rogers). [SpiritSH] (54) Spr-Sum 89, p. 14.
"Venice." [InterPR] (15:2) Fall 89, p. 126.
"Warsaw 1940." [SpiritSH] (54) Spr-Sum 89, p. 17.
"Watching." [InterPR] (15:2) Fall 89, p. 125.
"What Maxim Would Gorky Have to Say?" [SpiritSH] (55) Fall-Wint 89 [90 on cover], p. 21.
"Winter Vacation on Cape Cod." [FreeL] (2) Sum 89, p. 23.
4119. NIELSEN, A. L.
"Brown Coeds Nabbed." [Aerial] (5) 89, p. 156-157.
"Photo Opportunity." [WashR] (15:4) D 89-Ja 90, p. 18.
"Self Organizing Networks." [WashR] (15:4) D 89-Ja 90, p. 18.
4120. NIEVES MIELES, Edgardo
"Tres Lirios de Carne y un Ultimo Arcoiris para Ella." [Mairena] (11:27) 89, p. 60.
4121. NIGHTINGALE, Barbra
"Miranda's Crisis with Words." [Vis] (31) 89, p. 47.
4122. NIMMO, Dorothy
"For Annekate Friedlander." [BelPoJ] (39:3) Spr 89, p. 29.
4123. NIMMO, Kurt
"Criminality." [Lactuca] (12) F 89, p. 30.
"Southern Vacation." [Lactuca] (12) F 89, p. 30-31.
4124. NIMS, John Frederick
"The Dream of Augustine" (Selections: "Now You Are the Only Beast," "Carla," tr. of Mario Santagostini). [Poetry] (155:1/2) O-N 89, p. 149-150.
"Dropping the Names." [NewL] (56:2/3) Wint 89-Spr 90, p. 202-203.
"Freight." [GettyR] (2:3) Sum 89, p. 478-482.
"Niagara." [NewL] (56:2/3) Wint 89-Spr 90, p. 196-201.
"The Observatory Ode" (Harvard, June 1978). [NewL] (56:2/3) Wint 89-Spr 90, p. 193-195.
"Poetry Workshop (First Semester)." [AmerS] (58:2) Spr 89, p. 208-209.
"The Six-Cornered Snowflake." [Poetry] (155:3) D 89, p. 191-202.
"The Wine of Astonishment." [SewanR] (97:2) Spr 89, p. 189-194.
4125. NIMTZ, Steven
"The Contract." [BambooR] (41) Wint 89, p. 23-24.
"The Wind." [BambooR] (41) Wint 89, p. 25-26.
NIORD, Chard de
See DeNIORD, Chard
4126. NISETICH, Frank
"Ten Goodbyes to a Brief Affair / A Sonnet Sequence" (Selection: #1). [KanQ] (21:1/2) Wint-Spr 89, p. 273.
4127. NISKALA, Brenda
"A Cry Too Far." [Grain] (17:1) Spr 89, p. 52.
4128. NOBLE, Anita
"And Then." [BlackWR] (15:2) Spr 89, p. 112.
"December 1887." [NowestR] (27:2) 89, p. 55.
"Like This." [BlackWR] (15:2) Spr 89, p. 113.
"So What." [StoneC] (17:1/2) Fall-Wint 89-90, p. 32.
"The Ten Gates" (Selections: 11 poems, First Prize). [Nimrod] (33:1) Fall-Wint 89, p. 1-11.
4129. NOBLE, Claude Mary
"Moon Anesthesia." [Nimrod] (32:2) Spr-Sum 89, p. 81.
"Night Activity at a Campsite." [Nimrod] (32:2) Spr-Sum 89, p. 81.
4130. NOBLES, Edward
"Astronomy." [Boulevard] (4:1, #10) Spr 89, p. 179-180.
"The Letter." [NoDaQ] (57:3) Sum 89, p. 104-105.

"Natural History." [TarRP] (29:1) Fall 89, p. 11.
"A Violent Inheritance." [MinnR] (NS 32) Spr 89, p. 71.
4131. NOGUER, Eduardo G.
"El Eclipse." [Mairena] (11:27) 89, p. 84.
4132. NOGUERAS, Luis Rogelio
"At the Designated Hour" (For Juan Antonio Bardem in flight Madrid-Prague, tr. by
    Lourdes González). [Pig] (15) 88, p. 69.
4133. NOGUERE, Suzanne
"The Scribes." [LitR] (32:2) Wint 89, p. 226.
4134. NOLAN, Husam
"The Shaker at Hancock House." [PassN] (10:1) Wint 89, p. 8.
"Snowflake or Bone." [PassN] (10:2) Sum 89, p. 28.
4135. NOLAN, James
"Bread and Onions." [MissR] (18:1, #52) 89, p. 74-75.
"Sum." [ChatR] (10:1) Fall 89, p. 24.
4136. NOLAN, Patricia
"The Circle." [Event] (18:3) Fall 89, p. 62-63.
"Into Temptation." [Event] (18:3) Fall 89, p. 64.
NOORD, Barbara van
    See Van NOORD, Barbara
4137. NORBERG, Viktoria
"Appetite." [PacificR] (7) 89, p. 6.
4138. NORDFORS, Douglas
"A Dog's Life." [Iowa] (19:2) Spr-Sum 89, p. 159.
"The Slaughter of Elephants." [Iowa] (19:2) Spr-Sum 89, p. 160-161.
"Twenty-Four Hours." [Iowa] (19:2) Spr-Sum 89, p. 162.
4139. NORDHA, Jean
"The Dream of Packing." [HolCrit] (26:4) O 89, p. 18.
4140. NORDHAUS, Jean
"Opening Oysters" (for Roland Flint). [PassN] (10:2) Sum 89, p. 23.
"Traveler." [AmerPoR] (18:6) N-D 89, p. 46.
4141. NORDSTROM, Lars
"I Believe" (1987, after Chernobyl, tr. of Inger Tapio, w. Ralph Salisbury). [CharR]
    (15:2) Fall 89, p. 76.
"Snow Flakes" (tr. of Inger Tapio, w. Ralph Salisbury). [CharR] (15:2) Fall 89, p.
    74.
"Summer Morning" (tr. of Inger Tapio, w. Ralph Salisbury). [CharR] (15:2) Fall
    89, p. 75.
4142. NORRIS, Kathleen
"Calentures." [SoDakR] (27:1) Spr 89, p. 120.
"God's Boredom." [Witness] (3:1) Spr 89, p. 106.
"How I Came to Drink My Grandmother's Piano." [PraS] (63:2) Sum 89, p. 81-82.
"The Ignominy of the Living." [NewYorker] (65:15) 29 My 89, p. 40.
"LaVonne's Mantlepiece." [Witness] (3:1) Spr 89, p. 104.
"A Letter to Paul Carroll, Who Said That I Must Become a Catholic So That I Can
    Pray for Him." [ChiR] (36:3/4) 89, p. 25-26.
"My Favorite Woman in the World." [Salm] (84) Fall 89, p. 61-62.
"On the Land." [SoDakR] (27:1) Spr 89, p. 121.
"The Sky Is Full of Blue and Full of the Mind of God" (for Odo Muggli, O.S.B.).
    [PraS] (63:2) Sum 89, p. 80.
"St. Mary of Egypt Speaks to a Gentleman in a Victorian Whorehouse." [Witness]
    (3:1) Spr 89, p. 105-106.
4143. NORRIS, Leslie
"Early Frost." [NoDaQ] (57:2) Spr 89, insert p. 33-35.
"Elegy for David Beynon." [NoDaQ] (57:2) Spr 89, insert p. 36-37.
"Sonnets to Orpheus" (Selections: I: 15, 26, II: 3, 19, tr. of Rainer Maria Rilke, w.
    Alan Keele). [QW] (28) Wint-Spr 89, p. 93-96.
"Water." [NoDaQ] (57:2) Spr 89, insert p. 32-33.
4144. NORTH, Charles
"Chain." [HangL] (55) 89, p. 25.
"Nocturnes" (Selections: 4-7). [HangL] (55) 89, p. 23-24.
"On the Road" (after Colin Muset). [HangL] (55) 89, p. 22.
"Sunrise with Sea Monster." [Pequod] (28/29/30) 89, p. 198.
4145. NORTH, Mick
"The Pheasant Plucker's Son." [Stand] (30:4) Aut 89, p. 14-15.

4146. NORTH, Oliver L.
"Howls" (From "The Found Poetry of Lt. Col. Oliver L. North," compiled by John W. Hart III). [Harp] (279:1673) O 89, p. 30.
4147. NORTON, Scott
"Feast." [US1] (22/23) Spr 89, p. 38.
4148. NOSOW, Robert
"Congregation Leaving the Service." [CarolQ] (42:1) Fall 89, p. 70.
4149. NOSTRAND, Jennifer
"Hunting Scenes at the Carlyle." [KanQ] (21:3) Sum 89, p. 28-29.
4150. NOTLEY, Alice
"Mother Mask." [BrooklynR] (6) 89, p. 56-57.
"Mother Mask." [Ploughs] (15:4) Wint 89-90, p. 153-154.
4151. NOVAK, Helga M.
"Pill" (tr. by Sammy McLean). [MissR] (18:1, #52) 89, p. 105-106.
"Ready" (tr. by Sammy McLean). [MidAR] (9:1) 89, p. 42.
4152. NOWAK, Maril
"Dependable Imperfections." [SenR] (19:2) Fall 89, p. 43-44.
4153. NOWAK, Tadeusz
"Pastoral Psalm" (for Zosia, tr. by Stanislaw Baranczak and Clare Cavanah). [Trans] (21) Spr 89, p. 60-61.
"Psalm with No Answer" (tr. by Stanislaw Baranczak and Clare Cavanagh). [SenR] (19:2) Fall 89, p. 26.
4154. NOWLIN, Linda
"Chrysalides" (for K.S.). [CimR] (89) O 89, p. 104.
"Revisiting Bonnard: The Nudes." [NewRep] (200:17) 24 Ap 89, p. 36.
4155. NOWLING, Will
"John Morrow." [EmeraldCR] (1989) c1988, p. 83.
4156. NUÑEZ, Lorgio
"Valvula de Espejo." [Mairena] (11:27) 89, p. 84.
4157. NURKSE, D.
"Beyond the Breakwater." [HangL] (55) 89, p. 27.
"The Car Bomb." [HangL] (55) 89, p. 29.
"The First House." [MSS] (6:3) 89, p. 24.
"Half Past Dawn." [YellowS] (29) Spr 89, p. 10.
"The Hidden Fighters." [AmerPoR] (18:4) Jl-Ag 89, p. 32.
"The Invisible Faction." [HangL] (55) 89, p. 28.
"The Left Hemisphere." [BlueBldgs] (11) 89, p. 29.
"Linked Fates." [YellowS] (29) Spr 89, p. 10.
"Matched Hands." [YellowS] (29) Spr 89, p. 10.
"The Next World." [WestB] (25) 89, p. 23.
"Rumors." [AmerPoR] (18:4) Jl-Ag 89, p. 32.
"The Scab." [HangL] (55) 89, p. 26.
"The Screen." [HangL] (55) 89, p. 30.
"The United States Embassy in Salvador." [WestB] (25) 89, p. 22.
"Visiting Hours." [SoCoast] (5) Spr 88, p. 21.
4158. NUSHOLTZ, Jody
"Circling." [Amelia] (5:3, #14) 89, p. 92.
4159. NYE, Naomi Shihab
"Eating in Berkeley." [Witness] (2:2/3) Sum-Fall 88, p. 266-267.
"The Edge of a Country." [IndR] (13:1) Wint 89, p. 66-67.
"Here." [IndR] (13:1) Wint 89, p. 65.
"What Brings Us Out." [GeoR] (43:1) Spr 89, p. 159-160.
4160. NYHART, Nina
"Stern Visage" (after a painting by Paul Klee). [Ploughs] (15:4) Wint 89-90, p. 155-156.
4161. NYSTROM, Debra
"Reading Late." [Ploughs] (15:1) 89, p. 91.
"The Viewer." [Ploughs] (15:1) 89, p. 89-90.
4162. NYSTROM, Karen L.
"After the Talons Are Removed." [DenQ] (23:3/4) Wint-Spr 89, p. 114.
4163. O CRUALAOICH, Gearóid
"Anger" (tr. of Máirtín O Direáin). [Trans] (22) Fall 89, p. 37.
"Swan-Woman" (tr. of Máirtín O Direáin). [Trans] (22) Fall 89, p. 37.
4164. O DIREAIN, Máirtín
"Anger" (tr. by Gearóid O Crualaoich). [Trans] (22) Fall 89, p. 37.
"Aran 1947" (tr. by Valentin Iremonger). [Trans] (22) Fall 89, p. 36.

"Berkeley" (tr. by Douglas Sealy and Tomás MacSíomóin). [Trans] (22) Fall 89, p. 35.
"Grief's Dignity" (tr. by Douglas Sealy and Tomás MacSíomóin). [Trans] (22) Fall 89, p. 32.
"Invitation to the Virgin" (tr. by Douglas Sealy and Tomás MacSíomóin). [Trans] (22) Fall 89, p. 31.
"Spring in the West" (tr. by Douglas Sealy and Tomás MacSíomóin). [Trans] (22) Fall 89, p. 33.
"Stout Oars" (tr. by Douglas Sealy and Tomás MacSíomóin). [Trans] (22) Fall 89, p. 34.
"Swan-Woman" (tr. by Gearóid O Crualaoich). [Trans] (22) Fall 89, p. 37.
4165. O MUIRTHILE, Liam
"Portrait of Youth I" (for Annie Bowen/Julia Brien, tr. by Ciaran Carson). [Trans] (22) Fall 89, p. 128-129.
4166. O RIORDAIN, Seán
"Claustrophobia" (tr. by James Gleasure). [Trans] (22) Fall 89, p. 47.
"The Duck" (tr. by Cosslett Quinn). [Trans] (22) Fall 89, p. 45.
"Fever" (tr. by Richard Ryan). [Trans] (22) Fall 89, p. 46.
"Freedom" (tr. by Cosslett Quinn). [Trans] (22) Fall 89, p. 43-44.
"Frozen" (tr. by Valentin Iremonger). [Trans] (22) Fall 89, p. 40.
"The Moths" (tr. by E. Ní Loinn). [Trans] (22) Fall 89, p. 48.
"My Mother's Burying" (tr. by Valentin Iremonger). [Trans] (22) Fall 89, p. 38-40.
"Turnabout" (tr. by David Marcus). [Trans] (22) Fall 89, p. 42.
"The Women's Christmas Night" (tr. by David Marcus). [Trans] (22) Fall 89, p. 41.
4167. O SEARCAIGH, Cathal
"Seasons" (tr. by Thomas McCarthy). [Trans] (22) Fall 89, p. 152.
"Words of a Brother" (tr. by Thomas McCarthy). [Trans] (22) Fall 89, p. 152.
4168. O TUAIRISC, Eoghan
"Kyrie -- From Mass for the Dead Who Died at Hiroshima" (tr. by the author). [Trans] (22) Fall 89, p. 56-57.
4169. O TUAMA, Seán
"Christy Ring" (tr. by the author). [Trans] (22) Fall 89, p. 68-69.
"An Ecologist" (tr. of Biddy Jenkinson). [Trans] (22) Fall 89, p. 114.
"A Gaeltacht Rousseau" (tr. by the author). [Trans] (22) Fall 89, p. 66.
"Greek Waters" (tr. by the author). [Trans] (22) Fall 89, p. 67.
"In the Convent of Mercy" (tr. of Michael Davitt). [Trans] (22) Fall 89, p. 120.
"Love-Game" (tr. by the author). [Trans] (22) Fall 89, p. 66.
"The Poet to His Wife" (From a 3-act play *Four Cheers for Cremation*, tr. by the author). [Trans] (22) Fall 89, p. 65.
"She Being 78, He Being 84" (tr. by the author). [Trans] (22) Fall 89, p. 64.
4170. OANDASAN, William
"Acoma." [Pig] (15) 88, p. 53.
"Journeys to Myself." [Pig] (15) 88, p. 53.
4171. OATES, Catherine
"Absence." [PaintedB] (37) 89, p. 8.
"Fin de Siecle." [PaintedB] (37) 89, p. 7.
4172. OATES, Joyce Carol
"American Merchandise." [Agni] (28) 89, p. 233.
"Don't Bare Your Soul! [Agni] (28) 89, p. 236-237.
"Edward Hopper, *Nighthawks*, 1942." [YaleR] (78:3) Spr 89, p. 415-416.
"Falling Asleep at the Wheel, Route 98 North" (in memoriam, John Gardner). [MichQR] (28:1) Wint 89, p. 75-76.
"First Death, 1950" (in memory of my grandfather John Bush). [NewL] (56:2/3) Wint 89-Spr 90, p. 204-205.
"Half-Cracked Poetess." [AmerPoR] (18:5) S-O 89, p. 14.
"Honeymoon: 40 Years." [AmerPoR] (18:5) S-O 89, p. 14.
"I Can Stand There in the Corner" (for Norman Sherry). [Agni] (28) 89, p. 234-235.
"Love of the Parrots." [SouthwR] (74:4) Aut 89, p. 488.
"Marsyas Flayed by Apollo." [Pequod] (28/29/30) 89, p. 67.
"Night-Driving." [MassR] (30:3) Aut 89, p. 450.
"Nightmare, Mid-Summer." [NewL] (56:2/3) Wint 89-Spr 90, p. 207.
"Orion." [GettyR] (2:4) Aut 89, p. 575.
"The Present Tense." [NewL] (56:2/3) Wint 89-Spr 90, p. 206.
"Sleepless in Heidelberg." [MichQR] (28:1) Wint 89, p. 77-78.
"Through the Night." [NewL] (56:2/3) Wint 89-Spr 90, p. 208.
"The Time Traveler" (Selections: 3 poems). [OntR] (31) Fall-Wint 89-90, p. 49-50.

"Welcome to Dallas!" [WestHR] (43:1) Spr 89, p. 48-49.
"Young Love, America." [Atlantic] (264:1) Jl 89, p. 60.
"Your Blood in a Little Puddle, on the Ground." [GrandS] (8:3) Spr 89, p. 62-63.
4173. OBADIAH, Silas
   "The Counsel." [Obs] (3:3) Wint 88, p. 56.
4174. OBATALA, T.
   "Poem Written in View of the Christ." [ChangingM] (20) Wint-Spr 89, p. 24.
4175. OBENZINGER, Hilton
   "New York on Fire" (Selections). [WilliamMR] (27) 89, p. 25-35.
4176. OBERMAN, Sheldon
   "Interference." [Grain] (17:3) Fall 89, p. 58.
4177. OBERMEYER, Jon M.
   "Omnipresent." [GreensboroR] (46) Sum 89, p. 97.
4178. O'BRIEN, Geoffrey
   "007." [CentralP] (15) Spr 89, p. 10.
   "Water Music." [NewYRB] (36:12) 20 Jl 89, p. 7.
4179. O'BRIEN, Michael
   "Earring." [Bomb] (27) Spr 89, p. 73.
   "In the Elevator." [Bomb] (27) Spr 89, p. 73.
   "Poem: The world and its likeness given at once." [Bomb] (27) Spr 89, p. 73.
   "Seacoast." [Bomb] (27) Spr 89, p. 72.
   "Sundown" (in memory of George Quinan). [Bomb] (27) Spr 89, p. 72.
4180. O'BRIEN, Michael J.
   "Drought." [MidwQ] (30:2) Wint 89, p. 205.
4181. O'CONNELL, Patrick
   "I would Tell You Silence." [PraF] (10:1, #46) Spr 89, p. 55.
   "Lisa." [AntigR] (77/78) Spr-Sum 89, p. 34.
   "Who Could Be More Wonderful Than You." [PraF] (10:1, #46) Spr 89, p. 54.
4182. O'CONNELL, Richard
   "Epigrams from Martial" (4 epigrams). [ApalQ] (31) 89, p. 47.
4183. O'CONNOR, Deirdre
   "At the Psychic Reader's in Allentown, New Year's Day." [PoetL] (84:2) Sum 89,
      p. 22.
   "Hospital." [PoetL] (84:1) Spr 89, p. 45.
   "Pretending." [PoetL] (84:1) Spr 89, p. 43-44.
4184. O'CONNOR, Mark
   "Aboriginal Literacy." [Descant] (20:3/4, #66/67) Fall-Wint 89, p. 186.
   "Dinosaur Dreamtime" (a fantasy for Mt Stegorsaurus and the Centre). [Descant]
      (20:3/4, #66/67) Fall-Wint 89, p. 184-185.
   "Extinction of the Huia" (for Belinda Gillies). [Descant] (20:3/4, #66/67) Fall-Wint
      89, p. 180-181.
   "The Fruit Salad Jungle." [Descant] (20:3/4, #66/67) Fall-Wint 89, p. 182-183.
   "The Glass Cage." [Descant] (20:3/4, #66/67) Fall-Wint 89, p. 187-189.
4185. O'CONNOR, Sheila M.
   "How We Survive." [SingHM] (16) 89, p. 49.
4186. O'DALY, William
   "The Sea and the Bells" (Selections: 5 poems, tr. of Pablo Neruda). [PoetryE] (27)
      Spr 89, p. 134-138.
   "The Separate Rose" (Selections: IV, VII, XII, tr. of Pablo Neruda). [PoetryE] (27)
      Spr 89, p. 124-126.
   "Still Another Day" (Selections: I, V, XVII, tr. of Pablo Neruda). [PoetryE] (27) Spr
      89, p. 127-129.
   "The Winter Garden" (Selections: 3 poems, tr. of Pablo Neruda). [PoetryE] (27) Spr
      89, p. 130-133.
4187. ODAM, Joyce
   "As Soon As It Gets Light We Will Go Back to Bed." [PoetC] (21:1) Fall 89, p. 6.
   "Childless" (Honorable Mention). [StoneC] (17:1/2) Fall-Wint 89-90, p. prelim. p.
      2.
   "Dancer Among the Dancers." [ChamLR] (3:1, #5) Fall 89, p. 7.
   "In the House Are Many Souls." [ChamLR] (2:2, #4) Spr 89, p. 44.
   "In Whispered Rooms." [Interim] (8:2) Fall 89, p. 45.
   "The Lady Who Collects Elephants." [Lactuca] (13) N 89, p. 42.
   "The Phone Call." [Bogg] (61) 89, p. 21.
   "A Safe Walk Through the Garden." [KanQ] (21:1/2) Wint-Spr 89, p. 55.
   "Spells Against the Season." [PoetC] (20:2) Wint 89, p. 24.
   "The Stolen Child." [StoneC] (16:3/4) Spr-Sum 89, p. 48.

"Time Passing." [KanQ] (21:3) Sum 89, p. 158.
"Winter." [PoetC] (20:2) Wint 89, p. 22-23.
4188. O'DONNELL, Dianne
"New York" (Creative Writing Club Contest, 3rd Place). [DeKalbLAJ] (22:1/4) 89,
p. 79.
4189. O'DONNELL, Hugh
"Lady in Waiting." [FourQ] (2d series 3:2) Fall 89, p. 32.
4190. O'DONNELL, Mary E.
"Cot Death." [Vis] (29) 89, p. 37.
"The Tooth Fairy." [Vis] (29) 89, p. 36.
"The Widest River." [NoDaQ] (57:1) Wint 89, p. 113-115.
4191. O'DRISCOLL, Ciaran
"Cinecamera, 1944." [NoDaQ] (57:1) Wint 89, p. 117.
"A Veteran Recalls the Trojan War." [NoDaQ] (57:1) Wint 89, p. 116-117.
"Winter." [NoDaQ] (57:1) Wint 89, p. 116.
4192. OESTREICHER, Deb
"Discussion with Howie." [KanQ] (21:1/2) Wint-Spr 89, p. 257.
"In the Dark." [KanQ] (21:1/2) Wint-Spr 89, p. 258.
"The Marriage: For Worse." [PoetC] (20:3) Spr 89, p. 42-43.
4193. OFFEN, Ron
"Remembering / Remembered" (to James Baldwin, tr. of Jacques Dauphin).
[StoneC] (17:1/2) Fall-Wint 89-90, p. 42.
4194. OFNER, Terry
"Coming Home: Tanglefoot Lane." [WorldO] (21:3/4) Spr-Sum 87, c89, p. 62.
"Starting." [WorldO] (21:3/4) Spr-Sum 87, c89, p. 23.
4195. OGDEN, Hugh
"At the Intersection, Route 2, Route 17." [PacificR] (7) 89, p. 74-75.
"The Better Way Cafe, Near Goshen." [CinPR] (20) Fall 89, p. 36-37.
"Fingers." [CinPR] (20) Fall 89, p. 38-39.
"Let the Mind Become." [Blueline] (10:1/2) 89, p. 64.
"Stellwagen" (for Ted Paullin and the Friends of Hartford Monthly Meeting).
[PacificR] (7) 89, p. 72-73.
"When I Come to Dinner." [Blueline] (10:1/2) 89, p. 63.
4196. O'GRADY, Desmond
"A Willow Sprig" (for Professor Kelleher . . . on the occasion of his retirement from
Harvard, 1986). [NoDaQ] (57:1) Wint 89, p. 118-120.
4197. O'GRADY, Jennifer
"Geography" (After Chekhov's letters). [SouthernR] (25:3) Sum 89, p. 624-625.
4198. O'HARA, Deborah
"Trapeze Artists." [HighP] (4:1) Spr 89, p. 89.
4199. OHE, Brucette
"A Small Elegy for Myself" (tr. of Georgina Herrera). [Pig] (15) 88, p. 63.
4200. OHNESORGE-FICK, M. (Marlon)
"Looking for Small Bodies." [Pig] (15) 88, p. 49.
"A Slow Figure in the Key of Minor Sleep." [KanQ] (21:1/2) Wint-Spr 89, p.
166-167.
4201. OHRBOM, Mary Elizabeth
"Going Out of Business." [EmeraldCR] (1989) c1988, p. 124.
4202. O'KEEFE, Daniel
"How It Is." [HarvardA] (124:1) N 89, p. 30.
"The Rain Man." [HarvardA] (123:4) My 89, p. 8.
4203. O'KEEFE, Michael
"A Popular Myth." [Bomb] (30) Wint 89-90, p. 78.
"The Woman I Am With." [Bomb] (30) Wint 89-90, p. 76-77.
OKIKAZE, Fujiwara no (ca. 910)
See FUJIWARA NO OKIKAZE (CA. 910)
4204. OKU, Princess (7th c.)
"Even when we wandered together" (tr. by Sam Hamill). [PoetryE] (28) Fall 89, p.
200.
4205. OLAH, János
"Bundás." [Hawai'iR] (13:1, #25) Spr 89, p. 52.
"May Dog Dundas" (tr. by Nicholas Kolumban). [Hawai'iR] (13:1, #25) Spr 89, p.
53.
4206. OLANDER, Renee
"Sarah's Rites and Reflections." [Amelia] (5:3, #14) 89, p. 67.

4207. OLDER, Julia
"Daughters." [NewL] (56:2/3) Wint 89-Spr 90, p. 209.
"Pebbles." [NewL] (56:2/3) Wint 89-Spr 90, p. 210.
"Threads." [Vis] (30) 89, p. 6.
"Two Clans." [NewL] (56:2/3) Wint 89-Spr 90, p. 212.
"The Whistle, Dying." [NewL] (56:2/3) Wint 89-Spr 90, p. 211.
4208. OLDKNOW, Antony
"The Dog" (tr. of Paul Eluard). [WebR] (14:1) Spr 89, p. 16.
"Fish" (tr. of Paul Eluard). [WebR] (14:1) Spr 89, p. 17.
"In Order to Live Here" (tr. of Paul Eluard). [WebR] (14:1) Spr 89, p. 17.
"Me and the Big Bang." [SoDakR] (27:4) Wint 89, p. 74.
"Trees." [SoDakR] (27:4) Wint 89, p. 72-73.
4209. OLDS, Sharon
"The Bathrobe." [NewYorker] (64:49) 23 Ja 89, p. 36.
"Earliest Memory." [Poetry] (153:4) Ja 89, p. 208.
"Outdoor Shower." [Atlantic] (264:5) N 89, p. 110.
"Znamenskaya Square, Leningrad, 1941." [Poetry] (153:4) Ja 89, p. 207.
4210. O'LEARY, Dawn
"Surviving." [AntR] (47:3) Sum 89, p. 320-321.
"The Undoing." [JINJPo] [11] 89, p. 21.
4211. O'LEARY, Patrick
"I Knew." [PoetryE] (28) Fall 89, p. 15.
"Stuck." [PoetryE] (28) Fall 89, p. 16.
4212. OLEJNISZYM, Alexandra
"III. I have this poor sick head again" (tr. of Maria Korusiewicz). [Verse] (6:1) Mr
89, p. 40.
4213. OLES, Carole
"Day Trip." [ColR] (NS 16:2) Fall 89-Wint 90, p. 78.
"Echo Cardiogram." [ColR] (NS 16:2) Fall 89-Wint 90, p. 79-80.
"For Evelyn." [Poetry] (153:4) Ja 89, p. 194-195.
"The Gambler" (En route via Reno, Nevada). [Poetry] (153:5) F 89, p. 288-289.
"The Girl on the Red Velvet Swing" (Evelyn Nesbit, 1884-1967). [ColR] (NS 16:2)
Fall 89-Wint 90, p. 81-83.
"Letter to a High-School Friend, a Re-formed Radical." [ColR] (NS 16:2) Fall
89-Wint 90, p. 77.
"Love Poem Because." [DenQ] (24:1) Sum 89, p. 67.
"Stunts." [ColR] (NS 16:2) Fall 89-Wint 90, p. 76.
4214. OLES, Carole Simmons
"Tangier Repeats." [HolCrit] (26:3) Je 89, p. 19.
4215. OLINKA, Sharon
"The Broken Column: Frida Kahlo Speaks." [PaintedB] (37) 89, p. 22-23.
"Making a Sale." [WillowS] (23) Wint 89, p. 55.
"The Man in the 1986 Thunderbird." [WillowS] (23) Wint 89, p. 54.
"Oyster House." [HayF] (5) Fall 89, p. 66-67.
4216. OLIVE, Harry
"Light, Precious As the Sun." [Plain] (9:3) Spr 89, p. 25.
"Silk, the Time Was." [Interim] (8:2) Fall 89, p. 9.
"Woods, Black Crosses Stain the Snow." [Plain] (10:1) 89, p. 10.
4217. OLIVER, Louis Littlecoon
"My Haunt." [Nimrod] (32:2) Spr-Sum 89, p. 120.
"Salute to Alexander Posey." [Nimrod] (32:2) Spr-Sum 89, p. 121.
4218. OLIVER, Mary
"Little Owl Who Lives in the Orchard." [Ploughs] (15:4) Wint 89-90, p. 157-158.
"White Owl Flies Into and Out of the Field." [NewYorker] (64:46) 2 Ja 89, p. 26.
4219. OLIVER LABRA, Carilda
"The Boy Who Sells Greens" (tr. by Daniela Gioseffi, w. Enildo Garcia). [Contact]
(9:50/51/52) Fall-Wint 88-Spr 89, p. 39.
"Declaration of Love" (1963, October Cuban Missile Crisis, tr. by Daniela Gioseffi,
w. Enildo Garcia). [Contact] (9:50/51/52) Fall-Wint 88-Spr 89, p. 38.
"The Last Conversation with Rolando Escardo" (tr. by Daniela Gioseffi, w. Enildo
Garcia). [Contact] (9:50/51/52) Fall-Wint 88-Spr 89, p. 41.
"Of the Word" (tr. by Daniela Gioseffi, w. Enildo Garcia). [Contact] (9:50/51/52)
Fall-Wint 88-Spr 89, p. 40.
"When Papa" (tr. by Daniela Gioseffi, w. Enildo Garcia). [Contact] (9:50/51/52)
Fall-Wint 88-Spr 89, p. 40.

4220. OLLER, Walter
"Elegiac Lullaby." [Screens] (1) 89, p. 178.
"Sled Dog." [Screens] (1) 89, p. 177-178.
4221. OLMSTED, Katya
"And Schubert on the water, and Pushkin living on rations" (tr. of Aleksandr
Eremenko, w. John High). [FiveFR] (7) 89, p. 97.
"Portrait" (tr. of Ivan Zhdanov, w. John High). [FiveFR] (7) 89, p. 74.
"Still-Life" (tr. of Nina Iskrenko, w. John High). [FiveFR] (7) 89, p. 54.
"Talking to my crested hen" (tr. of Nina Iskrenko, w. John High). [FiveFR] (7) 89,
p. 55.
"To Beat or Not to Beat" (tr. of Nina Iskrenko, w. John High). [FiveFR] (7) 89, p.
56-57.
"To talk with you is like burning in the marsh" (tr. of Nina Iskrenko, w. John High).
[FiveFR] (7) 89, p. 53.
4222. OLSAN, Lea
"Pecan." [FloridaR] (16:2/3) Fall-Wint 89, p. 217.
4223. OLSEN, Lance
"Paw." [Shen] (39:3) Fall 89, p. 65.
"Taking Off." [CreamCR] (13:2) Fall 89, p. 111.
4224. OLSEN, William
"Big Language." [NewRep] (201:8) 21 Ag 89, p. 38.
"Black Storm." [Crazy] (37) Wint 89, p. 13-15.
"Fireflies in the New World." [PoetryNW] (30:4) Wint 89-90, p. 13-15.
"Happiness" (after Leonard Gardner and John Huston). [Crazy] (37) Wint 89, p.
16-17.
"In the Light of Dimmed Exteriors" (partial eclipse, Houston, 1984). [PoetryNW]
(30:4) Wint 89-90, p. 16.
"Painter's Wife's Island." [IndR] (12:3) Sum 89, p. 51-54.
"Richard Hakluyt's Notebooks of His Last Bedridden Summer." [IndR] (12:3) Sum
89, p. 48-50.
4225. OLSON, Charles
"The chain of memory is resurrection I am a vain man." [Sulfur] (9:2, #25) Fall 89,
p. 4-9.
4226. OLSON, Kirby
"Epitaphs" (3 poems, tr. of Philippe Soupault). [Rampike] (6:1) 87, p. 65.
"Homewards" (to M. P. Bons d'Anty, tr. of Henry J. M. Levet). [PartR] (56:1)
Wint 89, p. 122.
"Outwards" (to Francis Jammes, tr. of Henry J. M. Levet). [PartR] (56:1) Wint 89,
p. 121-122.
4227. OLSON, Marian
"Tracking." [Kalliope] (11:3) 89, p. 56.
4228. O'MELVENY, Regina
"Artichokes." [YellowS] (29) Spr 89, p. 19.
"Mongoose, Armadillo." [YellowS] (29) Spr 89, p. 19.
"She Considers Love with a Man Who Is Already Pregnant by Another Woman."
[YellowS] (30) Sum 89, p. 13.
"She Does the Red Dress Dance." [YellowS] (29) Spr 89, p. 18.
4229. O'NEILL, Alexandre
"Among Rocks, Words" (tr. by Richard Zenith). [MalR] (89) Wint 89, p. 97.
"Creation" (tr. by Richard Zenith). [MalR] (89) Wint 89, p. 99.
"The Hanged Man" (tr. by Richard Zenith). [MalR] (89) Wint 89, p. 98.
"St. Francis' Empty Sandal" (tr. by Richard Zenith). [MalR] (89) Wint 89, p. 96.
"Table" (tr. by Richard Zenith). [MalR] (89) Wint 89, p. 100.
4230. O'NEILL, Brian
"Late March, Driving West of Paris Crossing, Indiana." [OhioR] (44) 89, p. 60-61.
"One Month After" (for my father). [OhioR] (44) 89, p. 62-63.
4231. ONO NO YOSHIKI (D. 902)
"My love grows" (tr. by Sam Hamill). [PoetryE] (28) Fall 89, p. 203.
4232. ONYSHKEVYCH, Larissa M. L.
"The Winds of Saburtalo" (tr. of Serhiy Paradjanov). [Agni] (28) 89, p. 210-211.
4233. OPENGART, Bea
"Niangua, the Drought." [Shen] (39:2) Sum 89, p. 27.
"Summer Flowers in a Plastic Glass." [Shen] (39:2) Sum 89, p. 28-29.
4234. OPPEN, George
"The Circumstances" (A Selection from Uncollected Writing, ed. by Rachel Blau Du
Plessis). [Sulfur] (9:2, #25) Fall 89, p. 10-43.

4235. ORAVECZ, Imre
"After We Broke Up" (tr. by Bruce Berlind with Mária Körösy). [TriQ] (77) Wint
89-90, p. 296.
"Autumn in the Midwest" (tr. by Bruce Berlind and Mária Körösy). [ArtfulD]
(16/17) Fall 89, p. 66.
"It Was Still Summer" (tr. by Bruce Berlind with Mária Körösy). [TriQ] (77) Wint
89-90, p. 297.
"When Now and Then We Run Into Each Other" (tr. by Bruce Berlind with Mária
Körösy). [TriQ] (77) Wint 89-90, p. 295.
"You Are Asking Me" (tr. by Nicholas Kolumban). [PoetryE] (28) Fall 89, p. 179.
4236. ORBAN, Ottó
"A Blade of Grass" (tr. by Jascha Kessler). [Jacaranda] (4:1) Spr-Sum 89, p. 48.
"A Nice Little War" (tr. by Jascha Kessler). [Jacaranda] (4:1) Spr-Sum 89, p. 47.
"Photograph" (tr. by Jascha Kessler). [Jacaranda] (4:1) Spr-Sum 89, p. 49.
"Poverty" (tr. by Jascha Kessler, w. Maria Körösy). [Margin] (9) 89, p. 36.
4237. OREN, Miriam
"Advice" (tr. by Ruth Whitman). [AmerPoR] (18:6) N-D 89, p. 46.
"Exile" (tr. by Ruth Whitman). [AmerPoR] (18:6) N-D 89, p. 46.
ORIANS, Judith Nichols
See NICHOLS-ORIANS, Judith
4238. ORLEN, Steve
"Acrobatics" (For Gibb Windahl). [HighP] (4:2) Fall 89, p. 72-73.
"Conversation with the Dead" (Carol Marcus 1946-1969). [Colum] (14) 89, p. 190.
"Shame." [Poetry] (154:6) S 89, p. 323.
4239. ORLOWSKY, Dzvinia
"Four in the Morning." [Jacaranda] (4:1) Spr-Sum 89, p. 26.
"Yellow Jacket." [Jacaranda] (4:1) Spr-Sum 89, p. 25.
4240. ORMOND, John
"Ancient Monuments" (for Alexander Thom). [NoDaQ] (57:2) Spr 89, insert p.
44-46.
"Definition of a Waterfall." [NoDaQ] (57:2) Spr 89, insert p. 48.
"My Grandfather and His Apple Tree." [NoDaQ] (57:2) Spr 89, insert p. 46-47.
4241. ORMSBY, Eric
"Bee Balm." [Blueline] (10:1/2) 89, p. 28.
"My Mother in Old Age." [NewYorker] (65:28) 28 Ag 89, p. 32.
"Wood Fungus." [Blueline] (10:1/2) 89, p. 29.
4242. ORMSHAW, W. P.
"Descent." [Quarry] (38:4) Fall 89, p. 71.
"Jerusalem War Cemetery." [Quarry] (38:4) Fall 89, p. 69-70.
"Poem for Mom and Her Birds." [Quarry] (38:4) Fall 89, p. 68.
4243. ORNSTEIN, Nancy MacDonald
"A House." [Footwork] 89, p. 35.
"Remembrance 1951." [US1] (22/23) Spr 89, p. 41.
4244. O'ROARK, Frances
"The Anarchy Notebooks." [PoetryE] (28) Fall 89, p. 137-138.
"Island." [PoetryE] (28) Fall 89, p. 136.
4245. O'ROURK, Maury
"Lorna Lamé." [MissR] (17:3, #51), p. 66-67.
4246. OROZCO, Olga
"After Days" (tr. by Mary Crow). [BlackWR] (15:2) Spr 89, p. 109, 111.
"Después de los Días." [BlackWR] (15:2) Spr 89, p. 108, 110.
"In the End Was the Word" (tr. by Mary Crow). [LitR] (32:4) Sum 89, p. 555.
"The Other Side" (tr. by Mary Crow). [LitR] (32:4) Sum 89, p. 554.
"Reference Point" (tr. by Mary Crow). [LitR] (32:4) Sum 89, p. 552-553.
"Wailing Wall" (tr. by Mary Crow). [LitR] (32:4) Sum 89, p. 556.
4247. ORR, Ed
"The Obvious Not So." [YellowS] (31) Aut 89, p. 35.
4248. ORR, Pam
"Birth Throes." [Pembroke] (21) 89, p. 160.
4249. ORR, Priscilla
"For My Unborn Daughter." [SouthernPR] (29:1) Spr 89, p. 36-37.
4250. ORR, Verlena
"The Quiet Room." [MidwQ] (31:1) Aut 89, p. 56.
"Seven-Mile Grade, August 1948." [PoetC] (21:1) Fall 89, p. 27.
4251. ORTEGA, Julio
"Baroque Body" (tr. by James Hoggard). [StoneC] (16:3/4) Spr-Sum 89, p. 23.

"Cuerpo Barroco." [StoneC] (16:3/4) Spr-Sum 89, p. 22.
4252. ORTH, Kevin
"The Age of Steam." [Journal] (12:2) Fall-Wint 88-89, p. 48.
"From the Industrial North." [HighP] (4:2) Fall 89, p. 26-27.
"Now" (tr. of Manuel Nadian). [Vis] (31) 89, p. 15.
ORTIZ COFER, Judith
See COFER, Judith Ortiz
4253. ORTOLANI, Al
"Conversation with an Arkansas Farmer." [MidwQ] (30:2) Wint 89, p. 191.
4254. OSAKI, Mark
"Snow." [Hawai'iR] (13:1, #25) Spr 89, p. 78-79.
4255. OSBORN, Karen
"Gathering Wildflowers." [KanQ] (21:1/2) Wint-Spr 89, p. 216.
4256. OSBORNE, Alex
"One Day Old" (tr. of Biddy Jenkinson). [Trans] (22) Fall 89, p. 115.
"Spray" (tr. of Biddy Jenkinson). [Trans] (22) Fall 89, p. 116.
4257. OSHEROW, Jacqueline
"Letter to Rainer Maria Rilke." [WestHR] (43:3) Aut 89, p. 160-166.
4258. OSHIRO, Willis
"Bad Cookies." [Hawai'iR] (13:2, #26) Sum 89, p. 14.
4259. OSIELSKI, Jill
"The Hands of a Blind Man." [Mildred] (3:1) Spr-Sum 89, p. 37.
4260. OSING, Gordon
"Chloroquine" (Bangkok). [NoDaQ] (57:4) Fall 89, p. 36.
"A Clove of Garlic Poem" (for Sayre and Owen). [Vis] (29) 89, p. 19.
"Department Store TV's." [ColEng] (51:5) S 89, p. 481.
"Job" (for John Fergus Ryan). [SouthernHR] (23:1) Wint 89, p. 65.
"Lines Composed Over a Brandy at Punch 'n Judy's After a Long Walk and a Play .
. ." (again, St. Paul's, Covent Garden). [OxfordM] (5:1) Spr-Sum 89, p. 68.
"A Postcard from China" (Guangzhou). [SoCoast] (7) Spr-Fall 89, p. 48.
"The Queen of the Farm Courtyard" (tr. of Liu Xiaofang, w. Li Xijian). [BelPoJ]
(40:2) Wint 89-90, p. 14-15.
"Smoke from the Kitchen Chimneys in My Hometown" (tr. of Yang Mu, w. Li
Xijian). [BelPoJ] (40:2) Wint 89-90, p. 16-17.
4261. OSMAN, Jena
"Over-Painting." [Notus] (4:2) Fall 89, p. 69-73.
"Small System." [CentralP] (15) Spr 89, p. 164.
4262. OSMOND, R. K.
"Dancing with Rope." [AntigR] (79) Aut 89, p. 136.
4263. OSSMANN, April
"News Bulletin." [CimR] (87) Ap 89, p. 87.
4264. OSTRIKER, Alicia
"Alice Before Her Widowhood." [OntR] (30) Spr-Sum 89, p. 72.
"Anecdotes without Flowers, 1919." [Shen] (39:3) Fall 89, p. 90.
"Bitterness." [PraS] (63:1) Spr 89, p. 66.
"The Circus." [Nat] (248:12) 27 Mr 89, p. 424.
"The Eighties: A Poem to Aphrodite." [US1] (22/23) Spr 89, p. 4.
"Fifty." [OntR] (30) Spr-Sum 89, p. 74.
"George in the Hospital." [OntR] (30) Spr-Sum 89, p. 73.
"Happy Birthday." [PraS] (63:1) Spr 89, p. 65.
"Helium." [Poetry] (154:4) Jl 89, p. 226.
"I Can't Speak." [Poetry] (154:4) Jl 89, p. 225.
"Migrant." [US1] (22/23) Spr 89, p. 5.
"The Story of Joshua." [US1] (22/23) Spr 89, p. 5.
"Sunlight" (for C. M.). [Shen] (39:3) Fall 89, p. 89.
"Windowglass." [Shen] (39:3) Fall 89, p. 91.
4265. O'SULLIVAN, Derry
"Stillborn 1943: A Call to Limbo" (tr. by Michael Davitt). [Trans] (22) Fall 89, p.
100-101.
4266. O'SULLIVAN, Michael
"At Sea, at Land." [Vis] (31) 89, p. 31.
4267. OTERO, Blas de
"Man" (tr. by Francis Golffing). [SpiritSH] (54) Spr-Sum 89, p. 33.
4268. OTEY, Wili
"Abreaction." [Plain] (9:2) Wint 89, p. 10-11.
"Hinc Meae Lacrimae (Hence My Tears)." [Plain] (9:3) Spr 89, p. 19.

4269. OTIS, Emily
"Nocturne." [WestB] (23) 89, p. 9.
"Proverb." [WestB] (23) 89, p. 9.
4270. OTOMA NO KATAMI (ca. 750)
"Across Kasuga Moor" (tr. by Sam Hamill). [PoetryE] (28) Fall 89, p. 201.
4271. O'TOOLE, Jean M.
"Point of View." [Footwork] 89, p. 40.
4272. OTT, Gil
"A crew procedures us." [Screens] (1) 89, p. 134.
"Lost another year." [Screens] (1) 89, p. 132.
"Status." [PaperAir] (4:2) 89, p. 99-101.
"Stingere." [RedBass] (14) 89, p. 54-56.
"Transparence." [Screens] (1) 89, p. 135.
"Up short on him." [Screens] (1) 89, p. 133.
4273. OTTEN, Charlotte F.
"Two Sons Dead" (2 Samuel 21). [Comm] (116:8) Ap 21, 89, p. 241.
4274. OTTEN, Nick
"Grasses" (tr. of Po Chu-yi, w. Chuan Y. Fu). [RiverS] (30) [89], p. 79.
"Premier of Shu" (tr. of Tu Fu, w. Chuan Y. Fu). [RiverS] (30) [89], p. 78.
4275. OUELLETTE, Connie
"Ira's Blue Gift." [Vis] (31) 89, p. 38.
4276. OUGHTON, Libby
"The Fullerbrushman Calls." [MalR] (87) Sum 89, p. 75-77.
4277. OVERLAND, Patty
"Fever." [SinW] (39) Wint 89-90, p. 80-81.
4278. OVERTON, Ron
"26. While touring the studios of the TV network, a woman." [MinnR] (NS 32) Spr
89, p. 87.
"56. The train moves across the nightscape, a delirious snake." [MinnR] (NS 32)
Spr 89, p. 88.
"74. It's a hot hardboiled May Friday night." [MinnR] (NS 32) Spr 89, p. 87-88.
4279. OVID
"Epistulae ex Ponto: Book III" (tr. by David Slavitt). [TexasR] (10:1/2) Spr-Sum 89,
p. 48-49.
"The Epistulae ex Ponto: Book III" (tr. by David R. Slavitt). [SouthwR] (74:2) Spr
89, p. 220-224.
"Letter from the Black Sea" (1. To Brutus, tr. by David R. Slavitt). [Trans] (22) Fall
89, p. 219-221.
4280. OWEN, Eileen
"Ballooning over the Reformatory into a Field of Cows." [SoDakR] (27:3) Aut 89,
p. 116.
"Walls Tumbling Down." [SoDakR] (27:3) Aut 89, p. 117.
4281. OWEN, H. H., Jr.
"Junk." [GrahamHR] (12) Spr 89, p. 19.
4282. OWEN, Jan
"Saxophone." [Verse] (6:3) Wint 89, p. 78.
4283. OWEN, Maureen
"Crime Story." [Contact] (9:50/51/52) Fall-Wint 88-Spr 89, p. 32.
"The flax in blossom, bluebuttons." [Contact] (9:50/51/52) Fall-Wint 88-Spr 89, p.
31.
"Friday night, having a headache." [Contact] (9:50/51/52) Fall-Wint 88-Spr 89, p.
33.
"Might." [Contact] (9:50/51/52) Fall-Wint 88-Spr 89, p. 30.
"Prairie Song" (for Willa Cather). [Contact] (9:50/51/52) Fall-Wint 88-Spr 89, p.
31.
"Rain dents a steady robust." [Contact] (9:50/51/52) Fall-Wint 88-Spr 89, p. 31.
"Sunday dusk." [Contact] (9:50/51/52) Fall-Wint 88-Spr 89, p. 33.
4284. OWEN, Stephen
"Broken Boat" (tr. of Tu Fu). [LitR] (32:3) Spr 89, p. 427.
4285. OWEN, Sue
"A is for Apocalypse." [Journal] (13:1) Spr-Sum 89, p. 63.
"The Cutting Board." [Journal] (13:1) Spr-Sum 89, p. 60.
"Sorrow and Woe Poem." [Journal] (13:1) Spr-Sum 89, p. 62.
"Soul Searching." [Journal] (13:1) Spr-Sum 89, p. 61.
"Total Darkness." [Poetry] (155:3) D 89, p. 205.
"The Wand of Time." [Journal] (13:1) Spr-Sum 89, p. 59.

"Written in Blood." [Poetry] (155:3) D 89, p. 204.
4286. OWENS, Derek
"Grandfather." [Amelia] (5:3, #14) 89, p. 23.
4287. OWENS, Rochelle
"The First Person" (from "Discourse on Life & Death"). [Temblor] (10) 89, p. 4-17.
4288. OWENS, Scott
"The Event Rightfully Remembered." [SouthernPR] (29:1) Spr 89, p. 48-49.
"Preserving the Horn." [SouthernPR] (29:1) Spr 89, p. 48.
4289. OWENS, Suzanne
"As in an Hour of Generations." [SenR] (19:2) Fall 89, p. 80-83.
"A Kiss a Cactus a Betrayal" (For my daughter, just turned thirteen). [Interim] (8:2)
     Fall 89, p. 19-21.
4290. OWER, John
"Honeymoon on Maui" (for S. H.). [Poem] (62) N 89, p. 53.
"Love's Promise" (for S. H.). [Poem] (62) N 89, p. 52.
4291. OZSVATH, Zsuzsanna
"Jewel" (tr. of Janos Pilinszky, w. Martha Satz). [WebR] (14:1) Spr 89, p. 30.
"Silence" (tr. of Endre Veszi, w. Martha Satz). [WebR] (14:1) Spr 89, p. 30.
"Waiting for Miracles" (tr. of Attila Szepesi, w. Martha Satz). [WebR] (14:1) Spr
     89, p. 29.
4292. PACE, Rosalind
"The Fighter Continues to Speak About His Fear." [OntR] (31) Fall-Wint 89-90, p.
     24-25.
"The Fighter Speaks About His Fear." [OntR] (31) Fall-Wint 89-90, p. 23-24.
"The Young Model (Puberty)" (from a lithograph, 1894, by Edvard Munch). [DenQ]
     (24:2) Fall 89, p. 84.
4293. PACERNICK, Gary
"August." [PoetryE] (28) Fall 89, p. 145.
4294. PACK, Robert
"Cosmic Recycling." [KenR] (NS 11:2) Spr 89, p. 32-33.
"Place." [KenR] (NS 11:2) Spr 89, p. 30-31.
4295. PADEL, Ruth
"Byzantium Remembers Waiting." [Pequod] (26/27) 89, p. 119-120.
"Gar Sur." [Pequod] (26/27) 89, p. 120.
4296. PADGAONKAR, Mangesh
"Salaam" (tr. by Vinay Dharwadker). [TriQ] (77) Wint 89-90, p. 211-214.
"Seven Forty-five in the Morning" (tr. by Vinay Dharwadker). [TriQ] (77) Wint
     89-90, p. 210.
4297. PADGETT, Ron
"August 17, 1971." [Pequod] (28/29/30) 89, p. 217.
4298. PADHI, Bibhu
"Midnight Consolings." [Poetry] (155:3) D 89, p. 219.
4299. PADILLA, Heberto
"De Me a Ti" (tr. of Alastair Reid). [LindLM] (8:4) O-D 89, p. 3.
"Hard Times" (tr. by Anthony Kerrigan). [Salm] (82/83) Spr-Sum 89, p. 321.
"Juego de Espejos" (tr. of Alastair Reid). [LindLM] (8:4) O-D 89, p. 3.
"Una Leccion de Musica" (tr. of Alastair Reid). [LindLM] (8:4) O-D 89, p. 3.
"The Old Bards Say" (tr. by Anthony Kerrigan and Jeanne Cook). [Salm] (82/83)
     Spr-Sum 89, p. 320.
"Por Ella" (tr. of Alastair Reid). [LindLM] (8:4) O-D 89, p. 3.
"A Swim Off Havana" (tr. by Anthony Kerrigan and Jeanne Cook). [Salm] (82/83)
     Spr-Sum 89, p. 320.
4300. PAGE, Carolyn W.
"Clothesline." [Pembroke] (21) 89, p. 130-131.
4301. PAGE, Joanne
"Black Ice." [Quarry] (38:4) Fall 89, p. 14.
"Shut Out in the Garden." [Quarry] (38:4) Fall 89, p. 15-16.
"White on White." [Quarry] (38:4) Fall 89, p. 17.
4302. PAGE, Susan Roxie
"Hymn Sung in a High Meadow." [CumbPR] (9:1) Fall 89, p. 39.
"Now." [CumbPR] (9:1) Fall 89, p. 38.
4303. PAGE, William
"The Movie." [KanQ] (21:1/2) Wint-Spr 89, p. 184.
"Under the Star." [KanQ] (21:1/2) Wint-Spr 89, p. 183.
4304. PAGIS, Dan
"The Art of Minimalism" (tr. by Tsipi Keller). [PoetryE] (28) Fall 89, p. 178.

"Ein Leben" (tr. by Stephen Mitchell). [NewYorker] (65:7) 3 Ap 89, p. 85.
"A Moment at the Louvre" (tr. by Stephen Mitchell). [NewYorker] (65:13) 15 My
89, p. 42.
PAHLITZSCH, Lori Storie
See STORIE-PAHLITZSCH, Lori
4305. PAINCHAUD, Alain-Arthur
"1. Sensibles aux écolos moqueurs." [Rampike] (6:2) 88, p. 56.
"2. Mon lot de vie quotidienne." [Rampike] (6:2) 88, p. 56.
"3. Image furtive noire et grise." [Rampike] (6:2) 88, p. 56.
"4. Que la caresse de ton esprit." [Rampike] (6:2) 88, p. 56.
4306. PAINO, Frankie
"1965" (for Gerrie). [Crazy] (37) Wint 89, p. 30-31.
4307. PAIR, Grant
"Doorway" (tr. of Rainer Maria Rilke). [Jacaranda] (4:1) Spr-Sum 89, p. 62.
4308. PALACIOS MORE, René
"Dije que el día en que me amase." [Mairena] (11:27) 89, p. 85.
4309. PALANDER, John
"Autumn" (from Paroles, tr. of Jacques Prévert). [AntigR] (79) Aut 89, p. 73.
"On Leave" (from Paroles, tr. of Jacques Prévert). [AntigR] (79) Aut 89, p. 71.
"To Paint the Picture of a Bird" (tr. of Jacques Prévert). [AntigR] (77/78) Spr-Sum
89, p. 93, 95.
"Would You Believe It?" (From Rêves à Vendre, tr. of Félix Leclerc). [AntigR]
(77/78) Spr-Sum 89, p. 91.
4310. PALEN, John
"In a Public Park." [WebR] (14:1) Spr 89, p. 71.
"Leaving Home" (First Prize, 1989 Poetry Competition). [PassN] (10:2) Sum 89, p.
3.
"Music Room." [PassN] (10:1) Wint 89, p. 18.
"Old Ferd." [WebR] (14:1) Spr 89, p. 71.
4311. PALEOS, Kalliopy
"The Offer." [Footwork] 89, p. 74.
4312. PALLADAS
"Like a heard of swine, we're all fed under guard" (tr. by James Michie). [GrandS]
(8:4) Sum 89, p. 83.
4313. PALLISTER, Jan
"Game" (tr. of Mbaya Gana Kebe). [Pig] (15) 88, p. 50.
"The Little Signare" (tr. of Mbaya Gana Kebe). [Pig] (15) 88, p. 50.
"Words" (tr. of Mbaya Gana Kebe). [Pig] (15) 88, p. 50.
4314. PALMA, Michael
"Drinker's Delight (and Wisdom)" (tr. of Giorgio Caproni). [Poetry] (155:1/2) O-N
89, p. 35.
"The Elevator" (tr. of Giorgio Caproni). [Poetry] (155:1/2) O-N 89, p. 30-32.
"I Am Awakened" (tr. of Maurizio Cucchi). [Poetry] (155:1/2) O-N 89, p. 124.
"Inviolate" (tr. of Tiziano Rossi). [Poetry] (155:1/2) O-N 89, p. 93.
"The Knives" (tr. of Giorgio Caproni). [Poetry] (155:1/2) O-N 89, p. 33.
"Sorrow" (tr. of Maurizio Cucchi). [Poetry] (155:1/2) O-N 89, p. 125.
"The Words" (tr. of Giorgio Caproni). [Poetry] (155:1/2) O-N 89, p. 35.
"Youth" (tr. of Tiziano Rossi). [Poetry] (155:1/2) O-N 89, p. 92.
PALMA, Ray di
See DiPALMA, Ray
4315. PALMER, David
"The Man in the Park" (for my Father). [PassN] (10:1) Wint 89, p. 10.
4316. PALMER, Justin
"Theseus." [CumbPR] (8:2) Spr 89, p. 91.
4317. PALMER, Michael
"In C." [Talisman] (3) Fall 89, p. 8.
"Six Hermetic Songs" (for Robert Duncan). [Sulfur] (9:2, #25) Fall 89, p. 197-201.
4318. PALMER, Winthrop
"At Some Distance." [Confr] (39/40) Fall 88-Wint 89, p. 276.
"Bride." [Confr] (39/40) Fall 88-Wint 89, p. 277.
"The Buildings of New York." [Confr] (39/40) Fall 88-Wint 89, p. 277.
"Credo." [Confr] (39/40) Fall 88-Wint 89, p. 270.
"Festival." [Confr] (39/40) Fall 88-Wint 89, p. 277.
"Park Avenue." [Confr] (39/40) Fall 88-Wint 89, p. 276.
4319. PALMQUIST, Tira
"Being Caught Coming and Going." [TriQ] (77) Wint 89-90, p. 269-270.

"Manifest Destiny." [TriQ] (77) Wint 89-90, p. 267-268.
PANDEYA, Sudama
      See DHOOMIL
4320. PANDIRI, Thalia A.
      "Holy Ewe-Lamb, Madonna of the Pressure Cooker" (Selections: 10 poems, tr. of
            Athina Papadaki). [TriQ] (74) Wint 89, p. 170-179.
4321. PANKEY, Eric
      "Anniversary Ode." [Journal] (13:1) Spr-Sum 89, p. 20.
      "Expulsion from the Garden." [Journal] (13:1) Spr-Sum 89, p. 21.
      "Fool's Gold." [CinPR] (19) Spr 89, p. 40-41.
      "Icon." [Antaeus] (62) Spr 89, p. 177.
      "The Map." [Antaeus] (62) Spr 89, p. 178.
      "Memory of Heaven." [Poetry] (155:3) D 89, p. 226.
      "Ode on the Present Tense." [CinPR] (19) Spr 89, p. 39.
      "Ox." [RiverS] (30) [89], p. 67.
      "When the Wood Is Green." [NewYorker] (65:19) 26 Je 89, p. 40.
4322. PANOFF, Doris
      "This Ring." [WestB] (23) 89, p. 59.
4323. PAOLA, Suzanne
      "At Oakland Cemetery, with Bruce." [KanQ] (21:1/2) Wint-Spr 89, p. 85.
      "The Harrowing of Hell." [MissouriR] (12:2) 89, p. 28.
      "Intensive Care." [OntR] (30) Spr-Sum 89, p. 36.
      "June Prayer." [OntR] (30) Spr-Sum 89, p. 35-36.
      "Plague" (A Letter to Raymond of Capua, confessor and confidant to St. Catherine).
            [DenQ] (24:1) Sum 89, p. 68-69.
PAOLI, Francisco Matos
      See MATOS PAOLI, Francisco
4324. PAPADAKI, Athina
      "Holy Ewe-Lamb, Madonna of the Pressure Cooker" (Selections: 10 poems, tr. by
            Thalia A. Pandiri). [TriQ] (74) Wint 89, p. 170-179.
4325. PAPALEO, Joe
      "American Dream: First Report." [Footwork] 89, p. 19.
      "My Mother's Blindness." [Footwork] 89, p. 19.
      "Picasso at Ninety One." [Footwork] 89, p. 20-21.
      "Sister Mary Olympia at Eighty." [Footwork] 89, p. 20.
PAPPAS, Rita Signorelli
      See SIGNORELLI-PAPPAS, Rita
4326. PAPPAS, Theresa
      "One Night, Years from Now." [SouthernHR] (23:1) Wint 89, p. 53.
      "Possession." [NoDaQ] (57:3) Sum 89, p. 222-223.
      "Red Dress with Flower" (after a painting). [PoetL] (84:3) Fall 89, p. 32.
4327. PARADIS, Philip
      "Fall Planting" (for Marj). [PoetC] (20:3) Spr 89, p. 23.
      "In a Used-Books Store." [PoetC] (20:3) Spr 89, p. 21.
      "Ode to My Old Shoes." [PoetC] (20:3) Spr 89, p. 22.
      "Out Walking." [SouthernHR] (23:3) Sum 89, p. 254.
4328. PARADJANOV, Serhiy
      "The Winds of Saburtalo" (tr. by Larissa M. L. Onyshkevych). [Agni] (28) 89, p.
            210-211.
4329. PARENZEE, Donald
      "Something I Saw" (Umtata, Transkei). [AmerPoR] (18:4) Jl-Ag 89, p. 33.
4330. PARHAM, Robert
      "Life Is Clutter." [GeoR] (43:3) Fall 89, p. 569.
      "Rising in the Cold." [SouthernPR] (29:1) Spr 89, p. 59.
      "Teaching the Natives About the Sonnet." [HampSPR] Wint 89, p. 39.
4331. PARINI, Jay
      "Good Friday in Amalfi." [KenR] (N 11:4) Fall 89, p. 48.
4332. PARISH, Barbara S. (Barbara Shirk)
      "Beginning." [SmPd] (26:3 #77) Fall 89, p. 13.
      "Farm Hand." [Plain] (10:1) 89, p. 36.
      "Final Reunion." [Plain] (9:2) Wint 89, p. 35.
      "Hill-Shaded House." [Plain] (10:1) 89, p. 35.
4333. PARISI, Philip
      "A Dawn" (tr. of Alfonso Gatto). [Journal] (13:1) Spr-Sum 89, p. 54.
      "For the Martyrs of Piazzale Loreto" (tr. of Alfonso Gatto). [Journal] (13:1)
            Spr-Sum 89, p. 52-53.

"Returning at Dawn through San Vittore" (tr. of Alfonso Gatto). [Journal] (13:1)
Spr-Sum 89, p. 51.
4334. PARK, Donna M.
"Leftovers." [Kalliope] (11:2) 89, p. 54.
"Massacre." [Kalliope] (11:2) 89, p. 55-56.
4335. PARK, Hye Yung
"In the City." [Footwork] 89, p. 65.
4336. PARK, Tony
"Holding On." [SouthernR] (25:3) Sum 89, p. 619-620.
"Poem for Wesley Who Moos." [HampSPR] Wint 89, p. 20-21.
"Porcupine Quills." [GeoR] (43:2) Sum 89, p. 373.
4337. PARKER, Alan Michael
"Alchemy." [NewYorker] (65:12) 8 My 89, p. 38.
"Gents." [GrandS] (8:4) Sum 89, p. 165-169.
4338. PARKER, Aleksandra
"Atlantyda" (tr. of Stanislaw Baranczak, w. Michael Parker). [Verse] (6:1) Mr 89, p.
39.
"A Question of Rhythm" (tr. of Stanislaw Baranczak, w. Michael Parker). [Verse]
(6:1) Mr 89, p. 38.
"Some Time, Years Later" (tr. of Stanislaw Baranczak, w. Michael Parker). [Verse]
(6:1) Mr 89, p. 38.
4339. PARKER, Melinda
"The Anniversary." [Wind] (19:65) 89, p. 21-22.
4340. PARKER, Michael
"Atlantyda" (tr. of Stanislaw Baranczak, w. Aleksandra Parker). [Verse] (6:1) Mr
89, p. 39.
"A Question of Rhythm" (tr. of Stanislaw Baranczak, w. Aleksandra Parker).
[Verse] (6:1) Mr 89, p. 38.
"Some Time, Years Later" (tr. of Stanislaw Baranczak, w. Aleksandra Parker).
[Verse] (6:1) Mr 89, p. 38.
4341. PARKER, Pat
"Legacy" (Selection: Prologue, For Anatasia Jean). [Calyx] (12:1) Sum 89, p.
93-94.
"Love Isn't." [Calyx] (12:1) Sum 89, p. 91-92.
"Love Isn't." [SinW] (39) Wint 89-90, p. 1-2.
"Where Will You Be." [Cond] (16) 89, p. 168-171.
4342. PARKER, Susan
"3 Girls Bass Ackwards." [Rampike] (6:2) 88, p. 69.
"Dog Star." [Rampike] (6:2) 88, p. 69.
4343. PARKER, Trudi
"Tongue Trip." [Writer] (102:12) D 89, p. 26.
4344. PARKINSON, Thomas
"Goodbye, Margaret of Liverpool." [Rampike] (6:2) 88, p. 63.
4345. PARKS, Deb
"More Hair." [EvergreenC] (5:1) Fall 89, p. 21.
4346. PARKS, Richard
"Deformed." [BlackWR] (16:1) Fall-Wint 89, p. 83.
"Obsidian." [BlackWR] (16:1) Fall-Wint 89, p. 82.
4347. PARLATORE, Anselm
"Detroit Quiescence." [Caliban] (6) 89, p. 207-209.
4348. PARRIS, Erin
"On the Road Alone." [PoetC] (21:1) Fall 89, p. 20.
4349. PARSHCHIKOV, Aleksei
"In the savage bathroom, a razor blade glitters" (tr. by John High). [FiveFR] (7) 89,
p. 29.
"Mudflats" (tr. by Michael Molnar). [MichQR] (28:4) Fall 89, p. 727.
"An Overture Spoken to the Work Tools" (tr. by John High). [MichQR] (28:4) Fall
89, p. 724-726.
"Prelude, Spoken to My Work Tools" (tr. by John High). [FiveFR] (7) 89, p.
30-31.
"Two Women Make-Up Artists" (A variation on Michael Lermontov's poem, "In
noon's heat . . .", tr. by John High). [FiveFR] (7) 89, p. 32.
4350. PARSON, Julie
"Eclipse." [SingHM] (16) 89, p. 36.
"Valentine." [SingHM] (16) 89, p. 34-35.

4351. PARSONS, Jeff
"11:02, Boo-Hoo Tuesday." [SlipS] (9) 89, p. 70.
"Big Boned Girls." [WormR] (29:1, #113) 89, p. 8.
"How Many Wrongs Make It Right?" [WormR] (29:1, #113) 89, p. 9.
"It Reminded Me." [WormR] (29:1, #113) 89, p. 9-10.
"Jesus, Jim-Bob, Ya See That." [WormR] (29:1, #113) 89, p. 8.
"Oh, That's What It Is." [WormR] (29:1, #113) 89, p. 9.
"Paper Heroes." [SlipS] (9) 89, p. 69.
"Parsons' Dictionary." [WormR] (29:1, #113) 89, p. 10.
4352. PARTRIDGE, Dixie
"For Harrison, 80, Living Alone." [KanQ] (21:3) Sum 89, p. 110.
"That Moment." [KanQ] (21:3) Sum 89, p. 109.
"Turning to Rain." [Kalliope] (11:1) 89, p. 75.
"Versions." [Kaleid] (18) Wint-Spr 89, p. 15.
"Watermark: The Reservoir." [Comm] (116:4) F 24, 89, p. 118.
"A Woman Dreams of Her Daughter, Born with Down's Syndrome." [CrabCR]
        (6:1) 89, p. 24.
4353. PASOLINI, Pier Paolo
"The Fan" (tr. by David Stivender and J. D. McClatchy). [Poetry] (155:1/2) O-N 89,
        p. 50.
"Flesh and Sky" (tr. by David Stivender and J. D. McClatchy). [Poetry] (155:1/2)
        O-N 89, p. 51.
"Frammento Epistolare, al Ragazzo Codignola." [Poetry] (155:1/2) O-N 89, p. 46.
"Part of a Letter to the Codignola Boy" (tr. by David Stivender and J. D.
        McClatchy). [Poetry] (155:1/2) O-N 89, p. 47.
"Il Pianto della Scavatrice (The Lament of the Excavator)" (Selection: V., tr. by
        David Stivender and J. D. McClatchy). [Poetry] (155:1/2) O-N 89, p. 48-49.
4354. PASS, John
"Breezes And." [MalR] (87) Sum 89, p. 95-96.
"Delicious." [MalR] (87) Sum 89, p. 92.
"For the Animals." [MalR] (87) Sum 89, p. 93-94.
"Godlike." [Event] (18:3) Fall 89, p. 38-39.
"Now Almost." [Event] (18:3) Fall 89, p. 40-41.
4355. PASSER, Jay
"Insect Lord Speaks." [Caliban] (6) 89, p. 179.
"The Shortcomings of Homomorphism." [Caliban] (6) 89, p. 178.
4356. PASTAN, Linda
"At the Equestrian Museum." [Poetry] (154:2) My 89, p. 83.
"Cousins." [GeoR] (43:1) Spr 89, p. 35-36.
"Crocuses." [Atlantic] (263:5) My 89, p. 66.
"The Happiest Day." [KenR] (N 11:4) Fall 89, p. 25.
"The Hat Lady." [Poetry] (154:2) My 89, p. 92.
"The Keeper." [GeoR] (43:1) Spr 89, p. 36.
"The Myth of Perfectability." [Poetry] (155:3) D 89, p. 209.
"An Old Song." [KenR] (N 11:4) Fall 89, p. 26.
"Only Child." [PraS] (63:1) Spr 89, p. 67.
"Possibilities." [PraS] (63:1) Spr 89, p. 68.
"Sometimes in Winter." [Poetry] (155:3) D 89, p. 210.
"Subway." [Poetry] (154:2) My 89, p. 81.
"There Are Tracks." [GettyR] (2:3) Sum 89, p. 393.
"To a Lover Not Taken." [PraS] (63:1) Spr 89, p. 69.
"Waku." [Poetry] (154:2) My 89, p. 84.
"The Way the Leaves Keep Falling." [Poetry] (155:3) D 89, p. 208.
4357. PASTERNAK, Boris
"The Image" (tr. by Mark Rudman and Bohdan Boychuk). [Pequod] (28/29/30) 89,
        p. 273-274.
4358. PASTIOR, Oskar
"On My Sleep" (tr. by John Linthicum). [LitR] (33:1) Fall 89, p. 126.
"Reading with Desert Plinth Desert" (Selection: 2, tr. by John Linthicum). [LitR]
        (33:1) Fall 89, p. 127.
"Reading with Distorter" (Selection: 13, tr. by John Linthicum). [LitR] (33:1) Fall
        89, p. 128.
4359. PASTOOR, Brian
"Early." [AlphaBS] (5) Jl 89, p. 70.
4360. PATILIS, Yannis
"Hot Afternoon" (Selections, tr. by Stathis Gourgouris). [Jacaranda] (4:1) Spr-Sum

89, p. 61.
4361. PATTAY, Ricq
"Loam." [GreensboroR] (47) Wint 89-90, p. 91.
4362. PATTEN, Karl
"Imagining Lost Ancestors in Nova Scotia." [CinPR] (20) Fall 89, p. 8-9.
"Provincial Letter." [CinPR] (20) Fall 89, p. 7.
"Under Cover of Night" (tr. of Robert Desnos). [PaintedB] (38) 89, p. 61.
4363. PATTEN, Leslie
"Ritual." [Mildred] (3:2) 89, p. 64.
"Trying to Pray." [CrabCR] (6:1) 89, p. 7.
4364. PATTEN, Tom
"Aurora Borealis." [Farm] (6:1) Wint-Spr 88-89, p. 88.
4365. PATTERSON, Ian
"So Laid Out on a Cold Marble Day." [Pequod] (26/27) 89, p. 121.
"Time How Short." [Pequod] (26/27) 89, p. 122.
4366. PATTERSON, J. Yvonne
"Of Night." [DeKalbLAJ] (22:1/4) 89, p. 65.
4367. PATTERSON, Veronica
"Angel of Quandaries." [MalR] (89) Wint 89, p. 34.
"The Commando Taking a Shower" (for Jim Disney, painter and climber). [Caliban]
(7) 89, p. 133.
"Landlocked." [Caliban] (7) 89, p. 134.
"The No Poem." [MalR] (89) Wint 89, p. 35.
4368. PATTON, Dina
"Stranded." [EmeraldCR] (1989) c1988, p. 128.
4369. PAU-LLOSA, Ricardo
"The Intruder" (after the painting by Julio Larraz). [DenQ] (23:3/4) Wint-Spr 89, p.
115.
4370. PAUL, Marian O'Brien
"Ice Pearls." [Plain] (9:3) Spr 89, p. 33.
4371. PAUL, Matthew
"Envoy." [SpiritSH] (55) Fall-Wint 89 [90 on cover], p. 47.
"From This Point." [SpiritSH] (55) Fall-Wint 89 [90 on cover], p. 47.
4372. PAULENICH, Craig
"The Still Changes." [KanQ] (21:3) Sum 89, p. 29.
4373. PAULOVICH, Karen
"Life." [Confr] (39/40) Fall 88-Wint 89, p. 219.
4374. PAULUS SILENTIARIUS
"My name is -- Who cares? -- My birthplace" (tr. by James Michie). [GrandS] (8:4)
Sum 89, p. 85.
4375. PAUP, Frederick P.
"A Splurge" (dedicated to P.B. Shelley and H. Weinhard). [BellArk] (5:1) Ja-F 89,
p. 17.
"Vehicle with a Capital V." [BellArk] (5:1) Ja-F 89, p. 3.
4376. PAVLICH, Walter
"A Brother on Mars." [LaurelR] (23:2) Sum 89, p. 65.
"Flying to the Fire with the Doors Off." [Comm] (116:16) S 22, 89, p. 501.
"The Hand Beginning to Burn." [Comm] (116:16) S 22, 89, p. 501.
"Hardhat Pillow." [Comm] (116:16) S 22, 89, p. 501.
"Lost Comedy" (Laurel and Hardy filming at the seashore). [NowestR] (27:1) 89, p.
67.
"Oliver Hardy, a Little Tired." [Manoa] (1:1/2) Fall 89, p. 147.
"Oliver Hardy Near the End." [Manoa] (1:1/2) Fall 89, p. 148.
"On the Life and Death of Stan Laurel's Son." [Manoa] (1:1/2) Fall 89, p. 145.
"Stan Laurel, Retired, at His Oceana Apartment, 1962." [Manoa] (1:1/2) Fall 89, p.
146.
"Stan's." [NowestR] (27:1) 89, p. 66.
4377. PAWELCZAK, Andy
"Going Home." [Footwork] 89, p. 46.
"Jotting." [Footwork] 89, p. 47.
4378. PAWLAK, Mark
"Counterinsurgency: Theory & Praxis." [Pig] (15) 88, p. 86.
"Keepsake" (for Studs Terkel). [SlipS] (9) 89, p. 58-59.
"Orden: Organización Democrática Nacionalista." [Pig] (15) 88, p. 87.
"Subversive." [Pig] (15) 88, p. 86.

4379. PAYNE, Gerrye
"My Sister Is Bones." [Kalliope] (11:1) 89, p. 49.
4380. PAYNE, Johnny
"After the Wrench." [CapeR] (24:1) Spr 89, p. 38.
"Burial Papyrus" (tr. of Gonzalo Rojas). [SenR] (19:1) 89, p. 46-47.
"Don't You Copy Pound" (tr. of Gonzalo Rojas). [SenR] (19:1) 89, p. 43-44.
"For Vallejo" (tr. of Gonzalo Rojas). [SenR] (19:1) 89, p. 45.
"Goodbye to Hölderlin" (tr. of Gonzalo Rojas). [SenR] (19:1) 89, p. 48-49.
"Rimbaud" (tr. of Gonzalo Rojas). [SenR] (19:1) 89, p. 50.
"Running a Red Light in Seymour, Indiana." [CapeR] (24:1) Spr 89, p. 39.
4381. PAYNE, Robert
"How to End a Conversation (Method #33)." [Hawai'iR] (13:1, #25) Spr 89, p.
104-105.
4382. PAZ, Helena
"Melusina II" (A Elena Garro). [Lyra] (2:1/2) 88, c89, p. 10-11.
4383. PEABODY, Richard
"Amnesia." [Kalliope] (10:3) 88, p. 60-61.
"This Year's Girl." [Kalliope] (10:3) 88, p. 61.
4384. PEACOCK, Molly
"Don't Think Governments End the World." [CrossCur] (8:2) Ja 89, p. 56-57.
"Don't Think Governments End the World." [NewL] (56:2/3) Wint 89-Spr 90, p.
219.
"Good Girl." [NewL] (56:2/3) Wint 89-Spr 90, p. 218.
"In a Long Line of Horses." [CrossCur] (8:2) Ja 89, p. 55.
"Joy." [CrossCur] (8:3) Apr 89, p. 11-12.
"A Kind of Parlance." [NewL] (56:2/3) Wint 89-Spr 90, p. 213-215.
"Peacock's Superette." [NewL] (56:2/3) Wint 89-Spr 90, p. 216-217.
"Waking Up." [ParisR] (31:112) Fall 89, p. 24.
"Why I Am Not a Buddhist." [ParisR] (31:112) Fall 89, p. 25.
4385. PEALSTROM, Frank
"The Hunt." [BlueBldgs] (11) 89, p. 12.
4386. PEARL, Dan
"The Molecular Economy." [BellArk] (5:6) N-D 89, p. 9.
4387. PEARN, Victor
"Plaza Major Madrid 1974." [Pembroke] (21) 89, p. 33-34.
4388. PEARSON, Marlene
"The Growing Up and Learning the Truth About Hope and Glory Poems"
(Selections: "2. Revelations," "3. The Lesson"). [Calyx] (12:2) Wint 89-90, p.
15-17.
"To Document a 20-Second Hug Between 2 Women in a Mental Hospital w/o Saying
the 'L' Word." [Calyx] (12:2) Wint 89-90, p. 18-19.
4389. PEARSON, Ted
"Stanzas from a Work in Progress" (Selections: VIII-XXI). [Temblor] (10) 89, p.
18-21.
"Work in Progress: 1-VII." [Screens] (1) 89, p. 84-90.
4390. PECK, Gail J.
"Capricorn." [NegC] (9:2) 89, p. 26.
"Grieving." [WilliamMR] (27) 89, p. 88.
4391. PECKHAM, Robert Shannan
"Smoke." [Verse] (6:2) Je 89, p. 28.
4392. PECZYNSKI, Joseph
"Father and Son." [Lactuca] (12) F 89, p. 40.
4393. PEDEN, Margaret Sayers
"Ode to a Pantheress" (tr. of Pablo Neruda). [NewOR] (16:2) Sum 89, p. 62-63.
"Ode to a Ship in a Bottle" (tr. of Pablo Neruda). [NewOR] (16:2) Sum 89, p.
86-87.
4394. PEDERSEN, Pat
"Her Real Name." [CrabCR] (6:1) 89, p. 25.
4395. PEDERSON, Miriam
"Woman on a Sled" (on my 40th birthday). [PassN] (10:1) Wint 89, p. 18.
4396. PEDRICK, Jean
"Hospital Visitors." [SouthernPR] (29:1) Spr 89, p. 51.
4397. P'EI, Ti
"Deer Park" (w. Wang Wei, tr. by Joseph Lisowski). [LitR] (32:3) Spr 89, p. 422.
"Frost Bamboo Ranges" (w. Wang Wei, tr. by Joseph Lisowski). [LitR] (32:3) Spr
89, p. 421.

"Lakeside Pavilion" (in Chinese & English, tr. by Joseph Lisowski). [KanQ] (21:3) Sum 89, p. 72.
"Magnolia Enclosure" (w. Wang Wei, tr. by Joseph Lisowski). [LitR] (32:3) Spr 89, p. 422.
"Meng Wall Cove" (w. Wang Wei, tr. by Joseph Lisowski). [LitR] (32:3) Spr 89, p. 421.

4398. PEIRCE, Kathleen
"Crane." [Farm] (6:1) Wint-Spr 88-89, p. 105.
"Hunger." [Farm] (6:1) Wint-Spr 88-89, p. 102-103.
"Love." [Farm] (6:1) Wint-Spr 88-89, p. 104.

4399. PELL, Derek
"Gestures of Arousal." [Rampike] (6:3) 88, p. 69.

4400. PELLAROLO, Silvia
"I. El Duelo de *Requiem para (Mi?) Infancia RIO-plat-ENSE*." [Mester] (18:1) Spr 89, p. 53-54.
"III. The Desperadoes Queman las Naves de *Requiem para (Mi?) Infancia RIO-plat-ENSE*." [Mester] (18:1) Spr 89, p. 55.

4401. PELLETIER, Gus
"Speaking of Poets: Bookjacket Talk." [PoetC] (20:2) Wint 89, p. 49-50.

4402. PELOT, John
"Florida Sunset." [GreensboroR] (46) Sum 89, p. 138.
"Grilling Quail." [GreensboroR] (46) Sum 89, p. 138.

4403. PEMBER, John
"All Day for a Dime: The IRT." [JINJPo] [11] 89, p. 22-23.

4404. PENCE, Amy (Amy S.)
"Down to the Cathedral." [NegC] (9:2) 89, p. 76-77.
"For My Mother." [AntR] (47:4) Fall 89, p. 451.
"Transparent Diary." [NewAW] (5) Fall 89, p. 118.

4405. PENDARVIS, Edwina D.
"Before the Flood" (Pikeville, 1956). [Wind] (19:64) 89, p. 23.
"Speaking in Tongues." [Wind] (19:64) 89, p. 23-24.

4406. PENG, Jianpu
"Poem: The bluebird bites a grape" (tr. by James F. Maybury). [NewOR] (16:3) Fall 89, p. 28.

4407. PENGILLY, Gordon
"Urban Erotic." [Dandel] (16:2) Fall-Wint 89, p. 25.

4408. PENNA, Sandro
"Down There" (tr. by William Jay Smith). [Poetry] (155:1/2) O-N 89, p. 17.
"Interior" (tr. by William Jay Smith). [Poetry] (155:1/2) O-N 89, p. 15.
"Interno." [Poetry] (155:1/2) O-N 89, p. 14.
"Laggiù, Dove una Storia." [Poetry] (155:1/2) O-N 89, p. 16.
"Life, Is Remembering Having Wakened" (tr. by William Jay Smith). [Poetry] (155:1/2) O-N 89, p. 15.
"The Little Venetian Square" (tr. by William Jay Smith). [Poetry] (155:1/2) O-N 89, p. 15.
"Nuotatore." [Poetry] (155:1/2) O-N 89, p. 16.
"Swimmer" (tr. by William Jay Smith). [Poetry] (155:1/2) O-N 89, p. 17.
"La Veneta Piazzetta." [Poetry] (155:1/2) O-N 89, p. 14.
"La Vita, E Ricordarsi di un Risveglio." [Poetry] (155:1/2) O-N 89, p. 14.

4409. PENNANT, Edmund
"Sisera." [HangL] (55) 89, p. 32.

4410. PENNEY, Darby
"The Error of Light." [Blueline] (10:1/2) 89, p. 39.
"Still in November, Trout." [Blueline] (10:1/2) 89, p. 40.

4411. PENNEY, Scott
"Brooklyn Canal." [KanQ] (21:3) Sum 89, p. 191.

4412. PENNY, Michael
"Caveat Pellagra." [Event] (18:3) Fall 89, p. 88.
"Pellagra Knocked Out." [Event] (18:3) Fall 89, p. 89.

4413. PEPPERSHTEIN, Pavel
"Untitled: The daring dreams of willful admissions" (tr. by Gary Kern). [MichQR] (28:4) Fall 89, p. 733.

4414. PERCHIK, Simon
"90. Again my eyes." [PoetC] (21:1) Fall 89, p. 34-35.
"147. From this anvil its lost cry." [HighP] (4:1) Spr 89, p. 88.
"206. From a rowboat: a letter." [HolCrit] (26:2) Ap 89, p. 19.

"214. What I hear, flat, off key." [ColR] (NS 16:2) Fall 89-Wint 90, p. 64.
"218. From this door my jacket." [Pembroke] (21) 89, p. 16.
"As I lean." [Os] (29) 89, p. 18.
"As If." [BallSUF] (30:4) Aut 89, p. 62.
"As if they were just born, my kisses." [SoDakR] (27:3) Aut 89, p. 42.
"Bells know this, they have so much room." [BelPoJ] (39:4) Sum 89, p. 12.
"Bells know this, they have so much room." [SoDakR] (27:3) Aut 89, p. 44.
"Between these two fingers the air." [SoDakR] (27:3) Aut 89, p. 43.
"Four Corners." [ChatR] (9:3) Spr 89, p. 47.
"From nowhere, a star overflows." [Os] (29) 89, p. 19.
"He Will Inhale." [CrabCR] (6:1) 89, p. 12.
"I Can Mimic This Fork." [CreamCR] (13:2) Fall 89, p. 74.
"No hardhat and this stubborn doctor." [HiramPoR] (46) Spr-Sum 89, p. 21-22.
"Sniffing its footprints, this pebble." [ArtfulD] (16/17) Fall 89, p. 53.
"So many thorns :these markers sting." [NewL] (55:3) Spr 89, p. 110.
"There's a fragrance to light." [Os] (28) 89, p. 8.
"This ledge and my leather jacket." [BlackWR] (16:1) Fall-Wint 89, p. 103.
"What I hear, flat, off key." [BlackWR] (16:1) Fall-Wint 89, p. 104.
PEREA, Roberto Ramos
   See RAMOS-PEREA, Roberto
4415. PEREC, Georges
   "Three Epithalamia" (tr. by Harry Mathews). [ParisR] (31:112) Fall 89, p. 68-77.
4416. PERELMAN, Bob
   "Captive Audience" (Excerpt). [PaperAir] (4:2) 89, p. 23-27.
   "Chronic Meanings" (for Lee Hickman). [Temblor] (10) 89, p. 223-225.
   "Quite Frankly, You Enjoyed It." [NewAW] (5) Fall 89, p. 69.
   "Voice Play." [Screens] (1) 89, p. 75-79.
PERES CONDE, Gil
   See CONDE, Gil Peres
4417. PEREZ, Anthony
   "Desiring." [LindLM] (8:4) O-D 89, p. 15.
4418. PÉREZ, Hiram
   "Our Garden." [LindLM] (8:3) Jl-S 89, p. 5.
   "Rosa." [LindLM] (8:3) Jl-S 89, p. 5.
4419. PEREZ, Nola
   "All We Need to Know." [Poem] (62) N 89, p. 55.
   "Driving Home." [Poem] (62) N 89, p. 56.
   "Someone Drowning." [CapeR] (24:2) Fall 89, p. 1.
   "Someone Drowning." [Kalliope] (11:3) 89, p. 62.
   "Someone Drowning." [Poem] (62) N 89, p. 54.
   "Trees, Old Men." [Poem] (62) N 89, p. 57.
   "Wise Fig." [CapeR] (24:2) Fall 89, p. 2.
4420. PÉREZ-BUSTILLO, Camilo (Pérez, Camilo)
   "The Promised Land" (Selection: Section 35, tr. of Clemente Soto Vélez, w. Martín
      Espada). [MinnR] (NS 33) Fall 89, p. 39-42.
4421. PEREZ FIRMAT, Gustavo
   "A Likely Story." [LindLM] (8:1) Ja-Mr 89, p. 8.
   "The Operation." [LindLM] (8:1) Ja-Mr 89, p. 8.
4422. PEREZ SARDUY, Pedro
   "Farewell Not Tinged with Sadness" (tr. by Jean Stubbs). [Pig] (15) 88, p. 76.
4423. PERILLO, Lucia
   "On a Streetcorner in Mérida." [NowestR] (27:2) 89, p. 17.
4424. PERKINS, James Ashbrook
   "Autoerotic Poem for One Hand Accompanied." [Footwork] 89, p. 37.
   "Druid's Winter Night." [Footwork] 89, p. 36-37.
   "Nada." [Footwork] 89, p. 36.
   "No Mas Poem." [US1] (22/23) Spr 89, p. 15.
4425. PERKINS, Michael
   "The Hour of Passionate Speech." [Talisman] (2) Spr 89, p. 81.
4426. PERLBERG, Mark
   "The Floating World" (for Anna). [Hudson] (42:1) Spr 89, p. 93-94.
4427. PERLONGO, Bob
   "Memo: Atlantic." [Talisman] (3) Fall 89, p. 117.
4428. PERRAULT, John
   "Les Enfants Terribles." [KeyWR] (2:1/2) Fall-Wint 89, p. 169.
   "Icon." [KeyWR] (2:1/2) Fall-Wint 89, p. 168.

"North Country." [PoetL] (84:2) Sum 89, p. 51.
4429. PERREAULT, George
"O'Keeffe's *Untitled #3*." [HighP] (4:2) Fall 89, p. 24-25.
4430. PERRICONE, C.
"Castrati." [RiverC] (9:1) Spr 89, p. 17.
"Firefighter." [RiverC] (9:1) Spr 89, p. 16.
4431. PERRICONE, Evelyn
"In Pennsylvania Station New York." [RagMag] (7:1) 89, p. 60.
4432. PERROW, Michael
"Pantoum." [WillowS] (23) Wint 89, p. 14-15.
4433. PERRY, Elaine
"Entropy." [BlueBldgs] (11) 89, p. 8-9.
"Shooting the Final Scene with Sharecroppers." [YellowS] (29) Spr 89, p. 41.
4434. PERRY, Pamela
"Night Watchman of the Dawn" (tr. of Nikolai Kantchev, w. Bradley R. Strahan).
[Vis] (30) 89, p. 4.
4435. PERRY, Stephen
"En Passant and Mate." [YellowS] (30) Sum 89, p. 39.
"Real Reresa "oses in Winter" (For Susan). [YellowS] (30) Sum 89, p. 36-38.
4436. PESEROFF, Joyce
"Bluebird." [NewL] (56:2/3) Wint 89-Spr 90, p. 222.
"October." [NewL] (56:2/3) Wint 89-Spr 90, p. 220.
"Orange." [NewL] (56:2/3) Wint 89-Spr 90, p. 221.
"Sheba's Wisdom." [NewL] (56:2/3) Wint 89-Spr 90, p. 223-225.
4437. PETER
"Today is a very special day for me" (with photograph by Billy Howard).
[JamesWR] (6:4) Sum 89, p. 17.
4438. PETERS, Patrick
"Migration" (for Lisa). [PoetryE] (28) Fall 89, p. 7.
4439. PETERS, Robert
"Death of the Maiden." [FreeL] (2) Sum 89, p. 14.
"Fish" (From *Love Songs for Robert Mitchum*). [FreeL] (2) Sum 89, p. 15.
4440. PETERSEN, Karen
"Madame D'Ovary." [Rampike] (6:2) 88, p. 64-65.
4441. PETERSEN, Keith S.
"Are You OK?" [BellArk] (5:5) S-O 89, p. 3.
"In the Family Photo Album." [BellArk] (5:5) S-O 89, p. 9.
4442. PETERSEN, William
"Lesson." [NewEngR] (11:4) Sum 89, p. 391.
"Turn It Over." [NewEngR] (11:4) Sum 89, p. 391.
4443. PETERSON, Allan
"Avoiding Morning." [CinPR] (19) Spr 89, p. 20.
"Bridges." [EmeraldCR] (1989) c1988, p. 105-106.
"Decoys." [BelPoJ] (39:3) Spr 89, p. 5.
"Dressing for Dreams." [BlackWR] (15:2) Spr 89, p. 46.
"Multiple Lives." [BlackWR] (15:2) Spr 89, p. 47-48.
"The Salmon for Instance." [BlackWR] (16:1) Fall-Wint 89, p. 99-102.
"Talking with Clothes." [BlackWR] (15:2) Spr 89, p. 45.
"Taproots." [SoCoast] (5) Spr 88, p. 29.
"What Matters." [CapeR] (24:2) Fall 89, p. 36.
"Wooly for Cold." [NegC] (9:2) 89, p. 17.
PETERSON, Allen
See PETERSON, Allan
4444. PETERSON, Jim
"The Closet-Man." [SouthernPR] (29:1) Spr 89, p. 33-34.
"The Other." [Poetry] (154:1) Ap 89, p. 10-12.
"The Song." [CharR] (15:1) Spr 89, p. 65.
4445. PETERSON, Karen
"Advice for Anatomy Students." [SpoonRQ] (14:1) Wint 89, p. 47-48.
"Advice for Anatomy Students." [SpoonRQ] (14:4) Fall 89, p. 16-17.
"Bringing Children to Hiroshima." [SpoonRQ] (14:1) Wint 89, p. 49-54.
"Bringing Children to Hiroshima." [SpoonRQ] (14:4) Fall 89, p. 18-23.
"My Mother, in Indonesia." [SpoonRQ] (14:1) Wint 89, p. 42-46.
"My Mother, in Indonesia." [SpoonRQ] (14:4) Fall 89, p. 11-15.
"My Son at the Aquarium." [SpoonRQ] (14:1) Wint 89, p. 40.
"My Son at the Aquarium." [SpoonRQ] (14:4) Fall 89, p. 9.

"Passage North, at Dusk." [SpoonRQ] (14:1) Wint 89, p. 41.
"Passage North, at Dusk." [SpoonRQ] (14:4) Fall 89, p. 10.
"Secret." [SpoonRQ] (14:1) Wint 89, p. 55-56.
"Secret." [SpoonRQ] (14:4) Fall 89, p. 24-25.
4446. PETERSON, Lorinda
"Doing Your Time." [Quarry] (38:4) Fall 89, p. 40.
"Family Reunion." [Quarry] (38:4) Fall 89, p. 39.
4447. PETERSON, Nils
"William." [Mildred] (3:2) 89, p. 128-130.
4448. PETERSON, Susan
"Stealing a Life" (For Rita Gonzales). [CinPR] (20) Fall 89, p. 60.
4449. PETRARCH, Francesco
"Rime Sparse" (Selection: 52, tr. by E. Allen Tilley, Jr.). [Kalliope] (10:3) 88, p.
19.
4450. PETRI, Györsgy
"The Night Song of the Peeping Tom" (tr. by Nicholas Kolumban). [ArtfulD]
(16/17) Fall 89, p. 75.
4451. PETRIE, Paul
"Reflections." [CentR] (33:2) Spr 89, p. 135.
4452. PETROV, Aleksandar
"Poetry in Yiddish" (tr. by Lynne Ikach). [ColR] (NS 16:1) Spr-Sum 89, p. 99.
4453. PETROV, Krinka
"The Good Waters of Old Tales" (tr. of Radmila Lazic). [ColR] (NS 16:1) Spr-Sum
89, p. 98.
4454. PETRUNIS, Sergei
"Hieroglyphs" (tr. by Mary Jane White). [WillowS] (23) Wint 89, p. 62-72.
4455. PETTEE, Dan
"Ideal Love, or, Another View of It." [Bound] (16:2/3) Wint-Spr 89, p. 250-251.
4456. PETTEYS, D. F.
"Advice from Tao-chi." [Salm] (81) Wint 89, p. 102.
"Naked Singularity." [Boulevard] (4:1, #10) Spr 89, p. 94.
4457. PETTIT, Michael
"The Blue Angel." [IndR] (12:3) Sum 89, p. 7.
"Furnace Without End." [ThRiPo] (31/32) 88, p. 32.
"Hurricane Watson." [IndR] (12:3) Sum 89, p. 8.
"Los Alamos Rush Hour." [ThRiPo] (31/32) 88, p. 30-31.
4458. PEVEAR, Richard
"Ai" (tr. of Henri Volohonsky). [GrandS] (8:4) Sum 89, p. 209-211.
4459. PFEIFER, Michael
"Colander." [KanQ] (21:1/2) Wint-Spr 89, p. 230.
"Cold Frame." [PoetL] (84:2) Sum 89, p. 21.
"Elderberries." [KanQ] (21:1/2) Wint-Spr 89, p. 231.
4460. PHELPS, Dean
"Outside All the Time That Tears." [Poem] (62) N 89, p. 1.
"The Rose of Parma." [Poem] (62) N 89, p. 2.
"Yesterday and Today." [Poem] (62) N 89, p. 3.
4461. PHILBRICK, Stephen
"She Wakes, She Never Dreams, Her Smile, She Loves." [Talisman] (3) Fall 89, p.
118-119.
"The Snatch of Time." [KeyWR] (2:1/2) Fall-Wint 89, p. 39-40.
"To Heaven on Our Backs." [KeyWR] (2:1/2) Fall-Wint 89, p. 41-42.
4462. PHILIP, Marlene Nourbese
"Cyclamen Girl." [Obs] (4:1) Spr 89, p. 47-54.
4463. PHILIPS, Elizabeth
"Brothers and Outsiders." [Event] (18:3) Fall 89, p. 47.
"Florence." [Event] (18:3) Fall 89, p. 46.
"Four Small Poems for the Grasses." [MalR] (89) Wint 89, p. 66-69.
4464. PHILLIPPY, Patricia
"Everything About Love." [Salm] (84) Fall 89, p. 64-65.
4465. PHILLIPS, Bob
"I know we are all a part of something so large and so very wonderful" (with
photograph by Billy Howard). [JamesWR] (6:4) Sum 89, p. 19.
4466. PHILLIPS, Carl
"Africa Says." [PoetL] (84:4) Wint 89-90, p. 35-36.
"The Bulb Show." [Plain] (9:2) Wint 89, p. 17.
"Film Noir." [PoetL] (84:4) Wint 89-90, p. 37-38.

"From the Sun's Tower." [StoneC] (17:1/2) Fall-Wint 89-90, p. 46.
"With Love for the Night Patrol" (First Prize). [StoneC] (17:1/2) Fall-Wint 89-90, p. prelim. p. 1.
4467. PHILLIPS, David
"After Reading *The Centre*." [CapilR] (1st series: 50) 89, p. 43-44.
"The Carpenter" (For Ron & Pat, Nicole & Owen). [CapilR] (1st series: 50) 89, p. 45-48.
"The Path." [CapilR] (1st series: 50) 89, p. 49-50.
4468. PHILLIPS, Dayton
"Sidewinder." [TexasR] (10:3/4) Fall-Wint 89, p. 118.
4469. PHILLIPS, Dennis
"Arena" (Excerpt, from Part Nine. Pages missing, indexed from Table of Contents). [Temblor] (10) 89, p. 33-41.
4470. PHILLIPS, Frances
"Counting: One." [HangL] (54) 89, p. 39-42.
"Thanksgiving." [HangL] (54) 89, p. 38.
"Today in the New House." [HangL] (54) 89, p. 36-37.
4471. PHILLIPS, Frank Lamont
"Aries." [Obs] (4:2) Sum 89, p. 88.
"Love Song." [Obs] (4:2) Sum 89, p. 89.
"Shiloh." [Obs] (4:2) Sum 89, p. 87-88.
4473. PHILLIPS, Kathy (Kathy J.)
"Kannon Submits to Freedom in the Tea Ceremony." [BambooR] (44) Fall 89, p. 29-30.
"Kuan Yin Faces Charges." [ChamLR] (2:2, #4) Spr 89, p. 79-80.
"Kuan Yin in Europe." [BambooR] (44) Fall 89, p. 28.
"Lesson in Ink." [ChamLR] (2:2, #4) Spr 89, p. 81.
"Ryozen's White-Robed Kannon." [BambooR] (44) Fall 89, p. 27.
"This Isn't a Picture I'm Holding." [BambooR] (44) Fall 89, p. 31.
4474. PHILLIPS, Louis
"A Bout de Soufflé." [RiverC] (10:1) Fall 89, p. 116.
"A Bout de Souffle." [WestB] (24) 89, p. 99.
"& There & There & There." [Vis] (30) 89, p. 47.
"A Final Conversation with My Muse." [WestB] (24) 89, p. 100.
"Fitzgerald, Keats, & Marriage." [RiverC] (10:1) Fall 89, p. 117.
"My Mother's Wedding Photo." [Footwork] 89, p. 10.
"Public Demands Upon the Private Self." [CentR] (33:2) Spr 89, p. 135-136.
"Some Sources of the Chinese Tradition." [Hawai'iR] (13:2, #26) Sum 89, p. 118-119.
"We Have Built Planets Out of Less." [OxfordM] (5:1) Spr-Sum 89, p. 70.
4475. PHILLIPS, Michael Lee
"Cape Sounion." [YellowS] (30) Sum 89, p. 34.
"Children Left in the Palm of Your Hand." [YellowS] (30) Sum 89, p. 34.
"Scorpion Love." [PoetryNW] (30:1) Spr 89, p. 25.
4476. PHILLIPS, Pat
"Alley." [Sulfur] (9:2, #25) Fall 89, p. 68.
"Child." [Sulfur] (9:2, #25) Fall 89, p. 66.
"Features." [Sulfur] (9:2, #25) Fall 89, p. 67.
4477. PHILLIPS, Robert
"After the Fact: To Ted Bundy." [OntR] (31) Fall-Wint 89-90, p. 90-92.
"Avant-Garde Music Comes to America" (Charles Ives, 1874-1954). [Hudson] (42:2) Sum 89, p. 274-275.
"Ghost Story." [Hudson] (42:2) Sum 89, p. 276.
"The Hole." [Boulevard] (4:1, #10) Spr 89, p. 131-132.
"A Little Elegy for Howard Moss" (1922-1987). [Hudson] (42:2) Sum 89, p. 273-274.
"Scouting Days." [Hudson] (42:2) Sum 89, p. 271-272.
"Walnuts." [Hudson] (42:2) Sum 89, p. 272-273.
4478. PHILLIPS, Rod
"On Finding a Stone Arrowhead on the Banks of the Looking Glass." [KanQ] (21:1/2) Wint-Spr 89, p. 86.
4479. PHILLIPS, Walt
"Gertrude Stein and Her Friend Out West." [Wind] (19:64) 89, p. 20.
4480. PHILLIS, Randy
"Amsterdam, with a Friend." [PoetryE] (28) Fall 89, p. 154-155.
"Oklahoma." [FloridaR] (16:2/3) Fall-Wint 89, p. 218-220.

4481. PHILLIS, Yannis
"A Sonata in Pursuit of the Galaxy." [StoneC] (17:1/2) Fall-Wint 89-90, p. 48-49.
4482. PHILPOT, Tracy
"Playing House." [WillowS] (23) Wint 89, p. 29.
4483. PICCIONE, Anthony
"At the Tomb of Li Bai" (tr. of Bai Juyi, w. Carol Zhigong Chang). [LitR] (32:3)
Spr 89, p. 392.
"Autumn and a Woman's Room" (tr. of Li Yu, w. Li Young Lee and Carol Zhigong
Chang). [LitR] (32:3) Spr 89, p. 390.
"Drinking at a Lake on a Clear Day Followed by Rain" (tr. of Su Shih, w. Carol
Zhigong Chang). [LitR] (32:3) Spr 89, p. 391.
"Evening River Song" (tr. of Bai Juyi, w. Carol Zhigong Chang). [LitR] (32:3) Spr
89, p. 392.
"Now That We Know Where We Are." [PaintedB] (39) 89, p. 79.
"Past Thoughts" (tr. of Li Yu, w. Li Young Lee and Carol Zhigong Chang). [LitR]
(32:3) Spr 89, p. 390.
"Rising Late" (tr. of Meng Hao-jan, w. Li Young Lee and Carol Zhigong Chang).
[LitR] (32:3) Spr 89, p. 389.
"Separation" (tr. of Su Shih, w. Li Young Lee and Carol Zhigong Chang). [LitR]
(32:3) Spr 89, p. 389.
4484. PICKARD, Deanna
"The Story of Butter." [Chelsea] (48) 89, p. 136.
4485. PICKETT, James Carroll
"Dream Man." [Tribe] (1:1) Wint 89, p. 34-58.
4486. PIECZYNSKI, Therese
"Daddy and I Dance in a Hurricane." [RiverC] (10:1) Fall 89, p. 122.
4487. PIEPHOFF, Bruce
"Ghost Fiddler." [Pembroke] (21) 89, p. 167-169.
"Greetings from Holden Beach." [GreensboroR] (46) Sum 89, p. 98-99.
"Molly Jane, They Oughta Name a Hurricane After You." [Pembroke] (21) 89, p.
165-166.
"Nobody." [Pembroke] (21) 89, p. 166-167.
4488. PIERCE, Deborah
"In Aroostook." [Comm] (116:11) Je 2, 89, p. 348.
4489. PIERCE, Pamela
"Birth Control." [Calyx] (12:1) Sum 89, p. 18.
4490. PIERCY, Marge
"Beaver Shot." [Footwork] 89, p. 5.
"Cast Skins." [Vis] (30) 89, p. 29-30.
"Cousin, Cousine." [KeyWR] (2:1/2) Fall-Wint 89, p. 18-19.
"Dreaming the Frog's Sleep." [PoetryE] (28) Fall 89, p. 135.
"The Ex in the Supermarket." [KeyWR] (2:1/2) Fall-Wint 89, p. 16.
"First Day Out of Bed." [AmerPoR] (18:4) Jl-Ag 89, p. 18.
"Havdalah" (For a Reconstructionist Siddur project sponsored by Pnai Or).
[Kalliope] (11:3) 89, p. 6-7.
"Hot, Hotter." [YellowS] (29) Spr 89, p. 4.
"January, 3 P.M." [PoetryE] (28) Fall 89, p. 134.
"Meditation on Reading the Torah" (For a Reconstructionist Siddur project
sponsored by Pnai Or). [Kalliope] (11:3) 89, p. 8.
"Peeled After Flu." [KeyWR] (2:1/2) Fall-Wint 89, p. 17.
"Persimmon Pudding." [AmerPoR] (18:4) Jl-Ag 89, p. 18.
"The Same Place Struck Again." [Footwork] 89, p. 5.
"Shad Blow." [PoetryE] (28) Fall 89, p. 131-133.
"Waking Up with My Ears Ringing." [Vis] (30) 89, p. 28.
4491. PIERMAN, Carol J.
"After Church." [RiverS] (30) [89], p. 59.
"Le Côte d'Azur." [ThRiPo] (31/32) 88, p. 34-35.
"How the World Has Changed." [BlackWR] (15:2) Spr 89, p. 28-29.
"How We Learned About Friction." [ThRiPo] (31/32) 88, p. 33.
"Natural Science." [RiverS] (30) [89], p. 61.
"Perestroika." [BlackWR] (15:2) Spr 89, p. 32-33.
"Summer Flood." [ThRiPo] (33/34) 89, p. 19-20.
"Things As They Are." [RiverS] (30) [89], p. 60.
"Visiting the Shrine" (Where a Mass Has Been Said for Your Mother Who Was Not
Catholic). [BlackWR] (15:2) Spr 89, p. 30-31.
"The Winding Sheet." [ThRiPo] (31/32) 88, p. 36.

PIERO, W. S. di
    See Di PIERO, W. S.
4492. PIERSANTI, Umberto
    "Quando l'Ottobre Lento Trascolora." [Poetry] (155:1/2) O-N 89, p. 118-122.
    "When Slow October Changes Color" (tr. by Stephen Sartarelli). [Poetry] (155:1/2)
        O-N 89, p. 119-123.
4493. PIGNO, Antonia Quintana
    "Cancion de Segadores." [Ploughs] (15:4) Wint 89-90, p. 159-162.
4494. PIJEWSKI, John
    "Taking Out the Trash." [Agni] (28) 89, p. 278.
4495. PILINSZKY, Janos
    "Jewel" (tr. by Zsuzsanna Ozsvath and Martha Satz). [WebR] (14:1) Spr 89, p. 30.
4496. PILKINGTON, Kevin
    "Plymouth." [Verse] (6:2) Je 89, p. 41.
4497. PINARD, Mary
    "Black and White Autopsy." [MinnR] (NS 32) Spr 89, p. 72.
4498. PINDAR
    "Age" (tr. by Friedrich Hölderlin and David Rattray). [Temblor] (10) 89, p. 198.
    "The Asylums" (tr. by Friedrich Hölderlin and David Rattray). [Temblor] (10) 89, p.
        198.
    "The Enlivener" (tr. by Friedrich Hölderlin and David Rattray). [Temblor] (10) 89,
        p. 199.
    "The Faithlessness of Wisdom" (tr. by Friedrich Hölderlin and David Rattray).
        [Temblor] (10) 89, p. 196.
    "The Infinite" (tr. by Friedrich Hölderlin and David Rattray). [Temblor] (10) 89, p.
        198.
    "Of Peace" (tr. by Friedrich Hölderlin and David Rattray). [Temblor] (10) 89, p.
        196.
    "Of the Dolphin" (tr. by Friedrich Hölderlin and David Rattray). [Temblor] (10) 89,
        p. 197.
    "Of Truth" (tr. by Friedrich Hölderlin and David Rattray). [Temblor] (10) 89, p.
        196.
    "The Supreme" (tr. by Friedrich Hölderlin and David Rattray). [Temblor] (10) 89, p.
        197.
4499. PINE, Red
    "1. I made my home west of the Sha" (tr. of Stonehouse). [LitR] (32:3) Spr 89, p.
        356.
    "76. It's a lonesome hut this new fall night" (tr. of Stonehouse). [LitR] (32:3) Spr
        89, p. 356.
    "143. Life in the mountains depends on a hoe" (tr. of Stonehouse). [LitR] (32:3) Spr
        89, p. 356.
    "144. I fix my hoe my hut can lean" (tr. of Stonehouse). [LitR] (32:3) Spr 89, p.
        356.
4500. PINES, Paul
    "11/11/87: A Snowy Veterans Day." [Contact] (9:50/51/52) Fall-Wint 88-Spr 89, p.
        35.
    "The Hotel Madden Poems." [Contact] (9:50/51/52) Fall-Wint 88-Spr 89, p. 34.
    "Hotel Madden Poems" (Excerpt). [Talisman] (2) Spr 89, p. 10.
    "I'd sooner be in Merida." [Contact] (9:50/51/52) Fall-Wint 88-Spr 89, p. 35.
    "Mingus at the Five Spot." [Contact] (9:50/51/52) Fall-Wint 88-Spr 89, p. 34.
    "New Year, 1988 faces me like." [Contact] (9:50/51/52) Fall-Wint 88-Spr 89, p. 35.
PING, Ding Yu
    See DING, Yu Ping
PING, Du Wei
    See DU, Wei Ping
4501. PINGARRON, Michael
    "Autumn's Silent Announcement with Wind." [Lactuca] (13) N 89, p. 61.
    "Imposing Questions." [Lactuca] (13) N 89, p. 63.
    "The Innocent" (for Bertha, my sister Pat and David Cope). [Lactuca] (13) N 89, p.
        62.
    "Jealousy and Anger." [Lactuca] (13) N 89, p. 61-62.
    "The Left Hand, the Right Hand." [LindLM] (8:3) Jl-S 89, p. 25.
    "Making Some Sense Out of This Is Our Lives." [Lactuca] (13) N 89, p. 60.
    "The Marriage." [LindLM] (8:3) Jl-S 89, p. 25.
    "Names've Been Changed." [Lactuca] (13) N 89, p. 63.
    "Our Earnings on Account." [Lactuca] (13) N 89, p. 64.

"Pretentious Poets." [LindLM] (8:3) Jl-S 89, p. 25.
"Unrighteous Facts of Our Politics in 1988." [Lactuca] (13) N 89, p. 59-60.
4502. PINK, David
"Door to the River" (Selections: 4 poems). [Nimrod] (33:1) Fall-Wint 89, p. 66-69.
4503. PINKEL, Sheila
"Consume Her." [Acts] (10) 89, p. 95.
"Consumer." [Acts] (10) 89, p. 37-40.
4504. PINKERTON, C. F.
"A Short Walk in the Garden" (after Ashbery). [NewRep] (200:25) 19 Je 89, p. 43.
4505. PINSKER, Sanford
"At the Grave of Bessie Smith" (September 26, 1987). [OxfordM] (5:1) Spr-Sum
89, p. 20.
"Just a Smack at the Deconstructionists." [KanQ] (21:3) Sum 89, p. 28.
"Lines for a Ghost of My Hungry Graduate Student Heart" (for John Logan).
[PaintedB] (39) 89, p. 14.
"Lines in Early Morning." [KanQ] (21:3) Sum 89, p. 27.
4506. PINSKY, Robert
"Dreamer." [NewRep] (201:11) 11 S 89, p. 36.
"The Ghost Hammer." [ParisR] (31:112) Fall 89, p. 190-192.
"Immortal Longings." [ParisR] (31:112) Fall 89, p. 193.
"Pilgrimage." [Antaeus] (62) Spr 89, p. 179-181.
"Shirt." [NewYorker] (65:16) 5 Je 89, p. 34.
4507. PIOMBINO, Nick
"Aftermath." [Temblor] (9) 89, p. 139-140.
4508. PIRIE, Donald
"Beyond the window there is rain, a glass of tea on the table" (tr. of Bronislaw Maj).
[Verse] (6:1) Mr 89, p. 34.
"It was all rather different to the way they later said it was" (tr. of Bronislaw Maj).
[Verse] (6:1) Mr 89, p. 35.
"No one has claimed it: homeless and untouched" (tr. of Bronislaw Maj). [Verse]
(6:1) Mr 89, p. 34.
"Who will bear witness to these times?" (tr. of Bronislaw Maj). [Verse] (6:1) Mr 89,
p. 35.
4509. PITCHFORD, Kenneth
"Sonnet to Billy." [Ploughs] (15:4) Wint 89-90, p. 165.
"The Weed Flower" (to Alma Graham). [Ploughs] (15:4) Wint 89-90, p. 163-164.
4510. PITKIN, Anne
"Blue Herons." [MalR] (86) Spr 89, p. 98.
4511. PIUCCI, Joanna A.
"Generations." [Kalliope] (11:1) 89, p. 46.
4512. PIZARNIK, Alejandra
"For Janis Joplin" (fragment, tr. by Susan Bassnett). [LitR] (32:4) Sum 89, p. 566.
"Fragments to Overcome Silence" (tr. by Susan Bassnett). [LitR] (32:4) Sum 89, p.
565.
"I don't hear the orgasmic sounds of certain precious words" (tr. by Susan
Bassnett). [LitR] (32:4) Sum 89, p. 567.
"Privilege" (tr. by Susan Bassnett). [LitR] (32:4) Sum 89, p. 565.
"Speaking Your Name" (tr. by Susan Bassnett). [LitR] (32:4) Sum 89, p. 566.
"Your Voice" (tr. by Susan Bassnett). [LitR] (32:4) Sum 89, p. 566.
4513. PLANTENGA, Bart
"Radio Silence." [SlipS] (9) 89, p. 9.
4514. PLANTIER, Therese
"No One Writes Me" (tr. by Frances Driscoll). [WillowS] (23) Wint 89, p. 26.
"So That Fur and Water and My Dreams Surround You" (tr. by Frances Driscoll).
[WillowS] (23) Wint 89, p. 28.
"This Being the Season" (tr. by Frances Driscoll). [WillowS] (23) Wint 89, p. 27.
4515. PLATIZKY, Roger S.
"Memorial Day." [ChangingM] (20) Wint-Spr 89, p. 20.
4516. PLATO
"Aster" (tr. by James Michie). [GrandS] (8:4) Sum 89, p. 79.
"Aster, my star, you raise" (tr. by James Michie). [GrandS] (8:4) Sum 89, p. 79.
4517. PLATT, Donald
"20/20 Vision." [PoetryNW] (30:4) Wint 89-90, p. 5.
"Blackout." [PoetryNW] (30:4) Wint 89-90, p. 6-7.
"Carolina Steel Co. Canticle." [PoetryNW] (30:4) Wint 89-90, p. 3-4.
"Inventing Water." [PoetryNW] (30:4) Wint 89-90, p. 6.

"The Other Side of Sound." [PoetryNW] (30:4) Wint 89-90, p. 7-8.
4518. PLATZ, Judith
      "North Country." [AnthNEW] (1) 89, p. 19.
      "Wrong Tense." [AnthNEW] (1) 89, p. 20.
4519. PLEASE, Roger
      "Tightened in Snow." [HiramPoR] (46) Spr-Sum 89, p. 23.
PLESSIS, Rachel Blau du
      See DuPLESSIS, Rachel Blau
4520. PLOTIN, Stephanie
      "Marathoner." [HangL] (54) 89, p. 59-60.
4521. PLUMB, Hudson
      "The Largest Thing." [WebR] (14:1) Spr 89, p. 83.
4522. PLUMLY, Stanley
      "Birthday." [OhioR] (44) 89, p. 41.
      "Boy on the Step." [Antaeus] (62) Spr 89, p. 182-188.
      "Coming into LaGuardia Late at Night." [NewYorker] (64:49) 23 Ja 89, p. 30.
      "Four Appaloosas." [NewYorker] (65:21) 10 Jl 89, p. 91.
      "Men Working on Wings." [OhioR] (44) 89, p. 42-44.
4523. PLUMMER, Deb
      "Corolla." [KanQ] (21:3) Sum 89, p. 62-63.
4524. PLUMPP, Sterling D.
      "No Chasers" (for James Baldwin). [BlackALF] (23:3) Fall 89, p. 519-521.
4525. PLYMELL, Charles
      "The grass talks in small equations." [AlphaBS] (6) Wint 89-90, p. 21.
      "The Shoe Store Man." [AlphaBS] (6) Wint 89-90, p. 20-21.
PO, Chu-i
      See BAI, Juyi
PO, Chü-yi
      See BAI, Juyi
PO, Li
      See LI, Po
4526. POBO, Kenneth
      "Always Thrilling." [CumbPR] (9:1) Fall 89, p. 22.
      "Clock Poem." [CimR] (87) Ap 89, p. 27.
      "Father." [CentR] (33:1) Wint 89, p. 55-56.
      "For Amphibians." [CumbPR] (9:1) Fall 89, p. 21.
      "Gardens Come Upon Suddenly." [Grain] (17:3) Fall 89, p. 45.
      "Gator." [Outbr] (20) 89, p. 45.
      "Louie, Louie." [WestB] (25) 89, p. 24-25.
      "Minnows Under the Boat." [MidwQ] (30:4) Sum 89, p. 450.
      "Noises at Night." [Grain] (17:3) Fall 89, p. 44.
      "Old Woman's Windowbox." [CimR] (87) Ap 89, p. 28.
      "Pineapple Glaze." [ChamLR] (3:1, #5) Fall 89, p. 21.
      "Ruth." [Plain] (9:2) Wint 89, p. 26.
      "Silk Tree." [Confr] (39/40) Fall 88-Wint 89, p. 25.
      "A Split Man." [Nimrod] (33:1) Fall-Wint 89, p. 91.
      "Storm." [WestB] (23) 89, p. 35.
      "We Are in Philadelphia Driving." [SmPd] (26:2 #76) Spr 89, p. 22.
4527. POE, Edgar Allan
      "The City in the Sea." [SouthernR] (25:1) Wint 89, p. 34-36.
4528. POETHEN, Johannes
      "Back Then I Owned an Ocean" (tr. by John Linthicum). [LitR] (33:1) Fall 89, p.
            70.
      "The Face in the Water" (tr. by John Linthicum). [LitR] (33:1) Fall 89, p. 68-69.
      "On a Bright Afternoon Occasionally" (tr. by John Linthicum). [LitR] (33:1) Fall 89,
            p. 70.
      "The Self Made of Words" (tr. by John Linthicum). [LitR] (33:1) Fall 89, p. 69.
POL, Miquel Marti i
      See MARTI i POL, Miquel
4529. POLITE, Frank
      "Alter and Illuminate." [FreeL] (3) Aut 89, p. 2-3.
      "As Time Goes By" (For R. Pawlowski). [FreeL] (3) Aut 89, p. 13-16.
      "The Flamingo." [FreeL] (1) 89, p. 10-21.
4530. POLITO, Robert
      "Doubles." [Agni] (28) 89, p. 106-109.

4531. POLITTE, Ann
"Oils." [Vis] (31) 89, p. 18.
4532. POLIZZI, M. A.
"Ausable Chasm." [JINJPo] [11] 89, p. 25.
"Circling the Tanglewood." [JINJPo] [11] 89, p. 24.
"A Cow without Remembrance." [JINJPo] [11] 89, p. 26.
4533. POLKINHORN, Harry
"Easy Art Makes People Forget the Violence." [Rampike] (6:3) 88, p. 30-31.
4534. POLKOWSKI, Jan
"Hymn" (tr. by Stanislaw Baranczak and Clare Cavanagh). [PartR] (56:2) Spr 89, p. 290.
"My Sweet Motherland" (tr. by Stanislaw Baranczak and Clare Cavanagh). [PartR] (56:2) Spr 89, p. 289.
"The Restaurant 'Arcadia,' Central Square, Nowa Huta" (tr. by Stanislaw Baranczak and Clare Cavanah). [Trans] (21) Spr 89, p. 81.
4535. POLLAK, Felix
"The Divorce" (tr. of Hans Magnus Enzensberger, w. Reinhold Grimm). [LitR] (33:1) Fall 89, p. 19.
"The Dresses" (tr. of Hans Magnus Enzensberger, w. Reinhold Grimm). [LitR] (33:1) Fall 89, p. 22.
"Shit" (tr. of Hans Magnus Enzensberger, w. Reinhold Grimm). [LitR] (33:1) Fall 89, p. 21.
"Short History of the Bourgeoisie" (tr. of Hans Magnus Enzensberger, w. Reinhold Grimm). [LitR] (33:1) Fall 89, p. 20.
4536. POLLITT, Katha
"Collectibles." [NewYorker] (65:18) 19 Je 89, p. 32.
"Happiness Writes White." [GrandS] (8:2) Wint 89, p. 59.
"Rereading Jane Austen's Novels." [NewRep] (201:6/7) 7-14 Ag 89, p. 35.
"Two Cats." [YaleR] (78:3) Spr 89, p. 481-482.
"What I Understood." [YaleR] (78:3) Spr 89, p. 482.
4537. POLSON, Don
"Baptism." [CrossC] (11:2) 89, p. 14.
4538. PONSOT, Marie
"Autumn Clean-Up." [Ploughs] (15:4) Wint 89-90, p. 167.
"Doorways. Windows. Fences. Verges." [Ploughs] (15:4) Wint 89-90, p. 166.
4539. PONTE, Pero da
"Song About a Dead and Living Ass" (Galician-Portuguese Troubadour poem, tr. by Richard Zenith). [SenR] (19:1) 89, p. 78.
"Song About a Lost Crusade" (Galician-Portuguese Troubadour poem, tr. by Richard Zenith). [SenR] (19:1) 89, p. 77.
4540. POOLE, Dave
"Remembering Gallup." [Plain] (10:1) 89, p. 23.
4541. POOLOS, James
"For the Bloodline of a Shadow." [ParisR] (31:110) Spr 89, p. 183.
4542. POPE, Aurora
"Para el llamado del silencio." [Mairena] (11:27) 89, p. 82.
4543. POPKIN, Louise
"Little Cambray Tamales (5,000,000 Bite-Size Tamales)" (for Eduardo and Helena, tr. of Claribel Alegria). [TriQ] (77) Wint 89-90, p. 273-274.
"Snapshots" (to Eliseo Diego, tr. of Claribel Alegria). [TriQ] (77) Wint 89-90, p. 275.
4544. PORRITT, Ruth
"Pente." [TarRP] (29:1) Fall 89, p. 18-19.
4545. PORTA, Antonio
"First Day in Los Angeles" (tr. by Paul Vangelisti). [Temblor] (10) 89, p. 166.
4546. PORTER, Anne
"In Chartres." [Comm] (116:3) F 10, 89, p. 88.
"In Storm-Watch Season" (For Anne Robertson). [Comm] (116:20) N 17, 89, p. 640.
"Living Things." [Comm] (116:10) My 19, 89, p. 297.
4547. PORTER, Mary Jane
"Eclipse." [Bound] (16:2/3) Wint-Spr 89, p. 360.
"Journey." [Bound] (16:2/3) Wint-Spr 89, p. 359.
"Supreme Court." [Bound] (16:2/3) Wint-Spr 89, p. 361.
"Undertow." [Bound] (16:2/3) Wint-Spr 89, p. 357-358.

4548. PORTER, Pamela Rice
    "Vespers." [OxfordM] (5:2) Fall-Wint 89, p. 55-56.
PORTER, Patricia McKenzie
    See McKENZIE-PORTER, Patricia
4549. PORTER, Peter
    "Frogs Outside Barbischio." [Descant] (20:3/4, #66/67) Fall-Wint 89, p. 160.
    "Hanged for a Sheep." [RiverC] (9:1) Spr 89, p. 1.
    "Porter's Retreat." [Descant] (20:3/4, #66/67) Fall-Wint 89, p. 157-158.
    "Servants of the Servant of the Muse." [Descant] (20:3/4, #66/67) Fall-Wint 89, p.
        159.
    "Sun King Sulking." [Poetry] (153:6) Mr 89, p. 335-336.
4550. PORTERFIELD, Kay Marie
    "Cabin Fever." [SoDakR] (27:4) Wint 89, p. 75.
4551. PORTIA
    "Mother's Colors." [AntR] (47:4) Fall 89, p. 458-459.
4552. PORTNAY, Linda
    "Anatomy Lesson." [Kalliope] (11:2) 89, p. 58.
4553. POSEY, E. Carol
    "For Billy." [EmeraldCR] (1989) c1988, p. 106-108.
4554. POSTON, Jane
    "Barkless Dog's Emotional Reaction to Abandonment Measured by Apparatus."
        [BelPoJ] (39:4) Sum 89, p. 14.
    "Bats / Fragments from a Slide Show Script." [BelPoJ] (39:4) Sum 89, p. 10-11.
    "The Hat Your Father Wore." [BelPoJ] (39:4) Sum 89, p. 20-22.
    "The Man Afraid: A Fable." [BelPoJ] (39:4) Sum 89, p. 16-17.
    "Manta Rays" (for JLP). [BelPoJ] (39:4) Sum 89, p. 18-19.
    "Mouse Discriminating Between Two Cards." [BelPoJ] (39:4) Sum 89, p. 15.
    "Sea Anemone." [BelPoJ] (39:4) Sum 89, p. 13.
    "Spectrograph." [BelPoJ] (39:4) Sum 89, p. 12.
4555. POSWIATOWSKA, Halina
    "Evenings" (tr. by Marek Labinski). [WillowS] (23) Wint 89, p. 60.
    "In My Barbaric Language" (tr. by Marek Labinski). [PoetryE] (28) Fall 89, p. 175.
    "These Words Have Always Been" (tr. by Marek Labinski). [PoetryE] (28) Fall 89,
        p. 176.
4556. POTOKAR, Jure
    "Their Genius" (tr. by Michael Biggins). [NewEngR] (11:3) Spr 89, p. 244.
4557. POTTER, Carol
    "Herding the Chickens." [Iowa] (19:1) Wint 89, p. 22-23.
    "What We Did with the Chickens." [Iowa] (19:1) Wint 89, p. 23-25.
4558. POTTS, Randall
    "Medicine Show." [AntR] (47:4) Fall 89, p. 452-453.
4559. POULIN, A., Jr.
    "Calco di Cadevere di Donna: Pompeii" (for John Logan). [PaintedB] (39) 89, p.
        17-19.
4560. POUND, Ezra
    "The Jewel Stairs' Grievance" (tr. of Li Po). [LitR] (32:3) Spr 89, p. 301.
    "The River-Merchant's Wife: A Letter" (tr. of Li Po). [LitR] (32:3) Spr 89, p. 302.
4561. POW, Tom
    "Galloway Tale." [NewYorker] (64:47) 9 Ja 89, p. 81.
    "Ghosts I." [SoCoast] (5) Spr 88, p. 44-45.
    "Ghosts II." [SoCoast] (5) Spr 88, p. 46.
    "Halloween." [SoCoast] (5) Spr 88, p. 43.
    "Russian Still-Life" (Kiev-to-Moscow Sleeper). [NewYorker] (65:29) 4 S 89, p.
        105.
4562. POWELL, Amanda
    "Ice." [Ploughs] (15:4) Wint 89-90, p. 168-170.
    "Separation." [Agni] (28) 89, p. 267.
4563. POWELL, Craig
    "The Ocean Remembers It Is Visible: Poems 1966-1989" (for Gwen Harwood in
        friendship, 47 poems). [QRL] (9:28-29) 89, 66 p.
POWELL, Dannye Romine
    See ROMINE-POWELL, Dannye
4564. POWELL, Donna Fleming
    "Pop." [EngJ] (78:2) F 89, p. 96.
4565. POWELL, Douglas
    "One for Your Scrapbook." [Mildred] (3:1) Spr-Sum 89, p. 96.

4566. POWELL, Jim
"The Crooked House." [Poetry] (153:4) Ja 89, p. 205.
"Napoleon Reviendra." [Poetry] (153:4) Ja 89, p. 206.
4567. POWELL, Lynn
"Adam's Needle." [US1] (22/23) Spr 89, p. 37.
"At Ninety-Eight." [Footwork] 89, p. 66.
"Great-Grandmother." [Footwork] 89, p. 66.
"In the Garden." [US1] (22/23) Spr 89, p. 37.
"Postcard to an Emperor, from the Freer Gallery." [US1] (22/23) Spr 89, p. 37.
4568. POWELL, Patricia A.
"Guess What?" [Obs] (4:3) Wint 89, p. 69-70.
4569. POWELL, Shirley
"Grammarian's Poem." [AlphaBS] (5) Jl 89, p. 40.
4570. POWER, Marjorie
"Like the Daffodil." [CapeR] (24:2) Fall 89, p. 8.
4571. POYNER, Ken
"Freedom." [WestB] (24) 89, p. 48-49.
"The Last Maniacal Stand of the Theoretical Physicists." [GreensboroR] (47) Wint
89-90, p. 52.
4572. POZZI, Antonia
"L'Anticamera delle Suore." [BlueBldgs] (11) 89, p. 33.
"Deserted" (tr. by Deborah Woodard). [PoetryE] (28) Fall 89, p. 183.
"Fields" (tr. by Deborah Woodard). [PoetryE] (28) Fall 89, p. 182.
"The Nun's Antechamber" (tr. by Deborah Woodard). [BlueBldgs] (11) 89, p. 32.
"Sicilian Landscape" (tr. by Deborah Woodard). [PoetryE] (28) Fall 89, p. 184.
4573. PRATT, Charles W.
"Graduation Speech for Tim, Who Turned Out OK." [Comm] (116:11) Je 2, 89, p.
327.
4574. PRATT, Minnie Bruce
"Crime Against Nature" (Selections: 1, 3, 5). [Ploughs] (15:4) Wint 89-90, p.
171-174.
"My Life You Are Talking About." [SinW] (37) Spr 89, p. 66-69.
"Sounds from My Previous Life." [AmerV] (14) Spr 89, p. 3.
4575. PRATT, Pamela
"Bump." [SinW] (39) Wint 89-90, p. 51-52.
PREE, Don Keck du
See DuPREE, Don Keck
4576. PRELLBERG, Gail Sorenson
"A band of wind-blown birds." [SpoonRQ] (14:1) Wint 89, p. 29.
"Drawing room blues." [SpoonRQ] (14:1) Wint 89, p. 31.
"Fog paws." [SpoonRQ] (14:1) Wint 89, p. 28.
"The hour engaged." [SpoonRQ] (14:1) Wint 89, p. 29.
"How can I." [SpoonRQ] (14:1) Wint 89, p. 28.
"I feel as small as a star looks." [SpoonRQ] (14:1) Wint 89, p. 29.
"I think I have." [SpoonRQ] (14:1) Wint 89, p. 29.
"I will go out." [SpoonRQ] (14:1) Wint 89, p. 28.
"It was as if." [SpoonRQ] (14:1) Wint 89, p. 30-31.
"Looking at stars." [SpoonRQ] (14:1) Wint 89, p. 30.
"The mist is a visible mood." [SpoonRQ] (14:1) Wint 89, p. 29.
"Moon." [SpoonRQ] (14:1) Wint 89, p. 30.
"A parrot is a bird who has flown through a rainbow." [SpoonRQ] (14:1) Wint 89,
p. 29.
"These are the dictations." [SpoonRQ] (14:1) Wint 89, p. 28.
"Where is the answer to why?" [SpoonRQ] (14:1) Wint 89, p. 30.
"The world was a naked wall." [SpoonRQ] (14:1) Wint 89, p. 28.
4577. PREST, Peter
"Waltham Forest and Math 23." [Dandel] (16:1) Spr-Sum 89, p. 48.
4578. PRETTYMAN, Quandra
"Carousel." [StoneC] (16:3/4) Spr-Sum 89, p. 51.
4579. PRÉVERT, Jacques
"L'Automne" (from *Paroles*). [AntigR] (79) Aut 89, p. 72.
"Autumn" (from *Paroles*, tr. by John Palander). [AntigR] (79) Aut 89, p. 73.
"On Leave" (from *Paroles*, tr. by John Palander). [AntigR] (79) Aut 89, p. 71.
"Pour Faire le Portrait d'un Oiseau." [AntigR] (77/78) Spr-Sum 89, p. 92, 94.
"Quartier Libre" (from *Paroles*). [AntigR] (79) Aut 89, p. f70.
"To Paint the Picture of a Bird" (tr. by John Palander). [AntigR] (77/78) Spr-Sum

89, p. 93, 95.
4580. PRICE, Caroline
"Chagall Windows." [Stand] (30:4) Aut 89, p. 70-71.
4581. PRICE, Elizabeth (Elizabeth A.)
"Billy." [DenQ] (24:1) Sum 89, p. 70.
"Desire." [Iowa] (19:1) Wint 89, p. 26.
"Timbuktu." [TarRP] (28:2) Spr 89, p. 24.
"When It Is Winter." [DenQ] (24:1) Sum 89, p. 71-72.
"When Things Were Just Getting Interesting." [KanQ] (21:3) Sum 89, p. 30.
4582. PRICE, Laura A.
"The Visit." [PoetL] (84:3) Fall 89, p. 21.
4583. PRICE, Reynolds
"The Eel." [TriQ] (75) Spr-Sum 89, p. 168-170.
"A Heron, A Deer -- a Single Day." [Poetry] (155:3) D 89, p. 225.
"The Resident Heron." [Poetry] (155:3) D 89, p. 224.
4584. PRIEST, Robert
"A Cultural Nightmare." [CrossC] (11:2) 89, p. 11.
4585. PRIESTER, Katie
"A Ghost Poem." [Mildred] (3:1) Spr-Sum 89, p. 34.
4586. PRIESTLY, Tom
"Arrivals II" (tr. of Maja Haderlap). [ColR] (NS 16:1) Spr-Sum 89, p. 93.
"As You Become" (tr. of Jozica Certov). [ColR] (NS 16:1) Spr-Sum 89, p. 92.
"Universitatsstrasse" (tr. of Jozica Certov). [ColR] (NS 16:1) Spr-Sum 89, p. 91.
4587. PRIGOV, Dmitri
"So here I am crushing cockroaches . . ." (tr. by Andrew Wachtel). [Sequoia] (33:1)
Sum 89, p. 60.
4588. PRIGOV, Dmitrii
"Forty-Fifth Alphabet Poem (tsa-tsa)" (Moscow, 1985, tr. by Gerald Janecek).
[MichQR] (28:4) Fall 89, p. 728-730.
4589. PRINCE, James Dale
"Marie Claudel in the Asylum at Montdevergues." [JamesWR] (7:1) Fall 89, p. 13.
4590. PROKOP, Jan
"Song of a Crust of Bread Thown to Sparrows on Victory Square . . ." (tr. by
Stanislaw Baranczak and Clare Cavanagh). [SenR] (19:2) Fall 89, p. 27.
"Song of Four-Egg Enriched Ribbon Noodles" (tr. by Stanislaw Baranczak and
Clare Cavanah). [Trans] (21) Spr 89, p. 62.
4591. PROPER, Stan
"High Dive." [Lactuca] (12) F 89, p. 31.
"Insect Husk." [StoneC] (17:1/2) Fall-Wint 89-90, p. 63.
"Jimmy Jack." [Lactuca] (12) F 89, p. 31.
4592. PROPERTIUS
"IV.7. I do believe in ghosts! And death is not, after all" (tr. by Diane Arnson
Svarlien). [Trans] (22) Fall 89, p. 222-225.
4593. PROPP, Karen
"Autumn Night." [AntR] (47:1) Wint 89, p. 57.
"The Woman of Lake Wenatchee" (for my sister). [RiverC] (9:1) Spr 89, p. 88.
4594. PROSPERE, Susan
"Party Per Pale." [NewYorker] (65:25) 7 Ag 89, p. 40.
4595. PROVOST, Sarah
"As If I Knew." [SouthernPR] (29:1) Spr 89, p. 21-22.
4596. PRUNTY, Wyatt
"Dr. Williams' Garden" (for Paul Mariani). [SouthernR] (25:3) Sum 89, p. 601.
"Falling Through the Ice." [SouthernR] (25:3) Sum 89, p. 600.
"The Lake House." [YaleR] (78:3) Spr 89, p. 410-413.
"Learning the Bicycle" (for Heather). [AmerS] (58:1) Wint 89, p. 122.
"Playing by Ear." [KenR] (NS 11:3) Sum 89, p. 49.
"The Shortwave Radio." [Boulevard] (4:1, #10) Spr 89, p. 17.
"The Starlings." [Boulevard] (4:1, #10) Spr 89, p. 18.
"The Wild Horses." [KenR] (NS 11:3) Sum 89, p. 50-51.
"With Others." [KenR] (NS 11:3) Sum 89, p. 51-52.
4597. PUGSLEY, Susan
"Rooms Waiting." [PassN] (10:1) Wint 89, p. 7.
4598. PULCINI, Robert
"Guardian Angels." [WindO] (52) Wint 89-90, p. 4.
"The Resurrecting." [WindO] (52) Wint 89-90, p. 3-4.

4599. PULTZ, Constance
"Voyage." [StoneC] (16:3/4) Spr-Sum 89, p. 49.
4600. PURDY, James
"The Black Boy I Met Half a Year Ago." [Lactuca] (12) F 89, p. 44.
"Blossoms." [Contact] (9:53/54/55) Sum-Fall 89, p. 30.
"Do You Wonder Why I Am Sleepy?" [Lactuca] (12) F 89, p. 45.
"Fighting in a Wood." [Contact] (9:53/54/55) Sum-Fall 89, p. 30.
"From Rivers, and from the Earth Itself." [Contact] (9:53/54/55) Sum-Fall 89, p. 31.
"In a Deep Slumber." [Contact] (9:53/54/55) Sum-Fall 89, p. 29.
"Men of Bangladesh." [Contact] (9:53/54/55) Sum-Fall 89, p. 32.
"Men of Bangladesh." [Lactuca] (12) F 89, p. 45-46.
"Untitled: The axles creaking under the wagons." [Contact] (9:53/54/55) Sum-Fall
    89, p. 31.
"White Sheep." [Contact] (9:53/54/55) Sum-Fall 89, p. 31.
"White Sheep." [Lactuca] (12) F 89, p. 44.
"White Yellow Orange." [Contact] (9:53/54/55) Sum-Fall 89, p. 29.
4601. PURDY, Richard
"The Official Ratings Against Absolute Truth." [Rampike] (6:2) 88, p. 51.
4602. PURPURA, Lia
"Anger." [Colum] (14) 89, p. 86-87.
"Mourn That We Hear." [DenQ] (24:2) Fall 89, p. 85-86.
4603. PUSHKIN, Aleksander
"The Faun and the Shepherdess" (tr. by Chester Kallman). [SouthwR] (74:2) Spr
    89, p. 214-217.
4604. PUTALLAZ, Brian
"Family Ties." [Mildred] (3:1) Spr-Sum 89, p. 36.
4605. PYBUS, Rodney
"Dumbka." [Stand] (30:3) Sum 89, p. 14-15.
QI-JIAO, Cai
    See CAI, Qi-jiao
QING, Xiao
    See XIAO, Qing
4606. QUAGLIANO, Tony
"Bio-Politics of Molokai." [ChamLR] (2:2, #4) Spr 89, p. 14.
"Fierce Meadows." [Hawai'iR] (13:1, #25) Spr 89, p. 107.
"The Leper Eye." [ChamLR] (2:2, #4) Spr 89, p. 13.
"One for WCW at the Post-Nuclear Philosophy Conference in Manoa." [ChamLR]
    (3:1, #5) Fall 89, p. 98.
4607. QUART, Alissa
"Horse Dream Sequence." [HangL] (54) 89, p. 61.
"Simple Harmonic Motion." [HangL] (54) 89, p. 62.
"Surrealism." [HangL] (54) 89, p. 63.
"Two in One." [HangL] (54) 89, p. 64.
4608. QUAYLE, Amil
"Empyrean, Nebraska." [MidwQ] (30:2) Wint 89, p. 198.
4609. QUESSEP, Giovanni
"Lectura de William Blake." [LindLM] (8:2) Ap-Je 89, p. 3.
4610. QUETCHENBACH, Bernard
"When That Time Comes." [Wind] (19:65) 89, p. 24.
4611. QUEVEDO, Francisco de
"A Sonnet in Dialogue" (tr. by Sharon King). [Jacaranda] (4:1) Spr-Sum 89, p. 59.
4612. QUIG, Steven
"In the Cellar." [RiverC] (9:1) Spr 89, p. 72.
4613. QUIJANO, Mauricio
"A Partir de Cero." [Inti] (29/30) Primavera-Otoño 89, p. 268.
"Comenzar de Nuevo." [Inti] (29/30) Primavera-Otoño 89, p. 268.
"Extravagancias." [Inti] (29/30) Primavera-Otoño 89, p. 268.
"Inventario." [Inti] (29/30) Primavera-Otoño 89, p. 268.
4614. QUINLAN, Linda
"Ruth Wiseman" (my mother's partner). [SinW] (37) Spr 89, p. 71-72.
"Summer of 53." [SinW] (37) Spr 89, p. 70.
4615. QUINN, Bernetta
"End of Autumn." [GreensboroR] (46) Sum 89, p. 156.
4616. QUINN, Cosslett
"The Duck" (tr. of Seán O Ríordáin). [Trans] (22) Fall 89, p. 45.
"Freedom" (tr. of Seán O Ríordáin). [Trans] (22) Fall 89, p. 43-44.

4617. QUINN, Fran
"Heaven's Floor." [PaintedB] (39) 89, p. 89.
4618. QUINN, John
"Dogs Dreams & Donkeys Years." [ColEng] (51:4) Ap 89, p. 387.
"Dust" (for Lovell & Sweet). [Interim] (8:2) Fall 89, p. 16.
4619. QUINN, John Robert
"Blackberries." [Wind] (19:65) 89, p. 23-24.
"The Dream." [PoetL] (84:3) Fall 89, p. 17.
"Landscape with Cow." [Wind] (19:65) 89, p. 23.
"Memento." [Wind] (19:65) 89, p. 23.
"Memories of Alexandria, Virginia." [SpiritSH] (54) Spr-Sum 89, p. 37.
"Tall, Thin Sonnet." [SpiritSH] (54) Spr-Sum 89, p. 37.
"Wood Thrush at Dusk." [SpiritSH] (54) Spr-Sum 89, p. 38.
4620. QUINN, Nancy
"Transmission Chunks." [NewRena] (7:3, #23) 89, p. 70.
4621. RAAB, Lawrence
"The Agent." [SouthernPR] (29:2) Fall 89, p. 34-35.
"Dead Elms." [NewEngR] (12:1) Aut 89, p. 20.
"Evidence of Memory." [NewEngR] (12:1) Aut 89, p. 17-19.
"The Last Castle in England." [SouthwR] (74:1) Wint 89, p. 98-99.
"Old Times" (for my wife's mother). [ParisR] (31:110) Spr 89, p. 96.
"The Secret Life." [Poetry] (154:1) Ap 89, p. 5-9.
"Since You Asked" (for a friend who asked to be in a poem). [ParisR] (31:110) Spr
89, p. 97.
"What I Forgot to Mention." [NewYorker] (65:31) 18 S 89, p. 124.
"What the Dead Know." [SouthwR] (74:1) Wint 89, p. 99-100.
4622. RABINOWITCH, Joseph
"Time of the Bear." [CrossC] (11:2) 89, p. 7.
4623. RABINOWITZ, Anna
"Of Pine." [PoetryNW] (30:1) Spr 89, p. 42.
4624. RABINOWITZ, Sima
"Passover April 1985." [EvergreenC] (4:4) Sum 89, p. 26.
4625. RABONI, Giovanni
"Chair" (tr. by Vinio Rossi and Stuart Friebert). [NewL] (55:3) Spr 89, p. 21.
"Città dall'Alto." [Poetry] (155:1/2) O-N 89, p. 88.
"City from Above" (tr. by David Stivender and J. D. McClatchy). [Poetry] (155:1/2)
O-N 89, p. 89.
"Codicils" (tr. by Vinio Rossi and Stuart Friebert). [NewL] (55:3) Spr 89, p. 20-21.
"Figures in the Park" (tr. by David Stivender and J. D. McClatchy). [Poetry]
(155:1/2) O-N 89, p. 90.
"My Daughter's Birthday" (tr. by David Stivender and J. D. McClatchy). [Poetry]
(155:1/2) O-N 89, p. 91.
"Untitled: I have my father's years, I have his hands" (tr. by Vinio Rossi and Stuart
Friebert). [CentR] (33:1) Wint 89, p. 58-59.
4626. RACHEL, Naomi
"Bear Chase." [HampSPR] Wint 89, p. 6-7.
"The Ice Blink." [HampSPR] Wint 89, p. 5.
4627. RADAVICH, David
"A Season in Cancer." [Farm] (6:2) Fall 89, p. 87-92.
4628. RADDEN, Viki
"Not Black America." [SinW] (37) Spr 89, p. 93.
4629. RADNOTI, Miklós
"Elegy on the Death of Gyula Juhász" (tr. by Lászlo Komlósi and Len Roberts).
[IndR] (12:2) Spr 89, p. 97.
4630. RADUL, Judy
"The Dream of the Audience." [Rampike] (6:2) 88, p. 72.
4631. RAE, Mary
"Dream" (tr. of Juan Ramón Jiménez). [NewRena] (7:3, #23) 89, p. 69.
4632. RAFFA, Joseph
"Wino in Residence." [Wind] (19:65) 89, p. 25.
4633. RAGAN, Jacie
"Autumnal Equinox." [MidwQ] (31:1) Aut 89, p. 59.
"Midday Shadows." [MidwQ] (31:1) Aut 89, p. 58.
"Mississippi Sundown." [MidwQ] (31:1) Aut 89, p. 57.
4634. RAGAN, James
"Out of Context." [AntR] (47:3) Sum 89, p. 330-331.

4635. RAIMUND, Hans
"August 27th, Night" (tr. by David Chorlton). [Os] (29) 89, p. 15.
"Che Solo Puoi Afferrare Bricioli di Ricordi" (Auf Distanz Gegangen, Baden bei
Wien, 1985. In German). [Os] (29) 89, p. 16.
"Che Solo Puoi Afferrare Bricioli di Ricordi" (tr. by David Chorlton). [Os] (29) 89,
p. 17.
4636. RAINE, Craig
"Retirement." [NewYorker] (65:42) 4 D 89, p. 72.
"Scrap." [GrandS] (8:4) Sum 89, p. 20-22.
4637. RAINER, Jacki
"The First Three Months of Love." [FiveFR] (7) 89, p. 69.
4638. RAISOR, Philip
"Let Me Go Where the Laughter Is." [OxfordM] (5:1) Spr-Sum 89, p. 19.
4639. RAJAN, Tilottama
"Spotlight / Searchlight." [MassR] (30:1) Spr 89, p. 101.
4640. RAMIREZ, Orlando
"August 31." [Zyzzyva] (5:3, #19) Fall 89, p. 63.
4641. RAMIREZ, Tino
"Circling the Island." [BambooR] (41) Wint 89, p. 27.
4642. RAMKE, Bin
"After Hawthorne." [ParisR] (31:110) Spr 89, p. 92.
"Cinéma Verité." [Pequod] (28/29/30) 89, p. 266.
"Elegy As Algorithm: Seasonal Lamentation." [WestHR] (43:1) Spr 89, p. 56-57.
"Elegy As Origin." [DenQ] (23:3/4) Wint-Spr 89, p. 33-36.
"Figure in Landscape." [Pequod] (28/29/30) 89, p. 264-265.
"In a Manner of Speaking." [MissR] (18:1, #52) 89, p. 25-27.
"The Little Flowers." [ColR] (NS 16:2) Fall 89-Wint 90, p. 74.
"An Old Philosopher." [ParisR] (31:110) Spr 89, p. 89-91.
"Summer on the Coast." [Boulevard] (4:1, #10) Spr 89, p. 92-93.
"War Crimes." [NewRep] (201:15) 9 O 89, p. 34.
"Words Fail Me." [ColR] (NS 16:2) Fall 89-Wint 90, p. 72-73.
4643. RAMNATH, S.
"Apartheid." [Lactuca] (13) N 89, p. 56.
"News Poem." [Lactuca] (13) N 89, p. 57.
"Rebel." [Lactuca] (13) N 89, p. 57.
4644. RAMOS-PEREA, Roberto
"La Ira Dulce." [Mairena] (11:27) 89, p. 88.
4645. RAMSEY, Jarold
"Hand-Shadows" (for our children Kate, Sophie, and John, 45 poems). [QRL]
(9:28-29) 89, 61 p.
4646. RAMSEY, Martha
"The Garden." [PassN] (10:2) Sum 89, p. 18.
"Mother in Rain." [AmerV] (14) Spr 89, p. 61-62.
4647. RAMSEY, Patrick
"An Afternoon in the Park." [NoDaQ] (57:1) Wint 89, p. 121.
"A New Year's Tableau." [NoDaQ] (57:1) Wint 89, p. 122.
4648. RAMSEY, Paul
"City As Museum." [PoetC] (20:3) Spr 89, p. 20.
"The Desert Maker." [Hawai'iR] (13:1, #25) Spr 89, p. 55.
4649. RAMSEY, William
"In Medias Res (The Poem)." [PoetryNW] (30:2) Sum 89, p. 22-23.
4650. RANAN, Wendy
"Academic Pursuits." [GrahamHR] (12) Spr 89, p. 15.
"Insomniacs of the Sea." [GrahamHR] (12) Spr 89, p. 16-17.
"On the Sixth Day." [GrahamHR] (12) Spr 89, p. 13.
"Orchard in Late Fall." [GrahamHR] (12) Spr 89, p. 18.
"Strength in Numbers." [GrahamHR] (12) Spr 89, p. 14.
4651. RAND, Lydia
"An Explosion of Light." [Vis] (30) 89, p. 14.
4652. RANDAHL
"Deer Season in Deer Canyon." [SoCoast] (7) Spr-Fall 89, p. 52.
4653. RANDALL, Belle
"Donner" (Selection: "In Praise of Proper Names"). [TriQ] (74) Wint 89, p.
196-200.
4654. RANDALL, Julia
"In Memory of Francis Fergusson (1904-1986)." [Ploughs] (15:4) Wint 89-90, p.

175-176.
"Twenty-One Turkeys." [Ploughs] (15:4) Wint 89-90, p. 177.
4655. RANDALL, Mary Carol
"Delicate As." [SinW] (37) Spr 89, p. 88-89.
4656. RANDOLPH, Robert
"Eddies." [GeoR] (43:2) Sum 89, p. 242-243.
4657. RANKIN, Paula
"Fifteen." [ThRiPo] (31/32) 88, p. 37.
"Mantises." [ThRiPo] (31/32) 88, p. 38-39.
4658. RAPANT, Larry
"All Questions." [Mildred] (3:2) 89, p. 21.
"Calling." [Mildred] (3:2) 89, p. 23.
"The Promise." [Mildred] (3:2) 89, p. 22.
4659. RAPHAEL, Dan
"Changing the Clocks on the Wrong Day." [BellR] (12:1, #25) Spr 89, p. 22-24.
"Graceful As 3 Blocks in a Winter Downpour." [FreeL] (2) Sum 89, p. 11.
"In Saxophone Shadow." [FreeL] (2) Sum 89, p. 12-13.
"Inforestation." [Aerial] (5) 89, p. 158.
4660. RASH, Ron
"Chester County Fair: October, 1960." [Poem] (61) My 89, p. 47.
"Copperhead." [KanQ] (21:1/2) Wint-Spr 89, p. 154.
"The Disaster Drill." [SouthernPR] (29:2) Fall 89, p. 41.
"Fishing at Night" (for Tom Rash). [KanQ] (21:1/2) Wint-Spr 89, p. 155.
"Fishing Beyond the Pale." [Poem] (61) My 89, p. 48.
"Luna." [Poem] (61) My 89, p. 46.
"A Preacher Who Takes Up Serpents Laments the Presence of Skeptics in His
   Church." [SouthernR] (25:4) Aut 89, p. 936-937.
"Sunday Evening at Middlefork Creek Pentecostal Church." [SouthernR] (25:4) Aut
   89, p. 937.
4661. RASULA, Jed
"Accidental Research, Less." [Screens] (1) 89, p. 27.
4662. RATCH, Jerry
"The Loss of Virginity, III." [WashR] (14:5) F-Mr 89, p. 16.
4663. RATCLIFFE, Stephen
"Present Tense" (Excerpt). [NewAW] (5) Fall 89, p. 87-88.
4664. RATTRAY, David
"Age" (tr. of Pindar, w. Friedrich Hölderlin). [Temblor] (10) 89, p. 198.
"The Asylums" (tr. of Pindar, w. Friedrich Hölderlin). [Temblor] (10) 89, p. 198.
"The Enlivener" (tr. of Pindar, w. Friedrich Hölderlin). [Temblor] (10) 89, p. 199.
"The Faithlessness of Wisdom" (tr. of Pindar, w. Friedrich Hölderlin). [Temblor]
   (10) 89, p. 196.
"The Infinite" (tr. of Pindar, w. Friedrich Hölderlin). [Temblor] (10) 89, p. 198.
"Of Peace" (tr. of Pindar, w. Friedrich Hölderlin). [Temblor] (10) 89, p. 196.
"Of the Dolphin" (tr. of Pindar, w. Friedrich Hölderlin). [Temblor] (10) 89, p. 197.
"Of Truth" (tr. of Pindar, w. Friedrich Hölderlin). [Temblor] (10) 89, p. 196.
"The Supreme" (tr. of Pindar, w. Friedrich Hölderlin). [Temblor] (10) 89, p. 197.
4665. RAWLEY, Donald
"City of Men." [YellowS] (32) Wint 89, p. 6-7.
"Mulholland Drive." [YellowS] (30) Sum 89, p. 6-7.
4666. RAWLINGS, Jane B.
"Voice" (Commended). [StoneC] (17:1/2) Fall-Wint 89-90, p. prelim. p. 9.
4667. RAWLINS, C. L.
"All Souls Day." [WeberS] (6:1) Spr 89, p. 68.
"Burning the Fields" (Cache Valley, Utah). [OxfordM] (5:2) Fall-Wint 89, p. 34.
"Drinking in the Space." [Sequoia] (33:1) Sum 89, p. 42-43.
"Elegy" (for Edward Abbey). [Sequoia] (33:1) Sum 89, p. 44.
"Fires" (Salt Lake City, Utah). [OxfordM] (5:2) Fall-Wint 89, p. 32-34.
"Lots with a View" (Woodside-La Honda, California). [OxfordM] (5:2) Fall-Wint
   89, p. 31-32.
"A Song in Trade" (a jeremiad for John D.). [ChiR] (36:3/4) 89, p. 76-79.
4668. RAWLINS, Susan
"Notes from a Plague Year." [PoetC] (21:1) Fall 89, p. 3-4.
"The Queen of Hearts Says *Hit Me, Not Too Hard*." [AnotherCM] (19) 89, p. 172.
4669. RAWN, Michael David
"Interludes." [Pig] (15) 88, p. 45.

4670. RAWORTH, Tom
        "One Two Six." [Acts] (10) 89, p. 89-94.
4671. RAWSON, JoAnna
        "The Border" (Moshav Neot Hakikar, Negev Desert). [AmerPoR] (18:5) S-O 89, p.
            6.
        "Flaming June" (Lord Frederick Leighton, 1896). [AmerPoR] (18:5) S-O 89, p. 6.
        "From Across the Eel Marsh, Watching the Boathouse Burn." [AmerPoR] (18:5)
            S-O 89, p. 5.
        "Up in the Attic with the Antique Electric Organ." [AmerPoR] (18:5) S-O 89, p. 7.
4672. RAY, David
        "Address to a Child in India." [SouthernPR] (29:1) Spr 89, p. 6.
        "Apologia." [PoetC] (20:2) Wint 89, p. 31-32.
        "Buddha." [NewL] (56:2/3) Wint 89-Spr 90, p. 230.
        "Class." [ColEng] (51:3) Mr 89, p. 277.
        "A Commissioned Poem." [NewL] (56:2/3) Wint 89-Spr 90, p. 229.
        "The Customs Man Melville Greets the Expatriates." [KanQ] (21:4) Fall 89, p.
            88-89.
        "Diary Entry in New Zealand." [SouthernPR] (29:1) Spr 89, p. 5-6.
        "E. L. Mayo." [KanQ] (21:1/2) Wint-Spr 89, p. 33.
        "Fatalities." [ColEng] (51:6) O 89, p. 577.
        "Field of Snails." [ColEng] (51:6) O 89, p. 579.
        "For Sam on His Birthday." [ColEng] (51:3) Mr 89, p. 279.
        "The Foreigner Has His Meal Abroad." [LaurelR] (23:2) Sum 89, p. 68.
        "Fresh Start." [KanQ] (21:1/2) Wint-Spr 89, p. 33.
        "The Ghosts of Lake Como." [HeliconN] (20) 89, p. 45-47.
        "The Giant Bird That Could Not Fly Away From Its Destiny" (After Allen Curnow).
            [CreamCR] (13:2) Fall 89, p. 141.
        "Good News at the Alpine Villa." [KanQ] (21:3) Sum 89, p. 51.
        "Holladay's Sin" (Honorable Mention Poem, 1988/1989). [KanQ] (21:1/2) Wint-Spr
            89, p. 31-32.
        "The Humpbacks." [GrahamHR] (12) Spr 89, p. 100-101.
        "Incident in N.Y." [NewL] (56:2/3) Wint 89-Spr 90, p. 228.
        "Letter from Abroad." [PoetC] (20:2) Wint 89, p. 33.
        "Letter to One Long Mourned." [PoetC] (20:2) Wint 89, p. 34-36.
        "News Item." [WestB] (23) 89, p. 12.
        "The Nursing Home." [WestB] (23) 89, p. 12.
        "The Overcast Lake." [GrahamHR] (12) Spr 89, p. 99.
        "The Pace of Life" (after Prabhakar Barwe's paintings). [GrahamHR] (12) Spr 89,
            p. 98.
        "The Papers Are Full." [ColEng] (51:3) Mr 89, p. 278.
        "Progress on the Block." [KanQ] (21:1/2) Wint-Spr 89, p. 32.
        "Quite Enough." [ColEng] (51:6) O 89, p. 580.
        "A Regret." [ColEng] (51:6) O 89, p. 578-579.
        "Saltambiques." [Pequod] (28/29/30) 89, p. 251.
        "So Now How Do You Feel." [NegC] (9:2) 89, p. 25.
        "Thanksgiving." [ColEng] (51:3) Mr 89, p. 279.
        "Thoreau on the Merrimack." [KanQ] (21:4) Fall 89, p. 89-90.
        "Throwing the Racetrack Cats at Saratoga." [NewL] (56:2/3) Wint 89-Spr 90, p.
            226-227.
        "The Tourist." [NewL] (56:2/3) Wint 89-Spr 90, p. 228.
        "A Visit." [KanQ] (21:3) Sum 89, p. 50.
        "Walking on Shore: Villanelle." [KanQ] (21:3) Sum 89, p. 52.
4673. RAY, Judy
        "Centenarians of Dunedin, New Zealand." [AmerV] (14) Spr 89, p. 40-42.
4674. RAY, Pratima
        "Marriage Vessel" (tr. by Paramita Banerjee and Carolyne Wright). [NewEngR]
            (11:4) Sum 89, p. 459.
4675. RAY, Sunil B.
        "Full Moon" (tr. of Nabaneeta Dev Sen, w. Carolyne Wright and the author).
            [NewEngR] (11:4) Sum 89, p. 456.
        "To Be Worthy" (tr. of Vijaya Mukhopadhyay, w. Carolyne Wright and the author).
            [NewEngR] (11:4) Sum 89, p. 458.
        "Welcome Angel" (tr. of Nabaneetä Dev Sen, w. Carolyne Wright and the author).
            [MalR] (89) Wint 89, p. 31-33.
4676. REA, Charles
        "Summer." [CanLit] (120) Spr 89, p. 64.

4677. REA, Susan
"Fourteenth Anniversary." [NewRena] (7:3, #23) 89, p. 175.
"North American Rare Bird Alert." [LaurelR] (23:2) Sum 89, p. 21.
"Portrait of Aunt Ellen." [AmerS] (58:4) Aut 89, p. 543-544.
"Volcanoes" (for Demian). [AmerS] (58:4) Aut 89, p. 542-543.
4678. REAL, Damienne
"Watching the Weather." [PassN] (10:1) Wint 89, p. 13.
4679. REBOA, Daniela
"I Don't Know What It Is About You." [Footwork] 89, p. 13.
"In the Sweetness of It All." [Footwork] 89, p. 13.
4680. RECIPUTI, Natalie
"The Catalpa Tree." [BellArk] (5:1) Ja-F 89, p. 10.
"Epithalamium" (to honor the marriage of Bob and Mary). [BellArk] (5:4) Jl-Ag 89,
        p. 4.
"In One Long Sentance." [BellArk] (5:1) Ja-F 89, p. 1.
"Listening to the Clock." [BellArk] (5:5) S-O 89, p. 7.
"Magician in Love." [BellArk] (5:4) Jl-Ag 89, p. 7.
"Prairie Schooner." [BellArk] (5:4) Jl-Ag 89, p. 5.
4681. RECTOR, Liam
"Hans Reading, Hans Smoking." [NewRep] (201:19) 6 N 89, p. 126.
"Saxophone." [Epoch] (38:2) 89, p. 136-137.
RED PINE
        See PINE, Red
4682. REDHILL, Michael
"Lovers Breaking." [Quarry] (38:2) Spr 89, p. 59.
4683. REECE, Spencer
"Frozen Music." [KeyWR] (2:1/2) Fall-Wint 89, p. 166.
"On Frank O'Hara." [KeyWR] (2:1/2) Fall-Wint 89, p. 167.
4684. REED, Jeremy
"I Am from There" (tr. of Mahmoud Darwish, w. Lena Jayyusi). [PoetryE] (27) Spr
        89, p. 72.
"Left Hand." [Stand] (30:4) Aut 89, p. 48.
"Life Expectations." [Poetry] (153:6) Mr 89, p. 320.
"Slate." [Verse] (6:2) Je 89, p. 44.
"There Is a Night" (tr. of Mahmoud Darwish, w. Lena Jayyusi). [PoetryE] (27) Spr
        89, p. 93.
"To Celebrate John Ashbery." [Verse] (6:3) Wint 89, p. 31.
4685. REED, John R.
"Baudelaire." [OntR] (31) Fall-Wint 89-90, p. 19.
"Verlaine." [OntR] (31) Fall-Wint 89-90, p. 17-18.
"Winter Cats." [BelPoJ] (40:2) Wint 89-90, p. 38.
4686. REED, Lesley
"Confessions." [PoetL] (84:4) Wint 89-90, p. 31.
"Plums." [PoetL] (84:4) Wint 89-90, p. 30.
4687. REED, W. A.
"Between Father and Child." [Farm] (6:2) Fall 89, p. 25-27.
"The Temperature of Conversation." [Farm] (6:2) Fall 89, p. 23.
4688. REES, Elizabeth
"During." [NowestR] (27:1) 89, p. 34-35.
"Monsoon." [NowestR] (27:1) 89, p. 33.
4689. REESE, Leslie A.
"Freedom Music" (to the tune of unused lyrics). [Obs] (2:1) Spr 87, p. 83-84.
4690. REEVE, F. D.
"Duke of the Air." [SewanR] (97:1) Wint 89, p. 30-32.
"A New House in April." [VirQR] (65:3) Sum 89, p. 449-450.
4691. REEVES, Trish
"Van Gogh Aims for Own Heart and Misses." [HeliconN] (20) 89, p. 28.
4692. REFFE, Candice
"American" (for Paige and Cathleen). [AntR] (47:1) Wint 89, p. 74-75.
"Summer in the Dordogne." [Thrpny] (38) Sum 89, p. 30.
4693. REGAN, J. M.
"In the Confessional." [JamesWR] (5:2 [i.e. 6:2]) Wint 89, p. 14.
"Weapon Effects on a Wood Frame House." [JamesWR] (6:3) Spr 89, p. 12.
4694. REGE, P. S. (Purushottam Shivram)
"The Green Dress" (tr. by Vinay Dharwadker). [TriQ] (77) Wint 89-90, p. 194-195.
"Mirror" (tr. by Vinay Dharwadker). [TriQ] (77) Wint 89-90, p. 192.

"Poem at Midnight" (tr. by Vinay Dharwadker). [TriQ] (77) Wint 89-90, p. 196.
"The Visit" (tr. by Vinay Dharwadker). [TriQ] (77) Wint 89-90, p. 197.
4695. REGIER, Gail
"Acid." [SouthernHR] (23:2) Spr 89, p. 141.
"Divorce." [SouthernHR] (23:3) Sum 89, p. 216.
4696. REIBER, James T.
"Clearing After Rain, Early Spring in the North" (tr. of Zhu Xiang). [WebR] (14:1)
Spr 89, p. 35.
"Long-Awaited Spring" (tr. of Zhu Xiang). [WebR] (14:1) Spr 89, p. 35.
"Tranquil Summer Evening" (tr. of Zhu Xiang). [WebR] (14:1) Spr 89, p. 35.
4697. REID, Alastair
"De Me a Ti" (tr. into Spanish by Herberto Padilla). [LindLM] (8:4) O-D 89, p. 3.
"Juego de Espejos" (tr. into Spanish by Herberto Padilla). [LindLM] (8:4) O-D 89,
p. 3.
"Una Leccion de Musica" (tr. into Spanish by Herberto Padilla). [LindLM] (8:4) O-D
89, p. 3.
"Por Ella" (tr. into Spanish by Herberto Padilla). [LindLM] (8:4) O-D 89, p. 3.
4698. REID, Bethany
"The Coyotes and My Mom" (Selections: 5 poems). [BellArk] (5:2) Mr-Ap 89, p.
4-6.
REID, Bill
See REID, William A. (Bill)
4699. REID, Christopher
"Contretemps." [Pequod] (26/27) 89, p. 123.
4700. REID, D. C.
"After It Aches, Loneliness Glows." [AntigR] (79) Aut 89, p. 121.
"Peeking in to Someone Else's Summer." [Dandel] (16:2) Fall-Wint 89, p. 34.
"Saying Yes to Suicide." [AntigR] (79) Aut 89, p. 122.
4701. REID, Ian
"The Arrest." [Descant] (20:3/4, #66/67) Fall-Wint 89, p. 216.
"The Losing." [Descant] (20:3/4, #66/67) Fall-Wint 89, p. 215.
"The Measure." [Descant] (20:3/4, #66/67) Fall-Wint 89, p. 214.
"The Meeting." [Descant] (20:3/4, #66/67) Fall-Wint 89, p. 216.
4702. REID, Joan
"Rent." [AlphaBS] (6) Wint 89-90, p. 55.
"Sandra." [AlphaBS] (6) Wint 89-90, p. 53-54.
"The Utopian's Daughter." [AlphaBS] (6) Wint 89-90, p. 51-52.
4703. REID, Monty
"A Perfect Audience." [Dandel] (16:1) Spr-Sum 89, p. 50-51.
"What We Call It." [Dandel] (16:1) Spr-Sum 89, p. 52.
4704. REID, William A. (Bill)
"Newton Farms." [Rampike] (6:2) 88, p. 69.
"Subterfuge." [Rampike] (6:3) 88, p. 44-45.
4705. REIDEL, James
"Devils Night." [TriQ] (74) Wint 89, p. 189.
4706. REIMER, Dolores
"At Susan's Veg Shop." [AntigR] (77/78) Spr-Sum 89, p. 32.
"I Want to Know, My Sisters." [Event] (18:2) Sum 89, p. 62.
"Mother and Daughter." [AntigR] (77/78) Spr-Sum 89, p. 33.
"*Sati* Means Good Wife" (for Roop Kanwar). [Event] (18:2) Sum 89, p. 63.
4707. REIMONENQ, Alden
"A Pleonastic *Ne*." [BlackALF] (23:3) Fall 89, p. 466.
"A Tree Died in France." [BlackALF] (23:3) Fall 89, p. 466-467.
4708. REINFELD, Linda
"Blurb Ls" (Excerpt). [Screens] (1) 89, p. 56-58.
4709. REINKE, Steve
"Three Angels Contained by Architecture." [Rampike] (6:2) 88, p. 61.
4710. REINKING, Victor
"The Smile" (tr. of Abdellatif Laabi). [Vis] (31) 89, p. 45.
REIS, Siri von
See Von REIS, Siri
4711. REISS, James
"Finding Jung's Castle." [FreeL] (1) 89, p. 34-35.
"Guatemalan Worry Dolls." [Poetry] (153:4) Ja 89, p. 219.
"Jerusalem." [DenQ] (23:3/4) Wint-Spr 89, p. 116.
"Mexico." [Agni] (28) 89, p. 238-240.

4712. REITER, David (David P.)
"Clippings." [Grain] (17:2) Sum 89, p. 32-33.
"From Scratch." [BellR] (12:1, #25) Spr 89, p. 4-5.
"Grand Final at Palenque." [Grain] (17:2) Sum 89, p. 33.
"Voices from the Flood of '94." [Dandel] (16:1) Spr-Sum 89, p. 17-18.
4713. REITER, Jendi
"Danger: Watch Out for Falling Semicolons." [HangL] (54) 89, p. 65-66.
"The Revolt of Mouse(tm), Patent #474,325,865." [HangL] (54) 89, p. 67-68.
"Service Includes Free Lifetime Updating." [HangL] (55) 89, p. 63-64.
"So It's Goodbye, Mr. Postman." [HangL] (54) 89, p. 69-70.
4714. REITER, Käte
"Alone in Your House of Skin" (tr. by John Linthicum). [LitR] (33:1) Fall 89, p. 78.
"The Angel" (tr. by John Linthicum). [LitR] (33:1) Fall 89, p. 78.
"The Child Has Gray Eyes" (tr. by John Linthicum). [LitR] (33:1) Fall 89, p. 79.
"Is There More Wood" (tr. by John Linthicum). [LitR] (33:1) Fall 89, p. 79.
"The Sun" (tr. by John Linthicum). [LitR] (33:1) Fall 89, p. 79.
4715. REITER, Lora K.
"Three Meals Two Miles from Tacambaro" (Michoacan, Mexico. For Marguerita).
[SingHM] (16) 89, p. 50-53.
4716. REITER, Thomas
"Backbone Park: The Way Down." [ThRiPo] (31/32) 88, p. 40.
"Free Gift and a Home Demonstration." [Journal] (13:1) Spr-Sum 89, p. 49-50.
"Leaving a River Town in Early Spring." [GettyR] (2:3) Sum 89, p. 533-534.
"Seed Starters." [PoetryNW] (30:3) Aut 89, p. 14.
4717. REMICK, J. L.
"Memory of Wood." [HeavenB] (6) Wint-Spr 89, p. 23.
"Memory of Wood." [HeavenB] (7) Wint 89, p. 30.
"The Root of the Horde." [HeavenB] (6) Wint-Spr 89, p. 3.
4718. RENDLEMAN, Danny
"Shooting Nine-Ball with My Father at the Rainbow Bar." [PassN] (10:2) Sum 89,
p. 22.
4719. RENJILIAN, Jerry
"Wads of Gum." [EngJ] (78:3) Mr 89, p. 90.
4720. RENKL, Margaret
"Love and the Ten O'Clock News." [CrossCur] (8:3) Apr 89, p. 86-87.
"Out from the Dark of Trees at Night." [BlackWR] (15:2) Spr 89, p. 9-14.
"The Way In." [TexasR] (10:1/2) Spr-Sum 89, p. 86-87.
4721. RENSCHLER, Norman G.
"I was aiming at the intuitive level, I wanted to." [Grain] (17:1) Spr 89, inside front
cover.
4722. REPLANSKY, Naomi
"In the Hospital." [Ploughs] (15:4) Wint 89-90, p. 178.
4723. REPOSA, Carol Coffee
"Amadeus." [Wind] (19:65) 89, p. 27.
"Miss Emily." [Wind] (19:65) 89, p. 26-27.
4724. REPP, John
"For Fanny Goldberg, Who Asked God to Bless Me." [KenR] (NS 11:1) Wint 89,
p. 83.
"Personal Essay." [Interim] (8:1) Spr 89, p. 8.
4725. RESS, Lisa
"Broadcast." [Farm] (6:2) Fall 89, p. 68.
"Dream Jungle: El Salvador." [Farm] (6:2) Fall 89, p. 67.
"The Landscape Around Vienna" (tr. of Ingeborg Bachmann). [GrahamHR] (12) Spr
89, p. 48-50.
"Playing on the Block." [Farm] (6:2) Fall 89, p. 69.
4726. RESTREPO, Elkin
"Cuando estamos acostados hay cosas que no digo a él." [LindLM] (8:2) Ap-Je 89,
p. 4.
4727. RETSOV, Samuel
"Daphnis and Chloe" (for Elaine). [Talisman] (2) Spr 89, p. 59.
"Former Care." [Talisman] (3) Fall 89, p. 107.
"Gültepe." [Talisman] (3) Fall 89, p. 98.
4728. RETTBERG, Georgeann Eskievich
"Timing." [SoCoast] (6) Fall 88, p. 14-15.
4729. REVARD, Carter
"Driving in Oklahoma." [Nimrod] (32:2) Spr-Sum 89, p. 88.

"November in Washington, D.C." [Nimrod] (32:2) Spr-Sum 89, p. 86-87.
4730. REVELL, Donald
"Apart from Solitude." [OhioR] (44) 89, p. 126-127.
"Connecticut." [OhioR] (44) 89, p. 124-125.
"Heliotrope: Years and Years after the Revolution." [WillowS] (23) Wint 89, p. 12-13.
"The Inns of Protest." [Antaeus] (62) Spr 89, p. 189-190.
"Martinmas." [SouthernPR] (29:2) Fall 89, p. 22.
"The Night Orchard." [Poetry] (154:4) Jl 89, p. 211-213.
"The Old Causes." [Boulevard] (4:1, #10) Spr 89, p. 118-119.
"Open City." [Crazy] (37) Wint 89, p. 56-57.
"Production Number." [Pequod] (28/29/30) 89, p. 241.
"A Prospect of Youth." [Pequod] (28/29/30) 89, p. 240.
"The Season to Scale." [ParisR] (31:111) Sum 89, p. 86-88.
"Swan Autumn." [GrandS] (9:1) Aut 89, p. 228.
"Tabard and Terrace." [NewRep] (200:10) 6 Mr 89, p. 34.
"The World's Fair Cities." [Agni] (28) 89, p. 80-81.
REVUELTA, Gutierrez
See GUTIERREZ REVUELTA, Pedro
REVUELTA, Pedro Gutierrez
See GUTIERREZ REVUELTA, Pedro
4731. REXROTH, Kenneth
"All Year Long" (tr. of anonymous Chinese poem (Six Dynasties)). [LitR] (32:3) Spr 89, p. 304.
"Winter Dawn" (tr. of Tu Fu). [LitR] (32:3) Spr 89, p. 303.
4732. REYNOLDS, Craig A.
"Biodance." [ChangingM] (20) Wint-Spr 89, p. 20.
4733. REYNOLDS, Lawrence Judson
"Molyneux's Wake." [GreensboroR] (46) Sum 89, p. 169-170.
4734. REYNOLDS, Oliver
"From Unknown Tongues." [Verse] (6:2) Je 89, p. 3-4.
"Necropolis." [Pequod] (26/27) 89, p. 124-126.
4735. REYNOLDS, Thomas
"Fingertips." [CapeR] (24:1) Spr 89, p. 18-19.
4736. RHENISCH, Harold
"The House." [CanLit] (120) Spr 89, p. 143-144.
"Mani." [Grain] (17:4) Wint 89, p. 43.
"The Night of My Conception." [Event] (18:3) Fall 89, p. 74-75.
"The War of the Angels." [Event] (18:3) Fall 89, p. 76-79.
4737. RHOADES, Lisa
"Into Grace" (Winner, 1989 Ratner-Ferber-Poet Lore Competition). [PoetL] (84:2) Sum 89, p. 7.
4738. RHODENBAUGH, Suzanne
"Country Song: White Chenille." [Journal] (13:1) Spr-Sum 89, p. 18-19.
"Keeping the Faith." [FloridaR] (16:2/3) Fall-Wint 89, p. 178-179.
"Making a Christ of the Average Jesus." [Journal] (13:1) Spr-Sum 89, p. 16-17.
"My People." [NewEngR] (12:2) Wint 89, p. 151-152.
"Questioning the Remains." [NegC] (9:2) 89, p. 63.
4739. RHODES, Martha
"Fall Visit." [FloridaR] (16:2/3) Fall-Wint 89, p. 120.
"Her Future." [FloridaR] (16:2/3) Fall-Wint 89, p. 123.
"In the Sick Room." [FloridaR] (16:2/3) Fall-Wint 89, p. 121.
"Like Today." [FloridaR] (16:2/3) Fall-Wint 89, p. 122.
4740. RICE, H. William
"Jagged." [ChatR] (9:3) Spr 89, p. 43.
4741. RICE, Paul
"Love and the Jersey Shore." [PoetL] (84:3) Fall 89, p. 10.
"Ossahatchee" (for Levi Walker). [ChatR] (9:4) Sum 89, p. 69-70.
4742. RICE, Stephen B.
"Seathunder Beyond." [Writer] (102:12) D 89, p. 26.
4743. RICH, Adrienne
"6/21." [TriQ] (74) Wint 89, p. 202.
"The Desert As Garden of Paradise." [AmerPoR] (18:2) Mr-Ap 89, p. 5-7.
"Harpers Ferry." [AmerPoR] (18:2) Mr-Ap 89, p. 3-4.
"Living Memory." [AmerPoR] (18:2) Mr-Ap 89, p. 4-5.
"Sleepwalking Next to Death." [Zyzzyva] (5:2, #18) Sum 89, p. 109-113.

"The Slides." [TriQ] (74) Wint 89, p. 201.
4744. RICHARDS, Marilee
"Cows in Your Window." [CinPR] (20) Fall 89, p. 11.
"Guest House." [CapeR] (24:1) Spr 89, p. 49.
"Having It All." [CinPR] (20) Fall 89, p. 10.
"Rabbits." [CapeR] (24:1) Spr 89, p. 48.
"The Town Where I Spent My Summer." [SoCoast] (5) Spr 88, p. 53.
4745. RICHARDSON, James
"How It Ends." [YaleR] (78:4) Sum 89, p. 654.
4746. RICHETTI, Peter
"Bury the Dead." [RiverS] (28) 89, p. 14.
"Fair Play." [BlueBldgs] (11) 89, p. 25.
"Into the Light." [RiverS] (28) 89, p. 11.
"The Last Time." [RiverS] (28) 89, p. 12-13.
4747. RICHEY, Joe
"Chronicles: A Central American Travel Journal" (Part II). [HeavenB] (7) Wint 89,
p. 18-28.
"Chronicles: Travel Journal Notes '87-'88" (Chapter One of a Four Part
Manuscript-in-Progress). [HeavenB] (6) Wint-Spr 89, p. 16-22.
4748. RICHMAN, Elliot
"Ariel's Night Song to the Stars Above Arles" (from *Blastin' Out of Abilene*).
[Bogg] (61) 89, p. 31.
"At a Poor Man's Zen Garden." [Bogg] (61) 89, p. 12.
"The Ballad of an Old Vietnamese Woman Who Lives Along the Saranac and Picks
Wild Flowers That She Plants in the Snow." [Lactuca] (12) F 89, p. 33.
"The Decoy." [Lactuca] (12) F 89, p. 33.
"A Meeting with an Old Lover" (After a Poem by Tu Fu). [HiramPoR] (46) Spr-Sum
89, p. 24.
"A Night by a Distant Lake -- 1988" (After a Poem by Tu Fu). [HiramPoR] (46)
Spr-Sum 89, p. 25.
"The Ocean of the 38th Caliber." [SlipS] (9) 89, p. 46.
"On First Reading Tu Fu" (from *Blastin' Out of Abilene*). [Bogg] (61) 89, p. 31.
"Seven Sketches from the Tao." [Mildred] (3:2) 89, p. 114-115.
"Toward Eternity." [CentR] (33:3) Sum 89, p. 248.
"Zuzu's Petals." [Contact] (9:50/51/52) Fall-Wint 88-Spr 89, p. 20-21.
4749. RICHMAN, Heath
"Freedom." [WindO] (51) Spr 89, p. 44.
4750. RICHMAN, Robert
"The Fossil." [AmerS] (58:4) Aut 89, p. 585.
4751. RICHMAN, Steven
"The Burden of Sisyphus." [CapeR] (24:2) Fall 89, p. 26.
"A Good Day." [JINJPo] (11) 89, p. 27.
4752. RICHMOND, Michael L.
"Written on a Computer." [Kaleid] (19) Sum-Fall 89, p. 39.
4753. RICHMOND, Steve
"Gagaku." [Bogg] (61) 89, p. 49.
"Gagaku." [WormR] (29:1, #113) 89, p. 38.
"Gagaku: forget it." [Lactuca] (12) F 89, p. 41.
"Gagaku: it's better they call me." [Lactuca] (12) F 89, p. 42.
"Gagaku: sex like a demon." [Lactuca] (12) F 89, p. 41.
"Gagaku: the surprise is yellow blouse." [Lactuca] (12) F 89, p. 41.
"The Human." [WormR] (29:1, #113) 89, p. 39.
"It's Hard." [WormR] (29:1, #113) 89, p. 37.
"What's." [WormR] (29:1, #113) 89, p. 39.
4754. RICHTER, Greg
"August Shadow" (Excerpt, tr. of Larissa Vassilieva). [CharR] (15:1) Spr 89, p. 67.
"Vassilisa" (Excerpt, tr. of Larissa Vassilieva). [CharR] (15:1) Spr 89, p. 68.
"Whiteness in February" (tr. of Larissa Vassilieva). [CharR] (15:1) Spr 89, p. 68.
4755. RICHTER, Harvena
"The Snake" (from "The Yaddo Elegies"). [Chelsea] (48) 89, p. 142.
4756. RICKEL, Boyer
"The Bloated Goldfish" (for Mike Hendershot). [HayF] (4) Spr 89, p. 67.
"The Exposure of Form." [PraS] (63:1) Spr 89, p. 100-101.
"Spring Sonata" (Robert O'Connor, 1896-1986). [PraS] (63:1) Spr 89, p. 101-102.
"The Watchers." [PraS] (63:1) Spr 89, p. 102-103.

4757. RIDDELL, John
"Columns." [Rampike] (6:2) 88, p. 44-45.
4758. RIDL, Jack
"Bus Driver." [PoetryE] (28) Fall 89, p. 59-60.
"The Chair" (For Carrie and Tom Andrews). [FreeL] (1) 89, p. 22-23.
"Coach Wonders If He Could Have Been Anything Else." [ChamLR] (3:1, #5) Fall
89, p. 97.
"Halftime Entertainment." [WindO] (51) Spr 89, p. 18.
"History Class, Coach Teaching." [Wind] (19:64) 89, p. 33.
"Leafing Through His Daughter's Physics Book Coach Begins to Dream." [WindO]
(51) Spr 89, p. 19.
"Ref." [PoetryE] (28) Fall 89, p. 56-57.
"Scrub." [CharR] (15:2) Fall 89, p. 88.
"Scrub Dreams of Injuries." [CharR] (15:2) Fall 89, p. 89.
"Thinking Again of My Daughter." [FreeL] (1) 89, p. 23.
"Vendor." [PoetryE] (28) Fall 89, p. 58.
4759. RIDLAND, John
"Winslow Homer Sketches the Lake." [PoetC] (20:3) Spr 89, p. 12-14.
4760. RIEKE, Susan
"Poor Fools." [Wind] (19:64) 89, p. 22.
"The Winter Sun." [Wind] (19:64) 89, p. 22.
4761. RIFENBURGH, Daniel
"Finale for a Marriage." [PoetryE] (28) Fall 89, p. 48.
"LSD & All." [PoetryE] (28) Fall 89, p. 47.
4762. RIGGS, Dionis Coffin
"In the Home for the Aged" (tr. of Özcan Yalim, w. the author and William Fielder).
[StoneC] (16:3/4) Spr-Sum 89, p. 35.
"Moon Shadows." [StoneC] (16:3/4) Spr-Sum 89, p. 61.
4763. RIGSBEE, David
"Atomic Future." [SouthernPR] (29:1) Spr 89, p. 39-41.
RIHAKU
See LI, Po
4764. RILEY, Joanne M.
"Curse of the Bee Tree." [BallSUF] (30:4) Aut 89, p. 54.
"The Dark Side of the Butterfly." [ThRiPo] (33/34) 89, p. 41-42.
"Tornado and the County Fair." [BallSUF] (30:4) Aut 89, p. 67.
"Wintering." [BallSUF] (30:4) Aut 89, p. 44.
4765. RILEY, Matthew
"Beautiful Place." [WorldO] (22:1/2) Fall-Wint 87-88, c90, p. 31.
4766. RILEY, Michael D.
"Ballet Lesson." [CumbPR] (9:1) Fall 89, p. 47.
4767. RILEY, Peter
"Ospita" (Selections: I, II, IX, X). [Pequod] (26/27) 89, p. 127-128.
4768. RILKE, Rainer Maria
"Doorway" (tr. by Grant Pair). [Jacaranda] (4:1) Spr-Sum 89, p. 62.
"The Fifth Duino Elegy" (tr. by Bernhard Frank). [WebR] (14:1) Spr 89, p. 5-7.
"The Fishmonger's Stall" (Naples, tr. by Stephen Mitchell). [GrandS] (9:1) Aut 89,
p. 116-117.
"For Veronika Erdmann" (tr. by Stephen Mitchell). [ParisR] (31:111) Sum 89, p.
270.
"Little Tear-Vase" (tr. by Stephen Mitchell). [ParisR] (31:111) Sum 89, p. 253.
"Night Drive" (St. Petersburg, 1901, tr. by Derek Mahon). [Trans] (22) Fall 89, p.
180.
"Sonnets to Orpheus" (Selections: I: 15, 26, II: 3, 19, tr. by Leslie Norris and Alan
Keele). [QW] (28) Wint-Spr 89, p. 93-96.
4769. RIMBAUD, Arthur
"Ophelia, I" (tr. by Nathaniel Smith). [WebR] (14:1) Spr 89, p. 21.
4770. RIND, Sherry
"Rosh Hashana." [PoetryNW] (30:4) Wint 89-90, p. 29.
RIORDAIN, Seán O
See O RIORDAIN, Seán
4771. RIOS, Alberto
"Hers Is the Noise, Also, of the Dogs Asleep and in Dream." [Manoa] (1:1/2) Fall
89, p. 49-50.
"Marvella, For Borrowing." [Ploughs] (15:4) Wint 89-90, p. 179-181.
"Teodoro Luna's Old Joke." [Ploughs] (15:4) Wint 89-90, p. 182.

4772. RIOS, Soleida
"After the Drums and the Steps" (tr. by Lourdes González). [Pig] (15) 88, p. 72.
"Ancient" (tr. by Lourdes González). [Pig] (15) 88, p. 72.
"Another's Bolero" (tr. by Lourdes González). [Pig] (15) 88, p. 74.
"Bolero for Albino" (tr. by Lourdes González). [Pig] (15) 88, p. 73.
"Dreaming" (tr. by Lourdes González). [Pig] (15) 88, p. 73.
4773. RISI, Nelo
"The Muses Are Weary" (tr. by Richard Zenith). [PoetryE] (28) Fall 89, p. 177.
4774. RISSET, Jacqueline
"Seven Passages from a Woman's Life" (tr. by Rosmarie Waldrop). [Verse] (6:2) Je
89, p. 14-16.
4775. RISTAU, Harland
"Off the Avenue." [SmPd] (26:2 #76) Spr 89, p. 8.
4776. RISTOVIC, Aleksandar
"Happiness" (tr. by Charles Simic). [ParisR] (31:110) Spr 89, p. 171.
"Landscape with Snow" (tr. by Charles Simic). [ParisR] (31:110) Spr 89, p. 170.
"Old Motif" (tr. by Charles Simic). [ParisR] (31:110) Spr 89, p. 169.
"Out in the Open" (tr. by Charles Simic). [ParisR] (31:110) Spr 89, p. 172.
"To a Fool" (tr. by Charles Simic). [ParisR] (31:110) Spr 89, p. 168.
4777. RITCHE, Robert
"Green" (Mainstreet Elementary Poetry Contest, 2nd Grade, 1st Place).
[DeKalbLAJ] (22:1/4) 89, p. 102.
4778. RITCHIE, Elisavietta
"Annunciations, October." [Vis] (30) 89, p. 48.
"Education." [Amelia] (5:3, #14) 89, p. 27.
"Sorting Laundry." [Poetry] (153:5) F 89, p. 274-275.
4779. RITSOS, Yánnis
"Accented-Unaccented" (tr. by Edmund Keeley). [PoetryE] (27) Spr 89, p. 54.
"After the End" (tr. by Minas Savvas). [SenR] (19:1) 89, p. 9.
"And One More Night" (tr. by Minas Savvas). [AmerPoR] (18:5) S-O 89, p. 8.
"Death Portrait" (tr. by Edmund Keeley). [Caliban] (6) 89, p. 151.
"Description" (tr. by Edmund Keeley). [Caliban] (6) 89, p. 150.
"Farm Woman" (tr. by Stratis Haviaras). [Trans] (22) Fall 89, p. 260-261.
"Freedom" (tr. by Edmund Keeley). [PoetryE] (27) Spr 89, p. 57.
"The Hats" (tr. by Minas Savvas). [SenR] (19:1) 89, p. 8.
"Healing" (tr. by Edmund Keeley). [PoetryE] (27) Spr 89, p. 58.
"Hesperos" (tr. by Minas Savvas). [SenR] (19:1) 89, p. 7.
"In the Hallway Underground" (tr. by Minas Savvas). [AmerPoR] (18:5) S-O 89, p.
8.
"Insomnia" (tr. by Edmund Keeley). [PoetryE] (27) Spr 89, p. 51.
"The Meaning of Simplicity" (tr. by Edmund Keeley). [PoetryE] (27) Spr 89, p. 55.
"Mode of Acquisition" (tr. by Edmund Keeley). [PoetryE] (27) Spr 89, p. 56.
"Refutation" (tr. by Minas Savvas). [AmerPoR] (18:5) S-O 89, p. 8.
"Second Coming" (tr. by Edmund Keeley). [Caliban] (6) 89, p. 151.
"Sketch" (tr. by Edmund Keeley). [PoetryE] (27) Spr 89, p. 53.
"Slowly" (tr. by Edmund Keeley). [PoetryE] (27) Spr 89, p. 52.
"Toward Saturday" (tr. by Edmund Keeley). [PoetryE] (27) Spr 89, p. 50.
"Variation" (tr. by Edmund Keeley). [Caliban] (6) 89, p. 150.
"We Wait" (tr. by Edmund Keeley). [PoetryE] (27) Spr 89, p. 48.
"Women" (tr. by Edmund Keeley). [PoetryE] (27) Spr 89, p. 49.
4780. RITTY, Joan
"Kinds of Speech." [Plain] (9:2) Wint 89, p. 17.
4781. RIVARD, David
"Arrival Song." [Agni] (28) 89, p. 56-57.
"Earth to Tell of the Beasts." [Crazy] (36) Spr 89, p. 13-14.
"I Am a Pilgrim & a Stranger." [Crazy] (36) Spr 89, p. 15-16.
"Pilgrim Lake" (for John Logan, 1923-87). [Crazy] (36) Spr 89, p. 11-12.
"The Road Out." [Agni] (28) 89, p. 55.
4782. RIVARD, Ken
"Arms." [Dandel] (16:1) Spr-Sum 89, p. 49.
"Heart and Head." [AntigR] (77/78) Spr-Sum 89, p. 145.
4783. RIVERA, Diana
"Good-bye, My Loved One." [Americas] (17:1) Spr 89, p. 59-61.
"Here, in the House of Memories." [Americas] (17:1) Spr 89, p. 64.
"Here, in the House of Sorrows." [Americas] (17:1) Spr 89, p. 62-63.
"Learning to Speak." [Americas] (17:1) Spr 89, p. 54-58.

4784. RIVERA, Etnairis
"Decimas a la Luna." [Mairena] (11:27) 89, p. 81.
4785. RIVERA, Tomás
"Searching at Leal Middle School." [Americas] (17:3/4) Fall-Wint 89, p. 51-53.
4786. RIVERO, Mario
"Sisifo." [LindLM] (8:2) Ap-Je 89, p. 3.
4787. RIVERS, Ann
"Picking a Tune." [SpiritSH] (55) Fall-Wint 89 [90 on cover], p. 44-45.
4788. RIVERS, J. W.
"Respite." [Poetry] (154:3) Je 89, p. 137-139.
RIVIERE, Gladys M. la
See LaRIVIERE, Gladys M.
4789. RIXEN, Gail
"A Modern Judgement" (On seeing Bruegel's "The Triumph of Death"). [Vis] (30) 89, p. 13.
4790. ROBARDS, Brooks
"Fossils." [StoneC] (17:1/2) Fall-Wint 89-90, p. 17.
4791. ROBBINS, Anthony
"Theories of Decline" (Selections: 4 poems). [Temblor] (10) 89, p. 126-129.
4792. ROBBINS, Doren
"Could You Have Understood This, Marc Chagall? The Male Soul Was My Whipping-boy." [WillowS] (23) Wint 89, p. 7-9.
"Drawn to and Confounded." [Sulfur] (9:1, #24) Spr 89, p. 133.
"Not." [Sulfur] (9:1, #24) Spr 89, p. 134.
4793. ROBBINS, Martin
"Bone Blessing." [Pembroke] (21) 89, p. 129.
"Dot Painting." [Os] (29) 89, p. 2.
"Double Stars." [CapeR] (24:1) Spr 89, p. 50.
"Fishing." [Pembroke] (21) 89, p. 129.
"One Illness, Long Life: A Cancer Chronicle" (Selections: 2 poems). [StoneC] (16:3/4) Spr-Sum 89, p. 18-19.
4794. ROBBINS, Richard
"About Us." [HayF] (4) Spr 89, p. 11.
"Brief History of Going Back." [SoDakR] (27:2) Sum 89, p. 97.
"The East Shore." [ChrC] (106:33) N 8, 89, p. 1006.
"Political Poem #3." [HayF] (4) Spr 89, p. 10.
"Toward Mankato." [SoDakR] (27:2) Sum 89, p. 95-96.
"The Trapper." [SpoonRQ] (14:2) Spr 89, p. 7.
"The Whale." [HayF] (4) Spr 89, p. 9.
"Yard 1." [SoDakR] (27:2) Sum 89, p. 98.
"Yard 4." [SoDakR] (27:2) Sum 89, p. 99.
4795. ROBERSON, Ed
"Elegy for a White Cock" (after Mei Yao-ch'en, ca. 1002-1060). [Callaloo] (12:1, #38) Wint 89, p. 81-84.
4796. ROBERTS, Beth K.
"Rowing in Late September." [PassN] (10:1) Wint 89, p. 17.
4797. ROBERTS, Dorothy
"Sledding to Sunset." [AntigR] (79) Aut 89, p. 48.
4798. ROBERTS, Kim
"The Edge of the World" (for my Father). [Interim] (8:1) Spr 89, p. 28.
"The Plastic Cup." [NewL] (55:3) Spr 89, p. 22.
4799. ROBERTS, Len
"Apparition" (tr. of Sandor Csoori). [InterPR] (15:2) Fall 89, p. 23.
"Burning the City." [NewEngR] (12:2) Wint 89, p. 141-142.
"Darkly from the Darkness" (tr. of Sandor Csoori). [InterPR] (15:2) Fall 89, p. 24.
"The Day Has Passed (Elmút a nap)" (tr. of Sándor Csoóri, w. László Vertes). [IndR] (12:2) Spr 89, p. 100.
"Elegy on the Death of Gyula Juhász" (tr. of Miklós Radnóti, w. Lászlo Komlósi). [IndR] (12:2) Spr 89, p. 97.
"Esztergom Summer" (tr. of Sandor Csoori, w. Anita Senyi). [InterPR] (15:2) Fall 89, p. 26.
"Farewell to Finland" (tr. of Sandor Csoori). [InterPR] (15:2) Fall 89, p. 22.
"Fog, I Hear the Crack of Bullets" (tr. of Zsuzsa Takács, w. Mária Kurdi). [IndR] (12:2) Spr 89, p. 98-99.
"In the Night Corral." [PoetryE] (28) Fall 89, p. 71.
"Learning to Dance on Olmstead Street." [ThRiPo] (33/34) 89, p. 24.

"My Father's Forecast." [FreeL] (2) Sum 89, p. 6.
"The Naming Field." [WorldO] (22:1/2) Fall-Wint 87-88, c90, p. 21.
"November, Wassergass." [PraS] (63:3) Fall 89, p. 24-25.
"The Old Marriage." [SouthernR] (25:3) Sum 89, p. 630-631.
"On the Hill." [FreeL] (2) Sum 89, p. 5.
"Postponed Nightmare (Elmaradt lázálom)" (tr. of Sándor Csoóri, w. László Vertes).
    [IndR] (12:2) Spr 89, p. 101.
"R.R.R." [PraS] (63:3) Fall 89, p. 26.
"Removing the Mole." [WorldO] (22:1/2) Fall-Wint 87-88, c90, p. 22.
"Running the Trains at High Speed." [MichQR] (28:3) Sum 89, p. 342-343.
"Shoveling While the Snow Keeps Falling." [PraS] (63:3) Fall 89, p. 23-24.
"Ten Below." [SouthernPR] (29:1) Spr 89, p. 38.
"Winter's Voice Has Softened" (tr. of Sandor Csoori, w. Calduia Zimmermann).
    [InterPR] (15:2) Fall 89, p. 25.
"Working the Counter at the Cohoes Drive-In." [ThRiPo] (33/34) 89, p. 23.
4800. ROBERTS, Michael Symmons
    "Navigation." [Verse] (6:2) Je 89, p. 43.
4801. ROBERTS, Stephen R.
    "Brittle's Exhibitionist." [SmPd] (26:1, #75) Wint 89, p. 27.
    "Delgado's Hailstorm." [SmPd] (26:1, #75) Wint 89, p. 28.
4802. ROBERTS, Susan
    "Fuse" (Excerpt. Corrected reprint from #15). [CentralP] (16) Fall 89, p. 188.
    "Fuse" (Excerpts). [CentralP] (15) Spr 89, p. 27.
    "Under Sensation" (Excerpts). [Notus] (4:1) Spr 89, p. 49-59.
4803. ROBERTS, Teresa Noelle
    "Apotheosis of the Kitchen Goddess I." [BellArk] (5:5) S-O 89, p. 1.
    "Apotheosis of the Kitchen Goddess II." [BellArk] (5:5) S-O 89, p. 1.
    "Starting Seeds on the First Day of Spring." [BellArk] (5:5) S-O 89, p. 4.
    "Two Different Thin Men." [Kalliope] (10:1/2) 88, p. 102.
4804. ROBERTSON, David
    "Bleeding Kansas." [SewanR] (97:1) Wint 89, p. 33.
    "Carnal Knowledge." [SewanR] (97:1) Wint 89, p. 33.
4805. ROBERTSON, Harry
    "Night Rain at the Lake." [CimR] (86) Ja 89, p. 38-39.
4806. ROBERTSON, Maureen
    "Moved to Protest" (tr. of Li He). [LitR] (32:3) Spr 89, p. 394.
    "Parting on a Moonlit Night" (tr. of Li Yeh). [LitR] (32:3) Spr 89, p. 395.
    "Playing with a White Deer in the Mountains" (tr. of Shih Chien-wu). [LitR] (32:3)
        Spr 89, p. 394.
    "Thinking of Our Spring Excursions in Kouyang and and Moved by Memories of
        Times Long Past . . ." (tr. of Li Chung). [LitR] (32:3) Spr 89, p. 393.
    "Waking Up Sober" (tr. of Li Chung). [LitR] (32:3) Spr 89, p. 393.
4807. ROBERTSON, Michael J.
    "The Food Chain." [Writer] (102:6) Je 89, p. 27.
4808. ROBERTSON, Michael V.
    "Southern Sawgrass." [EmeraldCR] (1989) c1988, p. 116-117.
4809. ROBERTSON, Robin
    "The Flood." [GrandS] (9:1) Aut 89, p. 247.
    "Mandelstam." [QW] (28) Wint-Spr 89, p. 92.
    "Tokens." [GrandS] (9:1) Aut 89, p. 248.
4810. ROBERTSON, William B. (Wm. B.)
    "August's Gravity." [Dandel] (16:1) Spr-Sum 89, p. 9.
    "Buying It Back." [Quarry] (38:4) Fall 89, p. 46.
    "Cancer." [Quarry] (38:4) Fall 89, p. 47.
    "Every Father's Dream for His Daughter." [Quarry] (38:4) Fall 89, p. 48-49.
    "Mid-City Harvest." [Dandel] (16:1) Spr-Sum 89, p. 5.
    "Much to Say." [Dandel] (16:1) Spr-Sum 89, p. 7-8.
    "To a Father Who Has Lost a Young Son." [Dandel] (16:1) Spr-Sum 89, p. 6.
4811. ROBINSON, Deborah
    "After Work." [Wind] (19:64) 89, p. 25.
4812. ROBINSON, Elizabeth
    "Norte." [Caliban] (7) 89, p. 42.
    "Temple of the Mariposa." [Caliban] (7) 89, p. 41.
4813. ROBINSON, James E.
    "Post-Genesis." [KanQ] (21:3) Sum 89, p. 120-121.

4814. ROBINSON, Peter
"More About the Weather." [Pequod] (26/27) 89, p. 129.
"These Few Words." [Pequod] (26/27) 89, p. 130.
4815. ROBINSON, Roland
"The Frog Who Was King" (Aboriginal narrative of New South Wales, collected by Roland Robinson, related by Tom Whaddy, Gumbangirr Tribe). [PraS] (63:3) Fall 89, p. 77-78.
"Uncle Abraham Whose Blackfeller's Name Was Minah" (Aboriginal narrative of New South Wales, collected by Roland Robinson, related by Percy Mumbulla, Wallaga Lake). [PraS] (63:3) Fall 89, p. 78-82.
4816. ROBINSON, Sondra Till
"Largo Ma Non Troppo." [WebR] (14:1) Spr 89, p. 72-73.
4817. ROBSON, Ruthann
"The Last Decade of Patriarchy." [Kalliope] (10:1/2) 88, p. 143-147.
"She-Bear." [SingHM] (16) 89, p. 75.
"White and Black Photography" (Honorable Mention). [Nimrod] (33:1) Fall-Wint 89, p. 53-57.
4818. ROCA, Juan Manuel
"El Hechizado." [LindLM] (8:2) Ap-Je 89, p. 4.
ROCCA, Lennie della
See Della ROCCA, Lennie
4819. ROCHELLE, Belinda
"The Island of Lost Soldiers." [Obs] (3:3) Wint 88, p. 54.
"Mothers of South Africa." [Obs] (3:3) Wint 88, p. 55.
4820. RODEFER, Stephen
"April in the Free World." [Talisman] (3) Fall 89, p. 110-111.
4821. RODGERS, Don
"Mirror, Mirror." [Verse] (6:1) Mr 89, p. 17.
4822. RODITI, Edouard
"Arbitrary Fate" (tr. of Robert Desnos). [Caliban] (7) 89, p. 117.
4823. RODRIGUEZ, Claudio
"Ahí Mismo." [InterPR] (15:2) Fall 89, p. 34, 36.
"Una Aparición." [InterPR] (15:2) Fall 89, p. 30, 32.
"Elegy from Simancas" (Towards History, tr. by Louis Bourne). [InterPR] (15:2) Fall 89, p. 39-45.
"Elgia desde Simancas" (Hacia la Historia). [InterPR] (15:2) Fall 89, p. 38-44.
"Just a Smile" (tr. by Louis Bourne). [InterPR] (15:2) Fall 89, p. 33, 35.
"The Poppy's Shadow" (tr. by Louis Bourne). [InterPR] (15:2) Fall 89, p. 31.
"Right There" (tr. by Louis Bourne). [InterPR] (15:2) Fall 89, p. 35, 37.
"Sin Adios." [InterPR] (15:2) Fall 89, p. 36, 38.
"Sombra de la Amapola." [InterPR] (15:2) Fall 89, p. 30.
"A Startling Sight" (tr. by Louis Bourne). [InterPR] (15:2) Fall 89, p. 31, 33.
"Tan Sólo una Sonrisa." [InterPR] (15:2) Fall 89, p. 32, 34.
"With No Good-Bye" (tr. by Louis Bourne). [InterPR] (15:2) Fall 89, p. 37, 39.
4824. RODRIGUEZ, Florencio
"Dusty's Cantina." [Americas] (17:2) Sum 89, p. 51.
"Harvest." [Americas] (17:2) Sum 89, p. 50.
4825. RODRIGUEZ, Luis J.
"Running to America." [Americas] (17:3/4) Fall-Wint 89, p. 63-65.
"String Bean." [RiverS] (29) [89], p. 13-14.
RODRIGUEZ, Monica Amador
See AMADOR RODRIGUEZ, Monica
4826. RODRIGUEZ, Norman
"III. La Muerte." [Mairena] (11:27) 89, p. 56.
"IV. Momento en la Eternidad." [Mairena] (11:27) 89, p. 56.
"V. El Poeta." [Mairena] (11:27) 89, p. 57.
4827. RODRIGUEZ, Reina María
"Signals" (tr. by Bonnie Jefferson). [Pig] (15) 88, p. 75.
4828. RODRIGUEZ, Victorino
"Fluir Esencial." [Mairena] (11:27) 89, p. 75.
"Formula Sustancial." [Mairena] (11:27) 89, p. 75.
"Palabras de Hombre Sencillo." [Mairena] (11:27) 89, p. 75.
"Ser al Margen." [Mairena] (11:27) 89, p. 75.
4829. RODRIGUEZ-FLORIDO, Jorge J.
"Birthday Cake." [LindLM] (8:3) Jl-S 89, p. 3.

4830. RODRIGUEZ MILANÉS, Cecilia
"Gull No. I." [KeyWR] (2:1/2) Fall-Wint 89, p. 79.
4831. ROE, Margie McCreless
"Turning." [ChrC] (106:22) Jl 19-26, 89, p. 686.
4832. ROESKE, Paulette
"Daughter, Diving." [SpoonRQ] (14:3) Sum 89, p. 57.
"Duet" (2nd Prize, 3rd Annual Contest). [SoCoast] (6) Fall 88, p. 8.
"Planting." [Ascent] (14:3) 89, p. 46.
4833. ROESSLER, Marjorie Dorothy
"This Canine Wind." [Grain] (17:3) Fall 89, p. 31.
4834. ROFFMAN, Rosaly D. (Rosaly DeMaios)
"Fanatic Trying to Revive Interest in a Girl He Once Rejected." [ApalQ] (31) 89, p.
      51.
"Marie: Taking the Final." [LaurelR] (23:1) Wint 89, p. 102-103.
"On His Journey." [Wind] (19:65) 89, p. 9.
"When the Ceiling Falls." [Wind] (19:65) 89, p. 8.
4835. ROGAL, Stan
"Bearded Eros" (for Louis Zukofsky). [Rampike] (6:3) 88, p. 46-47.
4836. ROGERS, Bertha
"Gauguin's 'Why Are You Angry?'" [BlueBldgs] (11) 89, p. 18-19.
"Your Smile." [Plain] (9:2) Wint 89, p. 13.
4837. ROGERS, Bobby Caudle
"Burning the Walls." [GeoR] (43:1) Spr 89, p. 133-134.
"Peony." [Shen] (39:1) Spr 89, p. 87.
4838. ROGERS, Daryl
"Greyhound." [SlipS] (9) 89, p. 13-14.
"Meeting at the Reststop." [Wind] (19:64) 89, p. 26.
4839. ROGERS, David
"At Madison Wilbur's Grave." [SewanR] (97:4) Fall 89, p. 511.
"Words on a Winter Night." [SewanR] (97:4) Fall 89, p. 510-511.
4840. ROGERS, Jean
"Dreaming of Castlerigg Circle." [SpiritSH] (55) Fall-Wint 89 [90 on cover], p. 16.
4841. ROGERS, Linda
"Woman at Mile Zero" (Selections: 3 poems). [MalR] (86) Spr 89, p. 52-54.
4842. ROGERS, Pattiann
"Earth-Night Errors." [PoetryNW] (30:2) Sum 89, p. 5-6.
"Elinor Frost's Marble-topped Kneading Table." [NewEngR] (11:4) Sum 89, p.
      436-437.
"The Fear of Non-being." [LaurelR] (23:2) Sum 89, p. 46-47.
"The God of Sunday Evening, June 7, 1987." [PoetryNW] (30:2) Sum 89, p. 6-7.
"Grandmother's Sister" (for Emma and Edna). [RiverC] (10:1) Fall 89, p. 2-3.
"The Greatest Grandeur." [PoetryNW] (30:2) Sum 89, p. 3-4.
"In an Open Field on a Clear Night." [PoetryNW] (30:2) Sum 89, p. 4-5.
"Next to Sleep." [RiverC] (10:1) Fall 89, p. 1.
"Repeat and Repeat." [LaurelR] (23:2) Sum 89, p. 45-46.
"That's Why." [GettyR] (2:1) Wint 89, p. 142-142.
"Under the Big Top." [GettyR] (2:1) Wint 89, p. 144-145.
"When at Night." [NewEngR] (11:4) Sum 89, p. 435-436.
4843. ROGERS, Peter A.
"2AM." [SpiritSH] (55) Fall-Wint 89 [90 on cover], p. 19.
4844. ROGERS, Robert C.
"Cupid Shot." [Writer] (102:3) Mr 89, p. 25.
4845. ROGERS, Thorold
"In the Long Run." [Stand] (30:4) Aut 89, p. 49.
4846. ROGOFF, Jay
"Documentary." [PoetryNW] (30:4) Wint 89-90, p. 8-10.
"Strown Bliss, Scattering Bright." [NewRep] (200:16) 17 Ap 89, p. 34.
4847. ROJAS, Gonzalo
"Alcohol and Syllables" (tr. by Ben Belitt). [Salm] (82/83) Spr-Sum 89, p. 300.
"Bed with Mirrors" (tr. by Ben Belitt). [Salm] (82/83) Spr-Sum 89, p. 299-300.
"Burial Papyrus" (tr. by Johnny Payne). [SenR] (19:1) 89, p. 46-47.
"Don't Copy Pound" (tr. by Ben Belitt). [Salm] (82/83) Spr-Sum 89, p. 297-298.
"Don't You Copy Pound" (tr. by Johnny Payne). [SenR] (19:1) 89, p. 43-44.
"For Vallejo" (tr. by Johnny Payne). [SenR] (19:1) 89, p. 45.
"Goodbye to Hölderlin" (tr. by Johnny Payne). [SenR] (19:1) 89, p. 48-49.
"Latin and Jazz" (tr. by Ben Belitt). [Salm] (82/83) Spr-Sum 89, p. 298-299.

"Rimbaud" (tr. by Johnny Payne). [SenR] (19:1) 89, p. 50.
4848. ROKUNYO
"Spotting Plum Blossoms by the Road" (tr. by Burton Watson). [LitR] (32:3) Spr 89, p. 439.
"When My Beloved Japanese Spaniel Died" (tr. by Burton Watson). [LitR] (32:3) Spr 89, p. 438.
"Winter Day: Scene on the Road to Otsu" (tr. by Burton Watson). [LitR] (32:3) Spr 89, p. 439.
4849. ROLLINS, Cal E.
"Basilica de Guadalupe / Mexico City." [WorldO] (22:1/2) Fall-Wint 87-88, c90, p. 36.
"Musing about My Rights" (for Vanessa and Birgit). [WorldO] (22:1/2) Fall-Wint 87-88, c90, p. 30.
4850. ROMA-DEELEY, Lois
"Truth" (Ursa Minor). [OxfordM] (5:1) Spr-Sum 89, p. 51.
4851. ROMANO, Edward
"Concerto for the 20th Century." [JINJPo] [11] 89, p. 29.
"When I Think That This Banana." [JINJPo] [11] 89, p. 28.
4852. ROMANO, Rose
"Chinatown Morning." [Footwork] 89, p. 68.
"Out of Context." [Footwork] 89, p. 68.
4853. ROMELL, Karen
"Blackberries." [AntigR] (77/78) Spr-Sum 89, p. 54-55.
"The Fat Woman Next Door." [AntigR] (77/78) Spr-Sum 89, p. 52-53.
4854. ROMERO, Armando
"De los Asesinos." [LindLM] (8:2) Ap-Je 89, p. 4.
"The Militiaman Speaks" (tr. of Manuel Díaz-Martínez, w. Pat Carrothers). [Pig] (15) 88, p. 69.
"Parabola" (tr. of Pablo Armando Fernández, w. Pat Carrothers). [Pig] (15) 88, p. 75.
4855. ROMERO, Kelly
"A Wednesday Night in 1969." [Hawai'iR] (13:1, #25) Spr 89, p. 109-111.
4856. ROMERO, Leo
"Marilyn Monroe Indian." [SoDakR] (27:4) Wint 89, p. 5-11.
4857. ROMINE-POWELL, Dannye
"The Absence of Bounty." [GettyR] (2:4) Aut 89, p. 703.
"Hope, Dead But Well Preserved, Now Crumbles." [GettyR] (2:4) Aut 89, p. 704.
"Mothers, Attend the Women Your Sons Marry." [Shen] (39:3) Fall 89, p. 85-86.
4858. RONKOWITZ, Ken
"The Hole." [EngJ] (78:4) Ap 89, p. 100.
4859. ROONEY, Olive
"Selling Buttons." [Vis] (29) 89, p. 24.
4860. ROOT, Judith
"Architecture of a Cold August." [WilliamMR] (27) 89, p. 21.
"Good Friday" (Barranca del Cobre). [Comm] (116:11) Je 2, 89, p. 348.
"Running the Irrigation Ditch." [WilliamMR] (27) 89, p. 53.
"Two Couples on a Quilt in Indian Summer." [GreensboroR] (46) Sum 89, p. 134.
4861. ROOT, William Pitt
"With No Other Witnesses" (for Yannis Ritsos). [Comm] (116:1) Ja 13, 89, p. 15.
ROSA, Alexis Gomez
See GOMEZ ROSA, Alexis
ROSA, Pablo La
See La ROSA, Pablo
4862. ROSAS, Yolanda
"Hay Días." [Americas] (17:1) Spr 89, p. 65-66.
"Ruta Espiral." [Americas] (17:1) Spr 89, p. 67.
4863. ROSBERG, Rose
"Joseph Campbell on TV in Miami." [Kalliope] (11:3) 89, p. 35.
"Night Rock and Roll." [Wind] (19:65) 89, p. 42.
4864. ROSCHER, Marina
"Damnation" (tr. of Sarah Kirsch, w. Charles Fishman). [WebR] (14:1) Spr 89, p. 12.
"Gentle Hunt" (tr. of Sarah Kirsch, w. Charles Fishman). [WebR] (14:1) Spr 89, p. 15.
"Heartstone" (tr. of Sarah Kirsch, w. Charles Fishman). [WebR] (14:1) Spr 89, p. 14.

"Ravens" (tr. of Sarah Kirsch, w. Charles Fishman). [WebR] (14:1) Spr 89, p. 14.
"The Sleeper" (tr. of Sarah Kirsch, w. Charles Fishman). [WebR] (14:1) Spr 89, p. 13.
"The Trochel" (tr. of Sarah Kirsch, w. Charles Fishman). [WebR] (14:1) Spr 89, p. 15.
4865. ROSE, Jennifer
"Harvard Square Postcard" (to Michael Sagalyn). [Agni] (28) 89, p. 286-287.
4866. ROSE, Midred A.
"There Must Be Reasons." [Grain] (17:4) Wint 89, inside front cover.
4867. ROSE, Wilga
"Botticelli Rising." [Bogg] (61) 89, p. 14.
4868. ROSEDAUGHTER, Stefanie Prather
"Catwise." [BellArk] (5:1) Ja-F 89, p. 3.
4869. ROSEN, Kenneth
"Gulf." [Ploughs] (15:1) 89, p. 92-93.
"Lies." [Agni] (28) 89, p. 276-277.
4870. ROSEN, Michael J.
"Groundwork, a New House." [KenR] (NS 11:1) Wint 89, p. 60-62.
"Palpable and Mute." [Journal] (13:1) Spr-Sum 89, p. 30-31.
"Penn's Would-Be 35th Anniversary." [PraS] (63:2) Sum 89, p. 90-91.
"A Story of Gordon and Sylvie, with Accompaniments." [WestHR] (43:2) Sum 89, p. 134-141.
4871. ROSENBERG, Liz
"Pittsburgh." [SouthernHR] (23:1) Wint 89, p. 35.
"The Poem of My Heart." [AmerPoR] (18:5) S-O 89, p. 13.
"A Vanished World" (Selections: 6, 15-16, 21, 42, 46, 49, based on the book by Roman Vishniac). [SouthernHR] (23:4) Fall 89, p. 356-357.
4872. ROSENBLATT, Sarah
"Yoyo." [PoetryE] (28) Fall 89, p. 157.
4873. ROSENFELD, Natania
"Flight" (for my Lithuanian mother). [LaurelR] (23:1) Wint 89, p. 95-97.
4874. ROSENQUIST, Karl
"Family." [Ploughs] (15:4) Wint 89-90, p. 183-184.
4875. ROSENSTOCK, Gabriel
"Rust and Rampart of Rushes" (for Máire, tr. of Michael Davitt, w. Michael Hartnett). [Trans] (22) Fall 89, p. 126-127.
4876. ROSENWASSER, Rena
"Basium." [FreeL] (3) Aut 89, p. 11.
4877. ROSENZWEIG, Geri
"From Dublin to the Midlands." [Vis] (29) 89, p. 19.
"Military Cemetery: Jerusalem" (for a young widow). [Verse] (6:1) Mr 89, p. 58.
4878. ROSKOLENKO, Harry
"Classical Journey -- 1956-1957." [SoDakR] (27:4) Wint 89, p. 89-116.
4879. ROSS, Joe
"Up the Alps." [NewAW] (5) Fall 89, p. 119.
4880. ROSS, Stuart N.
"After a Passover Seder." [Footwork] 89, p. 67.
"The Couple Upstairs." [US1] (22/23) Spr 89, p. 17.
4881. ROSSELLI, Amelia
"I Fiori Vengono in Dono e Poi Si Dilatano." [Poetry] (155:1/2) O-N 89, p. 84.
"The Flowers Come As Gifts" (tr. by Beverly Allen). [Poetry] (155:1/2) O-N 89, p. 85.
"In Ancient China" (tr. by Beverly Allen). [Poetry] (155:1/2) O-N 89, p. 87.
"There's Something Like Pain in the Room" (tr. by Beverly Allen). [Poetry] (155:1/2) O-N 89, p. 86.
4882. ROSSER, J. Allyn
"Advice for the Unadvisable." [Poetry] (153:5) F 89, p. 282.
"Clippings." [Poetry] (153:4) Ja 89, p. 222-223.
"Disbelief." [Crazy] (36) Spr 89, p. 32-33.
"An Open Fire." [Hudson] (42:3) Aut 89, p. 450.
"Remains." [Poetry] (153:4) Ja 89, p. 224-225.
"Timeline." [Poetry] (153:5) F 89, p. 283-284.
"What Was Clear." [Hudson] (42:3) Aut 89, p. 451.
4883. ROSSI, Lee
"Personals" (Selections: I, III). [Jacaranda] (4:1) Spr-Sum 89, p. 20-21.

4884. ROSSI, Tiziano
"Giovani." [Poetry] (155:1/2) O-N 89, p. 92.
"Inviolate" (tr. by Michael Palma). [Poetry] (155:1/2) O-N 89, p. 93.
"Youth" (tr. by Michael Palma). [Poetry] (155:1/2) O-N 89, p. 92.
4885. ROSSI, Vinio
"Chair" (tr. of Giovanni Raboni, w. Stuart Friebert). [NewL] (55:3) Spr 89, p. 21.
"Codicils" (tr. of Giovanni Raboni, w. Stuart Friebert). [NewL] (55:3) Spr 89, p. 20-21.
"Untitled: I have my father's years, I have his hands" (tr. of Giovanni Raboni, w. Stuart Friebert). [CentR] (33:1) Wint 89, p. 58-59.
4886. ROSSI-SNOOK, Elena
"As I walk across the dance floor." [Mildred] (3:1) Spr-Sum 89, p. 34.
4887. ROSSINI, Clare
"Ideology." [Poetry] (155:3) D 89, p. 211.
4888. ROSSINI, Frank
"Charles on Wheels." [SilverFR] (16) Spr 89, p. 15.
4889. ROSU, Dona
"Din Noaptea" (tr. of Mihai Eminescu, w. W. D. Snodgrass and Radu Lupan). [AmerPoR] (18:6) N-D 89, p. 32.
"Sonnets" (I, II, III, tr. of Mihai Eminescu, w. W. D. Snodgrass and Radu Lupan). [AmerPoR] (18:6) N-D 89, p. 32.
4890. ROTAR, Braco
"Hunger II" (tr. by Michael Biggins). [NewEngR] (11:3) Spr 89, p. 245.
4891. ROTELLA, Alexis
"After School." [Footwork] 89, p. 15.
"Black Cow." [Footwork] 89, p. 15.
"My Mother's Vanity." [Footwork] 89, p. 15.
4892. ROTELLA, Guy
"Florida: Still Life." [DenQ] (24:2) Fall 89, p. 87.
4893. ROTENBERG, Bettina
"Worst Asylum." [Screens] (1) 89, p. 180.
4894. ROTH, Susan H. (Susan Harned)
"Minding the Store." [PoetL] (84:1) Spr 89, p. 39.
"Natural History." [PoetL] (84:1) Spr 89, p. 37-38.
"Wife Admires Husband's Insomnia." [Footwork] 89, p. 41.
4895. ROTH-NATALE, Nanci
"I Heard the Geese Fly Home Today." [BellArk] (5:5) S-O 89, p. 4.
"Sunday Morning Rituals." [BellArk] (5:4) Jl-Ag 89, p. 10.
4896. ROTHENBERG, Jerome
"The Dispersal." [Sulfur] (9:2, #25) Fall 89, p. 99-102.
"Eleventh Gematria." [Screens] (1) 89, p. 171-174.
"Gematria Five." [PaperAir] (4:2) 89, p. 11.
"Gematria Four." [PaperAir] (4:2) 89, p. 10.
"Gematria One." [PaperAir] (4:2) 89, p. 8.
"Gematria Six." [PaperAir] (4:2) 89, p. 11.
"Gematria Three." [PaperAir] (4:2) 89, p. 9.
"Gematria Two." [PaperAir] (4:2) 89, p. 8-9.
"Night: Suite for Piano & Poet's Voice" (tr. of Federico Garcia Lorca). [ParisR] (31:110) Spr 89, p. 20-24.
4897. ROTHMAN, David J.
"Four Ponies." [TarRP] (28:2) Spr 89, p. 5.
4898. ROTHSCHILD, Douglas
"2nd Person." [Rampike] (6:2) 88, p. 59.
4899. ROUBAUD, Jacques
"Some Thing Black" (Selections: 9 poems, tr. by Rosmarie Waldrop). [Conjunc] (14) 89, p. 54-60.
"Some Thing Dark" (Selections, tr. by Rosmarie Waldrop). [Verse] (6:2) Je 89, p. 9-13.
4900. ROUSE, Ann
"Big." [Verse] (6:3) Wint 89, p. 80.
4901. ROUSE, Nancy Frost
"Mother, in the Kitchen." [ChatR] (9:4) Sum 89, p. 68.
4902. ROUX, Saint Pol
"The Aviary" (tr. by Robin Magowan). [Margin] (8) 89, p. 93.
"Birds" (tr. by Robin Magowan). [Margin] (8) 89, p. 94.

4903. ROWE, Vivienne
"View from a Window in Derbyshire." [Thrpny] (36) Wint 89, p. 16.
4904. ROY, Lucinda
"Needlework" (The Baxter Hathaway Prize in Poetry). [Epoch] (38:2) 89, p. 79-89.
4905. ROZEWICZ, Tadeusz
"The Poet Grows Weaker" (tr. by Stanislaw Baranczak and Clare Cavanah). [Trans]
(21) Spr 89, p. 36-37.
4906. RUBIN, Anele
"October" (for Joan). [Footwork] 89, p. 11.
4907. RUBIN, Larry
"The 366th Day." [Poem] (62) N 89, p. 32.
"The Puritan, Returning" (Aboard the Liner). [Poem] (62) N 89, p. 33.
"Reconciliation." [Poem] (62) N 89, p. 31.
"Unheated Miami Schools, Circa 1940." [TexasR] (10:1/2) Spr-Sum 89, p. 53.
4908. RUBIN, Mark
"De Soto." [LaurelR] (23:1) Wint 89, p. 18-22.
"Genesis." [AmerV] (15) Sum 89, p. 39-44.
"Lepidoptera." [CinPR] (20) Fall 89, p. 57.
"New York, New York." [Nimrod] (33:1) Fall-Wint 89, p. 70-71.
"Soul Train." [BlackWR] (16:1) Fall-Wint 89, p. 36.
"The Way They Want." [BlackWR] (16:1) Fall-Wint 89, p. 37.
4909. RUBINSHTEIN, Lev
"From Thursday to Friday" (Excerpt, tr. by Gerald Janecek). [MichQR] (28:4) Fall
89, p. 741-742.
"Momma Washed the Floor" (Excerpt, tr. by Michael Molnar). [MichQR] (28:4) Fall
89, p. 739-740.
4910. RUCKER, Trish
"Impressionists in Hurt Park." [ThRiPo] (33/34) 89, p. 25.
"Sea Creature." [CentR] (33:3) Sum 89, p. 249.
4911. RUDDER, Sonja M.
"City Block Summer." [BlackALF] (23:3) Fall 89, p. 490-491.
4912. RUDMAN, Mark
"Changes in the Atmosphere." [Ploughs] (15:4) Wint 89-90, p. 187-188.
"Courbet." [Pequod] (28/29/30) 89, p. 68-74.
"Facts of Life" (4 selections). [Agni] (28) 89, p. 197-204.
"The Image" (tr. of Boris Pasternak, w. Bohdan Boychuk). [Pequod] (28/29/30) 89,
p. 273-274.
"Material." [Ploughs] (15:4) Wint 89-90, p. 185-186.
"On Location." [DenQ] (23:3/4) Wint-Spr 89, p. 42-44.
"The Retreat." [DenQ] (23:3/4) Wint-Spr 89, p. 40-41.
"The Second Quarter." [Thrpny] (37) Spr 89, p. 14.
"The Unveiling." [Boulevard] (4:2, #11) Fall 89, p. 81-88.
4913. RUEFLE, Mary
"Arturo's Song." [SouthernHR] (23:4) Fall 89, p. 340.
"Ecce Homo." [ColEng] (51:7) N 89, p. 702.
"A Few Words to Let in Doubt." [ColEng] (51:7) N 89, p. 703.
"Lilies of the Nile" (for Kate Cleaver). [SouthernHR] (23:4) Fall 89, p. 341.
"The Pedant's Discourse." [ColEng] (51:7) N 89, p. 701.
"White Tulips." [ColEng] (51:7) N 89, p. 703.
4914. RUFFILLI, Paolo
"Malaria" (in Italian & English, tr. by Felix Stefanile). [Poetry] (155:1/2) O-N 89, p.
138-147.
4915. RUFFIN, Paul
"Fever." [SouthernR] (25:3) Sum 89, p. 608.
"Floundering." [MidAR] (9:2) 89, p. 134-135.
"How a Poem Begins" (For Genevieve). [SouthernR] (25:3) Sum 89, p. 609-610.
"My Daughter Gathers Shells." [MidwQ] (31:1) Aut 89, p. 60.
"Petrified Log." [SouthernR] (25:3) Sum 89, p. 609.
4916. RUFINUS
"Armed against Love, reason my shield" (tr. by James Michie). [GrandS] (8:4) Sum
89, p. 84.
RUGERIS, C. K. de
See De RUGERIS, C. K.
4917. RUGGIERO, Greg
"The Dinner Guest." [Lactuca] (13) N 89, p. 29.

RUIZ, José O. Colón
    See COLON RUIZ, José O.
4918. RUKEYSER, Muriel
    "In Our Time" (Original draft). [PoetryE] (27) Spr 89, p. 66.
    "We pride ourselves as a nation on dealing with facts" (journal entry). [PoetryE] (27)
        Spr 89, p. 64-65.
4919. RUMENS, Carol
    "A Meeting of Innocents: A Birthday Sequence" (For my daughters). [GrahamHR]
        (12) Spr 89, p. 61-67.
4920. RUNGREN, Lawrence
    "Pentecost." [MidwQ] (31:1) Aut 89, p. 61.
4921. RUNNING, Thorpe
    "Asking Oneself, Every Once in a While" (tr. of Alberto Girri). [LitR] (32:4) Sum
        89, p. 493-494.
    "On Opening Your Eyes and Not Hearing" (tr. of Alberto Girri). [LitR] (32:4) Sum
        89, p. 492-493.
    "The Poem as Unstable" (tr. of Alberto Girri). [LitR] (32:4) Sum 89, p. 494-495.
    "Simplistic, Convincing Version" (tr. of Alberto Girri). [LitR] (32:4) Sum 89, p.
        491-492.
4922. RUSH, Jerry
    "Diary of A Brief Friendship." [Grain] (17:1) Spr 89, p. 39.
    "An Early Morning Dream of Late Evening." [Grain] (17:1) Spr 89, p. 38.
    "For Jim Stafford." [Grain] (17:1) Spr 89, p. 40.
    "Greeting the Family." [Grain] (17:1) Spr 89, p. 37.
    "Hear the Sea Roll In." [Grain] (17:1) Spr 89, p. 38.
    "Shadows." [Grain] (17:1) Spr 89, p. 36.
    "Untitled Fragment: Down in the valley, silence swallows us whole." [Grain] (17:1)
        Spr 89, p. 36.
4923. RUSHIN, Kate
    "Comparative History: Our Stories." [Callaloo] (12:2, #39) Spr 89, p. 290-291.
    "The Tired Poem" (Last Letter from a Typical Unemployed Black Professional
        Woman). [Cond] (16) 89, p. 57-60.
4924. RUSHMER, David
    "The Book" (for Edmond Jabes). [SpiritSH] (55) Fall-Wint 89 [90 on cover], p. 46.
4925. RUSS, Biff
    "Fossils." [MidwQ] (31:1) Aut 89, p. 62.
    "Heirloom" (in memory of my grandfather). [StoneC] (16:3/4) Spr-Sum 89, p. 52.
    "To a Small Silver Christ on an Argentinian Crucifix during the Days of the
        Disappeared." [StoneC] (16:3/4) Spr-Sum 89, p. 54.
    "Uragami Tenshudo Church, Nagasaki" (didicated to my niece). [StoneC] (16:3/4)
        Spr-Sum 89, p. 53.
4926. RUSS, Don
    "Men." [PoetL] (84:4) Wint 89-90, p. 39-40.
4927. RUSSELL, CarolAnn
    "Breasts." [PoetryNW] (30:3) Aut 89, p. 37-38.
    "Carnival." [PoetryNW] (30:3) Aut 89, p. 36-37.
    "Reading Hugo's Gravestone." [CharR] (15:2) Fall 89, p. 92.
    "Skin." [PoetryNW] (30:3) Aut 89, p. 35-36.
RUSSELL, Gillian Harding
    See HARDING-RUSSELL, Gillian
4928. RUSSELL, Henry W.
    "T. E. Lawrence: Two Poems." [SouthernR] (25:1) Wint 89, p. 179-180.
    "Traveling Companions." [SouthernR] (25:1) Wint 89, p. 178-179.
4929. RUSSELL, Jonathan
    "Artemis in Acapulco." [Poem] (61) My 89, p. 59.
    "November 11th in Europe." [Plain] (10:1) 89, p. 34.
    "The Tally Man." [Poem] (61) My 89, p. 58.
4930. RUSSELL, Norman
    "And I Have Looked Out Windows." [Nimrod] (32:2) Spr-Sum 89, p. 29.
    "I Am Beautiful." [Nimrod] (32:2) Spr-Sum 89, p. 26.
    "Life Songs." [Nimrod] (32:2) Spr-Sum 89, p. 28.
    "The Martian Painting." [Caliban] (6) 89, p. 187.
    "The Martian Times." [Caliban] (6) 89, p. 187.
    "A Story About an Ugly Man." [Nimrod] (32:2) Spr-Sum 89, p. 27.
    "Such a Pig Is the Earth!" [Nimrod] (32:2) Spr-Sum 89, p. 27.

361

4931. RUSSELL, Paul
   "Rain in Germany." [WilliamMR] (27) 89, p. 23.
4932. RUSSELL, Sandra
   "New Orleans." [Amelia] (5:3, #14) 89, p. 100.
   "Unravelling Riddles in the Eternal City." [Amelia] (5:3, #14) 89, p. 98-99.
   "The Women." [Amelia] (5:3, #14) 89, p. 99.
4933. RUSSELL, Thomas (Tom)
   "Cow People." [DenQ] (24:2) Fall 89, p. 88-89.
   "Mother's Visit." [NowestR] (27:2) 89, p. 58-59.
   "A Rosy Man." [AmerPoR] (18:6) N-D 89, p. 42.
   "The Yoke Woman at the Mall." [AmerPoR] (18:6) N-D 89, p. 42.
4934. RUSSELL, Timothy
   "In Deceptio Visus." [WestB] (23) 89, p. 62-63.
4935. RUSSELL, Valerie (Valerie J.)
   "The Fire Tower." [CreamCR] (13:2) Fall 89, p. 114-115.
   "Successions." [MissouriR] (12:2) 89, p. 138-139.
4936. RUTH, Barbara
   "Breakup." [SinW] (39) Wint 89-90, p. 118.
   "Pelvic Mass Etiology" (for all the people who say or think, "Barbara, why are you
      doing this? Again?"). [SinW] (39) Wint 89-90, p. 11-13.
4937. RUTSALA, Vern
   "Empty Rooms." [AmerPoR] (18:5) S-O 89, p. 27.
   "Finns Have Long Memories" (-- L. Reino Inala). [Zyzzyva] (5:2, #18) Sum 89, p.
      132-134.
   "The Hard Market." [KanQ] (21:3) Sum 89, p. 205.
   "Killing Flies in Georgia." [Ploughs] (15:1) 89, p. 94-99.
   "Letting Things Slide." [SenR] (19:2) Fall 89, p. 84-85.
   "The Lost Barn." [Stand] (30:1) Wint 88-89, p. 64-65.
   "Making Lists." [AmerPoR] (18:5) S-O 89, p. 27.
   "The Rest of Your Life." [SouthwR] (74:1) Wint 89, p. 78-79.
   "Specter." [GeoR] (43:3) Fall 89, p. 458-459.
4938. RUTTER, Mark Francis
   "Moss." [Stand] (30:1) Wint 88-89, p. 60.
4939. RUVINSKY, Joan
   "Andean Holiday." [AntigR] (79) Aut 89, p. 60-62.
4940. RUZESKY, Jay
   "Young at Art." [Event] (18:2) Sum 89, p. 76.
4941. RYAN, Dan
   "The Man Who Drank Everything." [PoetL] (84:1) Spr 89, p. 26.
4942. RYAN, Gregory A.
   "The Fall of Numbers." [SenR] (19:1) 89, p. 66.
4943. RYAN, Kay
   "Flamingo Watching." [AntR] (47:4) Fall 89, p. 466.
   "Poetry Is a Kind of Money." [Epoch] (38:2) 89, p. 165.
   "Reach and Grasp." [SoCoast] (5) Spr 88, p. 36.
4944. RYAN, Michael
   "A Burglary." [Ploughs] (15:1) 89, p. 114-121.
   "County Fair." [Poetry] (154:4) Jl 89, p. 205-206.
   "The Crown of Frogs." [AmerPoR] (18:4) Jl-Ag 89, p. 16.
   "The Ditch." [Thrpny] (36) Wint 89, p. 7.
   "Her Report." [AmerPoR] (18:4) Jl-Ag 89, p. 17.
   "Houseflies." [VirQR] (65:3) Sum 89, p. 442.
   "Meeting Cheever" (Iowa City, 1973). [VirQR] (65:3) Sum 89, p. 440-441.
   "Milk the Mouse." [Nat] (249:3) 17 Jl 89, p. 99.
   "Smoke." [Thrpny] (37) Spr 89, p. 11.
   "Stone Paperweight." [TriQ] (75) Spr-Sum 89, p. 10.
   "TV Room at the Children's Hospice." [AmerPoR] (18:4) Jl-Ag 89, p. 17.
   "Two Rides on a Bike." [AmerPoR] (18:4) Jl-Ag 89, p. 15.
4945. RYAN, Richard
   "Fever" (tr. of Seán O Ríordáin). [Trans] (22) Fall 89, p. 46.
   "Wulf and Eadwacer" (from the Exeter Book, tr. of anonymous Old English poem).
      [Trans] (22) Fall 89, p. 235-236.
4946. RYDER, Salmon
   "The Vietnam Veterans Memorial." [US1] (22/23) Spr 89, p. 46.
4947. RYMKIEWICZ, Jaroslaw Marek
   "Mandelstam Street" (tr. by Stanislaw Baranczak and Clare Cavanagh). [SenR]

(19:2) Fall 89, p. 28.
"When I Woke Up" (tr. by Stanislaw Baranczak and Clare Cavanah). [Trans] (21)
    Spr 89, p. 64-65.
4948. SAARIKOSKI, Pentti
"The conditions for life to begin" (tr. by Anselm Hollo). [PoetryE] (27) Spr 89, p.
    156.
"A free enterprise economy and the right to say" (tr. by Anselm Hollo). [PoetryE]
    (27) Spr 89, p. 159.
"Had my last cup of tea" (tr. by Anselm Hollo). [PoetryE] (27) Spr 89, p. 154.
"High poetry, the sun sets, the sun rises" (tr. by Anselm Hollo). [PoetryE] (27) Spr
    89, p. 148.
"I live in Helsinki" (tr. by Anselm Hollo). [PoetryE] (27) Spr 89, p. 146.
"The new suburbs surrounded by woods" (tr. by Anselm Hollo). [PoetryE] (27) Spr
    89, p. 158.
"No need to decide" (tr. by Anselm Hollo). [PoetryE] (27) Spr 89, p. 152-153.
"Not sure" (tr. by Anselm Hollo). [PoetryE] (27) Spr 89, p. 160.
"Out Loud" (tr. by Anselm Hollo). [PoetryE] (27) Spr 89, p. 144-145.
"Parliament has been dissolved" (tr. by Anselm Hollo). [PoetryE] (27) Spr 89, p.
    155.
"Sun, hot through the window" (tr. by Anselm Hollo). [PoetryE] (27) Spr 89, p.
    149-151.
"This started two years before the wars" (tr. by Anselm Hollo). [PoetryE] (27) Spr
    89, p. 147.
"The Tiarnia Trilogy" (Selections: XLIII, XVIV, XLVIII, LII, tr. by Anselm Hollo).
    [PoetryE] (27) Spr 89, p. 161-166.
"What are they talking about" (tr. by Anselm Hollo). [PoetryE] (27) Spr 89, p. 157.
4949. SABA, Umberto
"Insomnia on a Summer Night" (tr. by Christopher Millis). [MissouriR] (12:1) 89,
    p. 53.
"Sapling" (tr. by Christopher Millis). [MissouriR] (12:1) 89, p. 54.
"Trieste" (tr. by Christopher Millis). [MissouriR] (12:1) 89, p. 55.
4950. SABETAY-WILCOX, Edie
"Condena." [Mester] (18:1) Spr 89, p. 56.
4951. SACKHEIM, Eric
"Frontier Song" (tr. of Hsiang Yü). [LitR] (32:3) Spr 89, p. 420.
"Grief Song" (tr. of Princess Wu-sun). [LitR] (32:3) Spr 89, p. 420.
4952. SACKS, Peter
"Above Maser." [AmerPoR] (18:4) Jl-Ag 89, p. 35.
"April." [Boulevard] (4:1, #10) Spr 89, p. 178.
"Hymn for the New Year." [PartR] (56:3) Sum 89, p. 448.
4953. SACUTA, Norm
"The Job Inteview." [Grain] (17:1) Spr 89, p. 64.
"Missing Voice." [Grain] (17:1) Spr 89, p. 63.
4954. SADLER, Janet
"The Wind Has Been Up to Something." [MidwQ] (31:1) Aut 89, p. 63.
4955. SADOFF, Ira
"August." [ThRiPo] (31/32) 88, p. 42.
"The Bath." [AmerPoR] (18:4) Jl-Ag 89, p. 6.
"Incest." [Antaeus] (62) Spr 89, p. 191.
"My Sister's Room." [ThRiPo] (31/32) 88, p. 41.
"Ode to Experience." [ThRiPo] (31/32) 88, p. 43.
"When You Asked Me, 'Were You a Needy Child?'" [PoetryNW] (30:3) Aut 89, p.
    23.
4956. SADOW, Stephen A.
"We, the Generation in the Wilderness" (Selections: 1, 7-11, 14, tr. of Ricardo
    Feierstein, w. J. Kates). [Pig] (15) 88, p. 96.
4957. SAGAN, Miriam
"52 Dharmas per Second." [LitR] (32:2) Wint 89, p. 231.
"Among Friends." [Agni] (28) 89, p. 285.
"Basic English." [Bogg] (61) 89, p. 34.
"Las Cruces: The Stone Woman." [Bogg] (61) 89, p. 32-33.
"The Geology of Mercury." [Bogg] (61) 89, p. 32.
"Santa Fe, New Mexico" (January-December). [BallSUF] (30:4) Aut 89, p. 21-22.
4958. SAGARIS, Lake
"At Half Mast / A Media Asta" (tr. of Carmen Berenguer). [Rampike] (6:1) 87, p.
    64.

"Fragrance." [Grain] (17:4) Wint 89, p. 35.
"The Great Speech (MM)" (Selection: "The Crazy Woman from the Alley / La Loca
del Pasaje," tr. of Carmen Berenguer). [Rampike] (6:1) 87, p. 64-65.
"Modern Muses." [Grain] (17:4) Wint 89, p. 34.
4959. SAHAY, Raghuvir
"Our Hindi" (tr. by Vinay Dharwadker). [TriQ] (77) Wint 89-90, p. 135-136.
"Sanskrit" (tr. by Vinay Dharwadker). [TriQ] (77) Wint 89-90, p. 138.
4960. SAIL, Lawrence
"Perspective." [Stand] (30:2) Spr 89, p. 42.
SAINT ...
    See also ST. ... (filed as spelled)
4961. SAINT, Assotto
"De Profundis" (for eleven gay men in my building." [JamesWR] (5:2 [i.e. 6:2])
Wint 89, p. 1.
"The Memory of Suffering." [JamesWR] (5:2 [i.e. 6:2]) Wint 89, p. 1.
"The Quilt." [JamesWR] (5:2 [i.e. 6:2]) Wint 89, p. 1.
SAISEI, Muro
    See MURO, Saisei
4962. SAJE, Natasha
"In My Father's Garden." [PoetL] (84:2) Sum 89, p. 42.
"To the Mother Tongue." [PoetL] (84:2) Sum 89, p. 43-44.
4963. SAKNUSSEMM, Kristopher
"Destiny." [TarRP] (28:2) Spr 89, p. 34-35.
"Heat Lightning." [Nimrod] (33:1) Fall-Wint 89, p. 109.
"Joplin, MO." [CharR] (15:2) Fall 89, p. 81.
"Second Honeymoon." [Caliban] (6) 89, p. 203.
4964. SAKUTARO, Hiagiwara
"Homecoming" (tr. by Graeme Wilson). [Jacaranda] (4:1) Spr-Sum 89, p. 73-75.
"Red Light District" (tr. by Graeme Wilson). [Jacaranda] (4:1) Spr-Sum 89, p. 76.
4965. SALA, Jerome
"Ding Dong the Witch Is Dead." [AnotherCM] (19) 89, p. 186.
"For Art Blakey." [AnotherCM] (19) 89, p. 187-188.
"A Pleasant Life in the Carpathian Mountains." [BrooklynR] (6) 89, p. 52.
"Where the Movement Began." [AnotherCM] (19) 89, p. 189-190.
4966. SALADO, Minera
"Reportage from Viet Nam, Especially for International Woman's Day" (tr. by
Daniela Gioseffi, w. Enildo Garcia). [Contact] (9:50/51/52) Fall-Wint 88-Spr
89, p. 46.
"Today's Interview" (tr. by Daniela Gioseffi, w. Enildo Garcia). [Contact]
(9:50/51/52) Fall-Wint 88-Spr 89, p. 47.
4967. SALAMONE, Karen
"Alone in a Room Looking Through Rain." [BellArk] (5:6) N-D 89, p. 1.
"Appearances." [BellArk] (5:1) Ja-F 89, p. 1.
"The Daily Quest." [BellArk] (5:4) Jl-Ag 89, p. 10.
"Dance of Whiteness." [Plain] (9:2) Wint 89, p. 28.
"Passing the Night." [Plain] (9:3) Spr 89, p. 17.
"Tempting Fate." [BellArk] (5:4) Jl-Ag 89, p. 5.
"Vistas Dormant with Joy." [BellArk] (5:6) N-D 89, p. 8.
4968. SALAMUN, Tomaz
"The Fish" (tr. by Michael Biggins). [NewEngR] (11:3) Spr 89, p. 248-249.
"Grass" (tr. by Michael Biggins). [ColR] (NS 16:1) Spr-Sum 89, p. 102.
"Shepherd" (tr. by Charles Simic and Sonja Kravanja-Gross). [WestHR] (43:1) Spr
89, p. 64.
"The Tree of Life" (tr. by Sonja Kravanja-Gross). [Field] (40) Spr 89, p. 75-76.
"Untitled: Dürer's hare hisses and falls from a great height" (tr. by Charles Simic).
[Field] (40) Spr 89, p. 73-74.
"Untitled: Peace to the people of this earth" (tr. by Anselm Hollo and the author).
[Field] (40) Spr 89, p. 74-75.
"Vacation Time" (tr. by Anselm Hollo and the author). [ColR] (NS 16:1) Spr-Sum
89, p. 103.
"The Wheel" (tr. by Michael Biggins). [ColR] (NS 16:1) Spr-Sum 89, p. 101.
"When There Is No More" (tr. by Michael Biggins). [NewEngR] (11:3) Spr 89, p.
250.
4969. SALASIN, Sal
"With mothers pushing forward children." [Talisman] (3) Fall 89, p. 120.

4970. SALEMI, Joseph S.
"III.75. For a long time now, Lupercus" (tr. of Martial). [ArtfulD] (16/17) Fall 89,
p. 10.
"VI.26. Our friend Sotades is in peril of his head" (tr. of Martial). [ArtfulD] (16/17)
Fall 89, p. 10.
"XI.104. Wifey dear" (tr. of Martial). [ArtfulD] (16/17) Fall 89, p. 11.
4971. SALERNO, Joe
"Drinking Tea Among Craggy Peaks." [WormR] (29:4, #116) 89, p. 136-137.
"Essay on Hair." [PoetC] (20:2) Wint 89, p. 39-40.
"The Gift." [WindO] (52) Wint 89-90, p. 8.
"Late November Afternoon, Falling Asleep in a Chair with a Handful of Basil Seeds
in My Shirt Pocket." [PoetC] (20:2) Wint 89, p. 37-38.
"To Beverly, After Fifteen Years." [WindO] (52) Wint 89-90, p. 9-10.
"Written after Reading the Tanka of Tachibana Akemi." [WormR] (29:4, #116) 89,
p. 137-140.
4972. SALGADO, Porfirio
"Last Night" (tr. by Diane Kendig). [Pig] (15) 88, p. 88.
4973. SALINAS, Luis Omar
"Love Rushes By." [MissouriR] (12:2) 89, p. 52-53.
4974. SALINAS, Pedro
"Another You" (tr. by David Garrison). [InterPR] (15:2) Fall 89, p. 55.
"Juice" (tr. by David Garrison). [InterPR] (15:2) Fall 89, p. 57.
"Otra Tu." [InterPR] (15:2) Fall 89, p. 54.
"Vocación." [InterPR] (15:2) Fall 89, p. 58.
"Vocation" (tr. by David Garrison). [InterPR] (15:2) Fall 89, p. 59.
"El Zumo." [InterPR] (15:2) Fall 89, p. 56.
4975. SALING, Joseph
"Jason on a Grey Day at the Coast." [Amelia] (5:3, #14) 89, p. 78.
4976. SALISBURY, Ralph
"I Believe" (1987, after Chernobyl, tr. of Inger Tapio, w. Lars Nordstrom). [CharR]
(15:2) Fall 89, p. 76.
"Snow Flakes" (tr. of Inger Tapio, w. Lars Nordstrom). [CharR] (15:2) Fall 89, p.
74.
"Summer Morning" (tr. of Inger Tapio, w. Lars Nordstrom). [CharR] (15:2) Fall
89, p. 75.
4977. SALLIS, James
"Conclusions." [SpoonRQ] (14:2) Spr 89, p. 12.
"June 6, 1984." [SpoonRQ] (14:2) Spr 89, p. 10-11.
"Nimbus." [SoDakR] (27:2) Sum 89, p. 57.
"To My Daughter." [SpoonRQ] (14:2) Spr 89, p. 13.
4978. SALTER, Mary Jo
"I Lose You for an Instant" (Guilin, China). [CrossCur] (8:2) Ja 89, p. 25-27.
"The Upper Story." [Atlantic] (263:1) Ja 89, p. 70-71.
4979. SALTMAN, Benjamin
"Cloudy and Isaac" (1988 John Williams Andrews Prize Winner). [PoetL] (84:1)
Spr 89, p. 5-22.
4980. SAMARAS, Nicholas
"Nuclear Medicine." [IndR] (13:1) Wint 89, p. 39.
4981. SAMBERG, Ken
"Am I in Love? and Peripheral Matters." [AntigR] (77/78) Spr-Sum 89, p. 144.
SAMPER, Cristina Caballero
See CABALLERO SAMPER, Cristina
4982. SAMPSON, Dennis
"Coming Home Late and Alone." [AmerS] (58:3) Sum 89, p. 420.
"If My Friend Were in Heaven" (for Larry Moffi). [TarRP] (28:2) Spr 89, p. 29-30.
"Past the Remaining Animals." [OhioR] (44) 89, p. 106-107.
4983. SAMSON, Sue
"Open Windows." [Farm] (6:2) Fall 89, p. 70.
4984. SAMUELS, Virginia
"Look up, O, Sadness." [HarvardA] (124:1) N 89, p. 25.
4985. SANAZARO, Leonard
"Two Movies from Childhood." [DenQ] (23:3/4) Wint-Spr 89, p. 117-118.
4986. SANCHEZ, Ricardo
"En-Ojitos: Canto a Piñero" (recuerdos dejan huellas en las humosas palabras, El
Paso, 10 Nov. 88). [Americas] (17:1) Spr 89, p. 35-36.
"Horizontes y Ensueños." [Americas] (17:1) Spr 89, p. 45-47.

"Notas a Federico García Lorca (con Disculpas y Festejos)." [Americas] (17:1) Spr
89, p. 37-44.
4987. SANCHEZ, Sonia
"Fragment 2." [Callaloo] (12:2, #39) Spr 89, p. 351.
"Summerpoem, 1986." [Callaloo] (12:2, #39) Spr 89, p. 350.
4988. SANDERS, Anthony
"Sicitur ad Astra." [Boulevard] (4:1, #10) Spr 89, p. 183-184.
4989. SANDERS, Catherine Marie
"Flamingo" (For Pedro James Rodriguez). [CentralP] (16) Fall 89, p. 34-36.
4990. SANDERS, David
"Amish." [Stand] (30:3) Sum 89, p. 39.
"A Wash." [WestB] (23) 89, p. 81.
4991. SANDERS, Edward
"The Ocean Étude." [RiverS] (29) [89], p. 71-79.
4992. SANDERS, Jo
"Basket." [Plain] (10:1) 89, p. 11.
"Bouquet." [Plain] (9:3) Spr 89, p. 29.
4993. SANDERS, Mark
"Assets." [KanQ] (21:3) Sum 89, p. 119.
"The Ball Game, 1975." [CharR] (15:2) Fall 89, p. 72-73.
"The Cowley County Murders, 1958" (The Deputy's Report). [CharR] (15:2) Fall
89, p. 71.
"The Cowley County Murders, 1958 (The Deputy's Report)." [Event] (18:3) Fall
89, p. 80-81.
"Hands" (for Travis). [RiverC] (10:1) Fall 89, p. 110-111.
"James River Inlet: Nixa, Missouri." [SouthernHR] (23:3) Sum 89, p. 263.
"The Lost Book." [Plain] (9:3) Spr 89, p. 32-33.
"Missouri Barns." [CharR] (15:2) Fall 89, p. 73.
"My Father and I Sit Down to Talk." [SpoonRQ] (14:3) Sum 89, p. 56.
"On Modern Poetry." [Plain] (10:1) 89, p. 9.
"These Children." [MidwQ] (30:4) Sum 89, p. 451.
"The Trilobite." [Event] (18:3) Fall 89, p. 82.
"A Vigil at a Missile Silo (Near Warrensburg, Missouri)." [PoetryE] (28) Fall 89, p.
115-116.
"Virginia Beach." [KanQ] (21:3) Sum 89, p. 118-119.
"Windows." [RiverC] (10:1) Fall 89, p. 112-113.
"The World." [CharR] (15:2) Fall 89, p. 74.
4994. SANDERS, Tony
"Heart Island." [GrandS] (8:2) Wint 89, p. 172-175.
4995. SANDERSON, Rachel
"Relic." [Wind] (19:64) 89, p. 13.
4996. SANDFORD, Christy Sheffield
"Balzac Robed, Balzac Nude." (After Sculptures by Rodin with Quotes from *Pere
Goriot*, tr. by Henry Reed). [NegC] (9:2) 89, p. 70-71.
4997. SANDFORT, Lolly
"Yesterday's Linens." [EmeraldCR] (1989) c1988, p. 119.
4998. SANDSTROEM, Yvonne
"Warm Rooms and Cold" (tr. of Lars Gustafsson). [Field] (40) Spr 89, p. 72.
4999. SANDY, Stephen
"Father and the Minneapolis Chacmool" (January 1986). [SouthwR] (74:4) Aut 89,
p. 533.
"Mexican Head." [SouthwR] (74:4) Aut 89, p. 532.
SANEKATA, Fujiwara no (d. 998)
See FUJIWARA NO SANEKATA (d. 998)
5000. SANER, Reg
"How." [Poetry] (155:3) D 89, p. 207.
"Meanwhile." [Poetry] (155:3) D 89, p. 206.
"Red Letters" (for Elizabeth, 52 poems). [QRL] (9:28-29) 89, 71 p.
5001. SANFORD, Christy Sheffield
"Black Hawk ('My' Antonia)." [MinnR] (NS 32) Spr 89, p. 84-86.
"Lady of the Valentine (With Dangerous Suggestions)." [HeliconN] (20) 89, p. 63.
"Magnolia Grandiflora L." [KanQ] (21:1/2) Wint-Spr 89, p. 215.
"Painted Man." [Kalliope] (10:1/2) 88, p. 73.
5002. SANFORD, Jim
"About the Hall at Ryusho-Ji" (tr. of Ikkyu). [LitR] (32:3) Spr 89, p. 358.
"Beneath the Trees, Among the Boulders, a Rustic Hut" (tr. of Ikkyu). [LitR] (32:3)

Spr 89, p. 358.
"A Natural Way" (tr. of Ikkyu). [LitR] (32:3) Spr 89, p. 358.
"Night Journey to the Eastern Brook" (tr. of Wang Chi). [LitR] (32:3) Spr 89, p.
357.
"Written on the Tavern Wall" (tr. of Wang Chi). [LitR] (32:3) Spr 89, p. 357.
5003. SANGUINETI, Edoardo
"Erotopaegnia" (Selection: "He Slept in You Like a Dry Fibroma," tr. by Charles
Tomlinson). [Poetry] (155:1/2) O-N 89, p. 78.
"Erotopaegnia" (Selection: "In Te Dormiva Come un Fibroma Asciutto). [Poetry]
(155:1/2) O-N 89, p. 78.
"Hell's Purgatory" (Selection: "Through Hebecrevon, Lessay, Portbail," tr. by
Charles Tomlinson). [Poetry] (155:1/2) O-N 89, p. 79.
5004. SANT, Indira
"Her Dream" (tr. by Vinay Dharwadker). [TriQ] (77) Wint 89-90, p. 208.
5005. SANTAGOSTINI, Mario
"The Dream of Augustine" (Selections: "Now You Are the Only Beast," "Carla," tr.
by John Frederick Nims). [Poetry] (155:1/2) O-N 89, p. 149-150.
"Il Sogno di Agostino" (Selection: "Sei Ormai l'Unica Bestia"). [Poetry] (155:1/2)
O-N 89, p. 148.
5006. SANTEK, Jerry
"2:13 A.M., Drunken Long-Distance Call from JR's Bar and Grill." [Ploughs]
(15:4) Wint 89-90, p. 191.
"Sudden Departure." [Ploughs] (15:4) Wint 89-90, p. 189-190.
SANTIAGO, José Luis Colon
See COLON SANTIAGO, José Luis
5007. SANTIAGO, Leida J.
"Hoy en Tu Ausencia." [Mairena] (11:27) 89, p. 90.
5008. SANTIAGO-BACA, Jimmy
"Drawing Light." [Colum] (14) 89, p. 210.
5009. SANTOS, Sherod
"Augury." [WestHR] (43:1) Spr 89, p. 31.
"Cheeveresque" (Mr. and Mrs. Stone's Vacation). [GettyR] (2:2) Spr 89, p.
328-329.
"Hysteria." [WestHR] (43:1) Spr 89, p. 30.
"Ideology." [PacificR] (7) 89, p. 7.
"In the House on North Gate Heights." [IndR] (12:2) Spr 89, p. 102-103.
"The Limestone Cave." [GettyR] (2:2) Spr 89, p. 326-327.
"A Modern Goddess." [PacificR] (7) 89, p. 8.
"The New Republic." [PacificR] (7) 89, p. 10.
"On Style." [VirQR] (65:4) Aut 89, p. 649.
"Quai Saint Bernard." [Antaeus] (62) Spr 89, p. 209.
"South Wing." [VirQR] (65:4) Aut 89, p. 650-651.
"Still Life with Minnows." [VirQR] (65:4) Aut 89, p. 650.
"Wednesdays." [PacificR] (7) 89, p. 9.
"The Wing Dike at Low Water." [NewYorker] (65:20) 3 Jl 89, p. 32.
SAOI, Máire Mhac an t
See Mhac an tSAOI, Máire
5010. SAPIA, Yvonne
"Palm Reading, 1968." [CinPR] (19) Spr 89, p. 56.
"Releasing the Reptile." [Kalliope] (11:3) 89, p. 57.
"Submissions." [SouthernPR] (29:2) Fall 89, p. 59-60.
"To a Deaf Cousin." [CinPR] (19) Spr 89, p. 57.
"When Valentino Died" (1960 -- After an interruption by a regular, the barber
continues his confession). [ApalQ] (32) 89, p. 17-26.
5011. SAPPHO
"Ode" (tr. by Francis Golffing). [SouthwR] (74:2) Spr 89, p. 213.
"To a Supine Lady" (tr. by Francis Golffing). [SpiritSH] (55) Fall-Wint 89 [90 on
cover], p. 30.
5012. SARDUY, Severo
"The Fallow Deer" (in Spanish and English, tr. by Michael Johnson). [Mildred] (3:2)
89, p. 13.
5013. SARGENT, Robert
"A Problem in Hermeneutics." [Pembroke] (21) 89, p. 13-14.
5014. SARRACINO, Carmine
"The Idea of the Ordinary." [WestB] (24) 89, p. 124.

5015. SARRIS, Nikos
"The Almond of the World" (tr. of Odysseus Elytis, w. Jeffrey Carson). [PartR] (56:1) Wint 89, p. 125-132.
5016. SARTARELLI, Stephen
"Poem of the Dawn and the Night" (tr. of Rodolfo Di Biasio). [Poetry] (155:1/2) O-N 89, p. 95, 97.
"To Diderot" (tr. of Fabio Doplicher). [Poetry] (155:1/2) O-N 89, p. 99-103.
"Tutto Perso, Tutto Parificato? (All Lost, All Made Equal?)" (Selections: 4 poems, tr. of Mario Luzi). [Poetry] (155:1/2) O-N 89, p. 27-29.
"When Slow October Changes Color" (tr. of Umberto Piersanti). [Poetry] (155:1/2) O-N 89, p. 119-123.
"You Had Breath, a Body" (tr. of Stefano D'Arrigo). [Poetry] (155:1/2) O-N 89, p. 45.
"You Who Still Possess Speech" (tr. of Stefano D'Arrigo). [Poetry] (155:1/2) O-N 89, p. 43, 45.
5017. SASANOV, Catherine
"Demolitions." [MalR] (87) Sum 89, p. 70.
"Demolitions II." [MalR] (87) Sum 89, p. 71.
"Demolitions III." [MalR] (87) Sum 89, p. 72.
"Excavations: The Pigs of Gardara / The Bones in a Wall." [HayF] (4) Spr 89, p. 104.
"Leaving the Emergency Room." [MalR] (87) Sum 89, p. 69.
5018. SASSEEN, Sue B.
"Zone 3: Alert" (Honorable Mention). [Nimrod] (33:1) Fall-Wint 89, p. 58-59.
5019. SASTRY, Sailaja
"The Promise." [Footwork] 89, p. 52.
5020. SATER, Stephen
"Mom's Vigil." [SpiritSH] (54) Spr-Sum 89, p. 19.
"On a Painting by Jackson Pollack." [SpiritSH] (54) Spr-Sum 89, p. 18.
"On Van Gogh's Painting of the Yellow Chair." [SpiritSH] (54) Spr-Sum 89, p. 19.
5021. SATHERLEY, David
"Dear reader." [Quarry] (38:1) Wint 89, p. 5.
"Puzzling." [AntigR] (77/78) Spr-Sum 89, p. 72-73.
"The Rape." [Quarry] (38:1) Wint 89, p. 57-58.
"The Seal Men." [Event] (18:2) Sum 89, p. 18-19.
5022. SATTERFIELD, Leon
"Burying the Dog: An Anti-Poem." [Plain] (9:3) Spr 89, p. 38.
"Upon Being Recognized for a Quarter Century on the Faculty." [Plain] (10:1) 89, p. 28.
5023. SATZ, Martha
"Jewel" (tr. of Janos Pilinszky, w. Zsuzsanna Ozsvath). [WebR] (14:1) Spr 89, p. 30.
"Silence" (tr. of Endre Veszi, w. Zsuzsanna Ozsvath). [WebR] (14:1) Spr 89, p. 30.
"Waiting for Miracles" (tr. of Attila Szepesi, w. Zsuzsanna Ozsvath). [WebR] (14:1) Spr 89, p. 29.
SAUCEDO, Jaime Garcia
See GARCIA SAUCEDO, Jaime
5024. SAUER, Ronald
"Good God" (for Wilhelm Reich). [Sequoia] (33:1) Sum 89, p. 20.
5025. SAUNDERS, Geraldine
"Out of Atlanta." [SingHM] (16) 89, p. 14-15.
5026. SAVARD, Jeannine
"The Daughter's Brooch." [Ploughs] (15:1) 89, p. 122.
"Fireweed." [MissR] (18:1, #52) 89, p. 69.
5027. SAVARD, Michel
"Bivalve" (in French). [AntigR] (79) Aut 89, p. 42.
"Bivalve" (tr. by Neil B. Bishop). [AntigR] (79) Aut 89, p. 43.
"L'Hiver les mouches se reposent les pinsons." [AntigR] (79) Aut 89, p. 46.
"In winter the flies rest, a few bad whistles" (tr. by Neil B. Bishop). [AntigR] (79) Aut 89, p. 47.
"Observe attentively observe this season" (tr. by Neil B. Bishop). [AntigR] (79) Aut 89, p. 45.
"Observe attentivement observe cette saison." [AntigR] (79) Aut 89, p. 44.
5028. SAVARESE, Ralph
"State of the Union." [SewanR] (97:3) Sum 89, p. 404-405.

5029. SAVINES, Jaime
"1. La Luna." [Inti] (29/30) Primavera-Otoño 89, p. 269-270.
"2. En Serio." [Inti] (29/30) Primavera-Otoño 89, p. 270.
"Yo No Lo Sé de Cierto." [Inti] (29/30) Primavera-Otoño 89, p. 270-271.
5030. SAVVAS, Minas
"After the End" (tr. of Yannis Ritsos). [SenR] (19:1) 89, p. 9.
"And One More Night" (tr. of Yánnis Ritsos). [AmerPoR] (18:5) S-O 89, p. 8.
"The Hats" (tr. of Yannis Ritsos). [SenR] (19:1) 89, p. 8.
"Hesperos" (tr. of Yannis Ritsos). [SenR] (19:1) 89, p. 7.
"In the Hallway Underground" (tr. of Yánnis Ritsos). [AmerPoR] (18:5) S-O 89, p. 8.
"Refutation" (tr. of Yánnis Ritsos). [AmerPoR] (18:5) S-O 89, p. 8.
5031. SAWYER-LAUÇANNO, Christopher
"Ode to Salvador Dalí" (tr. of Federico Garcia Lorca). [AmerPoR] (18:3) My-Je 89, p. 5-6.
5032. SAXENA, Sarveshvar Dayal
"To Father Gone to Heaven" (tr. by Robert A. Hueckstedt). [Pig] (15) 88, p. 15.
5033. SAYA, Tom
"The Farmer." [MidwQ] (30:2) Wint 89, p. 180-183.
"The Farmer II." [MidwQ] (30:2) Wint 89, p. 211-214.
5034. SAYRE, Cecil
"Soul of the Wolfman." [NewRena] (7:3, #23) 89, p. 52.
5035. SCALAPINO, Leslie
"At Dawn Fishing Among the Tules: a Play." [Screens] (1) 89, p. 127-131.
"Fin de Siècle, III: a Play." [Temblor] (10) 89, p. 76-80.
"The Pearl" (Selection: IV). [Notus] (4:2) Fall 89, p. 43-46.
"The Series -- 3." [Conjunc] (13) 89, p. 62-66.
5036. SCALF, Sue
"Hester and Arthur in the Twentieth Century." [Plain] (10:1) 89, p. 22.
"Live Coals." [CarolQ] (41:3) Spr 89, p. 69-70.
"A Scent of Green." [SoCoast] (7) Spr-Fall 89, p. 55.
"A Sea Journey" (an elegy). [NegC] (9:2) 89, p. 64-65.
5037. SCALISE, Gregorio
"Authority Has Played" (tr. by Adria Bernardi). [Poetry] (155:1/2) O-N 89, p. 106.
"La Mente e il Corpo Sono Angeli." [Poetry] (155:1/2) O-N 89, p. 104.
"The Mind and Body Are Angels" (tr. by Adria Bernardi). [Poetry] (155:1/2) O-N 89, p. 105.
"Now to Reopen a Text" (tr. by Adria Bernardi). [Poetry] (155:1/2) O-N 89, p. 105.
"Ora Riapre un Testo." [Poetry] (155:1/2) O-N 89, p. 104.
"Saying Again That Flowers" (tr. by Adria Bernardi). [Poetry] (155:1/2) O-N 89, p. 107.
5038. SCAMMACCA, Nat
"I Love My Wife Because She Has ONE Head!" [Footwork] 89, p. 31.
"The Madonie" (tr. of Pietro Attinasi). [Footwork] 89, p. 31.
"Sicily." [Footwork] 89, p. 30.
5039. SCAMMELL, Michael
"Hostages" (tr. of Veno Taufer). [ColR] (NS 16:1) Spr-Sum 89, p. 89-90.
"Lipizzaners" (tr. of Edvard Kocbek, w. Veno Taufer). [ColR] (NS 16:1) Spr-Sum 89, p. 95-97.
"Red and Black Fish Circle Between Us" (tr. of Veno Taufer). [Vis] (31) 89, p. 37.
5040. SCANZELLO, Charles J.
"A Little Thing Without Wings." [Wind] (19:64) 89, p. 17.
5041. SCARANO, Laura R.
"Libro de las Epifanias" (Selections: 2, 5). [Mairena] (11:27) 89, p. 62.
5042. SCARBROUGH, George
"Small Poem." [SpiritSH] (55) Fall-Wint 89 [90 on cover], p. 4.
"Summer Revival: Brush Arbor." [SpiritSH] (55) Fall-Wint 89 [90 on cover], p. 3-4.
5043. SCATES, Maxine
"The Drunkard: Our Song." [PoetryE] (28) Fall 89, p. 128-129.
"Forgiveness." [PoetryE] (28) Fall 89, p. 124-127.
"The Garden." [NowestR] (27:2) 89, p. 14-15.
5044. SCHAEFFER, Susan Fromberg
"Small" (Second Award Poem, 1988/1989). [KanQ] (21:1/2) Wint-Spr 89, p. 25.
5045. SCHAFFNER, Michael A.
"Opechancanough's Latter Day Sketch." [Vis] (31) 89, p. 9.

5046. SCHAIN, Eliot
"White Blues." [AnotherCM] (19) 89, p. 191-193.
5047. SCHALLER, Thomas
"Dream in Exile" (tr. of Reiner Kunze, w. Thomas S. Edwards, Ken Letko, and Jeff Gearing). [Nimrod] (33:1) Fall-Wint 89, p. 111.
"On the Danube in the Fog" (tr. of Reiner Kunze, w. Thomas S. Edwards, Ken Letko, and Jeff Gearing). [Nimrod] (33:1) Fall-Wint 89, p. 111.
"The Silhouette of Lübeck" (tr. of Reiner Kunze, w. Thomas S. Edwards, Ken Letko, and Jeff Gearing). [Nimrod] (33:1) Fall-Wint 89, p. 111.
5048. SCHAUBLE, Virginia
"Moving into Light." [Comm] (116:17) O 6, 89, p. 526.
5049. SCHECHTER, Ruth Lisa
"Nothing Changes." [Footwork] 89, p. 128-129.
"Where Is Mercy Street?" (for Anne Sexton, 1928-1974). [Footwork] 89, p. 127.
"Who's Afraid of Maurice Schwartz?" [Footwork] 89, p. 128.
5050. SCHEELE, Roy
"Junk Sculpture: Still Rings." [Plain] (9:2) Wint 89, p. 27.
"One Traveler." [Wind] (19:64) 89, p. 24.
"Produce Wagon." [Wind] (19:64) 89, p. 24.
5051. SCHEINOHA, Gary
"Expatriate." [Lactuca] (12) F 89, p. 66.
"Frogman Rising." [Lactuca] (12) F 89, p. 65.
"Houdini of the Heart." [Lactuca] (12) F 89, p. 65.
"Soul of the Keyboard." [Lactuca] (12) F 89, p. 64.
"Test of the Hunter." [Lactuca] (12) F 89, p. 65.
5052. SCHENDLER, Revan
"Pedestrian, Walk!" [NewYorker] (65:11) 1 My 89, p. 36.
"Reparations of Spring." [NewYorker] (65:6) 27 Mr 89, p. 46.
5053. SCHENK, Johannes
"Knife Beneath the Fig Tree" (tr. by John Linthicum). [LitR] (33:1) Fall 89, p. 99-100.
"The Lily-Eater" (tr. by John Linthicum). [LitR] (33:1) Fall 89, p. 100-102.
5054. SCHENKER, Donald
"Beef Tune." [Iowa] (19:3) Fall 89, p. 108.
"Cows in the Rain." [Iowa] (19:3) Fall 89, p. 107.
"Pink" (for Jack Hurth). [Iowa] (19:3) Fall 89, p. 106.
5055. SCHERTZER, Mike
"Lamb." [Grain] (17:3) Fall 89, p. 32.
5056. SCHIFF, Jeff
"Diamond District." [CinPR] (19) Spr 89, p. 60-61.
"The Garden." [RiverC] (10:1) Fall 89, p. 104-105.
"Go Know." [ChiR] (36:3/4) 89, p. 33.
"Hoppers." [WritersF] (15) Fall 89, p. 102-103.
"Learning to Take the Blame." [ChiR] (36:3/4) 89, p. 34.
"Plainly Now." [RiverC] (10:1) Fall 89, p. 103.
5057. SCHIFFER, Wolfgang
"The Following Dream" (tr. by John Linthicum). [LitR] (33:1) Fall 89, p. 39.
"Living" (tr. by John Linthicum). [LitR] (33:1) Fall 89, p. 38.
"My Son" (tr. by John Linthicum). [LitR] (33:1) Fall 89, p. 38.
"Taking the Things" (tr. by John Linthicum). [LitR] (33:1) Fall 89, p. 40.
"Wait, My Friend?" (tr. by John Linthicum). [LitR] (33:1) Fall 89, p. 39.
"Yes, Your Honors" (tr. by John Linthicum). [LitR] (33:1) Fall 89, p. 40.
5058. SCHLOSS, David
"Blue Pools." [IndR] (13:1) Wint 89, p. 35.
"In Autumn." [ThRiPo] (31/32) 88, p. 45.
"The Pearl." [ThRiPo] (31/32) 88, p. 44.
"Testimony of the Man on the Ledge." [OxfordM] (5:1) Spr-Sum 89, p. 13.
5059. SCHMIDT, Jan Zlotnik
"Steely Dan Man." [Plain] (9:2) Wint 89, p. 7.
5060. SCHMIDT, Paul
"Holy Pictures: Poem for Robert Mapplethorpe." [Bomb] (27) Spr 89, p. 74-75.
5061. SCHMITT, Peter
"Class Clown." [SouthernR] (25:4) Aut 89, p. 909-910.
"Glance." [SouthernR] (25:4) Aut 89, p. 908.
"Harbinger." [SouthernR] (25:4) Aut 89, p. 914-915.
"Homecoming." [Nat] (248:24) 19 Je 89, p. 861.

"Intimacies." [KeyWR] (2:1/2) Fall-Wint 89, p. 25.
"Just Married." [SouthernR] (25:4) Aut 89, p. 912-913.
"Letter to a Homesick Niece." [SouthernR] (25:4) Aut 89, p. 913-914.
"Nature Hike." [SouthernR] (25:4) Aut 89, p. 910-912.
"Old Fashioned Juice Squeezer." [KeyWR] (2:1/2) Fall-Wint 89, p. 24.
"Tin Ear." [Poetry] (153:6) Mr 89, p. 341-342.
5062. SCHMITZ, Dennis
  "Anna Karenina." [Field] (41) Fall 89, p. 88-89.
  "Ball." [Zyzzyva] (5:2, #18) Sum 89, p. 79-80.
  "Birds." [Field] (41) Fall 89, p. 86-87.
  "Catfishing." [HayF] (4) Spr 89, p. 127.
5063. SCHNACKENBERG, Gjertrud
  "The Paperweight." [SouthwR] (74:4) Aut 89, p. 519.
5064. SCHNEIDER, Karen Warren
  "Migratory Notions" (for Christine). [HeliconN] (20) 89, p. 88-89.
5065. SCHNEIDRE, P.
  "Falsetto Returns." [AntR] (47:3) Sum 89, p. 325.
5066. SCHOEBERLEIN, Marion
  "The Farmer." [MidwQ] (30:2) Wint 89, p. 187.
  "New Bread." [MidwQ] (30:2) Wint 89, p. 206.
5067. SCHOENBERGER, Nancy
  "The Girls with Their Tall Combs." [MissouriR] (12:1) 89, p. 174-175.
  "Revolt of Our Late Spring Flowers." [RiverS] (28) 89, p. 54-55.
5068. SCHOFIELD, Don
  "On Assignment (Beirut)." [StoneC] (17:1/2) Fall-Wint 89-90, p. 53.
5069. SCHOLL, Diane
  "Easter Sunday in Eyam, Derbyshire." [ColEng] (51:1) Ja 89, p. 46.
  "Scrooby Village, Nottinghamshire." [ColEng] (51:1) Ja 89, p. 45.
5070. SCHOONOVER, Amy Jo
  "Old Valentine." [HiramPoR] (46) Spr-Sum 89, p. 26.
  "Renounced." [HiramPoR] (46) Spr-Sum 89, p. 27.
5071. SCHORB, E. M.
  "The Big Crunch." [OxfordM] (5:2) Fall-Wint 89, p. 54.
  "Hadewijch in Wall Street." [HampSPR] Wint 89, p. 51.
  "Murderer's Day." [HampSPR] Wint 89, p. 50-51.
5072. SCHORR, Laurie (Laurie J.)
  "Desert Rain Chant." [CarolQ] (41:3) Spr 89, p. 20.
  "Home Again." [ThRiPo] (31/32) 88, p. 46.
  "The Problem." [AntR] (47:2) Spr 89, p. 205.
  "Unburied." [CarolQ] (41:3) Spr 89, p. 21.
5073. SCHOTT, Barbara
  "Babushka." [PraF] (10:3, #48) Aut 89, p. 27.
  "Knives." [PraF] (10:3, #48) Aut 89, p. 26.
  "The Smoker." [PraF] (10:3, #48) Aut 89, p. 25.
5074. SCHOTT, Penelope Scambly
  "At Princeton Airport." [Footwork] 89, p. 9-10.
  "Granddaddy's Garden." [StoneC] (16:3/4) Spr-Sum 89, p. 63.
  "Moving Among Snow Women." [Footwork] 89, p. 10.
  "My Daughter Calls, Hurting." [Footwork] 89, p. 10.
  "My Lover's Grandparents." [US1] (22/23) Spr 89, p. 14-15.
  "Nothing Is Moving." [SouthernPR] (29:1) Spr 89, p. 14-15.
  "The Women We Have Become." [AmerV] (16) Fall 89, p. 48-49.
5075. SCHOULTZ, Solveig von
  "Scent of Apples" (tr. by Anne Born). [Verse] (6:1) Mr 89, p. 47.
  "Three Sisters" (tr. by Anne Born). [Verse] (6:1) Mr 89, p. 47.
5076. SCHRAMM, Darrel G. H.
  "The Long Dance Over the Fields." [EvergreenC] (5:1) Fall 89, p. 36-38.
5077. SCHREIBER, Ron
  "Isthmus." [EvergreenC] (4:4) Sum 89, p. 24.
  "Legal Seafoods, Kendall Square." [EvergreenC] (4:3) Spr 89, p. 24.
5078. SCHREINER, Steven
  "Backrub." [PassN] (10:1) Wint 89, p. 12.
  "Niagara Falls." [CinPR] (19) Spr 89, p. 21.
  "The Thousand Evenings." [DenQ] (23:3/4) Wint-Spr 89, p. 119.
5079. SCHROEDER, Gary
  "Night Shift: Another Elegy." [PassN] (10:2) Sum 89, p. 28.

5080. SCHRÖER, Rolfrafael
"Age of the Ants" (Two Passages, tr. by John Linthicum). [LitR] (33:1) Fall 89, p. 136-137.
"The Last Circus" (tr. by John Linthicum). [LitR] (33:1) Fall 89, p. 138.
"Songsong" (tr. by John Linthicum). [LitR] (33:1) Fall 89, p. 139.
5081. SCHUBERT, Ninon
"Arrivals: Hamburg" (tr. by Ron Butlin). [Verse] (6:2) Je 89, p. 29.
"Divided Islands" (tr. by Ron Butlin). [Verse] (6:2) Je 89, p. 29.
5082. SCHUG, Lawrence
"Barber's Son." [RagMag] (7:1) 89, p. 49.
"Hobo Camp." [RagMag] (7:1) 89, p. 48.
"School Bell." [Plain] (10:1) 89, p. 13.
5083. SCHULDT
"Life & Death in China" (3 selections). [CentralP] (15) Spr 89, p. 85-87.
5084. SCHULMAN, Grace
"False Move." [NewL] (56:2/3) Wint 89-Spr 90, p. 239.
"The Marsh." [NewL] (56:2/3) Wint 89-Spr 90, p. 232.
"The Movie." [WestHR] (43:4) Wint 89, p. 267-268.
"Rescue in Pescallo." [GrandS] (8:3) Spr 89, p. 51-56.
"Rescue in Pescallo." [NewL] (56:2/3) Wint 89-Spr 90, p. 233-238.
"The Stars and the Moon." [NewL] (56:2/3) Wint 89-Spr 90, p. 231-232.
5085. SCHULTZ, Lee
"The Vets in Creative Writing Class." [PacificR] (7) 89, p. 76-77.
5086. SCHULTZ, Robert
"The Shape of a Leaf." [PoetC] (20:3) Spr 89, p. 33.
5087. SCHULTZ, Susan (Susan M.)
"Articles of Amazement" (words for Ariel). [RiverC] (9:1) Spr 89, p. 71.
"On Reading Ovid's *Metamorphoses*." [ChiR] (36:3/4) 89, p. 74-75.
"Prospero in Milan." [Verse] (6:2) Je 89, p. 42.
5088. SCHULTZ, Wes
"It Is Too Bad That." [RagMag] (7:1) 89, p. 47.
5089. SCHUSTER, David
"Linking." [Mildred] (3:1) Spr-Sum 89, p. 106.
5090. SCHUYLER, James
"Advent." [AmerPoR] (18:6) N-D 89, p. 3.
"Ajaccio Violets." [BrooklynR] (6) 89, p. 7-8.
"A Cardinal." [AmerPoR] (18:6) N-D 89, p. 3.
"Haze." [NewYorker] (65:24) 31 Jl 89, p. 28.
"Noon Office." [AmerPoR] (18:6) N-D 89, p. 4.
"Reserved Sacrament." [AmerPoR] (18:6) N-D 89, p. 4.
"A View." [AmerPoR] (18:6) N-D 89, p. 3.
"White Boat, Blue Boat." [NewYorker] (65:41) 27 N 89, p. 100.
"Yellow Flowers." [NewYorker] (65:30) 11 S 89, p. 42.
5091. SCHWARTZ, Hillel
"Above Me, Always." [Wind] (19:64) 89, p. 27-28.
"Available Light." [Boulevard] (4:2, #11) Fall 89, p. 79-80.
"Cosmos." [PoetryNW] (30:4) Wint 89-90, p. 47.
"Dumplings and Heart." [MalR] (86) Spr 89, p. 92.
"Fat Man at Standard Royal, 240 WPM, Picture Perfect." [Thrpny] (37) Spr 89, p. 29.
"For the Nine Women at the County Fair Dancing to 'Lola' in Pink and Blue Chiffon with Green Sequins." [NewEngR] (11:3) Spr 89, p. 322.
"From the Lone Pine." [Grain] (17:1) Spr 89, p. 54.
"Monkey's Uncle." [NewRena] (7:3, #23) 89, p. 56-58.
"Pieces of Seven." [MalR] (86) Spr 89, p. 93.
"Settling." [CarolQ] (41:2) Wint 89, p. 18.
"Visiting the Bathroom." [Grain] (17:1) Spr 89, p. 55.
"Wax Works." [NewEngR] (11:3) Spr 89, p. 323-324.
5092. SCHWARTZ, Howard
"The Fire in the Ferns." [RiverS] (30) [89], p. 72.
"Mississippi John Hurt Buried in the Pepper." [RiverS] (30) [89], p. 71.
5093. SCHWARTZ, Leonard
"Between Perception." [CentralP] (16) Fall 89, p. 72-74.
"From: Ulysses" (tr. of Benjamin Fondane, w. E. M. Cioran). [PartR] (56:1) Wint 89, p. 120-121.
"Mtasipol" (tr. of Benjamin Fondane). [Pequod] (28/29/30) 89, p. 188-194.

5094. SCHWARTZ, Mimi
"Grow Up, Will You?" (To my Dad who left too soon). [US1] (22/23) Spr 89, p. 28.
5095. SCHWARTZ, Naomi
"Making Time." [Pequod] (26/27) 89, p. 22-23.
5096. SCHWARTZ, Ruth
"Father, After the Divorce." [HayF] (4) Spr 89, p. 126.
5097. SCHWAUSS, Waldemar B.
"I.Q. Test 4Four Doodlers?" [Rampike] (6:3) 88, p. 65.
5098. SCHWER, Martha
"The Student." [HiramPoR] (46) Spr-Sum 89, p. 30-31.
"The Uses of Cartography." [HiramPoR] (46) Spr-Sum 89, p. 28-29.
5099. SCOBIE, Stephen
"Guillaume (by that I mean, Apollinaire) always insisted that his bed be perfectly made." [CanLit] (121) Sum 89, p. 41.
"Hermit, used as a verb, meaning: to wait, invisible, at the mouth of a cave." [CanLit] (121) Sum 89, p. 39.
"In the kitchen at Rue de Fleurus, Alice is setting down a stock of tea-dishes on the draining board." [CanLit] (121) Sum 89, p. 39.
"An old hardcover book, the binding broken, the dry glue cracking like twigs in autumn." [CanLit] (121) Sum 89, p. 40.
"The prisoner escaped, at prairie midnight, follows the railway tracks home." [CanLit] (121) Sum 89, p. 40.
"Tilting at windmills, you said, looking around for some windmills to tilt at." [CanLit] (121) Sum 89, p. 41.
"What it amounts to, what it comes back to." [CanLit] (121) Sum 89, p. 40.
"You look at the word pencilled, graffiti-like, eye-level on the washroom wall." [CanLit] (121) Sum 89, p. 41.
5100. SCODOVA, Cynthia
"Re-Membering." [WestB] (25) 89, p. 21.
5101. SCOTT, Caitlin
"Prague January, 1987." [MSS] (6:3) 89, p. 43-44.
5102. SCOTT, Dennis
"Crossing" (for August Wilson). [Vis] (31) 89, p. 6-8.
"Frostsong: for Joy." [Vis] (30) 89, p. 7.
"Scabsong." [Vis] (30) 89, p. 6.
"Strategies." [Vis] (30) 89, p. 8.
"Visa." [Vis] (31) 89, p. 8.
"Weaponsong." [Vis] (30) 89, p. 7.
5103. SCOTT, Herbert
"Evening, Milking." [Shen] (39:2) Sum 89, p. 29.
5104. SCOTT, Jim
"Postcards" (for Michael Poling). [EvergreenC] (5:1) Fall 89, p. 39.
5105. SCOTT, L. E.
"A Death in the Family" (For James Baldwin). [Obs] (3:3) Wint 88, p. 47-53.
5106. SCOTT, Peter Dale
"Coming to Jakarta" (Selections: II.iv, II.xvii, III.xi, IV.iv, IV.x). [Witness] (2:1) Spr 88, p. 54-65.
5107. SCOVILLE, Jane (Jane A.)
"Milestones." [BellArk] (5:5) S-O 89, p. 9.
"Moving On." [SmPd] (26:1, #75) Wint 89, p. 29.
5108. SCRIMGEOUR, J. D.
"Dean's Truck." [TarRP] (29:1) Fall 89, p. 23-24.
5109. SCRUTON, James
"Drought." [Farm] (6:2) Fall 89, p. 18.
"Drought." [StoneC] (17:1/2) Fall-Wint 89-90, p. 68.
"Kerry Glass." [StoneC] (17:1/2) Fall-Wint 89-90, p. 69.
5110. SCUTELLARO, Guy E.
"When You Get to the Top of the Mountain, Keep Climbing" (Zen Buddhist saying). [StoneC] (17:1/2) Fall-Wint 89-90, p. 37.
5111. SEA, Gary
"Desecration" (tr. of Jesse Thoor). [WebR] (14:1) Spr 89, p. 10.
"Harmony" (tr. of Christoph Mangold). [StoneC] (17:1/2) Fall-Wint 89-90, p. 51.
"Sonnet in Summer" (tr. of Jesse Thoor). [WebR] (14:1) Spr 89, p. 8.
"Sonnet of Modern Naïveté" (tr. of Jesse Thoor). [WebR] (14:1) Spr 89, p. 9.
"Suite No. 6" (tr. of Christoph Mangold). [StoneC] (17:1/2) Fall-Wint 89-90, p.

50-51.
"Talking in the Wind" (tr. of Jesse Thoor). [WebR] (14:1) Spr 89, p. 11.
5112. SEABURG, Alan
"After Intercourse." [BallSUF] (30:4) Aut 89, p. 50.
"The Hardness the Softness." [PoetC] (21:1) Fall 89, p. 26.
"The Right of Way." [BallSUF] (30:4) Aut 89, p. 52.
"Tributes Around the Heart." [BallSUF] (30:4) Aut 89, p. 51.
5113. SEALY, Douglas
"Berkeley" (tr. of Máirtín O Direáin, w. Tomás MacSíomóin). [Trans] (22) Fall 89,
p. 35.
"Grief's Dignity" (tr. of Máirtín O Direáin, w. Tomás MacSíomóin). [Trans] (22)
Fall 89, p. 32.
"Invitation to the Virgin" (tr. of Máirtín O Direáin, w. Tomás MacSíomóin). [Trans]
(22) Fall 89, p. 31.
"Spring in the West" (tr. of Máirtín O Direáin, w. Tomás MacSíomóin). [Trans] (22)
Fall 89, p. 33.
"Stout Oars" (tr. of Máirtín O Direáin, w. Tomás MacSíomóin). [Trans] (22) Fall 89,
p. 34.
SEARCAIGH, Cathal O
See O SEARCAIGH, Cathal
5114. SEARLES, George J.
"Letter to Farrell." [Footwork] 89, p. 55.
"La Nostalgie du Bon Vieux Temps." [Footwork] 89, p. 55.
5115. SEARS, Donald A.
"Flown" (with a fragment from Sappho). [SoCoast] (7) Spr-Fall 89, p. 47.
5116. SEATON, J. P.
"At 'Be Careful Bank'" (tr. of Yüan Mei). [LitR] (32:3) Spr 89, p. 415.
"Dog Days" (tr. of Yüan Mei). [LitR] (32:3) Spr 89, p. 415.
"Drunken Villagers" (tr. of anonymous Chinese poem). [LitR] (32:3) Spr 89, p.
413.
"House Cricket" (tr. of Tu Fu). [LitR] (32:3) Spr 89, p. 414.
"Night Thought" (tr. of Yüan Mei). [LitR] (32:3) Spr 89, p. 416.
"Song of the Bound Chicken" (tr. of Tu Fu). [LitR] (32:3) Spr 89, p. 414.
"Talking Art" (tr. of Yüan Mei). [LitR] (32:3) Spr 89, p. 416.
"When the Clouds Come" (tr. of Yüan Mei). [LitR] (32:3) Spr 89, p. 416.
5117. SEATON, Maureen
"America Loves Carney." [MassR] (30:1) Spr 89, p. 81-82.
"Glory Days." [WestB] (24) 89, p. 24-25.
"The Kill." [PoetryE] (28) Fall 89, p. 121.
"Rhapsodies of Fire" (after Wallace Stevens). [WestB] (24) 89, p. 25.
"Robin's Egg Blue." [PoetryE] (28) Fall 89, p. 122-123.
"Sonnets for a Single Mother." [Ploughs] (15:4) Wint 89-90, p. 192-193.
5118. SECOR, Laura J.
"Poem for Margaret." [HangL] (55) 89, p. 65-66.
5119. SEFERIS, George
"Diary Entries" (tr. by Athan Anagnostopoulos). [Pequod] (28/29/30) 89, p.
105-107.
5120. SEGALEN, Victor
"To the Ten Thousand Years" (tr. by Dorothy Aspinwall). [WebR] (14:1) Spr 89, p.
18.
5121. SEGALL, Pearl Bloch
"Deja-Vu." [Amelia] (5:3, #14) 89, p. 117.
5122. SEI, Shonagon
"Who's There?" (tr. by Graeme Wilson). [Poetry] (153:5) F 89, p. 298.
5123. SEIBLES, Tim
"The Shit Didn Hit Nuttin But Net" (for brothers everywhere). [BlackALF] (23:3)
Fall 89, p. 480.
"The Word 1964-1981." [BlackALF] (23:3) Fall 89, p. 481.
5124. SEIDEL, Frederick
"The Last Poem in the Book." [AmerPoR] (18:6) N-D 89, p. 19-20.
5125. SEIDMAN, Hugh
"1968-1969." [Pequod] (26/27) 89, p. 15.
"Edge." [Ploughs] (15:4) Wint 89-90, p. 194-197.
"Embarkment." [NewL] (56:2/3) Wint 89-Spr 90, p. 243-244.
"For the Victims." [Pequod] (26/27) 89, p. 16-17.
"The Front." [NewL] (56:2/3) Wint 89-Spr 90, p. 242-243.

"Jurasic." [NewL] (56:2/3) Wint 89-Spr 90, p. 249.
"The Mother." [NewL] (56:2/3) Wint 89-Spr 90, p. 240-241.
"Mother's Day, Coney Island: Metropolitan Jewish Geriatric Home." [NewL]
    (56:2/3) Wint 89-Spr 90, p. 245-246.
"Mother's Day, Coney Island: Metropolitan Jewish Geriatric Home." [Pequod]
    (26/27) 89, p. 18-19.
"The Point of the Story Is." [NewL] (56:2/3) Wint 89-Spr 90, p. 246-248.
"Triads (1)" (10 poems). [Boulevard] (4:1, #10) Spr 89, p. 35-38.
5126. SEIFERLE, Rebecca
    "The Dancer or the Dance." [TriQ] (77) Wint 89-90, p. 298-301.
5127. SEILER, Barry
    "Train Time." [NewEngR] (12:2) Wint 89, p. 156.
5128. SEITZER, Carol
    "Can They Really See Me?" [SlipS] (9) 89, p. 57.
    "A Good Place in the Galaxy." [HolCrit] (26:1) F 89, p. 16.
    "Myths." [BallSUF] (30:4) Aut 89, p. 16.
5129. SELAWSKY, John T.
    "Appointment" (for Peter). [CapeR] (24:1) Spr 89, p. 36.
    "August." [Wind] (19:64) 89, p. 40.
    "From the Hillside Overlooking Borgo alla Collina." [Poem] (61) My 89, p. 28.
    "Groundwork." [CapeR] (24:1) Spr 89, p. 37.
    "Late Summer." [Poem] (61) My 89, p. 30.
    "Reunion." [WestB] (23) 89, p. 14.
    "Solstice." [Poem] (61) My 89, p. 29.
    "Summer." [StoneC] (17:1/2) Fall-Wint 89-90, p. 56-57.
    "Talisman." [Wind] (19:64) 89, p. 40.
5130. SELBY, Martha Ann
    "The Purchase." [Prima] (13) 89, p. 41.
5131. SELBY, Spencer
    "Barricade" (Selections: 3, 6, 10, 12). [Screens] (1) 89, p. 60-63.
    "Instar" (Excerpts). [CentralP] (16) Fall 89, p. 152.
5132. SELCH, A. H.
    "Blank Verse for Bob." [GreensboroR] (46) Sum 89, p. 94.
5133. SELEMI, Joseph S.
    "The Epigrams of Martial" (Selections, tr. of Martial). [CumbPR] (9:1) Fall 89, p.
        11-12.
5134. SELLIN, Eric
    "The Girls of Tangier" (tr. of Tahar Ben Jelloun). [Pig] (15) 88, p. 38.
    "Take Me Between Your Eyelashes" (tr. of Rabah Belamri). [Pig] (15) 88, p. 37.
    "Time's Stake" (tr. of Mohammed Dib). [Pig] (15) 88, p. 37.
5135. SELMAN, Robyn
    "The Children of Abergavenny." [Ploughs] (15:4) Wint 89-90, p. 200-201.
    "Past Lives." [Ploughs] (15:4) Wint 89-90, p. 198-199.
5136. SEMANSKY, C. (Chris)
    "Hit & Run." [SoCoast] (6) Fall 88, p. 35.
    "Learning to See in the Dark." [SoCoast] (6) Fall 88, p. 36.
    "The Map Is Not the Territory." [ColEng] (51:4) Ap 89, p. 389.
    "Present Forecast." [WebR] (14:1) Spr 89, p. 60.
5137. SEMENOVICH, Joseph
    "Hit-and-Run Victim." [SlipS] (9) 89, p. 90.
    "To My Step-Father Otto Treffeisen." [SlipS] (9) 89, p. 91.
5138. SEMONES, Charles
    "A Ceremony of Barns." [Wind] (19:65) 89, p. 29-30.
    "Picture" (in memory: D.T.S.). [Wind] (19:65) 89, p. 28.
    "The Ravisher" (for D.D.). [YellowS] (29) Spr 89, p. 36.
    "The Talbott" (estab. 1779, Bardstown, Kentucky). [Wind] (19:65) 89, p. 29.
SEN, Nabaneetä Dev
    See DEV SEN, Nabaneetä
5139. SENGUPTA, Mallika
    "The Carriers of Fire" (tr. by Paramita Banerjee and Carolyne Wright). [NewEngR]
        (11:4) Sum 89, p. 460.
    "Home" (tr. by Paramita Banerjee and Carolyne Wright). [Iowa] (19:2) Spr-Sum 89,
        p. 120.
    "Ritual Sacrifice" (tr. by Paramita Banerjee and Carolyne Wright). [Iowa] (19:2)
        Spr-Sum 89, p. 120-121.

5140. SENYI, Anita
"Esztergom Summer" (tr. of Sandor Csoori, w. Len Roberts). [InterPR] (15:2) Fall 89, p. 26.
5141. SERCHUK, Peter
"Looking Out from Herring Cove." [PoetC] (20:2) Wint 89, p. 5-7.
"A Papal Mass at Auschwitz Forty Years After the Holocaust" (June 8, 1979). [PoetC] (20:2) Wint 89, p. 3-4.
5142. SERENI, Vittorio
"The Beach" (tr. by William Jay Smith). [Poetry] (155:1/2) O-N 89, p. 19.
"First Fear" (tr. by William Jay Smith). [Poetry] (155:1/2) O-N 89, p. 23.
"It's Perhaps the Boredom" (tr. by William Jay Smith). [Poetry] (155:1/2) O-N 89, p. 21.
"Paura Prima." [Poetry] (155:1/2) O-N 89, p. 22.
"Paura Seconda." [Poetry] (155:1/2) O-N 89, p. 22.
"Sarà la Noia." [Poetry] (155:1/2) O-N 89, p. 20.
"Second Fear" (tr. by William Jay Smith). [Poetry] (155:1/2) O-N 89, p. 23.
"La Spiaggia." [Poetry] (155:1/2) O-N 89, p. 18.
5143. SERPAS, Martha
"Southern Women." [TarRP] (28:2) Spr 89, p. 6.
5144. SESHADRI, Vijay
"Beginner." [Agni] (28) 89, p. 88.
"The Refugee." [Agni] (28) 89, p. 87.
5145. SETLAK, LeAnne
"Buying Family Heirlooms at Auction." [WestB] (24) 89, p. 84.
"Nuptial Primer." [WestB] (24) 89, p. 85.
"The Tailor." [WestB] (24) 89, p. 83.
5146. SEVERANCE, Judy
"Moving On" (by Cookie Schwarz). [BellR] (12:2, #26) Fall 89, p. 43.
5147. SEXTON, Tom
"The Coldest Snow." [Zyzzyva] (5:2, #18) Sum 89, p. 51.
"Dark Hands Webbing Time." [HayF] (5) Fall 89, p. 40.
"December 22nd." [HayF] (5) Fall 89, p. 39.
"Father." [Zyzzyva] (5:2, #18) Sum 89, p. 54.
"June 22nd." [HayF] (5) Fall 89, p. 38.
"Open Season." [Zyzzyva] (5:2, #18) Sum 89, p. 52.
5148. SEYFRIED, Robin
"Poem with Questions Following." [Poetry] (153:6) Mr 89, p. 326.
5149. SHADOIAN, Jack
"Armenian Mother." [Hawai'iR] (13:1, #25) Spr 89, p. 54.
5150. SHAEFFER, Susan Fromberg
"Departures" (Selection: 4). [ConnPR] (8:1) 89, p. 7-8.
5151. SHAFARMAN, Gail
"The Last Loneliness." [HeavenB] (6) Wint-Spr 89, p. 48.
5152. SHAFFER, Eric Paul
"Six Terminal Words." [SoCoast] (5) Spr 88, p. 40-41.
SHAN, Han
See HAN, Shan
SHANG-YIN, Li
See LI, Shang-yin
SHANGYIN, Li
See LI, Shang-yin
5153. SHANKS, Armitage
"Loving Small Blanks." [Bogg] (61) 89, p. 46.
5154. SHANNON, Jeanne
"A Disappearance in Tennessee" (September 23, 1980, For David Lang, wherever he may be). [CrabCR] (6:2) Wint 89, p. 5.
"Toward the Blue Rooms of What We Remember." [CrabCR] (6:2) Wint 89, p. 5-6.
5155. SHANNON, Lisa
"Highway Rest Stop: Little Amsterdam." [HayF] (5) Fall 89, p. 46-47.
"Living in Vacationland." [HayF] (5) Fall 89, p. 45.
5156. SHAO, Yan-Xiang
"I'll Always Remember" (tr. by Edward Morin and Dennis Ding). [DenQ] (24:2) Fall 89, p. 69.
5157. SHAPIRO, Alan
"The Lesson." [TriQ] (77) Wint 89-90, p. 286-294.
"Two Elegies." [Thrpny] (39) Fall 89, p. 8.

"Underground." [Poetry] (154:1) Ap 89, p. 18-19.
"Virgil's Descent." [Poetry] (154:1) Ap 89, p. 19-20.
5158. SHAPIRO, Daniel E.
"She Dreams, Bali" (for Seow Ah Gek). [YellowS] (29) Spr 89, p. 22.
5159. SHAPIRO, David
"After a Lost Original." [Boulevard] (4:1, #10) Spr 89, p. 177.
"A Book of Glass." [Pequod] (28/29/30) 89, p. 83.
"Realism." [Pequod] (28/29/30) 89, p. 82.
5160. SHAPIRO, Gregg
"Roy's." [RagMag] (7:1) 89, p. 62.
5161. SHAPIRO, Harvey
"Belief Systems." [PoetryE] (28) Fall 89, p. 161.
"The Boast." [PoetryE] (28) Fall 89, p. 160.
"Celebrations." [Boulevard] (4:2, #11) Fall 89, p. 41.
"Evening." [PoetryE] (28) Fall 89, p. 158.
"Portrait." [PoetryE] (28) Fall 89, p. 159.
5162. SHAPIRO, Karl
"Whitman." [AmerS] (58:2) Spr 89, p. 210.
5163. SHAPIRO, Myra
"Over and Over." [Kalliope] (10:1/2) 88, p. 100.
"This Frame, Heart-Shaped." [Kalliope] (10:1/2) 88, p. 101.
SHARAT CHANDRA, G. S.
    See CHANDRA, G. S. Sharat
5164. SHARPE, Peter
"Armorica." [SouthernR] (25:3) Sum 89, p. 613-616.
5165. SHATTUCK, Roger
"Cahier de 1947" (Selections, tr. of G. Braque). [Salm] (81) Wint 89, p. 6-18.
5166. SHAVIT, Dean
"Dressing the Dead." [PoetL] (84:2) Sum 89, p. 45-47.
5167. SHAW, Alan
"Adult Books." [GrandS] (8:4) Sum 89, p. 116.
"Bar." [GrandS] (8:4) Sum 89, p. 116.
5168. SHAW, Catherine
"Melding." [Kalliope] (10:1/2) 88, p. 99.
5169. SHAW, Robert B.
"Camera Obscura." [CrossCur] (8:2) Ja 89, p. 82-83.
"The Post Office Murals Restored." [YaleR] (78:3) Spr 89, p. 370-378.
"Vanishing Act." [CrossCur] (8:2) Ja 89, p. 84-85.
5170. SHAWGO, Lucy
"Arrangement in Light and Dark." [SoCoast] (5) Spr 88, p. 8.
"A Fall Too Far." [HolCrit] (26:2) Ap 89, p. 16.
"A Hoax of History." [SoCoast] (5) Spr 88, p. 4.
"While Lions Only Roar." [SoCoast] (6) Fall 88, p. 9.
5171. SHCHERBINA, Tat'iana
"The Thousandth Anniversary of the Christianization of Rus" (tr. by J. Kates).
    [MichQR] (28:4) Fall 89, p. 737.
5172. SHEA, Marilyn
"Time, That Old Bird." [MidwQ] (31:1) Aut 89, p. 64.
5173. SHEARD, Norma Voorhees
"Domestic Artifacts" (Honorable Mention). [Nimrod] (33:1) Fall-Wint 89, p. 60-63.
"Elegy for My Mother." [Footwork] 89, p. 38-39.
"Mrs. McGuffie Is Making Wreaths." [US1] (22/23) Spr 89, p. 44.
"Spring." [Footwork] 89, p. 37.
5174. SHECK, Laurie
"Rush Hour." [ParisR] (31:111) Sum 89, p. 121-123.
5175. SHECTMAN, Robin
"The Comet Visits the City." [KenR] (NS 11:1) Wint 89, p. 84.
"The Death of a Friend" (For Mary). [KenR] (NS 11:1) Wint 89, p. 85.
"House of the Black Glass." [KenR] (NS 11:1) Wint 89, p. 84.
"January First, From Pasadena." [SenR] (19:2) Fall 89, p. 88.
5176. SHEEHAN, Marc J.
"The Library at Alexandria." [MinnR] (NS 32) Spr 89, p. 82-83.
"My Father's Singing." [CinPR] (19) Spr 89, p. 17.
SHEKERJIAN, Regina deCormier
    See DeCORMIER-SHEKERJIAN, Regina

5177. SHELDEN, Pam
"Listen." [EmeraldCR] (1989) c1988, p. 114-115.
5178. SHELDON, Glenn
"Comforting Mother Because Her Therapist Killed Himself." [Lactuca] (12) F 89, p. 43.
"Day After My Divorce." [Lactuca] (12) F 89, p. 42.
"In Springfield." [Lactuca] (12) F 89, p. 42.
5179. SHELLER, Gayle Hunter
"Dust to Dust" (for my grandmother, Pauline Nelson Adams). [BellArk] (5:6) N-D 89, p. 4.
"First Man, Boxer Man." [BellArk] (5:4) Jl-Ag 89, p. 4.
5180. SHELNUTT, Eve
"Alberte" (November 4, 1987). [Nimrod] (33:1) Fall-Wint 89, p. 121.
"At Little Sisters of the Poor." [Confr] (39/40) Fall 88-Wint 89, p. 122.
"Cafe of the Spirits." [PoetC] (20:3) Spr 89, p. 7-8.
"I Met You Here Many Times." [Nimrod] (33:1) Fall-Wint 89, p. 123.
"Matisse, 1919." [Shen] (39:1) Spr 89, p. 64.
"Taking the Crow to Market." [Nimrod] (33:1) Fall-Wint 89, p. 122.
"Where Are the Old Fates?" [Hawai'iR] (13:2, #26) Sum 89, p. 64-65.
5181. SHELTON, George
"At Sunset." [Iowa] (19:3) Fall 89, p. 58.
"The Body Is Beautiful." [Iowa] (19:3) Fall 89, p. 56.
"March." [Iowa] (19:3) Fall 89, p. 56-57.
"Three Foxes." [Iowa] (19:3) Fall 89, p. 57.
5182. SHELTON, Richard
"Those Who Name Birds." [Manoa] (1:1/2) Fall 89, p. 173-174.
5183. SHELTON, Roswitha M. Petretschek
"Black Birds." [WorldO] (22:1/2) Fall-Wint 87-88, c90, p. 23.
"The Stranger." [WorldO] (22:1/2) Fall-Wint 87-88, c90, p. 24.
SHEN, Huang
See HUANG, Shen
5184. SHEPARD, Keith
"Earth Freedom." [Lactuca] (13) N 89, p. 58.
5185. SHEPARD, Neil
"The Missing Ear." [Chelsea] (48) 89, p. 114-116.
"Morning Composition." [DenQ] (24:2) Fall 89, p. 90.
"One Night." [BellR] (12:2, #26) Fall 89, p. 20-21.
5186. SHEPARD, Roy
"Great Blue Heron." [Comm] (116:13) Jl 14, 89, p. 402.
"Hubris in March." [Comm] (116:6) Mr 24, 89, p. 178.
"The Interloper." [Comm] (116:19) N 3, 89, p. 590.
5187. SHEPHERD, J. Barrie
"I'm Dreaming." [ChrC] (106:37) D 6, 89, p. 1141.
"Temple Cleansing." [ChrC] (106:10) Mr 22-29, 89, p. 304.
5188. SHEPPARD, S. R.
"Signals." [SmPd] (26:2 #76) Spr 89, p. 17.
5189. SHER, Steven
"The Atlantic As Origin of Life." [InterPR] (15:2) Fall 89, p. 122.
"Deep Water." [KanQ] (21:3) Sum 89, p. 87.
"Swimming the Neversink." [Pembroke] (21) 89, p. 132-133.
5190. SHERBONDY, Ellen
"Aging in America." [CentR] (33:2) Spr 89, p. 137-138.
"On Growing Begonias." [CentR] (33:2) Spr 89, p. 138-139.
5191. SHERLOCK, Karl
"A Stalinist Building and Its Reasons." [FreeL] (1) 89, p. 32-33.
"A Stalinist Building and Its Reasons." [Jacaranda] (4:1) Spr-Sum 89, p. 32.
5192. SHERMAN, Charlotte Watson
"A Season." [PaintedB] (37) 89, p. 55-58.
5193. SHERRILL, Jan-Mitchell
"Waiting to Go Home." [SoCoast] (6) Fall 88, p. 18.
5194. SHERRILL, Steven
"It Was Always Cold." [FloridaR] (16:2/3) Fall-Wint 89, p. 151.
5195. SHERRILL, Susan Tryon
"Not so unusual." [EmeraldCR] (1989) c1988, p. x-xi.
5196. SHERRY, James
"Our Nuclear Heritage" (Selections from Appendix B: "Nukeman"). [CentralP] (15)

Spr 89, p. 29-32.
SHERWIN, Judith Johnson
        See JOHNSON, Judith E. (Judith Emlyn)
5197. SHEVIN, David
        "Napoleón and Adolfo." [Pig] (15) 88, p. 89.
        "Overdue Letter." [MidAR] (9:1) 89, p. 140-149.
5198. SHIELDS, Bill
        "There Are Those Nights When." [Footwork] 89, p. 53.
5199. SHIELDS, Carol
        "Entry." [Quarry] (38:4) Fall 89, p. 5.
5200. SHIH, Chien-wu
        "Playing with a White Deer in the Mountains" (tr. by Maureen Robertson). [LitR]
                (32:3) Spr 89, p. 394.
SHIH, Su
        See SU, Shih
SHIH-WU
        See STONEHOUSE
SHIMPEI, Kusano
        See KUSANO, Shimpei
SHIN, Su
        See SU, Shih
5201. SHINDER, Jason
        "Bordeaux." [AmerPoR] (18:3) My-Je 89, p. 33.
        "From Magritte's Notebooks." [Pequod] (28/29/30) 89, p. 103-104.
5202. SHINGYO, Hannya
        "Maha Prajna Paramita Hridaya Sutra" (tr. by Gary Snyder). [AlphaBS] (6) Wint
                89-90, p. 38-39.
5203. SHIPLEY, Betty
        "Boy with Kiowa Eyes." [Nimrod] (32:2) Spr-Sum 89, p. 65.
5204. SHIPLEY, Vivian
        "The Cellar House." [OxfordM] (5:1) Spr-Sum 89, p. 12.
5205. SHIPP, R. D.
        "For Reason's Sake." [NowestR] (27:2) 89, p. 60-61.
5206. SHIRAISHI, Kazuko
        "Al's Inside His Sax and Won't Come Out" (tr. by Sally Ito). [Rampike] (6:2) 88, p.
                67.
        "March" (tr. by Sally Ito). [Rampike] (6:2) 88, p. 67.
        "Sheep's Eye" (tr. by Graeme Wilson). [ConnPR] (8:1) 89, p. 20.
5207. SHIVELY, Bill
        "Stone Cold Days." [Bogg] (61) 89, p. 13.
5208. SHOAF, Diann Blakely
        "Cézanne at Aix, 1886." [SouthernHR] (23:4) Fall 89, p. 372.
        "The Lesson." [OxfordM] (5:1) Spr-Sum 89, p. 17.
        "Solstice." [Verse] (6:1) Mr 89, p. 52.
        "Summer Sublet." [AntR] (47:2) Spr 89, p. 204.
        "Tinea Versicolor." [DenQ] (24:2) Fall 89, p. 91.
        "Unfinished Sketch of an American Woman" (-- John Singer Sargent, London,
                1891). [SouthernHR] (23:2) Spr 89, p. 120.
        "Vintage." [WestB] (23) 89, p. 82.
        "Widow at Thirty." [TarRP] (29:1) Fall 89, p. 35.
5209. SHOLL, Betsy
        "The Argument." [WestB] (25) 89, p. 41.
        "The Hospital State." [HangL] (54) 89, p. 43-44.
        "Joining the Circus." [Field] (41) Fall 89, p. 64-65.
        "Pick a Card." [Field] (41) Fall 89, p. 62-63.
        "Thinking of You, Hiroshima." [WestB] (25) 89, p. 42-43.
        "Three Deaths." [Field] (41) Fall 89, p. 66-67.
        "What the Moon Won't Let Me Forget." [WestB] (25) 89, p. 43-44.
5210. SHOMER, Enid
        "Datelines: Jacqueline Cochran at War's End" (9 poems). [ApalQ] (32) 89, p. 1-12.
        "First Sunset at Outler's Ranch." [SilverFR] (16) Spr 89, p. 41.
        "From the Wailing Wall." [Kalliope] (10:1/2) 88, p. 119.
        "Kaffeeklatsch in Chungking." [PoetL] (84:3) Fall 89, p. 51-52.
        "The Mirror Divides" (New York City). [PoetL] (84:3) Fall 89, p. 53-55.
        "Pool Party." [ApalQ] (31) 89, p. 49-50.
        "Refusing the Call" (For Henry Roth, author of *Call It Sleep*). [Kalliope] (11:3) 89,

p. 63.
5211. SHORB, Michael
"A Flower Responds to Certain Criticisms Advanced by the Cathedral." [Comm]
(116:9) My 5, 89, p. 273.
5212. SHORE, Jane
"The Legend of the Trouble Dolls." [Pequod] (28/29/30) 89, p. 29-30.
5213. SHORT, Gary
"After My Brother's Death." [PoetryE] (28) Fall 89, p. 72.
SHPANCER, Brittany Newmark
See NEWMARK-SHPANCER, Brittany
5214. SHRAEDER, Deanna
"The Rules Changed." [CrossCur] (8:3) Apr 89, p. 104-105.
5215. SHU, Ting
"Perhaps" (for the loneliness of an author, tr. by Carolyn Kizer). [LitR] (32:3) Spr
89, p. 320.
"The Singing Flower" (7 selections: I, II, IV, V, VIII, X, XVI, tr. by Carolyn
Kizer). [LitR] (32:3) Spr 89, p. 318-320.
5216. SHUMAKER, Peggy
"Hunting Scorpions." [HayF] (5) Fall 89, p. 101-102.
"Mask Making." [Ploughs] (15:1) 89, p. 123.
"Occupied Territory." [HayF] (5) Fall 89, p. 99-100.
"The Provider." [Manoa] (1:1/2) Fall 89, p. 160-161.
5217. SHUMATE, Kathleen
"The Excavation." [MissouriR] (12:2) 89, p. 50-51.
5218. SHUMWAY, Mary
"The Golden Goose Lays Another Egg in My Mailbox." [Northeast] (ser. 5:1) Wint
89-90, p. 8.
"Modulation." [Northeast] (ser. 5:1) Wint 89-90, p. 7.
"Mysteries." [Northeast] (ser. 5:1) Wint 89-90, p. 9.
5219. SHURIN, Aaron
"Blue Shade." [Notus] (4:1) Spr 89, p. 72.
"Breath." [Notus] (4:1) Spr 89, p. 73.
"Connection." [Temblor] (10) 89, p. 29.
"Continuous Thunder." [Temblor] (9) 89, p. 71.
"His Promise." [Temblor] (10) 89, p. 27.
"Honor Roll." [Acts] (10) 89, p. 20.
"Into Distances." [Sulfur] (9:2, #25) Fall 89, p. 180-185.
"On Low." [Temblor] (10) 89, p. 126.
"One Evening." [Temblor] (10) 89, p. 28.
"Sailed." [Temblor] (10) 89, p. 30.
"Sweeping." [Acts] (10) 89, p. 19.
"Temptation." [Temblor] (9) 89, p. 72.
"The Third Floor." [Temblor] (10) 89, p. 25.
"A Union." [Screens] (1) 89, p. 170.
5220. SHUTTY, Jane
"After You" (Prose Poem Winter, the First Short Grain Contest). [Grain] (17:3) Fall
89, p. 74.
5221. SIDOLI, Graziella
"The Green Rose" (Selections: 2 poems, tr. of Paolo Valesio). [Screens] (1) 89, p.
184-189.
5222. SIEDLECKI, Peter
"Lesson." [StoneC] (17:1/2) Fall-Wint 89-90, p. 31.
5223. SIEFKIN, David
"Summer Morning" (tr. of Francois Jacqmin). [Vis] (31) 89, p. 30.
5224. SIEGEL, Jane
"Missed Children." [PassN] (10:2) Sum 89, p. 23.
5225. SIEGEL, Joan I.
"Our Father." [WestB] (24) 89, p. 64.
5226. SIEGEL, Robert
"Bronze Horses." [CreamCR] (13:2) Fall 89, p. 123.
"Muskellunge." [Verse] (6:1) Mr 89, p. 54-55.
"Tiger." [Verse] (6:1) Mr 89, p. 55-56.
5227. SIEGENTHALER, Peter
"HIV Poem." [Os] (28) 89, p. 4.
"She grew into a flame." [Os] (28) 89, p. 5.

5228. SIEMS, Lawrence
  "California Song, and Variation on a Theme." [SouthernPR] (29:1) Spr 89, p.
    23-25.
5229. SIEVERS, Kelly
  "Samples" (Johanna Mulvihill McMahon, 1850-1913). [GreensboroR] (47) Wint
    89-90, p. 40.
5230. SIGNORELLI-PAPPAS, Rita
  "Christmas Eve." [ColEng] (51:5) S 89, p. 479.
  "A Sister's Wedding." [ColEng] (51:5) S 89, p. 478.
5231. SIGURDSSON, Olafur Johann
  "Folk Verse" (tr. by Alan Boucher). [Vis] (31) 89, p. 19.
5232. SILAS, Paul (Paul N.)
  "Pieces of Night" (From "Poems from Prison"). [MidwQ] (30:4) Sum 89, p. 452.
  "Pieces of Night" (from "Poems from Prison, 123). [BelPoJ] (39:3) Spr 89, p.
    26-27.
  "Pieces of Night: Poems from Prison" (Selection: 31). [SouthernPR] (29:1) Spr 89,
    p. 29.
  "Pieces of Night: Poems from Prison" (Selection: 92). [Outbr] (20) 89, p. 19-20.
  "Pieces of Night, Poems from Prison #35." [Hawai'iR] (13:2, #26) Sum 89, p. 20.
  "Pieces of Night: Poems from Prison, 103." [MassR] (30:2) Sum 89, p. 338-340.
  "The Prison Poems, #188." [Witness] (2:2/3) Sum-Fall 88, p. 13.
5233. SILBER, Kathy
  "On a Picture of Self with Hoe, Cultivating Plum Blossoms in Moonlight" (tr. of Wu
    Tsao). [LitR] (32:3) Spr 89, p. 397.
  "Song in Sixteen Words" (tr. of Wu Tsao). [LitR] (32:3) Spr 89, p. 396.
  "To the Tune of 'Tung Hsien Ko'" (tr. of Wu Tsao). [LitR] (32:3) Spr 89, p. 396.
5234. SILESKY, Barry
  "Blue Rising" (after "Le Couple" by Nancy Spero). [AnotherCM] (20) 89, p. 85-86.
  "Nightgown with Tulips." [SouthernPR] (29:1) Spr 89, p. 26-27.
5235. SILK, Dennis
  "Stingy Kids: Prose Poems About the Situation." [GrandS] (8:2) Wint 89, p. 81-93.
5236. SILKIN, Jon
  "Amber." [Bogg] (61) 89, p. 8-10.
  "Famine" (for Kevin and Trisha Fitzpatrick). [Bogg] (61) 89, p. 5-8.
5237. SILLIMAN, Ron
  "Oz" (Selection, being a part of The Alphabet, for Fred Glass & Maureen Katz).
    [Screens] (1) 89, p. 106-109.
  "Toner" (Excerpt). [MinnR] (NS 32) Spr 89, p. 51-54.
  "Toner" (Selections). [Talisman] (3) Fall 89, p. 76-79.
  "Toner" (Selection: "Brucebook"). [Sulfur] (9:1, #24) Spr 89, p. 13-35.
  "Toner" (Selections. Brucebook). [Zyzzyva] (5:1, #17) Spr 89, p. 73-85.
5238. SILVA ACEVEDO, Manuel
  "Tres Imágenes y una Diosa Blanca." [Inti] (29/30) Primavera-Otoño 89, p.
    257-259.
5239. SILVERSTEIN, David
  "In Such Tumbling Does Love Begin Its Fall." [YellowS] (32) Wint 89, p. 5.
  "A More Ordinary Provocation." [YellowS] (31) Aut 89, p. 33.
5240. SIMAS, Jospeh
  "The Tiresome Ambiguities of Action." [Screens] (1) 89, p. 126.
5241. SIMIC, Charles
  "Babylon." [Field] (41) Fall 89, p. 56.
  "Beyond Appearances." [GrandS] (8:3) Spr 89, p. 69.
  "Crepuscule with Nellie." [GrandS] (8:3) Spr 89, p. 71.
  "Happiness" (tr. of Aleksandar Ristovic). [ParisR] (31:110) Spr 89, p. 171.
  "The Initiate." [Antaeus] (62) Spr 89, p. 210-212.
  "Landscape with Snow" (tr. of Aleksandar Ristovic). [ParisR] (31:110) Spr 89, p.
    170.
  "A Letter." [GrandS] (8:3) Spr 89, p. 72.
  "Madonnas Touched Up with a Goatee." [NewL] (56:2/3) Wint 89-Spr 90, p. 252.
  "Midpoint." [NewL] (56:2/3) Wint 89-Spr 90, p. 251.
  "Misfortune on the Way." [Field] (41) Fall 89, p. 57.
  "The North." [Field] (41) Fall 89, p. 53.
  "Old Motif" (tr. of Aleksandar Ristovic). [ParisR] (31:110) Spr 89, p. 169.
  "Old Mountain Road" (for Goody and Maida Smith). [NewL] (56:2/3) Wint 89-Spr
    90, p. 250.
  "Out in the Open" (tr. of Aleksandar Ristovic). [ParisR] (31:110) Spr 89, p. 172.

"Pyramids and Sphinxes." [Field] (41) Fall 89, p. 55.
"The Scarecrow." [WestHR] (43:2) Sum 89, p. 97.
"Shelley" (for M. Follain). [NewL] (56:2/3) Wint 89-Spr 90, p. 255-256.
"Shepherd" (tr. of Tomaz Salamun, w. Sonja Kravanja-Gross). [WestHR] (43:1)
    Spr 89, p. 64.
"St. Thomas Aquinas." [NewL] (56:2/3) Wint 89-Spr 90, p. 253-254.
"To a Fool" (tr. of Aleksandar Ristovic). [ParisR] (31:110) Spr 89, p. 168.
"Untitled: Dürer's hare hisses and falls from a great height" (tr. of Tomaz Salamun).
    [Field] (40) Spr 89, p. 73-74.
"The White Room." [NewL] (56:2/3) Wint 89-Spr 90, p. 257-258.
"Whose Eyes to Catch, Whose Eyes to Avoid." [WestHR] (43:2) Sum 89, p. 96.
"The Window." [Field] (41) Fall 89, p. 54.
"A Word." [GrandS] (8:3) Spr 89, p. 70.
5242. SIMISON, Greg
    "Postcards from Arcadia." [Dandel] (16:2) Fall-Wint 89, p. 35-37.
5243. SIMKO, Daniel
    "Against Our Forgetting." [GrahamHR] (12) Spr 89, p. 34-37.
    "Autumn Evening" (to Karl Rock, tr. of Georg Trakl). [DenQ] (23:3/4) Wint-Spr 89,
        p. 124.
    "A Field of Red Poppies." [GrahamHR] (12) Spr 89, p. 33.
    "Hymns for a Rosary" (tr. of Georg Trakl). [DenQ] (23:3/4) Wint-Spr 89, p.
        122-123.
    "Psalm" (tr. of Georg Trakl). [AmerPoR] (18:1) Ja-F 89, p. 37.
    "Transformation of Evil" (tr. of Georg Trakl). [AmerPoR] (18:1) Ja-F 89, p. 38.
5244. SIMMERMAN, Jim
    "Beast Zoo." [Journal] (12:2) Fall-Wint 88-89, p. 51-52.
    "Cheers." [NewL] (56:2/3) Wint 89-Spr 90, p. 266.
    "The Dead Madonnas of Santiago." [NewL] (56:2/3) Wint 89-Spr 90, p. 259-260.
    "Distance." [Poetry] (154:4) Jl 89, p. 228-229.
    "Inside Out." [Journal] (12:2) Fall-Wint 88-89, p. 49.
    "Kite." [Poetry] (154:4) Jl 89, p. 227.
    "My Old Man." [NewL] (56:2/3) Wint 89-Spr 90, p. 260-262.
    "Night of the Living Dead." [SouthernPR] (29:1) Spr 89, p. 28-29.
    "Outside In." [Journal] (12:2) Fall-Wint 88-89, p. 50.
    "Yoyo." [NewL] (56:2/3) Wint 89-Spr 90, p. 263-265.
5245. SIMMIAS of Rhodes (c. 300 B.C.)
    "Axe" (tr. by Stanley Lombardo). [Temblor] (10) 89, p. 201.
    "Egg" (tr. by Stanley Lombardo). [Temblor] (10) 89, p. 202.
    "Wings" (tr. by Stanley Lombardo). [Temblor] (10) 89, p. 200.
5246. SIMMONS, James
    "Nigerian Cattleman's Song." [MissouriR] (12:2) 89, p. 26-27.
    "Sex, Rectitude, and Loneliness." [NoDaQ] (57:1) Wint 89, p. 123-126.
5247. SIMMONS, Patricia
    "The Welsh Curse." [NewRena] (7:3, #23) 89, p. 183.
5248. SIMON, John Oliver
    "Adentro." [Lactuca] (12) F 89, p. 12.
    "Anahuac" (for David Huerta). [Lactuca] (12) F 89, p. 8-9.
    "Blue Tryptich" (tr. of Alberto Blanco). [Lactuca] (12) F 89, p. 14-15.
    "Campiento de Chajul." [Lactuca] (12) F 89, p. 11-12.
    "The Drowned Man." [Lactuca] (12) F 89, p. 10-11.
    "Green Tryptich" (tr. of Alberto Blanco). [Lactuca] (12) F 89, p. 16-17.
    "Insomnia VII / Calle Garcisalo." [Caliban] (7) 89, p. 82.
    "Of Fierce Origin" (tr. of Raúl Antonio Cota). [Caliban] (7) 89, p. 78.
    "The Possible Myth" (tr. of Raúl Antonio Cota). [Caliban] (7) 89, p. 79-81.
    "Red Tryptich" (tr. of Alberto Blanco). [Lactuca] (12) F 89, p. 13-14.
5249. SIMON, Josef
    "High-Flats and TV Screens" (tr. by Jarmila and Ian Milner). [Verse] (6:2) Je 89, p.
        63.
5250. SIMON, Louise
    "Church Service" (Prose Poem Winter, the First Short Grain Contest). [Grain]
        (17:3) Fall 89, p. 71.
5251. SIMON, M. B.
    "Influence." [Writer] (102:6) Je 89, p. 28.
5252. SIMON, Maurya
    "Breakwater." [SouthernR] (25:1) Wint 89, p. 176-177.
    "Cannibal Galaxies." [SwampR] (1:4) Sum 89, p. 8.

"Cloud Watching on Mt. Baldy." [SwampR] (1:4) Sum 89, p. 9.
"Ensenada." [SwampR] (1:4) Sum 89, p. 10.
"Evening Triads." [SwampR] (1:4) Sum 89, p. 7.
"The Palmist." [Salm] (81) Wint 89, p. 100-101.
"Post Meridien." [Poetry] (153:5) F 89, p. 253.
"Rattlesnake." [LaurelR] (23:2) Sum 89, p. 84-85.
"Snails." [SwampR] (1:4) Sum 89, p. 60.
"The Surreal Man." [Salm] (81) Wint 89, p. 99-100.
"Theme and Variations." [Poetry] (153:5) F 89, p. 254.
"The View from Here." [Poetry] (153:5) F 89, p. 251-253.
5253. SIMONIDES
"For the Spartan Dead at Thermopylae" (tr. by James Michie). [GrandS] (8:4) Sum
89, p. 79.
5254. SIMONSON, Michael
"My Daughters of War." [RagMag] (7:1) 89, p. 50.
"Romanov Necklace." [RagMag] (7:1) 89, p. 51.
"That Moon." [RagMag] (7:1) 89, p. 52.
5255. SIMONSUURI, Kirsti
"March Fires" (tr. by Jascha Kessler). [MidAR] (9:1) 89, p. 161.
5256. SIMPSON, Batista
"I Know You Don't Like Me to Act Stupid." [RagMag] (7:1) 89, p. 55.
"Last Request from a Deserter." [RagMag] (7:1) 89, p. 54.
5257. SIMPSON, Grace
"Unnatural Aging of Things." [CumbPR] (8:2) Spr 89, p. 66.
5258. SIMPSON, Louis
"The Book of the Opera." [SouthernR] (25:1) Wint 89, p. 133.
"Colonial Education." [SouthernR] (25:1) Wint 89, p. 134-135.
"Harry and Grace." [Witness] (3:1) Spr 89, p. 84-85.
"Jabez." [SouthernR] (25:1) Wint 89, p. 135-136.
"The Magic Carpet." [Hudson] (41:4) Wint 89, p. 635-644.
"The Naturalist and the Volcano." [NewL] (56:2/3) Wint 89-Spr 90, p. 268-269.
"Neptune's Daughter." [SouthernR] (25:1) Wint 89, p. 132.
"The Peace March." [NewL] (56:2/3) Wint 89-Spr 90, p. 267.
"Riverside Drive." [SouthernR] (25:1) Wint 89, p. 136.
"Saudi Arabia." [NewL] (56:2/3) Wint 89-Spr 90, p. 270.
"Trouble." [NewL] (56:2/3) Wint 89-Spr 90, p. 271-273.
"Villa Rosalinda." [SouthernR] (25:1) Wint 89, p. 138-139.
"Volksgrenadiers." [SouthernR] (25:1) Wint 89, p. 137.
5259. SIMPSON, Megan
"B Movie." [BlackWR] (16:1) Fall-Wint 89, p. 84.
5260. SIMPSON, Michael
"Happy New Year." [Hawai'iR] (13:2, #26) Sum 89, p. 135.
5261. SIMPSON, Nancy
"Titian." [TexasR] (10:1/2) Spr-Sum 89, p. 93.
5262. SIMPSON, Richard
"Cubs vs. Giants, Cable TV, Candlestick." [LaurelR] (23:1) Wint 89, p. 27-28.
5263. SINCLAIR, John
"Hell Hound on My Trail" (for Celia Sinclair, from "Fattening Frogs for Snakes,"
Delta Sound Suite). [Notus] (4:1) Spr 89, p. 74-77.
5264. SINCLAIR, Marcia
"Too Much." [Lactuca] (12) F 89, p. 43.
5265. SINCLAIR, Marjorie
"Birthday." [MissouriR] (12:1) 89, p. 28.
"Lonely" (tr. of Difan Zou, w. the author). [BambooR] (44) Fall 89, p. 8.
"To My Mother" (tr. of Difan Zou, w. the author). [BambooR] (44) Fall 89, p. 7.
5266. SINDALL, Susan
"The Old Man at Pushkin's Funeral." [HeliconN] (20) 89, p. 79.
"The Wake." [KenR] (NS 11:2) Spr 89, p. 12.
"White Skiff." [KenR] (NS 11:2) Spr 89, p. 13.
5267. SINE, Georgia
"Tornado Warning." [ThRiPo] (33/34) 89, p. 52.
SINGDE, Nalan
See NALAN SINGDE
5268. SINGER, Frieda
"Ways of Dying" (After viewing Claude Lanzmann's film, *Shoah*). [NegC] (9:2) 89,
p. 68-69.

5269. SINGH, Kedarnath
"An Argument About Horses" (tr. by Vinay Dharwadker). [TriQ] (77) Wint 89-90,
p. 149-150.
"The Carpenter and the Bird" (in Hindi). [TriQ] (77) Wint 89-90, p. 147.
"The Carpenter and the Bird" (tr. by Vinay Dharwadker). [TriQ] (77) Wint 89-90, p.
145-146.
"On Reading a Love Poem" (tr. by Vinay Dharwadker). [TriQ] (77) Wint 89-90, p.
143-144.
"Signature" (tr. by Vinay Dharwadker). [TriQ] (77) Wint 89-90, p. 140-141.
5270. SINGLETON, Martin
"Covetousness" (From "The Seven Deadly Sins"). [CrossC] (11:1) 89, p. 18.
"Gluttony" (From "The Seven Deadly Sins"). [CrossC] (11:1) 89, p. 18.
5271. SINHA, Kabita
"Curse" (tr. by Enakshi Chatterjee and Carolyne Wright). [Trans] (21) Spr 89, p.
150.
"The Diamond of Character" (tr. by Swapna Mitra and Carolyne Wright). [Trans]
(21) Spr 89, p. 153.
"The Last Door's Name Is Sorrow" (tr. by Swapna Mitra and Carolyne Wright).
[Trans] (21) Spr 89, p. 151-152.
"Waterfall" (tr. by Enakshi Chatterjee and Carolyne Wright). [Trans] (21) Spr 89, p.
149.
5272. SIPE, D. D.
"A Living Legend" (Largemouth Bass). [Wind] (19:65) 89, p. 31.
5273. SJÖBERG, Leif
"Aniara" (Selections: V, XXIX, tr. of Harry Martinson, w. Stephen Klass).
[Pequod] (26/27) 89, p. 35-36.
"Autumnal Journey" (tr. of Johannes Edfelt, w. David Ignatow). [Pequod] (26/27)
89, p. 26.
"This Is You" (tr. of Johannes Edfelt, w. David Ignatow). [Pequod] (26/27) 89, p.
26.
5274. SKAU, Michael
"After the Bomb" (XXI, XXIV, XXV). [Sequoia] (33:1) Sum 89, p. 30-32.
"News." [CarolQ] (41:2) Wint 89, p. 29.
"Roommates." [CarolQ] (41:2) Wint 89, p. 28.
5275. SKEATH, Meredith Briggs
"Bridget McGonagle Briggs (1887-1913)." [VirQR] (65:4) Aut 89, p. 659.
"Outside the Orchard." [VirQR] (65:4) Aut 89, p. 659-660.
5276. SKEEN, Anita
"The Artist Travels the Kansas Turnpike, Wichita to Topeka, on Valentine's Day."
[KanQ] (21:3) Sum 89, p. 17.
"Note Tossed Out in a Bottle" (Seaton Honorable Mention Poem). [KanQ] (21:3)
Sum 89, p. 16.
"Vespers" (with Carol Barrett). [SoCoast] (5) Spr 88, p. 13.
"What It Would Be Like." [Ploughs] (15:4) Wint 89-90, p. 202-205.
5277. SKEEN, Tim
"She Asks If I Love Her." [Sonora] (17) Spr-Sum 89, p. 10.
5278. SKILLMAN, Judith
"Attic Windows." [SenR] (19:2) Fall 89, p. 47-48.
"The Bird in the Attic Window" (for Win). [SenR] (19:2) Fall 89, p. 45-46.
"Estrangement Suites." [CrabCR] (6:2) Wint 89, p. 28.
"Improvisations for Echo." [PoetryNW] (30:3) Aut 89, p. 21-23.
"In the Parlor of Elliptical Billiards." [MidwQ] (31:1) Aut 89, p. 66-68.
"The Indoor Garden." [NowestR] (27:2) 89, p. 16.
"The Mist As Subject." [MidwQ] (31:1) Aut 89, p. 65.
"Pot Made from a Hillside" (for Ruth). [CrabCR] (6:2) Wint 89, p. 29.
"The Rabbi's Wife." [CrabCR] (6:2) Wint 89, p. 29.
"Roofers." [CumbPR] (8:2) Spr 89, p. 34.
"Studying the Abstraction." [BellR] (12:2, #26) Fall 89, p. 13-14.
"The Woman Who Thinks She Is Me." [MalR] (86) Spr 89, p. 50-51.
5279. SKINNER, Douglas Reid
"The Fig Tree" (in memoriam Sydney Clouts." [AmerPoR] (18:4) Jl-Ag 89, p. 39.
5280. SKINNER, Jeffrey
"The Dangerous Teaching." [Poetry] (154:6) S 89, p. 311-312.
"Like Water." [Poetry] (154:1) Ap 89, p. 17.
"Living Poets" (For Michael Collier). [Poetry] (154:6) S 89, p. 312-313.
"Thanksgiving Over the Water." [CrossCur] (8:2) Ja 89, p. 141.

"Those Who Insist They've Returned" (For Gail Gorham). [Poetry] (154:1) Ap 89,
p. 16-17.
"To John Donne and His Dogs." [CrossCur] (8:2) Ja 89, p. 139-140.
5281. SKINNER, Knute
"The Next Day." [Vis] (29) 89, p. 35.
5282. SKLAN, Susan
"Singing the Blues." [Kalliope] (11:3) 89, p. 55.
"A Sister's Visit." [SingHM] (16) 89, p. 74.
5283. SKLOOT, Floyd
"Blanche Morton." [Shen] (39:3) Fall 89, p. 87-88.
"Brain Scan." [NowestR] (27:3) 89, p. 33.
"The Fury." [PraS] (63:3) Fall 89, p. 91-93.
"In the Coast Range." [Shen] (39:2) Sum 89, p. 69.
"The Light That Streams Through." [SilverFR] (16) Spr 89, p. 10-13.
"The Melody Girl." [ThRiPo] (31/32) 88, p. 47.
"Music Appreciation." [PoetryE] (28) Fall 89, p. 8.
"Neighbor's Complaint." [WestB] (24) 89, p. 23.
"The Pure Tongue." [Shen] (39:2) Sum 89, p. 68-69.
"The Search." [Shen] (39:3) Fall 89, p. 88.
"Strike It Rich." [SilverFR] (16) Spr 89, p. 14.
"Widow's Morning." [PraS] (63:3) Fall 89, p. 93-95.
"Wild Light." [PraS] (63:3) Fall 89, p. 90-91.
"Wild Light" (Collection of 17 poems. For My Mother and Father). [SilverFR] (18)
89, 32 p.
5284. SKOYLES, John
"Small Diary." [NoAmR] (274:4) D 89, p. 40.
5285. SKRUPSKELIS, Viktoria
"Coffee House, with Pigeons" (tr. of Judita Vaiciunaite, w. Stuart Friebert). [Field]
(41) Fall 89, p. 71.
"Untitled: I'll freeze, a column of salt" (tr. of Judita Vaiciunaite, w. Stuart Friebert).
[Field] (41) Fall 89, p. 69.
"Wild Plum in Bloom" (tr. of Judita Vaiciunaite, w. Stuart Friebert). [Field] (41) Fall
89, p. 68.
"Winter II" (tr. of Judita Vaiciunaite, w. Stuart Friebert). [Field] (41) Fall 89, p. 70.
5286. SLADE, Giles
"Concerning Fireflies and Gravity." [Rampike] (6:2) 88, p. 76.
5287. SLAVEN, Amy
"Disassembling." [HayF] (4) Spr 89, p. 69.
"Effects of Gin and Childhood on My Sister." [HayF] (4) Spr 89, p. 68.
5288. SLAVEN, Fred
"Our Last Day." [PaintedB] (38) 89, p. 59.
5289. SLAVENS, Kerry
"Genie's Birds." [PraF] (10:4, #49) Wint 89-90, p. 42.
5290. SLAVITT, David (David R.)
"The Epistulae ex Ponto: Book III" (tr. of Ovid). [SouthwR] (74:2) Spr 89, p.
220-224.
"Epistulae ex Ponto: Book III" (tr. of Ovid). [TexasR] (10:1/2) Spr-Sum 89, p.
48-49.
"Job's Wife." [PraS] (63:1) Spr 89, p. 63-64.
"Letter from the Black Sea" (1. To Brutus, tr. of Ovid). [Trans] (22) Fall 89, p.
219-221.
"Sentence." [Shen] (39:3) Fall 89, p. 23.
"Vlad." [Shen] (39:3) Fall 89, p. 24-25.
"Vlad's Nocturne." [LaurelR] (23:1) Wint 89, p. 57.
"Vlad's Serenade." [LaurelR] (23:1) Wint 89, p. 56.
5291. SLAVUTYCH, Yar
"The Firebird" (tr. by Orysia Ferbey). [CanLit] (120) Spr 89, p. 90.
"Poem: It was when you arrived in white" (tr. by Orysia Ferbey). [CanLit] (120) Spr
89, p. 115.
5292. SLAYTON, Ann
"Ghost Dancers." [PoetL] (84:2) Sum 89, p. 48.
5293. SLEIGH, Tom
"Afterwords." [Agni] (28) 89, p. 48-50.
"Aubade." [YaleR] (78:4) Sum 89, p. 625-626.
"Fish Story." [GrandS] (9:1) Aut 89, p. 118-120.
"Marché aux Oiseaux." [WestHR] (43:1) Spr 89, p. 43.

"Stone." [WestHR] (43:1) Spr 89, p. 44-45.
5294. SLOAN, Gerry
"Floods." [WritersF] (15) Fall 89, p. 45.
"Raising Crazy Horse." [WritersF] (15) Fall 89, p. 44-45.
5295. SLOAN, Margy
"The One the Other Will Contain." [Acts] (10) 89, p. 82-87.
SLOMKOWSKA, Luisa
See SLOMKOWSKA, Lusia
5296. SLOMKOWSKA, Lusia
"The Eel Catchers" (Poland, Summer 1977). [TarRP] (29:1) Fall 89, p. 25-27.
"Persistence of Memory" (after Dali). [QW] (29) Sum-Fall 89, p. 145-146.
"The Polka Hour." [QW] (29) Sum-Fall 89, p. 143-144.
5297. SLOTA, Richard
"Elegy: A Ten Year Old White Female with a Defective Pituitary." [BlueBldgs] (11)
89, p. 28.
5298. SLOWINSKI, Stephanie
"The Catch." [SouthernPR] (29:2) Fall 89, p. 20.
"Housewarming." [CreamCR] (13:2) Fall 89, p. 73.
"My Sister's Overdose." [CreamCR] (13:2) Fall 89, p. 72.
5299. SMAILS, William
"I Love the Backwards of Rowing." [BellArk] (5:3) My-Je 89, p. 1.
"Ocra." [BellArk] (5:3) My-Je 89, p. 5.
"The Pacific Electric Power Plant." [BellArk] (5:6) N-D 89, p. 3.
"Poem on My 38th Birthday for Margaret, My Mother." [BellArk] (5:6) N-D 89, p.
10.
5300. SMALL, Abbott
"Recovering the Powers of Speech." [Wind] (19:64) 89, p. 44.
5301. SMALLFIELD, Edward
"At the Hospital." [Margin] (9) 89, p. 78.
"The Book." [Margin] (9) 89, p. 78.
"Cattaraugus Creek" (for Bill). [Zyzzyva] (5:1, #17) Spr 89, p. 126.
"Fennel." [Margin] (9) 89, p. 76.
"Insomnia." [Margin] (9) 89, p. 74.
"Radio." [FiveFR] (7) 89, p. 4.
"The Room." [FiveFR] (7) 89, p. 5.
"War of Attrition." [Margin] (9) 89, p. 77.
"The Window." [Margin] (9) 89, p. 75.
5302. SMART, Carolyn
"Buffalo." [Event] (18:2) Sum 89, p. 13.
"Christmas in the Bosom of the Family." [Event] (18:2) Sum 89, p. 12.
"Driving Through the Drakensberg." [Event] (18:2) Sum 89, p. 8-9.
"For My Mother, Who Loved Southern Africa Although She Never Went There."
[Event] (18:2) Sum 89, p. 7.
"Outside the Teahouse of the Blue Lagoon." [Event] (18:2) Sum 89, p. 10-11.
5303. SMIEJA, Florian
"For Alicja Martyred by the Immigration Office." [CanLit] (120) Spr 89, p. 5.
5304. SMITH, Arthur
"Ordinary Crambles." [GeoR] (43:4) Wint 89, p. 750.
"Rue." [PraS] (63:2) Sum 89, p. 112.
"The Sun Sessions." [PraS] (63:2) Sum 89, p. 113-114.
"Wedding on the West Coast." [PraS] (63:2) Sum 89, p. 111.
5305. SMITH, Barbara
"Oddly American." [PoetL] (84:2) Sum 89, p. 29-31.
5306. SMITH, Beatrice
"Julia." [US1] (22/23) Spr 89, p. 6.
5307. SMITH, Bruce
"Eve of Geneva." [Agni] (28) 89, p. 91.
"I Pray for No More Reagans." [Agni] (28) 89, p. 89-90.
5308. SMITH, Carolyn Reams
"Allergic Reaction." [EngJ] (78:2) F 89, p. 97.
5309. SMITH, Carolyn Steinhoff
"Housework." [Nimrod] (33:1) Fall-Wint 89, p. 98.
"Useless." [Nimrod] (33:1) Fall-Wint 89, p. 99.
5310. SMITH, Charlie
"Aquarium." [ParisR] (31:111) Sum 89, p. 215-216.
"Ex Regis." [SouthernR] (25:3) Sum 89, p. 621-623.

"Figurative Marriage." [Pequod] (28/29/30) 89, p. 271-272.
"Number Six Shot." [Crazy] (36) Spr 89, p. 35-36.
"Omnipotence." [Colum] (14) 89, p. 88.
"Renewal: A Version." [AmerPoR] (18:2) Mr-Ap 89, p. 55.
"Self Defense." [Crazy] (36) Spr 89, p. 34.
"This Holy Enterprise." [ParisR] (31:111) Sum 89, p. 214.

5311. SMITH, Claude Clayton
"Stopping for Gas" (In the Gambia). [Pig] (15) 88, p. 49.

5312. SMITH, D. J.
"Parting." [EmeraldCR] (1989) c1988, p. 146.

5313. SMITH, Dave
"An American Roadside Elegy." [VirQR] (65:1) Wint 89, p. 66-67.
"Before Ground Roses." [KenR] (NS 11:3) Sum 89, p. 136.
"Bible School" (for Sidney Burris). [SouthernHR] (23:2) Spr 89, p. 165-167.
"The Canoe in the Basement." [KenR] (NS 11:3) Sum 89, p. 133-135.
"Deer in the Yard." [SouthwR] (74:3) Sum 89, p. 357.
"The Early Flames." [VirQR] (65:1) Wint 89, p. 69-70.
"Fallen Tree." [Antaeus] (62) Spr 89, p. 217-218.
"Graduation." [Verse] (6:1) Mr 89, p. 12.
"Hawk Walking to Hunt" (Homage to Richard Hugo). [Antaeus] (62) Spr 89, p. 214-216.
"Jumper." [VirQR] (65:1) Wint 89, p. 67-68.
"Pulling a Pig's Tail." [VirQR] (65:1) Wint 89, p. 68-69.
"Shoveling the Walkway." [Antaeus] (62) Spr 89, p. 213.
"Some Last Things." [SouthwR] (74:3) Sum 89, p. 358.
"Southern Crescent." [NewEngR] (11:3) Spr 89, p. 298-303.
"Summer Garden." [NewEngR] (11:3) Spr 89, p. 304.
"Wharf-End" (Windmill Point, Virginia). [WilliamMR] (27) 89, p. 16-18.

5314. SMITH, David-Glen
"We (Ourselves) Make the Spirits Breathe" (for Lynwood and Turlough). [YellowS] (30) Sum 89, p. 27.

5315. SMITH, David James
"Young Men Hitch Out of the San Joaquin Valley Towards Glory." [WritersF] (15) Fall 89, p. 89.

5316. SMITH, Donald
"After All, Why Not" (for Wade). [Plain] (10:1) 89, p. 26.
"Try Crows." [Plain] (10:1) 89, p. 26.

5317. SMITH, Douglas Burnet
"In Another Station of the Metro" (Prose Poem Winter, the First Short Grain Contest). [Grain] (17:3) Fall 89, p. 69.
"The Knife-Thrower's Partner." [MalR] (88) Fall 89, p. 36-58.

5318. SMITH, Iain Crichton
"Autumn." [Stand] (30:1) Wint 88-89, p. 17.
"Farewell My Brother." [Stand] (30:1) Wint 88-89, p. 17-18.
"A Message to the Bard" (tr. of William Livingstone). [Stand] (30:1) Wint 88-89, p. 12-14.
"Napoleon, on St. Helena." [Stand] (30:1) Wint 88-89, p. 16.
"O Apple-Tree, O" (from "Eilean Fraoich," tr. of anonymous Gaelic poem). [Stand] (30:1) Wint 88-89, p. 15.
"Raf, Cyprus." [Stand] (30:1) Wint 88-89, p. 16.
"When I Was Young" (tr. of Mary MacPherson). [Stand] (30:1) Wint 88-89, p. 14-15.

5319. SMITH, J. D.
"Nocturne." [Kaleid] (18) Wint-Spr 89, p. 35.
"Shortness." [Kaleid] (18) Wint-Spr 89, p. 35.

SMITH, James Sutherland
See SUTHERLAND-SMITH, James

5320. SMITH, Jared
"Behind." [ArtfulD] (16/17) Fall 89, p. 112.

5321. SMITH, Jennifer (Jennifer E.)
"Black Art." [Obs] (4:1) Spr 89, p. 26-27.
"Eulogy of a Torch." [Obs] (3:1) Spr 88, p. 50.
"We Workers." [Obs] (4:1) Spr 89, p. 25-26.
"Words." [Obs] (3:1) Spr 88, p. 49.

5322. SMITH, John
"The Book" (for Ruth). [US1] (22/23) Spr 89, p. 8.

5323. SMITH, Jonathan Cedric
"Narrative of the Miraculous Escape." [Obs] (4:1) Spr 89, p. 37-38.
5324. SMITH, Jordan
"AM Classical." [YaleR] (79:1) Aut 89, p. 127-128.
"Calling." [KenR] (NS 11:1) Wint 89, p. 35.
"First Baptist" (for Harry Marten). [WestHR] (43:1) Spr 89, p. 39-42.
"The Household of Continuance." [WestHR] (43:4) Wint 89, p. 231-234.
"Memorial Day Exercises, 1971." [YaleR] (79:1) Aut 89, p. 126-127.
"On the Beach at Truro." [NewEngR] (12:2) Wint 89, p. 150.
"On the Resemblance of Poetry to Prayer." [KenR] (NS 11:1) Wint 89, p. 33-34.
"A Song of Dowland's on the Stereo." [KenR] (NS 11:1) Wint 89, p. 33.
"Summer." [NewEngR] (12:2) Wint 89, p. 149.
"The Verities." [NewEngR] (12:2) Wint 89, p. 148-149.
"Witness." [KenR] (NS 11:1) Wint 89, p. 34-35.
5325. SMITH, Keith
"Later, West of Mount Symmetry." [Timbuktu] (3) Wint-Spr 89, p. 56.
"Where Is God?" [Timbuktu] (3) Wint-Spr 89, p. 56.
"Why I'm Happy as a Minor Artist." [Timbuktu] (3) Wint-Spr 89, p. 57.
5326. SMITH, Ken
"The Five Hour Drive Home." [WashR] (15:2) Ag-S 89, p. 12.
"Towards Morning." [WashR] (15:2) Ag-S 89, p. 12.
"Wall." [Margin] (9) 89, p. 88-89.
5327. SMITH, Kevin
"From Heaven." [NoDaQ] (57:1) Wint 89, p. 128.
"Ghosts." [NoDaQ] (57:1) Wint 89, p. 127.
5328. SMITH, Kevin J.
"My Biggest Fear Is That I'll Live Too Long" (Overheard at a senior citizens'
center). [Farm] (6:1) Wint-Spr 88-89, p. 122.
5329. SMITH, Lawrence R.
"Living in the USA" (for Jerry Vizenor). [NewAW] (5) Fall 89, p. 71.
5330. SMITH, Lonna Lisa
"Mermaid." [Writer] (102:3) Mr 89, p. 24.
5331. SMITH, Loueva
"Swimmers" (From a Lecture on Modern Poetry). [Kalliope] (11:1) 89, p. 20.
5332. SMITH, Michael C.
"Last Call." [Jacaranda] (4:1) Spr-Sum 89, p. 158.
5333. SMITH, Nathaniel
"Ophelia, I" (tr. of Arthur Rimbaud). [WebR] (14:1) Spr 89, p. 21.
5334. SMITH, Pat
"Lauds" (from "A Book of Ours"). [Temblor] (10) 89, p. 54-56.
5335. SMITH, Patricia
"Your Man." [TriQ] (76) Fall 89, p. 96-97.
5336. SMITH, R. T.
"Alter All." [CarolQ] (42:1) Fall 89, p. 10.
"Bible Alice, Gulf-Bound." [GettyR] (2:3) Sum 89, p. 436-437.
"Cardinal Directions." [CarolQ] (42:1) Fall 89, p. 9.
"The Cardinal Heart." [GeoR] (43:3) Fall 89, p. 570-571.
"Comfort." [ChatR] (9:4) Sum 89, p. 65.
"Heraclitus Called." [Journal] (13:1) Spr-Sum 89, p. 25-27.
"Kitchen Window." [GettyR] (2:1) Wint 89, p. 59.
"Last Things." [GettyR] (2:1) Wint 89, p. 62.
"Potamic Ammons Letter to Shelby Stephenson, And It Stormed All Afternoon."
[Pembroke] (21) 89, p. 77-78.
"Saint Patrick's." [GettyR] (2:1) Wint 89, p. 60-61.
"Signifiers." [CumbPR] (8:2) Spr 89, p. 57-58.
5337. SMITH, Renée
"A Big Kiss." [Bogg] (61) 89, p. 27.
5338. SMITH, Robert L.
"In the City." [StoneC] (16:3/4) Spr-Sum 89, p. 50-51.
"Song About a Dog" (tr. of Sergei Esenin). [Sequoia] (32:2) Wint-Spr 89, p. 30.
5339. SMITH, Robert Lavett
"Elegy for a Spanish Poet." [Pembroke] (21) 89, p. 35.
"Sacred Music" (Ely Cathedral, 1982). [BallSUF] (30:4) Aut 89, p. 25.
5340. SMITH, Rod
"A Common Tack on a Tender." [Aerial] (5) 89, p. 159.
"Or Jazz." [Aerial] (5) 89, p. 159.

"Tibet Series" (Selections: 2 poems). [Screens] (1) 89, p. 105.
"What one determines turns trickulable." [Aerial] (5) 89, p. 160.
5341. SMITH, Ron
"Approaching the Great Divide" (U.S. Route 36, June). [Journal] (13:1) Spr-Sum
89, p. 68-69.
"Nashville Rendezvous with My Parents in the Dead of Winter." [PoetryE] (28) Fall
89, p. 118-120.
5342. SMITH, Samuel Random
"What Happens to Old Men at Sundown." [HighP] (4:2) Fall 89, p. 92-93.
5343. SMITH, Sheila K.
"He Said: She Said" (for Skins). [Obs] (2:3) Wint 87, p. 43.
"On the Phone with Alonzo." [Obs] (2:3) Wint 87, p. 44.
"Stranger on the Road." [Epoch] (38:3) 89, p. 198-211.
5344. SMITH, Slade
"Dream #2." [Colum] (14) 89, p. 148-149.
5345. SMITH, Stephen E.
"Loose Talk." [SpoonRQ] (14:1) Wint 89, p. 62.
"The Poet's Photograph." [ApalQ] (31) 89, p. 40-41.
5346. SMITH, Steven
"A Butcher at Les Halles, 1927." [CrossC] (11:2) 89, p. 6.
5347. SMITH, Tom
"Talaria." [SpiritSH] (55) Fall-Wint 89 [90 on cover], p. 43.
5348. SMITH, William Jay
"The Beach" (tr. of Vittorio Sereni). [Poetry] (155:1/2) O-N 89, p. 19.
"Down There" (tr. of Sandro Penna). [Poetry] (155:1/2) O-N 89, p. 17.
"First Fear" (tr. of Vittorio Sereni). [Poetry] (155:1/2) O-N 89, p. 23.
"Interior" (tr. of Sandro Penna). [Poetry] (155:1/2) O-N 89, p. 15.
"It's Perhaps the Boredom" (tr. of Vittorio Sereni). [Poetry] (155:1/2) O-N 89, p.
21.
"Life, Is Remembering Having Wakened" (tr. of Sandro Penna). [Poetry] (155:1/2)
O-N 89, p. 15.
"The Little Venetian Square" (tr. of Sandro Penna). [Poetry] (155:1/2) O-N 89, p.
15.
"Poetry" (tr. of Nina Cassian). [NewYorker] (64:50) 30 Ja 89, p. 71.
"Second Fear" (tr. of Vittorio Sereni). [Poetry] (155:1/2) O-N 89, p. 23.
"Swimmer" (tr. of Sandro Penna). [Poetry] (155:1/2) O-N 89, p. 17.
5349. SMITH-BOWERS, Cathy
"After Being Commissioned to Write a Poem for the Centennial Celebration of
Springs Cotton Mills . . ." [PoetL] (84:3) Fall 89, p. 23-24.
"After Reading It Is Only a Myth That a Person Looking Up from the Bottom of a
Well . . ." [SouthernPR] (29:2) Fall 89, p. 40-41.
"Aphasia." [GeoR] (43:2) Sum 89, p. 279-280.
"Bone." [SouthernPR] (29:1) Spr 89, p. 37.
"Namesake" (for Cathy Fiscus, 3 1/2, who died in an abandoned well the summer of
1949). [GeoR] (43:2) Sum 89, p. 278-279.
"Thunder." [PoetL] (84:3) Fall 89, p. 22.
5350. SMITHER, Elizabeth
"A Book of Louisiana Plantation Houses." [Verse] (6:3) Wint 89, p. 3.
"Error on a Quizz Programme." [Descant] (20:3/4, #66/67) Fall-Wint 89, p. 171.
"The French Translation." [Descant] (20:3/4, #66/67) Fall-Wint 89, p. 171.
"The French Translation." [Verse] (6:2) Je 89, p. 4.
"Listening to Handel's Water Music." [Verse] (6:3) Wint 89, p. 4.
"My Mother's Black Dogs." [Descant] (20:3/4, #66/67) Fall-Wint 89, p. 172.
"Nine Postcards on a Wall." [Descant] (20:3/4, #66/67) Fall-Wint 89, p. 173.
"The Race Meeting." [Descant] (20:3/4, #66/67) Fall-Wint 89, p. 174.
"Stubble Fields." [Descant] (20:3/4, #66/67) Fall-Wint 89, p. 173.
5351. SMITS, Ronald
"The Pennsylvania Turnpike." [KanQ] (21:4) Fall 89, p. 16.
"The Whale-Rocks." [Hawai'iR] (13:2, #26) Sum 89, p. 91.
5352. SMOLDAS, Ivo
"Hour of the Wolf" (tr. by Jarmila and Ian Milner). [Verse] (6:2) Je 89, p. 63.
5353. SMUKLER, Linda
"Lover." [Ploughs] (15:4) Wint 89-90, p. 206.
"Monkey Boy." [Ploughs] (15:4) Wint 89-90, p. 207-208.
5354. SMYTH, Richard
"The Cripple Dance." [TampaR] (2) 89, p. 39.

5355. SNEFF, Priscilla
"Ars Memoriae." [Sulfur] (9:2, #25) Fall 89, p. 176-179.
"The Bells." [Screens] (1) 89, p. 176.
"Chemo." [YaleR] (79:1) Aut 89, p. 39-40.
"The Daimon." [SouthernR] (25:1) Wint 89, p. 165.
"Fugue." [Screens] (1) 89, p. 176.
"O This Is a Golden Age." [Sulfur] (9:2, #25) Fall 89, p. 175.
"The Way to Things by Words and to Words by Things." [SouthernR] (25:1) Wint
    89, p. 164.
5356. SNIDER, Clifton
"Letting Go." [PaintedB] (37) 89, p. 62.
"Surrender." [Vis] (30) 89, p. 47.
5357. SNIVELY, Susan
"The Balloon." [MassR] (30:1) Spr 89, p. 16.
"The Crash." [PoetryE] (28) Fall 89, p. 37-38.
"Family Practices." [PoetryE] (28) Fall 89, p. 32.
"Frequent Sneezing Enlarges Bust." [PoetryE] (28) Fall 89, p. 33.
"The Novelist." [PoetryE] (28) Fall 89, p. 39-41.
"Old Sick Crazy Lover." [PoetryE] (28) Fall 89, p. 35.
"Out Among the Screwdrivers." [PoetryE] (28) Fall 89, p. 34.
"Property." [Shen] (39:1) Spr 89, p. 23.
"Rapture Placemats." [PoetryE] (28) Fall 89, p. 31.
"Seeing Adrienne Rich in the Supermarket." [PoetryE] (28) Fall 89, p. 42-43.
"The Shape." [PoetryE] (28) Fall 89, p. 29.
"The Shopping Gene." [PoetryE] (28) Fall 89, p. 36.
"A Woman Holding a Balance." [PoetryE] (28) Fall 89, p. 30.
5358. SNODGRASS, Ann
"Austerlitz." [AmerPoR] (18:3) My-Je 89, p. 47.
"Matisse's *Goldfish*." [AmerPoR] (18:3) My-Je 89, p. 47.
"Pierrot in the Park." [AmerPoR] (18:3) My-Je 89, p. 47.
5359. SNODGRASS, W. D.
"Dance Suite" (after the paintings by DeLoss McGraw: Selections: 4 poems).
    [SouthernR] (25:1) Wint 89, p. 148-161.
"Din Noaptea" (tr. of Mihai Eminescu, w. Dona Rosu and Radu Lupan). [AmerPoR]
    (18:6) N-D 89, p. 32.
"Dog After Love" (tr. of Yehuda Amichai). [GrandS] (9:1) Aut 89, p. 264.
"If Boughs Tap" (tr. of Mihai Eminescu). [SenR] (19:2) Fall 89, p. 76.
"The Midnight Carnival" (part of a long sequence related to paintings by DeLoss
    McGraw). [Salm] (81) Wint 89, p. 90-92.
"The Midnight Carnival" (Selections: 3 poems). [AmerPoR] (18:1) Ja-F 89, p. 26.
"Sonnets" (I, II, III, tr. of Mihai Eminescu, w. Dona Rosu and Radu Lupan).
    [AmerPoR] (18:6) N-D 89, p. 32.
"Star" (tr. of Mihai Eminescu). [SenR] (19:2) Fall 89, p. 77.
SNOOK, Elena Rossi
    See ROSSI-SNOOK, Elena
5360. SNOW, Anthony
"I observed ragged shadows." [Mildred] (3:1) Spr-Sum 89, p. 35.
5361. SNOW, Barbara
"The Goddess Broods Under Auburndale at Christmas." [Kalliope] (11:1) 89, p. 63.
5362. SNOW, Carol
"Bridge." [AmerPoR] (18:3) My-Je 89, p. 32-33.
5363. SNYDAL, James
"The Beginnings of a Style" (After Cezanne's "Clos des Mathurins"). [CrabCR]
    (6:1) 89, p. 7.
5364. SNYDER, Gary
"At Maple Bridge" (Two Poems Written at Maple Bridge Near Suzhou). [LitR]
    (32:3) Spr 89, p. 446.
"At Tower Peak." [Zyzzyva] (5:1, #17) Spr 89, p. 100-101.
"Bamboo Lane House" (tr. of Wang Wei). [LitR] (32:3) Spr 89, p. 444.
"Building." [Witness] (2:2/3) Sum-Fall 88, p. 242-243.
"Maha Prajna Paramita Hridaya Sutra" (tr. of Hannya Shingyo). [AlphaBS] (6) Wint
    89-90, p. 38-39.
"Maple Bridge Night Mooring" (Two Poems Written at Maple Bridge Near Suzhou,
    tr. of Zhang Ji). [LitR] (32:3) Spr 89, p. 446.
"Parting with Hsin Chien at Hibiscus Tavern" (tr. of Wang Ch'ang-ling). [LitR]
    (32:3) Spr 89, p. 445.

"River Show" (tr. of Liu Tsung-yüan). [LitR] (32:3) Spr 89, p. 445.
"Saying Farewell" (tr. of Wang Wei). [LitR] (32:3) Spr 89, p. 444.
"A Set of Path Poems." [Sulfur] (9:1, #24) Spr 89, p. 9-12.
"Some Critic Tried to Put Me Down" (tr. of Han Shan). [LitR] (32:3) Spr 89, p. 443.
"When Men See Han-Shan" (tr. of Han Shan). [LitR] (32:3) Spr 89, p. 443.
5365. SNYDER, Jennifer
"Concerning Music." [PoetryNW] (30:3) Aut 89, p. 8-9.
"The Day Fish Fell from the Sky" (Otto in Honduras, 1971 -- for my grandfather). [PoetryNW] (30:3) Aut 89, p. 6-7.
"Whales" (1989 National Collegiate Poetry Fellowship Competition). [IndR] (12:3) Sum 89, p. 103.
5366. SNYDER, Kirtland
"Soldiers of Fortune." [Notus] (4:2) Fall 89, p. 57-65.
5367. SOARES, Martim
"Song About Lopo the Jester (Cantiga d'Escarnho)" (tr. by Richard Zenith). [PoetryE] (28) Fall 89, p. 197.
"Song to an Unbelieving Lady (Cantiga d'Amor)" (tr. by Richard Zenith). [PoetryE] (28) Fall 89, p. 195-196.
SOARES de TAVEIROS, Pai
    See TAVEIROS, Pai Soares de
5368. SOBIN, Anthony
"Epithalamium Catalogue of the Folklore of the Origins of the Double Wedding Ring Quilt" (For A.G.). [KenR] (NS 11:2) Spr 89, p. 87-89.
"Negative." [MissR] (17:3, #51), p. 102.
"Oil on Board: Pennsylvania Farm, ca. 1840." [MissR] (17:3, #51), p. 98-99.
"Painter's Light: Long Island." [KenR] (NS 11:2) Spr 89, p. 90-92.
"Toward Pocatello." [MissR] (17:3, #51), p. 100-101.
5369. SOBSEY, Cynthia
"Separations." [StoneC] (16:3/4) Spr-Sum 89, p. 72.
5370. SOCOLOW, Elizabeth (Elizabeth A., Elizabeth Anne)
"Daughter Cells and Viola D'Amore." [Ometeca] (1:1) 89, p. 15-17.
"Hearing the Russian Writer Lecture." [US1] (22/23) Spr 89, p. 24-25.
"In a Villa." [US1] (22/23) Spr 89, p. 24.
"Income Bracket." [Footwork] 89, p. 58.
"What Women Want." [US1] (22/23) Spr 89, p. 25.
5371. SOIFER, Mark
"Greenbacks and Holsteins." [Pembroke] (21) 89, p. 131.
"The Lights of the Prison." [Pembroke] (21) 89, p. 132.
"Local Color." [Pembroke] (21) 89, p. 131-132.
5372. SOLARI, Patrica
"Saviours." [Writer] (102:9) S 89, p. 23.
5373. SOLHEIM, James
"All That Is." [PoetryNW] (30:2) Sum 89, p. 13-15.
"Cambrian Night." [PoetryNW] (30:2) Sum 89, p. 16.
"The Lost Kings of Maryville." [KenR] (NS 11:3) Sum 89, p. 1-10.
"The Stick Woman." [PoetryNW] (30:2) Sum 89, p. 11-13.
5374. SOLLFREY, Stacey
"Sitting on Newsprints of Paper." [AlphaBS] (5) Jl 89, p. 70.
5375. SOLNICKI, Jill (Jill Newman)
"In the Middle of a Day." [Quarry] (38:1) Wint 89, p. 36.
"Metamorphosis." [Grain] (17:3) Fall 89, p. 15.
"Necropolis." [CrossC] (11:2) 89, p. 8.
"Teenage Boys." [Grain] (17:3) Fall 89, p. 14.
5376. SOLOMON, Carl
"Further Tales of the City." [AlphaBS] (5) Jl 89, p. 1-2.
5377. SOLOMON, Marvin
"Why All the Nickels Are Black in Port Sulphur, LA." [PoetL] (84:3) Fall 89, p. 35.
5378. SOLOMON, Sandy
"Revision." [Ploughs] (15:1) 89, p. 124-125.
5379. SOLONCHE, J. R.
"For One in Hospital." [LitR] (32:2) Wint 89, p. 233.
"Poem on the Winter Solstice." [SmPd] (26:3 #77) Fall 89, p. 10.
"Water Lilies." [SmPd] (26:3 #77) Fall 89, p. 11.
5380. SOMERVILLE, Jane
"Drowning the Slug." [OhioR] (44) 89, p. 109.

391

"How to Open a Combination Lock." [SmPd] (26:2 #76) Spr 89, p. 26.
"I Think Sometimes." [Kalliope] (11:1) 89, p. 18.
"It's Worth Seeing: A Cruise in the Greek Isles." [Interim] (8:1) Spr 89, p. 9.
"The Leaf." [OhioR] (44) 89, p. 108.
"On Fans as Fences." [Interim] (8:1) Spr 89, p. 10.
"Red Rover, Red Rover." [SmPd] (26:2 #76) Spr 89, p. 25.
"The Social Scientist Surveys Our Attitudes About the Stars: He Asked Her If She'd
      Ever, and She Said Yes." [Kalliope] (11:1) 89, p. 56.
"Telling Your Story." [PoetryE] (28) Fall 89, p. 117.
5381. SOMMER, Piotr
"Indiscretions" (tr. by Stanislaw Baranczak and Clare Cavanagh). [SenR] (19:2) Fall
      89, p. 29.
"Medicine" (tr. by Stanislaw Baranczak and Clare Cavanah). [Trans] (21) Spr 89, p.
      79.
5382. SONG, Cathy
"Field of Vision." [Shen] (39:2) Sum 89, p. 89.
"Heaven." [BambooR] (42/43) Spr-Sum 89, p. 211-212.
"Immaculate Lives." [BambooR] (41) Wint 89, p. 28-29.
"Immaculate Lives." [BambooR] (42/43) Spr-Sum 89, p. 213-214.
"Living Near the Water." [BambooR] (42/43) Spr-Sum 89, p. 200-202.
"The Miracle of Trees." [Shen] (39:2) Sum 89, p. 90-91.
"A Pale Arrangement of Hands." [BambooR] (42/43) Spr-Sum 89, p. 197-199.
"Pearls." [BambooR] (41) Wint 89, p. 31-32.
"Shadow Figures." [BambooR] (42/43) Spr-Sum 89, p. 203-206.
"Stamp Collecting." [MissouriR] (12:1) 89, p. 56-57.
"The Tower of Pisa." [BambooR] (42/43) Spr-Sum 89, p. 207-210.
"The Woman Who Loved Him" (for Kenny and Maura). [BambooR] (41) Wint 89,
      p. 30.
5383. SONG, Ci
"Crime and Punishment" (tr. by Dong Jiping). [Footwork] 89, p. 29.
"Shadow and Crime" (tr. by Dong Jiping). [Footwork] 89, p. 28.
"The Steps We Face To" (tr. by Dong Jiping). [Footwork] 89, p. 28-29.
5384. SONIAT, Katherine
"#2 Yellow Wooden Pencil, 1953." [RiverC] (10:1) Fall 89, p. 64.
"Distance and Design." [KenR] (N 11:4) Fall 89, p. 94.
"October." [NoAmR] (274:4) D 89, p. 57.
"Picturing the Landscape: 'The Grand Teton Block'." [CarolQ] (42:1) Fall 89, p. 27.
"Short Street" (for Betsy). [ColEng] (51:8) D 89, p. 837.
"Smile." [SpoonRQ] (14:1) Wint 89, p. 32.
"Some Vegetables and Stars." [TarRP] (29:1) Fall 89, p. 8.
"Standing Wet and Close." [TarRP] (29:1) Fall 89, p. 7.
5385. SONNENBERG, Ben
"Vitale" (i.m. Virgil Thomson). [Nat] (249:20) 11 D 89, p. 728.
5386. SONNENSCHEIN, Dana
"Four Seasons" (photographs by Man Ray). [YellowS] (30) Sum 89, p. 9.
"The Lady in 314." [NowestR] (27:1) 89, p. 73.
5387. SONNEVI, Göran
"Aby, Öland, 1982" (tr. by Rika Lesser). [SouthwR] (74:2) Spr 89, p. 227-229.
5388. SORBY, Angela
"Zinaida Remembers, 1917." [DeKalbLAJ] (22:1/4) 89, p. 66.
5389. SORELLA, Naja
"I Want to Love You Hot" (For Frieda). [SinW] (39) Wint 89-90, p. 70-71.
5390. SORESCU, Marin
"And Everything Slips Easily Away" (tr. by Adriana Varga and Stuart Friebert, w.
      Gabriela Dragnea). [Timbuktu] (4) Sum-Fall 89, p. 25.
"Between Stars" (tr. by Stuart Friebert and Adriana Varga, w. Gabriela Dragnea).
      [MalR] (88) Fall 89, p. 79.
"Casa." [Timbuktu] (4) Sum-Fall 89, p. 30.
"Un Cleste" (in Rumanian). [Os] (29) 89, p. 8.
"Dream" (tr. by Adriana Varga and Stuart Friebert, w. Gabriela Dragnea).
      [Timbuktu] (4) Sum-Fall 89, p. 27.
"Game" (tr. by Adriana Varga and Stuart Friebert, w. Gabriela Dragnea). [Timbuktu]
      (4) Sum-Fall 89, p. 29.
"Hide and Seek" (tr. by Stuart Friebert and Adriana Varga, w. Gabriela Dragnea).
      [Field] (40) Spr 89, p. 40.
"Horoscop." [Timbuktu] (4) Sum-Fall 89, p. 34.

SORESCU

392

"Horoscope" (tr. by Adriana Varga and Stuart Friebert, w. Gabriela Dragnea).
[Timbuktu] (4) Sum-Fall 89, p. 35.
"The House" (tr. by Adriana Varga and Stuart Friebert, w. Gabriela Dragnea).
[Timbuktu] (4) Sum-Fall 89, p. 31.
"Hyena" (tr. by Stuart Friebert and Adriana Varga, w. Gabriela Dragnea). [Field]
(40) Spr 89, p. 42.
"Laocoon" (in Rumanian). [Timbuktu] (4) Sum-Fall 89, p. 28.
"Laocoon" (tr. by Adriana Varga and Stuart Friebert, w. Gabriela Dragnea).
[Timbuktu] (4) Sum-Fall 89, p. 29.
"Launching" (tr. by Stuart Friebert and Adriana Varga, w. Gabriela Dragnea).
[MalR] (88) Fall 89, p. 83.
"Lightning Passed" (tr. by Stuart Friebert and Adriana Varga, w. Gabriela Dragnea).
[Field] (40) Spr 89, p. 41.
"The Mountains" (tr. by Adriana Varga and Stuart Friebert). [Iowa] (19:2) Spr-Sum
89, p. 167-168.
"Paintings" (tr. by Stuart Friebert and Adriana Varga, w. Gabriela Dragnea). [Field]
(40) Spr 89, p. 38-39.
"Paper" (tr. by Stuart Friebert and Adriana Varga, w. Gabriela Dragnea). [MalR]
(88) Fall 89, p. 80-81.
"Passport" (tr. by Stuart Friebert and Adriana Varga, w. Gabriela Dragnea). [MalR]
(88) Fall 89, p. 78.
"Perspectiva" (in Rumanian). [Os] (29) 89, p. 6.
"Perspective" (tr. by Adriana Varga and Stuart Friebert). [Os] (29) 89, p. 7.
"Pliers" (tr. by Adriana Varga and Stuart Friebert). [Os] (29) 89, p. 9.
"The Sacred Fire" (tr. by Adriana Varga and Stuart Friebert). [Iowa] (19:2) Spr-Sum
89, p. 166-167.
"Si Totul Imi Aluneca Usor." [Timbuktu] (4) Sum-Fall 89, p. 24.
"Spiral" (tr. by Stuart Friebert and Adriana Varga, w. Gabriela Dragnea). [MalR]
(88) Fall 89, p. 82.
"Subiectivism." [Timbuktu] (4) Sum-Fall 89, p. 32.
"Subjectivism" (tr. by Adriana Varga and Stuart Friebert, w. Gabriela Dragnea).
[Timbuktu] (4) Sum-Fall 89, p. 33.
"Vibratii." [Timbuktu] (4) Sum-Fall 89, p. 32.
"Vibrations" (tr. by Adriana Varga and Stuart Friebert, w. Gabriela Dragnea).
[Timbuktu] (4) Sum-Fall 89, p. 33.
"Village Museum" (tr. by Adriana Varga and Stuart Friebert). [Iowa] (19:2) Spr-Sum
89, p. 165-166.
"Vinat." [Timbuktu] (4) Sum-Fall 89, p. 28.
"Vis." [Timbuktu] (4) Sum-Fall 89, p. 26.
"Vision" (tr. by Stuart Friebert and Adriana Varga). [Vis] (30) 89, p. 5.
"Whim" (tr. by Adriana Varga and Stuart Friebert). [Iowa] (19:2) Spr-Sum 89, p.
168.
5391. SORESTAD, Glen
"Fifty Thousand Coyotes Can't Be Wrong." [AntigR] (77/78) Spr-Sum 89, p.
70-71.
"Whatever Happened to Jane Jayroe?" [AntigR] (77/78) Spr-Sum 89, p. 68-69.
5392. SORKIN, Adam J.
"Only the Blank Page" (tr. of Anghel Dumbraveanu, w. Irina Grigorescu). [NewOR]
(16:2) Sum 89, p. 92.
"Runes" (tr. of Anghel Dumbraveanu, w. Irina Grigorescu). [NewOR] (16:2) Sum
89, p. 96.
5393. SORNBERGER, Judith
"From the Art Museum's Oriental Wing" (for Kris Vervaecke). [DenQ] (24:1) Sum
89, p. 73-75.
"Lamp Man." [TarRP] (28:2) Spr 89, p. 21-22.
"The Split." [Kalliope] (11:2) 89, p. 50.
5394. SORRENTINO, Gilbert
"Dark Discovery." [Screens] (1) 89, p. 163.
"Days." [Screens] (1) 89, p. 162.
"New Attachment." [Screens] (1) 89, p. 162.
"Seven Gaudy Poems" (for William Bronk). [Talisman] (2) Spr 89, p. 11-17.
5395. SOSEI, the monk (ca. 890)
"In the dark godless month" (tr. by Sam Hamill). [PoetryE] (28) Fall 89, p. 200.
"Where is the dark seed" (tr. by Sam Hamill). [PoetryE] (28) Fall 89, p. 203.
5396. SOSIS, Phil
"Maturian I." [US1] (22/23) Spr 89, p. 28.

5397. SOSSAMAN, Stephen
"Night Fishing with an Old Friend." [BallSUF] (30:4) Aut 89, p. 69.
5398. SOTERES, Kip
"Committee Landmarks" (for my grandfather, Spiros Soteres). [Shen] (39:1) Spr 89,
p. 90.
5399. SOTO, Gary
"Apple." [Witness] (2:1) Spr 88, p. 134-136.
"The Asking." [Zyzzyva] (5:, #20) Wint 89, p. 103-106.
"The Dictionaries." [Poetry] (154:2) My 89, p. 74-76.
"The Family in Spring." [Witness] (2:1) Spr 88, p. 139-141.
"Magnets." [MissouriR] (12:1) 89, p. 58-59.
"Pink Hands." [Witness] (2:1) Spr 88, p. 137-138.
5400. SOTO MÉNDEZ, Nilda
"En la tierra simiente preñada por los siglos busco." [Mairena] (11:27) 89, p. 85.
5401. SOTO VÉLEZ, Clemente
"The Promised Land" (Selection: Section 35, tr. by Martín Espada and Camilo
Pérez-Bustillo). [MinnR] (NS 33) Fall 89, p. 39-42.
5402. SOTOBA, Layman
"The Mountain -- Buddha's Body" (tr. by Lucien Stryk). [LitR] (32:3) Spr 89, p.
359.
5403. SOUAID, Carolyn-Marie
"Nobody, Not Even My Mother, Came to the Wedding." [Quarry] (38:1) Wint 89,
p. 59-61.
5404. SOUMAGNE, Ludwig
"End" (tr. by John Linthicum). [LitR] (33:1) Fall 89, p. 131.
"Envious" (tr. by John Linthicum). [LitR] (33:1) Fall 89, p. 131.
"Latest Report" (tr. by John Linthicum). [LitR] (33:1) Fall 89, p. 130.
"Litany" (tr. by John Linthicum). [LitR] (33:1) Fall 89, p. 129.
"Talent" (tr. by John Linthicum). [LitR] (33:1) Fall 89, p. 131.
"Tell Me Everything" (tr. by John Linthicum). [LitR] (33:1) Fall 89, p. 129.
"Transplantation" (tr. by John Linthicum). [LitR] (33:1) Fall 89, p. 130.
5405. SOUPAULT, Philippe
"Epitaphs" (3 poems, tr. by Kirby Olson). [Rampike] (6:1) 87, p. 65.
5406. SOUTH, Karen
"Before the Illness." [StoneC] (16:3/4) Spr-Sum 89, p. 36.
"Hearing Peeps." [ThRiPo] (33/34) 89, p. 30.
"Letter Home." [StoneC] (16:3/4) Spr-Sum 89, p. 37.
"X-Ray." [ThRiPo] (33/34) 89, p. 28-29.
5407. SOUTHWICK, Marcia
"Arrest." [CinPR] (19) Spr 89, p. 8-9.
"Brothers." [RiverS] (28) 89, p. 9.
"Finding Horseshoes." [CinPR] (19) Spr 89, p. 10-11.
"The Rain's Marriage." [RiverS] (28) 89, p. 10.
"Voices from the Afterlife." [CinPR] (19) Spr 89, p. 12.
"Why the River Disappears." [RiverS] (28) 89, p. 5-8.
5408. SPACKS, Barry
"Bachelard on Art" (Composed of freely rearranged phrases from Gaston
Bachelard's *The Right to Dream*). [Poetry] (153:6) Mr 89, p. 311-312.
"Carver's Medallion." [CumbPR] (9:1) Fall 89, p. 28.
"Gates." [Hudson] (42:2) Sum 89, p. 282.
"In a Funky Motel." [OntR] (31) Fall-Wint 89-90, p. 94.
"Mortal Coil." [OntR] (31) Fall-Wint 89-90, p. 93.
"Praising Pasta." [Salm] (81) Wint 89, p. 103.
"Puma." [NoDaQ] (57:3) Sum 89, p. 145.
"Soft Core." [Interim] (8:1) Spr 89, p. 25.
"Sunday Service." [KanQ] (21:1/2) Wint-Spr 89, p. 84.
"The Wools." [KanQ] (21:1/2) Wint-Spr 89, p. 84.
"Wordworker." [ConnPR] (8:1) 89, p. 16.
5409. SPADY, Susan
"Emily Between." [Calyx] (12:2) Wint 89-90, p. 4.
"Nursling." [Calyx] (12:2) Wint 89-90, p. 5.
5410. SPATOLA, Adriano
"Little Exhortation" (tr. by Paul Vangelisti). [Temblor] (10) 89, p. 3.
5411. SPAZIANI, Maria Luisa
"If It Were a Sea, This Immense Wind" (tr. by Beverly Allen). [Poetry] (155:1/2)
O-N 89, p. 67.

"Se Fosse un Mare Questo Vento Immenso." [Poetry] (155:1/2) O-N 89, p. 66.
"Sunday in the Provinces" (tr. by Beverly Allen). [Poetry] (155:1/2) O-N 89, p. 69.
"Your Life Is a Baby Not Yet Born" (tr. by Beverly Allen). [Poetry] (155:1/2) O-N 89, p. 68.
5412. SPEAKES, Richard
"Manners" (for Rick Simpson). [RiverC] (9:1) Spr 89, p. 82.
5413. SPEAR, Roberta
"Armona." [MissouriR] (12:1) 89, p. 180-182.
5414. SPECK, Heidi
"Lost Victory." [WindO] (51) Spr 89, p. 50.
5415. SPECK, Ryan
"Foul Language." [WindO] (51) Spr 89, p. 52.
5416. SPECKTER, Wanda Thomason
"Salt and Stone." [ChatR] (9:2) Wint 89, p. 42.
5417. SPECTOR, Donna
"Family Photos." [Footwork] 89, p. 17-19.
"Reading the Bones." [BellR] (12:2, #26) Fall 89, p. 4.
"The Woman Who Married." [PoetC] (20:3) Spr 89, p. 40-41.
5418. SPEER, Laurel
"Completely Dead Wench." [TarRP] (28:2) Spr 89, p. 7.
"Dead Dogs." [PraS] (63:2) Sum 89, p. 115.
"Empty Alcatraz." [Confr] (39/40) Fall 88-Wint 89, p. 212.
"I Tell You My Dear Phoebe, Whom I Adore and Wish to Take to Bed This Minute . . ." [HeavenB] (7) Wint 89, p. 56.
"J. Joyce." [LaurelR] (23:2) Sum 89, p. 69.
"Memory Is a Fish" (Hortense Calisher). [Outbr] (20) 89, p. 34.
"Raworth." [ConnPR] (8:1) 89, p. 28.
"Sandwich." [PraS] (63:2) Sum 89, p. 114-115.
"Schubert at 4." [CentR] (33:2) Spr 89, p. 137.
"Very Frightened Men." [BrooklynR] (5) 88, p. 24.
5419. SPEIDEL, Joanne
"The Musician." [NewRena] (7:3, #23) 89, p. 42.
"Night Creature." [NewRena] (7:3, #23) 89, p. 41.
SPEK, Corneil van der
See Van der Spek, Corneil
5420. SPENCE, Michael
"Poem on Your 33rd Birthday" (for Sharon Hashimoto). [CharR] (15:1) Spr 89, p. 54.
5421. SPENCER, Anne
"Life-Long, Poor Browning." [Obs] (3:2) Sum 88, p. 9.
5422. SPENCER, Linda Moore
"Good Friday." [Kalliope] (11:3) 89, p. 36-37.
5423. SPERA, Gabriel
"Traveler's Advisory." [GreensboroR] (47) Wint 89-90, p. 119.
5424. SPERANZA, Jim, Jr.
"Liberate This Man, Dear Brother, Who Is No One But You." [ChangingM] (20) Wint-Spr 89, p. 48.
5425. SPHERES, Duane
"Watertower." [BellArk] (5:5) S-O 89, p. 20.
5426. SPICER, Bob
"Garden of Love." [AntigR] (79) Aut 89, p. 80.
5427. SPICER, David
"The Scab." [Ploughs] (15:1) 89, p. 126-127.
"The Watermelons." [Ploughs] (15:1) 89, p. 128-129.
5428. SPIELBERG, Peter
"Trading Off." [OxfordM] (5:2) Fall-Wint 89, p. 41.
5429. SPINA, Vincent
"Black Legend." [Pembroke] (21) 89, p. 113.
5430. SPINELLI, Eileen
"About Nights." [ChrC] (106:39) D 20-27, 89, p. 1197.
"Welcome Song for a New Baby." [Footwork] 89, p. 52-53.
5431. SPINNER, Bettye T.
"For All the Silent Fathers." [EngJ] (78:6) O 89, p. 92.
"My Father's Hands." [Footwork] 89, p. 35.
"The Woman of the Street." [EngJ] (78:7) N 89, p. 93.

395

SPIRENG

5432. SPIRENG, Matthew J.
"Matamorphosis." [CapeR] (24:2) Fall 89, p. 50.
"Thrush Flying Against a Window." [CapeR] (24:2) Fall 89, p. 49.
5433. SPIRES, Elizabeth
"For Someone One." [SouthwR] (74:3) Sum 89, p. 356.
"January 1: Key West." [Epoch] (38:2) 89, p. 169.
"Josephine." [AmerPoR] (18:1) Ja-F 89, p. 36.
"Primos" (off Land's End). [AmerPoR] (18:1) Ja-F 89, p. 36.
5434. SPIRO, Peter
"Death for the First Time." [Lactuca] (13) N 89, p. 25.
"Stopping By for the Last Time." [Lactuca] (13) N 89, p. 26.
5435. SPISAK, Jill
"Taking Rachel Home." [SinW] (38) Sum-Fall 89, p. 32.
5436. SPIVACK, Kathleen
"The Bureau." [NewL] (56:2/3) Wint 89-Spr 90, p. 276.
"For Gail in Fort Defiance." [NewL] (56:2/3) Wint 89-Spr 90, p. 274-275.
"The Geometry Lesson." [Kalliope] (10:1/2) 88, p. 48.
"The List of Wedding Gifts." [NewL] (56:2/3) Wint 89-Spr 90, p. 278-279.
"The Sleeping Dog." [Ploughs] (15:1) 89, p. 130-131.
"The Visit." [NewL] (56:2/3) Wint 89-Spr 90, p. 277.
5437. SPIVACK, Susan Fantl
"After Hysterectomy." [Kalliope] (10:1/2) 88, p. 103.
"Pig Gift Ceremony (Learning the Labyrinth)." [Kalliope] (11:3) 89, p. 32-33.
"The Unevenness of Happiness." [Mildred] (3:2) 89, p. 131.
"Winter Walk to Schuyler Lake" (for Jay). [Blueline] (10:1/2) 89, p. 53-54.
5438. SPRAGUE, Cherie
"Agravaine, Let Us To." [HeavenB] (7) Wint 89, p. 31.
5439. SPRAYBERRY, Sandra
"After Reading 'Two Views of a Cadaver Room'." [PacificR] (7) 89, p. 97.
5440. SPRIO, Peter
"Subway Station Restroom." [RagMag] (7:1) 89, p. 56-57.
"When I Die." [RagMag] (7:1) 89, p. 58.
5441. SPRUNT, Haines
"The Weed Garden." [CarolQ] (41:3) Spr 89, p. 72.
ST. . . .
See also Saint . . .
5442. ST. ANDREWS, B. A.
"Blake for the Over-Educated." [ChamLR] (3:1, #5) Fall 89, p. 109.
"Divorce." [DeKalbLAJ] (22:1/4) 89, p. 68.
"Elegy." [Jacaranda] (4:1) Spr-Sum 89, p. 144.
"Explaining the Addiction." [CrossCur] (8:3) Apr 89, p. 170.
"Helga's Wyeth." [BellR] (12:1, #25) Spr 89, p. 6-7.
"Ritual." [ChamLR] (3:1, #5) Fall 89, p. 110.
"Semi-Sweet Solid Sin Sonnet." [HighP] (4:1) Spr 89, p. 50.
5443. ST. CLAIR, Philip
"Shirt." [PoetryNW] (30:3) Aut 89, p. 25.
5444. ST. CYR, Napoleon
"Hunting the Big Game. Hunting, the Big Game." [SmPd] (26:3 #77) Fall 89, p. 34.
"Leaving the Flag Out All Night." [SmPd] (26:3 #77) Fall 89, p. 32.
"Post Office Box." [SmPd] (26:3 #77) Fall 89, p. 37.
"The Rattle of an Ordinary Can." [SmPd] (26:3 #77) Fall 89, p. 35.
"Spring Paper Drive." [SmPd] (26:3 #77) Fall 89, p. 36.
"While the Partner Is Out at an Organization Meeting." [SmPd] (26:3 #77) Fall 89, p. 33.
5445. ST. GERMAIN, Sheryl
"Paw-paw's Hogshead Cheese" (in memory, August Frank, September 6, 1909-March 8, 1971). [RiverS] (29) [89], p. 57-58.
"Poet in a White Silk Suite" (for Galway Kinnell). [Footwork] 89, p. 14.
ST. GERMAINE, Sheryl
See ST. GERMAIN, Sheryl
5446. ST. JOHN, David
"I Know." [Antaeus] (62) Spr 89, p. 219.
"Last Night with Rafaella." [GettyR] (2:1) Wint 89, p. 111-113.
"Stairways and Fountains" (Poetry Chapbook: 8 poems). [BlackWR] (16:1) Fall-Wint 89, p. 49-64.

"The Unsayable, the Unknowable, and You." [DenQ] (23:3/4) Wint-Spr 89, p. 52.
5447. ST. JOHN, Susan Lee
"Getting Groceries." [BambooR] (42/43) Spr-Sum 89, p. 217-218.
"John S.W. Lee." [BambooR] (42/43) Spr-Sum 89, p. 219.
5448. STAFFORD, Darrell
"Communion at Coldwater Baptist Church." [KenR] (NS 11:2) Spr 89, p. 59.
"Horses." [KenR] (NS 11:2) Spr 89, p. 60-62.
"Travis Cox Dies on a Light Pole." [KenR] (NS 11:2) Spr 89, p. 60.
5449. STAFFORD, William
"1940." [Field] (41) Fall 89, p. 44.
"Anticipation." [ChamLR] (2:2, #4) Spr 89, p. 15.
"The Anxiety of Influence." [Interim] (8:2) Fall 89, p. 7.
"Ask Me." [Field] (41) Fall 89, p. 34.
"At the Bomb Testing Site." [Field] (41) Fall 89, p. 8.
"Bonuses." [CimR] (89) O 89, p. 105.
"By the Chapel." [PaintedB] (39) 89, p. 23.
"Deep Light." [CimR] (89) O 89, p. 105.
"Doing My Part." [Footwork] 89, p. 5.
"If Only." [NewL] (56:2/3) Wint 89-Spr 90, p. 282-283.
"Knowing." [Field] (41) Fall 89, p. 37.
"Listening at Little Lake Elkhart." [CrabCR] (6:1) 89, p. 6.
"Maybe." [NewL] (56:2/3) Wint 89-Spr 90, p. 281.
"A Memorial: Son Bret." [AmerS] (58:3) Sum 89, p. 370.
"Owls at the Shakespeare Festival." [Field] (41) Fall 89, p. 46-47.
"Pieces of Summer." [Interim] (8:2) Fall 89, p. 3-5.
"Populis Deltoides." [NewL] (56:2/3) Wint 89-Spr 90, p. 283.
"Reading with Little Sister: a Recollection." [MSS] (6:3) 89, p. 70.
"Remarks on My Character." [GeoR] (43:3) Fall 89, p. 545.
"Remembering Brother Bob." [NewL] (56:2/3) Wint 89-Spr 90, p. 280.
"Robert Bly's Working-with-things Project." [CrabCR] (6:1) 89, p. 5.
"Something to Declare." [Antaeus] (62) Spr 89, p. 220.
"Spirit of Place: the Great Blue Heron." [Caliban] (6) 89, p. 15.
"Things I Learned Last Week." [Field] (41) Fall 89, p. 41.
"Thinking for Berky." [Field] (41) Fall 89, p. 11.
"Waking at 3 A.M." [Field] (41) Fall 89, p. 29.
"Where Is Tomorrow?" [ChamLR] (2:2, #4) Spr 89, p. 16.
"Winnemucca, She." [NewL] (56:2/3) Wint 89-Spr 90, p. 282.
"With Apologies All Around." [Interim] (8:2) Fall 89, p. 6.
"With Kit, Age 7, at the Beach." [Field] (41) Fall 89, p. 25.
"You Forget." [TampaR] (2) 89, p. 15.
5450. STAHLECKER, Elizabeth
"Three Flights Up." [CumbPR] (9:1) Fall 89, p. 24.
5451. STAINSBY, Martha
"In the Air." [Event] (18:2) Sum 89, p. 14.
"Sweetmeats." [Event] (18:2) Sum 89, p. 15.
"What an Elephant Knows." [Event] (18:2) Sum 89, p. 16-17.
5452. STAMATIS, William
"Bicycle Summer." [Vis] (31) 89, p. 23.
5453. STAMM, Geoffrey
"Atrocities: Vietnam Poetry" (To Those Who Served and Know). [HirmaPoR]
(Supplement No. 10) 89, 55 p.
5454. STANDINGBEAR, George Eugene
"Spring Song." [Nimrod] (32:2) Spr-Sum 89, p. 42.
5455. STANDISH, Lorraine
"Grandmother's Attic." [EmeraldCR] (1989) c1988, p. 88-89.
5456. STANFORD, Ann
"The Birds and Columbus." [Atlantic] (263:6) Je 89, p. 46.
5457. STANHOPE, Patrick
"Wind." [KanQ] (21:3) Sum 89, p. 158.
5458. STANIZZI, John L.
"Farmer." [PassN] (10:1) Wint 89, p. 10.
"Green Hill Beach" (Rhode Island, July, 1983). [BlueBldgs] (11) 89, p. 14-15.
"October Fishing." [BlueBldgs] (11) 89, p. 16.
5459. STANLEY, Jean W.
"Drift." [Contact] (9:53/54/55) Sum-Fall 89, p. 27.
"Early Along the Waterway." [InterPR] (15:2) Fall 89, p. 128.

"Emily." [Contact] (9:53/54/55) Sum-Fall 89, p. 27.
"The Glass That Separates." [InterPR] (15:2) Fall 89, p. 130.
"July Thoughts." [InterPR] (15:2) Fall 89, p. 128- 130.
"Leavetaking." [CapeR] (24:2) Fall 89, p. 13.
"Too Holy Here." [InterPR] (15:2) Fall 89, p. 131.
"Where the Sun Strikes." [InterPR] (15:2) Fall 89, p. 131-132.

5460. STANTON, Joseph
"The Child Descends the Stair." [ChamLR] (3:1, #5) Fall 89, p. 103.
"Edward Hopper's *New York Movie.*" [Poetry] (154:4) Jl 89, p. 200-201.
"Edward Hopper's *Rooms by the Sea.*" [ChamLR] (3:1, #5) Fall 89, p. 99-100.
"Obasute." [BambooR] (44) Fall 89, p. 32.
"Subterranean Termite Blues." [ChamLR] (2:2, #4) Spr 89, p. 107-108.
"The Third Man." [ChamLR] (3:1, #5) Fall 89, p. 101-102.

5461. STANTON, Maura
"Breadfruit." [Journal] (12:2) Fall-Wint 88-89, p. 12-13.
"Kalaloch." [Journal] (12:2) Fall-Wint 88-89, p. 14-15.
"School Morning." [PoetryNW] (30:3) Aut 89, p. 34-35.

5462. STARBUCK, George
"Grace." [NewL] (56:2/3) Wint 89-Spr 90, p. 295.
"Magnificat in Transit from the Toledo Airport." [NewL] (56:2/3) Wint 89-Spr 90, p. 284-288.
"Offshoreoilrigworker Hammerclaviersonate" (for the Piano of G.W. Beiswanger). [NewL] (56:2/3) Wint 89-Spr 90, p. 296.
"The Universe Is Closed and Has REMs" (to Celia and Wally, to Milly and Gene). [NewL] (56:2/3) Wint 89-Spr 90, p. 289-294.

5463. STARK, Jonathan
"Credo." [StoneC] (17:1/2) Fall-Wint 89-90, p. 21.

5464. STARKEY, David
"Among the Homeless at the Santa Monica Public Library, I Browse." [Wind] (19:64) 89, p. 7.
"Emigrants." [RiverC] (9:1) Spr 89, p. 24.
"Grandfather's Dictionary." [Interim] (8:1) Spr 89, p. 24.
"Insurance." [SoCaR] (21:2) Spr 89, p. 46.
"Miyajima." [HighP] (4:1) Spr 89, p. 46.
"Tree Logic." [BellArk] (5:1) Ja-F 89, p. 10.
"True Love Apparent in Kountze, Texas." [BellArk] (5:1) Ja-F 89, p. 5.
"Unheard Confession." [RiverC] (9:1) Spr 89, p. 26-27.
"Vanitas Vanitatum." [RiverC] (9:1) Spr 89, p. 25.
"Women's Studies." [CumbPR] (9:1) Fall 89, p. 6-7.

5465. STARKMAN, Elaine
"The Tai Chi Master & I." [Kalliope] (11:3) 89, p. 17.

5466. STARR, Jean
"Tales from the Cherokee Hills" (Selections: 4 poems). [Nimrod] (32:2) Spr-Sum 89, p. 17-25.

5467. STARZEC, Larry
"The Senior Citizens Picnic." [SpoonRQ] (14:2) Spr 89, p. 38.

5468. STATMAN, Mark
"From Sea to Shining Sea." [Notus] (4:1) Spr 89, p. 46.
"Open and Close." [Notus] (4:1) Spr 89, p. 48.
"Weapons." [Notus] (4:1) Spr 89, p. 47.

5469. STAUFFER, Grant
"Thoughts on a Judge's Order." [NewL] (55:3) Spr 89, p. 24-25.

5470. STEARNS, Catherine
"Conversation with The-Poem-Not-Yet-Born." [NoDaQ] (57:4) Fall 89, p. 83.
"Domestic Life." [Shen] (39:1) Spr 89, p. 89-90.

5471. STECEWICZ, Miroslaw
"Music As It Is" (tr. by Leslaw Ludwig). [BelPoJ] (40:2) Wint 89-90, p. 22-31.

STEEG, Jennie ver
See VERSTEEG, Jennie

5472. STEELE, Frank
"Early Summers." [Wind] (19:64) 89, p. 29.
"May." [Wind] (19:64) 89, p. 29.

5473. STEELE, Janet
"Indication." [ChamLR] (3:1, #5) Fall 89, p. 87.

5474. STEELE, Timothy
"Cosmos." [GreensboroR] (46) Sum 89, p. 136.

"Decisions, Decisions." [CrossCur] (8:2) Ja 89, p. 15.
"Last Tango." [SouthwR] (74:4) Aut 89, p. 527-528.
"On Wheeler Mountain." [GreensboroR] (46) Sum 89, p. 135.
"Practice." [CrossCur] (8:2) Ja 89, p. 16.
5475. STEFANILE, Felix
"Malaria" (tr. of Paolo Ruffilli). [Poetry] (155:1/2) O-N 89, p. 138-147.
STEFANO, John de
See De STEFANO, John
STEFANO, John di
See De STEFANO, John
5476. STEFFAN, Paula
"Clear Fall Morning, North Station." [SlipS] (9) 89, p. 83.
5477. STEFFEY, Duane
"Castleman in February, Thawing." [Wind] (19:65) 89, p. 32.
"Discussing Rain with a Child." [Wind] (19:65) 89, p. 32-33.
5478. STEFFLER, John
"At the Pigi Café, Ano Potamia." [MalR] (88) Fall 89, p. 100.
"Leaving Deer Lake by Air." [MalR] (88) Fall 89, p. 98.
"The Point of Combustion." [MalR] (88) Fall 89, p. 99.
"That Night We Were Ravenous." [MalR] (88) Fall 89, p. 101-103.
5479. STEIN, Agnes
"Portrait of the Artist's Mother." [RiverC] (10:1) Fall 89, p. 114.
5480. STEIN, Hannah
"Anniversary" (after Chagall). [YaleR] (78:3) Spr 89, p. 483.
"The Distance to the Ocean." [PraS] (63:2) Sum 89, p. 46-49.
"Grace." [PoetryNW] (30:4) Wint 89-90, p. 35-36.
"Madame Monet in the Garden." [CharR] (15:1) Spr 89, p. 60.
5481. STEIN, Jill
"Explaining the Passing Through." [US1] (22/23) Spr 89, p. 22.
"Roaches." [US1] (22/23) Spr 89, p. 22-23.
5482. STEIN, Kevin
"Cheating." [Poetry] (153:4) Ja 89, p. 217-218.
"The Music Time Makes" (With a line borrowed from Plutarch). [BlackWR] (16:1)
    Fall-Wint 89, p. 105-106.
"Portraits." [Ploughs] (15:1) 89, p. 134-135.
"The Shrine." [Crazy] (37) Wint 89, p. 32.
"The Virgin Birth." [NoAmR] (274:3) S 89, p. 41.
"What I Know about the Eye." [Ploughs] (15:1) 89, p. 132-133.
5483. STEINARR, Stein
"Running Water" (tr. by Alan Boucher). [Vis] (31) 89, p. 36.
5484. STEINBERG, Alan
"Loon Calls." [Blueline] (10:1/2) 89, p. 78.
"Weathered." [Blueline] (10:1/2) 89, p. 79.
5485. STEINBERG, David
"After James' Death" (For Harry Kelley, and to the memory of James Meade).
    [JamesWR] (6:4) Sum 89, p. 11.
5486. STEINBERGH, Judith
"Questions at Kezar Lake." [StoneC] (17:1/2) Fall-Wint 89-90, p. 13.
5487. STEINER, Donna
"Chambers of the Heart." [SinW] (38) Sum-Fall 89, p. 97.
5488. STEINGLASS, Matt
"Lafayette Park." [HarvardA] (123:4) My 89, p. 19.
5489. STEINGRABER, Sandra
"Epithalamion." [DenQ] (24:1) Sum 89, p. 76.
"Life After." [TriQ] (76) Fall 89, p. 104.
"Post-Op, January Ice Storm." [TriQ] (76) Fall 89, p. 105.
"Waiting Room." [TriQ] (76) Fall 89, p. 106.
5490. STEINMAN, Lisa M.
"Shelley to Byron, On Being Given an Already Named Boat." [Thrpny] (38) Sum
    89, p. 21.
5491. STELMACH, Marjorie
"Confirmation." [Chelsea] (48) 89, p. 95.
"Ghazals for the Color Gold." [Chelsea] (48) 89, p. 94.
"Here Be Dragons." [RiverS] (30) [89], p. 62-63.
"Pentecost." [Chelsea] (48) 89, p. 91-93.
"Self-Portrait Under a Portrait of the Moon." [Chelsea] (48) 89, p. 90-91.

"To Yourself." [Chelsea] (48) 89, p. 88-90.
5492. STEPANCHEV, Stephen
"Inspiration." [Poetry] (153:6) Mr 89, p. 349.
"One and Many." [Confr] (39/40) Fall 88-Wint 89, p. 58.
5493. STEPHENS, Jack
"Instantly." [NegC] (9:2) 89, p. 72.
"Rooms without Windows." [PraS] (63:4) Wint 89, p. 15-16.
"Surprise." [Journal] (12:2) Fall-Wint 88-89, p. 16.
"Transient Patterns in Light & Surf." [CinPR] (19) Spr 89, p. 18.
5494. STEPHENS, Phil
"Green Corn Moon." [MidwQ] (30:2) Wint 89, p. 207.
5495. STEPHENSON, Victoria
"By the Heels." [SoCoast] (5) Spr 88, p. 22-23.
5496. STEPTOE, Lamont (Lamont B.)
"Grand Daughter of Mama" (for LaMer). [PaintedB] (37) 89, p. 61.
"Something Broke Loose." [PaperAir] (4:2) 89, p. 115.
5497. STERLE, Francine
"Bosch's Harp." [Vis] (30) 89, p. 11.
"In the Pictures." [BelPoJ] (40:2) Wint 89-90, p. 4-5.
"Undressing." [Vis] (31) 89, p. 39.
"Wolf Woman." [Nimrod] (33:1) Fall-Wint 89, p. 100.
5498. STERLING, Phillip
"Crickets." [PassN] (10:2) Sum 89, p. 23.
"Relearning Sleep." [Plain] (9:3) Spr 89, p. 6.
5499. STERN, Gerald
"Bread Without Sugar" (In memory of Harry Stern, 1897-1969. Dedicated to Ted
Solotaroff). [GeoR] (43:2) Sum 89, p. 231-241.
"First Day of Spring." [Iowa] (19:2) Spr-Sum 89, p. 25-29.
"The Founder." [Antaeus] (62) Spr 89, p. 221-222.
"I Sometimes Think of the Lamb." [ThRiPo] (33/34) 89, p. 78.
"R for Rosemary." [Iowa] (19:2) Spr-Sum 89, p. 30-31.
"Saving My Skin from Burning." [Iowa] (19:2) Spr-Sum 89, p. 30.
"Three Hearts." [Iowa] (19:2) Spr-Sum 89, p. 29.
5500. STERN, Robert
"If I Make." [AntigR] (77/78) Spr-Sum 89, p. 128.
"The Stars Look Down." [AntigR] (77/78) Spr-Sum 89, p. 128.
"Totem." [AntigR] (79) Aut 89, p. 114.
5501. STERNBACH, David
"I Feel Free." [Screens] (1) 89, p. 45.
5502. STERNBERG, Ricardo
"For Now." [Nat] (249:19) 4 D 89, p. 693.
5503. STERNLIEB, Barry
"Right of Way." [GettyR] (2:3) Sum 89, p. 447-448.
5504. STESSEL, Edward
"The Cart." [MSS] (6:3) 89, p. 180.
5505. STETLER, Charles
"He Writes the Songs, or He Writes the Song." [Wind] (19:64) 89, p. 30-31.
"Pure Love." [Wind] (19:64) 89, p. 30.
5506. STETSER, Virginia M.
"The Bungler." [Kaleid] (18) Wint-Spr 89, p. 13.
"Columbine." [Kaleid] (18) Wint-Spr 89, p. 13.
5507. STEVEN, Ida
"Try Touching River Fog." [WritersF] (15) Fall 89, p. 66.
5508. STEVEN, Kenneth C.
"Summer." [Verse] (6:3) Wint 89, p. 41.
5509. STEVENS, C. J.
"The Remedies." [SoCoast] (6) Fall 88, p. 16.
5510. STEVENS, Jadene Felina
"A Marble Game in 1955." [Kalliope] (11:1) 89, p. 22-23.
5511. STEVENS, James R.
"Waters." [SoDakR] (27:4) Wint 89, p. 68-70.
5512. STEVENS, Lois Prante
"Daffy Dimensions." [Amelia] (5:3, #14) 89, p. 79.
5513. STEVENS, Shirley S.
"Bally Ferriter." [PoetL] (84:2) Sum 89, p. 10.

5514. STEVENSON, Anne
"And Even Then." [Pequod] (26/27) 89, p. 131.
"Call Them Poppies." [Pequod] (26/27) 89, p. 132.
"Inquit Deus." [Pequod] (26/27) 89, p. 134.
"Letter to Sylvia Plath" (Grantchester, May 1988). [GrahamHR] (12) Spr 89, p.
    9-12.
"*Portrait of a Lady* by Francis Bacon." [Pequod] (26/27) 89, p. 133.
"Stone Fig." [Atlantic] (264:2) Ag 89, p. 40.
5515. STEVENSON, Diane
"Descartes." [Poetry] (154:4) Jl 89, p. 189-190.
"Discovering Paradise." [OhioR] (44) 89, p. 64.
5516. STEVENSON, Richard
"Big Al's Trick." [Dandel] (16:1) Spr-Sum 89, p. 57.
"Expatriate Stories" (Maiduguri, Nigeria, 1980). [CrossC] (11:3) 89, p. 5.
"Henry, in Mid-Leap." [Grain] (17:2) Sum 89, p. 72.
"Supply Teacher / Relief Janitor." [Dandel] (16:1) Spr-Sum 89, p. 55-56.
"The World According to Reuter." [Grain] (17:2) Sum 89, p. 73.
5517. STEWARD, D. E.
"June." [MinnR] (NS 32) Spr 89, p. 112-121.
"March." [Conjunc] (14) 89, p. 245-255.
"Spring Semester Lecture Series." [SlipS] (9) 89, p. 50.
"Troopers." [SlipS] (9) 89, p. 35.
5518. STEWART, Caroline
"Plugged In." [EmeraldCR] (1989) c1988, p. 130.
5519. STEWART, Christine
"Sri Lanka 1983-1984." [Event] (18:2) Sum 89, p. 72-73.
5520. STEWART, Deborah
"Gloria's Husband." [AnthNEW] (1) 89, p. 22.
"The Road." [AnthNEW] (1) 89, p. 21.
5521. STEWART, Frank
"Giving Her Up to Emergency." [ColR] (NS 16:2) Fall 89-Wint 90, p. 27.
"A Night Drinking Song." [SwampR] (1:4) Sum 89, p. 61.
"Song." [SwampR] (1:4) Sum 89, p. 14.
"St. Agnes, and the Stars Come In." [ColR] (NS 16:2) Fall 89-Wint 90, p. 24-26.
"Summer Aubade." [HayF] (4) Spr 89, p. 12.
"The Vulture of This World." [ColR] (NS 16:2) Fall 89-Wint 90, p. 22-23.
5522. STEWART, Jack
"Cartersville." [Poem] (62) N 89, p. 7.
"Dispensations." [Poem] (62) N 89, p. 12.
"Hell." [Poem] (62) N 89, p. 8-9.
"The Old Channel" (White Lake, Michigan, for Bruce). [Poem] (62) N 89, p. 10-11.
5523. STEWART, Pamela
"The Crickets of Amherst." [Crazy] (37) Wint 89, p. 45-46.
"Naive Reading." [Crazy] (37) Wint 89, p. 47.
5524. STICKNEY, John
"Her Life." [Caliban] (7) 89, p. 55.
"Léger." [Caliban] (7) 89, p. 55.
5525. STIFFLER, Randall
"The Clearing." [StoneC] (16:3/4) Spr-Sum 89, p. 31-32.
"Fish Bone." [StoneC] (16:3/4) Spr-Sum 89, p. 30-31.
5526. STIGALL, John
"As Told in the Tombs." [Obs] (3:3) Wint 88, p. 115-117.
"Gigolo." [Obs] (3:3) Wint 88, p. 117-118.
"Morning." [Obs] (3:3) Wint 88, p. 119.
"The Scope." [Obs] (3:3) Wint 88, p. 118.
5527. STILL, Gloria
"The Good Distance" (for T. Z. and C. D.). [IndR] (13:1) Wint 89, p. 29-33.
5528. STILLER, Nikki
"Two by Van Gogh." [Prima] (13) 89, p. 42.
5529. STINSON, Susan
"Summer Office." [YellowS] (29) Spr 89, p. 6.
5530. STITT, Linda
"The Intuitive Rose." [KeyWR] (2:1/2) Fall-Wint 89, p. 115.
"Youth, Passing." [KeyWR] (2:1/2) Fall-Wint 89, p. 116.
5531. STIVENDER, David
"City from Above" (tr. of Giovanni Raboni, w. J. D. McClatchy). [Poetry] (155:1/2)

O-N 89, p. 89.
"The Fan" (tr. of Pier Paolo Pasolini, w. J. D. McClatchy). [Poetry] (155:1/2) O-N
89, p. 50.
"Figures in the Park" (tr. of Giovanni Raboni, w. J. D. McClatchy). [Poetry]
(155:1/2) O-N 89, p. 90.
"Flesh and Sky" (tr. of Pier Paolo Pasolini, w. J. D. McClatchy). [Poetry] (155:1/2)
O-N 89, p. 51.
"My Daughter's Birthday" (tr. of Giovanni Raboni, w. J. D. McClatchy). [Poetry]
(155:1/2) O-N 89, p. 91.
"Part of a Letter to the Codignola Boy" (tr. of Pier Paolo Pasolini, w. J. D.
McClatchy). [Poetry] (155:1/2) O-N 89, p. 47.
"Il Pianto della Scavatrice (The Lament of the Excavator)" (Selection: V., tr. of Pier
Paolo Pasolini, w. J. D. McClatchy). [Poetry] (155:1/2) O-N 89, p. 48-49.
5532. STOCK, Norman
"The Broken Doorbell." [ColEng] (51:3) Mr 89, p. 284.
"Change of Plans." [ColEng] (51:3) Mr 89, p. 285.
"The Dead Horse of Poetry." [ColEng] (51:1) Ja 89, p. 48.
"How to Get Out of Bed." [ColEng] (51:1) Ja 89, p. 48.
"Nursery." [ColEng] (51:3) Mr 89, p. 285.
"This Must Be My Stop." [ColEng] (51:1) Ja 89, p. 47.
"Trying to Remember Himself at 18." [ColEng] (51:3) Mr 89, p. 284.
5533. STOCKWELL, Jeff
"Serial Killers." [NoAmR] (274:2) Je 89, p. 47.
5534. STOKES, Denis
"Frozen Smoke." [AntigR] (77/78) Spr-Sum 89, p. 27.
5535. STOKES, Terry
"I See the Girl on T.V. Who Has Lost Her Memory." [WestHR] (43:2) Sum 89, p.
132-133.
5536. STOKESBURY, Leon
"The Lamar Tech Football Team Has Won Its Game." [ThRiPo] (31/32) 88, p. 55.
"Señor Wences and the Man in the Box" (L.B. Stokesbury, 1924-1987).
[NewEngR] (12:1) Aut 89, p. 82-83.
"Unsent Message to My Brother in His Pain." [ThRiPo] (31/32) 88, p. 54-55.
5537. STOLOFF, Carolyn
"Emptying the Bowl." [Contact] (9:50/51/52) Fall-Wint 88-Spr 89, p. 16.
5538. STONE, Alison
"Bad New York Poems." [ArtfulD] (16/17) Fall 89, p. 33.
"Beneath the Beautiful." [Poetry] (154:4) Jl 89, p. 221-222.
"Dojo." [StoneC] (17:1/2) Fall-Wint 89-90, p. 34-35.
"Ink Threads." [ParisR] (31:111) Sum 89, p. 217-218.
"Nightclub." [SlipS] (9) 89, p. 8.
"Starving for God." [Poetry] (154:4) Jl 89, p. 220.
5539. STONE, Arthur
"My Lunch with Bukowski." [SouthernPR] (29:2) Fall 89, p. 76.
5540. STONE, Carole
"The Persistence of Memory." [WestB] (24) 89, p. 50.
"Souvenir." [HayF] (4) Spr 89, p. 75.
"Welcome to New Smyrna Beach." [HayF] (4) Spr 89, p. 76.
5541. STONE, Frances
"Sounds of Silents" (Derived from Charlie Chaplin's One-Man Show by Dan
Kamin). [SmPd] (26:3 #77) Fall 89, p. 6.
5542. STONE, Ruth
"As I Remember." [AmerPoR] (18:2) Mr-Ap 89, p. 37.
"That Day." [AmerPoR] (18:2) Mr-Ap 89, p. 37.
5543. STONEHOUSE
"1. I made my home west of the Sha" (tr. by Red Pine). [LitR] (32:3) Spr 89, p.
356.
"76. It's a lonesome hut this new fall night" (tr. by Red Pine). [LitR] (32:3) Spr 89,
p. 356.
"143. Life in the mountains depends on a hoe" (tr. by Red Pine). [LitR] (32:3) Spr
89, p. 356.
"144. I fix my hoe my hut can lean" (tr. by Red Pine). [LitR] (32:3) Spr 89, p. 356.
5544. STORACE, Patricia
"War Movie: Last Leave, 1944." [Ploughs] (15:4) Wint 89-90, p. 209-210.
5545. STORIE-PAHLITZSCH, Lori
"Coming Out." [CapeR] (24:2) Fall 89, p. 41.

"Tree Work." [PoetryNW] (30:2) Sum 89, p. 40-41.
"Wanting Whole Memory" (for Michelle, who was my student). [PoetryNW] (30:2)
  Sum 89, p. 39-40.
5546. STORTONI, Laura Anna
  "Atlantis" (On the Greek island of Santorini). [MidwQ] (30:4) Sum 89, p. 453-454.
5547. STOTTS, Ann
  "The Proletarian Weed." [Farm] (6:2) Fall 89, p. 39.
STOWALL, Phyllis
  See STOWELL, Phyllis
5548. STOWELL, Phyllis
  "#100 and 6." [FiveFR] (7) 89, p. 60.
  "Definition of a Shadow." [Ascent] (14:3) 89, p. 47-48.
5549. STRAHAN, B. R. (Bradley R.)
  "Night Watchman of the Dawn" (tr. of Nikolai Kantchev, w. Pamela Perry). [Vis]
    (30) 89, p. 4.
  "Talisman." [HolCrit] (26:2) Ap 89, p. 15.
5550. STRAK, Andrzej
  "The King and the Poet" (tr. by Jerzy Jarniewicz). [TampaR] (2) 89, p. 69.
5551. STRAND, Mark
  "The Continuous Life." [NewYorker] (64:47) 9 Ja 89, p. 34.
  "Fiction." [YaleR] (78:4) Sum 89, p. 625.
  "From a Lost Diary." [Antaeus] (62) Spr 89, p. 223.
  "The Idea." [NewYorker] (65:17) 12 Je 89, p. 120.
  "Life in the Valley." [NewYorker] (65:7) 3 Ap 89, p. 38.
  "A Little Chekhov." [Antaeus] (62) Spr 89, p. 224-225.
  "Orpheus Alone." [NewYorker] (65:3) 6 Mr 89, p. 42-43.
  "Translation." [Antaeus] (62) Spr 89, p. 226-229.
  "Velocity Meadows." [NewRep] (200:21) 22 My 89, p. 35.
5552. STRATFORD, Philip
  "The Villon Legacy" (tr. of Félix Leclerc). [CanLit] (121) Sum 89, p. 107-114.
5553. STRATIDAKIS, Eileen
  "Oz." [Vis] (31) 89, p. 12.
5554. STRATTON, R. E.
  "Hors d'Oeurves." [Plain] (10:1) 89, p. 35.
  "Innovative Strategies in Developmental Education." [Plain] (9:2) Wint 89, p. 38.
  "Sam Alexander, the Two-Faced Man." [Plain] (9:3) Spr 89, p. 16.
5555. STRAUSS, Nancy
  "Waiting." [CinPR] (19) Spr 89, p. 13.
5556. STRICKER, Meredith
  "The Lightning Hive." [Epoch] (38:3) 89, p. 177-197.
5557. STRINGER, A. E.
  "Closures." [Journal] (12:2) Fall-Wint 88-89, p. 31.
  "Half-Life Matters." [Journal] (12:2) Fall-Wint 88-89, p. 28-29.
  "Hello, I Must Be Going." [Journal] (12:2) Fall-Wint 88-89, p. 27.
  "Sheer Flight." [Journal] (12:2) Fall-Wint 88-89, p. 30.
5558. STRITCH, Jerry
  "Woodful" (tr. of Biddy Jenkinson). [Trans] (22) Fall 89, p. 117.
5559. STROBLOVA, Jana
  "Circus" (tr. by Jarmila and Ian Milner). [Verse] (6:2) Je 89, p. 60.
  "The Slaughterhouse" (tr. by Jarmila and Ian Milner). [Verse] (6:2) Je 89, p. 61.
5560. STROMBERG, Scott
  "Love Song of Billy Morning." [Mildred] (3:1) Spr-Sum 89, p. 89.
  "My Little Gray Aunt." [Mildred] (3:1) Spr-Sum 89, p. 88.
5561. STRONG, Eithne
  "Bald." [FourQ] (2d series 3:2) Fall 89, p. 20.
  "The Learning Process." [NoDaQ] (57:1) Wint 89, p. 148.
5562. STRONG, K. Scott
  "Epitaph." [KeyWR] (2:1/2) Fall-Wint 89, p. 120.
  "Meditation." [KeyWR] (2:1/2) Fall-Wint 89, p. 120.
  "Sunrise." [KeyWR] (2:1/2) Fall-Wint 89, p. 121.
5563. STRUTHERS, Ann
  "Norwegian Spring." [PoetC] (21:1) Fall 89, p. 42.
  "Sarah Orne Jewett." [AmerS] (58:3) Sum 89, p. 354.
  "Weaving Like Dancing Basketmakers." [SouthernHR] (23:2) Spr 89, p. 122.
  "When Passion Fades." [Kalliope] (10:1/2) 88, p. 41.
  "William Cullen Bryant." [PoetC] (21:1) Fall 89, p. 40-41.

"Writing *Moby Dick*." [Poetry] (153:6) Mr 89, p. 319.
5564. STRUTHERS, Betsy
"High Tide" (Editors' Second Prize Winner, Poetry). [CrossC] (11:1) 89, p. 17.
5565. STRYK, Dan
"Mouse." [SmPd] (26:3 #77) Fall 89, p. 9.
"Netting Butterflies." [PoetryNW] (30:3) Aut 89, p. 12-13.
"Prayer Rug Fading." [BelPoJ] (40:2) Wint 89-90, p. 34-35.
5566. STRYK, Lucien
"Joshu Exclaimed, 'Dog's No Buddha'" (tr. of Ichigen). [LitR] (32:3) Spr 89, p.
359.
"Light." [Poetry] (154:3) Je 89, p. 148.
"The Mountain -- Buddha's Body" (tr. of Layman Sotoba). [LitR] (32:3) Spr 89, p.
359.
"Song and Singer: A Note for John Logan." [PaintedB] (39) 89, p. 24-25.
5567. STUART, Dabney
"Gospel Singer." [SouthernR] (25:2) Spr 89, p. 485-486.
"Umpire." [SouthernPR] (29:1) Spr 89, p. 31-32.
5568. STUART, Judith
"For Mono Mills Alice, B. 1857-." [Quarry] (38:1) Wint 89, p. 34.
"Island / Point of View." [Quarry] (38:1) Wint 89, p. 35.
"Passchendaele, Again." [Quarry] (38:1) Wint 89, p. 33.
5569. STUBBS, Jean
"Farewell Not Tinged with Sadness" (tr. of Pedro Pérez Sarduy). [Pig] (15) 88, p.
76.
5570. STUDER, Constance
"Same Flesh, Same Bone" (For Patricia Ann Bush, Nagshead, 1987). [CreamCR]
(13:2) Fall 89, p. 245-246.
"The Small Head, Damp Against the Chest." [HighP] (4:2) Fall 89, p. 46-47.
5571. STULL, Dalene Workman
"Physical Realities." [KanQ] (21:3) Sum 89, p. 60.
"Winter Song." [KanQ] (21:3) Sum 89, p. 61.
5572. STULL, Richard
"Adoration of the Golden Calf." [Pequod] (28/29/30) 89, p. 185.
5573. STUMP, Sheldon
"When They Speak." [CumbPR] (9:1) Fall 89, p. 8-9.
5574. STURDIVANT, Kay
"The Body as a Volume of Desire." [DenQ] (24:2) Fall 89, p. 92-93.
5575. STYLE, Emily
"Rachel's Fourteenth Birthday Poem, Written September 15, 1988." [Footwork] 89,
p. 45-46.
5576. SU, Shih
"Drinking at a Lake on a Clear Day Followed by Rain" (tr. by Anthony Piccione and
Carol Zhigong Chang). [LitR] (32:3) Spr 89, p. 391.
"Lotus Viewing" (tr. by Burton Watson). [LitR] (32:3) Spr 89, p. 435.
"Mid Autumn Festival" (tr. by Julie Landau). [MSS] (6:3) 89, p. 71.
"Separation" (tr. by Anthony Piccione, Li Young Lee, and Carol Zhigong Chang).
[LitR] (32:3) Spr 89, p. 389.
"Ten Years Living Dying Alone" (tr. by Cid Corman). [LitR] (32:3) Spr 89, p. 375.
SU, Shin
See SU, Shih
SU, Tung-p'o
See SU, Shih
5577. SUBACH, Karen
"Coal." [CimR] (89) O 89, p. 99-100.
"Don't Tell Me" (tr. of Georges Hausemer). [Vis] (31) 89, p. 41.
"Rabbits at Iraklion." [AmerPoR] (18:6) N-D 89, p. 19.
5578. SUBLETT, Dyan
"Francis of Assisi." [WestHR] (43:1) Spr 89, p. 58-59.
5579. SUBRAMAN, Belinda
"Brain/Cow Poem." [RagMag] (7:1) 89, p. 61.
5580. SUDERMAN, Elmer
"Defined by Barbed Wire." [KanQ] (21:1/2) Wint-Spr 89, p. 165.
"Mennonite Country Church." [KanQ] (21:1/2) Wint-Spr 89, p. 165.
"Thoughts in the Cemetery Where My Parents Are Buried." [Wind] (19:64) 89, p.
32-33.
"Unless It Rained." [MidwQ] (30:2) Wint 89, p. 186.

"Wheat Chaff Settled." [MidwQ] (30:2) Wint 89, p. 190.
SUEUR, Meridel le
    See LeSUEUR, Meridel
5581. SUK, Julie
    "Family." [MidwQ] (31:1) Aut 89, p. 69.
    "Heartwood." [SouthernHR] (23:4) Fall 89, p. 320.
5582. SUKNASKI, Andrew
    "Vitpalno." [CanLit] (120) Spr 89, p. 21-41.
5583. SULLIVAN, A. D.
    "Nothing But Clover." [CreamCR] (13:2) Fall 89, p. 29.
5584. SULLIVAN, Anita T.
    "A Mention of Birds." [SoCaR] (21:2) Spr 89, p. 54.
5585. SULLIVAN, Chuck
    "Radio Hanoi Is Still Playing Our Song." [GreensboroR] (46) Sum 89, p. 171-172.
5586. SULLIVAN, David
    "Storyville" (Selections: 5 poems). [BelPoJ] (40:2) Wint 89-90, p. 6-12.
5587. SULLIVAN, James
    "The Dissolution of Memory." [BelPoJ] (39:3) Spr 89, p. 1.
5588. SULLIVAN, Mary Jane
    "The Double Becoming." [Vis] (29) 89, p. 41.
    "The Gaunt Cove at Carna." [Vis] (29) 89, p. 42.
    "Leaning on Ritual." [Vis] (29) 89, p. 42.
5589. SULLIVAN, Sally
    "Cinderella: An Unabridged, Updated Version." [Pembroke] (21) 89, p. 161-165.
    "On Love and Lisianthus" (To J.W.). [Pembroke] (21) 89, p. 160-161.
5590. SUMRALL, Amber Coverdale
    "Daybreak." [Kaleid] (19) Sum-Fall 89, p. 33.
    "Listening to the Language of Birds." [Kaleid] (19) Sum-Fall 89, p. 33.
    "Moving Through Silence." [Kaleid] (19) Sum-Fall 89, p. 32.
    "Night Muse." [Kaleid] (19) Sum-Fall 89, p. 33.
5591. SUNDAHL, Daniel James
    "Buffalo." [CreamCR] (13:2) Fall 89, p. 109-110.
    "Hiroshima Maidens: Imaginary Translations from the Japanese." [Hawai'iR] (13:1, #25) Spr 89, p. 94-95.
    "The Persistence of Memory: Part II." [MidAR] (9:1) 89, p. 40.
    "Rabbinical Legends: Necessity and Grace." [PassN] (10:1) Wint 89, p. 7.
    "Ransford Dodo at the Depot" (circa 1955). [Verse] (6:1) Mr 89, p. 51.
    "Sketch of a Young Woman Picking Fruit." [Comm] (116:16) S 22, 89, p. 502.
    "Summer Work, Iowa, 1968." [BambooR] (44) Fall 89, p. 33.
    "Summer Work, Iowa, 1968." [SouthernPR] (29:2) Fall 89, p. 26.
5592. SUPERVIELLE, Jules
    "Heavy" (tr. by Geoffrey Gardner). [SenR] (19:2) Fall 89, p. 68.
    "The Little Forest" (tr. by Geoffrey Gardner). [SenR] (19:2) Fall 89, p. 63.
    "The Room Next Door" (tr. by Geoffrey Gardner). [SenR] (19:2) Fall 89, p. 65.
    "The Sick Man" (tr. by Geoffrey Gardner). [SenR] (19:2) Fall 89, p. 64.
    "Without God" (tr. by Geoffrey Gardner). [SenR] (19:2) Fall 89, p. 66-67.
5593. SUPRANER, Robyn
    "By Appointment Only." [PaintedB] (38) 89, p. 68.
    "Hurricane Alice." [BlueBldgs] (11) 89, p. 39.
    "The Second Time." [Confr] (39/40) Fall 88-Wint 89, p. 135.
5594. SURNAMER, Shulamith
    "Passover Villanelle." [SingHM] (16) 89, p. 41.
5595. SURVANT, Joe
    "A Ceremony of Deer." [Farm] (6:1) Wint-Spr 88-89, p. 39.
    "Edaithi." [Chelsea] (48) 89, p. 34-35.
    "Euthanasia." [PoetC] (20:3) Spr 89, p. 37.
    "Finding Lost River." [Farm] (6:1) Wint-Spr 88-89, p. 38.
    "The Man Who Loved Trees." [Farm] (6:1) Wint-Spr 88-89, p. 40.
    "Polo in the Tang." [Chelsea] (48) 89, p. 35-36.
5596. SURVE, Narayan
    "Lifetime" (tr. by Vinay Dharwadker). [TriQ] (77) Wint 89-90, p. 205.
5597. SUSSKIND, Harriet
    "Custom." [HeliconN] (20) 89, p. 80-81.
5598. SUSUMU, Kamaike
    "A Batch of Late Poems" (9 poems, tr. of Kusano Shimpei, w. Cid Corman). [Sulfur] (9:1, #24) Spr 89, p. 60-69.

5599. SUTHERLAND, W. M.
"The Van Gogh Letters." [Rampike] (6:2) 88, p. 19.
5600. SUTHERLAND-SMITH, James
"Birds." [LaurelR] (23:2) Sum 89, p. 88.
"Clouds in Libya." [GrahamHR] (12) Spr 89, p. 104-105.
"The Donkey." [MinnR] (NS 32) Spr 89, p. 78.
"Fate Theme." [LitR] (32:2) Wint 89, p. 234.
"The Fossil." [KanQ] (21:1/2) Wint-Spr 89, p. 156.
"History on the Coast." [LaurelR] (23:2) Sum 89, p. 87.
"Old Tattooed Man at a Carnival." [WindO] (51) Spr 89, p. 42.
"Tayamoum." [WindO] (51) Spr 89, p. 43-44.
"To Persephone." [GrahamHR] (12) Spr 89, p. 102-103.
5601. SUTTER, Barton
"A Little Litany for Moving Day." [NoDaQ] (57:4) Fall 89, p. 57-58.
"No Fish." [NoDaQ] (57:4) Fall 89, p. 59.
5602. SUTZKEVER, Abraham
"The Batman" (tr. by Ruth Whitman). [GrahamHR] (12) Spr 89, p. 56.
"Black Grapes" (tr. by Ruth Whitman). [GrahamHR] (12) Spr 89, p. 53.
"In a Chinese Antique Shop" (tr. by Ruth Whitman). [MassR] (30:1) Spr 89, p. 7-9.
"It's Obvious" (tr. by Ruth Whitman). [MassR] (30:1) Spr 89, p. 10-11.
"The Kiss" (tr. by Murray Wolfe). [PartR] (56:1) Wint 89, p. 114.
"Prayer for a Sick Friend" (tr. by Ruth Whitman). [NewYorker] (65:8) 10 Ap 89, p. 40.
"Sifting Through" (tr. by Ruth Whitman). [MassR] (30:1) Spr 89, p. 9.
"Song About Caves, Sung in Darkness" (tr. by Ruth Whitman). [GrahamHR] (12) Spr 89, p. 54-55.
"Tall Violincellos" (tr. by Ruth Whitman). [GrahamHR] (12) Spr 89, p. 57.
SUTZKEVOR, Abraham
See SUTZKEVER, Abraham
5603. SUVIN, Darko R.
"Shipwreck in Pannonia: A Sonnet with a Tail." [Pig] (15) 88, p. 36.
5604. SVARLIEN, Diane Arnson
"IV.7. I do believe in ghosts! And death is not, after all" (tr. of Propertius). [Trans] (22) Fall 89, p. 222-225.
5605. SVEHLA, John
"Brief Stars." [Wind] (19:65) 89, p. 25.
"Brown Leaf Twigs." [DeKalbLAJ] (22:1/4) 89, p. 67.
"Brown Leaf Twigs." [Wind] (19:65) 89, p. 14.
"Driving." [Wind] (19:65) 89, p. 14.
"Leaf Crabs." [DeKalbLAJ] (22:1/4) 89, p. 67.
"Motor Bikes." [Wind] (19:65) 89, p. 34.
"Shoe Bubbles." [DeKalbLAJ] (22:1/4) 89, p. 67.
5606. SVENDSEN, Sharon E.
"News of Dark Matter." [CapeR] (24:2) Fall 89, p. 28.
5607. SVENOLD, Mark
"Poverty Music." [MSS] (6:3) 89, p. 111.
"Relearning Winter." [MSS] (6:3) 89, p. 109.
5608. SVOBODA, Terese
"All Happy Families." [Ploughs] (15:4) Wint 89-90, p. 211-217.
"As the Birds." [AmerPoR] (18:5) S-O 89, p. 48.
"Betty's Silence." [MassR] (30:2) Sum 89, p. 336.
"Brothers." [PraS] (63:3) Fall 89, p. 98-99.
"Cowboy." [NewEngR] (11:4) Sum 89, p. 442-443.
"For Shirley." [PraS] (63:3) Fall 89, p. 95-97.
"His Dark." [DenQ] (24:1) Sum 89, p. 77-78.
"Nothing Beautiful Except in Things." [MassR] (30:2) Sum 89, p. 336-337.
"Pink." [NewYorker] (65:37) 30 O 89, p. 97.
"The Sixties." [MassR] (30:2) Sum 89, p. 335.
"Snow Cold." [PraS] (63:3) Fall 89, p. 99-100.
"Tuba Sonnet." [PraS] (63:3) Fall 89, p. 98.
5609. SWAIM, Alice MacKenzie
"Violet-Starred Grass" (Honorable Mention, 3rd Annual Contest). [SoCoast] (6) Fall 88, p. 10-11.
5610. SWAN, Allison
"Unmailed Letter." [BellR] (12:1, #25) Spr 89, p. 25.

5611. SWANBERG, Christine
"The English Teacher's Sonnet." [EngJ] (78:3) Mr 89, p. 89.
"Oppenheimer, After Forty Years" (The Seattle Post-Intelligencer, June 16, 1985).
[Amelia] (5:3, #14) 89, p. 124-125.
5612. SWANEY, George
"Xenobia." [Jacaranda] (4:1) Spr-Sum 89, p. 19.
5613. SWANGER, David
"Evening Television." [CharR] (15:2) Fall 89, p. 87.
"How Does Music Measure Time?" [PoetryNW] (30:2) Sum 89, p. 17-18.
"Love." [PoetC] (20:2) Wint 89, p. 25-26.
"Oedipus Irvington." [PoetryNW] (30:2) Sum 89, p. 17.
"Sloth: The Deadliest Sin." [GeoR] (43:4) Wint 89, p. 708.
"Where Wind Learns About Itself." [PoetC] (20:2) Wint 89, p. 27-28.
"White Out." [CharR] (15:2) Fall 89, p. 86.
5614. SWANN, Brian
"Aerealist." [SouthernPR] (29:2) Fall 89, p. 18.
"Ancient Evenings." [NewAW] (5) Fall 89, p. 110.
"Back." [NewL] (56:2/3) Wint 89-Spr 90, p. 300-301.
"Connected." [NewL] (56:2/3) Wint 89-Spr 90, p. 302.
"Countdown." [PoetryNW] (30:1) Spr 89, p. 18.
"Epithalamium." [Caliban] (6) 89, p. 143.
"Exist." [ParisR] (31:110) Spr 89, p. 33.
"The Horse." [ColEng] (51:8) D 89, p. 838.
"In Memory of Raymond Brown" (1927-1983). [Poetry] (154:4) Jl 89, p. 230-231.
"Late Spring." [NewL] (56:2/3) Wint 89-Spr 90, p. 297-299.
"Looted." [PoetryNW] (30:1) Spr 89, p. 18-19.
"Lost Constellations." [Ploughs] (15:1) 89, p. 137.
"Of Hell." [Agni] (28) 89, p. 281.
"The Party." [Caliban] (6) 89, p. 143.
"Poetry Makes Nothing Happen." [Ploughs] (15:1) 89, p. 138.
"Tomorrow, Today." [Ploughs] (15:1) 89, p. 136.
"Where the Woods Begin." [PoetryNW] (30:1) Spr 89, p. 19.
"Wipeout." [NewL] (56:2/3) Wint 89-Spr 90, p. 301-302.
5615. SWANN, Roberta
"Stay." [Ploughs] (15:1) 89, p. 139-140.
"Uncle Alice." [Ploughs] (15:1) 89, p. 141.
5616. SWANSON, Catherine
"Many Volatile Acts Have Passed As Love." [NoDaQ] (57:3) Sum 89, p. 221.
"Zuni" (for Lisa). [PassN] (10:2) Sum 89, p. 28.
5617. SWARD, Robert
"Basketball's The American Game Because It's Hysterical." [FreeL] (3) Aut 89, p.
24-25.
5618. SWARTS, Helene
"Like Artists." [NegC] (9:2) 89, p. 73.
5619. SWEENEY, Michael
"Ars Poetica" (for Bill Evans). [BrooklynR] (5) 88, p. 11.
"Celtics' Last Stand." [BrooklynR] (5) 88, p. 9.
"Fat Franky." [BrooklynR] (5) 88, p. 10.
5620. SWEENEY, Richard
"The Glory of Divorced People" (For Kathllen Platt). [WestB] (23) 89, p. 61.
5621. SWEENEY, Teresa
"Waiting Tables." [KanQ] (21:3) Sum 89, p. 64.
5622. SWENSEN, Cole
"The Civil Servant." [Colum] (14) 89, p. 62.
"The Evening News." [Colum] (14) 89, p. 63.
"Ghazal with Something Missing." [NewL] (55:3) Spr 89, p. 109.
"Washing Hands." [Zyzzyva] (5:1, #17) Spr 89, p. 65.
5623. SWENSON, Karen
"Trekking the Hills of Northern Thailand." [DenQ] (24:1) Sum 89, p. 79.
5624. SWENSON, May
"A Rescue." [Ploughs] (15:4) Wint 89-90, p. 218-221.
5625. SWERDLOW, David
"In Memory of Eugene O'Neill." [Confr] (39/40) Fall 88-Wint 89, p. 107.
"Looking Out the Window, Drawing Nudes." [PoetL] (84:2) Sum 89, p. 13-14.
5626. SWIFT, Joan
"Chiton." [Poetry] (154:5) Ag 89, p. 276.

"Spoon." [PoetryNW] (30:3) Aut 89, p. 24.
"Stockings." [WillowS] (23) Wint 89, p. 35-36.
5627. SWILKY, Jody
"At Any Time." [HeavenB] (7) Wint 89, p. 15.
5628. SWIR, Anna
"Poems on My Father and My Mother" (15 poems, tr. by Czeslaw Milosz and
Leonard Nathan). [AmerPoR] (18:1) Ja-F 89, p. 23-25.
5629. SWISS, Thomas
"The Dream Life." [TarRP] (29:1) Fall 89, p. 21.
5630. SWIST, Wally
"Euterpe Singing." [PoetryE] (28) Fall 89, p. 70.
"Life Pulse" (6 of 12 tanka for each of the compositions performed by Kodo on their
One Earth Tour '89 . . .). [Os] (28) 89, p. 25-27.
"Shells." [Os] (29) 89, p. 3.
"Sweet Woodruff" (for Robert Francis). [PaintedB] (37) 89, p. 90.
5631. SWOFFORD, Michael
"Swift Flight" (Chet Baker, 1929-88). [NewL] (55:3) Spr 89, p. 85.
5632. SYLVESTER, Janet
"Heat." [Journal] (12:2) Fall-Wint 88-89, p. 19.
"The Mangle." [Journal] (12:2) Fall-Wint 88-89, p. 18.
5633. SYVERTSEN, Paul
"Identical Twins." [StoneC] (16:3/4) Spr-Sum 89, p. 78.
5634. SZABADOS, Béla
"Crossing with Jello." [PraF] (10:1, #46) Spr 89, p. 20.
"Epilepsy." [PraF] (10:1, #46) Spr 89, p. 21.
"Tongues." [Dandel] (16:2) Fall-Wint 89, p. 9-10.
5635. SZE, Arthur
"Axolotl." [Chelsea] (48) 89, p. 110.
"The Great White Shark." [Chelsea] (48) 89, p. 109.
"In Your Honor." [Chelsea] (48) 89, p. 111.
"Slanting Light." [Manoa] (1:1/2) Fall 89, p. 48.
5636. SZEPESI, Attila
"Waiting for Miracles" (tr. by Zsuzsanna Ozsvath and Martha Satz). [WebR] (14:1)
Spr 89, p. 29.
5637. SZÖCS, Géza
"An American Indian on the Hungarian Radio" (For the poet Willima Least Heat
Moon, tr. by Nicholas Kolumban). [NoDaQ] (57:4) Fall 89, p. 12-13.
"On a January Morning" (from Romania, tr. by Nicholas Kolumban). [PoetryE] (28)
Fall 89, p. 180-181.
5638. SZUMOWSKI, Margaret
"Born Again at the Golden Nozzle." [MassR] (30:2) Sum 89, p. 239.
"The Color of Jungle Birds." [MassR] (30:2) Sum 89, p. 240.
"Schermerhorns' Fish." [Calyx] (12:1) Sum 89, p. 6-7.
"The Woman Who Gave Up a Good Thing." [WillowS] (23) Wint 89, p. 10-11.
"Zampiceni's Marketplace." [Calyx] (12:1) Sum 89, p. 8.
5639. SZYMBORSKA, Wislawa
"Clothes" (tr. by Stanislaw Baranczak and Clare Cavanagh). [SenR] (19:2) Fall 89,
p. 20.
"The Great Man's House" (tr. by Stanislaw Baranczak and Clare Cavanah). [Trans]
(21) Spr 89, p. 42-43.
"In Broad Daylight" (tr. by Stanislaw Baranczak and Clare Cavanagh). [PartR]
(56:2) Spr 89, p. 278-279.
"Into the Ark" (tr. by Stanislaw Baranczak and Clare Cavanagh). [SenR] (19:2) Fall
89, p. 21-22.
"Our Ancestors' Short Lives" (tr. by Stanislaw Baranczak and Clare Cavanagh).
[PartR] (56:2) Spr 89, p. 277-278.
"Possibilities" (tr. by Stanislaw Baranczak and Clare Cavanagh). [SenR] (19:2) Fall
89, p. 23-24.
"A Tale Begun" (tr. by Stanislaw Baranczak and Clare Cavanagh). [PartR] (56:2)
Spr 89, p. 280-281.
SZYMBORSKA, Wistawa
See SZYMBORSKA, Wislawa
5640. TABAK, Ayelet
"They have been quiet for a long time now." [FiveFR] (7) 89, p. 1.
5641. TABLADA, Jose Juan
"Nocturno Alterno." [LindLM] (8:2) Ap-Je 89, p. 7.

5642. TAFDRUP, Pia
"White Fever" (Selection: "Seen (Set)," tr. by Monique M. Kennedy and Thomas E. Kennedy). [Pequod] (26/27) 89, p. 195.
5643. TAFT, Mark
"The mountains' soft harp-like." [Mildred] (3:1) Spr-Sum 89, p. 35.
5644. TAGG, John
"Equilibrium." [Poem] (62) N 89, p. 43.
"War Play." [Poem] (62) N 89, p. 42.
5645. TAGGART, John
"The Face of Love." [Sulfur] (9:1, #24) Spr 89, p. 52.
"For Instance." [Sulfur] (9:1, #24) Spr 89, p. 53.
"Free Gifts." [Sulfur] (9:1, #24) Spr 89, p. 54.
"In and Under." [Epoch] (38:1) 89, p. 25.
"The King of Eynan." [Epoch] (38:1) 89, p. 21.
"Milk and Seed." [Caliban] (7) 89, p. 83.
"Question No Question." [Screens] (1) 89, p. 175.
"Ready or Not." [Caliban] (7) 89, p. 84.
"Rereading." [Temblor] (10) 89, p. 68-75.
"Take Away." [Epoch] (38:1) 89, p. 22-24.
"Three Words from Thomas Bernhard." [Notus] (4:1) Spr 89, p. 78-80.
"Vaguely Harmless." [Conjunc] (14) 89, p. 261-266.
5646. TAGLIABUE, John
"A Request Related to William Carlos Williams." [Chelsea] (48) 89, p. 104-105.
5647. TAGORE, Rabindranath
"I Am Lost" (tr. by Monish R. Chatterjee). [InterPR] (15:2) Fall 89, p. 86.
T'AI-PO, Li
See LI, Po
5648. TAJIMA, Princess (ca. 687)
"Men love to gossip" (tr. by Sam Hamill). [PoetryE] (28) Fall 89, p. 204.
5649. TAKACS, Nancy
"For the Neighbor." [ColR] (NS 16:2) Fall 89-Wint 90, p. 68-69.
"Not Burning the Leaves." [ColR] (NS 16:2) Fall 89-Wint 90, p. 67.
5650. TAKACS, Zsuzsa
"Fog, I Hear the Crack of Bullets" (tr. by Mária Kurdi and Len Roberts). [IndR] (12:2) Spr 89, p. 98-99.
TAKARA, Kathryn Waddell
See WADDELL-TAKARA, Kathryn
5651. TAKSA, Mark
"The Flowers Fade Before We Eat Them." [CapeR] (24:1) Spr 89, p. 22.
"From the Non-Hero." [LaurelR] (23:1) Wint 89, p. 101.
"Love on the Avenue." [BallSUF] (30:4) Aut 89, p. 58-59.
"Marble Circumference." [Interim] (8:1) Spr 89, p. 26.
"The Parent and the Haunting Lake." [Contact] (9:50/51/52) Fall-Wint 88-Spr 89, p. 17.
"Skyscrapers Are Quiet in Our Tanks." [Interim] (8:1) Spr 89, p. 27.
"The Smiling Stone." [CinPR] (20) Fall 89, p. 69.
"Speculative Cradle." [CinPR] (20) Fall 89, p. 68.
"Trampled Courage." [WritersF] (15) Fall 89, p. 102.
"Versus Tired Feet." [ArtfulD] (16/17) Fall 89, p. 34.
"Wearing Her Husband's Shirt." [LaurelR] (23:1) Wint 89, p. 100-101.
5652. TALAL, Marilynn
"The Egyptian Museum of Antiquities." [Poetry] (154:1) Ap 89, p. 26.
5653. TALENTINO, Arnold
"The Deer at the Waterworks." [PoetC] (21:1) Fall 89, p. 31.
"In New Light." [PoetC] (21:1) Fall 89, p. 30.
5654. TALLANT, Kay
"Sex at Seventeen." [US1] (22/23) Spr 89, p. 27.
5655. TALLEY, Jere
"An African American Woman's Praisesong Celebration." [Obs] (4:2) Sum 89, p. 83.
5656. TAM, Reuben
"A'a." [ChamLR] (2:2, #4) Spr 89, p. 28.
"Ghost Dogs of Halaula." [BambooR] (42/43) Spr-Sum 89, p. 65.
"Inside the Island." [ChamLR] (2:2, #4) Spr 89, p. 29.
"The Sand Crab Trap." [BambooR] (42/43) Spr-Sum 89, p. 66.
"Waimea Canyon." [BambooR] (42/43) Spr-Sum 89, p. 67.

5657. TAMARA
"Death of a Secretary" (for me-n-Eleanor). [BlackALF] (23:3) Fall 89, p. 456-457.
"Holy Ghost." [BlackALF] (23:3) Fall 89, p. 457-459.
"Xmas Poem" (for the Children). [BlackALF] (23:3) Fall 89, p. 455-456.
5658. TAMMARO, Thom
"The Man Who Never Comes Back." [NoDaQ] (57:3) Sum 89, p. 203-204.
5659. TAMMEN, Johann P.
"Catching Breath" (tr. by John Linthicum). [LitR] (33:1) Fall 89, p. 44.
"Last Report" (tr. by John Linthicum). [LitR] (33:1) Fall 89, p. 44-45.
"A Modest Request That the Weathercock Be Released" (tr. by John Linthicum).
[LitR] (33:1) Fall 89, p. 45.
"No More Songs" (tr. by John Linthicum). [LitR] (33:1) Fall 89, p. 47.
"When Nothing Else Is Left" (for Miroslav Holub, tr. by John Linthicum). [LitR]
(33:1) Fall 89, p. 46.
5660. TANA, Patti
"Old Habits Die Hard: Milk." [HiramPoR] (46) Spr-Sum 89, p. 33.
"Touched by Zero." [HiramPoR] (46) Spr-Sum 89, p. 32.
5661. TANIGUCHI, Chris K.
"One Long Blast." [Hawai'iR] (13:3) Fall 89, p. 24-25.
5662. TANNER, Sara
"Hestia." [CumbPR] (8:2) Spr 89, p. 63-64.
"Plainsong." [CumbPR] (8:2) Spr 89, p. 65.
5663. TANNY, Marlaina
"Foreign Soil." [WorldO] (22:1/2) Fall-Wint 87-88, c90, p. 25.
5664. T'AO, Ch'ien
"The Friends Who Know Me" (tr. by Cid Corman). [LitR] (32:3) Spr 89, p. 379.
"Moving I" (tr. by Cid Corman). [LitR] (32:3) Spr 89, p. 380.
"Moving II" (tr. by Cid Corman). [LitR] (32:3) Spr 89, p. 380.
"My Home Here" (tr. by Cid Corman). [LitR] (32:3) Spr 89, p. 379.
T'AO, Hsüeh
    See HSÜEH, T'ao
TAO, Xue
    See HSÜEH, T'ao
5665. TAPIO, Inger
"I Believe" (1987, after Chernobyl, tr. by Lars Nordstrom and Ralph Salisbury).
[CharR] (15:2) Fall 89, p. 76.
"Snow Flakes" (tr. by Lars Nordstrom and Ralph Salisbury). [CharR] (15:2) Fall
89, p. 74.
"Summer Morning" (tr. by Lars Nordstrom and Ralph Salisbury). [CharR] (15:2)
Fall 89, p. 75.
5666. TARDIEU, Jean
"Child Left at the Roadside" (tr. by James Gill). [MissR] (17:3, #51), p. 86-87.
"The Mask" (tr. by James Gill). [MissR] (17:3, #51), p. 83.
"The Young Man and the Sea" (tr. by James Gill). [MissR] (17:3, #51), p. 84-85.
5667. TARN, Nathaniel
"Amicus Curiae" (Architextures 22-28). [Temblor] (10) 89, p. 91-97.
"Home, One to Seven." [Conjunc] (13) 89, p. 170-175.
"The Mothers of Matagalpa." [Acts] (10) 89, p. 32-36.
5668. TARRANT, John
"The Lost Science of Atlantis." [Thrpny] (37) Spr 89, p. 19.
5669. TATE, Allen
"Girls." [SouthernR] (25:1) Wint 89, p. 88-89.
"Profs." [SouthernR] (25:1) Wint 89, p. 90-91.
5670. TATE, James
"Anatomy." [MassR] (30:2) Sum 89, p. 188.
"Beaucoup Vets." [Caliban] (6) 89, p. 87.
"Black Monday." [Caliban] (6) 89, p. 86.
"Certain Nuances, Certain Gestures." [MassR] (30:2) Sum 89, p. 190.
"City at Night." [Poetry] (154:4) Jl 89, p. 191.
"Consolations After an Affair." [MassR] (30:2) Sum 89, p. 192.
"Crimes Against the Lyric." [MassR] (30:2) Sum 89, p. 187.
"Distance from Loved Ones." [DenQ] (23:3/4) Wint-Spr 89, p. 120.
"Haunted Aquarium." [MassR] (30:2) Sum 89, p. 191.
"Mimi." [MassR] (30:2) Sum 89, p. 189.
"No Spitting Up." [Poetry] (154:4) Jl 89, p. 191.
"Peggy in the Twilight." [DenQ] (23:3/4) Wint-Spr 89, p. 121.

"Taxidermy." [Caliban] (6) 89, p. 87.
"Trying to Help." [Poetry] (154:4) Jl 89, p. 192.
5671. TATTER, John D.
"Smoke." [HiramPoR] (46) Spr-Sum 89, p. 34.
5672. TAUFER, Veno
"Artist and Model" (tr. by Michael Biggins). [NewEngR] (11:3) Spr 89, p. 246-247.
"Hostages" (tr. by Michael Scammell). [ColR] (NS 16:1) Spr-Sum 89, p. 89-90.
"Lipizzaners" (tr. of Edvard Kocbek, w. Michael Scammell). [ColR] (NS 16:1)
    Spr-Sum 89, p. 95-97.
"Red and Black Fish Circle Between Us" (tr. by Michael Scammell). [Vis] (31) 89,
    p. 37.
5673. TAVEIROS, Pai Soares de
"Song to a Lady in Simple Clothes" (Galician-Portuguese Troubadour poem, tr. by
    Richard Zenith). [SenR] (19:1) 89, p. 79.
5674. TAYLOR, Eleanor Ross
"At the Altar." [GrandS] (8:2) Wint 89, p. 12-13.
"Balance Brought Forward." [NewYorker] (64:48) 16 Ja 89, p. 32.
"Dog in 'The Quiet Man'." [KeyWR] (2:1/2) Fall-Wint 89, p. 21.
"Dust." [KeyWR] (2:1/2) Fall-Wint 89, p. 20.
"Hatchways." [KeyWR] (2:1/2) Fall-Wint 89, p. 22-23.
"No Need." [BostonR] (14:3) Je 89, p. 21.
"On the Writing of Poems." [Shen] (39:2) Sum 89, p. 93.
"Salting the Oatmeal." [NewYorker] (64:51) 6 F 89, p. 94.
5675. TAYLOR, Joan Imig
"Falling Water Elegy." [WorldO] (22:1/2) Fall-Wint 87-88, c90, p. 34-35.
5676. TAYLOR, Keith
"Everything I Need." [Witness] (2:1) Spr 88, p. 40-43.
5677. TAYLOR, Kent
"Flooding the Labyrinth." [SwampR] (1:4) Sum 89, p. 21.
"Hide-and-Seek." [SwampR] (1:4) Sum 89, p. 22.
5678. TAYLOR, Leah
"Explaining the Color of Dusk to a Child, Rochester, Minnesota." [PassN] (10:1)
    Wint 89, p. 21.
"Walking Through a Miniature, 1641." [PassN] (10:2) Sum 89, p. 18.
5679. TAYLOR, Linda
"Adults-Only Condominiums." [KanQ] (21:1/2) Wint-Spr 89, p. 170.
"At the Boston Aquarium." [Nimrod] (33:1) Fall-Wint 89, p. 101.
"Sunday in the Forest." [MassR] (30:3) Aut 89, p. 465-466.
"Trying to Have Children with the Wrong Man." [OhioR] (44) 89, p. 77.
5680. TAYLOR, Marilyn
"I Know a Bank Where the Wild Thyme Blows." [Kalliope] (11:2) 89, p. 64.
5681. TAYLOR, Michael
"Third Poem, Odes Book I" (tr. of Horace). [Zyzzyva] (5:3, #19) Fall 89, p.
    121-122.
5682. TAYLOR, Ross
"Falling." [AntR] (47:3) Sum 89, p. 315.
5683. TAYLOR-GRAHAM
"The Necessary Edge: Potter Bluff." [BallSUF] (30:4) Aut 89, p. 49.
TE-HO, Li
    See LI, Te-Ho
5684. TEASLEY, Lisa
"Jokers Wild." [Rampike] (6:2) 88, p. 60.
5685. TEICHMANN, Sandra Gail
"Concerto." [WestB] (25) 89, p. 98-99.
"Generations in Masquerade" (tr. of Graciela Guzmán). [InterPR] (15:2) Fall 89, p.
    53.
"Note to the Model." [WritersF] (15) Fall 89, p. 65-66.
"Pretext for Comfort from the Agony" (tr. of Graciela Guzmán). [InterPR] (15:2)
    Fall 89, p. 51.
"Useless Offsprings of a Body" (tr. of Graciela Guzmán). [InterPR] (15:2) Fall 89,
    p. 51.
5686. TEIGEN, Sue
"Inside the Wolf." [PoetL] (84:2) Sum 89, p. 19-20.
5687. TEILLIER, Jorge
"Afternoon Story" (tr. by Carolyne Wright). [IndR] (12:3) Sum 89, p. 63.
"Cuento de la Tarde." [IndR] (12:3) Sum 89, p. 62.

"End of the World" (tr. by Carolyne Wright). [IndR] (12:3) Sum 89, p. 67.
"Fin del Mundo." [IndR] (12:3) Sum 89, p. 66.
"I Have Trusted in the Night" (tr. by Carolyne Wright). [Chelsea] (48) 89, p. 24-25.
"Immobile Rain" (tr. by Carolyne Wright). [Chelsea] (48) 89, p. 24.
"In Memory of a Closed House" (tr. by Carolyne Wright). [OhioR] (44) 89, p. 32.
"Now That Once Again" (tr. by Carolyne Wright). [OhioR] (44) 89, p. 33-34.
"Poema de Invierno." [IndR] (12:3) Sum 89, p. 64.
"Story of a Prodigal Son" (tr. by Carolyne Wright). [MassR] (30:2) Sum 89, p.
    298-300.
"Tango Lyric" (tr. by Carolyne Wright). [OhioR] (44) 89, p. 34.
"To a Child in a Tree" (tr. by Carolyne Wright). [Chelsea] (48) 89, p. 25.
"Winter Poem" (tr. by Carolyne Wright). [IndR] (12:3) Sum 89, p. 65.
5688. TEJADA, Roberto
    "Boat. Banner. Leagueless Opportunity." [Notus] (4:1) Spr 89, p. 81-90.
    "The Gauntlet" (for Susana). [Acts] (10) 89, p. 69.
5689. TEJEDA, Manuel
    "Hace tiempo que se fueron algunos." [Mairena] (11:27) 89, p. 54-55.
5690. TEJERA, Nivaria
    "Afuera la Vida." [LindLM] (8:1) Ja-Mr 89, p. 4.
    "El caballo asoma su distancia por la ventana." [LindLM] (8:1) Ja-Mr 89, p. 4.
    "Eternidad está en mis pies." [LindLM] (8:1) Ja-Mr 89, p. 4.
    "Muebles de Nogal." [LindLM] (8:1) Ja-Mr 89, p. 4.
5691. TEMES, Peter S.
    "Battlefield of glass." [Contact] (9:50/51/52) Fall-Wint 88-Spr 89, p. 13.
    "Heavy rocks cut from the oldest tunnels." [Contact] (9:50/51/52) Fall-Wint 88-Spr
        89, p. 13.
5692. TEMME, Leonard A.
    "Lucky at Cards." [EmeraldCR] (1989) c1988, p. 86-87.
    "Songs of Passion." [EmeraldCR] (1989) c1988, p. 83-86.
5693. TEMPLE, Thea
    "Modern Love." [YellowS] (30) Sum 89, p. 12.
    "Sweet Bisque Kisses." [YellowS] (30) Sum 89, p. 12.
5694. TENEBAUM, Molly
    "In Love with Time and Stars." [PoetL] (84:3) Fall 89, p. 43-44.
5695. TENENBAUM, D. G.
    "Arnold Is Obese." [Rampike] (6:3) 88, p. 59.
5696. TENENBAUM, Molly
    "In the Atlas: Hydrology." [PoetryNW] (30:4) Wint 89-90, p. 30-31.
    "Wherever the Story May End." [PoetryNW] (30:4) Wint 89-90, p. 31-32.
5697. TENEYCK, Richard
    "Poetic Justice." [EngJ] (78:5) S 89, p. 97.
5698. TENNENT, Cheryl Ervin
    "A Clockwork Dream." [CapeR] (24:2) Fall 89, p. 6.
    "An Old Friend Is Pulled from the River." [CapeR] (24:2) Fall 89, p. 7.
    "Saturday on the Pond, Painted." [CapeR] (24:2) Fall 89, p. 5.
5699. TERENCE, Susan
    "Those from El Salvador." [NegC] (9:2) 89, p. 78-79.
    "Visitor." [SouthernPR] (29:2) Fall 89, p. 31-32.
5700. TERMAN, Philip
    "The Bris." [LaurelR] (23:2) Sum 89, p. 89-90.
    "The Used Car Lot." [KenR] (N 11:4) Fall 89, p. 6-9.
    "What Survives." [SouthernPR] (29:2) Fall 89, p. 12-16.
5701. TERRANOVA, Elaine
    "Dinner at the Holiday Inn." [Kalliope] (11:2) 89, p. 21-22.
    "Songs of the Maid and the Madam" (from a South African t.v. documentary on
        apartheid). [Kalliope] (11:2) 89, p. 18-20.
5702. TERRILL, Richard
    "Taking a Walk." [SouthernPR] (29:2) Fall 89, p. 74-75.
5703. TERRIS, Virginia R.
    "Apparitions" (Honorable Mention). [StoneC] (17:1/2) Fall-Wint 89-90, p. prelim.
        p. 5.
5704. TERRY, Patricia
    "For Mary Ann." [Hudson] (42:3) Aut 89, p. 449.
5705. TETI, Zona
    "External Souls." [NoAmR] (274:3) S 89, p. 23.
    "I Was Less Than a Flower." [KanQ] (21:3) Sum 89, p. 192.

412

"Near Naxos" (for M. L. Lord). [ConnPR] (8:1) 89, p. 33.
5706. TETTE, Sharan Flynn
"County Mayo Guide." [PaintedB] (38) 89, p. 7.
5707. THALMAN, Mark
"Power Break." [Footwork] 89, p. 51.
5708. THAM, Hilary
"Grandmother's Left Eye." [Wind] (19:65) 89, p. 34.
"Mrs. Wei in America." [Pig] (15) 88, p. 15.
"My Father's Orchids Are Beautiful." [Vis] (31) 89, p. 40.
5709. THENIOR, Ralf
"Alterer's" (tr. by John Linthicum). [LitR] (33:1) Fall 89, p. 132.
"The Invaders" (tr. by John Linthicum). [LitR] (33:1) Fall 89, p. 135.
"Portrait" (tr. by John Linthicum). [LitR] (33:1) Fall 89, p. 132.
"Simple Things" (tr. by John Linthicum). [LitR] (33:1) Fall 89, p. 134.
"Snow" (tr. by John Linthicum). [LitR] (33:1) Fall 89, p. 134.
"Yellow-lit Crosswalk Stripes" (tr. by John Linthicum). [LitR] (33:1) Fall 89, p. 133.
5710. THEOBALDY, Jürgen
"Chorus of the Hunters" (tr. by John Linthicum). [LitR] (33:1) Fall 89, p. 24.
"German Song" (tr. by John Linthicum). [LitR] (33:1) Fall 89, p. 24-25.
"Occasional Poem" (tr. by John Linthicum). [LitR] (33:1) Fall 89, p. 25.
5711. THEOCRITUS
"Daphnis, the boy with the fair skin" (tr. by James Michie). [GrandS] (8:4) Sum 89, p. 80.
"Syrinx" (tr. by Stanley Lombardo). [Temblor] (10) 89, p. 203.
5712. THESEN, Sharon
"Bear Bracelet." [CapilR] (1st series: 50) 89, p. 53.
"Boat of the Dead." [CapilR] (1st series: 50) 89, p. 51.
"For Carson McCullers at 30." [CapilR] (1st series: 50) 89, p. 52.
5713. THOMAS, Ann
"Chemin des Dammes." [Verse] (6:3) Wint 89, p. 83.
"Zookeepers." [Verse] (6:3) Wint 89, p. 82.
5714. THOMAS, Christopher
"Pubescence and Pulse." [EvergreenC] (4:3) Spr 89, p. 32.
5715. THOMAS, Colette
"Delta Sestina." [PoetL] (84:2) Sum 89, p. 33-34.
"Letter Against the Dusk." [PoetL] (84:2) Sum 89, p. 35-36.
"Unleaving." [PoetL] (84:2) Sum 89, p. 37.
5716. THOMAS, D. F.
"Cabin Fever." [Bogg] (61) 89, p. 13.
5717. THOMAS, Delaina
"Cranes of Luck." [BambooR] (41) Wint 89, p. 33-34.
5718. THOMAS, Denise
"Colorado." [CinPR] (20) Fall 89, p. 20.
"The Devil Walks a Lonely Road." [Ascent] (14:3) 89, p. 52-53.
"Quilting." [Ascent] (14:3) 89, p. 53.
"Since the Fire." [CinPR] (20) Fall 89, p. 21.
"Waco, 1951." [TexasR] (10:3/4) Fall-Wint 89, p. 101.
"A Woman in Texas." [TexasR] (10:3/4) Fall-Wint 89, p. 100.
5719. THOMAS, Jamila
"If I Could Fly" (Mainstreet Elementary Poetry Contest, 1st Grade, 3rd Place). [DeKalbLAJ] (22:1/4) 89, p. 102.
5720. THOMAS, Jim
"Birdnapper." [KanQ] (21:1/2) Wint-Spr 89, p. 227.
5721. THOMAS, Julia
"Certain Words." [Hawai'iR] (13:1, #25) Spr 89, p. 102-103.
5722. THOMAS, Larry D.
"In Maine" (for Andrew Wyeth). [TexasR] (10:3/4) Fall-Wint 89, p. 117.
"The Live Oaks." [CapeR] (24:2) Fall 89, p. 31.
"A Sunday Morning." [CapeR] (24:2) Fall 89, p. 32.
5723. THOMAS, Linda
"The Mexicanas on Salad Bar." [Vis] (31) 89, p. 13.
5724. THOMAS, Lorenzo
"Back-Ordered Tears." [Ploughs] (15:4) Wint 89-90, p. 222.
5725. THOMAS, R. S.
"Confrontation." [LitR] (32:2) Wint 89, p. 139.

"Countering." [LitR] (32:2) Wint 89, p. 137.
"Cures." [LitR] (32:2) Wint 89, p. 138.
"Destinations." [LitR] (32:2) Wint 89, p. 135.
"The Empty Church." [NoDaQ] (57:2) Spr 89, insert p. 22.
"The Fly." [LitR] (32:2) Wint 89, p. 133.
"Good." [NoDaQ] (57:2) Spr 89, insert p. 23.
"He and She." [LitR] (32:2) Wint 89, p. 137.
"Jerusalem." [LitR] (32:2) Wint 89, p. 136.
"Pardon." [LitR] (32:2) Wint 89, p. 134.
"Questions." [LitR] (32:2) Wint 89, p. 136.
"Reservoirs." [NoDaQ] (57:2) Spr 89, insert p. 22.
"The Small Country." [NoDaQ] (57:2) Spr 89, insert p. 24.
"Song." [LitR] (32:2) Wint 89, p. 134.
"Welsh Landscape." [NoDaQ] (57:2) Spr 89, insert p. 21.
"The White Tiger." [NoDaQ] (57:2) Spr 89, insert p. 23.
5726. THOMAS, Robert
"Squid." [Chelsea] (48) 89, p. 112-113.
5727. THOMAS, Scott E.
"Trailing Arbutus." [Plain] (9:2) Wint 89, p. 6.
5728. THOMPSON, Dorothy Perry
"My Fancy Tea Room" (for Bertha West Nealy). [BlackALF] (23:3) Fall 89, p.
498-499.
5729. THOMPSON, Earle
"Ceremony." [Pig] (15) 88, p. 54.
"Origin." [Pig] (15) 88, p. 54.
"She Wakes in Morning Clover." [Contact] (9:50/51/52) Fall-Wint 88-Spr 89, p. 15.
"Spirit." [Pig] (15) 88, p. 54.
5730. THOMPSON, Edgar H.
"America Pie." [Wind] (19:64) 89, p. 34-35.
"Contraries." [Wind] (19:64) 89, p. 34.
5731. THOMPSON, Frederika (Fredrika)
"Grandma." [SpoonRQ] (14:3) Sum 89, p. 17.
"The Liar." [SpoonRQ] (14:3) Sum 89, p. 18.
"The Missionary." [PassN] (10:1) Wint 89, p. 22.
"Mother of the Disappeared" (Argentina, 1976). [SpoonRQ] (14:3) Sum 89, p. 16.
5732. THOMPSON, Gary
"Impatiens." [SoCoast] (5) Spr 88, p. 5.
"Mornings." [SoCoast] (5) Spr 88, p. 14.
5733. THOMPSON, Julius E.
"Cats & Dogs." [Obs] (4:2) Sum 89, p. 84-85.
"Du Bois' Greatest Hour." [Obs] (4:2) Sum 89, p. 86.
"Oxford, Jackson, Natchez." [Obs] (2:1) Spr 87, p. 57-58.
"Preserving the Memory" (For Hoyt W. Fuller, 1923-1981). [BlackALF] (23:3) Fall
89, p. 500.
5734. THOMPSON, Phyllis Hoge
"A Childhood." [Writer] (102:11) N 89, p. 24.
5735. THOMPSON, Raymond
"Homeless Parks." [FiveFR] (7) 89, p. 13.
"What It Is." [FiveFR] (7) 89, p. 14.
5736. THOMPSON, Sidney R.
"In His Hands" (for Noel Eubanks). [MidwQ] (30:2) Wint 89, p. 188.
5737. THOMPSON, Sue Ellen
"How to Tell a True Love Story." [GeoR] (43:1) Spr 89, p. 45-46.
5738. THOOR, Jesse
"Desecration" (tr. by Gary Sea). [WebR] (14:1) Spr 89, p. 10.
"Sonnet in Summer" (tr. by Gary Sea). [WebR] (14:1) Spr 89, p. 8.
"Sonnet of Modern Naïveté" (tr. by Gary Sea). [WebR] (14:1) Spr 89, p. 9.
"Talking in the Wind" (tr. by Gary Sea). [WebR] (14:1) Spr 89, p. 11.
5739. THORNTON, Don
"Eirene." [Kalliope] (10:3) 88, p. 20.
5740. THORNTON, Jerome E.
"Beloved." [Obs] (4:1) Spr 89, p. 34.
"A Memory: Sana'a." [Obs] (4:1) Spr 89, p. 35-36.
"Sunday Morning." [Obs] (4:1) Spr 89, p. 34-35.
5741. THORPE, Allison
"The Propensity of Mountains Toward Flight." [Wind] (19:65) 89, p. 35.

5742. THORPE, Michael
"Before the Deluge: Three Vignettes." [AntigR] (79) Aut 89, p. 90-01.
TI, P'ei
See P'EI, Ti
T'IAO-YU, Yen
See YEN, T'iao-yu
5743. TIBBETTS, Frederick
"At Tree Line." [US1] (22/23) Spr 89, p. 45.
5744. TICKNOR, Kerrie
"Crossing the Mainland" (2nd Runner Up, Poetry Award). [NewL] (56:1) Fall 89,
p. 110-111.
"In the Church of Broken Crosses" (2nd Runner Up, Poetry Award). [NewL] (56:1)
Fall 89, p. 106-108.
"In the Dark City" (2nd Runner Up, Poetry Award). [NewL] (56:1) Fall 89, p.
108-109.
"In the Town of Asnan." [AntR] (47:2) Spr 89, p. 200-201.
"Sometimes in Dreams I See the Word *Pig*" (2nd Runner Up, Poetry Award).
[NewL] (56:1) Fall 89, p. 103-105.
"The Space Between." [PoetL] (84:2) Sum 89, p. 15-16.
5745. TIDWELL, Pat
"Dialogue with an Old Mennonite Woman" (At the Rebecca Home for Delinquent
Girls). [TexasR] (10:1/2) Spr-Sum 89, p. 74.
"Lambent Lass Between Heaven and Charing Cross Station." [TexasR] (10:1/2)
Spr-Sum 89, p. 75.
5746. TIERNEY, Diane
"The Habit of Tending." [WestB] (23) 89, p. 103.
5747. TIERNEY, Karl
"After His Death." [Contact] (9:50/51/52) Fall-Wint 88-Spr 89, p. 14.
"Design in Blue." [Contact] (9:50/51/52) Fall-Wint 88-Spr 89, p. 15.
"Turning 30." [Contact] (9:50/51/52) Fall-Wint 88-Spr 89, p. 14.
5748. TIGER, Madeline (Madeline J.)
"Babies." [Mildred] (3:1) Spr-Sum 89, p. 72-73.
"Late Fall" (rotogravure). [SoCoast] (7) Spr-Fall 89, p. 54.
"The Medea Complex: A Sestina for Sabina" (and a coda). [NegC] (9:2) 89, p.
15-16.
"Selves." [US1] (22/23) Spr 89, p. 16.
"The Wind Poem." [Footwork] 89, p. 49.
5749. TILLEY, E. Allen, Jr.
"Dream: After a Conference." [Kalliope] (10:3) 88, p. 18-19.
"Rime Sparse" (Selection: 52, tr. of Francesco Petrarch). [Kalliope] (10:3) 88, p.
19.
5750. TILLINGHAST, Richard
"Xiphias." [NewEngR] (12:1) Aut 89, p. 91-92.
TING, Shu
See SHU, Ting
5751. TIPTON, Carolyn (Carolyn L.)
"Botticelli" (Arabesque, tr. of Rafael Alberti). [Sequoia] (32:2) Wint-Spr 89, p. 22.
"Now it is Autumn." [ChamLR] (3:1, #5) Fall 89, p. 23.
"Postcard from Lanikai." [ChamLR] (3:1, #5) Fall 89, p. 22.
"Two Visions." [ChamLR] (3:1, #5) Fall 89, p. 24-25.
5752. TIPTON, James
"Geographical Dyslexia." [HighP] (4:3) Wint 89-90, p. 127-128.
"Mightier Than the Word." [HighP] (4:3) Wint 89-90, p. 125-126.
"There Never Really Was a Blue of Course." [HighP] (4:3) Wint 89-90, p. 124.
5753. TODARO, Brenda
"Living Together." [Sonora] (17) Spr-Sum 89, p. 12-13.
"The Meteorologist." [Sonora] (17) Spr-Sum 89, p. 14-15.
"The Only Part of Bean Avenue That's Not Alley." [Sonora] (17) Spr-Sum 89, p.
11.
5754. TODD, Theodora
"The Elgin Marbles." [BelPoJ] (39:3) Spr 89, p. 6-8.
TOEWS, David Waltner
See WALTNER-TOEWS, David
5755. TOKARCZYK, Michelle M.
"Well Tonight Thank God It's Them Instead of You." [MinnR] (NS 32) Spr 89, p.
67-68.

415

5756. TOKUNO, Ken
"Bindings." [BellArk] (5:6) N-D 89, p. 5.
"Donut Holes." [BellArk] (5:6) N-D 89, p. 7.
"I Went to See My Adviser." [BellArk] (5:4) Jl-Ag 89, p. 9.
"Nisei Marriage" (to my Mother and Father). [BellArk] (5:4) Jl-Ag 89, p. 7.
"Onomatopopper." [BellArk] (5:1) Ja-F 89, p. 3.
5757. TOLIVER, Suzanne
"Narrow Paths" (tr. of Annemarie Zornack). [NewOR] (16:4) Wint 89, p. 82.
5758. TOMAS, Consuelo A.
"Somos latinoamericanos." [Mairena] (11:27) 89, p. 63.
5759. TOMKIW, Lydia
"Studies in Red." [Talisman] (3) Fall 89, p. 108-109.
"What You Want." [PaintedB] (38) 89, p. 51.
5760. TOMLINSON, Charles
"Along the Mohawk." [ParisR] (31:110) Spr 89, p. 31.
"Apples Painted." [ParisR] (31:110) Spr 89, p. 32.
"Chance." [Hudson] (42:2) Sum 89, p. 265.
"Chronochromie." [Hudson] (42:2) Sum 89, p. 265-266.
"Erotopaegnia" (Selection: "He Slept in You Like a Dry Fibroma," tr. of Edoardo
Sanguineti). [Poetry] (155:1/2) O-N 89, p. 78.
"For a Godchild." [Hudson] (42:2) Sum 89, p. 362.
"The Garden." [Hudson] (42:2) Sum 89, p. 261-263.
"Harvest." [Hudson] (42:2) Sum 89, p. 266.
"Hell's Purgatory" (Selection: "Through Hebecrevon, Lessay, Portbail," tr. of
Edoardo Sanguineti). [Poetry] (155:1/2) O-N 89, p. 79.
"Letter to Uehata." [Hudson] (42:2) Sum 89, p. 267.
"A Ruskinian Fable Retold: Courtesy." [Hudson] (42:2) Sum 89, p. 264.
5761. TOMLINSON, Rawdon
"Creede, 1931" (R.E.T. 1884-1948). [RiverC] (10:1) Fall 89, p. 124-125.
"Teenage Funeral." [TarRP] (29:1) Fall 89, p. 13-15.
"Under the Hackberry." [RiverC] (10:1) Fall 89, p. 123.
5762. TOPAL, Carine
"Dogs Watching My Mouth." [BlueBldgs] (11) 89, p. 46-47.
"Should I Have a Baby?" [Interim] (8:1) Spr 89, p. 42-43.
5763. TORRE, Stephan
"After Bacon and Eggs with Duane." [MalR] (87) Sum 89, p. 107.
"Coming Home." [Grain] (17:3) Fall 89, inside back cover.
"June 6." [PraF] (10:1, #46) Spr 89, p. 50.
"Neighbor Upriver." [WillowS] (23) Wint 89, p. 56-57.
"Rocky Creek Switchback Song." [MalR] (87) Sum 89, p. 105-106.
"Water Calling." [PraF] (10:1, #46) Spr 89, p. 51.
TORRE, Stephen
See TORRE, Stephan
5764. TORRES, Raquel
"Researching zeal." [AlphaBS] (5) Jl 89, p. 69.
5765. TORRESON, Rodney
"The Bethlehem Nursing Home." [CapeR] (24:2) Fall 89, p. 9.
"Homecoming." [Northeast] (ser. 5:1) Wint 89-90, p. 19.
"Twelve." [CapeR] (24:2) Fall 89, p. 10.
5766. TOSTESON, Heather
"Il N'Est Pire Aveugle Que Celui Qui Ne Veut Pas Voir." [SouthernR] (25:1) Wint
89, p. 173-174.
"Woman Devoured by Fishes." [SouthernPR] (29:2) Fall 89, p. 42-43.
5767. TOURÉ, Askia M.
"A Canopic Jar / 2 (Requiem for a Lady)." [Obs] (2:1) Spr 87, p. 29-30.
"Rebellion Suite / Straight. No Chaser" (for Thelonious Sphere Monk and the Bebop
Rebellion). [Obs] (2:1) Spr 87, p. 30-33.
TOV, S. Ben
See BEN-TOV, S.
5768. TOVT, Giovanni
"Doune's Old Railway 1987" (Doune by Stirling, 1987, Scotland). [AlphaBS] (5) Jl
89, p. 44.
"Five Rooms" (w. Christophe Beauregard, inspired by the paintings of Yvonne
Hawker, Edinburgh, 5.12.87). [AlphaBS] (5) Jl 89, p. 44.
5769. TOWNSEND, Ann
"Pattern for a Sweater." [QW] (28) Wint-Spr 89, p. 91.

"Pyromania." [MissouriR] (12:1) 89, p. 151.
5770. TOWNSEND, Cheryl
"When You Lick." [AlphaBS] (5) Jl 89, p. 68.
5771. TRAINA, Joe
"Turning Cures." [Wind] (19:65) 89, p. 35.
5772. TRAKL, Georg
"Autumn Evening" (to Karl Rock, tr. by Daniel Simko). [DenQ] (23:3/4) Wint-Spr
89, p. 124.
"Hymns for a Rosary" (tr. by Daniel Simko). [DenQ] (23:3/4) Wint-Spr 89, p.
122-123.
"Psalm" (tr. by Daniel Simko). [AmerPoR] (18:1) Ja-F 89, p. 37.
"Transformation of Evil" (tr. by Daniel Simko). [AmerPoR] (18:1) Ja-F 89, p. 38.
"Twilight Land" (tr. by John Logan). [PaintedB] (39) 89, p. 64-65.
TRAN, Kha
See KHA, Tran
5773. TRANSTRÖMER, Tomas
"Berceuse" (tr. by Robin Fulton). [Verse] (6:3) Wint 89, p. 22.
"Female Portrait, 19th Century" (tr. by Robin Fulton). [Verse] (6:3) Wint 89, p. 23.
"The Inheritance" (tr. by Robin Fulton). [Verse] (6:3) Wint 89, p. 21.
"Leaflet" (tr. by Robin Fulton). [Verse] (6:3) Wint 89, p. 22.
"Medieval Motif" (tr. by Robin Fulton). [Verse] (6:3) Wint 89, p. 23.
"Six Winters" (tr. by Robin Fulton). [Verse] (6:3) Wint 89, p. 21-22.
"Vermeer" (tr. by Samuel Charters). [Quarry] (38:2) Spr 89, p. 81-82.
5774. TRANTER, John
"Anyone Home?" [Verse] (6:1) Mr 89, p. 13-15.
"Con's Cafe." [Verse] (6:3) Wint 89, p. 13.
"Haibun: Bells Under Water." [Verse] (6:3) Wint 89, p. 12.
"Haibun: Cellar." [Verse] (6:3) Wint 89, p. 11.
"Haibun: Dizzy." [Verse] (6:3) Wint 89, p. 14.
5775. TRASK, Haunani-Kay
"Waikiki." [Hawai'iR] (13:1, #25) Spr 89, p. 37-38.
5776. TRAVIS, Jennifer
"My Mother Married a Man Like Her Mother." [PoetryNW] (30:3) Aut 89, p. 19-21.
5777. TRAWICK, Leonard
"How Technology Came to the Arts in Okeepoka." [RiverC] (9:1) Spr 89, p. 38.
"Jacqueline du Pré" (Jan. 26, 1945 -- Oct. 19, 1987). [LaurelR] (23:1) Wint 89, p.
68.
"The Raccoons." [LaurelR] (23:1) Wint 89, p. 69.
5778. TRAXLER, Patricia
"The Widow's Words" (4 selection). [Ploughs] (15:4) Wint 89-90, p. 223-228.
5779. TREGEBOV, Rhea
"At Three or Four or Five AM." [PraF] (10:4, #49) Wint 89-90, p. 29.
"Extremities." [Dandel] (16:1) Spr-Sum 89, p. 16.
"Ideology." [CanLit] (120) Spr 89, p. 4-5.
"Not God's Order" (For Harley Ayearst, February 1987-October 1987). [CanLit]
(120) Spr 89, p. 61-62.
"Nothing Will Let Go." [Dandel] (16:1) Spr-Sum 89, p. 14.
"Villa d'Este." [Dandel] (16:1) Spr-Sum 89, p. 15.
5780. TREITEL, Margot
"Bronzed Court Scenes" (Benin Expedition, 1897). [PaperAir] (4:2) 89, p. 13-14.
"An Entry in the Journal." [Pig] (15) 88, p. 38.
"Guide to the African Exhibit, 1974." [Pig] (15) 88, p. 38.
"The Lost Wax Process." [PaperAir] (4:2) 89, p. 15.
"The Year of Divine Illumination" (Ibadan, Nigeria 1964). [Pig] (15) 88, p. 39.
5781. TREITEL, Renata
"On the Death of Phoebus Delphi" (tr. of Margherita Guidacci). [InterPR] (15:2) Fall
89, p. 75.
"To Phoebus Beyond the Border" (tr. of Margherita Guidacci). [InterPR] (15:2) Fall
89, p. 75.
"To Say" (tr. of Amelia Biagioni). [MidAR] (9:1) 89, p. 163-164.
"The Water Spring." [OxfordM] (5:1) Spr-Sum 89, p. 55-56.
5782. TREMBLAY, Bill
"Trusting the Music." [IndR] (12:3) Sum 89, p. 9.
5783. TREMMEL, Robert
"The Art of Waiting by the Water" (a Plainsongs Award Poem). [Plain] (9:3) Spr 89,
p. 4.

"Jumpshooting a Pond." [KanQ] (21:1/2) Wint-Spr 89, p. 46.
"Opening Day Fantasy: Driving Past Alf Landon's House." [KanQ] (21:1/2)
    Wint-Spr 89, p. 47.
"When You're in Love, Your Mind Becomes a Dangerous Animal." [Plain] (10:1)
    89, p. 15.
TRETHEWAY, Eric
    See TRETHEWEY, Eric
5784. TRETHEWEY, Eric
    "A Brief History of the Ironic Mode." [Journal] (13:1) Spr-Sum 89, p. 48.
    "The Colors." [CentR] (33:3) Sum 89, p. 243.
    "Echoes." [ColEng] (51:7) N 89, p. 705-706.
    "Family Tree." [KanQ] (21:1/2) Wint-Spr 89, p. 133.
    "Irony in the Teaching of *Oedipus Tyrannus*." [Journal] (13:1) Spr-Sum 89, p. 47.
    "Portent." [ArtfulD] (16/17) Fall 89, p. 35.
    "Raising Steel." [MissouriR] (12:1) 89, p. 26-27.
    "Walking Home." [CumbPR] (9:1) Fall 89, p. 37.
TRIBBLE, John
    See TRIBBLE, Jon
5785. TRIBBLE, Jon
    "All You Need Is Ten Dollars and Someone Who Loves You" (Honorable Mention,
        1989 Poetry Competition). [PassN] (10:2) Sum 89, p. 8.
    "And There Is Many a Good Thing." [Ploughs] (15:1) 89, p. 142-143.
    "Fathers." [Poetry] (154:3) Je 89, p. 149.
    "My Brother, Betting on *Ray's Hope*." [Ploughs] (15:1) 89, p. 144-145.
5786. TRINIDAD, David
    "Hockney: Blue Pool." [Pequod] (28/29/30) 89, p. 218.
    "Lines." [NewAW] (5) Fall 89, p. 114.
    "The Portrait of a Lady." [NewAW] (5) Fall 89, p. 115.
    "Reruns" (Excerpts). [Colum] (14) 89, p. 147.
5787. TRIVELPIECE, Laurel
    "North of the Crocuses." [Zyzzyva] (5:1, #17) Spr 89, p. 112.
    "Playground." [PraS] (63:4) Wint 89, p. 16-17.
5788. TRIVERS, Mildred Raynolds
    "The List." [BallSUF] (30:4) Aut 89, p. 45-48.
5789. TROUPE, Quincy
    "Poem for My Father" (for Quincy Trouppe, Sr.). [Ploughs] (15:4) Wint 89-90, p.
        229-230.
5790. TROWBRIDGE, William
    "Great Big Crybabies." [GeoR] (43:3) Fall 89, p. 572.
    "The Kiss" (V-J Day, Times Square, 1945). [BlackWR] (16:1) Fall-Wint 89, p. 34.
    "The Lewis Chessmen" (a 12th Century set of humorously-carved figures discovered
        in 1831 on the Isle of Lewis). [CharR] (15:1) Spr 89, p. 71.
    "Living with Solar Keratosis." [Poetry] (154:5) Ag 89, p. 271-272.
    "Million Dollar Winners." [BlackWR] (16:1) Fall-Wint 89, p. 35.
    "Shoah." [BlackWR] (16:1) Fall-Wint 89, p. 31-33.
5791. TROY, Jack
    "Some Words (Like Doves) to Fly After You" (For the National Theatre of the Deaf).
        [WestB] (23) 89, p. 34.
5792. TRUCULENTO, Guillermo
    "Veinte Centavos." [Americas] (17:2) Sum 89, p. 54-55.
5793. TRUHLAR, Richard
    "Closures" (for Misha Chocholak). [Rampike] (6:1) 87, p. 60.
    "Three Native Texts for Richard Huelsenbeck." [CapilR] (1st series: 50) 89, p. 120.
5794. TRUITT, Samuel
    "Axes" (Selections: I-IV, XI, XXVIII-XXX, XXXIV). [WashR] (14:6) Ap-My 89,
        p. 16.
5795. TRUSSELL, Donna
    "Dreams, Indexed" (a found poem). [NewL] (55:3) Spr 89, p. 89.
    "On Sky-Vue Boulevard." [Poetry] (153:5) F 89, p. 276.
    "Presence" (after *The Secret House*). [ChiR] (36:3/4) 89, p. 22.
    "To Miss Candace Mayes, Lost on the Titanic." [Poetry] (153:5) F 89, p. 227.
TSAO, Wu
    See WU, Tsao
tSAOI, Máire Mhac an
    See Mhac an tSAOI, Máire

5796. TSUJIMOTO, Joseph
"Party Line." [ChamLR] (3:1, #5) Fall 89, p. 53-54.
5797. TSUMORI, Kunimoto (1023-1103)
"Like an old love-letter" (tr. by Sam Hamill). [PoetryE] (28) Fall 89, p. 203.
TSUNG-YÜAN, Liu
See LIU, Tsung-yüan
5798. TSURAYUKI (883-946)
"All this summer night" (tr. by Sam Hamill). [PoetryE] (28) Fall 89, p. 199.
"Angry river winds" (tr. by Sam Hamill). [PoetryE] (28) Fall 89, p. 202.
TU, Fu
See DU, Fu
TUAIRISC, Eoghan O
See O TUAIRISC, Eoghan
TUAMA, Seán O
See O TUAMA, Seán
5799. TUCKER, Richard
"The Sixth Day." [MidwQ] (30:2) Wint 89, p. 209-210.
5800. TUGWELL, Judith A.
"The Room Smells of Sleep." [WorldO] (22:1/2) Fall-Wint 87-88, c90, p. 30.
5801. TULLIS, Rod (Rodney Wayne)
"Driving to Town for Coffee (Pattonsburg, Missouri)." [Farm] (6:2) Fall 89, p. 22.
"The Final Cut (Haying)." [Farm] (6:2) Fall 89, p. 20-21.
5802. TULLOSS, Rod
"Antique Song: Mary Feeding the Birds." [Footwork] 89, p. 66.
"Cut Tulips" (iii.17.84 Sign of the Sorrel Horse, Haycock Township, PA, for
Mary). [US1] (22/23) Spr 89, p. 32.
"Exercise" (iii.11-16.80, Princeton/Roosevelt, for Salmon Ryder). [US1] (22/23)
Spr 89, p. 33.
"Die Kunst der Fuge." [Footwork] 89, p. 65.
"Sitting on a Porch in Chatham." [Footwork] 89, p. 66.
"Sushi" (iv.30.86 Joshu-Ya, Berkeley, for the sushi chef who taped the napkin on
which this was written to the wall). [US1] (22/23) Spr 89, p. 32.
"Sushi #2" (5.ix.86, Holmdel, NJ, for Keiji chef of Yoshi's). [US1] (22/23) Spr
89, p. 32.
5803. TULLY, John
"City Mouse." [HolCrit] (26:1) F 89, p. 17.
TUNG, Mu
See MU, Tung
TUNG-P'O, Su
See SU, Shih
5804. TURCOTTE, Gerry
"The Double Hook." [CanLit] (122/123) Aut-Wint 89, p. 8-9.
5805. TURCOTTE, Huguette
"Poetique du Désert, Essai 1." [Rampike] (6:2) 88, p. 58-59.
5806. TURNAGE, Sheila
"Autumn Dance." [YellowS] (29) Spr 89, p. 40.
5807. TURNBULL, Becky
"At the Mecca Bar with Seth." [PaintedB] (38) 89, p. 52.
5808. TURNER, Clement
"Weekend Astronomer." [KanQ] (21:1/2) Wint-Spr 89, p. 258-259.
5809. TURNER, Doug
"Reprieve." [Hawai'iR] (13:2, #26) Sum 89, p. 66-67.
"Space." [Hawai'iR] (13:2, #26) Sum 89, p. 68.
5810. TURNER, Frederick
"37,000 Feet Above the Atlantic." [SouthernR] (25:4) Aut 89, p. 944.
"April Wind" (for Ann Weary). [SouthernR] (25:4) Aut 89, p. 942-943.
"The Blackness of the Grackle." [CrossCur] (8:2) Ja 89, p. 107-108.
"On the Anthropic Principle." [SouthernR] (25:4) Aut 89, p. 943.
5811. TURNER, Larry
"The Bed." [KanQ] (21:1/2) Wint-Spr 89, p. 83.
5812. TURPIN, Mark
"Laborer's Code." [Thrpny] (36) Wint 89, p. 6.
5813. TUSIANI, Joseph
"La Gloria del Momento." [Mairena] (11:27) 89, p. 87.
5814. TWARDOWSKI, Jan
"The Jesus of Nonbelievers" (tr. by Stanislaw Baranczak and Clare Cavanah).

[Trans] (21) Spr 89, p. 18.
5815. TWICHELL, Chase
"The Blade of Nostalgia." [NewEngR] (11:4) Sum 89, p. 412-414.
"The Condom Tree." [GeoR] (43:1) Spr 89, p. 64.
"The Cut" (winning entry, 9th Annual Competition in Narrative Poetry). [NewEngR]
    (12:1) Aut 89, p. 3-8.
"In the Exploded View." [GeoR] (43:1) Spr 89, p. 62.
"The Man Who Practices Next Door." [OntR] (31) Fall-Wint 89-90, p. 52.
"A Minor Crush of Cells." [NewEngR] (11:4) Sum 89, p. 415-416.
"O Miami." [OntR] (31) Fall-Wint 89-90, p. 51-52.
"One Physics." [NewEngR] (11:4) Sum 89, p. 416-417.
"Six Bélons." [GeoR] (43:1) Spr 89, p. 63.
5816. TYLER, Robert L.
"Boredom." [Wind] (19:65) 89, p. 36-37.
"Gestures of Reassurance." [Wind] (19:65) 89, p. 36.
"Surprise." [Bogg] (61) 89, p. 44.
"Under Glass." [Wind] (19:65) 89, p. 37.
5817. TYLER, Valerie R.
"Brother." [BlackALF] (23:3) Fall 89, p. 469.
5818. TYRRELL, Patricia A.
"Role Switching." [Writer] (102:9) S 89, p. 22.
TZU, Lao
    See LAO, Tzu
TZU-LUNG, Ch'en
    See CH'EN, Tzu-lung
5819. UCHMANOWICZ, Pauline
"Visiting Rights." [MassR] (30:1) Spr 89, p. 99-100.
5820. ULLMAN, Leslie
"Ambition." [PraS] (63:3) Fall 89, p. 113-116.
"Amethyst." [Poetry] (153:5) F 89, p. 271.
"Mauve." [Poetry] (153:5) F 89, p. 267-270.
5821. ULMER, James
"Marguerite." [ThRiPo] (33/34) 89, p. 45-46.
5822. UMPIERRE, Luz Maria
"Bella Ilusion Que Fugaz." [LindLM] (8:4) O-D 89, p. 9.
"For Ellen." [LindLM] (8:4) O-D 89, p. 9.
5823. UNDER, Marie
"Äraminejad" (in Estonian). [InterPR] (15:2) Fall 89, p. 6.
"Between Night and Day" (tr. by Leonard Fox). [InterPR] (15:2) Fall 89, p. 15.
"Käik Valgusse" (in Estonian). [InterPR] (15:2) Fall 89, p. 12.
"The Kiss" (tr. by Leonard Fox). [InterPR] (15:2) Fall 89, p. 11.
"Langes Üks Täht" (in Estonian). [InterPR] (15:2) Fall 89, p. 18.
"Lightward Movement" (tr. by Leonard Fox). [InterPR] (15:2) Fall 89, p. 13.
"Öö Ja Päeva Vahel" (in Estonian). [InterPR] (15:2) Fall 89, p. 14.
"Puu Lindudega" (in Estonian). [InterPR] (15:2) Fall 89, p. 8.
"Shooting Star" (tr. by Leonard Fox). [InterPR] (15:2) Fall 89, p. 19.
"Suudlus" (in Estonian). [InterPR] (15:2) Fall 89, p. 10.
"The Time of Parting" (tr. by Leonard Fox). [InterPR] (15:2) Fall 89, p. 7.
"The Tree of Birds" (tr. by Leonard Fox). [InterPR] (15:2) Fall 89, p. 9.
"Valveaeg" (in Estonian). [InterPR] (15:2) Fall 89, p. 16, 18.
"Vigil" (tr. by Leonard Fox). [InterPR] (15:2) Fall 89, p. 17, 19.
5824. UNDERWOOD, Robert
"Cherry's Hair Villa." [WormR] (29:1, #113) 89, p. 14.
"The Smudge Pot." [PacificR] (7) 89, p. 79.
"There." [WormR] (29:1, #113) 89, p. 14.
"Xu Wei's 'Flowers in Four Seasons'." [PacificR] (7) 89, p. 78.
5825. UNGAR, Barbara Louise
"Athena." [Kalliope] (11:3) 89, p. 51.
"The Kvetch" (To Steven Mitchell, for his translation of The Book of Job).
    [Kalliope] (11:3) 89, p. 50-51.
5826. UNGER, Barbara
"Chava." [CreamCR] (13:2) Fall 89, p. 183.
"The Fog of the Forties." [SoCoast] (7) Spr-Fall 89, p. 30-31.
"The March." [Mildred] (3:1) Spr-Sum 89, p. 113.
"Penelope." [SouthernHR] (23:2) Spr 89, p. 119.
"The Radium Girls." [SouthernHR] (23:2) Spr 89, p. 142.

"Solo Flight." [Lactuca] (13) N 89, p. 26.
"Sparing the Children." [Mildred] (3:1) Spr-Sum 89, p. 114.
5827. UNGRIA, Ricardo M. de
"Answering Machine." [Manoa] (1:1/2) Fall 89, p. 47.
"Lanai Soliloquy." [RiverS] (28) 89, p. 45-46.
"No Man's Land." [RiverS] (28) 89, p. 47-48.
"Villager" (after Stevens). [RiverS] (28) 89, p. 43-44.
5828. UNTERECKER, John
"Arroyo: Flash Flood." [Poetry] (154:5) Ag 89, p. 269.
"In Five Minutes." [Wind] (19:64) 89, p. 36.
"Obake Song" (for Ernest Morgan). [Wind] (19:64) 89, p. 36.
5829. UPDIKE, John
"Back Bay." [Manoa] (1:1/2) Fall 89, p. 118-119.
"Charleston." [OntR] (31) Fall-Wint 89-90, p. 48.
"Frost." [OntR] (31) Fall-Wint 89-90, p. 47.
"In Memoriam Felis Felis." [GrandS] (8:4) Sum 89, p. 137-138. Corrected reprint
        [GrandS] (9:1) Aut 89, p. 268-269.
"Orthodontia." [NewRep] (200:7) 13 F 89, p. 35.
"Squirrels Mating." [Atlantic] (264:1) Jl 89, p. 60.
"To a Box Turtle." [NewYorker] (65:30) 11 S 89, p. 38.
5830. UPTON, Lee
"Bedtime Story." [DenQ] (23:3/4) Wint-Spr 89, p. 55.
"Cleopatra's Spectacle." [DenQ] (24:1) Sum 89, p. 85.
"The Compliment." [DenQ] (24:1) Sum 89, p. 80-81.
"Courtesy." [DenQ] (24:1) Sum 89, p. 82.
"Fortune Readings." [DenQ] (24:1) Sum 89, p. 83.
"Occasional Poem." [DenQ] (24:1) Sum 89, p. 84.
"Pity for Blondes." [DenQ] (23:3/4) Wint-Spr 89, p. 56.
5831. URDANG, Constance
"Emergency Ward, St. Vincent's." [NewYorker] (65:25) 7 Ag 89, p. 72.
"Green Study in a Dry Climate." [WestHR] (43:2) Sum 89, p. 98-99.
5832. USCHUK, Pamela
"Barranca de Cobre." [SoCoast] (6) Fall 88, p. 30-32.
"Red Cat Near Old Snow." [Comm] (116:9) My 5, 89, p. 266.
5833. USUI, Masami
"In This Country." [Hawai'iR] (13:2, #26) Sum 89, p. 42.
"Tokyo Rose." [Hawai'iR] (13:2, #26) Sum 89, p. 40-41.
5834. UU, David
"Not Far from the Old Melon Patch." [Rampike] (6:2) 88, p. 68.
"Western / Separation." [Rampike] (6:2) 88, p. 68.
5835. UYEMATSU, Amy
"Inaka / Country Girl." [BambooR] (44) Fall 89, p. 34.
"Letting the Body Speak." [Mildred] (3:2) 89, p. 5-7.
5836. VAETH, Kim
"Friendship Among Women." [Ploughs] (15:4) Wint 89-90, p. 231-238.
5837. VAICIUNAITE, Judita
"Coffee House, with Pigeons" (tr. by Viktoria Skrupskelis and Stuart Friebert).
        [Field] (41) Fall 89, p. 71.
"Untitled: I'll freeze, a column of salt" (tr. by Viktoria Skrupskelis and Stuart
        Friebert). [Field] (41) Fall 89, p. 69.
"Wild Plum in Bloom" (tr. by Viktoria Skrupskelis and Stuart Friebert). [Field] (41)
        Fall 89, p. 68.
"Winter II" (tr. by Viktoria Skrupskelis and Stuart Friebert). [Field] (41) Fall 89, p.
        70.
5838. VAKY, James Russell
"Athlete Verus Aesthete." [Writer] (102:9) S 89, p. 23.
5839. VALDES, Eduardo A.
"Llamame." [Mairena] (11:27) 89, p. 64.
5840. VALDÉS GINEBRA, Arminda
"Tiempo de Luz" (Del libro Por una Primavera). [Os] (28) 89, p. 30.
5841. VALENCIA, Guillermo
"There Is an Instant" (tr. by Joe Bolton). [Pig] (15) 88, p. 92.
5842. VALENTIN, Marta I.
"La Salsa Is Still Very Much Alive in Me." [Pig] (15) 88, p. 58.
5843. VALENTINE, Jean
"For Patrick Henisse, Dead of AIDS, in Memory." [AmerV] (16) Fall 89, p. 4.

"Ikon." [Field] (40) Spr 89, p. 36.
"Still Life: In the Epidemic." [Field] (40) Spr 89, p. 34-35.
"The Summer Was Not Long Enough." [NewYorker] (65:38) 6 N 89, p. 102.
"Trust Me." [Field] (40) Spr 89, p. 80-81.
5844. VALERO, Roberto
"Los ánsares abandonaron el otoño" (A Tze-yeh que fue Mila durante la dinastía
Chin). [Mairena] (11:27) 89, p. 58.
"Son muchas las estrellas que limitan las tierras" (A Va-D'hia, Princesa de
Shouhsiang, 618-701). [Mairena] (11:27) 89, p. 58.
5845. VALESIO, Paolo
"The Green Rose" (Selections: 2 poems, tr. by Graziella Sidoli). [Screens] (1) 89, p.
184-189.
5846. VALLEJO, César
"Trilce XIII". [StoneC] (16:3/4) Spr-Sum 89, p. 38.
"Trilce XV" (tr. by Joe Bolton). [Pig] (15) 88, p. 90.
"Your Sex" (tr. by Joe Bolton). [StoneC] (16:3/4) Spr-Sum 89, p. 39.
5847. VALLOTTON, Jean Pierre
"It Is True" (tr. by James Gill). [MissR] (17:3, #51), p. 88.
5848. Van BRUNT, Lloyd
"Eudaemonia." [SouthernPR] (29:2) Fall 89, p. 73.
"On the Serengeti." [AnotherCM] (19) 89, p. 213.
"The Stars Like Minstrels Sing to Blake." [Witness] (2:2/3) Sum-Fall 88, p.
268-269.
"Waking Up in Rabun Gap, 1988" (In Memoriam, Edie Christy, 1939-1988, dear
companion). [PoetL] (84:2) Sum 89, p. 52.
5849. Van der Spek, Corneil
"This Is a Recording." [Rampike] (6:2) 88, p. 75.
5850. Van DUYN, Mona
"The Block." [RiverC] (9:1) Spr 89, p. 2-3.
"Gardens." [NewYorker] (65:35) 16 O 89, p. 44.
"Headlines." [GrandS] (8:2) Wint 89, p. 108-109.
5851. Van HOOSE, Susanna
"The Last Strafings -- 4/30/85." [NegC] (9:2) 89, p. 74.
5852. Van HOUTEN, Lois
"Cicadas." [Footwork] 89, p. 42.
"The Creation of Night and Day." [StoneC] (16:3/4) Spr-Sum 89, p. 58.
Van ITALLIE, Jean-Claude
See ITALLIE, Jean-Claude van
5853. Van NOORD, Barbara
"My Grandmother." [Kalliope] (11:2) 89, p. 37-38.
"On Things to Hang On To, Like Bleach." [MinnR] (NS 33) Fall 89, p. 20.
5854. Van STEENBURGH, B.
"The End of a Love Affair." [SpoonRQ] (14:1) Wint 89, p. 61.
5855. Van WERT, William F.
"Dorothea Lange." [LitR] (32:2) Wint 89, p. 229.
5856. Van WINCKEL, Nance
"All the Livelong Day." [PoetryNW] (30:4) Wint 89-90, p. 17-18.
"Boy Soprano." [Iowa] (19:3) Fall 89, p. 104-105.
"Cheers." [SpoonRQ] (14:3) Sum 89, p. 12.
"Elixir." [Journal] (13:1) Spr-Sum 89, p. 22.
"Irregular Moons Over the Metro." [BlackWR] (15:2) Spr 89, p. 80-81.
"Levitation." [PoetryNW] (30:2) Sum 89, p. 19-20.
"Séance without Table." [Journal] (13:1) Spr-Sum 89, p. 23.
"What Kind of Hairdo Is That?" [PoetryNW] (30:2) Sum 89, p. 18-19.
"Women Talking in Doorways." [PoetryNW] (30:4) Wint 89-90, p. 18-19.
5857. VANCE, Richard
"Chance Perfume." [AntigR] (77/78) Spr-Sum 89, p. 25.
"Communion in Autumn." [InterPR] (15:2) Fall 89, p. 127.
"In the Blink of an Eye." [OxfordM] (5:2) Fall-Wint 89, p. 11.
"My Turn." [AntigR] (77/78) Spr-Sum 89, p. 26.
"A Restored Shaker Village in Kentucy." [AntigR] (77/78) Spr-Sum 89, p. 24.
5858. VANDENBERG, Peter
"Meeting Yourself on Vacation -- Day Three" (a Plainsongs Award Poem). [Plain]
(10:1) 89, p. 4.
5859. VanderMOLEN, Robert
"Chairs in the Water." [ArtfulD] (16/17) Fall 89, p. 107.

"The Generals." [Caliban] (6) 89, p. 159.
"Pissarro." [Caliban] (6) 89, p. 157-158.
"The Family." [ArtfulD] (16/17) Fall 89, p. 108-109.
5860. VANDERSEE, Charles
"The Desert." [Timbuktu] (4) Sum-Fall 89, p. 66.
5861. VANGELISTI, Paul
"Alephs Again" (for Adriano Spatola). [Temblor] (10) 89, p. 163-165.
"First Day in Los Angeles" (tr. of Antonio Porta). [Temblor] (10) 89, p. 166.
"Little Exhortation" (tr. of Adriano Spatola). [Temblor] (10) 89, p. 3.
"Loose Shoes, or An Account for a Son." [Temblor] (9) 89, p. 141-143.
5862. VANIER, Denis
"Le Droit de Saintete." [Rampike] (6:2) 88, p. 57.
5863. VARELA, Blanca
"Not Dated" (for Kafka, tr. by Carin Clevidence). [Field] (41) Fall 89, p. 58-59.
5864. VARELA, Franklyn P.
"The End of Time." [Americas] (17:1) Spr 89, p. 70-71.
"Manhattan, circa 1958." [Americas] (17:1) Spr 89, p. 68-69.
5865. VARGA, Adriana
"And Everything Slips Easily Away" (tr. of Marin Sorescu, w. Stuart Friebert and
Gabriela Dragnea). [Timbuktu] (4) Sum-Fall 89, p. 25.
"Between Stars" (tr. of Marin Sorescu, w. Stuart Friebert and Gabriela Dragnea).
[MalR] (88) Fall 89, p. 79.
"Dream" (tr. of Marin Sorescu, w. Stuart Friebert and Gabriela Dragnea).
[Timbuktu] (4) Sum-Fall 89, p. 27.
"Game" (tr. of Marin Sorescu, w. Stuart Friebert and Gabriela Dragnea). [Timbuktu]
(4) Sum-Fall 89, p. 29.
"Hide and Seek" (tr. of Marin Sorescu, w. Stuart Friebert and Gabriela Dragnea).
[Field] (40) Spr 89, p. 40.
"Horoscope" (tr. of Marin Sorescu, w. Stuart Friebert and Gabriela Dragnea).
[Timbuktu] (4) Sum-Fall 89, p. 35.
"The House" (tr. of Marin Sorescu, w. Stuart Friebert and Gabriela Dragnea).
[Timbuktu] (4) Sum-Fall 89, p. 31.
"Hyena" (tr. of Marin Sorescu, w. Stuart Friebert and Gabriela Dragnea). [Field]
(40) Spr 89, p. 42.
"Laocoon" (tr. of Marin Sorescu, w. Stuart Friebert and Gabriela Dragnea).
[Timbuktu] (4) Sum-Fall 89, p. 29.
"Launching" (tr. of Marin Sorescu, w. Stuart Friebert and Gabriela Dragnea).
[MalR] (88) Fall 89, p. 83.
"Lightning Passed" (tr. of Marin Sorescu, w. Stuart Friebert and Gabriela Dragnea).
[Field] (40) Spr 89, p. 41.
"The Mountains" (tr. of Marin Sorescu, w. Stuart Friebert). [Iowa] (19:2) Spr-Sum
89, p. 167-168.
"Paintings" (tr. of Marin Sorescu, w. Stuart Friebert and Gabriela Dragnea). [Field]
(40) Spr 89, p. 38-39.
"Paper" (tr. of Marin Sorescu, w. Stuart Friebert and Gabriela Dragnea). [MalR]
(88) Fall 89, p. 80-81.
"Passport" (tr. of Marin Sorescu, w. Stuart Friebert and Gabriela Dragnea). [MalR]
(88) Fall 89, p. 78.
"Perspective" (tr. of Marin Sorescu, w. Stuart Friebert). [Os] (29) 89, p. 7.
"Pliers" (tr. of Marin Sorescu, w. Stuart Friebert). [Os] (29) 89, p. 9.
"The Sacred Fire" (tr. of Marin Sorescu, w. Stuart Friebert). [Iowa] (19:2) Spr-Sum
89, p. 166-167.
"Spiral" (tr. of Marin Sorescu, w. Stuart Friebert and Gabriela Dragnea). [MalR]
(88) Fall 89, p. 82.
"Subjectivism" (tr. of Marin Sorescu, w. Stuart Friebert and Gabriela Dragnea).
[Timbuktu] (4) Sum-Fall 89, p. 33.
"Vibrations" (tr. of Marin Sorescu, w. Stuart Friebert and Gabriela Dragnea).
[Timbuktu] (4) Sum-Fall 89, p. 33.
"Village Museum" (tr. of Marin Sorescu, w. Stuart Friebert). [Iowa] (19:2) Spr-Sum
89, p. 165-166.
"Vision" (tr. of Marin Sorescu, w. Stuart Friebert). [Vis] (30) 89, p. 5.
"Whim" (tr. of Marin Sorescu, w. Stuart Friebert). [Iowa] (19:2) Spr-Sum 89, p.
168.
5866. VARN, Jim
"Adulterous Sonnets." [CharR] (15:2) Fall 89, p. 31.

5867. VARNES, Katherine
"When Life's Unbearable and Left to Chance." [CrabCR] (6:2) Wint 89, p. 18.
5868. VASQUEZ, Robert
"Night-Song in Verano" (for Peter and Phil). [MissouriR] (12:1) 89, p. 173.
VASSEUR, Jeanne le
See LeVASSEUR, Jeanne
5869. VASSILAKIS, Nico
"Love Quake." [HeavenB] (7) Wint 89, p. 15.
5870. VASSILIEVA, Larissa
"August Shadow" (Excerpt, tr. by Greg Richter). [CharR] (15:1) Spr 89, p. 67.
"Vassilisa" (Excerpt, tr. by Greg Richter). [CharR] (15:1) Spr 89, p. 68.
"Whiteness in February" (tr. by Greg Richter). [CharR] (15:1) Spr 89, p. 68.
5871. VAZQUEZ DIAZ, René
"La Ciudad Entera Murmura." [LindLM] (8:3) Jl-S 89, p. 17.
"Hay Oficios Que Son." [LindLM] (8:3) Jl-S 89, p. 17.
VEAUX, Alexis de
See De VEAUX, Alexis
5872. VEGA, Garcilaso de la
"Four Sonnets" (in Spanish and English, tr. by H. Gaston Hall). [BallSUF] (30:3)
Sum 89, p. 28-30.
5873. VEGA, Janine Pommy
"Bagarchap" (Bagarchap, Nepal, Sept. 16/88). [AlphaBS] (6) Wint 89-90, p. 56.
"Lattar" (Lattar, Nepal, Sept. 22/88). [AlphaBS] (6) Wint 89-90, p. 57.
5874. VEGRI, Sasa
"Relics: The Family" (tr. by Michael Biggins). [NewEngR] (11:3) Spr 89, p. 251.
5875. VEIGA, Marisella
"On a River, Insects Compose." [Pig] (15) 88, p. 59.
5876. VEINBERG, Jon
"The Beginning of Ritual." [MissouriR] (12:2) 89, p. 56.
"The Voyeur." [MissouriR] (12:2) 89, p. 57.
VÉLEZ, Clemente Soto
See SOTO VÉLEZ, Clemente
5877. VELTEN, Kathe
"Bend to Me." [SoCoast] (6) Fall 88, p. 12-13.
5878. VENRIGHT, Steve
"Counting Cars." [Rampike] (6:2) 88, p. 68.
5879. VENUTI, Lawrence
"After Marx, April" (tr. of Giuseppe Conte). [Poetry] (155:1/2) O-N 89, p. 129.
"Cruel Fair Adheres" (tr. of Cesare Viviani). [Poetry] (155:1/2) O-N 89, p. 133.
"He Who Has Dared" (tr. of Milo De Angelis). [Poetry] (155:1/2) O-N 89, p. 153.
"The Narrator" (tr. of Milo De Angelis). [Poetry] (155:1/2) O-N 89, p. 155.
"The Sky Overtook the Fading Light" (tr. of Cesare Viviani). [Poetry] (155:1/2) O-N
89, p. 133.
"This Is Exactly What She Told Me" (Excerpt, tr. of Giuseppe Conte). [Poetry]
(155:1/2) O-N 89, p. 127.
"Trans-Europe-Express" (tr. of Giuseppe Conte). [Poetry] (155:1/2) O-N 89, p.
131.
"Will You Put on the Blindfold?" (tr. of Milo De Angelis). [Poetry] (155:1/2) O-N
89, p. 153.
"Year" (tr. of Milo De Angelis). [Poetry] (155:1/2) O-N 89, p. 151.
"Yearbook" (tr. of Milo De Angelis). [Poetry] (155:1/2) O-N 89, p. 155.
5880. VERDE, Thomas
"Nantucket Girl." [AnthNEW] (1) 89, p. 23.
5881. VERDICCHIO, Pasquale
"Three for Pier Paolo Pasolini." [Temblor] (10) 89, p. 124-125.
5882. VERGIL
"The Golden Bough" (Aeneid Book VI, tr. by Seamus Heaney, in memory of Jack
and Máire Sweeney). [Trans] (22) Fall 89, p. 197-201.
5883. VERMA, Shrikant
"Khyber" (in Hindi). [TriQ] (77) Wint 89-90, p. 174-175.
"Khyber" (tr. by Vinay Dharwadker). [TriQ] (77) Wint 89-90, p. 172-173.
"Process of Change" (tr. by Vinay Dharwadker). [TriQ] (77) Wint 89-90, p.
170-171.
5884. VERNIER, Tom
"Call of the Mail Train." [Wind] (19:65) 89, p. 22.

5885. VERNON, William (William J.)
"Freezing Weather." [PassN] (10:1) Wint 89, p. 10.
"Once Something." [PoetL] (84:1) Spr 89, p. 42.
"Snow As a Blanket" (-- Robert Gibb). [StoneC] (16:3/4) Spr-Sum 89, p. 79.
5886. VERSÉNYI, Sue Lipsiner
"East Rock Park." [SenR] (19:1) 89, p. 67-68.
5887. VERSTEEG, Jennie
"A Witch, Five Years Barren, to Her Husband." [CrabCR] (6:2) Wint 89, p. 4.
5888. VERSTEEG, Tom
"Beyond the Last Fence." [CimR] (86) Ja 89, p. 75.
5889. VERTES, László
"The Day Has Passed (Elmút a nap)" (tr. of Sándor Csoóri, w. Len Roberts). [IndR] (12:2) Spr 89, p. 100.
"Postponed Nightmare (Elmaradt lázálom)" (tr. of Sándor Csoóri, w. Len Roberts). [IndR] (12:2) Spr 89, p. 101.
5890. VERTREACE, Martha (Martha M.)
"Aquarelles." [AnotherCM] (19) 89, p. 214-215.
"Glassworks." [HampSPR] Wint 89, p. 40-41.
"Leaving Thirtieth Street Station, Philadelphia." [ChiR] (36:3/4) 89, p. 20-21.
"Maize." [MidwQ] (30:4) Sum 89, p. 455.
"My Uncle Speaks of Bees." [Farm] (6:1) Wint-Spr 88-89, p. 124.
"Night Cafe." [ClockR] (5:2) 89, p. 15-16.
"Patterns of Observed Vision Disturbances" (after Edvard Munch). [AnotherCM] (19) 89, p. 216-217.
"Silver Maple." [ClockR] (5:2) 89, p. 14.
"Somerset, Kentucky." [ClockR] (5:2) 89, p. 13.
5891. VESPER, Guntram
"The Cry of the Owl" (tr. by John Linthicum). [LitR] (33:1) Fall 89, p. 62.
"Old Comrade" (tr. by John Linthicum). [LitR] (33:1) Fall 89, p. 60.
"Strong As Death" (tr. by John Linthicum). [LitR] (33:1) Fall 89, p. 61.
5892. VESZI, Endre
"Silence" (tr. by Zsuzsanna Ozsvath and Martha Satz). [WebR] (14:1) Spr 89, p. 30.
5893. VICENTE GARCIA, Luis Miguel
"Insomnio." [Mester] (18:1) Spr 89, p. 58.
"Los Busco y los Encuentro en Medio de Mi Alma." [Mester] (18:1) Spr 89, p. 57.
5894. VIDAS, Gregory
"Golden As Wheat." [Confr] (39/40) Fall 88-Wint 89, p. 73.
"I Was Running After You" (Federsee, January 1st, 1984). [KanQ] (21:1/2) Wint-Spr 89, p. 238.
5895. VIERAVÉ, Alfredo
"And Now on to Sensible Explanations" (tr. by Carlos and Monique Altschul). [LitR] (32:4) Sum 89, p. 593.
"Description of the Monster She or the Cannon Woman" (tr. by Carlos and Monique Altschul). [LitR] (32:4) Sum 89, p. 592.
"History and Sociology" (tr. by Carlos and Monique Altschul). [LitR] (32:4) Sum 89, p. 588-590.
"Madame Bovary" (tr. by Carlos and Monique Altschul). [LitR] (32:4) Sum 89, p. 591-592.
"Poem: Claudia Cardinale bird of imperial plumage and her breasts" (tr. by Carlos and Monique Altschul). [LitR] (32:4) Sum 89, p. 590-591.
5896. VIERECK, Peter
"By the Way, Mr, Eichmann." [NewL] (56:2/3) Wint 89-Spr 90, p. 305.
"Courage and Sleep." [Salm] (84) Fall 89, p. 42-49.
"Ore." [NewL] (56:2/3) Wint 89-Spr 90, p. 303-304.
"The Shaggy Somnambulists" (The Moscow Circus bear dance in 1988 at Radio City, NYC). [NewL] (56:2/3) Wint 89-Spr 90, p. 306-307.
"The Three Furies at Age Sixteen." [NewL] (56:2/3) Wint 89-Spr 90, p. 307-308.
5897. VILA BARNÉS, Gladys
"Elegia por un Pintor" (A Richard Pagán). [Mairena] (11:27) 89, p. 80.
5898. VILLA, Carlo
"Cento di Questi Fogli." [Poetry] (155:1/2) O-N 89, p. 80.
"Donne" (tr. by Rebecca Messbarger). [Poetry] (155:1/2) O-N 89, p. 82.
"One Hundred of These Pages" (tr. by Rebecca Messbarger). [Poetry] (155:1/2) O-N 89, p. 81.
"Women" (tr. by Rebecca Messbarger). [Poetry] (155:1/2) O-N 89, p. 83.

5899. VILLALONGO, Jose
"Stormy Garden." [Footwork] 89, p. 76.
"Who Will Remember Me." [Footwork] 89, p. 75-76.
5900. VILLANUEVA, Tino
"Fight Scene: Final Frames." [Agni] (28) 89, p. 295-296.
"Fight Scene, Part II." [Agni] (28) 89, p. 293-294.
"Fight Scene Beginning." [Agni] (28) 89, p. 291-292.
5901. VILLEGAS, Penny
"Life Line." [Mildred] (3:1) Spr-Sum 89, p. 97.
"My Mother" (in dedication to my mother, who died December 27, 1988). [Mildred]
(3:1) Spr-Sum 89, p. 97.
5902. VINCIGUERRA, Theresa
"Love as Remembrance" (for Patrick). [YellowS] (30) Sum 89, p. 35.
VINCK, Christopher de
See DeVINCK, Christopher
5903. VINE, Scott
"The headline screams to me to answer." [HiramPoR] (46) Spr-Sum 89, p. 35.
5904. VINOGRAD, Julia
"Blues." [FiveFR] (7) 89, p. 41.
"Safe Sex." [FiveFR] (7) 89, p. 39.
"San Francisco." [Sequoia] (32:2) Wint-Spr 89, p. 28.
"When Someone Dies." [FiveFR] (7) 89, p. 40.
5905. VINZ, Mark
"Living on the Edge of Dakota." [SoDakR] (27:1) Spr 89, p. 133.
5906. VIRGA, Michael Jeffrey
"Song for a King: MLK." [Sequoia] (32:2) Wint-Spr 89, p. 76.
VITO, E. B. de
See De VITO, E. B.
5907. VIVIANI, Cesare
"Il Cielo Passava l'Ultima Luce e i Fiori." [Poetry] (155:1/2) O-N 89, p. 132.
"Cruel Fair Adheres" (tr. by Lawrence Venuti). [Poetry] (155:1/2) O-N 89, p. 133.
"Fera Aderisce, Come Era Caldo l'Abito." [Poetry] (155:1/2) O-N 89, p. 132.
"The Sky Overtook the Fading Light" (tr. by Lawrence Venuti). [Poetry] (155:1/2)
O-N 89, p. 133.
5908. VLASOPOLOS, Anca
"Bird Snobs." [SpiritSH] (54) Spr-Sum 89, p. 22.
"Sex and War." [Interim] (8:1) Spr 89, p. 30.
"Sifting through Ashes." [Interim] (8:1) Spr 89, p. 29.
"Voodoo on Former Landlords." [Interim] (8:1) Spr 89, p. 31-32.
"A Walk with My Mother." [Interim] (8:1) Spr 89, p. 32.
"A Walk with My Mother." [SpiritSH] (54) Spr-Sum 89, p. 23.
5909. VODUSEK, Bozo
"City by Night" (tr. by Michael Biggins). [NewEngR] (11:3) Spr 89, p. 252-253.
5910. VOGELSANG, Arthur
"Kern County." [Ploughs] (15:1) 89, p. 148-149.
"Material." [DenQ] (23:3/4) Wint-Spr 89, p. 58-59.
"Skip Tracers." [Ploughs] (15:1) 89, p. 146-147.
5911. VOIGT, Ellen Bryant
"At the Movie: Virginia, 1956." [NewL] (56:2/3) Wint 89-Spr 90, p. 316-317.
"Blue Ridge." [NewL] (56:2/3) Wint 89-Spr 90, p. 309-311.
"Dancing with Poets." [NewL] (56:2/3) Wint 89-Spr 90, p. 315-316.
"For My Mother." [NewL] (56:2/3) Wint 89-Spr 90, p. 313.
"Sweet Everlasting." [NewL] (56:2/3) Wint 89-Spr 90, p. 312.
"The Trust." [NewL] (56:2/3) Wint 89-Spr 90, p. 314.
5912. VOLDSETH, Beverly
"The Death of the Boxelder." [RagMag] (7:1) 89, p. 64.
5913. VOLEK, Bronislava
"Spot." [Vis] (30) 89, p. 38.
5914. VOLKMAN, Karen
"Arms." [FloridaR] (16:2/3) Fall-Wint 89, p. 150.
5915. VOLKMER, Jon
"Centralia, PA." [CarolQ] (42:1) Fall 89, p. 16.
5916. VOLKOVA, Bronislava
"Here in Charlottesville the roads ring" (tr. by the author and Andrew Durkin).
[InterPR] (15:2) Fall 89, p. 20.
"I am homesick" (tr. by the author and Judy Miner). [InterPR] (15:2) Fall 89, p. 21.

"If My Hands Could Undress the Moon" (a variation on Lorca's theme, tr. by the
    author and Wilis Barnstone). [InterPR] (15:2) Fall 89, p. 20-21.
5917. VOLLMER, Judith
    "My Grandmother's Rags." [MinnR] (NS 32) Spr 89, p. 73.
5918. VOLOHONSKY, Henri
    "Ai" (tr. by Richard Pevear). [GrandS] (8:4) Sum 89, p. 209-211.
5919. VOLZ, James
    "Potatoes." [PassN] (10:2) Sum 89, p. 18.
5920. Von BUCHLER, Judith Lewis
    "In the Moment of the Candles." [BallSUF] (30:4) Aut 89, p. 8.
    "Yellow Iris." [BallSUF] (30:4) Aut 89, p. 60.
5921. Von MALTZAHN, Nicholas
    "Alders." [MalR] (87) Sum 89, p. 110.
    "Marriage Song." [MalR] (87) Sum 89, p. 111.
5922. Von REIS, Siri
    "L'Ange Gardien" (after the Haitian painter Wilmino Domond). [RiverS] (29) [89],
        p. 40.
    "La Bélaittée" (after the Haitian painter Louverture Poisson). [RiverS] (29) [89], p.
        41.
    "Scène Familial" (after the Haitian painter Fernand Pierre). [RiverS] (29) [89], p. 42.
Von SCHOULTZ, Solveig
    See SCHOULTZ, Solveig von
5923. VONIER, Sprague
    "A Captive Audience Listens to Borodin's Second String Quartet." [CreamCR]
        (13:2) Fall 89, p. 181-182.
5924. VORHEES, Duane
    "Soundlessly Scarlet Fruits" (tr. of Sung Bok Yi). [MidAR] (9:1) 89, p. 41.
5925. VOSS, Fred
    "8 Hours at Goodstone Aircraft Company." [WormR] (29:1, #113) 89, p. 18.
    "Air Force Contractor." [WormR] (29:1, #113) 89, p. 20.
    "The Aristocrats." [WormR] (29:1, #113) 89, p. 19.
    "A Bright Future." [WormR] (29:1, #113) 89, p. 25.
    "Confidence." [WormR] (29:1, #113) 89, p. 28.
    "Disadvantage." [WormR] (29:1, #113) 89, p. 15.
    "The Edge." [WormR] (29:1, #113) 89, p. 26.
    "Etiquette." [WormR] (29:1, #113) 89, p. 29.
    "Excretion." [WormR] (29:1, #113) 89, p. 31.
    "Fringe Benefit." [WormR] (29:1, #113) 89, p. 33.
    "Gasket Factory." [WormR] (29:1, #113) 89, p. 22.
    "High Priority." [WormR] (29:1, #113) 89, p. 27.
    "Hot Potato." [WormR] (29:1, #113) 89, p. 21.
    "The Inspection." [WormR] (29:1, #113) 89, p. 25.
    "Integrity." [WormR] (29:1, #113) 89, p. 18.
    "It Figures." [WormR] (29:1, #113) 89, p. 27.
    "Keep the Faith." [WormR] (29:1, #113) 89, p. 32.
    "Kings for a Minute." [WormR] (29:1, #113) 89, p. 26.
    "Labor of Love." [WormR] (29:1, #113) 89, p. 28.
    "A Learning Experience." [WormR] (29:1, #113) 89, p. 23.
    "Lingo." [WormR] (29:1, #113) 89, p. 29.
    "The Loser." [WormR] (29:1, #113) 89, p. 24.
    "Making the World's Most Advanced Bomber." [WormR] (29:1, #113) 89, p. 20.
    "Mental Patient." [WormR] (29:1, #113) 89, p. 33.
    "Occupational Hazard." [WormR] (29:1, #113) 89, p. 17.
    "Paperwork." [WormR] (29:1, #113) 89, p. 32.
    "Pride." [WormR] (29:1, #113) 89, p. 23.
    "Progress." [WormR] (29:1, #113) 89, p. 19.
    "Relief." [WormR] (29:1, #113) 89, p. 26.
    "Rough Job." [WormR] (29:1, #113) 89, p. 17.
    "Safety Net." [WormR] (29:1, #113) 89, p. 24.
    "Self-Preservation." [WormR] (29:1, #113) 89, p. 16.
    "Sleepworking." [WormR] (29:1, #113) 89, p. 30.
    "Solidarity." [WormR] (29:1, #113) 89, p. 22.
    "Spirit." [WormR] (29:1, #113) 89, p. 16.
    "The Standard of Excellence." [WormR] (29:1, #113) 89, p. 15.
    "The Stud." [WormR] (29:1, #113) 89, p. 21.
    "T.G.I.F." [WormR] (29:1, #113) 89, p. 34.

"Tool of the Trade." [WormR] (29:1, #113) 89, p. 30.
"Uptight." [WormR] (29:1, #113) 89, p. 34.
"The Vice-President Gives His Monthly Shop Talk." [WormR] (29:1, #113) 89, p. 31.
"What You Got for Your Tax Dollars." [WormR] (29:1, #113) 89, p. 27.

5926. VOVAKES, Christine
"Lunar Findings." [CapeR] (24:1) Spr 89, p. 46.
"Watching Seven Crows Fly." [CapeR] (24:1) Spr 89, p. 47.

5927. VRAGOLOV, Zoran
"Challenger." [Footwork] 89, p. 61.
"The Stars Are of Long Watching." [Footwork] 89, p. 61.

VRIES, Judith A. de
See DeVRIES, Judith A.

5928. WACHTEL, Andrew
"So here I am crushing cockroaches . . ." (tr. of Dmitri Prigov). [Sequoia] (33:1) Sum 89, p. 60.

5929. WADDELL-TAKARA, Kathryn
"C's Cafe." [Hawai'iR] (13:1, #25) Spr 89, p. 121-123.
"Elegy." [Hawai'iR] (13:2, #26) Sum 89, p. 136-137.
"Trekking Friends." [Hawai'iR] (13:1, #25) Spr 89, p. 124-126.

5930. WADDINGTON, J.
"Victory Square, Vancouver." [Grain] (17:1) Spr 89, p. 27.

5931. WADDINGTON, Miriam
"An Evening in the Old People's Home" (tr. of Rohel Korn). [CanLit] (120) Spr 89, p. 20.

5932. WADE, Sidney
"Among Friends on the Metaphysical Farm." [GrandS] (8:4) Sum 89, p. 33-34.
"Aurora Borealis and the Body Louse." [GrandS] (8:4) Sum 89, p. 35-36.
"Leaving Rome." [GettyR] (2:3) Sum 89, p. 546.
"Raveliana in Brown." [GettyR] (2:2) Spr 89, p. 300.
"Repast in the Shadows." [GrandS] (8:4) Sum 89, p. 31-32.

5933. WADSWORTH, William
"The Marriage of Edgar and Cordelia." [NewRep] (201:18) 30 O 89, p. 30.

5934. WAGNER, Robert
"After All Saints'." [SmPd] (26:2 #76) Spr 89, p. 19.
"Exchanging Pleasantries." [SmPd] (26:2 #76) Spr 89, p. 18.
"Khafre on the Throne." [Bogg] (61) 89, p. 35.

5935. WAGNER, Shelly
"The Blue Chair." [PoetryE] (28) Fall 89, p. 93-94.
"The Foxes." [PoetryE] (28) Fall 89, p. 91-92.
"The Gold Sofa." [PoetryE] (28) Fall 89, p. 95-96.
"The Grocery Store." [PoetryE] (28) Fall 89, p. 89-90.
"The Oak Tree and the Two Swings." [PoetryE] (28) Fall 89, p. 85-87.
"The Pearl." [PoetryE] (28) Fall 89, p. 88.

5936. WAH, Fred
"Music at the Heart of Thinking" (Selections: Ninetyone-Ninetyfour). [Temblor] (10) 89, p. 81-82.
"Three Artknots" (Selections: 18-20). [Temblor] (10) 89, p. 83.

5937. WAHLE, F. Keith
"John and Marsha: Their Life Together." [YellowS] (29) Spr 89, p. 5.

5938. WAKEFIELD, Kathleen
"Why She Cannot Hear the Sound of Her Own Weeping." [CumbPR] (9:1) Fall 89, p. 46.

5939. WAKOSKI, Diane
"The Bowl of Apples." [AnotherCM] (19) 89, p. 219.
"Kelly As The Mage." [AlphaBS] (5) Jl 89, p. 47-49.
"Meditation on the King of Wands." [AlphaBS] (5) Jl 89, p. 45-46.
"Rosenkavalier." [Caliban] (6) 89, p. 152-154.
"Star." [AnotherCM] (19) 89, p. 218.
"Young Men Fighting or Playing with Green Poles." [Witness] (2:2/3) Sum-Fall 88, p. 232-234.

5940. WALCOTT, Derek
"Achille in Africa" (from "Omeros," Book III). [Agni] (28) 89, p. 13-28.
"A Castle in the Olives." [NewYorker] (65:12) 8 My 89, p. 44-45.
"Homer in the Underground." [NewRep] (200:12) 20 Mr 89, p. 38-39.
"Polonaise." [NewYorker] (65:34) 9 O 89, p. 52-53.

5941. WALDMAN, Anne
"Athens Airport" (tr. of Mahmoud Darwish, w. Lena Jayyusi). [PoetryE] (27) Spr 89, p. 80.
"Couchette" (on "The Orient Express," from 1978). [AlphaBS] (6) Wint 89-90, p. 47.
"Helping the Dreamer." [AmerPoR] (18:6) N-D 89, p. 17-18.
"Horses Neighing on the Slope" (tr. of Mahmoud Darwish, w. Lena Jayyusi). [PoetryE] (27) Spr 89, p. 84.
"Kill or Cure." [AmerPoR] (18:6) N-D 89, p. 16-17.
"Putting Makeup on Empty Space" (Excerpt, NYC '81). [AlphaBS] (6) Wint 89-90, p. 48.
"To Jesse Helms et Al." [NewAW] (5) Fall 89, p. 70.

5942. WALDOR, Peter
"Ahh. He Is the Pear of My Nose." [Iowa] (19:2) Spr-Sum 89, p. 122.
"Future." [Iowa] (19:2) Spr-Sum 89, p. 122.

5943. WALDREP, Shelton
"Cracked Actor." [Jacaranda] (4:1) Spr-Sum 89, p. 148-149.

5944. WALDROP, Jason
"Cathedral." [NewL] (55:3) Spr 89, p. 111.
"The Materiality of Light." [PoetryNW] (30:4) Wint 89-90, p. 32-33.
"Second Sight." [PoetryNW] (30:4) Wint 89-90, p. 33.

5945. WALDROP, Keith
"Any order precludes some other: one function." [Talisman] (2) Spr 89, p. 77.
"Transcendental Studies" (Excerpts). [Temblor] (9) 89, p. 103-106.

5946. WALDROP, Rosmarie
"The Book of Resemblances" (Selections, tr. of Edmond Jabes). [Temblor] (10) 89, p. 182-191.
"Dawn" (Excerpt, tr. of Joseph Guglielmi). [Notus] (4:2) Fall 89, p. 36-39.
"In Providence, you can encounter extinct species." [Conjunc] (13) 89, p. 238.
"Lawn of Excluded Middle" (Excerpts). [Temblor] (9) 89, p. 133-134.
"My love was deep and therefore lasted only the space of one second." [Conjunc] (13) 89, p. 238.
"The Picture" (for William Bronk). [Talisman] (2) Spr 89, p. 54.
"Rhapsody." [Witness] (3:1) Spr 89, p. 124-125.
"Seven Passages from a Woman's Life" (tr. of Jacqueline Risset). [Verse] (6:2) Je 89, p. 14-16.
"Some Thing Black" (Selections: 9 poems, tr. of Jacques Roubaud). [Conjunc] (14) 89, p. 54-60.
"Some Thing Dark" (Selections, tr. of Jacques Roubaud). [Verse] (6:2) Je 89, p. 9-13.
"This is not thinking, you said, more what colors it, like a smell." [Conjunc] (13) 89, p. 238.
"We know that swallows are drawn to window panes." [Conjunc] (13) 89, p. 237.
"What's left over if I subtract the fact that my leg goes up from the fact that I raise it?" [Conjunc] (13) 89, p. 237.
"Words too can be wrung from us like a cry from that space." [Conjunc] (13) 89, p. 237.

5947. WALEY, Arthur
"The Little Cart" (tr. of Ch'en Tzu-lung). [LitR] (32:3) Spr 89, p. 305.
"On Board Ship: Reading Yüan Chen's Poems" (tr. of Po Chü-yi). [LitR] (32:3) Spr 89, p. 305.

5948. WALFER, Michael
"To My Brothers." [FiveFR] (7) 89, p. 43-44.

5949. WALKER, A. A.
"Adoration." [HeavenB] (7) Wint 89, p. 43.

5950. WALKER, Anne F.
"Love Poem." [PraF] (10:4, #49) Wint 89-90, p. 14.

5951. WALKER, Brian
"Three Views." [BallSUF] (30:4) Aut 89, p. 75.

5952. WALKER, Jeanne (Jeanne Murray)
"Birth" (For Wendy Weger). [Poetry] (153:4) Ja 89, p. 189-190.
"Blind Genius Discovers Infinity." [Shen] (39:2) Sum 89, p. 52.
"Carpenter Sets His Own House on Fire." [Boulevard] (4:1, #10) Spr 89, p. 181-182.
"February." [Nimrod] (33:1) Fall-Wint 89, p. 102.
"Going Home." [Poetry] (153:4) Ja 89, p. 192.

"I Won't Read the Alphabet Book Once More." [Poetry] (153:4) Ja 89, p. 190-191.
"Man Survives Nine Days in Rubble of Collapsed Bakery." [WestB] (24) 89, p.
   42-43.
"Man's Thumb Bleeds for Three Years." [WestB] (24) 89, p. 41-42.
"Meteorite the Size of a House Falls in Farmer's Field." [Shen] (39:2) Sum 89, p.
   50-51.
"My Grandmother Called Me by Everything But My Own Name." [Nimrod] (33:1)
   Fall-Wint 89, p. 103.
"Sweethearts Vanish in Tunnel of Love." [WestB] (24) 89, p. 44.
"Whacky Gardener Weds Head of Lettuce." [Shen] (39:3) Fall 89, p. 25-26.
5953. WALKER, John David
"Burial of Twin Babies, Florence, Texas." [MSS] (6:3) 89, p. 37.
"Gentle Time." [MSS] (6:3) 89, p. 39.
5954. WALKER, John V.
"At the Movies" (from "City Magic -- A Naked Lunch"). [AlphaBS] (5) Jl 89, p. 69.
5955. WALKER, Leon
"For a Neighbor Departed." [Plain] (9:3) Spr 89, p. 28.
5956. WALKER, Rodney
"How sweet, to know again, this tender joy." [EmeraldCR] (1989) c1988, p. 137.
5957. WALKER, Sue
"If We Penetrate Nature's Secrets, We Come to an Animal with a Knowledge of All
   His Relatives and Their Habits." [Kalliope] (11:3) 89, p. 34.
"Live Copy" (For Bobby). [NegC] (9:1) 89, p. 11.
"Second Hand Dealer." [SoCoast] (5) Spr 88, p. 35.
5958. WALL, Kathleen
"How Simple Lives Need No Sense of Humor" (1972, 1984). [BlueBldgs] (11) 89,
   p. 38-39.
5959. WALLACE, Aurelia D.
"Darwin at Datona." [NegC] (9:2) 89, p. 80.
5960. WALLACE, Bruce
"Choke Cherries." [Plain] (9:3) Spr 89, p. 27.
"If, By Thought Alone." [Plain] (9:2) Wint 89, p. 13.
"Twenty-Four Hours of Sunlight, Sweden 1982." [Plain] (9:2) Wint 89, p. 12.
5961. WALLACE, D. M.
"Babies in the Mexico City Earthquake." [Lactuca] (13) N 89, p. 41.
"The Jewel" (for Julian). [Lactuca] (13) N 89, p. 42.
"Opening and Closing." [SilverFR] (16) Spr 89, p. 8.
"The Sister." [SilverFR] (16) Spr 89, p. 9.
5962. WALLACE, Naomi
"The Bath." [Chelsea] (48) 89, p. 99.
"The Farewell" (for Bruce). [HayF] (4) Spr 89, p. 43.
"Judas in the Field of Aceldama." [Chelsea] (48) 89, p. 98.
"Notes on an Old Priest's Death." [Chelsea] (48) 89, p. 96-97.
"Purpose." [AntR] (47:1) Wint 89, p. 58.
"Traveling the Same Place." [HayF] (4) Spr 89, p. 42.
"A Troubled Man's Sestina." [NegC] (9:2) 89, p. 81-82.
5963. WALLACE, Ronald
"Basketball." [Shen] (39:1) Spr 89, p. 24.
"The Inaccessible." [CinPR] (19) Spr 89, p. 68.
"Love and Sex." [Poetry] (153:5) F 89, p. 287.
"Nightshade." [SouthernPR] (29:1) Spr 89, p. 27.
"Peace." [PoetryNW] (30:4) Wint 89-90, p. 24.
"The Poetry Report." [Poetry] (153:6) Mr 89, p. 330.
"Quick Bright Things." [Nat] (249:20) 11 D 89, p. 732.
"State Poetry Day." [GeoR] (43:3) Fall 89, p. 586.
"Turkeys." [Nat] (248:21) 29 My 89, p. 750.
5964. WALLACE, Rudy
"Journey to Heritage" (3rd Runner-up in the Minority Book Prize Contest,
   Selections: 7 poems). [Obs] (3:2) Sum 88, p. 82-88.
5965. WALLACE, T. H. S.
"So the Old Beggar with the Bow Can Shoot as Straight as Death." [CumbPR] (8:2)
   Spr 89, p. 85.
5966. WALLACE-CRABBE, Chris
"The Ibis." [Verse] (6:2) Je 89, p. 8.
"Loss." [Verse] (6:2) Je 89, p. 7.
"River Run" (for Kevin Hart). [Verse] (6:2) Je 89, p. 7.

"Thirteen Ways of Looking at Europe" (for Peter Porter). [Descant] (20:3/4, #66/67) Fall-Wint 89, p. 201-203.

5967. WALLENSTEIN, Barry
"A Public Man." [AntigR] (77/78) Spr-Sum 89, p. 12.

5968. WALLS, Doyle Wesley
"She of the Cochineal Nose." [Amelia] (5:3, #14) 89, p. 64.
"X." [CimR] (87) Ap 89, p. 57-58.

5969. WALLS, Jan
"On Climbing Baogong Pagoda" (tr. of Wang An-shih). [LitR] (32:3) Spr 89, p. 363.
"Reversible Verse" (Readable left to right from top to bottom, and right to left from bottom to top, tr. of Wang An-shih). [LitR] (32:3) Spr 89, p. 362.
"Twenty Poems in the Style of Han Shan and Shi De" (16, tr. of Wang An-shih). [LitR] (32:3) Spr 89, p. 363.
"Written in Reply to Chen Zhengshu Using His Own Rhymes" (First of Two, tr. of Wang An-shih). [LitR] (32:3) Spr 89, p. 361.

5970. WALLUM, Robert
"Jesus' Injunction to His Disciples and the Importance of Sparrows." [Plain] (10:1) 89, p. 31.
"The Sheep of Sebago Bay" (a Plainsongs Award Poem). [Plain] (9:3) Spr 89, p. 36.

5971. WALSH, J. K.
"The Poet Speaks with His Beloved on the Telephone" (tr. of Federico Garcia Lorca, w. Francisco Aragon). [ChamLR] (3:1, #5) Fall 89, p. 76.
"The Poet Tells the Truth" (tr. of Federico Garcia Lorca, w. Francisco Aragon). [ChamLR] (3:1, #5) Fall 89, p. 75.
"Sonnet of the Sweet Complaint" (tr. of Federico Garcia Lorca, w. Francisco Aragon). [ChamLR] (3:1, #5) Fall 89, p. 77.

5972. WALSH, Joy
"If Your Right Hand Offends You." [AlphaBS] (6) Wint 89-90, p. 12-19.
"Introductory Dialogue" (from "Mary Magdalen Sings the Mass in Ordinary Time"). [AlphaBS] (5) Jl 89, p. 7-9.

5973. WALSH, Margaret B.
"Dacotah Winter." [SoDakR] (27:1) Spr 89, p. 119.

5974. WALSH, Marty
"After Making Love." [StoneC] (17:1/2) Fall-Wint 89-90, p. 30.
"Crow Shouts at the Game from the Sidelines." [BelPoJ] (39:4) Sum 89, p. 35.
"I am the Stranger." [Poem] (61) My 89, p. 55.
"The Iron Ikon." [Poem] (61) My 89, p. 56-57.

5975. WALSH, Michael
"Cry, Totem." [ChamLR] (2:2, #4) Spr 89, p. 47-48.
"Five Masks." [ChamLR] (2:2, #4) Spr 89, p. 49-50.

5976. WALTERS, LaWanda
"Marilyn Monroe." [Ploughs] (15:4) Wint 89-90, p. 239-240.

5977. WALTHALL, Hugh
"You Judge the Bees" (for MT). [WashR] (15:3) O-N 89, p. 15.

5978. WALTNER-TOEWS, David
"Saskatoon Revisited" (for ABR, on her 19th birthday). [Grain] (17:2) Sum 89, inside back cover.

5979. WALTON, Anthony
"First Fall in New York." [IndR] (12:2) Spr 89, p. 48.
"Logos." [IndR] (12:2) Spr 89, p. 44-45.
"Longing." [IndR] (12:2) Spr 89, p. 46-47.
"Summer Plaint." [IndR] (12:2) Spr 89, p. 43.

5980. WANG, An-shih
"On Climbing Baogong Pagoda" (tr. by Jan Walls). [LitR] (32:3) Spr 89, p. 363.
"Reversible Verse" (Readable left to right from top to bottom, and right to left from bottom to top, tr. by Jan Walls). [LitR] (32:3) Spr 89, p. 362.
"Twenty Poems in the Style of Han Shan and Shi De" (16, tr. by Jan Walls). [LitR] (32:3) Spr 89, p. 363.
"Written in Reply to Chen Zhengshu Using His Own Rhymes" (First of Two, tr. by Jan Walls). [LitR] (32:3) Spr 89, p. 361.

5981. WANG, Ch'ang-ling
"Parting with Hsin Chien at Hibiscus Tavern" (tr. by Gary Snyder). [LitR] (32:3) Spr 89, p. 445.
"Silent at Her Window" (tr. by Sam Hamill). [LitR] (32:3) Spr 89, p. 350.

5982. WANG, Chi
"Night Journey to the Eastern Brook" (tr. by Jim Sanford). [LitR] (32:3) Spr 89, p. 357.
"Written on the Tavern Wall" (tr. by Jim Sanford). [LitR] (32:3) Spr 89, p. 357.
5983. WANG, Jiaxin
"Autumn" (tr. by Dong Jiping). [Footwork] 89, p. 25.
"Landscape" (tr. by Dong Jiping). [Footwork] 89, p. 25.
"A Praise" (tr. by Dong Jiping). [Footwork] 89, p. 25.
5984. WANG, Jun
"Scene" (tr. of Cheng Gu). [Vis] (31) 89, p. 10.
5985. WANG, Wei
"Bamboo Lane House" (tr. by Gary Snyder). [LitR] (32:3) Spr 89, p. 444.
"Composed on Horseback for My Younger Brother Cui the Ninth on His Departure to the South" (tr. by Willis and Tony Barnstone w. Xu Haixin). [LitR] (32:3) Spr 89, p. 337.
"Deer Park" (w. P'ei Ti, tr. by Joseph Lisowski). [LitR] (32:3) Spr 89, p. 422.
"Frost Bamboo Ranges" (w. P'ei Ti, tr. by Joseph Lisowski). [LitR] (32:3) Spr 89, p. 421.
"Going to the Country in the Spring" (tr. by Willis and Tony Barnstone w. Xu Haixin). [LitR] (32:3) Spr 89, p. 338.
"In the Mountains" (for J. E., tr. by Matthew Flannery). [StoneC] (17:1/2) Fall-Wint 89-90, p. 43.
"In the Mountains" (in Chinese). [StoneC] (17:1/2) Fall-Wint 89-90, p. 43.
"Lady Pan" (tr. by Willis Barnstone, Tony Barnstone, and Xu Xaixan). [CentR] (33:3) Sum 89, p. 250.
"Lakeside Pavilion" (in Chinese & English, tr. by Joseph Lisowski). [KanQ] (21:3) Sum 89, p. 73.
"Magnolia Enclosure" (w. P'ei Ti, tr. by Joseph Lisowski). [LitR] (32:3) Spr 89, p. 422.
"Meng Wall Cove" (w. P'ei Ti, tr. by Joseph Lisowski). [LitR] (32:3) Spr 89, p. 421.
"Missing the Loved One" (tr. by Willis Barnstone, Tony Barnstone, and Xu Xaixan). [CentR] (33:3) Sum 89, p. 250.
"Moaning about My White Hair" (tr. by Willis and Tony Barnstone w. Xu Haixin). [LitR] (32:3) Spr 89, p. 337.
"Saying Farewell" (tr. by Gary Snyder). [LitR] (32:3) Spr 89, p. 444.
"The Stillness of Meditation" (tr. by Willis and Tony Barnstone w. Xu Haixin). [LitR] (32:3) Spr 89, p. 338.
"Written in My Garden in Spring" (tr. by Willis Barnstone, Tony Barnstone, and Xu Xaixan). [CentR] (33:3) Sum 89, p. 250.
5986. WANIEK, Marilyn (Marilyn Nelson)
"Annunciation." [Ploughs] (15:4) Wint 89-90, p. 241.
"Balance." [SouthernR] (25:4) Aut 89, p. 954-955.
"The Ballad of Aunt Geneva." [Ploughs] (15:4) Wint 89-90, p. 243-244.
"Chopin." [Ploughs] (15:4) Wint 89-90, p. 242.
"Chosen." [SouthernR] (25:4) Aut 89, p. 955.
"Diverne's House." [SouthernR] (25:4) Aut 89, p. 950-951.
"Diverne's Waltz." [SouthernR] (25:4) Aut 89, p. 953-954.
"The Fortunate Spill." [Ploughs] (15:4) Wint 89-90, p. 245.
"The House on Moscow Street." [SouthernR] (25:4) Aut 89, p. 948-949.
"Life on the Mississippi." [SouthernR] (25:4) Aut 89, p. 956-957.
"Mrs. Jacobs' Tiger." [Obs] (3:3) Wint 88, p. 43-45.
"Sestina with All the Time in the World." [Obs] (3:3) Wint 88, p. 45-46.
"To Market." [SouthernR] (25:4) Aut 89, p. 952-953.
5987. WARD, Dave
"In the Streets." [Bogg] (61) 89, p. 23.
5988. WARD, Jerry W., Jr.
"I Dream of Lear." [Obs] (3:1) Spr 88, p. 67.
5989. WARD, Robert (Robert R.)
"The Blue Mouse" (from *Premonitions of Death by Cancer -- 5 Dreams*). [HayF] (5) Fall 89, p. 80.
"Early Sunday Morning" (after a painting by Edward Hopper). [SilverFR] (16) Spr 89, p. 20-21.
"Firing the Fields." [BellArk] (5:2) Mr-Ap 89, p. 7.
"Incidental Reflections." [Interim] (8:2) Fall 89, p. 13.
"Life Is Not Much Like a Razor Blade." [BellArk] (5:2) Mr-Ap 89, p. 7.

"Reflections Unfold Upon the Face of a Wave." [SoCoast] (7) Spr-Fall 89, p. 21.
"Relativity, Special and General." [BellArk] (5:2) Mr-Ap 89, p. 7.
"Some Definitions Transcend Coordinate Systems." [SoCoast] (7) Spr-Fall 89, p. 22.
5990. WARING, Belle
"Breeze in Translation." [Crazy] (37) Wint 89, p. 58.
"To Come Back." [Crazy] (37) Wint 89, p. 59-60.
5991. WARN, Emily
"Icarus." [PoetryE] (28) Fall 89, p. 156.
5992. WARREN, Nagueyalti
"Deep River." [Obs] (4:3) Wint 89, p. 76.
"Piano Player" (to my absentee father who played by ear). [Obs] (4:3) Wint 89, p. 76-77.
"Quilt Pieces: a Feminine Legacy." [Obs] (4:3) Wint 89, p. 74-75.
"Till's Death Did Us Part." [Obs] (4:3) Wint 89, p. 75-76.
5993. WARREN, Rebecca
"Winter Trees." [GreensboroR] (46) Sum 89, p. 188-189.
5994. WARREN, Robert Penn
"Tell Me a Story." [GeoR] (43:3) Fall 89, p. 446.
5995. WARREN, Rosanna
"Agonies and More" (tr. of Max Jacob). [SenR] (19:2) Fall 89, p. 72.
"Christ at the Movies" (tr. of Max Jacob). [PartR] (56:1) Wint 89, p. 123-125.
"The Cormorant" (for Eunice). [Boulevard] (4:2, #11) Fall 89, p. 90-91.
"Eskimo Widow." [Boulevard] (4:2, #11) Fall 89, p. 89.
"In the Brouhaha of the Fair" (tr. of Max Jacob). [SenR] (19:2) Fall 89, p. 71.
"Infernal Vision in the Form of a Madrigal" (tr. of Max Jacob). [SenR] (19:2) Fall 89, p. 69-70.
"Man, That Is Born of Woman." [NewYorker] (65:44) 18 D 89, p. 44.
"Pornography." [WestHR] (43:1) Spr 89, p. 29.
5996. WARREN, Shirley
"Uncle, Good-Bye." [StoneC] (16:3/4) Spr-Sum 89, p. 15.
"Walking the Dog" (For my firend, the Stand-up Comedian). [StoneC] (16:3/4) Spr-Sum 89, p. 14-15.
5997. WARROCK, Anna M.
"What Gets Said in the Car." [Mildred] (3:1) Spr-Sum 89, p. 74-75.
5998. WARSHAWSKI, Morrie
"Boys and Girls." [YellowS] (29) Spr 89, p. 7.
"Figure Ground" (Excerpt). [HayF] (5) Fall 89, p. 44.
"Party Man." [ApalQ] (31) 89, p. 44-45.
5999. WARWICK, Ioanna-Veronika
"Amalia Freud to Her Son Sigmund" (1st Place, Poetry Award). [NewL] (56:1) Fall 89, p. 5-6.
"Lenin to His Mistress, Inessa Armand" (the village of Poronin, Tatra Mountains. 1st Place, Poetry Award). [NewL] (56:1) Fall 89, p. 12-14.
"Letter from Kafka." [NegC] (9:2) 89, p. 83-85.
"Letter from Kafka" (1st Place, Poetry Award). [NewL] (56:1) Fall 89, p. 7-9.
"Nietzsche, Sils-Maria" (for Don Lewis, 1st Place, Poetry Award). [NewL] (56:1) Fall 89, p. 10-12.
6000. WARWICK, John
"The Calling: To Flannery O'Connor." [ChatR] (10:1) Fall 89, p. 62-63.
WARWICK, Julia Menard
See MENARD-WARWICK, Julia
6001. WASHINGTON, Jerome
"One-Crow, One-Buddha." [HeavenB] (6) Wint-Spr 89, p. 26-28.
6002. WATERHOUSE, Philip A. (Philip Anthony)
"Overbite." [SmPd] (26:2 #76) Spr 89, p. 24.
"Time of My Life." [Nimrod] (33:1) Fall-Wint 89, p. 105.
6003. WATERS, Mary Ann
"Seizure." [PoetryNW] (30:2) Sum 89, p. 42-43.
"Tail" (for Alia). [PoetryNW] (30:2) Sum 89, p. 43-44.
6004. WATERS, Michael
"Boy and Sycamore." [RiverC] (9:1) Spr 89, p. 77.
"Gibberish." [RiverS] (29) [89], p. 1.
"Hummingbirds." [Poetry] (153:5) F 89, p. 293.
"Miles Weeping" (Koh Samui, Thailand). [AmerPoR] (18:6) N-D 89, p. 55.
"Paradys." [Poetry] (154:5) Ag 89, p. 281-282.

"The return" (for John Logan). [PaintedB] (39) 89, p. 35.
"The Sadness of Barges." [QW] (28) Wint-Spr 89, p. 85.
"Singing for Elizabeth." [Shen] (39:1) Spr 89, p. 99.
"Snake Skin." [RiverC] (9:1) Spr 89, p. 76.
"The Torches" (Nicaragua). [AmerPoR] (18:6) N-D 89, p. 55.
6005. WATKINS, Sherrin
"Porch-Sitting." [Nimrod] (32:2) Spr-Sum 89, p. 43.
6006. WATKINS, William John
"Dead Man's Feet." [WindO] (51) Spr 89, p. 6-7.
"The Disciplined Prey." [JINJPo] [11] 89, p. 30-31.
"It is three a.m." [JINJPo] [11] 89, p. 32.
"Longlost Joe Comes Home for Chad's College Graduation." [WindO] (51) Spr 89,
    p. 5-6.
"Lowell and I Wear the Same Size Shoe." [SouthernPR] (29:1) Spr 89, p. 63.
"Sound Sculpture." [HighP] (4:1) Spr 89, p. 19.
6007. WATSKIN, Linda
"Of a Little Thing" (For D.A.L.). [Footwork] 89, p. 53.
6008. WATSON, Burton
"Lotus Viewing" (tr. of Su Tung-p'o). [LitR] (32:3) Spr 89, p. 435.
"Love Long-Enduring" (tr. of Po Chu-i). [LitR] (32:3) Spr 89, p. 436.
"A Question Addressed to Liu Shih-Chiu" (tr. of Po Chu-i). [LitR] (32:3) Spr 89, p.
    436.
"Spotting Plum Blossoms by the Road" (tr. of Rokunyo). [LitR] (32:3) Spr 89, p.
    439.
"Spring Outing" (tr. of Po Chu-i). [LitR] (32:3) Spr 89, p. 437.
"When My Beloved Japanese Spaniel Died" (tr. of Rokunyo). [LitR] (32:3) Spr 89,
    p. 438.
"Winter Day: Scene on the Road to Otsu" (tr. of Rokunyo). [LitR] (32:3) Spr 89, p.
    439.
"Written When Drunk" (tr. of Chang Yüeh). [LitR] (32:3) Spr 89, p. 435.
6009. WATSON, Craig
"Found Drown" (for Patricia McGee). [Screens] (1) 89, p. 66-73.
"Fourth Wall." [Temblor] (9) 89, p. 98-102.
"Learning to Disappear." [Temblor] (9) 89, p. 88-89.
"One Inch Over One Mile" (for Mary Beath). [PaperAir] (4:2) 89, p. 72-77.
"White Days." [Temblor] (9) 89, p. 90-97.
6010. WATSON, Lynn
"The Agony." [ChamLR] (3:1, #5) Fall 89, p. 91.
"Writer's Confession" (for Pam). [ChamLR] (3:1, #5) Fall 89, p. 92.
6011. WATSON, Randall (Randall H.)
"Diary of a Skull." [GeoR] (43:3) Fall 89, p. 548-549.
"A Gift Without Landscapes." [FloridaR] (16:2/3) Fall-Wint 89, p. 62.
6012. WATSON, Robert
"Bangladesh." [GreensboroR] (46) Sum 89, p. 87.
"The Cure." [GreensboroR] (46) Sum 89, p. 86.
"Duplicating Machine." [GreensboroR] (46) Sum 89, p. 88.
"Going Nowhere Alone at Night." [GreensboroR] (46) Sum 89, p. 42-43.
"My Father Breaks His Hip at Eighty-One." [GreensboroR] (46) Sum 89, p. 84-85.
"Please Write: Don't Phone." [GreensboroR] (46) Sum 89, p. 19-20.
6013. WATSON, Ron
"Randolph County Gets a Dog Sniffing Dog." [Wind] (19:65) 89, p. 13.
6014. WATSON, Stephen
"Exposure." [AmerPoR] (18:4) Jl-Ag 89, p. 34.
6015. WATTEN, Barrett
"Frame" (Selections: I-XII). [MinnR] (NS 32) Spr 89, p. 58-61.
6016. WATTERSON, William Collins
"On Reading Cavafy." [KenR] (NS 11:1) Wint 89, p. 63-64.
"Teaching My Son to Talk." [KenR] (NS 11:1) Wint 89, p. 64-65.
"Thinking of Jackson Pollock." [KenR] (NS 11:1) Wint 89, p. 66.
6017. WATTS, Bob
"Child of Age." [SouthernPR] (29:1) Spr 89, p. 16.
6018. WATTS, David
"Wind." [Footwork] 89, p. 54.
6019. WAUGAMAN, Charles A.
"Ours Is a Noble Line" (On viewing "The Annunciation" by van Eyck). [Wind]
    (19:65) 89, p. 38.

"A Prayer for Any Friday, Good or Not." [Wind] (19:65) 89, p. 38-39.
6020. WAUGHTEL, Michelle
"The Other One." [PaintedB] (38) 89, p. 39.
6021. WAYBRANT, Linda
"If I Had a Child My Sister & I Would Have 4 Altogether, 4 and a Half If We
Counted the One Growing in Her Now." [Event] (18:2) Sum 89, p. 65.
"The Pollen Has Landed & I Didn't Tell My Brother." [Event] (18:2) Sum 89, p. 64.
6022. WAYMAN, Tom
"Birds, in the Last of the Dark." [Hudson] (41:4) Wint 89, p. 691-692.
"Defective Parts of Speech: Doing the Word's Laundry." [MinnR] (NS 33) Fall 89,
p. 32-35.
"Greed Suite: Economic Meditations." [Hudson] (41:4) Wint 89, p. 689-691.
"Greed Suite: The Emptiness of Business." [Hudson] (41:4) Wint 89, p. 688-689.
"Hard Time." [Hudson] (41:4) Wint 89, p. 687-688.
"Initial Report" (after Yehuda Amichai). [NoDaQ] (57:3) Sum 89, p. 146-147.
"RVs." [Quarry] (38:2) Spr 89, p. 7.
"The Valley." [Quarry] (38:2) Spr 89, p. 5-6.
6023. WAYNE, Jane O.
"The Finishing Touches." [Poetry] (154:2) My 89, p. 94-95.
"Gaps." [Confr] (39/40) Fall 88-Wint 89, p. 127.
"Horror Vacui." [TarRP] (28:2) Spr 89, p. 11.
"In Praise of Zigzags" (For a Girl Failing Geometry). [TarRP] (28:2) Spr 89, p. 12.
"Inheritance." [Poetry] (154:2) My 89, p. 95-96.
6024. WAZYK, Adam
"The Offspring of Heraclitus" (tr. by Stanislaw Baranczak and Clare Cavanah).
[Trans] (21) Spr 89, p. 16.
6025. WEARNE, Alan
"Charley" (for Robert Langsford." [Descant] (20:3/4, #66/67) Fall-Wint 89, p.
217-218.
"Charley, Alistair, Barbara" (from "Seeing Other People"). [Descant] (20:3/4,
#66/67) Fall-Wint 89, p. 220.
"Vivienne." [Descant] (20:3/4, #66/67) Fall-Wint 89, p. 219.
6026. WEATHERFORD, Carole B.
"Slave Castles." [Obs] (2:1) Spr 87, p. 49-50.
6027. WEAVER, Margaret
"Lo, They Shall All Grow Old As a Garment: The Moth Shall Eat Them Up" (--
Isaiah 50:9. Commended). [StoneC] (17:1/2) Fall-Wint 89-90, p. prelim. p.
10.
6028. WEAVER, Michael S.
"Bathsheba." [Obs] (3:3) Wint 88, p. 17.
"David." [Obs] (3:3) Wint 88, p. 18.
"The Falling Angel." [Obs] (3:3) Wint 88, p. 18-19.
"In Paris on a Humble" (for Josephine Baker). [BlackALF] (23:3) Fall 89, p. 492.
"Neo-African Sculpture." [BlackALF] (23:3) Fall 89, p. 493.
"The Picnic, an Homage to Civil Rights." [Callaloo] (12:3, #40) Sum 89, p.
474-475.
"The Praying Jew." [Obs] (3:3) Wint 88, p. 19-20.
6029. WEBB, Bernice Larson
"Heavy Hole." [StoneC] (17:1/2) Fall-Wint 89-90, p. 30.
6030. WEBB, Charles
"Nice" (Special Section: 17 poems). [WormR] (29:4, #116) 89, p. 117-134.
"Night at Jade Light." [Wind] (19:64) 89, p. 37-38.
"The Wise Man Sees Another Dire Prophecy Fulfilled." [Wind] (19:64) 89, p. 37.
6031. WEBB, Don
"I Won't Dance Close to the Surface." [Rampike] (6:2) 88, p. 32.
6032. WEBB, Harri
"Epil y Filiast." [NoDaQ] (57:2) Spr 89, insert p. 31.
"Synopsis of the Great Welsh Novel." [NoDaQ] (57:2) Spr 89, insert p. 29.
"Thanks in Winter." [NoDaQ] (57:2) Spr 89, insert p. 30.
6033. WEBB, Phyllis
"As Rare as Hens' Teeth." [MalR] (87) Sum 89, p. 11.
"Cornflowers & Saffron Robes Belittle the Effort." [MalR] (87) Sum 89, p. 8.
"Diplomatic Paouch." [CapilR] (1st series: 50) 89, p. 57.
"Evensong" (even song syllabics). [MalR] (87) Sum 89, p. 7.
"Gate Crashing." [MalR] (87) Sum 89, p. 13.
"Hanging Fire." [MalR] (87) Sum 89, p. 12.

435

WEBB

"Imprint." [CapilR] (1st series: 50) 89, p. 60-61.
"'Krakatoa' and 'Spiritual Storm'" (Dedicated to Dorothy Livesay and Bill Bissett).
   [CapilR] (1st series: 50) 89, p. 54-56.
"Long Suffering." [MalR] (87) Sum 89, p. 14-15.
"Miasma." [MalR] (87) Sum 89, p. 6.
"The Mills of God." [MalR] (87) Sum 89, p. 10.
"The Mind of the Poet." [MalR] (87) Sum 89, p. 5.
"The Salt Tax." [MalR] (87) Sum 89, p. 16.
"Seeking Shape, Seeking Meaning." [CapilR] (1st series: 50) 89, p. 58-59.
"Sliding Doors." [MalR] (87) Sum 89, p. 9.
"You Have My Approval." [MalR] (87) Sum 89, p. 17-18.
6034. WEBER, Maria
"Lost Riches." [Footwork] 89, p. 64.
"Marco Island." [Footwork] 89, p. 64.
6035. WEBSTER, Diane
"Haiku: Dust motes." [BallSUF] (30:4) Aut 89, p. 11.
"Nursing Home." [NewRena] (7:3, #23) 89, p. 84.
6036. WEDGE, George (George F.)
"First Time Out" (For Jack. Seaton Honorable Mention Poem). [KanQ] (21:3) Sum
   89, p. 18.
"Heroic Versus." [CinPR] (19) Spr 89, p. 35.
"Shades of Art Tatum." [ClockR] (5:2) 89, p. 44-45.
6037. WEDGE, Philip
"Car Keys." [Amelia] (5:3, #14) 89, p. 123.
"Home on Leave" (for Jim Carothers). [StoneC] (17:1/2) Fall-Wint 89-90, p. 29.
"In Retrospect." [StoneC] (17:1/2) Fall-Wint 89-90, p. 28.
6038. WEEKS, Robert Lewis
"Exquisite Is Like a Death Watch." [Poem] (61) My 89, p. 68.
"Modern History." [SouthernPR] (29:2) Fall 89, p. 70.
"Promiscuity." [WestB] (25) 89, p. 112.
"Reentering the Dream." [Nimrod] (33:1) Fall-Wint 89, p. 104.
"Ritual Bagpipes." [WestB] (25) 89, p. 113.
"Theatricals." [SewanR] (97:3) Sum 89, p. 406-407.
"There's Someone in the Other Room." [Poem] (61) My 89, p. 66-67.
"A Vacant Lot in Red Bank." [SoCoast] (5) Spr 88, p. 50-51.
WEI, Hsü
   See HSÜ, Wei
WEI, Wang
   See WANG, Wei
6039. WEIGHTMAN, Sharon
"Thinking about Thinking about Spring in a House by the Torrent." [StoneC]
   (17:1/2) Fall-Wint 89-90, p. 70.
"Under." [CapeR] (24:1) Spr 89, p. 13.
6040. WEIGL, Bruce
"A Brief Ontology." [IndR] (13:1) Wint 89, p. 81.
"The Confusion of Planes We Must Wander in Sleep." [KenR] (N 11:4) Fall 89, p.
   93.
"The Hand That Takes." [OhioR] (44) 89, p. 37-40.
"Meditation at Las Cruces." [IndR] (13:1) Wint 89, p. 83.
"On the Dictatorship of the Proletariat." [IndR] (13:1) Wint 89, p. 82.
6041. WEIL, Eric
"One Halloween." [GreensboroR] (46) Sum 89, p. 167.
6042. WEIL, James L.
"Imperatives Composed for Bill's Voice." [Talisman] (2) Spr 89, p. 80.
6043. WEILLER, Rosa
"Women." [YellowS] (31) Aut 89, p. 22.
6044. WEINBAUM, Batya
"The Importance of Learning." [KeyWR] (2:1/2) Fall-Wint 89, p. 81.
6045. WEINER, Rebecca
"Water." [Pequod] (28/29/30) 89, p. 35.
6046. WEINFIELD, Henry
"Buried within the Language." [DenQ] (24:2) Fall 89, p. 94.
"The Lives of the Poets." [Talisman] (2) Spr 89, p. 56-58.
6047. WEINGARTEN, Roger
"Dance of the Mourning Child." [KenR] (NS 11:2) Spr 89, p. 72-73.
"A February Thaw Should Be Played Slowly." [KenR] (NS 11:2) Spr 89, p. 73.

"From the Temple of Longing." [KenR] (NS 11:2) Spr 89, p. 74.
"The January Thaw." [MissR] (18:1, #52) 89, p. 28-29.
"Ornamental Agony of December." [Ploughs] (15:1) 89, p. 152-153.
"A Poet's Prayer." [PoetryE] (28) Fall 89, p. 44-46.
"Saturday Morning" (for Michael Trombley). [Ploughs] (15:1) 89, p. 150-151.
"The Spectral Illumination of Moonshine." [MichQR] (28:3) Sum 89, p. 344-346.

6048. WEINMAN, Paul
"Fire in Circle." [DeKalbLAJ] (22:1/4) 89, p. 68.
"Making It to First." [Wind] (19:65) 89, p. 40-41.
"Rock at Bottom." [Wind] (19:65) 89, p. 40.

6049. WEINRAUB, Richard
"Among Friends (At the Municipal Gallery)." [HampSPR] Wint 89, p. 42.
"In the bath." [Amelia] (5:3, #14) 89, p. 83.
"In the hot garage." [Amelia] (5:3, #14) 89, p. 83.
"On Bricklieve Mountain." [HampSPR] Wint 89, p. 42.

6050. WEIS, Lyle
"Farm on the Block." [Grain] (17:2) Sum 89, p. 62.
"The Kiss." [Grain] (17:2) Sum 89, p. 63.

6051. WEISNER, Ken
"Above Tree-Line." [BrooklynR] (5) 88, p. 35.
"I Recently Slept for Eighteen Hours." [BrooklynR] (5) 88, p. 30-31.
"Inner Dog." [BrooklynR] (5) 88, p. 32.
"Ode." [BrooklynR] (5) 88, p. 33-34.

6052. WEISS, Irving
"Eighteen." [Rampike] (6:1) 87, p. 62.

6053. WEISS, Jason
"Then You Know." [Rampike] (6:2) 88, p. 67.

6054. WEISS, R.
"A Place to Stand" (w. T. Weiss). [Nat] (249:16) 13 N 89, p. 576.

6055. WEISS, Sigmund
"Back Street, Chicago 1919." [Lactuca] (12) F 89, p. 34.
"The Invitation." [Lactuca] (12) F 89, p. 34-35.

6056. WEISS, T. (Theodore)
"A Parisian Air" (after Marcel Duchamp and one of his Readymades, a 50 cc glass
ampul, "Air de Paris"). [Pequod] (28/29/30) 89, p. 255-256.
"A Place to Stand" (w. R. Weiss). [Nat] (249:16) 13 N 89, p. 576.

6057. WEISSMILLER, Jan
"From a Distance." [RiverS] (29) [89], p. 38.
"The Ghost of the Matriarch." [RiverS] (29) [89], p. 37.
"Narcissus in the Gray Afternoon." [RiverS] (29) [89], p. 39.

6058. WELBOURN, Cynthia
"Lawn Chairs." [CrossCur] (8:3) Apr 89, p. 135.

6059. WELBURN, Ron
"Deer Dancer." [Mildred] (3:2) 89, p. 11.
"In the Absence of Gourds." [Pig] (15) 88, p. 53.
"An Intention." [Mildred] (3:2) 89, p. 11.

6060. WELCH, Don
"The Broken Bird." [TarRP] (28:2) Spr 89, p. 8.
"The Christmas Wreather." [EngJ] (78:8) D 89, p. 91.
"Lot's Wife." [LaurelR] (23:2) Sum 89, p. 71-72.
"My Neighbor, the August Hunter." [Plain] (10:1) 89, p. 18.
"The Plea of Anne Greenslade Pudeator, Ancestor" (Salem, MA, 1692). [Plain] (9:3)
Spr 89, p. 12.

6061. WELCH, John
"Bow." [Vis] (31) 89, p. 25.

6062. WELCH, Liliane
"Stones." [AntigR] (79) Aut 89, p. 89.

6063. WELCH, Phillip
"Artifact of Christ." [Shen] (39:4) Wint 89, p. 21.
"Introspective." [Shen] (39:4) Wint 89, p. 23.
"Spell." [Shen] (39:4) Wint 89, p. 22.

6064. WELISH, Marjorie
"Curio." [Conjunc] (14) 89, p. 45.
"Epitaph." [Pequod] (28/29/30) 89, p. 93.
"Hercules As Inkstand." [Pequod] (28/29/30) 89, p. 94.
"Street Cries" (Selections: 1, 6). [ParisR] (31:111) Sum 89, p. 124-125.

"Tableau-Tableau." [Conjunc] (14) 89, p. 44.
6065. WELLS, Will
"Last Peaches, Chalfont St. Giles, 1665." [ChiR] (36:3/4) 89, p. 72.
"A Ringing." [ChiR] (36:3/4) 89, p. 71.
"Shells." [LitR] (32:2) Wint 89, p. 215.
6066. WEN, T'ung
"Echoing Mountain Recluse Ho Ching's Poem on *Hai-T'ang* Blossoms" (tr. by Jonathan Chaves). [LitR] (32:3) Spr 89, p. 433.
"Irritated by the Insects" (tr. by Jonathan Chaves). [LitR] (32:3) Spr 89, p. 434.
"Late Winter -- Describing Scenes" (tr. by Jonathan Chaves). [LitR] (32:3) Spr 89, p. 433.
6067. WEN, Yi-duo
"Night Song" (tr. by Robert Dorsett). [LitR] (32:3) Spr 89, p. 345.
"Spring Glow" (tr. by Robert Dorsett). [LitR] (32:3) Spr 89, p. 344.
"You Point to the Sun and Swear" (tr. by Robert Dorsett). [LitR] (32:3) Spr 89, p. 344.
6068. WENDELL, Julia
"Matisse's Chapel, Venice." [MissouriR] (12:2) 89, p. 25.
"What Changes Us." [CinPR] (19) Spr 89, p. 36-38.
6069. WENDEROTH, Joe
"The Artist As an Avatar." [AmerPoR] (18:2) Mr-Ap 89, p. 25.
"Conclusion." [AmerPoR] (18:2) Mr-Ap 89, p. 23.
"Day Passing Without Snow." [AmerPoR] (18:2) Mr-Ap 89, p. 24.
"False Idols." [AmerPoR] (18:2) Mr-Ap 89, p. 24.
"How It Is." [AmerPoR] (18:2) Mr-Ap 89, p. 25.
"The Man Under the Bridge." [AmerPoR] (18:2) Mr-Ap 89, p. 23.
"October, Last Light" (a version). [AmerPoR] (18:2) Mr-Ap 89, p. 24.
"Passages to a Place in a World." [AmerPoR] (18:2) Mr-Ap 89, p. 24.
6070. WENDERS, Wim
"Reverse Angle: NYC March '82." [AnotherCM] (20) 89, p. 73-76.
6071. WENNER, Mary
"Coming Back." [BellArk] (5:5) S-O 89, p. 9.
6072. WEÖRES, Sándor
"The Colonnade of Teeth" (tr. by Edwin Morgan). [Field] (40) Spr 89, p. 62-63.
"Moon and Farmstead" (tr. by Edwin Morgan). [Field] (40) Spr 89, p. 66.
"Renaissance" (tr. by Edwin Morgan). [Field] (40) Spr 89, p. 67-68.
"Signs" (tr. by Edwin Morgan). [Field] (40) Spr 89, p. 64-65.
6073. WERDINGER, Roberta
"Going." [YellowS] (29) Spr 89, p. 4.
WERT, William F. van
See Van WERT, William F.
6074. WERTMAN, Carl A.
"Sand Roses." [BallSUF] (30:4) Aut 89, p. 26-28.
6075. WESLOWSKI, Dieter
"The Angelus Hour." [Caliban] (6) 89, p. 204.
"Don't Be Fooled." [Nimrod] (33:1) Fall-Wint 89, p. 106.
"For the Carlini Brothers' Angel." [WebR] (14:1) Spr 89, p. 64.
"The Logician Extemporaneous." [PoetryE] (28) Fall 89, p. 69.
"Palabras para un Noviembre Final." [Caliban] (7) 89, p. 113.
"Rooster." [MalR] (89) Wint 89, p. 50.
"Sanctuary." [MalR] (89) Wint 89, p. 51.
6076. WEST, Allen C.
"Mushrooms." [KanQ] (21:3) Sum 89, p. 204.
6077. WEST, Ann J.
"Again." [NewOR] (16:4) Wint 89, p. 54.
6078. WEST, Michael Lee
"The Evolution of Mermaids." [Prima] (13) 89, p. 56-58.
"Myth of the Now-Extinct Southern Virgin." [SingHM] (16) 89, p. 16-18.
6079. WEST, Paul
"Hermann Goering, Nuremberg, 1946." [Conjunc] (13) 89, p. 261-262.
"John Clare Walking to the Horizon." [Conjunc] (13) 89, p. 259-260.
"Josef Goebbels." [Conjunc] (13) 89, p. 263.
"Nixon in China." [Conjunc] (13) 89, p. 260-261.
"Pelé." [Conjunc] (13) 89, p. 259.
"Virginia Woolf by the River Ouse." [Conjunc] (13) 89, p. 262.

6080. WESTBROOK, Max
"Enough Is Genug." [Interim] (8:1) Spr 89, p. 46.
"Outer Darkness." [TexasR] (10:1/2) Spr-Sum 89, p. 90-91.
6081. WESTBURY, Debbie
"Dapto Dressing Up." [AntigR] (76) Wint 89, p. 34.
6082. WESTERFIELD, Nancy G.
"The Columbarium." [Poem] (62) N 89, p. 61.
"How the Past Holds All of It." [Plain] (9:2) Wint 89, p. 16.
"In the Button-Box." [Poem] (62) N 89, p. 62.
"Kentucky, from a Kitchen Door." [BallSUF] (30:4) Aut 89, p. 22.
"Looking into an Ear." [CumbPR] (8:2) Spr 89, p. 93.
"Motherland." [FourQ] (2d series 3:1) Spr 89, p. 54.
"The Neighbor in the Next Lot." [Poem] (62) N 89, p. 60.
"On Railroad Street." [PoetL] (84:1) Spr 89, p. 47.
"A Romance of Widows." [ChrC] (106:38) D 13, 89, p. 1165.
"The Suicide Note." [Plain] (9:3) Spr 89, p. 25.
"Summer Storm." [BallSUF] (30:4) Aut 89, p. 69.
"Summoning the Night Nurse." [FourQ] (2d series 3:1) Spr 89, p. 53.
"Tightening Clotheslines." [ChrC] (106:3) Ja 25, 89, p. 76.
"Waiting." [CumbPR] (8:2) Spr 89, p. 94.
6083. WESTERGAARD, Diane
"Peonies." [PraS] (63:2) Sum 89, p. 49-50.
"Rules of the Cemetery." [Lactuca] (12) F 89, p. 19-20.
"Taung Child" (*Australopithecus* fossil found at Taung, South Africa in 1924 by
Raymond Dart). [PraS] (63:2) Sum 89, p. 51-52.
6084. WESTLAKE, Wayne
"Dogo." [Hawai'iR] (13:3) Fall 89, p. 42.
"Flawed Intelligence." [Hawai'iR] (13:3) Fall 89, p. 43.
6085. WEXELBLATT, Robert
"Assistant Oxygen Therapist." [CapeR] (24:1) Spr 89, p. 28.
6086. WEXLER, Evelyn
"The Tutor" (Budapest, 1936, for Vörös Ur). [CapeR] (24:2) Fall 89, p. 16.
WF. H.
See H., Wf.
6087. WHADDY, Tom
"The Frog Who Was King" (Aboriginal narrative of New South Wales, collected by
Roland Robinson, related by Tom Whaddy, Gumbangirr Tribe). [PraS] (63:3)
Fall 89, p. 77-78.
6088. WHALEN, John
"Flocking." [HolCrit] (26:3) Je 89, p. 19.
6089. WHALLEY, Karen
"The Blue Bowl." [BellArk] (5:2) Mr-Ap 89, p. 3.
"Elegy for Vincent." [BellArk] (5:2) Mr-Ap 89, p. 3.
"Mail Order Sweet Peas." [BellArk] (5:2) Mr-Ap 89, p. 3.
"Sounds That Come to Her Porch in Evening." [BellArk] (5:2) Mr-Ap 89, p. 3.
"Waking to Winter Weather." [BellArk] (5:2) Mr-Ap 89, p. 3.
"White Butterflies." [BellArk] (5:2) Mr-Ap 89, p. 3.
6090. WHEALE, Nigel
"Elousa." [Pequod] (26/27) 89, p. 136.
"Kardiotissa." [Pequod] (26/27) 89, p. 135.
6091. WHEATCROFT, John
"Definition." [NewRena] (7:3, #23) 89, p. 91.
"Infidel in Rome." [LitR] (32:2) Wint 89, p. 176-177.
6092. WHEDON, Tony
"While Fishing on Paradise Pond, a Woman's Face Floats Up from the Weeds and
Accuses Me." [HampSPR] Wint 89, p. 53-54.
6093. WHEELER, Charles B.
"Dies Irae." [CumbPR] (8:2) Spr 89, p. 16-17.
"Girls' Dormitory." [CumbPR] (8:2) Spr 89, p. 18-20.
"Wrong Number." [KanQ] (21:3) Sum 89, p. 176-177.
6094. WHEELER, Lesley
"Crocus." [Interim] (8:2) Fall 89, p. 12.
"Stones." [Interim] (8:2) Fall 89, p. 11-12.
6095. WHEELER, Robert L.
"Lichen." [Comm] (116:7) Ap 7, 89, p. 207.

6096. WHEELER, Sylvia Griffith
"Mother in the Rock Shop." [ClockR] (5:2) 89, p. 29.
6097. WHIPPLE, George
"Apples." [AntigR] (76) Wint 89, p. 104.
6098. WHISLER, Robert F.
"Year of the Dragon." [KanQ] (21:3) Sum 89, p. 63.
6099. WHITE, Calvin
"BMX Jump." [Grain] (17:4) Wint 89, p. 24.
"The Victim." [Grain] (17:4) Wint 89, p. 22-23.
6100. WHITE, Carolyn
"House Keeper." [MichQR] (28:3) Sum 89, p. 323.
6101. WHITE, Claire Nicolas
"Two Metamorphoses." [GrandS] (8:2) Wint 89, p. 215.
6102. WHITE, Gail
"Alibi." [SouthernPR] (29:1) Spr 89, p. 30-31.
"Bavarian Baroque." [Plain] (9:2) Wint 89, p. 15.
"The Engulfed Cathedral." [WestB] (24) 89, p. 63.
"Nightpieces." [Northeast] (ser. 5:1) Wint 89-90, p. 1-2.
"The Nursery Falls from Grace." [CrabCR] (6:2) Wint 89, p. 22.
"Private Fantasy #12: Singapore." [WestB] (24) 89, p. 63-64.
"The Remains of the Dead King." [WestB] (24) 89, p. 62.
6103. WHITE, Howard
"The Made Bed." [Event] (18:3) Fall 89, p. 84-85.
"Oolachon Grease." [Event] (18:3) Fall 89, p. 86-87.
6104. WHITE, J. K.
"Brinkmanship." [SpoonRQ] (14:3) Sum 89, p. 13.
6105. WHITE, J. P.
"The Son of a Sailor." [Poetry] (154:3) Je 89, p. 128.
6106. WHITE, Mark Arvid
"21 Haiku for the Second World War." [WebR] (14:1) Spr 89, p. 68-70.
6107. WHITE, Mary Jane
"Evenings." [WillowS] (23) Wint 89, p. 73-74.
"Hieroglyphs" (tr. of Sergei Petrunis). [WillowS] (23) Wint 89, p. 62-72.
6108. WHITE, Michael K.
"/Lesser Light/." [Wind] (19:65) 89, p. 42.
6109. WHITE, Mike
"The Dream." [MissouriR] (12:1) 89, p. 131.
"Fish Creek Falls" (for Jackie Bromstedt). [MissouriR] (12:1) 89, p. 132.
"The *Narcissus* Moored" (after Conrad). [MissouriR] (12:1) 89, p. 126-127.
"Near Light." [AntR] (47:1) Wint 89, p. 60.
"Near Light." [MissouriR] (12:1) 89, p. 130.
"The Story." [MissouriR] (12:1) 89, p. 125.
"This Water" (Collection of 6 poems. Dedicated to the memory of Tom McAfee).
[SilverFR] (17) 89, 18 p.
"Underway." [MissouriR] (12:1) 89, p. 128-129.
6110. WHITE, Mimi
"February Dark." [StoneC] (16:3/4) Spr-Sum 89, p. 63.
"Indian Summer." [NegC] (9:2) 89, p. 86-87.
"To Wander" (for Matthew). [Vis] (30) 89, p. 37.
6111. WHITE, Patrick
"The Benjamin Chee Chee Elegies" (Excerpt). [CrossC] (11:2) 89, p. 11.
"The Benjamin Chee Chee Elegies" (Selection: V). [CrossC] (11:3) 89, p. 10.
6112. WHITEHEAD, James
"The District Attorney Considers Resignation." [SouthernR] (25:3) Sum 89, p. 602.
6113. WHITEHILL, Karen
"The Behavior of Matter." [VirQR] (65:1) Wint 89, p. 77-78.
"Children's Rehabilitation Center." [VirQR] (65:1) Wint 89, p. 76-77.
6114. WHITING, Nathan
"Blindritations." [Chelsea] (48) 89, p. 106.
"Butchering Giant Gelados." [HangL] (55) 89, p. 57.
"Can Odor Pollution Make You Sick?" [HangL] (55) 89, p. 55.
"Contact the Oval Window." [Chelsea] (48) 89, p. 108.
"An Inside Outside Cascade." [Mildred] (3:2) 89, p. 118.
"Quantum Weirdness." [Chelsea] (48) 89, p. 107.
"Reducing Head Shape." [HangL] (55) 89, p. 54.
"Stream Structure." [HangL] (55) 89, p. 56.

"The Sugar Boat *Empresa*." [SoCoast] (5) Spr 88, p. 55.
"Vanishing Fishes of North America." [ColEng] (51:4) Ap 89, p. 390.
"Without a Transmitter." [Mildred] (3:2) 89, p. 117.

6115. WHITMAN, Ruth
"Advice" (tr. of Miriam Oren). [AmerPoR] (18:6) N-D 89, p. 46.
"The Batman" (tr. of Abraham Sutzkever). [GrahamHR] (12) Spr 89, p. 56.
"Black Grapes" (tr. of Abraham Sutzkever). [GrahamHR] (12) Spr 89, p. 53.
"Chamber Music in Early December." [Ploughs] (15:4) Wint 89-90, p. 246-247.
"Exile" (tr. of Miriam Oren). [AmerPoR] (18:6) N-D 89, p. 46.
"In a Chinese Antique Shop" (tr. of Abraham Sutzkever). [MassR] (30:1) Spr 89, p. 7-9.
"In a Mirror." [WestB] (23) 89, p. 37.
"It's Obvious" (tr. of Abraham Sutzkever). [MassR] (30:1) Spr 89, p. 10-11.
"Prayer for a Sick Friend" (tr. of Abraham Sutzkever). [NewYorker] (65:8) 10 Ap 89, p. 40.
"Sifting Through" (tr. of Abraham Sutzkever). [MassR] (30:1) Spr 89, p. 9.
"Song About Caves, Sung in Darkness" (tr. of Abraham Sutzkever). [GrahamHR] (12) Spr 89, p. 54-55.
"Tall Violincellos" (tr. of Abraham Sutzkever). [GrahamHR] (12) Spr 89, p. 57.
"Visitation." [WestB] (23) 89, p. 36.

6116. WHITMAN, Walt
"Democratic Vistas" (Excerpt). [PoetryE] (27) Spr 89, p. 61.
"I Sit and Look Out." [PoetryE] (27) Spr 89, p. 62.

6117. WHITNEY, Thomas P.
"The Muscle of Water" (tr. of Yunna Moritz). [WestB] (24) 89, p. 45.

6118. WHITT, Laurie Anne
"Christina's World" (-- Andrew Wyeth). [StoneC] (16:3/4) Spr-Sum 89, p. 62.

6119. WHITTAKER, Steven
"Epiphany 2A6." [Event] (18:3) Fall 89, p. 44-45.
"Father and Son." [MalR] (89) Wint 89, p. 52.

6120. WHITTINGTON, Janice D.
"Mesquites in February." [MidAR] (9:2) 89, p. 30.

6121. WIDERKEHR, Richard
"Clarity." [CrabCR] (6:1) 89, p. 8.
"Disappearances." [PassN] (10:2) Sum 89, p. 17.
"The End of the Field." [CrabCR] (6:1) 89, p. 9.
"Into the Rain." [CrabCR] (6:1) 89, p. 9.
"Islands." [CrabCR] (6:1) 89, p. 8.
"The Mask." [Vis] (31) 89, p. 12.

6122. WIEBE, Dallas
"Inside / Outside." [Pig] (15) 88, p. 63.

6123. WIEDER, Laurance
"Your Melodies." [Boulevard] (4:2, #11) Fall 89, p. 157-158.

6124. WIEDER, Laurence
"Art History." [Pequod] (28/29/30) 89, p. 197.

6125. WIELAND, Liza
"Any Promise Made." [MissouriR] (12:2) 89, p. 175.

6126. WIENER, Carl
"Bartok in New York." [CumbPR] (9:1) Fall 89, p. 3.
"Elegy (of the Freighters)." [CumbPR] (9:1) Fall 89, p. 1-2.
"The Light Remaining." [CumbPR] (9:1) Fall 89, p. 4.
"The Mountain's Crown." [CumbPR] (9:1) Fall 89, p. 5.

6127. WIER, Dara
"For a Book about Legendary Indian Maidens." [ThRiPo] (31/32) 88, p. 50-51.
"Happy Dance and Wild Party of All the Skeletons." [ColR] (NS 16:2) Fall 89-Wint 90, p. 37.
"A Life Based on a Worthless Dare." [ColR] (NS 16:2) Fall 89-Wint 90, p. 38.
"Miracle at Medzhegoria." [ThRiPo] (31/32) 88, p. 48-49.

6128. WIGGINS, Jean
"The Original Hippies." [Interim] (8:2) Fall 89, p. 8.

6129. WIGINGTON, Nan
"On the Shores of Hades." [AntR] (47:4) Fall 89, p. 464-465.

6130. WILBORN, William
"Amiss." [CumbPR] (9:1) Fall 89, p. 23.
"The Girls." [SewanR] (97:1) Wint 89, p. 34-35.
"Nighthawks" (After Hopper). [WebR] (14:1) Spr 89, p. 61.

"Nightwatch." [SewanR] (97:1) Wint 89, p. 35.
"Pipes." [WebR] (14:1) Spr 89, p. 61.
"Reel to Reel." [SewanR] (97:1) Wint 89, p. 34.
6131. WILBUR, Frederick
"The Espionage of Alcohol." [HampSPR] Wint 89, p. 22-23.
6132. WILBUR, Richard
"A Prayer to Go to Paradise with the Donkeys" (tr. of Francis Jammes, to Máire and
Jack). [Trans] (22) Fall 89, p. 258-259.
"A Wall in the Woods: Cummington." [NewYorker] (65:16) 5 Je 89, p. 40.
6133. WILBURN, Paul
"Coonie." [EmeraldCR] (1989) c1988, p. 78-79.
"Street People." [EmeraldCR] (1989) c1988, p. 77.
6134. WILCOX, Adam A.
"Insomnia." [SpiritSH] (54) Spr-Sum 89, p. 21.
WILCOX, Edie Sabetay
See SABETAY-WILCOX, Edie
6135. WILCOX, Patricia
"Death Valley Suite" (for M. B.). [DenQ] (23:3/4) Wint-Spr 89, p. 60-74.
6136. WILD, Marillyn
"Upon Making the Acquaintance of Miss Emily Dickinson." [SingHM] (16) 89, p.
48.
6137. WILD, Peter
"Adulterous Farmers." [Mildred] (3:2) 89, p. 15.
"Evenings in Missoula." [HiramPoR] (46) Spr-Sum 89, p. 36.
"In Oregon." [Wind] (19:64) 89, p. 39.
"Indian Circle." [LitR] (32:2) Wint 89, p. 219.
"Meredith." [ClockR] (5:2) 89, p. 10.
"The Polish Baker." [SouthernPR] (29:2) Fall 89, p. 9.
"Roofers." [Wind] (19:64) 89, p. 39-40.
"Settling." [Outbr] (20) 89, p. 33.
6138. WILDE-MENOZZI, Wallis
"Along the Back Roads" (to H.B.). [Pequod] (28/29/30) 89, p. 221-222.
"Eating near Caiano with a Priest." [MissR] (17:3, #51), p. 96-97.
"Explanations." [Pequod] (28/29/30) 89, p. 219-220.
"Pages." [SouthwR] (74:4) Aut 89, p. 489-490.
6139. WILDER, Arwen
"Exuviae." [Prima] (13) 89, p. 7.
6140. WILDES, Doretta
"Blow Ball." [YaleR] (78:3) Spr 89, p. 479-480.
6141. WILDING, Margo
"First Kids." [MidAR] (9:2) 89, p. 61-62.
"Learning to Dance." [MidAR] (9:2) 89, p. 63.
"My Sister's Stutter." [MidAR] (9:2) 89, p. 64-65.
"Voyeur." [MidAR] (9:2) 89, p. 66.
6142. WILER, Jack
"Letter to Mack in Osaka." [US1] (22/23) Spr 89, p. 33.
6143. WILHARM, Evelyn S.
"Seasons of Love." [EmeraldCR] (1989) c1988, p. 144-145.
6144. WILHELM, Kate
"Absence of Light." [KanQ] (21:3) Sum 89, p. 190.
"Thoughts Preceding a Death." [KanQ] (21:3) Sum 89, p. 189.
6145. WILJER, Robert
"Esthetic Surgery." [Poetry] (153:5) F 89, p. 297.
6146. WILKINS, W. R.
"Consider the Tao." [StoneC] (17:1/2) Fall-Wint 89-90, p. 49.
6147. WILKINSON, Claude
"By Night." [Poem] (61) My 89, p. 10.
"Psalm for Don and Frank." [Poem] (61) My 89, p. 6-9.
6148. WILKINSON, John
"Back on the Slopes." [Pequod] (26/27) 89, p. 137-138.
6149. WILLARD, Nancy
"A Hardware Store as Proof of the Existence of God." [KenR] (NS 11:2) Spr 89, p.
71.
6150. WILLEY, Edward
"Blindworld." [KeyWR] (2:1/2) Fall-Wint 89, p. 98.

6151. WILLIAMS, Barbara
"God-Speed" (for Tom York). [NegC] (9:1) 89, p. 128-130.
6152. WILLIAMS, Beryle
"Study in Archaeology" (To My Daughter, Blythe). [LakeSR] (23) 89, p. 14.
6153. WILLIAMS, Bob
"Honeysuckle: Showy Flower Rich in Nectar." [JamesWR] (6:4) Sum 89, p. 4.
6154. WILLIAMS, David
"Bright Weight and Sight." [Sonora] (17) Spr-Sum 89, p. 72-73.
6155. WILLIAMS, Denise
"Long Island Railroad -- Great Neck to Manhattan." [PacificR] (7) 89, p. 40-41.
"The Winnowing." [PacificR] (7) 89, p. 42.
6156. WILLIAMS, Dianne
"The Fish." [BellArk] (5:4) Jl-Ag 89, p. 6.
"The Fish." [BellArk] (5:5) S-O 89, p. 4.
"Kourion" (1600 years ago on Cyprus a powerful earthquake destroyed the Roman
city, Kourion). [BellArk] (5:3) My-Je 89, p. 6.
"The Lost Garden." [BellArk] (5:5) S-O 89, p. 9.
"Oregon Coast Idyll" (a Mother's Day poem). [BellArk] (5:5) S-O 89, p. 7.
"The Siletz River" (for my brother). [BellArk] (5:3) My-Je 89, p. 18.
"Spring" (for Scott). [BellArk] (5:3) My-Je 89, p. 5.
6157. WILLIAMS, Faith
"Bather by a River." [PoetL] (84:4) Wint 89-90, p. 28.
"Endings." [PoetL] (84:1) Spr 89, p. 48.
"Translating Poetry." [PoetL] (84:1) Spr 89, p. 49.
6158. WILLIAMS, Gwyn
"Easter Poem." [NoDaQ] (57:2) Spr 89, insert p. 16.
"Pelagius." [NoDaQ] (57:2) Spr 89, insert p. 15.
"Under Orion" (For D.). [NoDaQ] (57:2) Spr 89, insert p. 16.
6159. WILLIAMS, Haare
"Bellbird and Flax Flower." [Descant] (20:3/4, #66/67) Fall-Wint 89, p. 47-48.
"E Ma." [Descant] (20:3/4, #66/67) Fall-Wint 89, p. 39-40.
"Koha." [Descant] (20:3/4, #66/67) Fall-Wint 89, p. 45.
"Patches Hide No Scars." [Descant] (20:3/4, #66/67) Fall-Wint 89, p. 46-47.
"Te Kooti." [Descant] (20:3/4, #66/67) Fall-Wint 89, p. 49-50.
6160. WILLIAMS, Joe
"Igues sthey want metoac tlike." [BlackALF] (23:3) Fall 89, p. 494.
6161. WILLIAMS, Larry
"Sixteenth Birthday Lament." [LakeSR] (23) 89, p. 12.
6162. WILLIAMS, Maurine
"Consequence." [DeKalbLAJ] (22:1/4) 89, p. 69.
6163. WILLIAMS, Miller
"An August Evening Outside of Nashville." [NewEngR] (12:2) Wint 89, p. 139.
"Before." [SouthernR] (25:3) Sum 89, p. 604-605.
"The Book." [SouthernR] (25:3) Sum 89, p. 603.
"The Gift of Prophecy Lost." [NewL] (56:2/3) Wint 89-Spr 90, p. 320.
"The Journalist Buys a Pig Farm." [NewL] (56:2/3) Wint 89-Spr 90, p. 321-322.
"The Ones That Are Thrown Out." [NewL] (56:2/3) Wint 89-Spr 90, p. 320.
"Rituals." [NewEngR] (12:2) Wint 89, p. 137-138.
"Rock." [NewL] (56:2/3) Wint 89-Spr 90, p. 318-319.
6164. WILLIAMS, Philip Lee
"Which Beasts Shall I Become." [Poem] (61) My 89, p. 72.
6165. WILLIAMS, Rynn
"Breasts." [BelPoJ] (39:4) Sum 89, p. 39-40.
"What It Means." [BelPoJ] (39:4) Sum 89, p. 38.
6166. WILLIAMS, Sandra
"Scars." [Thrpny] (37) Spr 89, p. 35.
6167. WILLIAMS, Sherley Anne
"An Afro-American Returns: A Market in Ghana." [Callaloo] (12:2, #39) Spr 89, p.
346-349.
6168. WILLIAMS, Tyrone
"Full House." [ArtfulD] (16/17) Fall 89, p. 54.
"Halfwayhome." [ColR] (NS 16:1) Spr-Sum 89, p. 57-60.
6169. WILLIAMS, Windell
"Salvador Dali Hangs on the Wall." [Obs] (4:3) Wint 89, p. 65.
6170. WILLIAMSON, Alan
"Love and the Soul." [ParisR] (31:110) Spr 89, p. 93-95.

6171. WILLIAMSON, Don (Don T.)
"Night-fishing." [Plain] (10:1) 89, p. 14.
"Nude Poem Ascending Staircase." [Plain] (9:3) Spr 89, p. 13.
"Summer Rental." [PassN] (10:2) Sum 89, p. 16.
6172. WILLIS, Elizabeth
"H-YRDN." [Sulfur] (9:2, #25) Fall 89, p. 44-50.
6173. WILLIS, Irene
"I Cash." [US1] (22/23) Spr 89, p. 37.
6174. WILLIS, Kerrie A.
"After Keats' 'When I Have Fears That I May Cease to Be'." [Plain] (9:3) Spr 89, p.
11.
6175. WILLOW, Morgan Grayce
"Obsidian." [EvergreenC] (4:4) Sum 89, p. 16-17.
"The Rose and the Panther" (To Cora). [EvergreenC] (4:4) Sum 89, p. 18.
6176. WILLS, Ora
"Wouldn' min' dyin' got to go by myself." [EmeraldCR] (1989) c1988, p. 82.
6177. WILMER, Clive
"St. Francis Preaching to the Birds." [Pequod] (26/27) 89, p. 139.
"Three Brueghel Paintings" (The Massacre of the Innocents, The Conversion of St.
Paul, Hunters in the Snow). [Pequod] (26/27) 89, p. 140.
6178. WILNER, Eleanor
"Conversation with a Japanese Student." [TriQ] (74) Wint 89, p. 211-213.
"Infection in the Ear." [Calyx] (12:1) Sum 89, p. 19.
"It's a Boy" (message sent by Edward Teller when the first H-bomb was
successfully tested). [Calyx] (12:1) Sum 89, p. 20-21.
"It's Not Cold Here" (for Bob). [TriQ] (74) Wint 89, p. 209-210.
"Kazuko's Vision." [IndR] (13:1) Wint 89, p. 91.
"Out of the Hellespont." [IndR] (13:1) Wint 89, p. 94-96.
"Those Who Come After." [IndR] (13:1) Wint 89, p. 92-93.
"Two Pairs of Eyes" (for Leah Kosh). [Calyx] (12:1) Sum 89, p. 22-23.
6179. WILSON, Alan R.
"47" (From "Counting to Zero"). [CrossC] (11:1) 89, p. 10.
"Counting to 100" (Selections: 32, 33, 41). [Grain] (17:1) Spr 89, p. 70-71.
"Windows." [CanLit] (122/123) Aut-Wint 89, p. 107.
6180. WILSON, Barb
"Drinking Tea with My Mother." [ThRiPo] (33/34) 89, p. 21.
6181. WILSON, Barbara H.
"A Place Inside a Child." [SouthernPR] (29:1) Spr 89, p. 10.
6182. WILSON, David
"Smash Saturday." [Bogg] (61) 89, p. 41.
6183. WILSON, Elizabeth (Betty)
"4. My island is a ghetto" (from *Paroles pour solder la mer*, tr. of Edouard
Maunick). [Callaloo] (12:3, #40) Sum 89, p. 504.
"Beirut, Lebanon" (for Adonis, from *Paroles pour solder la mer*, tr. of Edouard
Maunick). [Callaloo] (12:3, #40) Sum 89, p. 501.
"Lvov, Ukraine" (for the Ivan Franko faithful, from *Paroles pour solder la mer*, tr.
of Edouard Maunick). [Callaloo] (12:3, #40) Sum 89, p. 502-503.
"Milan in Lombardy" (for Maretta Campi, from *Paroles pour solder la mer*, tr. of
Edouard Maunick). [Callaloo] (12:3, #40) Sum 89, p. 503.
"Parole 47" (from *Ensoleillé vif*, tr. of Edouard Maunick). [Callaloo] (12:3, #40)
Sum 89, p. 505.
"Rome, Piazza Navona" (for Claude Couffon, from *Paroles pour solder la mer*, tr. of
Edouard Maunick). [Callaloo] (12:3, #40) Sum 89, p. 502.
6184. WILSON, Gisela
"Weather Vein." [PoetryNW] (30:4) Wint 89-90, p. 38.
6185. WILSON, Graeme
"Homecoming" (tr. of Hiagiwara Sakutaro). [Jacaranda] (4:1) Spr-Sum 89, p.
73-75.
"Japanese Garden" (tr. of Emperor Meiji). [ConnPR] (8:1) 89, p. 19.
"Maiden Flower" (From the First Imperial Anthology, Kokinwakashu, of 905, tr. of
Bishop Henjo). [Jacaranda] (4:1) Spr-Sum 89, p. 72.
"Party Ending" (tr. of Hsu Tsai-ssu). [DenQ] (24:1) Sum 89, p. 86.
"Plum Scent" (From the First Imperial Anthology, Kokinwakashu, of 905, tr. of
anonymous poem). [Jacaranda] (4:1) Spr-Sum 89, p. 72.
"Proximity" (tr. of anonymous Japanese poem). [DenQ] (24:1) Sum 89, p. 87.
"Railway Train" (tr. of Muro Saisei). [ConnPR] (8:1) 89, p. 21.

"Red Light District" (tr. of Hiagiwara Sakutaro). [Jacaranda] (4:1) Spr-Sum 89, p. 76.
"Second Thoughts" (From the First Imperial Anthology, Kokinwakashu, of 905, tr. of anonymous poem). [Jacaranda] (4:1) Spr-Sum 89, p. 72.
"Sheep's Eye" (tr. of Shiraishi Kazuko). [ConnPR] (8:1) 89, p. 20.
"Who's There?" (tr. of Shonagon Sei). [Poetry] (153:5) F 89, p. 298.

6186. WILSON, John
"A Manifesto." [HeliconN] (20) 89, p. 84.

6187. WILSON, Joseph
"Bird Fantasy." [SpoonRQ] (14:2) Spr 89, p. 64.

6188. WILSON, Joyce
"Grammar Lesson." [DenQ] (24:2) Fall 89, p. 95.

6189. WILSON, Larry
"Choices." [TexasR] (10:1/2) Spr-Sum 89, p. 57.
"On Being Compared to Don Quixote." [TexasR] (10:1/2) Spr-Sum 89, p. 56.

6190. WILSON, Ralph
"Sleeping Dogs." [PassN] (10:1) Wint 89, p. 8.

6191. WILSON, Rob
"Fukuzawa Blue." [BambooR] (44) Fall 89, p. 35.
"Travelling" (for Russell Banks). [Hawai'iR] (13:1, #25) Spr 89, p. 77.

6192. WILSON, Steve
"Empirical Proof" (for Bruce Cutler). [MidwQ] (30:4) Sum 89, p. 456.

6193. WILSON, Walter
"Amber." [SpiritSH] (54) Spr-Sum 89, p. 26.
"Mother's Wake." [SpiritSH] (54) Spr-Sum 89, p. 25.
"Out of the Oak Climax." [SpiritSH] (54) Spr-Sum 89, p. 27.
"Thaw." [SpiritSH] (54) Spr-Sum 89, p. 24.
"The Ulster Way." [SpiritSH] (54) Spr-Sum 89, p. 28.

6194. WIMAN, Christian
"Is That You." [Shen] (39:1) Spr 89, p. 50.

6195. WIMP, Jet
"Left on the Refrigerator." [WestB] (25) 89, p. 80-81.

6196. WINANS, A. D.
"For Jack Spicer." [Bogg] (61) 89, p. 53.
"Strange Happenings." [Outbr] (20) 89, p. 72.

6197. WINANS, Janet
"Becoming." [CentR] (33:1) Wint 89, p. 58.
"Economy." [SoCoast] (5) Spr 88, p. 7.

WINCKEL, Nance van
    See Van WINCKEL, Nance

6198. WIND, Chris
"Adam's Apple." [Grain] (17:3) Fall 89, p. 26.
"The Thinker." [Bogg] (61) 89, p. 16.

6199. WINDER, Barbara
"Betting the Blue Chip." [KanQ] (21:4) Fall 89, p. 14-15.
"Malinche, My Indian Name." [SouthernPR] (29:1) Spr 89, p. 18-19.

6200. WINFIELD, William
"The Word." [BlueBldgs] (11) 89, p. 7.

6201. WING, Linda
"Bridges Across." [LakeSR] (23) 89, p. 23.
"Glass." [LakeSR] (23) 89, p. 22.

WING, Tek Lum
    See LUM, Wing Tek

6202. WINN, Howard
"Belief." [WindO] (52) Wint 89-90, p. 5.
"Instruction in Philosophy." [WindO] (52) Wint 89-90, p. 5.
"Jane Austin in China." [DeKalbLAJ] (22:1/4) 89, p. 69-70.
"Man in a Beard." [LaurelR] (23:1) Wint 89, p. 66-67.
"Robert Frost in Costa Rica." [DeKalbLAJ] (22:1/4) 89, p. 71.

6203. WINSLOW, Hall
"Hostilities." [Poem] (62) N 89, p. 41.
"Missing Boys." [Poem] (62) N 89, p. 38-39.
"Parthenon 512 A.D." [Poem] (62) N 89, p. 40.

6204. WINTERS, Bayla
"Janis Joplin and the Folding Company." [FreeL] (3) Aut 89, p. 19.
"Like a Second Skin, a Third Eye." [Footwork] 89, p. 72.

"My Kahlua Runneth Over." [Vis] (30) 89, p. 44.
"The *Nuclear* Winter of Our Discontent." [CreamCR] (13:2) Fall 89, p. 30.
6205. WINWOOD, David
"Cows." [WritersF] (15) Fall 89, p. 101-102.
"Warthogs." [SenR] (19:1) 89, p. 75.
6206. WIRPSZA, Witold
"Mendacity" (tr. by Stanislaw Baranczak and Clare Cavanah). [Trans] (21) Spr 89,
p. 19.
6207. WIRTH, Eric
"Block Party Consul." [Aerial] (5) 89, p. 23.
"Commencement Bay, Tacoma, Wash." [Aerial] (5) 89, p. 22.
"Swift and Beautiful." [Aerial] (5) 89, p. 24.
6208. WISEMAN, Christopher
"Autumnal." [Dandel] (16:1) Spr-Sum 89, p. 60.
"Effects" (for M.W.). [CrossC] (11:2) 89, p. 5.
"Sketch, by Son and Nephew." [Dandel] (16:1) Spr-Sum 89, p. 61-62.
6209. WISENBERG, S. L.
"In 1882 Oscar Wilde Stopped in Chicago on His Lecture Tour and Dazzled
Everybody." [SpoonRQ] (14:2) Spr 89, p. 42-44.
"In Hell, We Pass by Sidewalk Cafes." [SpoonRQ] (14:2) Spr 89, p. 41.
WIT, Johan de
See De WIT, Johan
WIT, Sonja de
See DeWIT, Sonja
6210. WITEK, Terri
"I Tell You Another Story." [Poetry] (154:4) Jl 89, p. 204.
6211. WITHERUP, William
"Walking Mt. Vision Trail" (For Blue Bear). [HighP] (4:1) Spr 89, p. 86-87.
6212. WITT, Bana
"Two Halves." [Sequoia] (32:2) Wint-Spr 89, p. 29.
6213. WITT, Harold
"American Lit: Anaïs Nin." [WritersF] (15) Fall 89, p. 43.
"American Lit: Interim." [Interim] (8:1) Spr 89, p. 2.
"American Lit: Peg." [WritersF] (15) Fall 89, p. 44.
"American Lit: Studs Lonigan." [PoetC] (21:1) Fall 89, p. 39.
"American Lit: Sylvia Plath." [PoetC] (21:1) Fall 89, p. 38.
"Cowden." [BellArk] (5:1) Ja-F 89, p. 20.
"Dactyls." [CharR] (15:1) Spr 89, p. 61.
"Danse Russe." [KanQ] (21:4) Fall 89, p. 34.
"Elmer Gantry." [CharR] (15:1) Spr 89, p. 61.
"Is There Any Culture or Love of Beauty in Grover's Corners?" [BellArk] (5:4)
Jl-Ag 89, p. 9.
"The Long Hot Summer." [KanQ] (21:4) Fall 89, p. 34.
"Martin Eden." [CharR] (15:1) Spr 89, p. 62.
"Miss Lonelyhearts." [CharR] (15:1) Spr 89, p. 63.
"The Postman Always Rings Twice." [BellArk] (5:6) N-D 89, p. 8.
"Richard Wilbur." [BellArk] (5:1) Ja-F 89, p. 3.
"Robert Nathan." [BellArk] (5:4) Jl-Ag 89, p. 7.
"Sea Anemones." [Confr] (39/40) Fall 88-Wint 89, p. 59.
"Stephen Crane." [CharR] (15:1) Spr 89, p. 62.
"Willa Cather" (from American Lit). [ThRiPo] (31/32) 88, p. 52.
"William Stafford" (From the *American Lit.* series). [FreeL] (1) 89, p. 36.
WITT, Howard
See WITT, Harold
WITT, Jim de
See DeWITT, Jim
6214. WITT, Sandra
"Flight Control." [ChamLR] (2:2, #4) Spr 89, p. 119.
6215. WITTE, Francine
"Lottery." [PoetC] (21:1) Fall 89, p. 5.
6216. WITTE, George
"The Vantage Point." [Confr] (39/40) Fall 88-Wint 89, p. 90.
6217. WITTE, John
"Blue School." [OhioR] (44) 89, p. 100-101.
"Meteorite." [ParisR] (31:110) Spr 89, p. 186-187.
"Snail." [ParisR] (31:110) Spr 89, p. 184-185.

6218. WOEHRLEN, Sara Heikoff
"The Foundling" (tr. of Jose Elgarresta). [WindO] (52) Wint 89-90, p. 33.
"It Frequently Happens" (tr. of Sergio Badilla). [SoDakR] (27:2) Sum 89, p. 85.
"The Red Shoes" (For Marylin, tr. of Marjorie Agosin). [CumbPR] (9:1) Fall 89, p. 54-55.
"Skin" (tr. of Sergio Badilla). [SoDakR] (27:2) Sum 89, p. 86.
"The Suicide" (tr. of Jose Elgarresta). [WindO] (52) Wint 89-90, p. 33, 35.

6219. WOERNER, Margaret K.
"Listen!" [EmeraldCR] (1989) c1988, p. 124.

WOFFORD, Jan Bailey
See BAILEY-WOFFORD, Jan

6220. WOHMANN, Gabriele
"Head Start" (tr. by John Linthicum). [LitR] (33:1) Fall 89, p. 103.
"I Don't Want to Die in the Evening" (tr. by John Linthicum). [LitR] (33:1) Fall 89, p. 104.
"Time for the Good Things" (tr. by John Linthicum). [LitR] (33:1) Fall 89, p. 105.

6221. WOJAHN, David
"Armageddon: Private Gabriel Calvin Wojahn, 1900-1918." [DenQ] (23:3/4) Wint-Spr 89, p. 125-126.
"Azimuth." [YaleR] (78:3) Spr 89, p. 459.
"Diary Pages: Amsterdam." [NoAmR] (274:2) Je 89, p. 32-33.
"Double Exposures." [Ploughs] (15:1) 89, p. 154-156.
"Mystery Train: Janis Joplin Leaves Port Arthur for Points West, 1964." [Iowa] (19:3) Fall 89, p. 110.
"The Naming." [Poetry] (153:6) Mr 89, p. 323-324.
"The Novelist" (For D.Y.). [Poetry] (153:6) Mr 89, p. 321-323.
"Photographer at Altamont: The Morning After, 1969." [Iowa] (19:3) Fall 89, p. 111.
"Posthumous Life" (London: Hampstead Heath). [YaleR] (78:3) Spr 89, p. 460-462.
"The Recent Work." [Ploughs] (15:1) 89, p. 157-161.
"The Resurrection of the Dead: Port Glasgow, 1950" (A Painting by Sir Stanley Spencer, Tate Gallery). [GettyR] (2:1) Wint 89, p. 146-148.

6222. WOLF, Joan
"Hepatica." [SwampR] (1:4) Sum 89, p. 27.

6223. WOLF, Michele
"Toilette." [Hudson] (42:3) Aut 89, p. 452.

6224. WOLF, Mindy
"Born Henry." [SoCoast] (6) Fall 88, p. 3.

6225. WOLF, Naomi
"The Pied Piper." [Verse] (6:1) Mr 89, p. 53.

6226. WOLFE, Murray
"The Kiss" (tr. of Abraham Sutzkevor). [PartR] (56:1) Wint 89, p. 114.

6227. WOLFF, Daniel
"Work Sonnets" (Selection: "We live off air. And since that's true"). [Talisman] (2) Spr 89, p. 63.

6228. WOLK, Joel
"The Horses Who Joined the Mother." [WritersF] (15) Fall 89, p. 100.

6229. WOLOCH, Cecilia
"Conception." [Interim] (8:1) Spr 89, p. 19.
"The Honeymoon." [Interim] (8:1) Spr 89, p. 18.

6230. WOMONGOLD, Marcia
"Womongold's Cosmic Alphabet." [Hawai'iR] (13:2, #26) Sum 89, p. 32.

6231. WONG-MORRISON, Tamara
"08-31-1987." [Hawai'iR] (13:3) Fall 89, p. 56.
"Continental Drift" (for Nell). [Hawai'iR] (13:3) Fall 89, p. 57.

6232. WONSON, Carolyn
"A Prayer to the Rain God." [KeyWR] (2:1/2) Fall-Wint 89, p. 99.
"Soliloquy." [KeyWR] (2:1/2) Fall-Wint 89, p. 100.

6233. WOOD, Peter
"Afterword." [Footwork] 89, p. 56.
"Local Talent in a Western Town." [PaintedB] (37) 89, p. 25.
"Weeds." [Footwork] 89, p. 56.

6234. WOOD, Renate
"Blood." [PraS] (63:1) Spr 89, p. 29-30.
"Digging for Treasure" (Selections: "2. Knives," "3. For M.G."). [Calyx] (12:2)

Wint 89-90, p. 10-11.
"The Tree" (Astrakhan, 1895). [PraS] (63:1) Spr 89, p. 30.
"Wilderness." [PraS] (63:1) Spr 89, p. 31.
6235. WOOD, Tex
"Bomb Shell Memory." [StoneC] (16:3/4) Spr-Sum 89, p. 40.
"Touring Ruins in Spain." [GreensboroR] (46) Sum 89, p. 168.
6236. WOODARD, Deborah
"Deserted" (tr. of Antonia Pozzi). [PoetryE] (28) Fall 89, p. 183.
"Fields" (tr. of Antonia Pozzi). [PoetryE] (28) Fall 89, p. 182.
"The Nun's Antechamber" (tr. of Antonia Pozzi). [BlueBldgs] (11) 89, p. 32.
"Sicilian Landscape" (tr. of Antonia Pozzi). [PoetryE] (28) Fall 89, p. 184.
6237. WOODFORD, Bruce P.
"The Great Leap." [Wind] (19:64) 89, p. 41-44.
6238. WOODFORD, Keisha Lynette
"Mill Street." [Footwork] 89, p. 15-16.
"This Written After Viewing Cry Freedom." [Footwork] 89, p. 15.
6239. WOODRUFF, William
"Anima." [PacificR] (7) 89, p. 80-81.
"Gently polishing." [WormR] (29:4, #116) 89, p. 116.
"Imbedded in a tire track." [WormR] (29:4, #116) 89, p. 116.
"In a ditch, tires up." [WormR] (29:4, #116) 89, p. 116.
"In a waiting room." [WormR] (29:1, #113) 89, p. 5.
"Its linen kept fresh." [WormR] (29:4, #116) 89, p. 116.
"Keeping me awake." [WormR] (29:4, #116) 89, p. 116.
"Me poking my rod." [WormR] (29:4, #116) 89, p. 116.
"Nailed to the blackened door frame of a gutted store." [WormR] (29:4, #116) 89, p. 116.
"On Heraclitus." [Lactuca] (12) F 89, p. 28.
6240. WOODS, Brien
"Hired Hand." [DenQ] (24:1) Sum 89, p. 88.
6241. WOODS, Christopher
"An Artificial Man." [KanQ] (21:3) Sum 89, p. 159.
"Buffaloes." [ChamLR] (3:1, #5) Fall 89, p. 119.
"Near Ucross, Wyoming." [Grain] (17:1) Spr 89, p. 32.
"A Poem Long in Coming." [ChamLR] (3:1, #5) Fall 89, p. 117-118.
"What Comes, What Goes." [KanQ] (21:3) Sum 89, p. 160.
6242. WOODS, Elizabeth
"Because." [CrossC] (11:2) 89, p. 9.
6243. WOODS, Gregory
"I Your You My First." [JamesWR] (5:2 [i.e. 6:2]) Wint 89, p. 14.
6244. WOODS, Linda
"The Girl on the Street." [AlphaBS] (5) Jl 89, p. 68.
"To the Victim Who Got Stabbed at Kaleigh Park, 4-9-88." [AlphaBS] (5) Jl 89, p. 67.
6245. WOODS, Macdara
"Miz Moon I." [Vis] (29) 89, p. 13.
"Miz Moon IV." [Vis] (29) 89, p. 14.
6246. WOODS, Phil
"The Good Journey." [CinPR] (19) Spr 89, p. 22-23.
6247. WOODSUM, Douglas H.
"Mulch." [DenQ] (24:2) Fall 89, p. 96.
6248. WOOI-CHIN, J-son
"The End of a Walk." [MissR] (18:1, #52) 89, p. 107-108.
6249. WOOLSEY, Wanda
"Sunday Morning." [EmeraldCR] (1989) c1988, p. 93-94.
6250. WOON, Koon
"The Aberdeen Poems" (6 poems). [BellArk] (5:2) Mr-Ap 89, p. 24-25.
"Far and Near." [BellArk] (5:5) S-O 89, p. 9.
"How to Cook Rice." [BellArk] (5:5) S-O 89, p. 20.
"A Moment in My Rented Room." [BellArk] (5:1) Ja-F 89, p. 1.
"Morphs." [BellArk] (5:1) Ja-F 89, p. 20.
"Playing Ping-Pong with Myself." [BellArk] (5:5) S-O 89, p. 7.
"Slivers." [BellArk] (5:6) N-D 89, p. 8.
"Under a Shaft of Light." [BellArk] (5:1) Ja-F 89, p. 9.
6251. WORLEY, James
"Accessible Tombs." [ChrC] (106:5) F 15, 89, p. 166.

"Monarch Butterfly." [ChrC] (106:29) O 11, 89, p. 901.
"Neither Here Nor There." [ChrC] (106:15) My 3, 89, p. 462.
"October." [ChrC] (106:30) O 18, 89, p. 924.
"On Refusing to Prune an Ancient Lilac." [ChrC] (106:23) Ag 2-9, 89, p. 723.
"Ruth Cleaves Again to Naomi." [ChrC] (106:19) Je 7-14, 89, p. 590.
"The Ultimate Barricade." [ChrC] (106:27) S 27, 89, p. 837.
6252. WORLEY, Jeff
"An American Romance." [AntigR] (77/78) Spr-Sum 89, p. 22-23.
"Emergency." [CinPR] (20) Fall 89, p. 32-33.
"The Magician's Assistant Dreams." [MalR] (86) Spr 89, p. 100.
"Mother Going for Groceries, 1953." [HolCrit] (26:1) F 89, p. 16.
"November." [ColEng] (51:1) Ja 89, p. 41-42.
"The Ordinary Sun" (after Kim). [LitR] (32:2) Wint 89, p. 225.
"The Poet Turns 40." [KanQ] (21:1/2) Wint-Spr 89, p. 232.
"Some Nights." [ColEng] (51:1) Ja 89, p. 42-43.
"Vagrant." [CinPR] (20) Fall 89, p. 31.
6253. WORMSER, Baron
"Pigeons" (From "Atoms, Soul Music and Other Poems). [Harp] (279:1672) S 89,
    p. 34.
6254. WOROSZYLSKI, Wiktor
"Fascist Nations" (tr. by Stanislaw Baranczak and Clare Cavanagh). [PartR] (56:2)
    Spr 89, p. 283-285.
"Indictment" (tr. by Stanislaw Baranczak and Clare Cavanagh). [PartR] (56:2) Spr
    89, p. 285-286.
"The Padlock Speaks" (From the "Diary of Internment, II," tr. by Stanislaw
    Baranczak and Clare Cavanagh). [PartR] (56:2) Spr 89, p. 286.
"Philately" (tr. by Stanislaw Baranczak and Clare Cavanah). [Trans] (21) Spr 89, p.
    58-59.
6255. WOROZBYT, Theodore (Theodore, Jr.)
"At Four Years." [ApalQ] (31) 89, p. 59-60.
"Chess." [Poetry] (153:5) F 89, p. 261-262.
"For Your Sins" (corrected reprint from 30/31 Spr 88). [MinnR] (NS 33) Fall 89, p.
    7-9.
"Haircut." [RiverC] (9:1) Spr 89, p. 78-79.
"Neighborhood Light." [Poetry] (153:5) F 89, p. 260-261.
"Someone Is Coming." [BlueBldgs] (11) 89, p. 48.
6256. WORTH, Dorothy Williamson
"Caveat Emptor." [DeKalbLAJ] (22:1/4) 89, p. 72.
"On Decatur Street." [DeKalbLAJ] (22:1/4) 89, p. 73.
6257. WORTH, Jan
"Message to My Neighbors on Seventh Street." [MichQR] (28:1) Wint 89, p.
    121-122.
"Walking Toward You, October Thursday." [PassN] (10:2) Sum 89, p. 15.
6258. WOSTER, Kevin
"Recovery." [SoDakR] (27:1) Spr 89, p. 131-132.
"Tourists in Summer." [SoDakR] (27:1) Spr 89, p. 124.
6259. WREGGITT, Andrew
"Builder, Broadview Road." [AntigR] (77/78) Spr-Sum 89, p. 149-150.
"Making Movies." [AntigR] (77/78) Spr-Sum 89, p. 151-152.
"Mine." [Quarry] (38:2) Spr 89, p. 24-25.
6260. WRENN, Charles P., Jr.
"Desire" (Creative Writing Club Contest, 2nd Place). [DeKalbLAJ] (22:1/4) 89, p.
    78.
6261. WRIGHT, Alvin (Alberta)
"How Aids Has Affected My Life" (with photograph by Billy Howard). [JamesWR]
    (6:4) Sum 89, p. 15.
6262. WRIGHT, C. D.
"Detail from What No One Could Have Told them" (after Taggart). [Sulfur] (9:1,
    #24) Spr 89, p. 57-58.
"Utopia." [FiveFR] (7) 89, p. 70.
"Weekend in the Country." [PoetryE] (28) Fall 89, p. 162-164.
"What No One Could Have Told Them." [Sulfur] (9:1, #24) Spr 89, p. 55-56.
6263. WRIGHT, Carolyne
"Afternoon Story" (tr. of Jorge Teillier). [IndR] (12:3) Sum 89, p. 63.
"Beginning and End" (in Bengali and English, tr. of Nabaneeta Dev Sen, w.
    Paramita Banerjee and the author). [BlackWR] (15:2) Spr 89, p. 82-83.

"The Carriers of Fire" (tr. of Mallika Sengupta, w. Paramita Banerjee). [NewEngR] (11:4) Sum 89, p. 460.
"Curse" (tr. of Kabita Sinha, w. Enakshi Chatterjee). [Trans] (21) Spr 89, p. 150.
"Death Beside the Ganges" (tr. of Sanjukta Bandyopadhyay, w. Paramita Banerjee and the author). [MichQR] (28:2) Spr 89, p. 230-231.
"The Diamond of Character" (tr. of Kabita Sinha, w. Swapna Mitra). [Trans] (21) Spr 89, p. 153.
"End of the World" (tr. of Jorge Teillier). [IndR] (12:3) Sum 89, p. 67.
"Engraving" (in Bengali and English, tr. of Anuradha Mahapatra, w. Paramita Banerjee and the author). [BlackWR] (15:2) Spr 89, p. 86-87.
"Full Moon" (tr. of Nabaneeta Dev Sen, w. Sunil B. Ray and the author). [NewEngR] (11:4) Sum 89, p. 456.
"Home" (tr. of Mallika Sengupta, w. Paramita Banerjee). [Iowa] (19:2) Spr-Sum 89, p. 120.
"I Have Trusted in the Night" (tr. of Jorge Teillier). [Chelsea] (48) 89, p. 24-25.
"If This Is Wednesday, It Must Be Vienna." [WestHR] (43:4) Wint 89, p. 265-266.
"Immobile Rain" (tr. of Jorge Teillier). [Chelsea] (48) 89, p. 24.
"In Memory of a Closed House" (tr. of Jorge Teillier). [OhioR] (44) 89, p. 32.
"Kitchen" (tr. of Sanjukta Bandyopadhyay, w. Paramita Banerjee and the author). [MichQR] (28:2) Spr 89, p. 229-230.
"The Last Door's Name Is Sorrow" (tr. of Kabita Sinha, w. Swapna Mitra). [Trans] (21) Spr 89, p. 151-152.
"Living in Disguise" (tr. of Anuradha Mahapatra, w. Paramita Banerjee). [Iowa] (19:2) Spr-Sum 89, p. 119.
"Marriage Vessel" (tr. of Pratima Ray, w. Paramita Banerjee). [NewEngR] (11:4) Sum 89, p. 459.
"Now That Once Again" (tr. of Jorge Teillier). [OhioR] (44) 89, p. 33-34.
"The Peacock" (tr. of Anuradha Mahapatra, w. Paramita Banerjee). [Iowa] (19:2) Spr-Sum 89, p. 118.
"Return" (in Bengali and English, tr. of Nabaneeta Dev Sen, w. Paramita Banerjee and the author). [BlackWR] (15:2) Spr 89, p. 84-85.
"Ritual Sacrifice" (tr. of Mallika Sengupta, w. Paramita Banerjee). [Iowa] (19:2) Spr-Sum 89, p. 120-121.
"Story of a Prodigal Son" (tr. of Jorge Teillier). [MassR] (30:2) Sum 89, p. 298-300.
"Talking Politics." [Witness] (3:1) Spr 89, p. 148-151.
"Tango Lyric" (tr. of Jorge Teillier). [OhioR] (44) 89, p. 34.
"To a Child in a Tree" (tr. of Jorge Teillier). [Chelsea] (48) 89, p. 25.
"To Be Worthy" (tr. of Vijaya Mukhopadhyay, w. Sunil B. Ray and the author). [NewEngR] (11:4) Sum 89, p. 458.
"Undesired" (tr. of Anuradha Mahapatra, w. Jyotirmoy Datta). [NewEngR] (11:4) Sum 89, p. 457.
"Village Nocturne" (tr. of Anuradha Mahapatra, w. Paramita Banerjee). [Iowa] (19:2) Spr-Sum 89, p. 117.
"Wander Luis" (Ouro Preto, Brazil: February 1972). [ApalQ] (32) 89, p. 13-16.
"Waterfall" (tr. of Kabita Sinha, w. Enakshi Chatterjee). [Trans] (21) Spr 89, p. 149.
"Welcome Angel" (tr. of Nabaneetä Dev Sen, w. Sunil B. Ray and the author). [MalR] (89) Wint 89, p. 31-33.
"Winter Poem" (tr. of Jorge Teillier). [IndR] (12:3) Sum 89, p. 65.
"You" (in Bengali and English, tr. of Anuradha Mahapatra, w. Paramita Banerjee and the author). [BlackWR] (15:2) Spr 89, p. 88-89.
6264. WRIGHT, Charles
"After Reading Tu Fu, I Go Outside to the Dwarf Orchard." [Field] (41) Fall 89, p. 98.
"After Reading Wang kWei, I Go Outside to the Full Moon." [NewRep] (201:24) 11 D 89, p. 34.
"At Zero." [SouthwR] (74:4) Aut 89, p. 515-516.
"Early One Morning in the Teatro Romano." [KenR] (NS 11:3) Sum 89, p. 137.
"An Evening Like So Many Others" (tr. of Giovanni Giudici). [Poetry] (155:1/2) O-N 89, p. 72-73.
"The Forties" (tr. of Luciano Erba). [Poetry] (155:1/2) O-N 89, p. 65.
"La Grande Jeanne" (tr. of Luciano Erba). [Poetry] (155:1/2) O-N 89, p. 63.
"A Journal of Three Questions." [Antaeus] (62) Spr 89, p. 231.
"Lines After Rereading T. S. Eliot." [GettyR] (2:2) Spr 89, p. 250-251.
"Lines on Seeing a Photograph for the First Time in Thirty Years." [Field] (41) Fall

89, p. 95-96.
"Looking Outside the Cabin Window, I Remember a Line by Li Po." [Field] (41) Fall 89, p. 97.
"Madame Bovary C'Est Moi" (Poem for one voice. Selection: I, tr. of Giovanni Giudici). [Poetry] (155:1/2) O-N 89, p. 71.
"Moving On." [SouthwR] (74:4) Aut 89, p. 525.
"Saturday Morning Journal." [Antaeus] (62) Spr 89, p. 230.
"Sitting Outside at the End of Autumn." [GettyR] (2:2) Spr 89, p. 252.
"Sunday at Home at the Beginning of Winter." [KenR] (NS 11:3) Sum 89, p. 138.
"Under the Nine Trees in January." [NewYorker] (65:9) 17 Ap 89, p. 89.
6265. WRIGHT, Franz
"The Drunk." [Field] (40) Spr 89, p. 29.
"Illegibility." [Field] (40) Spr 89, p. 31.
"Loneliness." [Field] (40) Spr 89, p. 32-33.
"The Needle: For a Friend Who Disappeared." [NewYorker] (65:35) 16 O 89, p. 84.
"Occurrence." [Field] (40) Spr 89, p. 30.
"Pawtucket Postcards." [Field] (40) Spr 89, p. 28.
"Poem: Per each dweller" (for Frank Bidart). [TriQ] (74) Wint 89, p. 188.
"Provincetown Postcards." [Field] (40) Spr 89, p. 27.
"The World." [TriQ] (74) Wint 89, p. 187.
"Writing at Night." [TriQ] (74) Wint 89, p. 186.
6266. WRIGHT, Howard
"Shanty." [AntigR] (77/78) Spr-Sum 89, p. 11.
6267. WRIGHT, James
"Melancholy inside Families" (tr. of Pablo Neruda, w. Robert Bly). [Quarry] (38:2) Spr 89, p. 76-77.
6268. WRIGHT, Jay
"Boleros" (Selections: 5, 7, 14, 25, 39). [Callaloo] (12:1, #38) Wint 89, p. 7-16.
6269. WRIGHT, Jeff
"Artemis." [BrooklynR] (5) 88, p. 6.
"Dense Flight." [BrooklynR] (5) 88, p. 3-5.
6270. WRIGHT, Lisa
"The Quote." [Amelia] (5:3, #14) 89, p. 32.
6271. WRIGHT, Stephen C.
"Gwendolyn's Givings: Celebration of the People." [ColR] (NS 16:1) Spr-Sum 89, p. 55-56.
"What Gwendolyn Might Have Me Say" (reflecting on grandmothers). [ColR] (NS 16:1) Spr-Sum 89, p. 54.
6272. WRIGLEY, Robert
"C. O." [Poetry] (154:3) Je 89, p. 135-136.
"Dust." [PoetryNW] (30:3) Aut 89, p. 42-43.
"February 3, Minus 22 Degress" (for Ed Hughes). [PoetryNW] (30:3) Aut 89, p. 42.
"The Grandmothers." [PoetryNW] (30:3) Aut 89, p. 41-42.
"My Father's Fingernails." [Poetry] (154:3) Je 89, p. 124-135.
"Night Calls." [Shen] (39:3) Fall 89, p. 68-70.
"Night Rising" (on the Lochsa). [Shen] (39:3) Fall 89, p. 67-68.
"Quail." [KenR] (NS 11:2) Spr 89, p. 10-11.
"Sea Flower." [KenR] (NS 11:2) Spr 89, p. 10.
"Sinatra." [KenR] (N 11:4) Fall 89, p. 78.
"So Long Sailor" (for Keith Browning). [Shen] (39:3) Fall 89, p. 66.
6273. WRONSKY, Gail
"Against Masculine Discourse." [AntR] (47:2) Spr 89, p. 199.
"Longings, Salt Lake City." [AntR] (47:2) Spr 89, p. 198.
6274. WU, Tsao
"On a Picture of Self with Hoe, Cultivating Plum Blossoms in Moonlight" (tr. by Kathy Silber). [LitR] (32:3) Spr 89, p. 397.
"Song in Sixteen Words" (tr. by Kathy Silber). [LitR] (32:3) Spr 89, p. 396.
"To the Tune of 'Tung Hsien Ko'" (tr. by Kathy Silber). [LitR] (32:3) Spr 89, p. 396.
6275. WU-SUN, Princess
"Grief Song" (tr. by Eric Sackheim). [LitR] (32:3) Spr 89, p. 420.
6276. WUEST, Barbara
"The Joyful Mysteries (I)." [ParisR] (31:112) Fall 89, p. 96.
"The Joyful Mysteries (III)." [ParisR] (31:112) Fall 89, p. 97.

6277. WYATT, Charles
"History." [BelPoJ] (40:2) Wint 89-90, p. 2.
"Killing Chickens." [Mildred] (3:2) 89, p. 120.
"Rain Is Older." [Mildred] (3:1) Spr-Sum 89, p. 102-104.
"Renaissance." [Mildred] (3:2) 89, p. 119.
"Two Beginnings." [CumbPR] (9:1) Fall 89, p. 44-45.
6278. WYTTENBERG, Victoria
"I Could Light a Candle or Each Birthday Take One Candle Away." [PoetryNW]
(30:1) Spr 89, p. 27-28.
"Something Old, Something New." [PoetryNW] (30:1) Spr 89, p. 26-27.
"Trying to Change Shape." [PoetryNW] (30:1) Spr 89, p. 28-29.
6279. XAIXAN, Xu
"Lady Pan" (tr. of Wang Wei, w. Tony Barnstone and Willis Barnstone). [CentR]
(33:3) Sum 89, p. 250.
"Missing the Loved One" (tr. of Wang Wei, w. Tony Barnstone and Willis
Barnstone). [CentR] (33:3) Sum 89, p. 250.
"Written in My Garden in Spring" (tr. of Wang Wei, w. Tony Barnstone and Willis
Barnstone). [CentR] (33:3) Sum 89, p. 250.
XI, Li Xuan
See LI, Xuan Xi
XIANG, Gao
See GAO, Xiang
XIANG, Zhu
See ZHU, Xiang
6280. XIAO, Qing
"Fate" (tr. by Dong Jiping). [Footwork] 89, p. 27.
"The Lost Horizon" (tr. by Dong Jiping). [Footwork] 89, p. 27.
"Time" (tr. by Dong Jiping). [Footwork] 89, p. 27.
XIAOFANG, Liu
See LIU, Xiaofang
XIJIAN, Li
See LI, Xijian
6281. XU, Haixin
"Composed on Horseback for My Younger Brother Cui the Ninth on His Departure
to the South" (tr. of Wang Wei, w. Willis and Tony Barnstone). [LitR] (32:3)
Spr 89, p. 337.
"Going to the Country in the Spring" (tr. of Wang Wei, w. Willis and Tony
Barnstone). [LitR] (32:3) Spr 89, p. 338.
"Moaning about My White Hair" (tr. of Wang Wei, w. Willis and Tony Barnstone).
[LitR] (32:3) Spr 89, p. 337.
"The Stillness of Meditation" (tr. of Wang Wei, w. Willis and Tony Barnstone).
[LitR] (32:3) Spr 89, p. 338.
6282. XU, Jingya
"The West" (tr. by Dong Jiping). [Footwork] 89, p. 28.
6283. XUE, Chun-jian
"Beginnings." [Quarry] (38:4) Fall 89, p. 41.
"Coal." [Quarry] (38:4) Fall 89, p. 42.
XUE, Tao
See HSÜEH, T'ao
XUELIANG, Chen
See CHEN, Xueliang
6284. YAKAMOCHI (718-785)
"Late evening finally comes" (tr. by Sam Hamill). [PoetryE] (28) Fall 89, p. 199.
"Light snow silently sweeps" (tr. by Sam Hamill). [PoetryE] (28) Fall 89, p. 202.
6285. YALIM, Özcan
"In the Home for the Aged" (tr. by the author, William Fielder and Dionis Coffin
Riggs). [StoneC] (16:3/4) Spr-Sum 89, p. 35.
"Yaslilarevinde." [StoneC] (16:3/4) Spr-Sum 89, p. 34.
6286. YAMADA, Leona
"Bed of Coal: Roses." [ChamLR] (2:2, #4) Spr 89, p. 30-31.
"Dear Jack." [ChamLR] (2:2, #4) Spr 89, p. 5-6.
"Godmother." [Hawai'iR] (13:1, #25) Spr 89, p. 119.
"Hurricane Near: Midnight." [ChamLR] (3:1, #5) Fall 89, p. 56.
"January 10, 1989: The New Year for a Teacher" (for Jack Unterecker, 1922-1989).
[ChamLR] (2:2, #4) Spr 89, p. 7-8.
"Lilies from Helen" (for Jack Unterecker). [ChamLR] (2:2, #4) Spr 89, p. 3-4.

6287. YAMANAKA, Lois-Ann
  "Lickens." [BambooR] (41) Wint 89, p. 35-36.
  "Tita: The Bathroom." [BambooR] (44) Fall 89, p. 36-37.
  "Under the Bonsai." [BambooR] (41) Wint 89, p. 37-38.
6288. YAMAZAKI, Toshiro
  "1. When I Read Shakespeare's Sonnets." [Caliban] (7) 89, p. 99.
  "The Brain." [Caliban] (7) 89, p. 102.
  "I'm Sending Lautréamont to Shakespeare in America." [Caliban] (7) 89, p. 100.
  "Untitled: If language lost identity?" [Caliban] (7) 89, p. 101.
6289. YAN, Yi
  "The Trolley Car Goes On" (tr. by Edward Morin and Dennis Ding). [MinnR] (NS
      32) Spr 89, p. 79.
YAN-BING, Ye
  See YE, Yan-bing
YAN-XIANG, Shao
  See SHAO, Yan-Xiang
6290. YAÑEZ, Adriana
  "Fragments flee" (tr. by Thomas Hoeksema). [RiverS] (28) 89, p. 52.
  "Gray emptiness" (tr. by T. Hoeksema and R. Enriquez). [Jacaranda] (4:1) Spr-Sum
      89, p. 63.
6291. YANG, Mu
  "Smoke from the Kitchen Chimneys in My Hometown" (tr. by Li Xijian and Gordon
      Osing). [BelPoJ] (40:2) Wint 89-90, p. 16-17.
6292. YANG, Wan-li
  "Don't Read Books!" (tr. by Jonathan Chaves). [LitR] (32:3) Spr 89, p. 429.
  "First Day of the Second Month: Rain and Cold" (tr. by Jonathan Chaves). [LitR]
      (32:3) Spr 89, p. 430.
  "Reading" (tr. by Jonathan Chaves). [LitR] (32:3) Spr 89, p. 428.
YANG-HAO, Chang
  See CHANG, Yang-hao
6293. YARBROUGH, Anne
  "Mary in Egypt." [ChrC] (106:1) Ja 4-11, 89, p. 7.
6294. YARROW, Douglas
  "I Want a Poem Built Strong." [EngJ] (78:1) Ja 89, p. 93.
YASUNARI, Kawabata
  See KAWABATA, Yasunari
6295. YATCHISIN, George
  "Film and Fiction of the Fifties" (after Nicholas Ray). [BostonR] (14:5) O 89, p. 3.
  "Market." [WestB] (25) 89, p. 99.
6296. YATES, Christopher
  "Is There." [Plain] (9:3) Spr 89, p. 31.
6297. YAU, John
  "Bare Sheets" (I-III, from *Radiant Silhouette*). [Screens] (1) 89, p. 29.
  "La Brea." [CentralP] (15) Spr 89, p. 124.
  "Cascade." [CentralP] (15) Spr 89, p. 125.
6298. YAVUZ, Hilmi
  "Mystery" (tr. by Feyyaz Fergar). [Trans] (21) Spr 89, p. 231.
6299. YAX, Larry
  "Old Man's Lament." [EmeraldCR] (1989) c1988, p. 135-136.
6300. YE, Yan-bing
  "The Circular Expressway and Straight Lines of the Ancient City" (tr. by Edward
      Morin, Dennis Ding and Dai Fang). [Pig] (15) 88, p. 6.
6301. YEATS, William Butler
  "Politics." [YellowS] (30) Sum 89, p. 49.
YEH, Li
  See LI, Yeh
6302. YEN, T'iao-yu
  "Traveler's Song" (adaption by Kenneth O. Hanson). [LitR] (32:3) Spr 89, p. 328.
6303. YENSER, Pamela
  "Farming in Poweshiek County" (for Susan and Cindy, living on the farm).
      [MidwQ] (30:2) Wint 89, p. 196.
6304. YERPE, Dale G.
  "The Momentum of Water." [Plain] (9:2) Wint 89, p. 30.
6305. YI, Sung Bok
  "Soundlessly Scarlet Fruits" (tr. by Duane Vorhees). [MidAR] (9:1) 89, p. 41.

YI, Yan
    See YAN, Yi
YI-DUO, Wen
    See WEN, Yi-duo
YIN, Liu
    See LIU, Yin
6306. YODER, Mimi
    "The Wytches Sabbathe." [EmeraldCR] (1989) c1988, p. 110.
YONG-YU, Huang
    See HUANG, Yong-yu
6307. YORK, Gary Page
    "Dutch Treat." [Bogg] (61) 89, p. 40.
6308. YOSANO, Akiko (ca. 1900)
    "All alone" (tr. by Sam Hamill). [PoetryE] (28) Fall 89, p. 204.
6309. YOSELOFF, T. R.
    "Sleep." [LitR] (32:2) Wint 89, p. 218.
YOSHIKI, Ono no (d. 902)
    See ONO NO YOSHIKI (D. 902)
6310. YOSHINO, Kenji
    "Apology." [HarvardA] (123:2) Ja 89, p. 12.
    "Fecundity." [HarvardA] (123:3) Mr 89, p. 15.
    "The Geometry of Passion." [HarvardA] (123:4) My 89, p. 14.
6311. YOUNG, Brian
    "Bad Water Experiment." [HayF] (4) Spr 89, p. 70.
6312. YOUNG, Carolyn
    "Quogue Beach." [Confr] (39/40) Fall 88-Wint 89, p. 234-235.
6313. YOUNG, David
    "Adolescence Ghazal." [AntR] (47:2) Spr 89, p. 192.
    "Another to the Tune 'All the Garden's Fragrance'" (tr. of Ch'in Kuan, w. William
        McNaughton). [LitR] (32:3) Spr 89, p. 374.
    "Easter Ghazal." [AntR] (47:2) Spr 89, p. 193.
    "Root Vegetable Ghazal." [AntR] (47:2) Spr 89, p. 191.
    "A Third to the Tune 'As Though Dreaming'" (tr. of Ch'in Kuan, w. William
        McNaughton). [LitR] (32:3) Spr 89, p. 373.
    "To the Tune 'As Though Dreaming'" (tr. of Ch'in Kuan, w. William McNaughton).
        [LitR] (32:3) Spr 89, p. 372.
    "To the Tune 'Welcome Spring Music'" (tr. of Ch'in Kuan, w. William
        McNaughton). [LitR] (32:3) Spr 89, p. 373.
    "Untitled Love Poem I" (tr. of Shang-yin Li). [Field] (41) Fall 89, p. 90.
    "Untitled Love Poem II" (tr. of Shang-yin Li). [Field] (41) Fall 89, p. 91.
    "Untitled Love Poem III" (tr. of Shang-yin Li). [Field] (41) Fall 89, p. 92.
    "Untitled Love Poem IV" (tr. of Shang-yin Li). [Field] (41) Fall 89, p. 93.
    "Untitled Love Poem V" (tr. of Shang-yin Li). [Field] (41) Fall 89, p. 94.
    "Visionary's Ghazal." [AntR] (47:2) Spr 89, p. 190.
6314. YOUNG, Dean
    "The Afterlife." [Ploughs] (15:1) 89, p. 164.
    "Beloved Infidel." [IndR] (12:3) Sum 89, p. 11-12.
    "A Bouquet on the Third Day" (for Robert Duncan). [Ploughs] (15:1) 89, p.
        162-163.
    "Comet." [IndR] (12:3) Sum 89, p. 10.
    "The Last Thing I Remember." [PoetryNW] (30:1) Spr 89, p. 35-37.
    "Other Obit." [IndR] (12:3) Sum 89, p. 13-14.
    "Rothko's Yellow." [NoAmR] (274:1) Mr 89, p. 61.
    "Transubstantiation." [OhioR] (44) 89, p. 58-59.
    "What to Call It." [AntR] (47:1) Wint 89, p. 61.
6315. YOUNG, Gary
    "I put asters in a small blue vase." [MissouriR] (12:1) 89, p. 52.
    "In August." [AmerPoR] (18:4) Jl-Ag 89, p. 40.
    "Our son was born under a full moon." [MissouriR] (12:1) 89, p. 52.
    "September Night." [AmerPoR] (18:4) Jl-Ag 89, p. 40.
    "The stillborn calf lies near the fence where its mother." [MissouriR] (12:1) 89, p.
        52.
    "Two girls were struck by lightning at the harbor mouth." [MissouriR] (12:1) 89, p.
        52.
6316. YOUNG, Geoffrey
    "His Unexampled Samples" (for Clark). [Talisman] (3) Fall 89, p. 5-6.

6317. YOUNG, Jenifer
   "Moon Over Montlake." [BellArk] (5:3) My-Je 89, p. 10.
   "On Whether Happiness Is Too Simplistic a Basis for Art." [BellArk] (5:3) My-Je
      89, p. 1.
6318. YOUNG, Kathryn
   "Apple Picking" (for C. Kierspie). [SpoonRQ] (14:3) Sum 89, p. 58-59.
   "The Birth of the Brother" (for J. Young). [Mildred] (3:1) Spr-Sum 89, p. 68-70.
   "Danelion" (for Michelle Young). [Mildred] (3:1) Spr-Sum 89, p. 67.
   "God Has a Name for All the Stars" (to Stephanie Corbett-Salling). [Mildred] (3:1)
      Spr-Sum 89, p. 65.
   "Primary Colors" (for William James Young). [Mildred] (3:1) Spr-Sum 89, p. 66.
6319. YOUNG, Kevin
   "Another Dream in Which You Spoke of White Leaves." [HarvardA] (123:2) Ja 89,
      p. 11.
6320. YOUNG, Patricia
   "The End of a Good Day." [Event] (18:2) Sum 89, p. 68.
   "See That Child." [Event] (18:2) Sum 89, p. 69.
6321. YOUNG, Ree
   "In a Field on Flint Hill." [GreensboroR] (46) Sum 89, p. 187.
   "What Counts." [FloridaR] (16:2/3) Fall-Wint 89, p. 197.
   "When Leland Left Elma." [SpoonRQ] (14:2) Spr 89, p. 56-57.
6322. YOUNG, Reggie
   "Saviors." [ChrC] (106:20) Je 21-28, 89, p. 623.
6323. YOUNG, Tom
   "Cookies" (companion piece to Decaf Coffee). [JamesWR] (6:3) Spr 89, p. 9.
   "Crutches on the Sun." [JamesWR] (6:3) Spr 89, p. 8.
   "For Herman Melville." [JamesWR] (6:3) Spr 89, p. 8.
   "Hey You." [JamesWR] (6:3) Spr 89, p. 9.
   "Holiday Psalm." [JamesWR] (6:3) Spr 89, p. 8.
   "Nuclear Babies." [JamesWR] (6:3) Spr 89, p. 8.
   "Sissy." [JamesWR] (6:3) Spr 89, p. 8.
6324. YOUNG, William
   "Leaving Wyoming." [SouthernR] (25:2) Spr 89, p. 501.
   "Noon at Bell Cemetery." [SouthernR] (25:2) Spr 89, p. 502.
6325. YOUNGS, Anne Ohman
   "Reward" (for Bryan and Linda). [MidAR] (9:2) 89, p. 133.
6326. YOUNT, Lisa
   "Elegy on the Death of a Favorite Chinese Restaurant." [Mildred] (3:2) 89, p. 123.
   "Listening Song." [MidwQ] (30:4) Sum 89, p. 457.
   "Visiting Home." [Mildred] (3:2) 89, p. 123.
6327. YOVU, Peter
   "Prelude." [CrabCR] (6:2) Wint 89, p. 3-4.
   "Weasel." [CrabCR] (6:2) Wint 89, p. 3.
6328. YOWS, Kristina
   "From the Terrace of the Temple." [Poetry] (154:4) Jl 89, p. 216.
   "Le Pont Neuf: A Night Photograph." [Poetry] (154:4) Jl 89, p. 217.
   "Red Dust." [Poetry] (154:4) Jl 89, p. 218.
   "To Anne." [Poetry] (154:4) Jl 89, p. 217.
6329. YRAGUI, Yvonne
   "In the Eye of the Hurricane." [CumbPR] (8:2) Spr 89, p. 55-56.
YU, Han
   See HAN, Yu
YU, Li
   See LI, Yu
YU, Lu
   See LU, Yu
6330. YU, Yu
   "Today" (tr. by Dong Jiping). [Footwork] 89, p. 29.
   "A View-Point to an International Congress" (tr. by Dong Jiping). [Footwork] 89, p.
      29.
6331. YÜAN, Hung-tao
   "On Receiving My Letter of Termination" (tr. by Jonathan Chaves). [LitR] (32:3)
      Spr 89, p. 431.
   "Things Seen on Spring Days" (tr. by Jonathan Chaves). [LitR] (32:3) Spr 89, p.
      432.
   "West Lake" (tr. by Jonathan Chaves). [LitR] (32:3) Spr 89, p. 431.

"A Woman's Room in Autumn" (tr. by Jonathan Chaves). [LitR] (32:3) Spr 89, p. 432.
6332. YÜAN, Mei
"At 'Be Careful Bank'" (tr. by J. P. Seaton). [LitR] (32:3) Spr 89, p. 415.
"Dog Days" (tr. by J. P. Seaton). [LitR] (32:3) Spr 89, p. 415.
"Night Thought" (tr. by J. P. Seaton). [LitR] (32:3) Spr 89, p. 416.
"Talking Art" (tr. by J. P. Seaton). [LitR] (32:3) Spr 89, p. 416.
"When the Clouds Come" (tr. by J. P. Seaton). [LitR] (32:3) Spr 89, p. 416.
6333. YÜCEL, Can
"Can'in Cani Cehenneme." [Talisman] (3) Fall 89, p. 14.
"To Hell with Saul's Soul" (tr. by Esra Mirze). [Talisman] (3) Fall 89, p. 114-115.
6334. YUEN, Dana Leilehua
"Live Radio Coverage." [BambooR] (41) Wint 89, p. 40.
"Maggie Don't Sweep." [BambooR] (41) Wint 89, p. 39.
"Rice Cookers." [BambooR] (42/43) Spr-Sum 89, p. 220.
6335. YUKE, Prince (7th c.)
"Like a tall ship" (tr. by Sam Hamill). [PoetryE] (28) Fall 89, p. 201.
6336. YUNGKANS, Jonathan
"Reverie." [Writer] (102:12) D 89, p. 24-25.
6337. YURKIEVICH, Saúl
"Off to Nevernever Land" (tr. by Cola Franzen). [PartR] (56:1) Wint 89, p. 118-119.
6338. YUSON, Alfred A.
"Andy Warhol Speaks to His Two Filipina Maids." [Manoa] (1:1/2) Fall 89, p. 55.
6339. YVON, Josée
"Dieu Tous les Jours à la Fenêtre avec Son Amant, ou Attention aux Anges Tombés." [Rampike] (6:2) 88, p. 57.
6340. ZAGAJEWSKI, Adam
"Sails" (tr. by Renata Gorczynski and Benjamin Ivry). [NewYorker] (65:36) 23 O 89, p. 56.
6341. ZAHNISER, Ed
"Comparitive [sic] Religion." [HeavenB] (7) Wint 89, p. 30.
6342. ZAJC, Dane
"You're Not" (tr. by Michael Biggins). [NewEngR] (11:3) Spr 89, p. 254.
6343. ZALAN, Tibor
"Ergo I'm Getting Warm. I May Even Eat Supper, . . ." (tr. by Nicholas Kolumban). [ArtfulD] (16/17) Fall 89, p. 73.
"Evenings When Silence Arrives in My Apartment with a Boom, . . ." (tr. by Nicholas Kolumban). [ArtfulD] (16/17) Fall 89, p. 72.
6344. ZALLER, Robert
"On an Inscription Against Two Tyrants of Eressos." [SoCoast] (5) Spr 88, p. 42.
6345. ZANDER, William
"Heading for the Beaverkill." [NewL] (55:3) Spr 89, p. 109.
"Portrait of the Poet as Pater Familias." [WritersF] (15) Fall 89, p. 130.
"Quis Est?" [NewL] (55:3) Spr 89, p. 108.
6346. ZANZOTTO, Andrea
"The Baby-Talk Elegy" (tr. by Beverly Allen). [Poetry] (155:1/2) O-N 89, p. 57-61.
"L'Elegia in Petèl." [Poetry] (155:1/2) O-N 89, p. 56-60.
6347. ZAPATA, Miguel Angel
"Cumulo Estelar." [Lyra] (2:1/2) 88, c89, p. 24.
"En el principio la luna no inspiraba los cantos." [Inti] (29/30) Primavera-Otoño 89, p. 273.
"Helga by the Tree, 1978 (Andrew Wyeth)." [Inti] (29/30) Primavera-Otoño 89, p. 274-275.
"Ländler." [Inti] (29/30) Primavera-Otoño 89, p. 274.
"La Luna." [Lyra] (2:1/2) 88, c89, p. 25.
"Saint-Saëns Caminando en el Muelle de Santa Bárbara." [Inti] (29/30) Primavera-Otoño 89, p. 275-276.
6348. ZARATE MACIAS, Rosa Marta
"Cantico de Mujer." [ChrC] (106:18) My 24-31, 89, p. 561.
"Woman Song" (tr. by Caroline M. Kisiel). [ChrC] (106:18) My 24-31, 89, p. 561.
6349. ZARENSKY, Hope F. T.
"Fort Knox, Kentucky (1944-45)." [Wind] (19:65) 89, p. 6.
6350. ZARIN, Cynthia
"Far Abbotsbury." [NewYorker] (65:18) 19 Je 89, p. 38.

6351. ZARUCCHI, Roy
"Seraphim." [Pembroke] (21) 89, p. 114.
6352. ZARZYSKI, Paul
"The Antler Tree" (For Matt Hansen -- In Memoriam -- and to his book pf poems,
Clearing). [Poetry] (153:4) Ja 89, p. 226-227.
"The Garnet Moon" (For Elizabeth Dear). [HighP] (4:1) Spr 89, p. 22-23.
"She Counts on the Turtle's Tree-Ring Scutes." [HayF] (4) Spr 89, p. 102.
"Wondering Where the Blind Boy Goes at Night." [HayF] (4) Spr 89, p. 103.
6353. ZAZUYER, Leah
"Lockport Gasport Brockport, with Stops in Medina Albion and Holley." [OntR]
(31) Fall-Wint 89-90, p. 95-97.
6354. ZDANYS, Jonas
"Children's Taste" (tr. of Nijole Miliauskaite). [Field] (40) Spr 89, p. 22.
"A cold evening, swollen painful" (tr. of Nijole Miliauskaite). [Field] (40) Spr 89, p.
20.
"Every spring as the meadows blossom" (tr. of Nijole Miliauskaite). [Field] (40) Spr
89, p. 21.
"In the damp places" (tr. of Nijole Miliauskaite). [Field] (40) Spr 89, p. 22-23.
"Look, then: how big this bag is on my back" (tr. of Nijole Miliauskaite). [Field]
(40) Spr 89, p. 20-21.
"On winter nights, when my grandmother went to work" (tr. of Nijole Miliauskaite).
[Field] (40) Spr 89, p. 21.
"These are lilacs" (tr. of Nijole Miliauskaite). [Field] (40) Spr 89, p. 19.
"You who led the way into the forest's cool shadows" (tr. of Nijole Miliauskaite).
[Field] (40) Spr 89, p. 19.
6355. ZEALAND, Karen
"Wedding with Lovers Within" (A chapbook of 11 poems). [ThRiPo] (33/34) 89, p.
9-18.
6356. ZEIGER, David
"The Infrastructure of Perfection." [WindO] (51) Spr 89, p. 11.
6357. ZEIGER, Gene
"Old Boats." [StoneC] (16:3/4) Spr-Sum 89, p. 70.
"Old Boats." [SwampR] (1:4) Sum 89, p. 15.
"Post and Beam Construction." [SwampR] (1:4) Sum 89, p. 16.
6358. ZEIGER, Lila
"Numbers." [FreeL] (3) Aut 89, p. 17.
"Perspective." [FreeL] (3) Aut 89, p. 18.
"Things That Bore Me . . ." [FreeL] (3) Aut 89, p. 17.
6359. ZEKOWSKI, Arlene
"Once a Time Upon the --." [SoDakR] (27:4) Wint 89, p. 117-121.
6360. ZELCER, Brook
"Accident." [WormR] (29:1, #113) 89, p. 8.
"After." [SlipS] (9) 89, p. 14.
"Louis Read Somewhere." [WormR] (29:1, #113) 89, p. 8.
"A Quiet Man." [WormR] (29:1, #113) 89, p. 8.
6361. ZELTZER, Joel
"And our first time." [RagMag] (7:1) 89, p. 63.
6362. ZEMAIDUK, Nick R.
"And Further Down." [Wind] (19:64) 89, p. 31.
6363. ZENICK, Robert
"Onyce." [Rampike] (6:2) 88, p. 46-49.
6364. ZENITH, Richard
"Among Rocks, Words" (tr. of Alexandre O'Neill). [MalR] (89) Wint 89, p. 97.
"Creation" (tr. of Alexandre O'Neill). [MalR] (89) Wint 89, p. 99.
"The Hanged Man" (tr. of Alexandre O'Neill). [MalR] (89) Wint 89, p. 98.
"The Muses Are Weary" (tr. of Nelo Risi). [PoetryE] (28) Fall 89, p. 177.
"Song About a Dead and Living Ass" (tr. of Galician-Portuguese Troubadour poem
by Pero da Ponte). [SenR] (19:1) 89, p. 78.
"Song About a Lost Crusade" (tr. of Galician-Portuguese Troubadour poem by Pero
da Ponte). [SenR] (19:1) 89, p. 77.
"Song About a Worsening World" (tr. of Pero Gomez Barroso). [SouthwR] (74:2)
Spr 89, p. 218-219.
"Song About Lopo the Jester (Cantiga d'Escarnho)" (tr. of Martim Soares).
[PoetryE] (28) Fall 89, p. 197.
"Song for a Lover What Went to Sea (Cantiga d'Amigo)" (tr. of Pai Gomes
Charinho). [PoetryE] (28) Fall 89, p. 194.

"Song of a Restless Heart (Cantiga d'Amigo)" (tr. of Lopo). [PoetryE] (28) Fall 89,
p. 198.
"Song of the Parting Flowers (Cantiga d'Amigo)" (tr. of Pai Gomes Charinho).
[PoetryE] (28) Fall 89, p. 192-193.
"Song of Thy My Money" (tr. of Galician-Portuguese Troubadour poem by Gil
Peres Conde). [SenR] (19:1) 89, p. 80.
"Song to a Lady in Simple Clothes" (tr. of Galician-Portuguese Troubadour poem by
Pai Soares de Taveirós). [SenR] (19:1) 89, p. 79.
"Song to an Unbelieving Lady (Cantiga d'Amor)" (tr. of Martim Soares). [PoetryE]
(28) Fall 89, p. 195-196.
"St. Francis' Empty Sandal" (tr. of Alexandre O'Neill). [MalR] (89) Wint 89, p. 96.
"Table" (tr. of Alexandre O'Neill). [MalR] (89) Wint 89, p. 100.
6365. ZETTELMEYER, Carl
"Hopper Landscape." [Jacaranda] (4:1) Spr-Sum 89, p. 18.
6366. ZHANG, Ji
"Maple Bridge Night Mooring" (Two Poems Written at Maple Bridge Near Suzhou,
tr. by Gary Snyder). [LitR] (32:3) Spr 89, p. 446.
6367. ZHAO, Li-hong
"The Pledge" (tr. by Edward Morin and Dai Fang). [CharR] (15:2) Fall 89, p. 60.
6368. ZHDANOV, Ivan
"But already sensing terror" (tr. by John High). [FiveFR] (7) 89, p. 73.
"Falling, a tree's shadow carries some of the leaves along" (tr. by John High).
[FiveFR] (7) 89, p. 72.
"I'm not the branch, only the prebranchness" (tr. by John High). [FiveFR] (7) 89, p.
71.
"Portrait" (tr. by John High and Katya Olmsted). [FiveFR] (7) 89, p. 74.
6369. ZHU, Xiang
"Clearing After Rain, Early Spring in the North" (tr. by James T. Reiber). [WebR]
(14:1) Spr 89, p. 35.
"Long-Awaited Spring" (tr. by James T. Reiber). [WebR] (14:1) Spr 89, p. 35.
"Tranquil Summer Evening" (tr. by James T. Reiber). [WebR] (14:1) Spr 89, p. 35.
6370. ZICKLER, Elaine Perez
"Mother Sounds." [SoCoast] (6) Fall 88, p. 6-7.
6371. ZIDE, Arlene
"Dinnertime." [Prima] (13) 89, p. 36-37.
"Mirrors." [Prima] (13) 89, p. 38-40.
6372. ZIMMER, Paul
"The Eisenhower Years" (for my father). [NewL] (56:2/3) Wint 89-Spr 90, p. 326.
"The Morning News." [NewL] (56:2/3) Wint 89-Spr 90, p. 327.
"Night Maneuvers." [NewL] (56:2/3) Wint 89-Spr 90, p. 328.
"Once As a Child I Had Bad Dreams" (for my mother). [NewL] (56:2/3) Wint
89-Spr 90, p. 323-324.
"Zimmer Imagines Heaven" (for Merrill Leffler). [NewL] (56:2/3) Wint 89-Spr 90,
p. 325.
6373. ZIMMERMAN, Alois
"The Power of Anatomy." [ArtfulD] (16/17) Fall 89, p. 96-97.
6374. ZIMMERMAN, Ken
"Billy Hightower." [BrooklynR] (5) 88, p. 40.
"Coriolis." [BrooklynR] (5) 88, p. 41-42.
6375. ZIMMERMAN, Thomas
"Sailing the West." [Plain] (9:2) Wint 89, p. 20.
6376. ZIMMERMANN, Calduia
"Winter's Voice Has Softened" (tr. of Sandor Csoori, w. Len Roberts). [InterPR]
(15:2) Fall 89, p. 25.
6377. ZIMMERSON, Ken
"Crying." [SilverFR] (16) Spr 89, p. 17.
6378. ZINKEL, Brian
"Blueberries." [KanQ] (21:1/2) Wint-Spr 89, p. 99.
"I See Through the Light of Yesterday's Dreams." [KanQ] (21:1/2) Wint-Spr 89, p.
100.
"Sunlight." [KanQ] (21:1/2) Wint-Spr 89, p. 100.
6379. ZINNES, Harriet
"My, Haven't the Flowers Been" (-- John Ashbery, "The Skaters"). [DenQ] (23:3/4)
Wint-Spr 89, p. 127-128.
6380. ZIOLKOWSKI, Thad
"Nov 59." [Sulfur] (9:1, #24) Spr 89, p. 151-152.

6381. ZOECKLEIN, Aliesa
"Night Blooming Jasmine." [PacificR] (7) 89, p. 43.
6382. ZOLA, Jim
"Letting Go." [FloridaR] (16:2/3) Fall-Wint 89, p. 148-149.
"The Singing Bone" (after an Italian folktale). [FloridaR] (16:2/3) Fall-Wint 89, p. 147.
6383. ZOLLER, James A.
"Rocking the House." [Blueline] (10:1/2) 89, p. 65.
6384. ZONAILO, Carolyn
"Infidelities of the Heart" (from *Poems of the Heart*, for Anna Akhmatova). [CanLit] (120) Spr 89, p. 99.
"Visiting Aunt Annie's." [CanLit] (120) Spr 89, p. 116.
6385. ZONTELLI, Patricia
"Black Car." [GettyR] (2:2) Spr 89, p. 347-348.
"Things" (Second Prize, 1989 Poetry Competition). [PassN] (10:2) Sum 89, p. 4.
6386. ZORACH, Rebecca
"Solitaire USA." [HarvardA] (124:1) N 89, p. 19.
6387. ZORNACK, Annemarie
"Narrow Paths" (tr. by Suzanne Toliver). [NewOR] (16:4) Wint 89, p. 82.
6388. ZOU, Difan
"Lonely" (tr. by Marjorie Sinclair and the author). [BambooR] (44) Fall 89, p. 8.
"To My Mother" (tr. by Marjorie Sinclair and the author). [BambooR] (44) Fall 89, p. 7.
6389. ZUCKER, Jack
"Dream Poem." [BallSUF] (30:4) Aut 89, p. 31-32.
6390. ZUJEWSKYJ, Oleh
"From a Simple Triptych." [CanLit] (120) Spr 89, p. 115.
6391. ZULAUF, Sander
"Third Sunday in Advent." [Footwork] 89, p. 49.
"Wednesday Morning." [Footwork] 89, p. 48.
ZURKO, Edward de
See DeZURKO, Edward
6392. ZURLO, Tony
"African Tragedy." [CinPR] (19) Spr 89, p. 26-27.
6393. ZWICKY, Jan
"At the Burn Barrel." [Event] (18:3) Fall 89, p. 83.
"The Back Kitchen." [MalR] (88) Fall 89, p. 73.
"Kleanza Creek" (for Laurie Whitt). [MalR] (88) Fall 89, p. 77.
"Practicing Bach." [MalR] (88) Fall 89, p. 74-75.
"The West Room." [MalR] (88) Fall 89, p. 76.
6394. ZYDEK, Fredrick (Frederick)
"Dog Dance." [WebR] (14:1) Spr 89, p. 58.
"Going Broke in Babylon." [WebR] (14:1) Spr 89, p. 59.
"The Grass on Recent Graves" (for Eileen). [CrossCur] (8:3) Apr 89, p. 9-10.
"The Last Three Lines." [CharR] (15:1) Spr 89, p. 69.
"Letter to Father Aloysius Peorkowski on the Tenth Anniversary of His Death." [Wind] (19:65) 89, p. 43.

Title Index

Titles are arranged alphanumerically, with numerals filed in numerical order before letters. Each title is followed by one or more author entry numbers, which refer to the numbered entries in the first part of the volume. Entry numbers are preceded by a space colon space (:). Any numeral which preceeds the space colon space (:) is part of the title, not an entry number. Poems with "Untitled" in the title position are entered under "Untitled" followed by the first line of the poem and also directly under the first line. Numbered titles are entered under the number and also under the part following the number.

Chanteuse with Dog, Walking : 3696.
The Chanticleer : 2995.
Charles Blackman in the Vicinity of Rue des
    Beaux Arts : 478.
Charles Darwin : 3717.
Charles on Wheels : 4888.
Charleston : 5829.
Charley : 6025.
Charley, Alistair, Barbara : 6025.
Charley-Bop : 1757.
Charlie Chaplin Impersonates a Poet : 1545.
Charlotte in the Slough : 3513.
The Charm : 2995.
The Charm Machine, 1965 : 454.
Charmed : 3864.
A Charmed Life : 1549.
Chartist Meeting : 2748.
Chase : 3188.
A Chaser : 3716.
Chasing the Water : 955.
Chava : 5826.
Che altro senso aggiunge un'ora di ghiaccio :
    which other sense adds hours of ice :
    2196.
Che Solo Puoi Afferrare Bricioli di Ricordi :
    974, 4635, 4635.
Cheap Sunglasses : 3735.
Cheating : 1581, 5482.
Check : 3602.
Checking the Medical Library for Mystery
    Show Television : 1712.
Checkpoint : 229.
Cheek to Cheek : 72.
Cheers : 5244, 5856.
Cheeveresque : 5009.
Chekhov : 2256.
Chemical Examination : 1635.
Chemin de Jerusalem : 1107.
Chemin des Dammes : 5713.
Chemists : 3235.
Chemo : 5355.
Cherephon [sic] to Pindar : 81.
Cherish : 882.
Cherries : 3143.
Cherry Street : 3841.
Cherry's Hair Villa : 5824.
Chess : 6255.
Chess Game in a Garden : 1599.
The Chessboard Is on Fire : 1789.
Chester County Fair: October, 1960 : 4660.
Chewing Thread : 1934.
Chi Ha Osato : 1300.
The Chicago Odyssey : 312.
Chichicastenango : 499, 2241.
The Chickadee : 3580.
Le Chien Englouti : 134.
Child : 2084, 4476.
The Child Born : 2377.
The Child Descends the Stair : 5460.
Child Frightened by a Monkey : 1872.
The Child Has Gray Eyes : 3332, 4714.
Child Left at the Roadside : 2005, 5666.
Child of Age : 6017.

A Child of Air : 1008.
Child of an Eye So Seldom Seen : 2911.
Child with Pillar Box and Bin Bags : 2720.
Childhood : 141, 1320, 3273.
A Childhood : 5734.
Childhood Impression, Tampa : 3354.
Childless : 4069, 4187.
Children : 295, 3372, 3964.
Children in School During Heavy Snowfall :
    3421.
Children Left in the Palm of Your Hand : 4475.
The Children of Abergavenny : 5135.
Children of Ham : 729.
The Children of Mechanics : 1952.
The Children of Suicides : 3586.
The Children of Tela : 3387.
The Children's Concert : 385.
Children's Poem: This Village : 2463.
Children's Rehabilitation Center : 6113.
Children's Taste : 3835, 6354.
Children's Ward : 1178.
A Chill at the Edge of an Intersection : 1665.
Chilton County Woods: Revisiting the Garden
    in Ruins : 3801.
Chimera : 3466.
Chimneys : 482.
China : 2407.
China Soup : 975.
Chinatown : 2406.
Chinatown Morning : 4852.
Chinese Fireworks Banned in Hawaii : 971.
Chinese Hot Pot : 3411.
Chinese New Year : 971.
Chinese Poem : 3797.
Chinese Poem by Li Ho (791-817) : 1374.
The Chinese Restaurant : 3308.
Chinese Tea : 1678.
Chiton : 5626.
Chivalry : 3866.
Chloroquine : 4260.
Choice : 1841.
Choiceless Pledge : 3940.
Choices : 426, 6189.
Choke Cherries : 5960.
Chokecherry : 514.
Choosing : 1225.
Chopin : 5986.
Chora in Hell, 2 : 3232.
Chora in Hell: Nine Days Old : 3232.
Chorus Girls, 2: A Brief History of the Muses :
    2750.
Chorus of the Hunters : 3332, 5710.
Chosen : 5986.
Christ : 3672.
Christ at the Movies : 2700, 5995.
Christa: A Monologue, Jan. 28, 1986 : 1203.
Christian Fowl Rhapsody : 2984.
Christina's World : 6118.
Christmas : 4100.
Christmas Conjuring : 3300.
Christmas Eve : 2578, 5230.
Christmas Eve: My Mother Dressing : 1358.
Christmas in September : 458.

Dogs : 243.
The Dogs : 2705.
Dogs Dreams & Donkeys Years : 4618.
A Dog's Life : 3550, 4138.
Dogs Watching My Mouth : 5762.
DogThought : 3990.
Doing Cartwheels : 1518.
Doing It Like the Animals : 1398.
Doing My Part : 128, 5449.
Doing the All-White Puzzle : 1740.
Doing What You Can with What You Have :
    3586.
Doing Your Time : 4446.
Dojo : 5538.
Doll Hospital : 3148.
Dolores : 1914.
Dolphins : 2184, 3105.
Domains : 2056.
Dome Car Scavenger Hunt : 3322.
Domestic : 765.
Domestic Artifacts : 5173.
Domestic Interiors : 426.
Domestic Life : 5470.
Domestic of Hope : 258.
Domestic of Terror : 258.
Domestic Weight : 3550.
The Dominie : 2442.
Dominion : 3621.
Don Giovanni's Dream : 690.
Donald in Love : 2697.
Donatien Alphonse Addresses the Ills of the
    World : 4055.
The Donkey : 5600.
Donna : 2710.
Donne : 3806, 5898.
Donner : 4653.
Don't Ask Me for That Love Again : 85, 1662.
Don't Bare Your Soul! : 4172.
Don't Be Afraid, Gringo : 1144.
Don't Be Fooled : 6075.
Don't Copy Pound : 402, 4847.
Don't Dwell on Things That Can't Be Known :
    1973, 3090.
Don't Jump : 592, 1845.
Don't Jump Out of Your Skin : 92, 3174.
Don't Look in the Garden : 2842.
Don't Read Books! : 951, 6292.
Don't Show Me Your Poem : 223.
Don't spy at the window : 317, 2447.
Don't Start Something You Can't Finish : 3451.
Don't Take My Love Like a Joke : 3255.
Don't Tell Me : 2361, 5577.
Don't Think Governments End the World :
    4384.
Don't Use the Word 'Exile' : 290.
Don't You Copy Pound : 4380, 4847.
Donut Holes : 5756.
The Door : 2740, 3080.
A Door Can Be Beaten Down from Either Side
    : 3357.
Door to the River : 4502.
Doors : 3979.
Doorway : 4307, 4768.

Doorways. Windows. Fences. Verges : 4538.
Dopo Marx, Aprile : 1096.
Doppelganger : 711.
Dorothea Lange : 5855.
Dostoevsky & Other Nature Poems : 1881.
Dot Painting : 4793.
The Double Becoming : 5588.
The Double Bow : 2731.
Double Digging : 699.
Double Exposures : 6221.
Double Helix : 183.
The Double Hook : 5804.
Double Jacquard Coverlet : 878.
The Double Portrait : 801.
Double Sonnet for Mickey : 762.
Double Stars : 4793.
Doubled Doris : 2413, 3332.
Doubles : 4530.
Doubts : 4116.
Dought, 1988 : 4118.
Doune's Old Railway 1987 : 5768.
Dove Cottage : 3735.
The Dover Sole : 551.
Down by the River : 897.
Down from the Mountain : 3740.
Down in the valley, silence swallows us whole :
    4922.
Down in the Well : 3736.
Down Old Greece Way : 1134.
Down on Mission : 458.
Down on the Yucatan : 2944.
Down River : 3021.
Down South Camp Meeting : 1546.
Down There : 4408, 5348.
Down to the Cathedral : 4404.
Downriver : 2047.
Downsizing : 883.
Downstream : 3844.
The Dowser : 3534.
Doxy : 693.
Dr. Goebbel's Novels : 3421.
Dr. Kilmer : 2518.
Dr. Korczak's Lie : 2113, 2865, 3110.
Dr. Williams' Garden : 4596.
Dracula's Bride : 3847.
Draft #7: Me : 1534.
Draft Animals : 563.
A Dragon of Tremendous Size : 2766.
Dragon Winter : 3432.
Dragonfly / Altered States : 1253.
Drawing a Broom : 336.
Drawing a Fish Bowl : 336.
Drawing a Spoon : 336.
Drawing an Umbrella : 336.
Drawing Light : 5008.
Drawing room blues : 4576.
Drawing the Sea : 336.
Drawing the Wind : 336.
Drawn to and Confounded : 4792.
Drayton Gardens, S.W. 10 : 2999.
Dream : 1118, 1485, 1859, 2761, 3940, 4631,
    5390, 5865.
The Dream : 4619, 6109.

Like Always Talking About the Weather : 815.
Like an old love-letter : 2267, 5797.
Like Artists : 5618.
Like Something from a Story : 2357, 3332.
Like the Daffodil : 4570.
Like This : 4128.
Like Today : 4739.
Like Tulipomania : 3021.
Like Two Pears : 777.
Like Water : 5280.
Like Wind : 937.
Like Years : 610.
A Likely Story : 4421.
The Lilac Age : 1696.
Lilacs : 2126.
Lilacs and Hail : 2908.
Lilies : 1137.
Lilies from Helen : 6286.
Lilies of the Nile : 4913.
Lilies of the Valley : 2104.
The Lily-Eater : 3332, 5053.
Lily Photographed by Moonlight, 1863 : 195.
The Lima Bean : 1144.
Limb for Limb : 240.
Limbo : 4109.
The Limestone Cave : 5009.
The Limestone Cowboy Sees God, and It's a
    Woman : 1976.
Liminal : 3477.
Limit's Eden : 2198.
Limpieza : 780.
Lin Chiang Hsien : 3146, 3289.
Lineal Answer : 3988.
Lines : 3077, 5786.
Lines After Rereading T. S. Eliot : 6264.
Lines Composed Over a Brandy at Punch 'n
    Judy's After a Long Walk and a Play . . . :
    4260.
Lines for a Ghost of My Hungry Graduate
    Student Heart : 4505.
Lines for Anne Pasternak : 1693.
Lines for Queen Gertrude : 3986.
Lines in Early Morning : 4505.
Lines on Seeing a Photograph for the First Time
    in Thirty Years : 6264.
Lines on Seeing the First Color Photograph of
    Planet Mars : 1051.
Lines to an Old Friend : 2804.
Lines to the Sun : 21.
Lingo : 5925.
Lingo Bistro : 2256.
Link : 3259.
Linked Fates : 4157.
Linking : 5089.
Lint : 1470.
Lionne Ailée : 520.
The Lions at the Gate : 2275.
The Lion's Tooth : 2709.
Lip : 2647.
The Lip-Reader : 414.
Lipizzaners : 3043, 5039, 5672.
Lips in Jail : 3540.
Lipstick : 2754.

Lisa : 4181.
Lisa, the Widow, and Poetry : 1813.
The List : 3603, 5788.
The List of Wedding Gifts : 5436.
Listen : 869, 5177.
Listen! : 6219.
Listen to the Summer Boarder : 3469.
Listening : 3894, 4009.
Listening at Little Lake Elkhart : 5449.
Listening In : 260.
Listening Song : 6326.
Listening to Frank Sinatra : 1546.
Listening to Handel's Water Music : 5350.
Listening to 'Ole' by John Coltrane : 478.
Listening to Sorrow : 690.
Listening to the Clock : 4680.
Listening to the Language of Birds : 5590.
Listening to the Poem : 1020.
Listening to your unconscious : 3104.
Litany : 3332, 5404.
Litany, Amy of : 890.
LI(teracy) Is a LI Word : 1319.
Literal Lives : 3229.
Literature : 4082.
Lithium for Medea : 3247.
Lithium Sonnet : 2056.
\Litter\ass\y : 1248.
Little America Confidential : 49.
Little Burger Blues Song : 2056.
Little by Little : 1859.
Little Cambray Tamales (5,000,000 Bite-Size
    Tamales) : 69, 4543.
The Little Cart : 952, 5947.
A Little Chekhov : 5551.
Little Crisis Framed in My Window : 1280.
Little Elegy for Gay : 3468.
A Little Elegy for Howard Moss : 4477.
Little Elegy for the Age : 3735.
Little Exhortation : 5410, 5861.
Little Fish : 1230.
The Little Flowers : 4642.
The Little Forest : 1933, 5592.
The Little Girl on the Bridge : 3739.
The Little Hats : 3057.
A Little Litany for Moving Day : 5601.
Little Mouths, Little Ghosts : 1889.
A Little Night Music: Armistice Day, 1987 :
    3382.
A Little Night Music for My Mother : 1606.
Little nightingale : 2267, 4051.
Little Nothings : 2527.
Little Ode : 1105.
Little Owl Who Lives in the Orchard : 4218.
A Little Poem About the Rain : 1608.
The Little Signare : 2902, 4313.
A Little Sonnet on Celibacy : 2013.
The Little Stones : 2084.
Little Tear-Vase : 3895, 4768.
Little Testament : 576.
A Little Thing Without Wings : 5040.
A Little Tooth : 3421.
The Little Venetian Square : 4408, 5348.
Liu 2 : 3184.

Memorial Day : 1123, 4515.
Memorial Day Exercises, 1971 : 5324.
Memorial Day Week : 3308.
Memorial for a River Fisherman : 557, 677.
A Memorial: Son Bret : 5449.
Memories : 3460.
Memories of Alexandria, Virginia : 4619.
Memories of an Old Fighter : 3542.
Memories of the Dispossessed : 2174.
Memories Rerun : 2315.
Memory : 395, 953, 1744.
The Memory : 3758.
Memory and the Blue-Eyed Man : 2726.
Memory Is a Fish : 5418.
Memory Li(n)es : 3274.
Memory of Heaven : 4321.
The Memory of Suffering : 4961.
Memory of Wood : 4717.
A Memory: Sana'a : 5740.
Memory's Hard Way Out : 832.
Men : 3908, 4926.
Men Holding Eggs : 2621.
Men in Aïda : 3779.
Men love to gossip : 2267, 5648.
Men of Bangladesh : 4600.
Men on Fire : 283.
The Men on the Moon : 3031.
Men Working on Wings : 4522.
Menage A Tois : 3308.
Mendacity : 290, 910, 6206.
Meng Wall Cove : 3341, 4397, 5985.
Mennonite Country Church : 5580.
Mennonites : 2877.
Men's Wiles: What We Teach Each Ohter :
    3914.
Menstruum of the Dragon : 920.
Mental Patient : 5925.
Mental Ward : 1297.
La Mente e il Corpo Sono Angeli : 5037.
A Mention of Birds : 5584.
Menu for a Last Supper : 1542.
Mercer's Pottery and Tile Works, Doylestown,
    Pennsylvania, 1964 : 1991.
Mercy : 302, 691, 691.
Meredith : 6137.
Mermaid : 5330.
The Mermaid : 2342, 4104.
The Mermaid and the Dragon : 427.
(Merton) : 3768.
Merwin's Inlet : 2641.
Mesquites in February : 6120.
Message : 1581.
Message from Herculaneum : 690.
Message from the Early Worm : 693.
Message to My Neighbors on Seventh Street :
    6257.
A Message to the Bard : 3350, 5318.
Messenger : 1449, 2056.
The Messenger : 2471.
The Messengers : 1660.
Messiah of the Black Heart : 1988.
Met Before : 112.
Metamorphosis : 5375.

Metamorphosis: At the Van Gogh Museum :
    2680.
Metaphor of Grass in California : 3574.
Metastasis : 1948.
Meteorite : 6217.
Meteorite the Size of a House Falls in Farmer's
    Field : 5952.
The Meteorologist : 5753.
Metropolitan Corridor : 1413.
Mexican Head : 4999.
Mexican World Mural 5 x 25 : 2452.
The Mexicanas on Salad Bar : 5723.
Mexico : 4711.
Miasma : 6033.
Michael : 2521, 2778.
Michelangelo in Frontier : 4058.
Michigan : 3235.
Mid Autumn Festival : 3146, 5576.
Mid-City Harvest : 4810.
Mid-January Thaw : 2539.
Mid-Winter Thaw, New England : 252.
The Midas Touch : 1060.
Midday Shadows : 4633.
Middle Age : 4099.
Middle-Aged : 779.
Middle-Aged Man Experiences Spring : 3335.
Middle-Aged Man with Crayons : 2916.
Middle Class Prayer : 1280.
The Middle Distance : 838.
The Middle Years : 3679.
Midlife : 934.
Midnight and Winter : 1420.
The Midnight Carnival : 5359.
Midnight Consolings : 4298.
Midnight denies poursuivant of the dawn :
    3401.
Midnight Gladness : 3259.
The Midnight Shark : 551.
Midpoint : 5241.
Midsummer : 1079.
Midwest : 1530.
Midwestern Town : 3014.
Midwifery : 122.
Midwinter in New Hampshire, 1967 : 2650.
Miedzryzecz : 2002.
Might : 4283.
Mightier Than the Word : 5752.
Migori : 2813.
Migrant : 4264.
The Migrants in Suburbia : 542.
Migration : 1138, 3761, 4438.
Migratory Notions : 5064.
Miguel a Osorio : 2729.
Mike Tyson : 1501.
Milan in Lombardy : 3617, 6183.
Milbert's Tortoiseshell : 2329.
Miles Weeping : 6004.
Milestones : 5107.
Milestones in a Life : 3068.
Military Cemetery: Jerusalem : 4877.
The Militiaman Speaks : 868, 1385, 4854.
Milk and Seed : 5645.
Milk Cartons : 1230.

Milk the Mouse : 4944.
Milkweed Summer : 3575.
The Milkweed Wife : 3371.
Mill Street : 6238.
Miller Canyon Trail No. 106 : 611.
Million Dollar Winners : 5790.
A Million Questions : 1741.
The Mills of God : 6033.
Mimi : 5670.
Mina Bell's Cows : 3738.
The Minarets, So Named, Not to be Parted With : 1016.
The Mind and Body Are Angels : 451, 5037.
The Mind of the Poet : 6033.
Mindfully : 1655.
Minding the Store : 4894.
Mine : 6259.
Mine Is No Ordinary : 1818.
The Mineral Kingdom : 1533, 2032.
Mingus at the Five Spot : 4500.
Minimal Audio Plays (1989) : 3068.
A Mining Town : 4002.
Miniota, Manitoba : 1103.
Minnows Under the Boat : 4526.
Minor Afflictions : 772.
A Minor Crush of Cells : 5815.
A Minor Gift : 784.
Minotaur : 3532.
Minotaur Grief : 1632.
Mio Amore Non Credere : 905.
Il Mio Risveglio E Stato Nel Tuo Nome : 1189.
The Miracle : 1346.
Miracle at Medzhegoria : 6127.
The Miracle of Trees : 5382.
The Miracle of Twenty-Third Street : 1971.
Mirages : 450.
Miranda's Crisis with Words : 4121.
Mirror : 1377, 3278, 4694.
The Mirror : 1293, 1682, 3996.
The Mirror Divides : 5210.
Mirror, Mirror : 4821.
Mirror of Actual Notice : 3807.
The Mirror to Deal With : 695.
The Mirror Wall : 4020.
Mirrors : 6371.
Mirrors in the Room : 3459.
Mirth : 2356.
Miscarriage Abroad : 2342, 4104.
Misfortune on the Way : 5241.
Mishima : 1847.
Misled by the Specificity of Prose : 3310.
Mismatched Shoes : 3054.
Miss Emily : 4723.
Miss Lonelyhearts : 6213.
Missed Children : 5224.
Missed Opportunity : 905, 1722, 1722.
Missing : 1449, 1470.
Missing Boys : 6203.
The Missing Ear : 5185.
Missing in Action : 2679.
Missing in Action and Presumed Dead : 2679.
Missing My Grandmother : 57.
Missing Person-1 : 2679.

Missing Persona Report : 773.
Missing the Dead : 3992.
Missing the Loved One : 317, 318, 5985, 6279.
Missing Voice : 4953.
Missionary : 549.
The Missionary : 5731.
Mississippi : 534, 1586.
Mississippi John Hurt Buried in the Pepper : 5092.
Mississippi River, Near Cape Girardeau, Mo. : 2690.
Mississippi Sundown : 4633.
The Missouri : 3097.
Missouri Barns : 4993.
Missouri Farmers at the Louvre : 1289.
The Mist As Subject : 5278.
The mist is a visible mood : 4576.
Mister . . . : See Mr. . . ., below.
Mistress : 1075.
Mitosis : 691.
Mixed Frequencies in the Golden West Saloon : 3819.
Miyajima : 5464.
Miyaki : 2283.
Miz Moon I : 6245.
Miz Moon IV : 6245.
Moaning about My White Hair : 317, 318, 5985, 6281.
Mobile Home : 1872.
Mobile Over Hecate Strait : 2922.
Mock & Shame : 2271.
Mockingbird : 865.
Mode of Acquisition : 2907, 4779.
The Model Child : 2939.
Model Home 3 : 3708.
Model Home 4 : 3708.
Modeling for de Kooning : 2797.
Modern Consciousness : 2256.
A Modern Goddess : 5009.
Modern History : 6038.
Modern Japanese Autobody Versus the Audience Cult, A Transition : 3025.
A Modern Judgement : 4789.
Modern Love : 5693.
Modern Muses : 4958.
Modern Notes : 2200.
Modern Times : 1458, 3716.
A Modest Proposal, Overtly Political : 3182.
A Modest Request That the Weathercock Be Released : 3332, 5659.
Modulation : 2838, 5218.
Mohnkuchen : 570.
Mokuahana : 268.
The Molecular Economy : 4386.
Molly Jane, They Oughta Name a Hurricane After You : 4487.
Molyneux's Wake : 4733.
Moment : 3099, 3332.
The Moment : 371, 3865.
The Moment After : 2740.
A Moment at the Louvre : 3895, 4304.
A Moment in My Rented Room : 6250.
Moment of Silence : 878.

Ode to Föhn : 2351.
Ode to Knees : 1587.
Ode to Michael Milken : 2121.
Ode to My Old Shoes : 4327.
Ode to Paperclips : 2930.
An Ode to Queen Mumbi : 3635.
Ode to Salvador Dalí : 1929, 5031.
Odradek : 1745.
Odysseus Recalls Cassandra : 1118.
Odysseus to Selena : 1682.
Odyssey : 476, 2559.
Oedipus Irvington : 5613.
Of : 1128.
Of a Little Thing : 6007.
Of Death and Beauty : 3977.
Of Fierce Origin : 1142, 5248.
Of Hell : 5614.
Of Learning What I Was Taught Was Taught :
    770.
Of Night : 4366.
Of Pairs : 2705.
Of Peace : 2532, 4498, 4664.
Of Pine : 4623.
Of Politics, & Art : 1503.
Of the Death of a Rhinoceros : 2268.
Of the Dolphin : 2532, 4498, 4664.
Of the Doubleness : 2056.
Of the Pleasures Which May be Discovered in
    Books, 1902 : 2352.
Of the River : 2200.
Of the Word : 1923, 2017, 4219.
Of Time and the River : 4100.
Of Truth : 2532, 4498, 4664.
Of Tulips and Trillium : 2234.
Of Two Minds : 1512.
Of Whitman, Reclining : 1120.
Of Women and Men : 1415.
Off My Foot : 3173.
Off the Avenue : 4775.
Off the Path : 647.
Off to Nevernever Land : 1845, 6337.
The Offer : 1675, 4311.
The Offering Stance : 2625.
Offertory : 4038.
An Office Overlooking the Green : 2334.
The Official Ratings Against Absolute Truth :
    4601.
Offshoreoilrigworker Hammerclaviersonate :
    5462.
The Offspring of Heraclitus : 290, 910, 6024.
Oh : 1161.
Oh, I've seen the sights of the Arctic nights :
    1309.
Oh Sefiroth de Mis Deseos : 4050.
Oh, That's What It Is : 4351.
Oh Yes He Wants to Feel Happier Help
    People : 3308.
Ohio Tops the List of License Plates Traded in
    for California Plates : 667.
Oigo Tu Fragil Vocecita Ahumada : 1396.
Oil Field Wife : 2030.
Oil on Board: Pennsylvania Farm, ca. 1840 :
    5368.

Oiled Feet Smoothing Certain Now Old Waves
    : 3256.
Oils : 4531.
The Oject of Desire : 3310.
Okavango Dawn : 1680.
Okeechobee Chicken Pen : 2842.
O'Keeffe's Black Iris : 1092.
O'Keeffe's Untitled #3 : 4429.
The Okinawa Nudes : 3448.
Oklahoma : 4480.
Oklahoma Patchwork : 3234.
Ol Time Religion : 1287.
Olana, Summer, 1872 : 3963.
Old Asian Hand : 964.
The Old Bards Say : 1100, 2950, 4299.
Old Boats : 6357.
Old Books : 1541.
The Old Causes : 4730.
The Old Channel : 5522.
Old Christmas : 1806, 3953.
Old Comrade : 3332, 5891.
An Old Counting-Game : 2542.
Old Dust : 2267, 3293.
Old Fashioned Juice Squeezer : 5061.
An Old-Fashioned Song : 2542.
Old Ferd : 4310.
Old Field : 1499, 2094.
Old Flames : 3736.
Old Friend : 2562.
An Old Friend Is Pulled from the River : 5698.
Old Friends : 2684.
Old German Wives' Tales : 2958.
Old Gold : 1233.
Old Habits Die Hard: Milk : 5660.
An old hardcover book, the binding broken, the
    dry glue cracking like twigs in autumn :
    5099.
Old House : 1286.
Old Iron : 2122, 3332.
Old Is This Road and Foxes : 3147.
An Old Joke: Christ and the Woman Take in
    Adultery : 2612.
Old Love : 3705.
Old Man Among His Flowers : 1132.
The Old Man and His Orchids : 1089.
The Old Man at Pushkin's Funeral : 5266.
An Old Man Remembers the Guitar : 378.
Old Man's Lament : 6299.
The Old Man's Tools : 1820.
Old Maps : 3865.
The Old Marriage : 4799.
Old Men Fishing at Brownwood : 3679.
Old Men with Penknives : 3561.
Old Metropolitan Cemetery : 3119, 3332.
Old Moons : 2110.
Old Motif : 4776, 5241.
Old Mountain Road : 5241.
Old Mrs. Bedell : 741.
Old Music : 141, 3273.
Old Neighborhood : 2405.
Old People's Spring : 1859, 3099.
An Old Philosopher : 4642.
Old Plum Trees : 972, 1098, 3470.

Putting in Iris During Hanukkah : 3484.
Putting Makeup on Empty Space : 5941.
Putting Out the Trash : 615.
Puu Lindudega : 5823.
Puzzle : 2067.
Puzzling : 5021.
Pygmalion : 551.
Pyracantha : 905, 1722.
Pyramid : 714.
Pyramids and Sphinxes : 5241.
Pyromania : 5769.
Qingping Market, Guangzhou : 3798.
Quai Saint Bernard : 5009.
Quail : 6272.
Quail Eggs : 3855.
Quaker Ellwood : 3986.
Quaking Aspen : 2867.
Qualcuno Mi Ha Detto : 909.
The Quality of Being Poor : 1546.
A Quality of Light : 3054.
Quando l'Ottobre Lento Trascolora : 4492.
Quantum Weirdness : 6114.
Quarantine in Room 202 at the Corinth Hotel in
    Mississippi : 2186.
The Quarry : 1227.
Quarryman at the Pandy, CLWYD : 279.
Quarter Section : 1103.
Quartier Libre : 4579.
Quasimodo : 2990.
Quatrains for Pegasus : 3797.
Que la caresse de ton esprit : 4305.
Que les Mots Fassent Souche dans l'Air : 1533.
The Queen Bee : 2702.
Queen City : 1683.
The Queen in a Coin : 1447, 2187.
The Queen of Hearts Says *Hit Me, Not Too
    Hard* : 4668.
The Queen of the Farm Courtyard : 3296, 3348,
    4260.
The Quest : 29.
Questi Piccoli Uccelli : 905.
A Question Addressed to Liu Shih-Chiu : 256,
    6008.
The Question Following the Statement : 4022.
Question No Question : 5645.
A Question of Rhythm : 290, 4338, 4340.
Questioning : 2658.
Questioning the Remains : 4738.
Questionnaire : 3021.
Questions : 2015, 5725.
Questions at Kezar Lake : 5486.
Quetzalcoatl : 1255.
Qui : 905.
Quick Bright Things : 5963.
Quiet Days Beside the Ocean : 1055.
A Quiet Man : 6360.
The Quiet Room : 4250.
The Quilt : 4961.
Quilt Pieces: a Feminine Legacy : 5992.
Quilting : 5718.
The Quiltmaker : 1617.
Quincunx : 1654.
Quinnipiac R. : 2128.

Quintet in C Major : 105.
Quis Est? : 6345.
Quit : 2658.
Quite Enough : 4672.
Quite Frankly, You Enjoyed It : 4416.
Quiveys' Spring : 2334.
Quogue Beach : 6312.
The Quorum : 351.
The Quote : 6270.
R for Rosemary : 5499.
R.R.R. : 4799.
Rabbinical Legends: Necessity and Grace :
    5591.
The Rabbi's Wife : 5278.
Rabbit Tobacco : 3865.
Rabbits : 4744.
Rabbits at Iraklion : 5577.
Raccoon : 1553.
The Raccoons : 5777.
Raccoons at the Window : 386.
The Race : 2342, 3562, 4104.
The Race Meeting : 5350.
Rachel : 1692.
Rachel's Fourteenth Birthday Poem, Written
    September 15, 1988 : 5575.
Radiance : 184.
Radiation Pressure : 3953.
Radio : 5301.
Radio Baseball : 2056.
Radio Hanoi Is Still Playing Our Song : 5585.
Radio Silence : 4513.
Radio Sky : 1503.
The Radiologist's Daughter : 2348.
The Radium Girls : 5826.
Raf, Cyprus : 5318.
Rahab Remembers : 1443.
Raik : 1413.
Railway Train : 4014, 6185.
Rain : 216, 441.
Rain and Memory : 542.
Rain & Snow : 3231.
Rain dents a steady robust : 4283.
Rain in Germany : 4931.
Rain Is Older : 6277.
Rain Last Night : 699.
The Rain Man : 4202.
The Rain of Stones Is Finished : 85, 1662.
Rain Revisited : 3061.
Rain Years : 468.
Rainbows and Circumcision : 3981.
Raincoat : 974.
Raindrops : 3671.
Rainmaker : 2739.
The Rain's Marriage : 5407.
Rainwind : 143.
Rainy Day Shoppers : 1805.
Raised Stones : 1533, 1724.
Raising Crazy Horse : 5294.
Raising Steel : 5784.
The Raker : 521.
Ramah : 3504.
Ramona Palace : 897.
Ranchman : 608.

Syzygy in Center Field : 2802.
T-Bone Steak : 3411.
T. E. Lawrence: Two Poems : 4928.
T.G.I.F. : 5925.
T.L. : 1823.
A T.S. Eliot Centennial Lecture : 1458.
Tabard and Terrace : 4730.
Tabasco's Bar : 2316.
Table : 4229, 6364.
Table for Two : 3461.
Tableau : 1818.
Tableau-Tableau : 6064.
Tabula Rasa : 3021.
Tadpoles in the Gutter : 2529.
Tae Kwon Do : 1895.
Tag Teams : 1243.
The Tai Chi Master & I : 5465.
Tail : 6003.
The Tailor : 5145.
Take a pitcher full of water and set it down on
      the water : 553, 2848.
Take Away : 5645.
Take Me Between Your Eyelashes : 397, 5134.
Take Out : 389.
Taking a Life : 247.
Taking a Walk : 5702.
Taking Heed : 3536.
Taking Her to the Open Market : 3411.
Taking Him from the Cell : 1323.
Taking in the Wild : 3311.
Taking Notice : 2223.
Taking Off : 3457, 4223.
Taking Out the Trash : 4494.
Taking Rachel Home : 5435.
Taking Stock : 1243.
Taking the Comfort with Us : 3370.
Taking the Crow to Market : 5180.
Taking the Cure : 4005.
Taking the Lambs to Market : 3116.
Taking the Things : 3332, 5057.
Taking the Train to Reading, PA : 4049.
Talaria : 5347.
The Talbott : 5138.
A Tale : 2056.
A Tale Begun : 290, 910, 5639.
Talent : 3332, 5404.
Tales from the Cherokee Hills : 5466.
Tales of the Forebears : 1414.
Talisman : 5129, 5549.
The Talk Show : 2056.
Talking Art : 5116, 6332.
Talking in the Wind : 5111, 5738.
Talking Politics : 6263.
Talking to my crested hen : 2468, 2677, 4221.
Talking with Charlot : 858.
Talking with Clothes : 4443.
Tall Stranger : 1092.
Tall, Thin Sonnet : 4619.
Tall Violincellos : 5602, 6115.
The Tally Man : 4929.
Tan Sólo una Sonrisa : 4823.
Tandem : 276.
Tangier Repeats : 4214.

Tango Lyric : 5687, 6263.
Tangy Taste in the Bramble Bush : 3929.
Tanks in Greenwich Village : 1916.
Tanners' Creek : 2404.
The Tanner's Pride : 3712.
Tanzanian Basket / Lost in Translation : 3636.
Tao : 1619.
Tao-Chi : 3895.
Tao of the Running Child : 2962.
Tao Te Ching : 3169, 3201.
Tapestries : 2796.
The Tapestries of Appetite : 4002.
Taproots : 4443.
Tar River Again : 3495.
Tarascon Diligence : 3526.
Una Tarde de Marzo, Educando a Luis : 1783.
Target : 3824.
Tarsane : 1122.
Tashkurghan, Afghanistan : 1084.
The Tattoo : 443.
The Tattooed Man : 224.
Taung Child : 6083.
Taxi : 1136.
Taxidermy : 5670.
Tayamoum : 5600.
Te Kooti : 6159.
Tea Ceremony : 4043.
Teach Me to Step Through Sorrow : 755.
Teacher at White Lake : 1140.
Teachers of Obscure Subjects : 3046.
Teaching Goldfish : 3794.
Teaching in Prison : 642.
Teaching My Son to Drive : 2531.
Teaching My Son to Talk : 6016.
Teaching the Natives About the Sonnet : 4330.
Teaching with Lint in My Pockets : 1403.
The Teachings of Lilacs : 1696.
Teanaway River, Two Passes : 3743.
Tears Are Invisible : 2911.
The Technology of Inertia : 3500.
Ted : 843.
Teen Blizzard : 2502.
Teenage Boys : 5375.
Teenage Funeral : 5761.
Teheran, January 1979 : 1828.
Telepathy: 17 Poems for My Sister : 2967.
Telephone Book : 4097.
Telephone Call : 559.
Television : 3880.
Tell 'Em I Ain't Home : 3635.
Tell Me : 2053.
Tell Me a Story : 5994.
Tell Me Everything : 3332, 5404.
Tell Me Zucchini : 2034.
Tell the Heroes to Wait : 2679.
Tell the President, It's My Day Off! : 43.
Telling Time : 1802.
Telling Your Story : 5380.
Tematica de Mercado con Utensilios de
      Mercado : 2074.
The Temperature of Conversation : 4687.
Temple : 3553.
Temple Cleansing : 5187.

We Never Close : 1026.
We Never Got Inside It : 3308.
We (Ourselves) Make the Spirits Breathe :
    5314.
We pride ourselves as a nation on dealing with
    facts : 4918.
We Rebuild Warsaw (Reprise, 1986) : 607.
We shall not have a face today : 758.
We, the Generation in the Wilderness : 1703,
    2881, 4956.
We Wait : 2907, 4779.
We Were Waking : 3751.
We Workers : 5321.
Wealth : 2462.
The Weaning of Baby Roy : 3236.
Weapon Effects on a Wood Frame House :
    4693.
Weapons : 5468.
Weaponsong : 5102.
Wearing Her Husband's Shirt : 5651.
Weary clear to his feet : 1885, 2267.
The Weary Pleasure Seekers : 1745.
Weasel : 6327.
Weather : 1462, 1818.
A Weather : 665.
Weather Eye : 134.
Weather Vein : 6184.
The Weathercock : 581.
Weathered : 5484.
Weaving Like Dancing Basketmakers : 5563.
Weaving Love-knots : 2606, 3012.
Weaving Love-knots #13 : 2606, 3012.
Web : 2612, 3663.
Webster's Bar : 2619.
The Wedding : 1358, 2428.
Wedding on the West Coast : 5304.
Wedding Song : 691, 3072.
Wedding with Lovers Within : 6355.
Wednesday Morning : 6391.
A Wednesday Night in 1969 : 4855.
Wednesdays : 5009.
The Weed Flower : 4509.
The Weed Garden : 5441.
Weeding (June 9) : 662.
Weeds : 3660, 6233.
A Week Off, Mathesen Bay, Canada, Fishing
    Trip : 1102.
The week that Margaret put herself to bed :
    2380.
Weekend : 384, 3332.
Weekend Astronomer : 5808.
Weekend in the Country : 6262.
Weekend Warrior : 1243.
The Weight of a Journal : 11.
Weightlessness : 114.
Weird Doctors : 3690.
Welcome Angel : 1368, 4675, 6263.
Welcome Song for a New Baby : 5430.
Welcome to Dallas! : 4172.
Welcome to New Smyrna Beach : 5540.
The Welder : 2585.
We'll Breathe Quietly : 607, 2558.
Well Tonight Thank God It's Them Instead of

You : 5755.
Wellington Letter: VIII : 2789.
The Welsh Curse : 5247.
Welsh Landscape : 5725.
Were You There When They Crucified My
    Lord? : 331.
The West : 1447, 6282.
West 22nd Street : 1426.
West Indian Primer : 76.
West Lake : 951, 6331.
West Monroe, Louisiana, 1972 : 3844.
West Palm : 2220.
The West Point Museum : 1932.
The West Room : 6393.
West Street : 1709.
A West Texas Oilfield : 2822.
West Third Street, the First Weekend in June :
    1545.
The Western : 987.
Western / Separation : 5834.
Wet, Awaiting Blue : 978.
Wet Pavement : 2165.
Wet Veteran : 419.
Whacky Gardener Weds Head of Lettuce :
    5952.
The Whale : 4794.
Whale Bone Man : 215.
The Whale-Rocks : 5351.
Whale Watching : 3150.
Whales : 5365.
Wharf-End : 5313.
What : 1161.
What a Little Moonlight Can Do : 3614.
What a Welcome : 820.
What About Those Old Faces in the Puffy
    Clouds of Summer? : 1628.
What an Elephant Knows : 5451.
What? Another Chinese Holiday?! : 971.
What Any Child Can Do : 2840.
What Anyone Really Wanted : 3743.
What Are Chores? : 1985.
What are they talking about : 2546, 4948.
What are you suffering? : 2829.
What Be and Ain't in Omaha : 722.
What Bird Song Remains : 1712.
What Blight : 972, 1098, 3470.
What Brings Us Out : 4159.
What Came to Me : 2943.
What Can I Say? : 2663.
What Can They : 290, 910, 2343.
What Can We Wish for and Believe We Can
    Have? : 2754.
What Changes Us : 6068.
What Comes, What Goes : 6241.
What Counts : 6321.
What Death? : 2913.
What Does Not Happen : 1647.
What Don Quixote Left Unsaid : 1860, 3332.
What Drives Us : 2908.
What Gets Said in the Car : 5997.
What Gwendolyn Might Have Me Say : 6271.
What Happens to Old Men at Sundown : 5342.
What Happens When You Recognize a Face :